# THE SEVEN BASIC PL

## Why we tell stories

# The Seven Basic Plots

## *Why we tell stories*

BY

CHRISTOPHER BOOKER

'We dance around in a ring and suppose;
But the Secret sits in the middle – and knows.'
Robert Frost

continuum
LONDON • NEW YORK

**CONTINUUM**
The Tower Building, 11 York Road, London SE1 7NX
15 East 26th Street, New York, NY 10010

*www.continuumbooks.com*

© Christopher Booker 2004

First published 2004
Reprinted 2004, 2005 (twice)

'Fire and Ice' by Robert Frost from *The Poetry of Robert Frost*, edited by Edward Connery Lathem and published by Jonathon Cape. Used by permission of the estate of Robert Frost and The Random House Group Ltd.

**British Library Cataloguing-in-Publication Data**
A catalogue record for this book is available from the British Library.

ISBN: 0-8264-5209-4 (HB)
ISBN: 0-8264-8037-3 (PB)

Typeset in Adobe Minion by Tony Lansbury, Tonbridge, Kent.
Printed and bound in Great Britain by The Cromwell Press, Trowbridge, Wiltshire.

*This book is dedicated to the memory of my parents,*
*John and Margaret Booker, who, between them, gave me*
*such a magical introduction to the world of storytelling.*

# Contents

## PART THREE: MISSING THE MARK

## PART FOUR: WHY WE TELL STORIES

# Introduction and Historical Notes

'He had likewise projected, but at what part of his life is not known, a work to show how small a quantity of REAL FICTION there is in the world; and that the same images, with very little variation, have served all the authors who have ever written.'

Dr Samuel Johnson, recorded in
Boswell's *Life of Johnson*

In the mid-1970s queues formed outside cinemas all over the Western world to see one of the most dramatic horror films ever made. Steven Spielberg's *Jaws*, which heralded the arrival of the most successful popular storyteller of the late-twentieth century, told how the peace of a little Long Island seaside resort, Amity, was rudely shattered by the arrival offshore of a monstrous shark, of almost super-natural power. For weeks on end the citizens are thrown into a stew of fear and confusion by the shark's savage attacks on one victim after another. Finally, when the sense of threat seems almost too much to bear, the hero of the story, the local police chief Brody, sets out with two companions to do battle with the monster. There is a tremendous climactic fight, with much severing of limbs and threshing about underwater, until at last the shark is slain. The community comes together in universal jubilation. The great threat has been lifted. Life in Amity can begin again.

It is safe to assume that few of the millions of sophisticated twentieth-century moviegoers who were gripped by this tale as it unfolded from the screens of a thousand luxury cinemas would have paused to think they had much in common with an unkempt bunch of animal-skinned Saxon warriors, huddled round the fire of some draughty, wattle-and-daub hall 1200 years before, as they listened to the minstrel chanting out the verses of an epic poem.

Yet just consider the story of that ancient poem which has survived to our own day mainly to be dissected in examination rooms by generations of bored and baffled students of Anglo-Saxon literature.

The first part of *Beowulf* tells of how the peace of the little seaside community of Heorot is rudely shattered by the arrival of Grendel, a monster of almost super-natural power, who lives in the depths of a nearby lake. The inhabitants of Heorot are thrown into a stew of fear and confusion as, night after night, Grendel makes his mysterious attacks on the hall in which they sleep, seizing one victim after another and tearing them to pieces. Finally, when the sense of threat seems almost too much to bear, the hero Beowulf sets out to do battle, first with Grendel, then with his even more terrible monster mother. There is a tremendous climactic

1

fight, with much severing of limbs and threshing about underwater, until at last both monsters are slain. The community comes together in jubilation. The great threat has been lifted. Life in Heorot can begin again.

In terms of the bare outlines of their plots, the resemblances between the twentieth-century horror film and the eighth-century epic are so striking that they may almost be regarded as telling the same story. Are we to assume that the author of *Jaws*, Peter Benchley, had in some way been influenced by *Beowulf*? Of course not. Even if he had read *Beowulf*, it is most unlikely that he could have conceived a story with the power of *Jaws* unless it had emerged spontaneously into his own imagination. Yet the fact remains that the two stories share a remarkably similar pattern – one which moreover has formed the basis for countless other stories in the literature of mankind, at many different times and all over the world.

So what is the explanation?

It is a curious characteristic of our modern civilisation that, whereas we are prepared to devote untold physical and mental resources to reaching out into the furthest recesses of the galaxy, or to delving into the most delicate mysteries of the atom – in an attempt, as we like to think, to plumb every last secret of the universe – one of the greatest and most important mysteries is lying so close beneath our noses that we scarcely even recognise it to be a mystery at all.

At any given moment, all over the world, hundreds of millions of people will be engaged in what is one of the most familiar of all forms of human activity. In one way or another they will have their attention focused on one of those strange sequences of mental images which we call a story.

We spend a phenomenal amount of our lives following stories: telling them; listening to them; reading them; watching them being acted out on the television screen or in films or on a stage. They are far and away one of the most important features of our everyday existence.

Not only do fictional stories play such a significant role in our lives, as novels or plays, films or operas, comic strips or TV 'soaps'. Through newspapers or television, our news is presented to us in the form of 'stories'. Our history books are largely made up of stories. Even much of our conversation is taken up with recounting the events of everyday life in the form of stories. These structured sequences of imagery are in fact the most natural way we know to describe almost everything which happens in our lives.

But it is obviously in their fictional form that we most usually think of stories. So deep and so instinctive is our need for them that, as small children, we have no sooner learned to speak than we begin demanding to be told stories, as evidence of an appetite likely to continue to our dying day. So central a part have stories played in every society in history that we take it for granted that the great story-tellers, such as Homer or Shakespeare, should be among the most famous people who ever lived. In modern times we have not thought it odd that certain men and women, such as Charlie Chaplin or Marilyn Monroe, should come to be regarded

2

as among the best-known figures in the world, simply because they acted out the characters from stories on the cinema screen. Even when we look out from our own world into space, we find we have named many of the most conspicuous heavenly bodies – Venus, Mars, Jupiter, Orion, Perseus, Andromeda – after characters from stories.

Yet what is astonishing is how incurious we are as to *why* we indulge in this strange form of activity. What real purpose does it serve? So much do we take our need to tell stories for granted that such questions scarcely even occur to us.[1]

In fact what we are looking at here is really one mystery built upon another, because our passion for storytelling begins from another faculty which is itself so much part of our lives that we fail to see just how strange it is: our ability to 'imagine', to bring up to our conscious perception the images of things which are not actually in front of our eyes.

If someone says to us 'the Matterhorn'… or 'a zebra'… or 'your kitchen table at home'… or 'a dragon breathing fire'… something very peculiar happens. Somewhere inside our heads, the words can trigger off a mental picture of each of these things. No one knows exactly where or how that image is produced or perceived. But we have this capacity to conjure up the inward images not only of places, people and things not present to our physical senses, but even of things, such as that fire-breathing dragon, which have never existed physically at all.

And it is of course this ability to conjure up whole sequences of such images, unfolding before our inner eye like a film, which enables us to have dreams when we sleep, and when we are awake to focus our attention on these mental patterns we call stories.

What this book sets out to show is that the making of these patterns serves a far deeper and more significant purpose in our lives than we have realised: indeed one whose importance can scarcely be exaggerated. And the first crucial step towards bringing this into view is to recognise that, wherever men and women have told stories, all over the world, the stories emerging to their imaginations have tended to take shape in remarkably similar ways.

꧁꧂

We are all familiar with the teasing notion that there may be 'only seven (or six, or five) basic stories in the world'. It is tantalising not least because, even though this suggestion has not infrequently been put forward in print, its authors never seem to carry it further by explaining just what those stories might be. But it is now more than 30 years since I began to realise that there might seriously be some truth in this idea.

---

1. In many conversations I had about this book during the years when it was being written, the explanation most commonly offered as to why we like stories was that they satisfy our need for 'escapism'. Certainly this describes the way we often use stories, as a means to escape out of the 'real world' into that realm of fantasy or imagination we find so beguiling. But in no way does it explain why we should be able to find diversion in this particular way. As soon as we begin to explore the psychology behind our ability to imagine stories, it becomes obvious that this 'explanation' in fact explains nothing.

While writing a book on a quite different subject, I found my attention focusing on a small number of particular stories. They included a Shakespeare play, *Macbeth*; Vladimir Nabokov's novel *Lolita*; a 1960s French film, Truffaut's *Jules et Jim*; the Greek myth of Icarus; and the German legend of Faust. On the face of it, these stories might not seem to have much in common. But what haunted me was the way that, at a deeper level, they all seemed to unfold round the same general pattern. Each begins with a hero, or heroes, in some way unfulfilled. The mood at the beginning of the story is one of anticipation, as the hero seems to be standing on the edge of some great adventure or experience. In each case he finds a focus for his ambitions or desires, and for a time seems to enjoy almost dream-like success. Macbeth becomes king; Humbert embarks on his affair with the bewitching Lolita; Jules and Jim, two young men in pre-First World War Paris, meet the girl of their dreams; Icarus discovers that he can fly; Faust is given access by the devil to all sorts of magical experiences. But gradually the mood of the story darkens. The hero experiences an increasing sense of frustration. There is something about the course he has chosen which makes it appear doomed, unable to resolve happily. More and more he runs into difficulty; everything goes wrong; until that original dream has turned into a nightmare. Finally, seemingly inexorably, the story works up to a climax of violent self-destruction. The dream ends in death.

So consistent was the pattern underlying each of these stories that it was possible to track it in a series of five identifiable stages: from the initial mood of anticipation, through a 'dream stage' when all seems to be going unbelievably well, to the 'frustration stage' when things begin to go mysteriously wrong, to the 'nightmare stage' where everything goes horrendously wrong, ending in that final moment of death and destruction. No sooner had I become aware of this pattern than many other well-known stories began to suggest themselves as following the same general shape. Not surprisingly, these included a good many dramatic and operatic tragedies, such as *Romeo and Juliet* or *Carmen*. They included myths and legends, such as that of Don Juan; novels, such as the dreams turned to nightmare of those two unhappy heroines, Emma Bovary and Anna Karenina, both ending in suicide; or films such as *Bonnie and Clyde*, describing the two young lovers who light-heartedly embark on a career as bank robbers and end up riddled with a hail of bullets. Again and again through the history of storytelling it was possible to see this same theme, of a hero or heroine being drawn into a course of action which leads initially to some kind of hectic gratification and dream-like success, but which then darkens inexorably to a climax of nightmare and destruction. And at this point two questions began to intrude.

Firstly, why was this so? Why has the imagination of storytellers seemed to form so readily and regularly round this theme? Why do we recognise it as such a satisfactory shape to a story?

Secondly, were there other patterns like this underlying stories, shaping them in quite different ways? After all, this cycle of self-destruction only describes a certain type of story, with an 'unhappy ending'. What about all those stories which have 'happy endings'? Were there any similar basic patterns underlying these too?

As soon as I began to look at stories in this light, a number of other possible basic plots began to suggest themselves. There were, for instance, all those stories about the overcoming of a 'monster', like *Jaws* or *Beowulf*, in which our interest centres on the threat posed by some monstrous figure of evil, who is then challenged by the hero and finally, after a climactic battle, killed. There were 'rags to riches' stories, like *The Ugly Duckling* or *Cinderella*, where our main interest lies in seeing some initially humble and disregarded little hero or heroine being raised up to a position of immense success and splendour. There were stories based on the theme of a great quest, like the *Odyssey* or *The Lord of the Rings*, where our interest centres on the hero's long, difficult journey towards some distant, enormously important goal.

I embarked on an almost indiscriminate course of reading and re-reading, through hundreds of stories of all kinds (soon recognising how little most of us actually remember in detail even about stories we think we know quite well). And it was not long before I began to make a startling discovery. Not only did it indeed seem to be true that there were a number of basic themes or plots which continually recurred in the storytelling of mankind, shaping tales of very different types and from almost every age and culture. Even more surprising was the degree of detail to which these 'basic plots' seemed to shape the stories they had inspired; so that one might find, for instance, a well-known nineteenth-century novel constructed in almost exactly the same way as a Middle Eastern folk tale dating from 1200 years before; or a popular modern children's story revealing remarkable hidden parallels with the structure of an epic poem composed in ancient Greece.

As one 'basic plot' after another emerged to view, each with its own particular structure, I eventually found myself with just one intractable pile of stories which did not seem to fit any of the patterns I had been looking at. I puzzled over them for some time. They seemed to be completely diverse: several were classic children's stories, like *Peter Rabbit*, *Peter Pan* and *Alice in Wonderland*; there were a long list of novels, from *Robinson Crusoe* to *Brideshead Revisited*; there were science fiction stories, like H. G. Wells's *The Time Machine*; there were films ranging from *The Third Man* and *The Wizard of Oz* to *Gone With The Wind*. Then the penny dropped that all these stories were in fact shaped by the same basic plot, one I had not even considered before (that which I have called 'Voyage and Return'). And at this point I found myself brought up against the possibility which is the basis of this book. Although I had long been familiar with that old teasing notion that there are only a handful of basic plots to stories, I had never taken it any more seriously than most people. I was now having to accept that, to a remarkable extent, it might actually be true.

Of course I could already see that the truth was by no means as simple as those lighthearted references to a limited number of basic stories might imply. Obviously it was not true that every story fits neatly and with mechanical regularity into one or another category of plot: otherwise we should all have noticed the fact long ago, and stories would scarcely be the endlessly varied and fascinating things that they are. There are extensive areas of overlap between one type of plot and another. Indeed, there are many stories which are shaped by more than one 'basic plot' at a time (there are even a very small number, including *The Lord of the Rings*, which include all seven of the plots which give this book its title). There are still other stories which are shaped only by part of such a plot. Again there are others, a great many, which show the story somehow 'going wrong', in terms of failing fully to realise the basic plot which lies behind it. As we shall see, the question of how and why stories can go wrong in this way, usually leaving us, the audience, with a dissatisfied sense that something has somewhere gone adrift, provides some of the most significant clues of all as to how stories work and what they are really about.

But the further my investigation proceeded, the more clearly two things emerged. The first was that there are indeed a small number of plots which are so fundamental to the way we tell stories that it is virtually impossible for any story-teller ever entirely to break away from them.

The second was that, the more familiar we become with the nature of these shaping forms and forces lying beneath the surface of stories, pushing them into patterns and directions which are beyond the storyteller's conscious control, the more we find that we are entering a realm to which recognition of the plots themselves proves only to have been the gateway. We are in fact uncovering nothing less than a kind of hidden, universal language: a nucleus of situations and figures which are the very stuff from which stories are made. And once we become acquainted with this symbolic language, and begin to catch something of its extraordinary significance, there is literally no story in the world which cannot then be seen in a new light: because we have come to the heart of what stories are about and why we tell them.

The perception that various basic themes and situations seem to recur through human storytelling is scarcely a new one. I shall end this introduction with a kind of technical note giving a brief background to how, over the past two centuries, a succession of writers, anthropologists, scholars and psychologists have approached this puzzle from many different angles, as they tried to explain why the same basic types of story should be found in the literature, folk tales and myths of different cultures all over the world.

Where this present book approaches storytelling in a quite different way from anything written on this subject before, however, is the extent to which it looks at all kinds of storytelling on the same level. We are not concerned here just with the well-known plays and novels of what is regarded as 'serious' literature. We shall be looking at every type of story imaginable: from the myths of ancient Mesopotamia and Greece to James Bond and *Star Wars*; from central European folk tales to *E.T.* and *Close Encounters of the Third Kind*; from P. G. Wodehouse to Proust; from the Marx Brothers to the Marquis de Sade and *The Texas Chainsaw Massacre*; from the Biblical story of Job to Orwell's *Nineteen Eighty-Four*; from the tragedies of Aeschylus to Sherlock Holmes; from the operas of Wagner to *The Sound of Music*; from Dante's Divine Comedy to *Four Weddings and a Funeral*. This is because, when we penetrate to the root of what our impulse to imagine stories is really about, we see there is in fact no kind of story, however serious or however trivial, which does not ultimately spring from the same source: which is not shaped by the same archetypal rules and spun from the same universal language.

To arrive at the point where all this can be finally seen in proper perspective, however, it is necessary to travel on a long and complex journey. And before we embark I should set out a brief route-map, so that it will become clear how the different stages of that exploration build on each other in working towards the eventual goal.

This book is divided into four parts.

Part one, 'The Seven Gateways To The Underworld', examines each of the seven 'basic plots' in turn. At first sight, each is quite distinctive. But as we work through the sequence, we gradually come to see how they have certain key elements in common; and how each is in fact presenting its own particular view of the same central preoccupation which lies at the heart of storytelling.

Part two, 'The Complete Happy Ending', looks more generally at what all these main story-types have in common. In particular we find that there are not only basic plots to stories but a cast of basic figures who reappear through stories of all kinds, each with their own defining characteristics. As we explore the values which each of these archetypal figures represents, and how they are related, this opens up an entirely new perspective on the essential drama with which storytelling is ultimately concerned. But we also come to see how there are certain conditions which must be met before any story can come to a fully resolved ending. This leads on in Part three to an investigation of one of the most revealing of all the factors which govern the way stories take shape in the human mind.

The third part of the book, 'Missing the Mark', which concentrates almost entirely on stories from the last 200 years, explores how and why it is possible, in a storyteller's imagination, for a story to 'go wrong'; or, as we say, 'lose the plot'. The first two parts of the book have been primarily concerned with those stories which express the archetypal patterns underlying them in a way which enables them to come to a fully resolved and satisfactory ending. In the third section of the book we see how, in the past two centuries, something extraordinary and highly significant has happened to storytelling in the western world. Not only do we look here at such an obvious question as why in recent times storytelling should have shown such a marked obsession with sex and violence. As we look at how each of the basic plots has developed what may be called its 'dark' and 'senti-mental' versions, we see how a particular element of disintegration has crept into modern storytelling which distinguishes it from anything seen in history before. But this in turn merely reveals one of the most remarkable features of how stories take shape in the human imagination; because we also see how those archetypal rules which have governed storytelling since the dawn of history have in no way changed. In fact these 'aberrant' stories not only obey the same rules; they even in themselves provide all the clues to understanding what has gone amiss, and why they cannot come to fully satisfactory endings. They thus show us just how and why in the collective psyche of our culture this element of disintegration should have arisen.

This third part of the book ends with a chapter on what are arguably the two most centrally puzzling stories produced by the Western imagination, Sophocles's *Oedipus Tyrannos* and Shakespeare's *Hamlet*. Only at this point have we at last completed the groundwork which is necessary to looking at the deepest questions of all. Just why in the course of our biological evolution has our species developed the capacity to create these patterns of images in our heads? What real purpose does it serve? And how do stories relate to what we call 'real life'?

These are the questions we look at in the fourth and final section of the book, 'Why We Tell Stories', which begins with two very significant types of story which we have not looked at before. This relates myths about the creation of the world and the 'fall from innocence' to the evolution of human consciousness and our relations with nature and instinct. In unravelling these riddles, what we see is how and why the hidden language of stories provides us with a picture of human nature and the inner dynamics of human behaviour which nothing else can present to us with such objective authority. We see how a proper understanding of why we tell stories sheds an extraordinary new light on almost every aspect of human existence: on our psychology; on morality; on the patterns of history and politics, and the nature of religion; on the underlying pattern and purpose of our individual lives.

The last two chapters, the longest in the book, attempt to use all we have learned about storytelling to reinterpret the psychological evolution of mankind since the dawn of civilisation. The first, 'Of Gods And Men', takes the story from the cave-paintings of Lascaux up to the French Revolution and the rise of Romanticism. The final chapter takes the story through the nineteenth and twentieth centuries up to the present day, ending with the film-version of *The Lord of the Rings* and the second Gulf War of 2003. The book then ends with a brief epilogue touching on one of the greatest stories ever written, Plato's *Parable of the Cave*.

By the time we have reached this point in exploring the real reasons why we tell stories, I hope I shall have conveyed something of why there can be few more important mysteries left for humanity to unravel on this earth.

## WHY DO SIMILAR STORIES APPEAR ALL OVER THE WORLD? A HISTORICAL NOTE ON PREVIOUS APPROACHES TO THIS QUESTION

The earliest instance which has come to light of an author observing that similar stories and situations may be found throughout literature appears in the late eighteenth century, in James Boswell's biography of Dr Samuel Johnson. In one of those poignant references to projects which Johnson talked of during his life but never got round to completing, a friend recalled to Boswell how the great man had once mentioned his intention to write a book showing (in the words quoted at the beginning of this Prologue):

> 'how small a quantity of REAL FICTION there is in the world; and that the same images, with very little variation, have served all the authors who have ever written.'

Dr Johnson was one of the best-read men of his age. He was familiar with virtually the whole of the surviving literature of classical times, not to mention most of the outstanding plays and novels written since the Renaissance (at least in English). It seems clear that his sharp and capacious mind had been so struck by the constant recurrence of certain images and situations in storytelling that he hoped one day to think about the matter more systematically. Alas, he leaves us with nothing more than this tantalising clue as to how far his observations might have taken him.

Another well-read near-contemporary of Johnson's whose thoughts seem to have turned in the same direction was Goethe (1749-1832), who several times in his *Conversations With Eckermann* touches on the same question: most notably in the remark often quoted since:

'Gozzi maintained that there can be but thirty-six dramatic situations; Schiller took great pains to find more, but was unable to find even as many as Gozzi.'[2]

Then, from quite another direction, in the second half of the nineteenth century, came the startling discovery by the growing army of anthropologists, ethnologists and students of folklore of the extent to which the same themes and *motifs* appeared through the myths and folktales of the entire world. It was not just that, as Sir James Frazer showed in *The Golden Bough* (1890), there were remarkable similarities in the central religious myths of different cultures, such as the idea of the god who dies and is reborn (as early as 1871 George Eliot's Mr Casaubon in *Middlemarch* had been engaged on 'a great work' to show that 'all the mythical systems or erratic mythical fragments in the world were corruptions of a tradition originally revealed': again, we are not given the slightest clue as to why Casaubon might have come to such a notion). The really startling thing was that the assiduous collectors of folktales were now coming across versions of the same basic story cropping up from places culturally and geographically so far apart that it no longer seemed possible that such stories could have sprung from just one original source. It was one thing for variants of, say, the 'Cinderella story' to be found all over Europe, from Serbia to the Shetlands, from Russia to Spain; at least all these countries did share some common cultural and linguistic traditions. But when the same story was found, in different guises, in China, in Africa and among the North American Indians, it was clear that its ubiquity could no longer be explained simply in terms of cultural contact, or of a common historical source, however archaic.

So where did the stories come from? One response of many of these late-nineteenth century writers was to suggest that somehow all these stories, myths and legends were simply attempts to explain and to dramatise natural phenomena, familiar to all mankind. One popular theory, particularly associated with the

---

2. Frustratingly, there is no reference to this in the extensive surviving correspondence between Schiller and Gozzi, the leading German and Italian playwrights of their day. At the beginning of the twentieth century George Polti was inspired by Goethe's reference to compile his own, somewhat laborious, survey, *The Thirty Six Dramatic Situations*. While he goes into elaborate detail about such *motifs* as 'Supplication of the Beloved By Those Dear to the Suppliant', Polti is not, however, concerned with actual plots so much as mere 'situations'; and only with 'tragic situations' at that.

philologist Friedrich Max Muller (1823–1900) was that stories of the god who dies and is reborn were 'solar myths', describing the setting and rising of the sun. It was suggested that the widespread folktales in which a heroine is eaten by a monster must have had something to do with the sun being 'eaten' by the moon in the course of an eclipse. Others held that the tales of 'dragons' and 'monsters' found all over the world originated in the discovery of dinosaur bones. But such theories were wholly inadequate to explain the astonishing universality, not just of the stories themselves, but often of the tiny details by which they were expressed – even though a more sophisticated version of these 'metaphors for nature' arguments has been advanced in more recent times by writers like the Canadian academic Northrop Frye, who attempted in his *Anatomy of Criticism* to relate the underlying forms of Tragedy and Comedy to the theme of 'death and resurrection' in the natural cycle of the year (Winter giving way to Spring, and so forth).

A second response, particularly popular among the experts on folklore themselves, has been to say in effect that there is simply no satisfactory, all-embracing explanation for the ubiquity of certain story-forms. Since Victorian times, the accumulation of parallels and links between the folk tales of hundreds of different cultures has turned into a major academic industry. Well over 1000 versions have been collected of the 'Cinderella story' alone. The 'literature', as scholars call it, now abounds in whole libraries-full of such items as 'Three Hundred and Forty Five Variants of Cinderalla, Catskin and Cap O'Rushes, abstracted and tabulated, with discussion of Mediaeval Analaogues and Notes'; or 'Tom-Tit-Tot: A Comparative Essay on Aarne-Thompson Type 500 – The Name of the Helper'; or 'A New Classification of the Fundamental Version of the Tar Baby Story on the basis of Two Hundred and Sixty Seven Versions'. Certainly the folklorists have established that the spreading of tales through cultural contact has been a far more complex process through history than might at first seem conceivable. Stories told to the Grimm brothers by German peasants in the early nineteenth century, for instance, have been traced back to Indian sources dating from well over a thousand years before, having entered Europe via trading routes or at the time of the Crusades, and been endlessly reworked by countless different storytellers in between. Stories collected in Africa and Asia in modern times as 'indigenous folk tales' have been traced back in turn to the Grimms, having been passed on by missionaries and dressed up in local clothing.

But one consequence of uncovering such complexities is that these busy collectors have been so overwhelmed by the Everest of material they have accumulated that they have finally despaired of finding any theory that actually might make sense of it all: that might discern a common ground in human psychology to account not just for the origin of the tales and their recurring features but also, just as important, for their continuing appeal through many generations to millions of outwardly quite different people, living in quite different cultural circumstances. In the words of Peter and Iona Opie:

> 'Happily such all-embracing theories are now regarded with scepticism. It is no longer felt that any one theory is likely to account satisfactorily for even the majority of the

tales. Their well-springs are certainly numerous ... their meanings – if ever they had meanings – are thought to be diverse. Each tale, it is now believed, should be studied separately.'[3]

The sigh of relief that one no longer has to think about such difficult matters is almost audible! However, the fundamental riddle remains.

A rather deeper approach to this whole problem in fact began to emerge more than a century ago when the German ethnologist Adolf Bastian (1826–1905) first put forward the theory that the human mind seems to be so constituted that it naturally works in certain forms or grooves, and round certain basic images. He accounted for the similarities he had discovered in the myths and folk tales of the primitive cultures he had studied by suggesting that such stories were based on what he called *elementargedenken* or 'elemental ideas', which somehow derive from the very nature of the human psyche, and which therefore all human beings have in common.

It was some years later that Sigmund Freud, in the 1890s, began to suggest that a great deal of human behaviour could be explained by the fact that enormous areas of our psychic activity lie in that part of the mind we call the unconscious, below the threshold of our conscious awareness. One of the most obvious ways in which we become aware of the existence of this is through our dreams, which spontaneously present to us sequences of pictures, like fragments of stories, without our being able to intervene consciously in controlling their contents in any way. And Freud was, of course, particularly struck by the parallels he observed between the contents of dreams and the themes of certain myths.

Perhaps in some way such myths were related to the very basis of the way we unconsciously perceive the world: to the inner patterns of our psychic development as individuals? Certainly the celebrated example of the 'Oedipal triangle', the perennial battle of the child to cope satisfactorily with the vast, overshadowing psychic presence of its parents, seemed to show a remarkable correspondence between an ancient myth and the experience of countless modern individuals whose problems seemed in large part to derive from this major hurdle on the road to establishing their own healthy, independent psychic identity. Perhaps all the other motifs of myth and folklore could be seen in the same Freudian light, as stories of 'rapacious mothers' (Hansel and Gretel), 'castration fears' (the sword which breaks) or the 'escape from the womb' (Jonah and the whale). After all, this was certainly relating stories to something universally experienced by mankind: our sexuality, our most fundamental human relationships, our memories of birth and fears of death. Over the past 100 years innumerable attempts have been made to interpret myths, folk tales and other stories in this way, from Ernest Jones's essay analysing Hamlet as another example of the Oedipal triangle to Dr Bruno Bettelheim's *The Uses of Enchantment* (1976) analysing the reasons for the appeal and value of the old fairy tales to the children of today.

3. Introduction to *The Classic Fairy Tales*, Peter and Iona Opie (Oxford University Press, 1974).

But still, as a comprehensive explanation of stories, such an approach seemed far from adequate: even in many instances grotesquely limited. However universal and important our relations with our parents or our sexuality may be, this surely was not the whole explanation of the complex structure of myths and tales all over the world, in all their myriad guises? Was there not a yet deeper level at which the meaning of these tales might be found: not necessarily one which rejected the Freudian explanation in its entirety, but one which transcended it, reflecting something much deeper and more universal altogether?

When I first came to this subject through my initial researches into the basic plots underlying stories, I discovered that in the previous 70 years yet another, much more fundamental, approach to myths and folk tales had been emerging which corresponded more closely to what I had begun to recognise as the real nature of stories. So much does my own approach lie in this tradition, and so much did it help me to understand all sorts of things about stories more clearly, that I will not even attempt to summarise it here, since it is implicit in much of the book which follows, and at certain points, where appropriate, I hope I shall make that debt explicit.

Suffice it to say that this tradition has in many ways built on that first perception by Bastian, over a century ago, that the human imagination seems to be so constituted that it naturally works round certain 'elemental' shapes and images; and on the further insight of Freud and others that, for an explanation of a great deal of what is most significant in human behaviour we must look into those parts of the psyche of which we cannot be directly aware, because they are below the threshold of our immediate consciousness. But whereas Freud became preoccupied with just a part of the picture, with sexuality and with the problems of the individual psyche, his Swiss colleague Carl Jung moved on to the much wider question of how, at a deeper level, we are all psychologically constructed in the same essential way. We all, at that deeper level, have the same psychological make-up, in much the same way as we are all genetically 'programmed' to grow physically: and it is only on, as it were, the more superficial levels of our psyche that our individuality emerges, and that each of us finds our own individual problems in coping with the 'programme' of development that our deeper unconscious has laid down for us.

If we are looking for an explanation of why certain images, symbols and shaping forms recur in stories to an extent far greater than can be accounted for just by cultural transmission, we must look first to those deeper levels of the unconscious which we all have in common, as part of our basic genetic inheritance. These work around what Jung called 'archetypes': 'the ancient river beds along which our psychic current naturally flows'; and it is only on this level of the archetypal structures that the basic meaning and purpose of the patterns underlying storytelling can be found.

Jung himself, of course, wrote much about myths and folk tales, as have many of his followers, such as Marie-Louise von Franz. Another author generally in the same tradition was the American Joseph Campbell who attempted in *The Hero With a Thousand Faces* and *The Masks of God* to relate an enormous amount of such storytelling to what he called 'the monomyth', a kind of universal story of which indvidual myths and tales merely present different aspects. Other authors have extended this kind of general approach to take in some of the better-known literary works of our culture, as did Northrop Frye in his *Anatomy of Criticism* and Leslie Fiedler in *Love and Death In The American Novel*, cited in the pages which follow. And I cannot conclude this brief summary of writers whose work I found illuminating without referring to an author much less well-known than any of these, John Vyvyan, whose little book *The Shakespearean Ethic* was not only an attempt to extend this kind of analysis to some of Shakespeare's plays, but is also the most original book about Shakespeare I have ever read.

The crucial point of departure, however, widening out these approaches in a way which allows us at last to see the activity of telling stories from a wholly new perspective, is the recognition that all kinds of story, however profound or however trivial, ultimately spring from the same source, are shaped around the same basic patterns and are governed by the same hidden, universal rules.

At this point our journey can begin.

# PART ONE

## The Seven Gateways to the Underworld

'When first we mean to build,
We first survey the plot, then draw the model.'
*Henry IV Pt.2*, I.iii

# Prologue to Part One

Imagine we are about to be plunged into a story – any story in the world. A curtain rises on a stage. A cinema darkens. We turn to the first paragraph of a novel. A narrator utters the age-old formula 'Once upon a time…'

On the face of it, so limitless is the human imagination and so boundless the realm at the storyteller's command, we might think that literally anything could happen next.

But in fact there are certain things we can be pretty sure we know about our story even before it begins.

For a start, it is likely that the story will have a hero, or a heroine, or both: a central figure, or figures, on whose fate our interest in the story ultimately rests; someone with whom, as we say, we can identify.

We are introduced to our hero or heroine in an imaginary world. Briefly or at length, the general scene is set. The purpose of the formula 'Once upon a time…', whether the storyteller uses it explicitly or not, is to take us out of our present place and time into that imaginary realm where the story is to unfold, and to introduce us to the central figure with whom we are to identify.

Then something happens: some event or encounter which precipitates the story's action, giving it a focus. In fact the opening of the story is governed by a kind of double formula: 'once upon a time there was such and such a person, living in such and such place… then, one day, something happened'.

We are introduced to a little boy called Aladdin, who lives in a city in China… then one day a Sorcerer arrives, and leads him out of the city to a mysterious underground cave. We meet a Scottish general, Macbeth, who has just won a great victory over his country's enemies… then, on his way home, he encounters the mysterious witches. We meet a girl called Alice, wondering how to amuse herself in the summer heat… then suddenly she sees a White Rabbit running past, and vanishing down a mysterious hole. We see the great detective Sherlock Holmes sitting in his Baker Street lodgings… then there is a knock at the door, and a visitor enters to present him with his next case.

This event or summons provides the 'Call' which will lead the hero or heroine out of their initial state into a series of adventures or experiences which, to a greater or lesser extent, will transform their lives.

The next thing of which we can be sure is that the action which the hero or heroine are being drawn into will involve conflict and uncertainty, because without some measure of both there cannot be a story. Where there is a hero there may also be a villain (on some occasions, indeed, the hero himself may be the villain). But even if the characters in the story are not necessarily contrasted in such black-and-white terms as 'goodies' and 'baddies', it is likely that some will be on the side of the hero or heroine, as friends and allies, while others will be out to oppose them.

Finally we shall sense that the impetus of the story is carrying it towards some kind of resolution. Every story which is complete, and not just a fragmentary string of episodes and impressions, must work up to a climax, where conflict and uncertainty are usually at their most extreme. This then leads to a resolution of all that has gone before, bringing the story to its ending. And here we see how every story, however mildly or emphatically, has in fact been leading its central figure or figures in one of two directions. Either they end, as we say, happily, with a sense of liberation, fulfilment and completion. Or they end unhappily, in some form of discomfiture, frustration or death.

To say that stories either have happy or unhappy endings may seem such a commonplace that one almost hesitates to utter it. But it has to be said, simply because it is the most important single thing to be observed about stories. Around that one fact, and around what is necessary to bring a story to one type of ending or the other, revolves the whole of their extraordinary significance in our lives.

One of the few general texts ever to have been written on stories was Aristotle's *Poetics*, left unfinished well over 2000 years ago, It was Aristotle who first observed that a satisfactory story – a story which, as he put it, is a 'whole' – must have 'a beginning, a middle and an end'. And it was Aristotle who, in the context of the two main types of stage play, first explicitly drew attention to the two kinds of ending a story may lead up to.

On the one hand, as he put it in the *Poetics*, there are tragic stories. These are stories in which the hero or heroine's fortunes usually begin by rising, but eventually 'turn down' to disaster (the Greek word *catastrophe* means literally a 'down stroke', the downturn in the hero's fortunes at the end of a tragedy). On the other hand, there are, in the broadest sense, comedies: stories in which things initially seem to become more and more complicated for the hero or heroine, until they are entangled in a complete knot, from which there seems no escape. But eventually comes what Aristotle calls the *peripeteia* or 'reversal of fortune'. The knot is miraculously unravelled (from which we get the French word *denouement*, meaning literally an 'unknotting'). Hero, heroine or both together are liberated; and we and all the world can rejoice.

This division holds good over a much greater range of stories than might be implied just by the terms 'tragedy' and 'comedy'. Indeed, with qualifications, it remains true right across the domain of storytelling. The plot of a story is that which leads its hero or heroine either to a 'catastrophe' or an 'unknotting'; either to frustration or to liberation; either to death or to a renewal of life. And it might be thought that there are almost as many ways of describing these downward and upward paths as there are individual stories in the world. Yet the more carefully we look at the vast range of stories thrown up by the human imagination through the ages, the more clearly we may discern that there are certain continually recurring general shapes to stories, dictating the nature of the road which the hero or heroine may take to their ultimate destination.

It is at the most important of these underlying shapes or 'basic plots' that we must now look.

*Chapter 1*

# Overcoming the Monster

'Legends of the slaughter of a destructive monster are to be found all over the world. The thought underlying them all is that the monster slain is preternatural and hostile to mankind.'

E. S. Hartland, *The Legend of Perseus* (1896)

In 1839 a young Englishman, Henry Austen Layard, set out to travel overland to Ceylon, the island now known as Sri Lanka. Halfway through his journey, when he was crossing the wild desert region then known as Mesopotamia, his curiosity was aroused by a series of mysterious mounds in the sand. He paused to investigate them, and thus began one of the most important investigations in the history of archaeology. For what Layard had stumbled on turned out to be the remains of one of the earliest cities ever built by humankind, biblical Niniveh.

Over the decades which followed, many fascinating discoveries were made at Niniveh, but none more so than a mass of clay tablets which came to light in 1853, covered in small wedge-shaped marks which were obviously some unknown form of writing. The task of deciphering this 'cuneiform' script was to take the best part of the next 20 years. But when in 1872 George Smith of the British Museum finally unveiled the results of his labours, the Victorian public was electrified. One sequence of the tablets contained fragments of a long epic poem, Dating back to the dawn of civilisation, it was by far the earliest written story in the world.

The first part of the Sumerian *Epic of Gilgamesh*, as we now know it, tells of how the kingdom of Uruk has fallen under the terrible shadow of a great and mysterious evil. The source of the threat is traced to a monstrous figure, Humbaba, who lives half across the world, in an underground cavern at the heart of a remote forest. The hero, Gilgamesh, goes to the armourers who equip him with special weapons, a great bow and a mighty axe. He sets out on a long, hazardous journey to Humbaba's distant lair, where he finally comes face to face with the monster. They enjoy a series of taunting exchanges, then embark on a titanic struggle. Against such supernatural powers, it seems Gilgamesh cannot possibly win. But finally, by a superhuman feat, he manages to kill his monstrous opponent. The shadowy threat has been lifted. Gilgamesh has saved his kingdom and can return home triumphant.

In the autumn of 1962, nearly 5000 years after the story of Gilgamesh was placed in the library at Niniveh, a period encompassing almost the whole of recorded human history, a fashionable crowd converged on Leicester Square in London for the premiere of a new film. *Dr No* was the first of what was to become, over the next 40 years, the most popular series of films ever made (even by 1980 it was estimated that one or more of the screen adventures of James Bond had been seen by some 2 billion people, then nearly half the earth's population). With their quintessentially late-twentieth century mixture of space-age gadgetry, violence and sex, anything more remote from the primitive world of those inhabitants of the first cities who conceived the religious myth of Gilgamesh might seem hard to imagine.

Yet consider the story which launched the series of Bond films that night in 1962. The Western world falls under the shadow of a great and mysterious evil. The source of the threat is traced to a monstrous figure, the mad and deformed scientist Dr No, who lives half across the world in an underground cavern on a remote island. The hero James Bond goes to the armourer who equips him with special weapons. He sets out on a long, hazardous journey to Dr No's distant lair, where he finally comes face to face with the monster. They enjoy a series of taunting exchanges, then embark on a titanic struggle. Against such near-supernatural powers, it seems Bond cannot possibly win. But finally, by a superhuman feat, he manages to kill his monstrous opponent. The shadowy threat has been lifted. The Western world has been saved. Bond can return home triumphant.

Any story which can make such a leap across the whole of recorded human history must have some profound symbolic significance in the inner life of mankind. Certainly this is true of our first type of story, the plot which may be called 'Overcoming the Monster'.

The realm of storytelling contains nothing stranger or more spectacular than this terrifying, life-threatening, seemingly all-powerful monster whom the hero must confront in a fight to the death.

We first usually encounter these extraordinary creations early in our lives, in the guises of the wolves, witches and giants of fairy tales. Little Red Riding Hood goes off into the great forest to visit her kindly grandmother, only to find that granny has been replaced by the wicked wolf, whose only desire is to eat Red Riding Hood. In the nick of time, a brave forester bursts in to kill the wolf with his axe, and the little heroine is saved. Hansel and Gretel are cruelly abandoned to die in the forest, where they meet the apparently kindly old woman who lives in a house made of gingerbread. But she turns out to be a wicked witch, whose only wish is to devour them. Just when all seems lost, they manage to push her into her own oven and burn her to death, finding, as their reward, a great treasure with which they can triumphantly return home. Jack climbs his magic beanstalk to discover at the top a new world, where he enters a mysterious castle belonging to a terrifying and bloodthirsty giant. After progressively enraging this monstrous figure by three successive visits, each time managing to steal a golden treasure, Jack finally arouses the giant to what seems like a fatal pursuit. Only in the nick of time does Jack manage to scramble down the beanstalk, and bring it crashing down with an axe. The giant falls dead to the ground, and Jack is left to enjoy the three priceless treasures he has won from its grasp.

The essence of the 'Overcoming the Monster' story is simple. Both we and the hero are made aware of the existence of some superhuman embodiment of evil power. This monster may take human form (e.g., a giant or a witch); the form of an animal (a wolf, a dragon, a shark); or a combination of both (the Minotaur, the Sphinx). It is always deadly, threatening destruction to those who cross its path or fall into its clutches. Often it is threatening an entire community or kingdom, even mankind and the world in general. But the monster often also has in its clutches some great prize, a priceless treasure or a beautiful 'Princess'.

So powerful is the presence of this figure, so great the sense of threat which emanates from it, that the only thing which matters to us as we follow the story is that it should be killed and its dark power overthrown. Eventually the hero must confront the monster, often armed with some kind of 'magic weapons', and usually in or near its lair, which is likely to be in a cave, a forest, a castle, a lake, the sea, or some other deep and enclosed place. Battle is joined and it seems that, against such terrifying odds, the hero cannot possibly win. Indeed there is a moment when his destruction seems all but inevitable. But at the last moment, as the story reaches its climax, there is a dramatic reversal. The hero makes a 'thrilling escape from death' and the monster is slain. The hero's reward is beyond price. He wins the treasure, or the hand of the 'Princess'. He has liberated the world – community, kingdom, the human race – from the shadow of this threat to its survival. And in honour of his achievement, he may well go on to become some kind of ruler or king.

There have been few cultures in the world which have not produced some version of the Overcoming The Monster story. But a civilisation we particularly associate with such stories is that of the ancient Greeks, whose mythology was swarming with monsters of every kind, from the original Titans overcome by Zeus or the one-eyed giant Polyphemus blinded by Odysseus to the mighty Python strangled by Apollo or the riddle-posing Sphinx who threw herself over the cliff when Oedipus proved to be the first man who could correctly answer her riddle (for which he was chosen to be king over Thebes).

One of the most celebrated of the Greek monster-slaying heroes was Perseus, who had to overcome not one monster but two, one female, one male. When, as a young boy, he is cast adrift in the world with his beautiful mother, the Princess Danae, the two fall under the shadow of the cruel tyrant Acrisius, who demands that Danae should succumb to his advances. In a desperate bid to save his mother from this fate, young Perseus offers to perform any task the tyrant should set him. The cruel Acrisius therefore sends the boy off to the end of the world to obtain the head of the dreadful Gorgon Medusa, the mere sight of whose face is sufficient to turn a man to stone. Perseus is equipped by the gods with magic weapons, a pair of winged sandals, enabling him to fly, a 'helmet of invisibility' and a brilliantly polished shield, in which he will be able to see the Medusa's reflection without having to look at her directly. 'By remote and pathless ways', as Ovid put it, Perseus reaches the Gorgons' lair at the Western edge of the world, and severs the Medusa's snake-covered head. It might seem that he has triumphantly concluded the task that has been set him; but we now learn that this was merely the essential preparation for a further immense task which awaits him on his journey home. As he flies back with his prize, he looks down to see a beautiful, weeping Princess, Andromeda, chained to a rock by the sea. She has been placed there as tribute to appease a fearsome sea-monster, which has been sent by Poseidon to ravage her father's kingdom. Perseus sees the huge reptile rising out of the deeps to seize Andromeda and swoops down to engage it in battle. He is able to use the trophy of his first victory, the head of Medusa, to turn the monster to stone. He is rewarded with the hand of the Princess, for liberating her father's kingdom from this awful threat. He returns home, where he uses the Medusa's head to turn the tyrant Acrisius to stone, and eventually goes on to become king of Argos.

Another celebrated monster-slayer was Theseus, who also grows up alone in the world with his mother. On coming of age he goes to rejoin his father, King Aegeus in Athens, having to kill a series of monsters and villains on the way. But when he arrives he finds his father's kingdom under a terrible shadow, cast by a rival kingdom across the sea in Crete, ruled over by the grim tyrant King Minos. Every ninth year the Athenians must pay a tribute to the tyrant, by sending the flower of their city's youth to feed the frightful monster the Minotaur, half-bull, half-man (another creation of Poseidon), which lives at the heart of the mighty Labyrinth, a dark, enclosed stone maze from which no one has ever found a way out. Theseus volunteers to lead the party of young men and maidens who are to be sacrificed to this creature; and on arriving in Crete he wins the love and support of the tyrant's daughter Ariadne, who secretly supplies him with the 'magic aids', a sword and a skein of thread, he needs to win victory. Finding his way to the centre of the Labyrinth, unravelling the thread, he confronts the Minotaur and kills it. Ariadne's thread enables him to retrace his way back through the maze of tunnels to the open air. It is true that, when they then flee together back to Athens, Theseus abandons his Princess on the island of Naxos. And as he comes within sight of the mainland, and forgets to hoist a white rather than a black sail to show his father that he has returned victorious, King Aegeus throws himself in grief into the sea which ever afterwards bore his name. But this also means that, like many another monster-slaying hero, Theseus succeeds to the kingdom, becoming the greatest ruler Athens ever had. He also eventually marries the Princess, by making Ariadne's sister Phaedra his queen.

Compared with the array of loathsome and supernatural monsters in Greek mythology (not forgetting the succession of horrors, like the many-headed Hydra, overcome by Heracles in the course of his twelve labours), the villain of the most familiar Overcoming the Monster story in Jewish legend might seem almost domesticated. But when the Philistine army invaded the kingdom of Saul, nothing could have seemed more terrifying to the children of Israel than the Philistines' towering, seemingly invincible champion, the boastful giant Goliath. When an obscure little shepherd-boy David stepped forward to challenge the giant, first his own brothers, then the Israelite army as a whole could not have been more scornful – until they saw the deadly aim with which he cast his 'magic' slingstones into the giant's forehead, sending the great figure toppling lifeless to the ground. And a detail of the story which might be overlooked is what happens to David after his victory. For being the saviour of his country, he is given the hand in marriage of King Saul's daughter, the Princess Michal; and eventually the young giant-slayer succeeds Saul to become his country's greatest king.

The hero's immediate reward for slaying the monster may not always be the winning of a 'Princess' and succession to a kingdom: but in some form or another these are rarely very far away.

Another notable constellation of monster-tales, for instance, were those which loomed up in the imaginations of the inhabitants of northern Europe, amid the mists and darkness of the first millennium of the Christian era. The world has rarely seen such a parade of giants, dragons, trolls, treacherous dwarves, foul fiends and 'loathly worms' as infested the Norse sagas and Germanic and Celtic epics of these times. And here the hero's immediate reward for slaying the monster was likely to be a fabulous treasure. One such tale, later to achieve wider currency from its adaptation by Wagner, was the episode in the *Volsunga Saga* which tells of how the young hero Sigurd, with the aid of his 'magic weapon', the great sword Gram, slays the horrible monster Fafnir, who sits in the middle of a wilderness brooding over a great treasure, which includes access to all sorts of runic knowledge, such as an understanding of the song of the birds. But he then goes on to discover 'the beauteous battle-maiden' Brynhild, lying asleep on a mountain top, guarded by a ring of magic flames which only 'the true hero' can enter; and it is the treasures and the secret knowledge he has won from his victory over Fafnir which enable him to waken her and win her love.

Another celebrated Overcoming the Monster story from the Dark Ages is that of Beowulf. Again we begin with the familiar image of a kingdom which has fallen under a terrible shadow: the little community of Heorot which is nightly menaced by the predatory assaults of the mysterious monster Grendel. The young hero Beowulf comes from across the sea and eventually, in a great nocturnal battle, deals the monster a mortal wound: only to discover, when he tracks the trail of Grendel's blood, that he must confront the monster's even more terrible mother, in the lair at the bottom of a deep lake where she is brooding over the body of her dead son. Although Beowulf's immediate reward for his victory over the two monsters is a rich hoard of 'ancient treasures and twisted gold' from the grateful king whose kingdom he has saved, he then returns home to become king over his own kingdom (many years later, at the end of his life, he has to confront a third monster, in a profoundly symbolic episode which we shall look at much later in the book).

Of the many Overcoming the Monster stories thrown up by Christian Europe in the Middle Ages, probably the most familiar is that of St George and the Dragon, which appears to be a Christian adaptation of the Perseus myth.[1] The

---

1. The story of St George and the Dragon first appears in the *Legenda Aurea*, the Golden Legend, of Jacobus de Voragine in the thirteenth century. A clear indication that it is derived from the Perseus myth is that it specifically places the battle with the dragon at much the same place on the coast of Palestine which in classical times had been associated with Perseus's freeing of Andromeda.

hero comes to a kingdom which is being ravaged by a dragon and, like Perseus, finds a beautiful Princess tethered by the edge of the sea, where she has been placed by her countrymen in a last desperate bid to buy off the monster's attacks. The monster approaches and George slays him; but, unlike Perseus, George is not then able to marry the Princess he has freed. Since this is rather self-consciously a 'Christian' version of the tale, his reward is simply to insist that all the inhabitants of the country should be baptised: in other words, that they should all succeed to another 'kingdom', the kingdom of Christ.[2]

During the centuries of diminishing faith in the supernatural which followed the Middle Ages and the Renaissance, the more obviously fantastic dragons and monsters of old slipped below the horizon of European storytelling (although they never faded away altogether). But then, in a way which to the rationalistic age of the Enlightenment or even through most of the literal, materialistic Victorian era would have seemed wholly improbable, fabulous and terrifying 'monsters' came back into vogue in a quite remarkable fashion.

It all happened quite suddenly, in the closing years of the nineteenth century. Over the previous 100 years there had been a number of premonitory signs, notably in the taste for 'Gothic horror' which had been such an important reflection of the rise of the Romantic movement, with stories such as *The Castle of Otranto* (1764) and Mary Shelley's *Frankenstein* (1817). But in the space of just a few years in the 1890s, there appeared in England a rash of stories of the kind which have played such a dominant part in popular entertainment ever since – ghost stories, tales of horror, science fiction – in which monsters of the most grotesque and improbable variety once again surged to the forefront of Western popular storytelling.

In 1894 a young Cambridge don, M. R. James, wrote a story called *Canon Alberic's Scrap Book*. Tales of ghosts and hauntings have been told since time immemorial, but with the first of his series of ghost stories James raised the form

---

2. Another mediaeval version of the Overcoming the Monster story we may note, because it introduces a rather more significant variation on the basic plot, is the fable of St Francis and the Wolf of Gubbio. The townsfolk of Gubbio were terrified by the ravages of an abnormally powerful, man-eating wolf, which lived in the forest outside the town. St Francis arrives to save them and ventures out alone to confront the wolf. Instead of killing it, he merely speaks to it, gently but firmly, in such a way that the wolf is tamed. It is no longer a 'monster' but becomes a friend to the people of Gubbio, who feed it on its regular visits to the town. Another example of the same variation is the story of Androcles (made the basis for Shaw's play *Androcles and the Lion*), who in the desert shows love to a fierce lion by pulling out a thorn from its paw. The resolution of the story comes years later when Androcles, as a Christian, has been thrown to the lions in Rome. When one approaches to eat him, it turns out of course to be the same lion to which he previously showed kindness and his life is saved. This form of the story which shows the true hero able to change the life-threatening monster's nature by a combination of courage and love is found not only in the Christian tradition but elsewhere in the world. A well-known Indian version is one of the legends associated with Buddha. This tells how 'Prince Five-Weapons' (an early incarnation of the Buddha) confronts, subdues and finally converts the fearful ogre Sticky-Hair. But this type of story really belongs to a later stage of the book (see Chapter 11, 'Rebirth') where we look at tales which show the monster going through a 'change of heart'.

onto a new plane of horror. In a 'decaying town' in the Pyrenees, an English scholar, Denniston, finds a folio of old mauscripts which belonged to a Canon of the local cathedral who had died in mysterious circumstances 200 years before. One drawing in particular catches his attention – a group of horrified soldiers at the court of King Solomon, surrounding a strange, shapeless creature. Late that evening, while he is examining the drawing in his lodgings, Denniston suddenly becomes aware of a terrible presence in the room:

> 'He flew out of his chair with deadly, inconceivable terror clutching at his heart. The shape ... was rising to a standing posture behind his seat ... coarse hair covered it, as in the drawing. The lower jaw was thin – what can I call it? – shallow, like a beast's; teeth showed behind the black lips; there was no nose; the eyes, of a fiery yellow, against which the pupils showed, black and intense, and the exulting hate and thirst to destroy life which shone there, were the two most horrifying features in the whole vision.'

Denniston grabs at a crucifix, as at a 'magic weapon': two servants rush in, and feel 'something' passing them out of the room. Denniston destroys the drawing; the 'monster' is overcome and appears no more.

Three years later, in 1897, an Anglo-Irish former civil servant, Bram Stoker, published *Dracula*. Again, stories of blood-drinking vampires had been told at various times before in history but Stoker's version was conceived on a new plane of horror. The story divided into two parts. In the first, the hero, a young English lawyer named Harker, makes a visit to a mysterious, ruined castle deep in the wolf-infested forests of Transylvania. There is an air of indescribable evil, both about the place and about his client, Count Dracula, a man with sharp, protruding teeth and unnaturally red lips. What follows makes any 'Gothic horrors' of a century before seem trivial. Harker discovers that he is trapped by a man who can crawl face downwards on the castle wall by moonlight; whom he finds one day lying as if dead, 'bloated' with blood, 'like a filthy leech, exhausted with his repletion'; who seems to be in command of a whole army of equally horrible supernatural spirits.

Just how the hero escapes from seemingly certain doom is never made clear, but the second part of the story tells of how Dracula 'invades' England, and in particular the battle by Harker and a group of friends to prevent the monster taking over two young girls, one of them Harker's intended wife Mina, to recruit them into his shadowy army of the living dead. The first of them, Mina's friend Lucy, falls fatally into Dracula's power:

> 'Far down the avenue of yews we saw a white figure advance ... Lucy Westenra, but yet how changed. The sweetness was changed to adamantine, heartless cruelty, and the purity to voluptuous wantonness ... (her) lips were crimson with fresh blood ... (her) eyes unclean and full of hell-fire.'

Having destroyed one 'Princess', Dracula then turns his nocturnal attacks on the other, the hero's fiancée Mina. Gradually we see her sinking away into the monster's deadly power. Harker and his friends eventually hunt Dracula down and pursue him back to his Transylvanian lair where, just in the nick of time before

Mina finally expires, they manage to operate their 'magic weapon' by plunging a stake into the monster's heart (the only way a vampire can be killed):

'Before our very eyes, and almost in the drawing of a breath, the whole body crumbled into dust and passed from our sight.'

Mina – and mankind – are saved!

In 1898, the year after *Dracula*, H. G. Wells published *The War of the Worlds*. Again, it was by no means the first science fiction story, but the comparatively cosy fantasies of Jules Verne had contained nothing like this. Puffs of fire are seen on Mars, huge meteorites flash across the sky, and some come to earth in southern England. The initial mood of excited curiosity changes to alarm, when it appears that these mysterious, half-buried cylinders contain life:

'As it bulged up and caught the light, it glistened like wet leather. The large, dark-coloured eyes were regarding us steadfastly. It was rounded, and had, one might say, a face. There was a mouth under the eyes, the brim of which quivered and panted and dropped saliva, The body heaved and pulsated convulsively. A lank, tentacular appendage gripped the edge of the cylinder, another waved in the air.'

The nightmarish realisation dawns that these huge 'fungoid' monsters climbing out of the cylinders are implacably hostile. They assemble great 'tripod machines' which stride across the countryside, armed with 'Heat Rays' and the deadly 'Black Smoke', against which mankind has seemingly no defence. Southern England is laid waste, as towns and cities burn, corpses pile up and the countryside is gradually submerged beneath the horrible 'Red Weed'. Can the world survive?

Then, as the hero cowers in a cellar in south London, all alone and imagining his wife to be dead, he hears floating across the deserted, half-ruined city a ghastly, wailing cry, 'Ulla, ulla, ulla'. He cautiously picks his way up to Primrose Hill, where he sees the great machines standing silent, the dead Martians hanging out of them as strips of decaying meat. The invading monsters have fallen prey to humble earthly bacteria, the one thing against which they had no defence. Mankind is saved; and the story ends on the image of the hero being joyfully reunited with his wife who turns out, like him, to have miraculously survived.

I have highlighted this little group of stories dating from the closing years of the nineteenth century in some detail because they represent one of the most remarkable developments in the entire history of stories: the sudden onset of that fascination with monsters of a near-supernatural power which was to become such a conspicuous feature of twentieth-century popular storytelling. In the latter-day Draculas, bug-eyed 'extra-terrestrials', triffids and other shapeless creature of the night which have swarmed in such numbers across the cinema screens and through the fantasy life of our time, we may see almost everything which characterised the most lurid monster-tales of the distant past. Since Perseus and Andromeda, for instance, has there been any more vivid image of the 'Princess' struggling in the clutches of the monster than the famous shot in the film *King Kong* showing the pretty young heroine being waved above the sky-line of New York in the grip of the gigantic ape?

What is certain is that it is by no means necessary to believe in the physical reality of such monsters for them to loom up, as it were unbidden, in the mysterious processes of the imagination which lie behind the creation of stories. Indeed, so fundamental is this phenomenon to an understanding of how stories work, that we must now look at it more closely.

## Chapter 2

# The Monster (II) and the Thrilling Escape From Death

'MONSTER ... something extraordinary or unnatural ... an animal deviating in one or more of its parts from the normal ... an imaginary animal having a form either partly brute and partly human, or compounded from elements from two or more animal forms ... a person of inhuman and horrible cruelty or wickedness.'  *Oxford English Dictionary*

What is this monster which, since time immemorial, has so haunted the imagination and fantasies of mankind? As we shall see, it is a question of deepest importance to the understanding of stories, relevant to tales of many kinds other than just those centred on the plot we have been discussing.

The question may be put in the singular – speaking of one 'monster' rather than many – if only because the essential characteristics of this creature are so unvarying, regardless of the variety of outward guises in which he (or she) appears.

For a start, throughout the world's storytelling, we find the monster being described in strikingly similar language. It tends, of course, to be highly alarming in its appearance and behaviour. It may be:

horrible, terrible, grim, mis-shapen, hate-filled, ruthless, menacing, terrifying.

As goes without saying, it is mortally dangerous:

deadly, bloodthirsty, ravening, murderous, venomous, poisonous.

It is a deeply deceitful and tricky opponent to deal with:

cunning, treacherous, vicious, twisted, slippery, depraved, vile.

There is also often something about its nature which is mysterious and hard to define. It may be:

strange, shapeless, sinister, weird, nightmarish, ghastly, hellish, fiendish, demonic, dark.

In other words, in its oddly elusive way, we see this 'night creature', whether it is a giant or a witch, a dragon or a devil, a ghost or a Martian, representing (often vested in a kind of dark, supernatural aura) everything which seems most inimical, threatening and dangerous in human nature, when this is turned against ourselves.

Then there are the monster's physical attributes. And here we must not be misled by the fact the monster is so often represented as an animal, or even a composite of several animals: e.g., the imaginary dragon, which we can only conceive of as made up from the organs of existing animals, such as a reptilian body, a bat's wings and the head of a giant toad or lizard. Such monsters may be animal in form, but they are invariably invested with attributes no animal in nature would possess, such as a peculiar cunning or malevolence. They are in fact preternatural, having qualities which are at least partly human.

Again, of course, there are many monsters in stories which are human, but invested with animal attributes: either directly, like the Minotaur, half-man, half-bull; or, more often, just in the way they are described (e.g., the comparisons of Dracula to a 'leech' and a 'bat'). In other words, they are seen as less than wholly human. And even when monsters are shown as entirely human in appearance, they tend to be in some way physically abnormal: abnormally large (giants), abnormally small (dwarves) or in some way deformed (e.g., missing an eye or a limb, or hunchbacked).

In short, whether it is animal, human or a mixture of both (or even, like John Wyndham's triffids, an intelligent plant), the monster will always have some human characteristics, but will never be represented as wholly human. By definition, the one thing the monster in stories can never be is an ideal, perfect, whole human being.

Then there are the monster's behavioural attributes. We invariably see it acting in one of three roles:

1. In its first 'active' role, the monster is Predator. It wanders menacingly or treacherously through the world, seeking to force or to trick people into its power. It may have a lair which it sallies out from, but primarily in this role it is looking for victims. It 'walketh about seeking whom it may devour', spreading fear and destruction, and casting a shadow wherever its influence is felt.
2. The monster's second, more 'passive' role is as Holdfast. It sits in or near its lair, usually jealously guarding the 'treasure' or the 'Princess' it has won into its clutches. It is in this role a keeper and a hoarder, broody, suspicious, threatening destruction to all who come near.
3. When its guardianship is in any way challenged, the monster enters its third role as Avenger. It lashes out viciously, stirring from its lair, bent on pursuit and revenge.

In fact we may often see the same monster acting out all three roles at different stages of the same story. In Jack and the Beanstalk, for instance, we first see the giant as Predator, prowling about, demanding human food. We next see him as Holdfast, brooding in miserly fashion over his treasures. We finally see him, when Jack steals the treasures, running angrily in pursuit, as Avenger. And the point about these three roles is that they represent all the main aspects of the way human beings behave when acting in an entirely self-seeking fashion. When people are at odds with the world, behaving selfishly or anti-socially, they are either 'after something', as Predators; wanting grimly to 'hold onto something', as Holdfasts; or, as Avengers, resentfully trying 'to get their own back'.

One may sum up by saying that, physically, morally and psychologically, the monster in storytelling thus represents everything in human nature which is somehow twisted and less than perfect. *Above all, and it is the supreme characteristic of every monster who has ever been portrayed in a story, he or she is egocentric.* The monster is heartless; totally unable to feel for others, although this may sometimes be disguised beneath a deceptively charming, kindly or solicitous exterior; its only real concern is to look after its own interests, at the expense of everyone else in the world.

Such is the nature of the figure against whom the hero is pitted, in a battle to the death. And we never have any doubt as to why the hero stands in opposition to such a centre of dark and destructive power: because the hero's own motivation and qualities are presented as so completely in contrast to those ascribed to the monster. We see the hero being drawn into the struggle not just on his own behalf but to save others: to save all those who are suffering in the monster's shadow; to free the community or the kingdom the monster is threatening; to liberate the 'Princess' it has imprisoned. The hero is always shown as acting selflessly and in some higher cause, in a way which shows him standing at the opposite pole to the monster's egocentricity.

And even though the monster wields such terrifying power that, almost to the end, its dark presence is the dominant factor holding sway over the world described by the story, it has one weakness which ultimately renders it vulnerable. Despite its cunning, its awareness of the reality of the world around it is in some important respect limited. Seeing the world through tunnel vision, shaped by its egocentric desires, there is always something which the monster cannot see and is likely to overlook. That is why, by the true hero, the monster can always in the end be outwitted: as was the mighty Goliath by little David, who was able to stay out of reach of the giant's strength by using his little slingstones; as was the Medusa by Perseus with his reflecting shield, which meant he did not have to look at her directly; as was Minos by his own daughter secretly presenting Theseus with the sword and thread; as were Wells's Martians by their overlooking even something as apparently insignificant as the destructive power of bacteria. It is this fatal flaw in the monster's awareness which is ultimately its undoing. Despite its power, the monster is shown not only as heartless and egocentric. It is also, in some crucial respect which turns the day, blind.

This shadowy figure is of the greatest significance in stories, not just because of the more obvious and lurid appearances it makes in myths, folk tales, horror stories and science fiction, but because to a greater or lesser extent these characteristics describe the dark, negative and villainous characters who appear in stories of almost every kind.

Indeed, once we have identified the monster's essential attributes, we can see how there are a great many types of story shaped by the Overcoming the Monster plot other than just the more literal examples we have so far been looking at.

## Melodrama

There were, for instance, many of those melodramatic tales beloved of the nineteenth century which may be caricatured as 'the hero having to rescue the beautiful maiden from the clutches of the wicked Sir Jasper'.[1] A familiar instance is Charles Dickens's *Nicholas Nickleby* (1838–1839). Like the hero of many a fairy tale, young Nicholas is left orphaned by the death of his father and having to provide for his penniless mother and sister. He is taken in hand by a seemingly kindly uncle, Ralph, who arranges a teaching post for him at the grim Northern school, Dotheboys Hall. And when we meet the tyrannical owner of this establishment, Mr Squeers (who, like Polyphemus, 'had but one eye, and popular prejudice runs in favour of two'), we might think we had met the story's chief 'monster'. But no sooner has Nicholas overcome this particular villain, by giving him a thrashing and escaping from the school, than it gradually emerges that the hero and his family are in fact threatened by a kind of mysterious, Hydra-headed conspiracy, of which Squeers had merely been one lesser 'head'.

In fact the chief monster at the centre of this web of evil is the wicked usurer, Uncle Ralph himself. The action centres first on the liberation of Nicholas's sister Kate from the predatory clutches of Ralph's disreputable friend Sir Mulberry Hawk, another 'Hydra-head'; then on the even more hazardous rescue of his own chosen 'Princess', the beautiful Madeleine Bray, from a vile plot to marry her off to yet another Hydra-head, the unpleasant old Arthur Gride. Finally all Ralph's wicked schemes are exposed and brought to naught. Nicholas, the triumphant hero, is free to marry his 'Princess' who, it is then discovered, has inherited a great 'treasure' from her father.

## War stories

A very different kind of tale shaped by the Overcoming the Monster theme is the war story, particularly those set at the time of the Second World War. In the past 60 years the immense drama of World War Two has inspired many more fictional stories than any other real-life episode in history. One reason for this was the way Hitler's Nazis, and to a lesser exent their Japanese allies, provided storytellers with such an extraordinarily rich store of 'monster-imagery'.

In countless films from the 1940s on, we saw Hitler's Germany cast as invading Predator, with all the diabolic paraphernalia of the blitzkrieg; as Holdfast, exercising ruthlessly tyrannical sway over Occupied Europe; or as Avenger, lashing out at resistance heroes, prison camp escapers or anyone else who dared challenge its murderous authority. The vast majority of such stories were based on the plot of Overcoming the Monster, with the underlying pattern of the story in almost every instance the same. At first there is a preparatory stage of anticipation, as of some great forthcoming ordeal. We see the seemingly insuperable power of the German war machine. There is then a gathering sense of danger, as battle is joined, and the

---

1. In fact, as we shall see much later in the book, this type of story was superbly caricatured even at the time, in W. S. Gilbert's parody of the melodramatic 'sensation novels' of the 1860s, where he called his wicked baronet-villain 'Sir Ruthven' (see Chapter 34).

heroes seem to have all the odds stacked against them. Then comes the climactic confrontation and, finally, the miraculous victory. The Nazi (sometimes Japanese) monster is overthrown. The dark armadas of the Luftwaffe (as in *The Battle of Britain*) are hurled back. The great Predator ship (as in *The Sinking of the Bismarck*) is destroyed. The invasion of Europe (as in *The Longest Day*) is success-fully achieved. The Nazis' counter-offensive (as in *The Battle of the Bulge*) is fought off. The beautiful city of Paris (in *Is Paris Burning?*), like a rescued Princess, is at the last moment saved.

But never far from the surface of these apparently modern, and even 'histor-ically accurate' accounts were the patterns and imagery of a story as old as the imagination of man. Alastair Maclean's *The Guns of Navarone* (1963), a typical fictional Second World War adventure story, tells how five heroes land on a closely-guarded Aegean island to destroy two huge German guns concealed in a clifftop cave, which Holdfast-like dominate a narrow strait. We are aware that this is the only way through which a large number of beleaguered Allied soldiers can be lifted to safety from a nearby island. Thousands of lives are at the mercy of these mighty engines of destruction. Painfully the heroes make their way across the island, narrowly escaping every kind of disaster, until at last they reach the cave and see, against the night sky:

> 'crouched massively above, like some nightmare monsters from another and ancient world, the evil, the sinister silhouettes of the two great guns of Navarone.'

Evading detection as they catch the sentries on their 'blind spot', the heroes fix their little explosive charges against the guns, like 'magic weapons' against some-thing so massive and overpowering. Finally, as the 'tremendous detonation tore the heart out of the great fortress', it is at one level not just the guns of Navarone which are being destroyed, but Humbaba, the Minotaur, Dracula and every other monster who has ever been. After the mounting suspense of the long ordeal, penned in at every moment by the prospect of sudden death, liberation is here! Life has triumphed over death! Humanity can breathe again!

## The Hollywood Western

So basic is the outline of the Overcoming the Monster plot that there is almost no limit to the variety of story-types it can give rise to. We can recognise it wherever our interest in a tale is centred on the steady build-up to a climactic battle between the hero and some dark, threatening figure, or group of figures, whether this be the wicked witch in a fairy tale or invading aliens from outer space, Spielberg's flesh-eating dinosaurs in *Jurassic Park* or the outlaw gang in a Western.

An obvious instance of a Western based on this plot is *The Magnificent Seven* (1960), inspired by Akira Kurosawa's *The Seven Samurai* (1954), his film version of a traditional Japanese legend. It begins in classic Overcoming the Monster style by showing a community living under the shadow of a monstrous threat: a little Mexican farming village being terrorised by an outlaw gang, led by the villainous Calveros, who regularly arrive at the village to rob the farmers of food. We see one such predatory visit, when one old farmer tries to protest. Calveros shoots him in front of the villagers, thus underlining just what a heartless and predatory tyrant he is. A wise old man living nearby advises the farmers that the only way to stop this reign of terror is that they should buy guns. Three of them ride over the American border where they see two professional gunmen (played by Yul Brynner and Steve McQueen) fearlessly standing up to the inhabitants of a small town in insisting that an Indian who has died in the town should be buried in its whites-only cemetery. This establishes that the two heroes are not racially prejudiced and are willing to fight against injustice. For a small sum of money, all they can afford, the Mexicans persuade the two gunmen to come back to their village to defend them against the outlaws. The two recruit another five, and the seven gunmen arrive in the village to train its inhabitants in self-defence.

When Calveros's gang next returns it is beaten off with heavy losses. But when the seven ride out into the countryside to see what the gang is up to, Calveros outwits them by secretly occupying the village in their absence. When they return they discover they have fallen into his clutches. In front of the cowed villagers, he removes their guns, and allows them to leave. Foolishly, however, showing the monster's blind spot, he allows their guns to be returned to them when they have left town. He cannot imagine that, as mere hired gunmen, they will not just ride away to avoid any further trouble, leaving him free to carry on oppressing the villagers. But, bruised by their humiliation, the seven ride back into town for a final climactic battle, in which Calveros and his gang are routed, not least because the villagers recover their courage and join in. Four of the seven are dead. One decides to remain in the village because he has fallen in love with a village girl, which allows the story to end on the image of a man and woman united in love. But the two original brave heroes ride off into the wide blue yonder, having overcome the 'monster' and saved the community.

Another classic Hollywood Western based on this plot was Fred Zinnemann's *High Noon* (1952), written by Carl Foreman. Again we see a community living under the shadow of a monstrous outlaw gang, the little town of Hadleyville in the old West. The story begins on the morning when the hero Will Kane (played by Gary Cooper), having resigned as town marshal, is getting married to Amy, a pretty young Quaker (Grace Kelly). No sooner is the ceremony over than Kane unpins his badge of office and he and his new bride prepare to leave the town for ever. But then shocking news arrives. Some years earlier Kane had been responsible for arresting Frank Miller, a psychopathic gang-leader who had terrorised the town, and now Miller has been released from prison. He is heading back to Hadleyville on the noon train, due to arrive in just two hours time. The three unsavoury members of his gang are already at the station waiting for him, and for the moment when they can settle their score with Kane and reimpose their reign of terror.

Scarcely have the newly-weds set out from town than Kane realises he cannot leave the townsfolk defenceless. He turns back, hoping to round up a posse of townsfolk to help defeat the gang. But the people are so cowed that they dare not help. Just like some of the villagers in *The Magnificent Seven*, they would much rather Kane left them, in the appeasing hope that trouble might be avoided. Amy herself, as a Quaker, refuses to have anything to do with bloodshed and leaves for the station to catch the same train. Suspense mounts, as clocks tick away the two hours, and Kane finds no one to support him. At last a distant whistle is heard from across the plain. The train approaches. Miller disembarks to join his gang and the four men swagger into the now-deserted town looking for a showdown with the solitary hero. The gun battle begins and Kane manages to kill first one of his opponents, then another. But finally he is trapped in a building, its exits covered by Miller and the other outlaw. It seems all is lost and he is at their mercy. Then a miracle takes place. A shot rings out from across the street, and a third villain lies dead. At the last minute Amy has jumped off the train and returned to town, and she is standing at a window with a smoking gun in her hand. Frank Miller seizes her, pushes her out in front of him into the street and tells the hero that, unless he comes out to surrender, she will be killed. As Kane emerges, Miller pushes Amy aside to fire; but bravely she jogs his arm, giving the hero a chance to get his shot in first. All four outlaws are dead. Hero and heroine embrace as the shamefaced townsfolk emerge from their hiding places to cluster round their saviours. The loving couple can at last ride happily off together to start their new life.

Beneath its comparatively modern trappings (guns, the train) there is nothing about this story which could not have been presented in the imagery of an ancient myth or legend: with the little town as a kingdom threatened by the approach of a terrifying dragon, and Kane as a princely hero who, against all odds, finally slays the monster – although, like Theseus, he only manages to do this with the help of a loving 'Princess', who unexpectedly comes to his aid just when all seems lost.

### The thriller

Another genre of story usually shaped by the Overcoming the Monster plot is the thriller: and here again we see how often thriller writers unconsciously fall back on the age-old stock of 'monster imagery', as they look for the kind of language which will help them to build up their hero's chief antagonist into a shadowy figure of immense menace and evil.

In that early thriller-adventure story Dumas's *The Three Musketeers* (1844), the action centres on the long struggle between the hero D'Artagnan and the evil Lady de Winter, who lures the hero's chosen 'Princess', the beautiful young Madame de Bonancieux, into her clutches. When we look at the imagery used to describe Lady de Winter, whose sinister influence extends all over France, we see her not only characterised explicitly as 'a monster' who has 'committed as many crimes as you could read of in a year', but as a 'panther', a 'tiger', a 'lioness' and several times as 'a serpent'.

When in *The Final Problem* Conan Doyle wished to create a villain who was at last a worthy match for the powers of his hero Sherlock Holmes, he conjured up the 'reptilian' Moriarty, like Dracula 'a fallen angel', a man of 'extraordinary mental powers' who has perverted them to 'diabolic ends'. 'For some years past' says Holmes, 'I have been conscious of some deep organising power which stands forever in the way of the law'. He realises that it is the shadowy Moriarty, eternally elusive, a master of disguise, 'the most dangerous criminal in Europe', who:

> 'sits motionless, like a spider in the centre of his web, but that web has a thousand radiations, and he well knows every quiver of them.'

The thrillers of John Buchan made lavish use of similar imagery. In *The Thirty Nine Steps*, for instance, the hero Richard Hannay learns of the materialising of some vast, shadowy threat to 'the peace of Europe': 'behind all the governments and the armies, there was a big subterranean movement going on, engineered by some very dangerous people'. When he tracks down the chief villain at the heart of this immense conspiracy to a remote Scottish moor, he is a German master-spy, described as 'bald-headed' like 'a sinister fowl'.

In those most successful of all twentieth-century thrillers, Ian Fleming's James Bond stories, the imagery again and again quite explicitly builds up the 'monster' with echoes of myth and fairy tales. Le Chiffre, the villain of *Casino Royale*, is 'a black-fleeced Minotaur'; Sir Hugo Drax in *Moonraker* has 'a hulking body' with 'ogre's teeth'; Mr Big in *Live and Let Die* has 'a great football of a head, twice the normal size and nearly round'; the villain of *Dr No*, bald and crippled, with steel pincers insteas of arms, 'looked like a giant venomous worm, wrapped in grey tin-foil'.

Indeed one of the key reasons for the initial success of the Bond stories, even before they were translated to the cinema screen (increasingly modifying Fleming's original versions), was precisely the way they tapped so unerringly into those springs of the human imagination which had given rise to similar stories for thousands of years. So accurately did the typical Bond novel follow the age-old archetypal pattern that it might almost serve as a model for any Overcoming the Monster story.

As conceived by Fleming, the basic Bond story (one or two vary the pattern slightly) unfolds through five stages rather like this:

1. *The 'Call' (or Anticipation Stage)*: The hero, a member of the British Secret Intelligence Service, is summoned by 'M', head of the service, and told of suspicious goings-on somewhere in the world which appear to pose a deadly threat to Britain, the West or mankind as a whole. Bond has been chosen to track down and confront the source of this evil, and the general mood of this opening phase is one of anticipation of the immense task to come. To prepare him for his ordeal, Bond may visit the armourer, 'Q', to be equipped with special weapons, such as a new gun, a sports car fitted with a smokescreen device or a rocket pack which will enable him to fly. These are exact modern equivalents to the 'magic weapons' of ancient myth, such as the sword, the 'helmet of invisibility' and the winged-sandals enabling him to fly with which Perseus was equipped by the gods before his journey to confront Medusa.

2. *Initial success (Dream Stage)*: Bond has first brushes with the 'monster's' agents or even the 'monster' himself, in which he is victorious (he catches Goldfinger or Drax cheating at cards or golf). There may be attacks on his life, but he survives these, and the general mood of this stage is a dream-like sense of

immunity to danger, with the full horror of the monster's power and ambitions not yet in full view.

3. *Confrontation (Frustration Stage)*: Bond eventually penetrates the monster's lair to get closer to his enemy and then suffers his first serious setback, when he falls into the monster's clutches. But this enables him to get a full view of his sinister and repulsive opponent for the first time.[2] Because the villain thinks he has Bond in his power, he reveals the full scale of his intentions, e.g., to rob Fort Knox or to drop a nuclear bomb on London. Bond's frustration at not being able to communicate this vital information back to the outside world is redoubled by knowing that the monster also has in his grip some beautiful girl or captive 'Princess'.

4. *Final ordeal (Nightmare Stage)*: Bond is now forced by the monster to face the 'terrible ordeal', which seems fiendishly designed to lead to his painful, long-drawn out death: e.g. having to endure a deadly obstacle race, crawling through a subterranean tunnel, where he has to run the gauntlet of poisonous spiders, roasting heat and finally a battle with a giant squid.

5. *The Miraculous Escape (and Death of the Monster)*: Bond survives the ordeal and then, by a miraculous feat of ingenuity and strength, manages in the nick of time to turn the tables, outwitting and killing the villain. He thus saves not only his own life but Fort Knox, London, mankind or whatever has been threatened with destruction. The monster is dead and Bond is free to end his adventure locked in fond embrace with the liberated 'Princess'.

## Science fiction

Just when Ian Fleming was publishing his first Bond novels, some of his British contemporaries were producing particularly striking examples of that type of story which in the past century has revived the imagery of archetypal monsters more grotesquely inhuman than anything seen in storytelling since the Dark Ages and the myths of ancient Greece. Since H. G. Wells had written his account of the invasion of Earth by leathery-skinned, tentacled Martians in *The War of the Worlds* at the end of the nineteenth century, science fiction writers had not come up with many repeat versions on this theme, apart from the celebrated episode in 1938 when the young Orson Welles first sprang to fame by broadcasting an Americanised adaptation of Wells's novel on radio, so vividly presented as a 'live news event' that it provoked a wave of panic among listeners who thought it was actually happening. In the early 1950s, however, as the world awaited the imminent arrival of the space age, two genres of science fiction story swept conspicuously into fashion: the first, following Wells, centred on deadly invasions

---

2. At this stage in *Dr No*, shortly after Bond has landed on the Caribbean island which is the monster's lair, the sense that we are about to confront the monster is heightened when Bond sees, coming across a lake at night:

> 'a shapeless thing, with two glaring eyes ... between them, where the mouth might be, fluttered a yard of blue flame. The grey luminescence of the stars showed some kind of a domed head, with two short, bat-like wings.'

This turns out to be merely a mechanical 'monster', built by Dr No to frighten off the local fishermen, but it prepares us for the first meeting with the real thing a few pages later.

of the earth by monsters from outer space; the other featuring some world-threatening catastrophe unleashed by mankind's own growing technological ability to interfere with nature.

A well-known example of this second genre was John Wyndham's *The Day of the Triffids* (1951), which began with a combination of two human experiments going disastrously wrong. A spectacular light show in the heavens turns out to be the unleashing of a secret weapon which renders the vast majority of the human race blind. This suspiciously coincides with the breaking loose of large numbers of triffids, genetically-engineered carnivorous plants which have a malevolent intelligence, the ability to move about and a deadly whiplash sting with which they can catch human beings as their prey.

The story begins in London, centred on a handful of survivors, including the hero and heroine, who have for various reasons retained their sight. They eventually manage to escape the city, where most of the population are helplessly falling victim to roaming bands of triffids. The 'frustration stage' begins when hero and heroine are separated, and much of the action is taken up with his quest to track her down, as he picks his hazardous way across the triffid-infested countryside of southern England. They are finally reunited in Sussex, where a determined band of survivors have holed up in a fortified farmhouse behind an electrified fence. The 'final ordeal' begins when an ever-growing mass of triffids lays siege to the farm, finally finding a way to break through the fence. But in the nick of time the survivors make their 'miraculous escape', to join others in the Isle of Wight. This has been established as a triffid-free sanctuary, from where humanity's counter-attack is to be launched to liberate the mainland from the monsters who have taken it over.

In his next book *The Kraken Wakes* (1953), Wyndham switched to the other genre, where the deadly threat to human survival is posed by a monstrous invasion from outer space. As in *The Day of the Triffids*, the story's power comes from the way the normality of everyday life is suddenly disturbed by the appearance of mysterious phenomena, the sinister nature of which is not initially clear. The action then unfolds through the familiar stages:

1. *Anticipation Stage*: Curiosity is aroused by reports from various parts of the world of 'mysterious fireballs' seen at sea.

2. *Dream Stage*: Rather more serious incidents take place, such as the unexplained sinkings of various large ships, and the discoloration of ocean currents, indicating some vast submarine activity in 'the Deeps'. But the real nature of the menace is not yet clearly in view, and it still seems too remote and mysterious to justify real alarm.

3. *Frustration Stage*: The first real shock. Various islands are mysteriously attacked, and when the hero and heroine visit the West Indies to investigate we actually see the 'monsters' in their full horror for the first time: huge 'sea tanks', crawling up from the shore and removing hundreds of people by means of deadly ribbon-like 'cilia' which stretch out into streets and houses to capture them. It seems mankind is powerless to deal with this threat. The attacks continue to worsen.

4. *Nightmare Stage*: The world's ice caps begin to melt, the sea-level rises catastrophically all over the globe, a large part of the world's population dies in various disasters and almost all social order breaks down.

5. *Miraculous Escape*: Humanity finds unspecified 'magic weapons' to kill off the monsters; the sea stops rising; humanity is saved; hero and heroine are happily united; life begins to return to normal.

The same year, 1953, just after the Queen's Coronation had prompted millions of Britons to install their first primitive television sets, the first serial on the new medium to catch the nation's imagination was Nigel Kneale's *The Quatermass Experiment*, with its hero a shrewd and robust scientist, Professor Bernard Quatermass. As head of the world's first manned space-flight project, Quatermass is horrified when the spaceship returns with only one of the three astronauts alive. Gradually it becomes clear that the survivor, Victor Caroon, has not only absorbed the personalities of his two dead colleagues but has been taken over by some diabolically ingenious extra-terrestrial power which is using his body as a vehicle to take over the earth. The 'frustration stage' sets in when Caroon appears to be turning into a cross between a cactus and a fungus, then disappears. When next sighted he has become a huge and fast-proliferating fungoid monster spreading over the interior of Westminster Abbey, about to throw out millions of spores which will wipe out humanity, allowing the aliens to take over. In this 'final ordeal', Quatermass confronts the monster and somewhat implausibly persuades the three human beings who are still mysteriously part of it to resist its influence, even though this will involve their own suicide. This leads to the 'miraculous escape' by which humanity is saved.

In the sequel *Quatermass II* (1955) our hero again saves mankind from extra-terrestrial invasion when he discovers that mysterious small meteorites dropping out of the sky contain an alien life-force which possesses any human being who comes near them. The only outward sign of what has happened is a mark on their skin. He then discovers that, with the aid of their new zombified human allies, the aliens have established a mysterious 'defence plant' in a remote part of northern England, The 'frustration stage' begins when Quatermass comes to London to alert people at the top of government that something astonishingly sinister seems to be going on. He is surprised to receive bland assurances that there is nothing to worry about. But then, in each case, observes that the senior figure to whom he is talking has the telltale mark on his arm. Frustration turns to nightmare when Quatermass manages to visit the plant with a delegation. One member separates from the group to look into a vast pressure dome. He comes out dying of ammonia-poisoning, uttering the one word 'slime'. Quatermass guesses the aliens are using the oxygen-free dome to reproduce, before emerging to take over the world The 'final ordeal' comes when the plant is stormed by an army of angry locals. As they engage in a shoot-out with zombified armed guards, Quatermass opens up the dome to oxygen, thus destroying the monsters within and saving mankind.

Kneale's third and most successful working of the theme, *Quatermass and the Pit* (1958), begins with the discovery on a London building site of a mysterious cylinder, at first taken to be an unexploded wartime bomb. Quatermass realises from surrounding fossil remains that in fact it must have been there for five million years. Through the now familiar sequence whereby initial dream-like curiosity leads first to frustration, then to a nightmare running out of control, it gradually emerges that the cylinder had originated from Mars. A civilisation threatened with extinction had used the spaceship to colonise the earth, by 'possessing from within' the prehistoric ancestors of mankind. The final 'nightmare stage' begins when Quatermass realises that most human beings are still unwittingly influenced by this 'Martian element' buried in their unconscious, and that this is now being activated by the unearthing of the buried space capsule. The Martian cylinder dissolves into a towering vision of a creature looking like the Devil and London is thrown into chaos, as crazed mobs launch a 'Wild Hunt', tracking down to kill any 'outsider' who has somehow escaped its influence. Finally, with half the city burning, Quatermass works out that the only way to destroy the monster is to short-circuit its electrical energy with a steel cable. He throws this earthing device into the heart of the spectral vision, there is a mighty electrical discharge, the vision disappears and its malign force ceases. Once again, thanks to our wise and indomitable hero, mankind has been saved in the nick of time from what looked like certain destruction.

Yet the underlying five-stage pattern of all these stories is only too familiar. As each of them begins with the arousal of curiosity, then continues with frustration as the monster's true deadly nature becomes apparent, leading to a 'nightmare stage' when catastrophe seems inevitable, finally ending in the 'miraculous escape', their pattern is exactly the same as that which we first came across in some of the simplest stories of our childhood, such as *Jack and the Beanstalk* or *Little Red Riding Hood* or *Goldilocks and the Three Bears*.

### Star Wars

As a last example, to underline just how fundamental a pattern to storytelling this is, we may look at what became the most successful science fiction film ever produced by Hollywood, George Lucas's *Star Wars* (1977).

The story is set in the distant future, when the many planetary worlds of our galaxy are ruled by one government. For centuries this had exercised benevolent sway as 'the Republic', with the aid of the brave and honourable Jedi Knights. But the government has now been seized by a conspiracy of power-crazed politicians, bureaucrats and corporations, headed by a shadowy 'Emperor'; and no-one, it seems, wields greater power in this tyrannical new 'Empire' than the ruthless 'Dark Lord' Darth Vader, once himself a Jedi knight, now, like Lucifer, a 'fallen angel'. Scattered across remote reaches of the galaxy dispossessed supporters of the old order, 'the rebel Alliance', are hoping one day to overthrow the dark Empire, to reclaim the universe for the forces of light.

The story opens with a rebel spaceship being attacked by an 'Imperial cruiser' captained by the terrifying Vader, whom we only see hidden in menacing black armour. As his Imperial forces take over the rebel ship, a tiny spacecraft escapes, containing See Threepio and Artoo Deetoo, two 'androids' or humanised computers, who land safely on the surface of a nearby planet, Tatooine. Still on the rebel ship is the beautiful Princess Leia, daughter of the leader of the rebel Alliance, whom Vader takes prisoner.

We thus begin with the familiar image of a Princess falling into the clutches of the 'monster'. But the one thing the 'Dark Lord' is desperate to discover is the whereabouts of the rebel organisation's secret headquarters, so he can destroy it, thus making the victory of the Empire complete. What he does not realise is that the resourceful Princess has programmed Artoo Deetoo with this vital information, along with an urgent appeal for help, before the androids bail out. By the fatal mistake of allowing them to escape, because he thinks their little craft is unmanned, the arrogant Vader has revealed a first 'blind spot'.

Only now do we at last meet the young hero of the story, Luke Skywalker, who lives with his uncle and aunt on a lonely farmstead on Tatooine, dreaming of future glory as a space-pilot. When the two androids arrive at the farm, Artoo lights up with a hologram of the Princess. Luke is at once smitten by her beauty. She utters the baffling message 'Obi-wan Kenobi, you're my only remaining hope', which Luke vaguely connects with a mysterious bearded hermit, 'a kind of sorcerer', who lives in an even more remote part of the desert. He and the androids set off to find him and, after Kenobi has miraculously intervened to save them from death at the hands of desert-dwelling monsters, they find themselves in the 'wizard's' cave. The old man reveals he is one of the last surviving Knights of the Jedi, with supernatural powers, and that Luke's lost father had been another, one of the bravest of all. Interpreting the Princess's cry for help, Kenobi asks Luke to accompany him on a hazardous mission to rescue her.

This marks the end of the 'Anticipation Stage'. The hero has received the 'Call', giving him and the story a focus. We can see now what the story is centrally to be about; and the hero's sense of being impelled towards this mysterious new destiny is reinforced when they return to the farmstead to find that the uncle and aunt who have brought him up have been vapourised by Imperial troops. There is nothing left to keep him at home.

Despite further threats, fought off with Kenobi's supernatural aid, Luke gradually assembles a team to make the journey; and in the nick of time, pursued by Imperial soldiers, they make a 'thrilling escape' in a deceptively battered old spacecraft, piloted, solely for the money, by a reckless mercenary Han Solo. This enables them to throw off their pursuers as they head off faster than light to their mystery destination. On the journey Kenobi imparts some of the ancient Jedi secrets to Luke, not least the importance of the mysterious 'force' with which the Knights learn to ally themselves, giving them supernatural powers. As the wise old man explains, this is 'an energy field, and something more. An aura that at once controls and obeys, a nothingness that can accomplish miracles.' During this phase of the story, the hero and his companions seem to enjoy a magical immunity to danger: the 'Dream Stage'. But we are reminded of the dark reality prevailing elsewhere, as we glimpse the Princess being subjected by Vader to horrific tortures, trying to force her into giving up the secret whereabouts of the rebel headquarters, the distant planet Alderaan.

Then suddenly, as they near their destination, they see the horrifying sight of a vast, mysterious man-made structure floating in space ahead of them. It is the Empire's own secret weapon, the Death Star, a spaceship so powerful it can destroy a whole planet. This is where the Dark Lord Vader is holding the Princess prisoner. Even as they approach, this monstrous engine of death pulverises Alderaan, including the Princess's father, to atoms. At the same time, the hero and his companions feel their own small spacecraft itself being sucked inexorably down a powerful beam into the heart of the Death Star. As their ship comes to rest it seems they are the monster's prisoners. Like Bond, when he penetrates the lair of one of his monstrous opponents and falls into his clutches, they have reached the 'Frustration Stage'.

Now begins the terrible ordeal of the 'Nightmare Stage' as, pursued all the way, threatened by one horror after another, they wander through the endless, dark, metallic labyrinth of this huge structure, first to track down and release the Princess from her prison cell; then to thread their way back to their own space-craft, having first immobilised the gravity beam which had taken it prisoner. Finally, thanks to old Kenobi sacrificing his life in a hand-to-hand struggle with his one-time pupil, the Dark Lord, they make their miraculous escape, with the freed Princess on board – hurtling through space to another unknown planet where, hidden beneath ancient ruins in a jungle, is the true secret command head-quarters of the rebel Alliance.

Here indeed begins the true 'Final Ordeal' of the story, as a small team of space pilots, including Luke, who has now captivated the Princess as surely as she had entranced him, set off for a final showdown with the Dark Empire, on which the whole future of the universe will rest. Thanks to Artoo having programmed himself with the entire layout of the Death Star, they have learned its vital secret. There is just one tiny aperture on the entire face of that immense, impregnable structure where a perfectly-aimed missile might penetrate to the central reactor which is its heart. After a deadly prolonged aerial battle between two groups of small spacecraft, more reminiscent of a World War Two dogfight than anything belonging to the space age, Luke and Darth Vader, hero and monster, finally come face to face. Just when it seems all is lost for the hero, he is miraculously saved. Han Solo, after refusing to risk his life in the battle because his only interest was money, has decided after all to intervene, arriving in the nick of time to blast Vader's craft helplessly out into space. Simultaneously, even more miracu-lously, Luke has become at one with Kenobi's supernatural 'force', unconsciously managing to launch his missiles at just the right split-second to hit the mark. Scarcely have Luke and Solo withdrawn to a safe distance than the whole artifi-cial planet explodes into a trillion fragments, in a sunburst which lights up that corner of the cosmos for days.

The monster has been overthrown. The victorious heroes return to a tumul-tuous welcome at the Alliance headquarters. In a vast temple hall, before a deli-rious crowd representing peoples from all over the universe, they walk up to a dais to be presented with gold medals by a radiant figure dressed in flowing white. As Luke receives his prize, he can scarcely hear the cheers. His thoughts are solely occupied by the smiling face of the Princess before him.[3]

## The thrilling escape from death

Again and again in all these expressions of the Overcoming the Monster plot we see a moment which is of fundamental significance to storytelling: one which, like the characteristics of the monster itself, is relevant to stories of many kinds other than just those shaped by this particular plot.

To the huge relief of the hero (and of ourselves as the audience, identifying with his fate), just when it seems all is lost and that his destruction is inevitable, he makes a miraculous escape. Always it is only in the nick of time, just when all seems lost, that Luke Skywalker escapes from the final deadly assault by Darth Vader; that Quatermass saves mankind from the extra-terrestrials; that the tiny band of survivors escape the clutches of the triffids; that James Bond escapes from the clutches of his villains; that Wells's invading Martians are killed by bacteria; that the guns of Navarone are blown up; that Gary Cooper in *High Noon* is saved by the unexpected shot fired by his wife; that Jack manages to scramble back down the beanstalk; that the forester bursts in to save Red Riding Hood from the devouring wolf; that Goldilocks scrambles out of the window to escape the three bears. From the constricting sense of imminent death, often physically represented by some dark, enclosing space in which the hero or heroine is trapped, they, and we the audience, are suddenly liberated.

So familiar is this moment of liberation, 'the thrilling escape from death', that in certain kinds of popular storytelling it has become a cliche, almost a joke: 'saved in the last reel by the US Cavalry', we say; or think of the hero of the old silent films galloping in to snatch away the heroine who has been tied down by the villain in the path of the oncoming train. Cartoon films like *Tom and Jerry* are made up of little else except one 'thrilling escape from death' after another, as cat and mouse are ironed out flat, or blow each other up in remorseless succession. Another famous instance was that legendary hero of a newspaper serial who was finally trapped by so many impossible dangers that not even his creator could think of a way to extricate him, until a colleague supplied the answer simply by writing in 'with one mighty bound Jack was free'.

Despite such caricatures, the significance of the thrilling escape from death runs very deep. It is one of the most consistent motifs in storytelling, cropping up again

---

3. This detail of the ending of the story is taken from Lucas's published version of the film's story. Two years after *Star Wars*, another Hollywood science fiction film *Alien* (1979) reflected the rise of late-twentieth-century feminism by providing a rare example of an Overcoming the Monster story in which the central role of 'monster-slayer' is played by a woman. The heroine, Ripley, is second-in-command of a space ship, far out in space, which is invaded by a peculiarly clever and ruthless alien. One by one it gruesomely destroys each of her six fellow-crew members, leaving her alone. She realises her only hope of escape is to bail out in a small spacecraft, and to blow up the main ship with the monster in it. No sooner is the mother-ship destroyed, however, than she realises the alien has escaped with her. There is a final battle in which the heroine blasts the monster out into space, and the film ends with her sleeping peacefully on her way back to earth.

and again in stories of every kind. And it is hardly surprising that we should find stories based on little else but the build-up to a thrilling escape.

An obvious example is Edgar Allan Poe's *The Pit and the Pendulum*. We know nothing of the hero of this short story, who he is or why he has been imprisoned. All we know is that he is tied down in some 'dark, enclosing space', a form of prison cell, undergoing a succession of mounting horrors. First he is attacked by giant rats. Then a huge, razor-sharp pendulum swings closer and closer to his body, although he uses this to sever his bonds. Then the metal walls of his prison become red-hot and begin to close in on him, driving him nearer and nearer to the edge of a bottomless well, until suddenly, just as the sense of oppression becomes unbearable:

> 'the fiery walls rushed back. An outstretched arm caught my own as I fell fainting into the abyss ... the French army had entered Toledo. The Inquisition was in the hands of its enemies.'

Poe explores the same theme in his *Descent into the Maelstrom*, in which the hero describes how his fishing boat had been sucked down into the black, roaring hole of the world's most notorious and deadly whirlpool. Deeper and deeper they spiral down the watery walls, until the hero notices that certain lighter pieces of driftwood are being carried not downwards, but upwards. He jumps out of the boat as it is being carried down to certain destruction and, miraculously, is carried up to safety.

There are other stories based on little more than this relentless build-up towards some inevitable doom, followed in the nick of time by miraculous deliverance. For instance, Daniel Defoe's *Journal of the Plague Year* and Camus's *La Peste* are both stories set in a city which has been attacked by a mysterious, deadly pestilence. From small beginnings, we feel the virulence of the plague becoming more and more obvious and terrifying until it seems no one can possibly survive: then suddenly, as by a miracle, it fades away. The mysterious plague in such stories is playing the part of the monster, all-conquering, deadly, remorseless in its power: except that we never see this particular monster face to face because it cannot be directly personified, but remains just a shadowy, increasingly threatening presence. Similarly the hero is not personally responsible for overcoming the monster; at the story's climax, the reversal comes when the threat suddenly recedes, as it does for Poe's hero in *The Pit and the Pendulum*. Indeed the same is true in other stories we have already cited under the heading of Overcoming the Monster. *The War of the Worlds*, for instance, is not strictly an Overcoming the Monster story, because the hero himself has nothing to do with the routing of the monsters; and the same is true of many of the stories which followed it in showing a deadly attack by some world-threatening monster from outer space, such as *The Kraken Wakes*. We experience such stories, in fact, much as we do those of Poe, Defoe and Camus: through the eyes of a hero who is merely a more or less helpless observer, sucked into a nightmare which seems certain to end in his death, until brought to an end by agencies beyond his awareness or control.

Stories on this pattern have again become familiar in recent times in the form of those 'disaster movies' so popular from the 1970s onwards, such as *The Towering*

*Inferno* (1974). This followed the experience of a disparate group of people who become trapped in a huge skyscraper, during the hours after an electrical fire breaks out in the bowels of the building. At first the fire is tiny and unnoticed. For a long time we know it is spreading behind the scenes, so that there is a sense of some enormous growing threat while, on the surface, life in the tower carries on as normal. But finally, by the time the fire has broken out into full view, it has become an unstoppable monster, raging uncontrollably through the whole building to a nightmare climax, when hundreds of victims are trapped on the upper floors, seemingly doomed to certain death. At this point they are miraculously lifted to safety.

*Airport* (1970) similarly centred on a group of passengers caught in the 'enclosing space' of a crowded airliner at night, threatened with imminent destruction by the presence of a madman armed with a bomb. At least here the threat is partly personified, and when the bomb explodes and the madman is sucked out into the darkness, it might seem the 'monster' has been 'overcome': except that the real source of the nightmare is not the madman himself, as it would be if he were a true monster, but simply the fear of the plane crashing; and this remains until, with enormous difficulty and to universal relief, the plane is at last brought safely to the ground.

In fact this story of the hero's deliverance from the nightmare of being trapped in some dark, enclosing space, threatening death, is one of the oldest in the world. An obvious example is the tale of Jonah, who falls overboard and is swallowed by the 'great fish'. For three days he lies in its cavernous interior, sure he is about to die:

> 'The water encompassed me round about, even to the soul; the depth closed me round about, the weeds were wrapped about my head. I went down to the bottom of the mountains; the earth with her bars was round me forever.'

Then miraculously his prayers are answered, and the fish 'vomited out Jonah on the dry land.'

Jonah does not, of course, kill his 'whale', which is why again his adventure cannot be considered strictly an Overcoming the Monster story. But this is only one of countless tales of a hero swallowed by a monster, found in mythology and folk tales from Europe, North America, Polynesia, Japan and almost all over the world, in many of which the hero does actually slay the monster from within. In *Hiawatha* Longfellow gives a North American 'Indian' version, where he describes how the hero goes to challenge 'the King of Fishes', Mishe-Nama:

> 'up he rose with angry gesture,
> quivering in each nerve and fibre,
> slashing all his plates of armour,
> gleaming bright with all his war-paint;
> in his wrath he darted upwards,
> flashing leaped into the sunshine,
> opened his great jaws and swallowed
> both canoe and Hiawatha.'

(Note the familiar anthropomorphisation of the animal 'monster' – 'armour', 'war-paint', 'wrath'.) In 'that darksome cavern' the hero 'groped about in helpless wonder' until he finds the fish's 'great heart beating' and slays it. The corpse drifts ashore, and Hiwatha, 'exulting from the caverns', cries out to the birds how he has killed the great monster, and they rescue him.

In the folklore of the Shetlands, the story was told as that of Assipattle, who is treated with contempt by his brothers (like the little shepherd boy David). But he alone is brave enough to challenge the great 'Mester Stoorwoorm', so huge that it stretches half across the world, to rescue from its clutches a captive Princess. Clutching a burning piece of peat, Assipattle allows himself to be swallowed, and places the live coal on the monster's liver: 'in troth, I think it gave the Stoorworm a hot harskit'. Then (as in many other versions) the hero is spewed out by the monster in its dying spasm, and wins the hand of the Princess.

### Overcoming the Monster: Summing up

One way in which a story seems naturally to form in the human imagination shows the hero being called to face and overcome a terrible and deadly personification of evil. This threatening figure is defined by the fact that it is heartless, egocentric and seemingly all-powerful, although we ultimately see that it has a blind spot which renders it vulnerable. As the story is usually presented, there is a long build-up to the final decisive confrontation, and the story is likely to to run through these five stages:

1. *Anticipation Stage and 'Call'*: We usually first become aware of the monster as if from a great distance, although in some stories we may be given some striking glimpse of its destructive power at the outset. Although initially we may see it as little more than a vaguely menacing curiosity, we gradually learn of its fearsome reputation, and how it is usually casting its threatening shadow over some community, country, kingdom or mankind in general. The hero then experiences a 'Call' to confront it.

2. *Dream Stage*: As the hero makes his preparations for the battle to come (e.g., as he travels towards the monster or as the monster approaches), all for a while may seem to be going reasonably well. Our feelings are still of a comfortable remoteness from and immunity to danger.

3. *Frustration Stage*: At last we come face to face with the monster in all its awesome power. The hero seems tiny and very much alone against such a super-naturally strong opponent. Indeed it seems that he is slipping into the monster's power (he may even fall helplessly into the monster's clutches), and that the struggle can only have one outcome.

4. *Nightmare Stage*: The final ordeal begins, a nightmare battle in which all the odds seem loaded on the monster's side. But at the climax of the story, just when all seems lost, comes the 'reversal'.

5. *The Thrilling Escape from Death, and Death of the Monster*: In the nick of time, the monster is miraculously dealt a fatal blow. Its dark power is overthrown. The community which had fallen under its shadow is liberated. And the hero emerges

in his full stature to enjoy the prize he has won from the monster's grasp: a great treasure; union with the 'Princess'; succession to some kind of 'kingdom'.

## Constriction and release

So powerful is the effect on us of one element in this plot – the growing sense of nightmare as the hero seems to be slipping into the monster's power, followed by the surge of relief at his thrilling escape from death – that a whole sub-group of tales has grown up which use just this element in the story to make a plot in itself. And this serves to introduce another very important general aspect of the way stories are constructed, and the way in which we all experience them.

At the most basic level, whenever we identify with the fate of a hero or heroine, we share their experience as the story unfolds in a particular sense. As they face ordeals, or come under threat, so we feel tense and apprehensive; even in extreme cases so terrified that we can scarcely bear to watch or listen. As the threat is lifted, we can relax. Our own spirits are enlarged. In other words, along with the story's central figure, we feel a sense either of constriction, or of liberation; either of being shut in and oppressed, or of being opened out. And in a story which is well-constructed, these phases of constriction and release alternate, in a kind of systole-diastole rhythm which provides one of the greatest pleasures we get from stories.

But of course these alternations are not evenly pitched throughout the story. As it unfolds, the swings from one pole to the other may become more extreme until usually the most violent of all comes just before the end, with the story's climax. This is the point where the pressure of the dark power is at its greatest and most threatening, followed by the miraculous reversal and release of the ending.

If again we take *Jack and the Beanstalk* as a simple example, we initially feel, as Jack and his mother become poorer and poorer, a vague sense of constriction. How are they going to escape from their plight? As we then follow Jack up the beanstalk and his exhilarated discovery of a whole new mysterious world at the top, our spirits expand. As Jack enters the castle, and begins to pass under the menacing shadow of the giant, we feel a more violent constriction setting in. Three times this happens, punctuated by Jack's escapes with the golden treasures (each more valuable than the last). But on the third occasion the giant is roused to angry pursuit; and, as Jack runs back to scramble down the beanstalk in a nightmare chase, it seems he is about to be caught by the giant thundering ever closer behind him. This is the climax of the story, when constriction is at its most acute, until in the nick of time Jack manages to bring beanstalk and giant crashing to destruction. The shadow is at last lifted. We feel a surge of liberation; and as it fades, we are left with the warming knowledge that, in the treasures he has won from the giant's grasp, the hero has won some much deeper hold on life which will last indefinitely into the future. As the phrase has it, he will 'live happily ever after'.

In other words, the inmost rhythm of our experience of the story is of an initial sense of constriction, followed by a phase of relative enlargement, followed by a more serious constriction. Then the story works up to its climax, when the threatening pressure on the hero is at its greatest. This is released in a final, much deeper act of liberation, coupled with the sense that something of inestimable and lasting value has been won from the darkness.

Such is the underlying structure of most Overcoming the Monster stories. But, as we shall see, this fundamental rhythm is so central to the way we tell stories that we find it, in different guises, almost all through storytelling.

We can now move on to our second plot.

*Chapter 3*

# Rags to Riches

'Though for the moment K. was wretched and looked down on, yet in an almost unimaginable and distant future he would excel everybody.'

Franz Kafka, *The Castle*

Again and again in the storytelling of the world we come across a certain image which seems to hold a peculiar fascination for us. We see an ordinary, insignificant person, dismissed by everyone as of little account, who suddenly steps to the centre of the stage, revealed to be someone quite exceptional.

An obscure little squire accompanies his master up to London for the solemn ceremonies surrounding the choice of a new king. A mighty stone has appeared in St Paul's churchyard, with a sword fixed in it and the inscription that anyone who can pull out the sword shall be king. All the great men of the nation try and fail. But to everyone's astonishment the unknown young squire steps forward and removes the sword effortlessly. He becomes King Arthur, the greatest king his country has ever known.

A little ungainly duckling, quite different in appearance from all his brothers and sisters, miserable at being ridiculed for his size and clumsiness, sets out into the world where he sees a sight which takes his breath away – some great white birds, more beautiful than anything he has ever known. They are swans, but they fly away for the winter, leaving the duckling more miserable than ever. Finally spring comes, and he see three swans on a lake. He swims towards the 'kingly' birds, fearing that, like everyone else, they will only mock him for his ugliness. He lowers his head in apprehension and catches sight of his reflection in the water. To his astonishment and joy, he sees that, without knowing it, he has become a swan himself – in the words of an onlooker, 'the most beautiful of all'.

A dirty, ragged little Cockney flower-seller, treated by passers-by almost as refuse, is picked up in the streets by a distinguished professor of phonetics. Hidden away from the world, she is scrubbed clean, given fine clothes and her tortured vowels are gradually moulded into the accents of the aristocracy. A few months later, she is brought into public for the first time, when she is taken to a grand ball, attended by the cream of London's fashionable society. As she enters, there are gasps of astonishment at her beauty and bearing, and she is taken by many present to be a princess.

Few images in the popular storytelling of our time have fixed themselves more vividly in the mind than the moment when Clark Kent, the weedy, bespectacled newspaper reporter, is suddenly transformed into 'Superman', the all-powerful righter of the world's wrongs'; or when Popeye, the shambling, ineffectual sailor-man, swallows his tin of spinach and swells up into a bulging-muscled hero, effortlessly despatching the bully who has been forcing his attentions on Popeye's helpless girlfriend. Few clichés of old pre-feminist Hollywood were so well-tried as the moment when the handsome hero removed the plain, bespectacled girl's glasses, let down her tightly-coiled hair, gazed at her with awe and exclaimed 'Gee ... but you're beautiful'.

In all these scenes, someone who has seemed to the world quite commonplace is dramatically shown to have been hiding the potential for a second, much more exceptional, self within. Somehow the moment of transformation when this other greater self emerges has a strange power to move us. And we begin with this transformation because it lies at the heart of our second plot, 'Rags to Riches'.

Early in our lives, most of us became familiar with a story which ran something like this.

Once upon a time there was a young hero or heroine, not yet embarked on adult life, living in lowly and very difficult circumstances. This humble little figure, almost certainly an orphan, was regarded as of little worth by most people around, and may even have been actively maltreated. But one day something happened to send our hero or heroine out into the world where they met with a series of adventures which eventually brought about a miraculous transformation in their fortunes. Emerging from the shadows of their wretched former state, they were raised to a position of dazzling splendour, winning the admiration of all who beheld them. The hero won the hand in marriage of a beautiful Princess; the heroine won the love of a handsome Prince. They succeeded to rule over a kingdom. And from that day forth they lived 'happily ever after'.

So familiar did this plot become to us in childhood that we take its almost unvarying regularity for granted. It is of course the story of how the little orphan Cinderella, dressed in rags and forced to sit in the ashes by her cruel stepmother and vain stepsisters, is enabled by her fairy godmother to go out to the the ball – which eventually wins her the hand in marriage of her Prince. It is the story of how the little orphan Aladdin is led out of the city by his wicked 'uncle', the Sorcerer, to retrieve the magic lamp, thus embarking on the strange series of adventures which transform him into a rich and admired national hero, winning the hand of the Princess and finally succeeding to the kingdom of her father, the Sultan. It is the story of how the unhappy little orphan hero of *Puss in Boots*, left with nothing in the world but his cat, is transformed by the cat's ingenious tricks into the magnificent Marquis of Carabas, complete with a great castle and estates – fit to win the hand of the King's daughter. It is the story of how the little orphan Dick Whittington comes up to London to live in poverty but, again with the aid of his cat, wins a fabulous fortune, marries a rich merchant's beautiful daughter and becomes 'thrice Lord Mayor of London'.

Most of the variations on this Rags to Riches story we met in childhood were adapted from folk tales, and it is perhaps not until we begin reading through folk stories from many different countries and cultures that we come to appreciate how universal this type of story is. The basic outline of the story we know as *Cinderella* is reckoned by the students of folklore to have given rise to well over a thousand different versions, found in every corner of Europe, in Africa, in Asia (the earliest known version dates back to ninth-century China) and among the indigenous peoples of North America. Other permutations on the Rags to Riches theme appear so often in folklore that on this score alone it must be regarded as one of the most basic stories in the world.

But the story of the humble, disregarded little hero or heroine who is lifted out of the shadows to a glorious destiny is by no means, of course, confined only to folk tales. We have already touched on such familiar examples as the opening episodes in the mediaeval story of King Arthur; or the modern fairy-tale trans-formation of the ragged little flower-girl Eliza Doolittle into a grand and beautiful lady which made one of the most popular stage and film musicals of our time, *My Fair Lady* (although without Shaw's original happy ending in *Pygmalion*, where Eliza finally marries and lives happily ever after).

We can find the Rags to Riches theme in almost every form in which stories have been told. It is as ancient as the biblical story of Joseph, the little dreamer so despised by his brothers that they want to kill him, who eventually rises to a position as the Pharaoh's chief minister, ruler over the mighty kingdom of Egypt. It is as modern as the countless versions produced in our own time by Hollywood, so that the very phrase 'rags to riches story' is these days likely to conjure up for many people the type of film which shows how a poor, obscure chorus girl dances her way to stardom or a poor boy from the slums battles his way to the top to become a world boxing champion.

Indeed there are certain categories of popular storytelling which seem so nat-urally drawn to the Rags to Riches plot, that we often think of this kind of story, with its 'fairy tale happy endings', as being essentially rather simple and sentimen-tal, the stuff of wish-fulfilment rather than great literature. The Rags to Riches theme has, for instance, traditionally been associated with that type of romantic fiction which was mainly written by and for women, telling of how some poor and beautiful (or plain and disregarded, but secretly admirable) heroine rises from obscurity to win the heart of a prince, dashing duke or millionaire. Quite apart from the well-known adaptations of folk tales, stories specially written for child-ren have always relied heavily on the Rags to Riches theme: we may think, for instance, of those Victorian school stories which told of how a new boy survived the initial ordeals of bullying and maltreatment to become Captain of the School; or those twentieth-century tales for girls which showed a little heroine eventually fulfilling her dream of dancing with a famous ballet company.

But equally the Rags to Riches plot has inspired some of the most serious and admired novels in Western literature. An obvious example is *David Copperfield*, in which we see how an unhappy, persecuted little orphan goes out into the world and eventually rises, after many adventures, to become a rich and famous writer, at last happily united in the closing pages to his 'true angel', Agnes Woodward. In *Jane Eyre* we again follow the fortunes of an unhappy, persecuted little Cinderella-like orphan as she goes out into the world, where she eventually becomes an heiress and, against all odds, marries her adored 'Prince' Mr Rochester. In each of these novels the fundamental plot shaping the story is precisely that of those childhood fairy tales: that of the unhappy and disregarded little child at the beginning gradually developing and maturing through the vicissitudes of life to the point at the end where he or she is raised up to a state of glorious happiness and fulfilment, united at last with a beloved 'other half'.

In general terms, such a story obviously makes some profound appeal to the human imagination. But when we come to look more closely at a wide cross-section of such stories, we find that they have much more in common than just a vague, generalised outline. Wherever we find the Rags to Riches theme in story-telling, we may be struck by how constantly certain of its features recur.

First of these is that, more consistently than in any other type of plot, the Rags to Riches story first introduces us to its hero or heroine in childhood, or at least at a very young age before they have ventured out on the stage of the world. As yet they are not fully formed, and we are aware that in some essential way the story is concerned with the process of growing up.

When we first see them in this initial state, it is always emphasised how the little hero or heroine are at the bottom of the heap, seemingly inferior to everyone around them. Often they are the youngest child, and disregarded for being so. They thus begin in the shadows cast by more dominant figures around them, who not only can see no merit in them but are usually deeply antagonistic to them.

These 'dark' figures who overshadow the hero or heroine in the early stages of the story fall into two main categories. Firstly they may be adult figures, often acting in the place of a parent, such as Cinderella's wicked stepmother, who replaces her loving real mother; or David Copperfield's cruel stepfather Mr Murdstone, and his grim sister Miss Murdstone, who replace his real parents when they die; or Jane Eyre's guardian Aunt Reed, and the fearsome Mr Brocklehurst, who takes her away to an orphanage. Secondly there are those figures nearer to the hero or heroine in age and status: Cinderella's vain, scornful stepsisters; Joseph's hostile older brothers, who want to kill him; the Ugly Duckling's fellow ducklings who, along with the other animals of the farmyard, jeer at him for his awkwardness and ugliness.

Whichever of these categories they fall into, these dark figures are always presented in the same light. In their scornful attitude to the hero or heroine, they are both hard-hearted and blind: they can neither feel for them nor perceive their true qualities. They are also, like Cinderella's stepsisters, wholly self-centred: vain, puffed-up, short-tempered, deceitful, concerned only with furthering their own interests. Later in the story, other 'dark' figures may emerge to stand between the hero or heroine and their ultimate goal: as we see in David Copperfield's rival for the hand of Agnes, the treacherous Uriah Heep; or in Jane Eyre's egregious suitor

St John Rivers. But these characters are typified by precisely the same negative qualities; they are defined by their egocentricity, their blinkered vision, their incapacity for true, selfless love.

What we see in the 'dark' figures of Rags to Riches stories is thus a combination of characteristics already familiar from our first plot, Overcoming the Monster. Psychologically, they share the same essential attributes as the monster, And against this we see the hero or the heroine themselves set in complete contrast. The hero or heroine begin the story largely unformed, in the shadows cast by the more dominant figures around them. But it is central to the story, as they gradually emerge from these shadows towards the the light, that the hero or heroine are not marked by these same hard, self-centred characteristics. We always see them as a positive against the overshadowing negative; and in this sense, as the story unfolds, they do not change their essential character. All that happens is that they develop or reveal qualities which have been in them, at least potentially, all the time: to the point where, by the end of the story, two things have happened. Firstly, all the dark figures have either been discomfited or have just faded away. And secondly, the hero or heroine have at last emerged fully into the light, so that everyone can at last recognise how exceptional they are. It is this which has essentially been happening in the story, and the fact that their material circumstances may also have gone through such a transformation – e.g., that they have exchanged their original poverty and rags for riches and fine clothes – is only an outward reflection of what has inwardly happened to them, lending it dramatic emphasis.

Even in the simplest folk-tale versions of the Rags to Riches plot, we can see how carefully this point is brought out. By the end of the story, no one ever doubts that the originally derided and humble little hero or heroine should be worthy of their final glorious destiny, however improbable it might have seemed from their circumstances at the beginning that they should eventually rise to such an elevated state, because they have already revealed along the way qualities which show their true inner worth. When Cinderella goes to the ball and meets her Prince for the first time, it is not just the magnificent clothes in which she has been dressed by her fairy godmother which catch every eye: it is her innate beauty and obvious sweetness of nature, which fine clothes have only helped to 'bring out' (it is a telling detail at the end that when the Prince finally sees her in her rags, he at once recognises her as the girl he loves; she does not need external trappings to be seen as beautiful in the eyes of the right person). Similarly, when Aladdin is decked out by the genie of the lamp in all sorts of splendour for his wedding to the Princess, the formerly scorned little urchin win all hearts by his generosity and noble bearing, and astonishes his prospective father-in-law the Sultan by his 'eloquence and cultured speech', 'his gallantry and wit'.[1] Even the hero of *Puss in Boots*, though it might be thought that he owed his elevation entirely to the ingenuity of his cat, has no sooner been dressed in fine clothes (which 'set off his

1. *Aladdin and the Enchanted Lamp*, from Tales of *The Thousand And One Nights*, translated by N. J. Dawood, Penguin Classics edition (1955).

good mien') than he impresses his future father-in-law the king by his 'fine quali-ties'. even though the 'well-made and very handsome young man' was originally only the son of a poor miller.[2] Likewise, Dick Whittington, who similarly owes everything to his cat, has no sooner become rich and put on his finery than he is revealed to all the world (as the narrator is careful to point out) as 'a thoroughly genteel young fellow'.[3]

Yet obviously these dazzling young heroes and heroines are not exactly the same people that we saw, unhappy, confused and rejected, in the earlier scenes of their stories. What has happened to them is that they have at last revealed or developed what was potentially in them all the time. They have matured. They have grown up. They have fully realised everything that was in them to become. In the best and highest sense, they have become themselves.

An example of a Rags to Riches story which makes this point particularly clearly – because, stripped down to this essence, the story consists of very little else – is Hans Christian Andersen's *The Ugly Duckling*. Being a duckling, the hero can hardly make the journey from literal rags to literal riches. But he is certainly looked down on by everyone at the beginning, and almost our entire interest in the tale centres round the contrast between that long initial period of misery and confusion when he suffers because he does not know who he really is, and that final moment of joyful self-realisation when he flowers into his true self as a beautiful swan.

In the majority of Rags to Riches tales, however, the joy and perfection of the central figure's final state are also expressed by those two other ingredients which equally have nothing to do with literal riches, but which are so fundamental to the world's storytelling that they are almost synonymous with our notion of a 'happy ending'.

The first is that, somewhere along the way, the hero should have met the girl of his dreams, a beautiful maiden or 'Princess'. The heroine has met her handsome 'Prince'. Nothing more profoundly conveys our sense of resolution at the end of a story that they should at last be united, a man and a woman brought together in perfect love.

The second is that the hero, or the newly united pair, should then succeed to some kind of a kingdom, inheritance or domain, over which they can rule. There we can leave them, with the sense that, after a long period when it seems that dark forces and uncertainty ruled the day, everything has at last been brought or restored to where it should be. We may at this point be told that 'they lived hap-pily ever after', and we do not necessarily need to know anything more about them: because we have reached that mysterious central goal in storytelling, where everything seems at last to be perfect and complete.

---

2. *Puss In Boots*, translated by Robert Samber (1729) from the French version of the traditional folk tale published by Charles Perrault in *Histoire ou Contes du Temps Passe* (1695), and reprinted in *The Classic Fairy Tales* by Peter and Iona Opie, OUP (1974).

3. *The History of Richard Whittington, Of His Lowe Byrthe, His Great Fortune*, published anonymously in 1605.

## The central crisis

At first sight it might seem that the process whereby the hero or heroine of a Rags to Riches story eventually reaches this goal is fairly simple. But the more systematically we examine such stories, the more we may be struck by the way the hero or heroine's emergence from the shadows is rarely presented as a simple, unbroken climb. In fact there is usually a particular moment in the story when, after an initial improvement in the hero or heroine's fortunes (sometimes so great that it might in itself seem the cue for a happy ending), they suddenly hit a new point of crisis, when all hopes of a happy ending seem to have been snatched away forever.

For a familiar example, let us go back to that classic English version of the Rags to Riches theme first recorded in 1605 under the title *The History of Richard Whittington, Of His Low Byrthe, His Great Fortune*. There is no more celebrated episode in this story that that when, about halfway through, the hero sets out to leave London, and is only called back by the sound of distant church bells proclaiming 'Turn again Whittington, Lord Mayor of London'.

At this point in the story, Dick is at his lowest ebb. He had arrived in the great city from the countryside, hoping to find the streets 'paved with gold'. He had initially met with terrible disillusionment and nearly died of hunger. But then his fortunes had begun to look up. A rich merchant, Alderman Fitzwarren, had taken pity on him and given Dick employment in his kitchens. He had even found at last a real friend and inseparable companion, his cat. It is only when he is forced to send his cat (as his only possession in the world) on one of his master's overseas trading ventures, and thus finds himself again, more than ever, alone and friendless, that Dick is finally overwhelmed by complete despair.

He decides to abandon London and all his dreams forever. It is, as we might put it, the worst crisis of Dick's life. But it is at precisely this moment, far away in the dark continent of Africa, that his fortunes are in fact being transformed. His cat has rid a kingdom of a terrible plague of rats and mice, and the king of that country has given an immense reward. Although Dick knows none of this, he is given by Bow bells a strange premonition of the almost unthinkable glories which life might still have in store for him. He returns to London to discover that he has become enormously rich. He marries his rich employer's beautiful daughter Alice (the person who had most obviously shown sympathy for him in his former lowly state) and becomes, as foretold by the bells, Lord Mayor of London, his equivalent of succeeding to a 'kingdom'.

Such a central moment of crisis and despair as Dick faced when he was separated from his cat is in fact so natural to the pattern of the Rags to Riches story that there are few examples where in some form or another it does not appear. Even in *The Ugly Duckling* there is no moment when the hero's spirits are at a lower ebb than after his first glimpse of the 'kingly' swans: a prevision of the unthinkable glories life might hold. But then the swans disappear, leaving the duckling alone to face the hardships of a long, terrible winter. He has never been so cold, short of food or miserable. It is only when he has been through this last, greatest ordeal that at last spring arrives, bringing with it the miraculous moment of his transformation into a 'kingly' swan himself, 'the most beautiful of all'.

Similarly in *Cinderella*, there is no moment when everything seems more hopeless for the heroine than after her third visit to the ball. Three times she has left her rags and ashes to dance with the Prince, winning universal admiration and catching a glimpse of the unthinkable happiness life might hold for her. Now, as she returns to her miserable, imprisoned life as a maid-of-all-work, with no prospect of ever seeing the Prince again, all seems blacker than ever. But of course, in her headlong flight from the palace on the third visit, she has left behind her dainty slipper; and, quite unknown to her, the Prince has found it, and sent out far and wide across the kingdom to see whose foot the slipper will fit. As with Arthur and the sword in the stone, the trying on of the slipper is a version of that motif familiar from many of the world's myths, legends and folk tales, 'the test which only the true hero, or heroine, can pass'. Cinderalla comes through her ordeal triumphantly (finally discomfiting on the way her two 'dark rivals', the Ugly Sisters). The Prince at once recognises her in her rags, and they proceed to the traditional happy ending.

In each of these examples we see the same essential structure to the story, as it falls into two distinct stages, separated in the middle by 'the central crisis'. First there is the initial rise in the hero or heroine's fortunes, as they are taken out of their original state of helpless misery, and may have a glimpse of the glorious state they might one day attain. Then comes the terrible crisis, when all seems lost again. Then comes the second half of the story, which shows them being prepared unwittingly for their final reversal of fortune, their final emergence into the light and the glorious state of completeness at which they arrive at the end.

We can already see this pattern at work in by far the earliest example of a Rags to Riches story of which we have record, the story of Joseph from the biblical book of *Genesis*. When young Joseph's jealous brothers, after first planning to leave him to die in the desert, then sell him into slavery in Egypt, he eventually rises to rule as an overseer over the household of Potiphar, the captain of the king's guard. This is an important position, and considering Joseph's earlier plight, when he faced death in the desert, it might seem like a miraculous happy ending to the story. But just then Joseph is falsely accused by Potiphar's temptress wife of attempting to seduce her. He is thrown into prison and his life seems irrevocably in ruins. Only after a long time of utter despair is Joseph's talent for interpreting dreams (the very thing for which he had nearly been murdered by his brothers) quite unexpectedly brought to the attention of Phaoroah himself. Through this he is eventually raised up to infinitely greater heights as chief minister, the second most powerful man in the kingdom. But even then, as Joseph enjoys his position of immense wealth and splendour, there is a crucial piece of unfinished business remaining before the story can come to a completely happy conclusion: Joseph's rift with his brothers. As famine stalks the land of Israel, they come to Egypt, pleading with this mighty, powerful figure to be given enough corn to survive. At first Joseph rejects them, until he is so moved by the sight of his youngest brother, 'little Benjamin', who had not been party to his earlier persecution, and by the thought of his aged father Jacob starving back in Israel, that he relents. He gives them the food they need. Only when he has passed this final test, and been reunited with his family in a state of love and forgiveness, can the story end on an image of complete resolution.

Equally it is by no means just in the older and more traditional forms of the Rags to Riches tale that we see this pattern of the story's division into two 'halves' interrupted by a 'central crisis'. We are just as likely to find it in versions as far removed from the world of the traditional folk tale or biblical legend as could be imagined.

An early instance of the fondness of Hollywood for the Rags to Riches theme was Charlie Chaplin's silent classic *The Gold Rush* (1921). The first half of the story shows Chaplin, in his familiar 'tramp' role, as an unsuccessful little Alaskan gold prospector, whose dreams of happiness centre on Georgia, a dance hall hostess he has met in a nearby town, and with whom he has fallen in love. He invites her to a New Year's Eve dinner in his shack, and all might seem set fair for a happy ending to his years of loneliness. But she had only accepted the invitation as a joke and fails to turn up. The central crisis has arrived. He has not discovered any gold; he has lost the girl who had become the dearest thing to him in the world; his life is in ruins. But then comes the second half of the story, when he helps his friend Big Jim to discover a lost gold mine and is rewarded with a share which makes him fabulously rich. We see him embarking on a ship back to San Francisco as a multi-millionaire, posing on the deck for photographers in his tramp's clothes. He slips and falls down onto a lower deck, where who should be first to see him but Georgia, travelling steerage on the same boat. From his clothes she imagines he must be a stowaway and offers to pay his fare. But, revealing his good fortune, he invites her to join him in first-class and the film ends with the couple in joyful embrace.

Another form of the Rags to Riches theme particularly beloved by Hollywood has been the story of the poor, struggling artist, inventor or scientist who for long is scorned by an uncomprehending world – but who is eventually recognised as a genius and ends in a blaze of universal acclaim (usually in fond embrace with the wife or girl he loves, who alone has stood by him during the years of rejection and apparent failure).

Typical of this genre was *The Benny Goodman Story*, made in 1956 about the life of the 1930s bandleader. And although the film was based, as they say, on 'a true story', it is fascinating to see how the scriptwriters chose to arrange their material to make it into a satisfactory story for the screen.

A poor Jewish boy, born into the Chicago slums in the early years of the twentieth century, takes up the clarinet and is early spotted by his wise old white-haired teacher to have remarkable talent. Growing up in the 'Jazz Age' of the 1920s, he is drawn to the unconventional new music and eventually, after various struggles and rebuffs, becomes leader of his own band. He enjoys initial success, rather as Cinderella enjoys her initial moments of success at the ball. But then comes the crisis. The band's new brand of 'swing music' has developed beyond the point where public taste seems ready to follow. As the musicians travel on a make-or-break tour across America, audiences dwindle, bookings fall off, money runs out and it seems the orchestra will have to disband. Failure stares Goodman in the face. When they reach California, they have just one last engagement left, at the Palomar ballroom in Los Angeles. A huge crowd of dancers has turned up, but when the band begins to play straight dance music, they seem bored. It seems like the final moment of rejection, until in a final gesture of defiance, Goodman decides to go down fighting, by switching to the hottest music his musicians can play. The dancers break off from dancing and cluster round the bandstand, simply to listen. Suddenly cheering breaks out. It is clear that 'swing' is just what America has been waiting for. Headlines pour across the screen recording the band's success, until the film ends with Goodman winning the hand of his 'Princess', his rich young impresario's beautiful upper-class sister, while the band faces its final test, a concert in Carnegie Hall, the first time a mere jazz orchestra has ever been permitted into the hallowed citadel of America's classical music. A close-up shows the feet of the heroine's elderly, conventional, rich parents surreptitiously beginning to tap to the rhythm of the music. The entire audience rises to give Goodman an ovation. The slum-born hero has triumphantly won his way into the 'kingdom'. [4]

We are now in a position to see how, as it unfolds in the mind of the storyteller, a story based on the Rags to Riches plot tends to take on a certain, quite specific shape. The longer and more fully developed such a story becomes, the more apparent this is likely to be, and this may be illustrated in some detail by way of two last examples. On the face of it, these stories could scarcely seem more dissimilar: one is the ancient Middle Eastern folk tale of Aladdin; the other a well-known nineteenth-century English novel, *Jane Eyre*. But as we follow the essence of what is happening to the central figure in each of these stories, we begin to see clearly what this structure of the Rags to Riches plot is really about.

The story of *Aladdin and His Enchanted Lamp* supposedly comes from that famous collection of Middle Eastern tales *The Thousand and One Nights* dating back to the eighth century (although it has recently been suggested that this story might have been written much later). [5]

The story begins with Aladdin as an unruly little good-for-nothing orphan, living alone with his mother in a great city. His father is dead and nothing can be done to control him. But one day a mysterious 'Sorcerer' appears, claiming to be the dead father's long-lost brother. Aladdin's new 'uncle' makes a great show of

---

4. We may note that when *The Benny Goodman Story* came to be made in 1956, the real-life event on which the scriptwriters chose to conclude the story, the Carnegie Hall concert of 1938, had taken place 18 years earlier. In other words, the special demands of fiction had taken over from factual biography, to provide them with a 'fairy tale ending' – the hero winning the 'Princess' and succeeding to the 'kingdom'; even though this meant omitting from the story everything which, in real life, had happened to Goodman subsequently. Such is the power of the underlying archetype to dictate the shape of a story.

5. Robert Irwin points out in *The Arabian Nights: A Companion* (1994) that the story of Aladdin first appeared in the French translation of *Les Mille et Une Nuits* published in Paris by Antoine Galland between 1704 and 1715. Before this there is no record of the story, so its origins remain a mystery.

taking a fatherly interest in the boy, and leads the young hero out of the city to a remote spot in the shadow of a great mountain. Here a mysterious hole appears in the ground. The Sorcerer gives Aladdin a magic ring to protect him in case of trouble, and the boy is sent down into the underground cave where he finds three rooms containing a fabulous treasure, jewels and finely worked gold and silver, shining in the darkness. But Aladdin has been instructed on no account to touch any of this. He must venture right to the back of the caves, where in a niche he will see an unprepossessing-looking old lamp. This he must bring back to the surface. When he does so, the Sorcerer turns out to be a wicked trickster. He asks Aladdin to hand the lamp up to him, but when the boy refuses, a rock closes over the entrance and the hero finds himself trapped. After three days of imprisonment in the darkness, he is just about to give up all hope when, in the nick of time, he inadvertently rubs the ring. A genie appears, who has the power to free him. Aladdin returns home, where he eventually discovers the much greater powers of the genie of the lamp. Thanks to the genie's help, he and his mother are now able to live in comfort for some years, while Aladdin, now in his teens, is quite transformed from the feckless child he was at the start of the story, spending time in earnest conversation with travellers from afar, learning about the world.

Such is the first part of the story, which shows the hero, with the aid of newly-discovered and mysterious powers, being turned from an unformed and unruly child into a serious young man on the verge of adult life.

The second stage of the story shows Aladdin falling in love, from a distance, with the most beautiful woman in the city, the Princess Badr-al-Budr, the daughter of the city's ruler. He hardly dares think he could ever be fortunate enough to win her, and indeed for a long time it seems certain that she will marry someone else – the arrogant son of the king's chief vizier. But eventually, with the aid of the genie of the lamp, Aladdin succeeds against all the odds in outwitting his dark rival, and wins the Princess's hand. He is transformed by the genie into a splendid and wealthy young man, whose qualities, including his good-hearted generosity, win universal admiration. The wedding takes place; the genie constructs for Aladdin a palace even more magnificent than the king's own; and, as general in charge of the king's army, he wins a great victory over the country's enemies. He has become a national hero.

Outwardly, by this point in the story, the young man seems to have the world at his feet. He has gone out onto the stage of the world, he has won the hand in marriage of the woman he has come to desire more than anything else, he is the most admired man in the kingdom. All might seem set for a happy, if somewhat straightforward ending to his story. But the storyteller is careful to emphasise just how much Aladdin's success is outward. He owes everything to the genies. And for the first time there is an ominous hint of impending trouble when Aladdin boasts to his father-in-law about the magnificence of his palace. He is getting carried away by the success that has come to him too easily, and we realise that a great deal more has to happen before his story can be properly and completely resolved.

Indeed it is now that the 'central crisis' arrives. While Aladdin is away from the city hunting, his attention all turned on the outside world, the shadowy Sorcerer creeps back into the city in disguise, offering 'new lamps for old'. The Princess falls for the trick and gives away the old lamp which has been the source of all her husband's success. In the twinkling of an eye, the Sorcerer has spirited Princess and palace away to darkest Africa. Aladdin returns to the city to find his world in ruins. Not only has he lost everything that was most dear to him, but the king is in a towering rage, threatening that unless Aladdin can return everything to where it was within forty days he will be put to death.

Faced with this unprecedented crisis, not knowing where to begin, Aladdin wanders out into the desert in suicidal despair. Resigning himself to death, he inadvertently rubs the ring, still on his finger, and the lesser genie appears. Aladdin appeals to him for help, and the genie says he can transport Aladdin to the place in Africa where the Princess and the palace have been taken. But beyond that he cannot help, because the powers of the genie of the lamp are too strong. From then on, it will be up to Aladdin alone.

This highly significant moment marks the beginning of the second half of the story. Just when all seems lost, Aladdin is rescued: but only on the crucial condition that, from now on, he must, in some entirely new way, learn to rely on himself and bring his own powers into play.

This new phase begins with Aladdin being carried to Africa, where he finds the Princess guarded day and night in the Palace by the dark powers of the Sorcerer. Disguising himself as a beggar (returning to the humble state in which he had begun), he enters the Palace and manages to reach the Princess, whom he supplies with a drug which she is to administer to the Sorcerer. When the Sorcerer has fallen into a state of unconsciousness, Aladdin breaks in and kills him. The monster is overcome. With the aid of the lamp, the hero then joyfully returns the Princess, himself and the palace back to China where they all belong.

Again this might seem to have all the makings of a happy ending (indeed it is here that many modern adaptations, such as pantomime versions, terminate the story). But in the full, original version, Aladdin now has to face a last testing ordeal, more nearly deadly than anything he has been through before, which provides the real climax to the story.

There arrives in the city the Sorcerer's brother, bent on revenge. The dark power represented by the Sorcerer has still not been finally overthrown. Originally we saw him, eager to obtain the lamp, in the role of Predator. We then saw him, defending his ill-gotten gains in Africa, as Holdfast. We now see him, transmuted as his 'brother' but otherwise identical, as Avenger.

The new Sorcerer secretly kills a famous 'Holy Woman' of the city and, putting on her disguise, inveigles himself into the Princess' confidence. Everyone is taken in, even Aladdin, who, at the false Holy Woman's suggestion, asks the genie of the lamp for the one thing necessary to make the palace perfect: the egg of the roc, a fabulous bird. The genie flies into a rage, saying that this is the one thing in the world it is not in his power to provide, because the roc is his mother. There is no way he can help Aladdin, apart from revealing to him that the Holy Woman is the Sorcerer in disguise. Aladdin realises the terrible danger they are all in, and that he is now completely on his own. Only by his own wits and courage can he overcome the dark power which has been arraigned against him since the beginning of the story. In a final climactic confrontation, he manages to outwit and kill the Sorcerer. Only when the dark power has thus been overthrown forever, does the awed and grateful Princess finally recognise his true worth ('I confess I have never done justice to our love'). They are at last truly and fully united, the king eventually dies, and Aladdin succeeds to the kingdom.

We can now see what the whole story was really about: the journey of a human being from unformed childhood to a final state of complete personal maturity. In the first half we see Aladdin, as he grows up from boyhood to adulthood, discovering that he has immense powers at his command, which bring him a dazzling marriage and glorious outward success on the stage of the world. But in no sense is he yet fully developed and mature; and this is symbolised in the way he has owed everything to the genies. He becomes forgetful of this and begins to behave hubristically, showing how immature he still is. Then the great crisis erupts and he loses everything, falling into total despair. We realise that, to become a true hero, he must cease to rely unthinkingly on these mysterious powers. He must go back to the beginning again and learn consciously how to stand on his own feet, and to become master of his own fate, his own character. Only when he has thus grown fully in inner stature, and become completely 'his own man' can the dark power which in one way or another has dogged him throughout the story be finally seen through and thrown off. Only now is he liberated to become completely united with his 'other half', the Princess, symbolising the state of personal wholeness he has reached: and only now is he truly fitted to succeed to rule wisely and justly over the kingdom. He has reached the end of his journey.

Let us now compare this fully-developed version of the Rags to Riches plot with our second, outwardly very different example, Charlotte Bronte's *Jane Eyre* (1847).

The story begins with the heroine as an unruly and miserable little orphan living with her mother's sister, Aunt Reed. Nothing can be done to control Jane when she is in one of her rages and one day the fearsome pillar of evangelical rectitude Mr Brocklehurst appears, making a show of only wanting to serve Jane's best interests, to take her off to the orphanage at Lowood. Her introduction to this strange new world is a terrifying ordeal, but when Jane has come through it she eventually settles down to several years of steady progress, blossoming into a serious-minded and accomplished girl in her late teens. This corresponds to the first phase of Aladdin's story, as it shows Jane being transformed from an unruly child into a serious young woman on the verge of adult life.

The second part of her story shows her going out into the wider world in a new way, when she takes up her first employment at the great house of Thornfield, as governess to the daughter of the rich and mysterious Mr Rochester. She conceives a deep but seemingly hopeless love for Rochester. She can hardly dare think she would ever be fortunate enough to marry him. Indeed for a long time it seems certain that he will marry someone else, a well-born, arrogant neighbour Blanche Ingram. But eventually, to Jane's astonishment, Rochester declares his love for his 'plain little governess', and asks her to marry him. It might seem an unthinkable happy ending was imminent, except that there are now abundant ominous signs that, behind the scenes, all is not well. The truth is that, even as preparations are going ahead for the wedding and Rochester is buying fine clothes to deck out his bride, she is inwardly not yet ready for this over-hasty transformation in her life and status. She is still an immature, undeveloped girl, who knows little of the dark side of life and the world: and then, even as she approaches the altar to be married, the central crisis of the story erupts.

A voice calls out from the back of the church that the wedding cannot take place because Rochester is already married. It turns out that for years he has been concealing his crazed first wife in an upstairs room at Thornfield Hall. Just as with Aladdin, at the moment when the Sorcerer snatches his Princess, palace and lamp away to Africa, Jane's seemingly glorious new world is in ruins. In despair she runs away from Thornfield, to wander distractedly over the bleak, inhospitable moors. After three days, cold, weak and starving, she falls down on a cottage doorstep to die – when, in the nick of time, she is rescued, by the seemingly kindly clergyman St John Rivers. Under the care of Rivers's sisters, Jane gradually recovers her strength: and we then see, as in *Aladdin*, a very significant new phase in her story. We see Jane setting up house on her own, opening a successful little school, and for the first time in her life learning to stand on her own feet, developing an inner strength and independence of spirit she has never known before: until, as a mark of her newly-won autonomy, she learns that she has mysteriously inherited a modest fortune, making her outwardly as well as inwardly independent.

But even now, like Aladdin when through his own efforts he has been able to recover the lamp and return home from Africa, Jane has to face one last terrifying ordeal, more nearly deadly than anything she has had to contend with before. The iron-willed, evangelical and hypocritical St John Rivers – a 'false Holy Man' – uses all his powers to force her to marry him, and to accompany him as a missionary to India, which Jane knows would certainly be fatal to her health. Although she tries to resist, she feels her powers of resistance slipping away and is on the verge of succumbing, when she hears a distant, mysterious voice calling her name, as if from half across the world. It is the voice of Rochester. An extraordinary new strength wells up in her (at last, as she puts it, 'my powers were in play'). She flees the house in the middle of the night and rushes across the countryside to Thornfield, where she finds that the house has recently burned down. The shadowy first Mrs Rochester has died in the fire. Her dark rival has gone. Jane finds Rochester, alone and blind, in the middle of a forest. She lovingly nurses him back to health and sight. They are at last married and completely united. They end up presiding over their little kingdom and, as nearly as a novel will allow, living 'happily ever after'.

What we thus see in *Jane Eyre* is a fundamental structure to the story strikingly similar to that of *Aladdin*: the process whereby a young central figure emerges step by step from an initial state of dependent, unformed childhood to a final state of complete self-realisation and wholeness. Obviously one of the most significant features of this type of story is the way it divides into two 'halves', punctuated by the 'central crisis'. In the first half we see the hero or heroine emerging from childhood to a state where they may seem outwardly successful, except that they are by no means yet fully mature. They then encounter a crisis which leads them on to the harder task of becoming much more fully-developed and self-reliant. This leads up to the ordeal which provides the story's climax, where they have a final confrontation with the dark figures and powers who, in one way or another, have overshadowed them through the story. Only when they have come through this test are they finally liberated to enjoy the state of wholeness and fulfilment which marks the conclusion of the tale.

The longer and more fully-developed a Rags to Riches story becomes, the more likely we are to see these steps to the ultimate goal spelled out in detail; as we do in the many other novels based on this plot such as *Moll Flanders, Great Expectations* or *David Copperfield*.

In the first half of *David Copperfield*, we see the little orphan hero going through essentially all the basic stages of development we have seen in *Aladdin* and *Jane Eyre*, up to the point where he marries his first wife, Dodie. But from her selfish, infantile nature and the sentimental nature of their marriage, it is clear that the hero has not reached his true goal, because he himself has not yet developed to full maturity, and when his child-wife sickens and dies in childbirth, he faces his central crisis. Then begins the second part of his story, where he becomes much more fully developed as a man, as he builds up his career as a successful writer. In this phase we see that his true 'other half', corresponding to his new depth and maturity, is the selfless, inspiring Agnes Woodward. But she is under the shadow of Copperfield's 'dark rival', the insinuating Uriah Heep, who is scheming to marry her (as a kind of cross between the Sorcerer and St John Rivers). Only when Heep's scheming is exposed and his power overthrown at the climax of the story are hero and heroine at last freed to come together in complete, loving union.

Even in simpler versions of the theme, however, we still see much the same essential structure, with the story dividing into two parts, separated by the central crisis, emphasising that the real task facing the hero or heroine is never a simple one. And in general the Rags to Riches plot can be summed up along the following lines:

**Rags to Riches: Summing up**

A second way in which a story naturally takes shape in the human imagination is that which shows how some young, unrecognised hero or heroine is eventually lifted out of obscurity, poverty and misery to a state of great splendour and happiness. But their upward progress is unlikely to be a continuous unbroken climb, and most Rags to Riches stories, except the very simplest versions, may well unfold through a recognisable series of stages like this:

1. *Initial wretchedness at home and the 'Call'*: We are first introduced to the young hero or heroine in their original lowly and unhappy state, usually at home. The most obvious reason for their misery is that they are overshadowed by malevolent 'dark' figures around them, who scorn or maltreat them. This phase ends when something happens to call or send them out into a wider world.

2. *Out into the world, initial success*: Although this new phase may be marked by new ordeals, the hero or heroine are here rewarded with their first, limited success, and may have some prevision of their eventual glorious destiny. They may make a first encounter with their 'Princess' or 'Prince', and may even outstrip 'dark rivals'; but only in some incomplete fashion, and it is made clear that they are not yet ready for their final state of complete fulfilment.

3. *The central crisis*: Everything suddenly goes wrong. The shadows cast by the dark figures return. Hero or heroine are separated from that which has become more important to them than anything in the world, and they are overwhelmed with despair. Because of the earlier lift in their fortunes, and because they are so powerless, this is their worst moment in the story.

4. *Independence and the final ordeal*: As they emerge from the crisis, we gradually come to see the hero or heroine in a new light. Although still unfulfilled, they are discovering in themselves a new independent strength. As this develops, it must at last be put to a final test, again usually involving a battle with some powerful dark figure who stands, as a dark rival, between them and their goal; and this forms the climax to the whole story. Only when this has been successfully resolved, and the shadow over their lives wholly removed, are they at last liberated to move to the final stage.

5. *Final union, completion and fulfilment*: Their reward is usually a state of complete, loving union with the 'Princess' or 'Prince'. They may also finally succeed to some kind of 'kingdom', the nature of which is not spelled out but which, from their mature and developed state, implies a domain over which they will rule wisely and well. The story thus resolves on an image which signifies a perfect state of wholeness, lasting indefinitely into the future ('they lived happily ever after').

As in the Overcoming the Monster plot, we see that, at its deepest level, the Rags to Riches story unfolds through alternating phases of constriction and expansion. We begin with the hero or heroine weighed down by the contempt and even persecution to which they are exposed in the opening scenes. This is followed by the sense of a gradual opening out and lifting of their hopes as they go out into the world and meet with their modest early successes. But this is abruptly ended by the shock of the central crisis, imposing a new sense of constriction. Again there is a gradual opening out, as they develop a deeper maturity, until this is put to a climactic test, when the sense of constriction is at its most severe. Only then can we see the final act of liberation which enables them to emerge triumphant at the end of the story, having won the prize which gives them a sense of complete fulfilment and a hold on life which will continue indefinitely into the future.

### The dark version

Once we are familiar with the essential outlines of this type of story we can recognise a variation on the theme which may be called the 'dark' version of the Rags to Riches plot. This is the sort of tale which shows a hero or heroine who attempts to follow the general pattern of the climb from rags to riches, but in some way fails to arrive at its fully rewarding conclusion.

An example of what may be regarded as the full 'dark' version of the Rags to Riches story is Stendhal's novel *Le Rouge et Le Noir* (1831). This introduces us to a little hero of humble origins living in an obscure provincial town in France in the years after the fall of Napoleon. Julien Sorel, a clever boy who enjoys reading books, is scorned by his practical, down-to-earth father and older brothers (we hear nothing of his mother, who appears to be absent). In this sense he starts off much like the heroes of many Rags to Riches folk tales, the little dreamer, his head apparently in the clouds, who is scorned and rejected by his unimaginative family. But Sorel is not like the traditional folk tale hero. He is profoundly ambitious. His dreams are of winning earthly glory, like his hero Napoleon, and in general his attitude towards the rest of the world is one of contempt. As he nears adult life, he goes out from home in a first, limited way, by having an affair with an older married woman in the town where they live, but eventually he contemptuously rejects her. He then goes off to a seminary for prospective priests, but only because he has calculated that the Church is the best stepping stone for a poor boy to further his worldly ambitions. Again his attitude towards his fellow students is one of heartless scorn. Eventually Sorel travels to the centre of all his ambitions, the great city of Paris, where he wins the post of private secretary to the magnificent Marquis de la Mole, the most powerful man in France. He unscrupulously worms his way into the heart of his employer's beautiful daughter Mathilde (whom he enjoys humiliating sexually) and seems on the verge of marrying her and succeeding to the 'kingdom' of immense power and riches. But at the last moment, disaster strikes. The unhappy mistress he had discarded years before comes back into his life, obsessed with her desire for revenge. In a desperate bid to hold onto his new prospects, he attempts to murder her – and ends up, not at the altar with his 'Princess', but disgraced and on the guillotine.

Obviously there is a huge difference between the heartless, self-seeking Sorel and the essentially good-hearted heroes and heroines of the Rags to Riches stories we have been looking at (who are so specifically contrasted with the self-seeking dark figures who are their main antagonists and rivals). When Sorel comes into any kind of opposition to others in his story, it is they who become victims of his egotism rather than the other way around. He himself is indeed a kind of 'monster'. Yet, outwardly, the ultimate goal he is seeking is remarkably similar to that central symbolic goal we see in more conventional Rags to Riches stories. What he aspires to is union with 'the beloved other' and succession to a position of great power: except that he is after these things only as a means to egotistical gratification, as expressions of his desire for power over others. And in the end his drive for that goal is not just frustrated; it brings about his complete destruction.

Another lesser 'dark' version of the Rags to Riches plot can be seen in the kind of story where the hero may actually achieve these goals, but only in a way which is hollow and brings frustration, because again he has sought them only in an outward and egocentric fashion. Budd Schulberg's Hollywood novel *What Makes Sammy Run?* (1940) shows its hero Sammy Glick as a ruthlessly egocentric little orphan from the New York slums pushing his way up the ladder of worldly success, first in the newspaper world, then in Hollywood. He ends up seemingly rewarded with the perfect traditional happy ending. He wins the hand of the beautiful, upper-class daughter of the all-powerful owner of a major film studio; and when his prospective father-in-law appoints him head of the studio (in place of the kindly father-figure who had consistently helped him on, and whom he had broken and humiliated), the hero 'succeeds to the kingdom'. But then comes the sting in the tail. No sooner has his glittering Hollywood wedding taken place, and the fashionable throng of celebrities returned to his mansion for the celebratory party, than the hero discovers his 'Princess' upstairs, making love to one of the studio's handsome young stars. She is as heartless and self-seeking as Glick himself, and has only married him to serve her own ambitions. He may outwardly have married the 'Princess' and 'succeeded to the kingdom'. But in no way has he reached that state of glorious completion and inner fulfilment which is the proper goal of the Rags to Riches story. The novel's whole point is to show its heartless little hero acting out the archetypal climb from Rags to Riches, yet in a way which leaves him at the end staring at a black hole of total emptiness; precisely because he has done it in a fashion which can lead to no other outcome.

We shall later see that the Rags to Riches plot is by no means the only type of story which can give rise to 'dark' versions like this. Yet what is significant is how these unfold to their self-destructive endings by precisely the same rules which govern the way in which the 'light' versions proceed to their happy endings. In coming to understand just how subtly and consistently this principle operates all through storytelling we shall uncover one of the most important secrets stories have to offer.

*Chapter 4*

# The Quest

'I have a journey, sir, shortly to go;
My master calls me, I must not say no.'
Kent in *King Lear*, v.iii

In the distant land of Mordor, says Gandalf, the old wizard, there is a mighty volcanic mountain. Your task, he tells Frodo, the young hero, is to journey to that far-off place, carrying a priceless ring, and cast it into the Cracks of Doom. When Squire Trelawney and Dr Livesey look at the parchment map the young hero Jim Hawkins has found in a dead man's chest, they see that it reveals the place on a far-off desert island where a fabulous pirate treasure is buried. They at once agree that they must sail in search of it. When Odysseus embarks with his men after the sack of Troy, his only desire is to return home to his far-off island kingdom of Ithaca and his beloved wife Penelope.

No type of story is more instantly recognisable to us than a Quest. Far away, we learn, there is some priceless goal, worth any effort to achieve: a treasure; a promised land; something of infinite value. From the moment the hero learns of this prize, the need to set out on the long hazardous journey to reach it becomes the most important thing to him in the world. Whatever perils and diversions lie in wait on the way, the story is shaped by that one overriding imperative; and the story remains unresolved until the objective has been finally, triumphantly secured.

Some of the most celebrated stories in the world are quests: Homer's *Odyssey*, Virgil's *Aeneid*, Dante's *Divine Comedy*, Bunyan's *Pilgrim's Progress*. The theme has inspired myths, legends, fairy tales and stories of all kinds, right up to such popular modern examples as Tolkien's *The Lord of the Rings*, Richard Adams's *Watership Down* or Steven Spielberg's *Raiders of The Lost Ark*.

On the face of it, stories based on the plot of the Quest could hardly seem more disparate. Consider, for instance, the variety of the goals the hero is seeking. It may be some fabulous buried treasure, as in Stevenson's *Treasure Island* or Rider Haggard's *King Solomon's Mines*. It may be some other, rather more mysterious priceless object, such as the Golden Fleece or the Holy Grail sought by King Arthur's knights, or the Golden Firebird, sought by the hero of one of the most famous of Slav folk tales, or the most sacred treasure in Jewish tradition, the 'Ark of the Covenant' in *Raiders of the Lost Ark*. It may be 'home', as in Odysseus's wanderings after the Trojan War. It may be some new home, as was sought by Aeneas, or by the Jews in their exodus from Egypt towards the 'promised land', or by the fleeing rabbits in *Watership Down*. It may be the secret of immortality, as was sought by Gilgamesh in his journey to the end of the world – or simply the distant 'freedom' dreamed-of by the escapers in so many Second World War prison-camp escape stories. It may be the Celestial City, Paradise itself, as in *Pilgrim's Progress* or the *Divine Comedy*.

Yet when we come to examine such tales more closely, we find that they reveal some startling similarities.

## The Call

We begin with the reason why the hero and his companions set out on their journey in the first place. The Quest usually begins on a note of the most urgent compulsion. For the hero to remain quietly 'at home' (or wherever he happens to be) has become impossible. Some fearful threat has arisen. The 'times are out of joint'. Something has gone seriously and terrifyingly wrong.

The story of Aeneas begins amid the roaring flames, billowing smoke and crashing masonry of his beloved Troy, as it is being sacked by the Greeks. Christian in *Pilgrim's Progress* has a nightmare vision in which he sees that the city he lives in 'will be burned with fire from heaven'. In *Watership Down*, one of the rabbits in Sandleford warren, the intuitive little Fiver, feels 'some terrible thing – coming closer and closer', and has a vision of the field where he and the other rabbits play 'covered with blood'. After living many years in Egypt, the Jews are being subjected to a savage persecution, their lives 'made bitter with hard bondage', their sons murdered.

In the midst of this fear and suffering comes the Call. Amid the smoking ruins of Troy, the ghost of Aeneas's lost wife Creusa looms up, 'larger than life', to tell him that across 'a great waste of ocean', in 'the Western land', he will find a new home. Christian meets Evangelist, who points out a distant 'shining light' and tells him that he must head for it. Fiver's premonitions of some great disaster overshadowing Sandleford warren become so acute that a small band of rabbits meet in the field and decide to flee into the gathering dusk. Moses has a terrifying vision of God in the Burning Bush, telling him that the Jews must flee Egypt, and that they will eventually be brought up into 'a land flowing with milk and honey'.

The Grail Quest begins with the arrival at King Arthur's court of a strange knight. He proves to be the only knight who can sit safely in the Siege Perilous, the 'Seat of Danger', at the Round Table: and this seemingly miraculous arrival of the young hero Sir Galahad is seen as the signal for the long-promised quest for the Holy Grail, 'to free our country from the enchantments and strange events which have troubled it so often and so long'. There is a terrible clap of thunder, the hall is lit by a ray of more than earthly light, and the knights are given an ethereal prevision of the Grail for which they are about to set off in search.

So subtly constructed is the *Odyssey*, with its flashbacks and shifts in the centre from which the narrative is related, that, as Homer arranges the story, we do not begin with Odysseus at all. The story begins with the terrible threat overhanging the kingdom of Ithaca, from which its king Odysseus has been absent for many years. Amid the riots and debauches of the suitors for the hand of his queen Penelope (who has all but given up hope that Odysseus will ever return), the Call comes in a visit by the goddess Athene to his son Telemachus. She sends him forth to search for his lost father, almost as if young Telemachus is himself the hero of the quest. It is not until some considerable time later that we finally join up with the real quest motivating the poem: that of Odysseus seeking to return home, which had of course begun long before, like that of Aeneas, in the smoking wreck of Troy.

Surrounded by this atmosphere of menace and constriction, the Quest hero and his friends feel under intense compulsion to get away. Even so, they may face every kind of discouragement and opposition before they can depart. Aeneas and his friends only escape from Troy by the skin of their teeth. Christian is universally scorned when he tells of his fearful premonitions, and announces his intention to leave. The little group of rabbits with Fiver are subject to a violent effort to stop them getting away by the leaders of the warren (it is only later they discover what a near thing their escape has been – shortly after their departure the whole warren is gassed and gouged out by bulldozers). The suitors make a determined effort to stop Telemachus by force. While the longest struggle of all is faced by the Jews in Egypt, who only escape the clutches of the tyrannical Phaoroah in Egypt after the land has been smitten with seven plagues. But at last, led on by visions of a goal which has become more precious and desirable to them than anything in the world, the hero and his companions set out.[1]

## The hero's companions

We can say 'the hero and his companions' because a distinctive mark of the Quest is the extent to which, more than in any other kind of story, the hero is not alone in his adventures. The story does ultimately centre round the single figure of the

1. There is sometimes a variation to this opening in versions of the Quest story based on the search for a buried treasure. As in *Treasure Island*, there is not necessarily the sense of any enormous threat looming up to force the hero and his companions to embark on their journey. But this is replaced in creating a sense of compulsion by the fact that the drive to reach the treasure becomes a race. In *Treasure Island*, as in other Quests based on a treasure-hunt, such as the films *It's A Mad, Mad, Mad, Mad World* or *Raiders of the Lost Ark*, the chief source of suspense driving the plot forward is the realisation that more than one group of people are trying to reach the treasure at the same time. The heroes have 'dark rivals' for their goal, like the Nazi treasure-hunters in Spielberg's film, desperate to find the lost ark for their own sinister reasons. In *It's A Mad, Mad, Mad, Mad World* several competing groups of motorists race each other across California to see who can first reach a buried cache of money. The same is true in *Treasure Island*, where much of the plot centres round who will reach the treasure first: the hero and his friends, or the pirate gang, led by the treacherous, one-legged Long John Silver, who becomes the story's chief 'monster'. Even so we still see in the opening scenes of Stevenson's novel the setting up of that brooding air of menace which is familiar at the start of an archetypal Quest story, with the sinister arrival at the remote Cornish inn of Black Dog and Blind Pew. This sets up a powerful sense of threat, even before we learn of the existence of the treasure.

hero. But more consistently than in any other type of story, we are also made aware of the presence and importance of the friends who accompany him.

In fact the relationship of the hero to his companions assumes one of four general forms: and since these basic types of relationship are also found, more sporadically, through stories of all kinds, they must be noted.

Firstly, the hero's companions may simply be a large number of undifferentiated appendages, few if any of whom we even know by name. Such are the twelve boatloads of men who set out from Troy with Odysseus, Aeneas's Trojans or the main body of the Jews who accompany Moses.

Secondly, the hero may have an alter-ego who has no real distinguishing mark except his fidelity. Christian, for instance, has Faithful; Aeneas's close friend is 'fidus Achates'; Frodo in *The Lord of The Rings* has the 'faithful Sam Gamgee'[2] (another instance of this relationship in a quite different type of story is Hamlet's with his 'faithful Horatio').

Thirdly, the hero may have a subtler type of alter-ego whose role is to serve as a foil, displaying qualities the opposite of those shown by the hero. In the story of the Jewish exodus, for instance, Moses is shadowed in this way by his brother Aaron. Whenever Moses is being particularly faithful to his commission to lead the Jews into the Promised Land (as when he is up on Mount Sinai, receiving the ten commandments), Aaron is likely to be embodying infidelity and disloyalty (as in inciting the Jews to worship the Golden Calf). When the hero in the *Epic of Gilgamesh* sets out to slay the giant Humbaba, he takes with him his friend Enkidu; whenever Gilgamesh expresses courage and confidence, it is Enkidu who expresses the opposite emotions, fear and doubt. Equally, whenever the hero is in negative mode, it may be the alter-ego's role to be positive: as when Christian is overcome with suicidal despair in the dungeons of Doubting Castle, and has to be reassured by Faithful's successor as his companion, Hopeful. This kind of relationship where the chief companion embodies compensatory qualities missing in the hero (though often in an 'inferior' or not fully-developed way) is of enormous importance in stories, and we shall come across many other examples: Don Quixote and Sancho Panza, Lear and the Fool, Don Giovanni and Leporello, Wooster and Jeeves, to name but a few.

Fourthly, in the most fully-differentiated form of the relationship between the Quest hero and his companions, the latter are each given distinct characteristics which complement each other, and add up to a 'whole'. In Watership Down, for instance, the hero and leader of the rabbits is Hazel. But he relies heavily on the physical strength of Bigwig, the rational planning capacities of Blackberry and the intuitive powers of Fiver; and without all their separate contributions combined, the Quest could not succeed. A strikingly similar balance can be seen in the group who set out on the Quest in King Solomon's Mines. Their leader and the story's hero is Allan Quatermain: his companions are the 'bull-like' Sir Henry Curtis, representing physical strength; the immaculate Captain Good, who

---

2. We shall not follow *The Lord of The Rings* in this chapter because its complex story is not based exclusively on the plot of the Quest. It is analysed in detail in Chapters 19 and 34.

represents rational calculation (it is he who saves them all by predicting a lunar eclipse from his nautical almanac); while the intuitive principle is represented by their mysterious, regal Zulu companion, Umbopa, who seems to have more hidden knowledge of the goal they are heading for than he lets on, for reasons which eventually emerge.

## The journey

The essential pattern of the journey in a Quest is always the same. The hero and his companions go through a succession of terrible, often near-fatal ordeals, followed by periods of respite when they recoup their strength, receiving succour and guidance from friendly helpers to send them on their way. In other words, after the initial feeling of constriction which dominates the start of the story, we now experience the journey itself as a series of alternating phases of life-threatening constriction followed by life-giving release. We shall now consider each in turn: first, the nature of the ordeals; then that of the hero's allies, who rescue him and help him towards his goal.

The first problem facing the hero and his companions is the nature of the terrain across which they have to make most of their journey. Its essence is that it is wild, alien and unfriendly: a desert or wilderness (the Jews, Allan Quatermain); a forest (e.g., 'the Waste Forest', 'vast and labyrinthine in its depths', in which the Grail-seekers have most of their adventures); moorland or mountainous country-side (Christian, Frodo); a countryside full of dangers from animals and men (*Watership Down*); or the wild and treacherous sea (Odysseus, the Argonauts, Aeneas, *Treasure Island*).

Some of the perils they encounter therefore are simply those of the hostile terrain itself. Odysseus and Aeneas are caught in great storms at sea. The Jews and Allan Quatermain face terrible ordeals through lack of food and water, from which they are miraculously saved, in 'thrilling escapes from death', by the fall of manna or the discovery of a waterhole. No sooner has Christian left his 'City of Destruction' than he is almost sucked down to his death in the Slough of Despond.

But rather more specific obstacles than these stand between the hero and his goal, and these fall into four general categories.

## 1. Monsters

Firstly the hero and his companions are likely to encounter 'monsters'. The episode in the *Odyssey*, for instance, in which Odysseus and his men are trapped in the cave of the man-eating, one-eyed giant Polyphemus, and finally make their 'thrilling escape' by blinding the Cyclops and concealing themselves under his sheep, may be read in isolation just like a miniature version of the Overcoming the Monster plot. But, inevitably, because such episodes are here playing only a sub-sidiary role in the whole story, they cannot usually be told at great length, and are often passed over much more sketchily.

Aeneas and his men have a fearsome battle with the Harpies, loathsome beasts, half-woman, half-bird. The Argonauts also encounter the Harpies, are set on elsewhere by a race of six-handed giants and, on the island of Babycos, one of them has to face in single-combat the dreaded King Amycus, who has previously challenged and killed every passer-by. Allan Quatermain and his friends have scarcely set out than they have to kill an enormous, deadly bull-elephant. Christian has his encounters with the dragon-like Apollyon and the Giant Despair. The Jews are threatened first by the pursuing armies of the Egyptians, then by the giant 'sons of Anak'. Frodo and his companions are threatened with death by a whole range of monstrous opponents, from the mysterious 'Black Riders' to the fearsome giant spider Shelob. While the Grail-seekers have on various occasions to fight tremendous battles in the forest with mysterious 'Black Knights', who are usually holding captive some beautiful maiden.

## 2. Temptations

The second specific peril the Quest hero has to face is rather more deceptive and treacherous: the 'Temptation'. This often, but not always, involves some beautiful and captivating woman. The essence of the Temptation is that it holds out the promise of some physical gratification. It may be sexually arousing. It may offer rich food and intoxicating wines. It may just offer the hero a time of ease and pleasure, in contrast to the hard and austere nature of the task he has been set. In fact to surrender to a Temptation may be as unambiguously deadly as confrontation with a Monster. But often the danger the hero runs is simply that he will be seduced and lulled into forgetting the great task he has undertaken, and will abandon his Quest under some beguiling spell. The most complete picture of the various forms the Temptation may take is given in the Odyssey:

(1) the beautiful but deadly Sirens who, like the Lorelei of German legend, lure sailors to their doom by their bewitching songs. Their only aim is to kill.

(2) the beautiful enchantress Circe, who imprisons all visitors to her island by turning them magically into animals (symbolising the way they have surrendered to their 'animal' appetites). But she does not kill them.

(3) Calypso, another beautiful enchantress, who falls in love with Odysseus and so captivates him that he stays seven years in her cave. But, although restive, he stays voluntarily.

(4) the simple, enervating captivation of the Land of the Lotus Eaters, which saps all will in an atmosphere of relaxed self-indulgence. This traps many of Odysseus's men until they are forcibly dragged back to their ships.

For Aeneas, the chief temptation is of the Calypso type: his love affair with Dido, the widowed queen of Carthage, which is brought to an abrupt end when the messenger of the gods, Mercury, is sent by Jupiter to ask the hero 'what can you possibly gain by living at wasteful leisure in African lands?', and to order him peremptorily back on his quest. Much the same temptation ensnares the Jews when they are lured into committing 'whoredom with the daughters of Moab', and the Argonauts when they arrive on the island of Lemnos to find that the women have killed all their menfolk and are avid for new lovers. It is Heracles who on this occasion strides angrily round the island with his club, sternly recalling Jason's men to their duty.

For the rabbits of *Watership Down*, the chief temptation turns out to be a cross between the Land of the Lotus Eaters and the deadly Sirens (the four aspects, or gradations of the Temptation are in fact more closely linked than might at first appear). They are made welcome at a strange warren which at first sight seems an ideal place for them to stay, with plenty of food, ample room and no apparent danger. But gradually (through the intuitive Fiver) they sense that there is something eerie and sinister about the life of ease lived by the sleek, well-fed but cowed rabbits in the new warren. They discover, to their horror, that it is in fact a kind of luxurious slave-camp, kept by the local farmer as a source of food: and that if they stay there they are sure to die. For Christian and Faithful, the town of Vanity Fair, offering 'all the delights of this world', proves to be much the same kind of deadly snare, in which Faithful loses his life, and from which Christian only narrowly escapes to continue the journey alone.

For the knights of the Grail, sworn to chastity, temptation is firmly of the Siren-type. When Sir Percival loses his horse, he meets 'a timid maiden' in the forest, who offers him another 'huge and black', which carries him off uncontrollably for 'three days or more'. Coming to a black river, burning with fire, Percival crosses himself, whereupon the horse throws him: and he wakes up trapped, foodless, on a precipitous island in the middle of the sea. In the heat of the day a handsome ship approaches, and sitting in it, under an awning, is the most beautiful woman he has ever seen. She erects a shady tent on the shore and invites Percival to an exquisite meal, with the most potent wine he has ever drunk: and then implores him to make love to her, saying 'you have not hungered to possess me half as much as I have wanted you, for you are one of the knights I was most passionately set on having' (as we have already seen, there is little new about the world of James Bond). As they are about to climb together into a great bed, Percival catches sight of the cross on his sword-hilt; he crosses himself, the tent vanishes in a puff of foul-smelling smoke, and the ship hurtles away at unnatural speed across the ocean, leaving a wake of fire rising from storm-tossed waves.

Of course the Temptation has much in common with the Monster, except that the latter threatens the hero by direct confrontation, while the former seeks to lure him to his doom by guile and seduction. The Sirens are only Predators in another guise. While the enchantresses who seek to imprison travellers by their spells, or the arts of love, are another version of Holdfast. Nevertheless, if they are mastered or overruled in some way, these Temptresses may completely change their nature, or rather their relationship to the hero. From being malign, destructive and a hindrance, they can become the most benign of allies. When Odysseus is given the magic herb by Hermes which enables him to withstand Circe's spells, he can persuade her to release all her victims from their enchantment. And though he stays with her, feasting and making love for another year, she in the end releases him with all sorts of aid and vital guidance for his journey. Similarly Calypso, at the behest of the gods, sends him on his way with every kind of equipment and good advice. The Temptresses have in fact been transformed into that other kind of crucially important figure the hero meets on his journey, the 'helper', whom we shall be looking at shortly.

### 3. The deadly opposites

A third familar type of ordeal is the need for the hero and his companions to travel an exact and perilous path between two great opposing dangers. For the Argonauts these are the mighty 'clashing rocks', the Symplegades, between which they have to sail at exactly the right moment to avoid being crushed to death. For Odysseus the 'deadly opposites' are the great whirlpool Charybdis and the six-headed monster, the Scylla, which stand on each side of a narrow gulf. To avoid the first Odysseus steers his ship too near Scylla, who seizes six of his men; later he returns on his own and this time has a 'thrilling escape' from Charybdis. For Christian, the 'straight and narrow way' he has to follow is emphasised like this on several occasions, as when he has to pass between two fierce lions, or tread a delicate path through the Valley of the Shadow of Death, avoiding a deep ditch on one side and a treacherous bog on the other. Lancelot, in the Grail Quest, also has to pass between two lions. For the Jews, the journey between the 'opposites' is represented by the occasion when the Red Sea rolls back like a great 'wall unto them, on their right hand and on their left', leaving a dry passage for them to cross over safely; while, when the armies of Phaoroah pursue them, the 'opposites' show their deadly nature by rushing together again, like the Symplegades, engulfing 'the chariots and the horsemen and all the host'. And there is no moment more hazardous for Allan Quatermain and his little party as that when, foodless and almost freezing to death, they have to cross the narrow, snowy pass exactly between two great symmetrical mountains, the Breasts of Sheba, which is the only way through from the desert to the lost land of Solomon which is their goal.

### 4. The journey to the underworld

A final, rather different kind of ordeal which the Quest hero may have to undergo before arriving at his goal is a visit to the underworld, inhabited by the spirits of the dead. In some cases, this is simply a horrific experience, as for Christian on his passage through the Valley of the Shadow of Death:

> 'we saw there hobgoblins, satyrs and dragons of the pit; we heard also in that valley a continual howling and yelling, as of people under unutterable misery... Death does always spread his wings over it ... dreadful ... utterly without order.'

In other instances, however, the journey through the underworld is not just a harrowing ordeal: it serves a deeper purpose, enabling the hero to contemplate the fate of those who have lived before, and also to consult them on matters vital to his future. When Odysseus is guided by Circe to the gate of the netherworld which lies beyond the River of Fear and the City of Perpetual Mist, on the very edge of the world, he meets the long-dead seer Teiresias, who gives him the advice which will enable him, alone of all his men, to reach his goal; predicting for the hero exactly how the rest of his journey and his life will unfold. When Aeneas finally arrives on the shores of Italy, his first duty (as he has been advised by a ghostly vision of his dead father Anchises) is to pay a visit to the maiden-priestess, the Cumaean Sibyl. Beside an echoing cavern in the mountainside, the Sibyl summons up the god of the oracle within:

'suddenly ... her hair fell in disarray ... her bursting heart was wild and sad, She appeared taller and spoke in no mortal tones.'

The prophetess gives him careful instructions as to how he can descend into the underworld (Aeneas first has to search 'the endless forest', with the aid of two doves, for the 'golden bough', which is protected in the dark of the forest by a little circle of light). They eventually make their their descent, witnessing every kind of monster and horror, and the shades of the damned enduring eternal punishment. Finally they come of the Land of Joy and the Fortunate Woods, where they find the wise old Anchises who, like Teiresias, reveals to Aeneas the nature of the ordeals he still has to face, his future life and the glorious prospects for his descendants when the new city of Rome has been founded. With this advice and guarantee of his eventual success, Aeneas is at last ready for the final stages of his Quest.[3]

## The helpers

In addition to all the negative figures the hero and his companions meet on the journey, they also, as we have seen, encounter some very different figures: the 'helpers' who give them positive assistance, ranging from periods of respite to crucial guidance. And among these two very important figures predominate, who are to be met with in countless guises, not just in Quest stories but through-out literature.

We have already begun to meet them in the characters of the old seers Teiresias and Anchises on the one hand, and that of the Sibylline priestess on the other. These are the figures of a benevolent, usually wise old man, and a beautiful young (though often mysteriously ageless) woman.

At the most basic level, the old man and the young woman may simply provide hospitality, rest, food, nursing care and other material assistance, as Odysseus receives from the kindly King Alcinous and his daughter, the Princess Nausicaa, when he is washed up exhausted on their island, after being shipwrecked. A similar pair appear to help Allan Quatermain and his friends when they arrive in the lost land of Solomon: the old man Infadoo who warns them of many dangers, and the beautiful Foulata.

In fact the 'old man' and the 'young woman' are of ever greater significance to the hero the nearer they come to being invested with supernatural powers. Their role is not so much to intervene in the action as to act as guides and advisers, drawing on supernatural wisdom and prescience. Perhaps the supreme example of

---

3. There is a curious echo of the 'journey through the underworld' in *King Solomon's Mines*. When the hero and his companions are at last on the verge of arriving in the land they have been journeying towards, they have to spend a night in a frozen cave high up on the mountain pass. When they wake in the morning, they find they have been sleeping in company with the perfectly-preserved corpse of the sixteenth-century Portugese explorer, whose ancient map has been their sole guide and inspiration on the journey. They thus make a kind of contact with the 'spirit from the past' who plays a crucial part in guiding them to their goal.

such a pair of guides in literature are the venerable sage Virgil and beautiful Beatrice who lead Dante on his journey up to Paradise in the *Divine Comedy*.

In the stories we are considering here, the supreme example of a 'wise old man' must be the mysterious figure who from start to finish guides the Jews on their hazardous journey to the promised land, the 'Ancient of Days', Jahweh himself. Not only does he appear to Moses at crucial moments of the story to reprimand, advise and warn him, but he gives many 'signs' to the Jews that they are on the right path, such as the miraculous 'pillar of fire' which leads them on through the trackless wilderness. It is no accident that in all attempts which have ever been made by artists or film-makers to personify this figure (as in paintings showing the handing down of the tablets of stone to Moses on Sinai), he is always represented as an immensely patriarchal, bearded, wise old man.

The outstanding example of a young but ageless feminine figure is she who assists Odysseus, the 'flashing-eyed goddess of wisdom' Athene, 'tall, beautiful and accomplished'; who watches over and guides her protégé through every peril, and fights for his cause in the counsels of the gods against the hero's chief opponent, the vengeful Poseidon (a similar, through less intimate role is played for Aeneas by Venus, the goddess of love).

In the Quest for the Grail, the part of the 'wise old man' is played by the succession of hermits and holy men, whose chief role is to interpret to the heroes the meaning of the great tests and ordeals they have just undergone, and to give warnings for the future. Similarly, at various points in the story, mysterious young women of unblemished virtue appear to guide the heroes on their way – particularly important being the beautiful maiden who at last appears to summon the three supreme heroes, Galahad, Percival and Bors, onto the ship which will take them over the sea to begin the closing stages of the Quest.

In *Pilgrim's Progress*, Christian is given supernatural guidance along his path by the grave 'wise old man' Evangelist, and by the three angelic 'Shining Ones'. He is also given more mundane assistance and hospitality by the three 'grave and beautiful damsels' who live in the Palace Beautiful: and it is they at last who point out to Christian on the horizon the Delectable Mountains, the final gateway to his mysterious goal.

In modern storytelling there is no more memorable an example of these archetypal figures than the two who play such a crucial role in guiding Frodo on his mighty Quest in *The Lord of the Rings*, the all-seeing old wizard Gandalf and his ally, the beautiful, ethereal, visionary queen Galadriel.[4]

## The final ordeals

At last the heroes of our Quest stories come to the edge of the great goal towards which, through so many perils and ordeals, they have been journeying so long. Odysseus at last reaches his island of Ithaca. Aeneas reaches Italy where he is to

4. We have already seen another striking modern example in the 'wise old man' Obi-Wan Kenobi and the beautiful Princess Leia, who play a key part in guiding the heroes on their journey in *Star Wars*.

make his new home. Jason arrives in Colchis, home of the Golden Fleece. After forty years in the wilderness, the Jews at last cross over the river Jordan and arrive in 'the promised land'. The rabbits reach Watership Down, which they decide is the perfect place to settle and to make their new home.

We now discover one of the most surprising things about the Quest plot. Most people, if one talks about a 'quest', will say 'Oh yes, a story about a journey' (the very word 'quest', from the Latin *quaere*, to seek, after all means 'a search') But in fact the journey in a Quest only makes up half the story.

It has taken Odysseus twelve books of the *Odyssey* to get back to Ithaca: but there are still twelve books to go before the story is finally over. Aeneas has reached Italy by the sixth book of the Aeneid: but the poem has twelve books in all. When the Jews reached their promised land 'flowing with milk and honey', or the rabbits reach Watership Down, there is still a huge part of the story left to unfold. In almost all the quests we have been looking at (and in many others), the journey turns out to have been only the first part of the tale. The second part, which begins when the hero is actually within sight of his goal, sees him having to face a final great ordeal, or series of ordeals, which may take as long to describe as everything which has gone before. It is this final struggle which is necessary for the hero to lay hold of his prize and to secure it.

The entire second half of the *Odyssey*, for instance, describes what follows when Odysseus arrives incognito back on his island, to find his kingdom in near-total disarray, overshadowed by the arrogance, greed and dissipation of the infesting army of suitors. We see him travel across the island to arrive at his palace, disguised as a beggar, treated by the suitors like dirt. His queen Penelope has finally despaired of ever seeing him again, and decreed that she will marry anyone who can bend Odysseus's mighty bow, and shoot an arrow through a row of axe-heads. The suitors all try and fail miserably. Finally Odysseus reveals himself in all his kingly majesty (in a way we have not seen at any time before in the story). He seizes the bow, passes the test with ease ('the test which only the true hero can pass'), and he and his son Telemachus then turn on the suitors and massacre them. Thus is he finally reunited with his loving Penelope, and thus does he triumphantly reclaim his kingdom.

No sooner has Aeneas returned from his visit to the underworld in the *Aeneid* than the Trojans recognise that they have in fact at last arrived at the very place, the mouth of the River Tiber, where the gods intend they should settle. And at first all seems set for a quick and happy ending to the story. They are warmly welcomed by the local king Latinius, because prophecy has long foretold that strangers would arrive, bringing great honour to his land: and that their leader would marry his daughter, the beautiful Princess Lavinia, who has been vainly wooed by every prince in Italy, above all by the great Turnus, king of the nearby Rutulians.

But when the Princess is promised to Aeneas, black jealousy seizes Turnus's heart: and gradually the storm clouds gather for Aeneas's last and most terrible ordeal. The entire second half of the poem is taken up with describing how the tribes gather from all over the surrounding countrsyide, to hurl the Trojan inter-lopers back into the sea; the mustering of two great armies; the first skirmishes;

a tremendous battle, which the Trojans survive only by the skin of their teeth; and finally the titanic single combat between Aeneas and his 'dark rival', which at first it seems the hero will lose. But it ends at last, with his protective goddess Venus hovering over him, in his total victory.

Again, when the Argonauts arrive in Colchis to claim the Golden Fleece, the evil King Aetes tells Jason that he must face three tests, far worse than anything the Argonauts had met on their journeyings. First he must yoke two monstrous, brazen-hoofed, fire-breathing bulls, which live in an underground cavern, and plough a great field. Then he must sow the field with dragon's teeth, from which will spring up an army of fierce warriors, and slay them. Finally, if he survives all this, he must somehow slip through the defences of the fearsome, unsleeping dragon which is coiled round the tree on which the shining fleece hangs, guarding it night and day.

It seems like mission impossible. But fortunately for Jason, just as happened when Theseus arrived in Crete to challenge the Minotaur, he has already won the love of a 'helper' of supernatural powers, the tyrant's beautiful daughter, the Princess Medea. Just as Ariadne provided Theseus with the magic thread, so Medea provides Jason with a magic salve, which enables him to withstand every onslaught of the mad bulls. When he has sown the field with dragon's teeth, and is confronted with the mass of armed warriors, he is again saved from seemingly inevitable death, this time by his own ingenuity, when he throws a rock into the middle of them, so that they all turn on each other. Finally, when Medea learns that her enraged father is treacherously planning to murder Jason and all his companions while they are sleeping, she secretly leads him by night to the sacred grove where the Golden Fleece hangs, armed with a magic drug which renders it unconscious. At last he can seize his prize.

When the Jews arrive in the Promised Land (without Moses or Aaron, whom God has decreed should die before the goal is reached, for allowing their faith in his protection to waver), they face a series of 'final ordeals' just as great as those confronting the other Quest heroes: a series of tremendous battles with the tribes who already live there, beginning with the great siege of Jericho, and culminating in their victory over 'the Thirty One Kings'.

Halfway through the story of the Holy Grail, when it is clear that only three knights, Galahad, Percival and Bors, are worthy to undertake the final stages of the Quest, there is a kind of complete scene-shift to mark the second part of the story from the first. We leave 'the Waste Forest' and travel with the three heroes across the sea, in a miraculous ship steered by a beautiful maiden. When the heroes disembark, they face their last great series of ordeals, including the bloodiest battle of the story, the capture of a grim castle in which, as usual, a Princess has been imprisoned. All this prepares them for the mystical climax when they arrive at another mysterious castle, to see the Holy Grail itself borne in by angels, with a vision of Christ's presence hovering above them.

When Allan Quatermain and his friends finally cross over the great mountain barrier, they have similarly reached the halfway point of their story. They have at last left behind the torturing heat of the desert, and they find themselves looking down on the breathtakingly beautiful, lush countryside of Solomon's lost kingdom, ringed by blue mountains. They are greeted by the natives as gods, and led along a great, ancient highway to the capital, where they find that the country is under the evil sway of the tyrranical King Twala, and his hideous old henchwoman, the witch Gagool, hundreds of years old.

They discover that their mysteriously regal companion on the journey, Umbopa, is in fact the true king of this land, returning to claim his throne from the usurper Twala; and again, like other heroes, they have to face three ordeals. In the first they fall into Twala's power, while attempting to rescue the beautiful Foulata, a local girl who has become attached to them. By cunning use of the almanac predicting a lunar eclipse, they terrify Twala's followers and make 'a thrilling escape from death'. Second is the great battle between the followers of Twala and those of Umbopa, which culminates in the tyrant's death. Thirdly, the climax to the whole story, is their journey with Gagool into the series of vast, mysterious caves in the heart of the mountains, which turns into a combination of 'visit to the underworld', 'overcoming the monster', 'liberating the treasure from the dark enclosing space' and 'thrilling escape from death' all in one. In one cavern they find the petrified corpses of the kings of the land, sitting round a stone table. In the last they come across the legendary treasure of Solomon, the richest hoard of diamonds the world has ever known, shining in the darkness. At this point, Gagool, the 'guardian of the treasure', creeps back 'like a snake' and 'with a look of fearful malevolence' swings shut the great stone door – but in the process crushing herself to death. The heroes are trapped in the eternal darkness and prepare to die. Only in the nick of time, like Aladdin trapped in his treasure cave, do they miraculously find a way out: threading their way, like Theseus, through the labyrinth of secret passages which lead them at last up and out into the cool, fresh air of the mountainside.

When the little band of male rabbits arrives on Watership Down, they are at much the same halfway point of their story as Aeneas and the Trojans when they arrive in Italy. They have reached their goal, but they must now face the task of finding some female rabbits with whom they can found a lasting community; and the rest of the book tells of their tremendous struggle with the fearful Efrafa, a warren some way off which is run like a totalitarian prison by the grim tyrant General Woundwort, where it just happens that a group of young female rabbits are imprisoned, led by the beautiful and intelligent Hyzenthlay. There is a 'thrilling escape', when these young 'rabbit princesses' are liberated. General Woundwort, as Avenger, comes hot in pursuit with a band of Efrafan thugs, to 'reclaim his own'. There is a great battle back on Watership Down, with Hazel and his friends seemingly trapped in the 'dark enclosing space' of their warrren. But just when all seems lost, Hazel ingeniously manages to enlist the help of a nearby farm dog, which puts Woundwort and his army to rout. The new warren is at last safely and securely established.

### The life-renewing goal

Thus does the great Quest come to an end, and we then we see perhaps the most surprising thing of all about this type of story, The heroes of all these very dissimilar tales have in fact arrived, by remarkably similar stages, at a remarkably similar goal. Odysseus has regained his Queen and his kingdom. Aeneas has won his Princess and his kingdom. Jason has won his Princess and, through her, succeeds to the kingdom of Corinth (the Golden Fleece itself by this time having come to be seen as purely symbolic of the 'treasure' that has been won). The Jews have won and established their new kingdom. The Grail heroes carry their great treasure, the golden Grail, to the city of Sarras, where Galahad becomes king, succeeding an evil tyrant, and is then received into the kingdom of heaven. Allan Quatermain and his friends, having established Umbopa as the rightful king over the lost and now found land of Solomon, in place of an evil tyrant, return home with their fabulous treasure. The rabbits of Watership Down, united with their 'princesses', have established their new kingdom – to the point where, in the closing pages, their 'King' Hazel can look round at a new generation of young rabbits playing in the sun, knowing that the future is assured. He is then called by a mysterious stranger, whose ears shine in the darkness of the burrow with 'a faint silver light', off to a rabbit heaven.

Of the Quests we have looked at in any detail, the only one which might not seem to follow this pattern is *Pilgrim's Progress*. But even Christian meets his most nearly fatal ordeal on the very edge of his goal, when he nearly drowns, amid hideous visions of 'hobgoblins and evil spirits', in the deep, dark river which surrounds the hill on which the Celestial City stands – and is then received to the sound of trumpets into the kingdom of heaven. And as if Bunyan subconsciously realised that, to make his story complete, Christian should there be united with a 'Princess', he promptly set about writing the second, much less well-known part of his tale, which tells of how his hero's wife Christiana makes her own long and hazardous journey to join him.

The real point about the ending of all these stories is that in essence it is so familiar. The real goal of the Quest emerges as remarkably similar to that happy ending we have seen in our previous types of story: the final coming together of hero and heroine, man and woman, and the succession to, or establishing of a kingdom. In each case it is this, in part or whole, which enables the Quest to end on an image of completion. And in each case what this also conveys to us is the sense that life, which in the opening stages of the story seemed so threatened, has in some profound sense been renewed. Odysseus has redemeed and brought his kingdom back to life, after the long, sterile years of the suitors' tyranny. Aeneas's city of Troy is dead: but on the Tiber it lives again, as new Rome, and will do so far into the glorious future. Jason returns home to redeem Iolcos from the sterile tyranny of his step-father King Pelias, and then sets up his own new dynasty in Corinth. As the Jews toiled across the dead wilderness there was no more regular promise of the new life that was to come than Moses' repeated striking of 'living waters' out of the rock: and from the years of harsh slavery in Egypt, where their sons, the promise of new life, had routinely been murdered, they are at last set free in the lush land 'flowing with milk and honey', where life abounds and is assured for the future.

And so on, with the Grail Quest, *Pilgrim's Progress, King Solomon's Mines, Watership Down*. In each case the story ends on a great renewal of life, centred on a new secure base, guaranteed into the future. And we can see at last (although it was by no means clear while the story was still unfolding) that this was what the Quest had really been about all along.

## The Quest: Summing up

A third way in which stories naturally shape themselves in the human imagination centres on the pull of the hero towards some distant, all-important goal. However much he becomes drawn into particular episodes along the way, we always know that these are merely subordinate to his overriding purpose, and that until that goal has been reached and properly secured, the story cannot be satisfactorily resolved. The basic Quest story unfolds through a series of stages like this:

1. *The Call*: Life in some 'City of Destruction' has become oppressive and intolerable, and the hero recognises that he can only rectify matters by making a long, difficult journey. He is given supernatural or visionary direction as to the distant, life-renewing goal he must aim for.

2. *The Journey*: The hero and his companions set out across hostile terrain, encountering a series of life-threatening ordeals. These include horrific monsters to be overcome; temptations to be resisted; and, probably the need to travel between two equally deadly 'opposites'. These each end with a 'thrilling escape', and the ordeals alternate with periods of respite, when the hero and his companions receive hospitality, help or advice, often from 'wise old men' or 'beautiful young women'. During this stage the hero may also have to make a 'journey through the underworld', where he temporarily transcends the separating power of death and comes into helpful contact with spirits from the past, who give him guidance as to how to reach his goal.

3. *Arrival and Frustration*: The hero arrives within sight of his goal. But he is far from having reached the end of his story, because now, on the edge of the goal, he sees a new and terrible series of obstacles looming up between him and his prize, which have to be overcome before it can be fully and completely secured.

4. *The Final Ordeals*: The hero has to undergo a last series of tests (often three in number) to prove that he is truly worthy of the prize. This culminates in a last great battle or ordeal which may be the most threatening of all.

5. *The Goal*: After a last 'thrilling escape from death', the kingdom, the 'Princess' or the life-transforming treasure are finally won: with an assurance of renewed life stretching indefinitely into the future.

We have so far illustrated the Quest story by looking at some of the best-known and most profound examples in the world; although the inclusion of *King*

*Solomon's Mines* and *Watership Down* showed how this theme may equally well be found in less serious forms of storytelling.

Even in so slight and charming an example as Jean de Brunhoff's *Babar and Father Christmas*, we see features of the archetypal structure at work. The little elephant-children in Babar's kingdom are very unhappy as they wonder why they are never visited by Father Christmas. King Babar decides to rectify matters by going in search of Father Christmas himself. On his journey he has three successive encounters with 'helpers', who give him advice: some mice, a flock of sparrows, finally a Professor whom, as we see him sitting below a bust of Socrates, we take for a 'wise old man'. This sage at last puts Babar on the right track and the hero sets out on the closing stages of his Quest, accompanied by his faithful companion, a dog. They enter a great snow-covered forest and come to a mountain where they face three ordeals. Firstly the dog is pelted with snowballs, and nearly suffocated by a small army of dwarves. Then the dwarves confront Babar himself, but he pushes them over with his trunk. Finally a violent blizzard blows up. Babar and the dog dig a hole in the snow for shelter, but they are so cold and tired that they are on the verge of giving up hope – when they have a 'thrilling escape from death'. The snow gives way under them, and they fall into a huge, brightly-lit underground cavern, a treasure house of toys, where they are warmly welcomed by the twinkling and venerable Father Christmas himself. He agrees to visit Babar's kingdom, which brings such joy to the children that, as he flies away, he promises to return every year (renewal of life assured indefinitely into the future!).

Another light and entertaining tale rather less obviously shaped by the Quest is Jules Verne's *Around the World in Eighty Days* (1873).The story's suspense hangs entirely on whether the hero, Phineas Fogg, can reach his distant goal in time to win a hefty bet. The fact that the goal of his Quest happens to be to arrive back exactly where he started is in this sense immaterial. Naturally much of the book consists of his journey, complete with ordeals and thrilling escapes, the most dramatic of which is in India where, with the aid of his servant and 'faithful companion' Passepartout, Fogg literally liberates a Princess, Aouda, the beautiful young widow of an Indian prince, just as she is about to be consumed by the flames of her husband's funeral pyre. The three travel onwards, shadowed by the detective Fix, who wants to arrest Fogg for having master-minded a huge robbery at the Bank of England. They arrive back in England just in time, when disaster strikes. Within sight of his goal, Fogg faces three unexpected ordeals. First he is arrested by Fix and imprisoned. In the nick of time it is discovered that he is perfectly innocent: but he has now missed the last train which could carry him back to London in time to win his bet. He hires a 'special' train, but it is held up on the way and arrives in London minutes too late. It seems all is lost, and next morning Fogg begins to make preparations for suicide. Then Passepartout happens to hear someone mention the date. Of course! By going round the world from west to east they had gained a day; and they now have just ten minutes for Fogg to get to his club to claim victory. The hero makes it with three minutes to spare. He has won his 'treasure': although, as the author is careful to emphasise, the real treasure he has gained from his journey is the 'Princess'. Just when all seemed lost, they had finally declared their 'sacred love' for each other, and can now get married.[5]

Although the Quest is such a distinctive type of story, it obviously has features in common with the two types of plot we looked at earlier, not least in terms of its basic structure. We saw how, at their deepest level, both Overcoming the Monster and Rags to Riches stories unfold by a kind of three-fold rhythm. They begin on a note of constriction, followed, when the hero or heroine respond to the 'Call', by a phase of expansion, as spirits and hopes are lifted. This leads eventually to a more serious constriction, leading to a phase when the hero or heroine are gradually being brought to a state of readiness for the final decisive confrontation with the dark forces which have so long oppressed them. When this arrives, providing the climax to the story, constriction reaches its height. Then comes the reversal, the triumphant liberation which paves the way to the happy ending.

We see the same fundamental rhythm at work in the structure of the Quest. There is the initial feeling of constriction which persuades the hero and his companions that they must leave. We then have a sense of enlargement as they set out into the world on their journey: although this contains within it lesser alternations of constriction and release, as each ordeal is followed by respite. We then come to the more serious constriction as the hero comes within sight of his goal, and has to face the final ordeals. Gradually the story works up to its climax, when he is pitted in a last decisive battle against the dark forces which have stood between him and his goal all along. At last we share his liberation from all opposition, as the darkness is overthrown, the goal secured and the story ends on the image of life gloriously renewed.

All the plots we have looked at so far share this same essential structure. Something else they have in common is that the dominant figures opposed to their heroes or heroines – the monsters, tyrants, witches, wicked stepmothers and

---

5. Further variations on the Quest plot are those which shape two different types of stories inspired by the Second World War. On one hand are those which are a cross with the Overcoming the Monster plot, where a small group of men have to travel on a long, perilous journey to destroy some particularly sinister and menacing concentration of the enemy's dark power. Well-known examples of this include films like *The Guns of Navarone* (which we have already looked at as an Overcoming the Monster story); *The Dirty Dozen*, in which a bunch of violent misfits redeem themselves when they are recruited to be dropped into occupied France to knock out a closely-guarded chateau which is the centre of the German army's information network; or *The Heroes of Telemark*, where a group of commandos are dropped into occupied Norway to join the resistance in knocking out a heavy-water plant which could enable the Nazis to develop a war-winning nuclear bomb. On the other hand are those prison camp escape stories, such as *The Wooden Horse*, *The Colditz Story* or *The Great Escape*, where the story's driving force is the contrast between the intolerable constriction in which the heroes begin as prisoners of war and their dream of the all-important distant goal of 'freedom'. The chief emphasis here, of course, is on the difficulty of getting away on the journey in the first place. The planning and execution of the escape itself inevitably takes up much of the story. Once the journey begins this follows the usual pattern of ordeals and 'thrilling escapes' alternating with periods of respite: and, again, one of the worst ordeals may be that which takes place when the goal is at last in sight, on the frontier. The plot in such stories thus depends for its suspense on a cross between the archetypes of the Quest and the Thrilling Escape.

rivals, from whose malevolence the sense of threat and constriction mainly emanates – are invariably dark figures; while the heroes and heroines themselves display qualities which put them unmistakably on the side of 'light'. They may in the earlier stages of the story show certain weaknesses and inadequacies (this is an important element, to which we shall return). But the whole underlying purpose of the action is to show us the hero or heroine maturing to the state where they are finally ready for that decisive confrontation with the archetypal power of darkness which can bring their complete liberation.

Nevertheless, just as we earlier saw a 'dark' variation on the Rags to Riches story, so there are 'dark' versions of the Quest. Perhaps the most obvious example in all literature is Herman Melville's *Moby Dick* (1851). The central figure, Captain Ahab, sets out on his obsessive quest across the oceans of the world to find the almost supernatural great white whale. Ahab looks on Moby Dick, as other quest heroes look on the Holy Grail or the Golden Fleece or the Firebird, as a prize of infinite value, worth any effort or sacrifice to seek out. Certainly the mysterious, numinous whale is an archetypal symbol for the essence of life. But there is nothing life-enhancing or light about the spirit in which Ahab pursues his goal. His only desire is to destroy it. He is not on the side of life but opposed to it. This is why the voyage which makes up his quest is so strained and sinister, fraught with omens of disaster. And when he does finally find the whale, it is of course Ahab himself who is slain. The reasons for this we shall explore more fully in Chapter 21. But once again, by those inexorable rules which govern the way in which stories unfold, all the clues as to why Ahab's quest can only end in disaster are there in this very sombre tale.

*Chapter 5*

# Voyage and Return

'THE DIVERTING HISTORY OF JOHN GILPIN, showing how he went further than
he intended and came safely home again.'

Title page of William Cowper's poem

'You know, coming home and finding things all right, though not quite the
same.'                Sam Gamgee in *The Lord of the Rings*, J. R. R. Tolkien

'I approached the very gates of death and set foot on Proserpine's threshold,
yet was permitted to return ... at midnight I saw the sun shining as if it were
noon; I entered the presence of the gods of the underworld.'

Apuleius, *The Golden Ass*

What do the stories of *Alice in Wonderland* or *Goldilocks and the Three Bears* have
in common with H. G. Wells's *The Time Machine* and a great deal of other science
fiction? What has Beatrix Potter's little nursery tale of *Peter Rabbit* in common
with Evelyn Waugh's *Brideshead Revisited*; or Coleridge's *The Rime of the Ancient
Mariner* with the parable of the Prodigal Son; or the Greek myth of Orpheus's
journey to the underworld with the film *Gone with the Wind*?

There is a second plot based on a journey, quite different from the Quest. It has
inspired such an extraordinary range of stories that it might seem impossible
that most of them could have anything in common – apart from the fact that
they include some of the most haunting and mysterious tales in the world. This is
the plot we may call the Voyage and Return.

The essence of the Voyage and Return story is that its hero or heroine (or the
central group of characters) travel out of their familiar, everyday 'normal'
surroundings into another world completely cut off from the first, where everything seems disconcertingly abnormal. At first the strangeness of this new world,
with its freaks and marvels, may seem diverting, even exhilarating, if also highly
perplexing. But gradually a shadow intrudes. The hero or heroine feels increasingly threatened, even trapped: until eventually (usually by way of a 'thrilling
escape') they are released from the abnormal world, and can return to the safety
of the familiar world where they began.

There are two obvious categories of story where the Voyage and Return plot is
particularly familiar. The first is that type stretching back to the dawn of story-

telling which describes a journey to some land or island beyond the confines of the known or civilised world. The other describes a journey to some more obviously imaginary and magical realm closer to home.

It is generally through stories of this second type that most of us first become acquainted with the Voyage and Return theme because, from C. S. Lewis's *The Lion, the Witch and the Wardrobe* to Frank Baum's *The Wizard of Oz*, it provides the basis for some of our best-loved stories of childhood.

Two classic instances are Lewis Carroll's Alice stories, *Through The Looking Glass* and *Alice's Adventures in Wonderland*. Bored and drowsy on a hot summer's day, a little Victorian girl suddenly finds herself transported underground into a totally strange 'wonderland'. Several times she finds herself altering in size. She meets a bewildering succession of animals and other creations, behaving like human beings but talking to her in riddles. Everything in this surreal dreamworld is like a parody or distortion of something familiar. But just as this dream seems finally to be turning into a death-threatening nightmare, with the Queen of Hearts in the courtroom scene angrily shouting 'off with her head' and all the cards rising up into the air and 'flying down upon her', Alice is jerked back to the reality of her familiar world by waking up, as if from a dream.

Almost identical in outline is the plot of that perennially popular Hollywood fairy tale, *The Wizard of Oz* (1939). Young Dorothy, who is staying with her uncle and aunt on their farm in Kansas, is upset when her dog Toto is taken off by Miss Gulch for chasing the rich, bad-tempered old spinster's cat. Toto manages to run back home but, terrified she will lose him again, Dorothy takes him off into the countryside, dreaming of escape into some far-off land 'over the rainbow'. On their way home, they are suddenly swept into the sky by a swirling tornado and find themselves falling abruptly down into the magical technicolor land of Oz, like Alice falling down her hole into Wonderland. Here Dorothy is greeted by a bewildering succession of characters, including the little Munchkins and the Good Witch Glinda, but provokes the deadly hostility of the Wicked Witch, the equivalent of Alice's Queen of Hearts (and a reincarnation of Miss Gulch). Dorothy escapes down the Yellow Brick Road to seek the help of the mysterious Wizard of Oz in getting home, On the way she is joined by three allies, the Scarecrow, the Tin Man and the Cowardly Lion, but eventually the Wicked Witch traps them all in her castle. Just when the nightmare is at its height, Dorothy in desperation throws a bucket of magic water over the witch, causing her to vanish. After their 'thrilling escape', they return to the Wizard, who turns out to be a fraud. But the Good Witch uses her magic to enable Dorothy to return home to Kansas, where she wakes up in bed as if emerging from a dream.

Another familiar childhood example of such a journey into an imaginary world is Barrie's *Peter Pan* (1904), the story of how the children of the Darling family fly off from their familiar nursery in the middle of the night, led by the little boy who cannot grow up, to the Never Never Land, a strange childhood dream realm inhabited by fairies, Red Indians, talking birds and pirates. Again the mood of their adventure is initially one of exhilaration. But increasingly it is shadowed by their awareness of the menacing presence of the pirate chief Captain Hook, a typical 'monster' figure, with his hook in place of a hand. Eventually the story works up to a nightmare climax, when Hook and his men take the children prisoner on board their ship and threaten to kill them. There is a final 'thrilling escape' when Peter Pan arrives in the nick of time and forces the monstrous Hook to jump overboard into the jaws of the crocodile; and the children return safely home to their nursery at home with their parents.

Some of the very earliest stories a child can grasp are simple versions of the Voyage and Return plot (long, for instance, before they can really appreciate the relative complexities of the Rags to Riches story, with its 'Princes', 'Princesses' and 'transformation scenes').

*The Tale of Peter Rabbit* tells of the little rabbit who ventures out of the familiar world of the burrow and the wood which are his home, into the forbidden world of Mr McGregor's kitchen garden. At first the new world is exhilarating. But gradually the mood changes. First Peter feels sick with overeating. Then he turns a corner and sees the terrifying Mr McGregor, who pursues him. The nightmarish chase continues until Peter thinks he is irrevocably trapped in the garden. But at last, by jumping up on a wheelbarrow, he sees the gate leading back to safety. He makes a heroic dash, with McGregor in hot pursuit, and in a 'thrilling escape' just manages to scramble out of the garden and back to the familiar, safe world of home and mother.

Similarly, little Goldilocks ventures out from home into the forbidden world of the great forest, where she eventually comes to the mysterious house belonging to the three bears. Again the initial excitement of exploring the empty house, with its steaming porridge bowls and inviting beds, gives way to a sense of growing menace as the bears return. As they begin to suspect her presence, the sense of threat comes nearer and nearer until finally they discover the little heroine asleep upstairs: at which moment Goldilocks wakes up, makes a 'thrilling escape' by jumping out of the window, and runs back to the safety of her mother and home.

But of course the Voyage and Return theme has shaped stories a good deal more complex than these simple versions of childhood. Here we move on to the second category in which such stories are most immediately familiar to us, those which involve a journey to some undiscovered realm beyond the confines of the known world.

We can find versions of this form of the Voyage and Return plot at almost every step along the history of storytelling. There were well-known Greek, Roman, Norse and mediaeval versions. There is even a strong Voyage and Return element in the closing episode of the earliest story ever recorded, the *Epic of Gilgamesh*, in the hero's journey to the far-off and mysterious land of Utnapishtim (although this is also a form of Quest, since he is seeking the secret of immortality). But this kind of tale became noticeably more evident in Western literature after the Renaissance, during the age of the great European voyages of discovery to every corner of the globe: and this was particularly true from the eighteenth century onwards.

Again these stories fall generally into two main types: those where the hero is marooned on some more or less deserted island; and those where the land he visits is the home of some strange people or civilisation.

In the early eighteenth century, two of the most famous of such stories were published, within a few years of each other: one in each category.

The first, in 1719, was that paradigm of all 'desert island' stories, *Robinson Crusoe*.[1] The plot of Defoe's novel follows the now familiar pattern. As a young sailor whose ship is wrecked, the hero suddenly finds himself all alone on a seemingly deserted tropical island. The first half of the story, after Crusoe has recovered from the initial shock, is dominated by his growing confidence as he comes to terms with his plight and with the simple wonders of his unfamiliar new world (e.g., discovering his ability to grow corn and bake bread). Then a shadow intrudes, when he sees the imprint of a strange human foot (not, as is popularly mis-recalled, that of Man Friday). As Crusoe realises that he may not be alone on the island, he begins to experience a sense of threat, which grows progressively more acute as he finds that his little kingdom is in fact regularly visited by bands of cannibals to pursue their horrid practices. The second half of the story is dominated by the measures Crusoe takes to protect himself; by his gradual recruitment of a little army of runaways (Friday being the first); and finally, as the climax of the tale, by leading his followers into a successful battle against the mutinous sailors on a Portugese ship which has anchored offshore. This culminates in his joyful release, when the grateful captain takes him off the island and back to civilisation.

The theme of the castaway or castaways cut off from civilisation so seized the European imagination that Defoe's novel was to find imitators in many countries (in Germany such tales were known as 'Robinsonismus'); and the desert island genre continued into the twentieth century, in examples ranging from J. M. Barrie's comedy *The Admirable Crichton* (1902), about an upper-class family and their servants wrecked on an island in the South Seas, to William Golding's *The Lord of the Flies* (1954). This is a model example of the Voyage and Return plot, with its description of a group of young, upper-middle-class English schoolboys marooned on a desert island by a plane crash. After an initial period of reasonably well-behaved excitement they gradually degenerate into bloodthirsty savages until, just as the nightmare has reached its murderous climax, they are plucked back to the normal world when they are miraculously rescued by the Royal Navy.

The other of these two categories of Voyage and Return stories, that which describes the hero's visit to some strange, unknown civilisation, found one of its most notable expressions just seven years after *Robinson Crusoe* with the publication in 1726 of Swift's *Gulliver's Travels* (although this too had its precursors, such as Thomas More's account in 1513 of the visit of the mariner Ralph Hythloday to

---

1. A century earlier Shakespeare had also set *The Tempest* on a kind of 'desert island', although the whole point about Prospero's isle was that it was inhabited. Few islands in stories turn out to be totally uninhabited: the true 'desert' (or 'deserted') island is more often found in cartoons. Of course the hero's visit to an island with strange and terrifying inhabitants appears in literature as far back as Odysseus's visits to the islands of the Cyclops, Circe, Calypso and others.

the imaginary country of Utopia). The travels of Lemuel Gulliver are made up of no fewer than four voyages, each to a separate land of freaks and marvels: the most famous of course being those to Lilliput and Brobdignag. Both episodes follow a classic Voyage and Return pattern, with the hero finding his initial sense of wonder turning to frustration as he realises that he is trapped. In Lilliput the tiny inhabitants finally turn against him when he helpfully puts out a fire in the king's palace by urinating on it. Gulliver is threatened with blinding and death, and only manages to escape in the nick of time, first to the neighbouring kingdom of Blefescu, then back to Europe. From Brobdignag, where Gulliver becomes the tiny plaything of giants, his escape is even more dramatic when his 'travelling box', in which his captors carry him about, is picked up by a monstrous eagle and dropped into the sea, from where he is rescued by a passing ship.

The eighteenth century, with its voyages of discovery to the southern hemisphere, made a particularly notable contribution to the literature of Voyage and Return stories, another haunting example being Coleridge's *Rime of the Ancient Mariner* (1797). The greybearded old sailor-hero tells of how, many years before, he had gone on an initially exhilarating voyage into the unexplored southern ocean ('we were the first that ever burst into that silent sea'), and how the greatest marvel they found there was the huge, beautiful white albatross which followed their ship. But then, in a reckless moment, the mariner had shot the albatross, at which a terrible curse had fallen over the voyage. The ship is becalmed, amid terrifying visions of sea monsters. Finally a spectral vision of another ship approaches, containing Death and her mate. The mariner see his shipmates all die, one by one, of hunger and thirst. Then, just when all seems lost, the mariner is looking down at a mass of sea-snakes crawling around the ship. He is so moved by the sight of the only living creatures left apart from himself that he croaks out a blessing on them. The ship returns to ghostly life, and a mysterious wind springs up, carrying it back within sight of home: at which point it sinks, leaving the mariner to be carried to shore, half-dead, but repentant of his crime.[2]

By the nineteenth century, as fewer and fewer places on the earth's surface remained unexplored, authors were having to push further and further afield to find terrestrial settings with the necessary remoteness for Voyage and Return

2. Two other well-known eighteenth-century novels shaped by the Voyage and Return theme were published in 1759: Samuel Johnson's *Rasselas* and Voltaire's *Candide*. Both show their heroes sallying forth from the comparatively cosy surroundings in which they have lived all their lives, to investigate the perplexing horrors of life in the great world outside. However, in *Rasselas*, by a reversal of the usual pattern, the Abyssinian prince-hero actually begins in a kind of 'never never land', a remote 'happy valley' shut off from the outside world, where the inhabitants know no evil. Accompanied by that archetypal pair, a beautiful young Princess and a 'wise old man', Imlac, Rasselas thus experiences the 'normality' of our familiar outside world (greed, folly, violence, deprivation) as highly novel and abnormal, before returning home enlightened. Candide has an even more salutary set of experiences in the outside world, which so signally fails to bear out his tutor Dr Pangloss's vacuously optimistic maxim that 'all is for the best in the best of all possible worlds'. Finally he decides to settle down with his equivalents of a 'Princess' and a 'wise old man', Cunegonde and Dr Pangloss, to 'cultivate his garden'. Although he does not return geographically to where he started, the end of the story has the familiar Voyage and Return feel of a return to humdrum normality after a highly abnormal adventure.

stories. Samuel Butler's imaginary country of *Erewhon* (1872) was situated on the far side of an unexplored range of mountains in New Zealand. In the twentieth century, Conan Doyle's *The Lost World* (1912) was set on a strange plateau in the Amazonian jungle, isolated from the rest of the 'normal' world by a geological freak which had preserved it as a wonderland still inhabited by dinosaurs and primitive cavemen. In Scott Fitzgerald's *The Diamond as Big as The Ritz* (1922), the young hero made his journey into a remote, closely guarded valley in the Rocky Mountains ('the only five square miles of land in the country which has never been surveyed'), where his host lived on top of a diamond so big that it made him 'the richest man that ever lived'. James Hilton in *Lost Horizon* (1933) set his imaginary paradise of Shangri-La, where no one grew old, in a remote, sealed-off valley in the Himalayas.

But already other authors had taken still more imaginative steps to surmount the shrinking availability of such settings on the face of the globe. Jules Verne set one of his most famous Voyage and Return adventures in an imaginary under-world deep below the earth's surface (*Journey to the Centre of the Earth*, 1864) and another, a few years later, below the surface of the sea (*20,000 Leagues Under the Sea*, 1872). H. G. Wells found a still more dramatic solution in *The Time Machine* (1895), taking his hero out of the familiar world in terms not of geography but of time. The Time Traveller invents a machine which transports him 800,000 years into the future, where he discovers the little, child-like Eloi, living in palaces in a seemingly paradisal landscape full of strange, exotic flowers and fruits. But then the familiar shadow intrudes. He gradually becomes aware that there is another semi-human race inhabiting this world, the sinister Morlocks who live under-ground, hating the light and coming up at night to prey on the defenceless Eloi for their food. The story winds to a familiar nightmare climax when the hero is chased and nearly caught by a gang of these horrible night-creatures, only managing in the nick of time to scramble back onto his machine, to return to the safe Victorian world he had left.

In the twentieth century, of course, countless authors were to venture still further along the path pioneered by Verne and Wells, setting their heroes travel-ling not just in time, but more frequently to other planets and still more remote parts of the universe. In fact a major factor contributing to the emergence of 'science fiction' was simply the need of storytellers in an over-explored world to find alternative or unfamiliar worlds in which to set Voyage and Return stories. For the essence of this plot is its central figure's confrontation with the unknown, that which seems abnormal precisely because it is in such contrast to and so cut off from the familiar world he or she naturally inhabits.

### The social Voyage and Return

We have so far looked at Voyage and Return stories almost entirely in terms of those where the hero or heroine makes some kind of *physical* journey into an unfamiliar world.

There are other, less obvious versions of this plot where the journey is of a rather different kind: as where, for instance, it takes its central figure into an unfamiliar *social* milieu. An author particularly drawn to this type of plot was Evelyn Waugh, several of whose best-known novels are shaped by the Voyage and Return theme. A fairly conventional example, not dissimilar to those we have already looked at in that it involves a physical journey into another country, is *Scoop* (1938) (which also has a Rags to Riches element, in showing how its obscure little hero, a shy writer of nature notes, finally pulls off an amazing journalistic scoop and becomes a national hero).

Waugh's first novel, *Decline and Fall* (1928), however, was an example of what may be called a purely 'social' Voyage and Return story. Paul Pennyfeather, a dull, ordinary undergraduate, suddenly finds himself ejected from his cosy, humdrum existence when he is helplessly caught up in the consequences of an upper-class brawl and sent down from Oxford. He first finds himself among the semi-grotesques of the seedy private school of Llanabba, and is then swept up into the even stranger and more exotic world of Margot Best-Chetwynde, a fabulously rich upper-class 'older woman' who somewhat implausibly decides she wants to marry him. Like Alice or the Time Traveller or many other central figures in Voyage and Return stories, Pennyfeather is caught up in events largely beyond his control – a bewildering dream which eventually turns to nightmare when he is convicted of having, quite unwittingly, been an agent in Mrs Best-Chetwynde's international 'white slave' ring. He is sent to prison, whence he is rescued by his now ex-fiancée to undergo an operation which gives him a new identity. He ends up returning to Oxford under a different name, to sink back into exactly the kind of dull, anonymous student existence from which he had been plucked at the start of the story.

In some ways a similar, though much more developed version of this story came twenty years later in Waugh's *Brideshead Revisited* (1945). Again a fairly ordinary middle-class Oxford undergraduate, Charles Ryder, finds himself abruptly plucked out of his humdrum routine into an exotic upper-class world, this time that of Lord Sebastian Flyte and his family's great house Brideshead. Ryder's initial exhilaration at being introduced to this romantic other-world is gradually overshadowed as Sebastian slides into incurable alcoholism; only to be revived by a second 'dream stage' when Charles embarks on a love-affair with Sebastian's sister Julia. This in turn becomes shadowed as Julia's father, the Earl Marchmain, dies, and Julia refuses to go ahead with her planned marriage to Charles. Thus rejected, the hero leaves the 'faery world' of Brideshead forever – until, in totally different circumstances, he unexpectedly finds himself back at the house as an army officer in World War Two, and recalls his Voyage and Return experience in a prolonged flashback.

Such a 'remembrance of times past', prompted by the activation of memory and conveyed through some kind of flashback, is not unfamiliar as the framework for a Voyage and Return story. The analogy between a journey into the past and one into another country is even made explicit in the opening lines of L. P. Hartley's *The Go-Between* (1953): 'the past is a foreign country; they do things differently there'. This serves to preface the aged narrator's recollection of the social Voyage and Return he had made 60 years before when, as a little middle-class schoolboy from a not very prosperous home, he had gone to stay with a rich, upper-class schoolfriend on his family's estate in Norfolk during a long, hot summer holiday. The boy Leo had found his initial shy exhilaration at being introduced to such a strange, grand, grown-up world increasingly shadowed as he becomes helplessly involved as a go-between in the secret affair between the daughter of the house, Marian, and her handsome, lower-class lover living in a humble cottage a mile away. The story had wound to a nightmarish climax when, as the heatwave broke in an immense thunderstorm, Marian's fearsome mother discovered the hapless lovers in an outhouse, in flagrante delicto. The semi-disgraced little hero had been abruptly packed off home, expelled from this wonderland for ever (until, 60 years later, he returns to meet Marian, now an old woman who, after the scandal, had never married).

A Voyage and Return story set in an alien social milieu of a different kind was the film *The Third Man* (1948), scripted by Graham Greene. The hero Holley Martins, a writer of Westerns, travels to the half-ruined city of Vienna during the post-war Allied occupation, to track down his old school friend Harry Lime. He is shocked to discover that his old friend has just been killed and buried in mysterious circumstances. But the more he tries to uncover what happened from the bizarre assemblage of people he meets in Vienna, ranging from Lime's seedy, mysterious friends and his enigmatic former mistress Anna to the laconic British military police officer Calloway, the more puzzled Martins becomes. He is here in a common predicament of the Voyage and Return hero, feeling he has been caught up in some strange, unreal dream world where everyone knows more than he does. The dream then begins to turn to nightmare when it turns out that Lime had not only been on the run from the authorities, for running a particularly nasty racket in deadly watered-down penicillin, but that he is still mysteriously alive. Eventually Martins makes contact with Lime and, when they talk on the great fairground wheel, is shocked by the cynical heartlessness with which Harry justifies his criminal activities. Martins has also fallen in love with Lime's erstwhile mistress, the enigmatic Anna, and is drawn by Calloway into a plot to trap his old friend on behalf of the authorities. The story winds to its nightmare climax in the chase through the half-lit tunnels of the Vienna sewers, with Martins firing the last fatal shot as his friend's fingers clutch for fresh air and life through the grille of a manhole cover. As Lime's body is at last genuinely buried the story ends, with the implication that, after such a horrific experience, Martins will now return to his normal, humdrum existence, although we no more see this at the end than at the beginning. The story is framed simply by his entrance to and exit from the alien world.

We must finally consider one more form of the Voyage and Return story, where the degree of the hero's translation into an unfamiliar realm might seem even more extreme than in the geographical or social journeys we have looked at so far. This is the kind of story where the hero temporarily undergoes a complete change of outward identity, while remaining himself behind his new persona. A well-known example was F. Anstey's Victorian novel *Vice Versa* (1882), in which a father

and his schoolboy son magically switch outward identities, with potentially catastrophic results in each case. But long before this such a form had already been
used rather more seriously in one of the most profound of all Voyage and Return
stories, in which the hero finds himself turned into an animal.

Lucius, the hero of the neo-Platonic allegory *The Golden Ass*, written by the
Roman North African author Apuleius in the second century AD, is a young man
obsessed with sex and the occult. He goes on a journey to Thessaly, home of the
black arts, where he finds lodgings in the house of a well-known sorceress and
embarks on a heady affair with her beautiful slave girl Fotis. But Lucius also has
a voyeuristic craving to spy secretly on her mistress, and to do this he asks Fotis
to turn him by magic into a bird. The spell goes horribly wrong. She turns him
by mistake into an ass, which is almost immediately stolen by a gang of robbers.
It seems Lucius is now trapped in his new persona with no hope of escape. After
a series of frightening adventures he is sold to a circus owner, who prepares to put
him on public show making love to a human murderess. Lucius finds this
prospect more horrifying than anything he has yet had to face, not least because
he suspects that, as the spectacle reaches its climax, the circus owner will release
onto the stage a wild beast to tear both him and the woman to pieces ('I was not
only appalled at the disgraceful part I was to play. I was in terror of death'). In the
nick of time, he manages to run away. Lying exhausted on a beach after his
'thrilling escape', he awakens in moonlight to see a shining vision of the goddess
Isis rising from the sea, 'with so lovely a face the gods themselves would have
fallen down in adoration of it'. She tells him she is 'Nature, the universal Mother,
mistress of all the elements … sovereign of all things spiritual … the single manifestation of all the gods and goddesses there are'. On her instructions, he attends
a great religious ceremony in her honour, and feels his ass's body melting away.
He has become human again. As a result of his miraculous deliverance he
remains a devoted follower of the cult of Isis, and the rest of the story (which we
shall consider later in more detail) shows him being initiated into its deepest
mysteries.

But first we must look rather more closely at what all these Voyage and Return
stories have in common. For behind the extraordinary variety of their outward
subject matter, they are all in a way describing the same shattering experience.

To see this plot in deeper perspective, we must consider three questions. First, how
do the heroes or heroines of these stories get into this 'other world' where their
adventures take place? Second, what is the real nature of this 'other world'?
Thirdly, what is really happening to them as they pass through it? How does it
affect them?

It is instructive to contrast the mood of the opening of a Voyage and Return
story with that at the start of the other type of story based on a journey, the Quest.
The Quest is altogether a more serious and purposeful affair. The hero of the
Quest realises he has to go on his journey. He is drawn by an overwhelming sense
of compulsion. He knows there is a specific goal he has to head for.

The heroes of the Voyage and Return story have no such sense of direction. It is true that in some instances, such as *Rasselas, Candide, The Time Machine, The Lost World*, the hero is consciously looking for something when he sets out, and we may call this a 'Quest element' in such stories. But much more often the point is that the adventure these heroes and heroines stumble into is totally unexpected. In some instances quite literally they fall into it. It is something which just happens to them.

At the same time, however, they are very much in a state of mind which lays them open for such a thing to happen. They may be just be bored and drowsy, like Alice, who falls asleep and is carried away into her Wonderland by a dream. They may be rather more actively craving some diversion, like Lucius in *The Golden Ass*, or Dorothy dreaming of 'somewhere over the rainbow' in *The Wizard of Oz*, or Wendy and the Darling children in *Peter Pan*. They may have exposed themselves to the risk that something dramatic and untoward may befall them simply because of their naivety, the restricted nature of their lives and their awareness, like Candide, or Holley Martins, or Waugh's Pennyfeather. Wittingly or unwittingly, what they have in common is that they are psychologically wide open for some shattering new experience to invade their lives and take them over.

One of the fullest pictures of the state of mind which allows a Voyage and Return hero to get into his strange predicament is that given in the opening pages of *Robinson Crusoe*. These describe how the young Crusoe was brought up by his father on the advice that if he wanted to live a full and happy life, he should head neither for the upper classes nor the lower, but should aim for a secure 'middle station' in life, between the opposites. He should settle down, have a sense of purpose: not become an aimless drifter, wandering about the world hoping that something would turn up. The realisation that he ignored this advice by going off to sea plays a large part in Crusoe's subsequent introspection, after his shipwreck. Even on his first voyage, he is nearly drowned in a terrible storm, and sees himself as the Prodigal Son, risking destruction by having recklessly ignored his father's kindly admonitions. Like all Voyage and Return heroes, he has laid himself open to the chance of falling into some extraordinary, unforeseen adventure: and eventually he does.

The first indication that something very unexpected is happening in a Voyage and Return story lies in the dramatic nature of the hero or heroine's entry into the 'other world'. The event which precipitates them into the abnormal world is often shocking and violent. It may be a shipwreck, as in *Robinson Crusoe, Gulliver's Travels, The Tempest, The Admirable Crichton*; or a plane crash, as in *The Lord of the Flies*. The heroines of *Alice in Wonderland* and *The Wizard of Oz* both have the sensation of falling into their 'other world' with a bump. Candide is literally propelled into his 'other world' by a violent kick on the backside, when he has been caught kissing the beautiful Cunegonde. The obscure little undergraduate Pennyfeather suddenly finds himself being debagged by a lot of drunken upper-class rowdies. Charles Ryder's introduction to his 'other world' begins when, on a similar occasion, Lord Sebastian Flyte suddenly leans through his ground-floor window and is violently sick into his room. Wells's time traveller, when he sets off into the future, has the sensation of being on a switchback, and when he finally stops his machine, it topples over, propelling him into the 'other world' in his own version of a shipwreck. Wendy and company also find their flight into the Never Never Land a bit like a switchback ride, and are greeted when they land by the deafening explosion of a pirate gun.

Even when the heroes or heroines do not land in their 'other world' quite so literally with a bang, it is always clear that something very queer is happening to them. They may simply sense that the reality of their familiar world is disconcertingly dissolving into something else, as when Alice finds herself passing through the mirror into the Looking Glass world beyond; or the horrified Lucius feels his arms growing hairy, and perceives he is changing into a donkey; or the children in *The Lion, the Witch and the Wardrobe* push their way through a cupboard full of fur coats and find themselves emerging from the back into the snow-covered forest of Narnia.

Of course it is hardly surprising that the experience of passing over from one world to another is disconcerting, because the very definition of the 'other world' is that it is totally strange and unfamiliar – and that the hero or heroine is trapped in it. Irrevocably cut off from the familiar world they have left, they now have to puzzle out the strange nature of this new world into which they have stumbled.

When we say the 'other world' is abnormal, what precisely do we mean? Our sense of normality, even of what is real, is to an enormous extent of course governed by what is familiar to us. We make sense of the world through a whole framework of largely unconscious assumptions of what is normal, based on everything we are used to – socially, culturally, morally, geographically and physically, in terms of scale, space and time. Such things play a central part in giving us our sense of outward identity in the world, telling us who we are. And the whole point of the Voyage and Return story is that, in some important respect, it takes the hero or heroine out of that framework of the familiar. It takes away some crucial defining point for their sense of reality and identity, which is why so many of their adventures are experienced as a kind of disconcerting and unreal dream.

One way or another these stories work every conceivable permutation on their heroes' and heroines' sense of what is normal, even in terms of the most basic assumptions we make about our identity as human beings. Both Alice and Gulliver, for instance, find their normal perspective on the world distorted by experiencing grotesque alterations in their relative size: Alice because she herself grows magically taller and shorter, Gulliver because he finds the people around him are either abnormally tiny or abnormally huge. Similarly the time traveller experiences a suspension of our normal co-ordinates of time (the hero of another Wells Voyage and Return adventure, *The New Accelerator*, finds his normal experience of time distorted in another way, when a new drug speeds up all the workings of his mind and body by thousands of times, so that he sees everything and everyone else around him frozen grotesquely still). Lucius has his whole centre of normal perspective on the world knocked for six by suddenly having to experience it in the body of an ass. Robinson Crusoe and the other heroes of 'desert island' versions of the plot lose their co-ordinates of identity in yet another way, finding themselves snatched out of the familiar constraints and framework of society into a world where all normal social assumptions are turned topsy-turvy (e.g., *The Admirable Crichton*, where the natural leader of the group wrecked on the island turns out to be the upper-class family's resourceful butler, who gradually assumes the role of 'king' over all his fellow-castaways.

Equally shattering in this 'other world' is the confrontation with those who already inhabit it, and who live by such different values; which is why much of the hero or heroine's time may be spent in trying to puzzle out the riddles posed by how they live and what they say: as when Alice is baffled by the quite literal riddles and nonsense talked by almost everyone in her two 'other worlds', or the agnostic Charles Ryder by the Flyte family's all-pervasive and seemingly illogical Roman Catholicism.

The 'other world' may initially seem to be full of beguiling promise. As Alice explored the hole she had plunged into, she caught her first glimpse of the wonderland she was about to enter when:

> 'she came across a low curtain she had not noticed before, and behind it was a little door … she knelt down and looked along the passage into the loveliest garden you ever saw. How she longed to get out of that dark hall and wander about among those beds of bright flowers and those cool fountains.'

As Charles Ryder set off to his first lunch invitation from the glamorously eccentric Lord Sebastian, he went:

> 'full of curiosity and the faint unrecognised apprehension that here, at last, I should find that low door in the wall which others, I knew, had found before me, which opened on an enclosed and enchanted garden, which was somewhere, not overlooked by any window, in the heart of that great city.'

But sooner or later the experience of being in the alien world becomes less and less pleasant. Our heroes and heroines never really become engaged with the alien surroundings in which they find themselves. They continue to experience everything in a kind of dream-like, semi-detached way. The 'other world' is never wholly real to them – even though the experience of being there may eventually seem to threaten their very survival. And it is here we come to the most important question of all about any Voyage and Return story. To what extent, when they finally emerge from their encounter with the 'other world', has it left any lasting mark on them? How has the experience changed them?

⁌⸙⸙⸵

Quite regardless of what outward form they take, Voyage and Return stories really fall into two distinct categories. There are those where the hero or heroine is transformed by the encounter with the mysterious 'other world'; and there are those where they are not.

Firmly of the latter type are the two adventures of Alice. 'Such a curious dream' remarks Alice, as she wakes up from her visit to Wonderland, and this is all it turns out to have been: just an incomprehensible dream, which she can look back on as no more than a memorably bizarre experience. Exactly the same are the visits of

Dorothy to Oz and of the Darling children to Never Never Land. Equally, the point about Waugh's two heroes Pennyfeather and Boot, in *Decline and Fall* and *Scoop*, is that they end up returning quite unaffected to the limited and obscure station in life where they began. So unaffected is the time traveller by his journey into the future (although he returns physically exhausted) that, no sooner has he recounted his bizarre experience to his friends, than he is off again on another journey. But this time he never returns. Such a 'Voyage without Return' can only be described as a 'dark' version of the Voyage and Return story; although, in this case, since we never discover what happened to him on his final journey through time, there is no story.[3]

On the other hand are all those stories where the central figure is affected by the experience of having been in the 'other world'. The degree to which they are affected varies considerably. In some instances, the chief effect is simply that the hero has been given a terrible shock, which leaves him shaken and in a rather more reflective state of mind. When Peter Rabbit returns home from his nightmare adventure in Mr McGregor's garden he is exhausted, and has to be put to bed: but whether he is truly repentant of his folly – i.e., whether he has really learned anything from his experience and is not just a naughty child who might well do it all over again tomorrow – is not altogether clear. Both Candide and Rasselas emerge from their adventures considerably chastened by what they have learned about the follies of mankind in general. The Ancient Mariner has been so shocked by the consequences of his own folly, in shooting the albatross, that he is marked for life. While few stories where a hero returns home repenting of his own folly have been more familiar over the centuries than the parable of the Prodigal Son from St Luke's Gospel. The younger of two brothers, after demanding his share of their inheritance from his father, travels into 'a far country' where he 'wasted his substance with riotous living'. Following the Voyage and Return pattern, his dream then turns to nightmare. After he has lost all his money, a great famine arises. He is on the verge of starving to death. But in the nick of time, he manages to crawl back home, prepared to throw himself on his father's mercy, begging to be allowed to perform the most menial tasks in return for enough to eat. So unconditional is the father's love that, on seeing his son approaching, he joyfully welcomes him home with honour.

There are other versions of the Voyage and Return story where the hero's transformation, as it progressively unfolds, becomes the real underlying theme of the whole story. The cumulative purpose of the satire in *Gulliver's Travels*, for instance, as Gulliver makes his four successive journeys to Lilliput, Brobdingnag, Laputa and

---

3. The truly 'dark' version of this plot is seen in those rare examples where we do see what happens to a hero who becomes fatally trapped in the 'other world'. Two examples we shall look at in more detail (in Chapter 23) are by Franz Kafka. In *The Trial*, the hero Josef K. suddenly falls out of his safe, normal world when he finds himself inexplicably under arrest for some mysterious offence. Like many another Voyage and Return hero, he cannot make head or tail of the nightmare world he has been plunged into. But he is finally executed without ever learning what he has been accused of. Kafka's short story *Metamorphosis* describes a hero who is plunged into his nightmare 'other world' when he wakes up one morning to find he has become a huge and hideous insect. Eventually, without changing back again, he dies: which is rather as if Lucius in *The Golden Ass* never found the remedy to undo his transformation, and had become fatally trapped in his new identity as a donkey.

the land of the Houyhnhnms, is to show the hero the real state of the supposedly civilised human beings he had left behind in a kind of Caliban's mirror, revealing their true nature as 'the most pernicious race of little odious vermin that nature ever suffered to crawl on the surface of the earth'. By the time he reaches the land of the Houyhnhnms, the wise, gentle, saintly horses who rule over the horrible, disorderly Yahoos (human beings seen in their 'true light'), Gulliver has conceived an almost total distaste for humanity. When he finally reaches home for the last time, he has been so profoundly changed that he finds the very presence of humans abohorrent, and desires only the company of horses.

A rather more positive personal transformation is the fundamental theme of that near-contemporary novel, *Robinson Crusoe*. At the beginining we see the hero as a thoughtless young man, rejecting the sage advice of his father and bent only on adventure (although even now the precedent of the Prodigal Son comes to his mind). Shocked to the core of his being by the ordeal he has to face when he finds himself cast away alone on the island, Crusoe eventually experiences feelings of pro-found repentance for his former frivolity. He comes to a belief in God who, despite the awful plight he finds himself in, has yet provided him with so many blessings, not least in sparing his life and providing him with so many vital necessities of life salvaged from the wreck. We see Crusoe gradually learning to become master of his little kingdom and of himself; so that by the time, in the second half of the story, he has to face the new ordeal of discovering that his island is the resort of a tribe of fearsome cannibals, his character has become strong enough to cope with it. By the end he is king over the island, a true leader over his little band of followers; and when he returns to England, the success of his inner transformation is outwardly symbolised by the discovery that an investment in land made long before has now matured. He is a prosperous man, able to settle down at last in that secure 'middle station' in life recommended by his father all those years before.

A similar prolonged personal transformation is the theme of Apuleius's *The Golden Ass*. We first meet the hero as a happy-go-lucky young man whose only interests are sexual adventure and a vague curiosity about the 'occult'. Shocked to the core of his being by finding himself suddenly a hairy, inarticulate ass, and consequently getting an extremely painful, ass's-eye-view of the darker side of human nature, Lucius slowly changes his whole perspective on the world. The degree to which he has inwardly changed is at last brought dramatically into the open when he is threatened with having to make love to a woman. He is pro-foundly disgusted by the thought of having to do something which would earlier have been his sole desire. He is finally 'ready' for his transformation back into a human being, but one very different from the Lucius who began the story. He sees his extraordinary vision of the goddess Isis, who calls him to a spiritual life. He is initiated into her mysteries (as Apuleius himself had been) and prepares to devote himself to her service for the rest of his days. We thus see the whole purpose of the work as having been to show a man who begins in a limited, purely sensual state of consciousness being lifted up through a series of ordeals to a much higher state of awareness, where his blind, illusory, self-destructive obsession with mater-ial appetites has given way to spiritual illumination.

The crucial episode in Lucius's final initiation is an experience so profound and mysterious that he can only refer to it in the sentences quoted at the head of this chapter. But this clearly hints at some kind of further Voyage and Return episode, a visionary 'journey to the underworld', where he has received the last extraordinary illumination which leaves him, by the end of the story, so changed:

> 'I approached the very gates of death and set foot on Proserpine's threshold … at midnight I saw the sun shining as if it were noon; I entered the presence of the gods of the underworld and the overworld, and I worshipped them.'

Such journeys to the underworld, or some 'land of the dead', are not uncommon in the world's literature (e.g., the episodes where Odysseus and Aeneas make their visits to Hades), and invariably they reflect many of the elements of a Voyage and Return story, such as the difficulty of communicating with the ghostly inhabitants and the topsy-turvy strangeness of everything ('at midnight I saw the sun shining as if it were noon'). A particularly haunting example is the Norse tale recorded by the twelfth-century Dane Saxo Grammaticus, of the journey made by King Gorm and the great hero Thorkill to 'the land of the non-dead', presided over by the terrible giant Geirrod, beyond the edge of the world in a land 'where the snows never melt and eternal night prevails'. To begin with all goes well with their journey, but gradually threats close in from all sides until they finally come to a huge, ghostly city, seemingly built of vapour and thronged by phantoms and grotesques. After a series of terrifying adventures they make a 'thrilling escape' and, miraculously, reach home, having lost all but 20 of their original 300 companions. At this point King Gorm 'sought not further adventures in distant lands beyond the perilous seas', but 'lived at peace after his sore travail, engaged in meditations regarding the mysteries of life and death'. Like Lucius, he had been deeply shaken – and transformed.

We can now see more clearly just what the Voyage and Return story is really about.

If we consider those examples where the hero is changed by his experiences in the 'other world', we see that, by definition, he has begun the story in a state of limited awareness. It is this which has plunged him into a realm of existence he had never previously imagined, an experience which leads to a nightmare threatening him with annihilation. But as a result he has learned something of fundamental importance. He has moved from ignorance to knowledge. He has reached a new and much deeper understanding of the world, and this has led to a complete change in his attitude to life.

Robinson Crusoe begins as a feckless young man, wandering the world, ignoring his father's sage advice and literally 'all at sea'. The shock of finding himself on the desert island gradually leads to a complete change in his view of the world. He learns to take responsibility for his own destiny. He becomes master of his little kingdom: to the point where, at the end, he can lead his little army of followers to victory, in the battle with the mutineers which forms the climax of the story. He has become a mature, self-reliant, 'kingly' figure, exercising just authority over everyone on the island.

Lucius in *The Golden Ass* begins as a feckless, self-centred young man whose only interests are promiscuous sexual gratification and the pseudo-spiritual titillations of the occult. He ends as a mature, disciplined, spiritually-illumined figure, dedicating his life to the goddess personifying selfless love and wisdom who has been his saviour and the inspiration of his enlightenment.

The Ancient Mariner begins as a feckless young man, like Crusoe 'all at sea', who blindly and heartlessly shoots the albatross. The consequences of this crime against the great numinous symbol of life which has been accompanying the ship are that he sees death closing in from every side, until he is seemingly all alone, frozen in a state of living death. The only other living creatures visible are the 'thousand, thousand creeping things', the water snakes: and when, almost with his dying breath, he whispers a blessing on them, this proves the turning point. He has at last begun to move from his original centre of awareness, his limited little ego, to another, much deeper centre in himself, from which he can recognise his kinship with all life. From this moment, as the frozen, deathly world around him begins to stir to life again, he is saved.

What we thus see in all these characters is that they have begun as selfish, not really recognising anything in the world outside themselves. In this state they exhibit very much the same blind egocentricity which in earlier plots we saw characterising those dark figures who were opposed to the hero or heroine. Here it is the hero himself who is initially presented as far from light; and it is precisely this which plunges him into the adventure which threatens to destroy him. But in the end he is saved, because his eyes have been opened and he has gone through a fundamental change of heart. He has made the switch from dark to light. Such is the case with Crusoe, with Lucius, with the Ancient Mariner, with the Prodigal Son. The real victory of such Voyage and Return heroes is not over the forces of darkness outside them. It is over the same dark forces within themselves.

In this respect, of course, this plot is rather different from the three types of story we have looked at earlier. And equally it does not share their general tendency to culminate in a final triumphant union of the hero with his 'Princess'. The complete happy ending of the Voyage and Return story is simply that the hero returns to his familiar world transformed. He has become a new man. By discovering a new, much deeper centre to his personality, he has 'seen the light'. And this in itself, the story suggests, is enough to guarantee that he will 'live happily ever after'.

But even though the Voyage and Return story does not end on that familiar concluding image of hero and heroine united in love, this is not to say that, during their dreamlike experience of the other world, relations with some figure of the opposite sex may not play an important part. Indeed such a relationship often marks the only real personal contact or point of engagement they have with the elusive other world. Yet, significantly, this is much more consistently true of those stories where the central figure returns again to the 'real world' without having been transformed, and without having won anything positive from the adventure. If he or she does form such a relationship in the other world, and it may seem of the highest importance to them, when they make their escape back to reality again, it has to be abandoned. When the hero returns, the girl is left behind.

In Wells's *The Time Machine*, for instance, the only identifiable personal contact the hero has with his other world of the distant future is his friendship with one of the Eloi, a pretty young girl called Weena, whom he rescues from drowning and who then slavishly follows him everywhere – until the final nightmare chase through the dark forest when she is snatched away by the shadowy Morlocks and presumably eaten. Similarly in *The Third Man* Holly Martins's only real point of engagement with another person in the unreal, nightmarish world of Harry Lime's Vienna is his friendship with the beautiful, enigmatic actress Anna, with whom he falls in love. But one of the most memorable scenes in the film comes right at the end, after Lime's funeral. Martins waits for Anna as she walks towards him down a long avenue in the wintry cemetery. Finally she reaches him and passes by without a look, leaving him to make his departure from Vienna friendless and alone. In *Brideshead Revisited*, Charles Ryder's only real personal engagement with the other world is his strangely intense friendship with Sebastian, later transmuted into his love for Sebastian's sister, Lady Julia. And of course the final cue for his 'expulsion' from the world of Brideshead is Julia's breaking off of their engagement. The only woman he has ever loved has to be left behind, and Ryder returns to his 'normal' world again to face the rest of his life, as he puts it, 'childless, middle-aged and loveless'.

Such is the position of the hero of one of the most famous of all Voyage and Return stories, Orpheus, who, after his journey through the underworld, has to leave behind him forever his great love Eurydice. Having gone there to bring her back, he is told he can do so on one condition: that, as he returns to the upper world, he keeps looking forward and does not look back. At the last moment, just before he steps out into the daylight, he looks back to see if Eurydice is following him. Instead of coming back joyful, with his life immeasurably renewed, Orpheus thus returns from his journey loveless, alone and untransformed. And it is no accident that the other heroes who must leave behind the woman who has become important to them during their time in the other world emerge similarly untransformed.[4]

A story which might seem to offer something of a variation on this pattern is Alain Fournier's novel *Le Grand Meaulnes*. Meaulnes, an uncouth teenage boy,

4. Another familiar example of an unhappy love story based on the Voyage and Return plot is the post-war British film *Brief Encounter* (1946), written by Noel Coward and directed by David Lean. The 'normal' world is represented by the humdrum home life of the heroine (played by Celia Johnson) married to Fred, her kindly, unimaginative, boring husband, who likes nothing better than to sit by the fire doing the crossword puzzle. In interior monologue, with a romantic Rachmaninov piano concerto blasting out of the gramophone, she unhappily reconstructs how some weeks before, in the station refreshment room in the nearby town, she had unexpectedly 'fallen into another world' by meeting a handsome, sensitive doctor (Trevor Howard), also married. She recalls how they fell in love, snatching several more surreptitious meetings, visits to the cinema, drinking champagne in a restaurant, walking in the country. Their affair goes through the familiar cycle of dream stage; frustration stage (as she feels growing guilt, lies to her husband, is spotted by friends in the restaurant); and nightmare stage (their attempt to make love in a friend's flat is aborted when he unexpectedly returns, they both realise the affair cannot last, he tells her he is about to leave with his family for a new job in South Africa). After they have made their final farewells on the station platform, she returns miserably home to the 'normal' world of Fred and his crossword, puts on the Rachmaninov and relives in her mind the whole sad story.

disappears one night in the French countryside. When he returns a few days later, exhausted and shaken, he has had a very strange adventure. He had got lost and, looking for somewhere to spend the night, he had come across a house blazing with light. On entering, he found himself plunged into a strange, dreamlike scene of revelry, involving a crowd of gay young people and children, dressed in clothes of a bygone age. He and the daughter of the house, Yvonne, found themselves mutually attracted. But suddenly the party had come to an end, the young people disappeared, and Meaulnes found himself all alone at a country crossroads. Has it all been a dream? So far it is a typical Voyage and Return adventure. But then comes the twist. Meaulnes eventually runs across Yvonne again in the 'real world', and marries her. Almost immediately, however, he has to go away and returns to find that she has died, in childbirth. In other words, although he has eventually been united with the girl he met in the other world, he still loses her. Their surviving child is the only proof that she ever really existed. But even he is now being brought up by someone else. At the end of the story Meaulnes is thus left 'childless, loveless' and alone.

A similarly hard-to-disguise bleak ending concludes another, even more famous twentieth-century story shaped by the Voyage and Return plot, *Gone With the Wind*, the novel by Margaret Mitchell which in 1939 became one of the most successful films ever made. We meet the heroine Scarlett O'Hara as a beautiful adolescent girl in the 'normal' world of her upbringing, the ante-bellum slave-owning Southern aristocracy and her home in her family's great house Tara. Like everyone else around Tara, she is then plunged into the 'abnormal' world of the American Civil War when, amid violence, deprivation and defeat, all familiar values and assumptions are turned upside down. Scarlett's story is centred on her love for two men, the weak, effeminate Ashley Wilkes and the 'over-masculine' Rhett Butler. As the shadows lengthen over her world, she finally embarks on a stormy marriage to Rhett and they produce a daughter. But the child dies in a riding accident. Scarlett miscarries a second pregnancy, and Rhett, having lost all love for her ('I don't give a damn'), abandons her for the last time. Scarlett returns to the half-ruined family mansion at Tara, where the story began, and forlornly wonders how she can win Rhett back. Anything is possible, she tries to persuade herself, ending the story on her brave declaration 'Tomorrow is another day!'. Her words seem to indicate that she is once again looking forward. But in fact, like Orpheus, she is really only looking back, to what she has lost forever. The truth is that, for all her wishful thinking, poor Scarlett is at last 'childless, loveless' and alone.[5]

5. Other well-known American examples of Voyage and Return stories where the central figure has to leave the 'other half' behind include *The Student Prince* (1924) and the Hollywood movie *Roman Holiday* (1953). The hero of Sigmund Romberg's operetta is a prince, bored with the formalities of life in his father's kingdom, who seeks diversion by making an incognito visit to the university town of Heidelberg There he has an exhilaratingly informal time surrounded by students, and falls in love with an innkeeper's daughter. News comes of his father's death and duty calls him home to take up his duties as king (where it has also been arranged that he should marry a princess for reasons of state). He cannot forget his true love and makes another secret visit to Heidelberg to say goodbye, but he must then sadly return to the 'normal' world, leaving her behind for ever. In some ways very similar is the story of *Roman Holiday*, starring Audrey Hepburn as a European princess on an official visit to Rome, likewise bored with all the stuffy formalities of her royal life. She secretly

What all these examples demonstrate is that, just as much in the Voyage and Return story as in the other types of plot we have looked at, the relations between the central figure and some feminine or masculine 'other half' may give us the essential key to what is going on in the story: except that here, where the central figure is the plaything of events beyond his or her control, what we see revealed by that relationship is likely to be some fundamental inadequacy in the central figure which is never rectified. In the earlier types of story, nothing more completely confirms the hero or heroine's worthiness to achieve a complete happy ending than the liberation of their 'other half' from the grip of darkness. But here the other half remains in the darkness of the 'other world'. And even though the hero or heroine themselves emerge from that other world, if their other half remains behind, the story ends on an unresolved, downbeat note which no amount of brave talk about tomorrow being another day can disguise. They have been through the tremendous experience of their confrontation with the mystifying, unknown realm, which has shaken them to the foundations of their previous identity. Yet they have emerged essentially untransformed, having learned or gained nothing. And what we have learned about them is that their understanding of the world is really no greater at the end of the story than it was at the beginning. They have been put to some very fundamental test – and they have failed.

### Voyage and Return: Summing up

A fourth way in which a story may take shape in the human imagination shows the hero or heroine being abruptly transported out of their 'normal' world into an abnormal world, and eventually back to where they began. The pattern of such a story is likely to unfold like this:

1. *Anticipation Stage and 'fall' into the other world*: When we first meet the hero, heroine or central figures, they are likely to be in some state which lays them open to a shattering new experience. Their consciousness is in some way restricted. They may just be young and naive, with only limited experience of the world. They may be more actively curious and looking for something unexpected to happen to them. They may be bored, or drowsy, or reckless. But for whatever reason, they find themselves suddenly precipitated out their familiar, limited exist-ence, into a strange world, unlike anything they have experienced before.

2. *Initial fascination or Dream Stage*: At first their exploration of this discon-certing new world may be exhilarating, because it is so puzzling and unfamiliar. But it is never a place in which they can feel at home.

---

escapes at night from the embassy where she is staying and, after walking the streets, falls asleep on a bench where she is picked up by an American journalist, played by Gregory Peck, in the city to cover her visit. He has no idea who she is but, concerned for her welfare, takes her back to the flat where he is staying. In the morning she asks him to show her the city, and she has an exhilaratingly informal day wandering incognito with him round Rome, with the inevitable result that, by night-fall, they are in love. But duty then calls her sadly back to her 'normal' world, leaving him behind. Now he is aware of her true identity, he momentarily contemplates selling the story of their time together. But when she appears at a press conference, he conveys to her that her secret is safe.

3. *Frustration Stage*: Gradually the mood of the adventure changes to one of frustration, difficulty and oppression. A shadow begins to intrude, which becomes increasingly alarming.

4. *Nightmare Stage*: The shadow becomes so dominating that it seems to pose a serious threat to the hero or heroine's survival.

5. *Thrilling Escape and return*: Just when the threat closing in on the hero or heroine becomes too much to bear, they make their escape from the other world, back to where they started. At this point the real question posed by the whole adventure is: how far have they learned or gained anything from their experience? Have they been fundamentally changed, or was it all 'just a dream'?

Again in the Voyage and Return story we see a parallel to that underlying structure we observed in the earlier plots. The story begins with the hero or heroine in that limited or incomplete state which leads to the initial sense of constriction as they are plunged into their adventure. This is followed, as they explore the new world they find themselves in, by a sense of expansion and widening horizons. But then, as the shadow approaches, there is a new sense of constriction. This eventually leads us up to the story's climax, where the sense of constriction is at its most acute; and here at last, if the story is to come to a full happy ending, we see the hero going through a life-changing reversal. At the opposite end of the spectrum, as in the stories by Kafka, are those rare examples of the Voyage and Return story in its darkest, most negative form, where the hero remains trapped in the other world, never coming back at all. Much more common, however, is the lesser dark form of the story where the hero or heroine do emerge again, but having learned nothing; and often having left behind in the other world some figure of the opposite sex who has become important to them. The complete happy ending is reserved for those stories, like *The Golden Ass* or *Robinson Crusoe*, where the hero has been fundamentally changed by his experience: from that limited, self-centred, potentially dark figure we saw at the beginning to the mature, fulfilled, light figure he has become by the end. And here, for the first time, we have seen a type of story which, to reach a fully resolved ending, requires its central figure to go through such an inner switch from darkness to light. We are now about to move on to another type of plot where this transformation is so central that the story cannot exist without it. Here we move firmly back into the realm of the complete happy ending as we have seen it in earlier plots, with a hero and heroine joyfully united; providing some of the most sunlit and glorious conclusions to stories in all literature.

*Chapter 6*

# Comedy

'Jack shall have Jill, naught shall go ill;
The man shall have his mare again, and all shall be well'.
*A Midsummer Night's Dream*

Figaro is planning to marry Susanna, but first he has to win the approval of his employer, the Count Almaviva, who has his eye on Susanna himself, much to the chagrin of his wife the Countess, who is adored by the young Cherubino, who is in turn loved by Barbarina. Just to make things even more straightforward, it also seems that Figaro is already contracted to marry the elderly Marcellina – until it is discovered that she is his long-lost mother.

As soon as we are presented with a situation like this we know we are faced with a type of story unlike any other and one which must be numbered high among the more improbable concoctions of the human imagination. We are entering a world of bizarre conventions, many of them scarcely altered in over 2000 years: the superficial spirit of which was perhaps best summed up by Groucho Marx when, in *A Night in Casablanca*, he was playing the new manager of a luxury hotel. Summoning his staff, he announces that he is going to change round the numbers on all the rooms. 'But the guests' protests one of his employees, 'they will go into the wrong rooms. Think of the confusion.' 'Yeah' replies Groucho, 'but think of the fun.'

Confronted by the kind of confusion which prevails at the beginning of *The Marriage of Figaro*, we may not be entirely surprised if this is made still more complicated by such further familiar sources of misunderstanding as:

- characters donning disguises or swapping identities;
- men dressing up as women, or vice versa;
- secret assignations when the 'wrong person' turns up;
- scenes in which characters are hastily concealed in cupboards or behind furniture, only for their presence to be inevitably and embarrassingly discovered.

Indeed we know that the general chaos of misunderstanding is likely only to get worse, until the knot the characters have tied themselves and each other up into seems almost unbearable. But finally, and to universal relief, everyone and everything will get miraculously sorted out, bringing a deliriously happy ending.

In fact Comedy is a very specific kind of story. It is not simply any story which is funny. Some very funny stories have quite different kinds of plot. Indeed, as we shall see, a story may follow the plot of comedy without it being intended to be funny at all. Even the fact that an author describes his story as a 'comedy' (e.g., Chekhov's *The Cherry Orchard*) does not necessarily mean that it is a Comedy in plot terms. But just what it is that shapes the plot of Comedy, that provides the common factor between say, a Marx Brothers film and a play by Shakespeare, an American musical and a novel by Jane Austen, a Mozart opera and a story by P. G. Wodehouse, requires a little careful unravelling. In fact it leads us on to one of the most rewarding puzzles literature has to offer.

## Comedy – Stage one: Aristophanes

Not the least unusual thing about Comedy is that, unlike any other kind of plot, we can actually see it taking shape historically. All the other basic types of story, when we first come across them in the history of storytelling, appear, as it were, fully formed. But when we look back over the history of Comedy we can see it evolving, through three distinct stages. Nevertheless, as we come to grasp the fundamental principle on which the plot rests, we can see that the basic plot itself has not really changed: all that has happened is that aspects of the story originally only implicit have been developed and brought out, to give a sharper focus on what the story is really about.

No one knows for certain whether Comedy began, as legend has it, in the village revels of ancient Greece[1] – although there is nothing inconsistent between a spirit of festive revelry and the mood which has prevailed at the conclusion of so many comedies since. What is certain is that, when we first come across specific examples, in the so-called 'Old Comedy' which, between 425 and 388 BC, made Aristophanes for nearly 40 years one of the leading playwrights in Athens, we still see the plot at an early stage of its development. We see some of the ingredients which later went to make up the fully-formed Comedy plot, but by no means all.

At the heart of Aristophanic comedy lay an *agon* or conflict between two characters or groups of characters. One is dominated by some dark, rigid, life-denying obsession. The other represents life, liberation and truth. The issue is ultimately decided, of course, in favour of the latter. In *Lysistrata* (the most popular of the comedies in recent times because of its 'feminist, anti-war' theme), the first group is represented by the men of Athens, full of martial ardour and always away from the city making war; the second by their unhappy wives, stuck at home, determined to cure their menfolk of their warlike obsession. The women hit on the device of retreating to the Acropolis and refusing to have anything to do with their husbands (in particular refusing them their 'conjugal rights') until the men agree to give up their love of war. For a time confusion reigns, until the men recognise where their inmost priorities lie and surrender to the women's demands. There is

---

1. The usual derivation given for 'comedy' (*cf.*, for instance, Skeat, *Etymological Dictionary of the English Language*) is from the old Greek κωμος, a banquet, a jovial festivity, a festal procession. But even Aristotle in the *Poetics* had difficulty in determining whether the original derivation was from κωμαξειν, to revel, or from κωμαι, the country word for a village.

a final scene of universal reconciliation, as each man is reunited with his 'other half', and all go off for a joyous celebration.

In *The Wasps* Aristophanes shows us the grim figure of Procleon, an old man who is obsessed with serving on juries, passing judgement on his fellow citizens and invariably finding them guilty. His son Anticleon determines to liberate him from this dark obsession. He persuades his father that he could much more conveniently indulge his favourite pastime if they were to set up a courtroom in their own home. The first 'prisoner' brought for judgement is a dog accused of stealing a leg of meat from the kitchen. Anticleon contrives so to confuse his father with his conduct of the case that Procleon inadvertently places his juryman's pebble in the wrong pot, thus for the first time in his life finding a prisoner not guilty. Initially he is furious at having been tricked into betraying his most deeply-cherished principle, but gradually he comes to recognise that his obsession with sitting in judgement was only a terrible imprisonment from which he has now been released. The conclusion of the play shows him happily discovering his new 'liberated' self, singing, drinking, going off to parties, pouring scorn on his old jury colleagues who are still stuck on the treadmill of their obsession, and in a final tour de force showing he can dance everyone else off the stage.

In the *Thesmophoriazusae (The Poet and the Women)* the characters possessed by dark, life-denying ill-humour are the women of Athens who, as they gather for their yearly festival, the Thesmophoria, are plotting to kill the playwright Euripides for the unfair way, as they see it, in which he presents women in his plays. Euripides smuggles his uncle Mnesilochus into the gathering, disguised as a woman, to plead his case. Inevitably his disguise is penetrated, and Mnesilochus is held prisoner while the women angrily decide his fate. He manages to get word of what has happened out to Euripides, who makes various absurd attempts to rescue him, disguised as a succession of heroes from his plays. Only when in desperation Euripides finally plucks up the courage to appear before them in his own identity, and threatens to reveal to their husbands the way they have been carrying on while their menfolk were away at the war, does the light dawn. The women recognise their true behaviour has been such that there is no way they would wish it to be exposed. There is a general return to good humour. Mnesilochus is released and all ends happily.

In each of these stories the eventual happy outcome hinges on a crucial turning point: the moment when the 'dark' characters, obsessed with their divisive desire to make war, to judge, to kill, are suddenly forced to recognise something so important about themselves that it completely changes their attitude, paving the way to reconciliation and celebration. It was this which Aristotle called anagnorisis or 'recognition', the moment when something previously not recognised or known suddenly becomes clear. 'Recognition', as Aristotle put it, 'means the change from ignorance to knowledge'. Something is discovered which transforms the situation. And although comedy was to go through many changes in the centuries which lay ahead, this transition 'from ignorance to knowledge' was to remain at the heart of the comic plot, as the central clue to what this type of story is about.

## Stage two – The 'New Comedy'

During the century after the heyday of Aristophanes, Comedy went through a change so marked as to amount almost to a mutation. As the 'Old Comedy' gave way to the so-called 'New Comedy', particularly associated with the Athenian Menander, and later with his Roman imitators Plautus and Terence, two new elements came to the fore in the plot, so fundamental they have come to be thought of as almost inseparable from Comedy ever since.

The most striking innovation was that Comedy became a love story. The action became centred for the first time on a hero and a heroine: and the chief effect of the confusion or conflict in the story is to keep the two apart until they can be brought triumphantly together in the closing scenes. In other words, the first thing we may observe about the 'New Comedy' is simply that it has arrived at the universal happy ending we are already so familiar with from other kinds of story: the final uniting of a hero and a heroine, in a way which symbolises completion, the end of division and the renewal of life.

There are two general ways in the New Comedy in which the lovers may be thus kept apart. In one type of story we see a hero and heroine who passionately desire to get married but are being prevented from doing so by a selfish and unrelenting father, until finally something comes to light which persuades him to withdraw his opposition to the match. In the other kind of story, the central conflict lies in a quarrel between the lovers themselves. This is invariably based on some dreadful misunderstanding (in the New Comedy it is invariably the hero who is guilty of wronging the heroine, by misjudging her in some way), until finally something comes to light which clears the misunderstanding up. The angry hero is contrite, the lovers are reconciled and unity is restored.

Apart from the important addition of the love element (which gives the story a much sharper, more personal focus), the actual shape of the New Comedy thus remains very similar to that of the Old Comedy. The story is still about the resolution of a conflict: some state of darkness and confusion giving way, through 'recognition' and a change of heart, to reconciliation and light. In Plautus's *Aurularia (The Pot of Gold)*, a typical story of two lovers prevented from marrying by an unrelenting father, we are still not far from the world of Aristophanes. Euclio is an obsessive old curmudgeon, reminiscent of Procleon in *The Wasps*, except that his obsession is with hoarding money rather than judging. His daughter wishes to marry the hero Lyconides, but the old miser is insisting that she marry one of his rich friends, for money. Euclio's state of darkness becomes even blacker when he loses his most precious possession, a pot of gold. But resolution begins when the gold is found by young Lyconides, who offers it to Euclio in return for permission to marry his daughter. In a change of heart similar to Procleon's the old miser 'sees the light', recognises that his greed has turned him into a monster of selfishness, and not only gives the couple his blessing but the gold as well.

The second, crucially important element which came to the fore in the New Comedy concerned the nature of the 'recognition' on which the resolution of the story turns: the nature of what it is that has to be discovered or made clear before a change of heart can pave the way to a happy ending. This centres on the revelation that someone's identity is different from what it seems.

In the *Epitrepontes (The Arbitration)* of Menander, who favoured the type of story based on a quarrel between the lovers themselves, we see a young husband and wife, Charisios and Pamphile, who have become violently estranged because, shortly after their wedding, Pamphile had given birth to a child. The baby has somehow been disposed of, but Charisios has been so enraged by this evidence of his wife's premarital carrying-on that he has left her. The action begins when a mysterious baby turns up, accompanied by various tokens, including a ring. The slaves of the estranged couple get together to discover the child's identity, and conclude that the baby's father can only be Charisios himself who, as his own personal slave remembers, gave this particular ring to an unknown girl he had made love to under cover of darkness at a public festival before his marriage. When the slaves confront Charisios with the proof that the baby is his, he is overwhelmed with remorse. He realises that he had dreadfully wronged his wife by berating her for a crime of which he had been just as guilty himself. But the slaves then tell him that, on the evidence of the other tokens, the mother of his child can be no one other than Pamphile: in other words, the girl he had ravished in the darkness was his future wife. The baby whose arrival had caused all the trouble had belonged to them both all the time. With this 'recognition', the couple are joyfully reconciled, the slaves are rewarded with their freedom and the play ends in the usual general celebration.

What we see emerging here as a crucial, and from now on increasingly familiar element in Comedy is that one of the chief sources of confusion in the story, and one of the chief obstacles to unity between the characters, is that they are in some way unaware of each other's true identity, or indeed their own. This had already been embryonically present in Aristophanes (e.g., the disguises adopted by Euripides and his uncle in the *Thesmophoriazusae*). But it now becomes much more explicit. One of the most important ingredients in the process of 'recognition' becomes the establishing of who people really are. Only when everyone's real identity has been sorted out can the way be made clear to the final union.

There is almost no moment we see more often in comedy than the discovery, to everyone's astonishment, that the true origins of one of the characters are in fact quite different from what had been generally supposed: usually that he or she is in fact the long-lost child of someone of elevated social position. When this device first appeared in the New Comedy, it was almost invariably the heroine who was belatedly discovered to be of higher social origin than anyone had been aware of, thus dispelling the objections to her union with the hero. In Terence's *Andria* (The Woman of Andros), for instance, the hero's father is violently opposed to his son marrying a poor courtesan, until it is revealed that she is the long-lost daughter of one of his rich friends. The father is of course delighted and at once withdraws his opposition to the match.

So important to the New Comedy was this element of ignorance as to people's true identity and the need to establish who everyone really is as a prelude to resolution that some plays were concerned with very little else: even the love interest taking second place, or disappearing altogether. Plautus's *Menaechmi*, for instance, the play on which Shakespeare was to base his *Comedy of Errors*, introduces perhaps the ultimate variation on the confusion arising from mistaken identity: the story of two identical twins being repeatedly taken for each other without either being aware of the other's existence. The hero arrives in a strange town, looking for his long-lost twin brother Sosicles, at just the moment when, after a row with his wife, Sosicles is storming out of his house to take refuge with his mistress. There follows a crescendo of increasingly contentious misunderstanding as the twins are constantly mistaken for each other by everyone else: Sosicles's wife, mistress, servants and friends. Only when the knot of confusion has reached strangulation point, with Sosicles about to be arrested as a madman, are the brothers finally brought face to face. 'Recognition' makes clear all that has happened, and the play ends on the usual note of rejoicing: although noticeably the central point of union is the bringing together of the two long-parted brothers, rather than the reconciliation of Sosicles with his wife.

By the end of the great age of classical stage Comedy in the second century BC, many of the basic features had already been established which were to be the mainstays of Comedy for the next two thousand years. Even the stories themselves were to be revived to entertain audiences of later ages. Molière was to adapt the *Aurularia* in his *L'Avare (The Miser)*; while the *Menaechmi's* direct descendants have included not only Shakespeare's version, but in the twentieth century a Laurel and Hardy film *Our Relations* and a successful Broadway musical, *The Boys from Syracuse*.

Before the Graeco-Roman world came to an end, however, there was a further landmark in the history of Comedy which was to have significance for later ages. This was the moment when, for the first time, the plot moved off the stage to become the inspiration for another kind of storytelling altogether. In the second and third centuries AD there was a vogue for a new kind of prose story. Sometimes described as 'the first novels', these were somewhat lurid tales of adventure, centred on a hero and heroine – but their plots followed a formula with a familiar ring. As one authority puts it:

> 'the usual pattern is that the hero and heroine fall in love with each other in the opening paragraphs, are separated by a long series of "moving accidents", and are finally reunited to provide the happy ending.'[2]

2. Paul Turner, introduction to *Daphnis and Chloe* (Penguin Classics edition). Despite the familiar overall shape of the plot, the 'moving accidents' which kept the hero and heroine apart in these novels might have seemed a far cry from the more mundane misadventures which had hitherto been the stuff of stage comedies, consisting as they did mainly of a series of violent and sensational 'thrilling escapes from death'. In *Anthia and Habrocomes* by Xenophon of Ephesus, for instance, the heroine 'is captured by pirates, captured by brigands, nearly raped, nearly made a human sacrifice, buried alive after she has drugged herself ... to avoid a distasteful marriage and buried in a pit with two fierce dogs'; while the hero, her lover, is 'shipwrecked on the coast of Egypt, captured by shepherds, sold into slavery, falsely accused of murdering his master, crucified on a rock overlooking the Nile, swept by a gale into the river, fished out again and condemned to be burned at the stake. Happily the Nile overflows and puts out the flames ... ' (*op. cit.*). It is only after yet further improbable adventures that hero and heroine are at last reunited to live happily ever after.

Easily the best-known (and least sensational) of these forerunners of the many novels and romances which in later times were to be based on the Comedy plot is Longus's *Daphnis and Chloe*. This begins with the discovery by shepherds on a country estate of two babies, each accompanied by tokens. The mere mention of such tokens, a device originally found in mythology and long preceding Comedy, of course signals that the resolution of the story will eventually hang on the discovery of the babies' true identities. The boy Daphnis and the girl Chloe are each adopted by a shepherd family. They grow up together in pastoral innocence, fall in love and from then on the entire suspense of the story lies in how they can overcome a long series of obstacles to their final union. First, each of the two are abducted in turn by a different set of kidnappers, and manage to escape. Then Chloe's parents advertise for a rich suitor for her hand, which seems to rule out the impoverished Daphnis – until he is told in a dream where to find the money necessary to win their approval. He does so and halfway through the story it seems as though the couple are about to get married. But then, just as in a Rags to Riches story (there is a strong Rags to Riches flavour about this tale), a 'central crisis' intervenes. The son of the rich owner of the estate arrives from the city, and Daphnis's foster-parents seize this opportunity to produce the tokens found with him as a baby. To the astonishment and delight of everyone except Daphnis and Chloe themselves, it is discovered that Daphnis is the estate owner's long-lost son. The lovers are heartbroken, because it seems they are about to be torn apart forever. Daphnis cannot now marry a mere shepherd girl. But just before the hero is taken away to the city to begin his grand new life, Chloe's foster-parents have the bright idea of producing her tokens, which seem to indicate that she may also be of high-born origin. She too joins the party for the city, where the estate owner holds a feast for all the richest men in town. Sure enough, when Chloe's tokens are handed round, the richest guest of all recognises that she must be his long-lost daughter. Thanks to the discovery of their true identities (a rare instance of both parties turning out to be of nobler birth than had been supposed), all obstacles to the union of the overjoyed couple have at last been removed.

With this delicately symmetrical essay on the importance of discovering who you really are as a precondition to living happily ever after, the classical world more or less bade farewell to the theme of Comedy. The third and final stage in the evolution of the plot was not to unfold for well over a thousand years.

## Stage three: Shakespeare

Although the Comedy plot by no means disappeared from Western storytelling during the Middle Ages (whose most famous poem, after all, was explicitly given the name of 'Comedy'), it was not until the conscious revival of the classical tradition in the pastoral romances and stage comedies of the Renaissance that it swept back to its earlier prominence. When it did so, an extremely important new dimension began to be added to the story which, in a sense, made the plot complete. Nowhere can we see this more clearly illustrated than in the 16 comedies of

Shakespeare (nearly half his dramatic output), who did more to explore the full range of the archetypal comic plot than any author before or since.

The first thing which may strike us when we look at the early comedies of Shakespeare after those of the classical world is how much richer and more complex their stories have become: like the textures of Renaissance polyphony after the single-line melodies of plainsong. We can see this particularly vividly in what was probably his first comedy, *The Comedy of Errors*, because we can contrast it directly with Plautus's *Menaechmi*, on which it was based. But what a transformation has been wrought in the original simple tale. Whereas Plautus concentrated on just a single thread of misunderstandings, culminating in the one reunion of the long-separated brothers, Shakespeare's version enriches this with such a tapestry of subsidiary themes and sub-plots that by the end he can present us with a positive cascade of additional unions and reunions. Ephesian Antipholus, the brother whose marital quarrel has lasted throughout the play, is reconciled with his wife. His twin, Syracusan Antipholus, has fallen in love with the wife's sister: so the play can end on the full resounding note of an impending wedding. Also reunited are the brother's two servants, another pair of identical twins who had been separated by the same shipwreck which parted their masters. In addition to all this the two Antipholuses are reunited not only with their long-lost father (whose life at the start of the play had been threatened and is now spared) but also with their equally long-lost mother, who makes a dramatic reappearance at the play's climax. Woven together at the end we thus see no less than seven different, deeply emotional unions or reunions (including that of an entire family), involving a group of people who had all previously been separated or divided from one another. The sense of a kind of cosmic gathering together of those who had been sundered and isolated could hardly be more complete.

It was really in his other early comedies, however, that Shakespeare began to explore that added dimension which was to extend the range of the plot in a way the classical world had not dreamed of.

In classical Comedy, it will be recalled, there had only been one central pair of lovers in a story, and their initial 'pairing off' had already taken place before the story opened (or at least, in the later romances, in 'the opening paragraphs'). We begin, in short, with a pair of already established lovers, and the chief problem of the story is to surmount some obstacle which has arisen – an unrelenting father or a quarrel – to the confirming of their union.

In plays like *The Taming of the Shrew* and *Love's Labours Lost*, however, we see something very significant happening. We no longer begin with a pair of established lovers. The focus has moved backwards, as it were, to an earlier stage of the process: to the wooing which brings the lovers together in the first place. At the start of the first of these two plays we meet the ill-tempered shrew Katharina who thinks no man good enough for her: and the story tells of how the hero, the imperturbable Petruchio, sets out to break her wilfulness, first to make her accept him as a lover and then to soften and tame her into a dutiful bride. In the second we see no fewer than four handsome young men, who have vowed to have nothing to do with women, being softened into breaking their vow when by chance they run into four attractive young women who, after an initial show of reluctance, finally accept them.

The main action of the story has thus shifted to the pairing off process itself; and in his two remaining early comedies Shakespeare takes this a crucial stage further. At least in *The Taming of the Shrew* and *Love's Labour's Lost* we are never in real doubt, once the action has begun, which young man is eventually going to end up with which young woman. But in *The Two Gentlemen of Verona* (based on an early sixteenth-century Italian romance), a further twist enters the plot. We begin with a pair of seemingly established lovers, Proteus and Julia; while Proteus's friend Valentine goes off to Milan and falls in love with the Duke's daughter Silvia. But then Proteus himself comes to Milan and also falls in love with Silvia. Thus both young men are now in love with the same young woman. Possessed by his new infatuation, Proteus then becomes a dark figure and proceeds doubly to betray his friend, by revealing to Silvia's father Valentine's plan to elope with her. Valentine is banished, leaving Proteus free to continue his wooing of the reluctant Silvia. The situation becomes still more complicated when Proteus's original love Julia arrives in Milan, disguised as a boy, and becomes his page. Silvia flees to join the man she really loves, Valentine, but is captured by robbers – and rescued by Proteus. Valentine is just about to concede Proteus the right to marry her when Julia speaks up in her true identity, reproaching Proteus for his lack of fidelity. This finally breaks the dark spell which has bewitched Proteus. He 'comes to himself', makes up his quarrel with Valentine, and the lovers can at last pair off properly and happily: Proteus with Julia, Valentine with Silvia.

If we have the sense that, in some important respect, Comedy is here at last coming into its own in a form in which we have known it ever since (incidentally giving rise to the most incomprehensible form of literature ever devised, the plot-summary of any play or comic opera based on a 'love tangle'), this is underlined by the last of Shakespeare's early comedies, *A Midsummer Night's Dream*, where we see the same kind of tangle handled with the effortless ease which showed him arriving at his full maturity as a storyteller.

When the story opens we meet two young men and two young women in a state of intense misery and confusion. The two young men, Lysander and Demetrius, are both in love with the same young woman, Hermia. Hermia loves Lysander and wishes to marry him, but her 'unrelenting' father Egeus wants her to marry Demetrius. Her friend Helena, on the other hand, loves Demetrius but is not loved in return. The foursome then enters the mysterious 'wood near Athens', where the fairy king Oberon and his mercurial agent Puck get to work sorting things out. But the first result of their enchantments is only to make things worse. By bungling his magic, Puck not only manages to persuade Demetrius to transfer his affections to Helena, but Lysander as well. This leaves Hermia loved by no one, and Helena convinced that all three must be playing a trick on her. Everyone is now at odds with everyone else. All that is required for a happy resolution, however, is for Puck to arrange that Lysander to switch his love back to Hermia. This leaves Demetrius loving Helena, who now accepts that his affection is genuine. The two couples, at last properly paired off, can emerge from the forest to join Duke Theseus and Hippolyta in the joyful prospect of a triple wedding.

What is new about this sort of dizzying merry-go-round is that so much of the story may now be taken up not just with how the lovers can be brought together, but in sorting out the even more basic question of who should end up with whom. In other words, compared with the simple formulae of the classical world, which were solely concerned with the pitfalls which may await lovers after they have established their love, Comedy has now been opened up to include all the possibilities for confusion which may arise before their final pairing off. On the one hand this may simply consist of the uncertainties attending the initial wooing of two lovers, as they first come to terms with their love and learn to accept each other. On the other, it may also include all the vastly greater complications which can arise when love proves inconstant or one-sided, such as when one person's love for another is initially unrequited; or when a lover begins by loving one person, then switches to another (and not infrequently back again); or when two men are in love with the same woman; or two women with the same man. What has happened, in fact, is that the range of Comedy has been extended, not just by Shakespeare, but in Renaissance literature generally, to include virtually every combination and permutation possible in the human experience of love. Its potential for confusion has, in effect, been made complete. As a result we can begin to see more clearly than ever before the true nature of the Comedy plot.

## Comedy: a first summary

What we are looking at when confronted by a fully developed Comedy is not unlike a jigsaw puzzle. By the time a jigsaw is complete, it seems obvious that there is only one way it could have ended up, with each piece in its proper place and fitting perfectly together with all the others. But it has not looked so obvious at an earlier stage when all the pieces were still muddled up and separate from each other, and when the significance of the fragment of picture on each piece was still unclear. What has had to be established is the precise nature of each piece: both what it stands for in itself and how it fits together with all the others, as part of a gradually emerging whole. In Comedy, the key to bringing this to light is the process of 'recognition'. And we can now see how the 'recognition' in a fully-developed comedy may involve four inter-related ingredients, all working together.

The first is that any characters who have become dark because they are imprisoned in some hard, divisive, unloving state – anger, greed, jealousy, shrewishness, disloyalty, self-righteousness or whatever – must be softened and liberated by some act of self-recognition and a change of heart. They must in effect become a 'new' or different person ('come to themselves') and if they do not change in this way, the only alternative, as we shall shortly see, is that they shall at least be shown up and paid out, by punishment or general derision, so they can no longer cause harm to others.

Secondly it may be necessary for the identity of one or more characters to be revealed in a more literal sense. They are discovered to be someone other than had been supposed.

Thirdly, where relevant, the characters must discover who they are meant to pair off with, their true 'other half', since until this is established they seem lost and incomplete. Recognition of their 'other half' thus becomes an essential part of discovering their own complete identity.

Finally and in general, wherever there is division, separation or loss, it shall be repaired. Families shall be reunited, lost objects found, usurped kingdoms re-established. Whatever is out of place or sick must be restored.

The 'change from ignorance to knowledge' thus becomes in each case a transition from division to wholeness, from darkness to light, and we can set out the 'before' and 'after' states of the four ingredients in Comedy like this:

| *Dark* | *Light* |
| --- | --- |
| One or more characters are trapped in some dark state which throws its shadow over others. | They either go through a change of heart or are exposed and punished. |
| The identity or true nature of one or more characters is hidden or unclear. | Their true identities or nature are revealed. |
| Lovers are still in a state of uncertainty: e.g., they are separated by a misunderstanding or are still in the process of pairing off. | Each lover is united with his or her 'other half'. |
| Families are divided and things are 'not as they should be'. | Families are reunited and everything is restored to its proper place |

In other words, for love and reconciliation to triumph, it must be discovered who all the characters really are and how they fit harmoniously together. The confusion which precedes this 'recognition' can thus be seen as a kind of twilight, marked by the fact that people are insufficiently aware of each other's and their own true identity: which is why such a conspicuous feature of Comedy is the obscuring of identities, not just through ignorance of birth, but through the whole repertoire of such devices as disguises, impersonations and characters being mistaken for each other.

The one thing of which we can be certain in a Comedy is that the happy ending cannot be reached until everyone has emerged into the full light of day, all disguises are thrown off and the characters no longer seem to be anything other than what they are. In the remainder of Shakespeare's comedies we see him developing this element in the plot in a particularly revealing way.

### The obscured heroine

A measure of just how richly Shakespeare developed the Comedy plot is to contrast his comedies with those of his contemporary Ben Jonson. Whereas the joy of a Shakespearean Comedy is to show a group of people all being finally lifted up into the light, as the powers of darkness in the story are dispelled, Jonson's plays derive their humour from concentrating far more obviously just on the devilry of the dark figures. In *Volpone*, a rich, elderly Venetian conspires with his confederate Mosca to trick a series of gullible fools by pretending that he is on his death bed. Each of the victims is persuaded to think he may be the chosen heir to Volpone's fortune, and therefore tries to ingratiate himself with the old rogue by giving him a present. Volpone then enjoys discomfiting them by announcing that he has made over all his estate to Mosca instead. But Mosca himself then tries to trick Volpone in turn, by blackmailing him. This so angers Volpone that he fool-ishly complains to the authorities, with the result that the whole story comes out. The play's ending simply shows both villains being paid out for their wicked game by being sentenced to fearful punishments.

*Volpone* is thus scarcely an example of Comedy, as we have been looking at it. The dark figures do not go through any change of heart as a prelude to the resolution. They are merely held up to ignominy and bundled off stage. Equally, there is no sense, as their dark powers are overthrown, of a whole community emerging from the shadows, joining together in joyful celebration round the loving union of a hero and heroine. Almost all Jonson's characters are shown as self-centred and dark. The focus of the story is entirely on how their greed, vanity, folly and deceit are finally exposed. In *The Alchemist* Jonson similarly shows a bunch of rogues, led by the cunning and cheeky Face, conspiring to trick various gullible fools into parting with their money, using as their headquarters the house of Face's master Lovewit during his temporary absence from London. Again the conspirators are eventually caught out, when Lovewit unexpectedly returns; although this time they escape punishment, partly because Lovewit lives up to his name by showing indulgent admiration for his servant's ingenuity; and partly because Face persuades him to accept one of the victims, the rich widow Pliant, as a wife. At least the play thus ends with a vestige of the conventional happy ending, as Lovewit and Pliant are happily brought together. But this final image of an impending marriage scarcely marks the triumphant resolution of everything the play has been about. It is merely tacked on at the end as a convenient device to round off the story.

Compared with the many-layered complexities of Shakespearean Comedy, the Jonsonian versions, by concentrating on just one aspect of the complete story, are little more than caricatures of the darker side of human nature. The glory of Shakespeare's comedies is not just that he so joyfully brings out the positive aspect of this plot, but how they may be read as a kind of anthology of almost every vari-ation the plot can offer. He constantly reshuffles the same basic situations and motifs in every conceivable combination, shedding light first on one aspect of the plot, then on another. From the middle of his career, however, we see a remark-ably consistent pattern emerging.

In what are often called the 'Middle Comedies' – *The Merchant of Venice, Much Ado About Nothing, As You Like It, Twelfth Night* – we are introduced to a group of characters, including a central pair of lovers who meet shortly after the story's opening. To begin with things go reasonably well, seeming to promise hope for the future. But then a threatening shadow intrudes: and at the heart of the story a particular opposition opens up between two of the characters. At one pole there is the play's chief dark figure, hard, bitter and vengeful; at the other is the heroine, who spends some crucial part of the story, particularly when the dark powers are most in the ascendant, in disguise: hidden, as it were, from complete view. Thus obscured, the loving heroine becomes the chief touchstone of the story, in one of two ways. Either from behind her disguise, she plays an active and dominant role in bringing about the play's resolution, in which case she is disguised as a man (Portia as the lawyer Dr Bellario, Rosalind as Ganymede, Viola as Cesario); or she is cast in a more passive role as the story's chief victim, passing into eclipse like Hero in *Much Ado*, when she is first taken for dead and then reappears at the end disguised as her cousin. Shakespeare often employed disguises in his earlier comedies, but only once, in *The Two Gentlemen of Verona*, had it been the heroine who adopted a disguise. Now his heroines do it consistently. And only as part of the general resolution and the routing of the dark powers does the heroine reappear in her proper identity: emerging from eclipse to bathe the play's ending in light.

The dark figure in these Middle Comedies is not one of the central characters but, as it were, an outsider or third party, whose egocentric and vengeful ill-humour throws the lovers into shadow. The supreme example of this is the embittered usurer Shylock; and it is notable that when he is finally put to rout by Portia, Shylock does not go through a change of heart. As is his nature, he remains unrelenting. He cannot therefore be admitted to the general rejoicing at the end, and thus becomes the first example we have seen in Comedy (apart from Jonson's grotesques in *Volpone*) of what may be called the 'unreconciled dark figure', who ends the story a broken object of derision: a kind of scapegoat or embodiment of all the negative, self-seeking qualities over which the ending of Comedy represents the victory.

In the next play in the sequence, *Much Ado About Nothing*, a similar part is played by Duke John, the treacherous brother of the lover Claudio. When his villainy is finally exposed he is unrepentant, and while Hero 'returns from the dead' to produce the happy ending, John remains off stage as the 'unreconciled dark figure', due for punishment.[3]

In *As You Like It* the dark figure is Frederick, whose usurpation of his brother's dominions eventually drives all the light characters into the mysterious, enchanted other-world of the Forest of Arden, He eventually does go through a change of heart, as a result of conversing with 'an old religious man', but this takes place off stage (simultaneously with the resolution of the confusion in the forest, as Rosalind throws off her disguise to be reunited with her lover Orlando and her father, the true Duke), and he therefore does not join the closing celebration.

---

3. The happy ending for Claudio and Hero is, of course, coupled with that of the sub-plot, the chequered relationship of Beatrice and Benedict who, after bickering their way so entertainingly through the play, finally recognise with disbelieving delight that they are actually meant for each other. This is a classic instance of two characters realising their own true identity through finally recognising their love for the 'other half' they have earlier dismissed or rejected (*cf.* also *Pride and Prejudice*).

Finally, in the intricate love-tangle of *Twelfth Night*, the role of dark figure is reserved for Malvolio, although the whole story is so light in tone that he scarcely offers a serious threat to the lovers. His offence is not so much active malevolence as merely the absurd self-love which deceives him into seeing himself as rival to 'Cesario' for Olivia's affections. Even so, Malvolio is still bundled derisively off stage as an unreconciled dark figure. In fact he is virtually the last such figure in Shakespeare's comedies,[4] because from now on we see an extremely significant shift taking place in the way Shakespeare looks at the story.

## The hero as dark figure

In *All's Well That Ends Well* we still encounter the familiar ingredients of a pair of lovers, with the central opposition between a 'dark figure' and a loving heroine who at a crucial moment passes into disguise. But now the dark figure is no longer some third party, like Shylock, but the hero himself. The confrontation between darkness and light has moved right to the heart of the story, dividing the two lovers themselves. The heroine Helen relentlessly pursues the arrogant Bertram through the entire story, with a deep unrequited love. And the hinge of the action, as in *Much Ado About Nothing*, is a midnight assignation, involving the hero in a confusion of identity between the heroine and another woman. Only this time it is the heroine who is disguised as the other woman, rather than the other way round; and the episode eventually leads to a happy resolution rather than, as in *Much Ado*, to darkness reaching its blackest point. Obviously where the hero himself is the chief dark figure he cannot remain unreconciled, or the story will not remain a comedy. Sure enough, Bertram's proud defences finally crumble, and he both accepts and returns Helen's love.

In his next comedy, *Measure for Measure*, Shakespeare pursues this theme of 'the hero as dark figure' in even more thoroughgoing fashion. Initially his hero Angelo seems the soul of virtue. But step by step he is exposed, behind this righteous persona, as a monster of vengeful hypocrisy; and once again the hinge of the action is a midnight assignation where the hero mistakes one woman in disguise for another. Despite the importance of this episode, however, it is now not so much the heroine who is the chief disguised figure in the play as the wise, all-seeing Duke of Vienna. At the play's outset he has pretended to go abroad, handing over the governance of Vienna to Angelo. But this has been a deliberate test, to see whether the virtuous young man is all that he seems. In fact the Duke has stayed in the city disguised as a humble friar, to observe and guide from behind the scenes all that follows. It is he who exposes Angelo's hypocrisy, and eventually confronts him with his guilt: to the point where Angelo is so contrite that he accepts that he must be put to death in punishment. This 'recognition' and change of heart allows the Duke to pardon him, paving the way to the happy ending

---

4. The only exception to this in the later plays is *Pericles*, where the two comparatively minor characters Cleon and Dionyza are punished off-stage.

where Angelo and the heroine can be united. And it was this motif which Shakespeare was finally to return to in *The Tempest*, where again we see the unfolding of the entire drama guided from behind the scenes by an all-seeing 'wise old man', the magician Prospero. But before that Shakespeare was to produce his last and most complex exploration of the theme of 'the hero as dark figure' and the heroine who passes into eclipse.

The first three acts of *The Winter's Tale* are so bleak and death-laden that, as has often been remarked, the story seems to be shaping up into a tragedy rather than a comedy. The hero, King Leontes, conceives a baseless suspicion that his wife Hermione is having an affair with his best friend, King Polixenes. He tries to have Polixenes killed and throws his wife into prison, where she gives birth to a daughter. Becoming more and more possessed by darkness, Leontes orders that the child be taken out and abandoned, and hardens his heart to every indication that his wife is blameless; until eventually his son dies of grief and Hermione seemingly follows suit. At last, thinking his entire family is dead, Leontes comes to himself and recognises the full horror of what he has quite unjustifiably set in train; and at this point, the scene changes in dream-like fashion to 'the sea coast of Bohemia'. We move at last out of the shadows of Tragedy into the recognisable world of Comedy. Leontes' little daughter Perdita, 'the lost one', has been found by shepherds, like Chloe in *Daphnis and Chloe*, and has grown up to fall in love with Florizel, the son of Leontes' old friend King Polixenes. Polixenes, now cast in the familiar role of 'unrelenting father', cannot agree to his princely son marrying a mere shepherd girl, and the lovers flee back to the court of Leontes, with angry father in pursuit. Here Perdita's true identity is discovered. Leontes is overjoyed to be reunited with his long-lost daughter (although this also revives his grief for his lost Hermione). And when Polixenes arrives it does not take long for him to make up his quarrel with Leontes, and for the two fathers to give joyful blessing to the union of their children. Finally Leontes is led to an uncannily lifelike statue of his dead wife. It turns out of course that Hermione had not died in prison but had merely been in hiding, and the statue is herself in disguise. Emerging from her long eclipse, she steps down to embrace her husband. Thus in every conceivable way the story ends happily.

In no other of his comedies has Shakespeare touched so sombrely on death and seeming death as a prelude to regeneration and the eventual victory of love and life. It was the conclusion of a long process of development in which he had steadily deepened his exploration of Comedy, making the issues at stake more and more serious, to the point where they had literally become a matter of life and death. Yet we may note that, at the very moment when Shakespeare reached such near-tragic depths, in a story about a husband separated by a terrible misunderstanding from his wife, he was in fact returning to the very theme which had launched the New Comedy nearly 2000 years before. The plays of Menander, such as the *Epitrepontes*, centred on precisely this basic situation of a husband and wife, or two lovers, rent apart by some dreadful misunderstanding – with the hero at last coming to recognise that he had done the heroine an appalling wrong. Indeed throughout the New Comedy no general theme had been more persistent than that of the heroine who spends much of the story misunderstood, rejected or otherwise under a shadow. The discovery at the end of so many comedies that this socially humble heroine was in fact the long-lost daughter of a rich man, thus raising her status from that of undervalued outcast to that of a pearl of great price, marked her 'emergence from eclipse' just as much as the throwing off of a disguise. There was nothing essentially new about the 'obscured heroine'. It was just that Shakespeare had found a new and subtle way to express a theme which had lain near the heart of Comedy for 1900 years.

### Above the line/below the line

A final very important aspect of Comedy which must now be introduced is again exemplified in *The Winter's Tale*. This is the way in which the process of regeneration in the story begins with the coming together of the two young lovers, Perdita and Florizel, in a socially humble setting, in another country, far removed from the darkened and divided world of King Leontes' court where we began.

If we turn from the comedies of Shakespeare to those of his later seventeenth-century successor Molière, the first thing which may strike us is how uncomplicated their stories are. We are almost back to the simplicities of the New Comedy. We may also be struck by how many of his plays are built round the same basic situation. Firstly, we see a father, the head of a household, who is in the grip of some foolish obsession. In *Le Bourgeois Gentilhomme* he is a rich tradesman and would-be social climber who wishes to pass himself off as a gentleman. In *Le Malade Imaginaire* he is a hypochondriac, with an exaggerated reverence for doctors. In *L'Avare*, taken straight from Plautus, he is a surly old miser trapped in his obsessive love for his money. In *Tartuffe* he is under the spell of the hypocritical religious fanatic who gives the play its name.

We then see this deluded paterfamilias cast in the role of selfish and unrelenting father. He has a daughter who is in love with some agreeable young man whom she wishes to marry. But for reasons directly stemming from his obsession, her father is opposed to the match and insisting that she marry some much less desirable person of his own choice: a nobleman, a doctor's nephew, a rich elderly friend, the appalling Tartuffe himself.

The fundamental situation of the play therefore is that we are presented with an impasse: on the one side stands the unyielding head of the household, in the grip of his dark obsession; on the other, cast under a shadow by his stern refusal to let them marry, are the young couple, representing life, hope and the way forward. The third ingredient is that, in each instance, a key part in breaking up the log jam, allowing the lovers to come together and life to flow again, is played by the paterfamilias's servants, the young couple themselves and even his wife. In other words a conspiracy is formed against his life-denying rule by all those around him whom he would regard as inferior, junior or subordinate. In *Le Bourgeois Gentilhomme* it is the blindly snobbish M. Jourdain's maidservant and his common-sensical wife who mastermind the ruse whereby the daughter's lover comes to ask for her hand in the socially dazzling disguise of 'the Grand Turk' (thus winning Jourdain's acceptance before the disguise is thrown off). In *Le Malade Imaginaire* it is the maidservant who dresses up as another doctor to expose the charlatanry of Purgon, thus helping to free Argan from his obsession and paving the way to the union of the lovers. In *L'Avare* it is the young valet who, by stealing the old miser's cash box, finally puts paid to Harpagon's dark, mean-minded scheme to marry off his two children to rich elderly friends. In *Tartuffe* it is Elmire, the wronged wife (aided and abetted by maidservant and young lovers) who stages the crucial assignation which exposes to her besotted husband Orgon what a vicious hypocrite Tartuffe really is (and when he is hauled off for punishment at the end Tartuffe represents as complete an instance of the 'unreconciled dark figure' as Shylock).

In fact this aspect of Molière's plays whereby the road to resolution lies through the 'inferior' figures in the story was by no means new in Comedy. Again and again, right back to Aristophanes, we see the characters in a comedy separated by, as it were, an unspoken dividing line. The characters above the line, like Moliere's fathers and their friends, represent the established order, an upper social level, the authority of men over women, fathers over their children. Those below the line, where the shadows fall, include servants, people of inferior class, wives and the rising generation. The chief source of darkness in the story, opposed to life, is on the upper level. The road to liberation lies through the 'inferior' level. In *The Wasps* it was young Anticleon who liberated his grim old father from his obsession with passing judgement. In *Lysistrata* it was the heroine and her fellow-wives who liberated their men from their ruling obsession with war. In the *Epitrepontes* it was the slaves to the various parties who, in a kind of below stairs conspiracy, got together to work out the identity of the newly-found baby, thus bringing love and reconciliation back to their master and mistress in the 'upper world'. Indeed for the slaves to be responsible for sorting out the confusion which had engulfed their social superiors was a regular feature of the New Comedy.

When we come to Shakespeare we almost invariably see a division into an 'upper' and a 'lower' world in social terms, and it is even occasionally servants or others on the lower level, as in *Much Ado*, who expose the vital truth which eventually brings about the triumph of love on the upper level. But much more often as we have seen, the same result is achieved by characters from the social upper level who move onto a shadowy, 'inferior' level in a different way, by concealing their true identity beneath a disguise. *The essence of Comedy is always that some redeeming truth has to be brought out of the shadows into the light.* This often requires a temporary descent into some obscured or 'inferior' state in order that the truth may be established, and the retreat behind a disguise is one of the most obvious ways in which this is achieved (e.g., Julia and Viola disguising themselves as pages, Rosalind as a poor country boy, the rich heiress Portia as a comparatively humble lawyer). Another form of 'descent' is into some shadowy 'other world', just as the lovers in *A Midsummer Night's Dream* cannot get themselves sorted out without their descent into the twilit world of the forest and the 'inferior' kingdom of the fairies; or the various light characters in *As You Like It* without their descent into the shadowy world of the Forest of Arden. The point is that the disorder in the upper world cannot be amended without some crucial activity taking place at a lower level, or in some other place beyond the consciousness of the 'upper world' character or characters who are in the grip of their life-denying state. It is from the lower level that life is regenerated and brought back to the upper world again, just as happens when Leontes is at his lowest ebb of spiritual exhaustion after the attack of darkness which dominates the first three acts of *The Winter's Tale*. The quickening of new life begins far away, amid the socially inferior surroundings where the young lovers are disguised as shepherds, until it eventually sweeps back up to the 'sick' King Leontes' court to turn winter into spring.

## Late eighteenth-century comedy

We can see a number of variations on this complex but extremely important aspect of Comedy in the memorable constellation of comedies which appeared in various European countries in the 1770s. For instance, in Goldsmith's *She Stoops to Conquer* (1773) we see an upper class young hero Marlow, who has a problem. He cannot relate to women unless they are of a lower station than his own. He is normally 'one of the most bashful and reserved young fellows in the world'; but confronted with a pretty barmaid he is suddenly seized with amorous confidence. He sets out into the country to meet the girl who has been chosen for him to marry, Miss Hardcastle, but is misled into mistaking her family's house for an inn. The whole visit thus becomes, in a sense, like a 'descent into an inferior realm', with the respectable house itself in effect in inferior disguise. And when the heroine herself enters into the spirit of the misunderstanding, by adopting the guise and manner of a serving girl, the hero is able to make ardent protestations of love to her. It is only at the moments when she reassumes her respectable 'upper world' identity that he again becomes tongue-tied. But finally 'recognition' takes place; all misunderstandings are cleared up; and the hero has won such confidence in the heroine's presence during the episodes when she is disguised, that he can at last happily approach her in her true 'upper world' identity.

In Sheridan's *The Rivals* (1775) we see almost the mirror image of this. Here it is the young heroine who romantically cannot imagine herself loving a man unless he is of lowly rank. When the hero, Captain Absolute, falls in love with her, he realises that his income and status are too high for her to reciprocate, so he woos her in the disguise of a poor ensign, with considerable success. But then the hero's father appears, representing the 'upper world', and proposes to the heroine's guardian-aunt a match between his son and her niece: so that Absolute in his proper identity has to become a rival for her affections to himself in his inferior disguise. Eventually, as in *She Stoops to Conquer*, 'recognition' takes place, and the heroine finds that she is now able to love the hero in his true 'upper world' identity.

In Sheridan's *The School for Scandal* (1777), the road to the happy ending via an inferior level is presented in a different way. We meet two young brothers who are both courting the same girl: one of them, Joseph Surface, apparently the more eligible, in that he is pious and respectable, while the other, Charles, is a reckless spendthrift. Nevertheless it is the outwardly 'inferior' of the two, Charles, that the heroine loves: and the brothers are then put to the test. Their rich uncle arrives incognito from abroad and approaches each of them in a different, lowly disguise, as a moneylender and as a poor and needy relative. As so often, the concealment beneath disguise of one character proves an admirable way to catch out and expose the true nature of others. Joseph is revealed as a treacherous hypocrite, while Charles emerges as honest and good-natured. The uncle finally returns to the 'upper world' by revealing his true identity, to reward Charles and pave the way to his union with the heroine; while the dastardly Joseph is bundled off-stage as an 'unreconciled' dark figure.

But it was in a play written at the same time in France that the theme of the redemption of an 'upper world' with the aid of socially inferior characters found perhaps its most celebrated expression: which is how we return to the story with which this chapter began, Beaumarchais's *The Marriage of Figaro*, mostly written by 1778 (though not staged until 1784), and translated into its better known form, with music by Mozart, in 1786.

## The Marriage of Figaro

If one had to choose one story to illustrate almost every point about Comedy which has emerged in this chapter, it might be *The Marriage of Figaro*. Indeed it is a story almost impossible to summarise briefly, precisely because it weaves so many familiar elements in the plot together. Yet what often passes on the stage as an almost impenetrable thicket of concealments, misunderstandings, stratagems, impersonations and disguises, succeeding each other in bewildering array, and only made acceptable by the continuous flow of some of Mozart's finest music, turns out to be one of the most perfectly constructed of all comedies, each character and episode interacting on all the others until, finally, everything is in place to turn disastrous confusion into a miraculously happy ending.

The fundamental situation presented by *The Marriage of Figaro* is one familiar from many earlier comedies, not least those of Molière. We see a household dominated by a 'dark paterfamilias', the Count Almaviva, who is blinded by an egocentric obsession: in this case his heartless compulsive philandering. In the shadows cast by his selfishness and ill-temper are his wife, the unhappy Countess, and a pair of young lovers, who are planning to get married, Figaro and Susanna. And if this were a conventional working out of the theme we should expect to see the story ending with the Count, as its chief dark figure, going through a change of heart, thus bringing him back together with his wronged wife and simultaneously paving the way for the union of the young lovers.

But *Figaro* presents us with a number of twists to the usual formula which lend a peculiar ambiguity to the relationships in the story, giving it unusual psychological force.

For a start there is the ambiguity of the young lovers' relationship to the couple at the head of the household. In a conventional comedy one of them would have been the child of the Count and Countess. Here they are not related to the Count and Countess at all, and it is implied that they may all be of similar age (although this is ambiguous). This means that, although Figaro and Susanna are servants and socially inferior, they are, in human terms, on much more of a level with the Count and Countess. Secondly, there is the mysterious and shadowy role played in the story by the two lesser couples: on the one hand the elderly Dr Bartolo and Marcellina; on the other the young Cherubino and Barbarina as a second, lesser pair of young lovers. Thirdly, there is the curious way in which the unfolding action. emphasises that the ultimate point of the story is not to bring Figaro and Susanna together, which happens some time before the end: but to bring the Count back into repentant and loving union with his Countess. It is the Count whose dark state poses the overwhelming problem of the story, casting a blight over everyone else, throwing his household into chaos. Until that is resolved, not even the union of the lovers can bring a truly happy ending.

When the story opens all seems sunny and normal, as Figaro and Susanna are busily engaged on mundane details of their forthcoming nuptials. But even the fact that they are both preoccupied with different things (he measuring the room for a bed, she dreaming of her hat) is a small subconscious sign that people in this world we have entered are shut off from one another; and gradually we learn that beyond the sunlit foreground a double shadow is looming over the happy pair. First Susanna reveals that the Count has amorous designs on her, which throws Figaro into a jealous rage against the Count. Then Figaro himself confesses that he has recklessly allowed himself to get into the position where, in return for an unpaid debt, he is contracted to marry the elderly Marcellina. In other words, he has passed into a curiously oblique echo of the classical Oedipal situation where a young man finds his way forward to a mature and independent relationship with his feminine 'other half' barred by the double obstacle of antagonism to a male rival, representing threatening masculine authority, and an equally retarding tie to a powerful older woman.

But the action of the first act is in fact dominated by another character altogether, the young page Cherubino: and as soon becomes apparent his role in the story is essentially symbolic. With his name resonant of a little boy god of love, Cherubino's only obvious characteristic is his insatiable, adolescent desire for love. He is like a personification of the restless love-urge, immature, unchannelled, egocentric (and therefore without any content of real love), which is precisely the problem which, in a much darker form, afflicts the Count and is the central problem of the whole story. The point of Cherubino's prominence in the first act (which afterwards diminishes considerably) is that he rattles about the household like a little inferior shadow of the Count's own weakness, drawing attention to it: which is precisely why the Count cannot stand him. And the chief effect of the first of the opera's three episodes of multiple misunderstanding (as characters hide behind the furniture, overhearing what they are not meant to hear) is to bring the Count's hatred for Cherubino to a head. First the Count learns that

Cherubino loves the Countess (which is what the Count himself ought to be doing). Then he thinks, erroneously, that Cherubino also loves Susanna (which is what the Count would like to be doing). We even learn that the Count has designs on Cherubino's own girl friend, Barbarina. Having worked himself up all round into a jealous fury, the Count tries to put an end to Cherubino's 'days of philandering' altogether by packing him off to be a soldier, little realising that by getting rid of his 'little shadow' he will do nothing to solve the real problem of the household which lies in himself.

If the point of the first act is to lay bare in a peculiarly subtle way the hidden source of everyone's troubles, the second opens with the beginning of an elaborate attempt to do something about it. For the first time we meet the Countess, and see the desperate state of misery to which she has been reduced by the Count's heartlessness. She is the ultimate helpless victim, consigned to the shadows by the state of darkness which has possessed him. Now with the aid of the much more 'active' Susanna and Figaro she is at last beginning to hatch a plot to trap the Count and expose him. This is just the sort of line-up we recognise from Molière: the dark and obsessed head of the household, representing a sick 'ruling order', being opposed by an 'inferior' alliance between wife, servants and lovers (except that here servants and lovers are the same).

The chief effect of the opera's second episode of multiple misunderstanding (with characters now hiding in cupboards and jumping out of windows) is, like that of the first, simply to get the Count into a greater state of angry confusion than ever. He is still looking for anyone other than himself to blame for the fact that everything seems to be going wrong. Only now his rage focuses on Figaro. For all sorts of dark and twisted reasons he determines to use his authority to thwart Figaro's plans to marry Susanna: and he thus passes obliquely into the familiar position of the 'unrelenting parent', bent on standing in the way of young love.

Act Three sees Figaro's problems coming to a head. It seems that there is nothing he can do to prevent the elderly Marcellina claiming her right to marry him – now with the full support of the Count. Confusion and darkness seem about to win their ultimate victory: when suddenly, to everyone's astonishment, it is revealed by way of a birthmark (the equivalent of 'tokens') that Figaro is in fact the long-lost son of Marcellina and Dr Bartolo. He has just been on the verge of being drawn into marriage with his own mother. This dramatic revelation of Figaro's true identity (totally improbable in any sense but that of psychological symbolism) has such a stunning effect on everyone that it completely pulls the rug from under the Count's feet. We are confronted with that potent image familiar from the end of so many comedies where suddenly everything comes right: a long-separated family is miraculously brought together; long-hidden identities are suddenly brought to light; the young lovers are finally free to get married; and preparations are made for Figaro's wedding to Susanna at once.

At this point, however, even while the wedding celebrations are in full swing, we are forcibly reminded of how far the story's title is misleading as to what it is ultimately about. The marriage of Figaro, at the end of Act Three, is by no means the end of the drama. The real problem overshadowing the whole story has yet to be brought to its head, and such is the theme of the fourth and concluding act.

For a third time the chief characters are plunged into a series of multiple misunderstandings, this time at night amid the shadowy surroundings of the garden, as the two leading ladies, the Countess and Susanna, disguised as each other, now take the final initiative in leading the Count a merry dance (so clearly is the focus now on the unshakeable feminine alliance between Susanna and the Countess that they even briefly fool Figaro as well). The Count is led into the final hypocrisy of a jealous attack on Figaro for supposedly making love to the Countess, when in fact Figaro is making love to his own wife and it is the Count who thinks he is making love to Figaro's. On this climax, bringing the Count's hypocrisy to its *reductio ad absurdum*, the doubly-wronged Countess can step from the shadows to bring home to him the full horror of the situation he has got into. We at last see the appalled Count going through the profound transformation we have been waiting for throughout the story. He has at last been forced to confront the truth about himself and his own behaviour. He recognises what a heartless monster of hypocrisy he has become, and pleads with his faithful loving wife for forgiveness. At last everyone in the story can properly pair off, and the four joyful couples sing out the moral of the tale:

> 'Let us all learn the lesson, forget and forgive,
> Whoever contented and happy would live'

and how, after this tempestuous day (the story's subtitle is 'The Day of Madness'), they are going 'to the sound of music to revel all night'.

The essence of what we see in *The Marriage of Figaro* is a situation familiar from countless other comedies. We see a group of people, a little community, reduced to complete confusion and misery primarily because one dominant figure in that community is totally egocentric and possessed by a state of 'darkness'. Because he is not 'centred' and right in himself, the repercussions of his inner disorder are felt in a domino-effect throughout the community. The chief source of power in the community is abusing his power. There is no longer a sense of harmonious order. No one quite knows who they are any longer. Everyone is set against everyone else. Nothing is clear.

What has happened by the end of *Figaro* is a weaving together of all the ingredients which we have seen making up almost any fully developed comedy. The figure who is the dominant source of 'darkness' in the story has finally been brought to recognise his blind and heartless egocentricity: he has moved to a different 'centre' of his personality or 'come to himself'. Power and authority in the community is at last being exercised properly and no longer abused. The terrible curse of egotism which has afflicted the community has been lifted. And as part of this same process of healing, of reconciliation and of everything being brought into the light, a number of other things have also happened at much the same time. All disguises have been thrown off. The need for concealment is at an end.

Everyone has emerged in or discovered their true identity. All the characters have finally recognised who they must properly pair off with. Everything has at last been brought into a harmonious state of order. Love and friendship are triumphant in all directions. And the story ends on a miraculous image of human wholeness; of everyone brought together, both outwardly and inwardly, in a way which gives us an exhilarating sense of life renewed.

In all these respects we may be struck by the parallels between *The Marriage of Figaro* and *The Winter's Tale*. As two of the most profound of all comedies, it is no accident that each is in the end describing a strikingly similar situation. The ruler of a kingdom or household has fallen under a great sickness of soul which casts all beneath him into shadow, particularly his wife, who becomes the 'obscured heroine'. Restoration begins in the shadows, 'below the line', with the bringing together of a pair of young lovers, representing youth, hope and new life. Eventually the spirit of renewal reaches up above the line, to thaw out the frozen heart of the sick ruler. And in each case the story ends with the 'obscured heroine' stepping out of the shadows, emerging from her long eclipse, as the real touchstone of the fact that her husband has at last 'come to himself'.

An aspect of both these stories very near the heart of Comedy is the dramatic contrast between the role played by the chief masculine and feminine characters. In each story it is a man who is the chief dark figure, abusing his power and spreading disorder and misery in all directions because he is unable to see straight and whole. In each case the other leading male characters – Figaro and Polixenes – also get infected by the confusion and fail to see things straight. It is the feminine characters – Hermione and Perdita, the Countess and Susanna – who remain faithful and unshakeable, standing at the heart of the story for true love and for seeing things straight and whole. And it is not until the men can go through the transformation which softens them and straightens them out, bringing them into harmony with the loving feminine, that the final image of wholeness which rounds off the story can be reached. This is the true significance of 'the obscured heroine'. So long as the male figures remain egocentric and confused by 'darkness', she will remain in the shadows. Whether she is 'passive' or 'active' (and these feminine pairings, Hermione and Perdita, the Countess and Susanna, each comprise an alliance of both) she is the light at the heart of the story, obscured by the darkness in others. Only when the male characters have eliminated the darkness in themselves can the light represented by the feminine at last shine out to illumine them all.

## Chapter 7

# Comedy (II): The Plot Disguised

'"Princess for God's sake!" he exclaimed, trying to stop her. "Princess!" She
turned round. For a few seconds they gazed silently into one another's eyes –
and what had seemed impossible and remote suddenly became possible,
inevitable and very near.'

Nikolai Rostov to Maria Bolkonskaya, *War and Peace*

More than with any of the other basic plots, it may be tempting to see Comedy
as a type of story arrived at by conscious contrivance. Compared with the great
primeval shapes of, say, the Quest or the Overcoming the Monster story, with
their misty origins in myth and legend, there seems to be something artificial
about Comedy. We have already seen how, unlike any of the other basic plots, that
of Comedy emerged in historical times and developed to its full extent only in a
series of stages. There has certainly been a self-conscious tradition in the writing
of comedies for the stage, in a way not true of any other kind of story. The playwrights of the post-Renaissance, such as Shakespeare and Molière, were very
much aware they were reviving a form and conventions established by their
Graeco-Roman forerunners. And when we consider such familiar situations and
devices of Comedy as 'the unrelenting father' or the belated revelation of someone's true identity through tokens or birthmarks, we might be tempted to conclude that later authors were merely writing 'in a tradition', consciously drawing
on a stockpile of comic conventions bequeathed them by their predecessors.

But to explain the emergence and staying power of the Comedy plot only in
this way is to beg two hugely important questions. The first is: why did this
particular kind of story establish itself so strongly, over such a long period, as
one of the central threads in the literature of Western civilisation? It must
have expressed something much deeper than can be accounted for just by the
force of convention.

The second question arises when we look at what happened when the Comedy
plot, more than ever before, began to move off the stage. How did it eventually
come to give rise to stories which seemed to owe little, if anything, to the tradition
established by writers for the theatre?

When the first recognisable modern novels began to appear in the eighteenth
century, it was perhaps hardly surprising that Comedy should have been one of
the plots to which their authors were most obviously drawn. For half a century
comedies had been the most prominent type of story on the stages of England
and France. One of the pioneers of the novel, Henry Fielding, had written many
comedies for the London stage, including translations of Moliere. And in the most

131

successful of his novels, *Tom Jones* (1749), we see how easily the traditional conventions of stage Comedy could be adapted to the new form.

The theme of the novel is that of a young hero, a 'foundling' born in mysterious circumstances, who is searching for his true identity in the world. Throughout the story he is shadowed by the chief dark figure of the tale; his adoptive brother Blifil, who apparently rejoices in every worldly advantage that Tom does not enjoy. In fact the pair are very like Charles and Joseph Surface in *The School for Scandal*. Blifil seems on the 'upper world' surface to be the respectable, well-behaved, successful one of the pair, legitimate and dutiful; while the high-spirited, illegitimate Tom, kind-hearted but constantly misunderstood, seems doomed to poverty and disgrace.

Almost as in a stage Comedy the action of the novel is divided into three main 'acts'. In the first, set in the countryside of Somerset, we see Tom and Blifil both setting their hearts on marrying the lovely heroine, Sophia Western. Secretly she loves Tom, but the parents on both sides are determined that she should marry Blifil; and the 'act' ends with Tom, thanks to Blifil's unscrupulous machinations, being driven from home to find his own way in the world.

The second 'act' shows Tom wandering aimlessly across the countryside and becoming involved in an inn at Upton-on-Severn in that central episode of multiple misunderstanding which is so reminiscent of the conventions of stage Comedy. He meets with a 'Temptress' and goes to bed with her. At just that moment, Sophia, who has been pursuing him, arrives to discover what he is up to, which turns her violently against him. Then her father also arrives and imagines Tom must be in bed with Sophia. This creates the greatest possible degree of misunderstanding all round, and the chief consequence of this 'act' is to set the hero and heroine at odds, thanks to Tom's moment of weakness: which means he is going to have to do a great deal more to prove himself truly worthy of her before any happy ending can be reached.

In the third and final 'act' all the main characters converge separately on London, where the denouement will eventually take place. We begin with Tom living in obscure, 'inferior' circumstances and, through various acts of kindness and courage, working his way back to the position where he can once again plausibly confront Sophia and seek a reconciliation. But just as this seems on the cards, he is caught out in a second act of weakness with a 'Temptress', the imperious and treacherous Lady Bellaston (whom he first woos at a masked ball imagining that she is Sophia in disguise). This lands him in what seems like a fatal catastrophe. Thanks to Lady Bellaston's scheming, he ends up in prison. Here he is told that the first 'Temptress' he made love to at Upton was in fact his own mother. He seems doomed to remain in the inferior underworld forever. Meanwhile, in the 'upper world', arrangements are being made for Sophia's marriage to Blifil. Then comes the dizzying series of revelations which comprise the 'recognition'. Tom discovers his true identity, as Blifil's elder brother. Blifil's real nature as an unscrupulous villain and hypocrite is finally exposed. Sophia recognises Tom's true worth and that, for all his moments of weakness, he has never ceased to love her. Their wedding is arranged, to universal rejoicing, while Blifil, as 'unreconciled dark figure', meets his come-uppance off stage.

Quite apart from Coleridge's oft-quoted claim that Fielding's novel had one of 'the three most perfect plots ever planned' (along with Jonson's *The Alchemist* and Sophocles's *Oedipus Tyrannus*), it is worth summarising *Tom Jones* in this way because it shows how little new there was to the treatment of Comedy when it moved off the stage into the pages of the novel. We see all the familiar devices: characters in disguise; 'unrelenting parents'; assignations where the heroine is confused with another woman; the discovery of someone's true identity as a crucial part of the 'recognition'. We see an unusually thorough working out of the contrast between an 'upper world' based on false values and the 'inferior' world where true worth is preparing for the moment when it can finally be revealed and brought up into the light: except that here it is the hero rather than the heroine who spends most of the story 'obscured', and Tom also has to work hard to prove his worth. Unlike the conventional 'wronged heroine' he is by no means wholly innocent.

We also see in *Tom Jones* how the novel was able to present the events leading up to this final emergence into the light as a more gradual process, taking place over a long period of time, corresponding more nearly to the processes of growth and development in human life. Fifty years later came another major step in the evolution of Comedy into a plot for the novel. Here, in an episode almost unique in the history of Comedy, we are given a rare glimpse of this plot – for all its overtones of artifice – springing directly from the circumstances of 'real life', showing how closely it could express the inmost patterns of an author's own psychology.

### Jane Austen: comedy as real life

In the 1790s a young girl in her late 'teens began writing novels in a Hampshire rectory. The sixth of seven children, most of whom were already married, Jane Austen had reached an age where her thoughts about the future were dominated by the possibility of her own marriage, and one of the most striking things about her novels is the way they reflected her personal situation. Quite apart from the fact that, as a woman, she centred her versions of the plot on a heroine rather than a hero, critics have noted how deeply she projected aspects of her own personality into her heroines. And at the very time when she was preoccupied with speculation as to how her own life might unfold, through a fog of uncertainty, to that central goal of finding her right 'other half', she was drawn to the plot which most naturally expresses this pattern.

Qualifying the impression of a plaster saint long fostered by her family after her early death (loved, as it was put on her tombstone, for 'the benevolence of her heart, the sweetness of her temper'), Jane Austen could be an ironical, often prickly and outspoken lady, with a tart tongue and shrewd eye for the pretensions and shortcomings of others. In her first completed novel, *Pride and Prejudice*, we see many of these characteristics, not least in her 'active', strong-minded heroine Elizabeth Bennett; and the essence of the story is the long gradual transformation which allows Elizabeth to come to terms with the rich, nobly-born hero Darcy, perhaps the most romantically conceived of all the versions of the ideal man she herself might have hoped to marry. At first Elizabeth considers Darcy to be insufferably proud and remote. But then her own pride is humbled by her folly in being taken in by the weak, unscrupulous Wickham. Step by step she softens towards Darcy, and we see him gradually proving himself in her eyes, as he shows himself beneath his aloof exterior to be both manly and generous-hearted: until finally both can 'recognise' and reveal their love.

What we see here is a story completely shaped by the underlying form of Comedy, but in a new kind of treatment where the conventions about misunderstandings, disguises, failure to recognise identity and 'dark' figures getting caught out are no longer presented in the terms of the old stage devices, but rather more subtly, in terms of the gradual revelation of people's true character from behind first mistaken impressions, and the discovery of true feelings, in a way which corresponds more to our experience of life.

In the other two of Jane Austen's early trilogy of mature novels, *Sense and Sensibility* and *Northanger Abbey*, we again see two heroines working their way through all sorts of misunderstandings and love-tangles towards eventual happy union with the hero. In the first, Elinor Dashwood represents another aspect of Jane Austen as the patient, high-principled young woman who quietly watches and waits while almost everyone else around her behaves foolishly or badly, until finally the erring hero can be freed from the little 'Temptress' who had him in her clutches and returns contritely to the admirable and constant Elinor. In the second we see the heroine Catherine Morland as herself a rather foolish girl who has to learn her lesson before she can be united with the admirable and constant hero Henry Tilney; and here it has been plausibly suggested that there is more of Jane Austen in the shrewd, ironical Tilney than in the heroine.

By the time her first three novels had been completed but not yet published, Jane Austen had been through the greatest disappointment of her life, when her one true love, James Lefroy, a penniless would-be lawyer, had been torn away from her by his family, on the grounds that, as an equally penniless clergyman's daughter, she would not be a suitable match. She then suffered a further devastating blow when her father retired, handing over the rectory which had been her home and workplace to her brother. Forced to move with her parents to lodgings in Bath, she felt so dislocated that she broke off from writing for a decade. But when she was finally able to settle down in a Hampshire cottage with her sister Cassandra, she embarked on the intensive burst of writing which between 1811 and 1816 produced three more novels, now reflecting the fact that she was no longer a young girl with every expectation of marriage but a spinster on the way to middle-age, who had seen her hopes of marriage dashed. Partly this was through the inadequacy of the men she had met; partly because of her own intimidating intelligence and sharp eye for other people's faults.

All three novels are still shaped perfectly round the Comedy theme, showing a heroine who against all odds finally achieves the happy ending of marriage, and again we see the same contrasted aspects of Jane's own personality projected into their three, very different central characters. Fanny Price, the poor little heroine introduced into the household of her rich cousins in *Mansfield Park*, is like a re-run of Elinor Dashwood, as the unshakeably moral young woman who watches while all the other young men and women around her behave foolishly and progressively get caught out; until finally the contrite hero Edmund comes to recognise what a rock of good sense and true feeling she had been, the only one who saw the world straight and did not betray herself.

The second of the three, *Emma*, is perhaps the most remarkable of all Jane Austen's variations on the Comedy plot, not least because, as in *The Taming of the Shrew*, we see the rare spectacle of the heroine as the chief 'dark' figure of the story. Emma Woodhouse, the only child of a weak, valetudinarian father, is a bossy, wilful girl of powerful personality, prone both to be severely critical of other people's weaknesses and to try to organise their lives. In this sense, as an 'active' heroine, she is like a darker, more interfering, more self-destructive version of Elizabeth Bennett. Only one person, Mr Knightley, has the strength of character to stand up to Emma and the shrewdness of heart to recognise that beneath her capacity for bossy self-deception there is a potentially sensitive, feminine and lovable girl being stifled by her domineering outward *persona*. The 'recognition' takes place when, as Emma is finally caught out in her match-making on behalf of Harriet, by trying to bring her young protégée together with Mr Knightley, she 'comes to herself' in realising what a fool she has been, and that it is really she herself who loves Mr Knightley. In her foolish *persona* she had completely overlooked the fact that he was her proper 'other half'. But equally, if she had not discovered her other, softer, repressed identity, he would never have accepted her. Her true inner feminine self has to be rescued from the shadows into which it has been repressed by her hard, superior *persona*, before the two of them can be brought together.

If Jane Austen was perhaps unconsciously reflecting here one reason why her own personality had made it difficult for her to find the right Mr Knightley, in her last completed novel *Persuasion* she expressed her melancholy in a more obvious way. Here we again see the constant heroine who quietly observes the antics of others, only this time Anne Elliott feels she is getting too old to hope for marriage: half-resigned to spinsterhood, half looking back with regret to her one real missed chance, when she had foolishly turned down Captain Wentworth at the urging of her tyrannical aunt, playing the role of 'unrelenting parent'. Then, almost unbelievably, Captain Wentworth turns up again, still looking for a wife; but Anne now has to watch him wooing others, much younger, more foolish and unsuitable than herself. The tangle becomes still worse when Anne herself is wooed by a man whom she might almost accept, to console her for her disappointment; until he reveals his true nature as a weak, treacherous trifler with ladies' affections (a recurring figure in Austen's novels, the ultimate 'dark' opposite to her admirable, strong and constant 'light' heroes and heroines). At last both hero and heroine are free to 'recognise' what has been subconsciously growing in each of them for a long time: that they still love each other and that nothing can any longer keep them apart. And so, for the last time in her stories (she was already sickening while she was writing *Persuasion* and died the following year), Jane Austen was able to imagine arriving at the happy ending which was always to elude her in life.

### The plot disguised: *Middlemarch, War and Peace*

By the mid-nineteenth century the Comedy plot had become so well established in its new incarnation that it crops up in novels all over the place (although Balzac's novel-sequence *La Comedie Humaine* is largely shaped by other plots). In many instances the familiar conventions of stage Comedy continued to appear, such as the last-minute discovery of someone's true identity as part of the 'recognition' (e.g., Dickens's *Our Mutual Friend*, Trollope's *Doctor Thorne*). But in some of the most familiar examples Comedy had by now travelled so far from its theatrical origins and become so successfully disguised in its new role that we might not even notice that the same archetypal plot is shaping the story.

We shall look briefly at two of these 'disguised Comedies', among the best-known novels of the age. The first is George Eliot's *Middlemarch* (1871–1872), which of course was written by a woman and centres on a heroine. The opening episodes of this long novel show the high-minded young Dorothea Brooke being drawn into marriage. But it is immediately clear that this is no prelude to a happy ending. Her husband, Dr Casaubon, is a dry-as-dust old clergyman and amateur scholar, old enough to be her father, and this 'father-daughter' balance turns out to be the key to the real nature of their unhappy relationship. Even before the marriage Dorothea has already met Casaubon's nephew, the handsome young artist Will Ladislaw, and this establishes the contrast between the tedious old pedant, representing death, and the romantic young painter, representing life. Dorothea's marriage is soon seen to be an empty imprisoning sham, as it becomes clear that the petty, pompous, jealous Casaubon, obsessed with his never-to-be-written book on myths, is an empty and self-important fraud. But eventually he dies, leaving a will which lays down that Dorothea can only inherit his considerable estate so long as she does not marry Ladislaw. Up to this point, the possibility of such a thing has not entered their heads, but now it begins to prey on each of them separately: although of course it cannot be, because of Casaubon's prohibition. Dorothea's dead husband thus, in effect, assumes from the grave the role of 'unrelenting father', standing in the way of the young lovers getting together. Other familiar elements of the Comedy plot appear: Ladislaw discovers the long-concealed truth of his parentage; Dorothea sees him holding hands with another woman and is miserably jealous, wrongly imagining they are having an affair. Finally 'recognition' comes when Dorothea realises that her love for Ladislaw transcends everything. The lovers confront each other, declare their love and walk liberated together into the future.

Cast on a much grander scale, another novel of the period shaped by the Comedy plot was Leo Tolstoy's *War and Peace* (1868). Among all the dozens of characters we meet in the opening chapters are four young people, all on the verge of embarking on the wider stage of the world. First there is the huge, awkward, introverted Pierre. Then, in the Rostov family, there are young Nikolai, extrovertedly looking forward to his career in the army, and his lively younger sister Natasha, Finally there is the shy, spiritual Maria, living at home in the country wtth her old father, the retired general Prince Bolkonsky. These are the main heroes and heroines of the story; although we must also include Maria's brother, the rather older Prince Andrew, already married and out on the stage of the world as a fast-rising young officer.

There is no doubt who occupies the role of chief dark figure in the story. The self-created Emperor Napoleon looms up like a distant cloud on the horizon in the opening line of the book. His insatiable ambition casts an ever-growing shadow over everyone, first coming to a head in the great confrontation between the Russians and the French in Austria in 1805 (although this is still at a reasonably comfortable distance from Russia itself); but finally, with the invasion of 1812, bursting right into the heart of Russia and the lives of all the main characters.

Across all this vast canvas and tumult of great events, what binds the whole narrative together is the working out of the destinies of the central four figures, with Prince Andrew, through every kind of misunderstanding, uncertainty and switch of love. We follow Pierre through the death of his father, his disastrous marriage to the temptress Helene Kuragin, his long and painful inner journey to discover 'the meaning of life'. We follow Nikolai through his adolescent love for little Sonia, and his character-forming adventures as an army officer. We see little Natasha blossoming into an adult, 'active' heroine, falling in love with Prince Andrew after the death of his wife, getting engaged to him and then falling into the disastrous folly of her infatuation with the unscrupulous fortune-hunter Anatole Kuragin. We have earlier seen the Princess Maria rejecting a cynical offer of marriage from the same dark figure, before sinking into a long 'passive' eclipse under the shadow of her tyrannical old father, imagining she will always remain a spinster.

Then comes Borodino and Napoleon's occupation of burning Moscow, the moment when darkness seems complete and all the characters are hurled about, willy-nilly, in the book's climactic episode of confusion. Pierre, who has already begun to sense a growing love for Natasha, is plunged into an 'inferior realm', firstly through his wandering about occupied Moscow in humble disguise, then through his hardships on the long march westward as a prisoner of war, daily expecting death, although it is in these depths that he meets the old peasant Platon whose wisdom transforms his life. Nikolai, in the chaos of the retreat to Moscow, meets and gives assistance to Princess Maria, before plunging into the further chaos of the ensuing battles. Natasha, in the chaos of the Rostovs' flight from Moscow, is reconciled with the dying Prince Andrew; and then begins to realise that she loves Pierre. Princess Maria, after her eventful meeting with Nikolai, begins to emerge from the shadow of her tyrannical old father, and realises that she loves Nikolai.

Finally the much greater shadow which has fallen over all of them begins to lift, when Napoleon orders the retreat from Moscow. With gathering pace, the chief dark figure of the story, with his battered legions, is bundled towards ignominious expulsion from the stage. As the light returns to Russia, the book moves towards a conclusion which, through most of its course, would have seemed totally improbable. Pierre and Natasha are reunited, declare their love and marry. Nikolai and Maria meet again, discover their love for each other, and also marry. Two unlikely couples have been brought together in a way which could not have happened without the vicissitudes and painful self-discoveries forced on them by the chaos, the suffering and uprooting of the war. And in their two joyful unions we see a microcosm of the greater fate of Russia itself, having come through the colossal crisis which had enabled her people to discover their inmost sense of national identity and now emerging into peace with a triumphant sense of life renewed.

But of course *War and Peace* does not end there. In Tolstoy's Epilogue we are carried forward a few years to be given a glimpse of the family life of the two couples after their marriage. Earlier authors of novels based on the Comedy plot, such as Fielding and Jane Austen, were able to remain within the archetypal framework and to end their stories quite happily on the great symbolic image of the wedding. But Tolstoy was so preoccupied with the 'realistic' and historical element in his story that he could not resist wanting to see what happened next, how the story continued after the archetypal ending; with the result that, as he explored the strains and disagreements which would inevitably be part of that aftermath, he was in danger of dissipating the impact of that final image of unity and life renewed, by allowing his story to peter out on an unresolved image of new disunity and uncertainty.[1]

This was merely one instance of the problems which were beginning to surround the Comedy plot in the mid-nineteenth century as it moved away from its original forms of expression. It was not that the plot was changing its structure; simply that it was being put to purposes which were threatening to detach it from its original archetypal foundations. And this was leading to a new phase in the history of the plot which has, in the past century or so, drastically altered its role in Western storytelling.

### The plot burlesqued

Ever since its beginnings one of the most remarkable things about Comedy was the way it had preserved a balance between the superficially light-hearted presentation of apparently quite implausible events and a core of fundamental seriousness. Part of the miracle of the comedies of Aristophanes or Shakespeare or Mozart is that, while constantly provoking their audiences to laughter, they manage to explore some of the deepest issues of human life. But in the nineteenth century, as Comedy moves into new forms of expression, there are signs that this balance is being lost. Tolstoy would never have thought of *War and Peace* as a 'comedy', even though unconsciously he was drawing on the archetypal outlines of the ancient

---

1. In fact, as we know, Tolstoy originally conceived *War and Peace* as a novel about the Decembrist rebellion of 1825. The story had begun to evolve in his mind merely as a way of showing the background to that moment of crisis in Russian life, and as a way of building up his characters to the point where they were confronted by the crisis: in which the liberal idealist Pierre and the conservative, loyal army officer Nikolai would find themselves on opposing sides. In light of this, it is even more interesting to see how Tolstoy's imagination became gradually possessed by a quite different type of story, based on the archetype of Comedy, leaving his First Epilogue as the only vestigial evidence of the story as it had originally occurred to him.

plot, because he was emphasising its serious, 'realistic' element to create one of the greatest and most profound novels ever written. And shortly we shall look at what was happening in the other direction, as Comedy began to be used in forms which preserved the lightheartedness while losing its core of seriousness, a tendency which first showed itself on the stage.

On the stage, in fact, Comedy had by the mid-nineteenth century fallen into relative eclipse since its prominence in the previous century. In 1868 (as it happens, the year Tolstoy began publishing *War and Peace*), it made a conspicuous re-appearance in a form which seemed to owe little to the tradition of the earlier operatic comedy of Mozart and Rossini. Wagner's *Die Meistersinger* is a unique opera. It is unmistakably shaped by the plot and conventions of Comedy (even to the extent of having a comic 'midnight assignation scene' where another woman impersonates the heroine), But it was intended by its composer as a fundamentally very serious work. And we shall consider it briefly in conjunction with another unusual opera, Richard Strauss and Hugo van Hofmannsthal's *Der Rosenkavalier* (1911), which even more obviously managed to preserve the balance between light-hearted exterior and serious core; although it was self-consciously placed in an eighteenth-century 'Mozartian' setting as if to recognise that by the time it was written in the early-twentieth century it was no longer possible to keep the traditional balance except in terms of pastiche.

Essentially, the two operas have much in common. Each is centred on four figures: a young hero and a young heroine; a boorish, insensitive dark figure who is a rival for the heroine's hand; and an older figure who selflessly masterminds from behind the scenes the hero's ultimately successful wooing of the heroine.

In *Die Meistersinger* the heroine Eva is established as the supreme prize for any man to win when her father, a prominent local citizen, announces that whoever wins the great song contest held by the Mastersingers of Nuremburg may be given her hand in marriage, There are three possible competitors: the chief dark figure Beckmesser, a leading Mastersinger who is obsessed with the Guild's traditional rules of song composition; the hero, Walther von Stolzing, an unknown newcomer to the city who sees Eva in the opening scene, falls in love with her and is deter-mined to win her; and a mysterious older figure, also a veteran Mastersinger, the wise, fatherly Hans Sachs. Initially the hero seems doomed because his first effort at a song breaks all the complicated rules laid down for songwriting by the Guild of Mastersingers, and he is grimly ruled out of order by Beckmesser. Only Sachs perceives that Walther's song in praise of love, spring and new life is in fact of exceptional beauty. The Mastersingers' rejection of Walther thus shows them to be an 'upper world' based on false values and limited awareness, while the hero, in the 'inferior realm', represents the life and truth which they (particularly Beckmesser) completely lack. As the action prcceeds, Beckmesser is more and more revealed as absurd, egocentric and anti-life. Eva dreads the possibility that he might win the contest and therefore her hand in marriage; and would like to hang on to her 'father-figure' Hans Sachs, But he tells her that he is too old for her, and that she must have faith and courage to move forward, to embrace the prospect of new life. Eventually the two chief competitors come before all the inhabitants of the city for the final test, Both are in fact intending to attempt the same song, because Beckmesser has stolen a copy of the song written by Walther, imagining that it is the work of the old master Sachs. Beckmesser makes a complete hash of it, because he is not in touch with life, and is laughed off the stage as an 'unreconciled dark figure' almost as memorable as Shylock. Walther triumphantly wins the contest and Eva's hand, and the opera ends with a universal hymn of praise to the wise Sachs who has guided the story to its happy conclusion.

In *Der Rosenkavalier* the part of the older figure is played by the Marschallin, an imposing lady portrayed as in early middle age (although she is in fact only 32), who has a young lover Octavian. The Beckmesser role is played by her boorish and lecherous cousin, Baron Ochs, who tells her he is hoping to marry a lovely young heiress Sophie. Can the Marschallin recommend a suitable young man to carry the traditional 'silver rose' to his fiancee, to demonstrate his intentions? The action of the story shows how the older woman selflessly sends her young Octavian to woo Sophie, nominally on behalf of Ochs, but with the predictable result that hero and heroine fall in love. Sophie's father, a nouveau riche who wishes his daughter to marry into the nobility, plays the traditional role of 'unrelenting father' in trying to force her into marriage with a man she detests; but the Marschallin master-minds the final routing of Ochs when he is lured into a midnight assignation with a young girl Mariandl, who turns out to be the hero in disguise. The foolish Baron is exposed and laughed off the stage as 'unreconciled dark figure'. With the Marschallin's blessing (albeit tinged with melancholy for the passing of her own youth), Octavian and Sophie are joyfully united.

Both these stories bring out with unusual subtlety a theme which had lain near the heart of Comedy ever since it first became centred on a pair of young lovers, as indeed it lies at the heart of so many other types of story: the handing on of the torch of life to a new generation. We see a ruling order which has become corrupt and out of touch with life, so often represented by the 'unrelenting parent' and here by Beckmesser and by the decadent aristocrat Ochs. We then see appearing in its shadow the seeds of new life, in the burgeoning love of the young hero and heroine; until eventually one or both are raised up from the shadows of the 'inferior realm', so that the story can end with them at last united centre stage. The transition to a new, healthy order, holding out hope for the future, is complete.

But if this is one of the most serious themes near the heart of Comedy, in the forty years between *Die Meistersinger* and *Der Rosenkavalier* the Comedy plot had swept into a new age of popularity on the European musical stage, in a form where the serious element in the story had been all but lost sight of. In Offenbach's Paris, Strauss's Vienna, Gilbert and Sullivan's London, this was the heyday of 'comic opera' or operetta. And here we suddenly see all the familiar ingredients of the plot being played with, in a way which seems simply like a burlesque of the traditional form.

Stories such as those of Strauss's *Die Fledermaus* (1874) and *The Gypsy Baron* (1885) are perfectly shaped by the pattern of the Comedy plot, and crowded with every sort of traditional device: disguises, assignations where the heroine is confused with another woman, startling revelations of true identity (including in

*The Gypsy Baron* the discovery that the gypsy heroine is in fact a princess, in *Die Fledermaus* that a mysterious Hungarian princess is in fact the heroine), and so forth. But in a way not true of Comedy before, there is never any intention that we should look for a serious message in the story. It is as if the medium of the Comedy plot, with all its familiar conventions, has itself become the only message.

These conventions were even more obviously caricatured in the contemporary British equivalents of Viennese operetta, the 'comic operas' of Gilbert and Sullivan. In *The Pirates of Penzance* (1880), for instance, the entire female chorus, the daughters of a major-general, fall in love with the male chorus, a gang of pirates. The major-general not unnaturally assumes the role of 'unrelenting father', pleading that he is an orphan and cannot let his daughters go, since they are the only joy left to him; but the pirates eventually emerge in their true identity as noblemen in 'inferior disguise', so the old soldier is only too happy to relent. In *HMS Pinafore* (1878) the hero, a humble seaman, falls in love with his captain's daughter, the heroine, who is also being wooed by the pompous, self-important Sir Joseph, 'ruler of the Queen's navee'. Eventually it is revealed that the hero and the captain had been switched as babies, so, highly improbably, they are now switched back again. The hero becomes a captain and the captain a humble seaman. Obviously the First Lord of the Admiralty cannot marry a mere seaman's daughter, so hero and heroine can at last be united.

This burlesquing of the Comedy plot was carried over to the non-musical stage in plays such as those of Oscar Wilde. *The Importance of Being Earnest* (1895) shows us two heroes, Jack and Algernon, a pair of rich and single upper-class young men. Jack, who when he is in London for some reason unexplained calls himself Ernest, wishes to marry the beautiful Gwendolen. But there is a formidable obstacle in their way in the shape of her fearsome mother Lady Bracknell who, as 'unrelenting parent', is refusing to allow the match. Algernon then discovers that his friend Jack is acting as guardian to a pretty little ward, Cecily, who lives quietly in the country, and at once hurries down to make her acquaintance, passing himself off as Jack's fictitious brother 'Ernest'. The predictable result is that both young couples are soon hopelessly in love (although, typically implausibly, the two heroines each wish to marry their man only because they are under the false impression that he is called Ernest). Lady Bracknell is forbidding Gwendolen to marry Jack, because he does not know who his parents were (he had been found as a baby abandoned in a handbag). Jack, in revenge, therefore assumes the role of 'unrelenting parent' in turn, by forbidding his ward's proposed marriage to Algernon. This double impasse is finally resolved thanks to the arrival of Cecily's governess Miss Prism, who inadvertently reveals Jack's true identity. He is in fact Algernon's elder brother, who had been lost as a baby when Miss Prism, as his nanny, had confused him with the manuscript of a three-volume novel and left him in the parcels office of a mainline London railway station. His true name, it then emerges from a reference book, has been Ernest all along. In this not even symbolically plausible fashion, all obstacles in the way of the two couples being united have been removed (except that Cecily never explains why she is prepared to overlook her previous insistence that she could only marry a man called Ernest).

## The twentieth-century divide

If the core of seriousness had already begun to drop out of Comedy, what happened in the twentieth century – when the plot continued to enjoy enormous
popularity in many different forms – was that Comedy tended to develop almost
into two different types of story. On one hand were those expressions of the plot
where the love interest took precedence, often without particular humour. On
the other were those which concentrated on the humour, or as we say the 'comic'
element, with the love interest either relegated to a subordinate place, or eliminated altogether.

Stories of the first kind, where the love interest predominates, became particularly popular in that home of sentimentality, Hollywood. An early example, featuring the leading hearthrob of the silent screen Rudolph Valentino, was *The
Sheikh* (1921), based on a novel published in England two years earlier by Edith
Hull, the wife of a Derbyshire pig farmer. The English heroine is shown falling into
an 'inferior realm' when she visits an Arab festival in disguise and is captured by
an Arab sheikh (played by Valentino). She secretly begins to fall in love with her
captor, but is then captured by a genuinely 'dark' figure, a villainous bandit chief.
She is rescued by her gallant sheikh and all is resolved when he turns out to be
really a European nobleman in disguise, adopted by Arabs when his parents had
been killed in the desert. His true identity revealed, showing him not be racially
'inferior' after all, the loving couple can happily return to the 'upper world' of
Europe to be married.

The love aspect of Comedy also came to the fore in that twentieth-century
successor to the tradition of 'light opera', the American stage and film musical.
Rogers and Hammerstein's *South Pacific* (1949), for instance, was an almost entirely
straight and sentimental love story. The heroine, an American naval nurse, arrives
during the Second World War on a Pacific island, where she falls in love with a
French planter. But he has had two children by a Polynesian woman, now dead; and
because of this supposedly 'inferior' racial link, the heroine is reluctant to marry
him. But thanks to his intimate knowledge of the islands, the planter is now recruited by the US Army to play a key part in a military operation. When he is smuggled
onto a Japanese-occupied island to spy on enemy military movements, he is
revealed to be a brave hero. The heroine at last sees him in his true light as a real
man, no longer 'inferior', and the story ends with her assuming the role of mother
to his half-Polynesian children as the couple look forward to their marriage.[2]

2. Another of many later stories to use 'non-white' characters in this way, to represent the 'below the
   line' element which must be brought up into the light to provide a happy ending, was Stanley
   Kramer's Hollywood movie *Guess Who's Coming to Dinner* (1967). The young white heroine
   returns home to San Francisco with a friend she has fallen in love with on holiday in Hawaii,
   planning to introduce him to her rich parents as the man she intends to marry. He (played by
   Sidney Poitier) is a highly-successful black doctor. Her mother (Katherine Hepburn) and father
   (Spencer Tracy), despite being the owner of a liberal newspaper which has long campaigned for
   racial equality, are horrified. Recognising that her daughter is deeply in love, mother is soon won
   round; but father remains adamantly opposed to the marriage. Since the lovers plan to fly off that
   night to Europe to be wed, the daughter invites to dinner his poor but respectable black parents, to
   break the news. They are equally shocked at the prospect of their son marrying a white girl; but his
   mother is similarly won round to supporting the match, leaving the two 'unrelenting fathers' united

We see a rather more obviously burlesqued version of the contrast between a 'lower' and 'upper' world in Frank Loesser's *Guys and Dolls* (1953), set in the underworld of New York's gambling fraternity. Nathan Detroit is desperate for money to rent a venue for an illegal crap game, because several big gamblers are in town, including the hero, Sky Masterson. Masterson casually boasts that there is not a woman in New York he could not persuade to accompany him to Havana, known in those pre-Castro days as the morally unconstrained 'fun city' where New Yorkers could let their hair down. Detroit makes this boast the basis of a wager. He points to the most unlikely woman he can imagine, Sister Sarah, the pretty but prim young organiser of the local Save-A-Soul Mission (in relative terms, therefore, since she is so moral and straitlaced, an 'above the line' character). Masterson propositions her, promising to produce 'twelve genuine sinners' at her next meeting if she will come to Havana with him, but she merely slaps his face in disgust.

Then, however, the fearsomely dragonish General Cartwright arrives from headquarters, threatening to close down the mission unless Sarah's next meeting is packed with repentant sinners. The heroine therefore accepts Masterson's bargain and agrees to accompany him to the 'inferior realm' of Havana, where she gets drunk in a nightclub and confesses that she loves him. She returns to New York and her straitlaced 'above the line' *persona*, appalled at her fall from grace. But Masterson keeps his side of the bargain. Her next meeting is packed with seemingly 'repentant' gamblers, General Cartwright is impressed and the mission is saved. But the heroine now learns to her horror that Masterson had only taken her to Havana for a wager. As the story moves to its climax, however, she then further discovers he has been telling everyone that he had lost his bet, and had not been able to persuade her to accompany him to Havana after all. She is so touched by his concern for her reputation that she rushes out to apologise for having misjudged him. They recognise their love for each other and the story ends, happily if implausibly, with their wedding.

However improbable and lightly treated the love element may be in such stories, it does at least provide the dominant thread of the tale. But we then come to that other modern derivation of the Comedy plot, the type of story where it is the humour which dominates, with the love interest playing only a rather embarrassed supporting role, if it survives at all.

## Playing it for laughs

When we use the term 'comedy' in the modern world we usually mean no more than something we are intended to find funny. It might seem odd to have taken so

---

in their opposition. A part in resolving the impasse is played by a wise, genial old Catholic priest, a friend of the family who is also invited to dinner. The denouement comes when the heroine's father announces that he wants to make a speech. Everyone expects him to reiterate his opposition to the match, but he reveals he has had a change of heart and now gives the marriage his blessing. Thus love triumphs over prejudice and all ends happily (although we are left only to guess whether the hero's black father has been similarly converted).

long to get round to what it is about Comedy which makes us laugh, because of course provoking an audience to laughter has always been inseparable from Comedy, right back to the days of ancient Greece. Only in comparatively recent times has this 'comic' element emerged as something which can be looked on as wholly separate, in its own right. But ever since Aristophanes, the essence of Comedy has lain in exposing as ridiculous the state of self-delusion which affects human beings who have become isolated from those around them by their ego-centricity. This is essentially what our human capacity for seeing something as funny is about. The chief function of humour is that it provides us with a more or less harmless way to defuse the social strains created by egotism. This is why comedy of any kind almost invariably centres on people who are in some way taking themselves too seriously, giving the rest of us the chance to see how foolish this makes them look. If a little old lady walking down the street trips up on a banana skin, we do not see this as funny. It arouses sympathy. If the same thing happens to a pompous man cocooned in self-importance we find it comical, precisely because we enjoy seeing his bubble of self-esteem being pricked, Almost all Comedy intended to make us laugh is thus centred on such a contrast between the self-regarding delusion of someone who is in some way blinded by egotism, and our capacity to see from outside what he is unable to see. We even do it, of course, when we laugh self-deprecatingly at ourselves.

Nothing seems funnier to us than the sight of someone imagining that he has the world around him organised and under control, when in fact we can see that it is nothing of the kind. This was why silent-film audiences in the 1920s found it funny to see Oliver Hardy, the earnest fat man in a bowler hat, trying to work out with his hapless partner Stan Laurel how to move a grand piano down a flight of steps, only to see it constantly slipping out of their grasp. This was why British television audiences in the 1970s laughed at the sight of Basil Fawlty, played by John Cleese in the series *Fawlty Towers*, desperately trying to preserve his *persona* as a coolly efficient hotel proprietor and to persuade his guests that everything is in perfect order, while behind the scenes it is only too obvious that all his establishment's arrangements are sliding into chaos. The same basic joke inspired Groucho Marx's role as a hotel manager in *A Night in Casablanca*. In the 1980s it was essentially the same joke which underlay the spectacle of Jim Hacker and Sir Humphrey Appleby engaging in their game of ruthless rivalry in *Yes Minister*, the British television series written by Antony Jay and Jonathan Lynn. The ambitious politician and the devious civil servant are each pursuing their own agenda behind an outward mask of civility and the pretence that their only concern is the public good. We see how, beneath the surface, the vain, gullible minister is really driven by egocentric calculations of how he might win plaudits or avoid criticism from the media and his colleagues. The outwardly deferential official is secretly trying to manipulate and out-manoeuvre his supposed master, to promote his own interests as head of his department. What makes us laugh is that we the audience are allowed to see both sides, self-delusion and reality. We can always see exactly what is going on behind the two men's respective *personas*, as each episode builds up some situation which promises to create maximum embarrassment for minister, civil servant or both.

We also know that eventually, in the nick of time, some form of 'recognition' will take place, allowing face to be saved and everyone to end happily.

Indeed, beneath the surface of these modern comedies which are primarily intended just to make us laugh, it is striking how far they are still shaped by those basic situations and rules of the Comedy plot going back thousands of years, as when Laurel and Hardy based one of their best-known films *Our Relations* on the plot of a comedy written in Rome in the third century BC. The only real difference lies in the extent to which the emphasis is placed on the 'comic' element at the expense of the rest of the underlying story. For instance, a typical Marx Brothers film when they were at the height of their fame in the 1930s and 1940s showed a little community of people working together (a circus, a sanitarium, a department store, a hotel), the future of which is threatened by a powerful dark figure engaged with his cronies in a conspiracy to pull off some villainous coup. This casts a shadow over all those threatened with disaster if the villainy succeeds. These invariably include a pair of young lovers wanting to get married who, in traditional Comedy terms, are technically the hero and heroine of the story. But our main attention is inevitably reserved for the fooling and wisecracking of the three stars themselves. Groucho is usually passing himself off raffishly as some figure with vaguely superior pretensions (such as a doctor, lawyer or hotel manager). Chico and Harpo play unashamedly 'inferior' lower-class characters. Between them they eventually manage, usually by spending some time in disguise or under assumed identities, to outwit the 'dark' figures and save the day. And this, of course, to provide the story with its archetypal ending, finally paves the way for the young lovers to get married.

This plot appeared, with slight variation, in the most popular of the Marx Brothers films, *A Night at The Opera* (1935). Groucho, as the supposedly well-connected Otis B. Driftwood, is trying to get the rich and gullible older woman Mrs Claypool (played by Margaret Dumont) into society. The ambitious Hermann Gottlieb who runs the New York Opera Company, greedy for her money, suggests that if she would pay 1000 dollars a night, they could hire the world's greatest tenor, Rodolphe Laspari. Groucho goes over to Europe to hire him, and Laspari turns out to be the chief dark figure of the story: arrogant, rude and condescending. They sail for New York on a luxury liner, with Laspari's leading lady, the heroine Rosa; while in an 'inferior realm' below decks as stowaways are Chico, Harpo and the hero Ricardo, also a tenor, with whom Rosa is in love. The stowaways manage to land by disguising themselves in beards as 'heroic foreign aviators', then go into hiding. When rehearsals begin Rosa is sacked, for failing to respond on stage to Laspari because he is so arrogant and unpleasant. The brothers scheme to ensure that the opera's first night is a shambles, as from behind the scenes they arrange that the scenery from several different operas should whizz on and off in bewildering array. Laspari is booed off the stage and Gottlieb is at his wits end; until Ricardo and Rosa emerge from the shadows to sing like angels and save the day. Their performance is wildly acclaimed. They are hired and can get married.

The love interest tended to play a similarly subordinate role in that other celebrated twentieth-century vehicle for so many of the traditional devices of Comedy, the novels of P. G. Wodehouse (who also, in his youth, wrote a number of American musicals). Nevertheless it is still usually there to play a crucial role in shaping the plot, as in *Leave it to Psmith* (1923). The hero has fallen in love with a girl who has just got a job cataloguing the library at Blandings Castle, the seat of the Earl of Emsworth. By improbably disguising himself as a Canadian poet, he himself wins an invitation to stay at the castle. Most of the fun-and games of the story then centres on the way the pair manage to outwit a hapless pair of disguised international jewel thieves who are trying to steal Lady Constance's diamond necklace. By the end of a sequence of entirely familiar Comedy situations, the dark figures have been exposed, all lost objects have been found (including the stolen necklace and the noble Earl's glasses) and the hero has re-emerged in his true identity to claim the heroine. But it cannot be said that the love interest serves any real purpose other than to lend theme to a hilarious farce; and this is even truer of most of the tales involving the silly-ass Bertie Wooster and his butler Jeeves, with the Lady Bracknell-like figure of Aunt Agatha invariably hovering disapprovingly in the background.

In the English-speaking world Jeeves has become the most famous servant in the history of Comedy. His role is the entirely familiar one of the socially 'inferior' figure who eventually redeems the disorder which is afflicting the 'upper world'. In *The Inimitable Jeeves* (1924), Wooster's friend Bingo Little, whose weakness is constantly falling romantically in love, develops an overwhelming passion for a humble teashop waitress. As usual, he immediately wishes to marry her; but the obstacle in the way is his rich and stuffy uncle, the source of Bingo's allowance, who will certainly oppose such a socially unsuitable match in the role of 'unrelenting parent' and thus deny Bingo his only means of income. Jeeves conceives a plan whereby Bingo will introduce his uncle to the works of an authoress named Rosie M. Banks, who specialises in sentimental romances in which girls of lowly origin marry men of superior station. Like most of Jeeves's schemes, it works like a treat, even to the point where Bertie is sent round to plead Bingo's case for getting married, implausibly impersonating Rosie M. Banks (Bingo has explained to his uncle that Wooster writes the novels he so admires under a pseudonym). So successfully is the uncle won over to the view that upper-class men should marry lower-class girls that he himself then proposes marriage to his cook. But all, alas, in vain because the waitress has now called off her affair with Bingo.

We then follow more of Bingo's ill-fated romances, including another journey into an 'inferior realm' where he disguises himself as a bearded revolutionary in order to woo Charlotte Corday Rowbotham, the daughter of the leader of a tiny revolutionary sect. He is eventually unmasked and his beard ripped off, just after he has directed a blast of revolutionary abuse at his uncle, now raised to the peerage, which not unnaturally leads to his allowance being finally cut off. The story comes to its climax when Bingo falls in love with yet another waitress and this time actually marries her. Bertie is again sent round to plead his case impersonating Rosie M. Banks, and the uncle is softened into receiving Bingo and his waitress to bless their marriage. But it then emerges that the waitress herself is none other than the real Rosie M. Banks, who had only adopted the disguise of a waitress to gather material for another novel (the heroine emerging from 'inferior disguise' in her true identity as an 'upper world' character). Only deft footwork by Jeeves, in conveying that Bertie is a lunatic who had misled everyone into thinking that he was Rosie M. Banks, saves the day so that Bingo's uncle renews his allowance (while Wooster, as the exposed 'dark' figure, discreetly leaves the stage).

## Married, divorced, remarried

Of course not all twentieth-century Comedy reflected this split between the romantic and comic elements in the plot. There continued to be many comedies where the two components were still woven together, as in Stanley Donen's musical *Singin' in the Rain* (1952). Set in Hollywood in 1927, when silent movies were giving way to the 'talkies' (and using songs, including the title number, originally written in that period), the story centres on two silent stars, Don Lockwood (Gene Kelly) and Lina Lamont (Jean Hagen). Lina, the chief dark figure of the story, is a shallow, self-centred monster, so deluded by the dream-world of Hollywood that she believes the romantic relationship they act out on the screen is meant to carry over into real life. But Don meets and falls in love with a young, serious actress, Kathy (Debbie Reynolds). The hinge of the plot comes when the studio decides it has to put its two romantic stars into a talking-picture. Lina's grating voice, inability to sing and painful Bronx accent threaten disaster until Don's song-and-dance partner Cosmo Brown (Donald O'Connor) has the clever idea of using Kathy to dub Lina's voice on-screen. It is the hero's joyous response to this proposal which prompts Kelly's famous tap-dance to the title song (originally written for *The Hollywood Revue* in 1929), which has become probably the best-known sequence in the history of the cinema. Thanks to Kathy's voice, the first 'Lockwood-Lamont musical' is a triumph, and the crafty Lina tries to blackmail the studio into keeping Kathy on anonymously in the shadows, as her secret 'screen voice'. But when she recklessly appears to sing before a packed live theatre audience she is in danger of being exposed, until Cosmo places Kathy behind a curtain to supply Lina's singing voice. The audience is fooled until, at a crucial moment, the curtain is drawn to reveal what is really going on (a perfect example of Aristotelian *anagnorisis*). The humiliated Lina flees the stage as 'unreconciled dark figure'. Kathy, the 'obscured heroine', emerges from the shadows as the real star. And the story ends with hero and heroine in loving embrace, in front of a billboard advertising their first film together.[3]

Seven years later, however, Hollywood produced perhaps its most celebrated example of the sending-up of the Comedy plot in Billy Wilder's *Some Like it Hot* (1959). Tony Curtis and Jack Lemmon play two dance musicians in the Chicago of the 1920s who unwittingly find themselves witnessing the St Valentine's Day massacre, in which the members of a criminal gang are machine-gunned by their

3. By a delightful twist of Hollywood unreality, both the speaking and singing voices of Debbie Reynolds, playing Kathy, themselves had to be dubbed in the film by other actresses. By an even greater irony, her speaking voice was dubbed by Jean Hagen, the actress playing Lina.

rivals. Realising that the murder gang will ruthlessly track them down to eliminate them, the pair disguise themselves as female dance musicians, Daphne and Josephine, and join an all-girl band heading for Florida. Here Curtis disguises himself back again as a man, posing as a millionaire in order to woo the prettiest of the girl musicians (Marilyn Monroe). Lemmon is in turn wooed in his female guise by a genuine but aged millionaire, Osgood E. Fielding III, who is so enamoured that, as the film ends, he proposes marriage. Trying one excuse after another to explain how this is totally out of the question, Lemmon finally pulls off his wig to reveal that he is a man. Even this does not deter the doting suitor, who merely replies 'well, nobody's perfect'.

Later in the book we shall consider just why the Comedy plot should have come to be so widely burlesqued in this way (a parallel development can be seen in the fate of the other basic plots). But in view of all these highly improbable marriages and unions at the end of modern comedies, it is perhaps hardly surprising that the only way in which the twentieth century could be claimed to have extended the range of the traditional Comedy plot was in the type of story where the hero and heroine have not only been married before the story opens, but also divorced. The interest of the plot then lies in seeing how they are eventually brought together again to remarry.

The earliest instance of such a story, regarded in its time as highly daring, was Noel Coward's play *Private Lives* (1933). The heroine goes off on honeymoon with her second husband, only to find that the next room in their hotel is occupied by her first husband, on honeymoon with his new wife. Plunged into this embarrassing situation, the heroine and her first husband gradually discover that they still love each other rather than their new partners, and by the end they are reunited.

Another instance of this twist to the plot was *The Philadelphia Story* (1940), originally written as a romantic comedy for Hollywood and later adapted to make the even better-known film musical *High Society* (1956). We meet the heroine, Tracy Lord (Katherine Hepburn/Grace Kelly), a rich, beautiful and frigid society girl, in her family's grand house (originally in Philadelphia, in the musical version at Newport, Long Island). Having been divorced from her first husband, Dexter Haven, she is making preparations for her wedding the following day to the new man in her life, a socially ambitious nouveau riche. When the relaxed and genial Dexter (Cary Grant/Bing Crosby) then strolls in to remind her teasingly of the happy romantic times when they were still in love, this begins to sow painful doubts in her mind. He tells her the only reason she has accepted her new fiancé is that he treats her like a goddess on a pedestal, and that her desire to be worshipped is her great weakness. At a lavish eve of wedding ball, Tracy gets drunk and recklessly wanders off to enjoy an amorous liaison with a handsome, raffish newspaperman (James Stewart/Frank Sinatra), who has been sent to cover the event for a vulgar gossip sheet. This descent into an 'inferior realm' thaws her out of her icy frigidity, and liberates her into becoming a different woman: with the result that she and her stuffy fiancé have a flaming row. With a crowd of fashionable guests already assembled for the wedding and the organ ready to strike up 'Here Comes The Bride', she decides to call the wedding off. She is nervously standing at the door, wondering how to explain it to the guests, when Dexter materialises at her shoulder, having recognised that the goddess has stepped down from her pedestal and become the warmer, softer, feminine girl he always knew she had it in her to be. He whispers to her what she is to say and, as she dutifully repeats his words to the guests, she suddenly realises that she is announcing that there is to be a wedding after all, and that she is about to remarry her first husband. Deliriously happy, she walks up the aisle, recognising that it is him she has really loved all along.

However novel this situation may seem, it is really only a contemporary version of that theme which has run through Comedy since the time of Menander: the lovers who are separated by a misunderstanding, and may even temporarily go off with other parties, but are eventually reconciled. It was precisely the situation that shaped that apparently revolutionary drama of the 1950's, *Look Back in Anger* (1956), which few would have dared at the time to describe as a mere 'comedy'. In a cramped flat in a dingy Midlands city, Jimmy Porter is perpetually arguing with his wife, Alison, until eventually he escapes with her friend Helen. He recognises that he is no better off and that it is Alison he really loves. He returns home, makes up his quarrel with Alison, and they end happily reunited in their childish fantasy of 'squirrels and bears'.

Only towards the end of the twentieth century, however, did modern Comedy finally manage to turn the outward conventions of the time-honoured plot completely on their head. The hero of the film *Four Weddings and a Funeral* (1994), played by Hugh Grant, is one of a group of young friends who, one after another, get married (or in one case, die). After the first wedding, he has a one-night affair with another guest, an American girl, but she returns to America. Eventually, as the sequence of weddings unfolds, the hero becomes so desperate at seeing all his friends married off that he proposes to another member of the group who is similarly on the shelf. As the guests all gather in church for what it seems will be the final wedding of the story, the hero sees in the congregation the American girl he has never been able to get out of his mind. The bride is already standing at the altar when the hero and his American friend manage to escape from the church and run off together into the rain. Declaring undying love for each other, they agree their love is so real that it would be a mistake for them ever to get married.

After more than 2000 years of comedies in which the climax was the moment when the hero and heroine could at last head off to their wedding, here was one which might have seemed the complete inversion: a story made up of a whole succession of weddings, but in which the resolution finally came with hero and heroine agreeing, as ultimate proof that their love was real, that they should not get married. However, it was only the outward form which had been stood on its head. The story still ended, after all their separations, misunderstandings and pairing off with the wrong partners, with hero and heroine coming together in recognition of their loving union. For all its seeming reversal of convention, the underlying power of the Comedy plot still brought the story to its irresistible archetypal conclusion.

## Comedy: Summing-up

Comedy cannot be summarised in quite the same way as the other basic plots because the very nature of the plot requires it to cover such a range of variations. But the essence of the story is always that:

(1) we see a little world in which people have passed under a shadow of confusion, uncertainty and frustration, and are shut off from one another;

(2) the confusion gets worse until the pressure of darkness is at its most acute and everyone is in a nightmarish tangle;

(3) finally, with the coming to light of things not previously recognised, perceptions are dramatically changed. The shadows are dispelled, the situation is miraculously transformed and the little world is brought together in a state of joyful union.

The key to Comedy is thus the transition between two general states. The first which persists through most of the story is a kind of twilight in which nothing is seen clearly; where people's true nature or identity may be obscured; and where there may be uncertainty as to who should end up with whom. The chief cause of the twilight is usually some central dark figure, who is in some way acting blindly and heartlessly. It is his (or her) egocentricity which is throwing everyone else into the shadows, and setting people at odds with one another. And nothing symbolises this state of division more powerfully than that it is keeping apart the hero and heroine of the story. The second state arrives with the 'recognition' and 'unknotting' when, at the climax of the story, the dark figure is in some way caught out, and all is at last seen clearly. Everyone's true nature and identity is revealed; everyone recognises who is his or her proper 'other half'; and the story ends, with darkness and division at an end, on the image of a great coming together. What was dark is now light. What was divided is now whole. And nothing symbolises this more completely than the union of hero and heroine.

During the first, twilit period, the world presented by the story is usually divided in some way into an 'upper realm', where the story's chief source of darkness holds sway, and a 'lower realm' in the shadows. It is 'below the line', in the 'inferior realm' that the seeds of life and truth, the potential for love and the ability to see whole are to be found: obscured from the dominant 'upper realm' until they are ready to be brought up into the light, to bring both halves of the world together.

Within the context of this general pattern, the great majority of stories shaped by the Comedy plot fall into two main types.

The first is where the chief source of darkness throwing a shadow over the proceedings is some character other than the hero (e.g., an unrelenting father or a 'dark rival') who dominates everyone else in a way which creates unhappiness and confusion and is opposed to the flow of life. In such a story the chief victims consigned to the shadows are likely to be the hero and heroine; and they can only be raised up into the light and brought together when the dark figure either has his eyes opened and goes through a change of heart, or is exposed and pushed off the stage.

The second is where the chief dark figure is the hero himself. It is then the wronged heroine, standing for true feeling and the ability to see whole, who is most obviously in the shadows. Here, to reach the happy ending, it is necessary for the hero to go through a change of heart and 'come to himself'. As he is liberated, so also is the heroine, so they can emerge together into the light. In those rare examples where the heroine is the dark figure, it is her own repressed inner feminity which is obscured. It is this which the loving hero perceives and brings out, so that she likewise goes through the change of heart necessary to bring about the happy ending.

There is a third type of Comedy where there is no obvious dark figure in the usual sense, and where the source of confusion is simply a general state of misunderstanding which has everyone in its grip (e.g., *The Comedy of Errors, A Midsummer Night's Dream, Guys and Dolls, Four Weddings and a Funeral*). But here the resolution can still only be reached when the redeeming truth is won from the shadows. And here we see more clearly than ever how the real preoccupation of Comedy is consciousness: what people are aware of. The real cause of confusion and conflict is always that the characters are not fully conscious of the truth, either about other people or about themselves; and while they are in this limited state of awareness they remain shut off from one another. What dispels the confusion is that their awareness is finally opened out so that they can see everything and everyone, including themselves, straight and whole. It is this which enables them to feel properly and to discover how they can all relate to each other in a state of unity and love: because they have at last 'seen the light'.

We can now look at the plot of Comedy in the context of the other types of story we considered earlier.

Like the other plots, it conjures up a world in which the threatening power of darkness is, through most of the story, in some way or other dominant. As in the others, this pressure is likely to reach its height just before the end, in the story's climax. As in the others, there then follows the reversal, the miraculous liberation, so that the story can end on an image of wholeness and completion.

In the first three plots, Overcoming the Monster, Rags to Riches and the Quest, we saw an essentially light hero or heroine, overshadowed by dark figures, moving towards the moment when the darkness is overthrown and they can at last emerge completely into the light. In the most fully developed examples of the Voyage and Return story, we saw a hero who begins by displaying some of the characteristics of a dark figure himself, but who is eventually liberated from the dark forces closing round him in the 'other world' by the fact that he has switched to become a light figure.

In Comedy we see both patterns at work. Sometimes, as in the earlier types of story, the hero and heroine are essentially light but overshadowed by some other dominant dark figure, who has to make the switch to light so that hero and heroine can be united. Sometimes, as in those Voyage and Return examples, the hero himself is dark and it is his switch to light which is necessary to pave the way to the happy ending. In either form, Comedy differs from the earlier types of story, where the dark figures opposed to the hero or heroine went through no change of heart but were simply cleared out of the way at the end by being discomfited or overthrown (although even in Comedy some vestige of this remains in those examples where the 'unreconciled dark figure' is caught out and pushed off the stage). Only in Comedy is it the general tendency for all the characters to be brought to light and reconciled, to produce the story's closing image of a little world wholly united.

Even so, what all the types of story we have looked at so far have in common is that they show the power of darkness itself having to be vanquished as the pre-condition of the hero or heroine being able to enjoy a happy ending. What we are now about to consider for the first time is what happens in stories when the central figure becomes dark and does *not* go through a change of heart, but remains dark right to the end. This produces a kind of story which in some respects is quite unlike any of those we have previously looked at. Except that ultimately, as we shall see, the fundamental rules which govern its unfolding are entirely consistent with those which govern the structure of the other plots.

In surveying the earlier plots we ended by looking briefly at the 'dark' versions of each type of story: examples where the underlying patterns fails to work out to its proper, happy conclusion. In the case of Comedy it might seem a contradiction in terms that there could be a 'dark' version, in that if 'recognition' and a change of heart fail to take place as the precondition of a happy ending, the story can scarcely be regarded as a Comedy. How then would we describe such a tale?

Let us consider a familiar example. We see a hero who falls in love with a beautiful heroine. She loves him and despite strong initial opposition from her father, who regards him as 'inferior', they get married. But the hero unwittingly gives offence to a jealous, embittered third party, who becomes the chief dark figure of the story. The dark figure determines to get his revenge, and begins to drop hints to the hero that his young wife is being unfaithful to him. The villain hatches a dark plot, involving a lost handkerchief, supposedly given by the heroine to her lover. The hero is taken in and becomes deranged with rage. If this were a Comedy, when confusion and misunderstanding have reached their height, this is where the process of 'recognition' would begin to clear things up. The true explanation of the lost handkerchief would come to light. The dark figure would be exposed for the villain he is. The hero would recognise he had dreadfully wronged his wife, and would be filled with contrition. Finally hero and heroine would be reconciled, and all would end happily. As we all know, however, the story does not end like that, precisely because there is no 'recognition'. *Othello* is not a comedy, and it leads us on to the next plot.

## Chapter 8

# Tragedy (I): The Five Stages

'For that – for that – I would give everything! Yes, there is nothing in the world
I would not give! I would give my soul for that!'

*Oscar Wilde, The Picture of Dorian Gray*

'He felt that all his powers, hitherto dissipated and scattered, were now concentrated and directed with terrible energy towards one blissful aim.'

*Vronsky in Anna Karenina*

'From that moment her whole existence was nothing but a maze of lies.'

*Gustave Flaubert, Madame Bovary*

'Have mercy, Jesu! Soft! I did but dream.
O coward conscience, how thou dost afflict me!
The lights burn blue. It is now dead midnight.
Cold tearful drops do stand upon my trembling flesh ...
All several sins, all us'd in each degree
Throng to the bar, crying all "Guilty! Guilty!"
I shall despair. There is no creature loves me.'

*Richard III (on the eve of his death)*

'So shall you hear
Of carnal, bloody and unnatural acts;
Of accidental judgements, casual slaughters,
Of deaths put on by cunning and forced cause;
And in this upshot, purposes mistook
Fall'n on the inventors' heads.'

*Hamlet, Act v. Sc.ii*

Sooner or later, in any attempt to explore the deeper patterns which shape story-telling, we are brought up against one central, overwhelming fact. This is the way in which, through all the millions of stories thrown up by the human imagination, just two endings have far outweighed all others. In fact we might almost say that, for a story to resolve in a way which really seems final and complete, it can only do so in one of two ways. Either it ends with a man and a woman united in love. Or it ends in a death.

On the face of it, this might not seem particularly odd. Nothing in human life, after all, might be considered more final than death, What could be more natural than that our imaginations should conjure up stories which conclude with their hero or heroine reaching old age and death?

But the point is that the number of stories which end like this, with their hero or heroine passing peacefully away in the fullness of years, is not very great. When we talk of a story ending in a death we do not usually mean that kind of death at

153

all. We mean a death that is violent, premature, a death that is 'unnatural'. In other words, we mean a death which shows that something has gone hideously or, as we say, tragically wrong.

₊˖✦˖₊

Of course the huge mass of stories which end in violent death do not by any means all have the same underlying shape. It is possible to arrive at such an ending by any of a number of routes. For a start, as we have seen from our glimpses of the 'dark' versions of other plots – the dark Rags to Riches story, the dark Quest and so on – it is possible for other basic types of story to lead up to such a conclusion, when we might talk of them having a 'tragic ending'. And even when we turn to that great family of stories which have for thousands of years been more specifically described as 'tragedies', we find considerable variety in their underlying shape and moral emphasis. Even more than with Comedy, we are venturing here into an area of storytelling which cannot be delineated in just one simple formula.

Nevertheless, all through the history of storytelling, we find one particular type of story which is shaped by a pattern so persistent and so distinctive as to make it unmistakable. This can be illustrated by five well-known examples, composed in a wide variety of cultural circumstances and for greatly differing purposes: the Greek myth of Icarus; the German legend of Faust; Shakespeare's *Macbeth*; Stevenson's nineteenth-century horror story, *Dr Jekyll and Mr Hyde*; and a modern novel, Nabokov's *Lolita*.

The story of Icarus tells of how he and his father, the inventor Daedalus, are enabled to escape from the island of Crete by means of feathered wings. Before they set out his father gives him an impassioned warning to fly neither too high, lest the heat of the sun melt the wax holding the wings together, nor too low, lest they fall into in the sea. They set off, and for a while all goes well – until eventually the temptation to ignore his father's advice to keep between the opposites proves too much for Icarus. He wishes to soar up higher and higher, towards the sun. His initial exhilaration turns first to anxiety, as the wax begins to melt, then to panic. The wings are giving way, Icarus can no longer keep up, and he plunges headlong to his death in the sea below.

The learned scholar Faust, eager for 'forbidden knowledge' and the mastery of occult powers, sells his soul to the devil. At first he is given glimpses of all sorts of marvels and wonders, and wins a great reputation. But gradually the insubstantiality of the visions he can conjure up begins to pall. Worse, Faust (in Marlowe's dramatisation *Dr Faustus*) senses that the time is drawing near when he must pay the price – until, amid mounting horror, he sees the moment arrive when he is carried down to hell by demons, to face everlasting punishment.

Macbeth, the victorious and ambitious general, is told by the witches of all sorts of honours which will come to him, including the improbable promise that he will one day be king of Scotland. When their lesser prophecies begin to come true, Macbeth is drawn by the temptation to make them complete, by murdering the reigning king Duncan and so succeeding him. At first all seems to go well, and

Macbeth becomes king; but he is not secure in his new state. First suspicion mounts around him, leading him to commit further crimes in a desperate effort to make his position safe. Then outright opposition gathers; until Macbeth is surrounded by his advancing enemies and killed.

Dr Jekyll, the outwardly respectable medical man with a dubious secret life, discovers a potion which will enable him to split into two personalities, one his normal 'light' self, the other the dark and deformed Mr Hyde. At first it is exhilarating to be able to escape at night into his Hyde-self, indulging in all sorts of nameless wickedness, then to return safely to his Jekyll-self by day. But gradually the Hyde-personality begins to take over, committing a succession of crimes, culminating in a particularly horrible murder. Jekyll has already found he is increasingly unable to control the switches between his light and dark personalities. Now he finds himself trapped forever in his alter-ego state, and on the run from the police, his friends, everyone. In a state of total despair he kills himself.

Humbert Humbert, the outwardly respectable scholar, has long nurtured a secret passion for very young girls. One day, when he is looking for lodgings, his obsession finds its ultimate focus when he sees sprawled on a suburban lawn the 'nymphet' of his dreams, Lolita. He takes a room in the house and marries Lolita's widowed mother, in order to be near the object of his 'dark' desires. The mother then discovers the secret diaries to which he has confided his obsession: she runs out of the house, distracted with horror, and is killed by a passing car. Humbert thus becomes Lolita's guardian, and he and his compliant ward then embark on a wild, dreamlike journey around America, enjoying forbidden sexual pleasure in a succession of motel rooms. But gradually the two fall to quarrelling and, as they settle in a little town where Lolita returns to her schooling, a mood of terrible frustration sets in. Humbert becomes dimly aware of another man hovering around, a playwright called Quilty, who seems to threaten his possession of Lolita like a kind of shadowy alter-ego. To get away, Humbert takes Lolita off on a second journey across America, this time more like a nightmare than a dream, as it seems increasingly obvious that the mysterious Quilty is following them; until one day Lolita disappears, kidnapped by Quilty. After some years of lonely misery Humbert eventually discovers what happened to them both. Lolita, grown up and married to someone else, no longer bears any relation to the little girl of his illicit fantasies. In a state of horror and distraction, Humbert vengefully tracks down Quilty, the alter-ego who had robbed him of his dream, and murders him in cold-blood. He is arrested and, after learning that Lolita has died in childbirth, himself dies in prison on the verge of his execution.

Each of these stories shows a hero being tempted or impelled into a course of action which is in some way dark or forbidden. For a time, as the hero embarks on a course, he enjoys almost unbelievable, dreamlike success. But somehow it is in the nature of the course he is pursuing that he cannot achieve satisfaction. His mood is increasingly chequered by a sense of frustration. As he still pursues the dream, vainly trying to make his position secure, he begins to feel more and more threatened – things have got out of control. The original dream has soured into a nightmare where everything is going more and more wrong. This eventually culminates in the hero's violent destruction.

In fact we can set out the general stages through which the pattern unfolds like this:

1. *Anticipation Stage*: the hero is in some way incomplete or unfulfilled and his thoughts are turned towards the future in hope of some unusual gratification. Some object of desire or course of action presents itself, and his energies have found a focus.

2. *Dream Stage*: he becomes in some way committed to his course of action (e.g., Faust signing his pact with the devil, Humbert causing the death of Lolita's mother which enables him to enter on his affair) and for a while things go almost improbably well for the hero. He is winning the gratification he had dreamed of, and seems to be 'getting away with it'.

3. *Frustration Stage*: almost imperceptibly things begin to go wrong. The hero cannot find a point of rest. He begins to experience a sense of frustration, and in order to secure his position may feel compelled to further 'dark acts' which lock him into his course of action even more irrevocably. A 'shadow figure' may appear at this point, seeming in some obscure way to threaten him.

4. *Nightmare Stage*: things are now slipping seriously out of the hero's control. He has a mounting sense of threat and despair. Forces of opposition and fate are closing in on him.

5. *Destruction or death wish Stage*: either by the forces he has aroused against him, or by some final act of violence which precipitates his own death (e.g., murder or suicide), the hero is destroyed.

If we look again at the familiar example of *Macbeth*, we can see how these five stages correspond exactly to the five acts into which Shakespeare divides the drama:

1. Act One (*Anticipation Stage*) shows the triumphant generals Macbeth and Banquo returning from winning a great victory. They meet the three 'dark sisters', who prophesy to Macbeth that he will hold three great titles, Glamis, Cawdor and King. This fires his ambition and when he hears that a grateful King Duncan has already rewarded him with the first two titles, he writes to his wife to tell her about the witches' prediction that he would one day hold the third as well. She eggs him on to make the prediction complete, and they find their 'focus' in the conspiracy to murder Duncan.

2. Act Two (*Dream Stage*) shows Macbeth comitting the 'dark deed' and subsequently killing the two grooms to cover up his crime. Initially things could not go better for the hero. Duncan's two sons flee to England, arousing suspicion that they had somehow been implicated in the crime, and Macbeth is chosen to be king.

3. Act Three (*Frustration Stage*) opens with Banquo soliloquising 'Thou hast it all now: King, Cawdor, Glamis, all, as the weird women promis'd; and, I fear, thou play'dst most foully for it'. The first inklings of suspicion are arising. Macbeth in turn is distrustful of Banquo because of the witches' prediction that it would be his descendants, not Macbeth's, who would sit on the throne of Scotland. He arranges for Banquo's murder. Macbeth expresses his growing frustration in such phrases as 'we have scotch'd the snake, not killed it', and this is heightened when

the murderers report that they have killed Banquo, but that his son Fleance escaped. At dinner that night Macbeth is confronted with Banquo's accusing ghost, and the act ends with the news that Macbeth's last supporter among the great Scottish lords, Macduff, has fled to England to join Duncan's sons.

4. Act Four (*Nightmare Stage*) opens with Macbeth's second, much more fearful visit to the witches, who give him three increasingly enigmatic warnings: that he should 'beware Macduff'; that he will only be overthrown by 'man not of woman born'; and that this can only happen when 'Birnam wood has come to Dunsinane'. Now in a state of mounting terror, Macbeth lashes out at the man who seems most to threaten him, the fled Macduff, by arranging for his wife and children to be brutally murdered. The second part of the act shows the horror with which this news is greeted by the exiles in England, and the coming together of an army to invade Scotland and overthrow the tyrant whose villainy is now clear for all to see.

5. Act Five (*Destruction Stage*) shows the nightmare closing in around Macbeth and deepening to its climax: with Lady Macbeth's guilty sleepwalking scene ('unnatural deeds do bring unnatural troubles'); the approach of the avenging army to Macbeth's lair at Dunsinane; Lady Macbeth's death; and finally the battle, when Macbeth learns that Macduff was 'not of woman born' just before Macduff slays him. The pattern is complete.

The pattern we have been looking at here is in fact so fundamental to the understanding of stories that its implications will be with us for the rest of this book. It is not just the starting point for exploring all that complex family of stories which we think of under the general heading of Tragedy, because it presents the tragic theme in its blackest and most basic form. It also, as we shall eventually see, provides one of the best starting points for exploring the profound link between the patterns which shape stories and those which shape events in what we call 'real life'.

Indeed, so important is it that we should become completely familiar with the workings of this tragic cycle that we shall shortly look in rather more detail at a further half-dozen examples; and these have been chosen, in addition to those already touched on, to build up a fuller picture of the range of basic situations from which a Tragedy can unfold.

We shall then, at the end of this chapter, take a look at the most obvious way in which storytellers may sometimes vary the emphasis of their presentation of the basic tragic theme: by concentrating only on the closing stages and beginning at the point, halfway through the complete cycle, where the mood of frustration is coming to be uppermost.

Finally we shall be in a position, in the two chapters that follow, to draw on all these and other examples to look at the essence of Tragedy in a deeper and more general way. What is really happening to the hero or heroine of a tragedy as they get drawn into their fatal course of action? Why does it seem to lead so inexorably to disaster? And what is it which distinguishes this type of story from all the others we have looked at, where the fundamental impulse is to lead the hero or heroine to a happy ending?

### The Picture of Dorian Gray

A story which expresses the basic plot of Tragedy with almost allegorical simplicity, like a kind of 'black fairy tale', is Oscar Wilde's novel, *The Picture Of Dorian Gray* (1890). We meet the hero, a languid and exceptionally beautiful young man, at just the moment when his artist friend Basil Hallward is completing a portrait of him. At this point the 'dark' figure of Lord Henry Wootton enters, and tempts the hero with two thoughts. The first is how wonderful it would be if Dorian Gray could always remain looking as young and beautiful as he does in the picture, while his portrait took on the ravages of the years instead. The second is how wonderful it would be to live a life of total physical self-indulgence, recognising that the most intense spiritual experiences in life come through the senses.

This is the moment of Temptation, or Focus. The young hero becomes possessed by these two related thoughts, and by the excitement of his 'dangerous' new friendship with Lord Henry. He takes his portrait home, and immediately plunges into the Dream Stage of his adventure by falling rapturously in love with a beautiful young actress, Sibyl Vane, whom he goes to see playing Shakespeare every night. He proposes to Sibyl; she accepts; and the following night she gives a thoroughly flat and wooden performance. She explains to Dorian that she had only been able to put her heart into acting because it was a substitute for real life, but now he has come into her life, her motivation as an actress has gone. Dorian is horrified and angrily tells her that he had only loved her for her brilliant *persona* on stage. He walks out on her, and she commits suicide. For the first time he notices a slight change in the portrait which he keeps at home: a new, cruel twist to the mouth. He hides the portrait away, but otherwise experiences no remorse for what has happened.

In a sense the Dream Stage of the story continues for a long time. Dorian throws himself into a relentless round of sensual gratification, sometimes aided and abetted by his friend Lord Henry, and seems able to indulge himself wherever his fancy leads him. But gradually we are made aware that a dark aura of scandal is surrounding his name. A growing succession of young men and women are being destroyed, even committing suicide, because of their association with him. We learn of his increasingly morbid fascination with historical tales about sexual excess, murder and insanity ('there were moments when he looked on evil simply as a mode through which he could realise his conception of the beautiful'); and although after many years he still looks outwardly as young and beautiful as on the day he was painted by Hallward, the portrait locked away in his house shows more and more signs of a terrible corruption.

The Frustration Stage is setting in, and eventually someone – Hallward himself – has the courage to confront Dorian with the shocking stories which are circulating about him. Gray reacts with cold rage and cold-bloodedly murders Hallward (like Macbeth's murder of Banquo, a new 'dark act' committed in an attempt to secure his position). An increasingly nightmarish atmosphere now shrouds the tale, as Gray blackmails a friend into dissolving Hallward's body in acid, fills the house with orchids to disguise the stench and heads off to the opium dens of east London ('dens of horror where the memory of old sins could be destroyed by the madness of sins that were new'). Here, in the fume-filled shadows, he is threatened with a revolver by Sibyl Vane's sailor brother, who has returned from years in Australia, bent on revenge.

Gray manages to extricate himself from this nightmare scene but is haunted by the mysterious figure of Jim Vane. Staying at a country house, he glimpses Vane peering through the conservatory windows and faints, and although Vane is accidentally killed the next day by a shooting party, Gray's thoughts are now in a ceaseless turmoil of horror and 'wild longing for the unstained purity of his boyhood' before he had embarked on corrupting and destroying so many people's lives. 'A new life! That was what he wanted ... he would never again tempt innocence. He would be good.'

So he muses, alone one night in his house, and decides to take another look at his portrait, which he finds not only looking 'more loathsome, if possible, than before' but shining with newly-spilt blood. If only he could 'kill this monstrous life-soul' he thinks, 'he could be at peace'. He takes up the knife with which he stabbed Hallward, to slash the picture. There is a tremendous crash and a cry, and his servants rush upstairs to find

> 'hanging on the wall, a splendid portrait of their master as they had last seen him, in all the wonder of his exquisite youth and beauty. Lying on the floor was a dead man ... with a knife in his heart. He was withered, wrinkled and loathsome of visage. It was not until they had examined the rings that they recognised who it was.'

## Carmen

Our next example is the story of Bizet's opera *Carmen* (1875), based on a novel by Prosper Merimée. When we meet the hero Don José, a corporal in the army, he is in love with a shy young girl, Micaela, and she with him. All might seem well, but our sense that something is about to disturb their happiness is aroused by the entry of the beautiful and imposing Carmen, a classic Temptress. She tries to flirt with Jose, at first in vain. She stalks off, but not before she has thrown down a blood-red flower at his feet. Wavering for a moment, he picks it up and places it next to his heart. Micaela returns, and José seems freed from Carmen's spell. A short time later, however, he is sent to restore order after a fight. Carmen has been involved and he has to arrest her. Once again she directs all her seductive charm at him, and this time he falls completely ('Carmen you have bewitched me'). Temptation has won. The Focus has been found.

Plunging recklessly into the Dream Stage, José allows Carmen to escape and tollows her to a tavern, where they ecstatically declare their love for one another. José gets involved in a fight over Carmen with one of his officers, and to avoid punishment for insubordination he deserts the army and flees to join Carmen and a gang of bandits in the mountains. No sooner has this dark act committed José irrevocably to his course than frustration sets in. The fickle Carmen begins to lose interest in José and transfers her admiration to the handsome bullfighter

Escamillo. The unhappy José feels increasingly trapped. He cannot now return to his former life, despite a pitiful attempt by young Micaela to win him back. He is still infatuated with Carmen, although it is becoming obvious to everyone except himself that he has lost her.

The nightmarish nature of his plight is now brought home to him when José meets Escamillo coming up the mountainside. Not recognising him, the bull-fighter recounts how Carmen used to love a soldier but that it is all over. José lashes out at his rival and the two have to be pulled apart by the bandits. The triumphant Escamillo invites them all to a bullfight, in which he will be the hero of the hour.

All that is left to unfold is the final stage. The 'pale and haggard' José, his eyes 'hollow' and 'glowing with a dangerous light', arrives at the bullfight to confront Carmen, who scornfully rejects him and tells him she now loves Escamillo. In the last paroxysm of desperation, José stabs her to death – thus ensuring his own immediate arrest and, presumably, execution.

### Bonnie and Clyde

Our third example is the film *Bonnie and Clyde* (1967), based like many fictional tragedies on an episode from 'real life': in this instance the story of two notorious young American 'gangsters' of the 1930's.

1. *Anticipation Stage*: the young hero Clyde arrives at a house in a little Texan town to make an amateurish attempt to steal a car. Through a window of the house he sees the heroine Bonnie, naked. She sees him, apparently doing something wild and daring, and their curiosity mutually aroused, they get together at a nearby drugstore where Bonnie dares Clyde to commit a real, grown-up robbery. This is the moment of Temptation and Focus.

2. *Dream Stage*: Clyde successfully holds up a grocery store, Bonnie is impressed and they drive off together. They begin to rob banks with seemingly dreamlike impunity; they recruit a third member to their gang, C. W. Moss, and the exhilarating series of robberies continues. But then they shoot a policeman dead after a bank hold-up, a 'dark act' which places them, as murderers, in a new, more serious league.

3. *Frustration Stage*: a series of incidents creates a mood of deepening frustra-tion. They capture a policeman who has been trailing them, insult him and let him go, in such a way that he is left swearing revenge. It transpires that Clyde is physically unable to make love to Bonnie: he works out his frustration through his obsession with guns. They hi-jack a couple's car, ask the man casually what he does for a living and he replies that he is an undertaker. Bonnie reacts hysterically, taking this as a terrible omen. The mood is becoming steadily darker and more threatening.

4. *Nightmare Stage*: there is a brief unreal interlude when the doomed couple fantasise in familiar fashion (*cf. Dorian Gray*) of escaping back to the days of innocence before all their troubles began. They take Bonnie's mother for a picnic

and Clyde talks about their settling down near her, to live a quiet life. But they remember they are now the most wanted criminals in the state, and have no alternative but to keep running. The nightmare deepens as they are spotted by the police and have to fight two gun battles, in which two members of the gang (now grown to five) are killed or injured.

5. *Destruction Stage*: as the police close in, the remaining trio, Bonnie, Clyde and C. W. Moss, take refuge with Moss's father. The atmosphere between them all is now fraught and quarrelsome. Eventually, in return for a promise of leniency to his son, the father betrays Bonnie and Clyde, who are tricked into their third and final confrontation with the police. Helpless and trapped, they are bloodily gunned down.

## Jules et Jim

Our fourth example is another well-known film of the 1960's, Francois Truffaut's *Jules et Jim* (1962).

1. *Anticipation Stage*: Jules and Jim, two high-spirited young men in pre-First World War Paris are full of nervous energy but lack direction, until a friend, Albert, shows them some lantern slides, including one of a female statue recently dug up on the Adriatic. A silent film-type caption tells us that they had never seen such 'a calm, tranquil smile' as that which appears on the statue, but that if they saw it again 'they would follow it'. It is the beginning of a Focus for their fantasy state, and when three strange girls shortly afterwards turn up for dinner they see that the third, Catherine, has exactly the smile of the statue. She is a bewitching madcap, given to impulsive pranks, and the two heroes are captivated. The Focus is complete.

2. *Dream Stage*: Catherine moves in to live with Jules, but the three become otherwise inseparable, enjoying a mad time all over Bohemian Paris. The sense of being drawn into a reckless, exhilarating dream is heightened when the three go off to the South of France together for the summer. 'After a long search they found the house of their dreams' says a caption. Here they play childish games together in the sun, Catherine always leading. 'I think we are lost children' she says, and a caption tells us 'she is an apparition'. They return to Paris, where Jules and Catherine decide to get married.

3. *Frustration Stage*: gradually the mood of the story darkens. The First World War approaches and the three are separated because Jules, as an Austrian, has to return with his wife Catherine to the other side of the great European divide created by the war. When hostilities are over, Jim travels to be reunited with his friends, who are living in a lonely chalet in the mountains with a little daughter, and finds all is not well with the marriage. They are all awkward together, talking in platitudes punctuated by silences; Catherine sleeping alone ('we lead a monastic life'); and the mood is darkened still further by the surrounding gloomy forests and mist-shrouded lakes and mountains. Their old friend Albert reappears in rather sinister, enigmatic fashion, living nearby (is he having an affair with

Catherine?). The sense that they may all be caught in some impending vortex is conveyed by the introduction of the film's theme song *Le Tourbillon*, 'the Whirlpool'. Jim finds he is slipping hopelessly into love with Catherine himself. Jules allows him to move into the chalet, though not without a warning: 'watch out'.

4. *Nightmare Stage*: as the three of them return to France the action of the film becomes more and more fragmented, as if they are all sleepwalking through some baffling nightmare, with many premonitory references to death. Catherine, becoming ever more withdrawn and enigmatic, with manic outbursts of fey gaiety, shuttles between the two men (with Albert making a last ominous, mysterious appearance). Jim makes a last desperate bid to escape from the vortex by returning to his old girl friend Gilberte, telling Catherine that he wants to marry and have children.

5. *Destruction Stage*: Catherine, with a strangely purposeful air, summons both Jules and Jim for a drive in the country in her little car. They stop at an inn for lunch. She calls Jim to her car, and deliberately drives it over a broken bridge into the river. Both are drowned, leaving a sadly uncomprehending Jules to superintend the burning of their coffins to ashes.

### Anna Karenina

For two final examples of Tragedy in its full five-stage form we may consider the stories of two of the most haunting tragic heroines in literature, Tolstoy's *Anna Karenina* and Flaubert's *Madame Bovary*.

The thousand-odd pages of *Anna Karenina* really tell two stories, interwoven but completely contrasting: that of Levin and that of Anna herself, each shaped by a quite different plot. We shall concentrate here entirely on the story of Anna.

When we meet Anna she is one of the most beautiful women in St Petersburg, married for some years to a senior and highly-esteemed government official. But living in the shadow of her husband's dry, intellectual high-mindedness, and preoccupation with his work, the passionate Anna feels a void in her life and heart. On a visit to Moscow, she briefly meets on her arrival at the railway station a handsome young cavalry officer, Count Alexei Vronsky. At a grand ball, they run into each other again, and both begin to be swept off their feet by violent mutual attraction. When they meet a third time, back in St Petersburg, Vronsky feels that 'all his powers, hitherto dissipated and scattered' have now become 'directed with terrible energy towards one blissful aim'. When Anna arrives home from their next encounter

'her face shone with a vivid glow, but it was not a joyous glow – it resembled the terrible glow of a conflagration on a dark night.'

Their mutual passion and sense of anticipation mount until at last they perform the irrevocable act which binds them together:

'That which for nearly a year had been Vronsky's sole, exclusive desire, supplanting all his former desires, but which for Anna had been an impossible, dreadful, but all the more bewitching dream of happiness, had come to pass.'

Firmly into the Dream Stage, they continue to meet more or less secretly, in a series of passionate encounters. But already others, including the increasingly chilly, unhappy Karenin, have some suspicion of what is going on. Tongues begin to wag, 'waiting for the scandal to break'; and the premonition of some ultimate disaster is heightened by an emotionally fraught incident at the race course when Vronsky, leading in a steeplechase on his beautiful English mare Frou-Frou, makes a stupid error, forcing his horse to stumble so that she has to be destroyed:

'for the first time in his life he experienced the worst kind of misfortune – one that was irretrievable, and caused by his own fault.'

Both Anna and Vronsky have the same terrible dream, of 'a peasant with a rough beard, small and dreadful', fumbling in a sack and muttering to hImself in French about 'battering' and 'iron': and gradually the story is drawn up to its first great climax. Anna has become pregnant and as she is delivered of a baby girl she falls desperately ill of puerperal fever. Thinking she is about to die, in her delirium she tells her husband how she has felt divided into two people:

'I am still the same ... but there is another in me as well, and I am afraid of her. It was she who fell in love with that other one, and I wished to hate you, but could not forget her who was before. That other is not I. Now I am the real one, all of me.'

The dying Anna and Karenin appear to be reconciled. Vronsky stumbles off in despair and attempts to shoot himself. It might seem that the story was, however messily, approaching a conclusion. But, at a deeper level, too much is still unresolved. Anna and Vronsky separately recover. Anna's old fatal yearnings return. She succumbs and leaves her husband forever, to throw in her lot irrevocably with Vronsky.

At this turning point in the story, Tolstoy opens Book Two with the biblical quotation 'Vengeance is mine; I will repay'. Vronsky and the now-totally compromised Anna flee from Russia for Italy:

'During this, the first period of her freedom and rapid recovery, Anna felt unpardonably happy and full of the joy of life...'

It might all seem like a new Dream Stage, after the nightmare of her illness, But when, at the book's ending, we look back over the whole story, we can see how this central period of turmoil in fact marks the Frustration Stage of the affair. Anna's abortive reconciliation with Karenin is her last attempt to erase all that had happened. Her running away with Vronsky is the final 'dark act' which commits her to her ultimate fate.

Indeed even when they are newly arrived in Italy, Vronsky, who has now thrown up his career for his passion:

'soon felt that the realisation of his longing gave him only one grain of the mountain of bliss he had anticipated. That realisation showed him the eternal error men make by imagining that happiness consists in the gratification of their wishes.'

Vronsky begins to feel bored and aimless, and after a while they return to Russia. Anna almost imperceptibly begins to feel her lover withdrawing from her and becomes increasingly obsessed with the little son Seryosha she has had to leave behind. She is refused permission to see him, but manages to snatch a brief meeting with him by penetrating Karenin's house in disguise. As we are told that, upon her son 'all Anna's unsatisfied capacity for loving was satisfied', it is a heartrending glimpse of all she has lost. She then throws all her energies into a protracted battle to get Karenin to grant her a divorce, so that she can marry Vronsky: a last pitiful attempt to make her now rapidly crumbling position secure. All ends in failure. Vronsky is becoming more and more openly cold towards her. She becomes prey to all sorts of jealous imaginings about his relations with other women. They fall to endless quarrelling. Feeling increasingly lost and desperate, Anna for the first time contemplates suicide. She again has her nightmare about the little old peasant, who seems to be doing something terrible to her with iron. After a final trivial misunderstanding with Vronsky, Anna drives across Moscow, her mind whirling with inconsequential thoughts. Almost without being aware of what she is doing, she arrives at the station where she and Vronsky first met, and on a sudden impulse throws herself under the wheels of an oncoming train:

'a little peasant muttering something was working at the rails. The candle, by the light of which she had been reading that book filled with anxieties, deceptions, grief and evil, flared up with a brighter light than before, lit up for her all that had before been dark, flickered, began to grow dim, and went out for ever.'

### Madame Bovary

In terms of the pattern we are looking at, one of the things which may strike us about *Madame Bovary* is how far we are into the story before the heroine finally becomes committed to the course of infidelity which ultimately destroys her. In *Anna Karenina* the heroine's inner restlessness which lays her open to her grand passion is deftly stated and she is already embarked on the heady early stages of the fatal affair with Vronsky within a short while of the story's opening. In *Madame Bovary*, however, the long-drawn out Anticipation Stage lasts for nearly half the book. This is not least because so much of Flaubert's intention is to show how Emma's fatal craving for excitement and romance builds up over a long period in her head, fuelled by her reading of romantic fiction, before she is finally drawn to act it out in real life.

To set the stage we first have to see the young Emma married to the limited and unambitious country doctor Charles Bovary: as incomplete an answer to her inward craving for passion as Karenin was for Anna. When the first pleasure of finding herself married wears off, the warning signs of distant danger begin to gather, as Flaubert puts it, like tiny rivulets gathering almost imperceptibly to make an eventually irresistible torrent:

> 'Emma tried hard to discover what, precisely, it was in life that was denoted by the words *joy, passion, intoxication*, which had always looked so fine in books.'

There is the excitement of the invitation to the local great house, when Emma is swept off her feet by the brief chance to mingle with such fashionable, titled people: the bright mysterious 'other world' which is beckoning her on. As months, even years go by, we are told that 'the void in her heart remained', that 'deep down in her heart she was waiting and waiting for something to happen'. But even when, thanks to her restlessness, Charles and Emma make the quite unnecessary move to Yonville, and she finds herself strangely exhilarated by her conversations with the young law student Leon, nothing is outwardly committed. Her dreams and desires are still only in her head. It is only when Leon leaves for Rouen and Emma meets the attractive, womanising local farmer Rodolphe that the dark anticipatory nervous energy seething within her at last finds its Focus. The two embark on a passionate secret affair. Emma has committed the irrevocable act which is to launch her on her fatal course

The Dream Stage lasts as long as the secret affair with Rodolphe:

> 'Never had Madame Bovary looked so beautiful as now. She went clothed in that indefinable loveliness which comes of joy, enthusiasm, success, and is produced by the perfect harmony of temperament and outward circumstances.'

It reaches its height when Emma lays plans to elope with her lover and leave her despised, 'repulsive' husband forever. But on the very verge of her leaving home, the Frustration Stage arrives like a thunderbolt. A note comes from Rodolphe:

> 'have you carefully weighed the consequences of your intended action? Have you realised the awful abyss to which I was dragging you, poor angel? No, ... you were going on, confident and heedless, imagining that all would be well, trusting in the future.'

Her lover is not going to elope with her. He had never thought of her as anything but a conveniently married mistress. Their 'grand affair of the heart' had only been in her head, a figment of her fantasy. Emma is so shocked that for several months she lies seriously ill; at the end of which her husband makes a last pathetic attempt to re-establish their marriage by taking her off on a brief holiday to Rouen. It is as doomed as the fragile reconciliation between Karenin and his wife at a similar stage in their story. For it is here, at the theatre, that Emma once again meets Leon. The concluding part of the story opens, like Book Two of *Anna Karenina* ('vengeance is mine'), on a note of dire foreboding.

To begin with, as when Anna and Vronsky flee to Italy, there is a last hectic echo of the Dream Stage, as Emma and Leon embark on their physical affair in the most dramatic and reckless way possible, driving round and round the daylit streets of Rouen in a darkened fiacre. Emma begins to find excuses, such as an imaginary course of piano lessons, to visit Rouen more and more often. She begins to borrow money recklessly from the unscrupulous M. Lheureux. Like Anna, with her recurrent nightmare of the little bearded peasant, Emma becomes haunted on her visits to Rouen by the sight of a hideous beggar ('in the place where his eyelids should have been, two gaping cavities all filled with blood') whose wailing cries go 'sheer down into the depths of her soul like a whirlwind in a chasm'. She is very nearly caught out by Charles in her 'cover story' about the piano lessons and adds one deceit to another ('from that moment her whole existence was a maze of lies'). She becomes more and more enmeshed in her tangle of debt to M. Lheureux. Even her relations with Leon become increasingly fraught and quarrelsome, as 'every day saw her calling for madder music and stronger wine'. Like so many tragic heroes and heroines, she dreams that she might escape back to happier, more innocent times, before the net began closing in. But the Nightmare Stage is inexorably nearing its climax:

> 'She was now always depressed, everywhere and about everything. Everything and everyone, herself included, was intolerable to her.'

Finally M. Lheureux forecloses, getting judgment for a sum of money that will involve selling everything she and Charles possess. Distractedly she runs to anyone she can think of to borrow from, ending up with Rodolphe. When he turns her away, she heads for the cupboard where the pharmacist keeps his poisons and takes a huge dose of arsenic. She has a final nightmare vision of the beggar from Rouen,

> 'thinking she saw the hideous features of the wretched being, rising up to strike terror to her soul, on the very threshold of eternal night'

and dies in agony. Sometime later the bankrupt Charles, ruined and turned into a wraith by her death, also dies.

## Julius Caesar, Antony and Cleopatra

On this sombre note we may conclude this introductory survey of stories which present the five-stage cycle of Tragedy in its entirety and move on to those – including some of the best-known tragic stories in the world – which concentrate only on the concluding phases of the cycle, picking it up, as it were, halfway through. The initial stages are already over before the story, as we see it, opens, and can only be reconstructed by means of flashback and sympathetic imagination.

We can see the difference between these two types of Tragedy clearly illustrated when we compare two of the tragedies of Shakespeare, *Julius Caesar* and *Antony and Cleopatra*. The first of these is of the type with which we are already familiar, portraying the complete five-stage pattern. In this sense *Julius Caesar* is essentially the tragedy of Brutus. It is he, 'the noblest Roman of them all', who has to be persuaded, as the conspirators gather together in the Anticipation Stage, to join the plot to kill Caesar. It is in Brutus's soul that we see the battle of temptation acted out, in Act II Scene i, when the other conspirators, led by the chief Tempter Cassius, call on him at night. When he finally succumbs, the Focus has been found and the Dream Stage follows, including the 'dark act' of the assassination itself, with Brutus as the conspirator who strikes the last fatal blow, and the heady aftermath, when it seems that the people of Rome are prepared to welcome Caesar's murder as the overthrow of an over-ambitious tyrant. But then the Frustration Stage begins, when the eloquence of Mark Antony presents a very different view of Caesar, as the people's friend. The crowd begins to turn against the conspirators. They are forced to flee from Rome and we see the triumvirate of Antony, Octavius and Lepidus assuming full authority, gathering their forces to avenge Caesar's death. The Nightmare Stage shows the conspirators on the run and beginning to fall out among themselves, with Brutus pursued by Caesar's ghost; and this culminates at Philippi in their total overthrow, first with the death of Cassius and finally Brutus's suicide.

In *Antony and Cleopatra*, we see the emphasis of the story falling quite differently. The essence of the situation is that the great soldier Antony has been caught between two poles: on the one hand his duty, his manly responsibilities as one of the triumvirs of Rome; on the other, his pleasure, his all-consuming infatuation with the Queen of Egypt. The basic question of the play, posed from its opening lines ('Nay, but this dotage of our general's overflows the measure ... the triple pillar of the world transform'd into a strumpet's fool') is: which pole will win?

The point is that we pick up the story of Antony's fatal love for Cleopatra halfway through. He has already embarked on the cycle of self-destruction which is to bring him down long before our story opens. Indeed we can reconstruct the moment when he was caught, the moment of Focus, when, in one of the play's most memorable speeches, Enobarbus recalls the occasion when the stern hero first set eyes on the voluptuous Temptress, on his arrival in Egypt:

'the barge she sat in, like a burnish'd throne burned on the water ....'

From there the Dream Stage follows, as Antony plunges into his affair with Cleopatra and begins to forget his soldierly responsibilities in endless nights of carousing. But eventually a series of threats to the security of Rome, such as that posed by the rebellious young Pompey, serve to remind Antony of his duty. An element of frustration has appeared, and it is only at this point, when Antony is being called back to his 'proper Roman self', that the play begins.

In terms of the complete five-stage cycle of Tragedy, in short, the play picks up the story at the Frustration Stage. The first two acts show the hero – rather like Anna Karenina at a similar stage in her story, when she attempts a last reconciliation with her husband – making a final effort to return to his Roman self, by going back to Rome to join Octavius and Lepidus in dealing with Pompey. To emphasise his determination to break with the past and make a fresh start, Antony even marries Octavius's sister. But, just as the unresolved lure of Vronsky had proved too much for Anna, the fatal lure of Cleopatra is too strong. Antony returns to Egypt, throwing him into final opposition to Octavius. There follows the battle of Actium, the beginning of the Nightmare Stage, when just as Antony thinks victory is in his grasp, Cleopatra leads her ships into headlong retreat, giving the day to Octavius. Octavius pursues Antony to Egypt and there is a second battle, in which again Antony sees victory torn from his grasp by the flight of Cleopatra's forces. Thirdly Antony falls out with Cleopatra, berating her for her treachery. She sends him word that she has killed herself, and in despair he commits suicide. Finally, when she sees what she has brought about by her foolish 'feminine' wiles, Cleopatra commits suicide herself.

### Don Giovanni

Another familiar tragic story we pick up at the Frustration Stage is that of Mozart and Da Ponte's *Don Giovanni*, derived via the version by Molière from the original 'Don Juan' play, the *Burlador de Sevilla*, by the pseudonymous 'Tirso de Molina'. Don Giovanni's reckless career as an insatiable and heartless seducer has obviously begun long before the story opens. Indeed, when Don Giovanni's servant Leporello recites a catalogue of his master's conquests (including the '1003' in Spain alone), it is clear just how long the Dream Stage of the adventure, when the hero was 'getting away with it', must have lasted. But as the opera begins, Don Giovanni is for the first time beginning to ran into serious trouble. He is embarking on a sequence of events which will first drive him into a mounting frenzy of frustration and ultimately destroy him. In the opening scene we see his latest attempted conquest, Donna Anna (who is engaged to Don Ottavio) struggling to get away from him. Her father, the Commendatore, intervenes and Don Giovanni kills him: the fatal 'dark act' which is going to be his downfall. From then on the whole story shows the hero getting enmeshed in an ever-tightening web of frustration, as he is driven on by his fatal weakness and only succeeds in arousing around him an ever-growing army of opponents. He attempts to seduce a woman in disguise, only to find to their mutual horror that she is one of his former conquests, Donna Elvira, whom he had cruelly thrown aside. He attempts to seduce the pretty young peasant girl Zerlina, and not only is frustrated by the intervention of Donna Elvira but also arouses the vengeful wrath of Zerlina's betrothed, Masetto. He now has on his trail both Masetto and Donna Anna's betrothed, Don Ottavio. He even falls out for a time with the only person who has hitherto always remained faithful to him, Leporello. Don Giovanni makes a last desperate attempt to seduce Donna Elvira's maid and is again frustrated. Everyone is now set against him, in a typical Nightmare Stage pursuit. And it is at this moment that, having fled into a graveyard, Don Giovanni finds himself confronted with the grim statue of the Commendatore, who seems, as in some nightmarish hallucination, to be addressing him. Mockingly he invites the statue to dinner and is horrified to hear it accept. Finally when he is sitting down to his supper table, the statue enters. After a terrifying exchange, the fires of hell blaze up in the darkness and the ghostly statue of his victim carries Don Giovanni off to his doom.

### The Devils

We end this chapter by looking at a story which presents a subtle variation on the basic shape of the tragic plot, not least because it mixes together both the forms of the plot we have been looking at: Dostoyevsky's great prophetic novel on the social and spiritual disintegration of late-nineteenth century, pre-Revolutionary Russia, *The Devils* (or *The Possessed*). For a long time – nearly 400 pages of a 700-page book – it is not entirely clear what plot is shaping the narrative, or even whether the book has a clearly defined plot at all. But when the plot does finally emerge we see that one reason why this novel is in some ways so puzzling is that it is made up of two quite distinct but interwoven tragedies which eventually converge. The first is a collective tragedy, drawing in a large group of people, and this has a very long Anticipation Stage which occupies the greater part of the book. The other is the personal tragedy of the character who becomes the story's 'dark hero', Nikolai Stavrogin – and this has already been through its initial stages before the opening of the story, as Dostoyevsky unfolds it.

The early chapters of the novel, as we are introduced to the life of a provincial Russian town, are in fact dominated by two middle-aged characters, the rich, indulgent widow Mrs Stavrogin and her weak, vain hanger-on Mr Verkhovensky, who likes to flatter himself that he is feared by the government in distant St Petersburg as a 'dangerous liberal'. But eventually we come to see these two primarily in their role as mother and father to the other two leading characters of the book, who return to the town after some years in the capital: Mrs Stavrogin's son Nikolai and Mr Verkhovensky's son Peter. The handsome Nikolai is a mysterious, romantic figure who returns with something of a scandalous reputation for having lived strangely and dissolutely, Outwardly he seems grave and well-mannered, but he shocks polite society in the town by one or two apparently inexplicable lapses, such as biting the ear of the provincial governor. His friend and admirer Peter Verkhovensky has apparently been associated with a secret society of revolutionaries.

Even after their return, life in the town continues for a long time to flow fairly placidly onwards, like a great river. But then odd little incidents occur, as if the surface is being disturbed by eddies, warning of the approach of some mighty cataract. A strange, crippled girl, Maria Lebyatkin, arrives, and it seems she may be married to Nikolai Stavrogin. A psychopathic criminal Fedka turns up in the town, and shortly afterwards everyone is scandalised by the theft of precious stones from a much-prized icon in the church. One night Fedka waylays Stavrogin and offers to murder his embarrassing wife for money, a suggestion Nikolai angrily dismisses. Finally there is a meeting of 15 people of loosely-assorted progressive or revolutionary views, organised by Peter Verkhovensky and attended by Stavrogin; and the outlines of the plot at last begin to emerge. We gather that Verkhovensky has a wild dream of unleashing chaos in the town as a preliminary to revolution. He is somehow inspired by a vision of Stavrogin as the charismatic figure of destiny who will then emerge as leader; but Stavrogin will apparently have none of this, and has already turned angrily on Verkhovensky, accusing him of wishing to arrange for the murder of his wife Maria and of another revolutionary Shatov, suspected of being a police spy, as a way to cement the revolutionaries' determination. What we are seeing, well over halfway through the book, is the culmination of a subtly sketched Anticipation Stage, where a whole mass of disparate dreams and vague fantasies about chaos, violence and some future revolution are at last being given their Focus round some specific plan.

But our attention is then abruptly switched to the much more personal tragedy which has already been unfolding for a long time in the life of Nikolai Stavrogin himself. He visits a wise old monk, Father Tikhon, and presents him with a written confession of a hideous episode which had taken place when he was living in St Petersburg. Finding himself alone one day in his lodgings with the daughter of the house, a 12-year old girl called Matryosha, he had on a sudden depraved impulse violently raped her. The girl had been reduced to such a state of shock that she had sat in a catatonic trance, only able to mutter 'I have killed God', and had eventually hanged herself. Stavrogin had found himself morally quite numb about the episode, but from then on had begun to act more and more strangely. For no apparent reason he had gone through a ceremony of marriage with the crippled and mentally defective Maria Lebyatkin. He had then abandoned her and travelled abroad for three years, where he had entered on an affair with Lisa Drozdov, a girl from the same town, and for a while contemplated bigamously marrying her, although he had then abruptly ended the affair (Lisa is now back home, and we have already met her as a friend of Mrs Stavrogin's). Eventually Nikolai had returned to their home town himself, where his strange behaviour now has some explanation. He has become plagued by hallucinations, often seeming to sense near him

'some evil creature, mocking and "rational", which took on a variety of personalities and characters, but which he knew was always the same creature'

and which he supposes to be the Devil. He has finally, in a desperate bid to free himself of his curse (or at least to come clean about it), had 300 copies printed of his 'Confession', which he is planning to distribute through the town. But at the end of their interview, Father Tikhon merely warns Stavrogin that he will probably 'feel driven to commit some new and still more heinous crime to avoid publication of the confession'. He has sensed that, like many tragic heroes wriggling on the hook in the Frustration Stage, Stavrogin may now be tempted into some new dark act, in a last effort at a cover up.

All is now set up for the concluding chapters of the novel which are as packed with incident as the earlier chapters seem uneventful. There are signs, such as a protest march of workers at the local factory, that some strange spirit of disorder is loose in the town which no one seems able to control. Everything comes to a climax at an absurd literary festival, organised by various local notables, with speeches and a ball. As this is unfolding, disorder breaks out, in a way which seems not so much planned as simply the breaking of the storm which has been brewing up throughout the preceding 500 pages of the book. The festival disintegrates into chaos. A great fire breaks out in part of the town and, in a house where the fire appears to have been started, the bodies of Maria and her brother are found. They have been murdered by Fedka the convict, in circumstances not altogether clear. What is clear, as the spirit of disorder takes charge in the town, is that Nikolai Stavrogin watches as if in a trance a horrifying sequence of events which he has no direct part in, but which in some terrible way he has inspired and made possible (as he admits about the first killings, 'I didn't kill them – I was against the killing, but I knew they were going to be killed and I didn't stop the killers'). Other deaths follow in chaotic profusion. Lisa, the other girl wronged by Stavrogin but who still loves him, is almost casually murdered by an angry mob. The convict Fedka is found murdered outside the town. Old Mr Verkhovensky makes a last pitiful attempt to run away from Mrs Stavrogin's suffocating clutches and dies on the journey. The growing nightmare finds a final focus round Peter Verkhovensky's organising of the cold-blooded killing of the unhappy Shatov by a group of would-be 'revolutionaries', which unleashes among those responsible a holocaust of remorse, confessions and suicide. At last Nikolai Stavrogin can take no more and hangs himself.

The overwhelming impression of *The Devils* – clearly intended from Dostoyevsky's opening quotation of the biblical story of the Gadarene swine – is of a whole group of people becoming possessed, for all sorts of disparate reasons, by a collective fantasy of violent 'revolutionary action'. For a long time they are merely swept along in a state of vague anticipation, talking and dreaming of the blood and chaos which is going to be unleashed on some day in the distant future. But finally the day arrives and it is not long before the Dream Stage of initial chaos spins rapidly out of control, until some of them are carried over the edge into a deadly vortex of destruction and self-destruction. Such, in a sense, is the greater Tragedy described by the book; and it was this which made the novel historically prophetic. But the greater Tragedy could not have taken place in the way it did without the much more personal and intense tragedy of Stavrogin, beginning with the rape and suicide of little Matryosha in St Petersburg. Without Stavrogin, the chief instigator of the collective Tragedy, Peter Verkhovensky would not have had his inspiration, his imagined leader. Verkhovensky would not have had his excuse to plot the murder of the crippled Maria, the event which more than any other eventually turns the town into a bloodbath, if it had not been for Stavrogin's reckless folly in marrying her. Stavrogin would not have got into the state where he was tempted into the quixotic and heartless gesture of marrying Maria if it had not been for the horrible preceding episode of Matryosha's death. Stavrogin could not have committed his crime against Matryosha, if he had not already lost his moral centre. And neither he nor Peter Verkhovensky would have lost their moral bearings and been reduced to the state where the 'devils' could so easily have possessed them in the first place, so Dostoyevsky's thread runs, without the initial weakness of their parents: Mrs Stavrogin's spoiling indulgence of her beloved Nikolai and Mr Verkhovensky's self-deluding fantasies about being a 'dangerous liberal'; which is why these two are placed in such a prominent position at the beginning of the story.

*The Devils* is one of the blackest of all literary portrayals of the spirit of Tragedy entering the ascendant, taking over men's hearts and minds and prompting them to unleash a torrent of death and destruction which eventually sweeps them away. In fact it provides an appropriate cue for us at last to stand back to look at this kind of story in more general terms: to examine what it is in the inner logic of storytelling which decrees that such disparate figures as Faust and Macbeth, Humbert Humbert and Dorian Gray, Anna Karenina and Emma Bovary, Don Giovanni and Nikolai Stavrogin, should all ultimately be trapped in the same black vortex and be carried down to the same violent end. So fundamental is this question to the whole of storytelling (and to the relationship of stories to what we call 'real life') that it may be reserved for a separate chapter.

## Chapter 9

# Tragedy (II): The Divided Self

'Since Cassius first did whet me against Caesar
I have not slept.
Between the first acting of a dreadful thing
And the first motion, all the interim is
Like a phantasma or a hideous dream;
The Genius and the mortal instruments
Are then in council; and the state of man,
Like to a little kingdom, suffers then
The nature of an insurrection.'

Brutus, *Julius Caesar*, ii.i

'Every kingdom divided against itself is brought to desolation; and
a house divided against itself falleth.'

Jesus, *St Luke's Gospel*, 11.17

One of the more illuminating ways to look at the pattern of Tragedy is to contrast it with the types of plot we discussed earlier.

In some respects the position of the hero or heroine at the beginning of a Tragedy is not dissimilar to that of the hero or heroine at the opening of, say, a Quest or a Rags to Riches story. We first meet them in some situation which does not give ease or satisfaction, which cries out for change. Then something happens which points the way forward. They receive some kind of 'Call' which leads them out of their dissatisfying state into the adventure which is going to transform their lives.

The great difference between Tragedy and other kinds of story begins with the nature of the summons which draws them into that adventure. When the hero of an Overcoming the Monster story or a Quest receives the 'Call' – however hazardous the course it opens out to him – we are in no doubt it is right for him to answer it. When the hero or heroine of Tragedy reaches the same point we are uneasy. We are aware that the 'Call' is not of the same nature; which is why it may more aptly be described as the 'Temptation'.

This is because of the peculiar way in which the summons to action is directed at one particular aspect of the hero or heroine's personality. We have already become aware that there is one part of them, one desire, one appetite, which is nagging at them to the point where the urge to gratify it is building up into an overwhelming obsession. This may be an appetite for power, as in the case of *Macbeth* or Marlowe's *Dr Faustus*, who dreams of winning 'power, honour and omnipotence' such as no man has ever enjoyed before. It may be a hunger for sex-

173

ual excitement or romantic passion, as with Humbert Humbert, or those two wives frustrated by their tedious, inadequate husbands, Anna Karenina and Emma Bovary. It may be a longing for sensation rather vaguer and harder to define, as in the examples of Dorian Gray or Bonnie and Clyde, committing bank robberies for 'kicks', where elements of sexual desire and the desire for power over others are mixed together.

But in every instance we are aware that what their obsession is drawing them into is something which violates and defies some prohibition or law or convention or duty or commitment or standard of normality. They are being tempted into stepping outside the bounds which circumscribe them.[1] Icarus wishes to defy the balance of the natural laws which govern his flight. Doctor Faustus wishes to step outside the bounds of conventional knowledge. Dr Jekyll and Dorian Gray wish to step outside the bounds of morality. Anna Karenina and Emma Bovary wish to step outside the bounds of their marriages. In every case, the tragic hero or heroine has come to sense the circumstances in which we originally discover them – Macbeth, Bonnie and Clyde, Humbert Humbert, Don José – as in some way irksome, restricting, tedious, inadequate.

And it is this sense of constriction from which the Temptation – whether it originates within themselves or is personified in the figure of a Tempter or Temptress who lures them on – seems to offer the promise of almost unimaginably exhilarating release.

This leads on to a second difference between the pattern of Tragedy and that of other kinds of story. When the hero of a Quest or an Overcoming the Monster story receives the 'Call', not only are we in no doubt that they should answer it: we know that they will have to commit themselves to their adventure totally, body, mind, heart and soul; and they usually leave no one else in any doubt as to their intentions. We are given the impression of someone completely and openly dedicated to the course he is embarking on.

When the heroes or heroines of Tragedy are faced with the Temptation it is a different matter. In many instances we see them struggling or wavering before they succumb, a sign that they are initially by no means single-minded about giving way. Faustus wrestles with himself before signing his pact with the Devil, as he hears the arguments of the 'Evil Angel' urging him on and the 'Good Angel' trying to call him back. Macbeth falters at the sight of the dagger in his hand, until Lady Macbeth as his 'evil angel' pushes him onward. Brutus wavers through the course of the stormy, ill-omened night before Caesar's murder, until the 'evil angel' Cassius finally persuades him. Don José is torn between his 'good angel' Micaela, and his 'evil angel' Carmen.

---

1. Hence the true meaning behind the Greek notion of *hubris*, originally derived from *hyper* meaning 'over'. We shall look later at why the ancient Greeks saw the tragic pattern as one of hubris followed by nemesis. Although in the modern world the term *hubris* is often understood to mean a kind of cosmic arrogance or pride (of the type inviting a fall), its derivation shows how it was originally meant to convey precisely that idea of 'stepping over the bounds' discussed here (see Chapter 20).

In each instance it is as if part of them is reluctant to commit the irrevocable act which another part of them has come to desire: as if, right from the start, the tragic hero or heroine is a 'divided self', one part of their personality striving against another.

A second way in which many heroes or heroines of Tragedy may be seen as 'divided' is in the need to keep their 'dark' impulses and actions hidden from the world behind a 'light' or respectable front. The main reason why *Dr Jekyll and Mr Hyde* has become one of the most celebrated stories of the English-speaking world is precisely because it crystallises this familiar motif so vividly, by making the central characteristic of the story the splitting of the hero into two quite distinct personalities, the respectable, law-abiding Jekyll and his secret 'shadow-self', the deformed and totally amoral 'night creature' Hyde. In *The Picture of Dorian Gray* the split is personified in the contract between the hero's perennially youthful beauty, unmarked by his crimes and moral excesses, and the portrait hidden away which carried the full burden of the moral and physical degeneration marking Gray's downward path. Professor Humbert, the great-grandson of two Dorset clergymen, for a long time manages to keep his secret obsession with little girls hidden behind the front of the respectable academic. He leads a 'double life', just as in their different ways, and for varying amounts of time, do the murderer Macbeth and the adulterous Anna Karenina and Emma Bovary.

In general we may speak of a split between the 'light' and 'dark' sides of all these characters: and it is, of course, their 'dark' side, initially hidden from the world, which is worked up into a state of anticipatory obsession by the Temptation. But sooner or later they succumb. The 'dark' energy finds its Focus. Macbeth screws up his determination to kill Duncan, Don José succumbs to the charms of Carmen, Anna Karenina succumbs to the charms of Vronsky, Humbert seduces the willing Lolita, Faustus seals his pact with Mephistopheles: they have passed the point of no return. And the first consequence is a flood of nervous excitement, marking their entry into a new stage. As Dr Jekyll puts it, when he first manages to effect the switch into his Hyde-self:

> 'I was conscious of a heady recklessness, a current of disordered sensual images running like a mill race in my fancy, a solution of the bounds of obligation...'

The bounds have been overstepped. Suddenly all seems possible. We are aware that our hero or heroine has left the comparative safety and security of the situation in which they began, like a boat launched out from the shore onto the unknown currents of a fast-flowing river. And to begin with it is fiercely exhilarating to be whirled along in this manner. But where is it going to lead them?

One of the most significant facts about stories, as we know, is their drive to work towards an ending: an ending which will give us the sense that everything set in train during the story has been resolved. In almost any story we see the hero or heroine leaving their initial state for a period of still greater uncertainty, when all seems more than ever unresolved. But where the story has a happy ending, we eventually see them arrive at a state where they can come to rest, on new and much more secure foundations. If a central part has been played in the story by some great threat or shadow, that shadow will have been lifted. If there is division between the characters, it will in some way or other have been resolved, usually in a general spirit of reconciliation. We have a profound sense that things are at least, in every way, complete. And symbolising that completion, at the heart of most happy endings, there is the spectacle of a hero and heroine united in love, with the future ahead of them.

The whole point of Tragedy, of course, is that it is not like that. It is somehow in the nature of the course the hero or heroine has embarked on that they are not going to reach that happy and secure point of rest. They may imagine that, if only they can reach such and such a place, they will be secure. Indeed a large part of their time is often spent striving towards just such a fondly imagined goal. But the trouble is that the ground keeps on giving way under their feet. From the moment they succumb to the Temptation and imagine that they are about to start enjoying their rewards, nothing turns out quite as they expected. Indeed, if we look closely at the unfolding of any of the tragedies we have been considering, we can see how the mood of the central figure is continually swinging between anticipation and frustration throughout the story. Nothing for the hero or heroine bent on a tragic course can even quite resolve. And for this there are two, closely related reasons.

The first is that, when they embark on their course, there is always something which they overlook. It is not for nothing that we apply the word 'reckless' to the mood in which they set out: they have their attention fixed so obsessively on one point, one object of desire, that they do not pay heed to other factors in the overall context in which they are operating which may therefore produce consequences which their restricted vision fails to foresee. When Icarus ascends upwards in his heady flight towards the sun he shuts his mind to the physical laws governing his flight. When Don José succumbs to his infatuation for Carmen, he has become blinded to the possibility that she may eventually switch her affections to someone else just as casually as she switches them to him. When Macbeth carries out the murder of Duncan his only conscious thought is that he is removing the one obstacle between himself and his heart's desire, the kingship. It does not enter his mind that his crime might one day be found out.

In fact we see the heroes and heroines of Tragedy becoming more and more ensnared in their predicament, precisely like the hero of one of those 'Stickfast' tales in folklore where, with every attempt to get free (like Macbeth murdering the suspicious Banquo) he only gets a little more trapped: except that when Brer Rabbit gets stuck to the Tar Baby he is falling into a trap laid for him by someone else, whereas the heroes and heroines of Tragedy are becoming ensnared by some obsessive desire which springs ultimately from themselves. In this respect it is no accident that we so often, in relation to the central figures of Tragedy, see reference to the words 'dream' and 'fantasy'. We naturally use such words to describe the state of mind of someone who has in some way lost touch with the reality of the world around him. And this is precisely what is happening to the hero and heroine of a Tragedy. They are being drawn into a kind of fantasy or dream-state, in which their obsession with gratifying one desire or appetite over-rules their capacity for wider judgement. Having entered into such a state of illusion, they slide further and further into it. Having made one false move, they are led into another and another in an increasingly desperate bid to shore up or retrieve their position. They are set more and more at odds with the reality of the world around them – until finally it begins to close in on them, demanding a reckoning.[2]

Nowhere do we see this inexorable process more clearly reflected – and this is the second reason why the course followed by the hero or heroine of Tragedy cannot reach a satisfactory resolution – than in the evolving nature of their relations with the other people around them in the story.

At the beginning of a full five-stage Tragedy, the central figure is always part of a community, a network of relationships, linked to other people by ties of loyalty, friendship, family or marriage. And one of the most important things which happens to such heroes and heroines as they embark on their tragic course is that they begin to break those bonds of loyalty, friendship and love (even if, initially, they may form other alliances). It is the very essence of Tragedy that the hero or heroine should become, step by step, separated from other people. Often they separate themselves in the most obvious, violent and final way possible, by causing other people's deaths. And here we must particularly note the kind of people around the hero or heroine who are most likely to die in a Tragedy.

In tragedies centred on a hero, we may single out four types of victim who are particularly likely to suffer as a result of the hero's reckless course. Two of these are male, two female – and we may describe them as:

the Good Old Man
the Rival or 'Shadow'
the Innocent Young Girl
the Temptress.

2. A story which perfectly reflects the pattern of how fantasy escalates out of control is the *Sorcerer's Apprentice*, made famous in modern times through the musical version by Paul Dukas (1897), based on a poem by Goethe (1779), and then used by Walt Disney for an episode in the film *Fantasia* (1940). The tale originated with the second-century Roman poet Lucian. An old sorcerer leaves his young apprentice to fetch water from the well. The boy remembers the spell used by his master to command a magic broomstick and orders the stick to do the work (Focus). For a while the stick fetches the pails of water and all goes well (Dream Stage). But when eventually enough water has been brought, the boy realises to his horror he does not know how to tell it to stop (Frustration Stage). As ever more buckets pile up, the boy in desperation takes an axe to the stick. This merely splits the stick in two, so that the two halves now fetch twice as much water as before (Nightmare Stage). The apprentice's use of the axe thus exemplifies how we so often in Tragedy see a hero or heroine driven to commit a second dark act in a desperate bid to avoid the consequences of the first. It is this which triggers off the Nightmare Stage and their eventual destruction. In this instance, the story does not follow the Tragic pattern to its conclusion because, just when it seems the house is about to be washed away by the flood, the Sorcerer returns and orders the broomstick to stop.

## The Good Old Man

This is a figure older than the hero, who in some way represents kingly or father-ly authority. Examples are Duncan, killed by Macbeth; Julius Caesar, killed by Brutus; the Commendatore, killed by Don Giovanni.

## The Rival or 'Shadow'

This is a figure in some way on a level with the hero (e.g., by age, rank or some other similarity) who comes to stand as a kind of 'opposite' and threat to him. An obvious example is Banquo, Macbeth's comrade in arms and fellow-general, who is promised that his descendants will succeed where Macbeth fails and who is the first to see through his old friend's crimes. Another instance is Jim Vane, the young brother of the actress Sibyl Vane, who is driven by a pure love for his wronged sister, just as Dorian Gray's love for her is impure. A third is Quilty, the lover who steals Lolita off Humbert Humbert. He stands as a threatening 'shadow' to the hero in the opposite way, precisely because he is so similar to Humbert, sharing his obsession; which is why Humbert feels eventually driven to murder him.

Even more significant than the hero's relations with these male figures are those between him and the chief feminine figures in the story: particularly when we bear in mind how important it is to a fully resolved happy ending that the hero should eventually be brought together with a heroine as his 'other half' in perfect, loving union.

The chief feminine figures in Tragedy also tend to polarise into two distinct types:

## The Innocent Young Girl

On the one hand, most poignant of all the hero's victims because she is so defence-less against his hard-hearted egotism, there is the innocent young girl. She stands in relation to the hero as 'good angel', but is inadequate to sway him. Sooner or later the hero brutally rejects her. And there is no moment in Tragedy more preg-nant with the horror of what is happening to the hero on his downward path than when the fate of such a girl is decided: as when little Matryosha, after being raped by Stavrogin, sits in her trance muttering 'I have killed God', before committing suicide. Sibyl Vane, rejected by Dorian Gray, does likewise. When little Micaela is finally rejected by Don José and creeps away into the shadows, we know he is doomed. The whole tragedy of Othello is contained precisely in the way that he blindly turns on the 'good angel' of his life, his 'other half' Desdemona, and stabs her to death.

## The Temptress

The other type of heroine in Tragedy is quite different, in that she is herself a 'dark' figure, leading the hero on. Even so, the Temptress almost invariably ends up dying a violent death, usually at much the same time as the hero. Bonnie, hav-ing drawn Clyde into his life of violent crime, is shot down with him in the closing moments of the story. Cleopatra, having lured Antony away from his manly 'Roman self' and played a crucial part in dragging him down to military humiliation, commits suicide shortly after he does. The most terrible symptom of the nightmare closing in on Macbeth is the onset of his wife's insanity, leading to her mysterious death shortly before his own.

At least these 'dark' heroines remain faithful to the man they have drawn down to destruction. In other versions of the theme the Temptress slips away from the hero in the closing stages, and nothing contributes more to his mounting sense of frustration than the fact that the woman for whom he has staked all proves ultimately elusive. Humbert loses Lolita. Carmen's abandonment of Don José drives him to final distraction. Catherine, the 'apparition' who bewitches Jules and Jim, ends up by slipping away from one and dragging the other down to his doom. And nowhere is this motif of the 'elusive feminine' presented more subtly than in *Doctor Faustus* where, as the last, supreme demonstration of his devil-given powers, the hero is permitted to conjure up the most beautiful woman who has ever lived, Helen of Troy. Faustus steps forward to seize and kiss her. She turns out to be just another insubstantial vision, and vanishes. At last he knows all is lost.

In every instance the hero finds himself unable to reach the fulfilment he craves, where he can achieve complete and lasting union with his desired 'other half'. Either she drags him down to share his destruction, or she skips away from him like a will o' the wisp. The same is true, in reverse, of tragedies centred on a heroine.

Both Anna Karenina and Emma Bovary leave the dull, inadequate security of their marriages for men who set them on fire with a fantasy of romantic passion. In each case they cannot reach the new security they dream of, where they can at last achieve the sense of total union with another man. In each case they begin to flounder and struggle: part of them still wishing to push onward, part now longing to get back to the dull security they so recklessly abandoned. In *Anna Karenina* there is that superb description of the 'divided self' when, at the height of the Frustration Stage, Anna tells her husband:

> 'there is another in me…I am afraid of her. It was she who fell in love with the other one…that other is not I.'

But it is the dark 'other self' which eventually wins, leading Anna to reject Karenin for the last time and to throw in her lot irrevocably with Vronsky. No sooner has she done so than her lover begins to slip away, a will o' the wisp, leaving her to disintegrate towards that terrible final moment when, all alone, she flings herself beneath the wheels of the advancing train.

The point about the heroes and heroines of Tragedy is that they end up utterly alone (even if, occasionally, like Bonnie and Clyde, hero and heroine die together), completely cut off from the rest of society. They have been drawn by some part of themselves into a course of action which is fundamentally selfish, putting some egocentric desire above every other consideration, isolating them both from reality and from other people. Initially, in the Dream Stage, they succeed in imposing their will on the world and the people around them. They have broken the rules and seem to be getting away with it, because they have seized the initiative and because other people are not yet fully aware of what they are up to.

But gradually the truth of what they are doing begins to dawn on others. Those around them begin to constellate in opposition. The hero or heroine having first set themselves against others, we now see the rest of society gradually setting itself against them.

Finally, having torn and trampled the network of relationships originally surrounding them into shreds, the hero or heroine is left alone. Whereas in other types of story the tendency is for a general gathering together at the end, round the central union of the hero and the heroine, in Tragedy exactly the reverse happens. The hero and heroine are divided in every way: split within themselves, split from their 'other self', split from the rest of society, which has gathered together only to encompass their destruction. Entirely isolated, all that is left is that their life should be violently extinguished.

In this image of an incomplete, egocentric figure who meets a lonely and violent end, we may recognise the essential characteristics of another deeply familiar figure from stories, whom we have already met in quite another context. We begin the next chapter by exploring some of the striking parallels which emerge between the hero or heroine of Tragedy and that figure we previously encountered, from a very different standpoint, as the Monster.

## Chapter 10

# Tragedy (III): The Hero as Monster

'I that am curtail'd of this fair proportion,
Cheated of feature by dissembling nature,
Deform'd, unfiinish'd, sent before my time
Into this breathing world, scarce half made up ...
Have no delight to pass away the time
Unless to spy my shadow in the sun,
And descant on mine own deformity.
And therefore, since I cannot prove a lover,
To entertain these fair, well spoken days,
I am determined to prove a villain.'

*Richard III*, i.1

When we hear these words spoken at the beginning of a story by a twisted hunch-back, exulting in his physical and moral deformity, we have little difficulty in recognising him at once as a 'monster'. Indeed Richard of Gloster, as portrayed by Shakespeare, is one of the most explicitly monstrous figures in all storytelling.

Since we are following the story, as it were, through his eyes, *Richard III* is a Tragedy. We see him, behind the 'light' mask of charm he wears to the world, plotting his way ruthlessly to the throne, over a mounting pile of corpses. In familiar tragic manner we see his mounting ambition and treachery casting an ever-longer shadow of fear and suspicion – until at last positive opposition to him begins to constellate round the figure of Henry Earl of Richmond.

But at this point, when we see Richmond landing in England, determined to seek out and destroy the 'wretched, bloody and usurping boar' who 'lives even now at the centre of this isle', it is as if we are being given a glimpse of another plot altogether. Henry is just like the brave young hero of an Overcoming the Monster story, setting out to confront and overthrow a towering figure of evil. On the eve of the battle of Bosworth we return to see events through Richard's eyes, the monster cornered at last, finally into the Nightmare Stage: a 'divided self' as he sees the fearful procession of his victims' ghosts. Stricken by 'coward conscience', he recognises how his foul crimes have left him all alone. The next day Richmond confronts Richard and kills him. exulting 'the day is ours, the bloody dog is slain'. Like many other monster-slayers, Richmond then succeeds to the kingdom and wins the hand of his chosen queen, the 'true' Elizabeth.

In other words, we see here how these two plots – Tragedy and Overcoming the Monster – may often be looking at the same basic pattern of events from two quite different points of view. If we were to look at the story of David and Goliath from

181

Goliath's point of view, it would seem like the end of a Tragedy. Conversely, what we are seeing in a certain kind of Tragedy, is the process whereby a human being may be transformed into a 'monster'. We are being shown how a 'monster' comes into being in the first place. The story of *Dr Jekyll and Mr Hyde* is the story of how a seemingly respectable doctor is transformed, step by step, into a hideous, deformed monster, Hyde. The story of *Macbeth* shows how a successful soldier, admired by everyone, is gradually transformed into the monster of the later stages of the play, with Macduff cast in the role of monster-slayer – even down to Macduff's last words to Macbeth, as they exit fighting:

> 'We'll have thee, as our rarer monsters are,
> painted upon a pole, and underwrit
> Here you may see the tyrant.'

Humbert Humbert, as he discloses his perverse love for little girls and the amoral heartlessness of his behaviour towards Lolita's mother, gradually reveals himself as the monster who can end up by committing the appalling cold-blooded murder of Quilty. The portrait in *The Picture of Dorian Gray* pitilessly reflects the gradual corruption of a beautiful young man into a monster 'hideous, wrinkled and loathsome' to behold. And if we recall the three chief modes of behaviour which, in an earlier chapter, we saw as typical of the 'Monster' in story-telling – the Monster as Predator, as Holdfast and as Avenger – we can see how closely this may correspond to the behaviour of the tragic hero, as he goes through the stages of his rise and fall. When we first meet Macbeth or Humbert Humbert, we see them turning into Predators, determined to get hold of some prize: the kingship, Lolita. We then see them, having won the object of their desire, deter-mined Holdfast-like to hang on to it. Finally we see their possession challenged, when they lash out blindly in the role of Avenger: Macbeth ordering the killing of Macduff's household, Humbert killing Quilty.

But at this point we must recognise, of course, that by no means all the heroes and heroines of Tragedy are such complete 'monsters'. It is hard to see Icarus, for instance, as anything more than a foolish boy, who harms no one but himself. Brutus, who killed Caesar not to gratify his own ambition but because he finally accepted that Caesar's ambition had become a threat to the public good, would hardly have been given by his opponents the epitaph 'the noblest Roman of them all' if they had seen him as a monster. Even Antony himself scarcely became a monster, although his actions must have led to the deaths of thousands. He was brought to his destruction as a 'divided self' by weakness and by a foolish love, rather than by that excess of ruthlessness inseparable from a true monster.

In fact we can now begin to look at Tragedy from a rather different perspective. So far we have been looking at it essentially in terms of the outlines of the plot. Now we must take into account the gradations which exist within the framework of that plot, according to the extent to which the hero or heroine is primarily the malevolent author of other people's sufferings, or is just a victim of his or her own folly. In an earlier chapter, and a different context, we distinguished between 'active' and 'passive' characters. Here we employ much the same distinction, and it is obviously the more 'active', aggressive tragic heroes – Macbeth, Richard III, Dorian Gray, Mr Hyde – who most completely correspond to the condition of the 'monster'.

On the other hand, those who are least monstrous fall into two groups. The first includes those heroes and heroines who, although egocentric, are most 'passive' and obviously victims, like Jules and Jim who seem simply unmanly and impotent as they are drawn down to destruction by the increasingly mad Catherine (it is she who becomes the monster, the chief dark figure of the story). The pitiful Don José is little more than a passive victim of Carmen's wiles, until the closing scene where he is turned into a raging monster by his desperate frustration at losing her. Even Faustus is much more a victim than an 'active' hero, because it is always Mephistopheles who is pulling the strings and making a fool of him, and he does no serious or obvious harm to anyone else (although in Goethe's version Faust is made to violate and then brutally reject an Innocent Young Girl, Margareta, whose consequent death marks the climax of Part One of the story).

The other category includes those heroes whose motivation is tinged by consideration for something higher and nobler than just their own personal gratification. Few of the examples we have looked at so far might seem to fall under such a heading, with the exception of Brutus: though even he, after a revealing inner moral struggle, puts his hand to the cold-blooded murder of one of his oldest friends, at the instigation of two others, the 'envious' Casca and the 'lean and hungry' Cassius, whose motivation may not be so obviously high-minded.

But here, as we consider the possibility of tragedies where there may be some redeeming feature to the hero, we are beginning to move on to another level of this plot altogether.

## Tragedies of redemption and fulfilment

The essence of Tragedy as we have seen it so far is that it shows a hero or heroine who commits some great offence and is then drawn down, step by step, into paying the price. We are never in much doubt in such stories as to where the balance lies between darkness and light. At the outset, the hero or heroine may be made up of both light and dark qualities. But their dark side prevails, and as they remain set on their disastrous course without serious deviation or change of course, they tend to become darker and darker, while the light in the story constellates more and more outside them: first and most poignantly in their innocent victims; finally, triumphantly, in those who gather in opposition to overthrow them. This is why some tragedies, such as *Macbeth* or *Richard III*, can even end on a note of solemn rejoicing. The great life-denying monster who has increasingly cast his shadow on all around has at last been overthrown. Life can begin to flow again. Ultimately the destruction of the dark hero has been a victory for light.

But we are about to look at some familiar examples of Tragedy where the balance between darkness and light falls rather differently. First we are going to look at two stories which begin in familiar tragic manner, but where the hero does not just plunge blindly on towards destruction. As the story progresses he begins to go through a real change of heart. Instead of becoming darker and darker as he gets further locked into egocentricity, he begins to turn into a light figure, even though it is not enough ultimately to save him from destruction. Next we shall look at another story which begins with the hero showing a fatal weakness: but here it is not so much a change of heart which alters the tone of the ending as his recovery of manly strength, which enables him to turn his death into a glorious victory. Then we shall look at a great Tragedy where the hero eventually manages to purge himself of the darkness which has infected him, and is released. Finally we shall look at two stories right at the other end of the spectrum from those in which the hero is a monster, the centre of darkness. These are tragedies where, by a complete inversion of the usual pattern, the hero or the hero and heroine are almost wholly light throughout the story, and where the darkness which finally engulfs them springs entirely from society outside them.

Each of these six stories presents the tragic theme with a slightly different emphasis. Between them they may serve to extend this introductory survey of Tragedy to include more or less the full range of basic variations of which this extraordinarily important plot is capable.

### King Lear

At the start of *King Lear* we are left in no doubt that the hero is about to make a potentially tragic error, His wishes to divest himself of the cares and responsibilities of kingship, while still wishing to enjoy the honours and privileges which attach to being a king. He plans to divide his kingdom between his three daughters, and puts them to a test by asking them how much they love him. But when Goneril and Reagan make flowery, empty protestations of their love, it is obvious that he is allowing himself to be deceived. When Cordelia, the youngest, makes a plain little declaration that she loves him no more and no less than is right and proper, he can no longer recognise the truth at all. He angrily rejects her, his 'good angel'; she goes off into exile with the equally honest Kent, and the seeds of Tragedy are sown.

Although it is Lear's judgement which has been darkened, and which has led him into acting heartlessly and rejecting true love, it is already evident that he is primarily a victim of his own weakness rather than an active monster. The real sources of darkness in the story, the monsters unleashed by his weakness, are his heartless, false daughters Goneril and Reagan who inherit the power in his kingdom; while as a shadow to the drama of filial treachery which is about to unfold we also see the ageing Gloucester being likewise fooled by the 'sweet words' of his villainous bastard son Edmund, as he rejects his loving and true son Edgar.

The Dream Stage of Lear's fantasy, while he can imagine that he still enjoys the honour of a king and the love of his two dark daughters, does not last long. Soon Frustration sets in, as Goneril and Reagan begin to treat their father with increasing contempt, until they reject him altogether.

The Nightmare Stage begins, with the poor, weak old man wandering through a stormy night on the desolate heath, accompanied only by the Fool and by the loyal Kent, who has returned from exile to serve his king in disguise. From now on the conflict between love and treachery, light and dark, carries the play into reaches of complexity such as are rarely touched on by the more straightforward type of Tragedy. Firstly, as a premonition of what is to come, we see the drama of Gloucester who, after rejecting his true son Edgar, rejoins the forces of light by ministering to the helpless Lear, for which he has his eyes torn out by the dark sisters. Now as helpless as Lear, he is rescued by his rejected but still loving son Edgar, who comes to him in disguise and cures him of his desire to commit suicide. Then, similarly, the rejected but still loving Cordelia arrives from France to rescue her father and nurse him back to sanity, in such a way that for the first time in the story Lear begins to see the truth and to recognise and feel real love.

Finally there is a battle, in which the forces of darkness seem to be victorious, with Lear and Cordelia taken prisoner. But almost at once the forces of darkness fall out amongst themselves. The three chief dark figures, Reagan, Goneril and Edmund, having been drawn down into the vortex of their own multiple treachery, all destroy each other. Unfortunately, as a last legacy of the evil that has possessed them, they have left the order by which Cordelia is hanged. The supreme, shining symbol of pure and selfless love, the 'good angel' of the entire story, has been put to death – and Lear dies broken-hearted. We end this bleakest of all Shakespeare's plays with the sense that, although love had begun its work to win some degree of redemption from the general catastrophe, it was not enough. The forces of darkness unleashed by Lear's initial act of heartless folly had proved too powerful. And although they themselves had ultimately brought about their own destruction, by the end they have extinguished 'light' with them, leaving only its shining memory behind.

### Tannhäuser

A very different tragedy which shows the hero going through a profound and positive change of heart is Wagner's opera *Tannhäuser*. Again, the move towards light is not enough to save the hero from catastrophe, but this time there is more of a hint of hope at the end.

When we first meet Tannhäuser, he is in the Frustration Stage of his story. For a year he has been living on the Venusberg, the mountain of Venus, enjoying with the goddess the delights of sensual love, in a prolonged Dream Stage. But he has found the dream insubstantial, and now he yearns for something more satisfying. Escaping back to the real world, he finds that a song contest has been arranged and that the prize is the hand of the pure and beautiful Elizabeth, who has long loved and waited for him. She is his 'good angel'. Tannhäuser enters the contest, but when his turn comes to sing he is still so infected with the poison of Venus, his 'evil angel', that he cannot help singing shamelessly of her delights. Everyone is outraged, except the faithful Elizabeth. When the hero 'comes to himself' again, he is filled with remorse, and Elizabeth's father orders him to go to Rome to seek full absolution from the Pope.

A long time elapses, and Elizabeth goes out to watch in vain for Tannhäuser's return. She gives up hope. Finally he appears, broken and weary, and we learn that

185

the Pope has decreed it would no more be possible for him to grant Tannhäuser forgiveness than for his papal staff to bring forth leaves. Tannhäuser, in despair, is for the last time tempted to return to his dream-life with Venus, who appears to him in a vision, but when he invokes the name of Elizabeth, the goddess disappears. In fact Elizabeth, equally despairing of ever being united with her love, had died of sorrow. Tannhäuser sees her body being carried past, embraces her and dies. Pilgrims enter, carrying the Pope's wooden staff. It has put forth both leaves and flowers. Tannhäuser's sin has been purged. He has at last been united with his 'good angel', if only in death.

Both *Tannhäuser* and *King Lear* show their hero going through a change of heart under the inspiration of his 'good angel', which begins to reverse the downward tendency of the plot, drawing it upwards again towards a happy ending – though neither quite reach it. In our next example, the downward tendency is similarly reversed, although this time not through the hero discovering his capacity for true love so much as through him recovering his masculine strength. Once again it is not enough to save him from the ultimate disaster which his initial weakness has set in train, but his 'return to himself' is sufficient to change the whole character of the story's ending.

## Samson

For twenty years Samson has been a judge over Israel. We know three things about him. The first is that he possesses superhuman strength, which is particularly important since his people are locked in continual conflict with their deadly rivals, the Philistines. The second is that he has long hair, in which somehow the secret of his strength resides; if it is ever cut, he will become as weak as any ordinary mortal. The third is that he already has another weakness, for women.

One day he goes out to sleep with a prostitute, and while he is with her he is nearly trapped by the Philistines. Only his superhuman strength enables him to escape. But it is a warning of what is to come. Next he falls in love with another woman, Delilah, and this time the Philistines are more cunning. They realise that it is no good tackling him on his superior function, his physical strength: they must go behind it, to his weakness, and they bribe Delilah to use her loving wiles to wheedle out of him the secret of where his strength lies. Three times she tries, and each time he brushes her aside with a misleading answer. But when she persists, throwing everything into her final attempt by the age-old device of pleading 'How can you say you love me when you won't tell me the truth?', he finally and fatally weakens. He reveals his secret, she waits until he is asleep and has his hair shaven off. When he wakes up, it is too late. He has fallen into the hands of the Philistines and is too weak to free himself.

From this Frustration Stage, Samson is quickly thrust into the Nightmare Stage, when the Philistines put out his eyes, bind him 'with fetters of brass' and 'he did grind in the prison house'. But what the Philistines forget is that, while he is in prison, Samson's hair will grow again.

They throw a great feast, to celebrate their capture of their deadly enemy. Three thousand Philistines gather in a great building, and when they are drunk they call for Samson to be brought in so they can mock him. He asks the boy who is leading him to guide his hand to the pillars of the building, so he can lean on them. Then, calling on his God, and with a final superhuman heave of his now recovered strength, Samson pulls the whole building down, killing everyone in it: 'so the dead which he slew at his death were more than they which he slew in his life'. It is his greatest victory.

There are important issues raised by this tale to which we shall have to return, because they have implications central to the nature of storytelling and the different psychological levels on which the basic stories can be told. As the story is presented to us, for instance, the Philistines are cast as wholly dark, unredeemedly evil; although they doubtless behaved little differently from the way the Israelites themselves would have done if they had caught the champion and strongman of the Philistines (e.g., the portrayal of Goliath). In this respect Samson's victory over 'evil' can only be seen in partial terms: we can hardly see it as a great life-renewing act, an absolute victory for life over death. But in our next example, one of the most profound tragedies in literature, we get right down to bedrock: with a play which looks head on at one of the most fundamental questions which Tragedy can pose.

### The Oresteia

It is a curious fact about Greek Tragedy that so few of the plays which have survived from its golden age in the fifth century BC present the tragic theme simply in its basic five-stage form. From Aristotle we know the general theory which the Greeks developed to account for the fact that they found themselves telling stories in this way: a central part of which was that tragedy should show a hero or heroine, otherwise noble in character, but with a fatal flaw which catches them out, leading to their destruction. This might seem a perfect summing up of the story of Samson; indeed of many of the tragedies we have been looking at. In practice, however, one of the strengths of the Greek tragedians (as of the Greek mind generally) was their capacity to appreciate the complexities of human existence. They were not satisfied with black-and-white answers. They were always looking round the corner for another question to ask. Despite Aristotle's dictum that a satisfactory story should have a beginning, a middle and an end, they were always asking 'what happened before the beginning?', 'what happened after the end?', which is why so many of the stories in their mythology seem to meander on interminably, with each episode before its conclusion sowing the seeds for the next. And one of the most basic questions posed by Tragedy is this: if a tragic hero arouses such opposition by his actions that he is eventually put to death by someone else (which is after all where the tragic pattern so often ends up), where morally does that leave the person who has killed him? Is it not possible that the avenger too, in killing another human being (for whatever reason), may not have become infected by something of the very evil he is trying to counter? Is it not possible that someone else, in further revenge, may wish to kill him in turn? Where does the killing stop? Where, in any episode involving an outbreak of evil and violent conflict, can the darkness be said to have been finally eliminated?

This is the question posed by the only complete trilogy of tragedies to have survived from ancient Greece, the *Oresteia* of Aeschylus.

We begin with the tragic cycle which is unleashed when the great king of Mycenae, Agamemnon, returns home victorious from the Trojan War. During the years he has been away, his wife Clytemnaestra has enjoyed a long adulterous affair with his cousin Aegisthus. At the prospect of her husband returning, she conceives a treacherous plan to murder him, succumbing to the fantasy that she will then be able to marry Aegisthus and settle down to many more peaceful years of life in Mycenae (Anticipation Stage). When Agamemnon returns, she promptly commits the dark deed, in peculiarly shocking manner. She gives him a lavish welcome, prepares a hot bath and stabs him three times as he lies in it (along with the Trojan prophetess Cassandra whom he has brought home with him). She then comes out of the palace to proclaim to the world what she has done, exultantly describing how her husband's blood had spurted forth at her blows. The first play of the trilogy, the *Agamemnon*, thus ends on the Dream Stage of her fantasy, as she and Aegisthus rejoice at their deliverance.

As the second play, the *Choeophori*, begins, the murderous pair are into the Frustration Stage. Clytemnaestra is being troubled by ominous dreams. Worse, her son by Agamemnon, Orestes, who as escaped into exile, has now returned secretly to Mycenae where he meets his sister Electra. They conspire to avenge their father: opposition is constellating against the murderers. Orestes wins admittance to the palace by arriving in disguise and promptly kills Aegisthus. After putting the villainess Clytemnaestra through a Nightmare Stage, by holding her beneath his sword while telling her at length what he thinks of her wickedness, he kills her too. The monster has been overthrown. The five-stage cycle which began with Clytemnaestra conceiving the plan to murder her husband is concluded.

But suddenly Orestes, the triumphant instrument of vengeance, finds himself surrounded by the Eumenides, the horrible, shrieking Furies, threatening him with destruction in turn. After all, he has committed one of the gravest crimes imaginable, by killing his own mother. Who is to say that this should not properly be the beginning of a new tragic cycle, and that he should not pay the price for his crime? Precisely this question is the theme of the concluding play of the trilogy, the *Eumenides*.

Pursued by the shrieking, taunting Furies, Orestes tries to take sanctuary in the holiest spot of the Greek world, the temple of Apollo at Delphi. Here he is told that he must go to Athens to see the goddess of wisdom Athene, who will finally decide where justice lies.

The play concludes with Orestes in effect on trial for his life, with the vengeful Furies leading for the prosecution. Orestes pleads in his own defence that he has committed a crime, but only in righteous punishment for one much more terrible. Furthermore he has already suffered grievously for it by having to endure the torments of the Furies (who also represent the torments of conscience). Athene finally agrees that, through his suffering and remorse, he has purged his sin and should be released. The Eumenides are conciliated by the promise of a permanent place of honour in Athenian life. The play ends with the sense of some huge shadow having at last been lifted, enabling life once again to flow free.

An important aspect of the argument in the *Eumenides* is the general admission that Orestes has committed a crime, but that he had been able to expiate it. In other words, in committing his act of vengeance, he has become a dark figure (though nothing like so dark as Clytemnaestra), and only by enduring his subsequent sufferings has he won his way through to become a light figure again.

What are we to make of tragedies where the central figure or figures are not dark at all? We come finally to two stories where the usual balance of darkness and light between the central figures and the world around them is completely reversed.

### Romeo and Juliet

The story of Romeo and Juliet unfolds precisely through the five stages of the tragic cycle. But the great difference between this and all the other tragedies at which we have looked lies in where we see the fundamental split or division which contains the seeds of catastrophe. It is not so much Romeo or Juliet themselves who present us with the spectacle of a 'divided self'. The split lies in the great feud dividing their two families. The desire of the hero or heroine is not to promote conflict but to escape from it. In other words, the fault which sets them at odds with those around them lies not in themselves but outside them.

As the play opens we are at once made aware of how deep and combustible is the rift between the Montagues and the Capulets by the casual suddenness with which a brawl between members of the two households breaks out in a Verona street. We are then drawn into the Anticipation Stage as we learn how Romeo is already detached from the conflict by lovesickness. He is actually hoping to gate-crash the Capulets' ball to catch sight of the girl he loves, Rosaline. At the same time the young daughter of the Capulets, Juliet, is being told by her mother that she must bend her thoughts towards marriage, with a young man called Paris. We might almost be in the opening stages of a Comedy, with both hero and heroine headed for the wrong partners. But then, at the ball, they meet, and at once fall in love. They have found their Focus. The height of the Dream Stage quickly follows when they declare their love for each other (the 'Balcony scene') and secretly get married under the auspices of the wise old Friar Laurence.

The Frustration Stage begins when the shadow of the great feud intrudes on their love. The hot-tempered young Capulet Tybalt comes looking for Romeo, furious at how he had gatecrashed the ball in disguise. Full of the spirit of love, Romeo has no wish to fight; but when Tybalt kills his friend Mercutio, Romeo is at last infected by the darkness and is drawn into killing Tybalt in reply. It is this dark act which precipitates the fatal conclusion. The frustration of the lovers quickly worsens as Romeo is banished and Juliet's father (in the guise of 'unrelenting father') prepares to marry her off to Paris (not knowing, of course, that she is already married).

The Nightmare Stage begins, as Juliet desperately tries to escape from the approaching threat of the false marriage. Friar Laurence masterminds the plan whereby she takes a drug which makes it seem that she is dead. She is taken to the family tomb, with the intention that Romeo will come secretly at night and carry her off. And if this were Comedy, with Juliet merely in eclipse, like those other heroines who feign death, Hermione in *A Winter's Tale* and Hero in *Much Ado*, such might be the happy denouement. But here there is to be no 'recognition'. The course of deception, once embarked on, leads only to the wrong people being deceived, and misunderstanding becomes fatal. Romeo is led to believe that Juliet is truly dead and commits suicide by her side. She wakes to find that he is dead and follows suit. They achieve their final union only in death.

If this were all there was to the story, we should feel that it had come to a very bleak conclusion indeed, with the forces of darkness triumphant. But, of course, what happens is that the two families, when they learn of the catastrophe, are so appalled that they go collectively through a profound change of heart. Reconciled in mutual grief, they call off their ancient feud. We see how, in their terrible deaths, Romeo and Juliet have redeemed the divided world of Verona, enabling the story to end on an image of wholeness restored and life renewed.

At least Romeo and Juliet could not have been drawn down to their catastrophe unless Romeo himself had eventually been infected by the darkness surrounding them, in his killing of Tybalt. But finally we come to a story where the hero is not infected by the darkness surrounding him at all. We have come, in short, right to the other end of the tragic spectrum from those stories which show the hero as a monster, to the point where he is completely a centre of light. Yet, interestingly, this is precisely the reverse of how he at first appears.

### The Snow Goose

The hero of Paul Gallico's little tale *The Snow Goose*, written in England in 1940 during the darkest days of the Second World War, is Philip Rhayader, a painter, who lives all alone in an abandoned lighthouse on the Essex marshes.

To the inhabitants of the nearby community, this mysterious solitary figure seems to be a monster. Rhayader is a hunchback, his left arm is 'crippled, thin and bent at the wrist, like the claw of a bird'. But we soon learn that in reality, despite his 'mis-shapen body and dark visage', Rhayader is as far from being a monster as it is possible to be, In every other sense he is a whole man, a superb sailor, strong and at the same time gentle, full of love for 'man, the animal kingdom and all nature'. He lives alone on the marshes because he is at home with the birds and the sea, which form the subject of his 'luminous' canvases.

In other words, as he is revealed to us, Rhayader is all light and the darkness in the story is all outside him, initially in his neighbours who regard the solitary hunchback out on the marshes with suspicion, hostility and fear.

But one day one of these neighbours comes to him, a frightened little girl carrying an injured snow goose she has found. He knows at once how to look after the bird, which he calls 'The Lost Princess', and the girl Frith comes regularly to visit him, to see how the bird is getting on. Eventually the snow goose, fully recovered, flies away. Frith's visits stop and Rhayader 'learned all over again the meaning of the word "loneliness"'. The child and the 'Princess' have become intertwined together, profoundly important to him.

The following year, to Rhayader's amazement and joy, the 'Princess' returns. He leaves a message for Frith, who resumes her visits until the bird again flies off for the summer – and this pattern continues for several years, with Rhayader enjoying alternations of happiness and loneliness, each time Frith and the great bird come back into his life for a while and then disappear again.

Then three things happen, more or less simultaneously. First, Rhayader realises that Frith is no longer just a wild little girl: she has grown up into a young woman. Second, the snow goose does not fly away as usual, but had obviously decided to stay at the lighthouse: 'the Lost Princess is no more. This is her home now – of her own free will.' Both Rhayader and Frith are aware of a tumult of new feelings, involving each other, which neither dares speak of. But thirdly, the darkness and conflict of the world outside suddenly intrude on them in a new and much more violent way.

It is 1940, the time of Dunkirk. Rhayader, the sailor, decides that he must answer the call for the 'little boats' to help in the evacuation, and sails off with the snow goose flying over him, like a guardian angel, straight into the nightmare of the Dunkirk beaches. Amid this deafening hell of smoke, gunfire, exploding bombs and death, he performs astonishing feats of heroism, rescuing hundreds of men, until finally he is machine-gunned. His boat is spotted drifting through the smoke and chaos, his body slumped over the tiller, with the great bird still watching over him – until the boat is blown to pieces by a mine. But for all who have encountered him in that hell, he has become an almost legendary, supernatural figure. For days Frith waits looking out for him, until the 'Princess' returns to circle round her, as if to tell her that Rhayader is not coming back. A few weeks later a stray German bomber blasts the lighthouse out of existence.

Obviously there is something profoundly positive even about this very bleak ending. We began by seeing Rhayader rejected and taken by everyone around him to be a 'monster', even though the fault lay only in themselves. By his selfless and heroic end, we finally see his true nature revealed to the world in such a way that he becomes a redeemer, he and his bird a vision of 'light' amid the terrible surrounding darkness. It is a story which triumphantly turns the usual theme of Tragedy inside out.

One of the subtler clues to the meaning of the tragic pattern lies in the origins of the word 'tragedy' itself, coming as it does from the Greek τραγως, a 'goat'. It is derived from the ancient ritual practice of the 'scapegoat', whereby a goat or some other creature could be sacrificed to restore health to the community. The animal (or human) scapegoat was regarded as symbolically carrying the sins of the tribe; with the idea that, in its death, those sins were purged and the tribe brought back to wholeness. The pattern this re-enacted was precisely that we see at the end of a tragedy, where a whole community has been cast into shadow by the darkness emanating from the central figure. The removal of that source of darkness brings the community back into the light.

We have come a long way since we first began to explore this strange pattern in storytelling which shows how human beings may get caught up in a course of action which leads eventually to their violent and unnatural death. We have been through some of the darkest stories in the world. We have seen people, possessed by some egocentric fantasy of love or power, gradually separating themselves from everyone around them, more and more submerged in the darkness which springs from their own split, disordered psyches, until finally the violent rejection they have shown to others turns in on themselves. But we have also seen how it is possible for this downward spiral into darkness to be reversed: how it is possible for the hero or heroine to begin to knot together again, within themselves and with others around them, so that light is again breaking in on their darkness.

So far, because we have been looking at Tragedy, we have only seen this return to the light able to operate partially, ultimately insufficient to prevail against the forces of darkness which have been unleashed, and which eventually sweep the hero or heroine away. But there are, of course, stories which show that climb upward from darkness reaching its ultimate triumphant conclusion, where the hero or heroine can re-emerge into the light altogether. This leads us on to the next and last of the basic plots.

## Chapter 11
# Rebirth

> 'It was on rotting prison straw that I felt the first stirrings of good in myself. Gradually it became clear to me that the line separating good from evil runs not between states, not between classes and not between parties: it runs through the heart of each and everyone of us, and through all human hearts. This line is not stationary. It shifts and moves with the passage of the years. Even in hearts enveloped in evil, it maintains a small bridgehead of good.'
> Alexander Solzhenitsyn, *The Gulag Archipelago*

Early in our lives we come across a type of story not quite like any other. In the form in which we first encounter it, in the stories of childhood, it usually centres round the familiar fairytale cast of young heroes and heroines, princes and princesses, who have fallen foul of dark enchanters, wicked witches or evil stepmothers. But this is not a conventional Rags to Riches or Overcoming the Monster story. It contains a crucial ingredient which marks it out from either.

In the folk tale *Sleeping Beauty*, a king and queen have a baby daughter. They invite seven fairies to the little Princess's christening, and six in turn bestow great blessings on her – beauty, grace, goodness of heart, and so on. But before the last can speak an old malevolent fairy bursts in, furious at not having been invited, and lays a deadly curse on the child: that she shall prick her finger and die before she grows up. The seventh good fairy can only commute this to a sentence of a hundred years of sleep, with the promise that eventually the Princess will be liberated.

The second stage shows the little girl growing up, endowed with all the 'light' gifts laid on her at her christening – while her parents do all they can to protect her by ordering that every needle in the kingdom shall be destroyed. But eventually the day arrives when the heroine is about to enter on her adult state. She wanders into a remote and overlooked corner of her father's castle, where she discovers a mysterious old woman at a spinning wheel. Blind to the danger she is running, she asks to try the wheel. The dark prophecy is borne out, the heroine pricks her finger and swoons into unconsciousness. The rest of the castle's inhabitants follow suit, and a hedge of impenetrable thorns springs up to seal them off from the outside world. We are thus presented with one of the most haunting images in storytelling of the state of living death: the flow of life frozen in suspension.

The third stage does not unfold until decades later. Many would-be heroes have tried to penetrate to the enchanted castle without success. Only when the right moment and the perfect hero arrives can the liberation take place. At last a prince from another land chances to pass the castle, makes his way effortlessly through the hedge of thorns, finds the Princess in her remote prison and wakes her with a kiss. The whole community of the castle – from servants, guards and animals up to the king and queen – stirs back into life. The Prince and the Princess he has 'won back from the dead' are married.

*Sleeping Beauty* is based on the type of plot we may call 'Rebirth'. A hero or heroine falls under a dark spell which eventually traps them in some wintry state, akin to living death: physical or spiritual imprisonment, sleep, sickness or some other form of enchantment. For a long time they languish in this frozen condition. Then a miraculous act of redemption takes place, focused on a particular figure who helps to liberate the hero or heroine from imprisonment. From the depths of darkness they are brought up into glorious light.

Another familiar version of this theme is *Snow White*. Again a king and queen have a baby daughter. Again, shortly after her birth, a terrible shadow falls over her when the little Princess's loving mother dies, and is replaced by the vain and heartless stepmother, the chief dark figure of the story. Her overriding obsession is to get rid of Snow White, as the challenge to her own supremacy as the chief feminine figure in the kingdom, and she orders that Snow White should be taken out into the forest and killed. Only in the nick of time is the heroine given a partial reprieve, when the huntsman who has been ordered to kill her merely abandons her.

The second stage begins when she finds her way to the mysterious cottage inhabited by the seven dwarfs, who spend their days digging out treasure from caves deep in the mountains, and here Snow White settles down happily to a new life as 'little mother' to the dwarfs. But eventually the dark shadow from the outer world again falls over her, when the wicked stepmother discovers Snow White's remote place of concealment and comes three times in disguise to offer her poisoned gifts. Each time in trusting ignorance Snow White succumbs to the temptation (like Sleeping Beauty, her naivety and limited awareness make her an unwitting party to her downfall), and each time she sinks into the state of living death. On the first two occasions the dwarfs are able to bring her back to life, but on the third - when Snow White chokes on the poisoned apple – their powers are no longer sufficient to save her. They assume she is dead, and place her on a mountaintop in a glass coffin.

Just as in *Sleeping Beauty*, the third and final stage of the story takes place only when many years have elapsed, when a prince arrives from a far-off land, sees the heroine in her state of suspended animation and falls in love with her. He orders that she should be taken down the mountain. As she is carried down, the apple is dislodged. Snow White awakens from her living death, falls in love with the perfect hero who has released her and they are married.

In each of these stories we see the heroine first falling under the shadow of the dark power when she is very young. For a while it still seems to be comfortably remote, although we are aware of it unresolved and menacing in the background. Then there is a mounting sense of threat as the dark power approaches, until finally it emerges in full force, freezing the heroine in its deadly grip. Only after a long time, when it seems that the dark power has completely triumphed, does the reversal take place; when the heroine is miraculously redeemed from her imprisonment by the life-giving power of love.

## Hero redeemed by heroine

Such is one version of the plot of Rebirth. But at much the same time that we first encounter these two fairy tales, we may come across another two familiar stories which present the theme of Rebirth in another way. We still see the heroine as the central figure. Everything still hinges on a final liberation by the power of love from a state of living death. But here it is the hero who is the central imprisoned figure of the story, trapped by dark enchantment, and it is the heroine who eventually liberates him. As the story unfolds, however, she herself also falls into a state of imprisonment, trapped by the hero when he is under the dark spell – so that we finally see each being liberated from the grip of the dark power by the other.

In *The Frog Prince*, a young Princess is out playing one day with her most precious possession, a golden ball, when it rolls away and sinks into a deep pool. She is in great distress, not knowing how to get it back, when a frog hops up and offers to recover it – on condition that she will take him home and allow him to share her food and her bed. She lightly gives her promise, the ball is recovered and the Princess goes happily off home, forgetting all about her promise to the frog. Eventually there is a knock at the palace door, the Princess opens it and is horrified to see the frog, come to claim his part of the bargain. In terror, the Princess slams the door, but when her father the king hears what has happened he sternly insists that she must fulfil her promise. With a sense of loathing she allows the repulsive little creature to eat from her plate, and even to share her bed – and when he disappears the next morning, she hopes she has seen the last of him. But her nightmare is not over. The frog returns, to share her bed for three nights; and only on the third morning does she wake up to find that he has turned into his true self as a handsome Prince. He explains that he had been placed under an evil spell by an enchantress, and turned into a frog; with the condition that he could only be released if he could persuade a Princess to let him share her bed for three nights. The Princess looks at the Prince she has unwittingly redeemed with almost disbelieving joy and love, and he takes her home to be married.

A second familiar folk tale which expresses this same basic outline with rather greater subtlety is *Beauty and the Beast*; and here it is more explicitly emphasised that the heroine actually has to show love for the hero before he can be released from his outwardly repulsive and dark state (although in *The Frog Prince* the Princess's sharing of her bed is obviously symbolically related).

We begin with the familiar situation of a father and three daughters. As in *Cinderella* and many other stories, the point is to contrast two of the children, vain, proud and hard-hearted, with the third, Beauty, who is not only outwardly attractive but also good-hearted and loving. The father goes on a journey and loses his way one night in a forest. He is drawn to a mysterious, empty castle, where he finds every kind of comfort and hospitality, although he never sees anyone until he is about to leave – when he is set upon by a terrifying monster, in semi-human shape.

195

The Beast only allows him to leave on condition that he sends back his youngest daughter to live at the castle (or, in some versions, the first person he sees when he arrives home – inevitably the loving Beauty, who rushes to welcome her father). Beauty comes to the castle, full of dread, and although she is splendidly looked after and even comes to like the friendly and kindly Beast, she cannot possibly accept his proposal that she should marry him. She feels terribly trapped; but eventually the Beast allows her to return home for a while to tend her father who has fallen sick, and she breaks her promise to come back. Then, in a dream, she sees the Beast dying of grief. She rushes contritely back to the castle, just in time to find him lying in the darkness in the garden, apparently dead. She is so overcome by the love which has been secretly growing in her that she flings herself down to embrace him. He stirs back to life, and says that he only wanted to see her once more: he can now die happy. She says that he must not die, she cannot live without him. At these words, the dark castle is suddenly filled with light, music plays and she sees standing before her a handsome Prince – who tells her that he had been turned into a monster by a wicked enchantress, and that he could only win his release if a beautiful virgin would freely consent to marry him. Beauty and the Beast have redeemed each other by the power of her love – although obviously he had only been a monster in outward form. Inwardly his true self had been there all along, waiting for the right woman to bring about the moment when all his outward deformations would fall away and he could at last emerge in his perfect, princely state, united with her forever.

## The Snow Queen

In all these examples of the Rebirth story based on folk tales and familiar from childhood, the central imprisoned figures have only become trapped in the state of living death through the agency of some dark figure outside them. But eventually we come across another children's story which takes the pattern of this plot a stage further. In Hans Christian Andersen's *The Snow Queen* we see a hero who initially passes under the spell of darkness through the action of an enchanter. But the consequence is that he becomes not just outwardly but inwardly infected by the power of darkness himself. It is this which draws him in turn into the power of another dark figure, the Snow Queen, and it is she who imprisons him in the state of living death.

The story begins with a prologue, which tells how a wicked Magician once constructed a most curious mirror. 'Everything good and beautiful, when reflected in it, shrank up almost to nothing, whilst those things which were ugly and useless were magnified and made to appear ten times worse than before.' The Magician's followers carried the distorting mirror up into the sky, where it fell from their grasp and shattered into millions of tiny fragments. Splinters of the mirror fell to earth all over the world. Some entered people's eyes, which caused them 'to view everything the wrong way'. Others entered people's hearts, which was even worse, for 'the heart became cold and hard, like a lump of ice'.

The story proper begins when we meet a little boy Kay and a little girl Gerda who live next door to each other in a big city. They play together and love each other. Both are innocent and sweet-natured. But one day, towards the end of summer, Kay feels shooting pains in his eye and heart. They have been entered by splinters of the magic mirror. The pain fades, but Kay's character begins to change. He begins to see the roses outside their windows as ugly, and tears them down. He scorns Gerda's tears, and starts to imitate people cruelly behind their backs. He now likes 'rational' games, such as looking at snowflakes through a magnifying glass, to delight in their cold, hard, crystalline perfection.

Winter has come and one day Kay takes his little sledge out into the square where he sees a large and handsome sledge passing by, driven by a mysterious figure all dressed in white. He attaches his own sledge behind the larger one, hoping for a ride, and finds himself being whirled along faster and faster through the streets, and eventually out into the snow-covered countryside. By now he is very frightened, but he cannot shake his sledge loose. He tries to say a prayer, but can only remember the multiplication table. At last they stop, miles from home, and the mysterious figure reveals herself as the Snow Queen. Kay sees her as beautiful: 'a more intelligent, more lovely countenance he could not imagine'. As they resume their journey, now flying over forests, lakes and seas, Kay sits beside her, his head filled with figures and statistics, until he falls asleep.

We then return to little Gerda, who is very unhappy at her friend's disappearance. The winter goes by, spring comes, still he has not returned. Some say he must be dead, but Gerda cannot believe it and she sets out to look for him. We now pass into the familiar territory of a Quest, as she embarks on her long journey into distant lands, with alternating episodes of ordeal and respite. For a time she passes into the power of an enchantress herself, who like Odysseus's Calypso tries to lull her into forgetfulness of her Quest. She meets helpers, a raven and a robber-maiden, who eventually sends her on the last part of her journey, on a reindeer. Then at last we see what has happened to Kay. Far to the north, in the land of everlasting cold, he is imprisoned in the vast ice palace of the Snow Queen. He sits most of the time all alone, doing 'Chinese puzzles' with splinters of ice. 'Kay could form the most curious and complete figures – this was the ice puzzle of reason – and in his eyes these figures were of the utmost importance ... but there was one word he could never succeed in forming. It was "Eternity." ' The Snow Queen had told him that if ever he can put that word together, he will become his own master and 'I will give thee the whole world'.

At last Gerda finds Kay, in the 'great empty hall of ice'. As he sits, 'cold, silent, motionless', he does not recognise her. She is so overcome by love and pity that she embraces him with hot tears, which wash the splinter of mirror from his heart. He then weeps too, which floats the splinter from his eye. At last he can feel and see straight again. 'Gerda, my dear little Gerda' he exclaims, as if waking from a long sleep, 'where have you been all this time? And where have I been?' They are both so filled with joy that even the ice fragments around them dance, and form the word 'Eternity' by themselves. Gerda and Kay set out on their long return journey, the world around them becoming ever warmer and more spring-like as they travel south. At last they arrive back in their old familiar streets, and as they come home the only alteration they can find is in themselves, for 'they saw that they were now fully grown up'. They gaze on each other happily, 'while all around them glowed warm, glorious Summer'.

From earlier stages of our journey through storytelling we have no difficulty in recognising what is happening to Kay in the course of this story. When the splinters of the mirror enter his eye and his heart, two things happen: he can no longer see straight and whole, and he can no longer feel for others. He becomes blind, heartless and egocentric. He has become 'dark' in exactly the same way in which we saw figures being possessed by darkness in earlier types of story, above all in Tragedy. And when Gerda finally finds her way to his lonely prison to liberate him, the transformation which takes place in him is precisely that which we saw in earlier types of story where a dark figure goes through a change of heart and becomes 'light'. As the splinters are washed from Kay's eye and heart, he regains both the powers he has lost: to see whole and to feel. He is once again able to love. He is restored to his true self. United with his 'other half' Gerda, he is complete. And, as the closing lines of the story make clear, he has 'fully grown up'.

But still the darkness which possesses Kay is personified outwardly, in the two dominant dark figures of the story who are ultimately responsible for placing him under the dark spell and consigning him to the state of living death, the Magician and the Snow Queen. We now move on to three more stories based on the Rebirth plot, written for an adult audience, where the dark power is no longer personified outwardly at all, but is shown as springing only from within the hero. What consigns him to his prison is seen as something which has happened solely within his own personality.

## A Christmas Carol

When we first meet the hero of Charles Dickens's *A Christmas Carol*, he is already in the state of living death. He does not yet recognise it as such, nor do we yet know how he got there – but both things are central to the way the story then unfolds.

It is Christmas Eve. A freezing fog shrouds the City of London but nothing is colder or less full of seasonal goodwill than the heart of the moneylender Scrooge. We see him in three encounters which underline how he has become imprisoned in a grasping, ill-tempered meanness which sets him at odds with all the world. First he contemptuously rejects an invitation to Christmas dinner from his cheerful nephew. Then he rejects the invitation of two gentlemen to contribute to a charity to provide Christmas cheer for the poor. Thirdly, he turns on his clerk Bob Cratchit, refusing him more coal for his fire and all but threatening to dock his wages for the following day's absence from the office. As Scrooge returns home that evening through the freezing streets, it is emphasised that it has become 'foggier yet, and colder! Piercing, searching, biting cold!' Arriving at his meagrely furnished lodgings, he sees the door knocker assume the ghostly features – 'livid ... horrible' – of his equally miserly former partner Jacob Marley, dead exactly seven years. Marley's ghost then appears, dragging a huge chain, to warn Scrooge of the punishment which awaits those who live only for themselves, and that he is about to receive visits from three more apparitions.

The first ghost, of Christmas Past, 'like a child, yet not so like a child as an old man', leads Scrooge through a series of flashbacks to his early life. He recognises himself as a solitary little boy, then in later years surrounded by loving relatives and cheerful Christmas scenes, up to the point where, as a young man, he was finally abandoned by the pretty young woman he had become engaged to because she felt that she had been replaced in his heart by 'an Idol'. ' "What idol?" ' the young Scrooge had asked. ' "A golden one" ' replied the girl, as she left him forever. We are seeing how Scrooge had originally been transformed from a pleasant young man into a cold, solitary monster, obsessed by money.

The second ghost, of Christmas Present, is a jolly giant, exuding plenty and good cheer. He shows Scrooge a series of visions of people enjoying all the sociable delights and generosity of spirit associated with Christmas. These festive groups include Scrooge's nephew and Bob Cratchit, each surrounded by a happy, laughing family. Nothing moves Scrooge more than the sight of Cratchit's little crippled son, Tiny Tim. In each case the only shadow over the merriment is cast by a mention of his own name.

The third ghost, of Christmas To Come, 'a solemn phantom, draped and hooded, coming like mist along the ground', shows Scrooge a sequence of mysterious, sinister visions in which it seems that someone has died. No one could care less about the passing of the dead man. It seems that he did not have a friend in the world. In a squalid hovel a group of grotesques are dividing his belongings, stolen from around his freshly-cold corpse. Then Scrooge sees the Cratchit family again. Tiny Tim is dead. Finally he is shown a bleak little gravestone recording the name of the man who has died, unmourned and unloved. It is of course his own. Scrooge is so horrified at everything he has seen that he has gradually been going through a transformation. He ends with a promise to the vanishing phantom that, if only he has the chance, he will utterly reform his life.

Scrooge awakes from his nightmare, imagining that he has somehow slept through three nights. He is amazed to discover that it is still only the morning of Christmas Day. He thus has a chance to express his new found self in a tornado of generosity and goodwill to everyone he meets and knows. He arranges for a vast turkey to be sent round to Bob Cratchit, rushes to offer the charitable gentlemen a contribution so generous as to be almost embarrassing and finally breaks in on his astonished nephew and his family to join their celebrations. The following morning he amazes Cratchit by raising his salary, and from that day forth Ebenezer Scrooge becomes like a second father to Tiny Tim, 'who did NOT die', and 'as good a friend, as good a master and as good a man as the old city knew'.[1]

1. Another story in which a benign spirit uses a nightmarish vision to bring about the hero's rebirth is Frank Capra's post-World War Two movie *It's a Wonderful Life* (1946). When George Bailey (played by James Stewart) is faced with bankruptcy in a little American town thanks to a theft of money by the story's villain, he first turns angrily on his wife and children, then gets drunk and contemplates suicide. A guardian angel Clarence is sent to save him. We first see scenes from George's life in which he has featured positively, from saving his brother Harry from drowning when they were boys, to setting up a loving family home. Clarence then leads George through

## Crime and Punishment

The action of *A Christmas Carol* centres almost entirely round the twofold process necessary to bring about Scrooge's 'rebirth'. The purpose of the succession of nightmarish apparitions is to open out his awareness, to allow him to see himself as others see him and to see the world from a new centre of perspective; and at the same time, as an inseparable part of this process, to awaken in him the ability to feel for others – just as Kay learned to see and to feel when the splinters of mirror were removed from his eye and his heart. And the central redeeming figure of the story who, more than anyone else, awakens his power to love is Tiny Tim, the son he never had, the Child.

Another nineteenth-century novel which presents the whole pattern of the Rebirth, from the moment when the hero first passes under the deadly spell of darkness through to his final liberation, is Dostoyevsky's *Crime and Punishment*. The opening scenes, in which we meet the hero Rodion Raskolnikov as a poor young student in St Petersburg, are directly akin to the opening of Tragedy. In his hopeless, drifting life in the great city, surrounded by human wreckage like the drunken civil servant Marmeladov, whose daughter Sonia has been driven into prostitution, Raskolnikov becomes obsessed by the fantasy that if only he can commit some vast crime he will somehow have demonstrated his superiority to the hundreds of thousands of ordinary human beings around him. Like Napoleon, he will have shown that he is not to be confined by the humdrum framework of morality appropriate to everyone else (as he says later 'I wanted to see whether I could step over or not').

He finds his Focus in the plan to murder an unattractive old woman who acts as the neighbourhood moneylender. For some time we see him going through 'an agonising inner struggle', very much a 'divided self' as he contemplates the enormity of what part of him desires. On the one hand he has a dream of himself as a young boy, watching with horror as a drunken peasant clubs his horse to death: young Raskolnikov rushes in at the last moment to kiss the dying horse on the lips. On the other, he sees 'signs' that he is right to proceed, as when he happens to overhear a student in a restaurant arguing that it would not be immoral to kill some 'stupid, senseless, worthless, wicked and decrepit old hag, who is of no use to anybody and who actively does harm to everybody'. Even when Raskolnikov is making his final preparations 'they all possessed one strange characteristic: the more final they became, the more absurd and horrible they at once appeared in

---

the town to show him just how different many people's lives would have been if he had never existed. As the hero walks through the familiar streets, unrecognised by his friends and family because they have never known him, he sees just how many sad and tragic things would have come about if he had not been there to influence the world for the better. This culminates in seeing the grave of his brother Harry, showing how, if George had not been there to rescue him, he would have died. Harry would therefore not have survived to become a national hero in World War Two for saving the lives of hundreds of American servicemen from a sinking ship. By the time Clarence returns George to the real world, the hero has seen how much good he has done in the world without knowing it. As the film ends, he is joyfully reunited with his wife and children under the Christmas tree, appreciative townsfolk pour into his home to rescue him from debt with gifts of money, and he has been reborn.

his eyes'. But he steels himself. He visits the old woman in her flat and hacks her to death with a hatchet, only to discover to his horror that her friend Lisaveta is also there and, unplanned, he has to kill her too.

Having committed his 'dark act' and managed to escape safely, leaving no clues, Raskolnikov does not, however, feel himself to be a great hero, liberated from the morality binding ordinary mortals. He finds himself more and more troubled. He is called to the police station about some quite different matter and hears talk of the murder of the two women. He faints. Everyone is now talking about the murders. Raskolnikov begins to see 'signs' that he is suspected, as when an unknown man comes up to him in the street and seems to call him 'murderer'.

An increasingly important part is now played in Raskolnikov's life and thoughts by Sonia Marmeladov, the meek young prostitute who, although she has become degraded to support her drunken father, consumptive mother and the rest of the family, is deeply religious. Indeed the inner structure of Raskolnikov's torment may now be charted through his alternating interviews with two figures, Sonia and a strangely authoritative, almost fatherly examining magistrate, Porfiry. In his first private conversation with Sonia, Raskolnikov for some reason asks her to read him the story of how Lazarus was brought back from the dead. He is then summoned by Porfiry for a routine interview, as one of the old moneylender's list of clients. The shrewd magistrate tells him that people who have committed such crimes will always eventually give themselves up, like moths coming to a candle. At his second meeting with Sonia, Raskolnikov confesses his crime. Pitying his terrible distress, she says she will never leave him. He then returns to Porfiry who says he knows that Raskolnikov has committed the crime and that he will eventually 'decide to accept suffering' by coming clean about it.

As the nightmare of other people's disordered lives closes in on him from all sides – the drunken Marmeladov has been run over and killed in the street, his wife is evicted from her rooms, goes mad and also dies, the admirer of Raskolnikov's sister Dunya shoots himself – Raskolnikov can at last take no more. He goes into the police station, gives himself up and is sentenced to seven years hard labour in a Siberian prison camp.

Even now, as he begins his sentence, Raskolnikov still has not faced up inwardly to the full extent of his guilt. But he is accompanied to Siberia by the faithful Sonia, who lives outside the camp, and becomes an almost saintly figure, a 'little mother', to his fellow prisoners. Finally Raskolnikov has a nightmare of the whole world being swept by a terrible disease, which gives all who are infected by it the conviction that they alone are right. Everyone is set against everyone else, until all are destroyed. It is the horrific vision of a world in which everyone has become like himself. Raskolnikov is moved to the core of his being, and when he next meets Sonia throws himself down to kiss her feet. She knows at last that he is beginning to come to himself and loves her. Later he picks up her little New Testament, from which she had read him the story of Lazarus, the man returned from the dead, and one thought flashes through his mind, 'is it possible that her convictions can be mine too, now?':

'But that is the beginning of a new story, the story of the gradual rebirth of a man, the story of his gradual regeneration, of his gradual passing from one world to another, of his acquaintance with a new and hitherto unknown reality ...'

## Silas Marner

In *A Christmas Carol* the central redeeming figure, Tiny Tim, was a child. In *Crime and Punishment* it is a young girl, Sonia. In a third nineteenth-century novel, George Eliot's *Silas Marner*, it is a combination of both.

The central figure Silas Marner is a weaver who, for 15 years, has lived all alone in a solitary cottage near the country village of Raveloe. He had grown up far away in a great manufacturing town, where as a young man he had been a member of an obscure religious sect, engaged to another, a girl called Sarah. But one day, almost as if he had passed under an evil spell, Marner had found himself falsely accused of stealing some money by a third member of the sect, who also had designs on Sarah. All Marner's protestations of innocence had been in vain, he had been framed and found guilty, and his treacherous accuser, the real thief, had completely won the day and the hand of Sarah. Marner had fled the scene, to end up in his lonely cottage.

Initially Marner and his new neighbours had got on reasonably well, but then they had begun to shun him, looking on the solitary weaver with fear and suspicion. He had turned in on himself, throwing himself wholly into his monotonous work, and gradually his life had become taken over by an obsession, his love of the gold he received for his weaving, which he hoarded away in his cottage and counted every night.

After many years of this embittered, miserly existence, Marner's life suddenly becomes intertwined in dramatic fashion with that of another family in the parish. Squire Cass of Raveloe has two sons. The elder, Godfrey, is a weak man, enamoured of the eligible Nancy Lammeter, but unable to propose because he has already been secretly and foolishly married to a girl of humble origin in a nearby town. He has also fallen into the blackmailing clutches of his younger brother, Duncan, an unscrupulous ne'er do well. Led by a series of typically reckless and selfish errors into desperation for money, Duncan finds himself one foggy night outside Marner's cottage. The door is open, the 'old miser' has gone out. Duncan cannot resist the temptation to steal his hoard of gold, and then disappears.

Silas returns and discovers his loss and it is as if he has been robbed of his life. As the first shock of what has happened fades, his neighbours begin to look more indulgently on him, as a poor hopeless creature, slightly crazed. He sinks into self-pitiful brooding. The Christmas season comes, everybody else is busy celebrating, it begins to snow and Marner's despair reaches its lowest point.

On New Year's Eve, a strange pathetic figure picks her way through the darkness and driving snow past Marner's cottage. It is Godfrey Cass's rejected wife, clutching their baby daughter, with which she plans to confront her husband and his family in the middle of their festivities. Weak and deranged by opium, she sinks down into the freezing snow to die. The little girl wanders off towards the light from the cottage door, finds it open and sinks down asleep in front of Marner's fire.

When he returns to the room it is some time before he notices the child, and when he does, it is her golden curls shining in the firelight which catch his attention. As if in a hallucination, he imagines that it is his lost gold which has been returned to him. But he then discovers that it is a little girl and the sight of the innocently sleeping child stirs in him feelings he has not known in all the years since he came to Raveloe, 'old quiverings of tenderness, old impressions of awe at the presentiment of some Power presiding over his life'.

Eventually the child's mother is found dead, and to everyone's astonishment Marner insists on keeping the little girl who had arrived so miraculously in his life. He has christened her Eppie, and we soon see what a transformation her coming has produced in him. 'Unlike the gold which needed nothing and must be worshipped in close-locked solitude ... Eppie was a creature of endless claims and ever growing desires, seeking and loving sunshine and living sounds and living movements.'

As the years go by and Eppie's life unfolds, Marner's 'soul, long stupefied in its cold, narrow prison, was unfolding too and trembling gradually into full consciousness'. He becomes open, friendly and liked by all: 'the little child had come to link him once more with the whole world'. After 16 years, when Eppie has become an attractive young woman, a pond near their cottage is drained and Duncan Cass's skeleton is found, with the bags containing Marner's lost gold: all is explained, and all is restored to him. Eppie agrees to marry a suitable young man of the village, but only on condition that they can both remain living with her beloved 'father', in the cottage which since her arrival has become surrounded by a beautiful garden. The story ends with Eppie exclaiming to Silas Marner 'I think nobody could be happier than we are'.

Each of these nineteenth-century novels describes its hero going through what is essentially the same kind of inward drama. In each we see:

(1) a hero who, as a young man, falls under the shadow of the dark power;
(2) as the poison gets to work, it takes some time to get the upper hand and to show its full destructive effect;
(3) eventually the darkness emerges in full force, plunging the hero into a state of total isolation;
(4) this culminates in a nightmare crisis which is the prelude to the final reversal;
(5) the hero 'wakes from his sleep', and is liberated through the power of love.

In fact this form of the Rebirth story finally brings us back to the point where we left off at the end of our exploration of Tragedy. As in a tragedy, we are looking from the inside at what happens to someone when he becomes possessed by the dark part of himself. We see him passing into the grip of an egocentric obsession, which renders him both unable to feel for others outside himself and also blind to the reality of what is happening to him. As he sinks ever further into the darkness, however, he does not, like the tragic hero, just plunge on to final destruction. What marks out the Rebirth plot is the way we see the central figure eventually frozen in his dark and lonely state with seemingly no hope of escape. And it is here, as light stealing in on the darkness, that the vision appears which inspires the stirring back to life, centred on a particular redeeming figure: invariably, where the story has a hero, a Young Woman or a Child.

Again, as in *The Snow Queen*, what we thus see happening to the hero is that familiar process which we have already seen in other types of story where the hero makes a switch from darkness to light. He is being put in touch with some deeper part of his personality which he has not previously been aware of. Firstly, this opens his eyes, enabling him to see the world from a wholly new, non-selfish perspective; it allows him for the first time to see everything straight and whole. Secondly, it enables him for the first time really to feel selflessly. As he finally moves securely to this new centre of his personality, love wells up in him like an unstoppable force, giving him a sense of extraordinary liberation, of being linked 'with the whole world' – and he experiences this as at last coming to his true, inmost self.

## Rebirth: Summing up

We can now sum up this type of story in all the main forms which it can take. Behind them all is the same basic sequence:

(1) a young hero or heroine falls under the shadow of the dark power;
(2) for a while, all may seem to go reasonably well, the threat may even seem to have receded;
(3) but eventually it approaches again in full force, until the hero or heroine is seen imprisoned in the state of living death;
(4) this continues for a long time, when it seems that the dark power has completely triumphed;
(5) but finally comes the miraculous redemption: either, where the imprisoned figure is a heroine, by the hero; or, where it is the hero, by a Young Woman or a Child.

The power of this type of story to move us lies in the contrast between the condition of the hero or heroine when we see them frozen in their isolated, imprisoned state and the moment when the liberation begins, as we see them being released from the dark power's icy grip. Again and again we see the same range of imagery being used to conjure up the former state, when the dark power is dominant:

coldness, hardness, immobility, constriction, sleep, darkness, sickness, decay, isolation, torment, despair, lack of love.

Finally, prevailing against that state as spring follows winter, we see the exactly corresponding imagery of

warmth, softness, movement, liberation, awakening, light, health, growth, joining together, happiness, hope, love.

On every count it marks the move from one universal pole of existence to the other, from death to life: hence the reason why we see this mighty transformation as 'rebirth'. But we can see this basic underlying drama presented in three different ways.

Initially, corresponding to the kinds of story we come across early in life, we may see the innocent but undeveloped young hero or heroine falling under the shadow of the dark power as it is personified in a mysterious, malevolent figure outside them. Nevertheless it is their own immature state and limited awareness which renders them unable to withstand the dark power, drawing them inexorably into its grip; and only after a long time are they ready to be released.

Eventually, corresponding to the kinds of story we are more familiar with in adult life, we may see the dark power represented much more directly as something springing entirely from within the hero or heroine's own personality: they have been unable to withstand the evil spell cast over them by the dark part of themselves.

In the middle, as a bridge between the two, we may see the kind of story where both these things happen: where the dark power is initially personified in magical figures outside the hero, who place him under a spell: but where its effect is to turn him into a dark figure himself.

Before we conclude this exploration of the Rebirth story we shall look at one more example of each of these basic forms which the plot can assume.

### Fidelio

The first example shows how it need not be only in fairy tales, or in stories written primarily for children, that we may see a hero who is trapped in a state of living death by a dark figure outside him. The profoundly moving story of Beethoven's opera *Fidelio* provides us with another instance of an imprisoned hero being released by a heroine, seen from the heroine's point of view. But we are not here looking, as in *Beauty and the Beast*, at a naive, relatively passive young heroine who achieves the hero's liberation unwittingly. Here, as in the adult version of Gerda in *The Snow Queen*, we see a heroine who is not just good hearted; she is the most 'active' figure in the story, determined, courageous and fully aware of what she is doing, as she sets out to rescue her hero from a physical and spiritual imprisonment which has reduced him to helpless impotence and despair.

The hero of the opera, Florestan, has been seized by an evil tyrant Pizarro, whose crimes he had been about to expose to the world, and thrown into the deepest, most secret dungeon of the fearsome prison of which Pizarro is governor. It is even generally assumed that the disappeared Florestan must be already dead (as in *The Snow Queen* it was assumed that Kay must have died when he disappeared), but Leonore his wife – like Gerda – refuses to believe it and determines to rescue him. First she disguises herself as a young man, like the 'active' heroines who play a chief liberating role in Shakespearean comedy, Portia, Viola or Rosalind, and talks herself into the post of assistant to the chief gaoler of Pizarro's prison, Rocco. After a comparatively cosy domestic opening, as if the opera were Comedy (with Rocco's daughter expressing her love for the 'young man'), we then meet the grim tyrant Pizarro himself, who learns that the mysterious 'Minister' is on his way to the prison to enquire into accusations that Pizarro has been exercising his authority unjustly. Realising that he dare not allow the Minister to discover Florestan, Pizarro makes preparations to kill his victim, ordering Rocco to dig the grave and arranging for a trumpet to sound to warn him of the Minister's approach. The first act ends with all the other prisoners allowed briefly up into the fresh air and sunlight, which they compare to emergence from the grave, before they are plunged down into the darkness again.

It is only at the beginning of Act Two that we are at last, amid the atmosphere of steadily gathering threat, allowed to see the hero himself – as we penetrate far beneath the earth to the squalid dungeon where Florestan is confined in perpetual darkness, in heavy chains. He is in the depths of despair, thinking he is about to die: but briefly imagines that he feels a 'gentle, soft stirring breeze' and sees his 'tomb illumined' by the vision of 'an angel, so like my wife Leonore, who leads me to freedom in the Heavenly Kingdom'. As he sinks down again, exhausted, Rocco and Leonore descend into the darkness to dig his grave. Even before she recognises the shadowy prisoner, Leonore is overcome with pity for his dreadful plight. When she sees who it actually is, she faints with shock, but recovers and manages to give him a crust of bread. Then the fearsome Pizarro enters to murder Florestan. He is about to stab his prisoner when Leonore rushes forward from the shadows to throw herself in front of her husband. Pizarro is about to leap forward to stab them both, when she pulls out a pistol – and just then the distant trumpet sounds. In the nick of time the Minister has arrived. Florestan is saved.

The story ends with everyone back above ground, in the open air and sunshine. The Minister orders the monster Pizarro to be taken away for punishment for all his crimes, and tells Leonore that it is her right alone to cut Florestan from his chains. The opera ends on a blazing choral celebration of Leonore's courage and fidelity, surrounding the central inexpressible joy of herself and Florestan at being again united – but also with a sense that all the other denizens of the prison have been redeemed by the victory of light over darkness which Leonore has brought about.[3]

### The Secret Garden

Our second example is of a story which, although written for children, reflects the more familiar adult version of the theme where the imprisonment is shown as

---

2. Another well-known version of the Rebirth story centred round the figure of a redeeming heroine is *The Sound of Music*, by Richard Rogers and Oscar Hammerstein, made into a successful film (1964). Maria, a beautiful young nun, leaves her convent to become governess to the seven children of Captain von Trapp, an autocratic Austrian aristocrat who has been left a widower. He is a cold disciplinarian who rules his children's lives with a rod of iron. As the lively new governess teaches them how to sing, play games and laugh, their father is initially furious to see them being liberated from the frozen prison he has built round them. But so infectious is their newfound delight in life that he himself eventually thaws out. As he joins in their songs and games, he and Maria fall in love and are married. When the Nazis take over the country in 1938, he falls under suspicion for his refusal to serve the tyrannical new regime. In the nick of time they make a 'thrilling escape' from Austria across the mountains, and the story ends with the family running over Alpine meadows to freedom, joyfully singing 'the hills are alive with the sound of music' to celebrate their liberation.

springing from within. In fact Frances Hodgson Burnett's *The Secret Garden* does not show us only one central character who is imprisoned. As the action unfolds we recognise no fewer than three main characters who have each become trapped in quite separate imprisonments of their own. The cumulative power of the story lies in the way the gradual liberation of one, the heroine, sets off a kind of chain reaction whereby each in turn is liberated: until by the end everyone involved in the story has been caught up in the general rebirth.

We first meet the story's heroine, Mary Lennox, when she is a little girl living in India with her parents, in the Edwardian heyday of the British Empire. Mary is a sour-tempered, sickly, selfish child who has been given no love by her equally selfish parents. Almost the only people she sees are the Indian servants, whom she treats badly. Then one day her parents and her nurse die in a plague, and Mary is sent half across the world to live in a remote mansion in Yorkshire, Misselthwaite Manor, which belongs to her uncle Archibald Craven.

Here, in this great, mysterious house, with the bleak moors outside, Mary finds herself in a strange, shadowy kingdom which itself seems to have fallen under a dark spell. Gradually she tries to unravel some of the mysteries which shroud the house. Why is her crook-backed uncle Mr Craven always away, so lost in himself and so unhappy? Why is there a special part of the garden locked away behind high walls, where no one is allowed to go? More sinister still, what is that strange crying which Mary thinks she hears in some far-off part of the house at night, when the wind is whistling off the moors?

A clue to these mysteries seems to lie in the terrible event which had fallen on the house 10 years earlier, when Mr Craven's beautiful young wife had fallen to her death from a tree in that 'secret garden', which is why it is now locked away and why Mary's uncle seems frozen in perpetual despair. But now even the staff of Misselthwaite Manor seem caught up in the same enchantment – the only one who ever smiles and behaves normally is Martha, the cheerful maid, who lives in a little cottage out on the moors, as one of a family of 12 children.

Although she is still a solitary, sour little girl, almost despite herself Mary begins to feel curiosity about all the unfamiliar things she sees in the gardens round the house, such as the friendly little robin who, like Martha, seems full of life and unaffected by the general air of gloom. Indeed it is the robin and Martha who first introduce Mary to the magical thread which is eventually going to lead her out of the labyrinth of misery which surrounds her. The robin digs up the rusty old key buried in a flowerbed which leads Martha through an ivy-covered door into the secret garden. She finds it wild and overgrown but the most beautiful place she has ever seen. She feels the urge to grow things there, but does not know how to begin. Martha suggests that the best person to help would be her young brother, Dickon – and from the moment Mary sets eyes on the boy, it is clear that he stands for everything the gloomy house of death and its abandoned, neglected secret garden is not. Cheerful, direct, without a hint of selfishness or guile, he is like the spirit of nature itself, constantly surrounded by birds and animals as he roams the moors, charming foxes and squirrels and jackdaws with his pipe – and he can 'make flowers grow out of a brick wall'.

Dickon is delighted to help Mary clear the garden and to plant seeds. Winter is turning to spring, soon there are bulbs pushing up on every side in their secret garden, birds building nests. Mary is now bright-eyed, amazing the servants by her ravenous appetite, for the first time in her life fired by real enthusiasm – and it is this which prepares her for the test which confronts her when she at last, one night, tracks down the source of the mysterious sobbing. Hidden away in a secret room at the heart of the house, she finds a crippled, sickly boy, Colin, Mr Craven's son. After Mary and his father, Colin is the third major prisoner of the story, and in some ways in the worst plight of all. A self-pitiful hypochondriac, who has spent most of his life in bed, fearing that he will shortly die, liable to fly into terrible rages, treating the servants like dirt, he is a little monster. But, buoyed up by her newfound spirit, Mary will have none of this selfish behaviour. She tells him about her secret garden and Dickon, she infects him with some of her own enthusiasm and has to promise to bring Dickon up to Colin's bedroom. From this moment on, the tendency of everything in the story is upward. As spring turns to summer, the secret garden becomes ever more full of life. Colin gets strong enough to make secret visits to the garden in a wheelchair with Dickon and Mary, and even ventures out of his chair to stand and walk: 'I shall get well. And I shall live for ever and ever and ever'. He creates for them all a kind of ceremonial in reverence for the 'magic', the healing power of life and nature which is bursting out everywhere around them and which he can feel transforming him with every day that passes. Eventually one of the servants is so amazed by these mysterious events that she sends a telegram to Mr Craven, who is on one of his long, miserable wanderings in foreign lands, suggesting that he come home. He returns unannounced to hear laughter from behind the wall, in the garden where nobody is supposed to have entered since his wife's death. As he opens the door, a tall, healthy looking boy rushes past him: Mr Craven stares in astonishment – it is his son, whom he last saw as an incurable invalid. The story ends with father and son walking together, straight, tall and happy, back to the house. The dark spell has at last been lifted. Everyone in the little kingdom of Misselthwaite has been redeemed and is at one – with each other, with nature and with the boundless power of life which, thanks to Dickon, is now pouring indivisibly through them all.

### Peer Gynt

For a final example of the Rebirth plot we return to the kind of story where, as in *The Snow Queen*, the hero falls under an evil spell cast by dark figures outside him, but with the result that he becomes a dark figure himself. He is completely possessed by darkness, both from without and within. In fact Ibsen's semi-allegorical *Peer Gynt* is not only the most complicated example of the Rebirth story we have looked at, but psychologically one of the most ambitiously complex stories ever written.

When we meet the hero, Peer Gynt, he is on the verge of adult life, 20 years old, and an incorrigible liar and romancer (in both senses, a fantasiser and a womaniser). He and his mother go off to a village wedding party, where Peer is jeered at by everyone, like the hero of a Rags to Riches story – although in his case the scorn is justified, because he is a boastful teller of tales. A demure young girl Solveig enters with her family, and Peer is at once smitten: 'How lovely! I've never seen anyone like her, with her eyes on the ground … and the way she … carried her prayer book wrapped in a kerchief'. But the incorrigible Peer still cannot resist trying to take the protesting bride off onto the mountainside and here, while she escapes from him, he meets a beautiful and mysterious Woman in Green. She takes him off into the subterranean palace of her father, 'the Hall of the Mountain King'. Peer has in fact descended into the kingdom of the trolls, where he is told that 'among us … black looks like white and ugly like fair' (an echo of the magician's mirror in *The Snow Queen*, or the 'dark sisters' in *Macbeth* – 'fair is foul and foul is fair'). The Troll King and his court try to turn Peer into a troll. One old courtier tells him 'Outside among men, where the skies are bright, there's a saying "Man, to thyself be true". But here among the trolls the saying runs "Troll, to thyself be – enough".' This is to be the theme of the whole story.

Taking the view that 'one *should* fit in with the local ways', Peer agrees to undergo various rites which will turn him into a troll, but he finally baulks at an operation which will remove his clear sight forever. The younger trolls set on him, rather like the moment in *Alice in Wonderland* when Alice is set on by the playing cards, and he is only saved in the nick of time by the sound of distant church bells which scatter the trolls in disorder. Peer suddenly finds himself alone on the mountainside, and there follows a curious scene in which Peer has an exchange in the darkness with a mysterious voice. 'Who are you?' asks Peer. 'Myself' answers the voice, 'can you say as much?' It is the shapeless Great Boyg, which tells Peer he has a long journey to go, and that he will have to 'go round about'. Peer returns to the world of men.

We next see him having built a hut in the forest and persuaded the lovely Solveig to abandon everything to come to live with him. All seems well: Peer says 'My royal princess! I have found her and won her'. But then an aged troll woman enters, the Woman in Green grown old, leading Peer's son, and she tells him that he will not be left alone to enjoy his love with Solveig. 'When you sit with that woman by the fire, when you're loving and want to embrace, I shall sit beside you and ask for my share.' When Peer angrily shouts at her 'you nightmare from hell', she replies that he has only been trapped by his own 'thoughts and desires'. He realises that his royal palace has crashed to the ground. A wall has grown up round Solveig, his 'purest treasure', and there is now no way which passes straight to her. As the Boyg foretold, he will have to 'go round about'. If only he could truly repent, everything might be all right, but there is no one in 'this savage forest' to teach him how. He will have to leave Solveig. She promises that, however long it takes, she will wait for him. He goes off down the forest path, leaving her at the door of the hut, and, after the death of his mother, sets off 'for the sea coast'.

When we next see Peer it is many years later. He has become middle-aged and enormously rich. He is sitting with four guests in Morocco and, in the expansively self-indulgent manner of a millionaire, asks them 'What ought a man to be? Well, my short answer is Himself … a thing he cannot be when burdened with other people's woes'. He elaborates that the 'self' is a mass of 'fancies, cravings and desires', in short 'what stirs inside my breast and makes me live my life as Me'. We learn that Gynt has made his millions in a fairly disreputable fashion, trading in slaves, arms, Bibles, anything that would make a profit, and has become totally self-righteous (indeed shortly afterwards, after his guests have disagreed with him, he is delighted to see their yacht sunk, by a thunderbolt). But he is still inwardly troubled by what it really means to 'be one's self'. In the desert he observes some lizards: 'they bask in the sun and scuttle about with no worries at all. How well they obey the Creator's behest, each fulfilling his own special immutable role. They are themselves through thick and thin: as they were at his first order, Be!' It is not long, however, before Gynt is dreaming of how he might flood the desert to produce a great new country, Gyntiana, which would bring him immortality ('a holy war against Death: that grisly miser shall be forced to free the gold that he has hoarded'). In fact the next role he tries, in his search for self-fulfilment, is that of Prophet, in the course of which he has an affair with the dancer Anitra. She leaves him, and he decides to say 'farewell to the pleasures of love' and to pursue instead 'the riddle of truth'. As one new interest leads hectically on to the next, he is finally taken on a visit to a lunatic asylum by his learned friend Begriffenfeldt, who observes that the inmates are all living for themselves. 'No one here sheds tears for another's sorrows, no one considers any one else's ideas', everyone here is 'enclosed in a barrel of self'. The effect on Gynt of seeing a world in which everyone is in a kind of caricature of his own ego-centric condition is like that of Raskolnikov's nightmare at the end of *Crime and Punishment*. Surrounded by the gibbering lunatics in this 'Empire of Self', Gynt finally sinks down insensible.

The final act begins with Gynt sailing back to Norway, determined to settle quietly on a farm, but still he cannot resist dreaming of building it up until 'it is like a castle'. The ship is wrecked, Gynt is rescued, and wanders up into the mountains. He is now plunged in deep reflection, but can find nothing in himself to hang on to. Suddenly he is passing a hut, which he vaguely seems to remember, and hears a voice singing within. It is Solveig, singing of how she is still patiently waiting. He goes pale: 'there is one who remembered and one who forgot, one who squandered and one who saved'. But there is no turning back. He realises that it was here, all those years before, that his 'empire was lost'.

He is now mocked by phantoms of his unfulfilled life: 'we are thoughts, you should have formed us', 'we are songs, you should have sung us', 'we are deeds, you should have performed us', 'we are tears that were never shed, otherwise we might have melted the ice spears which wound you'. From far off Gynt hears the voice of his dead mother, 'The Devil has deluded you...'.

Then the strange figure of the Button Moulder enters, who says that he has been sent by his 'Master' to melt Gynt down. Gynt retorts that he will allow no such thing, it would be the end of his selfhood, an 'affront to my innermost soul'. The Button Moulder tells him that he had no need to take on so badly – 'up to now you never have been yourself'. Gynt asks for the chance to find witnesses to prove that he has been himself.

The first person he runs into is the Mountain King, who tells him that, on that day in the mountains all those years before, Peer had in fact become a troll, without knowing it. 'The motto I gave you – "to thyself be enough" – enabled you to go through the world as a man of some substance'. Peer begins to realise with horror that he has lived as a troll, all along. The Button Moulder returns, asking for his witnesses, and Gynt, now in desperation playing for time, asks him whether he can first define what it means 'to be one's Self'. 'Being one's Self' comes the reply, 'means slaying one's self – but that answer's probably wasted on you'. Gynt then has a nightmarish vision of the Devil, and emerges in a mood of horrified remorse: 'Do not be angry, O lovely earth, if to no purpose I trampled on your grass... how lavish is Nature, how mean is the spirit'. He sees a group of church-goers singing a Whitsuntide hymn and shrinks away, imagining that he must be damned forever. It is very early in the morning, the world is still dark, and he sees a light shining in a hut up the mountainside. A woman is singing, and she comes out on her way to church: it is Solveig, now aged and nearly blind. She is full of joy at meeting Peer again, but he is now in total despair and tells her that there is a riddle; unless she alone can answer it, he is doomed to go down forever 'to the shadow land'. The riddle she must answer is 'where has Peer been since last we met?' She answers, smiling, 'oh, your riddle is easy... he has been in my faith, my hope and my love'. In other words, his true and inmost self had been with her all along, while he had lived in the world as a false self which was not himself at all. 'Oh purest of women' exclaims Peer. They joyfully embrace, and the sun comes up filling the world with light.

The long, tortuous story of Peer Gynt's eventual Rebirth from his lesser, egocentric troll-self into a deeper 'true Self', centred in the love of his faithful Solveig, is an apt point at which to end this introductory exploration of the main patterns underlying storytelling, because in a way it brings our journey full circle.

There are clear parallels between *Peer Gynt* and all the other types of story we have looked at. In that it centres on the hero's prolonged struggle with a monstrous figure who is the personification of egotism, it is like an Overcoming the Monster story, except for the obvious point that the only monster Peer has to overcome lies in himself.

Like a Rags to Riches story, it is based on a prolonged process of personal transformation. Like Peer Gynt, a Rags to Riches hero begins by seeming nothing very remarkable: indeed he often seems to the world contemptible. He then glimpses some glorious and elevated condition which he longs to attain more than anything in the world and which even seems to come within his grasp: as when Peer Gynt settles down in the forest with his 'princess'. But suddenly this vision of possibility is snatched away, just as Gynt sees his 'royal palace' crashing to the ground when he loses his 'purest treasure' Solveig. After this 'central crisis' the hero of the Rags to Riches story then has to undergo a further long period of testing, before he is finally ready to achieve the sense of self-fulfilment he has longed for. After a last great ordeal he finally discovers the deeper self that has lain buried within him; and this is marked by his being brought together in lasting union with the 'other half' who makes him complete.

Again we see how Peer's adventures are shaped by the pattern of a Quest. From the moment of his encounter with the Great Boyg, we see him embarking on a long search for that elusive prize of his 'true self'. Like the Quest hero he has to go through the worst series of ordeals on the edge of his goal. And his final re-union with Solveig may remind us of the moment when the most famous of all Quest heroes, Odysseus, is at last reunited with the loving woman who for so long has waited in obscurity for his return, the faithful Penelope. Like Odysseus, Peer has 'come home'.

But still there is missing that centrally important element which we did not come across fully in stories until we reached the plot of Voyage and Return. It was here we first began to see that fundamental shift in the emphasis of the plot which makes the hero himself the chief dark figure of the story. It was in the profounder versions of the Voyage and Return story such as the *Rime of the Ancient Mariner* and *The Golden Ass* that we first saw a hero, essentially self-centred and limited in his awareness, being recklessly drawn into a series of adventures which ultimately threaten him with destruction. Only as death stares him in the face does he go through that change of heart which liberates him from his limited, egocentric state of awareness and from the strange threatening world in which it has trapped him.

*Peer Gynt* certainly provides us with more than just echoes of such a Voyage and Return story. The hero begins in a state of limited self-awareness, which leads him to be plunged recklessly into the 'abnormal world' of the trolls. From here he makes a 'thrilling escape', in the nick of time, as he thinks, from being turned into a troll himself. In fact, as he only learns later, the trolls' dark magic has already done its work; with the result that he has to make the second, much longer Voyage and Return which begins when he abandons Solveig for far-off lands. Here, in this distant 'other world', the initial Dream Stage of his selfish, hard-hearted rise to great wealth turns first to frustration, then to the nightmare of his visit to the lunatic asylum. But even the second 'thrilling escape' of the shipwreck which lands him back in Norway only leads him to the final nightmare of his confrontations with the Button Moulder and the Devil, which force him at last to recognise what a monster he has become. He thinks there is no longer any part of him which remains uncorrupted, that he is now nothing but his hideous troll-self, a wrinkled and deflated balloon of egotism, deserving nothing but death. Only now does the reunion with Solveig finally teach him that all along there has been another quite different part of himself, identified with her as she remained in remote obscurity. He has come at last to that much deeper level of awareness which, as his 'other half' emerges from her long eclipse, shows him discovering his true self.

The next plot we came to, Comedy, gave even greater prominence to the hero who becomes the chief 'dark' figure of his own story; and who must be brought to 'recognition' of things hidden before he can achieve the happy ending. In this light, the story of Peer Gynt is entirely familiar. As in so many comedies, we see a hero and heroine who meet in the opening scenes and fall in love; but are then torn apart by a terrible misunderstanding, rooted in the hero's egotism. The heroine passes into eclipse, obscured in the shadows cast by his selfishness. Confusion continues to worsen until the impasse is finally resolved in the only way it can be: by the 'recognition' which brings the hero to see the nature of his error and the true, superior value of the heroine, thus bringing him to himself.

The essence of Tragedy, of course, is that it focuses on the process whereby the hero is transformed into the chief dark figure of the story more starkly than any other kind of plot. Indeed, as we saw, Tragedy can provide us with a kind of mirror image of an Overcoming the Monster story, seen from the point of view of the hero who has been transformed into the monster. Certainly the opening scenes of *Peer Gynt* present us with a situation similar to the opening of a tragedy. The hero is clearly a 'divided self', part drawn upwards by his 'good angel' Solveig, part drawn downwards by the troll Temptress and the tyrant Mountain King. The 'dark' side of Peer wins, he abandons his 'good angel' and is transformed into a monster of hard-hearted egotism. We only infer the long Dream Stage of his tragic course from the fact that he has risen to a position of enormous wealth and power. In fact, after a long gap in the story of his life, we pick it up again at the point where he is entering the Frustration Stage, as he begins to feel a sense of inadequacy and meaninglessness in his self-centred existence. He thrashes around more and more wildly for new realms to conquer, new roles to play: all of which ends in nightmare, despair and the threat of imminent destruction.

But then, because his story is not Tragedy, and because his 'good angel' is not one of the inadequate little rejected 'Innocent Young Girls' of so many tragedies but a strong, mature and wise woman in her own right, Gynt is enabled at the last minute to rediscover his 'light self' buried for so long beneath the outward monstrous shell of his egotism. He can move in the nick of time from the false centre of himself to his true centre. Like Raskolnikov redeemed by the love of Sonia, or Kay by Gerda, or the Beast by Beauty, he has been liberated to become himself. As he and Solveig embrace he is at last united with his missing 'other half' to make him whole.

⁂

Up to now we have been looking at the main plots underlying stories as much as possible in separate compartments. It is certainly true that, on one level, most stories are primarily shaped by one type of plot more than another; that each type of story serves its own special purpose and carries its own message. But the time has come to move on to a rather deeper level, where we look not so much at the peculiarities of each of the basic plot forms but at what they have in common. Here we see how they are all looking from different points of perspective at the same great basic drama.

## Chapter 12

# The Dark Power:
# From Shadow into Light

'The good ended happily and the bad unhappily. That is what fiction means.'
Oscar Wilde, *The Importance of Being Earnest*

So far in this book we have really been doing two things.

On one level we have been looking at hundreds of different stories, including many of the best-known tales in the world, seeing the remarkable extent to which these are formed round one or another of seven basic plots. What we have been exploring are seven of the central ways in which, when the human imagination conjures up a story, its contents naturally take shape. This does not mean, of course, that every story in the world falls neatly and exclusively into one of these categories. At this stage it would be easy to point to countless individual stories which in one way or another do not correspond precisely to any of these plots. Indeed a whole section of this book will later be devoted to looking at such stories and why they vary from the basic patterns. There are even a handful of other, more specialised plots – such as that behind 'creation myths' explaining how the world came into being, or the Mystery plot which underlies detective stories – which we have not yet touched on at all.

On another level, however, we have also through these past eleven chapters been building up a picture of something much deeper and more general than just a catalogue of story-types. We have been gradually laying bare a hidden landscape of figures, situations and images which run through stories of all kinds, regardless of which type of plot may on a more superficial level be directing our interest in the story. We have seen such motifs as 'the thrilling escape from death', the overthrow or redemption of the dark figure, the final union or separation of hero and heroine, appearing again and again, in one plot after another. And however far we continue our exploration of stories we shall find that they always return in one way or another to these same basic patterns and images. What we have been uncovering, in short, is the essential core of the way stories are made, how they work and what they are about. In this sense the real value of examining the seven central plots is that, between them, they provide a comprehensive introduction to all the fundamental elements from which a story can be made up.

The significance of this can hardly be exaggerated. For what it means is that whenever any of us tries to create a story in our own imagination, we will find that these are the basic figures and situations around which it takes shape. We cannot get away from them because they are archetypes. They are the elemental images around which the whole of the storytelling impulse in mankind is centred. And the reason for this is that these underlying patterns and images are somehow imprinted unconsciously in our minds, so that we cannot conceive stories in any other way.

This is why, when we are first introduced to stories in early childhood, we instinctively recognise what they are on about. The small child being told a story may be confronted with the images of all sorts of things which it has never seen in the real world, or which have never existed: bloodthirsty giants; animals which talk; dragons breathing fire. But the child can immediately accept and relate to such mythical beings, because the symbolic language in which stories are dressed up meets with an instinctual pattern of response which is already programmed into the child's own unconscious.

We have virtually no idea how this miraculous process works in neurological terms. We cannot explain physically how it is that we are able to conjure up these images in our 'mind's eye'. We cannot even locate precisely in which parts of our brain this hugely complex activity takes place. But what we can perceive is how, in the way these images present themselves to us, certain patterns persistently recur. The very fact that they do recur in this way means that, below the level of our conscious awareness, there is some shaping mechanism in the human psyche which not only assembles the images together into these patterns, but does so in a way which shows them unfolding according to entirely consistent rules. The only way we can uncover why evolution should have developed in us this capacity to imagine stories is to subject those patterns to systematic analysis: to decipher just what is the meaning of the symbolic language they embody, and what this can tell us about the real underlying purpose storytelling serves in our lives.

This is what we have begun to do in exploring the sequence of plots. And in doing so, we see how the central preoccupation of our need to conjure up the imaginary world of stories comes clearly into view.

## The universal plot

The most important thing we recognise from looking at the hidden structures of the basic plots is the extent to which they all revolve round the same fundamental conflict. This is the central problem posed by that component in human nature which we have seen symbolically represented in stories of all kinds as the 'dark power'. There is no better starting point from which to explore the underlying purpose of storytelling than to observe what is happening when a child is introduced to stories early in its life. If we watch carefully the types of story to which a child can first instinctively relate, we see how many of these tend to take shape round a remarkably similar pattern.

In its simplest form, some of these early nursery tales, such as *Peter Rabbit, Little Red Riding Hood* or *Goldilocks and the Three Bears*, show us a little hero or heroine who begins the story living at home with mother. They then go out into the mysterious outside world – Mr McGregor's garden, a great forest – where they encounter a terrifying and threatening figure (in the case of Goldilocks, three acting as one). This threat comes inexorably closer until it seems that, as in a nightmare, they are trapped, facing death. But then, at the story's climax, comes the 'thrilling escape', when they can run safely home to mother.

What all these stories are doing is to awaken the child's mind to the same basic message. As it is introduced to the central figure of each story, it sees and identifies with a child like itself, who begins surrounded by the security of home, living with a loving, protective mother. It then sees this little hero or heroine venturing out alone into the great world, beyond the protective setting of home, where they encounter a terrifying presence, so hostile that it spells death. In symbolic fashion, the listening child is being introduced to the idea that, somewhere in this unfamiliar new world it has come into, there is a mysterious and deadly dark power, far more frightening than anything it has ever outwardly encountered in real life. But in the end, the reassuring message of the story runs, it is possible to escape from this fearsome enemy. With a mighty sense of relief, the child identifying with the story can thus imagine returning to the safest place it knows, back home with mother.

Such is the simplest version of the story, and it is no accident that we associate it with tales intended to be told to very young children. But we then see a development of the pattern, in stories such as *Jack and the Beanstalk* or *Hansel and Gretel*. Again the child is introduced to a hero or heroine living dependently at home. Again they venture out into the mysterious outside world, where they fall under the shadow of a terrifying figure, the giant, the witch. Again the story builds to a climax, where it seems they are about to be killed. But the significant thing the child now sees is that it is up to the hero or heroine themselves to overcome the dark power. They must actually slay the giant or witch by their own efforts. And their reward in doing so, the message runs, is not only escape from death, but that they win a fabulous treasure.

Even now, however, because these are still only tales intended for young children, their heroes and heroines still return at the end to the familiar security of home. Only with a third step in the unfolding pattern does the story add a further important ingredient to the general message. In tales such as *The Three Billy Goats Gruff* or *The Three Little Pigs*, we again begin with little heroes living at home with mother: in each of these examples, three young brothers. Again, as they grow up, the heroes go out into the great world, where they encounter a terrifying dark figure: a fearsome troll guarding the bridge, a big bad wolf. Again, through courage and ingenuity, they themselves eventually manage to destroy this monstrous figure (even though, in the case of the little pigs, two are eaten). But we no longer see the victorious heroes having to retreat back home at the end of the story. The important thing now is that they can move forward rather than back. Having crossed the bridge, the goats can begin their new life feasting on the meadow of sweet grass up on the mountainside. The third little pig can live happily ever after in his home made of bricks, which has successfully withstood the wolf's assaults because, unlike his brothers, he has built it soundly, out of strong, secure materials. Thanks to their victory over the dark power, they have now established a secure new home for themselves in the outside world, where they are free to live their own independent life.

Finally we come to all those stories which show this pattern unfolding to its fullest state of development. In stories like *Aladdin* or *Snow White*, we again see the young hero or heroine going out into the world and being drawn into a struggle with the same dark power, which lasts through most of the story. Again they finally emerge triumphant. But their ultimate reward now takes a much more specific form, as we see them brought together in loving union with a beautiful Princess or handsome Prince, and in some way succeeding to rule over a kingdom.

We thus see them having completed perhaps the most fundamental transition in any human life. They have begun in the secure but dependent state of child-hood. They have gone out into the great world, to face all sorts of ordeals and adventures. But they end up having established an entirely new secure base of their own, united to a loving partner and presiding over their own little kingdom. The transition from childhood to maturity is complete. And the key to reaching this goal has been to emerge victorious from a series of battles with the dark power.

Indeed what we also come to recognise from such tales are those essential elements making up what Aristotle identified as the beginning, middle and ending of a story which, expressed in more sophisticated outward forms, remain central to our experience of storytelling for the rest of our lives.

### Beginning

The 'beginning' of almost any type of story shows us a hero or heroine who is in some way undeveloped, frustrated or incomplete. This establishing of their unhappy, immature or unfulfilled state sets up the tension needing to be resolved which provides the essence of the story.

### Middle

The 'middle' of the story shows them sooner or later falling under the shadow of the dark power, the conflict with which constitutes the story's main action. In the types of story we come to early in life this threatening presence is invariably personified as outside the central figure, although later we come to the type of story in which those same dark qualities are shown as lying in the hero or heroine themselves. Through most of the story we see its little world divided into an 'upper' realm, where the dark power holds sway, and an 'inferior' realm, where the forces of light remain in the shadows.

### Ending

The 'end' of the story provides its resolution. The action eventually builds to a climax, when the forces making for threat and confusion rise to their highest point of pressure on everyone involved, and this paves the way for the 'reversal' or 'unknotting', the moment when the dark power is overthrown.

The nature of the story's ending then depends entirely on how its hero or heroine have aligned themselves to the dark power. If the central figure has remained or ended up in opposition to the dark power, we see that, in this final act of liberation, there is a prize of infinite value to be won: a treasure to be won from the darkness; a captive 'Princess' or 'Prince' to be freed from its clutches; a community to be redeemed from its shadows. We see that the hero or heroine have ended up fulfilled and complete, in a way which through most of the story would have seemed unthinkable. They have reached some central goal to their lives.

If, on the other hand, the hero or heroine have become irrevocably identified with the dark power, the story will end in their destruction. But even this comes about according to the same rules which govern stories with a happy ending. So much have the central figures of Tragedy become the chief source of darkness in their story that only when they are removed by death can the light again emerge from the shadows. For all those forced to live in that shadow, this in itself can end the story on the familiar note of liberation. The wider community is restored to wholeness. Just as in a story which comes to a happy ending, it is a victory for life.

Thus in any story which is completely resolved, the basic pattern remains the same. In the end, darkness is overcome and light wins the day. In fact what ultimately distinguishes each of the basic plots is simply that each looks at this common theme from a different angle. Each lays emphasis on a particular aspect of that universal plot which lies behind them all.

## The road to self-realisation

The Overcoming the Monster story is in a sense the most basic of all the plots because it focuses attention on this conflict with the dark power to the exclusion of almost everything else. The word 'monster' comes from the Latin *monstrum*, meaning 'something put on show', as in our word 'demonstration'. It also came to mean 'a freak of nature', as in all those abnormal, deformed or just unfamiliar human beings or animals which in former times were put on show in fairgrounds, circuses or zoos. Whatever outward form it takes, the one thing the monster in stories can never be, as we have seen, is a whole, perfect human being. It is, by definition, a representation of human imperfection: and in no respect more than the way it is wholly egocentric, prepared to sacrifice anyone and everything else in the world to its own interests.

The essence of the monster, in short, is that, dressed up in symbolic form, it is a hugely magnified personification of the human capacity for egotism, which is invariably shown as immensely powerful, unfeeling for others but also in some crucial respect blind, lacking in understanding. Since this monster is invariably shown in a story as posing a deadly threat to a whole community of people, it is presented as a mortal enemy to the human race. As soon as we are made aware of the monster's existence, we know the only way the story can reach a satisfactory resolution is that it must be destroyed. That is why it is so important that, when the hero emerges, we are never left in any doubt as to why he is set in complete opposition to the monster, the positive to everything in which the monster is negative. He is not egocentric. He is always battling on behalf of the wider community. He is thus shown as representing the forces of life against death.

Yet at the same time it is crucial that, as the action of the story unfolds, we should see the hero himself growing in stature. When he first appears it might seem unthinkable that he should be able to confront the monster's awesome power. This is only reinforced when he finally confronts his opponent, even falling into its clutches. Towards the end, however, when the hero has worked out how to get the measure of his antagonist, we begin to see him in a new commanding light. Even James Bond invariably rises from his seemingly helpless position as the underdog who stumbles halfway through the story into the villain's clutches, to the moment where he is finally able by some superhuman feat to turn the tables. This transformation is still more obvious in those deeper versions of the story, set over a longer period of the hero's life, which, as the action unfolds, show him gradually emerging as an ever more masterful figure. Although we see young David, the disregarded little shepherd boy, winning the great victory over Goliath quite early in his story, we then see how this was merely a prelude to the transforming process which eventually qualifies him as the natural leader of his people, fit to succeed as a great king. We see Perseus gradually maturing from the young, untried boy who wishes to defend his mother's honour against the tyrant Acrisius into the mighty hero who, having slain the Medusa, then achieves his final victory by saving the Princess from the clutches of the sea-monster. It is this personal transformation which has qualified him, like David, to succeed to the kingdom.

In this sense, the Overcoming the Monster story is about the process of working towards maturity. This is presented even more obviously in the Rags to Riches plot, where the hero or heroine's personal transformation provides the central theme of the story. Much more often than in any other plot we are likely to meet the hero or heroine when they are still very young; so that what the story explicitly shows us is the pattern of someone growing up from childhood to maturity. So much does it concentrate our interest on their outward and inward development that, from the moment we first see them in their initial lowly, disregarded state, we know the one thing essential to bringing the story to a satisfactory resolution will be to see them finally emerging from obscurity into the light, where their true hidden self will finally become obvious for everyone to see. Yet the key to this transformation still lies in their struggle with the dark power, as we see symbolically represented even in those two very simple versions from early childhood, *Dick Whittington* and *Puss in Boots*. Here the crucial battle with the dark power is not even fought by the hero himself, but at arms length, by a 'helpful animal' who has become his special ally. In each story it is the cat which achieves the victory over the powers of darkness. However, it is the treasure won from this battle which is the key to the final reversal in the hero's own fortunes, leading to his union with the 'Princess' and his emergence in his true light as someone of exceptional qualities, worthy to rule over a 'kingdom'.

It is when we come to the fullest versions of the Rags to Riches story, such as *Aladdin*, *Jane Eyre* or *David Copperfield*, that we see most explicitly just how this plot is concerned with the process of developing from immaturity to maturity, and here the counterpoint between the hero or heroine's struggle with the dark power and their own inner transformation is portrayed much more directly. Each begins at home, as a young, unformed child. Their transformation begins when the shadow of the dark power falls over them, with the arrival of the Sorcerer, Mr Brocklehurst or the Murdstones, and they are sent out into the world to begin that long series of tests around which their inner growth takes place. At first we see them making considerable progress, as they develop through their adolescence to the point where they are ready to go out into the world in a new way, as young adults, searching for the 'other half' with whom to establish a permanent new centre to their lives. But just when it seems they might be about to achieve a happy ending, there intervenes that central crisis when the dark power reappears in even more fearsome guise, plunging them into the most desperate plight they face at any time in the story. The purpose of this, corresponding to that moment where the hero of an Overcoming the Monster story falls into his opponent's clutches, is to emphasise just how exceptional are the qualities they will now have to display to reach their final goal. They must learn to become reliant on their own inner strengths, in a way they have never done before. Only as they achieve this do we see them maturing to the point where they are ready for the decisive confrontation which enables them to throw off the dark power's grip forever. As they rescue their 'other half' from the shadows, they have finally realised everything they had it in them to become. They have at last reached the central goal of their lives.

It is of course this idea of a human life as a journey towards the ultimate goal of wholeness and self-realisation which provides the focus for the plot of the Quest. Our expectation in a Quest story is centred on the sense that somewhere in the world there is a distant, all-transcending prize, worth every effort to reach. As the tale opens, the hero becomes aware that he is in some 'City of Destruction', where it will be fatal for him to remain. The only way to escape is to embark on the journey towards that far-off, mysterious goal. In the first part, we see the hero and his companions making their journey, facing a succession of battles with the dark power. Even when their destination at last comes in sight, the hero finds he now faces a new set of challenges, so testing that to meet them will take up the entire second half of the story. It has been one thing to bring the prize into view. The ultimate test lies in knowing how to secure it. Yet when the hero does so, of course, we see how remarkably similar it is to that final goal reached by the hero or heroine in the earlier types of story. When Odysseus secretly advances in his humble beggar's rags towards his final showdown with the monstrous suitors, he is like the hero of a Rags to Riches story and an Overcoming the Monster story rolled into one. At last he throws off his disguise to reveal himself in all his kingly majesty, as he seizes the bow to put the suitors to rout. Like Cinderella when she throws off her rags for her final glorious transformation, his true self is at last revealed. Just like Aladdin, Jane Eyre, Perseus and so many others, Odysseus liberates his 'other half' from the shadows and succeeds to his kingdom. It turns out that the true goal of the Quest was precisely the same kind of ending we saw in the earlier plots.

Thus all the first three plots are really looking at a very similar basic story, except that each does so from its own distinctive angle. What we see symbolically represented, as was embryonically foreshadowed in those simple little versions we first hear in childhood, is the idealised pattern of how any human being can travel on the long, tortuous journey of inner growth, finally emerging to a state of complete self-realisation. The underlying impulse behind the three types of story is the same.

## The enemy within

Up to this point in the sequence of plots there is never any real doubt that the hero or heroine of the story stands in opposition to this external dark power which is presented as the main obstacle to them reaching their goal. When Cinderella is contrasted with her stepmother and ugly sisters, Jane Eyre with St John Rivers, Perseus with Medusa, David with Goliath, James Bond with Dr No, we never question for a moment that they stand for a different set of qualities to those which characterise their antagonists.

What we do see in the Quest, however, more than in the earlier types of story, are occasions where the hero and his companions themselves display weaknesses, making foolish errors which threaten to prevent them reaching the goal. Indeed one reason why the hero of a Quest is more commonly than in other types of story given companions is precisely that this allows us to see them making fatal mistakes without the hero himself being killed. And these invariably arise from their own lack of awareness, their failure to recognise the full truth of their situation, with the result that they fall into the deadly clutches of the dark power.[1]

Odysseus and his original twelve shiploads of companions make so many mistakes on their journey – invariably through some selfish act of folly, recklessness or greed – that by the time he arrives back in Ithaca only he himself is left alive. Christian and Faithful in *Pilgrim's Progress* fail to recognise the true nature of Vanity Fair, with the result that Faithful is killed and Christian only narrowly escapes with his life. Aeneas for a long time all but abandons his great task of finding a new homeland when he is bewitched by his love for Dido, and eventually has to be sternly recalled to his quest by Jupiter, the king of the gods. The rabbits in *Watership Down* make a near-fatal mistake when they fail to recognise the true nature of the strange warren in which they consider settling down: it is only in the nick of time that they are saved by Fiver's intuitive understanding that it is a place of death. Jason's Argonauts, the children of Israel, many of the knights on the Grail Quest, are similarly led into catastrophic misjudgements on their journeys, always by some appeal to their egocentric appetites, some failure to 'see whole'. And one

---

1. This only applies to the sort of Quest where the companions are seen as 'undifferentiated appendages' of the hero, and therefore expendable, as in the *Odyssey* or the Jewish Exodus. It does not apply in those, such as *Watership Down* or *King Solomon's Mines*, where the companions between them provide a balance of strengths, all of which are necessary for the Quest to succeed.

of the most important elements in the transformation which allows the hero and those who survive eventually to succeed in a Quest is that they gradually learn from their mistakes, and arrive at a state where they no longer make them.

In general, therefore, although the earlier types of plot show the dark forces which stand between the hero or heroine and the goal as being centred essentially outside them, nevertheless the more they themselves show the weakness and limited awareness of immaturity, the more likely they are to fall prey to the dark power. And of course we are now moving towards those types of story where it is made much more obvious that the dark forces the hero or heroine are having to contend with in fact lie within themselves.

## The maturing experience

As in the three earlier plots, the Voyage and Return story in its fullest expression is about the maturing process. But where it differs from the earlier plots lies in how it presents the transformation which the hero or heroine must go through if they are going to reach the goal. When we first meet them they are usually young and just on the verge of adult life, like Lucius in *The Golden Ass*, or Robinson Crusoe or the Ancient Mariner at the start of his fateful voyage. They are immature, feckless and self-centred, and this, directly or indirectly, is why they stumble in the first place into that new world which is so strange to them. They do not fully understand what they are doing or what is happening to them, which is why they become trapped in the shadow of the dark figures they meet in the other world, who eventually threaten them with destruction. What enables them eventually to escape from their thrall to the dark power is that they develop a wholly new understanding. They 'see the light' in a way which transforms their attitude; and it is this which eventually allows them to escape from the dark power and to return to the world where they began. But so changed have they been by their encounter with the unknown that their relationship to it is quite different. They have escaped from their original state of limited consciousness and learned to 'see whole'. They have discovered who they are. They have grown up.

We even see all this embryonically reflected in the children's tale of Peter Rabbit, who begins as a feckless, rebellious little child, which is what lands him in the appalling plight of being chased round the garden by Mr McGregor. Eventually, in the familiar nightmare climax, Peter finds himself completely trapped, without a clue as to what to do next. No one else can help him, he is completely on his own. But then he jumps up on a wheelbarrow from which, for the first time, he can see the whole garden. He has moved literally to a higher level of consciousness, which enables him to 'see whole'. It is this which, by showing him how to reach the gate of the garden without having to pass Mr McGregor, allows him to escape with his life from what had seemed certain death; even if he then, because this is still a tale designed for very young children, returns home to mother.

The Voyage and Return plot thus shows us, much more obviously than any of the previous plots, a hero who, in order to reach the goal, has to go through a complete shift in his psychological centre. Initially ego-centred, with his lack of feeling for other people and his limited vision, he begins with the potential characteristics of a dark figure, and it is precisely this which places him under the shadow of those external dark figures who threaten to kill him. But he then goes through the change of centre which allows him to 'see whole', saving his life and bringing him back into life-giving contact with others. It is this move from darkness to light which liberates him, and brings him to his happy ending.

## Comedy

The Voyage and Return is the first plot in the sequence where this fundamental shift of psychological centre is brought out as of central importance. Even more obviously does this shift provide the key to the next plot in the sequence, Comedy.

Again, the underlying shape of the Comedy plot is familiar. We begin with a hero or heroine who are in some way frustrated or incomplete. Usually they are just on the threshold of adult life and looking forward to marriage. But the reason for their frustration is that the little world they inhabit is under the shadow of the dark power, which may be centred either in some dominant figure who has power over the hero or heroine, such as an 'unrelenting parent' opposed to their marriage, or in the hero himself (less often the heroine). The essence of Comedy is that it shows how, when one person becomes possessed by egotism, this can place everyone around them in its shadow. No other type of plot so consistently portrays the effect on a whole community of people – a household, a circle of friends, neighbouring families – when one dominant figure in that community falls into the grip of the dark power. As his (or her) blinkered egocentricity imposes a dark pressure on everyone else, this makes it impossible for anyone to be fully themselves. The flow of life is blocked.

This is why everyone in a Comedy may seem to be in a kind of twilight, in which nothing can be seen clearly or whole; in which people are obscured and cut off from one another by pretences, disguises and misunderstandings. This general web of confusion works up to the nightmare climax, when everything seems more bewildering, oppressive and further from resolution than ever, threatening some final disaster. But suddenly comes the unknotting, the moment of recognition when everyone's true nature and identity is at last revealed. The chief dark figure of the story (if he is not merely exposed and bundled off the stage) goes through the fundamental psychological shift which brings him to himself. As he is liberated from his own dark prison, this also breaks the grip of the darkness which has oppressed everyone else. The heroine, or hero and heroine together, emerge from the shadows in which they have been obscured. Round their central loving union, the whole community is brought to unity and wholeness. Everyone has been freed to become his or her 'proper self'. Amid universal celebration, the little world of the story has again been connected with life.

## Tragedy

As we now see, the rules which dictate the outcome of Tragedy are no different from those which govern the unfolding of the other plots. Tragedy shows us what happens to a hero or heroine who have become possessed by the heartless, blind and egocentric part of their own personality, but cannot go through the inner transformation which could release them. As in the other plots, the story ends with the dark power being overthrown: except that here the hero or heroine have themselves become so completely identified with the darkness that it can only be eliminated by their own death.

In fact the actual shape of Tragedy bears many points of resemblance to that of the other types of story we have been looking at. We begin with a hero or heroine who is in some way dissatisfied, frustrated or incomplete. They then fall under the shadow of the dark power: except that this is not presented as something threatening to them but in the form of a Temptation, which arouses and gives dominance to the dark part of themselves. As in other types of story, the true nature of the dark power is not immediately apparent (the Dream Stage). But as the action unfolds, again as in other types of story, the real horror of the darkness finally comes clearly into view. Amid a mounting sense of threat, the story winds up to the familiar nightmare climax, that decisive confrontation between dark and light which culminates, as in the other plots, in the overthrow of the dark power and the final release which marks the ending of the story.

But because we are now seeing this familiar drama through the eyes of its chief dark figure, Tragedy focuses more intimately than the other plots on two things. First it shows us how someone is turned into a dark figure in the first place; and secondly we see just why the dark power eventually leads those who have passed under its spell to destruction. As we saw in Chapter Nine, *The Divided Self*, the tragic hero or heroine possessed by some fantasy of power or passion is trying to achieve something which cannot ultimately resolve into reality. Made heartless and blinded by the force of their egocentric obsession, they become more and more cut off from other people and from the reality of the world around them, until they are so far at odds with the entire context of their existence (including their own deeper selves) that the bubble of make-believe can no longer be sustained. And as we see happening to Othello or Dorian Gray, Stavrogin or Dr Jekyll, Anna Karenina or Emma Bovary, eventually the hero or heroine can tolerate the strain of this irresolution no longer. So disintegrated are they, inwardly and outwardly; so far has their original dream proved an illusion; so far off the rails has their blinkered vision taken them; so horrified has part of them become at what the dark component in their personality has led them to that, in self-disgust, they turn their violence on themselves, bringing about their own destruction. Thus do we see at the heart of Tragedy how the dark power, in rebellion against the whole, in the end works to bring about its own destruction.

In other tragedies we see how the hero possessed by darkness provokes his own destruction at the hand of others. In the early stages, as in other types of story, the chief dark figure seems to be getting his own way, just as does the monster in the early stages of an Overcoming the Monster story. But increasingly this drives the light figures into the shadows cast by his darkness. And as the action unfolds we gradually see a crucial polarisation taking place. 'Above the line' in the story is the dark figure, still dominant, but passing further and further into the grip of darkness and increasingly isolated. Meanwhile, in the shadows 'below the line', the forces of light are constellating in opposition to this unruly power which weighs so heavily on them all. This is the kind of situation we see so often in other plots, as in Overcoming the Monster stories, or in many comedies, such as *The Marriage of Figaro*. Eventually this polarisation leads to the climax of the story, the decisive confrontation. Just as in other plots, the power of darkness is finally over-thrown, the shadows are lifted. And for those who have won the day and emerged into the light, this is a moment of victory. The irruption of darkness which had blighted all their lives has passed away. Peace and wholeness are restored. Life can begin to flow again. Even though this is a Tragedy, we recognise it as a situation very similar to that which we see at the end of other types of story.

An obvious example of this type of tragedy is *Macbeth*.[2] We see the hero drawn into the grip of the dark power. As he becomes more and more dark, in his 'upper realm', so an ever growing number of those around him fall victim to his blind and deadly egotism. But for each of the chief victims he kills, Duncan, Banquo, Macduff's wife and children, there is another who escapes – Malcolm, Fleance, Macduff himself – and who flees the kingdom into England. Here, in the 'inferior realm', beyond Macbeth's limited field of awareness, the light forces concentrate their own power, until they are ready to invade the 'upper realm' and to close in on the monster for the climactic confrontation. When the reversal has taken place and the usurping tyrant has been overthrown, what we see is a kingdom restored to itself, under its rightful king. Indeed the play ends on a note of solemn rejoic-ing as they all head off to Scone for Malcolm's coronation. Just as in other types of story, as the kingdom is restored to wholeness, the great prize has been wrested from the grip of darkness. What essentially we are looking at, albeit from an unusual angle, is a version of the familiar happy ending.

### Rebirth

It is appropriate that the story of Rebirth should conclude this sequence because, in its simpler forms, it links back so clearly to the types of plot which began it, where the dark power is presented as something wholly outside the central figure. In the fairy tale versions of Rebirth we come across in childhood the chief source of darkness in the story is personified in some mysterious older figure with magical powers, such as the malign witches who in *Snow White* or *Sleeping Beauty* place the heroine under an imprisoning spell. Later we come to those versions, like *Crime and Punishment* or *Silas Marner*, where the darkness is presented as centred within the hero or heroine's own personality. And here, since they themselves have become dark, in order to be liberated they have to go through precisely that same psychic shift we see in Voyage and Return stories or Comedy (and even begin to see in some tragedies, like *King Lear*): the move from the restricted awareness centred on the ego to that deeper centre in the human personality which opens out their understanding and unites them with all the world.

2. I make no apology for the fact that we repeatedly return to *Macbeth* as an example because, of all Shakespeare's plays, it provides the most perfect expression of the five-stage cycle of Tragedy. The fact that it is such a pure distillation of the archetypal pattern may help explain why it has aroused such superstitition in actors that they are meant never to refer to it by name but only as 'the Scottish play'.

Finally in the two Scandinavian versions, *The Snow Queen* and *Peer Gynt*, we see both versions of the Rebirth story brought together. In each case the hero is placed under an imprisoning spell by the combination of two dark, older figures outside him, a wicked magician and a powerful witch. But in each case this has the effect of bringing out the dark side of the hero's own personality, which is what gradually draws him into nightmarish isolation. At last in each case he is released from his prison by a shining personification of the 'eternal feminine', a woman both strong and loving, who is all light. This is what finally inspires the shift from the limited centre of his personality in which he has spent most of the story, to that deeper centre which he consciously recognises to be his 'true self'. Thus it is that each hero can be shown ending his story in the warmth and light of a glorious summer's day, joyously alive because he is united with the 'other half' who has at last both set him free and made him whole.

## The underlying shape of stories: Summing up

We thus see that behind each of these seven central ways in which stories naturally form in the human imagination lies the same fundamental impulse.

Each begins by showing us a hero or heroine in some way incomplete, who then encounters the dark power. Through most of the story the dark power remains dominant, casting a shadow in which all remains unresolved. But the essence of the action is that it shows us the light and dark forces in the story gradually constellating to produce a final decisive confrontation. As a result, in any story which reaches complete resolution (and of course, for reasons we shall explore later, there are many which do not), the ending shows us how the dark power can be overthrown, with the light ending triumphant. The only question is whether the central figure is identified with the light, in which case he or she ends up liberated and whole; or whether they have fallen irrevocably into the grip of darkness, in which case they are destroyed. But, whatever the fate of the central figure, the real underlying purpose of the process has been to show us how, in the end, light overcomes the darkness. Such is the archetypal pattern around which our human urge to imagine stories is ultimately centred.

At its most basic level, the way we experience the unfolding of this pattern when we are following any story lies in the contrast between the moments when we sense the pressure of the dark power closing in on the central figure and those when we sense that pressure being relaxed. The pressure may be that of an actual threat to their life; or that of some other physical or spiritual imprisonment; or it may simply be the lack of any resolution to their situation, so that they feel lost and confused, cannot make sense of their surroundings and cannot see what do next. The release comes when that pressure is lifted: when the threat to their life recedes; when they escape from imprisonment; when they can again see clearly the way forward. In fact the fundamental rhythm of any story is determined precisely by this alternation between phases of constriction and liberation. And there is a common pattern to these alternations which we have seen in every type of story we have looked at.

Again and again through our sequence of plots we noted how they unfold through a basic structure consisting of five stages. The names given to these stages did not in every instance coincide, because what is happening in them may vary according to the specific demands of each type of plot. But we can now see how, on another level, there is a basic structure underlying them all, which shows the essence of how any fully resolved story takes shape.

(1) This begins with an initial phase when we are shown how the hero or heroine feel in some way constricted. This sets up the tension requiring resolution which leads into the action of the story.

(2) This is followed by a phase of opening out, as the hero or heroine sense that they are on the road to some new state or some far-off point of resolution.

(3) Eventually this leads to a more severe phase of constriction, where the strength of the dark power and the hero or heroine's limitations in face of it both become more obvious.

(4) We then see a phase where, although the dark power is still dominant, the light elements in the story are preparing for the final confrontation. This eventually works up to the nightmare climax, when opposition between light and dark is at its most extreme and the pressure on everyone involved is at its greatest.

(5) This culminates in the moment of reversal and liberation, when the grip of the darkness is finally broken. The story thus ends on the sense of a final opening out into life, with everything at last resolved.

The essential pattern underlying all this, the pattern of any properly constructed story, is therefore that of a threefold ebb-and-flow, in which the swings between the two poles become more pronounced until the climax is reached. The initial constriction and a first, limited opening out are followed by a new, more serious constriction. This is followed by a phase of preparation which culminates in the most acute constriction of all, the story's climax. This leads to the final liberation, with the release of the prize.

At such a moment we recognise, again and again, something which lies at the very root of our lifelong experience of storytelling, in all its myriad forms and guises: the sense, at the ending of a story, that only with enormous difficulty and after a long and painful struggle, something of inestimable life-giving value has at last been worked forth from a dark, imprisoning matrix which held it fast.

When we see the essence of stories in this light we are left with three overriding questions. What is this thing of priceless value which has to be won from the shadows? What is it which casts those shadows and creates that imprisonment in the first place? And, just as important as either of these, what is it that is required for this liberation to be successfully achieved?

Such are the questions we look at in the next part of the book. But before that we may pause, in an epilogue to Part One, to take an introductory look at an extraordinarily important element in storytelling which so far we have scarcely touched on.

# The Rule of Three
## (the role played in stories by numbers)

'Three definitely is the dynamic principle itself; and "three" says Balzac, "is the formula of all creation".'     R. Allendy, *Le Symbolisme des Nombres* (1948)

'One becomes two; two becomes three; and out of the third comes the fourth, the One.'                    The 'Axiom of Maria', in alchemical literature

It is impossible to reach a proper understanding of the unconscious structures of storytelling without recognising the archetypal significance of certain numbers.

In the beginning, in almost any story, there is an all-important 'one': the central figure of the story, the hero or heroine with whom we identify.

Then, sooner or later, there arises a sense of division, of a splitting into two, as in the opposition between the story's hero and its chief dark figure, or the opposition between 'light' and 'dark' generally: the conflict which creates most of the action of the story. But there is also that other very important 'two', the hero and the heroine, the central figure and that 'other half' who can make them whole.

The most obvious number we cannot help noticing in stories, however, because it occurs so insistently in the folk tales familiar from childhood, is 'three'. Again and again we see how things appear in threes: how things have to happen three times; how the hero is given three wishes; how Cinderella goes to the ball three times; how the hero or the heroine is the third of three children.

Few childhood tales are built more conspicuously round the number three than *Goldilocks and the Three Bears*. When the little heroine arrives at the mysterious house in the forest, she sees three chairs round the table, and three bowls of porridge. When she tries each of the bowls in turn, one is too hot, one too cold, only the third is just right, and she eats it all up. When she tries the chairs, one is too hard, one too soft, only one just right, and when Goldilocks sits on it she breaks it. Lastly she goes upstairs and tries the three beds. It now seems quite natural that the first is wrong in one way, the second in another, only the third and smallest just right, and that it is here Goldilocks lies down and goes to sleep. Everything is now set for the alarming shadow to intrude, as the three bears return. At first they are still downstairs, comfortably distant, as we begin the three-fold sequence all over again, with the three bears each discovering in turn that someone has been eating their porridge and sitting in their chairs. When Baby Bear finds his chair is broken, this builds up a sense of mounting apprehension. All the time the shadow is coming closer to the sleeping heroine, even more so when the bears come upstairs to examine the beds. For a third time we go through the sequence, Father Bear first, Mother Bear next, until finally Baby Bear looks at his bed and Goldilocks is still there! For the identifying child this is the fearful climax. And it is here, as we again reach the third in this cumulative sequence of threes, that the tension is at last released, as Goldilocks leaps through the window and scuttles off home.

A story rather more subtly built up around three is *Little Red Riding Hood*. When the heroine first encounters the wolf in the forest, he seems quite friendly. On his second appearance, we see him in his true dark colours, when he arrives at the house and eats the grandmother. In his third manifestation, when Red Riding Hood herself arrives at the house, he again initially seems benign, as he tries to pass himself off as the grandmother. But by another, more obvious process of three, the heroine expresses her mounting suspicion ('what big ears you've got', 'what big eyes you've got', 'what big teeth you've got') until, on the third exchange, the wolf jumps out of bed in his true black identity, attempting to eat her: and again of course, at this moment of climax, comes the 'thrilling escape', when the woodcutter bursts in to kill the wolf with his axe.

All the childhood tales we looked at the beginning of the last chapter are similarly built up around threes. In *Jack and the Beanstalk* this takes the form of the hero's three visits to the giant's castle, escaping with three golden treasures of ascending value: the gold (which is just itself), the goose which lays golden eggs (guaranteeing an indefinite supply into the future), the golden harp (which is somehow best of all, because it plays wonderful, inspiring music, touching the soul). And as usual it is the last in the sequence of three which leads to the climax, precipitating the reversal and the end of the story. The stories of the *Three Billy Goats Gruff* and *The Three Little Pigs* are each built up around two sequences of three. Each has three heroes, who each in turn must confront the dark figure. In the first, the goats are of ascending size, and it is important that the smallest and middle-sized goats each trick the troll into letting them past, until the biggest, strongest goat can at last tackle the troll head on, butting him to destruction, thus allowing all three to proceed up the mountain to their happy ending. In the second tale, it is equally significant that the pigs build houses of ascending strength, so that the wolf can easily blow down the first, made of straw, and slightly less easily the second, made of wood, but is defeated by the third, because it is made of brick. It is this which precipitates the wolf's destruction and, for the third pig, the happy ending.[1]

The role of 'three' in these old folk tales is so explicit that one cannot miss it. When we come to a more modern example, *Peter Rabbit*, this may not be quite so obvious. But, so unconsciously engrained is the archetype of 'three', we see it playing exactly the same role in building up tension towards the climax as in a

---

1. Again 'three' plays a central part in all the folk tales we looked at in the chapter on 'Rebirth'. *Sleeping Beauty* and *Snow White*, for instance, both unfold in three stages: the first when the heroine initially falls under the shadow of the dark power as a young child; the second when she arrives at the threshold of adult life and the dark power succeeds in imprisoning her in the state of living death; the third when, years later, she is finally redeemed and brought back to life by the Prince.

folk story. When the hero finally comes face to face with Mr McGregor, he first runs away and gets caught in a net by the buttons of his coat. He is about to be caught when he wriggles out of his coat and makes his first 'thrilling escape'. He is then pursued by Mr McGregor into a shed and hides in a watering can, but gives himself away by sneezing, thus having to make a second 'thrilling escape'. Only when he feels finally trapped does he leap up onto the wheelbarrow, giving him the vision to see how to make his third 'thrilling escape'. Once again it is the third which proves the charm, allowing him at last to run off home to his happy ending.

What we see in all these examples is how 'three' is the final trigger for something important to happen. Three in stories is the number of growth and transformation. Much as we say 'Ready, steady, go' to prepare and concentrate the runners at the start of a race, so the process of three conveys the steady build up to a moment of transformation which enables the hero or heroine to move on to the next stage. It conveys to us a sense that the miraculous developments which take place in stories do not just happen instantly and effortlessly; they require a steady accumulation of experience, concentration and effort, until everything is ready to allow the transformation to take place. And we see this rule of three expressed in four main ways:

(1) The 'simple' or 'cumulative three', where each thing is of much the same value, but all three have to be put together or succeed each other in sequence before the hero or heroine can move on, or come to their final transformation: e.g., Cinderella's three visits to the ball, the three treasure-caves Aladdin has to go through before he discovers the lamp.

(2) The 'progressive' or 'ascending three', where each thing is of positive value but each a little more important or valuable than the last: e.g., the ascending value of Jack's three treasures won from the giant (this idea is more explicitly expressed in those folk tales where the hero has to win three objects, made in turn of bronze, silver and gold). There is also the 'descending three', where each is of negative value, but similarly working up to a climax (e.g., Red Riding Hood's three questions to the wolf, leading to 'all the better to eat you with' as the wolf reveals his true deadly character).

(3) The 'contrasting' or 'double-negative three', where the first two are inadequate or wrong (essentially in the same way) and only the third one works or succeeds. We see an element of this in the three little pigs, two of whom get eaten, although it is most commonly seen in folk tales where the hero or heroine is the third child, contrasted with two identical others, usually older, who are dark. Cinderella's two 'ugly sisters' are as alike as identical twins. They are there merely to present a double-negative to Cinderella's positive, as do the heroine's two sisters in *Beauty and the Beast*.

(4) The final form of three, the one capable of the most sophisticated development, is what may be called the 'dialectical three' where, as we see reflected in *Goldilocks*, the first is wrong in one way, the second in another or opposite way, and only the third, in the middle, is just right. This idea that the

way forward lies in finding an exact middle path between opposites is of extraordinary importance in storytelling and, as we shall see, some of the ways in which it finds expression are of breathtaking subtlety.

So far in this introduction to the role of numbers in stories we have focused on those simple childhood tales where the 'rule of three' is obvious. But in earlier chapters we have already caught glimpses of how this rule plays the same function, rather less blatantly, in more sophisticated types of story. We saw how often in Quest stories, for instance, the hero has to face three final ordeals before he can secure his goal: as in the three tests imposed on Jason before he can win the Golden Fleece; or the three battles faced by Aeneas before he can marry the Princess and safely establish his new kingdom; or the three ordeals faced by Allan Quatermain and his friends in *King Solomon's Mines* before they can overthrow the Tyrant Twala and the Witch Gagool to secure the treasure. In *King Lear*, as in a folk tale, we see Cordelia as the third, light daughter, contrasted with the double-negative of her two dark, scheming sisters. In *A Christmas Carol* we see the character of Scrooge in his dark state initially defined by three acts of anti-social heartlessness; these trigger off the three successive nightmares centred on the spirits of Christmas Past, Present and Future which eventually trigger off his rebirth; and this is confirmed when, in his reborn, light self, he finally reverses each of the acts of rejection with which the story began.

Once we become aware of the archetypal significance of three in storytelling, we can see it everywhere, expressed in all sorts of different ways, large and small. It is something so fundamental to the way the human imagination works, that it often appears in ways of which not even the storyteller may have been conscious. It seems, for instance, quite natural that when Aladdin gets trapped in the cave after retrieving the lamp, he should be stuck there for three days. It seems the right number to convey the process of him gradually losing all hope until, when the third day is up, he at last despairingly rubs the ring on his finger and is confronted by the genie who releases him. It seems equally natural that when Charlotte Bronte describes Jane Eyre running away across the moors after her aborted wedding, she should have shown her heroine wandering distractedly for three days until she finally becomes so desperate that she throws herself on a doorstep to die. Only then is she discovered by St John Rivers and taken in to be restored to life.

The real point of this emphasis on three is the way it conveys to us, by a kind of symbolic shorthand, just how tortuous and difficult is the process whereby the hero or heroine is working towards their ultimate goal; and how there is only one, correct way for them to thread the path which will eventually lead them to their prize.

Indeed one of the more obvious ways in which this can be presented is in all those stories where, to reach the goal, the hero or heroine has to pass precisely between two equally deadly opposites, representing a 'double negative'. We saw this in all those Quest stories where a passage between the opposites was one of the ordeals the hero and his companions have to undergo, from Jason's Argo navigating between the clashing rocks to the 'straight and narrow' path to which Christian must keep to survive his perilous journey through the Valley of the Shadow of Death. In the version faced by Odysseus, when he has to sail exactly between Scylla and Charybdis, this emerges as more like a 'dialectical three', where each opposite poses a different threat, which is why Odysseus has to run the gauntlet twice. First he steers too near the monster Scylla, the second time too near the whirlpool Charybdis, so that he suffers the ill effects of both. But at least in the end he comes through; unlike Icarus who, ignoring his father's instruction to keep to the middle position, errs too far in one wrong direction, by flying too high, with the result that he is plunged into the opposite direction and is destroyed. Another explicit echo of the 'dialectical three' is the instruction given by his father to Robinson Crusoe that he must pursue a 'middle station' in life, not aspiring too high or sinking too low; which is where, after learning all the profound lessons his adventures have taught him, he finally reaches the happy ending of his story.

What all these different forms of the rule of three have in common is that they convey the gradual working out of a process, which will eventually lead to some kind of transformation. This can just as well be a transformation downwards as upwards. But most often we see it related to that essential theme of so many stories, the process of growth. It symbolises the slow process whereby the hero or heroine are striving towards some hugely important goal which, when it is finally achieved, we can see represents full maturity, the realisation of a state of fulfilment and wholeness. And this is why, as a story moves towards its ending, we are usually made aware of that which is needed for all the developments which we have seen taking place in the story to reach a state of completion: a word we use in two senses. Firstly it can mean that a process is complete, as when a sequence has unfolded to its conclusion. But secondly it can mean the putting together of all the component parts of something to make a complete whole.

A story which in very simple form presents this need to integrate all the parts in order to make a whole is a little tale from the Grimm brothers collection called *The Three Languages*. The hero is an apparently stupid boy who is sent off by his father for three successive years to be educated. After the first year he comes back having learned nothing but to understand what dogs are saying when they bark. In the second he learns nothing but the language of frogs. In the third he learns nothing but the language of birds. His father is enraged that the boy has so wasted his time. But together these skills have made a whole. The hero has learned the language of animals in all three elements, the dogs of land, the frogs of water, the birds of the air – and we recognise that somehow each of these skills will eventually have to be used in turn, to complete his transformation. Sure enough, after a while, the hero goes on a journey. His first skill enables him to win a great treasure, guarded by fierce dogs. The second enables him to interpret a prophecy by frogs that he will become the Pope, so he heads for the city of Rome, where he discovers the existing Pope has just died. The third, as the assembled cardinals are looking for a sign as to whom to choose to succeed, causes two snow-white doves to alight on the hero's shoulder (making a three) and whisper into his ear the words of the Mass. The hero is chosen. He has developed and integrated three elements in himself to make a 'whole', and the result is that he becomes a 'supreme ruler'.

### 'Four': The number of completion

At an even deeper level, as we saw at the end of Chapter Twelve, the whole of the way in which the human imagination unconsciously shapes a story is itself rooted in the 'rule of three', in that it follows that three-fold rhythm which provides stories with their most basic archetypal structure. Firstly, we see the central figure in some way constricted, but then enjoying a phase of limited enlargement. Secondly, we see the dark power closing in to impose a more severe sense of constriction (the 'central crisis'), which leads in turn to that gradual constellation of the light and dark elements in the story as they move towards their final showdown. Thirdly, in the story's climax, we see the most acute phase of constriction of all, as the prelude to that reversal which leads to the overthrow of darkness and the liberation of light.

Thus is the rule of three, as the pattern of growth and transformation, built into the very foundations of the way we imagine stories. But the nearer we get to the moment of completion or wholeness at the end of a story, the more likely we are somehow to see the number four appearing. In *Cinderella* the heroine is three times transformed from her rags into her finery, as she goes to the ball. Each time she returns to her rags and ashes, until she has gone through a second process of three, whereby the two ugly sisters try on the slipper and fail and she succeeds. Then at last, as the story reaches its conclusion, we see her make the fourth and final transformation back into her fine clothes. [2]

We see many similar examples of how some image of four emerges at the ending of stories. Hans Andersen's little ugly duckling, after his transformation, joins the three 'kingly swans' to make the fourth. At the end of *The Three Musketeers*, as the young outsider D'Artagnan finally emerges triumphant from his long battle with his monstrous opponent Lady de Winter, he is at last accepted by his close-knit trio of comrades as 'the fourth musketeer'. In *A Winter's Tale* and *The Marriage of Figaro*, we see the power of the Comedy ending reinforced by the bringing together not just of one couple but two, so that the stage can be dominated by four joyful figures, all at last at one with each other. In *The Secret Garden* the redeeming figure of Dickon triggers off three successive 'rebirths', those of Mary, Colin and finally Mr Craven, so that the closing image of the story is of all four standing joyfully together in the garden.

2. In the first published edition of the Cinderella story, included in Charles Perrault's collection of French folk-tales, *Histoires ou Contes du Temps Passé* (1697), he describes her as only going to the ball twice. This may have been because Perrault heard an already corrupted version; or that, in adapting the story for a French court audience, he shortened it because he did not understand the significance of the Rule of Three. But in almost all other folk-versions of the story (e.g., *Aschenputtel*, in the collection of German folk-tales by the Grimm brothers), the heroine sees the Prince-hero three times in her disguise, before the final fourth encounter which reveals her true identity.

Four in stories is the number of completion and perfection. Even during the earlier stages of the story, we often have a subconscious sense of the presence of four elements or figures which have not yet come together and revealed their potential, as when the hero of *The Three Languages* is waiting with his three skills for the moment of transformation. And in the next part of the book we shall see just how profoundly the number four as a symbol of totality provides the bedrock for the unconscious processes which create stories in the human imagination.

But of course the supreme symbol of completion in storytelling is the union of two people, hero and heroine, masculine and feminine, to make a whole: because they are seen as complementary in a more fundamental way than anything we know. Only when this has been achieved can hero and heroine together succeed to the kingdom: because the two have finally become one.

Such is the complete happy ending which lies at the heart of storytelling. What this really stands for is the theme of the next section of our book. And in exploring this we shall see how the hidden significance of numbers in stories opens up in a wholly new and dramatic way.[3]

3. Although the chief archetypal numbers around which stories are structured are one, two, three and four, other numbers which appear less often are those which combine and reinforce their significance, particularly compounds or multiples of three and four. Back into prehistory seven has taken on symbolic or magical significance as a combination of three and four, as in the mythical seven gateways to the underworld, the seven sages of the Greek world, the seven against Thebes, the seven ages of man, the seven deadly sins, the seven cardinal virtues. The Sumerians and later civilisations spoke of seven planets or 'heavenly wanderers', including the sun and the moon. Nine is significant as three times three, as in the nine Muses. Twelve is significant as three times four, making up a totality, as in the twelve apostles or the twelve supreme Greek gods on Olympus. Dante's *Divine Comedy*, which as we shall see in Chapter 33 is structured round the rule of three as comprehensively as any story in the world, is divided into three books each of 33 cantos, apart from the first which acts as prologue to the whole work, to make a round 100 in all.

# PART TWO

# *The Complete Happy Ending*

'The treasure which the hero fetches from the dark cavern is *life*: it is himself.'
C. G. Jung, *Symbols of Transformation*

# Prologue to Part Two

One of the most popular Hollywood films of the mid-1980s, *Crocodile Dundee* (1986), began with the dramatic arrival by helicopter in the remote Australian outback of a young American woman journalist. Sue Charlton was everything a thrusting professional woman in the post-feminist age was meant to be: forceful, resourceful, self-possessed. In addition she was the daughter of her New York paper's rich proprietor, and girl friend of its ambitious young editor, which in storytelling terms makes her the modern equivalent of a 'king's daughter' being wooed by a 'prince'.

The heroine has travelled to this tiny, dusty settlement in the back of beyond in the hope of interviewing a legendary local hunter, Mick 'Crocodile' Dundee. The first half of the story shows him taking her out into the bush, introducing her to all the dangers of the wild, from man-eating crocodiles to deadly snakes; and watching with wry amusement as her confident metropolitan *persona* crumbles when confronted with these fearsome monsters. She becomes a frail, helpless woman, looking for protection to this masterful hunter, with his teasing sense of humour. So completely does she fall under his spell that she decides to take him back to New York to show him life at the centre of modern urban civilisation. Here we meet her boyfriend, who treats Dundee with impatient disdain as some kind of primitive, 'below the line' freak. As the hero wanders through the city, the film contrasts his simple, unspoiled, good-hearted strength of character, as a 'natural man', with the unnatural state of the urban jungle around him, where perversion, violence and drug-taking rule, and where everyone seems morally and spiritually deformed. Such is the world represented by the heroine's boyfriend. Finally, as a grand 'above the line' party is thrown to announce the couple's engagement, Dundee cannot bear the thought of her marrying this pampered, vain monster who corresponds only to her outward career-girl persona. Next day he vanishes off into the city, disappearing down a subway. In a state of shocked 'recognition', the heroine heads off in desperate search for him, eventually descending into the 'inferior realm' of the subway station, where she sees him at the far end of a platform jammed with people. In the closing scene, by way of verbal messages passed along the packed crowd, the two proclaim their love for each other. The crowd is drawn into the spirit of this remarkable declaration, bursting into rapturous applause as Dundee walks on people's upturned hands to join her. As they finally come together it seems the whole world is at one with their joy.

In terms of its plot, *Crocodile Dundee* is a perfect example of Comedy – with the heroine seemingly doomed by her outward *persona* to marry the dark figure; until the recognition brings her to see, in the nick of time, that in her true feminine self she belongs with the true manly hero. Like countless stories before it, the film ends with its own modern version of the ancient fairy tale formula, 'they got married and lived happily ever after'.

We so take it for granted that this should provide a perfectly satisfactory happy ending to a story that we scarcely pause to reflect on just how odd this should be. Obviously in real life we do not look on marriage as an ending, certainly not in the all-resolving way in which it is presented as the conclusion to so many stories. It is more a beginning, a landmark along the road to a new state of life which may bring not only rewards but also all sorts of new challenges and problems.

Yet the fact remains that in stories the image of a wedding, or at least the bringing together of a man and a woman in a state of loving union, is the most complete form of happy ending we know. Something deep within us recognises this image as the moment of supreme fulfilment, when everything is at last complete and whole, when all the uncertainties of the story are resolved, when all its shadows have been lifted, and where hero and heroine are at last at one with each other and with life.

What we are about to look at in this second part of the book is what this great archetypal union really stands for, and why so many stories shape themselves towards this central concluding image. In fact what we are about to see is how, in order for the hero and heroine to reach this goal, they must be shown as representing a specific set of qualities. Only then, when we have built up a picture of the conditions which must be met for a story to come to a complete happy ending, can we move on, in the third part of the book, to see just why it is that so many stories should, in different ways, fail to reach such an all-resolving conclusion.

The first step towards this lies in focusing at last on a crucial element in storytelling which we have so far touched on only obliquely. Up to now we have concentrated on the structure of stories. What we must now look at in the same way are the characters who appear in stories. Just as we have seen how much of the seemingly almost infinite variety of storytelling resolves in the end down to providing variations on just a handful of plots, we now similarly see how all the host of characters who teem through storytelling ultimately resolve down to just a handful of basic archetypal figures. As we see what each of these figures stands for, and the nature of their fundamental relationships to the hero or heroine, so we arrive at the central key to understanding what stories are really about.

*Chapter 13*

# The Dark Figures

'The Shadow is the door to our individuality. Insofar as the Shadow is our first view of the unconscious part of our personality, it represents the first stage towards meeting the Self.'     Edward Whitmont, *The Symbolic Quest*

It is no accident that many of the stories we particularly respond to in childhood are based on the Rags to Riches plot, because no other type of story so consistently follows the growing up of its central figure from childhood into adult life. We begin with a little hero or heroine who, in the early stages of the story, usually at home, is powerless, ill-treated and unhappy. The main reason for this is that they are cruelly overshadowed by heartless older figures who look down on them with contempt and hostility. David Copperfield is the little orphan who, after losing his real parents, has fallen into the clutches of Mr and Miss Murdstone, who become his tyrannical step-parents. Jane Eyre is the little orphan who, miserable in the guardianship of her dead mother's sister and scorned by her young cousins, is sent off to the orphanage by the tyrannical pillar of rectitude Mr Brocklehurst. The little orphan Cinderella is tyrannised over by her wicked stepmother and ugly stepsisters. Joseph is despised and nearly killed by his older brothers. In fact, if we examine a whole range of Rags to Riches stories, we see how these overshadowing dark figures who surround the hero or heroine at the beginning of the story fall into three main categories:

**1. The Dark Father**

Firstly there is the older man who stands in some position of power or authority over the hero or heroine, usually in the place of a lost father: e.g., Copperfield's stepfather Mr Murdstone; Jane Eyre's Mr Brocklehurst; Aladdin's Sorcerer, who pretends to be the long-lost brother of the hero's dead father. This powerful, tyrannical figure, representing strong male authority in its most heartless, egotistical guise, is the Dark Father.

**2. The Dark Mother**

Secondly there is his female counterpart, the older woman who may stand in place of a lost mother: e.g., Copperfield's Miss Murdstone; Jane Eyre's Aunt Reed; Cinderella's stepmother, who has replaced her real, loving mother. This similarly heartless and oppressive figure is the Dark Mother.

241

### 3. The Dark Rivals

Thirdly there are the younger characters, of the same sex as the hero or heroine, and of roughly similar age and status, who also act as oppressors: e.g., Cinderella's stepsisters, Joseph's jealous brothers.

As the hero or heroine go out into the world, they may meet with more general scorn or persecution from society at large: e.g., the other animals who heap derision on the Ugly Duckling, or the bystanders who scorn the ragged, uncouth little flower seller Eliza Doolittle. But, as the story develops, the only other serious contender they are likely to encounter along the way is:

### 4. The Dark Other Half

This is a character of the opposite sex who seems to hold out the possibility of union with the hero or heroine, but is in fact self-seeking and treacherous, or in some other way inadequate: e.g., Potiphar's wife, the Temptress who tries to seduce Joseph; Jane Eyre's St John Rivers; Copperfield's silly and infantile first wife Dora Spenlow.

All the main characters we see opposed to the hero or heroine of a Rags to Riches story thus fall into one of these four categories: Dark Father, Dark Mother, Dark Rival and Dark Other Half.

In the earlier stages of the story, particularly while the hero or heroine are still very young, the Dark Father or Dark Mother are likely to be dominant. As the central figure moves into adulthood, the emphasis is likely to shift more towards the Dark Other Half and the Dark Rivals, who are now seen more directly as competitors for the hero or heroine's ultimate goal – as in the closing stages of *Cinderella* where, in the episode of the 'slipper test', we see her stepsisters hoping that it is they who will be chosen as the rightful 'other half' to the Prince. By the middle of the story indeed there may have emerged just one Dark Rival, posing such a particular threat that he or she comes to stand as a kind of Dark Alter-Ego to the central figure. An example is the emergence of Jane Eyre's shadowy rival for the hand of Mr Rochester, his crazed and malevolent first wife. In Aladdin this shift of emphasis is expressed with particular subtlety in the hero's changing relationship to the central dark figure who dogs him throughout the story. Initially, when Aladdin is still a young boy, the Sorcerer appears unmistakably as a Dark Father-figure. But later, when the hero has grown up, and the Sorcerer reappears to snatch Aladdin's Princess off to Africa, he has become a classic Dark Rival, or Dark Alter-Ego. Finally he reappears as an even more deadly Dark Rival, when he returns in disguise to try to kill Aladdin; and his death corresponds to the hero's final emergence into the light and union with the Princess.

Measured against these dark figures, the hero or heroine themselves provide a complete contrast. They are not cruel, treacherous, vain or self-seeking. Their real problem, at the beginning of the story, as underdogs in the shadows, is simply that they are lost and do not know what to do. Initially they seem at the mercy of fate and of the dark figures who so cruelly dominate their lives. That is why, in so many Rags to Riches stories, the first step towards their being drawn towards some ultimate happy ending is that they find a mysterious ally; either a 'helpful animal', as when Dick Whittington finds his cat or Aladdin his genies; or a 'light' Father or Mother-figure, as when Cinderella meets her fairy godmother or David Copperfield his kindly aunt Betsey Trotwood, who eventually adopts him. The first half of the story shows them, with the aid of their light allies, making considerable progress as they grow up outwardly and venture out on the stage of the world. They may even, by the halfway stage, seem within reach of a happy ending, either on the brink of marriage, like Jane Eyre, or married already, like Aladdin or David Copperfield.

But then comes the 'central crisis', when their world falls apart again. They lose all that is dear to them, and we see that inwardly they have not yet really matured at all. What the second half of the story shows is how they discover their own inner strengths, and learn to take charge of their own destiny. The final test invariably shows them confronting the dark power entirely on their own, relying on their own strength. Jane Eyre, as she reaches the climax of her potentially deadly struggle with the iron-willed St John Rivers, is inspired by inwardly hearing the mysterious voice of Rochester; but she feels at last that 'my powers were in play'. Aladdin finally overcomes the Sorcerer's brother entirely on his own, having been explicitly told by the genie that he can no longer expect any magical help. David Copperfield goes off alone for three years after the death of his wife Dora, initially miserable: but he emerges as a rich and famous writer, with his own position in the world, recognising at last with overwhelming certainty that he must track down his 'true angel' Agnes (who for so long has been in the shadow of the monstrous Dark Rival Uriah Heep), to rescue her from the shadows and marry her.

What all these stories in fact show is that, in order to reach their goal, the central figure eventually has to demonstrate a particular *balance* of qualities. Initially these heroes and heroines are shown as open to the path which is to lead to their eventual self-realisation because they are good-natured. They are not blinded and isolated from the world by egocentricity. They are not, like the antagonistic figures around them, dark. But although this may win them the invaluable help of their light allies, it is not enough in itself to bring them to their final goal. Ultimately, as the other half of the equation, they have to prove themselves in two other respects. They have to learn to stand on their own feet, to demonstrate inner strength and will power, to become self-reliant. Secondly they have to develop understanding. They have to see clearly and precisely what it is they have to do. It is this combination of qualities, that they are selflessly loving, strong and have a clear vision of what they must do, which finally wins them complete union with their 'other half'. And it is because they have become master or mistress of themselves, that we finally have the confidence when they succeed to rule over some kind of 'kingdom' that they will do it wisely, unselfishly and for the good of all.[1]

1. An exception to this usual pattern is the story of Joseph from the biblical book of *Genesis*. As a boy, isolated from his brothers by his gift for prophetic dreams, Joseph is in danger of having his ego inflated, as by the dreams which show his brothers bowing down to him. In this sense he is potentially a dark figure. When his brothers force him out into the world, by abandoning him to die in the wilderness, the fate from which he is rescued when he is sold as a slave into Egypt, his gift for interpreting the dreams of others eventually proves the key to his being raised to a position of immense power and wealth. As Phaoroah's chief minister he is already 'ruler over the kingdom'.

## Overcoming the Monster

In the Rags to Riches story, the dark figures are seen as relating to the hero or heroine in a very personal way, in the context of private and family life. In keeping with the more mythical resonances of the Overcoming the Monster plot, the figures who here personify the dark power tend to assume much grander and more terrifying proportions altogether.

Nevertheless, a good many dark figures in such stories still appear in familiar guise:

1. *The Dark Father-figure, or Tyrant*: this may again be the older man who has in some way replaced the hero's lost father: e.g., the Giant in *Jack and the Beanstalk*, who killed Jack's father and usurped his inheritance; or Sir Ralph Nickleby, brother of the hero's dead father in *Nicholas Nickleby*. On the other hand, because of the wider ramifications of this type of story, this figure may represent paternal or masculine authority in some more general way, as a tyrannical king (e.g., Minos) or some other kind of 'dark ruler' (e.g., Squeers, the tyrannical headmaster; Gessler, the tyrannical Austrian governor in the legend of William Tell; the Sheriff of Nottingham in the story of Robin Hood).

2. *The Dark Mother-figure, or Witch*: this is the treacherous, ruthless older woman who no longer just wants to repress the hero or heroine, as in Rags to Riches stories, but to kill them: e.g., the wicked stepmother who is transmuted into the witch in *Hansel and Gretel*. But again this category now runs wider to include all those powerful and deadly older women who feature in stories as 'the female monster': e.g., the Gorgon Medusa; Oedipus's Sphinx (literally 'the strangler'), the witch who casts her murderous shadow over the kingdom of Thebes; Lady de Winter, 'the most powerful woman in France', who is D'Artagnan's chief antagonist in *The Three Musketeers*; Rosa Klebb, the sadistic head of SMERSH in the James Bond story *From Russia with Love*.

3. *The Dark Rivals*: e.g., Moriarty, the 'Napoleon of Crime', who, as Sherlock Holmes's only intellectual equal, is his Dark Alter-Ego; the outlaw gang who are rivals to Sheriff Kane's authority over the town in *High Noon*.

But so potentially cosmic is the nature of the 'monster' in stories based on this plot – when we think of such examples as the Minotaur, Humbaba, Grendel, Dracula, the super-villains of Bond stories, with their ambitions to hold the entire world to ransom – that he often appears simply as a kind of huge, inflated 'dark opposite' to the hero, a grotesque abstract of the dark power in its most extreme form. He is the very personification of egotism, in all its greedy, aggressive, undisguised horror. He is twisted, treacherous, utterly malevolent. In his

---

But for the equation to be complete he also has to show, as a counterpoise to his outward power, that he is not heartless and selfish. Above all, for the story to be resolved, he has to be reconciled with his brothers. They come to him as underdogs, in a reversal of the situation at the start of the story. Now it is he who is 'above the line', they who are in the 'inferior realm', in his shadow. But inspired by his love for his youngest brother, 'little Benjamin', Joseph eventually treats them all with complete love and forgiveness, so that they are all joyfully at one. In this respect Joseph's story, although primarily shaped by the Rags to Riches plot, also contains a strong element of the Rebirth story: the strong man, inwardly frozen in an old grievance which hardened his heart, finally thawed out into a state of complete love and reconciliation.

physical and moral deformation, and his curious combination of human and animal attributes, he is, as we saw, anything but a complete, whole human being. He may have a strangely ageless, supernatural aura, as if he represents some ancient transcendent power. Above all the monster represents death. He is not just out to imprison the hero but to kill him. He has probably killed many others before. He may spread his shadow over a whole community, a whole kingdom, even over the world. And in setting out to challenge such a stupendously powerful being, the hero is bidding to become truly exceptional, seeking to succeed where many others have failed.

Superficially we might think all that is required for the hero to overcome this monstrous figure is sufficient courage and strength. Certainly the great monster-slayers of storytelling, from Perseus to Beowulf, from Siegfried to James Bond, have never lacked for such manly qualities. But when we come to see how the conflict is actually presented by stories, there is rather more to it.

For a start we have to see the hero as light, in complete contrast to the darkness of his opponent. For this we have to see that he is acting not just to further his own interests but on behalf of others; in particular, in the first half of the story, this means on behalf of the wider community which the monster is threatening. Gilgamesh sets out to challenge Humbaba because the monster is casting a shadow over his kingdom of Uruk; David challenges Goliath because the giant is threatening his country, Israel; Theseus journeys over the sea to challenge the Minotaur and his master, the tyrant Minos, because they are threatening his father's kingdom of Athens; Beowulf is called in from his own country because Grendel is threatening to destroy the kingdom of Heorot; Dracula is threatening to become master of England; James Bond's villains are threatening England, the West, all mankind; Darth Vader, in *Star Wars*, is threatening to impose his tyranny over the entire universe.

Once we have established some idea of the terrifying threat the monster poses to the world, and the courage of the hero in setting out to challenge it, the main thing the action of the story requires is simply that the two protagonists should be brought closer to one another until they are ready for the final decisive confrontation. Either the hero is travelling towards the monster, or the monster is approaching him, until at last the hero has the centre of darkness fully in view: at which point the monster's power seems so immense that it is hard to imagine how the hero in its shadow can possibly defeat it.

But as the story nears its climax, we may also become acutely aware that the monster is directly threatening another figure, the story's heroine. When Perseus sees the sea-monster, he sees that it is also bearing down on the Princess Andromeda, chained to her rock. St George rides into battle not just to save the town the dragon is threatening, but much more particularly the Princess tied to a stake. Dracula may be threatening England, but much more specifically he has set his sights on the hero's fiancée Mina, and is within an ace of destroying her. Dr No may be threatening the security of the Western world, but what matters more at the end of the story is that he has tied down the beautiful beach girl, Honeychile Rider, to be eaten alive by crabs. The central fact of which we are aware as *Star Wars* moves towards its climax is that Darth Vader, the would-be 'dark ruler of the universe', has imprisoned and is torturing the Princess Leia.

At such a moment, however little we may actually know about the heroine, we see her as a figure of extraordinary significance and numinosity. It is the most important thing in the world that she should be saved. In fact there are always three things we instinctively recognise in such a situation. On the one hand there is the hard, heartless, masculine strength of the monster. On the other, in total contrast, is the soft, vulnerable femininity of the heroine who is being threatened. The monster stands for strength without the balance of feeling, which means death. The heroine stands for feeling and life, but is without the strength to defend herself. But what we then see, as the hero comes between them to save her, is that he is a balance between the two. He is not only strong, fearless, utterly masculine. In responding to her helpless vulnerability he is inwardly open to the femininity which the heroine represents. The hero stands for strength transfigured and made life-giving by his capacity for selfless feeling. In balancing the opposites of masculine and feminine, the hero is potentially whole.

So much accounts for why we instinctively sense our support for the hero in his challenge to the monster. But it does not account for why he wins the battle: and here the reason is not usually that he is stronger than the monster. In purely physical terms, the monster may well be the stronger of the two, which is why he seems to have all the odds on his side. In straightforward hand-to-hand combat, Goliath would have beaten David any day. Perseus was probably puny compared to the sea-monster. Dracula had a whole array of magic powers at his command. The real secret of the hero's ultimate superiority is that the monster has a blind spot. That is why, by the true hero, he can be outwitted: as Goliath was by David's use from a safe distance of his slingstones; as the sea-monster was by Perseus's use of the Gorgon's head to turn him to stone; Dracula by the hero's knowledge of the one thing which could kill him, a stake to the heart. Luke Skywalker can eliminate the Death Star because he knows of the one spot in all its immense structure where it is vulnerable. In all three Quatermass stories, most of the action centres on the hero gradually puzzling out the true nature of the mysterious monster he is up against, which eventually gives him the necessary clues as to how it can be overcome. What ultimately puts the hero in charge of the situation is that, by the climax of the story, he can in some crucial respect see more clearly than the monster, and knows precisely what he is doing.

Thus the combination of qualities which the hero requires to overcome the monster is exactly the same as that required by the hero or heroine of a Rags to Riches story. He has to show that is acting selflessly, in some cause outside himself. He has to show himself inwardly strong, determined, totally self-reliant. In the end, as the final key in the lock, he has to have superior understanding, a clear vision of what he has to do.

Of course there are also Overcoming the Monster stories where the heroine is not just a passive potential victim waiting to be rescued from the shadows by the hero, but where she herself plays a much more active part in saving him and assisting him to his victory.

When Theseus sets out for Crete to liberate his country from the deadly shadow cast by King Minos and his dreadful creature, the Minotaur, the tutelary deity hovering protectively over him is Aphrodite, the goddess of love. It might seem a detail strangely irrelevant to so 'masculine' a contest. But when Theseus arrives, the first person to see him is Minos's daughter Ariadne, who falls in love with him. When he is led into the dark labyrinth to face the monster which lurks at its heart, it is Ariadne who secretly equips Theseus with the two 'magic weapons' which are to prove vital to his success: the sword with which he can slay the Minotaur, and the thread which will enable him to find the way out of the 'pathless maze'. It is the Princess's courage and strength of will which have enabled the hero to use properly his own masculine strength to win the victory. Where Theseus would otherwise have been reduced to impotence, it is the 'active' heroine who has given life to his strength and enabled him to see clearly his way out again into the light. Again we see a hero who, if he had not been open to the feminine, would not have succeeded in his immense task. It is Ariadne's own balance of love with inner strength which enables her to supply what Theseus needs in his desperate plight, enabling him to rise to his fully manly stature, allowing him to take charge of the situation and to see whole. Thus is he able to liberate his country, and on his return home to succeed as its king.[2]

We again see the heroine coming to the hero's rescue in his desperate hour of need in the film *High Noon*. When word comes that the murderous Miller gang is approaching to take over the town, Sheriff Kane seems wholly alone. No one will stand with him to resist the dark power. Fearing the worst, he persuades his new bride to leave town. As the climactic battle begins, he seems at the outlaws' mercy. But, just when all seems lost, a crucial shot rings out from an unexpected quarter. Inspired by the hero's bravery and her love for him, the heroine has returned, to provide just the element of strength needed to turn the battle. Thanks to her courage, he can complete the routing of the 'monster', and between them they have saved the 'kingdom'.

## The Quest

In no other type of story is the hero faced by such a range and variety of dark figures as in the Quest. But again these fall into familiar categories:

(1) *the Tyrant, or Dark Father-figure*: Odysseus's chief opponent through most of his journey, after he has blinded Polyphemus, is the giant's grimly vengeful father Poseidon, the 'dark lord of the sea'; Jason's chief antagonist is the tyrant-king Aetes; other examples are the cruel, overbearing figure of Phaoraoh, who tries to keep the children of Israel imprisoned in Egypt;

---

2. The strong-minded heroine who, from within the monster's camp, secretly switches to become the hero's closest ally is seen many times in storytelling. Another familiar instance in Greek mythology was Medea, the daughter of Jason's chief enemy, the tyrant-king Aetes, who helped him to win the Golden Fleece (again by providing him with the means of outwitting the monster, the serpent-guardian of the 'prize', by making it 'lose consciousness'). There are many instances in modern thrillers (e.g., *The Riddle of the Sands* by Erskine Childers), and this was a frequent motif in the James Bond stories, e.g., *From Russia with Love*, where the Russian agent Tatiana Romanova changes sides to help Bond win the 'treasure' he is after, the secret Soviet cipher-machine, before, like Ariadne or Medea, escaping with him for the journey home.

the evil King Twala, tyrant over the lost land of King Solomon's mines;

• General Woundwort, the 'dark ruler' over the hostile warren of Efrafa in *Watership Down*;

(2) *the Witch, or 'Dark Queen'*: Aeneas's chief opponent through most of his journey to Italy is the grimly vengeful 'Queen of Heaven' Juno; another instance is Gagool, the ancient witch-guardian of the treasure in *King Solomon's Mines*;

(3) *the Dark Rivals*: these again become increasingly prominent as the hero nears his goal: e.g., the suitors clustered threateningly round Penelope; Turnus, the hero's rival for the Princess and the kingdom in the *Aeneid*; the resident tribes who try to prevent the children of Israel from occupying the Promised Land.

When we come to the fourth category, however, we see a curious ambivalence emerging:

(4) *the Dark Other Half*: this is a figure who, in her guise as the Temptress, plays a particularly prominent part in Quest stories. But when we are confronted by such examples as Circe and Calypso in the *Odyssey*, it is difficult to pin down whether they are to be regarded as the beautiful women they first appear to be, or as ageless witches in disguise, armed with supernatural powers to imprison the hero and to hold him back from pursuing his quest (Circe, for instance, is explicitly described as 'a witch'). Similarly, when Aeneas falls in love with Dido (at the instigation of his real enemy, the dark goddess Juno), she is not represented as a young Princess whom he would easily marry. She is a widowed Queen, a mature woman with the power to bewitch him by her love, to enfeeble him and make him forget what he should be doing, which is to proceed on his journey.

In other words, when we consider the 'dark feminine' power which can hold back the hero of a story from his true purpose, we see a link beginning to emerge between the mature, beguiling Temptress as 'Dark Other Half' and the treacherous witch or Dark Mother-figure. When we consider the 'dark masculine' power standing rather more aggressively in the hero's path, we have already seen in Aladdin how the figure of the Dark Father can be transmuted into that of a Dark Rival. Similarly in *Watership Down* General Woundwort is not just a Tyrant and 'dark ruler': as leader of the rival warren he stands as an exact dark opposite and rival to the story's hero Hazel. Behind their variety of outward guises, the dark figures are more closely connected than they at first appear.

And of course we also begin to see in the Quest, more explicitly than in the earlier types of story, occasions where the hero and his companions themselves make potentially fatal errors, putting them at the mercy of their dark antagonists – and these invariably result from a failure of their own awareness.

When Odysseus sets out with his men for home there is no doubt about his manly strength and cunning. As a soldier he has been one of the great heroes of the Trojan War. What does come into doubt as soon as the journey begins is their ability to see clearly the nature of all the dangers they encounter on the way, and whether they have the self-control and willpower which will enable them to resist those perils. The essence of the journey is how again and again they make foolish errors, falling into one trap after another. They fall for almost every temptation placed in their way. To begin with they are beguiled and intoxicated by the pleasures of Lotus-eating. They then meet their first really serious disaster by failing to recognise the true nature of the island and the cave where Polyphemus lives. When Aeolus gives them bags holding all the contrary winds which enable them, still early in the journey, to come back within sight of Ithaca, Odysseus drowses off, losing consciousness. His men, blinded by greed into thinking the bags contain treasure, open them, leading to the worst disaster of all, when they are blown onto the island of the cannibal giants of Laestrygonia, who eat eleven of the twelve shiploads. They are fooled by the treachery of Circe, who seems to offer them feasting and ease, but in fact only wants to imprison them as animals. They fail to steer a proper course between the deadly 'opposites' of Scylla and Charybdis, suffering further losses to the monster Scylla.

Gradually, however, as the journey proceeds through one disaster and near-disaster after another, Odysseus develops clearer vision and greater self-control. Already, by the time they reach the island of Laestrygonia, Odysseus has become canny enough to remain behind, while the crews of the other eleven ships are tricked into their doom. When they arrive next on Circe's isle, he is again careful to send only half his surviving men ahead, and it is this which allows him to win the help of the god Hermes in overcoming the witch's powers and liberating all her victims. Once the Witch-Temptress has been mastered, she switches from dark to light to become an invaluable helper. And it is she who sends Odysseus on down to the underworld where the 'wise old man' Teiresias gives him a vision of what still lies ahead of him and what he must do to finish the journey. He survives the enchantments of the Sirens by the forethought of having himself strapped to the mast, although he cannot then stop his men from disobeying his strict orders not to interfere with the cattle of the Sun, which leads to their being struck by a thunderbolt. This leaves Odysseus at last all alone, to face yet another disaster when he steers this time too near the other 'opposite', the whirlpool Charybdis. At this point, literally 'all washed up', he is only too grateful to sink into the embraces of the beautiful Calypso for a seemingly interminable period of sensual ease and doing nothing, the longest episode of the entire journey. It takes Odysseus seven years to develop the strength and willpower to break loose from Calypso's enchantments (with the aid of the king of the gods, Zeus). But again, once he has developed the manly resolve to free himself from this unreal, twilit existence in the witch's cave, she switches to become a helper. After a last ordeal by shipwreck, he is washed up on the island of King Alcinous and his daughter, the Princess Nausicaa; and here he can tell the tale of all his adventures, as if he has returned to 'the real world'. Finally he lands back in Ithaca to begin the second half of the story. He has at last become master of himself and is ready for his final great test.

Through all the closing stages of the story, Odysseus can see – with the help of the goddess of wisdom Athene – exactly what he has to do, and is entirely in control of his actions. Outwardly, 'above the line', his kingdom is still triumphantly in the hands of the dark power, the loud-mouthed, swaggering, lecherous suitors, who infest his palace and press closer and closer round the increasingly despairing Penelope. But now, in the 'inferior realm', we see Odysseus, disguised as a humble beggar, moving inexorably through the shadows across the island, towards the final confrontation with his Dark Rivals. Again we see the story coming to the familiar three-cornered climax: on one hand, the overbearing 'masculine' power of the suitors, greedy, proud, quarrelsome, drunken, cruel, using their power only to indulge and to assert themselves; on the other, the helpless Penelope, the vulnerable feminine imprisoned in the shadows. Finally into their midst comes Odysseus, now stronger than ever because he is a man completely in charge of himself, who knows exactly what he has to do to take charge of the situation. At the same time his strength is balanced by his openness to the feminine and the fact that he is acting in a cause far greater than just his own. At the climactic moment he reveals himself in his true kingly majesty, as the only man able to bend the mighty bow. He fires his first arrow clean through the twelve axe-heads, to symbolise the twelve ordeals he has surmounted: there is no longer anything between him and his goal.[3] With contemptuous ease he puts the suitors to rout, dispelling the dark power forever. He liberates his 'other half' from the shadows. At last he is whole and can assume his rightful sovereignty over the kingdom.

Such is the essence of the Quest story (although there is no more complete and profound version than the *Odyssey*). It shows a hero who is initially 'all at sea' and at the mercy of events being gradually tempered by his ordeals into learning how to direct and to discipline his strength single-mindedly towards one end. He must develop his awareness and become master of himself until nothing can stand in his way. But at the same time he must show that he is entirely light, by his inward openness to the feminine, so that he is using his strength in the service of life and of the whole. Only when he has finally reached this state of complete balance and become fully himself is he ready to be united with his 'other half' and to claim the 'kingdom'. Thus does the Quest end at the same point as the earlier plots: because the fundamental impulse behind them all is the same.

## Voyage and Return

When the hero or heroine of a Voyage and Return story fall into the mysterious 'other realm', they may well find themselves in a landscape peopled by a familiar range of dark figures:

3. Whether or not Homer was conscious of the symbolism of the twelve axe-heads we cannot know. But certainly the first twelve books of the *Odyssey*, describing the hero's journey before finally arriving in Ithaca, show how the ordeals he had to survive after leaving Troy were twelve in number: the battle with the Cicones; the Land of the Lotus-Eaters; Polyphemus; the Laestrygonian giants; Circe; Hades; the Sirens; Scylla; the cattle of the Sun; Charybdis; Calypso; the final shipwreck on Alcinous's island. Since it was through these tests that he matured to the point where was ready for the final showdown with the suitors, it was thus symbolically appropriate that he should announce his presence to them by firing through the same number of axe-heads.

(1) *the Dark Father-figure, or Tyrant*: e.g., Mr McGregor, the terrifying denizen of the garden in *Peter Rabbit*, who has earlier killed and eaten the hero's father; Captain Hook, the would-be tyrant over the island in *Peter Pan*;

(3) *the Dark Queen, Witch, or Dark Mother-figure*: this is the tyrannical female version: e.g., the Queen of Hearts in *Alice In Wonderland* or the Red Queen in *Through The Looking Glass*; the Wicked Witch in *The Wizard of Oz*; Mrs Best-Chetwynde, the rich older woman who makes a plaything of Paul Pennyfeather, the hero of *Decline and Fall*;

(3) *the Dark Rivals*: e.g., the cannibals and the mutineers whom Robinson Crusoe encounters as rivals to his sovereignty of the island; the shadowy Morlocks who eventually capture the hero's little friend Weena in *The Time Machine*.

But the first thing we recognise about a Voyage and Return story, as we have seen, is how in the early stages, even more obviously than in the Quest, the emphasis is put on the limitations of the hero or heroine themselves. The essence of the deeper versions of this plot, such as *Robinson Crusoe*, *The Golden Ass* or the *Ancient Mariner*, is that we see a young man who falls into his horrific experience precisely because he is feckless, self-centred, uncaring – and because his awareness of the world is so severely limited. This is what puts him completely at the mercy of events, and why he suddenly finds himself plunged into the wholly strange 'other world'. What then happens?

Robinson Crusoe, aimlessly drifting round the world, 'all at sea', is suddenly pulled up short by the catastrophe of finding himself shipwrecked. The first part of the story shows him gradually coming to terms with his new situation, both outwardly and inwardly. He slowly wins control over his immediate environment, and also develops a wholly new attitude to life, coming to view his position realistically, without self-pity, grateful for what he has, learning to see objectively and whole. The second part of the story begins when we see his new-found qualities being put to the test. He becomes aware that he is not alone on the island and that it is under a deadly shadow cast by the visiting cannibals. Because Crusoe has won understanding and mastery of himself, and feels protectively towards their helpless victims, he can now act as a strong potential leader, becoming in the shadows the centre of light opposition to the dark power which dominates the island. First he is joined by Friday, whom Crusoe educates and trains to fight. Secondly, between them, they rout the cannibals, releasing more victims. Finally the ship which has been taken over by mutineers arrives, and Crusoe secretly reveals himself to the captain who accepts his complete authority. Crusoe masterminds the mutineers' overthrow and steps from the shadows as at last undisputed 'king' of the island. He can now return home, a king over himself, to live happily and prosperously for the rest of his life.

Lucius, the hero of *The Golden Ass*, also begins as an egocentric young drifter, only interested in sexual self-indulgence and the occult – in other words, with a dark, inferior desire for 'love', which he sees only in terms of physical self-gratification, and for 'secret knowledge', which he sees only as a way to win power for himself. It is precisely a combination of these two weaknesses which, by a catastrophic misjudgement, lands him in the horrific plight of being turned into an ass. He now finds himself entirely at the mercy of mindless, unfeeling human beings until, when he finally recoils from the degradation of having to perform the sexual act in a circus, knowing also that it will mean death, he is miraculously released by the mysterious goddess of wisdom Isis. Now his real transformation begins. Under the guidance of Isis and through intense self-discipline, he gradually comes to recognise the true meaning of selfless love and of that spiritual reality which is obscured to limited consciousness by physical appearances and appetites. His heart and his eyes are opened. His two original dark obsessions have each been transformed into their 'light' version. The story ends by showing him, as a devotee of Isis, a strong disciplined figure, at one with himself and with life.

When the Ancient Mariner, also a young man 'all at sea', casually shoots the great, friendly albatross which has been following the ship, he has committed an appalling crime. He has used his strength blindly, unfeelingly, selfishly, to kill a perfect symbol of wholeness, something immense, beautiful, mysterious, self-contained, floating entirely at one with the world of nature. He sinks down into the living death of his unfeeling egocentricity, seeing all the world around him drained of life. He sees the spectral ship approaching, containing the 'Nightmare Life-in-Death', the terrible 'Dark Mother' of final unconsciousness – until finally some deep impulse for life within him prompts him to croak out a blessing on the only other living creatures around him, the crawling water snakes. At last he is beginning to feel for life outside himself and to 'see whole' beyond the confines of his own ego. Both within him and outside him, life begins to flow again. He is at one with its power and, now master of his ghostly ship, he is carried home.

Even the story of Peter Rabbit, as we saw, is that of a feckless and selfish little hero at the mercy of his idle curiosity and his physical appetites who, by eventually coming to a higher level of consciousness and managing to 'see whole', wins a measure of conscious control over his destiny and escapes from death to life. In other words, in its fully resolved versions, the Voyage and Return story is still shaped by precisely the same fundamental impulse as the earlier plots – except that we are now seeing the hero much more clearly having to move from one 'centre' of his personality to another.

The essence of all these Voyage and Return stories is that they show their hero having to move away from the pole of limited 'ego-consciousness', which puts him at the mercy of events he does not understand, towards that other pole which connects him up to the world outside himself and gives him the wider vision which is necessary for his liberation. This winning of a wider vision is seen to be a process of the most profound importance, essential not just to the hero's survival in a limited, physical sense but, at least in the instances of Robinson Crusoe, Lucius and the Ancient Mariner, to his reaching an entirely new relationship with himself and the universe. The move from restricted ego-consciousness to the state of wider awareness means that he is at last, in some mysterious way, at one with life itself. And of course no type of story is more centrally dependent on the importance of this transition than Comedy: where coming to 'see whole' is what the process of recognition is all about.

## Chapter 14

# Seeing Whole
### The Feminine and Masculine Values

'I'm still defeated by the conundrum of God. But I have the devil clear.'
'And what's he?'
'Not seeing whole.'                          John Fowles, *Daniel Martin*

One of the parallels between a story and a piece of music is that each is based on a sequence of mental images which we unconsciously anticipate will come eventually to a point of perfect resolution. A movement in a Beethoven symphony develops through a succession of irresolutions each of which is then partly resolved. Only at the end does the pattern come to a full close, resolving all that has gone before.

For several months in 1984, millions of television viewers in Britain were held in suspense by a serialisation of Paul Scott's Raj quartet of novels *The Jewel in the Crown*. For weeks the story presented them with a complex drama of life in British India during the Second World War, introducing a large cast of characters whose lives were interwoven, full of mysterious and half-explained incidents. But as the plot developed, the one thing which eventually held interest more than any other was the central web of relationships between three characters – the attractive heroine, Sarah Layton, and two young men. The first of these, Merrick, a powerful, resentful, bullying police officer who had set his mind on marrying Sarah was the chief dark figure of the story. The other was a handsome and strong but sensitive and reserved army officer, Guy Perron. The question to which viewers wanted an answer was: which of the two would win the heroine? Would the Dark Rival get his way? Or would the light hero and heroine somehow manage to recognise their love and get together? Only in the closing scenes of the three-month long serialisation was the answer finally given, as Sarah and Guy at last came out into the open and declared their love. At this moment the whole of this enormously intricate drama, which had involved so many deaths and sub-plots, was resolved, in a way which seemed at last to make sense of almost everything that had previously happened in the story.

Again and again we have circled round the importance to stories of the elusive idea of being able to 'see whole' which runs through storytelling at so many levels and in so many ways. In that central struggle between darkness and light, for instance, we have seen how it is an absolutely consistent feature of all the monsters, villains, tragic heroes and other figures who embody the dark power that

253

they are in some crucial respect limited in their awareness. They have a blind spot; they are obsessive; they live in a fantasy world of wishful thinking; and this distortion of their vision is inextricably linked to their egocentricity. What stories show us is how it is in the very nature of egotism that it can only see the world in a subjective, restricted fashion. Wherever it holds sway it casts around it a shadow which also tends to obscure the vision of everyone else who is in that shadow.

Equally we have seen how it is an inseparable part of 'coming to the light' that this should bring a clearer vision. When, at the end of a story, characters are lifted out of the shadows, this is because they have been lifted out of all that obscures their vision. 'Seeing whole' does not mean they see and know everything. What it does mean is that they can see everyone and everything objectively, for what they really are. They have been liberated from the distortions of ego-consciousness, onto a different level which gives them a clearer understanding.

On another level, this transition between a long period of constricted vision and finally coming to a new centre of perspective which gives an uninterrupted view in all directions relates directly to one of the most fundamental satisfactions we ourselves get from following a story. Few things hold our interest in a story more compulsively than the desire to arrive at that point at the end where everything will finally be explained. Gradually we have been drawn deeper and deeper into a tangled knot of obscurity and uncertainty, setting up a tension in our minds which cries out for resolution. We long to know how it is all going to turn out; whether the hero and the heroine will finally be united; what unexpected twist at the end will suddenly make everything 'come out right'. In the earlier stages of a story all sorts of details may have been introduced which at the time seem puzzling, their significance not clear at the time. But if the story is properly constructed, by the time it reaches its conclusion the point and purpose of each will have been revealed. As in a piece of music, we have finally been lifted clear from the tangle of irresolution to the point where the pattern is complete; where we can see how everything in the end played its part in the whole. And no type of story illustrates this more subtly than Comedy, where the transition from baffling obscurity to a final phase of illumination when all is made clear is built into the very structure of the plot.

## Comedy

Three things mark out Comedy from other types of story. The first is that, more insistently than any other type of plot, Comedy is concerned not just with the individual fate of its central figure but with the network of relationships between a group of people. Initially we see these relationships all knotted up because something fundamental has gone wrong; at the end we see the 'unknotting' where everyone has at last been brought into the right relationship with everyone else.

The second unique feature of Comedy is the extent to which, except on those rare occasions where a dark figure remains unreconciled, it shows us all the characters in the story being brought at the end into the light. In this sense Comedy is the most idealised of the plots (although in this it overlaps with Rebirth) because it ends on a vision of a world entirely at one, from which no one is excluded.

The third distinguishing mark of Comedy is the emphasis it places on the fact that the fundamental reason why everyone is at odds through most of the story is that there is something very important that they do not know or cannot see; just as the miraculous coming together at the end results from the fact that something very important has been discovered. As Aristotle puts it, 'recognition is the change from ignorance to knowledge'. And this recognition is precisely what allows everyone to come into a new and quite different set of relationships to one another. Because everyone can at last see clearly and whole, because they have at last discovered who they and each other really are, and who belongs with whom, they can also feel properly. Everyone has at last 'seen the light' and thus been liberated to be their true, deeper selves; and for this reason everyone ends up happily integrated with everyone else in an image of complete individual and collective wholeness.

In other words, like an old 'Before and After' advertisement, Comedy shows us the contrast between two fundamental states of human nature. We are introduced to a little world – a household, a group of families, a city, a kingdom – which has fallen under the shadow of the dark power. The darkness may emanate primarily from the blind and heartless egotism of one dominant figure. But the result is that everyone is affected: everyone is stumbling about in a fog of frustration and confusion, divided off and obscured from one another, cut off from the flow of life. The fact that people cannot see clearly or whole and the fact that they cannot relate harmoniously to one another are seen as inextricably bound together as symptoms of the same fundamental condition.

But somewhere below the surface, hidden from the community's prevailing state of consciousness, events are constellating towards the moment when the revealing truth can suddenly emerge from the shadows. The distorting pressure of egocentricity is removed, the darkness is dispelled, everyone can 'see the light'; and every piece of the jigsaw falls naturally into place. The picture of unity is complete. The current of life can flow unimpeded.

### Dark masculine, light feminine

As we have seen, most comedies fall into two groups: those where the chief dark figure of the story stands opposed to the hero and heroine, and to the flow of life in general; and those where the chief dark figure is the hero himself (much less often the heroine).

Of stories in the first category, again the great majority are those where the dark figure is a Dark Father or Tyrant: some powerful older man, usually the head of a household, who is in the grip of some blinding, deadening obsession which casts a shadow over everyone around him, and usually in particular over the young lovers whose union he is opposing. We have seen this familiar figure running all through the history of Comedy, from Aristophanes's Procleon to George Eliot's Mr Casaubon, from the 'unrelenting fathers' of New Comedy to those of Molière, from King Leontes and Count Almaviva to the worlds of Wodehouse and the Marx Brothers.

Only rarely in Comedy do we see the Dark Mother-figure, but where we do she usually plays much the same tyrannical role as the Dark Father, invariably in the name of upholding the 'masculine' proprieties and the social order: e.g., Lady Bracknell, Gwendolen's 'unrelenting mother' in *The Importance of Being Earnest*, or Lady Catherine de Bourgh, Darcy's imperious, snobbish aunt who tries to prevent him marrying Elizabeth Bennett in *Pride and Prejudice*.

A rather more frequent figure, particularly in later Comedy, is the Dark Rival for the heroine's hand; e.g., Blifil in *Tom Jones*, Joseph Surface in *The School for Scandal*, Beckmesser in *Die Meistersinger*, Baron Ochs in *Der Rosenkavalier* (although as an older man and a friend of the heroine's father, he is also linked to the Dark Father).

We similarly see examples of the Dark Other Half. An obvious instance is Tom Jones's would-be seducer Lady Bellaston, a mature, beguiling Temptress (although, as an older married woman, she again shows links to the 'Dark Mother'). The novels of Jane Austen contain several examples, such as George Wickham, Henry Crawford, William Elliot: all false, unscrupulous triflers with the heroine's affections. Another striking pair of examples appear in *War and Peace*: Anatole Kuragin, the adventurer who tries to abduct Natasha, and his sister Helene, the imposing, heartless Temptress who marries, then abandons the rich and awkward (and motherless) Pierre. A more modern instance is the intolerable Lina Lamont in *Singin' In The Rain*.

With a handful of such exceptions, the dark figures in Comedy tend overwhelmingly to be male. They represent the hard, unfeeling, negative side of masculinity in such a way as to place the heroine, representing true feeling and the promise of life, firmly at the opposite pole and in the shadows. For life to triumph, it is the true value of the 'feminine' which has to be recognised and lifted up into the light, as was so often symbolised in the New Comedy of the Ancient World when the disregarded and scorned heroine of lowly status was finally discovered to be of high birth and therefore of great value after all. And ultimately this can only happen when the overshadowing dark figure – such as an unrelenting father – is either liberated from his egocentric prison by discovering a new centre of awareness and feeling within himself; or is exposed in his true colours and pushed off the stage.

In the type of Comedy where the hero himself is the chief dark figure, the same rules apply. Right back to Menander, we see the hero who has wronged the heroine and become divided from her by some misjudgement. Through an egocentric limitation on his awareness, he has failed in some way to recognise the truth of the situation. He reacts in a hard, unfeeling manner, rejecting the 'feminine' – often in the name of 'masculine' propriety and upholding the moral order. And eventually he gets caught out. Either, like Leontes in *The Winter's Tale*, he discovers that he has wronged the heroine by assuming that she has committed a crime when in fact she was innocent. Or, like Angelo in *Measure for Measure*, he is also exposed as a self-righteous hypocrite for having committed the same crime of which he has accused someone else.

Ultimately he can only be extricated from the trap he has made for himself by discovering that deeper centre of his personality which both brings him back in touch with true feeling and widens his perception so that he can see the world straight and whole again. And here we again see how the 'feminine value' which must be brought into play to redeem the situation represents both these things, inextricably intertwined; both true feeling for others *and* the wider awareness which permits true understanding, an appreciation of the totality of the situation and how everything is properly connected; whereas the 'dark masculine' represents precisely the opposite, a lack of true feeling and an inability to see things whole.

When we look at the handful of comedies which show the heroine herself as the chief dark figure, we see how the very reason she has become dark is that she is not in touch with the true feminine within herself, as we see in Katherina, the ill-tempered, aggressive virago in *The Taming of the Shrew*, or the bossy, interfering Emma Woodhouse, or the rich, spoiled Tracy Lord in *High Society*. Each has become imprisoned in a variation on essentially the same hard, egocentric state. They are neither alive to true feeling nor properly aware of the true situation around them (let alone how they look to everyone else). They are each in a state of self-deception. They need to be tamed, teased or thawed out into the soft, warm, alive state of femininity which is their true deeper self, buried under their tough, brittle exterior. Only at this point, when they become truly feminine, seeing the world straight (as with the heroine of *Crocodile Dundee*) can each recognise at last who is her true 'other half'.

Of course there are also those comedies, such as *Guys and Dolls* or *Four Weddings and a Funeral*, where there is no obviously dominant dark figure at all. In *A Midsummer Night's Dream* the darkness which engulfs all the characters is simply that of total confusion, based on the fact that no one can see things straight, although even here it is only the men who get confused. The two heroines remain models of firm, unswerving love. The true feminine is always a beacon of constancy.[1]

## The feminine value

What we thus see emerging is a fundamental polarity which is crucial to the structure of storytelling. At one pole is the power of darkness, centred on the ego, limited consciousness and an inability to see whole, making for confusion, division and ultimately death. At the other is the power of the feminine, centred on selfless feeling and the ability to see whole, making for connection, the healing of division and life. At the deepest level, it is around this opposition that the whole of the eternal conflict presented by stories revolves: and it is this which, in a sense, makes the light heroine the ultimate touchstone of storytelling. For it is she who above all and most directly embodies the feminine value. It is she who most often and most obviously has to be brought forth from the shadows in order for

1. It is true that on the 'fairy level' of the action, Titania is also confused by Puck's trickery into her infatuation with Bottom, thus becoming for a while the most poignantly absurd figure in the play. But the very absurdity of her plight points up how unusual in stories is the spectacle of the 'deluded feminine'. It is much more 'natural' that the male figures should be unable to see straight and whole. In this sense the journey into the dark wood and out again becomes a form of voyage and Return, where the male characters have needed the fall into a shadowy 'other world' for their limited awareness to be opened up to the point of transformation. They are only ready to emerge when they have all been brought into touch with that deeper feeling which can at last connect them up happily in all directions, with no one any longer rejecting or rejected by anyone else.

the complete happy ending to a story to be achieved. And this applies not just to those stories where a strong hero has to rescue a defenceless heroine, but just as much to those where an 'active' heroine has to emerge from the shadows to rescue a helpless hero, as in the myth of Theseus, *Jane Eyre*, *High Noon*, *The Merchant of Venice*, *Fidelio*.

But, as we have already explored in the previous chapter, in order for any story to reach that point where the heroine can emerge or be liberated from the shadows to produce the happy ending, there is another vital ingredient which is required to make the equation complete. And we see this brilliantly, if negatively illumined by the plot of Tragedy.

## The Dark Inversion

For obvious reasons, Tragedy occupies a unique place among the basic plots, because in a sense it turns the essential pattern of the other main types of story upside down. All these other types of story have their 'dark' versions, which we shall return to. But Tragedy is the only basic plot which is primarily concerned with showing what happens when the hero or heroine cannot muster the positive qualities necessary to wrest the life-giving feminine value from the shadows, but become so identified with the dark power that they cannot escape from it. It thus shows the process of transformation taking place in, as it were, a negative form: the hero or heroine are led ever further downwards and into the dark imprisonment, rather than upwards and away from it. And one of the corollaries of this is that we see the landscape familiar from other types of story appearing strangely inverted.

As the light part of the tragic hero or heroine falls further and further under the shadow of the darkness which has taken root in them, and they slip into ever greater egocentricity and lack of feeling for others, we see how their judgement, their ability to see the world straight and whole, becomes increasingly clouded. In fact their vision becomes so distorted that they actually come to see everything at the reverse of its true value. The light values increasingly become a threat to them; light characters come to seem only as obstacles to their egocentric desires. As Macbeth's Witches have it, 'fair is foul and foul is fair'; or as Albany puts it in *King Lear*, 'wisdom and goodness to the vile seem vile'. And one of the ways in which we see this inversion most strikingly exemplified is in the nature of the figures around the hero or the heroine whom they are most likely to see as hindrances in their path.

In an earlier chapter we saw how there were certain figures who were most likely to become the victims of the tragic hero on his downward course. In fact we can now see how these correspond to the characters who, in other types of story, are most likely to appear as dark figures: except that here, where the hero himself is dark, they appear as light. For instance, the first of the two male figures most likely to become the tragic hero's victims we saw as 'the Good Old Man', a king or father-figure, like Duncan in *Macbeth* or the Commendatore in *Don Giovanni*. He is the light version of the Tyrant or Dark Father-figure. Similarly, the tragic hero may turn on someone who comes to assume particular importance to him as his Rival, like Banquo – the hero's honourable counterpart or light alter ego, who comes to haunt him as a reproach to his crimes.

But it is when we come to the feminine figures whom the hero is most likely to kill or injure that we see the tragic inversion in its most revealing light. Nothing can more tellingly betray the horror of the dark state a tragic hero is getting into than the moment when he kills or rejects the 'Innocent Young Girl', his 'good angel'. When Othello kills Desdemona, when Lear sends Cordelia into exile, when Don José turns his back on Micaela, when Dorian Gray's rejection of Sibyl Vane brings about her suicide, when Stavrogin's violation of little Matryosha leads to her hanging herself, their ultimate fate is sealed. In violating or rejecting the feminine outside themselves, they have become catastrophically closed off to the feminine value within themselves, that which alone could allow them properly to feel and to see the world whole.

On the other hand, where the hero in other types of story must reject that other great female figure, the 'Dark Other Half', the Temptress, the tragic hero does the opposite. This is precisely where the seeds of so many tragedies are sown, as the hero succumbs to the bewitching embraces of the 'dark feminine': as Antony is bewitched by Cleopatra, Don José is bewitched by Carmen, Macbeth is bewitched by Lady Macbeth, Jules and Jim are bewitched by Catherine, Clyde is bewitched by Bonnie. It is the 'dark angel' who wins in the battle for the tragic hero's allegiance. And the result is not just that we see the hero losing touch with the true feminine value within himself. He is no longer a fully masculine figure either. As we see in all these examples, he has become literally un-manned. And so we see it confirmed, by this somewhat roundabout, negative route, how in order for the hero to succeed he must not only be in touch with the true feminine value within himself: he must also be truly a man, strong, alert, fully sovereign over himself and his actions. It is a definition of the hero of Tragedy that he always in some essential way shows himself to be weak. He gives way, he surrenders the masculine part of himself to some unreal fantasy. He is thus deficient both on the feminine side of himself and on the masculine. And one of the supreme rules of the way that stories work is that ultimately these two must go inextricably together. It is impossible fully to develop and make positive the one, without fully developing the other. Where one is deficient, so are they both.

We see this reflected in those two great stories centred on a tragic heroine, *Anna Karenina* and *Madame Bovary*. It is obvious that the husbands of both Anna and Emma Bovary are unimaginative, unfeeling men who lack the inner feminine which could form a living bridge to the feminine in their wives. But equally they are not fully men either. The work-obsessed bureaucrat and the failed provincial doctor are dried-up husks of undeveloped masculinity – and it is because they are inadequate on both the masculine and feminine sides that their unhappy, frustrated wives become prey to the 'Dark Other Half' who seems to promise all the fierce passion, mingling masculine strength and the feminine softness of love, which they lack in their marriages. But in each case the 'dark other' turns out to be an elusive phantom, spun largely out of the heroine's own fantasies. Finally, irrevocably cut off from the true, life-giving feminine within herself, the heroine is left wild, deranged and hopelessly alone, to throw herself into the oblivion of death.

And what happens in those tragedies of partial redemption, where there is an eventual turn upwards towards the light? We see such varied heroes as King Lear, Tannhäuser and Samson all initially bewitched by the 'dark feminine' – by the false Goneril and Reagan, by Venus, by Delilah – to the point where they are left unmanned and weak. But then in *King Lear*, even though it is too late to call back the monsters unleashed by his initial weakness, we see Lear first getting back in touch with his own inner feminine through his reconciliation with Cordelia; then, in the closing stages of the play, assuming once again some of his old kingly, manly stature. He may no longer be outwardly a king, but he is discovering a new sovereignty over himself. Tannhäuser, through the ordeal of his long, lonely pilgrimage to Rome, has found a new heroic stature. After the emasculation and enervation of his year on the Venusberg, he has become a man, worthy to be united in death with his 'good angel' Elizabeth. Samson, after being so hideously unmanned by Delilah, finally recovers his manly strength to such effect that he can die one of the greatest heroes of his nation.

### The masculine value

The true hero, if he is to succeed, must be fully a man. The way in which this is represented may seem straightforward enough in those types of story which require the hero to engage in direct physical conflict with the powers of darkness; where in order to overpower or outwit the 'monster', or to survive all the tests and ordeals of a Quest, he has to show such obvious manly qualities as outstanding physical and mental strength and stamina. The masculinity of such legendary heroes as Odysseus or Theseus, Gilgamesh or David, King Arthur or Robin Hood, Superman or James Bond, may never seem to be in doubt. As doughty fighters, they show it in their mastery of sword, bow, axe, spear or gun, in their powers of leadership, their courage and combative skill. They seem to be virile figures in every way. But what it is to be *fully* a man has rather more to it than just these qualities. And we can see this reflected still more clearly in the last of our seven plots, Rebirth.

The essence of the Rebirth story is, firstly, that it shows its central figure imprisoned by the dark power in any of its more familiar guises. We may, for instance, see the hero imprisoned by a Tyrant, like Florestan lying in Pizarro's dungeons. He may have fallen under a spell cast by a Witch or Temptress – like Kay imprisoned by the Snow Queen, or the prince imprisoned in the outward form of the Beast by an enchantress. We may see the hero trapped in a state of darkness which springs more obviously from within himself, like Scrooge or Raskolnikov. Indeed in *Peer Gynt* we see a hero who is the victim of all these things: the effect of his being enchanted by the 'dark king' and the Temptress from the subterranean troll king-dom being to bring out the dark part of Peer, his egotistical 'Gyntish self', which comes for so long to dominate his behaviour and to shape his life.

In each instance, what we see is a hero who is held back by his imprisonment from assuming his proper state as a man. He may be presented as a weak, passive figure, like the reclusive Silas Marner or little Kay in the Snow Queen's palace. On the other hand, he may be strong and powerful like the rich, tyrannical Scrooge or Peer Gynt, the amoral head of a great business empire. But in either case he is in the grip of a power which in some way stunts him and prevents him from living in easy sovereignty over himself. In terms of proper masculinity he has been reduced to a sad, two-dimensional caricature.

In fact, like the feminine, the masculine in stories has two aspects. The first of these is power or strength. This may be presented primarily as a matter of physical potency and presence, as with those heroes whose special combative power is associated with legendary weapons, like the great sword Excalibur or Robin Hood's bow. It may be presented as the holding of great position or the possession of great riches. It may be portrayed simply as a strength of will, personality or character which enables its possessor to exercise dominance: either over others, or over himself. And in this respect, which derives ultimately from a physical power, the masculine is something which gives mastery and independence.

The other masculine attribute is a sense of order. This may be presented as a consciousness of social order, of hierarchy, propriety, the need for discipline, for justice under the law. Or it may be seen, rather more subtly, as the whole capacity of the human mind to see the world in terms of orderly, rational patterns: that very thing which lies at the root of all our notions of order, whether social or intellectual: the need to see everyone or everything marshalled in proper place and relationship. In this respect, which derives ultimately from the need of the human mind for framework and comprehensibility, the masculine gives a sense of control through organisation.

Both these things, the physical and the mental, give an essential strength and firmness, a backbone and vigour to human life. Without them it remains weak, ineffectual, amorphous, chaotic, without discipline or direction, and it cannot survive. But in both its aspects the masculine is based on the principle of separation and division: the sense of power which enables one person or part to dominate over another; the sense of order which is rooted in the need to discriminate and to establish differences between one thing and another.

In both these respects the masculine is potentially hard and inflexible. And when we see a character possessed by the 'dark masculine', we see him in the grip of either or both of these things, in a way which is egocentric and life-denying. The Tyrant or Dark Father is a bully who uses his power and strength in an aggressive, cruel way to impose his will on others. He may also be doing so to preserve an established structure of authority and hierarchy, like the unrelenting fathers of Comedy who refuse to allow their sons to marry girls of humble origins. They wish to maintain a certain limiting notion of order which does not allow life to flow: like Shylock who remorselessly pursues justice under the law, at any human price; or like Beckmesser in *Die Meistersinger* who is so obsessed by the traditional rules of singing laid down by the Mastersingers that he cannot see that Walther has created a song of exceptional beauty, simply because his vision is constricted to that which lies within the rules.

In other words, while the masculine stands for the two great principles of power and order, if these are dark and one-sided they can only be turned to deadening and divisive purpose. The power can be used ultimately only to crush and to destroy. The order is a dead structure which becomes suffocating and oppressive and cannot resolve into life.

But equally, when a hero has fallen into the grip of the 'dark feminine', like Odysseus languishing on Calypso's isle, or Tannhäuser enjoying the sensual delights of the Venusberg, or Antony ensnared by 'the serpent of old Nile', we see him unable to become masculine enough. For the time being at least, he is not strong, disciplined or masterful enough to be a man. He has become beguiled into losing touch with his masculine power, he has become weak and dependent, no longer sovereign over his own actions. Worse still, his efforts to get in touch with the masculine in himself may become wild, rebellious and unresolved – like the increasingly desperate Don José, lashing out first at his victorious rival Escamillo, then fatally at Carmen herself; or the impotent, sexually frustrated Clyde, under the spell of Bonnie, trying to prove his manliness with the gun. If such a hero does have genuine masculine strength, the results when he falls under the sway of the 'dark feminine' may be most catastrophic of all, as when the tough, successful general Macbeth succumbs to the lures of the 'dark sisters' and his dominating wife: his strength is turned to dark ends, he kills the very thing he would like to become, the good legitimate king, the honourable bearer of true masculine authority, and becomes in consequence a Tyrant. In weaker men, their masculinity may remain all in the mind, as when little Kay first turns verbally aggressive and cynical and then, under the spell of the Snow Queen, sits all day spinning endless rational mental patterns of words and figures with ice splinters, but can never get them to resolve into the word 'eternity'.

The only way the hero can achieve a completely triumphant resolution is by fully developing his masculinity in a way which is positive: and this means in perfect balance with his inner feminine. It is this which alone can bring masculine strength fully to life by giving it the vital ingredient of connection, of joining up: through feeling, which gives a link to others and to the world outside the ego; through that intuitive insight which gives proper understanding, by allowing him to perceive the wholeness of things and their mysterious, hidden connections.

When these are brought into balance and harmony with the masculine, then what a transformation we see. When power is brought into conjunction with true sympathetic feeling for others; when the sense of order is brought into harmony with the capacity to see whole: then both are miraculously made life-giving. The strength of power becomes a force making for life, not death, serving the whole rather than the ego of he or she who possesses it. The patterns of the sense of order and structure are imbued with life because they are no longer just dead mental constructs spun out of the limited consciousness of the human ego, but connect up with a living totality. We thus see how each of the four elements – strength, order, feeling and intuitive understanding, or body and mind, heart and soul - is ultimately essential to all the others to make a living whole. And nowhere do we see the balances of this delicate equation expressed more subtly than in the workings of the plot of Rebirth.

## The four-sided totality

One of the first things we subconsciously pick up from those first Rebirth stories we meet in childhood, centred on a heroine, is that her femininity alone is not enough to save her from imprisonment. Sleeping Beauty and Snow White have neither the strength nor the judgement to withstand the spell cast over them by the 'dark feminine'. As they fall into their frozen sleep it seems they have lost everything. What is needed to return them to life is the strength of the masculine value, personified in the handsome prince who eventually releases them from their imprisonment.

Conversely, in *The Frog Prince* and *Beauty and the Beast*, when the immature young heroine first encounters the masculine value, it seems to her menacing, unattractive and deformed. Only when the heroine has developed her femininity to the point where she can show love to this representative of the masculine in its 'inferior' guise as a frog or a monster does it emerge in its proper fully-developed form as a handsome prince. Indeed at the end of these stories we see the feminine and the masculine liberating each other simultaneously. And such is the essence of Rebirth: that it shows us how it is impossible to develop one side of the human personality fully, masculine or feminine, unless this is also given positive counter-balance by the other. Initially a Rebirth story shows us someone who is imprisoned in such a way that it completely represses one side of his or her overall personality, while leaving the remaining, superior side stunted or deformed. Usually it is the feminine which is repressed, while the masculine is in some way deformed. But the hero or heroine then encounters some redeeming figure whose nature is such as to awaken the repressed, inferior side: with the result that the superior, deformed side can also at last assume its proper shape.

We learn of Scrooge, for instance, how as an originally sensitive and sociable young man his growing obsession with money had caused him to lose the girl who was going to marry him. He has lost touch with the softening feminine and thus passed into the deforming grip of the 'dark masculine', becoming heartless and tyrannical, obsessed with the power of riches and the endless calculation in his ledgers of how much he had lent and was owed. He comes to the crisis when he is confronted in a dream by the three spirits, like messengers from his unconscious, who by presenting him with the shocking objective truth of his state begin to give him back the capacity to see himself and others whole. Simultaneously his long dead capacity for sympathetic feeling is aroused by the plight of Tiny Tim, the little crippled, dying boy who represents the child he never had, stunted hope for the regeneration of life. Finally, having thus been brought back in touch with his inner feminine, Scrooge goes through the transformation which also awakens him back to his proper manly state, using his masculine power creatively and protectively to bring life to others.

The story of Peer Gynt is similar. He also loses touch with the feminine as a young man, when he abandons Solveig, and passes into the deforming grip of the 'dark masculine'. As a result, he becomes an immensely powerful figure, obsessed with using his power to dominate and reorganise the world. But nothing can ever resolve, or give him the satisfaction he craves. He then begins to find the capacity to see the objective truth of his deformed state through the mysterious figure of the Button Moulder. Finally, in his reunion with Solveig, he discovers not only true feeling but also his inmost identity as a man.

Both Scrooge and Peer Gynt are thus strongly masculine figures, whose masculinity has become dark and deformed because they have lost touch with the inner feminine. They are 'active' figures, because to be strong in the masculine qualities is what makes any character in a story 'active'.

The case of Silas Marner is different. His problem is not just that he has lost touch with the feminine (at the time when he had been falsely accused of stealing money and lost the girl he loved to a 'Dark Rival'). He has also lost the power of his masculinity (symbolised above all by the loss of his own money to another 'Dark Rival'). Dried-up, self-pitiful, completely closed in on himself, he thus becomes a passive figure – until the arrival of the redeeming child, Eppie, who not only awakens the lost feminine in him by giving him back the capacity to feel, but also, by calling him into the new role of father-protector, reawakens his masculine strength. He even recovers his money, which for years has lain like so much locked-up dead energy at the bottom of a pond, and can now put it to life-giving use in looking after Eppie.

Raskolnikov, the unhappy young student, is another hero weak on both the masculine and feminine sides of himself. In his disordered fantasies of proving himself to be a man he can only dream of some wild, rebellious action which will demonstrate his Napoleon-like power to transcend the moral order. In reality this turns out to be a hideous caricature of manliness, the heartless killing of two helpless old women. And at this point, if the story were Tragedy, we should see him spiralling down into the grip of darkness until he is destroyed. Instead he begins to pass mysteriously under the spell of two light figures: the magistrate Porfiry, a wise, all-seeing, 'father figure', who represents the true masculine authority and firmness which Raskolnikov lacks; and Sonia who, despite her outwardly fallen way of life, represents selfless, sympathetic feeling. Step by step, under their influence, Raskolnikov is drawn into facing up to the reality of his horrible crime, even though it is not until his nightmare shows him the objective truth of his state that he finally develops the capacity to see whole. It is this which brings him in touch with true feeling, in his spiritual union with Sonia, and we are thus led to suppose that at the end of the story he is at last on his way to becoming a whole man.

In The Snow Queen when one splinter of the magician's mirror enters Kay's eye he loses the capacity to see whole (everything is seen distorted and in a mocking, satirical light); when another enters his heart, it cuts him off from feeling (he rejects Gerda). This places him under the spell of the 'dark masculine', in terms of his newfound cerebral obsession with rational calculations and mental patterns. But he has no real masculine strength: it is all in the mind, as with Raskolnikov; and this also places him under the spell of the 'dark feminine' in the shape of the powerful, heartless Snow Queen. Kay is now completely imprisoned, both dead to the true feminine and stunted in his masculinity. At this point Gerda sets out to find him, representing in herself both the qualities he lacks: the femininity of her feeling and, in her courage and spirit, the masculine strength he needs as well. She is thus an 'active' heroine. And at the point of Kay's transformation, when she has liberated him, he recovers not only contact with the repressed feminine in himself, his ability to feel and to see whole, but also his independence and manly strength. Thus we learn at the end, when both have returned home, that the two former children have at last 'grown up'.

Finally, in *Fidelo*, we see the unusual case of a hero who, because of his special circumstances, has become stunted in his masculinity while remaining strong in his inner feminine. Florestan's imprisonment at the hands of the Tyrant reduces him outwardly to a weak, passive dependence. But he retains his secure link to the feminine in his unshakeable love for Leonore, and it is precisely this situation which her own balance of qualities is best equipped to redeem. Leonore is not only fully developed in her own femininity. She is also, in her fearless courage, irradiated with 'masculine' strength, as is conveyed by her donning a man's disguise. In this respect she brings to Florestan in his dungeon the very strength and spirit he has lost. She is able to defy and to outwit the Tyrant, and thus to make the equation complete whereby Florestan can be freed again to become a proper man. Like Ariadne, or Portia, or Jane Eyre, she is the 'active' heroine who is so often needed when the hero himself is for some reason rendered in masculine terms weak and lacking in power. The 'active' heroine is always a strong, independent figure, alive to the positive inner masculine qualities in herself, which is why she so often disguises herself as a man, or is associated with manly weapons (Ariadne bringing the sword to Theseus) or 'masculine' skills (Portia showing her mastery of the law). She is needed to redress the balance of the overall equation, where the hero has been reduced to impotence, by helping to pull him out of his imprisonment and restoring him to masculine strength. Because for any true, triumphant union to take place between the hero and heroine of a story, a complete balance of all four masculine and feminine qualities has somehow to be available between them: to bring about the final flowering which can enable both, in each other, to become whole.

We can now see the nature of the equation which lies at the heart of stories coming clearly into view.

## Chapter 15

# The Perfect Balance

'The heavens themselves, the planets and this centre,
Observe degree, priority and place,
Insisture, course, proportion, season, form,
Office and custom, in all line of order;
And therefore is the glorious planet Sol
In noble eminence enthron'd and sphered
Amidst the other; whose medicinable eye
Corrects the ill aspects of planets evil,
And posts, like the commandment of a king,
Sans check, to good and bad. But when the planets
In evil mixture to disorder wander,
What plagues and what portents, what mutiny,
What raging of the sea, shaking of earth,
Commotion in the winds, frights, changes, horrors,
Divert and crack, rend and deracinate
The unity and married calm of states
Quite from their fixtures.'
      Ulysses in Shakespeare's *Troilus and Cressida*, i.iii

'All happy families are alike, but each unhappy family is unhappy in its own way.'
The famous dictum with which Tolstoy opens *Anna Karenina* might well be
adapted to apply to stories. 'All stories which come to a happy ending are alike....'
And certainly, as we shall see when we come to look at what happens when stories
fail to reach a proper happy ending, there is a sense in which each does so in its
own way and for its own individual reasons. But what is remarkable when we consider the vast range of stories which do come to a complete happy ending is how
much they have in common. We can now, in this chapter, sum up what that is.

If we consider any of the examples we have looked at which do reach such a
positive resolution – from *Cinderella* to the *Odyssey*, from *The Marriage of Figaro*
to *Crocodile Dundee* – we can see how what has been going on in each of them is
fundamentally the same. In order to reach a full happy ending, the story must
culminate in an act of liberation from the dark power which produces a final
image of integration with life. This great prize can only be wrested from the darkness when the hero or heroine, or both together, have been transformed in such a
way that they are potentially whole. This means that, between them, they must
represent a balance of certain specific qualities: those qualities we can identify as
'masculine' and 'feminine'.

In fact what we have seen emerging in the last chapter is how stories present us with an ideal picture of human nature. What we see endlessly recurring is that same equation: how, to reach the fully happy ending, hero and heroine must represent the perfect coming together of those four values: strength, order, feeling and understanding. But, in the end, all these values represent simply two halves, masculine and feminine, which make up a whole. So long as either of these elements is lacking, the power of darkness and imperfection will still in some degree hold sway. For the characters in a story to emerge fully into the light, we must ultimately see both elements being brought together in perfect balance.

The process whereby this is achieved invariably requires a specific sequence of steps. First we see the hero or heroine in that incomplete, unresolved state which characterises the beginning of a story. Then something has to emerge which opens them out to the possibility that eventually they may achieve the distant state of wholeness. Thirdly, and this may comprise almost all the action of the story, they have to be shown as developing, or in some way being brought to the point where they are finally ready to realise that state. Only then, as in the opening of some complicated lock which requires all the tumblers to be aligned in exactly the right way before it will open, can we see the fourth, concluding step: the moment of final transformation and liberation from the dark power which releases the life-giving treasure and brings the story to its triumphant resolution.

So fundamental is this pattern that it shapes even some of the simplest stories in the world. In the little Russian folk tale, *The Turnip*, a man plants a seed which grows into an enormous turnip. When it is fully grown (or 'whole'), he tries to pull it out of the ground and cannot. We have the image of some great prize which cannot yet be secured because the hero is not yet adequate to the task. The man calls his wife, but even their combined strength is not enough. To help in the task, he then summons in turn a boy, a girl, a succession of animals, each adding to all the rest. The image is of the hero's original inadequate powers being gradually built up, until at last the smallest animal of all – a mouse (in some versions a beetle) – provides the final extra ounce of strength necessary to do the trick. The prize can finally be wrested from the earth, and they can all sit round together having a joyful feast. Indeed the turnip proves so large that it will continue to provide them all with food for a long time to come.

Two principles have been required to release the life-giving treasure. Obviously it needed the building up of a sufficiency of strength. But this could not have been achieved unless the hero had been able to join up with the other characters around him, in a state of mutual sympathy and co-operation. Only when the chain is absolutely complete (as is underlined by the way each link added to it is smaller and smaller) can the treasure be won.

In other words, the first essential principle is the masculine one of power and control. The second, allowing the state of potential wholeness to be reached, is the feminine one of connection and joining together. Such are the two elemental principles around which stories are constructed. If the hero of a story is destined fully to succeed, he must be shown to be fully masculine. He cannot be weak and ineffectual. But his masculine power must not be hard and inflexible. He must not be egocentrically closed off within himself. He must be open, in ways which connect him positively with others, with all that is beyond him, with the flow of life. Only when this potential state of balance has been achieved is the hero ready for the moment of liberation when the life-giving treasure is released.

In some stories we may see this process of coming to wholeness symbolised almost entirely in terms of what is happening to the hero himself. Even so, when we look carefully, we see how both the necessary elements are involved. The Ugly Duckling begins in a completely undeveloped, immature state. He then sees the swans, like a distant vision of some unattainable perfection and wholeness. He then goes through a long period of further testing and inward growth, until he is ready for his climactic transformation: and we then see his final, fully-developed state made up of two elements. On the one hand, he has reached a state of sovereign maturity as a 'kingly' swan, expressing the strength and autonomy of his fully-developed masculinity. On the other, he is also a beautiful, graceful creature, expressing within himself the instinctive perfection of nature in which the two parts of the equation, both strength and its life-giving balance, are never separated. He has reached a state of completeness which means that he is at last entirely at one with himself, with his fellow swans and with the world.

But in most stories this final image of wholeness is centred on the union of the hero with the heroine. And here, as we have seen, the action of the story is eventually reduced, as it nears its ending, to what is essentially a three-cornered struggle. Earlier we looked at this in terms of the dark power, on one hand, standing for the 'dark masculine'; the heroine, on the other, standing for the 'light feminine'; and the hero, coming between them, representing the balance between the two. We can just as well see it another way, with the hero on one side and the heroine on the other, representing the treasure, life, all that he needs to be complete: while the dark power stands between them, representing all that has to be overcome and transcended in order for that final state of wholeness to be achieved.

Whichever way we look at it, the only thing which matters is whether the right balance of qualities can be brought to bear to achieve the goal. And as the story nears its climax, this three-cornered struggle usually presents itself in one of three ways.

## (1) Balanced hero/passive heroine

The most basic form of this three-sided conflict is the type of story where we see the passive heroine somehow helpless in the clutches of the dark power – the Princess imprisoned by the monster – and where the hero has finally to prove himself by engaging in a battle to release her. Such a heroine may seem weak and helpless, but at this moment it is precisely her vulnerability which points up the essence of what is happening. In complete antithesis to the hard, aggressive, 'dark masculine' power which is threatening her, she stands for the soft, yielding, flowing, loving feminine: precisely the value which the threatening figure so completely lacks. Certainly to set her free the hero has to demonstrate his own masculine power. But just as important to us as we watch the unfolding of the action is the fact that he is seen as not just a tough, masculine figure: unlike his heartless opponent he is also irradiated with protective and sympathetic feeling, and it is this which allows us to see him as a light figure, worthy of his prize. His strengths are redeemed and made positive because they are being used in a cause which is not egocentric. Because he is open to the feminine value within him, he is able to join up with and liberate the feminine outside him. Because he represents not egotism and one-sidedness but a state of balance, he can see clearly what he has to do, and is thus able to rise above the limitations of the dark power and to be united with his 'other half'. And finally, to signify the state of inner and outer sovereignty he has achieved, we see him – like Aladdin, Perseus or Odysseus – succeeding to rule over the kingdom.

## (2) Balanced hero/active heroine

A second version of the story is that where the figure most obviously threatened by the dark power is the hero himself, and where the heroine plays a much more active role in liberating him. Here we see more explicitly how it is the life-giving power of the feminine which itself helps to draw the hero up to his final state of wholeness. When young Theseus arrives in Crete to face the final test of his burgeoning maturity, he is presented by the Tyrant Minos with two ordeals which show each of the aspects of the 'dark masculine' in its most deadly, negative guise. On the one hand, he has to face the Minotaur, half-man, half-bull, representing physical strength and power at its most heartless: on the other, he has to face the Labyrinth, with its maze of tunnels and dead ends, representing the ordering faculty of the human mind when it is cut off from life and the ability to see whole. What Theseus requires to rise above this double-test is the quality to turn each of these things into its positive, and it is this which he finds in his secure link to the feminine, in his loving bond with Ariadne. It is she who brings his strength to life by giving him the sword to slay the Minotaur; and she who gives him the vital thread which will liberate him from the deadly, suffocating Labyrinth, by enabling him to 'see whole' and thus connecting him back to life, light and the fresh air of the real world. Thus rooted in his link to the loving feminine, Theseus is finally able to rise to his full stature – fitting him on his return home to succeed to the kingdom.

## (1) and (2) from the heroine's point of view

We may see either of these types of story from the point of view of the heroine herself, in stories where she, rather than the hero, is the central figure. In such fairy tales as *Cinderella*, *Sleeping Beauty* or *Snow White*, we see a beautiful, gentle, entirely feminine heroine who is passively languishing in the shadows of the imprisonment where she has been placed by the 'dark feminine', a wicked stepmother, witch or bad fairy. What is required in each case to bring about her liberation is a handsome loving hero who can introduce into the equation precisely the element which is lacking, and which is necessary to override the negative, unbalanced, unloving power of the 'dark feminine' – namely masculine strength which is superior because it is balanced and open to the true feminine.

In stories where the heroine is 'active', such as *Jane Eyre*, *The Snow Queen* or *Fidelio*, and where it is the hero who has most obviously fallen into the state of imprisonment, it is the balanced heroine herself who introduces the element of strength which is necessary to release him and to restore him to his proper masculine state – even though she has only been brought up to her own full strength and stature by the inspiration of her love for the hero.

### (3) Dark hero/light heroine

The third variation arises when we come to those stories where the hero is himself the chief dark figure of the tale. Here the three-cornered battle has to be fought out essentially within his own divided personality. The hero may have most obviously fallen into the grip of the 'dark masculine', in which case he is strong, domineering and ruthless; he may have become possessed by the 'dark feminine', in which case he is most obviously weak and passive; or he may be in the grip of both, so that he behaves erratically, using his masculinity in a weak, treacherous way. In any respect, the one thing that is certain is that he is unable to make contact with the true feminine: he behaves egocentrically because has not got the capacity to feel for others or to see whole. And it is precisely through each of these deficiencies that, by the inexorable logic of storytelling, he gets caught up in the tragic downward spiral towards catastrophe. His inability to feel for others leads him to become progressively isolated and estranged from those around him, so that they (or those who survive) gradually constellate in opposition to him. His inability to see whole means that becomes enmeshed in that increasingly tortuous labyrinth of misjudgements which characterises any dark hero, as he is carried ever further from reality into the fantasy world of wishful thinking.

This is the real reason why any story in which the hero is dark shows him moving through mounting frustration into a state of nightmare. As his egocentricity drives him increasingly into outward and inward isolation, the reality of the world he has defied closes in on him until he is trapped. He faces the final crisis. And at such a moment his only hope of not plunging on to final disaster is that the terrifying pressure of his plight may at last force him out of the limited state of consciousness which has brought him to such a pass, and into contact with that deeper centre of his personality which can enable him to see the objective truth of his situation and to be brought back into living contact with others. If he can do this, like Leontes or Count Almaviva or Raskolnikov or Peer Gynt, we see that extraordinary moment of inward and outward transformation which marks the coming to wholeness. Liberated from the grip of the dark power within himself, he discovers that the heart of his identity, the inner self which has been liberated, is inextricably identified with the loving feminine, both within and outside him. At this moment his masculinity is no longer dark. And this is precisely the moment when his other half emerges from the shadows to join him up with all the world.

### (4) Dark heroine/light hero

More rarely, we see the same kind of story where it is the heroine who is dark and has become hard, self-centred and domineering, like Shakespeare's Shrew, Emma

Wodehouse, Tracy Lord or Mary Craven in *The Secret Garden*. Their personalities are strong, but they are heartless and blind, cut off from their inner feminine. What each of these heroines requires is a hero who is a perfect balance of masculine strength with a loving heart and the capacity to see whole (in particular to perceive the heroine's own repressed inner femininity). This is precisely what Petruchio, Mr Knightley, Dexter Haven and young Dickon represent. The result is that the heroine is liberated from the 'dark masculine' which has possessed her and isolated her from the world; her true feminine self emerges from the shadows to bring her alive and make her whole; and for the first time she is happily at one with all around her and with life.

So we come to the central goal around which – whether or not it can be reached – all storytelling ultimately revolves.

## The cosmic happy ending

The supreme moment of liberation in a story may well come at precisely that point where the hero and heroine are finally brought physically and spiritually together, melting into each other in an act of overwhelming love. We see such a moment when, after all his journeyings, all his ordeals, culminating in the great battle with the suitors, Odysseus can at last clasp his loving Penelope to him with no longer a trace of shadow between them:

> 'Penelope's surrender melted Odysseus's heart, and he wept as he held his dear wife in his arms, so loyal and so true.'

We see such a moment when the frozen statue of Hermione thaws into life and she steps down from her pedestal to embrace her contrite Leontes. We see such a moment when the Prince, having penetrated the hedge of thorns and found his way to the little hidden room at the heart of the castle, finally wakens the Sleeping Beauty with a kiss. But no sooner has the Prince done this than an extraordinary sequence of other events begins to unfold around them. All over the castle, every man, woman, child and animal that has also been frozen in sleep begins to stir. From the King and Queen downwards, the whole household awakens joyfully back to life.

Up to this point we have been looking almost entirely at what happens to the central characters in a story. We have concentrated on that great central theme of storytelling, as it may be seen from different angles: the working of the hero or heroine of the story towards some ultimate goal of wholeness and personal fulfilment. But a last enormously important element must now be brought in to complete the picture: and that is the wider context in which this individual drama of salvation is being worked out. For the outcome of the personal drama of the hero and heroine often has repercussions which affect many more people than just themselves.

In fact we are almost never presented in a story with a picture of the hero or the heroine in isolation. We usually meet them in the context of a group or community of others – a family, a household, a town, a city, a country, a kingdom. This is the 'little world' conjured up by the story, and it is almost invariably a world in which, in some way, 'the time is out of joint', something has gone badly amiss. The ruling order no longer exercises benign, harmonious or unchallenged sway. It may be that the king or the head of the household, the centre of authority, has become a Tyrant. It may be that he is weak, or has fallen sick, or is absent – or that his authority has been usurped by a Dark Rival. It may be that some monster or other force of darkness from outside the kingdom has intruded to threaten its security. The result is that things are in disarray, life is no longer flowing peacefully and happily. Whether we are looking at Odysseus's Ithaca or Phaoroah's Egypt, Beowulf's Heorot or Shylock's Venice, King Arthur's Britain or Robin Hood's England, the household of Cinderella or that of Count Almaviva, Robinson Crusoe's island or Sleeping Beauty's Castle, the Russia of *War and Peace* or the France of *The Three Musketeers*, the little 'kingdom' of Ebenezer Scrooge or that of Jimmy Porter in *Look Back in Anger*, the little community of Amity in *Jaws* or the entire galaxy in *Star Wars*, it is the same story. A state of conflict and confusion has arisen, division and disaffection rule. And this is because the little world presented by the story has fallen in some way under the shadow of the dark power.

Against this background of general disharmony we see the hero or the heroine of the story moving, consciously or unconsciously, towards their own moment of personal resolution. And almost every story we have looked at has centred round one of two general situations.

Firstly there is the type of story which shows us an essentially light hero or heroine who spends most of the story under the shadow of the dark power as it emanates from some source outside them. They are struggling, developing and working towards that eventual climactic moment when the scales can be finally tipped, the dark power can be overthrown and they can at last emerge from the shadows into the light.

The other type of story is that which shows the hero or the heroine as themselves the chief dark figure, casting a shadow over others. In this case also, the light, redeeming element eventually emerges from the shadows to overthrow the darkness and to end the story on a final image of wholeness.

In other words, from whichever perspective we view the drama, the essence of what is happening in the story remains the same. We see a world polarised between a dominant 'upper realm' in which for most of the story the dark power has the upper hand – with its egocentricity, heartlessness and limited consciousness; and an inferior 'shadow realm' which contains the potential for wholeness. Eventually, when all has been properly constellated, the scales tip and the centre of light in the story emerges from the shadows to redeem the corrupted upper world, to end division and to bring everything at last into a state of perfect balance and harmony. And this means not just for the hero and heroine themselves, but for everyone else around them in the world of the story who has been thrown into shadow (so long as they have survived).

We are thus left with two overriding images of the general state of things which stories can describe. The first shows human affairs under the shadow of the dark power, in a state of irresolution, uncertainty and incompleteness; and such a state may be characterised by four things:

(1) the aggressive and oppressive use of power;
(2) disorder and things not being as they should be;
(3) things being obscured or hidden, so that no one can see clearly or whole;
(4) a lack of proper feeling, love or mutual affection.

And when human affairs fall into such a state of sickness they have a tendency not just to remain static but to sink further into chaos and negativity until either they reach a catastrophe, or something happens to break the dark spell and to reverse the tendency upwards.

If this happens we may then see the other general state, that vision which is held out to us at the end of so many stories where the shadows are dispelled and where everything has suddenly and miraculously come out right. This means that:

(1) power is at last being exercised wisely and justly, under proper authority;
(2) a true harmonious state of order has emerged out of chaos;
(3) things obscured, hidden or not recognised have come to light;
(4) human beings are joined together in a joyful community of reconciliation, friendship and love.

In other words, what we see emerging at the end of such a story is a transformation from darkness to light, from negative to positive, on all four of the counts which go to make up a state of perfect balance: power, order, awareness and feeling. And in terms of the wider community, the 'world' of the story, this means that:

(1) either the existing ruler has once again been enabled to exercise his power properly; or a new ruler has emerged to do so in his place – as when the hero 'succeeds to the kingdom';
(2) the framework of order which had either become oppressive or had disintegrated has again knit together in a living, all-embracing way, so that all members of the community are in proper relationship with one another; families are reunited; everything out of place or lost has been restored to where it should be;
(3) everyone can at last see clearly and whole because nothing important any longer remains hidden; people have discovered everything they need to know, including their own true identities;
(4) the egotism and division which lay at the root of everyone's problem has at last been transcended, in a spirit of universal harmony and love.

If a story *can* reach the point where all these things have happened together (and they are so interdependent that they can only happen more or less together), we are given a momentary glimpse of a community of human beings entirely at one, liberated from every trace of shadow. And at the heart of this transition from incompleteness to wholeness has lain the transformation of just one individual, the central figure of the story. It has been around his or her working towards a state of individual balance and self-realisation that everything else has centred: so that nothing more completely symbolises the extraordinary thing that has happened to the wider world than the bringing together of a man and a woman to make a new and perfect whole, the microcosm of some infinite state of union, shining with life, light and hope for the future.

Such is the most completely positive ending that stories can aspire to. What does it mean that the human imagination has down the ages so consistently shaped stories in this way? To begin to answer this we must look again at those great shadowy presences who appear between the hero or heroine and their goal in so many stories, and who somehow have to be transcended if the goal is to be reached. We are now in a position to examine what these figures – the Dark Father, the Dark Mother, the Dark Rivals, the Dark Other Half – really stand for; how they fit together; and how they actually relate to the hero or the heroine's transformation during the story. In fact we can now see the real function and purpose which the dark figures serve in storytelling.

*Chapter 16*

# The Unrealised Value

'The light needs the dark to become articulate.'
Laurence Whistler, *Scenes and Signs on Glass*

A striking feature of the myths and folk tales of the world is how often their central figure is an orphan. In particular, at the beginning of a story, we often meet a little hero without a father or a heroine without a mother. Aladdin, Perseus, Theseus, the hero of *Jack and the Beanstalk* are all familiar examples of heroes with dead or absent fathers, who begin their story living alone with mother. Cinderella and Snow White are instances of heroines who lose their mothers, shortly before or after the story begins.

We thus begin the story with a family scene in which one major figure is conspicuously absent: in all these examples, the parents of the same sex as the central figure. What happens next?

In *Aladdin* a mysterious older man appears, the Sorcerer, who claims to be the dead father's long-lost brother, and who seems initially to be a replacement for the hero's lost father. He says he will look after the boy as his father would have wished. But this shadowy figure then turns out to be the hero's chief antagonist throughout the tale. Perseus finds himself with a wicked would-be stepfather, the tyrant king Polydectes, who is trying to force his attentions on Perseus's mother Danae. It is he who sends the boy off on the trail of perilous ordeals which make up the story. Theseus eventually finds himself confronted by the tyrant king Minos. Jack climbs the beanstalk and is faced by the towering, threatening figure of the giant, who he learns has killed his real father and dispossessed Jack of his rightful inheritance.

The central key to the story thus lies, in each case, in the struggle between the young hero and a fully-grown man who, as a Dark Father-figure or Tyrant, is a negative version of the father absent at the beginning. And when, after a long period of struggle, the hero at last comes to the end of his adventures, what happens? In each case the hero finally manages to overthrow this dark figure: Aladdin kills the Sorcerer; Perseus kills Polydectes; Theseus kills Minos's terrible representative, the Minotaur, Jack kills the giant. And we then see Aladdin, having at last grown up into a fully mature man, fully united with the Princess he has liberated and succeeding to her father's kingdom. Perseus and Theseus have likewise

277

liberated their Princesses from the shadow of the dark power and succeeded to their kingdoms. Jack has won the Giant's treasures and, even though he returns at the end to live with mother (which merely shows that this is a version of the story intended to be told to very young children) we no longer see him as the idle, good-for-nothing, dependent boy he was at the beginning, but as an independent, powerful young man in his own right, who has redeemed his father's lost inheritance, won a great treasure and is now capable of protecting and looking after his mother.

In each case we have seen a young boy whose most conspicuous lack was a strong, loving father. He has then been confronted with the negative version of this, a powerful but egocentric, unloving male authority-figure. And at the end, having killed off this figure, he has himself been transformed into a light and positive version of the figure he has overthrown. The hero has become a powerful, independent, fully-grown man, but at the same time – unlike his dark antagonist – he is whole, both strong and loving.

In the stories of *Cinderella* and *Snow White*, where the heroine is the central figure, once they have lost their true, loving mothers, we see the familiar pattern in the arrival of the wicked stepmother, cruel, treacherous and vain, who then becomes the chief dark figure of the story. Again, as a fully-grown woman, mother or queen, she represents the negative, unloving, egocentric version of what the heroine herself is eventually destined to grow up into. When, at the end, the heroine has been through her long maturing transformation and is finally liberated from the grip of the dark power by the Prince, she has at last become a perfect potential mother and queen in her own right, fit to succeed alongside her prince to rule over the kingdom.

In all these stories the chief dark figure thus signals to us the shadowy, negative version of precisely what the hero or heroine will eventually have to make fully positive in themselves. In fact, as we shall see, this principle whereby the nature of the dark figures gives us a direct, unconscious clue as to what needs to be transformed into its positive, light version for the story to reach a happy ending applies in stories of every kind. It is the key to the function played by the dark figure throughout storytelling. And once we learn to recognise how subtly and consistently this principle works, the drama which lies at the heart of storytelling opens up in a remarkable new way.

### The archetypal family drama

There are few themes more familiar to stories than that which traces the growing up of a little hero or heroine from immature, dependent childhood to some ultimate state of independent maturity, where he or she is united with a perfect 'other half'. There we can leave the newly-established couple with the reassurance that some profoundly important pattern has come to its proper resolution.

On a literal level, as we have noted, it might seem odd that we should find this so satisfying an ending to a story, since in real life marriage is far from being an ending. It is a new beginning, which may be merely the preface to the longest period of a human life.

Nevertheless, in terms of our deepest instincts, this obviously corresponds to one of the most basic and universal patterns in life. If we look around the natural kingdom, we see one impulse in every form of life which transcends everything else. From the protozoa to the higher primates, the central underlying concern of each species is to reproduce its kind, so that the chain of life can continue. And in the majority of life-forms this requires an absolutely fundamental process. Each individual creature, once it is born, must evolve and mature to the point where it can mate with another of the opposite sex, to ensure the birth of the next generation; and, in the higher life forms, must then ensure that those newly-born young are nurtured and provided with the conditions which can enable them in turn to grow up to the point where they are ready to continue the process. Both the drive to do this and the framework of 'knowledge' necessary to achieve it are instinctively programmed into every species which relies on sexual reproduction, as the central fact of its genetic inheritance. To this the human race is obviously no exception.

Every human being born into the world begins as a child, with a father and a mother. If the genetic imperative is to be fulfilled and the chain of life is to continue, the child must grow up, leave home and eventually find a mate with whom to establish a new home as a new centre for the generation of new life. In every generation, for life to be handed on, this is the drama which must be enacted: the son emerging from the shadow of his parents, to be united with a wife and take on the role of father; the daughter emerging from the shadow of her parents, to be united with a husband and become a mother.

We thus see essentially four characters in the drama, with a changing interplay of roles as the process unfolds: first the father and mother; then the child, growing up to adulthood; and finally the 'other half', necessary to bring the whole process back to its starting point, with the creation of a new child. Here, embedded in a web of our deepest and most powerful instinctual drives, are the most basic of all human relationships. And when we consider the main 'dark figures' who continually recur in stories, we have already begun to see how they correspond to each of the four figures in this primordial drama.

First there is the older man whom we see as the Dark Father-figure or Tyrant. He is powerful, often holding authority as the head of a household or a ruler, but he is heartless, using his power only to dominate others. He is thus seen as completely opposed to the flow of life.

Secondly there is the older woman whom we see as the Dark Mother-figure, Dark Queen or Witch. She is a more complex figure because outwardly she may seem to have 'feminine' attributes. She may make a show of being caring or protective. She may in her guise as a Witch have visionary, intuitive powers, the capacity to see behind the immediate surface of things to some hidden reality. But she no more possesses the real 'feminine' attributes of selfless feeling for others and the ability to 'see whole' than the Dark Father. Her 'feminine' facade is thus treacherous. Underneath, like the Dark Father, she is totally egocentric, possessed by the 'masculine' drive to power and domination.

Thirdly there are the Dark Rivals or the Dark Alter-Ego, of the same sex as the hero or heroine, who stand in some way more directly as competitors for the same goal, or as a 'dark opposite'.

Fourthly there is the Dark Other Half, the Temptress or False Wooer, who selfishly seeks to seduce or beguile the hero or heroine from their true path by offering a treacherous, false or inadequate version of the complete, perfect union they are striving towards.

We can see how these four types of dark figure correspond in a shadowy way to the four key roles in the most basic drama of human life. But once we grasp the significance of the 'unrealised value', the role of the dark figures in representing that which needs to be turned into its light version for the story to come to a happy ending, we can see how the real purpose of each of these dark figures is to present the hero or heroine of a story with a specific challenge. Each poses a particular negative threat which the hero and heroine must surmount by showing themselves as its positive equivalent.

On the face of it, the simplest of these challenges to identify is that posed by the Dark Father or Tyrant, because he usually makes no pretence of his true nature. He is simply a full-grown man, full of strength and power but self-evidently brutal and oppressive. In other words, he represents the fully-developed masculine values, in terms of his power and the fact that he embodies the ruling or dominant order, but completely without the life-giving feminine balance: and whenever the hero of a story comes up against such a figure (or turns into one himself) it is a sign that his ultimate task, if he is to succeed, is to become a positive, light version of the same figure.

The same is true when the hero encounters a strongly masculine 'Dark Rival'. In either case, he must show himself to be not just their match in masculine terms, but selfless where they are egocentric; good-hearted where they are heartless; able to see whole where their vision is limited. That is why the hero's ultimate prize from his struggle with the 'dark masculine' is that he can release the life-giving feminine from its deadly grip, and can replace the Dark Father as a potential light father or 'king'.

But to reach the point where he is ready to do this, he must first have shown his true masculinity: which is why, when the hero comes up against the 'dark feminine', the Dark Mother or the Temptress, his challenge has a different emphasis. Although, like the 'dark masculine', the 'dark feminine' is fundamentally egocentric and out for power, she works in a different way because she approaches the hero on his own softer, more feminine side. The 'dark masculine' is obviously aggressive and combative. But the 'dark feminine' works through a superficial show of feminine qualities, by appearing to feel and to care. She gets her way by guile, seduction, placation, deception. She disguises her true predatory intent beneath a pretence that she is serving the hero's best interests, like Circe or the Witch in *Hansel and Gretel* who offers the children gingerbread as a lure. It is only later that her real nature and purpose emerges, that she really wishes to imprison or devour her victims. The Dark Mother/Temptress promises the hero ease and self-gratification, that he does not have to make any effort or show firmness, that there is a short cut to becoming a man. She seeks to flatter his vanity or to gratify his physical appetites – for food, sex, comfort, relaxation. Always she appeals in some way to the hero's ego-centric desires, as a way of furthering her own. And here, in order to resist her wiles, the hero's task is to show himself as fully masculine. He has to show strength, judgement, the ability to discriminate. He has to remain his own man. The purpose of the 'dark feminine' is to unman him, to make him weak and dependent, to turn him into 'the boy hero who cannot grow up'. His way to resist her is certainly to hold onto true feeling and ability to 'see whole'. But even more directly it requires him to summon up all his masculine strength, will-power and self-reliance, as Odysseus does when he finally manages to break free from the enchantments of Calypso. That is why the great prize won by the hero from the battle with the 'dark feminine' is his independent manliness.

We also here come to a complication, in that it is perfectly possible for a male character in a story to remain unrealised in a positive sense on *both* sides of his personality at the same time. He lacks masculinity as well as the inner feminine. Although this makes him outwardly weak, it does not mean that he is not driven by the urge to exert power over others. But because he is unable to show his desire to dominate openly, he resorts to acting in the manner of the 'dark feminine', by guile and treachery. Such a character may pretend to be concerned for the interests of others, like Aladdin's Sorcerer or those Dark Rival figures, Blifil, the 'goody-goody' and 'sneak' in *Tom Jones*, Joseph Surface in *A School For Scandal*, Molière's Tartuffe; but this is only a hypocritical front for his ruthless self-seeking.

In fact the most extreme form of this outwardly male character who works through the insinuating manner of the 'dark feminine', trying to get a hold over the hero by pretending to be acting in his interests, represents the ultimate type of dark figure in stories, the Tempter. This figure, who is extremely dangerous because he is so deceptive, is most commonly seen in Tragedy. An obvious example is Mephistopheles in *Dr Faustus*, pretending to offer Faustus all sorts of illusory powers and the ability to know and see 'hidden things' (i.e., to see whole), when in fact he is appealing only to the weak, deluded Faustus's ego and seeking to destroy him. Iago is a similarly devilish example, pretending to be serving Othello's best interests, but in fact seeking only to trap and destroy him. Lord Henry Wootton plays the same role in luring Dorian Gray onto his path to self-destruction.

The Tempter is in fact the supreme 'dark opposite' in stories because he stands at the ultimate pole from the state of wholeness. He represents in its most extreme form egotism pretending to be its opposite. As such, if the hero is weak in judgement and self-control, he can become the most dangerous adversary of all.

In those stories where the central figure is the heroine, the emphasis of the challenges presented by the dark figures is reversed. When a heroine comes up against the 'dark masculine', like Leonore against the Tyrant Pizarro or Portia against Shylock, it is her strength which has to be called primarily into play, her 'masculine' qualities (although coupled with an unshakeable hold on her femininity). When she is up against the 'dark feminine', like Cinderella faced by her wicked stepmother and the ugly sisters, it is her own genuine femininity, her innocence, beauty and goodness of heart, which is the most obvious measure of her superiority, and it is this which in the end attracts the 'light masculine' figure of the hero to release her. But, like the hero, the heroine may also come up against that most 'inferior' figure of all, a male figure working through his 'dark feminine' wiles, like St John Rivers trying to lure Jane Eyre into a marriage which we know would first imprison and then kill her. St John Rivers is the Tempter as Dark Other Half, like those weak, treacherous false wooers who attempt to seduce several of Jane Austen's heroines, or Anatole Kuragin, the would-be seducer of Natasha in *War and Peace*. The Tempter, as the ultimate 'dark opposite' of the state of wholeness, is thus just as much the most dangerous enemy to the heroine as he is to the hero, and like him she needs to summon up all her potential for wholeness to resist him; just as does Jane Eyre does in her final struggle to free herself from succumbing to Rivers.

## The four basic figures

What we thus see is just how directly our human need to imagine stories is related to the most central instinctive drive in human life. Each of us born into a family unit soon becomes conscious that we are the third and youngest of a 'three': 'Daddy, Mummy and me', the primal triad. We are aware that, as the 'third' of that 'three', we are the central focus of a process of growth and transformation which naturally preoccupies us more than anything else in the world. From this beginning, as we gradually become aware, the deepest instinctive drive programmed into any of us is that we should eventually find that 'other half' who can complete the process by enabling us to repeat the continuation of life. We thus instinctively know that the original 'three' must become a 'four': in a way which also creates that new state of 'one-ness' which forms the core of a new family unit.

This essential pattern is programmed into our unconscious around a set of archetypes; which is why so many stories centre round the same little group of archetypal figures: father, mother, hero and heroine (whose symbolic roles are often enhanced, particularly in myths and folk tales, by giving them royal status as a King, a Queen, a Prince and a Princess). If a story manages to reach the complete happy ending, what it shows us is its hero and heroine finally coming together to become a potential new Father/King and Mother/Queen, reflecting that process central to human life whereby each new generation grows up to succeed to the one before it.

But stories are not concerned with this succession in its biological sense. Their concern is with its psychology. What they are showing us is those psychological qualities which are essential for the succession to take place in the right way. This is why the role of the dark figures in a story is to exemplify those negative qualities which the central figure must overcome in order to achieve the proper happy ending. In this respect, however many characters may appear in a story, its real concern is with just one: its hero or its heroine. It is he or she with whose fate we identify, as we see them gradually developing towards that state of self-realisation which marks the end of the story. Ultimately it is in relation to this central figure that all the other characters in a story take on their significance. What each of the other characters represents is really only some aspect of the inner state of the hero or heroine themselves.

This is why in so many stories we see a central figure who begins young, immature and single then falling in some way under the shadow of the dark power. For a long time the state of incompleteness which the dark power itself symbolises continues to hold sway, because this corresponds to the stage of development reached by the hero or heroine themselves. Only when they are finally ready to emerge to maturity can the dark power in the story be overthrown or fade away. We thus see the central figure developing through the story towards that moment of final emergence into the light, much as a butterfly evolves through all the incomplete stages of its development, first as a caterpillar, then as a chrysalis and only lastly in its complete state as a butterfly: *imago*, as it is called, the final perfect image of what it has been striving towards. Through all those phases of the story when hero or heroine are still psychologically incomplete, we see the dark figures looming over them, as negative symbols of the values they must still make positive in themselves before the story can reach its final resolution.

So central is this to understanding how stories take shape in the human imagination that it is time to look at how it works in practice. We begin with two of the most famous stories of the ancient world, each describing how its hero matures from immature boyhood to a final state of kingly manhood. We then see how a modern Hollywood version presents the same theme.

## From boy to king (Perseus)

The story of the great mythical hero Perseus begins even before he is born. It opens with a king, Acrisius, who has a daughter Danae. We thus begin with the image of a King/Father with a beautiful young woman by his side. He is then told by the oracle that one day in the distant future he will be killed by his grandson. In other words, he learns that he will one day have to die and that a new generation will succeed. Faced with this threat Acrisius turns dark and shuts up Danae in a tower, so that no man may reach her. It is a classic image of the dark power of the Tyrant imprisoning the light feminine in its shadow. Made selfish by the thought that he has to die, Acrisius has lost touch with the ability to feel or to see anything beyond his own self-interest.

Then the greatest king of all, Zeus, king of the gods, representing the power of masculine authority at its most numinous because it is serving the cause of life, comes to Danae disguised as a shining shower of gold and she becomes pregnant with the hero of the story, Perseus. When he is born, the fearful, enraged Acrisius turns loose the infant hero and his mother in a chest on the sea, whence they are eventually washed up alone together on a strange shore. The hero thus, like any human child, enters a new world close to his mother – but it is not long before a new presence enters their life in the shape of the king of the land they have come to, Polydectes. He tries to force his attentions on Danae and treats her cruelly, thus redoubling the shadowy image of the Dark King/Father which lies so heavily over the early stages of this story. The boy Perseus grows up to the verge of manhood, loving his mother and attempting to defend her against the tyrannical 'dark masculine' of Polydectes, and eventually, to buy him off, he promises the Tyrant he will do anything to save her from his clutches. This courageous declaration of loving unselfishness tells us that Perseus begins with a good relationship to the feminine; but in order to prove its worth he is first going to have to establish his manhood, for without the manly strength to back them up, such declarations are merely empty expressions of sentiment. The king sends him off to kill the dreadful Medusa. The terrible, once-beautiful Gorgon, with her deadly power to turn all who see her to stone, freezing the life and growth of all who fall into her shadow, is one of the most indelible images of the 'dark feminine' ever conceived. Eventually, after a long journey and much preparation, with the aid of the goddess of wisdom Athene and the god Hermes, Perseus manages to cut off her head. At the moment he does so, out of her body spring fleeting images of the shining warrior Chrysaor and the winged horse Pegasus, symbols of the bounding power of manhood which Perseus has released from his victorious struggle with the 'dark feminine'.

Now he has become a man, the only danger is that he will misuse his new-found power and strength for selfish purposes. He has one more task to become complete: to prove that his power has life-giving balance, by showing that it does not overshadow the 'light feminine'. This is precisely the test which awaits him when, on his journey home, he sees the beautiful Princess Andromeda chained to a rock as the terrible sea-monster sent by Poseidon approaches. The shadowy presence of Poseidon, grim king of the inferior realm beneath the sea, is always a sign in Greek mythology that the 'Dark Father' of unbalanced masculine power is at work. He is, for instance, the father of Polyphemus, the 'dark opposite' to Odysseus. He is the shadowy presence behind King Minos and his creature the Minotaur, the 'dark opposite' to Theseus. Here his sea-monster stands as the 'dark opposite' or 'Dark Rival' of Perseus, the representative of the 'dark masculine' with whom he is in competition for the Princess. By using the trophy of his new-found manhood, the head of Medusa, to outwit the monster, Perseus slays it, frees Andromeda and marries her. He returns to kill Polydectes, again using the Gorgon's head, to free his mother Danae. Finally, at a funeral games, he by mistake (and therefore innocently) kills the watching Acrisius, his grandfather – and at this point Perseus at last succeeds to the kingdom. The original oracle has been fulfilled. Perseus has succeeded in every sense. He has unravelled all the intricate series of challenges back to the beginning, turning darkness in each case to light. The story ends, as it began, on the image of a king, a proud, full-grown bearer of masculine authority, standing with a beautiful woman by his side. The torch has been passed to a new generation. The cycle of regeneration is complete.

### From boy to king (David)

Another instance of a young hero who grows up in the shadow of the Dark Father until he eventually succeeds to the kingdom is the biblical story of David, recorded from Jewish legend in the two books of Samuel and the first book of Kings. We look here at just the first part of his story, up to the point where he becomes king, because of its particularly subtle emphasis on the fact that, unlike his dark, one-sided antagonist, young David is in masculine and feminine terms so well balanced, and therefore always potentially whole.

The story begins with King Saul having just won a series of tremendous, bloody victories over his country's enemies, but incurring the wrath of God for his disobedience. Saul has failed. He is becoming a dark figure. God decides that his days as king are numbered. At this point we meet David as an obscure young shepherd boy, and almost the first thing we learn about him is that he plays the harp beautifully, a first intimation of his softer, feminine side. Then follows the most familiar episode of the story when the great enemies of Israel, the Philistines, invade, led by their champion, the boastful giant Goliath, representing 'dark masculine' strength at its most brutal. Alone of all the Israelites the little shepherd boy dares to step forward to challenge the giant. Goliath looks down in contempt, because it is emphasised that David was not only young but 'fair of countenance'; again the softer value. And of course it is not because David is stronger than Goliath that he wins the contest, but because he is cleverer and more imaginative. Like so many other little heroes confronted by giants in folklore, he catches Goliath out on the blind spot of his self-regarding stupidity, his limited awareness. David has the wider vision to use the little slingstones which enable him to attack from out of the giant's reach; and having slain Israel's greatest enemy by his combination of manly courage and intuitive imagination, he becomes his country's greatest hero.

At first Saul welcomes the emergence of David as his leading general. David marries his daughter, the Princess Michal, and becomes the inseparable friend of Saul's son Jonathan, a 'light alter-ego', emphasising that David is now almost a son to Saul himself. But increasingly Saul becomes jealous and bitter towards the happy, balanced, harp-playing young man. He turns more and more into a moody, scheming, heartless Dark Father, inwardly possessed by the 'dark feminine', making a succession of treacherous attempts to kill David. David is driven increasingly into the position of being a hunted outlaw, first in the wilderness of Israel itself, then in exile in the land of the hated Philistines. As Saul, 'above the line', sinks ever further into darkness, David is being polarised ever further into the shadows 'below the line'. But never for a moment does he lose his balance, his sense of loyalty, his true feeling and his ability to see whole. Even when he has a chance to kill the sleeping Saul in the darkness of the cave, he merely cuts off a piece of Saul's coat to show that he has no desire to cause Saul injury. In the 'shadow realm', in short, he is developing more and more completely into Saul's 'light opposite', integrated and whole, while Saul in the 'upper realm' becomes ever more dark and unbalanced. Finally the nightmare gathering round Saul comes to a climax. He and his army suffer a huge defeat at the hands of the Philistines, Jonathan is killed, Saul himself commits suicide in despair. David is recalled by popular acclamation from the 'inferior realm' of his exile, and the seemingly perfect hero becomes king.[1]

1. There is of course much more to David's story after this point, during the 40 years when he remains king of Israel; and part of the continuing psychological subtlety of the story is that he is by no means shown as remaining flawless in his conduct. He faces further tests of his character, such as the episode involving his adultery with Bathsheba and the ruthless fashion in which he disposes of her husband by ordering him into the front line of battle. But always his moments of weakness are resolved in greater understanding and recognition of his failings. Thus when he eventually dies 'stricken in years' (*Kings 1*), he hands on the kingdom to his son Solomon, who has remained legendary as 'the wisest king' of all.

### From boy to king (*The Lion King*)

One of the most popular Hollywood movies of recent times was the Disney Studio's animated version of this basic theme, *The Lion King* (1994).[2] This begins in Africa with different species of animals and birds congregating in the bush round Pride Rock, home of Mufasa, king of the lions and acknowledged lord of all the other animals. Their gathering symbolises the 'Circle of Life'. Mufasa, strong and mature, is presenting his young cub Simba as his heir, proudly watched by Simba's mother Sarabi. Deliberately absent from the ceremony is the king's younger brother Scar, disfigured by a scar over one eye, physically weaker than his brother but crafty and cruel. His dark hope that he might one day himself succeed as king has now been dashed.

Initially we see Simba, the story's hero, as foolish and immature, as he takes his little friend Nala, a young lioness, to the 'elephants' graveyard' where they have been told never to go. They are rescued from a pack of evil hyenas by Simba's father, the king, who has come to look for them. But then Simba's recklessness leads him to be nearly trampled to death by a stampeding herd of wildebeeste. After again coming to save his son, Musafa escapes up a cliff from which Scar, waiting at the top, pushes him to his death. Simba imagines he has been the cause of his father's death, and wanders miserably off into exile, leaving Scar, helped by the treacherous pack of hyenas, to claim the kingship.

We thus see the archetypally familiar situation of a good King/Father dying or being murdered, at a time when his immature young heir is not yet ready to succeed, so that the role of King/Father is taken on by a usurping dark brother (as in *Hamlet*, *Aladdin* and many other versions), leaving the son-hero disconsolate and dispossessed.

The lost and exiled Simba is taken into the care of a warthog and a meerkat, who become his friends, and he stays with them, enjoying a happily irresponsible life out in the bush, without noticing that he is gradually maturing into a full-grown lion (archetypally, this playful relationship with his friends echoes Prince Hal's friendship with Falstaff and Co.). But eventually a full-grown young lioness intrudes on their peace, who turns out to be Nala. The news from the kingdom could not be worse. Under the misrule of Scar and his hyenas (like Saruman and his orcs in *The Lord of the Rings*), all has gone to wrack and ruin. Food and water are exhausted. It seems the very survival of the Pride is in question. At first Simba seems apathetic, but thanks to Nala and a wise money Rafiki, he is called back to himself. This is emphasised when he looks at his reflection in water, to see that he now looks just like his father – who then appears in a heavenly vision to tell him 'you have forgotten who you are … the one true king'.

Simba leads his friends back to Pride Rock to challenge the evil Scar, who scornfully accuses him of having killed his father. But when Scar then tries to kill Simba in the same way, by pushing him off the cliff, he admits that it was he himself who had murdered Musafa. Simba manages to leap upwards to safety, outwrestles Scar

---

2. In many respects the Disney version echoed a Japanese animated film made 30 years earlier, *Kimba The White Lion* (1965), although the studio strongly denied that there was any link between the two.

in a fight and, when the 'dark king' is pushed over the cliff in turn, he is set on and devoured by the hyenas. To the joy of his mother and the other unhappy lionesses, Simba has, like Odysseus, triumphantly reclaimed his kingdom. He marries his loving Nala, and the story ends with a hymn to the 'Circle of Life' sung by all the animals, as the new king and queen hold up a new-born daughter to confirm that the continuance of life into the future is now assured.

## A version from the Stone Age

Once we begin to recognise the significance of the part played by the 'unrealised value' in stories, we see just how crucial it is to the unconscious logic by which they are constructed. All through a story the dark figures identify those negative qualities which must be redeemed into their positive opposites if it is to reach a happy ending. The whole story thus becomes the picture of a changing balance between the power of darkness initially dominant 'above the line' and the gradually developing centre of light 'below the line'; until finally the balance can tip, the shadows fade away and light can flood up 'above the line' to show hero and heroine united and at one with life.

This kind of coding is so firmly built into the structure of myths and folk tales that we find it in storytelling all over the world. No culture could be more remote from our own than that of the 'Stone Age' bushmen of southern Africa. Yet consider the outline of a typical traditional bushman children's story, from a collection made in the nineteenth century by Dr Wilhelm Bleek (later republished in *The Heart of the Hunter* by Laurens van der Post).

The story begins by describing how two of the little creatures of the veldt, a lizard and a black beetle, have a daughter. They keep her prisoner and force her to perform menial tasks, in such a cruel fashion that all the other creatures around are horrified. Eventually the other animals come together and resolve to liberate the little prisoner. First to attempt this heroic deed is a long-nosed mouse, but the lizard and the black beetle have no difficulty in killing him. A whole succession of other long-nosed mice try to succeed in his place, but all are killed. At last the mysterious Mantis, an insect which plays a central part in bushman mythology as a wise, far-seeing visionary, has a dream: with the result that a different creature, a striped mouse, sets out to free the unhappy young 'beetle woman'. He goes into battle and by a combination of courage and ingenuity he succeeds finally in slaying both the lizard and the black beetle, exclaiming as he does so 'I am, by myself, killing to save friends'. Not only is the young heroine liberated from her imprisonment, but all the slain mice come back to life as well. They march home in a triumphant column, at its head the victorious hero and by his side the young beetle woman: 'for he felt that he was the husband of the girl and that she was utterly his woman'.

Although this tale comes from what might be regarded as one of the most primitive cultures in the world, nothing about its structure is unfamiliar to us. We recognise the initially dominant dark power, keeping the 'light feminine' imprisoned in its shadow, so cruelly that the shadow of its tyranny falls over the whole surrounding community. We recognise the way the storyteller describes the first inadequate attempts from within the 'shadow realm' to free her, which only helps to build up our sense of what a colossal task it is going to be. We recognise the intervention of the mysterious seer, whose wider vision leads to the emergence of the true redeeming hero (like Merlin arranging for the emergence of King Arthur); and, again, the careful emphasis placed on the point that the hero is only 'killing to save friends' (he is not doing it for selfish reasons but for the general good). Finally we recognise the familiar climax of that selfless act of liberation, which leads to the hero both winning the supreme prize of his own perfect union with the heroine and at the same time liberating the wider community of all those who had fallen under the dark power's shadow.

What we may particularly note, however, is the way the story begins with the two overshadowing figures of a Dark Father and a Dark Mother and, after a long process of struggle, ends on the image of a fully-realised hero and heroine emerging together into the light. The essence of what has happened in the story is that the original dark and negative image we began with has been redeemed by the end into its light, positive opposite. The initial threatening presence of the Dark Father and Mother has been replaced by the young hero and heroine, who have emerged from the darkness to the point where they are themselves ready to become a Light Father and Mother. As in so many other stories, we see the older generation, characterised as being dark and life-denying, being succeeded by the new generation who are on the side of life. The very way in which the older generation are presented as dark provides a direct signal of the light values which the younger generation must embody, in order to show themselves as worthy to succeed.

But it is by no means only in the more overtly symbolic types of story, such as myths and folk tales, that we find the 'unrealised value' presented in this way. As we shall see in the rest of the book, it is absolutely integral to the way stories take shape in the human imagination.

## Chapter 17

# The Archetypal Family Drama
# (Continued)

'Therefore shall a man leave his father and his mother, and shall cleave unto his wife; and they shall be one flesh.'

*Genesis* 2.24

At the beginning of *David Copperfield* we see the little hero, as a young child, losing both his parents, so that, like the heroes of so many folk tales and myths, he becomes an orphan. He then falls under the shadow of that fearsome couple Mr and Miss Murdstone, who take on the roles in his life of Dark Father and Dark Mother. He embarks on the long, painful process of growing up, falling under the shadow of a succession of other dark figures on the way, until we see him at last ready to come together with his 'true angel' Agnes, at which point the whole immense story is resolved. The novel thus begins overshadowed by the towering image of a dark couple. It ends with hero and heroine finally stepping out of the shadows as a fully-realised light couple.

When, as a young boy, Nicholas Nickleby loses his father, he immediately falls under the shadow of the Dark Father, his uncle Ralph. All the dark figures he subsequently encounters are different expressions of his uncle's brooding presence over his life – until finally the Dark Father's power is overthrown. Having liberated his beloved Madeleine from his uncle's thrall, the hero can at last step out into the light, as a shining example of upright manliness in all the ways the evil, twisted Sir Ralph was not.

At the beginning of *Great Expectations* we see the little orphan Pip falling under the shadow of two seemingly dark and terrifying older figures, the convict Magwitch and the embittered old recluse Miss Havisham, with her bewitching little protégée Estella in her shadow. Finally, many years later, when Magwitch and Miss Havisham have both died violent deaths, we see the mature Pip coming together with the mature, still beautiful Estella in the garden of Miss Havisham's ruined house, and 'I saw no shadow of another parting from her'.

When the novel emerged to play such a dominant role in the popular storytelling of the eighteenth and nineteenth centuries, one of the elements it inherited from the tradition of the folk tale was the idea of tracing the story of the orphaned hero or heroine's life from early childhood all the way up to its eventual 'happy ending' in adult years. Dickens was particularly drawn to this type of tale. And whenever a story does begin with the hero or heroine's childhood in this way, there is likely to be a strong Rags to Riches element in the way it unfolds, which-ever type of plot may be primarily shaping the way the story is presented. This is because, in the language of storytelling, the process of growing up from childhood to adulthood naturally expresses itself in Rags to Riches terms. The shadows in which we first meet the disregarded little hero or heroine – usually those cast by dark parent-figures – correspond to the as-yet unrealised value of what they have it in them eventually to become; when they have at last realised that potential, as independent adults, the shadows finally drop away and they emerge fully into the light.

More often in stories, however, we do not begin with the hero or heroine in child-hood. When we first meet them they are already adults, or on the verge of becoming so. What they are not, yet, is wholly mature, settled, happy or complete. No situa-tion is more familiar at the start of a story than that its central figure is a young man or woman who is in the process of stepping out onto the stage of the adult world, but has not yet reached an established state; and who, above all, is still single. Just as in the versions which begin in childhood, therefore, the real question underlying the story is whether, by the end, we can see them having 'found themselves', which usually means happily united to the right 'other half' and having found a new, secure centre to their lives. There we can leave them, knowing that in some centrally important sense the pattern of their lives has been resolved. As always, the question is not simply 'can they get married'? It is, can they do so in the right way, showing that the fundamental problem of all human life, the problem posed by that imma-turity which is synonymous with egotism, has been confronted and overcome?

A plot which particularly lends itself to presenting the story in this way is Comedy. When we earlier traced the historical evolution of Comedy, we saw that this type of story was originally concerned with showing the transition from frag-mentation to wholeness only in more general terms. In the *Lysistrata* Aristophanes shows the city of Athens under a shadow because its ruling menfolk have become imprisoned in their obsession with making war. In their shadow the women, rep-resenting the feminine value, band together with masculine strength of will and organisation to win the men from the grip of the 'dark masculine'. The result is that, at the end, masculine and feminine are brought together in harmony and the community is restored to wholeness. In the *Thesmophoriazusae* it is the women of Athens who have become possessed by the 'dark masculine', in their obsessive desire for violent revenge on Euripides. It is he who, by putting them back in touch with their proper feeling and sense of proportion, wins them back to balance, so the play can end on an image of good-humoured reconciliation. In *The Wasps*, the tyrannical old Dark Father Procleon represents all those ageing, dried-up senior citizens who wish to uphold a lifeless vision of social order by their obses-sive desire to condemn others.[1] Here it is his son, representing youth and life, who

---

1. Procleon is a typical example of that stock character who was to become familiar in later Roman comedy as *senex*: the dried-up, judgemental old man, opposed to the flow of life, who has con-tinued to play the role of Dark Father or Tyrant through the history of storytelling. In fact *senex* characteristics are so well-defined that they constitute an archetype, which can affect older women just as much as men, as in the fearsome Granny-figure, constantly complaining about the younger generation and the modern world, made famous over many decades by the British cartoonist Giles.

liberates his father from his imprisonment by enabling him once more to feel, to see whole and to become once again his true living self.

What happened when the plot developed from these beginnings into the New Comedy was simply that it moved into the mainstream of storytelling and became anchored in that same archetypal family drama which is at the centre of other types of story. The focus of the story becomes the need to make that successful transition to a new generation which is centred on the union of the young hero and heroine. And in this context, as we have seen, Comedy took on two main forms, according to whether the main obstacle to their union lies in the older generation or the younger.

The first shows us the hero and heroine in love, longing to get married, but with the way ahead to their union barred by a Dark Father or a Dark Mother. We thus see a little world in which the road to future life is blocked by the fact that the ruling figure in that world has fallen into a state of darkness and become a Tyrant. The young hero is placed in the familiar situation of all those other types of story where the 'Princess' is in the grip of a tyrant or a monster; and in those other types of story he would now have to destroy the monster, in order to free the heroine from his clutches.[2] But in Comedy, where everyone in the end has to be brought round to playing his or her role in the archetypal drama properly and positively, it is the tyrant himself who has first to be liberated from his prison, in order for everyone else to be liberated. As his eyes are opened and he goes through a change of heart, he is discovering the 'unrealised value' in himself. He is transformed into a 'light Father'. This enables him to recognise the supreme value of the love between the hero and the heroine. The way to the succession has been cleared, and hero and heroine can step out into the light as the centre of life for the next generation.

The other type of Comedy is that where the problem lies in the younger generation. Either the young hero is not yet ready to succeed, because he has been cut off from his inner feminine by his own state of darkness; in which case it is he who must discover the 'unrealised value' in himself (exactly the same is true when the central figure is a dark heroine). Or we see one of those comedies where the problem simply lies in general confusion as to who should properly end up united to whom; in which case it is this uncertainty itself which symbolises the state of immaturity, until they are finally able to see clearly and all confusion is resolved.

Everything that Comedy develops into from these foundations is an extension of these basic themes. For human life to flourish, runs its essential message, each generation has to make the proper transition to the next. The representatives of

---

2. There are occasions when Comedy presents a situation remarkably similar to that familiar in Overcoming the Monster stories, where we see the 'Princess' locked away by the Tyrant in a tower, with the handsome hero arriving to free her. In Rossini's opera *The Barber of Seville* the young heroine Rosina is kept shut away by her grim guardian, Dr Bartolo, until the Count Almaviva and his ally Figaro manage by a series of stratagems to liberate her. In Mozart's *Il Seraglio* the beautiful young English heroine Constanze has been imprisoned by the Pasha Selim in his palace, and her lover Belmonte arrives to risk his life in rescuing her: until the Tyrant magnanimously recognises the force of their love and lets her go.

the older generation must play their part by not being negative and overbearing, clinging onto dominance and thus stifling the onward flow of life. The representatives of the younger generation must develop sufficient maturity for them to succeed. A proper balance must be achieved in all directions. And this means ultimately that the four roles involved in the archetypal process – father, mother, hero and heroine – must all be acted out positively. We thus arrive at a complete model of that drama which lies at the heart of storytelling.

### The archetypal family drama: Summing up

Nothing is more remarkable about the way stories naturally form in the human imagination than the way, beneath the surface, they unconsciously centre round this most fundamental of all dramas in human life, involving just four basic figures. In the dark versions of each of these figures we see a different negative aspect of that which has to be redeemed and made positive if the central figure of the story is ultimately to succeed.

This is why, initially standing over everything, are the grim figures of the Dark Father and/or the Dark Mother. They are not only the negative shadows of what the hero or heroine must eventually become. In the most cosmic sense they represent power, authority and the prevailing order of the human world when it has become most obviously oppressive and opposed to the flow of life. They symbolise the remorseless strength of the human ego when it is without love, or any connection to the world outside itself, and it is this which must be eliminated for life to be renewed.

Most obviously in their shadow languishes the young heroine, the light feminine. She embodies both the life-giving value which they lack and the supreme prize which must be redeemed to restore the world to wholeness. By definition, the selfless light feminine stands at the opposite pole to the blind power of the ego. This is why, while its power remains unchallenged, we see her so often presented in stories as a helpless prisoner or victim, either of a Dark Father or of a Dark Mother. More directly she may explicitly be shown as a daughter to one or other of them: as in all those familiar images of the strong, unloving Tyrant and his imprisoned daughter (Minos and Ariadne, Acrisius and Danae, Aetes and Medea, Shylock and Jessica, Prince Bolkonsky and Maria); or those equally familiar images of a daughter under the spell of an overbearing Dark Mother (Cinderella, Snow White).

The central challenge of stories is to see the heroine liberated from this imprisonment; and this implies she has found the right hero, both strong and loving enough to free her. It is this combination of qualities which enables him both to redeem the heroine and to succeed as ruler over the 'kingdom'. This is why we usually see the final stage of the drama as a confrontation between the hero and the one-sided dark masculine, either by a direct challenge to the Dark Father himself, or through a battle with a Dark Rival who represents the hero's own shadow in competing for the ultimate goal.

To make the challenge successfully, however, the hero must already have successfully developed both outward masculinity and inner femininity. His good relationship to the feminine may initially have been developed through a positive relationship to a 'light Mother'. But to become fully a man he must eventually escape from this dependence, or it will turn into the emasculating grip of the dark feminine. So long as the hero remains in any way under the spell of Mother, the older woman, the Temptress, he remains the weak 'boy hero who cannot grow up'. He cannot develop the masculine strength or firmness of character to rise to the challenge of contending for the true heroine in the first place. This will leave him frozen in an impotent posture of conflict with the Dark Father who, by the law of the 'unrealised value', thus comes also to represent the masculinity the hero cannot make positive in himself.

In such a situation, where the hero is not adequate to the challenge, the heroine herself must in some way remain in thrall to the dark masculine, and everything remains unresolved.

⁍

Once we come to recognise this central dynamic to the archetypal process which lies behind so much of storytelling, it is remarkable how many of the situations we see in stories it helps to show in a new light. To illustrate this this chapter ends by looking again at four examples of Comedy, each of which concentrates attention on some less familiar aspect of this four-cornered network of relationships.

The first two, *Tom Jones* and *Der Rosenkavalier*, focus in different ways on the problem of the hero in escaping the pull of 'Mother'. The others, *Die Meistersinger* and *Middlemarch*, centre on the problem for the heroine in finding her own strength to win independence from the pull of 'Father'.

### Tom Jones

In *Tom Jones* we see a hero whose chief problem, as a little foundling who has arrived in the world without any prospects of a proper, secure station in life, is to develop his masculine identity. From the beginning the kind-hearted, honest Tom shows a promising connection to the feminine, the centre of his inner identity, as is indicated by the fact that the heroine, Sophia Western, loves him rather than his Dark Rival, Blifil. But because he is *outwardly* only a poor orphan, the dominant power in their little world – the older generation, centred on Squire Western, the heroine's Dark Father – cannot conceive of allowing their match.

Tom's real task is to build up a secure sense of his own manliness, to give him strength of character, self-discipline and a defined position in the world. Thus most of the ordeals he faces, exposing his lack of self-control, centre round a series of encounters with Temptress or Dark Mother figures. These come to a head when he is briefly under the impression that he has actually made love to his own mother: a perfect instance of the sort of superficially inexplicable incident in stories, like Figaro's involvement with Marcellina, which only makes sense in terms of its deeper archetypal symbolism. But interspersed with these episodes, each of which threatens to destroy Tom and tear him apart from Sophia forever, he eventually, in the shadowy world of London, begins to prove himself as strong, resourceful and independent, capable of courageously intervening to sort out other people's problems. It is here in the 'inferior realm' that we see Tom developing towards maturity, as no longer just a bewildered, amiable young man weakly at the mercy of temptation and circumstance. This is why, when the moment of general 'recognition' arrives, we find it entirely satisfying to discover that Tom was the older (and superior) brother to the treacherous, unmanly Blifil all along. Tom has at last established his proper manly identity in the world, and the older generation, led by Squire Western, are at last only too happy to recognise him as worthy to be united to Sophia.

### Der Rosenkavalier

In *Tom Jones* the focus is on the hero's own efforts to break loose from the disintegrating pull of the dark feminine. In *Der Rosenkavalier* we see the same part of the overall drama focused quite differently: this time on the 'Mother-figure' who by voluntarily relinquishing her hold on the hero helps to push him forward into his proper state of manhood. We begin with a young, immature hero whose lack of masculinity is emphasised by the fact that he is having an affair with a powerful, older, woman (not to mention the fact that he is played by an actress). Octavian falls in love with the young heroine, only to find the way barred by a forbidding 'dark masculine' alliance between his older rival, the Baron Ochs, and Sophie's *nouveau riche* father, who wishes to force her into marriage with Ochs to improve his own social position. But salvation comes when the Marschallin, the central figure of the story, shows that she is not a Dark Mother who wishes to hold onto her 'son-lover' at all costs. It is she who cunningly masterminds the overthrow of the Dark Rival, in such a way as to open the eyes and heart of the Dark Father to the hero and heroine's true love. The opera comes to its moving climax as the Marschallin surrenders sadly but gracefully to the need for life to flow onward into a new generation, and she hands over Octavian to his true 'other half'. Like Calypso relinquishing Odysseus, she thus shows herself to be the Light Mother-figure who guides the hero forward to his manly destiny when the time is right.

### Die Meistersinger

In *Die Meistersinger* the focus of the story is not on the 'Mother-Son' part of the overall drama but on the 'Father-Daughter' relationship. When in the opening scene the young hero and heroine meet in church and begin to fall in love, we see all the signs of a new centre of wholeness beginning to form (emphasised by the setting and solemn holy music). But each has a long way to develop before they can be united. Eva is still under the shadow of her father, although he has promised to release her to the hero who proves his worthiness by winning the great song contest. Walther still has to prove his manhood, and he takes the first step by trying to enter the city's ruling body and centre of masculine authority, the Guild of Mastersingers, which has fallen under the dark influence of the order-obsessed Beckmesser. Walther is ruled out of order by his Dark Rival, and only Hans Sachs observes that Walther has all the potential for wholeness. He merely needs a little more maturity to control his abounding power and life.

As the great contest draws near we see the psychological crux of the story, when the still immature Eva clings fearfully to Sachs, hoping that somehow, if she has to marry anyone, it can be him; she is still reluctant to cut her tie to the protective, fatherly presence of an older man. But like the Marschallin pushing Octavian forward to manhood, Sachs urges the heroine forward to meet her proper feminine destiny. Finally Walther emerges in his true colours, demonstrating both his inner feminine through the incomparable beauty and truth of his song, and his mastery by winning the contest. All egocentricity has been transcended, symbolised by the sight of the humiliated Beckmesser being laughed off the stage. Walther and Eva can step to centre-stage, joined in perfect wholeness. And the opera ends on a hymn of praise to the wise father-figure Sachs who has guided the whole drama to its proper, life-renewing conclusion.

## Middlemarch

In fact it is not until we come to examples of the Comedy plot by women writers that we see this particular 'Father-Daughter' aspect of the overall picture explored in proper depth. The story of *Middlemarch* (like that of Jane Austen's *Emma*) is entirely centred round the long struggle of its heroine to break free from the dominance of the dark masculine which threatens to stifle her own inner, life-giving femininity. The intellectual Dorothea Brooke falls for the dried-up old father-figure Casaubon, imagining that she will be able to live happily in a continuing 'Father-Daughter' relationship with her husband, acting as the dutiful amanuensis serving his lofty intellectual ambitions. But already we see the more sensitive, artistic Will Ladislaw appealing unconsciously to the life and femininity within her; just as we see her discovering that Casaubon's outward parade of scholarship is just a lifeless, egocentric sham, a self-deceiving illusion, a mental labyrinth without Ariadne's thread. After Casaubon's death, leaving on her the curse by which he attempts to keep her imprisoned in his shadow forever, the rest of the story shows Dorothea gradually coming to terms with her inner feminine. Gradually, despite the curse, she escapes from Casaubon's deadening shadow, until finally the moment of 'recognition' arrives, when she and Ladislaw can openly admit their love to one another. She is at last happily liberated from the ghostly tyranny of the dark masculine.

## The Winter's Tale

Such is the universality of the Comedy plot that, in ways like these, it can be used to reflect every nuance of the archetypal drama. In the four examples we have just looked at, the key figure of the story has been, in turn, the hero, the mother-figure, the father-figure and the heroine: each of the four figures making up the family drama, and each presented as playing his or her part in bringing it to its proper conclusion in a way that is unusual. But some of the most complete versions of Comedy are those which show the intermingling of both the basic forms of the plot unfolding at the same time: so that the story ends not just on the image of a young hero and heroine joined together, surrounded by joyful parents and friends, but on that of two couples brought together out of the shadows, one representing the younger generation, the other the older.

In *The Winter's Tale* we begin with a King/Father, a Queen/Mother and their young son, representing the promise of new life. But at once Leontes falls into the state of darkness, grievously wronging his wife (and turning his best friend King Polixenes, by the tragic 'dark inversion', into an imagined Dark Rival). In the Tyrant's shadow everything now goes as wrong as could be. First he throws his feminine 'other half' Hermione into prison, where she gives birth to a daughter, Perdita, whom Leontes promptly orders to be abandoned to die. Then his son, representing the next generation, dies of grief for his mother's plight. Finally it seems Hermione has died also. At this point, where Leontes is stricken with remorse, we see him taking the first step towards recognising what a monster he has become. Sure enough we learn that little Perdita, the 'lost feminine' as her name implies, is not dead after all; she is just far away, in an 'inferior realm'. We then follow the psychological essence of the drama entirely in terms of her growing to maturity, the feminine value secretly developing, to the point where she falls in love with young Prince Florizel, representing a potential new centre of wholeness. Although the young lovers then fall under the shadow of the Dark Father, Polixenes – the dark masculine still holds some sway over the story at this stage – they flee to the sorrowing Leontes, whom we find already well on the way to complete inward transformation. He and Polixenes are then reunited in blessing the union of the young lovers. Finally, as the last piece of the jigsaw falling into place, Leontes is reunited with his lost 'other half' Hermione, so that the story can end on the ultimate four-cornered symbol of wholeness, father, mother, hero and heroine, all brought out of the shadows and joyfully united. Turned from darkness into light, the archetypal family is complete.

The crucial transforming role in *The Winter's Tale* is played by the shining figure of Perdita, originating when the darkness is at its height as a little new-born baby, growing secretly in strength until she can at last emerge triumphantly into the 'upper realm' of Leontes's court, to flood everyone with light. She is a perfect symbol of the feminine value, around whom everyone else in the story is ultimately drawn up into a state of wholeness. In this respect *The Winter's Tale* is as much a Rebirth as a Comedy. And, as we have seen, one of the outstanding features of the Rebirth plot is the centrally important role it gives to the redeeming figure, drawing the hero or heroine out of the shadows into light.

So far in looking at the symbolic figures who are central to storytelling we have concentrated on their dark aspects. It is finally time to turn to their opposites: those whose purpose is to lead and inspire the hero and heroine to their goal, the great figures of light.

*Chapter 18*

# The Light Figures

'While I was quietly thinking these thoughts over to myself and giving vent to my sorrow... I became aware of a woman standing over me. She was of awe-inspiring appearance, her eyes burning and keen beyond the usual powers of men. She was so full of years that I could hardly think of her as of my own generation, and yet she possessed a vivid colour and undiminished vigour. It was difficult to be sure of her height, for sometimes she was of average human size, while at others she seemed to touch the sky...

When she saw that it was not that I would not speak but that, dumbstruck, I could not, she gently laid her hand on my breast and said "It is nothing serious, only a touch of amnesia that he is suffering, the common touch of deluded minds. He has forgotten for a while who he is, but he will soon remember, once he has recognised me..."

The clouds of my grief dissolved and I drank in the light'.

Boethius meets Sophia, the Spirit of Wisdom,
in *De Consolatione Philosophiae*

Again and again in the storytelling of the world we meet two mysterious and haunting figures. They are not like any of the other characters we see constantly reappearing around the hero and heroine in stories. When either or both these figures appear, it is not so much to take a direct part in the action as to play a kind of guiding role from the wings. They may appear at critical moments to offer advice. They may intervene when things are going wrong, to bring the hero or heroine back to the right path. They can give vital help. Their chief concern is that the goal should be reached. One is male, the other female. They often appear in some way together, or in alliance. These are the archetypal figures identified by Jung, from his experience of seeing them emerging to the human imagination in myths, folk tales, dreams and paintings all over the world, as the Wise Old Man and the Anima.

We have already glimpsed the Wise Old Man a good many times in the course of this book. He appears as Teiresias in the *Odyssey*, as Anchises in the *Aeneid*, as Prospero in *The Tempest* and as the Duke in *Measure for Measure*, as Platon the old peasant whose wisdom transforms Pierre's life in *War and Peace*, as Hans Sachs in *Die Meistersinger*, as the magistrate Porfiry in *Crime and Punishment*, as Father Tikhon in *The Possessed*, as Merlin in the Arthurian legends, as Obi Wan-Kenobi in *Star Wars*. In the next chapter we shall see him as Gandalf in *The Lord of the Rings*, as Professor Dumbledore, the headmaster of Harry Potter's Hogwarts, as Sarastro in *The Magic Flute*. He may even not be human in his

297

appearance, as when he appears as Aslan the lion in C. S. Lewis's Narnia books, as Rafiki the monkey in *The Lion King,* or as Mantis in Bushman folklore. But the essence of the Wise Old Man is always the same: he is a male figure who represents a state of complete maturity. He is someone who has travelled the full road of personal inner development (he may not even be particularly old, although he is certainly not young). In fact, although outwardly a man, he represents the masculine and the feminine in human nature in perfect balance. He is strong, autonomous and authoritative. There is no doubt about his masculinity. But he also, to a marked degree, embodies the inner feminine qualities of protective feeling for others and intuitive understanding, the ability to see whole. The most usual physical attributes he is given (apart, often, from an imposing beard as a mark of his age and authority) are his keenly penetrating eyes. The word 'wise' comes from the same root as 'vision'. It means the depth and breadth of that inner vision which transcends the distortions and wishful thinking of consciousness centred only on the ego, and is able, from long experience, to see things and people for what they really are. The Wise Old Man has a more or less super-natural aura because he is somehow connected to the mysterious totality of life, beyond superficial or transitory appearances. He can see into the past and the future because he rises above the confines of the immediate present and knows the hidden rules of growth and decay which govern the outward transformation of things. He is in touch with some dimension of ultimate reality which tran-scends time and the physical world altogether. And we always have the sense (as, for instance, whenever Gandalf appears in *The Lord of the Rings*) that he is work-ing in the service of some immense cause and purpose which entirely transcends any selfish or personal interest.

The Wise Old Man's feminine counterpart we have encountered as Athene, the goddess of wisdom in the *Odyssey*; as the priestess Sibyl who guides Aeneas down into the underworld; in those mysterious 'young women' who play such an impor-tant role as guides in many other Quest stories; and as the awe-inspiring figure of the goddess Isis who redeems Lucius in *The Golden Ass*. In such supernatural manifestations, as when she appears to Frodo as Galadriel in *The Lord of the Rings* or to Dante as Beatrice in *The Divine Comedy*, the Anima-figure represents the 'eternal feminine' in her most numinous guise. But like the Wise Old Man, when she appears on her own in such manifestations, she also stands very obviously for a balance of feminine and masculine qualities. Outwardly a woman, with her grace and beauty, she represents protective feeling and the visionary power to see whole. But she is also imbued with the inner strength and authority of the masculine, which is why she is so often of imposing physical appearance, like the towering Sibyl; or clad in semi-masculine garb, like the tall 'flashing-eyed' Athene with her helmet and spear.

Indeed the way in which the Wise Old Man and the Anima are ultimately aspects of the same deep power in the human psyche can be seen in their tendency often to appear together in perfect alliance. In such instances they may appear in a Father-Daughter relationship, where the old man expresses the full weight of masculine authority and the young girl expresses the softer feminine in all its shining purity. We see a peculiarly moving expression of the power of this shaping archetype in the closing stages of *King Lear* where, as the king in the depths of his defeat finds a new inner sovereignty and clarity of vision, we see Lear and Cordelia in an evanescent constellation of this Wise Old Man and Anima relationship, united at last in their love and capacity to see the inner truth. An even stranger example is in the story of Theseus, where we see the extraordinary change coming over our image of Daedalus, the wicked old magician who had created the Minotaur and the Labyrinth. At last, at the moment when Daedalus gives Ariadne the magic thread which will lead Theseus out of the maze, we see him switching from the side of death to the side of life; and at that moment, in our inner mind's eye, we see Daedalus and Ariadne constellating in Theseus's hour of most desperate need into the Wise Old Man and the Anima, the twin symbolic figures presiding over the hero's salvation, leading him out of darkness into light.

The point about these two great archetypal figures is that they are the supreme personal expressions of that mysterious purposive power in stories which not only guides the hero himself towards the goal, but which is inherent in the very structure of the way stories form themselves in the human imagination, shaping the action towards some final image of perfect resolution. When we see Merlin appearing to Arthur, or Athene to Odysseus, when we see the old enchanter Prospero and his beautiful daughter Miranda waiting on the island for the shipwrecked travellers, or the twin figures of Porfiry and Sonia coming to exercise a strange growing influence over the tortured Raskolnikov, we are given a reassuring sign that, despite all indications to the contrary, there is some benign power behind the scenes, operating on a plane of consciousness beyond our comprehension, which is working to draw both hero and story towards some ultimate state of wholeness, when at last all will be made clear and when all the dark elements in the story have been dispelled.

But equally the point about these figures is that they cannot control what is going on in the story. They can understand what is happening, they can set things up, give guidance, point the way, proffer assistance. But in the end it is always up to the hero himself to show the qualities which will make him worthy of success. The more closely he can align himself with this mysterious power behind the scenes and everything it stands for, the more likely he is to achieve the goal.

And of course in most instances the central element in that goal is the hero's union with the heroine, who herself represents the 'eternal feminine' – although in a more immediate, personal guise. Athene may help to guide Odysseus to his goal, representing the eternal feminine of the Anima in its supernatural, impersonal, ideal aspect: but in the end it is Penelope who is Odysseus's goal, his personal *anima*-figure, corresponding directly to his own inner feminine, the inmost centre of his identity. The 'light' heroine in stories represents the *anima* in this personal sense, just as the more lofty, detached Athene-like figures hovering over the action represent the great universal power with which the hero must align himself if he is to win her. Such 'active' redeeming heroines as Ariadne, Portia, Leonora, are classic *anima*-figures representing the numinous power of the feminine when it is directly involved in the action of the story. But so too may be the seemingly more 'passive' heroines whom the hero has to win or redeem from the shadows, when he himself is 'active' and strongly masculine. The *anima*-figure reflects whatever is needed to complement the particular balance of qualities shown by the hero. So long as he is worthy of her and open to her, she stands for whatever he needs to make him whole. If he, for any reason, is rendered weak or powerless, she may have to be strong enough to supply him with the strength he lacks; if he is strong, she may merely need to represent the complementary softening feminine, necessary to ensure that his strength is life-giving. This is why, as the hero's 'good angel', the heroine is of such crucial importance in stories, and why it is so revealing when the hero wrongs or rejects her in any way. Because ultimately she stands in both a personal and a universal, supra-personal way for the heart and soul of man – the Latin *anima* means 'soul' – that mysterious 'other half' who enshrines both the centre of a man's identity and the essence of life itself. If the hero scorns or mistreats an *anima*-figure it is that aspect of his own nature which he is in effect rejecting.

When the heroine is herself the central figure of a story, then the same complementary role is played for her by the figure Jung termed the *animus*, the masculine figure whom the heroine needs to make her complete. We see such a figure in the Prince in such fairy tales as Cinderella, Sleeping Beauty or Snow White, in Jane Eyre's Mr Rochester, in Elizabeth Bennett's Mr Darcy and Emma Woodhouse's Mr Knightley. The positive *animus*-figure is a handsome, compelling man, unmistakably masculine, but softened and made still more attractive by his inner feminine characteristics, his sensitive and sympathetic feeling and his ability to perceive the heroine's true inner nature. He corresponds to the 'spirit' in woman (the Latin *animus* means 'spirit', from the Greek *anemos* or 'wind'): the vital power which is necessary to inspire her and to bring her femininity to life: as the Sleeping Beauty is brought to life or 'animated' by her Prince; as the femininity of Shakespeare's 'Shrew' is awakened by the masterful Petruchio; that of Emma Woodhouse by the inspiring presence of Mr Knightley; that of Tracy Lord by Dexter Haven in *High Society*; or that of the tough-minded Sue Charlton by the manly but sensitive hero of *Crocodile Dundee*.

### The 'light family'

The 'light other half' is the most compelling figure in storytelling simply because she or he is the 'centre' to whom the hero or the heroine is being drawn, consciously or unconsciously, throughout the story. In terms of the archetypal family drama their eventual union is the supreme goal which marks the culmination of all striving and uncertainty, symbolising both the final point of rest and the beginning of unimaginable new life.

Obviously the reason why we, the audience, can so easily identify with this overwhelming sense of attraction is that, whether we are a man or a woman, it triggers off a pattern of response coded into our own unconscious: that gravitational pull between the sexes which is rooted in one of the most powerful instinctive drives we know. But what is significant about this attraction is that it is far more than just a physical impulse. When a man and a woman are mutually attracted this may be because they evoke in each other a whole complex of responses, reaching far down into their psyche, and which can operate on any or all of four levels. It is true that their attraction may simply be physical. But it may also be mental, based on shared interests and values, a 'meeting of minds'. It may be emotional, springing from the feelings and the heart, inspiring love. It may be spiritual, inspiring a sense of that transcendent dimension we call the 'soul'. In an ideal loving relationship, all these levels of attraction may be at work simultaneously. This is because the couple have activated in each other an archetype: one of those complex structures of response programmed into our unconscious which lie latent until triggered off by a specific external stimulus. A man is attracted to a woman because she personifies his *anima*, that component of his psyche which represents his own inner feminine. A woman is drawn to a man because he evokes that power in her psyche which is her *animus*. It is equally the power of these archetypal complexes in us which we see at work when they are activated by a story.

However powerful their appeal, the *anima* and the *animus* are of course only two of the archetypes around which stories are shaped. Most obviously these also include those which relate to the other central roles in the family drama: those of Father, Mother and the Alter-Ego. We have already seen how this works in terms of the dark figures in storytelling; how instinctively we relate, for instance, to the image of the tyrannical, overbearing Dark Father or the treacherous, oppressive Dark Mother. But each of these represents only the negative aspect of its archetype. Each also has its light aspect, preconditioning us to all those qualities which archetypally represent the role of Father, Mother or alter-ego being acted out positively, in the right way. And these correspond to the light figures whom we may see appearing round the hero or heroine in a story, assisting or guiding them on the way to their goal:

1. *The Light Father, or Good King*: this is the archetypal father-figure, king or ruler whom we immediately recognise as acting out his role in an ideal fashion. What this means is that he combines the strength of the masculine with the love and understanding of the feminine. He thus represents masculine power and authority being exercised properly and selflessly. In many stories this figure stands in the background to the main action. He may most obviously come to the centre of the stage when the drama is reaching its conclusion: e.g., the mysterious 'Minister' who enters at the end of Fidelio to symbolise the overthrowing of the Tyrant Pizarro and the restoration of proper, just authority; or Richard the Lionheart, England's true king, who reappears from his exile abroad at the end of the story of Robin Hood. At the end of *A Midsummer Night's Dream*, we see him as Theseus, Duke of Athens, in the royal marriage which sets a symbolic seal on the resolution of the drama which has been unfolding in the 'inferior realm' of the forest.

In other stories where such a figure becomes more directly involved in the action, we are likely to see him playing a role in the hero or heroine's life which is the very opposite of that played by the Dark Father. When the hero of the Arthurian cycle comes into the world as a baby, his true father Uther Pendragon dies, leaving him an orphan. But unlike all those stories where such a gap is filled

301

by a Dark Father-figure, representing the 'unrealised value', here the baby is given two versions of a Light Father. First, Arthur is spirited away by Merlin, the Wise Old Man who represents the extreme light version of fatherhood, the 'realised value' of that balanced maturity which Arthur must one day attain to in himself. He then entrusts the baby to Sir Ector, who acts as 'good father' in bringing up Arthur as his own son. But Merlin continues to watch over the hero, guiding his destiny from the wings, until Arthur has achieved his own maturity as an idealised 'Good King'. At which point, halfway through the story, the Wise Old Man fades away. His work is completed, because Arthur has now begun to develop and integrate into himself those qualities which Merlin symbolised.

Similarly in *Star Wars* Obi-Wan Kenobi plays a fatherly role in teaching the hero Luke Skywalker how to align himself with 'the force'. But he then dies, in a duel with the Dark Father-figure, Darth Vader, just when the hero has developed the maturity to fight his own battles. In fact, as a mature older man guiding the 'son-hero' towards the goal, the Wise Old Man always represents the qualities of an ideal father: as Gandalf does for Frodo in *The Lord of The Rings*; as Platon for Pierre in *War and Peace*; as Sarastro for Tamino in *The Magic Flute*. This is because he represents that fully realised state of selfless manhood to which the hero himself must aspire. We also of course see this archetype represented in all those comedies and other stories where, at the end, a selfish Dark Father-figure has his heart and his eyes opened, transforming him into a Light Father.

2. *The Light Mother or Good Queen*: again this archetypal figure may remain more or less in the background as a symbol of light motherhood, providing the hero or heroine with a rock of loving security which they may both leave and return to: as in all those stories for young children which show the central figure leaving mother for their great adventure and then returning to her at the end, such as *Peter Rabbit* or *Red Riding Hood*.

As with the Father-figure, however, we may see her playing a more active guiding role in the action, when she is likely to appear as the feminine equivalent of the Wise Old Man, as a wise older woman. The most familiar instance of this in all storytelling is that which we recognise from the worldwide folk tale we know as *Cinderella*. When the heroine's true mother dies, she is first replaced by the Dark Mother, the wicked stepmother. But then the mysterious Fairy Godmother (or 'good Mother') appears. The Mother-archetype has split into its dark and light aspects, and from then on Cinderella's story is written in the conflict of the two, until the light version has guided the heroine to her goal. Similarly, in *Jane Eyre*, when the little heroine has lost her true mother she falls under the shadow of the Dark Mother, Aunt Reed; but eventually finds a 'light Mother' in the wise and kindly head of the orphanage, Miss Temple. When David Copperfield's true mother dies, he falls under the shadow of the Dark Mother, Miss Murdstone; and during this phase of the story the light elements of 'Mother' are personified in an 'inferior' form in the kindly servant Peggotty, who can give David love but lacks the power to transform his situation. Eventually, however, these two opposites, the strength of Miss Murdstone and the love of Peggotty, are brought together in the 'light Mother' figure of Betsey Trotwood, the firm, loving and shrewd (if eccentric) aunt who adopts David. It is this that launches him on the positive road which brings him eventually to his goal.

In other stories we see a powerful older woman who initially appears to the hero in the emasculating guise of Dark Mother or Witch, like Circe or Calypso, Marcellina or the Marschallin; but who eventually switches to the role of Light Mother, as she releases him from her shadow and urges him forward into independent manhood.

3. *Light Alter-Ego or Companion*: these are the figures of roughly similar age or status to the hero or heroine who stand as the light equivalents of the Dark Rivals or the Dark Alter-Ego. Here, of course, they are not rivals but friends and allies, who help the hero or heroine on their way towards the goal; and, as we saw in the chapter on the Quest, their relationship to the central figure may take various forms. To begin with the hero may be shown as the leader of a group of companions or followers who are not clearly differentiated from one another. Although they may provide him with vital assistance, they may also commit fatal errors, often against his advice, and as such they may be expendable, like the twelve shiploads of companions lost by Odysseus.

More obviously standing in the position of Alter-Ego to the hero, however, are those recognisable individuals who are much closer to him and here, as we saw, the relationship may take three forms. Firstly there is the close friend or ally who is not otherwise distinguished – David's Jonathan, Christian's Faithful, Hamlet's Horatio – except that he is a faithful, honourable companion. Secondly there is the Alter-Ego or ally who differs from the hero, often by displaying qualities compensatory to those of the hero himself. This figure may be presented as in some way 'inferior' to the hero (e.g., as a servant, like Man Friday), but in other ways he may well have attributes which the hero himself lacks and which are of vital assistance: e.g., Sancho Panza, Jeeves, Figaro in *The Barber of Seville*. Thirdly there are those instances where the hero has several companions who between them make up a whole. Sometimes these may simply be echoes of the hero, like D'Artagnan's three musketeers, or Sir Galahad's two fellow-knights, Percival and Bors, who accompany him in the closing stages of the Grail Quest. Sometimes they are carefully differentiated, so that each companion individually contributes to an overall balance of qualities which will be necessary for ultimate success; as in *Watership Down* or *King Solomon's Mines*, where in each case the hero is a protective leader, but has around him a tightly-knit team including one figure who represents physical strength, another who represents mental calculation and planning skills and a third who represents intuitive understanding, the power to see hidden realities beyond the immediate situation.

The real point of these allies, in all their different forms, is that they act to reinforce the hero's own powers and qualities. Their role in the story is to act as extensions of the hero himself.

## The Child

Thus do the chief light figures in stories correspond to the four central roles in the archetypal drama: Father, Mother, Hero/Heroine and 'Other Half'. There is one other light figure who occasionally appears to make the family drama complete. Since, on an instinctive level, the ultimate purpose of this process is that the hero should be united with the heroine to form a new centre of wholeness for the regeneration of life, then the final confirmation that the chain of life is to continue into the future is the birth of a child. At this stage of the drama the hero himself is transformed into a father, with a whole new focus for his love and protective feelings in the little defenceless being he has called into the world and who commands a new complex of instinctual responses. And as we have seen, in a certain type of story, the Child plays a numinous role, not just as the promise of new life but as a redeeming figure, capable of awakening the dormant inner feminine of a dark hero. This is the archetypal figure whom Jung called the *puer aeternus*, the eternal Child.[1]

Particularly where the hero is an older man, the Child can play much the same redeeming role in awakening his heart and soul as the *anima*-figure. The dried-up old miser Scrooge is brought alive and awakened to his inner feminine by the moving vision of the little crippled Tiny Tim. Silas Marner is similarly liberated from his narrow egocentric prison by the arrival of the little golden-haired child Eppie who, as she grows up into a young woman, gradually evolves from the role of Child to *anima*-figure. Perdita, the figure of redemption in *The Winter's Tale*, goes through a similar transformation, reflecting the steadily increasing influence of the feminine value in the story as she grows to maturity. And there is no more striking illustration of the way the Child can play the same liberating role as the *anima*-figure than the biblical story of Joseph, whose final reconciliation with his brothers is brought about around the redeeming symbol of his youngest brother, 'little Benjamin'.

By the end of his rise from rags to riches, Joseph has become an immensely powerful figure, but one important thing is missing. Neither he nor the story can end on an image of wholeness until he has mended his old quarrel with his brothers. This is achieved when Joseph orders his brothers to bring back their father's youngest son Benjamin, described as 'a child of his old age, a little one'. It is through the upwelling of love in his stern heart at the sight of his little brother that Joseph finally comes to forgive the others the great wrong they have done him. He reveals himself at last in his true identity, and he and his contrite brothers are joyfully reconciled. But the curious thing is that although Benjamin is constantly described as 'a lad' with emphasis on his youth, although he is almost invariably thought of

---

1. As with all archetypes, Jung saw the *puer aeternus* as having both light and dark aspects. In its light aspect, the 'eternal Child' – as represented in paintings of the Madonna and Child – is the archetype which shapes our basic emotional response to any new-born life. This instinctively-conditioned response is not only aroused by a human child. We can experience it when confronted by the sight of the new-born young of almost any species at the higher end of the evolutionary ladder, such as lambs, chicks, ducklings, calves or foals (prompting the exclamation 'aaah, how sweet!'). But in its dark aspect Jung uses the same term *puer aeternus* in a different context: to describe an adult male locked into immaturity by a psychological over-dependence on 'Mother' and his resulting inability to grow up into fully mature manhood. While it might seem entirely apt to describe someone suffering from this psychological condition as an 'eternal child', it may seem confusing to use the same term for what are essentially two quite distinct archetypes. This is why in this book the negative version of Jung's *puer aeternus* is generally described as 'the boy hero who cannot grow up'.

as 'little Benjamin', the internal evidence of the story shows that he cannot be anything of the sort. He was already alive before Joseph left home at the age of 17. Since then at least 22 more years must have elapsed before the brothers first arrived in Egypt (Joseph was 30 when he was released from prison, and subsequently there had been seven years of plenty and two of famine). It is something of a shock to realise therefore that Benjamin cannot be younger than his mid-twenties. Yet such is the unconscious pull of the Child-archetype that the storyteller turns him once again, for symbolic purposes, into a 'little one', in order to convey the awakening of Joseph's love in the most moving and convincing manner.

In considering the archetypal basis for human emotions, it is not for nothing that we are familiar with the phrase 'women and children first'.

## The 'Self'

The more we look at stories in this light, the more clearly we see the consistency with which they portray one great fundamental struggle. On one hand there are the forces making for disintegration, confusion, darkness and ultimately death. These are all centred on the ego. On the other are all those forces which are urging both central figure and story towards wholeness and light, to the point where he or she can at last realise their complete identity. What these have in common is that they are centred not on the ego but on something much deeper in the human personality, something all-connecting, something universal. This ultimate state of wholeness and the forces which work to bring it about comprise the archetype of totality which Jung and others have called the Self.[2]

The most obvious vision of what the Self stands for can be seen in the closing stages of any story which comes to a complete happy ending. It is synonymous with everything we see represented in such an ending. It is the point where everything comes together in perfect balance: power, order, feeling, awareness. It is the point of perfect unity, with no trace of division or egotism. It is the point of perfect light, with no shadow.

More specifically, as such an image of totality comes together, the Self may be represented by four things which happen more or less simultaneously:

(1) the story's central figure at last reaches a state of complete individual self-realisation;

(2) the hero and heroine come together in perfect union, each making the other whole;

(3) the archetypal family drama comes to its culmination, so that we see hero and heroine momentarily in equipoise between all four central roles. As

2. This term might seem open to confusion, in that we normally identify the idea of self, with a small 's', with the ego and with selfishness; whereas the archetype of the Self represents the very opposite. But at its root is the idea that, the more fully we realise our own individual identity, the more we come into contact with that ego-transcending level of the psyche which links us to the wider world. The Self is both the core of our individual identity and that which connects us with everyone and everything outside us. A great artist, like Beethoven or Shakespeare, is not so much different from other people as someone more directly in contact with that level of the psyche which is shared by all humanity in common. Hence we speak of their 'universality'. It is in this sense that the 'Self' is an appropriate term for this complex component of the psyche, which plays such an important role in the symbolism of storytelling.

they become the fully-realised Son/Hero and Daughter/Heroine, so they are simultaneously ready to succeed as perfectly balanced Father and Mother;

(4) the wider community or kingdom is redeemed, under proper sovereignty, at one with itself, with the world and with the power of life.

But it is not only in this closing image of totality and fulfilment that we see the power of the Self represented in a story. At earlier stages we see it in everything that is working to draw hero, heroine, community – and the story itself – towards this final point of resolution.

The numinosity of the Self may be symbolically evoked in many different ways as the distant life-renewing goal the central figure is heading for. We may see it symbolised for instance, as a treasure, a jewel or some other mysterious priceless object (e.g., the 'Golden Fleece', the 'Holy Grail', the silver rose in *Der Rosenkavalier*). It may be presented as a far-off shining city, as when the young Dick Whittington is told about faraway London, 'where the streets are paved with gold'; or Christian is told of the 'Celestial City'; or the hero of *Jude the Obscure* sees the distant vision of 'Christminster', the Self he will never attain. It may be symbolised as a great mountain, with its roots in the earth and its peak in the heavens, as in the opening stanzas of *The Divine Comedy* or in *Aladdin* where, in the shadow of such a mountain, the hero first goes down into the cave to fetch the lamp; itself a symbol of the Self.

More personally, the power of the Self may be seen in all the light figures who appear round the hero or heroine during the course of the story, inspiring or assisting them on to their goal. Each of these light figures represents a different aspect of the Self, the mysterious power which is drawing the central figure and the story towards the point where it can become fully realised. And, as we have seen, all the main characters in stories – both light and dark – represent different aspects of the four central roles in the family drama. Each of these roles can be split into its ego-centred dark aspects, which give rise to the dark figures, that negative version which the hero or heroine must overcome or transcend; and its light aspects, standing for the powers of life and wholeness.

In fact we can now draw up a cast list of all those archetypal figures who provide the key to the main characters in storytelling:

| *Negative/centred on the ego* | *Positive/centred on the Self* |
|---|---|
| Dark Father/Tyrant/Dark Magician | Light Father/Good King/Wise Old Man |
| Dark Mother/Dark Queen/Witch | Light Mother/Good Queen/Wise Old Woman |
| Dark Rival/Dark Alter-Ego | Light Alter-Ego/Friend and Companion |
| Dark Other Half/Temptress | Light Other Half (light *anima/animus*) |
| | Child |

In the negative version of the archetypal drama, the supreme image of darkness triumphant is the image of the 'light feminine', the *anima*, held prisoner in the shadow of the 'dark masculine', the Tyrant or Dark Father, representing the power of the human ego. We can now see why the image which stands at the opposite pole is that of the Wise Old Man and the Anima; because they represent the state of fully-realised masculinity and femininity, transcending the ego in perfect life-giving conjunction.

## The 'helpful animal'

To complete the list of archetypal figures in stories, two other, more specialised figures must be added: each of which serves also to underline an important general principle governing the way stories work.

One of the more familiar figures in the folk tales of the world is the 'helpful animal'. We meet a little hero who is very much alone in the world, and may well have fallen under the shadow of a Dark Father, Dark Mother or Dark Rivals. Just when he seems most alone he runs into a mysterious creature or creatures with strange powers who become his friend or ally. Dick Whittington and the hero of *Puss in Boots* meet their cats, Aladdin meets the genies, and so forth. Often the hero shows some significant act of kindness to this creature. There are innumerable folk tales where the hero gives a share of his food to a frog, a fox, a bird, a mysterious little man in the forest, usually when others, such as the hero's two brothers, have conspicuously failed to show such generosity. This action is significant because it shows that the hero has a good heart, a capacity for selfless feeling. From then on this creature becomes a powerful ally and proves in the end to be the key to the hero's salvation.

The point about these figures is that they only appear when the hero is young and undeveloped, before he has won real understanding of the world. But he has shown the vital prerequisite of his potential for eventual wholeness in the act of generosity which shows that he is not inwardly imprisoned in egocentricity. So long as that condition is met, showing that he is connected with life, the role of the 'helpful animal' is to symbolise all those mysterious instinctive powers in his psyche which will help to carry him to maturity. For a long time, provided that his heart is in the right place, he will be able to rely on these unconscious powers, beyond his conscious understanding, to carry him upwards. But the nearer he gets to his goal, the more he will have to show a conscious grasp of what he is doing. Not the least reason why the story of Aladdin is so profound is that it emphasises this point so explicitly, in how the genies eventually impress on him that he can no longer just rely on them to do everything and that he must begin to rely consciously on himself. In masculine terms, to reach complete union with the Self means developing complete self-reliance, self-mastery and self-understanding. It can only be achieved by the hero who has shown himself to be autonomous or self-controlled; who in the end can see exactly what he has to do.

In stories where the central figure is a hero, the 'helpful animal' thus stands for powers which he has not yet fully integrated into himself. Although these powers may be working for the hero's good, as aspects of the Self, so long as they are still operating semi-independently, or in a way which is beyond his conscious understanding, they appear in an 'inferior' form, as forces split-off from and outside him. Indeed it is by no means only in the form of the 'helpful animal' in folk tales that we see this principle at work in storytelling. Again and again, in different ways, we recognise in some ally or companion of the hero an 'inferior' version of some quality which the hero will eventually have to develop and integrate into himself - at which point the 'inferior' figure often vanishes from the story. One of the most celebrated instances of this is the role played by the Fool in *King Lear*: the wise idiot who sees the truth of what is happening more clearly than anyone else. But at the moment in the story where Lear himself begins to understand and to see clearly the Fool disappears, because he was the 'inferior' version of the Wise Old Man that Lear himself is now becoming.

The same motif may appear in tales where the central figure is a heroine, as in the seven dwarves who play such an important part in the adolescence of Snow White. As these little masculine figures spend their days mysteriously digging gold out of the mountains (symbolising the build-up of those life-giving instinctive powers which are unconsciously carrying her towards maturity), on a more conscious level she develops her loving, maternal femininity by looking after their household. But eventually there comes the crisis where the dwarves can help her no more. Frozen on her mountaintop, she has to wait for the emergence of her fully-developed masculine 'other half', in the shape of a loving Prince, to liberate her. In other folk tales such as *Beauty and the Beast, The Frog Prince* or *Snow White and Rose Red*, we again see the masculine appearing in the heroine's life in an 'inferior' form, except that here her initial reaction is one of fear or revulsion. Only when the heroine reaches the point where she can show love to this alarming creature does this prove to be the key to the Beast, frog or bear turning into a handsome Prince. This initially threatening presence is her *animus*, that which governs her relationship to the masculine both within her psyche and outside it. Only when the heroine has fully developed her femininity do we see the figure representing her inner masculinity emerging from his original negative, inferior disguise into his proper light identity.

In a wider sense this motif of the 'helpful animal' helps to underline one of the most important general principles of storytelling, which is that for a long time in a story the elements which will eventually prove to be the key to salvation may appear in some inferior, obscured or distorted form. Only when the hero or heroine are ready to achieve wholeness can these inferior elements disappear: either because they have been integrated, or because they have emerged into the light in positive, fully-developed guise to bring about the triumphant resolution.

### The Trickster

A last archetypal figure must be added to complete the list. In some ways, as we saw, the darkest figure of all in stories is the Tempter – Mephistopheles or Iago – who appears as a personification of the hero's dark ego-self or fantasy-self in its most 'inferior' form of all. The Tempter is 'inferior' in every respect, ruthlessly using his power in the treacherous manner of the 'dark feminine' by pretending to act in the hero's highest interests while in fact seeking to destroy him. The real purpose of the Tempter is always to blind the hero, to restrict his consciousness without him being aware of it.

However, we also occasionally see a light version of this figure, the Trickster, who is an aspect of the Self. Like the Tempter, his aim is to trick people into a different state of consciousness: but this time the other way round, to broaden and heighten their vision, to bring them into contact with the Self. Although the Trickster is widely found in certain traditions of folklore, two of the most familiar instances to us are seen in Shakespeare. The purpose of Puck in *A Midsummer Night's Dream* is to use his magic to trick the lovers out of the original confused and limited state of consciousness in which they begin and into that wider consciousness which enables them all to recognise their true 'other half', thus bringing the story to a triumphantly happy resolution. Similarly in *The Tempest*, as we shall see in the next chapter, the role of Ariel, as the 'tricksy spirit' of the Wise Old Man Prospero, is to use his magic to trick the two main dark figures of the play into the higher state of consciousness which can bring them back to their 'proper selves'.

As with the 'helpful animal', the Trickster is only one expression of a much more general principle of storytelling, which we have already seen again and again in this book: namely the vital part played in any character's switch from dark to light by that fundamental shift in consciousness from ego to Self. The Trickster is a personification of the power in the psyche which brings about that shift, by shaking the character out of one level of consciousness onto the other. In this sense, the three 'Christmas spirits' who visit Scrooge, like messengers from his unconscious, dragging him round into an entirely new perspective on the world, are examples of the Trickster archetype at work. So is the mysterious figure of the Button Moulder who plays such a crucial part in forcing Peer Gynt out of the prison of ego-consciousness into seeing himself and the world whole. So is the guardian angel in Frank Capra's *It's a Wonderful Life*, who uses his magic to tease the suicidal hero into recognising just how much good he has done in the world: thus bringing him to the rebirth which joyfully reunites him under the Christmas tree with his family and all the good people of the town.

In fact Hollywood has produced few more memorable examples of a Trickster-figure than that played in *Singin' in the Rain* by the hero's friend Cosmo Brown (Donald O'Connor). It is he who is the mastermind behind the key moves which lead eventually to the heroine Kathy being lifted out of the shadows and united with the hero, as a star in her own right. It is Cosmo who has the flash of inspiration that the studio should use Kathy's voice instead of Lina Lamont's. It is he who, like some latter-day Puck or Ariel, plays the magical trick at the end which exposes Lina for the fraud she is: by first placing Kathy behind the curtain to dub Lina's singing voice in front of a packed audience, then pulling it away to reveal her as the real star. Yet Cosmo is not a central figure in the story in his own right. He is there only as a kind of alter-ego to the hero, to set up that process of transformation which ensures that love is triumphant and gives the story its special, enduring appeal.

We have now completed this introduction to the principles which are involved in bringing a story to a complete happy ending. In the next chapter, to sum up, we look at a set of new examples: five well-known stories which illustrate how all these principles work in practice.

## Chapter 19

# Reaching the Goal

'When that which is perfect is come, then that which is in part shall be done away... for now we see through a glass, darkly; but then, face to face.'

*I Corinthians*, 13

We end this survey of the principles necessary to guide a story to a completely happy ending by looking at five well-known stories which illustrate everything this second part of the book has been about. We have not examined any of these stories in detail before, because none is shaped exclusively by just one of the basic plots we looked at in the first part of the book. But between them they show how an understanding of the underlying principles which shape stories takes us onto a deeper level altogether – where the particular significance of the plot-form guiding the action dissolves into the essence of that central drama which lies at the heart of storytelling.

On the face of it, these five stories could scarcely seem more disparate: a Slav folk-tale, *Prince Ivan and the Firebird*; a mediaeval English legend, *Robin Hood*; a modern pseudo-epic adventure story, Tolkien's *The Lord of the Rings*; Shakespeare's last and most mysterious play, *The Tempest*; and Mozart's last comic opera, *The Magic Flute*. But in the light of our theme in recent chapters, we can now see how each of these tales is shaped around the same essential drama. Each shows a kingdom or a world, having fallen under the shadow of the dark power, which is sick or in disarray. Each then shows an as-yet unfulfilled hero gradually moving through the shadows towards the point where, after a long and painful struggle, he can finally overthrow the dark power and step out into the light. As he does so, he redeems the kingdom. All these stories therefore culminate in that cosmic happy ending which shows a world divided and in shadow being brought to wholeness, round a hero who has reached the ultimate 'centre' of complete maturity.

The only thing which varies as we move through this sequence of stories is the emphasis in the way this central drama is presented. In *The Firebird* the focus is on the hero's lonely struggle towards self-realisation. In the legend of *Robin Hood* the emphasis is more general, on the redeeming of the kingdom. In *The Lord of the Rings* it is on both: on the hero's long and painful journey, but also on the cosmic implications of his eventual success in completing his task (except that, as we shall see, in order to show this fully, something very significant happens to the 'hero' as the story develops). In *The Tempest* we see the hero, as he redeems the kingdom, at last becoming a complete Wise Old Man. Finally, in *The Magic Flute*, we see a story which sums up everything which this part of the book has been about: a plot which, by a dazzlingly original trick of construction, manages to set out the inner workings of the archetypal family drama with an ingenuity which makes it unique in storytelling.

### The Firebird

It would be impossible to categorise the folk tale of *Prince Ivan and the Firebird* under any one of our original seven basic plots because it combines elements of all of them.[1] But the overall story which results perfectly exemplifies that central underlying theme to storytelling which has been emerging in the past few chapters. It tells of how a young hero matures until he is ready to succeed his father.

A certain king had a very beautiful garden. At its centre was a very rare tree, which every day bore a single fruit, a perfect golden apple. But every night the apple mysteriously vanished and one day the king called his three sons and told them that whichever could catch the thief would be given half the kingdom. The two older sons each watched in turn, but each fell asleep and when asked to explain the disappearance of the apple the following morning said that it had disappeared by itself. The third and youngest son, Ivan, was the only one who remained awake. At midnight he saw a golden bird fly down to steal the apple. He tried to seize it but it flew off, leaving just one golden feather in his hand – which proved to glow with such a light that it illumined the whole of the king's palace. The king was overjoyed with this treasure, which his courtiers told him must have come from the legendary Firebird. But the bird never returned and the king began so to long for a sight of it himself that he fell sick with grief. He called his sons to him again and said that whichever of them could find and bring him the Firebird would be rewarded with half the kingdom.

The initial situation the story presents us with thus sets up a polarity. On one hand there is the ageing King/Father who is losing his powers and whose kingdom has passed into shadow. On the other is the mysterious, elusive Firebird as a symbol of that which alone can restore it to wholeness again: the Self. To realise it is the task which now passes to the younger generation.

The three boys set out into the world, taking three different paths, and shortly after they have separated each is confronted by the same test. A little vixen emerges from the forest and – in a motif found in many folk tales – asks each of the princes for a share of his food. The two older sons shoot at the fox with their bows and it vanishes. Ivan willingly hands over half his food, and the vixen says she will reward him by helping him find the Firebird.

---

1. This eastern European folk-tale is not to be confused with the quite different story on which Stravinsky based his ballet *The Firebird* (1910). Probably the best-known version, *Prince Ivan, The Firebird and The Grey Wolf*, is that told in Russia and first published by Alexander Afnasev (1826–1871), the Russian counterpart of the brothers Grimm. But I shall here be referring to the rather more complex Czech version, found in most collections of Czech folk tales, in which the 'helpful animal' is not a wolf but a fox.

We have now, by the double-negative form of the Rule of Three, learned two important things about Ivan, in contrast to his older brothers. Firstly he keeps his eyes open: he is aware. When watching in the garden he did not fall asleep. Secondly, unlike his brothers, he is goodhearted. He is not blinded by egotism. In other words, he is open to the 'feminine' value. The result is that he wins a mysterious ally, a feminine 'helpful animal' who, like Dick Whittington's cat or Aladdin's genies, is going to prove crucial to the unfolding of his story.

The vixen leads Ivan to a mysterious remote castle made of bronze, where the Firebird lives in a room with two cages, one golden, the other of wood. The fox tells Ivan that he must go into the castle alone, and that whatever he does, he must put the Firebird into the wooden cage and not that of gold. Of course whenever such a prohibition is issued in a story (as when Peter Rabbit is told not to go into Mr McGregor's garden, or Bluebeard orders his wife not to go into a certain room in his castle, or Adam and Eve are told in *Genesis* not to eat the fruit of the Tree of Knowledge) we know it will be disobeyed. Otherwise there can be no story. Inevitably Ivan considers the Firebird too beautiful to be placed in the humble wooden cage. But no sooner has he placed it in that made of gold than guards rush in to take him before the owner of the castle, a fearsome and angry king. When Ivan explains that he was not trying to steal the Firebird on his own account but only to restore his father's health, the king says he will give him the Firebird; but only on condition that Ivan obtains for him in exchange another great treasure, the Horse with the Golden Mane.

This second episode is virtually a repeat of the first. The vixen leads Ivan to another remote castle, this time of silver, where again Ivan disobeys her prohibition and is brought before the castle's fearsome owner. Again he explains that he was not stealing on his own behalf, and he is told he can have the horse if he brings back to its owner a third great treasure, the Golden Princess from a faraway golden castle beside the sea.

So comprehensively structured round the Rule of Three is *The Firebird* that, when the vixen leads Ivan to the golden castle, his third great test turns out itself to consist of three more tests. The owner of the castle is the terrible 'Queen of the Sea' and she has three beautiful daughters, the third and youngest of whom is the Golden Princess. Now at last Ivan has learned from his previous experiences to do exactly as the vixen advises him, and this enables him to pass the first test by identifying the youngest daughter, as the one who is most plainly dressed. Once again here we see the familiar principle that whatever represents the Self, like Aladdin's plain old lamp in a cave of glittering jewels, is often the thing which least obviously catches the eye, because its value lies within and is not external. This turns out to be really the crux of the whole story, for although the enraged Queen imposes two further tasks on Ivan, each harder than the last, he passes both because the Princess is now secretly helping him. Finally in the nick of time he and the Princess manage to escape the avenging Dark Mother, and Ivan is only sad because he now loves the Princess more than anything in the world and cannot bear the thought of exchanging her for the Horse with the Golden Mane. But again the vixen comes to his aid, as the story unravels back the way it came. By magically disguising herself first as the Princess, then as the Horse, the little fox eventually helps Ivan to get away from the two Dark Kings with all three 'treasures' intact, and he can begin the final stages of his journey home.

Then, just as all seems on the verge of resolution, there intrudes the 'central crisis'. Ivan is about to emerge from the forest within sight of home when he makes a fatal mistake. Just like Odysseus when he is first about to reach Ithaca with the help of the wind-god Aeolus, he feels weary and falls asleep. At a crucial moment he has lost consciousness. His brothers come upon him in the forest, see his prizes and, as Dark Rivals, decide to steal them. They cut Ivan into a thousand pieces, leaving him in the forest, and bring the treasures home, thinking that one of them will marry the Princess and that they will share the kingdom. But when they arrive the Firebird does not sing, the Horse hangs its head and will not eat, and the Princess pines away. Their father, the king, believing his youngest son must be dead, falls sicker with grief than ever.

The purpose of the 'central crisis' is always to emphasise how the final stages of the maturing process are different from what came earlier. The hero's lapse into unconsciousness has seemed fatal. From now on he must develop his consciousness more fully than ever, as he learns to depend on his own powers. In fact, the little vixen does again come to the rescue, for the last time. After a complex episode which involves enlisting the help of another helpful animal, a raven, to fly to the distant sea to bring back the waters of life and death, the vixen puts the hero back together again and restores him to life. But, having told Ivan to go to his father's castle disguised as a humble stable boy, she disappears from the story, leaving him at last completely on his own. The climax of the story is approaching in a way which may remind us of the closing stages of the *Odyssey*, when Odysseus secretly approaches his palace disguised in beggar's rags. When Ivan arrives he finds the whole castle under a terrible shadow. All is sick and out of sorts. But thanks to his return everything gradually comes together again. First the Horse recognises the new 'stable boy' and begins to eat. The king hears of this miracle and sends for the stable boy to see whether he can do the same for the Firebird. It too recognises him and begins to sing. Finally the stable boy is brought before the Princess, She also recognises him with joy. The king is astonished until Ivan throws off his disguise and reveals his true identity. The heartless treachery of the two Rivals is exposed and they are beheaded. The king is restored to health. Ivan and his Princess are married and succeed to half the kingdom (a common motif in folk tales, to show that the hero is ready to inherit); and when the king eventually dies, they succeed to the whole and 'govern the kingdom wisely and well for the rest of their lives'.

Behind its fairy-tale symbolism, the essence of what *The Firebird* is describing is, of course, entirely familiar. As the story of a young man's growing up, we see how he can only do this by showing a balance of qualities, masculine and feminine. All the way through his journey it is as though he comes to a succession of doors, each of which must be opened in the right way. Initially he makes mistakes, but is saved by the fact that he is ultimately acting not for himself but in some greater, selfless cause. Eventually he learns to control his impulses and to trust his instincts, and it is this degree of self-mastery which, in his crucial encounter with the Dark Mother/Queen, wins him his unshakeable alliance with the *anima/* Princess. Nevertheless he still, at the critical moment when he is within sight of the goal, makes his worst mistake through a lack of awareness, and again it is only the 'helpful animal' of instinct which saves him. But he is now finally on his own. As he reaches the climax of the story he has to prove himself by relying on his own qualities; and on the fact that his previous heroism and good-heartedness have won him the total loyalty of his three mysterious 'allies' waiting for him in the castle. For the last time the Rule of Three operates in the last three 'tests'. Ivan himself is the 'fourth' who brings his three allies to life. As in many other stories, we see a 'three' becoming a 'four' at the end, to symbolise the final emergence of a perfect totality. The hero is revealed at last in his true identity, is united with his 'other half' and can succeed to his father, to rule wisely over the kingdom he has redeemed.

### Robin Hood

The legend of Robin Hood again presents us with the picture of a kingdom – twelfth-century England – which has fallen under a terrible shadow. The true, just ruler of the kingdom, Richard, has disappeared abroad. In his absence his rule has been usurped by his wicked brother John, both weak and tyrannical. Power in the kingdom is no longer being exercised in a just or orderly fashion, and a symptom of this is the way the Norman barons abuse their position, behaving arbitrarily and heartlessly. Our attention focuses on one corner of the kingdom where one local Norman lord, the Sheriff of Nottingham, has become a particularly noxious Tyrant, and where the ordinary people, the Saxons, are reduced to fear and misery under his cruel sway.

But in the shadows cast by this dark figure – more precisely in the shadowy world of the great forest of Sherwood – a little community has gathered round the hero of the story. Robin Hood, half-Norman, half-Saxon (thus representing both parts of the divided kingdom), is the dispossessed orphan son of a great noble, the Earl of Huntingdon. Having lost his father in childhood, he has grown up to be confronted with the Dark Father/Tyrant figure of the Sheriff of Nottingham as his particular 'dark opposite'. And he has now gathered round him a group of followers in the forest who represent a kind of 'inferior kingdom', under the rule of their shadowy 'king' Robin and his 'queen' Maid Marian. With their differentiation of skills and personalities, Little John, Will Scarlett, Friar Tuck and the rest add up to a kind of balanced community, an image of potential wholeness. But nothing about them is out in the open or properly resolved. They are outlaws, who can only show themselves to the outer world in disguise. Robin himself is having to live under an assumed name, disguising his true noble identity. We learn how he fell in love with Marian at an early stage in the story aud how they were almost married; but how, on the steps of the altar, their wedding was interrupted by the dark power, so that they are not yet properly and fully united (hence the fact that she is still a 'Maid'). Yet we are in no doubt that Robin and his followers are figures of light. Robin is an outstanding leader, wholly a man; yet at one with his inner feminine, exercising his strength selflessly on behalf of the poor and oppressed. His loving Marian, with her skill as an archer, is a perfect *anima*-figure, both entirely feminine and yet with the inner strength of the masculine. In other words, Hood's 'inferior kingdom' in the shadow-realm of the forest represents all the potential for wholeness and light which the upper-world kingdom in disarray so obviously lacks.

After many adventures which show Robin and his men gradually building up their power and determination in the shadow realm, the outlaw kingdom finally breaks out into the upper world and overthrows the Sheriff's tyranny; at just the moment when the true king, Richard the Lionheart, returns from abroad to seize back his throne from his usurping brother. Robin and his men throw off their disguises, emerge into the light and are greeted with honour by their King. Robin himself can at last assume his true upper-world identity as Earl of Huntingdon and can be properly married at last to his Marian. Everything in the kingdom is back where it should be. Merrie England has been restored to itself.

### The Lord of the Rings

In the early years of the twenty-first century, Peter Jackson's imaginative three-part screen version of Tolkien's *The Lord of the Rings* established itself as one of the most popular films ever made. One reason why we have not looked in detail before at this huge novel, originally conceived by Tolkien for his young son in the years around the Second World War, is that it is another instance of a story which is not shaped by a single basic plot but which contains elements of all seven woven together.

Tolkien's story begins in the cosy, safe world of 'the Shire' – in many ways like an idealised rural England of the pre-machine age, with the innocence of childhood – where there live some little near-human creatures called hobbits. But the Shire is only, as it were, the brightly-lit foreground. Beyond it, chiefly to the east and south, stretches a vast, mysterious world from where a great shadow has lately been emerging.[2] The 'Dark Lord', Sauron the Great, has taken up his abode again in the 'Dark Tower', in the far-off land of Mordor (with its echoes of *mort*, death). The shadow eventually lengthens as far as the Shire and the little hobbit-hero of the story, Frodo, receives the Call to a great Quest. There is a ring, of enormous magical power, but of ambivalent value: its power can be used both for good and ill, but mostly for ill. There is nothing in the world Sauron wishes to lay his hands on more, because it will make his power complete:

> 'One Ring to rule them all, One Ring to find them
> One Ring to bring them all and in the darkness bind them
> In the Land of Mordor where the Shadows lie.'

2. It was probably no accident that Tolkien should unconsciously have arranged the geography of his imaginary world of Middle Earth in this way, conceived as it was in Britain around the time of the Second World War. If 'the Shire' to the western edge of the map was identified with England, it was threatened from the east and south-east by the vast, world-threatening shadow of the dark power of Sauron, centred in Mordor. This reflected the way in which, at the time, Hitler's dark empire on the continent of Europe was casting a deadly shadow over Britain from the same general direction. Tolkien denied any conscious parallel between his story and contemporary political events (in his Foreword to the second edition of the book); but others, including his brother, have suggested otherwise.

Frodo's task, laid on him by the old wizard Gandalf, who comes from the mysterious world beyond the Shire, is to make a long and perilous journey to the heart of distant Mordor, where he must throw the ring into a bottomless cleft in a great volcano, Mount Doom.

Such is the goal of Frodo's quest, and the greater part of the story is taken up with his journey across the hazardous terrain to Mordor. This follows the usual Quest pattern. Frodo sets out with three hobbit companions, Merry, Pippin and his gardener, the faithful Sam Gamgee; and even before they have left the Shire, shadowed by the menacing 'Black Riders', they have already entered on that famil-iar Quest sequence of terrifying ordeals alternating with periods of respite and succour. They find allies to accompany them on the journey, until the 'Company' is nine strong, including representatives of all the races which inhabit the world of 'Middle Earth', an elf, a dwarf and two men, one of them the tall, mysterious 'Strider'. They have to confront an amazing array of enemies and deadly monsters. They have many 'thrilling escapes from death'. They meet with 'helpers', like the 'Good King' Elrond and Galadriel, the 'Lady of Lorien', 'tall and white and fair', 'above all the jewels that lie beneath the earth'. They are also guided at crucial points by Gandalf, who even, for one stretch of the journey, becomes part of the Company, although he then plunges over an underground precipice to seeming destruction, locked in a death-grip with a particularly terrible monster, the Balrog (like Sherlock Holmes plunging with Moriarty over the Reichenbach Falls). Eventually, like Holmes, Gandalf returns, in ghostly elusive form as the 'White Rider', to watch over the remainder of the Quest and even, at times, to intervene in the action.

Halfway through the journey, the Company is divided – and from now on the book itself splits, rather unmanageably, into two almost separate stories. One of these centres on Frodo the Ring-Bearer himself, with his faithful Sam, as they battle on alone across increasingly wild and menacing country towards the dark mountains which surround Mordor.[3] Here, in the pattern of the Quest, they face their worst ordeals on the edge of the goal. They confront the fearful monster Shelob in a labyrinth of caves. Frodo is taken prisoner by the horrible Orcs, and is only released by Sam with the aid of 'magic weapons', the sword Sting and the ring itself which, among its other powers, can confer invisibility on its wearer, like Perseus's helmet. Through all this second part of the journey they have been shad-owed by the treacherous, 'inferior' little monster Gollum, the weak and pathetic 'dark masculine' having to act through the sly, pleading, self-pitiful manner of the 'dark feminine', in his obsessive desire to get hold of the ring. The third and last of their final ordeals comes when Frodo and Sam finally drag themselves up the slopes of the volcano to the Cracks of Doom. Gollum launches a last crazed assault, biting the ring off Frodo's finger but immediately plunging with it to his death in the bottomless pit. The goal has been achieved. As Gandalf puts it 'the Ring-bearer has fulfilled his Quest'.

3. There are clear echoes here, as elsewhere in *The Lord of the Rings*, of the thrillers of John Buchan. With his stories of heroes battling across wild landscapes threatened by shadowy enemies, Buchan was one of the few modern fiction writers Tolkien admired.

But *The Lord of the Rings* is not just a Quest story. It is also an immense version of the Overcoming the Monster plot. Although the story teems with monsters and 'dark figures' of every description, Black Riders, the Barrowight, the Balrog, the dark wizard Saruman with his Orcs, Shelob and many others, they are all in the end agents of the supreme monster at the heart of it all: Sauron the Dark Lord of Mordor (his name, contrary to its pronunciation in the film-version, echoing 'Saurian', lizard-like, the ultimate prehistoric monster). He is portrayed as the ultimate source of everything that is menacing and deadly. Although we never see him directly, except as a great watching eye, he lies behind all the terrible things which happen in the story, all the threats, all the conspiracies. He is a supreme evocation of Evil. Seated in his Dark Tower, he is more than anything conjured up in imagery of darkness. Everything about him is dark, shadowy and powerful. He is Death. And the whole purpose of Frodo's Quest is to overthrow his power.

The nearer Frodo gets to Mordor, the more he feels himself being drawn under Sauron's spell through the ring, which is somehow intimately connected with Sauron. The 'Dark Lord's' powers are on the move, threatening the whole world with destruction. It is into Sauron's power that Frodo is falling when, as he feels himself being lulled and pulled from his purpose by the ring, he allows himself to be captured by the Orcs. But finally, when the ring disappears with Gollum into the Cracks of Doom, an incredible upheaval takes place throughout the world. It is clear that a cosmic victory has been won. The shadows recede. The black clouds lift. The forces of darkness are overthrown in all directions. Again, as Gandalf puts it, 'the realm of Sauron is ended'. The monster has been overcome.

In this respect, however, we can also look on *The Lord of the Rings* as a mighty Rebirth story. The impression given throughout the story is of a world slipping further and further into the eternal winter of some deadly imprisonment. By his victory, Frodo has redeemed it. Spring returns. Life has been renewed. As they sing in Gondor at the news, 'the tree that was withered shall be renewed, and he shall plant it in the high places, and the City shall be blessed. Sing all ye people!'

It is also a Voyage and Return story. We see Frodo and Sam, in a state of limited consciousness, setting out from their familiar little world into a much vaster, completely unfamiliar 'other world' which they do not really begin to understand. Although continually baffling, it is at first quite exhilarating; but the underlying shape of the story is of an ever-growing shadow threatening them, culminating in the nightmare of their journey across Mordor itself, surrounded by nameless horrors on all sides, until finally, on the topmost Crack of Doom, comes the ultimate 'thrilling escape'. At which point Frodo and Sam can return with relief to the safe, familiar world of the Shire.

As, like other Voyage and Return heroes, they come back transformed, we can also see in the change that has come over Frodo and Sam, now called 'Sam the Wise', a version of the Rags to Riches story. The essence of this plot is that an outwardly unremarkable little figure, treated as of little account by those around him, should eventually reveal a much deeper and more extraordinary self within. This is precisely what has happened to Frodo and his companion. Initially they are very ordinary little characters. But as the story progresses they reveal undreamed-of depths of courage, ingenuity and steadfastness, until by the end they have been transfigured into great heroes.

By its nature *The Lord of the Rings* cannot be centrally a Tragedy. But certainly we see the basic plot of Tragedy unfolding in the fate of one character, the 'dark wizard' Saruman, Gandalf's alter-ego, who had once been endowed with great magical powers for good but then perverted by the influence of Sauron. As the story develops we see this immensely powerful figure becoming more and more frustrated, until, in the nightmare of his master Sauron's overthrow, he journeys to the Shire to make a last pitiful bid, as Avenger, to create havoc. Here he is finally turned on and killed by his sly companion Wormtongue, who in the nick of time has made the switch from 'dark' to 'light'.

Thus six of the seven great themes we looked at earlier can all be seen unfolding simultaneously in the main plot of *The Lord of the Rings*. But we may then note two odd things about the story.

The first, very unusually, is that it is a Quest explicitly not to win some great prize, but to get rid of something, to throw something away. The explanation of this lies in the nature of the 'treasure' which has to be thrown away, the ring. The whole point of the ring – as in that other pseudo-mythic story centred on the appeal of a magical ring which confers enormous power on anyone who possesses it, Wagner's *Ring of the Nibelungen* – is that, despite its immense value and magical properties, it is ultimately a very dangerous and dark object.[4] Not only is it intimately connected with the 'Dark Lord' Sauron, but if he can get hold of it, the world is lost. It is in fact a symbol not of wholeness but of the ego, tempting anyone who possesses it to dreams of infinite power. No one realises this more clearly than those two great figures of 'light' in the story, Gandalf and Galadriel, the Wise Old Man and the Anima. Both are themselves momentarily tempted to possess the ring, although each has enough self-knowledge to recognise just how disastrous this would be. Frodo alone has been chosen to carry the ring, despite his frailty, because he is sufficiently awed by the solemn task which has been laid upon him not to fall prey to such temptation. And when the ring is finally returned to the depths of the earth whence it came, the world is restored to life and wholeness because the ego has at last merged back into union with the Self.[5]

4. Wagner drew the inspiration for his ring from a genuine myth, the Norse *Volsunga Saga*. This tells how the ring cursed by the dwarf Andvari, after being stolen by Loki, leads first to his own son Fafnir turning into a monster; then to Fafnir's death at the hand of the great hero Sigurd the Volsung (Wagner's Siegfried), who goes on to free and marry Brynhild; and finally to Sigurd's own death (we look at Wagner's Ring-cycle in Chapter 24 and the Norse myths in Chapter 34). Much of Tolkien's own story was, of course, inspired by his scholarly study of Norse sagas and Anglo-Saxon epics from the 'Dark Ages'.

5. A later parallel to the symbolism of these rings can be seen in *Harry Potter and the Philosopher's Stone*, the first of the books by J. K. Rowling which enjoyed such popularity at the end of the 1990s and at the beginning of the twenty-first century. In a story combining elements of Voyage and Return, Rags to Riches, Overcoming the Monster and Quest, the young orphan hero, persecuted by the suburban family who have adopted him after the death of his parents, suddenly finds himself transported into a mysterious 'other world' governed by magic and peopled by wizards, dragons, trolls and other fabulous creatures. Here it seems he is already famous because, when he was a baby, his parents, as two distinguished wizards, had been killed by this world's chief figure of darkness, Voldemort, who had been magically destroyed in trying to kill Harry himself. We thus realise how,

The other odd thing about Frodo's story is that when his Quest is concluded there is one supremely important element missing. There is no heroine, no 'Princess', no 'other half' to make him whole. This is part of the reason why he cannot ultimately seem a complete character, and why there is a strong sense of something missing about the story in general and his character in particular. He remains somehow unfulfilled, not fully developed, a hobbit rather than a man.

Nevertheless it would be surprising, where an author's imagination has been so profoundly stirred by so much of the basic material out of which stories are spun, if this enormously important element were not present somewhere in the story, and of course it is. The story's one hero of real majestic stature is the figure we first meet as the mysterious 'Strider', who then reveals himself, tall, strong and with 'a keen, commanding' light in his eyes, as 'Aragorn, son of Arathorn', descended from a long line of kings. Here is the one figure in the story of whom we can say that he is cast in truly heroic proportions, and so compelling did this become to Tolkien as the story unfolded in his imagination that he eventually separated Aragorn from his original hero Frodo, and found himself drawn into what amounted to a huge sub-plot, incidental to the main story, to allow him to follow the story of his new 'hero' to its proper conclusion.

It is this which accounts for the somewhat disconcerting way in which, at the point where Frodo and Sam begin their final approaches to Mordor, the book splits into two almost separate stories. For a long time, as the two of them set off in one direction and the remainder of the Company in another, it is not easy to hold the whole story together. We follow the immense drama which surrounds the capture of Merry and Pippin by the Orcs, the siege of Helm's Deep, its rescue by Gandalf and the Riders of Rohan, the rescue of Merry and Pippin by Treebeard and his walking forest of Ents, followed by their flooding of Saruman's grim city of Isengard round its dark tower. But the full significance of all this is not really clear, until at last a central new story-line emerges to run in parallel with the closing stages of Frodo's Quest. When it does, we see it taking on a very familiar shape.

We are introduced to a kingdom in disarray, Gondor, with its capital Minas Tirith, ruled by a weak regent because its 'true king' is absent, and therefore unable to withstand for much longer the attacks of the dark power emanating from Mordor. But in the shadows beyond the city walls, salvation is approaching, in the

---

in classic Rags to Riches fashion, the boy hero has been singled out for some special destiny. Harry is initiated into the magical world and sent to Hogwarts, a school for young would-be wizards. Here he finds himself caught up in a cosmic battle between light and dark which eventually centres on a race to secure the 'Philosopher's Stone', an object of immense magical power. The spirit of Voldemort needs this to become reincarnated, to carry on his evil work. But when, at the story's climax, Harry finally wins the Stone, it disappears. He is then told by Professor Dumbledore, the 'wise old man' who is the school's headmaster, that this is just as well because the powers of the Stone, like those of Tolkien's and Wagner's rings, can only really be used to serve dark and selfish ends. Like the rings, in short, it is a symbol not of the Self but of the ego. Harry had only been able to win it because he did not want it for himself but only in the name of a selfless, world-saving cause. Like Frodo's ring on Mount Doom, it can then disappear back into the 'One' from which it had been separated.

shape of Aragorn and his allies. We have already seen Aragorn in an increasingly heroic light, from his part in the siege of Helm's Deep. We now learn that this mysterious wanderer is in fact Gondor's true king. In the nick of time he throws off his disguise, emerging like Odysseus in royal majesty. He saves his city and redeems his kingdom. Aragorn's story then ends in his marriage to the beautiful Elvish Princess Arwen Evenstar.

In this sense, as the hero emerges from the twilight of disguise and obscured identity to his final glorious union with a heroine whose name indicates that she is all light, the book also contains elements of the seventh plot, Comedy. Yet the fact that Aragorn's own drama unfolds in a sense off centre-stage, and that it is not he but the much more limited, child-like Frodo who is the central figure of the book, leaves us at the end with the sense that there is still something lacking and that, for all its splendours, *The Lord of the Rings* is not a fully integrated, grown-up story.

What is interesting, in the context of our present concerns, is that a story which was originally conceived to entertain a child, and therefore had a rather child-like hero, should eventually have aroused in its author's unconscious all those deeper elements which are necessary to bring a story to the complete archetypal happy ending – showing a hero who has attained to complete maturity being united with his 'Princess' and succeeding to a kingdom. But this required the emergence of a new hero, equipped to become fully a man, because the original hero could never really develop into anything more than a child. Which is why, at the end of the book, Frodo departs for the Isles of the Blest across the western sea, still in the company of Gandalf: the father he could never himself become.

### Don Quixote

The examples we have so far looked at in this chapter all belong to the type of story we are likely to encounter in the earlier stages of life, where the hero or heroine are shown as pitted against dark forces centred outside them. Only later do we come more consistently to stories which present the drama from that other perspective which shows the hero or heroine having to contend with the same dark forces within themselves. In *Peer Gynt*, for instance – another story shaped by elements of all the seven basic plots – we saw how the dark figures the hero encounters at the beginning, the Dark King of the Trolls and the Temptress Woman in Green, are personifications of the dark powers which then come to possess the hero himself through almost the whole of the story. His real problem is to find that wider vision which will liberate him from his own monstrous and blind egotism, from the double grip of the 'dark masculine' and the 'dark feminine' which is separating him from the Self; until he is finally brought to that deeper state of consciousness, and the story can end on the image of Peer united with his *anima* Solveig, 'light masculine' and 'light feminine' in perfect balance.

In fact all archetypal stories – whether the darkness is shown as outside the central figure or within – are really preoccupied with the hero or heroine's inner state. By the principle of the 'unrealised value', their battles with the external world are merely reflections of what is going on inside them, and we never see them

321

satisfactorily overcoming the darkness outside them until they have eliminated the darkness within.

A story explicitly concerned to make precisely this point is that great seventeenth-century Spanish novel *Don Quixote*. The whole purpose of Cervantes's tale is to show the foolishness of a man who projects onto the outside world the struggle which should be fought inside him. Don Quixote is a man in middle life who for years has been obsessed with chivalric romances, stories of knights engaged in derring-do to save damsels in distress (the equivalent of the James Bond stories of our own time), without understanding their inner meaning. Full of blind and silly egotism, he decides to become a knight himself. He dedicates himself to the 'service' of a local girl, La Dulcinea Tobosa, as an external projection of his *anima*, takes up a rusty lance, as a projection of his masculinity, and rides out into the world to challenge all the powers of evil that he can find. But of course these manifestations of the dark power are purely illusory, projections of his own fantasies, as when he attacks the windmills imagining them to be hostile giants.

It is only after he has wandered through the world for a long time as an absurdly self-deceiving idiot (as is only too apparent to almost everyone he meets) that he finally recognises the central truth which has been eluding him all along: that all the blindness and egotism which he has been projecting onto the 'enemies' outside him are in fact his own problem. In the closing pages of the book, he flings away the silly romances which have snared him into such a false perspective and repents of his idiocy. He has at last won true self-knowledge, he has come to 'see whole'. And at this point, transformed from the foolish Don Quixote into 'Don Alonso the Good', he dies in old age, at peace with himself and all the world.

### The Tempest

At the end of *The Lord of the Rings* Frodo disappears into the sunset, still led by the Wise Old Man he could never become himself. Don Quixote at least attains to the beginning of wisdom just before his death. One of the few stories in the world which concentrate on the process of a hero actually being transformed into a Wise Old Man, representing the most complete state of maturity and inner development a man can reach, is the last complete play written by Shakespeare.

In *The Tempest* we are again confronted by the image of a kingdom where something has gone horribly amiss, where the true ruler is absent and where power has been usurped by his weak, tyrannical brother: even though, in the play itself, we do not actually see this 'upper world' in disarray at all. In this, the most inward of all Shakespeare's plays, we follow events entirely in the shadowy 'inferior' (or interior) realm, where, after many years, we see the forces of light at last constellating to put the world to rights.

The first image in the play, giving it the immediate feel of a Voyage and Return story, is of the group of characters from the sick 'upper world', the usurping Duke Antonio, his equally dark friend King Alonso and their followers, tumbling suddenly and violently into the 'inferior realm' as their ship is wrecked on Prospero's island. Here wait the denizens of the lower world to put them through the ordeals which will transform them: above all Prospero himself, who was exiled by

Antonio from his proper state as the true Duke of Milan. Now, after years of study and inward growth, Prospero has been almost completely transformed into a Wise Old Man; and with him we see his gentle daughter Miranda, a perfect, loving symbol of the *anima*. But even in Prospero's shadow-kingdom all is not yet fully redeemed and brought to the light, as we see from the shambling, shadowy presence of Caliban, son of the Dark Mother and Witch Sycorax. Prospero himself still has to make the last moves which will bring him back to his full state of kingship in the upper world. He still, in contrast to the innocent, compassionate Miranda, has some anger against those who have wronged him. Equally, among the upper world figures who have now fallen into Prospero's power, not all are wholly dark: they include two light figures, the Son-Hero Ferdinand, and the faithful old courtier Gonzalo, who had been responsible for saving Prospero and Miranda from death all those years before, and who himself observes the drama through sage eyes as a second Wise Old Man.

The first move in the great process of transformation which is now set in motion is the bringing together of the two representatives of the rising generation, Ferdinand and Miranda, a Prince and a Princess. In the instant burgeoning of pure, innocent love between them we see the first promise of hope and new life for the future. But before that can be realised, the whole complex of disordered relationships involving the older generation must be unknotted and brought into their proper life-giving state. The real problem which has to be sorted out is the chief source of the sickness and disorder, centred in the two dark kings, Antonio and Alonso. These, by the double-negative, are the 'dark Opposites' to the hero Prospero himself, symbolising all that holds him back from his own state of wholeness. And the key figure in the drama now becomes his servant Ariel.

Described by Prospero as 'my tricksy spirit', Ariel is the elusive, mischievous Trickster, whose archetypal role in stories is to stir up and bewilder people who are set in one mode of consciousness into another. Dancing round like a will-o'-the-wisp, using his magical powers, he convinces them that they are no longer sure of anything. He teases them out of their existing state of mind: firstly, into what seems like a state of madness, where nothing is any longer certain; but eventually into seeing the world straight and whole again.

Such is Ariel's role in *The Tempest*. First, by a bewildering display of tricks, visions and mysterious music, he drives the dark figures into a state of desperation. Then he confronts them with the reality of their terrible crime, the usurpation of Prospero, with the hint that such a crime must lead to death. 'You among men being most unfit to live' he tells them, 'I have made you mad; and even with such-like valour, men hang and drown their proper selves'. In other words, the heart of their crime is that they have not been true to their proper selves; they have violated the Self. Finally, as the horror of what they have done begins to sink in on them, Prospero confronts them and this shock – for they thought he was dead – is enough for them to beg for mercy and forgiveness. At the point where Prospero does forgive them, he at last reaches wholeness, as he emerges in his true upper world identity to reassume sovereignty over his rightful kingdom. Gonzalo rubs in the message that the whole effect of the adventure had been to bring everyone back to their proper selves, after a time when 'no man was his own'.

At last the young Son-Hero and Daughter-Heroine, Ferdinand and Miranda, can step to the centre of the stage, truly united, with the blessing of their fathers Alonso and Prospero. The royal road to the future is open and assured. And now that the real hero of the story, Prospero himself, has become whole, his kingdom fully redeemed, even the gross, drunken Caliban, the animal-man who has understood nothing (the very opposite of a Wise Old Man, and therefore Prospero's other 'dark opposite' in the play) has been swept up in the general redemption and says 'I will be wise hereafter and seek for grace'. Prospero ends alone in the middle of the stage, having completed his great spiritual work, which has all been ultimately concerned with the putting right of his own 'inner kingdom'. He is utterly drained and left in a state of complete religious humility: 'now my charms are all o'erthrown ... and my ending is despair, unless I be relieved by prayer'.

Thus in effect did Shakespeare conclude his own immense inner journey, reflected stage by stage through all the unfolding sequence of his plays. He could now retire from the world to end his days quietly in Stratford where he had begun. Like Prospero, he had reached his goal.

### The Magic Flute

There is no more appropriate story to conclude this summing-up of the principles which guide stories to a happy ending than the magical opera which Mozart wrote in the closing months of his own life in 1791, to a libretto by Emanuel Schikaneder. No story in the world lays out the essence of the archetypal family drama more completely or economically than *The Magic Flute*.

The plot is dominated by four characters: a Father-figure, Lord Sarastro; a Mother-figure, the Queen of the Night; a Son-Hero, Tamino; and a Daughter-Heroine, Pamina. Dressed in symbolic terms, *The Magic Flute* portrays all the key stages of a man's inner psychological development, from the moment of his birth, through his gradual enlightenment, to the point where he is at last consciously whole.

The opera begins with the young hero, Prince Tamino, being propelled violently onto the stage by a terrifying serpent. He falls helpless and unconscious to the ground. The serpent is killed by three ladies who look down at the boy adoringly and leave to tell their mistress, the Queen, of his arrival. Tamino then wakes up and finds himself in a wholly unfamiliar world. The first person he meets is the strange figure of the bird-catcher Papageno, covered in feathers. Tamino discloses that his father is a great king who rules over 'many lands and peoples'. But all this now seems very far away, and he is baffled by Papageno who seems to know nothing of who his own parents are, or where he comes from; merely that he lives 'by eating and drinking' and that he obtains his food by catching birds and presenting them to the mysterious ruler of this country, the Queen of the Night, whom he has never seen but who rewards him by giving him all he needs.

What we have seen so far is Tamino, as Everyman, enacting his birth into the world. Initially unconscious, like any newborn baby, he is surrounded, like any baby at its birth, by the joyful female presence of those who have assured his safe arrival. He then emerges to consciousness to find, again like any baby, that this new world he has entered is dominated by nature and instinct. To personify this is the role of Papageno, who describes himself as 'a child of nature'. Throughout the story he represents the unthinking, instinctive existence of someone very little different from the birds and animals, and who aspires to no higher state of consciousness or understanding. He simply depends on 'the Queen' to supply all his needs, as an animal depends instinctively on 'Mother Nature'. But Tamino's destiny is to be very different.

At this point the three ladies return to tell Tamino that their mysterious Queen is pleased with him and has a great task for him to perform. She has a beautiful daughter, the Princess Pamina. They show Tamino her picture, and he is at once smitten with love ('O image, angel-like and fair, no mortal can with thee compare'). Then, with three rolls of thunder, the Queen herself appears and tells Tamino how her beloved daughter has been abducted by an 'evil fiend'. Pamina has fallen into the clutches of the terrible Sarastro, and it is Tamino's task to release her from this imprisonment. The Queen then vanishes, but her ladies present Tamino, to aid him in his task, with the magic flute, which has the power to transform human passions from dark to light ('whene'er this power is asserted, all human passions are converted, the saddest man to smile will learn, the coldest heart with love will burn').

So far the imposing figure of the mysterious, kindly Queen seems the most light figure in the story. As a loving Mother she is the chief representative of the feminine in Tamino's life, and she has awoken his own inner feminine by sowing in his heart the desire for the *anima*-figure Pamina, whom he yearns for more than anything in the world. Like many young heroes, Tamino thus finds himself enjoying a good relationship with 'Mother' but aware that, to make him complete, he must one day be united with his own feminine 'other half'; and that she languishes in the grim clutches of a tyrannical male. Thus does the Dark Father enter as the main shadow over Tamino's future; and his only talisman in the great ordeal which lies ahead is the magic flute itself, as a symbol of the sovereign power of the Self to turn darkness into light.

Tamino sets off full of resolve to challenge the Tyrant in his lair and is separated from Papageno. We then for the first time see the lovely Pamina, and realise with horror that she is about to be brutally ravished by Sarastro's servant, the shadowy Moor, Monostatos. In the nick of time she is saved by the intervention of Papageno, who tells her about Tamino and his love for her. Meanwhile Tamino himself approaches Sarastro's dark temple and demands entry. 'Is this Sarastro's realm of terror?' he demands at the door. He is told that it is a 'temple of wisdom', but does not believe it. He shouts that he hates Sarastro for ever, as 'a tyrant and foe of men'.

At this point the shadow of the 'dark masculine' over the story reaches its height. We have seen the heroine about to be violated by the 'dark masculine' Monostatos, who represents the dark side of 'natural man' just as Papageno represents his light aspect. Indeed, for the moment, it is the impulsive intervention of the instinctively good-hearted Papageno which saves her. But Pamina is still a prisoner of Monostatos's far more terrible master Sarastro, and Tamino himself, as he stands at the temple gate, even believes that she must be already dead.

Now comes the dramatic reversal which gives this story its extraordinary psychological profundity. In musically one of the most moving moments of the opera, 'mysterious voices' from within the temple assure him that she is still alive. 'She lives, she lives' he exclaims in almost disbelieving relief; and the music conveys the sense of life flooding back into him. At his moment of greatest despair we can feel the life-giving *anima* stirring within him (much as, in Beethoven's *Fidelio*, we see the despairing prisoner Florestan joyfully returning to life when, in the gloom of his dungeon, he disbelievingly senses the presence of his 'angel Leonora'). Gradually the awe-inspiring air of the temple is beginning to sow doubts that Sarastro is quite the figure of total darkness he has been painted. Then, heralded by a solemn chorus in praise of his wisdom, we for the first time meet Sarastro himself. Pamina throws herself at his feet, begging for mercy and to be allowed to return to her mother; but Sarastro firmly explains he cannot release her, for her own good. If he had left her with her mother 'what would become of truth and right?' The Queen of the Night is 'all too proud. By man your course must be decided. For by herself a woman steps beyond her sphere and is misguided.'

This is the crux of the story. What Sarastro is saying is that, to bring about true human wholeness, the instinctive feminine value on its own is not enough. It must be strengthened, disciplined, given a firm framework of rational understanding by the masculine value: this is the only way that true wisdom and higher consciousness can be reached. Up to now we have seen the feminine value uppermost, as Tamino is in the familiar position of closeness to the feminine value represented by the Mother and hostility to the masculine values represented by the Father. But now the balance has to be redressed. Tamino has to realise his full masculinity. He therefore now begins to see the masculine values represented by Sarastro as light, as Sarastro becomes the Father-figure and Wise Old Man guiding him to his goal. Meanwhile the Queen of the Night, representing the natural world of unconscious dependence on instinct, switches over to become the chief dark figure through the rest of the story; because she now stands for the infantile state of dependence which is the chief thing Tamino has to escape from if he is to reach real self-knowledge and autonomy. Such is the theme of the second and final act.

To emphasise this, Act Two is almost entirely dominated by the contrast between Tamino and Papageno. Sarastro has set them a series of tests to prove their steadfastness and self-control. On each occasion Tamino passes the test triumphantly, emerging as a true man. Papageno, on the other hand, representing the instinctive impulsiveness of nature, fails miserably. He has no self-discipline and therefore never comes to any real understanding or higher state of consciousness; even though he is eventually rewarded, in the way of nature, with a little feathered and good-natured 'other half', Papagena, just like himself. And their only joint thought, in the way of nature, is to reproduce and to bring into the world dozens of little Papagenos and Papagenas.[6]

But for Tamino a very different destiny is in store, because he represents man who has truly risen above the state of nature, to the very highest state a man can aspire to. As we see him refined by his series of ordeals into a strong, austere, self-disciplined figure, entirely true to the great ego-transcending cause to which he has dedicated himself, he is at last united with his Pamina. They go through the final ordeal, the opposites of fire and water, together, showing that they have transcended all opposites and achieved a state of total unity: not just on an instinctive level, like Papageno and Papagena, but in full conscious understanding of their union with the unseen mystery of creation itself. Tamino has at last attained to the full state of wisdom.

At this point, in a rocky landscape in the darkness, we see the dark forces of nature, the Queen of the Night now allied with Monostatos, preparing to make their last terrifying assault on the Temple of Wisdom. Amid the raging of a great storm we see them plunging to destruction. Out of the darkness Sarastro's temple reappears as 'the Temple of the Sun' and he himself sings 'the sun's radiant glory has vanquished the night, the powers of darkness have yielded to light'. The magical notes of the flute have finally led us up to a perfect image of the consciously-realised Self.

Although it may be easy to be misled by the playful way *The Magic Flute* comes over almost like a pantomime, this is to miss the psychological subtlety with which the opera is constructed. Symbolically it finds a uniquely ingenious way to encompass both the light and dark aspects of 'Mother' and 'Father' in the archetypal family drama, as it presents such a luminous account of a man travelling the full road of inner human development, from birth to complete maturity.

⁕

In this second part of the book we have concentrated on the central drama of storytelling as it unfolds to its most positive conclusion. But what of those countless stories which are exceptions to this pattern; where the outcome is nothing like so happy or so certain?

---

6. The role played by Papageno in *The Magic Flute* helps to illumine the significance of that played by Caliban in *The Tempest*. Like Papageno, although he is much darker and less good-natured, Caliban stands for 'natural man': someone living more or less unconsciously and instinctively, understanding nothing. Papageno's darker side is split off and represented by Monostatos. Caliban's mother Sycorax 'was a witch and one so strong that could control the moon, make flows and ebbs'. Like the Queen of the Night, she is 'Mother Nature'. It is in this respect that Caliban is the opposite to Prospero, who lives on such a lofty plane of consciousness, understanding almost everything; although as master and servant the two are intimately connected, just as Monostatos is the shadow of his master, the Wise Old Man Sarastro. So long as Prospero himself is not yet completely whole, Caliban stands for the unregenerate remnant in Prospero's kingdom – i.e., in Prospero himself ('this thing of darkness I do acknowledge mine'). But at the moment when Prospero finally achieves wholeness, Caliban is brought to the light. The last vestige of natural, unconscious man has been purged by the arrival of complete understanding.

327

We must now turn to the other face of storytelling: to consider all those types of story which show the hero or the heroine in one way or another not managing to reach the central goal. Here we shall see that, far from being a different kind of story altogether, such stories are rooted in precisely the same central drama we have been looking at. Nothing is more revealing of the unconscious rules which govern the way stories take shape in the human imagination than their unfailing consistency.

## Chapter 20

# The Fatal Flaw

*'Cut is the branch that might have grown full straight.'*
Marlowe, *Doctor Faustus*

We end this second part of the book by looking again at the plot of Tragedy. Of the seven plots we looked at in Part One, one stood very obviously as the odd man out. Six lead naturally to a happy ending. Only Tragedy seems to stand at the opposite pole of storytelling, as it brings its central figure to a lonely, violent death. But when we return to it in the context of all that has emerged in recent chapters, we can see what is really going on in a Tragedy in a rather different light.

What is it that brings the hero or heroine of a Tragedy so inexorably to catastrophe? The first people consciously to ask this question were the ancient Greeks; and they had no doubt that all the great tragic figures in their mythology had something profoundly in common. They called it hubris, which we usually interpret as a form of overweening pride, a reckless arrogance. But the literal derivation of hubris was from the word *hyper*, meaning 'over'. It meant a 'stepping over the bounds', a defiance of the cosmic order, that state of perfect balance which ultimately holds the universe together (characterised in the motto 'nothing in excess', written up over the temple of Apollo at Delphi, the most sacred spot in the Greek world). By the rule of that same balance, anything which disturbed it would eventually meet with a violent shock as the state of balance and order was restored. The inevitable consequence of hubris was nemesis, from the root *nemein*, to 'allot a due portion', the same root from which sprang *nomos*, 'law'. Literally, nemesis was the 'due portion' required to restore the equilibrium of the cosmic order when it had been unbalanced by an act of hubris.

But the Greeks went further than this in providing a general answer to the question of why the tragic hero must come to ultimate disaster. As Aristotle put it in a famous passage in the *Poetics*, there was a specific reason why the heroes and heroines of tragedy – Prometheus, Oedipus, Medea, Agamemnon, Clytemnestra – should fall prey to hubris in the first place. The essence of a tragic hero or heroine, said Aristotle, is that they must not be shown as wholly good or bad, but that they must be shown as being brought from 'prosperity to misery' through some 'fatal flaw'. And the Greek word for this was *hamartia*, which means literally 'missing the mark', as an arrow fails to reach its target. The fatal flaw in the tragic hero

329

or heroine is that deficiency in their character or awareness which prevents them from 'reaching the goal'.[1]

In other words, the very nature of the 'fatal flaw' in these central figures of tragedy is that it is something which renders them unable to 'succeed', a word we use in two senses. The first means simply 'to be successful', as in reaching a goal of any kind. But we also use the word more precisely in the sense of people succeeding to their parents, succeeding to an inheritance, one generation following or succeeding to another. And through stories we can see how originally our two uses of the word were one. Those who truly 'succeed' in life are those who succeed in both senses: they reach the central goal of life which is true maturity, as they develop to the point where they can play their proper role in the succession of one generation to another.

The essence of the tragic hero or heroine, in short, is that they are held back by some fatal flaw or weakness from reaching that state of perfect balance which is presented by stories as the supreme goal of human existence. They are doomed to fall short of the goal because in some way they are stuck in a state of incompleteness or immaturity.

A simple example of this is seen in the myth of Icarus. We see Daedalus, in his light aspect as the ideal wise Father, telling his son that in order to hold onto life he must keep in a state of perfect balance. He must keep precisely between the opposites, by flying neither too high nor too low, because either will lead to disaster. But the immature boy is carried away by his egotism into imbalance and one-sidedness. Puffed up by his power to fly, he falls into the state of hubris, the cosmic pride which is the essence of egocentricity. Hubris defies the supreme law of balance and proportion which governs everything in the universe, and the inter-relatedness of all its parts. Blinded by the limitations of ego-consciousness to the sustaining framework of the laws of nature, out of harmony with the totality of which he is a part, Icarus recklessly flies up too near the sun, his wings fall off, and he plunges back into the sea of unconsciousness and death. In every sense he is 'the boy hero who cannot grow up'.

The story of Icarus might thus be regarded as a pure distillation of the spirit of Tragedy. But usually, of course, the events of Tragedy are set in a more social context. Indeed we see them rooted in precisely that same web of basic human relationships with which we are now familiar, in the archetypal family drama. The moment has come to see how the patterns of Tragedy relate directly to the central drama we have seen emerging in the last few chapters.

1. Aristotle was not of course alone in using the word *hamartia*. It also appears in the New Testament, where it has usually been translated into English as 'sin' – a word which itself may originally have derived from the same root as 'sinister', meaning everything that is done in the 'left' way, as opposed to the 'right' way (compare, for instance, the Russia phrase, *na levo*, 'on the left', applied to anything which is crooked, underhand, 'not quite right'). In the Lord's Prayer, *hamartia* was translated into sixteenth-century English as 'trespasses', or 'stepping over the bounds', linking it back to the original meaning of hubris. At the roots of language all these ideas – missing the mark, stepping over the bounds, not doing things in the right way, sin, error – are related.

To understand the essence of what is happening in Tragedy we must recall the two great principles of the Self which guide a light hero to the ultimate goal. He must show himself as perfectly balanced. Firstly he must be strong, in the positive masculine sense which gives him sovereignty over himself and proper authority over others. It is this which enables him at last to succeed to the 'kingdom'. Secondly he must be open to the feminine: that which connects him with the world outside him and with feeling for others. It is this which enables him at last to be fully united with the heroine. It is the balance between these things which allows him ultimately to reach the goal.

But what happens if a hero remains centred not in the Self but on the ego? Firstly, his masculine strength, instead of being turned inward to give him control over himself and his appetites, is turned outward. It becomes merely an egocentric desire to win power, to assert himself over others. Secondly, his inner feminine, that which connects him to others, instead of expressing itself in selfless, unbounded love, turns into the selfish, exclusive love of passion or erotic desire. The egocentric hero is still driven by the urge to reach a goal: indeed this is the very definition of the tragic hero, as he finds the Focus for his dark desires. And when we look at the nature of his goal we see how it invariably corresponds in an *outward* way to that of the hero who is centred in the Self. He may wish to win power, to rule over a 'kingdom', like Macbeth or Richard III. He may feel the overwhelming urge to be united with an obsessively desired 'other half', like Humbert Humbert or Don Giovanni. But because he wants to achieve his goal for egocentric reasons the jigsaw no longer fits together.

This is what Tragedy is really about. It shows us the hero or heroine trying to achieve the goal but in the wrong way. Because of that 'fatal flaw' they are unable to succeed. In fact Tragedy shows us everything we have become familiar with in the type of story which comes to a happy ending, but in an inverted form. The light hero is drawn up to his ultimate goal and finally liberated, by a balance between light masculine and light feminine. The dark hero is possessed and drawn downwards by the dark masculine and the dark feminine. Instead of seeing the world whole, the right way up, he is drawn into seeing it upside down, by that dark inversion which turns light into dark and dark into light: so that the people he is most obviously turned against are the very people who represent those values of the Self which he should be realising in himself. What we see in Tragedy, in short, is an exact reversal of the pattern which leads to wholeness. And if we recall the essential moves the light hero has to make to bring him to the Self, we can see how the plot of Tragedy shows each of them in a negative form.

The light hero is confronted by one or more of a series of dark figures, the 'shadow family', whom he must resist or overcome in order to emerge fully and wholly into the light. He must escape the clutches of the Dark Mother, representing the 'dark feminine'; he must overcome the Dark Father, representing the 'dark masculine'; he may then have to overcome each of these challenges again, in the shape of the Dark Rival and the Dark Other Half – until finally, having confronted each test in the right way, he can reach the supreme goal. He can be fully united with his 'light other half', the *anima*, and succeed to the kingdom.

In Tragedy we see a complete inversion of this scenario. When the tragic hero is confronted by the 'dark feminine' (or by the Tempter, who represents the 'dark feminine' in masculine guise), he does not resist: he succumbs, and falls fatally under its emasculating spell. If his masculine strength does emerge, it can only be in the inferior form of the 'dark masculine', compelling him to the loveless pursuit of power and domination over others. And as we saw earlier, there is then a familiar set of light figures who are most likely to be the tragic hero's chief victims on his downward course:

(1) first there is the Good Old Man, whom we can now see as the 'light Father' or 'good King', representing mature and positive masculine authority: the very thing the hero should be realising in himself;

(2) then there is the 'light Rival' or 'light Alter-Ego', who corresponds to the hero in some way, as in terms of age, status or situation, but who is positive where the hero is negative, and thus his 'light Opposite';

(3) above all there is the Innocent Young Girl, his 'Good Angel' or 'light Other Half', representing the supreme value of the 'light feminine': except that in Tragedy she is not sufficiently powerful or well-developed to sway the hero and turn him back towards the light. She is the figure whom we shall see, where the hero himself is not fully developed, as the 'inadequate' or 'infantile *anima*'.

Nothing more tellingly reflects the course of the tragic hero's inward spiritual disintegration than the way, when he is confronted by any of these light figures, or each of them in turn, he either kills or brutally rejects them. Each time he does so, he is in effect killing or rejecting that aspect of himself. Thus does he remain locked into the basic situation of the weak, immature hero, bewitched by the dark feminine, who cannot grow up. He turns on one component of his psychic kingdom after another, extinguishing the light, until the darkness finally kills his soul and he plunges to destruction.

As we saw earlier, Comedy is in a sense the most comprehensive of the 'light' plots because it can be used to encompass all or any of the various strands in the complex process whereby the archetypal family drama is brought to its proper light conclusion. Similarly Tragedy encompasses such a varied range of stories because it can reflect in so many different ways the same complex process in reverse, each individual story giving its own emphasis to different aspects of the same basic overall pattern. This is why Comedy and Tragedy have occupied such a special place in storytelling, because of all the plots they are the most all-encompassing in their ability to present the light and dark aspects of the archetypal drama.

The time has come to look again at some of the very different stories shaped by the plot of Tragedy we considered earlier, to see how these principles work in practice.

## *Macbeth*: The strong man unmanned

Since, by definition, all tragic heroes suffer from a fatal weakness, there are not all that many tragedies which show us a hero who, at least outwardly, seems initially to be strong in masculine terms, a successful leader of men, happy in the exercise of authority. An obvious example of such a hero is Macbeth.

At the beginning of the play we see Macbeth as a victorious general, apparently a strong man at one with the world. Behind this manly facade, however, all is not as it seems. Even before Macbeth appears, we have already seen, lying in wait for him in the darkness, the three 'black and midnight hags', with their occult powers and knowledge, personifications of the inner 'dark feminine' which is to be his downfall. From their dark, inferior realm 'beyond the light', they catch Macbeth on his hidden weak spot, arousing his ambitions and his ego. At this stage the upper world kingdom, under the rule of Duncan and his loyal general Macbeth, is still light. The darkness is all in the inferior realm. Indeed at first Macbeth is disposed to dismiss the witches' prophecy that he might one day be king himself. It is as though a tempting thought had floated up from his unconscious, only to be pushed away by his conscious mind as too improbable to be taken seriously. But then, almost casually, in a letter to his wife, Macbeth passes the infection on: and through her the poison of the dark feminine returns to tempt him much more strongly, sapping his manly will and sense of propriety. Gradually he succumbs to the temptation, although not without a struggle. Even on the verge of the fatal act, the killing of the 'good King' Duncan, Macbeth is still wrestling with his soul. But once the awful deed is done, he is immediately drawn, like many another tragic hero, into further crimes in an attempt to cover up the first – beginning with the murder of the sleeping grooms. As an outwardly strong man now inwardly in the grip of the dark feminine, Macbeth is already turning into a 'dark King' or Tyrant.

At this point the dark power has passed into dominance on the upper level, taking the kingdom into its grip; and the potential light forces – Duncan's sons Malcolm and Donalbain fleeing into exile into England – are beginning to be polarised into the inferior or shadow realm. Gradually Banquo emerges from the growing darkness as Macbeth's 'light Rival': his fellow general whose descendants, the witches promised, would one day occupy the throne instead of Macbeth. As Banquo's suspicion grows, Macbeth lashes out and kills his 'light Alter-Ego'. The result is that the most powerful figure still remaining in the kingdom, Macduff, abandons Macbeth and flees to join Malcolm in England, as Macbeth's new, much more menacing 'light Rival' or 'light Opposite'. The hero's only response is to lash out in even greater desperation by ordering the killing of Lady Macduff and her children.

Macbeth has now committed three major crimes. First, as Predator, he has killed the 'good King'. Second, as Holdfast, to secure his position, he has killed the 'light Rival'. Thirdly, as Avenger, he has killed the 'light feminine' and the Child. We now see how, as the trigger to final transformation, the Rule of Three can work downwards as well as upwards. Having killed off all the chief light components of his kingdom on the upper level – or driven them into the inferior realm as exiles – Macbeth's third dark act precipitates him into the Nightmare Stage. Firstly he has to watch powerless as his 'other half', Lady Macbeth, disintegrates through madness to 'dusty death'. Secondly, now irretrievably cut off from the Self, he himself moves into a twilight where he sees the universe and life as utterly meaningless, 'signifying nothing'. Lastly the forces of light – led by the now-towering figure of Macduff, and the son-king Malcolm who is destined to succeed – re-emerge into the upper realm, by invading Scotland and closing in to extinguish Macbeth's life forever.

### Dr Faustus: The weak man unmanned

The story of Faustus is that of the most brilliant man of his age who gained a great reputation for learning until the moment when:

> 'swol'n with cunning, of a self conceit,
> his waxen wings did mount above his reach,
> and melting, heaven conspir'd his overthrow.'

The super-intellectual Faustus is not physically powerful or a leader of men, like Macbeth. In manly terms he is essentially weak. Such strength as he has is all in the mind. But, cut off from his fellow men by his life of abstract speculation and disputation, the desire creeps up on Faustus for limitless power and knowledge, so that 'all things that move between the quiet poles shall be at my command'. What he dreams of, in compensation for his weakness, are the two aspects of the masculine value, power and knowledge. But he desires them only to gratify his ego and to assert himself against the world. There is no sign in Faustus of the rooting feminine that might connect him with other people or with the reality of the world outside himself. And where the light feminine is lacking, only the vacuum of the dark feminine remains. Through this void the Tempter Mephistopheles enters to offer him the treacherous bargain, a fantasy of omnipotence and omniscience in return for his soul. No sooner has the battle between the 'Good Angel' and the 'Evil Angel' for the hero's soul been lost, than it begins to become clear that the powers Faustus has been given are nothing more than empty illusions, such as being allowed to play silly irreverent tricks on the Pope, who as the 'Holy Father' is symbolically an aspect of the Self.

Finally Faustus conceives his supreme desire to make love to the most beautiful woman who ever lived, Helen of Troy. She appears and he dreams that she is his immortal 'other half', his *anima* – 'Sweet Helen, make me immortal with a kiss'. But when he does kiss her – 'her lips suck forth my soul, see where it flies'. The most famous lines of the play, 'was this the face that launched a thousand ships, and burn't the topless towers of Ilium', have already warned us that Helen is no light figure but the terrible Temptress, luring men on to war and destruction. And no sooner is their brief, empty love-making over (with a 'wise old man' coming on to pronounce Faustus's doom) than the hero is plunged firmly into the Nightmare Stage, when he realises that all is now irretrievably lost. He is about to pay the price of eternal punishment in hell.

### *Dr Jekyll and Mr Hyde*: the fantasy self

The extraordinary fame of the Jekyll and Hyde story rests on the unforgettably vivid way in which it exemplifies another general characteristic of the tragic hero, which is the split between the respectable, seemingly light *persona* he turns to the outer world and the hidden 'lower self' representing the deformed state of humanity when it is centred not on the Self but on the ego. All tragic heroes and heroines display some version of such a split, but in *Dr Jekyll and Mr Hyde* it becomes the central theme of the story. The point about Mr Hyde is that we are not told a great deal about his particular sins: he is merely portrayed as a monstrous, totally egocentric creature who knows no bounds, feels no scruples, whose sole motivation is the gratification of the ego in flouting all the values of the Self. Hyde is a personification of the 'ego self' or 'fantasy self', the essence of the untrammelled ego when it is split off from the Self and turned against the light.

Initially, so long as the respectable Dr Jekyll retains his power to switch back whenever he wishes into his outer or upper world *persona*, Hyde only emerges in secret, at night, hidden away from the world in the inferior realm. But the more Jekyll gives way to his fantasy self, again like any tragic hero, the more it begins to take over his whole personality, threatening to emerge into the outer world. As Jekyll enters the Frustration Stage, he makes a last desperate bid to escape from his fantasy self by putting the drug under lock and key and trying to remain in his Jekyll-self. But, as when Anna Karenina at a similar stage in the tragic cycle tries to give up Vronsky and return to her husband, the poison has already entered too deeply into Jekyll's system. He eventually weakens, succumbs to the drug for a last irrevocable time and returns to his Hyde-self. 'My devil had long been caged, he came out roaring.'

This leads to the central incident of the whole story, first described by a young maid who had been sitting one evening looking out of her window. 'Never had she felt more at peace with all men or thought more kindly of the world'. She sees coming down the street 'an aged and beautiful gentleman with white hair', whom we later learn is a venerable and respected MP Sir Danvers Carew. We see here, in the juxtaposition of the Innocent Young Girl and the Good Old Man, an embryonic constellation of the Wise Old Man and the Anima, twin symbols of the Self which is about to elude Jekyll forever. To her horror the girl sees the deformed creature Hyde emerge from the shadows and bludgeon the old man savagely to death. This murder is the final dark act. From then on Jekyll finds that he has completely lost control; he slips more and more helplessly into his Hyde-self until, at the moment when he realises that Hyde has taken over completely, he commits suicide.

### *Lolita*: The infantile *anima*

Humbert Humbert (with double echoes of 'humbug') is another version of the divided hero, split between the outwardly respectable *persona* of the scholarly academic and the hidden fantasy self driven by his erotic, daydreaming obsession with pre-pubescent little girls. Lolita is one of the most celebrated instances in literature of the 'infantile *anima*', an underdeveloped or in some way inadequate 'other half' whose presence always shows that the hero is not fully a man and has an unresolved tie to the Mother.

Sure enough, no sooner has Humbert set eyes on Lolita, the supreme goal of all his dark daydreams, than two things follow. Firstly, in pursuit of his obsession, he marries her mother, who turns out to be the Dark Mother, an empty, silly, suffocating woman who, thanks to Humbert's callousness, is quickly and violently got out of the way. He has only married her as a front to his real goal; and, secondly, now that the way is clear, we see that Lolita herself is not an innocent young girl but a raging Temptress. Like all characters driven by an obsession, Humbert is fundamentally weak. All dark characters in stories are defined by some sort of obsession. This always shows that the hero is not fully a man, in control of himself, that some component of his personality, ego-centred but driven by an autonomous will of his own, is leading him by the nose, ruling his life. Equally, however often it is gratified, no obsession can ever reach a satisfactory resolution, because it is at odds with the framework of reality and the Self. Humbert's obsession with Lolita cannot possibly come to a lasting resolution. He cannot marry her because she is under-age and his stepdaughter; and even if she did one day come of age, she would have lost her charms for him.

We thus see how the treacherous, bewitching, egotistical little Lolita represents in the most frustrating possible way all the possible aspects of the dark feminine. She is simultaneously:

(a) the 'infantile *anima*';
(b) the Temptress;
(c) in the background she is related to the Dark Mother;
(d) she is even that very rare figure in stories, the Dark Child, a child who promises not the hope of new life but only the frustration and denial of the forces of life.

As Humbert's obsession grows, so, heightening his frustration in a vicious spiral, does Lolita begin to slip away from him. She thus becomes in addition:

(e) the 'elusive *anima*'.

Finally the only other figure of importance in the story begins to come mysteriously into view, Quilty, the Dark Rival, in the grip of exactly the same obsession as Humbert himself. The shadowy, menacing Quilty is a projection of Humbert's own fantasy self. And when, eventually driven mad by jealous loathing, Humbert tracks down and kills his Rival in a long drawn out frenzy of cold violence, he is in effect killing himself. He is arrested and shortly afterwards dies in prison of a heart attack.

In these four stories we have seen the range of goals the weak, tragic hero is after in his state of fantasy:

(1) for Macbeth and Faustus the emphasis is on their desire for power over others: the dark inversion of the masculine urge to sovereignty;

(2) for Humbert, as it later becomes for Faustus, it is on the urge for erotic sexual union with the 'other half', a desire for possession: the dark inversion of the urge to union with the feminine which is the essence of selfless love;

(3) for Dr Jekyll, through his fantasy self Hyde, it is more generally characterised as an unbounded desire for egocentric gratification at the expense of everything and everyone in the world outside him. This is the dark inversion of the drive to realisation of the Self, which stands for the opposite, a state of conscious loving unity with all the world.

We shall now look again, briefly, at the other stories in Chapter 8, to see how each reflects in its own way these basic rules of the dark inversion.

*The Picture of Dorian Gray* shows us the split between the outward persona of a beautiful, completely egotistical young man who wishes never to grow older (i.e., never to grow up) and his hidden fantasy self, represented by the portrait. The cue for the weak, vain young hero to succumb to his fantasy is provided by the Tempter Lord Henry and, like his shadowy Mephistopheles, the hero thus becomes an amalgam of dark feminine and dark masculine, the complete opposite of a light, whole man.

As with Hyde, most of Gray's sins as he embarks on a life of sensual debauchery are only hinted at, although all, it is implied, involve a heartless and destructive flouting of loving human relationships. But three episodes in particular are described more explicitly. The first centres on the inadequate *anima*-figure of Sibyl Vane, the actress with whom Gray becomes infatuated. Gray loves her only as a fantasy figure, for the image she creates on stage in the role of various 'active' Shakespearean heroines, Rosalind, Portia, Beatrice; when she tries to show him the reality of herself he coldly rejects her, and she commits suicide. The second step in his downward course brought clearly into view is the attempt by his honourable older friend, Basil Hallward, a light Father-figure, to confront Gray with the horror of what he is becoming. Gray murders him in particularly gruesome and deliberate fashion. The last figure to emerge, on the edge of Gray's consciousness, is the 'light Rival', Jim Vane, the brother who truly loved Sibyl (although he has now turned dark and shadowy in his desire for vengeance). Vane is mysteriously shot at a country house, where Gray is basking flirtatiously in the admiration of an older woman, his hostess the Duchess of Monmouth, who alone seems fundamentally unworried by Gray's horrible misdeeds and cruel reputation. He has, in effect, killed off the *anima*, the Father and the light Alter-Ego: the only relationship he really enjoys, as the little boy hero who does not want to grow up, is with a doting, inwardly heartless, powerful older woman, the Dark Mother. Finally, in the Nightmare Stage of self-pity, Gray turns in rage on the hideously ravaged portrait and stabs it, like Humbert murdering his fantasy self. As with Humbert and Dr Jekyll, the hero's fantasy self is now all that is left of him, and in killing it Gray has killed himself.

The next three examples we looked at were all straightforward stories of weak and inadequate young heroes being destroyed by a Temptress.

In *Carmen* we initially see the hero as a soldier, happily in love with his inno-cent Micaela. But behind his soldierly exterior Don José is no real man, and she is only an inadequate little *anima*-figure. It does not take long for the real problem to be exposed when the imposing figure of the Temptress/Dark Mother Carmen sweeps the weak little hero off his feet into blind infatuation. Under her bewitch-ing spell Don José is soon cut off from the upper, masculine world, as he becomes a deserter from the army and sinks down into the treacherous, intoxicating infer-ior realm of taverns, gypsies and bandit gangs. Here there looms up the figure of Escamillo, the toreador, representing the masculinity which Don José never had, who supplants him as a Rival in the Temptress/Dark Mother's affections. Having for the last time rejected his infantile *anima*, Micaela, Don José sinks into the final stages of impotent nightmare, weak, self-pitying, totally alone. In a last desperate bid to free himself he lashes out and kills the Dark Mother who has destroyed him, but in doing so he has in effect killed himself.

In *Bonnie and Clyde*, the hero is a weak, sexually impotent young man lured by the heroine, a combination of Temptress and infantile *anima*, into his life of stealing, murder and guns as a substitute for his unrealised masculinity. The central episode of the story is when they capture a policeman, representing mas-culine authority, and dance round taunting him (like Faustus playing tricks on the 'Holy Father'). As frustration turns to nightmare, there is a brief, sickly-sentimental episode when they go for a picnic with Bonnie's mother – again the fantasy Mother-figure who will overlook all their naughty crimes and with whom they can dream of escaping back to the happy, irresponsible innocence of childhood where everything will be all right. But now the stern masculine world is closing in, as the police net tightens around them, representing the values of the Father against which they have been frozen in rebellion. Eventually they are betrayed by the Father-figure in their midst, the father of their accomplice C. W. Moss with whom they have taken refuge, and the police shoot them down.

The heroes of *Jules et Jim* are two feckless, charming, weak young men who can-not grow up, and who fall prey to the bewitching Temptress Catherine. Led on by her in the Dream Stage they like to imagine themselves as children, playing 'at the white house in the country', with the Dark Mother in Catherine concealed behind the facade of an 'elusive *anima*' who is always dancing on before them, always just out of reach. But slowly their world darkens – not least through the violent irruption of dark masculine values in the First World War – and they are gradually sucked down into nightmare, uncomprehending, never becoming manly or responsible or understanding anything. Jim makes a last pitiful attempt to break loose and to live a normal, grown-up life, with a wife and child – but the poison has entered too deep. Finally the dark *anima* drags him down into the whirlpool of destruction, leaving Jules all alone, staring still uncomprehendingly at their ashes.

In those two remarkably similar stories *Anna Karenina* and *Madame Bovary*, we see the same tragic pattern from the heroine's point of view. Each of these hero-ines is initially married to a man who is neither fully a man nor alive to the inner feminine. In each case, in the upper or outer world, the heroine is thus joined to an inadequate *animus*-figure, with the corollary that her own inner feminine is not brought alive and begins to turn dark. In each case the heroine then falls secretly for a fantasy *animus*-figure who seems to represent everything their husbands are not (the Dream Stage). Vronksy is seemingly both strong and sensitive. Emma's fantasy-*animus* divides into, firstly, the masculine but insensitive Rodolphe, then the unmasculine but sensitive Leon. In each case, under the spell of the fantasy-*animus*, the heroine first loses contact with the respectable upper world, representing the outward masculine value of social order (Frustration Stage) and then is drawn down into the inferior realm where she begins to lose her reason, her mental order (Nightmare Stage). Increasingly each is haunted by the nightmare vision of a horrible little deformed male creature – the peasant and the beggar – representing the true state of her inner *animus*. In each case as the heroine, having irrevocably lost touch with her own inner feminine, horribly destroys herself, the deformed *animus* – symbolising her 'fatal flaw' – looms up over her final conscious moments before she plunges into unconsciousness forever.

We next looked at two stories, *Antony and Cleopatra* and *Don Giovanni*, which in terms of the tragic 'fantasy cycle' begin in the Frustration Stage, when the hero's problem is at last completely obvious. In each of these stories, the root of the hero's problem is the same – his inability to relate maturely to the feminine – but it expresses itself in precisely opposite ways.

In Antony, the successful general, we return to the image of a hero who, in masculine terms, seems fully developed. But as a tough soldier, living one-sidedly by masculine values, he has never fully realised or integrated his inner feminine; and by the law which dictates that we eventually fall foul of the dark version of that which has not been realised, Antony has been pulled over by his meeting with Cleopatra onto the opposite, undeveloped side of his psyche. We meet Antony when the two poles pulling him apart are at last fully and painfully evident. He is torn between his masculine 'Roman self' and the soft, emasculating embraces of the Temptress, the Dark Queen surrounded by her women and eunuchs, ruling maternally over the 'inferior realm' of Egypt. In the upper Roman world, as the play begins, the hero's 'other half' is Octavia, his intended wife, the sister of his rival Octavius. But she is an inadequate *anima* because she is not feminine enough to draw Antony to her. This is not a marriage based on love but on the need to cement the social and political order (i.e., based on a masculine value). With her stern devotion to the male Roman virtues, Octavia is herself over-masculine – which is why Antony is drawn back to the soft, indulgent mother-world of Cleopatra. But once the die is cast, once he has irrevocably abandoned the inadequate Octavia and the masculine strength of Rome, we see Antony slipping more and more into the treacherous toils of the dark feminine, losing his soldierly masculine judgement and discipline, his capacity for firm leadership, his manly sovereignty both over himself and others, until finally he and the Dark Mother who has unmanned him are both destroyed.

Antony's problem is that, because he cannot fully realise his *anima*, he is drawn obsessively back to the Dark Mother. The story of Don Giovanni or Don Juan presents the most familiar paradigm in our culture of the hero who attempts to solve the same basic problem in the opposite way. Don Giovanni's compulsion is to find endless fantasy *anima*-figures who exist only in his own mind, because as soon as he has conquered them sexually and his ego is gratified, he sees the reality (like Dorian Gray confronted by the off-stage reality of Sibyl Vane) and his fantasy evaporates. As in *Antony and Cleopatra*, the story of Don Giovanni begins at the moment when the hero has been through the long Dream Stage of his adventures, when he seemed to be getting away with it, and when he is at last unexpectedly brought up against the heart of his problem, in a way which will decide once and for all whether he can turn back towards the light or is headed irrevocably for destruction.

The opera's opening scene shows Don Giovanni confronted by two figures, Father and Daughter: the honourable father-figure of the Commendatore, representing positive masculine authority; and Donna Anna, the pure and innocent *anima*. In each case his response is fatally negative. First he attempts to seize and possess the protesting *anima* by force. Then, when the father intervenes to protect her, the hero kills him. From then on we know that Don Giovanni is doomed. By the law of the 'unrealised value', he has killed off both the aspects of himself which he will never now realise. He will never become a mature, fully-developed man; he will never develop his inner feminine. He is a fatally immature man who can never grow up – and the rest of the story shows the inevitable disintegration that is the consequence.

By the Rule of Three he encounters three women in the story. Donna Anna, a straightforward, light *anima*-figure, he attempts to violate. Secondly he meets Donna Elvira, his rejected *anima*, who has turned in consequence into the dark feminine, the virago who is pursuing him across the world bent on vengeance. Thirdly there is the regression to fantasy-innocence, as he tries to seduce the pretty peasant girl Zerlina, a fetching little infantile *anima*. But increasingly the stern masculine world against which Don Giovanni is in rebellion, representing the manly values which he cannot make positive in himself, is closing in on him. Finally, in the graveyard, he is confronted by the statue of the Commendatore, the grim, cold, stone image of the Dark Father. Here we have travelled full circle from all those stories which begin by showing a little hero who is confronted by the Dark Father as the unrealised value of the fully-grown, strong man the hero will one day become. The Commendatore's statue represents the shadowy version of the mature man Don Giovanni has failed to become; and he is dragged down by his unrealised value to hell.

### The Devils

Finally, in *The Devils*, we saw a story which embodies all these principles and adds one more, to make our picture of the pattern behind Tragedy complete. Dostoyevsky's novel begins with the image of a Mother and a Father, both archetypally inadequate. Mrs Stavrogin, the rich powerful heiress, appears to be kindly and indulgent, but only so long as she gets her own way with all those who are dependent on her. In her shadow is the weak and pathetic old Mr Verkhovensky, her emasculated protegé, obsessively fantasising about his youth as a brave, rebellious liberal when he stood up against the masculine values of power and order represented by the Tsar and his government in St Petersburg. In other words, Mrs Stavrogin is the Dark Mother; Mr Verkhovensky is 'the boy hero who cannot grow up' as he decays into late middle age; and the story centres on the consequences for their two sons.

On one hand there is charming, enigmatic Nikolai Stavrogin, spoiled by his dominating mother, bereft of a father. He cannot grow up in one way: he is plagued by strange attacks of rebelliousness against the world of 'Father', as when he suddenly and inexplicably bites the ear of the town governor (like Faustus with the Pope). Worse, because he cannot become a true man and is still inwardly locked into his tie to Mother, he cannot properly realise his inner feminine – with the result that he first brutally violates the little infantile *anima*-figure of Matryosha, in such a way that she commits suicide, then marries the crippled Maria, representing his deformed *anima*, whose death will eventually precipitate the entire catastrophe in which the story ends.

On the other hand, locked into immaturity in another way, is Peter Verkhovensky. The dominant factor in shaping his personality is that he has not been given a proper model of strong, mature manhood by his weak, egocentric father. He has therefore become imprisoned in a kind of extreme parody of his father's rebellious liberalism – in the fantasy of taking part in some great collective movement which will rise up and violently overthrow the Czar, the government, the entire ruling framework of power and order, all the symbols of the world of 'Father'. But young Verkhovensky cannot see himself as the leader of this movement: that would require qualities of manly dominance which he does not possess. He sees himself as the 'brains' behind the movement, its organiser. He requires a front-man for his own lack of real masculinity; and this is the role in which he mentally casts the 'mother's boy' Stavrogin who, at least in his eyes, has the kind of confidence, charm and charismatic personality required.

There is another respect, however, in which Verkhovensky unconsciously compensates for his own individual lack of manhood. This is the way in which, as he conjures up in his fantasies that whole imaginary army of underdogs who are going to rise up with him to overthrow the world of 'Father', he projects his own ego into the collectivised ego of the group, 'the movement'.

One of the most important features of the emergence of the Self in stories is the way in which, as the light hero achieves his state of wholeness, we see the entire community redeemed and brought to wholeness around him. Verkhovensky represents here what, in real life, can become the most destructive form of dark inversion of all: where that drive to communal totality itself appears in a dark inferior form, hijacked into the service of a collectivised ego. As Verkhovensky infects his little group of followers with his revolutionary vision, so all their individual egos are merged and given a dark energy by a negative inversion of the power of the Self. They imagine – or Verkhovensky imagines for them – that by destroying all the existing corrupt social order, they are going to bring Russia in some distant future back to a glorious state of wholeness, even if this requires appalling bloodshed and the deaths of millions along the way. In *The Possessed* this collective fantasy based on the 'ego-Self confusion' is portrayed only in local terms and when it is unleashed, spreading chaos and anarchy through the town, it soon winds to a hideous catastrophe, leaving 'normality' to re-emerge. But in history this dark inversion of the power of the Self was not to remain localised in just one corner of Russia. It was to possess the whole country. It was Dostoyevsky's intuitive insight into the archetypal forces already at work beneath the surface of Russia's disintegrating society more than half a century before 1917 which gave his novel such immense prophetic power.

⁕⋆⁂⋆⁕

We have now seen how the psychological root of all tragedy, the 'fatal flaw' in all tragic heroes and heroines, is ultimately the same. They are stuck at a certain stage in the unfolding of the archetypal drama, in such a way that they cannot move forward to the point of Self-realisation. All of them are in some way held back by the dark feminine, so that they cannot grow up. They cannot develop either the masculine or the feminine aspects of themselves completely. Some, like Macbeth or Antony, may seem to be developed on the masculine side, although when the test comes, their dark feminine drags down and destroys even the masculine strength they possess. In almost every other example we have looked at, the hero is more obviously weak from the start: a boy hero who cannot grow up. And the more the dark feminine asserts its hold over them, the more they are drawn into conflict with the world of 'Father', the masculine values of strength, discipline, firmness and self-control which they cannot develop in themselves, and which would be essential for them to achieve the full state of manhood.

What lies at the heart of Tragedy therefore is always the same problem; and again it confirms the way in which the positive development of the masculine and feminine values must go together. A hero cannot be fully a man, fully strong, unless he is also selfless, inwardly feminine. So closely interdependent are the two that if he is not light in both respects, he must inevitably become dark in both respects.

We see this just as clearly in the stories centred on a heroine, *Anna Karenina* and *Madame Bovary*. Just as the dark hero is always inwardly possessed by the dark feminine, so these heroines appear to be victims of the dark masculine, the dark *animus*. But the very fact that each is inwardly possessed by the dark masculine turns her outwardly into the dark feminine. Both Anna and Emma are beautiful women whose personalities are taken over by a raging, wild, reckless egocentricity which gradually cuts them off from all the world. The true feminine values, feeling for others and the ability to see whole, cannot by definition be egocentric. Both these heroines are thus cut off by the dark masculine from contact with the feminine within them, until everything in them is dark.

⁕⋆⁂⋆⁕

The pattern behind all the examples we have looked at in this chapter is so engrained in the human psyche that stories have been endlessly repeating it for thousands of years. And, as we have seen, there is nothing inconsistent between

342

this pattern and those which shape the other kinds of story we have looked at, which show the hero or heroine finding their way at last to the state of wholeness which is the Self. The fundamental rules which govern each type of story are the same. In each case the cosmic values of the Self are always ultimately triumphant. The ego, in separating itself from the Self, must always end in frustration or destruction.

But does this imply that stories can *only* be told according to certain pre-ordained rules? Why should a storyteller only be able to imagine a story according to these 'rules'? Why should the 'values of the Self' always be triumphant? What happens if a storyteller, consciously or unconsciously, is not himself in harmony with those particular values, and sets out to shape a story in a quite different way?

We must now bring into account one of the most remarkable elements of all in the way the human imagination gives birth to stories. In the third part of this book we come at last to the extraordinary change which has come over story-telling in the Western world in the last two hundred years.

# PART THREE

# *Missing the Mark*

'I once made a note of a remark by Jonas Salk, the American biologist, to the effect that it is where life's normal structure is disturbed that we come to know the essential laws of the species.'  Kazimierz Brandys, *A Warsaw Diary*

## CHAPTER TWENTY-ONE

# The Ego Takes Over (I)

## *Enter the Dark Inversion*

'Where, I wondered with increasing dismay, had all the stories gone? Why this
decay of the great and meaningful orchestration of the story that had occurred
everywhere in the nineteenth and beginning of the twentieth centuries?'

Laurens van der Post, *Testament to the Bushman*

What about Spielberg's *Close Encounters of the Third Kind*? Or Beckett's *Waiting
for Godot*? Or Salinger's *Catcher in the Rye*? Or Orwell's *Nineteen Eighty-Four*? Or
Conan Doyle's Sherlock Holmes stories?

At this stage it would be easy to point to any number of individual stories
which, in terms of the archetypal structures we have been looking at, it might
seem difficult to place. But the vast majority of such stories date from the last
two hundred years. We must now, in the third part of the book, look at one of
the oddest and most revealing developments in the evolution of storytelling.

We cannot reach a proper understanding of how and why stories form as they
do in the human mind without appreciating the way in which, around two centuries ago, something very unusual began to happen to storytelling in the Western
world. In its early stages (although the first signs of what was to come had
appeared even earlier, way back into the eighteenth century), it was directly related
to that great convulsion in the European spirit which we associate with the rise of
Romanticism and with such historic events as the French Revolution and the rise
and fall of Napoleon. This psychic upheaval was reflected in philosophy, music,
painting and all the arts. But nowhere was its true nature revealed more tellingly
than in a profoundly significant change which began to emerge at that time in the
way writers conceived stories; and which has continued to have the most far-
reaching effect on the way stories have been told in our modern world ever since.

So far we have been looking at how stories present to us what amounts to a kind
of basic ground-map of human nature and behaviour, governed by an absolutely
consistent set of rules and values. These values, like the archetypal structures
which shape stories, are programmed into our unconscious in a way we cannot
modify or control. The essential message implicit in that programming is that
the central goal of any human life is to achieve the state of perfect balance which
we recognise as maturity; and how the central enemy in reaching that goal is
our capacity to be held back by the deforming and ultimately self-destructive
power of egocentricity.

For a storyteller to imagine a story which fully expresses this central theme implies that he or she is entirely in psychological harmony with those unconscious archetypal rules and structures which shape stories. Up to now we have been so focused on deciphering the meaning of this symbolic language that we have treated almost all the stories we have looked at in much the same way; as if all storytellers are similarly in tune with the basic archetypal process which gives rise to stories. But here and there, in exploring the structures of one plot after another, we have come across examples of stories which in some way did not realise the full purpose and content of their underlying archetypal pattern. For instance, we saw Rags to Riches stories where the hero was frustrated in trying to reach the full happy ending. We saw Voyage and Return stories which remained strangely empty: where the hero or heroine emerged from their journey into the unfamiliar world unchanged, having learned nothing. We saw comedies which were little more than burlesques of the archetypal message of the Comedy plot, playing with its outward form but without any deeper meaning.

What we are about to look at, in examining what has happened to storytelling over the past two centuries, is how, in countless modern stories, a fundamental shift has taken place in the psychological 'centre of gravity' from which they have been told. They have become detached from their underlying archetypal purpose. Instead of being fully integrated with the objective values embodied in the archetypal structure, such stories have taken on a fragmented, subjective character, becoming more like personal dreams or fantasies. Yet what is remarkable, as we shall see, is that in every case the story shows us precisely where this element of disintegration has crept in. And most remarkable of all is the way, even where a story falls short of realising its full archetypal form and purpose, the unconscious laws of storytelling still continue to dictate how it will unfold. It is this which makes the change which has come over storytelling in the modern world so crucial to a proper understanding of how our faculty for imagining stories works; and it is this which forms the theme of the next part of the book.

### *The Scarlet and the Black*: The hero as egotist

To see what happened we may begin by looking at four well-known novels dating from the first half of the nineteenth century.

One of the most famous of the novels produced by the rise of Romanticism was Stendhal's *The Scarlet and the Black* (1830). When we first meet the young hero, Julien Sorel, he is on the verge of adult life, living at home with his father and brothers in an obscure French provincial town, far from the distant, glamorous centre of France's national life, Paris. Working in the family timber yard, Sorel is scorned and even physically ill-treated by his practical, unimaginative family, not least for his reading of books.

It might seem the opening of one of those Rags to Riches folk tales which show the persecuted young hero marked out from the rest of his family by the fact that he is a good-hearted little dreamer. But we soon learn that Sorel is not like this at all. Far from being kindly, he is consumed by malevolence ('he hated both his brothers and his father'). He is hugely ambitious and obsessed by Napoleon. He originally dreamed of joining the army, but when a splendid new church is built in the town, with ornate marble columns, he realises that in these peaceful times the Church is a better road to power and position than soldiering. 'All at once Julien stopped talking about Napoleon. He announced his plan of becoming a priest.' And immediately he is revelling in 'dreams of one day being introduced to beautiful Parisian women, whose attention he would manage to attract by some remarkable feat or other'. All his ambitions are centred on distant Paris, recalling the way in which the far-off city so often appears in stories, drawing the hero towards it as a symbol of the Self.

Already, in the early pages, we have seen how Sorel's fantasies centre round those three familiar aspects of the central goal – winning power and position, union with the opposite sex and the idea of ultimate 'Self-realisation' – but only seen through the dark, inverting glass of his all-consuming egotism. We also note that, unlike the fairy-tale hero who has usually lost a father, Sorel is without a mother. There is no feminine influence in his life at all.

Nevertheless, like some fairy-tale hero who is equipped with 'charms' or 'magic weapons' to enable him to escape any danger, Sorel is also given two attributes which enable him to triumph in any social test: the first is his striking good looks, the second his phenomenal memory, which allows him to learn whole books by heart with ease.

His story unfolds, like so many, through three main stages. The first begins when he learns by heart the Latin New Testament and a book on the Papacy ('he believed one as little as the other'). Armed with this trick, he takes his first step into the world outside his home by becoming tutor to the children of the mayor of the town, M. Renal. He at once wins the admiration of all by reciting chunks of the New Testament, a trick he shortly repeats at a dinner of local notables. He also, with his 'almost girlish good looks', wins the heart of the mayor's wife Mme Renal, and they begin an affair.

An affair with a married woman, an older woman, or in this case both, is always a danger sign in a story. It invariably shows us that the hero is caught in a tie to 'Mother', in a state of arrested inner development: and in Sorel's case it echoes the fact that he has no real 'Mother' in the story at all. Mme Renal fills this gap. But of course their affair cannot lead to any 'happy ending', and when it begins to attract embarrassing attention, Sorel heartlessly throws her over.

He now moves onto the second stage of his climb up the social ladder, as he leaves town for a seminary in the provincial capital, Besancon. 'So here's this hell on earth from which I'll never be able to get out' is Sorel's greeting to the seminary: 'according to the rules of conduct he had drawn up for himself, he looked on his three hundred and twenty fellow students as enemies'. The young man is now more egocentric and heartless than ever, seeing his contemporaries only in terms of rivalry and domination. Eventually Sorel wangles an invitation to dinner with the bishop, a worldly prince of the Church, visiting from Paris. Inevitably he wheels on his party trick, by reciting lengthy passages from Horace. The bishop is impressed, and shortly afterwards Sorel obtains an opening beyond his wildest dreams, to travel to Paris to become secretary to 'the most powerful man in France', the fabulously rich Marquis de la Mole.

The third stage begins with the gauche young provincial arriving in Paris, and making one or two silly social gaffes amid his magnificent new surroundings. But naturally he soon redeems himself by impressing everyone at dinner with a recital of Horace. He has already been struck by the beauty of the daughter of the house, Mathilde, 'a young woman with the palest golden hair and a shapely figure'. The Marquis, as a kindly 'Father', entrusts him with ever more important and confidential business. He is admitted to the ranks of the most fashionable young men in Paris (there are even whispers that he is 'the natural son of a duke'). Above all, he wins the adoration of Mathilde who, needless to say, has herself now become 'the most admired young woman in Paris'. But the manner in which Sorel wins her love is portrayed only in terms of egocentric domination and subjection: 'you are my master', she tells him, 'reign over me forever, punish your slave severely whenever she seeks to rebel'. She becomes pregnant and the couple decide to elope; but the Marquis relents and agrees to settle on them a huge income. It seems all is set for a sickly and pasteboard 'happy ending', with Sorel united to his 'infantile *anima*' and destined to 'succeed to the kingdom' as the chosen heir to the Marquis's empire. Then suddenly, out of Sorel's past, disaster strikes. Mme Renal, his discarded mistress, writes a letter to the Marquis, blackening Sorel's character unmercifully. Enraged and frustrated, Sorel returns to his home town and attempts to shoot the vengeful 'Dark Mother', Mme Renal, in church. Inevitably he is arrested and sent to the guillotine. The story ends with an extraordinary funeral ceremony, celebrated by 20 priests in a cave high up in the mountains, 'lit by countless candles'. A sorrowing Mathilde buries Sorel's severed head. Three days later Mme Renal dies of grief.

The first thing which may strike us about this story is the extent to which, despite its ending, it is not like a conventional Tragedy. In its outward form it is much more like a Rags to Riches story which only switches abruptly to Tragedy in its closing scenes. Right from the start, Sorel is thoroughly ego-centred. He does not show any of the qualities necessary to bring the hero to a happy ending. He is a completely two-dimensional character, defined almost solely by his ruthless ambition. The only reason we are ever shown for his success is the mechanical party trick of his memory, which is wheeled on again and again to manoeuvre him up every step of the ladder (highly implausibly, since within a very short time his fellow dinner-party guests would surely have found these vainglorious recitals infinitely wearisome). Not for a moment is there any sign of that gradual inner transformation which marks out a proper Rags to Riches hero. Yet equally we do not see him going through the dark inner transformation of a truly tragic figure either. For nine-tenths of the story we see this cardboard creation going through all the outward motions of a successful climb from Rags to Riches: until suddenly the whole thing falls apart and, like Icarus, he plunges to destruction.

What we may then also observe is the remarkable fact that Stendhal himself did not see his hero in this dark and negative fashion at all. He took the germ of his story from the court reports of a celebrated real-life tragedy in the France of the 1820s. A humble blacksmith's son had left home to become tutor to a wealthy middle-class family, and had gone on to a seminary to become a priest.

His previous employer's wife had then written a vindictive letter to the head of the seminary, as a result of which he had been expelled. He tried to take his revenge by shooting her at Mass, and had been sent to the guillotine. Many people at the time, including Stendhal, saw the young man as the unfortunate victim of social hypocrisy and a rigid class system, driven into the position of an outcast only because of his lowly social origins.

Far from seeing his hero as a monster of egotism, in fact, Stendhal viewed him with the utmost sympathy. He saw him as the new, post-Napoleonic hero of humble birth, defying an oppressive class structure to battle his way upwards, in a world in which there were only the strong and the weak, and in which everyone was, fundamentally, equally egotistical. A fervent admirer of Napoleon, Stendhal did not see egotism in itself as anything to be ashamed of. He proudly called one of his volumes of autobiography *Souvenirs d'Egotisme*. He admiringly hailed Chateaubriand as '*le roi des egotistes*'. And when he came to create his favourite hero, Sorel, he told people 'Julien is myself'. Nor did this identification apply only to Sorel's outward social ambitions. Consciously or unconsciously, there was also a close correspondence between Sorel and his creator in terms of their inner state, as expressed in their attitudes to the opposite sex. Stendhal fantasised endlessly about his 'conquests' of women, in a way which is reflected in Sorel's sado-masochistic 'conquest' and humiliation of Mathilde. But in real life, his love affairs were usually short-lived and embarrassing, and the key to his inadequacy was reflected in his saying that he felt towards his mother, who had died when he was only a boy, 'like a lover'.

In all these respects, *The Scarlet and the Black* represented something almost entirely new in storytelling. Whereas earlier storytellers down the ages had imagined their stories in accordance with the values of the Self, here was an author quite consciously creating a hero to defy those values. Sorel was a projection of Stendhal's own egocentricity, as he identified with his hero's rivalry with all the world, and with his effortless climb up the social and sexual ladder.

Yet in the end this rise from humble obscurity to social success turns inexorably to tragedy, just as it had done in the real life version which originally drew Stendhal as the inspiration for his novel. And it does so precisely in accordance with those underlying rules which ultimately dictate how any story shall unfold. Like any other storyteller, he followed the inner logic of the story, as it developed in his imagination: with the result that, at the very moment when, on the conscious 'upper level' of the story the hero seems finally within reach of his goal, of union with the pasteboard infantile *anima*-figure, and succession to the 'kingdom' of great wealth and position, out from the 'inferior realm' emerges the vengeful 'Dark Mother' to snatch it all away. At the end we see the extraordinary ceremony of the 20 priests blessing Sorel's corpse in the candelit cave, the 'womb unconscious' from which he could never escape. Mathilde is left with the severed head, the only part of Sorel which the *anima* could ever get hold hold of, his head or imagination. Only when he is buried does the 'Dark Mother', Mme Renal, relinquish her fatal grip. Psychologically, and to this extent unconsciously, it was the story of the weak, vain, 'mother-fixated' Stendhal himself.

351

In other words, we see two very significant things having taken place in this story. The first is that a storyteller, for reasons directly reflecting his own psychology, has himself become subject to what we saw earlier as 'the dark inversion', siding with his egocentric hero against the values of the Self. His story has become an ego-centred fantasy, akin to a prolonged daydream. But the second is that we still see the hero, by those implacable rules, eventually bringing about his own destruction. The values of the Self remain triumphant, because by the logic of that unconscious power in the human mind which governs the shaping of stories, they cannot be successfully defied. If an author sets out to tell his story round a dark, egocentric hero, there is no way the plot can unfold to a fully-resolved happy ending. Sooner or later those hidden rules will come into play to ensure that the hero cannot realise his goal.

## Balzac: The storyteller as egotist

Four years after Stendhal's book appeared, Balzac published the first of his series of novels *La Comedie Humaine*, portraying life in contemporary France,

*Père Goriot* (1834) focuses on the rise to fame and fortune of a poor law student, Eugene de Rastignac. Just as in *The Scarlet and the Black*, the story is in some ways reminiscent of a Rags to Riches fairy tale. The ambitious young hero arrives from the provinces in Paris, like Dick Whittington arriving in London, without a penny to his name. The only card in his hand is his distant kinship to 'one of the queens of fashionable Paris', the immensely grand Vicomtesse de Beauseant. This powerful lady becomes in effect de Rastignac's 'fairy godmother', and determines to use her influence to launch him on a dazzling social career. She first arranges for him to meet a certain rich Countess. But this is no fairy tale 'Princess' whom it is intended de Rastignac should marry. The Countess is married already. The aim is simply that he should win social advancement by becoming her lover. When this proposed affair comes to nothing, thanks to a social gaffe by de Rastignac, the 'fairy godmother' propels him in the direction of the Countess's sister, an equally rich Baroness. This time the ruse is more successful, not least because de Rastignac has discovered the guilty secret of both the sisters' wealth. They are being privily supported by their old father Goriot, a little retired vermicelli manufacturer, who just happens to live in de Rastignac's humble lodgings; and whom de Rastignac just happens one day to see through the keyhole, melting down the last of the family silver (like some fairy-tale gnome in the forest) to provide his daughters with more funds. Goriot and the Baroness combine to set up de Rastignac in a lavish apartment. Having moved in,

> 'Eugene, completely overcome, lay back on the sofa, unable to utter a word or make sense yet of the way in which the magic wand had been waved yet again for this final transformation scene.'

But, again, the fairy-tale happy ending is not to be. Suddenly disaster strikes. The financial affairs of both sisters crash in ruins. Old Goriot himself dies. His heartless, snobbish daughters do not even deign to come to his funeral. De

Rastignac, his promised fortune snatched away from him, climbs the hill above Paris, looks down contemptuously on 'the splendid world he had wished to gain' and says, in bitter defiance, 'It's war between us now'.

Despite its explicit echoes of a Rags to Riches fairy tale, this bleak, two-dimensional story could scarcely be further from the timeless, almost metaphysical realm of the folk tale, where riches, 'Princesses' and transformation scenes stand for something altogether more symbolic and psychologically profound than just the amassing of hard cash and a succession of sexual conquests. As de Rastignac climbs his way ruthlessly up the social ladder, there are no signs of any inner transformation, any development towards wholeness and maturity: merely the acquisition of new and sharper weapons in the war of social self-aggrandisement, and the general hardening of a once relatively innocent heart. What we again see here is an author defying the archetypal rules by trying to imagine a wholly egocentric, pasteboard hero going through the pattern of an ascent from Rags to Riches without any of the essential qualities which could allow him to reach a successful resolution: with the result that the story ends on that chilling final image when de Rastignac issues his angry challenge to the 'hostile' city of Paris, symbolising the totality of the Self. In bidding defiance to the city, Balzac's hero is merely reflecting that most ominous psychic split of all: where, far from the conscious ego ending up in harmony with the deeper 'centre', the two are left seemingly irretrievably at odds.

As with Stendhal in *The Scarlet and the Black*, Balzac was drawn to the general theme of the Rags to Riches plot, but in way which had become completely detached from its original deeper archetypal purpose. The traditional Rags to Riches story, as we have seen it in folklore, in *Aladdin*, in *Jane Eyre*, in *David Copperfield*, was the expression of a pattern coded into the human unconscious which, when made conscious in the form of a story, gives us an idealised symbolic picture of a human being travelling the full road of psychological development, from immaturity to integrated maturity.

What was happening in these 'Romantic' versions of the Rags to Riches theme was that this pattern was being appropriated by the storyteller's ego. Instead of being held internally, as an expression of inward psychic events, it was being projected onto the outside world, to express the desire of the ego for external gratification. The Rags to Riches story was thus becoming not so much a reflection of the hero or heroine's inner growth towards eventual integration, but simply the vehicle for ego-centred fantasies or daydreams. As Somerset Maugham said of Balzac, whom he admired as the only novelist to whom he could 'without hesitation ascribe genius':

> 'from the beginning his aim had been to live in splendour, to have a fine house with a host of servants, carriages and horses, a string of mistresses and a rich wife.'

When, in *Père Goriot* and later novels, Balzac fondly imagines his heroes rising ever more gloriously in Parisian society, it was precisely that aim which, in his fantasy, he was pursuing: by dreaming, through the social triumphs of de Rastignac and others, his succession of 'fantasy selves', of winning all those social and sexual gratifications his ego desired.

353

But for all the significance of this shift of the source in the psyche from which stories were told, it did not mean that the old archetypal forms would now just fade away. Indeed the human mind is so constituted that no storyteller can escape from the archetypes, however hard he or she may try. They are still the basic coding of the human psyche, the only forms around which stories can be told. They can no more be escaped from than storytellers can escape from the greatest archetype of all, the hidden totality of the Self, the ultimate form which embraces all the others. However far we try, through the ego, to bury, ignore or defy the Self, it cannot be cheated in its remorseless, objective insistence on the deepest, unchanging truths about the way we and the world work (as opposed to the ways in which, through the wishful thinking of the ego, we might like it to work).

If the Self is denied, it will always try, in some form or other, to pass back to the ego the message as to where the disorder has arisen and how it can be rectified; as we see demonstrated nowhere more vividly than in stories. And for an illustration of this one needs look no further than to the curious fate of the Rags to Riches story, once this profound shift in the moral and psychological centre of story-telling had begun to take place. In the dawn of the Romantic era, as storytellers began to pass into the grip of the 'dark inversion', so they found it increasingly difficult to write stories with happy, all-reconciling endings. But this was not only reflected in stories inspired by the Rags to Riches theme. It began to appear in stories of all kinds.

### Frankenstein: The monster as hero

We now look at what happened when the same dark inversion took over the archetypal theme of the Overcoming the Monster plot.

Some years earlier, in the summer of 1816, one of the most remarkable episodes in the history of storytelling had taken place on the shores of Lake Geneva. It resulted from the first meeting between the two most rebellious spirits of English Romanticism: Percy Bysshe Shelley, accompanied by his mistress Mary Godwin and her half-sister Claire, and Lord Byron, accompanied by his young hanger-on Dr William Polidori. Over a wet fortnight at the end of June, this oddly assorted group of young people, already riven by all kinds of psychic stress, talked them-selves, with the aid of a German book of horror stories, *Fantasmagoria*, into a state of collective near-hysteria. It was agreed that each of them should produce a ghost story. Mary Godwin had a hideous dream, coloured by some of the topics they had all been discussing, like the bringing of corpses back to life. And she finally produced, from the inspiration of her nightmare, a book not only more widely known today than any single work by either of the two famous poets themselves, but in psychological terms one of the most significant of all the products of the European Romantic movement.

The story of *Frankenstein: A Modern Prometheus* tells how its hero had been born into a respectable, happy family in Geneva. The main figures in his life had been his kindly father; his loving mother; his little brother William; his close boyhood friend Clerval; and his cousin Elizabeth, beautiful and adored; 'a creature who seemed to shed radiance from her looks, and whose form and motion were

lighter than the chamois of the hills'; and whom, as they grew up, it was assumed
Frankenstein would one day marry. Here we see the hero happily surrounded with
light (albeit entirely two-dimensional) characters: Father, Mother, Child, faithful
Alter-Ego, and finally, the *anima*.

The action of the tale begins when Frankenstein is about to go out into the world,
as a young student at the University of Ingoldstadt. On the eve of his departure,
as an omen, his mother and Elizabeth, the two representatives of the feminine in
his life, both fall desperately ill. His mother dies, but Elizabeth eventually recovers.
At the university he falls under the spell of various occult treatises, and becomes
possessed by a Faust-like longing to 'penetrate the secrets of nature'. 'The raising
of ghosts or devils was a promise liberally afforded by my favourite authors, the
fulfilment of which I most eagerly sought'. Having found his 'Focus', the hero shuts
himself away for months during a glorious summer, to work on his shadowy task:
'who shall conceive the horrors of my secret toil, as I dabbled among the unhal-
lowed damps of the grave or tortured the living animal to animate the lifeless clay'.
At last, from the remains of corpses stolen from charnel houses in the hours of
darkness, he completes his 'creation', in the hideously deformed shape of a man.
Appalled by what he has done, he instantly takes refuge in unconsciousness by
falling asleep. But this is:

> 'disturbed by the wildest dreams. I thought I saw Elizabeth, in the bloom of health,
> walking in the streets of Ingoldstadt. Delighted and surprised, I embraced her, but as I
> imprinted the first kiss on her lips, they became livid with the hue of death; her features
> appeared to change, and I thought that I held the corpse of my dead mother in my
> arms; a shroud enveloped her form, and I saw the grave worms crawling in the folds of
> the flannel.'

He wakes from this nightmare to see 'the miserable monster whom I had created'
standing by the bed, grinning, trying to utter inarticulate sounds and stretching
out a hand in friendship. Frankenstein is horrified, rushes out into the street and,
when he returns next morning, the monster is gone.

Here is an opening unlike any before it in the history of storytelling. We see
the hero first in a happy, innocent 'upper world', surrounded by his light family;
then isolating himself as he plunges down into the dark 'inferior realm' where
he himself brings to birth a monster. At the moment where the monster is about
to come to life, his nightmare betrays the true nature of what is happening, as
he sees his *anima* Elizabeth, his hope of future wholeness and life, dissolving into
the horror of the 'Dark Mother', with whom he is locked in a deathly embrace. But
then something even more revealing happens. When he first sees the monster, it
smiles and puts out a friendly hand to him. Here is a complete inversion of
the usual relationship between hero and monster: here it is the hero who has
become dark and isolated, in his dream of winning power and occult knowledge;
while the monster, wishing only for friendship and fellow-feeling, represents, in
his hideous, inferior form, the Self. Frankenstein rejects the monster, which
disappears. The next day there unexpectedly appears in Ingoldstadt his cheerful
boyhood friend Clerval, full of news of Frankenstein's home and family, a picture

of kindly normality: he now represents the hero's innocent 'light Alter-Ego', the Self the hero might have been had he not been tempted into his dark and secret course.

Outwardly Frankenstein's life, under the ministrations of Clerval, returns to normal. All seems well. But beneath the surface, he has made his fatal surrender to the powers of darkness. From that first crucial act of rejection of the monster's friendly overture, everything else in his life is to follow. Unknown to Frankenstein, the monster has retired secretly into the mountains, where by eavesdropping on peasants he first learns how to speak, then manages to read the great books of mankind. He is determined to become a full, proper human being, imbued with the most noble and benevolent feelings towards all mankind. But when he finally dares to confront some human beings, they recoil from him in revulsion. Crushed by this second act of rejection, the monster is now fired with terrible feelings of vengeance against his creator. He comes down from the mountains, tracks down Frankenstein's little brother, William, and kills him. Frankenstein, fully aware of who must have committed the murder, heartlessly watches while the boy's loving nursemaid is tried and executed for the crime. The Child and the Innocent Young Girl have become the first victims.

Frankenstein then has a long interview with the monster, who explains that his only desire is to live virtuously without harming anyone. He asks his creator to fashion a female 'monster' as a companion for him, with whom he can disappear to some remote region of the world and never trouble Frankenstein again. The hero agrees, and retires to a cottage in the Orkneys where he sets to work. He has almost completed the monster's 'other half' when he sees the monster peering in at him through a window. At the thought of his two creations getting together to reproduce, and to people the world with monsters, he panics and destroys his handiwork.

The monster is heartbroken, and by the Rule of Three this third rejection, Frankenstein's final dark act, seals the hero's fate. First the monster murders Clerval, the light Alter-Ego. Then, when Frankenstein has married his beautiful, calm, loving Elizabeth, the monster murders her too, on their wedding night. Finally Frankenstein's father dies of grief. The hero has now been responsible, through his shadow, for the deaths of the Child, the Innocent Young Girl, the Alter-Ego, the Good Old Man/Father and, above all, his own 'other half', his *anima*. All the light aspects of himself have been killed off. All along, Frankenstein had been the only truly dark figure in the story: although, like Dorian Gray's portrait, the monster has become more and more evil as a reflection of the ever greater darkness engulfing the hero. Like Gray, Frankenstein at last in desperation determines to free himself from his hated shadow forever. In a nightmare chase, he pursues the monster half across the world, up into the frozen Arctic wastes – but there it is the monster which turns on him and destroys him, before vanishing forever across the ice.

The most obvious thing which may strike us about this nightmarish tale is how it takes the familiar, age-old pattern of the Overcoming the Monster plot and turns it in every conceivable way upside down. It begins with a hero who is dark and a monster who is light; and ends with the hero being overcome by the monster, rather than the other way around. The question which then arises is: how did such an extraordinarily dark, inverted story come into the mind of a young girl who had never written anything before in her life? A good deal of the answer, as various commentators have observed, lies in the personality of the man who was by far the most dominating presence in Mary Godwin's life, Shelley himself.

Not only did a great many of the scenes and details in *Frankenstein* spring directly from Mary's life with Shelley since they had first eloped together two years earlier. He himself took a profound interest in the story, making clear, when he reviewed it anonymously after its publication in 1817, how much he identified with the monster, as a hapless victim of circumstances whose wish only to live benevolently and at one with mankind had so continually been thwarted by persecution and rejection. 'Too often in society', as Shelley put it, such a cruel fate is meted out to 'those who are best qualified to be its benefactors and its ornaments'.

Certainly by this time in his life Shelley had found himself violently at odds with society in every possible way. On the masculine side of his personality, there had been the terrible battles with his father, the stiff, conventional baronet, and with authority-figures of every kind, from those running his university to government agents. With his dreams of revolution, overthrowing the established order, and his horror at the notion of a cruel, patriarchal God, Shelley seemed at war with the world of 'Father' in all its aspects. But in terms of his relations with the feminine, his chaotic love-life showed him equally at sea. Having eloped with his first wife Harriet, and then found it necessary to be involved emotionally with two women at the same time, he cast them both off and repeated the pattern, by eloping with Mary herself and her half-sister Claire (although by the time the story was written Claire was also flinging herself at Byron, by whom she immediately became pregnant).

Shelley may have consciously identified himself with the poor, rejected, would-be benevolent monster in *Frankenstein*: but from the outside it seems that he was much more like Frankenstein himself, possessed by a demonic, blind egotism which, as the years went by, plunged his own life and that of those around him ever further into chaos and nightmare. Only a few months after the episode in Switzerland, the deaths began: with the suicides, first of Mary's sister Fanny, with whom Shelley had had a brief affair, then of his abandoned and distracted wife Harriet. Two years later his little son by Mary, their beloved William, died at the age of four. Other deaths of those close to him followed, in an almost uncanny echo of the deaths of everyone around Frankenstein in the story: until finally came that fateful summer in Italy in 1821.

After weeks of manic-depression, shot through with fearful death-laden dreams, thoughts of suicide (and Mary's miscarriage of another child), Shelley recklessly took out his boat, the *Don Juan*, into the teeth of a violent Mediterranean storm, under full sail. The 'Modern Prometheus', the 'boy hero who could never grow up', had defiantly invited his own destruction, along with that of his two companions. Reading Richard Holmes's comprehensive account of those last years and weeks of his life in *Shelley: The Pursuit*, one may reflect that few people in history can have turned themselves into their own 'monster' more poignantly, more dramatically and more unwittingly than Shelley himself. In this sense his wife's nightmare story in 1816 was like a horrendous premonition of what was already happening to the man she loved; and of how their life together would, only five years later, come to its awful climax.

### *Moby Dick*: **The quest to slay the Self**

> 'When, on the last day, they confront each other, which is the Monster? Moby Dick in his "gentle joyousness", his "mighty mildness of repose", or Ahab screaming his mad defiance? In complete contempt of the three-thousand-year-old pattern of myth, Melville permits the dragon-slayer to be slain, the dragon to escape alive; but it is hard to tell whether he really stands the legend on its head, allows evil to survive and heroism to perish. Only Ahab believes that the whale represents evil, and Ahab is both crazy and damned ... it is Ahab who must die, precisely because he has sought the death of the Other ...'.
>
> Leslie Fiedler, *Love and Death in the American Novel*

Hermann Melville's *Moby Dick: or The White Whale* (1851) is a much weightier work of literature than any of the novels we have looked at previously in this chapter, which is what helps to make it one of the darkest stories ever written.

'Call me Ishmael'. The explosive opening line sets the book's dark tone by invoking the archetypical outcast from *Genesis* (XVI), 'whose hand is against every man, and every man's hand is against him'. But it eventually becomes apparent that the narrator Ishmael is not so much the story's central figure as just a curiously passive observer. A rootless drifter through the cities of East Coast America, he has resolved to escape the depressing aimlessness of his existence by signing on for a long whaling voyage across the oceans of the world. In this respect, the book begins like a Voyage and Return story: an incomplete, inadequate hero is laying himself open to some shattering, life-transforming experience.

The story really divides into two quite separate parts. The first, unfolding through the opening chapters, takes place on land, when Ishmael travels up to New England to find a whaling ship. It is dominated by his encounter with Queequeg, the dark-skinned tattooed South Sea islander with his phallic idol and his collection of shrunken human heads. When the fearsome 'savage' first bursts in at night to share his bed, in the inn owned by a man called Coffin, Ishmael is terrified. But by the time they have talked at length, and spent the night with 'Queequeg's arm thrown over me in the most loving and affectionate manner' so 'you had almost thought I had been his wife', they are a 'cosy, loving pair'.

In this bizarre opening we may see an echo of the oldest story in the world, the *Epic of Gilgamesh*, where the hero is not psychologically ready for his journey across the world to slay the monstrous Humbaba until he has met, fought with and finally learned to love the shadowy other half who is to be his companion on the journey: the 'wild man' Enkidu, who has lived among the animals in a state of nature. We also see an instance of that alliance between a white hero and a black or Indian companion which Leslie Fiedler identified as such a recurring theme in American literature (as in the friendship between Huckleberry Finn and the runaway black slave Jim). This duality almost invariably represents the coming together of two halves to make a potential whole. The 'civilised' white man, separated from nature, represents 'ego-consciousness', with all its limitations; his dark-skinned companion, closer to nature and the world of instinct, embodying the 'feminine' values of feeling and intuition, represents the 'dark unconscious' from which the hero has become split off. Both are necessary to achieve the whole. But in *Moby Dick* the new partnership of Ishmael and Queequeg is not a prelude to the process of Ishmael's maturing to eventual Self-realisation, which might have provided the central theme of the story. For at the moment where they sign on as crew-members of the *Pequod*, Ishmael and Queequeg more or less fade into the background. This is where the the real theme of the story begins to take over.

Few novels are more overtly shot through with the 'rule of three' than *Moby Dick*, from the moment Ishmael chooses the three-masted *Pequod*, the third of 'three ships up for three-year's voyages'. The ship has three white men as mates, each with his 'dusky' harpooner: Tashtego the North American Indian, Dagoo the black American, Queequeg the Polynesian. The crew is so cosmopolitan, representing all the races of the world, that it is a microcosm of humanity. But its central figure is the one-legged, 'monomaniac' Tyrant, Captain Ahab. The overwhelming power of his dark obsession, from the moment when, with 'three heavy-hearted cheers' from its crew, the ship 'blindly plunged like fate into the lone Atlantic', dominates the rest of the story.

We soon learn that the real shaping plot of the book is a combination of a Quest and Overcoming the Monster. When Ahab assembles his crew and nails to the mainmast a Spanish gold piece, he unfolds the real purpose of their journey: to track down and take vengeance on the 'accursed white whale' which years before had stove in three of Ahab's whaleboats and 'reaped away' his leg 'as a mower a blade of grass in the field'. The gold is to be the prize for he who first sights their goal. And when Ahab first tells them of Moby Dick, we are left in no doubt that this 'treacherous', hideously deformed creature, with its massive humped back, its misshapen jaw, three holes in its starboard fluke, is an archetypal monster. Calling up rum for the crew, Ahab summons the three mates with their harpooners and, in a parody of a religious ceremony, adjures them to a solemn oath:

> 'now three to three ye stand. Commend the murderous chalices ... drink and swear, ye men that man the deathful whaleboat's bow – Death to Moby Dick! God hunt us all if we do not hunt Moby Dick to his death!'

We gradually learn that this 'murderous monster against whom I and all the others had take our oaths of violence and revenge' is far more than any mortal creature. Not only is it 'a Sperm Whale of uncommon magnitude and malignity', which has caused injury or death to countless mariners in almost every part of the seven seas; it has inspired such superstitious dread that there was an:

359

'unearthly conceit that Moby Dick was ubiquitous; that he had actually been encountered in opposite latitudes at one and the same instant of time.'

Such an inversion of normality does this phantasmagoric creature represent that even its colour is a clue to its treacherous nature. As Ishmael recalls, 'it was the whiteness of the whale that above all things appalled me'; before holding forth on how the colour white, commonly associated with innocence, purity and light, can often be a mask to what is cruel, sinister and dark.

From here on, the narrative alternates between two themes in counterpoint. On the 'upper level' we follow the human drama of what is happening on the *Pequod*, as it continues across the ocean wastes in search of their elusive goal, driven by the demonic obsession of its captain; a journey fraught with every kind of omen and foreboding, like the moment when, as the boats are launched to chase their first whale, we see Ahab suddenly 'surrounded by five dusky phantoms that seemed fresh formed out of air'. These are the mysterious additional crew he has smuggled on board to man his own whaleboat, led by the strangely sinister Fedallah, 'tall and swart', with 'one white tooth evilly protruding' from his 'steel-like lips'.

But on a second 'below the line' level we gradually learn more about whales, these wondrous, mysterious creatures of the deeps inhabiting the 'inferior realm' below the surface, to whose death and destruction the whale hunters devote their lives. As we do so, the picture we are being given of whales subtly changes.

A highlight of the book, for instance, is the time when the crew find themselves caught up in and surrounded by a vast becalmed armada of whales, covering several square miles. On the outer rim, where they lower the whaleboats, the monsters are threshing about in panic and violent commotion. But when Queequeg harpoons a whale, it draws his and Ishmael's boat 'into the innermost heart of the shoal, as if from some mountain torrent we had slid into a serene valley lake'.

Here, in an 'enchanted calm', they have an almost mystical vision, as they see the mother whales and their young calves coming up so close to the boat that Queequeg is able to 'pat their foreheads'.

'But far beneath this wondrous world upon the surface, another and still stranger world met our eyes as we gazed over the side. For, suspended in those watery vaults, floated the forms of the nursing mothers of the whales, and those that by their enormous girth seemed shortly to become mothers.'

As they watch in amazement at these mothers 'quietly eying us', while their offspring gambolled around in the translucent waters,

'some of the subtlest secrets of the seas seemed divulged to us in this enchanted pond. We saw young Leviathan amours in the deep. And thus, though surrounded by circle upon circle of consternations and affrights, did these inscrutable creatures at the centre freely and fearlessly indulge in all peaceful concernments, yes, serenely revelled in dalliance and delight.'

It is a vision of peace, joy and innocence, all the more shocking because it is an almost unique glimpse of the world of the soft, loving feminine in this otherwise hard, dark, one-sidedly masculine story. So relentless is the masculine colouring of the book that it contains almost no female characters at all (apart from a busy-bodying 'Quaker woman' who tries to provide homely necessaries when they are still in port). Even the masculine-feminine balance in human relationships has to be squeezed into a solely masculine straitjacket, as in the almost overtly homo-sexual companionship between Ishmael and Queequeg, when they sleep in each other's arms like a 'cosy, loving' married couple. Only when we catch a glimpse of the mother whales and their offspring do we see the 'feminine' presented openly and unambiguously, although even here it is only in the 'inferior' form of an animal world seen below the surface of the sea.

In fact we almost immediately we have a rather different sight of the hidden lifegiving values the whales represent when, by a trick, the crew of the *Pequod* manage to wrest the stinking, decaying corpse of a whale off a French boat, on the suspicion that, buried in its depths, may be ambergris, that substance so precious that is worth 'a gold guinea an ounce'. Sure enough, suddenly, from the heart of this rotting mass, 'there stole a faint stream of perfume'. Out come handfuls of sweet-smelling ambergris, all the more powerful for the contrast with the reek of putrescence which surrounds it.

Again we move on to the strange scene where, having captured and decapitated a sperm whale, and removed the 'sperm' from its head, 'The Baling of the Heidel-burgh Tun, or Case', we see Ishmael and others sitting on deck, rolling and squeez-ing the soft sperm in their hands, so transported by their 'sweet and unctous duty' that it is like another mystical vision:

> 'As I sat there at my ease, cross-legged on the deck; after the bitter exertion at the windlass; under a blue tranquil sky; the ship under indolent sail and gliding so serenely along; as I bathed my hands among these soft, gentle globules of infiltrated tissues, woven almost within the hour; as they richly broke to my fingers and discharged all their opulence, like fully ripe grapes their wine; as I snuffed that uncontaminated aroma literally and truly like the smell of spring violets; I declare to you that for the time I lived as in a musky meadow; I forgot all about our horrible oath; in that inexpressible sperm, I washed my hands and my heart of it ... I felt divinely free from all ill-will, or petulance, or malice, of any sort whatever.'

But even this mystically joyous moment, when Ishmael imagines all the human race at one – 'let us squeeze ourselves universally into the very milk and sperm of kindness' – has been bought at the price of little Pip, the black cabin boy, losing his wits in terror during the chase of the whale which provided the sperm. The double-entendre of 'sperm' in itself carries homoerotic echoes. And we are soon back into that other harsh, bleak, pitiless man-centred world, preoccupied with death and destruction, chequered with foreboding, which dominates most of the narrative.

Much of the structure of the latter part of the story is built round the successive meetings with other whaling ships, each from a different nation, again convey-ing the sense that we are here meeting all the human race. Each is hailed by the increasingly mad Ahab in hope that it might have news of the whereabouts of Moby Dick. And each encounter in turn adds to the build-up towards the final climax. The American *Jereboam* had lost its first mate to Moby Dick, and its crew have been terrorised by a religious fanatic who warns of a similar death for Ahab. The English captain of the *Samuel Enderby* has lost an arm to Moby Dick, and shortly afterwards Queequeg falls seemingly mortally sick and orders his coffin to be made, before he miraculously recovers.

At last they emerge into 'the great South Sea'. It is not unlike that moment in *The Rime of the Ancient Mariner*, when 'we were the first that ever burst into that silent sea' (indeed there are profound symbolic echoes between the two stories, each centred on the image of killing a creature which stands for the majesty and perfection of nature). Ahab orders the blacksmith to forge a special harpoon, like the dark version of a 'magic weapon'. Dipping it in the blood of the three harpooners, he dedicates it to the devil and to the destruction of the 'White Fiend' in a fearful inversion of Christian symbolism:

> ' "*Ego non baptizo te in nomine patris, sed in nomine diaboli*" deliriously howled Ahab, as the malignant iron scorchingly devoured the baptismal blood.'

The next afternoon four more whales are killed, one by Ahab. As, 'floating in the lovely sunset sea and sky', Ahab's whale and the sun 'died together', 'such a sweetness and such plaintiveness, such inwreathing orisons curled up in that rosy air' it almost seems as though the wind has carried 'vesper hymns' from some far-off Spanish convent, lost in a dark, green valley. Again, there is the identification of whales and the world of nature with Christian symbolism: everything Ahab and his crew are now so explicitly set to defy. That night the sinister Fedallah prophesies to Ahab that, before he dies, 'two hearses must verily be seen by thee on the sea; the first not made by mortal hands'; the other made from wood grown in America.

There is a terrifying midnight thunderstorm, when the *Pequod* is struck by such fearsome lightning that each of its 'three tall masts' are seen 'burning like three gigantic wax tapers before an altar'. They encounter the *Rachel*, 'weeping for her children' as in the Bible, as its captain distractedly searches for the whaleboat lost to Moby Dick in which his 12-year old son had been among the crew. Ahab refuses the captain's plea to help in the search, and as the *Pequod* ploughs on, it meets the *Delight*, carrying the 'few splintered planks' of its smashed whaleboat. 'Hast seen the White Whale?' calls Ahab. The captain points to the remains of his boat, in which five men had just been lost to Moby Dick. As the corpse of the last is thrown into the sea, the *Pequod* sails on, But the *Delight*'s captain duly notes the portent of 'the strange lifebuoy' at its stern, Queequeg's coffin.

Thus does the great quest approach its climax, and in keeping with so many other Quest stories, this unfolds through three stages. But its prelude is the dawn of another perfect, peaceful day, when 'the firmaments of air and sea were hardly separable in that all-prevading azure'; the 'pensive air was transparently pure and soft, with a woman's look'; while 'hither and thither, on high, glided the snow-white wings of small, unspeckled birds' like the 'gentle thoughts of the feminine air' above 'the strong, troubled, murderous thinkings of the masculine sea'. In gender terms, never before in the story has the opposition of 'light feminine' and 'dark masculine' been made so explicit.

This leads into 'The Chase – The First Day', when the cry goes up 'There she blows! A hump like a snowhill! It is Moby Dick!' As the boats are launched, we finally catch our first glimpse of this fearsome, fabulous monster towards which all the story has been leading us – and what a shock it provides. Our first vision of the whale is one of inexpressible majesty and peace, as we see him sliding along, set in a ring of 'finest, fleecy' foam, attended by 'hundreds of gay fowl softly feathering the sea'. 'A gentle joyousness – a mighty mildness of repose' invests 'the gliding whale'. Not Jove himself 'did surpass the glorified White Whale, as he so divinely swam'. Far from being the fearful deformed monster we have been led to expect, Moby Dick is god-like: the image of a mighty creature at one with life and with nature; in perfect harmony with the great spirit that moves the universe; a complete symbol of the transcendent Self. And the total opposite to this is that dark, murderous embodiment of the human ego personified in the demonic madman now bent on his destruction.

Precisely because everything in Ahab's world is now possessed by the dark inversion, once the struggle begins we now see only the other side of that life force which Moby Dick represents, the dark, destructive side of nature itself. On the first day, three boats are launched, Ahab's in the lead, and the whale comes up underneath it, snapping it in two with his jaws. Ahab is thrown into the water, the others cling to the wreckage, until all are rescued. Next morning, in 'The Chase – The Second Day', Moby Dick is again sighted. Again three boats are launched and this time the three harpooners all land their darts in his side. The whale turns on them in fury, wrecking two boats and overturning the third, Ahab's, so that his ivory pegleg is shattered. As they are again picked up by the *Pequod*, Fedallah has vanished, and it is thought he had been tugged under by Ahab's own harpoon line.

In 'The Chase – The Third Day', the pursuit resumes in the afternoon, again with three boats, one captained by Ahab. As the enraged whale attacks and damages the two others, this reveals the body of Fedallah lashed to his side by the harpoon line, prompting Ahab to recognise this as the first hearse, 'not made with mortal hands', the dead man had prophesied. From the third boat Ahab hurls his harpoon, goading Moby Dick to roll against his boat, throwing three men overboard. Finally, maddened beyond endurance, the whale launches himself with full force against the *Pequod* itself, fatally crushing its hull. As the ship begins to sink, Ahab recognises it as 'the second hearse', made from wood grown in America. Ahab hurls another harpoon but, as the whale dashes forward, the rope catches him round the neck, plunging him into the depths. The *Pequod* sinks into a swirling vortex, carrying the rest of the crew with it, and 'the great shroud of the sea rolled on as it rolled five thousand years ago'.

In a brief epilogue, we learn that Ishmael had been one of the three men from Ahab's boat thrown overboard. As he swims in the water, up from the sinking ship floats Queequeg's coffin, the 'lifebuoy' to which Ishmael can cling for survival. After a day and night floating on 'a soft and dirge-like main' he is rescued by the *Rachel* which, in her 'search after her missing children, only found another orphan'. Ishmael is the lone survivor. Yet he is like the hero of one of those dream-like Voyage and Return stories who emerge from what should have been a life-transforming experience having learned nothing, completely unchanged. He is still just an 'orphan': the solitary, unformed child he was when the story began.

When Melville completed *Moby Dick*, he famously wrote to his friend Nathaniel Hawthorne 'I have written a wicked book and feel spotless as a lamb'. Without fully understanding how or why, he must have sensed that his imagination had become possessed by a story which tried to turn the archetypal foundations of storytelling on their heads. He had relished conceiving a tale in which the hero, Ahab, was all dark, setting out to destroy the 'White Whale' which was a symbol of all that is light; even though the hidden logic of the tale continued to insist this could only end in his hero's destruction. Somewhere from his unconscious Melville knew he had written 'a wicked book', a story which attempted to defy all the cosmic order of things. But at the same time he felt 'spotless as a lamb'. He did not wish to feel any remorse, because, like other Romantic writers of the age, he had the exhilarating sense he was venturing into wholly new, uncharted waters of the human spirit, where no storytellers had ever travelled before.

There are obvious parallels here between *Moby Dick* and *Frankenstein*. In both stories, although they are fundamentally shaped around the Overcoming the Monster plot, the hero, as an embodiment of dark, heartless, all-consuming egotism, is the true monster. In each case his 'opposite', as we originally see him, is presented, in an 'inferior' way, as light, an image of the Self. But eventually in each case, reflecting the hero's own state of darkness, this shadowy antagonist does indeed turn, like the statue of the Commendatore in *Don Giovanni*, into the monstrous embodiment of the 'unrealised value' who must destroy him.

It is no accident that each of these stories was written at a time, the first half of the nineteenth century, when a highly significant change was coming over the psychology of Western man. Already the tumultuous political and social upheavals at the time of the French Revolution and Napoleon had created the sense that some entirely new age was dawning for mankind. In the dramatic advance of scientific knowledge, of which the immense material changes being brought by the industrial revolution were only the most obvious outward sign, man had begun to step out of his natural frame in a way that had no precedent. His new technological power was giving him the sense that he now had the power physically to 'conquer' nature as never before. Unprecedented advances in scientific knowledge were giving him the sense he could conquer the mysteries of the universe intellectually. On all sides there was the exhilarating sense of stepping on to that escalator of 'progress' which was carrying the human race up out of the dark, primitive past into an ever more glorious future; and this reflected the most profound shift taking place in Western man's psychological centre of gravity.

In fact, in taking this further giant step out of the natural frame from which he had sprung, there was an immense unconscious price to pay, in the severing of his new, seemingly all-powerful consciousness from that deeper level of his being which linked him instinctively with nature. In becoming emancipated from the constraints of nature as never before, he was also becoming in a new way alienated: not just from the natural world outside him but from the deeper levels of his own nature. It was in this process of separation, this splitting off of conscious from unconscious, that the fundamental psychic shift was taking place which was beginning to produce such an earthquake in the nature of storytelling. In the next few chapters we shall see how this has continued to shape the way stories are told right up to the present day.

## CHAPTER TWENTY-TWO

# The Ego Takes Over (II)
## *The Dark and Sentimental Versions*

'The activities of our age are uncertain and multifarious. No single literary, artistic or philosophic tendency predominates. There is a babel of notions and conflicting theories. But in the midst of this general confusion, it is possible to recognise one curious and significant melody, repeated in different keys and by different instruments in every one of the subsidiary babels. It is the tune of our modern Romanticism.'

Aldous Huxley, *The New Romanticism* (1931)

'Never was any age more sentimental, more devoid of real feeling, more exaggerated in false feeling than our own ... the radio and the film are mere counterfeit emotion all the time, the current press and literature the same. People wallow in emotion, counterfeit emotion. They lap it up, they live in it and on it ... and at times they seem to get on very well with it all. And then, more and more, they break down. They go to pieces.'

D. H. Lawrence, *Apropos of Lady Chatterley's Lover* (1929)

A key to understanding the enormous change which has come over storytelling in the past 200 years is to recall that an essential feature of all the archetypal plots is how they show the central figure of the story being inwardly transformed. The stories of Odysseus and Perseus, Aladdin and Jane Eyre, Raskolnikov and Peer Gynt, all tell us how they develop the balance of inner qualities required to bring them to Self-realisation. At root this is what our capacity to imagine stories is about: to show how the inner state of any story's hero or heroine is such that it can either bring them to a happy ending or carry them down to destruction.

In the last chapter we began to explore what happens when a split opens up between a storyteller's ego and his unconscious, that hidden level of the psyche containing the archetypal structures which give stories their shape and meaning. One of the most significant consequences, as the ego takes over, is that all the internal symbolism through which the archetypes operate becomes projected outwards, onto the external world. We no longer see the hero or heroine going through the inner transformation which is the real theme of the archetypal pattern. Their transformation is all in their outward circumstances. In this respect, the story has become subtly detached from its archetypal roots. And this disintegration shows itself in three main ways.

## The dark version

The first is the one we have just been looking at: the full 'dark version', where a storyteller presents us with a hero trying to act out the archetypal pattern which leads to a happy ending but unable to do so because he is egocentric and dark. Because there is no inner transformation to give him the balance of qualities required to reach the complete happy ending, the logic of storytelling dictates that, like Julien Sorel or Captain Ahab, he must ultimately bring about his own destruction.

## The lesser dark version

The second form such a story can take is 'the lesser dark version'. This is where a dark or inadequate hero or heroine may seem outwardly to reach their goal; but, again, because they have not gone through the necessary transformation, there is a final twist to the tale which shows us they have not really achieved it. Either they end in some kind of frustration or defeat; or we are in some other way made aware that the story has not been properly resolved.

## The sentimental version

There is a third form such a story can take, not always so obvious, which has played a hugely important role in the storytelling of the past 200 years: not least through that medium which so dominated twentieth-century popular storytelling, the cinema. This is 'the sentimental version'. Superficially, the story may seem to go through the archetypal pattern, complete with a happy ending. But because it has all been presented in outward terms, without any inner transformation, the story has been emptied of its deeper archetypal meaning. What remains is just a sentimental shell: form without content. Furthermore, whenever we examine such a story in detail, we invariably find that something has gone subtly awry with its plot. In this way it reveals just how it has become detached from the underlying archetype.

In this chapter and those which follow, we draw on a wide range of novels, films, plays and operas to see how each of these aberrations from the fundamental archetypes works.

## Rags to Riches: The dark versions

A particularly obvious candidate for dark or sentimental interpretations is the plot of the Rags to Riches story, because this so easily lends itself to ego-based fantasies, which can give both storyteller and audience the pleasure of identifying with a hero or heroine who emerges from the crowd to win success and acclaim.

The most extreme way in which this plot can turn dark, as we saw in *The Scarlet and the Black*, is where the storyteller presents a dark hero who lacks those essential inner qualities; who attempts to climb from Rags to Riches in defiance of the archetypal rules, and is therefore finally destroyed. The heartless Julien Sorel is as two-dimensional as a character in a strip cartoon. In no way does he go through any internal transformation. We only see him egotistically seeking to compete with, impress or dominate every other character in the story. He is precisely the same pasteboard figure at the end as he was at the beginning. The story's only real psychological interest is the extent to which its hero was a fantasy projection of the emotionally immature author himself.

An example of the 'lesser dark version' of the plot is Guy de Maupassant's novel *Bel Ami* (1885). A penniless but good-looking young French ex-army officer, Georges Duroy, is strolling through Paris with 'the authentic air of the bold bad hero of romance', wondering how he can afford his next meal. He runs into a former fellow-officer Forestier, who has a well-paid job with a newspaper, *La Vie Francaise*, and says he will help Duroy to become a journalist. They visit the Folies Bergere, where Duroy goes off to spend the night with an attractive prostitute, Rachel. She is so taken by his looks that she is not concerned by his lack of money. He is taken on by the newspaper to write a series of articles, but finds himself incapable of putting anything together until Forestier's clever wife writes the first article for him. At dinner with the couple he meets Mme de Marelle, an attractive married woman with whom he begins an affair, while still continuing to see Rachel. Although we are given little idea of how learns to write, he becomes established as a journalist, specialising in gossip and politics, while Mme de Marelle rents an apartment where they can carry on their affair. Her young daughter Laurine is taken by Duroy and nicknames him 'Bel Ami'.

The whole story is presented as a kind of wish-fulfilment fantasy, seen through Duroy's eyes, in which he enjoys effortless success, both with women (invariably more than one at the same time) and in his new profession, without ever really providing any plausible evidence of why he achieves either. Eventually he is summoned to the south of France to attend Forestier's premature death-bed. No sooner has his friend expired than Duroy proposes to Mme Forestier. They are married and work together as a journalistic team, Duroy changing his name to the grander Du Roy, while he resumes his affair with Mme de Marelle. He then sets his sights on the middle-aged wife of his editor, Walter. No sooner has he finally overcome her resistance, rendering her besotted with love for him, than he tires of her infantile devotion and begins to fancy her teenage daughter Suzanne, while at the same time continuing his affair with Mme de Marelle. A new French government comes to power, closely linked to *La Vie Francaise*, which gives Walter and his newspaper enormous new political influence and importance. In a desperate bid to regain Du Roy's affection, Mme Walter reveals to him a secret Government plan to take over Morocco, out of which her husband and members of the Government are scheming to make a vast fortune by insider dealing.

Mme Forestier is then herself left a large legacy by a man who turns out to have been her long-established lover. Du Roy insists that, to prevent scandal, it should be announced that the money was left to them both, making him a franc millionaire. But this is nothing to the immense fortune made by his editor Walter from his financial coup on the Morocco affair, who has now bought himself a palatial mansion in the heart of Paris. Discovering that the Foreign Minister is now his wife's lover, Du Roy conceives his final coup. He arranges for the Commissioner of Police to catch his wife and her lover in the act of adultery, so he can divorce her; thus leaving him free to woo Suzanne, as heiress to one of the richest men in France. He uses the knowledge of how her father had come by his fortune to ensure his agreement to the match, to the horror of Suzanne's mother. As the climax approaches, 'Bel Ami' seems to have won every worldly prize life has to offer. M. Walter makes him editor-in-chief of *La Vie Francaise*, which Walter's wealth has now made the leading newspaper in France. He is rich. He is ennobled as the Baron Du Roy. And the story culminates in a spectacular wedding in the most fashionable church in Paris, attended by the cream of Parisian society. But at this very moment, having imagined that the 'Man-God' Christ himself 'was descending to earth to consecrate' his triumph and how it might only be a matter of time before he became President of the French Republic, Du Roy's inmost thoughts are only of one person in that vast congregation, with whom he has enjoyed a pregnant exchange of glances. Before his eyes, as he walks down the aisle into the brilliant sunlight, 'there floated the image of Mme de Marelle', looking into the mirror as she always did before getting out of the bed where they made love. It would not be long before he saw that sight again.

The story is a complete outward projection of the Rags to Riches archetype. In worldly terms, Duroy has won the hand of his 'Princess' and succeeded to the 'kingdom'. He has achieved all the external trappings of Self-realisation, seemingly sanctified by all the solemnities of religion itself. But, as in *The Scarlet and the Black*, this has all been presented in only the most relentlessly superficial fashion, centred on a wholly self-centred, unscrupulous cardboard hero to whom every prize – women, money, position, fashionable acclaim – falls with the relentless, mechanical ease of a wish-fulfilment daydream; although admittedly in a world in which everyone else is shown to be as self-centred and amoral as himself. There is not the slightest pretence that Duroy has grown up into a mature man. Inwardly he remains wholly unchanged, the 'boy hero who cannot grow up', caught between 'Mother', represented by the succession of adoring married women who are his mistresses, and the infantile *anima* figures of the child Laurine and his eventual bride Suzanne. As the daughter of the richest and most powerful man in France, Suzanne is almost a carbon copy of Sorel's Mathilde; except that here the outward show of the happy ending is complete, as the wedding finally takes place, while 'Mother', the married mistress, is still waiting faithfully in the shadows. But this leaves us in no doubt that the archetypal resolution of the story is only a hollow sham. We have not really arrived at a happy ending at all.

A similar example of the 'lesser dark version' of the Rags to Riches plot was Budd Schulberg's Hollywood novel *What Makes Sammy Run*. This centres on the dizzying upward climb, first in the world of New York gossip journalism, then in Hollywood, of the ruthlessly ego-driven Sammy Glick (although, unlike Stendhal and de Maupassant, Schulberg did not identify with his hero but with his story's narrator, a fellow writer who observes Glick's remorseless rise with wry dismay). Like *Bel Ami*, this outwardly echoes the fairy-tale pattern, not least in its climax where the hero again appears to have married the beautiful 'Princess' and 'succeeded to the kingdom'. When a New York multi-millionaire buys the Worldwide Studios where Glick works, the hero schemes to ensure that he is appointed all-powerful head of the studio, overthrowing the kindly father-figure who had previously been his champion and protector; and the story concludes with the spectacular Hollywood wedding in which Glick marries the new owner's 'aristo-cratic' daughter. But there is no way, with such a dark hero, this could be the end of the story. Finally comes the twist to the tale, where in the middle of the party to celebrate the wedding, Glick goes upstairs in his mansion to find his equally cold-hearted, self-centred bride enjoying sex with a stupid but handsome young film star. Unabashed, she tells him the marriage was just a mutually-advantageous social arrangement. Temporarily, Glick's fantasy world is in ruins. But as the book ends, he has already retreated behind the armour of his all-consuming ego-centricity, 'running' as hard as ever. As in *Bel Ami*, we realise the cardboard hero has not inwardly changed at all. In no way is the story finally resolved.

A 'lesser dark version' which even more overtly alluded to the symbolism of the fairy tale was that British best-seller of the late 1950s, John Braine's *Room at the Top* (1957). Joe Lampton, an orphaned young man, arrives to seek his fortune in a big Yorkshire town. He is as two-dimensional and egocentric as 'Bel Ami' and Sammy Glick, although without their talents for self-advancement. He soon spots from afar the 'Princess' who represents all his ambition requires, Susan, the pretty, silly young daughter of a rich local businessman. At first she seems quite out of reach, and he muses:

> 'Susan was a princess and I was the equivalent of a swineherd. I was, you might say, acting out the equivalent of a fairy story. The trouble was that there were more difficult obstacles than dragons and enchanters to be overcome, and I could see no sign of a fairy godmother.'

Almost immediately, however, a 'fairy godmother' (or at any rate a 'Mother') comes into Lampton's life, in the shape of Alice Aisgill, a warm-hearted, married older woman. She begins to 'transform' him, although of course only externally, by smoothing away some of his social gaucheries and teaching him to use hair cream; and soon he is taking his 'Princess' out to social occasions, while the affair with 'Mother' continues in the background:

> 'I was taking Susan not as Susan but as a Grade A lovely and the daughter of a factory owner, as the means to obtaining the Aladdin's cave of my ambitions.'

In fact Susan is a classic instance of the kind of infantile *anima* figure who might be fantasised into existence by someone suffering from 'Mother-dominated' emotional immaturity. She begins to respond to the advances of her 'Joekins' (reminiscent of the infantile Dora Spenlow's pet-name 'Doady' for David Copperfield), but throws him over when she discovers that he is still tied to Alice ('Mother'). Joe and Alice travel down to Dorset for four days of love-making ('that night and the nights that followed I learned all about a woman's body and my own'), ending with Joe's sickly declaration 'I do love you Alice. I'll love you till the day I die. You're my wife now. There'll never be anyone else.'

On their return to Yorkshire, Joe at once wins Susan back and makes her pregnant. Her father offers to find his now prospective son-in-law a highly paid new job:

> 'I was a Prince Charming – every obstacle had been magically smoothed from my path.'

'Prince Charming' tells 'Mother' what has happened, and that their affair is over. She gets drunk, runs her car off the road and is crushed to an unrecognisable pulp. Truly in such fantasies has the world of the fairy tale been turned in our time inside out.

## Rags to Riches: The sentimental version

When we talk of 'sentimentality', we mean the false version of something real; the counterfeit of something which can inspire proper human emotions. Sentimentality plays with our emotions. When we see a sentimental film or hear a sentimental song, our heartstrings may be tugged. We may be moved to tears. As Noel Coward said 'there is nothing so potent as cheap music'. But we may also be aware that our emotional responses are only being outwardly manipulated, in a way which does not correspond to any genuine personal reality.

The essence of sentimentality is that it arises from the capacity of the human ego to appropriate the values and properties of the Self. It is thus egotism in disguise, pretending to identify with something higher and beyond Self. If one of the most obvious attributes of the Self is selfless feeling, sentimentality is the outward show of such feeling without its reality. This is why we particularly associate it with such expressions of emotion as the romantic love between a man and a woman; love between parents and children; sympathetic feelings for the plight of other people in general; the love of country; of nature; of God. All these are naturally functions of the deeper, ego-transcending Self. But they can all be sentimentalised when the ego seeks to enjoy such feelings without letting go of itself.

In one sense all the dark, ego-centred versions of stories we have already looked at are sentimental, compared with stories which are fully integrated with the underlying archetypes. Hence the two-dimensional nature of all the characters who appear in them. But at least in the 'dark' versions it becomes obvious something has gone seriously adrift, and that the story cannot achieve its proper archetypal ending. What we must now look at are those stories where the ego manages to appropriate almost the entire outward form of the archetype, while emptying it of its inner significance; although even here, as we shall see, the result always somehow indicates that something has gone awry.

Nowhere in our time has been more obviously the home of Rags to Riches stories than the 'dream factory' of Hollywood: either in its real life role of transforming Norma Jean Mortensons and Archie Kerrs into Marilyn Monroes and Cary Grants, poor, anonymous little boys and girls into 'Princesses' and 'Princes'; or in the multitude of fictional versions which over the past century have poured out onto the screens and into the fantasies of the world. Every conceivable permutation has been worked on this theme, not least in that host of films which showed some unrecognised genius winning his way at last to fame and recognition.

An example we looked earlier was *The Benny Goodman Story* (1956), recreating the early career of the 1930s swing bandleader. Outwardly this story followed the exact pattern of the Rags to Riches archetype, right up to the happy ending, with the hero winning the hand of the beautiful 'Princess' and succeeding to the 'kingdom', as he wins a standing ovation in Carnegie Hall, the supreme citadel of American musical respectability where no mere jazz musician had ever been allowed to play before. But when we look more carefully, we see how the hero's success is all presented in external terms. We see no inner development in his character. The story is no more than a wish-fulfilment fantasy, originally centred on a small boy whose only real defining characteristic is his exceptional musical talent, rather like Julien Sorel's capacity to remember chunks of Horace, and his all-consuming will to succeed. Because the hero is a pleasant-enough cardboard figure, there is nothing obviously dark and inimical about him. It is therefore acceptable that he should eventually win through to worldly gratification and acclaim. But it is telling that the ultimate mark of his success is when the heroine's rich elderly parents are seen tapping their feet to his music and joining in the cheers in Carnegie Hall. Really he is still just the small boy who wants approval from the 'grown ups'. He has not matured to become fully grown-up himself, a king over his own inner kingdom, which is what the Rags to Riches archetype is about. In psychological terms, like all those other Hollywood versions of the Rags to Riches story showing the disregarded young artist who eventually draws the attention of the world to recognise what a clever fellow he is, *The Benny Goodman Story* arranges the facts of history to make no more than a pleasantly self-indulgent fantasy.

Not all Hollywood's fondly-imagined fairy tales adhere quite so closely to the archetypal pattern, not least in real life. For there is nothing more dangerous than to try to act out externally the patterns of the archetypes, which can only yield their true significance when taken inwardly, as the symbols of inner psychic growth. This is why, behind its fairy-tale facade, Hollywood, as a town where the *persona* rules supreme, has to this day proved such a graveyard for those who pass unconsciously into the grip of projected archetypes, leaving that trail of divorces, alcoholism, nervous breakdowns and even murders with which it has long been synonymous.

Even Hollywood's fictional fairy tales can often be seen on closer examination to betray the dark side of the psychic disorder bound to rage in a town and an industry so remorselessly dedicated to the self-deceiving world of the ego. A revealing instance was that Charlie Chaplin silent-screen classic of the 1920s, *The Gold Rush*. The first part of the story shows Charlie and two fellow prospectors, Black Larsen and Big Jim, out in the wilderness, where Jim has discovered an enormous lode of gold ('the treasure in the cave'). After experiencing blizzards and starvation, Charlie's two companions begin to fight. Larsen hits Jim over the head with a spade and is then killed by an avalanche. Jim disappears, having lost his memory and forgotten the whereabouts of his gold mine. Charlie, left alone, goes down into the nearby town, where he meets and falls in love with Georgia, the little dance-hall hostess, who only dances with him to spite her drunken and bullying lover. Charlie, imagining that she likes him, invites her back to his cabin with her friends for a New Year's Eve celebration dinner. They do not turn up.

So far, in light of its inner symbolism, any analyst who heard such a story recounted as a dream by one of his patients might fear his subject was heading for nervous breakdown. Clearly this is an extreme case of arrested development. Both the girl (an infantile *anima* figure) and the buried treasure (potential personality growth) are 'lost'. This is coupled with the death of one companion and the disappearance of the other (a severe case of violent repression of important elements in the psyche!).

In the second part of the story Big Jim returns, looking for Charlie as the one person who can help him retrace his steps back to the lost gold. When, by lucky chance, they find it, he rewards Charlie with a share and they both become millionaires. But Charlie is still miserable because he has lost the girl he loves. In other words, he has been able to compensate for his inability to relate to the *anima* by becoming successful in the world and building up an impressive outward *persona*. But in no way has he developed inwardly, he is still as immature as he was at the beginning of the story and his fundamental inadequacy still nags at him.

In part three Charlie, now rich through no effort of his own, is embarking on a ship back to civilisation, happily showing off as he poses for photographers in his old tramp's clothes. Suddenly he falls over a rail into the ship's lower depths, where it just happens that little Georgia is travelling steerage. Seeing him in his old rags, she imagines he is a stowaway on the run and offers to look after him. In other words, he has regressed into the unconscious, where he finds his infantile *anima* projection who will love him as he really is, in his undeveloped, immature state. The story concludes on the hope that the two little sexless 'babes in the wood' can get married and live happily ever after: i.e., in the wishful thinking that they can remain happy frozen in their infantile state forever. Analysed in this light, it is not really a very happy little tale at all; and anyone who wished to understand Chaplin's inner life need look no further than his film scripts for plenty of clues.

A friend of Chaplin, the journalist Alistair Cooke, in his book *Six Men* (1977), observed that Chaplin was:

> 'extremely attractive to women and instantly susceptible to them, to two types more than most: the femme fatale and the child woman. The gamut is represented at its polar opposites by Pola Negri ... and his first wife, Mildred Harris. Time and again he found himself involved with lusty, earthy women. But the ones he sought were nubile adolescents. He married three of them, Mildred Harris at 16, when he was 29; Lita Grey at 17, when he was 35; Oona O'Neill at 18, when he was 55. I state this as an interesting but probably inexplicable phenomenon.'

Far from being 'inexplicable', the pattern is in fact only too familiar among men who fail to achieve the full transition of their 'inner feminine' between 'Mother' and a mature *anima*; and who thus remain caught in uneasy fluctuation between the two, equally frustrating poles of the 'earthy femme fatale' (Mother) and the 'child woman' (inadequately developed *anima*). Few men, however, have had more extensive or public opportunities to display this basic symptom of arrested development than Chaplin.

No brief summary of Hollywood's innumerable variants on sentimentalising the Rags to Riches plot would be complete without a mention of that immensely popular 1960s musical *My Fair Lady*. Based on Bernard Shaw's play *Pygmalion*, it is revealing to note where the two versions differ.

From the heroine's point of view, both stories unfold in many ways like a fairy tale. A dirty, coarsely-spoken little flower girl, Eliza Doolittle, used to being treated like garbage, meets a mysterious older person with apparently supernatural powers (his astonishing knowledge of phonetics, which enables him in the opening scene to place everyone in the Covent Garden crowd to within a few streets of where they live, just by the way they speak). This strange 'Sorcerer' figure, Professor Higgins, offers, for a bet with his friend Colonel Pickering, to transform Eliza into a 'Princess'. She arrives at his house in Wimpole Street, where she undergoes a rite of initiation (being given a hot bath to wash away all the grime which symbolises her ragamuffin outward *persona*). She is dressed up in fine clothes, and as the first stage of the story ends, the long business of transformation has begun, with Eliza learning from Higgins how to talk like a lady.

By the beginning of the next act, the first stage of Eliza's outward transformation is complete. She is now ready to go out into the world, where in Shaw's version she undergoes the archetypal three tests: a visit to Professor Higgins's mother's 'at home' (where she is taken for a lady); an embassy ball (where she is taken for a Princess); and finally a Buckingham Palace garden party. In *My Fair Lady* these tests are reduced to two: Mrs Higgins receives her guests at Ascot races, and this is followed by the embassy ball. Eliza passes the tests triumphantly, but, like Cinderella, each time she has to return home, if not to rags at least to the domineering presence of Higgins, who continues to treat her coldly as a cross between her pitiful little former self and a mere scientific experiment.

In other words, as usual in the second stage of the Rags to Riches story, a split has opened up between the heroine's triumphant new outer Self, her *persona*, and her real, deeper self, which is in danger of being repressed altogether. But we have already caught a glimpse of her embryonic 'other half', the 'Prince' who loves her for herself, in the somewhat improbable guise of Freddie Eynsford-Hill, the upper-middle-class young man who, as a guest of Mrs Higgins, has been bowled over by Eliza's spirited charms.

The central crisis of the story arrives when, after her last triumphant test, Eliza finally explodes in rage at Higgins's condescending treatment of her and, after giving him a piece of her mind, storms out of the house. All might seem lost, except that she falls into the arms of the waiting and doting Freddie. They wander round London at night, until she is ready for her final confrontation with Higgins, again under the eye of his mother. At last Eliza has discovered who she really is. Like the moment when, as Jane Eyre finally breaks loose from St John Rivers and exclaims 'at last my powers were in play', it seems Eliza is finally ready to throw off her 'Sorcerer's' tyranny and come to full Self-realisation.

At this point the two versions diverge. In *My Fair Lady*, the story ends with Higgins finally recognising, after she has fled the house, how much Eliza has come to mean to him. She, equally missing him, steals back into the house and finds him

sadly listening to her recorded voice. There is a hopelessly unresolved, sentimental ending where it is conveyed that she will come back to live with him, but
in a relationship left wholly vague and unspecified. Companion? Housekeeper?
Daughter? Wife? We never know.

In Shaw's version, the ending is very different. Eliza, having finally declared her
independence of Higgins, goes off with Freddie to get married. As Shaw explains
in his Epilogue to *Pygmalion*, they then live more or less happily ever after. This
may be at least the semblance of a fairy-tale ending for Eliza. But what if we look
at it through the eyes of Higgins, who was, after all, a much more likely point of
identification for the play's author? Shaw's name for the play was not Galatea, the
ivory statue who was turned into a woman in the original myth, but *Pygmalion*,
the name of her creator. Higgins, like Shaw when he wrote the play, is a man
in early middle age. The Professor's 'supernatural powers' are no more magical
in their way than the gift for words which had made the mocking, iconoclastic
Mr Shaw the most successful playwright of his day. And Shaw's inmost problem,
like that of many men, was with his unresolved tie to his mother and therefore
to his own *anima*, that elusive central component in the male psyche which in
Shaw's case was never fully realised. This gave him endless trouble in his intimate
relations with the opposite sex; not least in his embarrassingly public infatuation
with Mrs Patrick Campbell, the commanding actress who played Eliza when
*Pygmalion* was first staged in 1914, an affair which began in the wake of his
mother's death when he was in his late 50s.[1]

This inability to relate securely to his inner feminine held Shaw back from ever
being able to relate properly with the life-giving internal realm of the spirit; indeed
from ever fully growing up and becoming a 'whole' man. At root Shaw remained
emotionally and spiritually retarded, a 'boy hero who cannot grow up', a rebellious
*puer aeternus*, at odds with both the masculine and feminine parts of himself.
And the repercussions of this were reflected in his political views, not least in his
foolish 'love affair' with Stalin's Russia, which he liked to portray as an idealised
heaven-on-earth, a projected symbol of the Self, ruled by its benign Father-figure,
just when the Soviet tyranny was at its murderous height. In *Pygmalion*, just as
Eliza has developed to the point where she is capable of becoming an impressive
woman in her own right, Higgins is quite unable to recognise it. The real reason is
betrayed in his earlier remark to his mother: 'oh, I can't be bothered with women.
My idea of a lovable woman is someone as much like you as possible.' Just as
the *anima* which could lead to wholeness emerges, the suffocating embrace of
'Mother' intervenes; the age-old beguiling obstacle which stands in the way of
a man who cannot go out into the world and become fully a man. Like a spoiled
little boy, Higgins is thus left alone with Mother, oblivious to the end of how

---

1. Michael Holroyd in his biography of Shaw brings out the tortured nature of Shaw's relationship
with his mother, whom he loved but who showed no love for him. She had a strong antipathy to
all men, particularly her husband. The one exception was her music teacher, George Vandeleur Lee,
who shared the family home in Dublin, taught Mrs Shaw to sing and may well have been her lover.
Shaw, according to Holroyd, based Eliza loosely on his mother and Higgins on the teacher who
had moulded her into a singer, much as Pygmalion had moulded and brought Galatea to life in the
original Greek myth.

callously and selfishly he has behaved. A story which may seem, at first sight, to be a touching and rather funny fairy tale, complete with happy ending, turns out to have a rather darker side altogether.

## Overcoming the Monster: The dark versions

It is revealing to see what the split between a storyteller's ego and the unconscious does to the plot of Overcoming the Monster, because in its archetypal form this is so directly focused on the battle against the power of the human ego. The hero challenges the monster of egotism in the name of the values of the Self. So what happens when this archetype is taken over by the ego itself?

In its darkest form we saw this in *Frankenstein* and *Moby Dick*, where the roles of hero and monster are reversed. At the beginning the hero himself appears as the story's chief dark figure, while the monster appears as 'light', representing in an inferior form the unrealised value of the Self which the hero will never achieve. As the hero darkens further, so does the monster: to the point where, as the hero is finally destroyed by the shadow of his own egotism, the monster disappears.

An example of the 'lesser dark version' of this plot, in its own way almost as revealing about the psychological one-sidedness of modern civilisation, was that Hollywood classic from the early days of sound-pictures, *King Kong* (1933). An American film director Carl Denham is working on an immensely important and secret new project. He has hired a ship in New York and is desperate to find a young girl to act as his star. Spotting a penniless but beautiful blonde, Ann Darrow (Fay Wray), stealing an apple from a stall, he intervenes to save her from arrest and brings her onto the ship, to the disgust of its all-male crew. Only one young officer, the hero Jack Denholm, overcomes his initial aversion to her femininity and falls in love with her.

The ship crosses half the world to arrive in dense fog at a mysterious, unknown island, which has a small peninsula inhabited by a primitive people, cut off by a massive, ancient stone wall from the dark, jungle-clad interior. The white men see painted tribesmen working themselves into a frenzy, to the throbbing of drums, while a small girl is garlanded with flowers to be offered up through a mighty gate in the wall as 'the bride of Kong'. The tribesmen see the blonde white woman as a more appropriate sacrifice, and come by night to the ship to kidnap her. She is dragged through the gate and tied between two pillars, where she is terrified to see bearing down on her the mysterious denizen of the island's interior, a monstrous ape the size of a house. But instead of eating her, Kong carries her gently off into the jungle: a first sign that something unusual is happening to the normal archetypal pattern.

Everything we have seen up to this point reflects the way Denham and his all-male crew represent the ego-consciousness of modern American civilisation, cut off from the instinctive world of nature. In the metal prison of the ship, surrounded with their weapons and camera equipment, they represent all the limitations of one-sided masculinity. When they arrive at the island its geography symbolises what is happening. The small, inhabited peninsula of consciousness is cut off by a mighty barrier from the dark interior of the unconscious, inhabited by the natural forces of instinct which, because they are repressed, seem shadowy and menacing. And now the feminine value, the *anima*, has passed into that unconscious realm, into the clutches of the shadow of the dark masculine from which she will have to be rescued if there is to be any happy resolution.

Back on the ship, the crew discover she is missing and, led by the hero, the only man among them open to the feminine value, a group of them set off in pursuit. By the Rule of Three, they are attacked in turn by three monsters, first two dinosaurs, then King Kong himself. Twelve men are killed, leaving only the hero alive. We and the hero, who has arrived at the spot where Kong is guarding the heroine, then see her being threatened by prehistoric monsters, again three in number: a tyrannosaur, a huge snake and a pterodactyl. Each time she is saved, after a mighty struggle, by Kong. After the second battle, high on a rocky mountain ledge, he holds her in his huge hand, removing strips of her gauze-like clothing, looking at her tenderly, even playfully. Despite seemingly being an archetypal monster in every other way, he reveals that he is open to the femininity the heroine represents. Thus, by shadowy inversion, he reflects precisely the unrealised value the one-sidedly masculine crew-members lack.

The one exception is the hero who, as Kong fights off the third monstrous attack, rescues the heroine and together they make a 'thrilling escape', by abseiling down a sheer cliff into the sea. Kong comes storming in pursuit of the woman he loves, bursts through the gates into the tribal village (unconscious elements irrupting into consciousness) and smashes up the houses while crunching several tribesmen in his jaws. He is finally knocked unconscious by the white men's gas bombs, enabling him to be taken prisoner.

The scene then switches to New York, where 'King Kong' is to be put on show in a Broadway theatre, as the 'Eighth Wonder of the World'. In some ways this provides an echo of another film, 50 years later, in which Mick 'Crocodile' Dundee, the integrated 'natural' man from the Australian outback, is also brought to New York, the supreme symbol of modern American civilisation, to highlight by contrast everything its effete, unnatural inhabitants have lost by being cut off from their instinctive roots. A fashionable crowd flocks into the theatre to see Denham unveil his prize. As Kong, imprisoned in steel chains, sees the photographers' flashlights popping round his beloved heroine, who is due to marry the hero the following day, he angrily bursts his shackles, storms out into the darkened streets of New York and runs amok, while vast, anonymous crowds flee before him in panic.

Having smashed an elevated train to pieces, and eaten more people, Kong finally climbs half way up the wall of a hotel where, through a lighted window, he sees the prize he is looking for, the *anima*. Seizing her, he climbs to the top of the highest tower in New York, the Empire State Building, which had only just been completed when the film was made as the supreme emblem of the hubris unleashed in America by the 1920s's boom (which, as Scott Fitzgerald noted in his essay *The Jazz Age*, crashed into depression just when New Yorkers could climb that tallest tower in the world and see on the distant horizon open countryside, showing that their city did not comprise the entire world after all). Then America's ego-consciouness hits back, when five aircraft are sent up to kill Kong, who has gently placed the heroine on a ledge at the very top of the tower. Again and again these anonymous little representatives of modern man, his pride inflated by the power of his technology, zoom down on the helpless monster with machine-guns blazing until, as he sways, mortally wounded, he reaches down to the heroine in a last gesture of tender farewell. He then topples down to become a lifeless heap in the street below, surrounded by the usual goggling crowd.

The hero emerges at the top of the tower to embrace the heroine saved from the monster's clutches, so that the story can end on that familiar archetypal image of man and woman united in love, with the monster/shadow finally overcome. Except that here we are left with a profound sense that we have not seen the proper archetypal ending at all. In his touching love for the *anima*, the monster was by no means wholly a monster; in some respects less so than those little modern men, trapped in their limited ego-consciousness, whose strength was all projected outward through their machines, while their sense of the feminine was non-existent. At the end of the story, the 'King' is dead. Despite the ritual coming together of the pasteboard central couple, there is no other King to take his place.

## Overcoming the Monster: The sentimental version

If the sentimental version of any archetypal story shows us its outline, complete with happy ending, but drained of its deeper significance, the Overcoming the Monster plot certainly lends itself to such treatment as much as any other. There are countless modern stories where we see 'goodies' setting out to challenge 'baddies' in the name of the community, humanity and life. When they have overcome this personification of all that is dark in human nature, it might seem as if the age-old archetype was being fully acted out. But when we examine these stories more closely we can see how something very significant has happened since this plot first centred on such great mythic prototypes as Gilgamesh or David, Perseus or Beowulf. The key is to recall how the archetype is not just concerned with the outward act of saving the community from the monster. It is also the personal story of the hero himself, showing how he develops inwardly through his struggle with the monster until we see him emerging to full Self-realisation, usually symbolised by his union with the *anima* and his succession to rule over a 'kingdom'.

One obvious way in which the story can fall short of its archetype is in all those 'monster' stories where the hero does not actually overcome the monster but where he simply makes a 'thrilling escape from death': *The Pit and the Pendulum*, *La Peste*, *Inferno*, *Jurassic Park* and many others. The point about such stories is that they are just playing sentimentally with the outward form of the archetype: the sensation to be derived from identifying with a hero who faces the mounting threat of death but finally makes a miraculous escape through no particular effort of his own. George Clouzot's film *La Salaire du Peur* (*The Wages of Death*, 1952) was a classic example of this type of story, where three truck drivers must take their lorries packed with highly dangerous nitro-glycerine across miles of precipitous unmade mountain roads. Inevitably two explode, leaving the hero, by the Rule of Three, to make it to safety in the nick of time. But though he may have shown admirable courage, he is scarcely a hero who has been through the full character-forming ordeal of confronting and slaying a living monster. In a sense, he has experienced his ordeal passively, just sticking doggedly to his task, trusting to luck until he comes through.

Another obvious way in which this story can become detached from its full archetypal form is where the monster is no longer presented as an abstract of all that is dark in human nature, but where its characteristics are projected outwardly onto some rival social or national group. There are elements of this, as we saw, even in the Bible, where Goliath, the champion of the Philistines, is invested through Jewish eyes with all the archetypal character of the monster. Samson, the Jewish strong man, on the other hand, is presented as a national hero; although, by the Philistines, he might have been viewed in much the same light as was Goliath by the Jews.

We see a similar tendency in those countless fictional versions of the Overcoming the Monster plot inspired by World War Two, where the Germans are invested with all the archetypal characteristics of the monster. This does not mean that Hitler and the Nazis did not in reality display such characteristics. But when this vast historical struggle came to be turned into fictional entertainment, as in *The Guns of Navarone* or *The Battle of the Bulge*, it was inevitable that these should be dominated by the outwardly projected battle with the 'monster'. We see the heroes of such stories as light, because they are shown behaving heroically, bravely, honourably and selflessly; and because their opponents are generally shown with all the dark and negative qualities displayed by dark figures in stories down the ages. But in acting out the outward pattern of the Overcoming the Monster story, the inward aspect of the original archetype, as the story of a hero's personal maturing to Self-realisation, has virtually disappeared.

An element of this outward projection remained in that series of tales which, first appearing in the early years of the Cold War, were to provide popular storytelling in the second half of the twentieth century with its most celebrated 'monster slayer'. The success of Ian Fleming's James Bond novels, and the films they subsequently inspired, lay precisely in the extent to which they managed to create a hero who, while wholly contemporary, nevertheless seemed to act out the archetypal role of the monster slayers of yore down to the tiniest outward detail. Even though his antagonists fitted the projections of the Cold War era, in that their conspiratorial schemes threatened the survival of Britain, America or 'the West', Fleming still managed to lift them onto a more timeless plane, by creating a succession of villains as cosmically evil as any monsters of myth.

But one feature of Fleming's stories so striking that in the film versions it was turned into self-parody is their endings. In almost every instance, when the climactic battle has been brought to its triumphant conclusion, Bond sinks into the arms of the beautiful heroine whom he has liberated from the monster's clutches. It might seem like the perfect archetypal conclusion, the image of hero and *anima* coming together in joyful union. Except that in every story it is, of course, a different woman, each given a flip, throwaway, *double-entendre*-type name such as Pussy Galore, Honeychile Rider, Tiffany Case. Such disposable images of womanhood, viewed only as fantasy objects of male erotic desire, can scarcely be taken as standing for 'the eternal feminine'. We may also then note that there is no sign of Bond having attained rule over any kind of a 'kingdom'. Indeed there has been no sign of his inwardly developing and maturing through the story at all. He is exactly the same cardboard figure he has been all along, through story after story; programmed like an automaton with exactly the same set of outward characteristics and responses, like wanting to seduce every pretty woman in sight, while demanding that his vodka-martinis be 'shaken not stirred'.

So obviously is Bond just a two-dimensional fantasy projection that we might wonder how and why Fleming came to conceive his hero in the first place. Considerable light was shed on this by the biography of Fleming published after his death by John Pearson. We learn how as a young man, obsessed with fast cars and chasing pretty girls, he first imagined the figure who was to become Bond in his daydreams before World War Two, during which he served for several years in Naval Intelligence. It was this projection of his fantasy-self whom he developed into the hero of *Casino Royale*, the first Bond novel published in 1953. Fleming relished being paid for imagining how his fantasy-self could enjoy all the egocentric gratifications he could have wished for: driving his sports cars; living the secret life of an intelligence agent; enjoying effortless sexual success with an endless stream of adoring women; outwitting and killing his opponents. Yet all this seemed somehow morally justified by the fact that he was doing it in the name of a higher cause: fighting for his country; battling for 'our side' against wicked villains plotting the downfall of Western civilisation. The values of the Self could thus be called in to sanctify what was essentially just ego-centred self-indulgence.

If this suggests that in real life Fleming was something of a 'boy hero who cannot grow up', or *puer aeternus*, this was borne out by the unhappy story of his relations with the opposite sex. A succession of women could testify how he took them up and cast them off just as callously as Bond. To the end of his days he never matured into a whole, emotionally secure man. And in this sense it is noticeable how Bond always remained in a curiously ambivalent, immature relationship to authority in the stories, in particular to the all-powerful figure who ultimately ruled his life, the head of the Secret Service, 'M' (although, like a perpetual schoolboy, he was always prepared to cock a secret snook at 'M' behind his back). One might think 'M' was thus the Father-figure whom Fleming so lacked in his life, his father having died in the First World War when he was still a boy. But, considering the difficulty he had in relating maturely with women, nothing in Pearson's biography was more illuminating than his account of the shadow cast over Fleming's life by the dominating personality of his mother. And most interesting of all was the revelation that he always referred to his mother as 'M'.

### *Star Wars*: Getting the archetype wrong

For a final example of the sentimentalisation of the Overcoming the Monster archetype, we may return to the science fiction film which exceeded even the Bond movies in popularity, George Lucas's *Star Wars* (1977). We saw earlier how effectively this story seemed to touch such a deep chord with its audience, by finding contemporary imagery to express so much of the basic symbolism which had inspired myths and legends since stories began. What only later came to light was how deliberately and consciously this had been arrived at, when, in an episode almost unique in popular storytelling, Lucas drew on the knowledge of Joseph Campbell, the distinguished American writer on the symbolic role of the hero in world myth and folklore, in an effort to ensure that his story matched up as faithfully as possible to their archetypal patterns and imagery. From this he developed such important ingredients in the power of his story as the relationship between the aspiring hero, Luke Skywalker, and the 'wise old man' Obi-Wan Kenobi who, like Merlin to Arthur or Gandalf to Frodo, initiates his young pupil into the mystery of bringing himself into harmony with 'the force': the cosmic force of life itself, expressing the irresistible power of the Self to overcome the powers of darkness.

But however carefully Lucas tried to shape his script around these archetypal ground rules, there were certain crucial respects in which the resulting story betrayed the fact that, as a conscious construct, it had not got the pattern right. It was not based on a proper understanding of the underlying archetype. Particularly significant is what happens when the hero and his companions penetrate the dark labyrinth of the Death Star to rescue the heroine, Princess Leia. They succeed in freeing her, but in doing so they leave her captor, the monstrous Darth Vader, still alive and in control of his dark kingdom. This misses the very essence of what the archetypal symbolism is about. The *anima* can only properly be liberated at the moment when the monster is finally overcome. It is precisely because the shadow has been eliminated that she can finally emerge into the light. It is only by killing the suitors that Odysseus can liberate his *anima* Penelope; only when Perseus has defeated Poseidon's sea-monster that he can be united with Andromeda; only when Aladdin has finally slain the Sorcerer that he can be fully united with his Princess.

An equally telling aberration appears right at the end of the film when, in the great hall of the Rebel Alliance, we see Luke Skywalker and his ally Han Solo walking up through a cheering crowd, to be decorated for their bravery in saving the universe by the Princess herself. Although in Lucas's book version we are told that the hero only has eyes for the beautiful Princess as she looks down at him, what we see in the film version is not the cosmic union between man and woman we see at the heart of a true happy ending. It is not the moment when Odysseus and Penelope melt into each other's arms; when Cinderella is finally at one with her Prince; when Leontes can finally once again embrace his Hermione. Luke cannot be united with his Princess, because he has not yet achieved full mature manhood. As he and Solo together come to the platform to be congratulated, they are more like boys walking up in front of their classmates to receive the approbation of their teacher, or even 'Mother'.[2]

---

2. In fact we learn from a later film in Lucas's *Star Wars* sequence that, although not his mother, Leia is the next best thing, as Luke's older sister! I have here treated the original *Star Wars* as a story standing alone in its own right, as was intended when it first appeared. But in the succession of sequels and 'prequels' Lucas was inspired by its success to produce over the following decades, he continued to play around extensively with the archetypal figures who appeared in the 1977 version, to the point where we eventually learn that Darth Vader was Luke Skywalker's father. As a young man, Vader had been one of the bravest of the Jedi Knights and Obi-Wan Kenobi's closest

In two significant respects, the conclusion to the original film of *Star Wars* thus tells us much about the society which created it. The first is the way it ended on the image of two male heroes standing together side by side. It was D. H. Lawrence, in his *Classic Studies in American Literature* (1924), who first pointed out how many American stories, since Fenimore Cooper's *The Last of the Mohicans* (1826) and Mark Twain's *The Adventures of Tom Sawyer* (1876), end not with the archetypal image of a man and a woman united in love but on two male figures, emotionally bonded in friendship by their adventures. Innumerable Hollywood films end on such an image: as we see, for instance, in *Casablanca* (1942) when, after the lovers have finally made their escape to safety, Humphrey Bogart leaves the airfield accompanied by his new friend and accomplice, the French police chief, to face a solitary and uncertain future in Vichy-ruled Morocco. Another famous example is *The Magnificent Seven* which ends with Yul Brynner and Steve McQueen, the two rootless hired guns, riding over the horizon to a future similarly unknown.

Equally revealing is the way *Star Wars* ends on the image of the two heroes walking up together through a roomful of cheering people, This reflects how, in the prevailing ethos of the American way of life, the highest prize may be not to achieve individual maturity but simply to earn the approbation of the crowd, the collective, one's own group, one's fellow citizens. It is again remarkable how many Hollywood movies end, as in *This Wonderful Life*, on the image of the hero or heroes being acclaimed by a crowd of their fellow-Americans. This profoundly important aspect of the American character originated in the rootless insecurity of a society which carried so much unconscious emotional bruising from the way it was originally forged: from the rebellious desire to escape from the oppressively 'grown-up' old world of Europe, and from the psychological one-sidedness of the struggle to impose the white man's will on that vast natural wilderness and on the original inhabitants who lived there. All this has engendered in American culture an endemic immaturity which we see reflected throughout its history, not just in the all-pervasive sentimentality of Broadway musicals and the celluloid dreams of Hollywood, but even in the stories of America's most admired novelists: Melville and Henry James, Ernest Hemingway and Scott Fitzgerald, Norman Mailer and J. D. Salinger, Philip Roth and John Updike. It is this which helps to explain the remarkable fact that so few stories conceived in America over the past two centuries have ever managed to resolve in an unambiguous image of the fully mature, fully realised Self.

---

friend. But he had then switched to the side of darkness, like other 'fallen angels' in the history of storytelling, from Lucifer in Milton's *Paradise Lost* to Saruman in *The Lord of the Rings*. In archetypal terms there is nothing odd about this since, even in the original movie, Luke's relationship to the 'Dark Lord' is entirely consistent with that of a Son-Hero to a Dark Father-figure.

## CHAPTER TWENTY-THREE

# The Ego Takes Over (III)
## *Quest, Voyage and Return, Comedy*

'Before us was a great excavation, not very recent, for the sides had fallen in
and grass had sprouted on the bottom ... all was clear ... the cache had been
found and rifled: the seven hundred thousand pounds were gone!'

R. L. Stevenson, *Treasure Island*

'When the Supreme Value and the Supreme Negation are both outside, the
soul is void.'

C. G. Jung

Continuing our survey of what happens to the archetypal plots when they are
appropriated by the ego, this chapter looks at dark and sentimental versions of the
Quest, Voyage and Return and Comedy.

The fundamental archetype of the Quest, as in the *Odyssey*, shows us the journey
of its hero towards a distant goal which, when it is reached, turns out to symbolise his Self-realisation. The inversion of this, as in *Moby Dick*, shows us a dark hero
whose life-journey is dedicated to destroying an outward projection of the Self,
bringing about his own self-destruction.

Such a truly dark form is very rare in storytelling. But we can see the essence of
the Quest archetype in a number of well-known stories which are shaped around
a dark hero's obsessive drive to reach some distant, all-important goal; but
which then turns out to be the destruction of some figure symbolising wholeness
and 'light'.

A powerful example was that early modern novel Samuel Richardson's *Clarissa*
(1748). Few books have caused more of a stir in the history of literature than this
immensely long story, originally published in eight huge instalments, providing an
early premonition of the earthquake which, over the century following, was about
to shake Western storytelling to its foundations.

The story centres on the obsessive desire of its dashing libertine hero, Lovelace,
to seduce the beautiful, virtuous, strong-minded heroine Clarissa. When she is locked
away by her family for refusing the man they want her to marry, Lovelace rescues
her and carries her off to London. But this only places her in his power, so he is free
to lay siege to her virtue by every trick and device he can think of. Withstanding
all his assaults, she remains a model of the idealised *anima*, the soul of chaste and
sovereign femininity; until, after many hundreds of pages, Lovelace finally manages
to drug and rape her. This leaves her so devastated that she begins to lose her reason. She finally escapes, to endure more horrors such as being thrown into prison,
but is rescued by Belfort, who represents Lovelace's 'light Alter-Ego'. Under his care,

she recovers her sanity but continues to decline physically, until at last, having made her peace with the world and with God, she dies. This tragic conclusion, showing a virtuous heroine gratuitously destroyed, aroused such horror when the novel was first appearing in successive instalments that readers all over Europe rushed to protest, imploring Richardson to provide a happier ending. But the deed was done. And, after her death, Lovelace is finally paid out for his crime when he is killed in a duel by Clarissa's cousin.

Since it is not concerned with an outward, physical journey, it may seem odd to suggest that *Clarissa* is shaped by the archetype of the Quest. But, on an inward level, this is what the story is about. As in a more conventional Quest, the suspense which sustains our interest in the story lies all in that one overriding question: will the hero reach that central goal to which everything else in his life has become subordinated? To overcome Clarissa's resistance and take her virginity has become his one all-consuming aim. Yet we are in no doubt that his purpose is entirely dark. As with Ahab, we know the hero is possessed by the desire to commit a deed which symbolically has become the ultimate cosmic crime: the violation of the *anima*, the destruction of the Self. The story's whole intention is to present the heroine as the hero's absolute antithesis: the shining and selfless 'light feminine' being first besieged, then finally destroyed by the utterly ruthless egocentricity of the 'dark masculine'.

In this respect we cannot escape the ambiguity of Richardson's own position as the story's creator. Although he built up Clarissa as an idealised personification of the feminine, he did so only in order to fantasise his hero attempting in every way to degrade and defile her; placing her in a brothel, physically assaulting her, raping her, consigning her to prison, finally imagining her death. In this sense, Clarissa became a prototype for what Mario Praz called in *The Romantic Agony* 'the persecuted maiden' who, from the late-eighteenth century onwards, was to become such a conspicuous feature of plays, operas and novels in the age of Romanticism: the beautiful, virtuous heroine whose chief role in the fantasies of so many authors was to be portrayed as imprisoned, persecuted, ill-treated or murdered; or just wasting away through consumption to a tragically early death, as in *La Traviata*, *La Dame Aux Camellias* or *La Boheme*.

Once we recognise the significance of this figure as symbolising the *anima*, the personification of the soul, what an insight this conveys of what was beginning to happen, spiritually, morally and psychologically, to the culture for which the image of the 'persecuted maiden' was to become such a central emblematic figure. Less than fifty years after Richardson created Clarissa, the Marquis de Sade wrote his openly pornographic novel *Justine; the Misfortunes of Virtue*. And here the unremitting succession of physical cruelties and sexual degradations which its author could enjoy imagining being inflicted on his helpless heroine until she finally met a gratuitously violent death was even more obviously beginning to take storytelling in the Western world towards a wholly new phase of its development.

Another story similarly shaped by a hidden version of the Quest archetype was Peter Shaffer's play *Amadeus* (1979, filmed 1984). The narrator, the eighteenth-century Viennese composer Salieri, describes his growing obsession with his contemporary and more successful rival, the young Mozart, whose music is so inspired that it seems to come straight from God. So dark does his obsession become that Salieri conceives it as the supreme purpose of his life to destroy Mozart. At the moment when he settles on his goal, he snatches down from the wall an image of the crucified Christ and hurls it into the fire. Eventually he reaches the goal of his quest when he succeeds in harrying Mozart to an early death. Salieri then loses his reason, and recalls the story in a lunatic asylum.

A startling feature of this story, particularly in its film version, was the contrast between the care lavished to ensure that every detail of its setting might seem historically plausible and the way it portrayed its central character, Mozart himself. The film was shot in Prague, as the most unspoiled baroque city in Europe. It was even emphasised that a magnificent chandelier shown in several scenes was the very one owned by Mozart's Salzburg patron, the Archbishop Colloredo, lovingly restored and lit with thousands of candles for the first time since the eighteenth century. Yet in the midst of all this riot of historical verisimilitude appeared the central figure, Mozart, shockingly presented as a giggling and ridiculous little dirty-minded grotesque. Here any pretence at historical accuracy was chucked out of the window. This bizarre creation bore not the slightest resemblance to the complex and fundamentally very serious real-life Mozart who emerges from his letters or descriptions by contemporaries. It was as if it was not only Salieri who was setting out on his Quest to destroy Mozart but the author himself: turning the composer into this embarrassing travesty to gratify some obscure purpose of his own psyche.

To support such a distortion of the facts, Shaffer cited a few mildly scatological passages from letters Mozart had written to his girl cousin when in his early twenties. But, ignoring almost everything else we know about the composer, these fragments had then been blown up to represent the whole man. Inevitably this raises the question: why? The explanation offered was that the play was trying to show how an artist and his work can be seen as wholly separate. There was no connection between the nobility of the music and the ignoble personality of its composer. He was merely, Salieri explained, the unworthy channel for art which derived from some quite separate source.

But this hardly explained the need to debase Mozart in a way which so defied historical reality. Was it any accident that this dark story was conceived in an age which, while recognising the divine perfection of Mozart's music, had nevertheless travelled so far from the fundamental values it represented that it was now totally at odds with them? So long as the music could be treated as quite separate from the culture and the values which had given rise to it, it could still be marvelled at. But this made it all the more important to contrast the music with everything which had originally inspired it. Thus, instead of recognising the human Mozart as all of a piece with music which is one of the supreme expressions in history of the values of the Self, the story sought to degrade him into an infantile caricature. By doing dirt on Mozart, it was unconsciously violating the Self. Such, as was symbolised in Salieri's God-defying act of hurling the crucifix into the fire, was the purpose of portraying his demonic quest to destroy the composer of some of the most sublimely ego-transcending music ever written: resulting in a story which, in its own way, carried echoes of the darkness of *Moby Dick*.

Three very different examples of dark quests in modern popular storytelling were the movie *Raiders of the Lost Ark* (1981) by Steven Spielberg and George Lucas, Frederick Forsyth's novel *The Day of the Jackal* (1971) and the post-war Ealing film comedy *Kind Hearts and Coronets* (1949).

*Raiders of the Lost Ark*, set in a *pastiche* version of the 1930s, full of period clothes, cars and aeroplanes, centres on a race between its archaeologist hero Indiana Jones and a rival team of Nazi archaeologists to find the long-lost Ark of the Covenant, the holiest treasure of the Jewish people because it contained historic evidence of their unique contact with God (and is therefore a symbol of the Self). After adventures set in several continents, Jones finally discovers the treasure hidden in an ancient snake-infested underground chamber in Egypt. But the Nazis steal it from him and take it to an Aegean island where, before returning to Germany to present it to Hitler, they open the mysterious box to check its contents. Because their Quest to possess this image of the Self has been driven by dark motives, the act of opening it unleashes dark supernatural forces which destroy them.

*The Day of the Jackal* features the obsessive quest of an English mercenary to assassinate the French President de Gaulle in 1963. As a revered ruler and father of his people, de Gaulle is also a kingly symbol of the Self. Most of the story is taken up with how the dark hero moves relentlessly through the shadows towards his goal, pursued by a French policeman, until he has the President in his sights and is ready to fire the fatal shot. In the nick of time, the light hero who has been tracking him bursts into the room and kills him.

The black comedy *Kind Hearts and Coronets* opens with its hero Louis Mazzini in a condemned cell in Edwardian London, writing out the story of his life on the morning when he is due to be hanged. He describes how he grew up in genteel poverty in South London alone with his mother, a Duke's daughter, callously thrown out by her family for having eloped with an Italian singer, who had died of a heart attack at his son's birth. She brings him up to be aware that he is twelfth in line of succession to the current Duke of Chalfont, head of the D'Ascoyne family. As a young man Louis is turned down by 'the captivating Sibylla', a little Temptress, in favour of a Mr Holland, whom she thinks socially superior. When his mother is killed in an accident, he is inspired to wreak vengeance on the family by embarking on a systematic plan to murder in turn each of the 12 remaining members of the D'Ascoyne family who stand between him and the dukedom, the goal of his Quest. As he ingeniously arranges one death after another, he meanwhile conducts an adulterous affair with Sibylla, although, as he nears his goal, he also proposes marriage to Edith, the high-minded widow of one of his victims. Sibylla's now-bankrupt husband then commits suicide, freeing Sibylla to marry the hero herself.

No sooner has Louis reached his goal by murdering the Duke, thus succeeding to a great castle, vast estates and almost kingly social position (all the outward trappings of attaining to the Self), than everything begins to fall apart. He is arrested on the charge of murdering Sibylla's husband, the one crime he has not committed. Thanks to her perjured evidence, his fellow-members of the House of Lords find him guilty and he is sentenced to death, although Edith marries him to proclaim her faith in his innocence. The night before his execution, Sibylla, who has guessed the truth of his crimes, gives him an ultimatum. She will show the authorities a note proving that her husband committed suicide, if Louis promises to murder Edith and marry her instead. 'Poor Edith' he replies. Next morning, in the nick of time, he is reprieved. As he leaves the prison he sees the two women each waiting for him in a separate carriage. As he hesitates over which of them to go to, a reporter asks him whether he would consider publishing his memoirs. With a shock of horror he recalls that he has left behind in his cell the incriminating document in which he has set out precisely how he committed all his genuine murders. On this teasing note, the story remains in every way unresolved. Louis is a classic 'boy hero who cannot grow up', trapped by the dark feminine, his *anima* split between two powerful women, both formerly married and thus evoking the 'Dark Mother'. This has set him fatally at odds with the world of 'Father', which now threatens his death.

## The Quest: The lesser dark and sentimental versions

An early example of the 'lesser dark version' of this type of story was one of the most celebrated quests of all: that of the children of Israel as they journeyed out of bondage in Egypt to seek the distant promised land. As recorded in *Genesis*, this tale has been retold times without number as one of the most inspiring adventures in history, with its miraculous happy ending when the tribes of Israel finally arrive safely in the 'land flowing with milk and honey'. When we look at the story more closely it is not so simple. From its honoured place in Judaeo-Christian legend, we might imagine that when the Israelites enter the land promised by God it is lying there empty and waiting for them. But, as we learn from the final speech made before his death by their leader Moses (*Deuteronomy* 7), the future land of Israel is already home to many tribes. In the first part of his speech, Moses recalls the commandments handed down by God on Mount Sinai, including 'thou shalt not kill', 'thou shalt not steal', 'thou shalt not covet thy neighbour's goods'. But he then dramatically changes tack, telling his followers that when they arrive in the promised land they will find it full of the tribes who already live there: they are to kill them, steal their goods and 'show them no mercy'. Those seeming moral absolutes handed down on Sinai are not absolute at all. They apply only within the 'in group' of the children of Israel themselves. When it comes to outsiders, no such rules apply. They must be treated absolutely ruthlessly; because on them the Jews have projected the shadow of their own collective egotism.

Sure enough, when they arrive near their goal, they face, like many another group of Quest heroes, a succession of tremendous battles, beginning with the siege of Jericho and ending in the 'Battle of the Thirty-One Kings'. At last they establish their sovereignty. But this is no complete happy ending, as the archetype dictates. There is no sign that the children of Israel are going to live happily ever after in their new kingdom. The whole of the rest of their history is to be dominated by other nations and peoples challenging their occupation of that land, beginning with the Philistines and ending with the Roman expulsion of the Jews in the second century AD which was to lead to their diaspora, or scattering, all over the the known world. In the twentieth century, of course, this tragic story was to be acted out all over again, with the reoccupation of Palestine by the Jews of the *diaspora*, leading first to an uneasy cohabitation with the Palestinians who already lived there and finally, with the setting up of the state of Israel, to their forcible dispossession and suppression.

When, in the original story, the children of Israel arrived at their goal, this could not symbolise a genuine triumph for the values of the Self, because they had collectively projected the archetype out onto the external world, as an expression of that collective ego which must always carry its shadow. Thus the story could never reach a complete and final happy ending. There would always remain that shadow, from which those elements of the whole which had been repressed would continually emerge to haunt them: exactly as was again to be the case in the twentieth century.

A much more domestic example of projecting the Quest archetype out onto the external world can be seen in George Orwell's novel *Coming Up For Air* (1939). The hero, George Bowling, feels himself trapped in middle age, a loveless marriage, a humdrum job with an insurance firm, a little house in an anonymous London suburb and a life which has become wholly meaningless. He might say, like Dante at the beginning of *The Divine Comedy*, 'midway on the journey of this life, I came to a place where the way was lost'; and like Dante he sets out on a quest to reach paradise. Except that in 'Fatty' Bowling's spiritually shrunken world, the heaven he seeks is a distant memory from his childhood in a small country town. As a small boy obsessed with fishing, he had once, all alone, penetrated a dark wood in the grounds of a large house outside the town, where he had come across a secret, deep, dark pool, surrounded by trees. Gleaming in its depths were huge, ancient golden carp, the biggest fish he had ever seen. Now, half a lifetime later, he decides he will escape all the oppressions of his empty life by setting out on a Quest, back to the world of his childhood, to fish for those numinous carp in their mysterious pool. It is a classic external projection of the symbolism of the Self.

George journeys to the town, which he finds swollen almost out of recognition by modern development. The surrounding fields he remembered from his boyhood have disappeared under rows of identical little houses and factories. His childhood home is now an unwelcoming tea shop. He glimpses the pretty girl he had loved in his youth, his lost *anima*, now aged into a shapeless hag. He finally reaches the country house, now a lunatic asylum, and walks on through the trees, nearing his ultimate goal. But suddenly he emerges into a housing estate. Much of the wood has been felled. When he asks after the secret pool, he is told by a resident he must be thinking of that hole over there which, long since emptied of water or fish, is filled with tin cans and all the rubbish of twentieth century civilisation. He has sought the outward symbol of the Self, only to find it an empty hole, crammed with the detritus of human egotism. He returns home to his nagging wife, defeated and broken.

The destructive onward march of the twentieth century across the English countryside also hangs like a dark shadow over one of the most haunting and successful of recent Quest stories, *Watership Down* (1972). On the face of it, this modern epic is an almost perfect recreation of the Quest archetype, as its heroes set out on their long hazardous journey, reach their goal, marry their 'Princesses' and see the survival of their 'kingdom' secured for the future. One of the book's most appealing qualities is the way it transforms a stretch of familiar, all-too domesticated Home Counties countryside into a vast, seemingly mythic realm, comparable with that wild, mysterious terrain familiar from many an older Quest journey. It takes a feat of imagination to translate contemporary rural England, with its broiler farms, barbed wire fences and motorways, back into such a faery-realm of romance and high adventure; creating the most successful pseudo-mythic landscape since the imaginary world conjured up by Tolkien.

But it could only do this by turning its heroes into little rabbits, whose worst enemies, with their cars, guns and traps, are the human race itself. The very reason the rabbits must set out on their Quest is that the warren where they live is about to be gassed and bulldozed, to make way for yet another human housing estate. And it is precisely because the heroes are animals and not human beings that they can be invested with purely human qualities. With James Bond, *Star Wars* and most latter-day adventure stories, set in a prison of space rockets, aeroplanes, fast cars and electronics, the modern epic hero has been all but dehumanised, turned by his technology into little more than an automaton. With the rabbits of *Watership Down*, we are firmly back in a pre-mechanical world, where Hazel and his friends can only survive by their direct exercise of primary, innate human qualities. But the very fact that, to conjure up such a human story, according to the age-old pattern of the Quest, the author had in effect to escape from our modern technologically-shaped world altogether, says much about the underlying message of the book. It was trying to preserve the essence of the archetype in a world where in human terms, it was implied, humanity's remorseless collective egotism had rendered this all but impossible. For all its virtues, the story was little more than an escapist and rather melancholy dream.

Such is the power of this archetype that it has never ceased to exercise its hold over the imagination of modern storytellers; although usually it has been trivialised on a level far removed from its original underlying purpose. That typically mid-1960s film *It's a Mad, Mad, Mad, Mad World* (1964) was a good example of such a tale, both dark and sentimental at the same time. A group of motorists in California are overtaken by a car being driving recklessly along a mountain road. It crashes over the edge and they reach the dying driver, a professional criminal, just in time to hear him reveal the whereabouts of a hoard of illicit money buried 200 miles away. At once they are all fired with greed for the money and, after failing to work out any way they can co-operate, they all speed off in deadly rivalry to see who can reach the treasure first. Unwittingly, their Quest is being observed by a local police chief, Captain Culpeper (Spencer Tracy), who has long been on the trail of the dead criminal and even more of his illicit gains. Despite running into every kind of obstacle on their journey, all parties arrive at the goal simultaneously, plus a few more who have heard the story on the way. No sooner have they dug up the treasure, still arguing to the last on how it should be divided, than Culpeper arrests them all for being in possession of stolen money. He then tricks them into driving away in one direction, while he disappears in the other with the 'evidence'. Realising they have been duped, they turn round and pursue him, in an exact reversal of the earlier part of the story where he and his men had been pursuing them. They finally trap him on the fire escape of a tall building, while a vast crowd gathers below to watch the drama. As the pursuers catch up with him, the suitcase full of dollar bills bursts open and all the money showers down to the crowd below. Everyone involved in the Quest, including the policeman, has been motivated entirely by greed. They are now all paid out for their egocentricity, as the treasure they have been seeking literally dissipates into thin air.

More conventionally sentimental Quest stories include several examples we looked at earlier where, in each case, because they are simply external projections of the archetype, we find that something has gone askew with the story's proper structure. One instance is Stevenson's *Treasure Island* where, when the heroes finally reach the site of the buried treasure they have travelled across the world to find, they discover it is gone. The hole is empty. The treasure has already been dug up by Ben Gunn, the 'natural man' who, like Robinson Crusoe, has become 'king' of the island; although, as reward for their rescuing him, he shares it out among them.

In Verne's *Around the World in Eighty Days*, the hero Phineas Fogg actually liberates the 'Princess', his *anima*-figure, half way through the journey, completely missing the archetypal point; although only at the end, when he has finally reached his goal, is he properly united with her. In Rider Haggard's *King Solomon's Mines*, although it makes such powerful use of archetypal imagery, the disintegrated nature of the ending betrays the extent to which the story is just playing with the archetypes. The black (therefore, in story terms, 'inferior') hero, Umbopa, remains behind, having succeeded to his 'kingdom'; while the three white heroes return home with their haul of gold and jewels, which is only a mere material treasure, nothing more profound.

In *Babar and Father Christmas*, the hero Babar successfully reaches the goal of his Quest by finding Father Christmas and bringing him back to Africa. But here the archetypes all get muddled up, because Babar is already the King and father of his people, so he can hardly succeed to the kingdom as reward for successfully concluding his Quest. Indeed, Father Christmas merely supplies an additional kindly father-figure to the equation, although he then disappears again, while promising to return. So slight and charming is this tale that it might seem churlish to quibble about its failure to match up precisely to the archetype. But the fact remains that, without that underlying archetype, the story would not strike the responsive chord in children that it does. In this sense it is only the sentimentalised version of a story which, in its proper role, serves a much more serious function in the human imagination altogether.

## Voyage and Return: The dark version

According to its full archetype, the Voyage and Return story begins with an incomplete or inadequate hero or heroine being taken out of their original state of limited consciousness and plunged into an unfamiliar realm representing a world of which they were previously unaware. It is through this confrontation with 'unconscious elements' that, like Robinson Crusoe or Lucius in *The Golden Ass*, they learn that which is necessary to make them whole. Their final return to the normal world, inwardly transformed, marks the happy ending of the story.

The most completely dark version of this pattern, as we saw, is in those rare stories where the hero enters the abnormal world and remains trapped, never returning. Kafka's *The Trial* (1920) begins with its hero Joseph K. finding 'one fine morning' that 'without having done anything wrong', he has been arrested. He is at once plunged into a mysterious world where he knows he is under investigation for some shadowy and serious crime but is never told what it is. Outwardly, on the conscious level, he tries to continue living his normal life, as senior manager in a bank. But all the time he is aware that, on this mysterious unconscious level, the investigation by the mysterious 'Court' is continuing and that more and more people he knows or meets are somehow connected to it. Despite many knowing hints and innuendos, no one will tell him directly what is going on. Even when he visits an old bedridden lawyer who is meant to be his 'Advocate' in the case, nothing is ever properly explained. But here K. makes his only direct contact with anyone he encounters in the twilight world, the young maid Leni, who kisses, fondles and claims to love him; although he is later told she falls in love with any accused man who visits her employer. Finally, after an interview with a priest in a cathedral, still without any idea of what he is accused, K. receives a visit from two men who lead him out into the countryside, take out a butcher's knife and stab him, 'like a dog', through the heart.

What has caught people's imagination about this story, popularising the term 'Kafka-esque' even among those who have never read his books, is the sense it conjures up of someone feeling totally alone in a wholly baffling world, where he feels increasingly threatened by guilt while never being given enough information to understand what is happening to him. In this sense K. is like the central figure of other Voyage and Return stories, such as Alice in Wonderland (who also ends up being mysteriously put on trial and found guilty). A similar echo of many Voyage and Return stories is the haunting presence of Leni, the elusive *anima*, as the only character in the unconscious world to whom the hero can relate. But, unlike these other stories, K. is doomed never to escape from his shadow world and ends up dying a premature death without ever knowing why.

In this respect it may not be irrelevant that Kafka wrote his story during the early stages of the consumption which, four years later, was to kill him. On one level, in this picture of a man threatened by a shadowy, inexorable process which ends in his death without apparent reason, we may see a personification of the shadowy, fatal disease which already had him in its grip. For a time Kafka had a peculiar horror of his physical body, which may account for the even darker version of a Voyage without Return conveyed in his short story *Metamorphosis*. This begins with the hero, Gregor, waking up one morning to find he has turned into a monstrous, repulsive insect. Since his parents and young sister wholly depend on his earnings as a hard-working commercial traveller, they cannot understand why he has not got up for work, and remains behind the locked door of his room. Eventually the door is opened, and everyone sees with horror what has happened. At first, only his sister, his *anima*-figure, is at all sympathetic. But as weeks go by and he remains trapped in his disgusting state, even she, like every-one else, turns against him, until he finally starves to death.

From these nightmarish visions, it may seem a far cry to that novel which enjoyed such cult status among students in the 1950s and 1960s, J. D. Salinger's *Catcher in the Rye* (1951). The hero Holden Caulfield, in his late teens, is plunged into his other world when, after making a complete mess of his work and human relationships, he is sent home from from yet another smart, East Coast prep school, his fourth expulsion. Not daring to tell his parents what has happened, he heads for New York where he drifts through the city, meeting a succession of strangers, as in his brief embarrassing encounter with a young prostitute, and rather desperately trying to arrange dates with various girls he knows from school holidays. A parallel which emerges between Holden's adventures and the world of Joseph K. is that he never makes real contact with any of the people he meets: the empty-headed girls in a bar; two earnest nuns; the sad little hooker; snobbish Sally Hayes, whom he takes to a Broadway play. Like a psychotic, he is constantly divided between his contempt for almost everyone else in the world as irritating, embarrassing, stupid 'phoneys'; and then, as if trying to make up for it, wanting to throw in an extravagant reference to how much he likes them or misses them after all. Beneath his brash, cocky, dismissive *persona*, Holden becomes increas-ingly lost and desperate, until the only two people in the world he wants to see are his younger sister Phoebe, who lives with their parents in a smart, high-rise apartment, and Mr Antolini, the only teacher he has ever respected. As he nears the end of his tether, it is a faint evocation of that great archetypal duality, the Wise Old Man and the Anima. Late at night he calls on Antolini, who welcomes him in and, after giving him sage fatherly advice, puts him to bed. But Holden then wakes up to find Antolini stroking his head in an erotic fashion and flees in shocked horror. The next day, he meets young Phoebe, now the only person he loves and trusts in the world, his infantile *anima*, and after wandering about, they end at a funfair where, in the rain, he watches her going round and round on an old-fashioned carousel:

> 'I felt so damn happy, if you want to know the truth. I don't know why but she looked so damn nice, the way she kept going round and round, in her blue coat and all. God, I wish you could've been there.'

It is a chilling final image: the *anima*, instead of being a central fixed point of light, just revolving in endless neurotic motion. From the brief epilogue, addressed from a psychiatric hospital a few months later, we gather Holden then had a prolonged nervous breakdown. From the moment of his expulsion into the 'other world' he had never managed to return to normality. Perhaps, like the novel's reclusive author who, after writing two more books, shut himself away from the world for decades without producing another, he never would.

For a final example in this sequence we look at that curious little story produced by Evelyn Waugh in his middle age, *The Ordeal of Gilbert Pinfold* (1957). We saw earlier how Waugh was particularly drawn to the Voyage and Return plot. To the outside world, one of the novelist's more obvious characteristics, as someone who had escaped from his original middle-class suburban background onto the fringes of the world of the English upper classes, was the way he hid his personal insecurities behind an armour-plated *persona*, fabricated out of snobbery and a sentimentalised Roman Catholicism, combined with cantankerous impatience towards anyone who did not fit socially into his very limited world-view. The trouble with the persona is that it is only an outward mask: suppressed behind it, its owner's true personality becomes increasingly lost. In Waugh's case this was unconsciously reflected in the way both *Decline and Fall* and *Brideshead Revisited* showed a rather limited little middle-class hero finding himself drawn into a glamorous, upper-class 'other world' in which he is never wholly at ease or at home, and from which he is eventually rejected, sad and alone. But none of Waugh's stories was more directly self-revelatory than that of Gilbert Pinfold: portrayed as, like its author when he wrote it, a successful novelist with social pretensions who, in his early fifties, suddenly finds his life empty, suffocating and meaningless.

Pinfold decides to take a cruise to Ceylon, but no sooner has he boarded the good ship *Caliban* (echoing 'the shadow') than he hears an almost continuous babble of sounds, irritating dance music and voices, which he imagines must be emerging from some shipboard internal communication system. As he identifies the voices, what they are saying seems more and more to be directed at him personally, in an accusatory fashion. Much of their abuse is on a crude, rather babyish level, reflecting the ethos of the public school-educated English upper-middle class, accusing him of being a Jew, an enemy agent, a homosexual, a drunk. But he is so convinced of the reality of his paranoid delusions that they make it impossible for him to relate rationally to his fellow-passengers or the crew who, although initially polite, eventually shun him as a sad eccentric. Eventually one voice stands out from the babble, that of a young woman called Margaret, with whom Pinfold imagines he is establishing a kind of relationship. He also learns she is called 'Miss Angel'. She claims to love him, and in a particularly embarrassing scene they agree a midnight assignation, whereby she will come to his cabin to make love. But of course the elusive *anima* never appears, and eventually Pinfold abandons the ship and makes his way back to meet his wife in a London hotel, where the voices finally leave him. The last he hears is that of the *anima*, Miss Angel, repeating 'I do love you Gilbert. I don't exist but I do love ... Good-bye ... love ...'. He is then alone with his wife. He has made his Voyage and Return and comes back having understood nothing.

Three features in particular characterise all these examples of the dark Voyage and Return. In each case their hero, Joseph K., Gregor, Holden Caulfield and Pinfold, is almost wholly egocentric, trapped in his own limited awareness and lack of feeling for other people. In each case, when confronted by the challenge of the 'other world', this only heightens his isolation, in that he cannot properly communicate or establish a relationship with any of the people he meets there. But in each case, the one exception is the girl who represents the feminine: Leni, Gregor's sister, Caulfield's sister, Pinfold's Miss Angel, She tantalises the hero as his elusive anima, representing precisely that central value which is missing in his life: the sense of connection; the feeling and understanding of the inner feminine which, if only he could get properly in touch with it, might enable him to become a full man. But this cannot be. The hero remains trapped in his egotistical prison. Whether he stays trapped forever in his other world, like Kafka's heroes, or at least outwardly seems to return to where he started, like Pinfold, he has failed the challenge. Frozen in a state of arrested development, he is unable to grow up.

In this sense, these stories are typical of all those versions of the Voyage and Return plot we saw earlier, where the hero or heroine emerges from the other world basically unchanged. In some, the sentimental versions, like *Alice in Wonderland* or *The Wizard of Oz*, the experience has been just like some strange dream. It has not touched their lives; they can carry on as if it never happened. In other examples, the lesser dark versions, like *Le Grand Meaulnes*, *Gone with the Wind*, *Brideshead Revisited*, the hero or heroine lose the 'other half' they have encountered in the other world, and face the rest of their life 'childless, loveless and alone'. The whole purpose of this archetype is to show us a solitary individual being faced with the ultimate challenge. Confronted with the unknown world which symbolises the limitation of their ego-consciousness, are they ready, like Lucius, to go through that colossal transformation which will eventually enable them to reach Self-realisation, at one with their *anima* and with all the world? If not, they have failed the test and must remain trapped in the ego forever.

## Comedy: The dark and sentimental versions

What happens when the ego takes over the archetype of Comedy? A truly dark version of this lightest of plots might seem a contradiction in terms. In fact such stories have played a much more important role in the development of storytelling over the past 200 years than might be supposed. The only reason why this is not generally appreciated is that, when Comedy turns truly dark, we no longer recognise it as Comedy. We saw earlier how *Othello* is a play which in plot terms shows many of the ingredients of a Comedy; although when there is no 'recognition', and the hero thus ends up smothering his *anima* and turning his dagger on himself, it becomes arguably the darkest play Shakespeare ever wrote. For similar reasons, we shall not be looking at some of the best-known examples of what happens to Comedy when it turns dark until the next chapter.

The most obvious fate of Comedy when, like the other plots, it became detached from its true archetypal foundations was what we saw happening in the plays and light operas of the later nineteenth and early twentieth centuries. In the operettas of Johann Strauss and Lehar, in Gilbert and Sullivan, the plays of Wilde and Feydeau and many later examples, we see the outward form of the plot preserved but emptied of its deeper significance, so that Comedy becomes a mere burlesque of itself.

In this sense, *Die Fledermaus* or *The Importance of Being Earnest* or *The Merry Widow* represent the sentimentalisation of Comedy, enjoying the superficial fun it can provide without bothering about its more serious message.

What also happened to Comedy, as we saw earlier, was that it split into two separate types of story. On one hand are those which so concentrate on its 'comic' element that this becomes an end in itself, producing stories which concentrate just on its potential to make us laugh. Here we have all that vast range of comic films, novels, plays and TV 'situation comedies', from the films of Laurel and Hardy to such popular British television series as *Fawlty Towers, Yes, Minister, Dad's Army, Till Death Do Us Part* or *Steptoe and Son*, all of which are still essentially based on the humour to be derived from exposing the contrast between reality and the self-deluding pretensions of egotism.

Entertaining though such modern comedy may be, it has travelled a long way from the archetype's original purpose, which is to show not just the puncturing of the illusions of the human ego, but also the liberating effect of the shift to that other, deeper centre in the psyche, the Self. This was why, after its beginnings in the Athens of Aristophanes, the Comedy plot became so centred on the bringing together of a man and a woman, hero and *anima*, heroine and *animus*, as the ultimate image of human wholeness. Similarly, nothing is more illuminating in Comedy than how it shows the effect of one person's egotism on everyone else around. We see how the blind egotism of an Almaviva or Leontes throws a whole household or community into shadow, so that no one is free to relate properly to anyone else. Then, when recognition comes and the dominating source of egocentricity is removed, we see how the shadows lift and the whole community can emerge into the light.

It was all this which tended to get lost when the humorous element in Comedy became split off from its more serious foundations, although these too, as we saw, took on a life of their own by turning into stories of romantic love without much necessity for humour. Since this has produced many profound and important stories, not least the novels of Jane Austen or *War and Peace*, it can hardly be said in itself to have marked any fatal trivialisation of the plot; although even in *War and Peace* there are traces of sentimentality, notably in the somewhat implausible pairing-off of the two central couples. We also see in the book's messily unresolved ending how Tolstoy was losing touch with the basic archetype.

But we still see many modern comedies where the two elements remain unified, even though, where the desire to make the audience laugh becomes too obviously predominant, as in the novels of Wodehouse or the films of the Marx Brothers, they may persist only in rather uneasy and unequal relationship, with the 'love element' retained only as a kind of appendix: an organ surviving beyond the point where anyone can remember what was its original purpose.

Equally we see comedies which manage to retain that original combination of light-hearted humour with romantic love, but where there is no sense at the end of any real access of self-awareness: that fundamental moment of 'recognition' in the true comic archetype where we feel the story's centre of gravity finally moving from the claustrophobia of the ego to the liberation of the Self. In *Four Weddings and a Funeral* we see a group of middle-class young people stumbling through their lives in modern London in a fairly limited state of awareness; trying to work out who they should pair off with; attending each other's weddings; getting drunk (although for once external reality breaks into their muddled haze when one of their number dies, and is revealed to have been a homosexual). We finally see the hero and heroine coming to the climactic moment of 'recognition', when they are in a crowded church for his wedding to someone else. In the most embarrassing circumstances they suddenly realise that they are meant for each other after all, with a love they imagine to be so special and unique that it transcends any need to go through the mere outward, social ritual of a wedding. We duly respond in our archetypally programmed way by finding this a touching conclusion. But we hardly have the sense that they have reached that transcendent state of cosmic, selfless union, bringing together a whole community in joy and loving reconciliation, which, at the end of a Shakespearian comedy, can send an audience out of the theatre feeling that they are walking on air and that all the world has been renewed. The hero and heroine of *Four Weddings* are still the same rather limited, egocentric couple they have been all along. In this sense the film provides yet another illustration of what happens when Comedy is taken over by the ego and turned into only a sentimental vestige of itself.

What we shall see in the next chapter, however, is what happens when the plot of Comedy is both sentimentalised and turns dark at the same time; when it becomes so far removed from its proper roots that we no longer recognise it as related to Comedy at all. Yet in this guise, as we shall see, it helped shape some of the most celebrated stories of our modern civilisation.

## CHAPTER TWENTY-FOUR

# The Ego Takes Over (IV)
## *Tragedy and Rebirth*

'Don Giovanni ... is the most ambiguous of hero-villains. The pursuit of
happiness and the pursuit of love, which had once seemed so simple and life-
giving, have become complex and destructive; and his refusal to repent, which
makes him heroic, belongs to another phase of civilisation.'

Kenneth Clark, Civilisation (1967)

As with the other plots it might seem a contradiction in terms that Tragedy could
be viewed through the eyes of the ego, since the whole purpose of this archetype
is to show what happens when a hero or heroine gives way to the ego-centred part
of themselves. We see them going through the inexorable pattern which leads to
their destruction. But when we see this pattern portrayed by storytellers like
Shakespeare or Tolstoy, we see it presented objectively, viewed from the detached
standpoint of the Self. We may look on Lear or Anna Karenina with pity, as they
are drawn down to their doom. But we are in no doubt that they have been
deceived by the ego into a web of their own weaving; that what we are looking at
is the essential process whereby any such rebellion against the whole must unfold,
until hubris is followed by nemesis and the state of balance has been restored.

One obvious consequence when the ego takes over this type of story is that it
is no longer seen like this, from the viewpoint of the wider whole. We see the
doomed central figure presented, not as the author of his or her own misfortunes,
but as a heroic victim, caught up in the toils of a malevolent fate.

One early sign of the approaching age of Romanticism in the eighteenth century
was the so-called *Sturm und Drang* movement of the early 1770s, and in particular the extraordinary reception given to the first novel by the 25-year old Goethe,
*The Sorrows of Young Werther* (1774). The young hero paints an idyllic picture of
the little town in which he is living, in which one summer day arrives the most
wonderful, beautiful girl he has ever seen. Charlotte is a paragon of all the feminine virtues, strong-minded, sensitive, loving, soulful: a perfect personification
of the *anima*, with whom Werther at once falls madly in love. Furthermore, she
seems to like him, and their friendship soon becomes very close. But this Dream
Stage then gives way to the first hint of a Frustration Stage, when Werther learns
that Lotte is engaged to another man. Even when her decent but dull Albert
arrives, however, it initially seems the three of them can still get on very happily
together. But eventually, despite Lotte's continued apparent pleasure in Werther's
company, she and Albert are married. At last her new husband begins to show

impatience at Werther's continued presence. The hero feels his 'angel' slipping away from him. He begins to fall apart.

> 'Ill humour and listlessness became more and more deeply rooted in Werther's soul until finally they took possession of his entire personality ... his anxiety destroyed all the remaining forces of his intellect, his liveliness, his wit.'

He is into the Nightmare Stage. At last, on a winter's night, he has a final emotional interview with his beloved. He reads out to her at enormous length his translation of the sentimental songs of Ossian, showers her with passionate kisses and storms off into the night. At midnight, using pistols borrowed from Albert, he shoots himself.

The outward form of this story corresponds exactly to the five-stage pattern of the tragic archetype. But we are not expected to view Werther objectively as a foolish, immature young man, in the grip of an adolescent infatuation he has not the self-awareness or self-control to resist. Since we see much of the story through his own eyes, as its narrator, we are invited to identify with him as a romantic hero, so idealistic that he is prepared to sacrifice life itself for his noble dream of love. Certainly this was how Goethe's story was received when it first appeared, as all over Europe young admirers rushed to copy Werther in donning blue frock coats and yellow waistcoats, or buy perfumes bearing Werther's name. Indeed some were so carried away by the story's self-glorifying sentimentality that it even inspired a rash of sympathetic suicides.

Fifteen years later when Mozart and da Ponte created *Don Giovanni* (1789), subtitled *Il Dissoluto Punito*, this also centred on a hero bringing about his own destruction in the pursuit of love, but in a very different way. Giovanni's offence was not besottedly to project his *anima* onto just one woman, as representing the 'eternal feminine'. It was the ruthlessly indiscriminate way he degraded his *anima* by projecting it onto an endless succession of women. But despite Kenneth Clark's bid to promote him as another precursor to the age of Romanticism, in 'his refusal to repent, which made him heroic', we have no sense at the end of *Don Giovanni* that we are meant to sympathise with him. When he has been carried down by the Commendatore to the flames of hell, the blazing out of Mozart's joyful closing sextet proclaims the delight of those who remain that such a monster of egotism has been removed from the earth. They are celebrating a victory for light over darkness, life over death. In this respect Don Giovanni belongs not, as Clark had it, to the new 'phase of civilisation' that was coming to birth, but uncompromisingly to a much older and more deeply-rooted view.

Over the next half-century, however, all this was to change. As the age of Romanticism arrived in earnest, and storytelling became increasingly engulfed in the kind of sentimentalism foreshadowed by *Young Werther*, this was particularly reflected in two ways. The first was that, for the first time in the history of storytelling, it became fashionable for stories to have dark, tragic endings without any redeeming sense that the forces of life had triumphed. The other was the number of stories which ended in the violent death of an innocent heroine. We are here firmly into the pattern first heralded by Richardson's *Clarissa* as early as 1748. We see how, in the heyday of Romanticism, storytelling became conspicuously dominated by the haunting figure of 'the persecuted maiden': the poor, misunderstood, cruelly mistreated *anima*. And nowhere was this more vividly expressed than through that form of storytelling in which the nineteenth-century imagination was so notably prolific: the opera.

In general, one of the more marked changes which came over opera as it moved into the age of Romanticism was the way in which, in all senses, it darkened. The predominant form in late-eighteenth-century opera had been comedy. Now it became tragedy. The balance swung from the happy endings and brilliantly lit daylight scenes so often associated with Mozart or Rossini (of course there were exceptions) to the gloomy stages, night scenes and catastrophic endings we associate with Verdi or Wagner. We pass from the sunlit blue skies under which the heroines wish their boyfriends calm seas and a tranquil voyage in *Cosi Fan Tutte* to the rocky midnight gorge where we see 'the tempestuous, eerie and headlong "Ride to Hell"' in the *Damnation of Faust*, or the world-ending apocalypse of *Gotterdammerung*. We move musically from the clear, open, uncomplicated harmonies of the classical age to the swirling, hectic, heart-tugging emotionalism and complex chromaticism of the great Romantics. But just as revealing as any of this was the startling change which came over their operas' plots.

One of the first notable tragic operas to centre on the plight of 'the persecuted maiden' was Donizetti's *Lucia di Lammermoor* (1835), loosely based on a novel by that leading Romantic novelist Sir Walter Scott. But when we look at its plot we see something very significant has happened. It is not like that of a conventional Tragedy at all. With its stratagems, confusions and misunderstandings, it is much more like the plot of Comedy: but comedy which has gone hideously and tragically wrong.

The heroine's brother Lord Enrico is at once established as the central dark figure. Not only has he wrongfully usurped the estates of the light hero, Edgardo, with whose family his own has a long-standing feud; he is also under suspicion of treason against the king. He conceives as the only hope of reviving his fortunes a scheme to marry his sister Lucia to another powerful lord, Arturo. But Lucia has already established a secret love with Edgardo, with whom she exchanges rings and vows of eternal fidelity. When Edgardo leaves for France, Enrico forges a letter to make her think Edgardo has fallen in love with someone else. Devastated by this, and to save her brother from death for treason, Lucia nobly agrees to marry Arturo. The wedding ceremony takes place. But no sooner has Lucia signed the marriage contract, than Edgardo bursts in to protest, crying for vengeance. In despair at her brother's treachery, Lucia hands back her ring to Edgardo, who flings it down, cursing all her family, and storms out. Not long afterwards, while the wedding celebrations are still continuing, word comes from off-stage that Lucia has lost her reason and killed her husband. She then enters for her famous 'mad scene', in which she goes through an imaginary wedding ceremony with Edgardo. Unaware of this, Edgardo goes to the tombs of his ancestors, wishing he could join them because he has nothing left to live for. He then learns that Lucia has lost her wits and is dying. A bell tolls for her death and, promising her spirit that nothing can part them, he stabs himself.

As in *Othello* or *Romeo and Juliet*, this is Comedy without the saving grace of recognition'. Trapped by wicked deceit into their fatal misunderstandings, the innocent lovers are torn apart and die despairing lonely deaths without ever knowing the truth. But, unlike in the Shakespearian versions, there is no redeeming note at the end; whereby we might at least see the dark author of their misfortunes, like Iago, being taken off for punishment; or, as by the death of Romeo and Juliet, the feuding families being reconciled and harmonious order restored. Out of this black ending there is no victory for light. Only the dark inversion has triumphed. And thus, in a fundamental sense, the story remains unresolved.

When we move on to the operas of Verdi, we see this strange perversion of the plot of Comedy developed still further. A long succession of similarly black tales are based on misunderstandings, confusions of identity, disguises: all those devices familiarly used in Comedy to obscure the identities of characters from each other and themselves. But here the light of 'recognition' never breaks in on the twilight (or not until it is too late). And again and again these stories end in the heart-rending death of their heroine, although sometimes their hero and sometimes both. A typical instance of how relentlessly the tricks of misunderstanding or obscured identity could be piled on another to bring these stories to their melodramatic conclusions is the plot of *Rigoletto* (1851), based on a story by Victor Hugo, which so impressed Verdi that he called it 'the greatest subject, and perhaps the greatest drama of modern times'.

Immediately established as the central dark figure of the story is the Duke of Mantua, Tyrant and libertine, the epitome of the 'dark masculine' (as defined by the cruel exercise of power and the indiscriminate pursuit of sexual gratification). Set against him as the hero is Rigoletto, his court jester, who by dark inversion is made a hunchback. At first Rigoletto is infected with his master's darkness, addressing cruel, derisive remarks, first to the unhappy husband of a young woman whom the Duke is planning to seduce; then to the unhappy father of a girl the Duke has already dishonoured, who pronounces a curse on him.

But we now see the other side of Rigoletto, as he secretly comes at night to visit his beloved daughter Gilda, the *anima*, who is not allowed to know her father's name or position. Before she joyfully greets him, he curses the fate which has placed him in the power of the tyrannical Duke, whom he detests. When her father departs, the Duke himself arrives, in disguise, to woo Gilda, who had caught his fancy when he saw her in church. He pretends he is a poor student, and she falls in love with him. When he in turn leaves, his hateful courtiers arrive at the house to kidnap her, imagining she is Rigoletto's secret mistress. Rigoletto returns and, by pretending they have come to kidnap someone in the next house, the woman the Duke had earlier been planning to seduce, they blindfold the jester and persuade him to help them. He thus unwittingly assists in the kidnapping of his own daughter, whom they drag back to the Duke's palace. When Rigoletto enters the house to find her gone, he is heartbroken, remembering the curse. He heads for the palace, where the Duke has been overjoyed to see her, and she explains to her father that she and the Duke are in love. His only thought is that he must somehow murder the Duke and flee with her from Mantua.

He waits for an opportunity to revenge himself on the Duke, and at the same time to expose to his daughter her lover's true nature. The two of them watch through a crack in the wall of a derelict inn, while the Duke, again in disguise, first sings the famous aria '*La donna e mobile*' ('womankind is fickle'), then receives Maddalena, the sister of the Duke's resident paid assassin Sparafucile. Rigoletto tells Gilda to go home and put on a male disguise, so that when he has finished with the Duke, they can escape together to Verona. Sparafucile is unaware of the disguised Duke's true identity, and Rigoletto bribes the assassin to kill him, saying he will come back at midnight to collect the body. Maddalena begs her brother not to kill her handsome young wooer, but Sparafucile only agrees so long as a substitute victim can be found before midnight, to provide him with a corpse. This turns out, of course, to be Gilda, when she returns at the height of a great storm, disguised as a man. Sparafucile stabs her and places her body in a sack which, when Rigoletto returns as midnight strikes, is presented to him. Rigoletto drags his prize to a nearby riverbank, triumphantly imagining he is about to get rid of the hated Tyrant forever, when he hears the Duke's mocking voice singing '*La donna e mobile*'. In horror Rigoletto opens the sack and discovers his daughter who, with her dying breath, declares that she still loves the Duke. Recalling again the fatal curse, the jester collapses over her body.

Everything about this story is deliberately made so dark that it contains no element of redemption at all. The *anima* has been slain. The 'dark masculine' is triumphant. The dissolute remains unpunished. Every misunderstanding and disguise, instead of helping ultimately to lead to the revelation of the truth, as it would in Comedy, is used simply to push the plot further downwards towards its black conclusion.

We see similarly convoluted plots in one Verdi opera after another, usually ending likewise in the violent or painful death of the hapless heroine. In *La Traviata* ('The Frail One', 1853), when the consumptive heroine Violetta seems to reject her beloved Alfredo, he has no idea she has done this only to pave the way selflessly for his sister's happiness; but when, after further misunderstandings, they are finally reunited, this is only to provide a cue for her to expire from her dreadful disease. *La Forza del Destino* (1862) begins with the hero Alvaro deciding to elope with his beloved Leonore, because her 'unrelenting father' will not consent to the match. But, by mistake, Alvaro kills the father, launching her brother Don Carlos on a lifelong Quest for vengeance. After being separated on their flight and going through many adventures, the hero ends up as a monk, the heroine as an anchorite living alone in a remote hermitage. Finally the 'Dark Rival' Carlos tracks down Alvaro and tries to kill him in a wild, rocky landscape, but is mortally wounded in return. The hero calls for help at a nearby hermitage where he is astonished to find Leonore. She hurries to aid her dying brother who manages to stab her, so that no sooner has she been reunited with her lover than she is dying in his arms.

At the end of *Il Trovatore* (1853) the heroine Leonora takes poison, thinking that, by surrendering to the advances of the evil Count, she has at least bought the release of her beloved Manrico. Entering the dungeon where he is imprisoned, she dies in his arms. But then the Count orders Manrico's execution, only to find too late that he has murdered his own brother. At the end of *The Sicilian Vespers* (1855), when the hero dies with his father, resisting their enemies, the heroine, not to be left alone, stabs herself. At the end of *Aida* (1871), when the hero Radames is buried alive in a dungeon, he welcomes death, because he thinks at least his beloved Aida has escaped their deadly enemies; but at the last minute she slips into the prison to die in his arms. It was perhaps not surprising that Verdi should eventually have been drawn to produce his own version of that original dark comedy-turned-tragedy, *Otello* (1887), where the hero suffocates the heroine before plunging a dagger into his own heart.

What must strike us about these stories is what concoctions of artifice they are; how unrelated to any genuine outward or inward reality; how wilfully their familiar archetypal imagery is manipulated to play on the emotions of their audience, with its effect reinforced at every point by music of memorably emotive power. They provide a perfect definition of what is meant by sentimentality in its most sensational guise: using an outward show of much of the most basic symbolism programmed into the human imagination to trigger off the desired emotional response. Yet most revealing of all is how nothing more effectively achieves such a response than the spectacle of a beautiful, virtuous heroine, the embodiment of the feminine value, the *anima* and soul of mankind, being oppressed, imprisoned, degraded and finally put violently to death.

### Wagner: World ending without redemption

Another mid-nineteenth-century opera composer who expressed this darkness in a very different way, was Richard Wagner, Verdi's almost exact contemporary. The single most ambitious achievement of nineteenth-century opera was the four-part Ring cycle, *Der Ring des Nibelungen*, that extraordinary creation inspired by Norse and Teutonic myths, which Wagner nevertheless transmuted through the force of his fantasy into something entirely his own.

The prologue, setting the underlying theme of the story, is *Das Rheingold*. In the mysterious, half-lit world below the waters of the Rhine, the unconscious, the three Rhinemaidens sing of the glowing golden treasure, consciousness. Whoever can make a ring from the gold will be master of the world, but to possess it must forego love. The dwarfish Alberich agrees and seizes the gold. As in that later pseudo-mythic epic Tolkien's *The Lord of the Rings*, the ring, which gives its bearer untold power without love, is the power of the ego. But, despite the claim that the holder of the ring will exercise such power, it is notable that not one of those who possess it in the drama which follows seems able to use it to any effect whatever. Its power is all an illusion: its symbolism strangely empty.

We then see Wotan, the king of the gods, with his wife Fricka, gazing in wonder at the new home of the gods, Valhalla, but knowing that a terrible price must be paid to the giants, Fafner and Fasolt, who built it. The giants must be given Freya, the goddess of eternal youth. Wotan tricks the ring from Alberich and persuades the giants to accept it and the gold instead. So great is the greed the ring inspires, they immediately fight over it. Fafner kills Fasolt and disappears to brood over his accursed treasure. The story proper can now begin. At the start of *Die Valkure*, the first of the three main dramas, we learn that Wotan still dreams of getting the ring back, although it plays no part in the action which follows. This begins when we see Wotan's son Siegmund, on the run from his enemies, taking refuge in the hut of Hunding and his wife Sieglinde. She and Siegmund drug Hunding into unconsciousness with a potion and run away together. When Hunding awakes, determined to pursue Siegmund and kill him, Wotan orders the battle-maiden Brunnhilde, one of the Valkyries, to protect Siegmund, but Hunding manages to kill him. Wotan then kills Hunding. Brunnhilde tells Sieglinde to escape into the forest, and Wotan punishes her by decreeing that she is no longer a goddess, but must fall into a trance surrounded by a ring of fire. She can only be woken by a hero fearless enough to penetrate the flames.

At the start of *Siegfried*, the second drama, we learn that Sieglinde has died giving birth to the hero, Siegfried, who is without fear. Siegfried grows up and slays Fafner, now transformed into a monstrous dragon, thus winning the ring and also the knowledge that he must rescue Brunnhilde. Because he is fearless, Siegfried can penetrate the flames. He wakes Brunnhilde with a kiss and they joyfully declare their love. Much of this central episode, the victory of the hero over the monster, thus winning the treasure and union with the *anima*, is taken directly from the story of Sigurd slaying the dragon Fafnir and winning Brynhild in the Norse *Volsunga Saga*.

At the start of *Gotterdammerung*, the third and final drama, the three Norns, daughters of the earth goddess, spin the golden rope which binds together knowledge of past, present and future in an unbroken whole, as typifies the unreflective world of instinct. But when human consciousness emerges, that instinctive continuum is broken, as happens now when the Norns' rope becomes tangled and snaps. Siegfried cannot rest in happy union with his *anima*, but must go back into the world in search of new adventures, leaving the ring with Brunnhilde as a token of his love.

We then see the hatching of the greed-inspired plot which is to bring the story to its devastating conclusion, as Alberich's son Hagen schemes with his half-brother Gunter to win back the ring. Again by means of a drug, they trick Siegfried into unconsciousness. He forgets Brunnhilde and falls in love with Gunter's sister Gutrune. In the original Norse version, this fatal potion was supplied by their witch-like mother Grimhild: thus making it much more explicit that the hero loses touch with his *anima* because he has passed under the spell of the Dark Mother. Now bound by brotherhood to Gunter, Siegfried agrees to disguise himself as Gunter and to woo Brunnhilde on his behalf. Since only he can penetrate the flames, he is able to bring her to the hall where they are all assembled, where she sees Siegfried, now wearing her ring, about to marry Gutrune. Swearing vengeance at him for his betrayal, she now herself becomes the 'dark feminine', plotting with Hagen to murder Siegfried. As he dies, he remembers who Brunnhilde is and what she means to him. Hagen then kills Gunter as they fight for possession of the ring. Brunnhilde rides her horse into Siegfried's funeral pyre, the flames blaze up, the Rhine overflows, the Rhinemaidens seize the ring and vanish back into the swirling waters. Hagen, desperately trying to grab the ring, is drawn down into the depths after them. As the world dissolves into the opposites of fire and water, we see the apocalypse stretching up to Valhalla itself, as Wotan and his fellow gods are engulfed by the flames. The twilight of the gods darkens into eternal night.

So final and so all-embracing does this triumph of the power of darkness appear to be that it is fascinating to see how insistently those under Wagner's spell have sought to discern in it some positive, life-giving element: an indication that, even in this world-consuming apocalypse, the forces of light have still somehow won the day. Particular attention is paid to the music which hovers above the final orgy of death and destruction, the so-called 'redemption motif', although Wagner himself described this motif as 'the glorification of Brunnhilde'. The implication is that Brunnhilde's self-immolation in Siegfried's funeral pyre, to be reunited with her hero, by symbolising the power of eternal love, somehow redeems all that has happened. It was even suggested by the late Professor Robert Donington, whose *Wagner's 'Ring' and Its Symbols: The Music and the Myth* interpreted the operas from a Jungian viewpoint, that the 'redemption motif' should be called the 'transformation motif'; implying that, since the destruction of an old order of consciousness is part of the transformation necessary to allow a new one to emerge, we should regard the ending of the story as pregnant with hope.

The fact remains there is not the slightest evidence for this in the way Wagner presents his story. It is salutary in this respect to go back to the Norse mythology from which he drew his inspiration. In the original version, the climax comes in the world-ending catastrophe of Ragnarok, when the earth is swallowed up in an apocalyptic vision of destruction, along with all that is beneath it and above it, including the gods in Valhalla. But it has long been foreshadowed that, once the old order has been destroyed, a new, unimaginably better world will emerge: centred on the figure of the perfect hero Baldur who, like Siegfried, has been killed by treachery, but who must die in order that he may be resurrected to rule over the new world.

In Wagner's version, there is none of this. All we see is the story of how, once the treacherous, heartless power of egotism comes into the world, symbolised by the ring, everyone is corrupted by it. We see nothing but an endless vicious cycle of greed, rivalry, deceit, trickery and murder, until ultimately the self-destructive power of egotism destroys first the hero, then the *anima*, finally the entire world: leaving behind only an empty darkness. Beyond egotism, from the ego's point of view, there is nothing. Only that archetypal awareness buried deep in our unconscious that, even as the dark power in a story brings about its own destruction, the light must always re-emerge, leads people to want to imagine that they see a glimmer of light in the ending to the strange, dark story of the Ring of the Nibelungen. It is not there.

## The lost *anima*: Bizet and Puccini

In 1875, the year before Wagner finally brought the central work of his life, on which he had worked for more than a quarter of a century, to its first performance at Bayreuth, an outwardly rather more conventional opera had its premiere in Paris. We earlier looked at Bizet's *Carmen* as a perfect example of a story shaped by the five-stage archetypal pattern of Tragedy. Although the weak little hero José is in love with an infantile *anima*-figure, Micaela, he becomes infatuated with the Temptress, Carmen. Throwing off his soldier's uniform, as a symbol of losing his outward manhood, he rejects his loving *anima* and passes completely under the emasculating spell of the Dark Mother. There then looms up the bullfighter Escamillo, the shadow of the masculinity he will never realise; and finally, in futile, self-destructive rage, he lashes out at the Dark Mother, who symbolises his impotent immaturity. As in *Rigoletto* or the Ring cycle, there is very little sign of any redeeming victory for light.

It is interesting to look at this story in the context of Bizet's own psychology. He was another of those nineteenth-century artists, like Stendhal, with a mother complex, who therefore had serious difficulty both with his own inner feminine and with his masculinity. He wanted, as Robert Donington tells us, to live next door to his mother, yet have 'his mistresses come and go in spite of her, almost as it would seem by proxy for her'. In his severe attacks of angina pectoris, he had visions of his mother laying her hand on his chest, when 'the agony would increase. I would suffocate, and it seemed to me that her hand, weighing on me so heavily, was the true cause of my suffering.' Bizet was liable to ungovernable rages, and once in Venice when he received a letter from his mother addressed from hospital, he fell into such acute anxiety that, at the mere sight of the letter unopened, he 'attacked a gondolier as if to strangle him.'

He must unconsciously have recognised this central problem of his own identity when he chose Merimée's story to provide the basis for his last and most famous opera. When it finally went into production, at the Paris Comedie Francaise, Bizet entered a psychosomatic crisis. Three months later, the singer playing Carmen, at the scene where her death is foretold in the cards, was filled with such foreboding that she fainted in the wings. Next day came the news that the composer had died that same evening, at the age of 36.

A composer whose operas continued those of Verdi in reflecting the obsession of nineteenth-century storytellers with the tortured, persecuted *anima* was Puccini. At the end of *Manon Lescaut* (1893), the heroine dies on a vast, desolate plain, singing of how she is 'alone, lost and abandoned'. At the end of *La Boheme* (1896), Mimi dies painfully of consumption in the garret where she had once enjoyed the greatest happiness of her short life. In *Tosca* (1900), the heroine, having heard the groans of her lover being tortured in the next room on the orders of the Tyrant Scarpia, desperately tries to save him by betraying their friend. When Scarpia then deceitfully offers to spare her lover's life if she will submit to his sexual advances, she agrees, only to stab the villain when he tries to embrace her. Having committed this fatal act, at least she imagines she has managed to save her lover. But she then sees this was only a trick played on her and that he has been executed. Finally, as a policeman bursts in to arrest her, Tosca flings herself out of the window to her death, vengefully proclaiming that she and the Tyrant must now meet before God.

But there are few stories in which the plot is more poignantly centred on the persecution of the loving *anima* than Puccini's *Madame Butterfly* (1904). When the American officer Lieutenant Pinkerton arranges to marry the pretty little 15-year old Japanese girl Cio-Cio-San, Butterfly, he is warned he must not treat his new wife too lightly. But he just cynically drinks to the day when he can eventually marry 'a real American girl'. After their wedding, Butterfly is cursed and abandoned by her family for marrying a foreigner of another religion. Her beloved husband must now be her entire life, and Act One ends with her submitting joyfully to his embraces.

Act Two opens three years later when she has given birth to a son, but is now waiting anxiously with her faithful maid Suzuki for her husband to return after a long absence. Her only dream is the day when he will come back, and at last his ship is sighted coming into the harbour. She excitedly fills the house with flowers, puts on her wedding dress and prepares to welcome him. All night she waits, but he never arrives; until the following morning when he enters the house, having left the American wife he has married hidden in the garden. Butterfly is resting, after her sleepless night, and he tells Suzuki he has only come to take away his son. When Butterfly awakens and sees the strange woman in the garden, she soon puzzles out what is happening. She tells Pinkerton he may come to fetch his son in half an hour. She takes up the knife with which her father had committed suicide on the orders of the Mikado. Her little boy runs in and she says goodbye to him, binding his eyes and giving him an American flag to hold. She goes behind a screen, the knife clatters to the floor and, as Pinkerton enters, she dies.

The whole unconscious purpose of this story is to exploit the audience's archetypal emotional response to the heart-tugging spectacle of the loving *anima* being rejected in the most humiliating fashion by the heartless egocentric 'dark masculine'. Yet, when this offence against the light has been remorselessly pressed to its dark conclusion, there is no redeeming element. At least Tosca was able to take the Tyrant Scarpia with her before she died. Here light is extinguished and only darkness remains, having seemingly won the day. Seeing the archetypal pattern thus turned inside out, we may sense this is scarcely a complete resolution to the story. But, so slight and uninteresting is the cardboard cut-out figure of Pinkerton, it does not even seem to matter what might happen to him subsequently. The story's only real purpose has been to play the degradation of its central figure for maximum sentimental effect. Once we have seen the image of the faithful, tortured *anima* committing suicide, the lemon has been squeezed. What remains is really of no interest or significance whatever.

### The tragic hero glamorised

Returning in a sense to where this chapter began, a final obvious fashion in which Tragedy can both turn dark and be sentimentalised is where we see its hero, or central figures, acting out the archetypal self-destructive pattern, but in a way which invites us to see them somehow as attractive and glamorous, as they rebel in the name of vitality, excitement and freedom against a stuffy and oppressive social order.

In *The Portrait of Dorian Grey*, we may objectively be left in no doubt that the hero must in fact be a very dark character indeed, as he embarks on his life of debauchery and nameless wickedness. But at the same time we cannot avoid the impression that we are intended to see this beautiful, decadent young man as a glamorous hero; and it is no accident that the fundamental philosophy by which he lives, seeing life as a work of art achieved through gratifying the senses, was one with which his creator Oscar Wilde himself sympathised, delighting as he shocked the bourgeois proprieties of late Victorian society by doing so. When the beautiful young hero finally kills himself, turning instantly into the ravaged and bloated monster of his portrait, there is something deeply narcissistic about this; as if the real tragedy of the story is not all the cruelty and degradation he has inflicted on other people, but simply the way he has suddenly lost those beautiful, epicene good looks.

In that typical cult film of the early 1960s, *Jules et Jim*, we are not expected to view the obsession of the two young heroes with the fey, beguiling Temptress who leads them on to destruction as simply a sign of their weakness and immaturity; as showing how they lack either masculine strength of character or feminine understanding. The film's whole appeal was that the two good-looking young men were seen as glamorous and attractive, unshackled by bourgeois convention, losing themselves in a heady, wild, romantic adventure of precisely the kind the 1960s liked to fantasise about. And when the dark *anima* finally drives Jim off the bridge to their deaths, leaving Jules to stare bewilderedly at their ashes, we are meant to share his incomprehension; thinking how sad that malign fate should have brought such a terrible end to such a beautiful, if confusing dream.

In that typical cult film of the later 1960s, *Bonnie and Clyde*, we are not expected to view the young hero and heroine who egg each other on into a life of crime 'for kicks' as being led by their immaturity into something horrifyingly destructive and evil. We are invited to see their driving around the sunlit roads of America in vintage cars, occasionally stopping to rob a bank or blast off at someone who has got in their way, as another typical, wild, exhilarating, sixties-style adventure. When we finally see their car and bodies being riddled with bullets in dream-like slow motion, we are meant to think how sad that such daring defiance of humdrum normality in the name of freedom should have had to come to such a depressing end.

The point of what happens when the archetype of Tragedy is taken over by the human ego is not that it ceases to be tragic. It is that the balance of the story becomes inverted. Instead of presenting an objective portrayal of how the imbalance of egotism ultimately works to bring about its own destruction so that cosmic balance can be restored, the story now has no interest in seeing how the wider whole is restored. We do not see, as at the end of a tragedy like *Macbeth*, that solemn mood of celebration as the world returns to peace and normality after the terrible irruption of darkness has been purged. Its concern is solely internal, with what is going on inside the tragic pattern itself. Which is why, at the end of a romantic tragedy like *Young Werther* or *Bonnie and Clyde*, or the Ring cycle, or a Verdi or Puccini opera when we have seen the *anima* brought to her cataclysmic end, there is nothing left but a very lonely and silent darkness. Because, outside the world of the ego which has shaped such a tale, there is nothing else.

### Rebirth: A dark and sentimental version

Again it might seem a contradiction that the ego could take over the plot of Rebirth, since this is concerned with showing how its central figure moves from being centred on the ego to the deeper centre of the Self. The only example we shall look at here manages to present the Rebirth theme in both dark and sentimental guise at the same time.

By the time Ian Fleming came in 1963 to write his last completed James Bond novel, *You Only Live Twice*, the books he had been turning out every year for a decade had already made him rich. When his stories began to be adapted for the screen, with *Dr No* (1962) and *From Russia With Love* (1963), they were about to make Bond one of the most famous fictional characters of the twentieth century. But in some ways Fleming was by now deeply weary of the fantasy-hero who had dominated his daydreams since adolescence. Churning out yet another Bond adventure each year had become a kind of addictive slavery. He had developed a kind of love-hate identification with his creation which, in the eyes of those who knew him well, had become seriously unhealthy. Indeed, for reasons not unrelated to the resulting strain, he was now physically ill, with the disease which was soon to kill him.

*You Only Live Twice* is darker than any of the Bond stories which preceded it. For a start, we learn that, before the story opens, the relentlessly promiscuous hero had finally got married; only to see his wife murdered the day after their wedding, by the super-villain who had already emerged in two earlier stories as Bond's greatest shadowy antagonist of all. Blofeld, head of the sinister terrorist organisation SPECTRE, is like a supreme enemy to all mankind. After his wife's death, Bond had gone to pieces: drunk, unreliable, his health failing. But now he is summoned by 'M', head of the secret service, to a last great adventure.

On the far side of the world, in Japan, a mysterious figure has appeared, calling himself 'Dr Shatterhand'. He lives in a huge, remote, impregnable castle, and has surrounded himself with a 'Garden of Death', full of volcanic pools and every kind of poisonous and deadly plant, snake, insect and fish. Bond sets out for Japan, where he goes through a long period of briefing and preparation from his old friend Tiger Tanaka, head of the Japanese secret service. He learns that Shatterhand is 'a collector of death', and that people are being attracted from all over the world to commit suicide in his gardens. He is described as 'an eccentric of the most devilish nature ... a monster ... a fiend in human form ... either a great madman or a great criminal'.

Bond then sees a photograph of this shadowy monster and at once recognises him as his old enemy Blofeld, re-emerged in new guise (as we are told when Sauron reappears at the beginning of *The Lord of the Rings*, 'always after a defeat the

Shadow takes another shape and grows again'). Bond travels across Japan towards the distant 'dark' fortress, its owner being built up all the time as someone who operates 'on the scale of a Caligula, of a Nero, of a Hitler, of any other great enemy of mankind'. Bond sees himself as 'David spurred on to kill his Goliath', as 'St George approaching the dragon'.

So far, the story is as complete an example of the Overcoming the Monster plot as Fleming ever wrote. But at this point a strange new element intrudes, which will eventually return to take over the final stages of the story. For a last period of preparation for his crowning ordeal, Bond is sent to a primitive Japanese fishing village, to be taken under the tutelage of two figures: a spiritually wise Shinto priest and a beautiful young girl, Kissy Suzuki, once improbably a Hollywood actress but who has now come back to her remote native village to live as a simple fisher-girl. Suddenly looming up in the middle of a James Bond story we see those great archetypal figures, the Wise Old Man and the Anima; enough in itself to warn us that something unusual is afoot. Bond lives austerely in the village, almost like a novice monk, going on diving expeditions with the girl to bring up valuable shells from the seabed. At last she leads him to a local shrine, to ask six ancient stone figures, the Guardians, for their blessing. The girl waves goodbye, and Bond sets off on the last stage of his journey, emerging from the sea to climb into the 'Castle of Death'.

Hiding in the suicide garden, he witnesses the horrific deaths of several other visitors, being eaten alive by piranha fish or thrown by 'Black Guards' into bubbling volcanic pools. He enters the castle where, inevitably, he is captured and brought before the Monster himself for the ritual confrontation. Blofeld first makes sport with his victim, by having him tortured. Bond is placed on a stone seat which has been built on top of a geyser, and learns he has just 11 minutes left before it erupts with gigantic force to blow him away. He manages, as 'with one mighty bound', to break free, strangles Blofeld with his bare hands, closes down a valve to block off the top of the geyser and runs up onto the castle battlements, where a conveniently tethered helium balloon allows him to escape before the geyser erupts. How he has achieved all this in less than 11 minutes is a mystery. But as he floats out over the sea, there is a world-shattering explosion and he sees the 'Castle of Death' disintegrating in a vast fireball. Caught in the blast, his balloon falls into the sea and Bond feels himself sinking into warm water, 'down towards peace, towards the rippling feathers of some childhood dream of softness and escape from pain'. We next read *The Times* obituary of 'Commander James Bond', reporting that he has 'died on active service'. In the same book, not only has Fleming at last arranged for his hero to get married; he has also killed him off.

We then learn that our hero is not in fact dead at all. He has been rescued from the sea, inevitably by the loving Suzuki, his soul-carrying *anima*, and in a lonely cave behind the shrine of the Guardians she has tended him gently back to health. But Bond has completely lost any memory of his former life or identity. Under guidance from the Wise Old Man, Suzuki gives the hero a new name, Todo Todoroki. They happily begin a new, simple life together by the sea shore. It is an idyllic picture of a man completely reborn, having conquered Death, left his old life behind and at last found his inmost identity.

But of course Bond has not really discovered his identity. He may have acted out the external pattern of a rebirth, but he has not been through any inward transformation. He has merely covered up his old identity with an outward disguise. Like everything else about James Bond, it is just 'some childhood dream of escape'. And sure enough, he eventually comes across a scrap of newspaper on which he can make out the word 'Vladivostok'. He knows this somehow has deep significance for him; and when Suzuki tells him it is a place in Russia, he is sure that, if only he can get there, he will somehow learn who he truly is. The story ends with Bond setting off on a new journey across the sea to the Soviet Union. What Suzuki cannot tell him, because she does not know who he really is, is that when he arrives there he will fall into the hands of his real enemies, and that from this voyage there will be no return.

This death-wish laden fable was Fleming's last completed book. Less than a year later, and only a month after the death of his dominating mother, he himself was dead, at the age of only 56. In light of the peculiar strains of his last years, associated with the fantasy-figure who, like Frankenstein's monster, had taken over his life, he had become James Bond's only real-life victim.

As we end this introductory résumé of some of the main ways in which so many stories have in the past 200 years taken on these dark and sentimental forms, the time has come to look from a fresh angle at the process which lay behind this fundamental change in the character of Western storytelling. One of its more conspicuous features, as we have seen (not least in our last example from Ian Fleming), was the way stories became more like personal dreams, reflecting the particular psychological inadequacies and imbalances of their creators. No storyteller provides a clearer illustration of this process than the novelist who forms the subject of our next chapter, Thomas Hardy.

CHAPTER TWENTY-FIVE

# Losing the Plot
## *Thomas Hardy – A Case History*

'The Sea of Faith
Was once, too, at the full, and round earth's shore
Lay like the folds of a bright girdle furl'd.
But now I only hear
Its melancholy, long, withdrawing roar,
Retreating, to the breath
Of the night-wind, down the vast edges drear
And naked shingles of the world.'
Matthew Arnold, Dover Beach (1867)

It might seem odd, as we explore the way in which storytelling has over the past two centuries become detached from its archetypal roots, to devote a whole chapter to the works of just one author. But the seven major novels written by Thomas Hardy between 1872 and 1895 provide such rich insight into this process of disintegration that it is worth pausing to examine them in some detail. We have seen many examples of the types of story which represent the end-result of that process. What Hardy's novels show us is the pattern of disintegration actually taking place. We see an author whose stories begin apparently still securely anchored in the archetypal framework: but who then gradually loses touch with it, in a way corresponding directly to the crumbling apart of his own inner world.

When in the late 1960s a film version of *Far from the Madding Crowd* (1967) launched Hardy's stories back into vogue, one explanation offered for this was that these colourful evocations of life in the English countryside before it was disrupted by all the disintegrative pressures of the modern world appealed to the late-twentieth century's almost insatiable appetite for nostalgia. But obviously the last thing that can be said about Hardy's books is that they convey any cosily nostalgic view of the past. On the contrary, there are few stories so bleak in the English language: a sense of gathering gloom and despair hangs over the sequence of novels like a cloud.

In general there are two features we may note in his major stories which give us a particular clue as to what is happening. The first is the way the world they describe is so sharply polarised. On the one hand there is the timeless, rooted world of the Dorset countryside in which Hardy himself had grown up. This is personified in the rustic characters who appear in the early novels like a comic chorus: the carol singers of Mellstock in *Under the Greenwood Tree*, the bucolic drinkers in the Weatherbury malthouse in *Far from the Madding Crowd*. It is reflected in Hardy's beautifully observed descriptions of nature: the flowers and insects of Egdon Heath in *The Return of the Native*; the trees which whisper and rustle and sigh through almost every chapter of *The Woodlanders*. Above all this rooted natural world is summed up in those three almost interchangeable figures, Gabriel Oak in *Far from the Madding Crowd*; Diggory Venn in *The Return of the Native* and Giles Winterborne in *The Woodlanders*. Each of these rock-like characters, representing the timeless virtues of unselfish goodness and practical common sense, is cast in the role of looking on, shrewdly but sadly, while others in the story get carried away by self-deceiving fantasies, recklessly encompassing their own destruction.

At the other pole, intruding into this rooted world like a growing shadow, is the repeated appearance of a very different type of male figure: a predator on women, dark, heartless, promiscuous, without roots or moral centre, who inflicts misery and destruction on all those who fall under his spell: Sergeant Troy in *Far from the Madding Crowd*; Damon Wildeve in *The Return of the Native*; Edred Fitzpiers in *The Woodlanders*; Alec D'Urberville in *Tess of the D'Urbervilles*.

Making up a third significant group in the novels are the tragic characters caught between these two poles: those who have gone out into the wider world, lost their centre and their roots, and then make doomed attempts to put them down again: Clym Yeobright in *The Return of the Native*; Michael Henchard in *The Mayor of Casterbridge*; Grace Melbury in *The Woodlanders*.

The other notable feature of Hardy's novels is the remarkable extent to which they are centred on their characters' hopeless search for the right partner: the 'other half' who would make them whole. Tess, Jude, Giles Winterborne, Mayor Henchard, Grace Melbury, Eustacia Vye, Sue Bridehead, Farmer Boldwood: the list of Hardy characters who seek vainly for their true 'other half' is almost endless. No other writer has ever been so obsessed with mismatches, with the hero or heroine whose life seems blighted through having been landed by a malevolent fate with the wrong woman or the wrong man. And in both these general features of the novels we can see, thanks not least to the illuminating biography by Robert Gittings, just how Hardy's stories reflected the unfolding of his own inner life: as a deeply melancholy, insecure man who for 50 years, having been estranged from his own rustic roots and youthful faith, wandered through an inward world in an ever-increasing confusion of bitterness and despair, seeking an innocence, a sense of certainty and wholeness which would never come again.

### The rooted beginning

Hardy was born in 1840 in the little thatched cottage near Dorchester which is still preserved today much as it was: a perfect picture-postcard image of old rural England before the modern world broke in. His father, a respected local stone-mason, was known for his rustic fiddle-playing, in church and at village weddings. Through his childhood and teens, the country people, scenes and customs of this remote corner of Dorset were all the world Hardy knew. But already he was marked out by his intelligence, his avid reading and his sense of separateness for a very different destiny. With the simple religious faith of his upbringing, he dreamed of being a clergyman; although he then began to study as an architect, and even spent a short time in the distant great city of London. He showed his susceptibility to the opposite sex in a series of intense, unconsummated passions for various girls. Gittings shows how 'mother-dominated' Hardy was, and how ill at ease in his relationships with the opposite sex. In his late twenties, he gravitated towards his career as a writer. He met and fell in love with Emma Gifford, the socially superior daughter of a west country solicitor. And in his early thirties he at last wrote his first successful novel.

*Under the Greenwood Tree* (1872), the happiest and most innocent of his books, is like a charming retrospective snapshot of his own youthful state. In plot terms, it is a romantic Comedy. It centres on how its handsome young hero, Dick Dewy, marked out from all the other villagers he has grown up with, falls in love with Fancy Day, the pretty, independent-minded young farmer's daughter, socially a cut above him, who has moved into the schoolhouse to run the village school. But before he can win her hand, in keeping with the Comedy plot, two rivals loom up in his way. Her father, like so many 'unrelenting fathers' before him, is determined she should not marry her young lover but someone of higher social status, a well-off fellow-farmer, Mr Shinar the churchwarden. She is also proposed to by Mr Maybold, the new, modern-minded young clergyman. These two also play a key part in the story's main sub-plot, their determination to end the age-old practice of having the music in church accompanied by a rustic orchestra, and to install a modern new organ played by Fancy Day. The heartless way in which the vicar consigns the village musicians to the scrapheap is a symbol of how Hardy saw the new world of the future breaking in on the traditional ways of country life, and it is telling that this innovation is identified with both Dick's rivals for Fancy's hand. But in the end the way is clear and in the final pages the young couple are married, presumably to live happily ever after.

In the light of what was to come, this romantic Comedy reads like nothing more than a simple wish-fulfilment fairy tale. Two years later, just before Hardy's own marriage, came *Far from the Madding Crowd* (1874). This was the last novel he wrote in the cottage of his birth, still surrounded by his family and the rustic world of his youth. Again the basic plot is that of Comedy. Again we see the hero and heroine meeting early in the story, and much of the action is again taken up with the problems posed by two rivals for her hand in marriage. But although the story still comes eventually to a happy ending, this is no longer achieved with anything like the fairy tale ease of *Under the Greenwood Tree*.

The hero Gabriel Oak, strong, good-hearted and self-contained, a maturer version of Dick Dewy, is as complete a man as any character in Hardy. We first see him as a self-reliant young farmer in his late twenties, at the moment when he encounters the story's beautiful but vain and headstrong young heroine, Bathsheba Everdene. Again, like a more developed version of Fancy Day, she is just arriving to settle in the parish. They have further meetings, exchanging teasing badinage, and it is not long before Oak is in love. He even dares propose marriage. But Bathsheba says she is too independent. She needs someone to 'tame' her, and tells him he is not strong enough to do it. Shortly afterwards she disappears, to take over a farm she has inherited, and Oak is struck by disaster, when all his sheep plunge to destruction over a quarry face. He has lost his livelihood, his farm, everything. He is cast into the shadows, doomed to live 'below the line' as he seeks work as a lowly shepherd. Crossing the country by night, he sees an ominous blaze of flame. It is a wheat-rick on fire, threatening to destroy others. Farmhands are rushing around in confusion, but Oak at once takes charge and the potentially disastrous fire is extinguished. Impressed by his cool common sense, the farm's owner orders that he be taken on to run the farm as manager. Only then do the two discover each other's identities, and that his new employer is Miss Everdene.

The greater part of the story is then taken up with how Gabriel, from his subservient position in the shadows, has to watch while, 'above the line', his impulsive, imperious mistress makes one mistake after another. The first is her leading on of a rich, older neighbour Farmer Boldwood, when she has no intention of marrying him. So forthright is Oak in remonstrating with her for such folly that Bathsheba dismisses him. But almost immediately a crisis arises on her farm, when her sheep become fatally distended from eating clover. She has to plead with Oak to return, as again the only man with the strength of character and practical knowledge to save her.

Her next, much more catastrophic mistake comes with the arrival in the neighbourhood of the dashing philanderer Sergeant Troy. Swept off her feet by his 'dark masculine' charms, Bathsheba stumbles recklessly into marriage. On the night of the great party to celebrate their wedding and the bringing in of the harvest, only Gabriel observes the approach of a storm. The entire harvest, piled in unprotected ricks, is in danger of being lost. Troy contemptuously dismisses his warnings, ordering all the womenfolk home so that he can urge on all the men into a drunken stupor. When the strange behaviour of various animals provides three successive portents that the storm is likely to be of awesome proportions, Gabriel works demonically to get the ricks covered. As the first lightning flashes appear, he is joined by Bathsheba. Together they work on through the heavenly bombardment until, in the nick of time, just as the rain arrives, the task is complete. For a third time, by the Rule of Three, Bathsheba has been saved by Gabriel showing himself in a crisis to be a whole man: strong, disciplined, intuitively aware, unselfish; the very opposite of his weak shadow lying drunkenly asleep in the barn, Bathsheba's husband.

Indeed we now see just what a dark figure Sergeant Troy truly is, in his callous treatment of Fanny Robin, the frail, unhappy village girl he has promised to marry, who has borne his child and whom he has cruelly abandoned to live off Bathsheba. This infantile *anima*-figure is Hardy's first 'persecuted maiden'. The story moves in melodramatic crescendo towards its climax. The feckless Troy begins to gamble away his wife's money. The rejected, desperately ill Fanny crawls through the night to die, with her baby, on the steps of the workhouse. When her body is returned for burial in the village, it is brought to lie overnight in Bathsheba's house and, from looking into the coffin to see the two corpses, she discovers her husband's dreadful secret. Troy distractedly exhibits in death all the love towards the infantile *anima* he had failed to show in life. He disappears from home, swims out to sea and is taken to be dead. Eventually Farmer Boldwood, still dreaming in his broken state that he may one day win Bathsheba's hand, throws a Christmas party, to which she is invited as honoured guest. In the middle of the festivities, a mysterious stranger arrives in disguise. It is the dark figure of Troy, come to lay claim to his horrified wife. Boldwood shoots him and is sentenced to be hanged, although at the last minute this is commuted to life imprisonment.

Shattered by all that has happened, Bathsheba spends months withdrawn from the world, scarcely speaking. When the following summer she begins to venture out again, she encounters Gabriel, who tells her he will have to leave her employ. The threatened loss of the one solid figure in her life on whom she has come totally to depend finally works the trick which at the beginning of the story had seemed unthinkable. She has finally been tamed; softened into her inner femininity as completely as Katherina by Petruchio, or as Emma by Mr Knightley. Recognition dawns that she only wishes to be married to Gabriel, the honest, true, selfless man who has all along been as sturdy in her support as the tree whose name he bears. The story ends with the loving couple being joyfully greeted on their return from church by the chorus of rustic musicians, playing the same ancient instruments which had celebrated the victories of Marlborough a century and a half before. Not only have hero and heroine found wholeness in each other: they are united with the timeless world of the Dorset countryside where their new life can begin.

## Disintegration: The first stage

In bringing his manly hero to such a triumphant happy ending, we might think Hardy was imagining the kind of man he would like to have been himself: a countryman at one with his natural surroundings and with every admirable human quality. But between completing the novel and its publication, Hardy went through the most dramatic watershed of his life. Now engaged to be married to Emma, he moved away from Dorset and up to London. Here, in the literary circle around his new editor Leslie Stephen, he met various intelligent, lively, liberated young women, including his illustrator Helen Paterson, with whom he was so taken that even at the end of his life he was still wondering whether he should have married her. He abruptly severed all links with the world of his upbringing (no member of his family was invited to his wedding). Yet for all the heady excitements of his new life, he was far from finding anything in the outside world to compensate for the simple certainties of the world he had left behind. Quite suddenly he lost his religious faith. Even before his marriage, he was already beginning to be haunted by the possibility that he could have chosen better for himself than the naive, provincial Emma Lavinia. And as Gittings observes of Oak's acceptance by Bathsheba: 'no Hardy hero from that time onwards ever comes to such an assured and happy ending. From this moment on, the tragic and defeated hero arrives in Hardy's novels for good.'

In 1876 Hardy returned with Emma to Dorset: not to the simple life of a peasant, but to live in a new, middle-class, red-brick villa in the little town of Sturminster Newton, far apart from his family. His return to his native county inspired him to write *The Return of the Native*, describing how the wanderer Clym Yeobright returns from the sophisticated world of Paris to try to rediscover his roots on the great wilderness of Egdon Heath. But the attempt does not work. The mould has been broken. From its opening paragraph the book is shot through with a gathering darkness, often a quite literal darkness, as in all the scenes which take place at night or in twilight, which is quite new in Hardy's writing.

The story begins with four main characters, two masculine, two feminine. The contrast between the two men is not unlike that between the two central male characters in *Far from the Madding Crowd*. Diggory Venn, like Oak, is strong, good-hearted, self-contained and solitary. Damon Wildeve is as much a dark, heartless philanderer as Sergeant Troy. Similarly the restless, neurotic Eustacia Vye, longing to escape from this suffocating rural backwater, is as much a forceful opposite to the gentle, passive Thomasin Yeobright as Bathsheba had been to the infantile *anima* figure of little Fanny Robin. As the narrative opens Wildeve has been carrying on a secret affair with Eustacia, while Venn, the reddleman, moves mysteriously about the heath, nurturing a hopeless love for Thomasin. But, in a fit of caprice, to hurt Eustacia, Wildeve woos and marries Thomasin himself. With all its pent-up emotion and potential misunderstandings, it is like the start of a particularly black comedy. And the trigger for it to unfold to its black conclusion is the return to the heath of Thomasin's cousin Clym Yeobright, after several years in Paris (where Hardy had spent his honeymoon).

Desperately wounded by her lover's marriage to Thomasin, Eustacia sets her sights on the newcomer, hoping he will sweep her away from this claustrophobic little world back to Paris. To the horror of his mother, as strong-minded and dogmatic as Hardy's own, they get married. But Clym shows no sign of wanting to leave the heath and, as his eyesight fails, becomes a humble furze-cutter. The marriage begins to disintegrate, tempting Eustacia to resume her secret affair with Wildeve. When Clym's mother, after a sequence of misunderstandings in vainly trying to bring about a reconciliation between her son and his wife, exhausts herself and dies of a heart attack, this precipitates the climactic catastrophe in which the two 'dark' lovers try one stormy night to elope and are swept to their deaths by drowning. The weak, mother-dominated Yeobright is left motherless, wifeless and alone, to wander the countryside as an eccentric preacher.

At least there appears to be a partial happy ending to the story, as the two 'rooted' characters, Diggory Venn and Thomasin Yeobright, are finally brought together in marriage. But even this, Hardy tells us, was not his original intention, whereby Thomasin was to remain a widow and Venn was simply to vanish mysteriously from the heath. Their wedding was only concocted at the last minute while the story was being serialised, because Hardy's dismayed publishers felt the unrelieved hopelessness of his original ending might have been too much for readers to take.

### Disintegration: The second stage

What we see here is how Hardy's novels were beginning to follow a similar pattern to that we saw emerging in nineteenth-century opera, with Donizetti and Verdi.

The underlying plot is still that of Comedy. But now it is Comedy without any recognition or breaking in of the light. In contrast to his earlier books, Hardy's imagination could no longer encompass the kind of story which ends in a hero and heroine being brought triumphantly together. From now on, the characters rising up from his unconscious seem increasingly trapped in a kind of twilight, fatally mismatched with the wrong man or the wrong woman. And in this inability to bring masculine and feminine into balance, we see the reflection of a fundamental split which had opened up in Hardy himself.

As we have seen, the archetypal ending of stories where a hero and heroine come together in perfect union symbolises something much deeper than just a marriage. It is the image of complete human integration, where the two become in every sense one: physically, mentally, emotionally and spiritually. The hero, become a fully mature man, is at last integrated with his *anima*, that mysterious defining component in human identity we call the 'soul'. And it was precisely this point of maturity which Hardy, unable to become fully a man and therefore unable to realise his inner feminine, was unable to reach: as his fiction came increasingly to reflect. Whenever in a story there is outward trouble between a hero and heroine, we can be sure that something has gone awry in the hero's relations with his inner feminine; and that this may equally well express what is going on inside the author whose unconscious has created that character. It was no accident, for instance, that shortly after Tolstoy had, in *Anna Karenina*, conjured up one of the most haunting of all portraits of a beautiful woman throwing herself to destruction, he should have entered on the most profound spiritual crisis of his life. The world had become totally meaningless to him, he wished to kill himself and actually wrote that he felt he had lost his soul.

Coincidentally, the very years when Tolstoy was entering this crisis, 1878 and 1879, were also a time when Hardy himself was entering on one of the unhappiest phases of his life. His relations with his own outward 'other half' Emma were sharply deteriorating. They left Dorset again for London, where he produced three curiously artificial, superficial novels which might have come from a different author. He then returned to Dorset, to the town of Dorchester where he designed a rather ugly house for himself, and here he wrote easily his bleakest book to date, *The Mayor of Casterbridge* (1886). Again this was on the theme of a rootless hero trying to put down new roots for himself; quite specifically in Dorchester. But it was also of a man who has committed an offence against his feminine 'other half' so deep that it can never be expiated.

At the beginning of the story, in a fit of drunken bragadoccio, the hero Michael Henchard actually sells his wife and child; and it turns out that, in doing so, he has sold his soul. Initially he is filled with remorse and tries to make amends. He arrives in the far-off town of Casterbridge (Dorchester), where he builds up a considerable fortune and becomes the leading citizen of the community. He is even reunited with his wife and what he imagines to be his child. But he then gets sucked into an ever deeper mire of deception and self-deception; and, when his wife dies, the tragic reversal begins to close in on him. He discovers that his imagined daughter, his beloved Elizabeth-Jane, is not his child at all. Hardy is remorseless in showing how everything Henchard has built up is gradually stripped from him by Donald Farfrae, his former protégé and partner, who has now become his shadow. He loses his business, his home, his good name. He loses to Farfrae the woman he had hoped to make his second wife. He turns to drink and is humiliated in every way.

Finally he loses to Farfrae the one thing he has come to prize above all else; Elizabeth-Jane, the shining *anima*-figure who has remained in his life like a reborn version of his lost wife. In this sense she turns out to be as illusory a vision as Helen to that other hero who had sold his soul, Faustus. Robbed of all he has ever hoped for, Henchard wanders out into the wilderness to die: leaving, as a wedding present for the daughter he has lost, at her marriage to the man who has usurped everything he once proudly owned, a little goldfinch in a cage. Eventually the 'little creature' is found in its 'wire prison', dead: an outward and visible sign of what has already happened to the soul of poor Henchard himself. And when, next to his corpse, they find his pitiful last will and testament, scrawled on a scrap of paper, asking that no one should mourn his death or even remember him, its lost, despairing words are as chilling as anything Hardy had yet written.

His next book was *The Woodlanders* (1887), in which he returns to the countryside to describe the polarisation between the rustic, rooted world and that of the rootless, intrusive outsiders more starkly than ever. On one hand is the natural world of the trees and the woodland folk who live among them; above all Giles Winterborne, the man of the trees, and little Marty South. On the other is the world represented by the weak, vain young Edred Fitzpiers, his head full of dreams of experimental science; by the rich, spoiled Mrs Charmond, who has taken the big house; and also, alas, by Grace Melbury, the woodland village girl whose ambitious father had sent her off to school in the outside world and given her ideas above her station, or certainly above any such absurd idea as that she should marry Giles Winterborne, whom she has loved since childhood. In a now familiar tangle of mismatches, Grace returns to marry Fitzpiers, who then begins an affair with Mrs Charmond, leaving Grace to run off for sanctuary to Winterborne's cottage, which leads in turn to his death. Selflessly watching all this egocentric confusion, Giles and Marty are like a kind of replay of Diggory Venn and Thomasin Yeobright. But this time there can be no happy ending even for them, let alone for anyone else.

The death of Winterborne, as a projection of Hardy's own lost, rooted self, is symbolically a terrible moment. At least in the previous books it had been only the rootless ones who died, while Winterborne's previous incarnations, Dick Dewy, Gabriel Oak and Diggory Venn, had each come to a happy ending. One of the most moving moments in all Hardy is that where Grace Melbury realises, only after Giles is dead, that it had all along been plain little Marty South, with her hair shorn off, who was Giles's true mate: 'You and he could speak in a tongue that nobody else knew ... the tongue of the trees and fruits and flowers themselves'. That, and Marty's final farewell over Giles's grave ('No, no, my love, I can never forget 'ee; for you was a good man, and did good things') are Hardy's elegy for the instinctive world he had lost for ever, where man is at one with nature and faith is the knowledge of that fact.

## Disintegration: The final stage

As the sequence of Hardy's novels neared its conclusion, it is interesting to note how their changing mood had reflected the pattern of the fantasy cycle. Having begun with the youthful 'anticipation stage' of *Under the Greenwood Tree*, they had continued with a 'dream stage' in the eventual imagined happiness of *Far from the Madding Crowd*. They had worked up through the 'frustration stage' of *The Return of the Native* to the gathering nightmare of *The Mayor of Casterbridge* and *The Woodlanders*. Now they were to culminate in the two most terrible self-revelations of all.

*Tess of the D'Urbervilles* (1888), subtitled *A Pure Woman*, was the only one of Hardy's major novels to centre round the fate of a heroine rather than a hero. Tess Durbeyfield, a beautiful country girl from a poor and simple Dorset home, becomes bewitched by her father's story that she belongs to a great and ancient family. Going out into the world, she successively falls prey to the two socially superior men, the 'dark masculine' seducer Alec D'Urberville and the weak, moralistic, hypocritical Angel Clare, with whom, in different ways, she is so fatally mismatched. We have seen both these types before, in the predatory Troy/Wildeve figure and the religiose Clym Yeobright. But now there is no strong, good-hearted, male figure, like Gabriel Oak, to provide 'light' contrast to their darkness. He has finally dropped out of Hardy's inner landscape with the death of Winterborne. Now, for Tess, there is nothing left but these two oppressive dark male opposites competing to destroy her: until the nightmare finally becomes so intense that she is driven to murder the cruel monster who was originally responsible for her downfall and is hanged for the crime.

It is not surprising that Tess was Hardy's own favourite character, for she really was the deepest projection of all of his own inner feminine. And once we see her in that light, how even more poignant does her story become. We see Tess, the 'persecuted maiden', Hardy's *anima*, wandering blindly and distractedly across the face of an ever bleaker and more inhospitable Dorset countryside, looking for a home and a resting place where she might be whole, but eventually so tortured that she kills and is killed. In Hardy's oft-quoted phrase at the close of the book, 'the President of the Immortals' had 'ended his sport with Tess'. But of course the real power manipulating Tess from one improbable coincidence to the next, remorselessly stacking up the odds against her to such deadly conclusion, was not some vengeful deity, that God in whom the atheist Hardy no longer believed. It was Hardy himself. Even in the story we can only too easily see aspects of Hardy in both the men, unworthy of her, who make her their victim. D'Urberville is that recurring, heartless predator who represents the shadow of his unrealised masculinity. Angel Clare is the weak, high-minded progressive, first foreshadowed in Yeobright, who echoes what Hardy himself had been in his own youth. The story Hardy was unconsciously recording was nothing less than that of the stifling of his own soul.

His last major novel, *Jude the Obscure* (1895), was a fitting conclusion to the sequence of stories he had written in just over 20 years, because it was little more than an unconscious spiritual autobiography. It is the only one to be set almost entirely away from Dorset. But in the eagerly self-improving young country boy, of firm religious faith, whom we meet at the beginning in a little Berkshire village, it is not difficult to see the young Hardy of 30 years before. Jude Fawley's great ambition is to journey to the university city of Christminster (Oxford), shining on the horizon: the place where he would be able to realise himself to the full, in the company of scholars and men of intellect and distinction, just as Hardy himself had dreamed of when he was young. But on his way to the distant city, in an echo of what happened in Hardy's own life, he foolishly gets lured into marriage with a gross, stupid girl who in no way measures up to his lofty spiritual aspirations. Arabella abandons him, and he meets his soulmate Sue Bridehead, an idealised version of one of those liberated young women who had so taken Hardy's fancy in the London of the 1870s, when he was already engaged to his future wife.

From then on Jude's story is one of growing agony and disillusionment. Although he has arrived in Christminster, it in no way lives up to his idealised expectations. After seeming to have won Sue, the love of his life, she then, as an elusive *anima*, slips away from him again, to marry his academic mentor Phillipson. He wins her back again and they have two children. But just when Jude has a last moment of hope that he and Sue might now remain together, this is shattered by the last of those horrendous, inwardly symbolic moments which chequer Hardy's last novels. Jude's young son by Arabella, 'Old Father Time', stabs the two babies, then hangs himself, leaving the message 'Done because we are too menny'. It is the final catastrophe: the death of the children Hardy himself never had. Abandoned by Sue for the last time, Jude loses himself in an alcoholic haze. He is drawn back to live in poverty with the raddled Arabella and, before reaching the age of 30, dies a lonely, miserable death, amid the most alien surroundings imaginable.

When Jude was published it provoked uproar. Described by one reviewer as 'Jude the Obscene', it was castigated as 'indecent' 'degenerate' and 'nihilistic'. By now Hardy's outward estrangement from his roots and the world of his upbringing was so complete that when he bicycled through the village outside Dorchester where many of his relatives lived and they crowded to their cottage doors to wave to the great man, he stared stonily ahead and cycled on. The row over the book also marked his final estrangement from the increasingly evangelical and strait-laced Emma Lavinia (who signed letters to the papers 'An Old-Fashioned Englishwoman'). His only solace lay in an absurd series of infatuations with fash-ionable ladies up in London, would-be writers like Mrs Henniker and Agnes Grove. The scene was set for the last 30 years of his life, dominated creatively by that great flood of poems of nostalgia and loss which reached its climax after Emma's mis-erable and painful death in 1912: poems in which he sought to recapture that con-tact with the feminine which had proved so elusive through his life, and whose presence, as in Sergeant Troy's outpouring of grief over the corpse of Fanny Robin, never seemed so real to him as in death.

The other great task of Hardy's last years was the attempt to build up, through the biography he dictated to his second wife Florence, the picture of himself he wanted the world to see; in which, for instance, he portrayed his father, quite untruthfully, as feckless, and himself as the son who had single-handedly restored the fortunes of a once-important Dorset family, long in decline. This exercise in polishing up his *persona* was futile: partly because, despite his efforts to erase them, sufficient of the external facts about his father, his family and his life have survived for us to be able to see just what a sad, self-centred caricature the biography presented; and partly because he had left such a luminous record of his true inner life in the novels and poems. To devote so much time to such a pretence was hardly the sign of a man at ease with himself and the world; or of a man who had ever really come to terms with all those disintegrated components of his personality he had projected into his novels. Ultimately there was no apter epitaph on Hardy's life than the gruesome fate of the great man's mortal remains when he died in 1928. His cremated body was interred amid empty pomp in Westminster Abbey, just as his life out in the great world had long since turned to ashes. His heart was returned to be buried in Dorset where he had grown up: to the place his heart and his soul, his unrealised inner feminine, had never really left.

The way in which the gradual disintegration of Thomas Hardy's inner world was reflected in his novels gives us a particularly vivid picture of a process which was more generally taking place all over the Western world in the nineteenth and early twentieth centuries. As Europe and America were carried by the advance of science and technology ever faster towards the modern world, as hundreds of millions moved from the countryside into the newly industrialised cities, as ancient ways of life vanished, as social hierarchies began to break down, as old forms of religion and morality began to dissolve, people were losing touch on an unprecedented scale with that framework which had given them so much of their sense of outward and inward identity. In psychological terms, they were losing contact with much of that which had helped root human existence in the Self. What we see reflected in stories is a perfect model of what then happens, as the ego comes increasingly to the fore.

In the next two chapters we shall look at two of the most revealing ways in which the storytelling of the past hundred years has reflected this split between Self and ego. The first of these, as we shall see in the works of such twentieth-century storytellers as Chekhov and Proust, Pirandello and Samuel Beckett, is how, once the split has taken place, the ego eventually comes to a point where it has no sense of belonging to anything greater than itself. We see how it is in fact the framework of the Self which ultimately gives human life its sense of structure, meaning and purpose; and how, once contact with that is lost, the isolated ego is at last left facing nothing but a dark and empty void.

CHAPTER TWENTY-SIX

# Going Nowhere: The Passive Ego

## The Twentieth-Century Dead End – From Chekhov to Close Encounters

'All these clever people are so stupid, I have no one to talk to. I am so lonely, always so lonely, no one belongs to me, and ... who I am, what I exist for, nobody knows.'    Charlotta, in Chekhov's *The Cherry Orchard*

'One does not know, and one will never know; one searches desperately among the unsubstantial fragments of a dream ... a life hagridden by people who have no connection with one, full of lapses of memory, gaps, vain anxieties, a life as illusory as a dream.'

Marcel Proust, *The Captive, À La Recherche du Temps Perdu*

'Where I am I don't know, I'll never know, in the silence you don't know, you must go on, I can't go on, I'll go on.'    Samuel Beckett, *Malone Dies*

> '*Vladimir:* Well? Shall we go?
> *Estragon:* Yes, let's go.
> (They do not move).
> CURTAIN.'
> Samuel Beckett, end of *Waiting for Godot*

'Gatsby believed in the green light, the orgastic future that year by year recedes before us. It eluded us then, but no matter. Tomorrow we will run faster, stretch out our arms further ... so we beat on, boats against the current, borne back ceaselessly into the past.'

Scott Fitzgerald, end of *The Great Gatsby*

In this chapter and the next we shall be looking at two of the most significant things which happened to the nature of stories in the twentieth century. Each of these in its own way expressed a natural consequence of that profound psychological shift which had been taking place in storytelling since the dawn of Romanticism.

One, which will be the theme of the next chapter, was how, particularly in the century's closing decades, films, plays and novels became so obsessively preoccupied with images of sex and violence. But before we come to that we must first consider another development in modern storytelling which, although less blatant, was equally revealing. This was the way in which the works of so many twentieth-century playwrights, novelists and film-makers seemed to express the sense of having arrived at a kind of cosmic and spiritual dead end.

425

There was no more celebrated instance of this kind of story than a play which was first staged in a tiny theatre in Paris midway through the century, and again to even greater acclaim in London two years later: a drama so unusual that it was immediately recognised as something quite new in the history of storytelling. This was not least because *Waiting for Godot* (1953) had virtually no story. Two tramps are waiting by the side of a road for the promised arrival of a mysterious character called Godot. Eventually two more men arrive, one driving the other in front of him like an animal. After a series of exchanges, the newcomers then move on. A second act more or less echoes the first. At the end the two tramps are still waiting in vain for the elusive Godot, who never appears.

But to see how that change which had come over stories in the nineteenth century was eventually to lead to the limbo world of Samuel Beckett, we must first go back to the work of a dramatist who had been writing half a century earlier.

## Anton Chekhov: The disappearance of the Self

Just when Thomas Hardy was nearing the end of his career as a novelist in England, a young doctor at the other end of Europe was embarking on a sequence of plays which, psychologically, were to take storytelling into a new phase of its evolution. What we see in each of the five major plays written by Anton Chekhov between 1887 and his early death from tuberculosis in 1904 is a little group of people, somewhere in provincial Russia, who are going nowhere. They are trapped in a peculiar web of frustration and futility. Almost all his characters are defined by their yearning for something which does not exist. If they are young, they are dreaming of an imaginary future where life will somehow be better. By the time they are middle-aged or old, they are harking back to something they have lost: love, life, the enthusiasms and energy of youth. Away from this cycle of false hope souring into disillusionment and despair there is little else. And each time we then see them drifting towards a final shocking event which brings home just how hopeless and empty their lives have become.

The first of the sequence, *Ivanov* (1887), centres on a middle-aged landowner in the depths of what we would call a mid-life crisis. He has frittered away all his talents, energy, hopes and money. He is bored and irritated by all around him, but hates himself just as much, for being constantly 'bad-tempered, rude and petty-minded'. He did once love his wife Anna. She recalls how, when they first met, his 'eyes used to glow like burning coals when he talked with passion'. But no longer. Now, when he learns she is ill with TB, the news leaves him cold. As the young doctor Lvov bluntly tells him, he has been reduced to a state of nothing but 'heartless egotism'.

The action begins when Ivanov pays a visit to his neighbours, where their young daughter Sasha declares that she loves him, precisely because he seems such a lost soul. It is her mission to redeem him. They kiss and are seen by Ivanov's horrified wife, Anna. Back home, the self-hating Ivanov tells Lvov 'at 26 we are all heroes, we undertake anything, we can do anything; but at 30 we are tired already, and good for nothing'. When Sasha comes over to visit Ivanov, Anna accuses him of lying. He vindictively hits back by telling her she is going to die, and is immediately filled with remorse: 'how wicked I am'. In the final act, a year later, we learn that Anna has indeed died, and the guests are arriving for Ivanov's wedding to Sasha. No one is happy about what is about to happen, not least Sasha and Ivanov themselves. He finally tells her the wedding is off, and shoots himself.

What Chekhov introduces us to in *Ivanov*, veiled in that peculiar, sweet melancholy lit with flashes of mordant humour which hangs over his plays, is a little world not quite like anything seen in storytelling before. No one is presented as particularly dark: not even the heartless but self-despising Ivanov (although Chekhov's plays always feature one dominant personality, like Ivanov or Liuba in *The Cherry Orchard*, whose egotism casts a shadow over everyone else). But at the same time none of the other characters is particularly light either. All are essentially trapped in the same moral twilight. Each is isolated and shut off from everyone else, because they are all to a greater or lesser extent bound up in their own individual form of egotism. No longer is there any hint of that other dimension we have previously seen as so fundamental to the great archetypal stories: that life-giving force which can ultimately weld a story together by bringing light, recognition, transformation and wholeness. The values of the Self have all but vanished below the horizon. And without them, all that can happen – as we began to see developing in later Hardy – is that a story's characters are doomed to drift slowly downwards, like water draining away down a plughole, until finally may come that shocking event which shows the bath is empty. At least this gives the story the semblance of having come to a conclusion. But nothing has really been resolved or understood.

In Chekhov's next variation on the theme, *The Seagull* (1896), the dominant personality is Arkadina, the fading middle-aged actress, dreaming of the days when she was winning applause on the stage of the local provincial centre, Kharkhov. Behind theatrical shows of caring for others, she is wholly egocentric. Now she has come out to the family's country estate, accompanied by the successful but empty middle-aged writer Trigorin, where her son Trepliov has planned to put on a play in the garden, with Nina, the daughter of a neighbour. The nature of his dramatic fragment is telling. It conjures up a vision of the world 200,000 years into the future, when all the myriad forms of life on earth have become subsumed into a single World-Soul, opposed by the only other creature surviving in the universe, the Devil. Although presented as a kind of parody avant-garde play, this haunting image of a mysterious totality symbolising the spiritual unity of all life, and played by the innocent young Nina, is in fact the nearest thing to an evocation of the Self anywhere in Chekhov. But of course it is only an immature dream, set in some impossibly remote future. And such pretentious fantasy is all far too boring and 'decadent' for the uncomprehending mother, provoking her to sarcastic interventions so crushing to the poor young author that he brings proceedings to an abrupt end.

Once the son's inability to escape the suffocating grip of the 'Dark Mother' is established as the central problem, events then again gradually spiral down to a violent conclusion. In the wake of his humiliation over the play, Nina, who says she has been drawn to the household 'like a seagull', loses interest in young Trepliov and gravitates instead to the famous writer Trigorin. Trepliov, deeply hurt, shoots a seagull and presents it to her. The heartless Trigorin, cocooned in his self-important persona as a great writer, jots down notes for a story which he tells her is about 'a young girl like you' who is 'happy and free as a seagull. But a man chances to come along, sees her, and having nothing better to do, destroys her, just like this seagull here.' Nina's crush on Trigorin develops to the point where she refers him to a line in one of his own books: 'if you ever need my life, come and take it'. Trepliov and his mother have a row, in which he expresses utter contempt for everything she and Trigorin in their false 'above the line' world stand for. As the two of them prepare to leave, Trigorin and Nina privately exchange a long passionate embrace.

In the final act, two years later, we see Trepliov recounting how Nina had followed Trigorin to the city. They had an affair, she had given birth to a child which died, Trigorin abandoned her and she had become an unsuccessful actress. Then Arkadina and Trigorin arrive at the house. Trigorin is patronisingly complimentary about a story Trepliov has had published in a magazine. When the great man presents him with a copy, he finds Trigorin has cut the pages of a story written by himself but has obviously not even read Trepliov's contribution, the pages of which are still uncut. Nina turns up, and tearfully recalls to Trepliov their lost youth and those happy, innocent days when they were putting on their play. As Arkadina, Trigorin and others are heard approaching from outside the room, Trepliov quietly leaves and, when they have all come in, there is a shot offstage. The crushed and humiliated boy has committed suicide. So ends what Chekhov described as 'a comedy in four acts', although anything further removed from the archetype of Comedy would be hard to imagine.

In *Uncle Vanya* (1899) the dominant figure is Serebriakov, a distinguished art-historian, who has returned to live on his country estate in his retirement with his second wife Yeliena. But the central character is his brother-in-law by his first marriage, Voinitsky ('Vanya') who has for years worked tirelessly to run the estate while Serebriakov lived away in the city. Vanya has cheerfully sacrificed his life under the impresssion that his late sister's husband was a respected scholar, even a genius. But now Serebriakov has come back home, Vanya belatedly realises the man he has given his life for is a fraud, a nonentity who knows nothing about art: 'not a word of his writings will survive him'. Among those in the shadows cast by Serebriakov's egotism is the young local doctor Astrov, who despairs at the way, thanks to the stupidity and laziness of the Russian people, their beautiful land is going to rack and ruin ('The Russian forests are literally groaning under the axe, the homes of animals and birds are being laid waste, the rivers are getting shallow and drying up, the wonderful scenery is disappearing for ever.'). Yeliena notes that Sonia, her husband's daughter by his first marriage and Vanya's niece, is falling for Astrov. But when she tactfully tries to suggest a proposal, Astrov embarrassingly proclaims his love for Yeliena herself. Serebriakov then suddenly shocks everyone by announcing that he intends to sell the estate which Vanya has devoted his life to building up, even though it is Sonia's inheritance from her mother. This revelation of Serebriakov's mindless selfishness (even he himself recognises he is 'an egotist, a despot. But haven't I the right to be selfish in my old age? I love success. I like being a well-known figure') is finally too much for Vanya. He pours out his contempt for Serebriakov and tries to shoot him. But, for the first time, the act of violence is not the end of the story. A final act shows everything apparently back to normal, as Serebriakov and Yeliena prepare to leave the estate. When they are gone, all that is left is for young Sonia, left alone with her uncle, to conjure up a vision of how, after they have worked thanklessly and without rest for many more years, they will finally arrive in heaven:

> 'we shall hear the angels, we shall see all the heavens covered with stars like diamonds, we shall see all earthly evil, all our suffering swept away by the grace which will fill the whole world, and our life will become peaceful, gentle and sweet as a caress. I believe it. I believe it … we shall rest … we shall rest!'

But of course Chekhov is only mocking Sonia's self-deluding religiosity. What he is really conveying about human existence is that, behind such sentimental make-believe, there is nothing left but that black and empty void.

The one thing everyone remembers about the heroines of *The Three Sisters* (1901) is that the three girls, trapped in a dreary provincial town where their father had been commander of the military garrison until his death a year earlier, are perpetually dreaming of the day when they might return to Moscow. As so often in stories, the great city teeming with life and significance (Paris in so many French novels, New York in American stories, London in Dickens or *Tom Jones* or *Dick Whittington*) is an externally projected symbol of the Self: the 'centre' to which little provincial heroes and heroines aspire as the place where they will 'find themselves'. It is no accident that all Chekhov's plays are set in the provinces. The remoteness of their characters from the 'centre' is an external reflection of the fact that none have any inner centre. And nowhere is this more obvious than in the symbolic role played by Moscow in *The Three Sisters*. As Olga, the schoolmistress, puts it to her sisters at the play's beginning: 'if only we could go back to Moscow'. They are obsessed with the thought of that distant place where they imagine they might at last find life, love, meaning, purpose: everything they are deprived of in this suffocating little corner of nowhere.

The draining away of their hopes is symbolised in the decay of their brother Andre whom they have imagined to be so talented that, if only they could reach Moscow, he would surely be made a professor. But after he marries the boorish, insufferable Natasha she becomes the play's dominant figure, taking over the household like a monstrous cuckoo. She treats the family's old nurse Anfisa like dirt. She pushes Olga out of her bedroom, to make a nursery for the baby Bobik she dotes on with such mawkish sentimentality; then drives her from the house altogether. Meanwhile her pitiful husband, running up gambling debts, falls to pieces.

The only palliative for the girls' misery is the presence of the officers from the garrison, filling the house with their genial chatter. Masha, though married to a dull schoolmaster, falls for the equally unhappily married Vershinin, the new garrison commander, given to rambling on about how, in the distant future, 'life will be different. It will be happy'. Irena eventually agrees to marry Baron Toozenbach, as a way out of her misery. Then comes the order that the soldiers are to leave town. On the eve of their departure, Toozenbach fights a duel and is killed. Irena and Masha have each lost the only man who had given them hope. Echoing the general despair, the doctor asks rhetorically 'What does it matter? Nothing matters.' To which Olga replies, in the closing words of the play, 'if only we knew. If only we knew!'

In his final 'comedy' *The Cherry Orchard* (1904), written just before his early death, the dominant figure is the ageing Liuba Ranyevskaia, returning to her Russian estate after five years away in France. She has run up a mountain of debt living carelessly abroad with a drunken lover, her feckless brother and her daughter, and returns to find reality staring her in the face. Lopakhin, the former estate serf who has become a successful businessman, tells her the only hope of paying off her debts is to sell the once-magnificent cherry orchard in front of the house, to build a mass of summer villas for newly-prosperous city dwellers. The canny *nouveau riche* Lopakhin is the most positive character in Chekhov, because at least he is focused on becoming rich, according to the hard, down-to-earth commercial reality which is shaping Russia's future. Liuba, with her empty, wasted life, represents the past whose day is over. Despite all Lopakhin's friendly efforts to get her to face reality, she simply cannot do so. How could she possibly agree to the felling of the beautiful cherry orchard; the pulling down of the old house in which she grew up, with all its bittersweet memories? Surrounded by her family and dependents, she is lost in a dream world. Even after the auction, when the house and the whole estate are sold, inevitably to Lopakhin, she is still completely insulated from reality; until the moment when it is time for them all to leave the doomed house for the last time, and the play ends on the sound of an axe being taken to the cherry trees.

### 'Life's but a walking shadow'

What is new about this world conjured up by Chekhov is that for the first time we get a real preview of what was to lie at the end of that road which storytelling had begun to take in the dawn of Romanticism.

Certainly a central clue to the peculiar, stifling, trapped air which surrounds almost all the unhappy people in his plays is that none are ever strong enough to take control of their own lives (as a friend of mine once impatiently remarked 'if those girls really wanted to go to Moscow why didn't they just go down to the railway station and buy tickets?'). None of them ever look inwards, to know and change themselves. There is no growth in Chekhov's characters, except that of foolish dreams and decay. No one even begins to embark on that voyage of internal discovery which leads to transformation. We merely see weak, static figures, creatures of circumstances, without self-knowledge, doomed to the eternal round of youthful energy and optimism pinned on false, external goals, slowly souring into non-comprehending exhaustion and futility. It all echoes the view of human existence Chekhov expressed in a comment to Gorky: 'the Russian is a strange creature ... in his youth he fills himself greedily with anything he comes across, and after 30 years nothing remains but a kind of grey rubbish'. In the end, since there is no hope of maturity or wholeness, the only escape lies either in some despairing act of violence, or in fantasising about some distant future state, whether in this world or the next, where 'life will be different. It will be happy.' Human beings, as Chekhov portrays them, are little more than wraiths chasing shadows, hoping for a dawn which never comes.

In itself, however, this was not the first time a storyteller had given expression to such a bleak view of human nature. Nowhere is that sense of nihilistic futility which runs through Chekhov's plays more eloquently summed up than in one of the most familiar soliloquies in literature:

'Tomorrow and tomorrow and tomorrow
Creeps in this petty pace from day to day;
To the last syllable of recorded time;
And all our yesterdays have lighted fools
The way to dusty death. Out, out, brief candle!
Life's but a walking shadow, a poor player
That struts and frets his hour upon the stage,
And then is heard no more; it is a tale
Told by an idiot, full of sound and fury,
Signifying nothing.'

Macbeth's words might seem a perfect mirror to the world of Chekhov. But the point is that Shakespeare sets this despairing view in a very specific psychological context. He puts it into the mouth of the blackest of his tragic heroes, at a precise moment in his downward course. The reason why Macbeth sees the world like this is that he is at just the point in the Nightmare Stage of his Tragedy where all the self-defeating futility of his tragic adventure is finally being brought home to him. He has long since cut himself off from the Self. He has become totally isolated in his own egotism. And now external reality is finally crashing in on him, he can see nothing more than the end of the road to which egocentricity must eventually lead: a world devoid of meaning.

What Shakespeare was saying was that this is how the world must eventually look to someone who has inwardly lost contact with anything outside his own ego. The human psyche is so constituted, as he recognised with all the intuitive understanding of a great artist, that for anyone who views human existence from this shrunken perspective it will eventually come to seem exactly as Macbeth saw it: wearisome, unreal and utterly pointless, 'signifying nothing'. But, of course, no one knew better than Shakespeare that this represents only one, very limited aspect of human experience. It is possible to view life from a quite different, much deeper perspective. Only then does it take on colour and meaning, revealing its true patterns and purposes.

In Chekhov, however, beneath the apparently beguiling surface of his plays, he concentrates on that particular limited perspective to the exclusion of almost everything else. The little world he presents is one of people who may not be so obviously dark as Macbeth, but who still only really exist in terms of their ego. And the significance of this, at the start of the twentieth century, was that it reflected the onset of a further shift in that psychological 'centre of gravity' which, over the next 100 years, was to find expression in some of the best-known stories of the age.

### Proust: The little boy-hero who couldn't grow up

Not long after Chekhov's death, a doctor's son in his mid-30s retired from the world and took to his bed in a cork-lined room in Paris, to begin writing what was eventually to become the longest story ever published. Nearly a hundred years later, the 3,300-odd pages of Marcel Proust's *À La Recherche Du Temps Perdu* were to be widely described as 'the greatest novel of the twentieth century'.

One cannot see Proust's mountain of words in proper perspective without recognising the extent to which it reflected his own obsessively self-absorbed personality and the story of his own life. He was born in Paris, in the middle of the Prussian siege of 1870, into a typical *haut-bourgeois* French family. His imposing, bearded father was a distinguished pillar of the French medical establishment. But young Marcel's closest relationship, shaping his personality more than anything else, was that with his doting Jewish mother, who called him '*mon petit loup*'; and the peculiar degree to which this affected his character was notably illustrated, when he was seven, by what his biographer George Painter called 'the most important event in Proust's life'.

This took place on an evening when his parents were out in the garden, entertaining a guest, and his mother failed to come up to her son's bedroom to give him his usual goodnight kiss. The anguished child watched the grown-ups from his window, could not sleep, and pleaded in vain with a family servant to call his mother upstairs. Eventually he leaned out and called 'ma petite maman, I want you for a second'. When she entered the room, he broke into a fit of hysterical weeping, which he was to remember for the rest of his life as a sobbing inside him which had 'never ceased': the moment when he pleaded for his mother's love and she had not come. Two years later he terrified his father with the first of the asthmatic attacks which again were to haunt him for the rest of his life; and which Painter was to link with his hysterical weeping fits as unconscious pleas for 'his father's pity and his mother's love'. The fact was that Proust had already become the victim of a particularly acute 'mother-complex': a sickly, spoiled, hypochondriac little boy who, even when he was briefly separated from his mother at the age of 16, fell into such melodramatic sobbing that his great-uncle contemptuously dismissed it as 'sheer egotism'.

As a teenager, although he sometimes amused his schoolfriends with his clever remarks, he irritated them even more by his embarrassing attempts to curry favour and win their approval. As one, Daniel Halevy, put it:

'there was something about him we found unpleasant. His kindnesses and tender attentions seemed mere mannerisms and poses, and we took occasion to tell him so to his face.
Poor, unhappy boy, we were beastly to him.'

But one or two of his well-connected schoolfriends, including the orphaned son
of the composer Bizet, were to prove useful to him as an entrée to Parisian high
society. And at the age of 18, as a young dandy with a drooping moustache, a gift
for flattery and some wit, young Monsieur Proust began to be invited to fashionable salons and the grand dinner parties of the intensely snobbish and decadent
French aristocracy. In his mid-teens he had developed a crush on Marie de
Bernardaky, a teenage girl he had met playing in the Champs Elysées. But now
his transient passions for the opposite sex, which remained almost wholly in his
own mind, were largely inspired, as Painter describes it, by women 20 years older
than himself: either respectably married or 'unattainable high class cocottes' like
Laura Hayman, who called him 'my little porcelain psychologist'. When, aged 19,
he volunteered for a year in the army, he enjoyed what Painter described as 'the
discipline and love of comrades which to certain neurotics are so welcome'. But he
and his mother still wrote to each other every day.

By the age of 22 Proust was thus a classic case of the 'boy hero who cannot grow
up', imprisoned in the shadow of the 'Dark Mother', abnormally stunted on both
the masculine and feminine sides of his personality, and thus typically driven to
projecting the search for his 'other half' onto 'mother-substitutes', older women
of strong personality. Indeed he now took a familiar final step in this psychological progression when, under the spell of a new friendship with the flamboy-
antly camp Count Robert de Montesquiou, he entered the homosexual *demi-
monde* he was later to describe as 'Sodom and Gomorrah, the Cities of the Plain'.
He formed liaisons with young men like the musician Reynaldo Hahn and the
novelist Alphonse Daudet's son Lucien, who called him 'little Monsieur Proust'.
It was a twilight world in which the longing for love and to be liked constantly
foundered in jealousy and mistrust. Still supported financially entirely by his
indulgent father, Proust gave lavish and pretentious dinner parties, or took his
friends out to restaurants where he would order for them only the most expensive
dishes or fruits out of season. The bemused Dr Proust would in turn give way to
occasional outbursts of impatience at his son's affectations, as when a friend
told Marcel 'your father always tells everybody there's nothing whatever the
matter with you. He says your asthma's pure hypochondria.' To the composer
Debussy, Proust was 'long-winded, precious and a bit of an old woman'. But still
at the centre of Marcel's life was his suffocatingly close tie to his mother, with
whom he spent a famous holiday in Venice, accompanied by his friend Reynaldo
Hahn. Then his father died, and this was followed not long afterwards by the
death of his mother. It was the most traumatic experience of Proust's life.
Although, with her departure, he for the first time felt free to find his sexual
partners among young men from the working-class, the moment was nearing
when, in 1907, he began more and more to withdraw from society, sleeping away
the hours of daylight only to spend his nights obsessively scribbling away at his

life's work: the novel in seven volumes which he was not to complete until just before his death in 1922.

Seen through the eyes of its author-narrator, who only twice in a million-and-a-half words gives away that his name is 'Marcel', *Remembrance of Times Past* took the development of storytelling centred on the ego into a new dimension. The opening chapter, 'Overture', is based on Proust's memories of the scenes of his own childhood, introducing his parents, his grandmother and the family servant Francoise, whose earthy, female common sense is to remain such a supportive background presence through most of the book. We then we come to an elaborated version of the 'goodnight kiss' episode, when the narrator has to wait in agony all through the evening for his mother to come upstairs, because their usual goodnight rituals have been interrupted by the arrival of his parents' dinner guest, Monsieur Swann, their mysterious neighbour in the little town of Combray. When she finally comes up to his room, she reads to him, then agrees to spend the rest of the night sleeping in an adjoining bed. All this, laying the emotional foundation for what is to come, takes 18 pages to describe. The 'overture' ends with the often-quoted episode years later in his adulthood, when his mother offers him a cup of tea and a little scallop-shaped madeleine cake. He bites into it and is overcome with a strange joy, as the taste conjures up a flood of memories of his happy, long-lost childhood. On this note of 'once upon a time' the story proper can begin.

The central key to the immense narrative, with its huge cast of recurring characters, lies in three particular episodes, each describing a love affair. The first, in the volume entitled 'Swann's Way' and set at a time before the main narrative begins, describes how Charles Swann, the part-Jewish social outsider whose mysterious connections to powerful and fashionable people seem also to make him very much an 'insider', falls in love with Odette de Crecy. Everything about their prolonged love affair is presented in a kind of enigmatic twilight. The two characters are observed almost wholly from the outside. We know remarkably little about them. When Swann first meets Odette at a salon, he does not think she is his type. He then falls in love, and woos her. After the episode where he rearranges some orchids, 'cattleyas', on her dress (this detail was originally inspired by Proust seeing the Countess Greffuhle, the leading Parisian society beauty of the 1890s, festooned in these orchids at some grand occasion), it is suggested that the couple for the first time make love. But Swann then finds her becoming strangely elusive. Has she another lover (Forcheville)? Can he really trust her? Has he not caught her out in telling lies about where she has been, and whom she has been with? Is she in fact a cocotte, taking many lovers? Enmired in this growing morass of suspicion and distrust, Swann begins to wonder whether he really loves Odette after all. After wavering in one direction, then another, he finally decides that he doesn't. She is not for him. He never wishes to see her again. We then astonishingly discover, many pages later and for reasons which are never explained, that Swann and Odette did eventually get married after all, and now have a young daughter, Gilberte.

What is interesting is that this is the one really substantial episode in the book not centred on the narrator himself and seen through his eyes. But in significant respects it is like a precursor to the book's other two main love affairs, each of which do involve the narrator, and in each of which we see him, like Swann, perpetually tortured by uncertainties. During Swann's wooing of Odette she slips away from him as a classic 'elusive *anima*' figure, just as the narrator's own two girlfriends are to do later. The difference is that Swann's love affair does ultimately, albeit for reasons unexplained, reach a happy conclusion, when we see that he and Odette have married. It is as if, in creating the character of Swann, Proust was somehow imagining the elusive masculine part of himself eventually achieving a successful union with a woman. Certainly Swann is certainly a stronger, more masculine figure than the narrator ever manages to be, despite the merry dance his elusive *anima* leads him during their courtship. But when in the next volume, 'Within a Budding Grove', Proust moves on to imagine 'Marcel' himself falling in love with members of the opposite sex, there can be no such happy resolution.

The narrator's first love, whom he sees playing in the Champs Elysées when he is a teenager, is a lively girl with reddish hair whom he discovers is Gilberte Swann. He develops a powerful teenage crush on her, much as Proust had done for her original, Marie Bernardaky. He tries to join her street games as often as he can, hoping against hope that she will like him (much as Proust had done with his teenage schoolfriends). Gradually they develop a closer friendship and the young narrator becomes a regular visitor to her grand home, where Gilberte's parents receive the polite young boy kindly, imagining he might be a good influence on their daughter. But, in terms of love, the relationship is wholly one-sided, existing entirely in the narrator's mind. He is tortured by Gilberte's casual treatment of him, as he waits for letters which never come and rarely finds her at home when he calls (significantly he seems to spend more time with her mother Odette than with Gilberte herself). He tries to convince himself that he must forget her, his infatuation eventually fades and she drops out of his life (although years later they become friends and talk about the now long-distant past).

Much more substantial, in that it lasts on and off through 2000 pages of the novel, is the love which begins when the narrator, now a young man, takes a holiday with his grandmother and the faithful Francoise in the seaside resort of Balbec. He one day sees a lively band of girls playing games on the esplanade. His eye is particularly caught by one tomboyish, dark-haired girl pushing a bicycle, whom he cannot get out of his mind, and to whom he is eventually introduced as Albertine Simonet. As he gradually gets to know her and the other girls, his friendship with Albertine is soon sufficiently established for her to invite him alone up to her bedroom when she has to spend a night in the Grand Hotel where he is staying. By now besotted, he tries to kiss her, only to see her, to his horror, angrily sounding a bell to summon help. Again he has been cruelly rejected.

Most of the next 650 pages, in the volume entitled 'The Guermantes Way', are based on the time when, after leaving school, Proust was received as a young outsider into the world of the French upper class. As we are led interminably through their Parisian dinner parties and receptions, two impressions predominate. One is of the claustrophobic snobbery of this aristocracy which, cut off from any genuine social role, has become utterly decadent, obsessed with 'birth', titles and family histories stretching back centuries into the past, like that of the Guermantes themselves, "fourteen times connected to the French royal family". The other is of the unremitting triviality and self-regarding tedium of their conversations, so that when we are finally treated, at great length, to an example of the 'legendary Guermantes wit', a joke admiringly repeated round the fashionable salons of Faubourg St Germain for weeks, it is merely the awful pun by which the Duchesse de Guermantes describes someone as a 'teaser Augustus'. Yet this world of all-consuming egotism, where nothing seems to exist beyond the social masks of its inhabitants, Proust lovingly describes through his narrator as a magical realm, because it is the world into which he himself had been welcomed, and which had flattered his ego by treating him as someone interesting and of unusual talent. In the midst of all this heady social success, Albertine unexpectedly comes back into his life. She arrives one afternoon when he is in bed, complaisantly submits to his caresses and they make love.

By the time even the narrator is beginning to weary of the vapidity of this closed aristocratic world, the book's mood begins to change and darken. There is the strange interview with Baron de Charlus, the older man who seems to have taken the young narrator under his wing as a protégé, but then subjects him one night to an extraordinary petulant, threatening, snobbish tirade which reveals a new, much darker side to his character. This is a prelude to the scene where the narrator discovers that de Charlus is a homosexual (when he overhears him having sex with Jupien), and to the tortuous, opaque passage which opens the next volume, 'The Cities of the Plain', describing those who are condemned to live in the shadowy underworld of Sodom and Gomorrah: male and female homosexuals. Proust is here referring obliquely to the time when he himself had entered the twilight world of the homosexual *demi-monde*; and this now colours much of the rest of the novel, as in the scene where we see de Charlus, Morel and the Prince de Guermantes in a brothel – even though in the foreground the narrator's own sexual proclivities are presented almost entirely in terms of his tortured relationship with the sexually ambiguous Albertine.[1] We never really know very much about Albertine. She is a shadowy, cardboard figure, seen entirely through the narrator's eyes. She represents all the difficulty Proust had in realising his own inner anima: except that in real life he ended up projecting it onto men; whereas Albertine, for decorum's sake, remains outwardly, if at times ambivalently, feminine. Although his relationship with her finally becomes more or less established, he is afflicted by perpetual uncertainty. Can he trust her? Is she lying to him? Is she really a secret lesbian, engaging in affairs with other women? Should he marry her? After twitching one way, then another, like Swann before him, he eventually

---

1. Another episode in Proust's own life presented only obliquely is the year he spent in the army. But this is reflected through another significant character in the novel, Robert Saint-Loup, the dashing, confident young aristocrat, popular with women, who serves as an army officer, and who cuts the kind of manly figure the masculine part of Proust might have liked to be (his name echoing the pet name Proust was given by his mother). In this sense, like Swann, Saint-Loup represents his (and the narrator's) 'split-off' manhood, although eventually we see him too entering the sexual twilight zone, first in his love affair with the prostitute 'Rachel When From The Lord', and finally when he also becomes at least in part homosexual.

decides that this would be madness. But almost immediately he decides that he does love Albertine after all, after 'kissing her, as I used to kiss my mother at Combray, to calm my anguish'. We finally see the real heart of his problem. He has just told his mother that he is definitely not going to marry Albertine. But next day, after hearing him crying in the night, his mother comes into his room and says 'remember your Mamma is going away today and couldn't bear to leave her big pet in such a state'. He takes his mother's head in his arms, still weeping, and says 'I know how unhappy I'm going to make you'. But he has been thinking it over all night, and 'I absolutely must ... I absolutely must marry Albertine'.

The next volume, 'The Captive', centres on the period where Albertine is living in the narrator's flat in Paris, both being looked after by the faithful Francoise (as usual, Marcel is wholly dependent on others for all the practical necessities of life). Again the narrator's love for Albertine switches on and off, punctuated by fits of jealousy and the constantly recurring suspicion that she has been lying to him and secretly engaging in lesbian affairs. So cocooned is he in his own self-centredness that, in wondering whether marriage to Albertine might not spoil his life, 'by making me assume the too arduous task of devoting myself to another person', he even suggests that it is 'physical desire which alone makes us take an interest in the existence and character of another person'. All we see of their love play is that it is fairly infantile; and Albertine gives the narrator no greater pleasure than the 'soothing power' of her presence every evening by his side,

> 'the like of which I had not experienced since the evenings at Combray long ago when my mother, stooping over my bed, brought me repose in a kiss.'

Nevertheless, as time drags by, it becomes clear their affair is going nowhere, and that our weak, neurotic hero will never be decisive enough to propose marriage. Finally, after a petulant scene when he has yet again interrogated Albertine about her supposed lesbian affairs, he decides to break off their relations forever. He returns to the flat to be told by Francoise '*Mlle Albertine est disparue*'. She has already packed her bags and left. He is distracted. The 'captive' *anima* has become 'The Fugitive', the title of the next volume. He sends his friend Saint-Loup out into the countryside in an attempt to find her. Eventually word comes that Albertine has been killed in a riding accident. The *anima* is dead.

From his initial shock and grief, the narrator then retreats back into total self-absorption, as moves through what are described as his 'three stages on the road to indifference' about her death. The third of these appropriately is Proust's reconstruction of his visit to Venice with his mother and his friend Reynaldo. In the novel, while he and his mother are there, he receives a telegram from Albertine, appearing to tell him that she is still alive. But this gives him 'no joy'. Happily back in the company of his beloved mother, he chillingly reflects that 'the Self' in him which loved Albertine is dead, and there is thus no reason for him to be moved, although subsequently it turns out he has misread the telegram. It had not been from Albertine at all. She really is dead.

In 'Time Regained', the final volume, years have gone by and France is in the middle of the First World War. Saint-Loup has married Gilberte; but even this does not provide at least some faint echo of a happy ending, since he too had then started to have affairs, first with other women, then with men. Even this shadow of the narrator's masculinity has finally been sucked down into the twilit sexual under-world, where we glimpse the now ageing, pro-German Baron de Charlus being thrashed for sexual pleasure by a soldier in a dubious hotel, from which the narra-tor has just seen Saint-Loup emerge. But at least Saint-Loup's manhood survives sufficiently for him to die as an officer at the front. Everyone else the narrator has known, like the Duc de Guermantes, is growing old and decrepit. He has another 'madeleine-like' flash of happy memories of the past, set off by the uneven paving stones in the courtyard of the Guermantes' house, musing that 'the true paradises are the paradises one has lost'. As he feels time running out, and death approaching, he realises at last that the true purpose of his life is that he must become a writer and put it all down on paper. He must rememember everything that has happened to him since his far-off distant childhood; every person he has known; every minute detail, however trivial: for this 'was my life, it was in fact me'.

Thus ends the greatest monument to human egotism in the history of story-telling: a book so preoccupied with the ego-life of its author that it is not so much a story as a case study: the self-portrait of a man so frozen in immaturity by the unresolved tie to 'Mother' that he is incapable of making any contact with the deeper Self. Because he cannot make any genuine connection with anyone else, or see anything of significance outside the unfolding of his own life, it becomes a story which cannot have any resolution: which can go nowhere except back to its own beginning, like the mythical *ouroboros*, the snake which ends up eating its own tail.

## The three 'Pseudo-Endings': Either with a bang or a whimper

The most obvious thing which happens when storytelling moves exclusively into the world of the ego is that stories no longer centre round the archetypal oppos-ition between darkness and light. The characters thus appear in a kind of twilight, cut off from one another, living on dreams which can lead only to disillusionment. Above all, they cannot go through any real inner transformation. And because they cannot develop those personal qualities which will bring them to wholeness, it is impossible for such stories to come to a full archetypal conclusion. Where there is no real light or dark, the story cannot culminate in a climactic confronta-tion between them. But this does not eliminate the need of any story for an end-ing. What happens therefore is that the storyteller falls back on a 'pseudo-ending': some device which appears to round off the story, even though in reality nothing has been resolved. And these 'pseudo-endings' take three main forms (sometimes seen in combination).

(1) As we saw in Chekhov, the story may end in some shocking act of violence, erupting more or less from nowhere. At least, by bringing home the emptiness of the characters' lives, this appears to give the story a dramatic conclusion, even though nothing has really been resolved.

(2) As we saw in Proust, the story may become circular, with its ending referring back in some way to its beginning. The hope is that simply by retracing the events which have led up to this concluding moment, this may in itself give a semblance of meaning to all that has happened, even though again nothing has really been resolved. Another example is the film *Brief Encounter*. This begins just after the breaking off of a love affair which had ended up going nowhere. But this is then recalled in flashback, eventually leading back to the scene of non-communication between husband and wife which has been the story's starting point.

(3) A third type of 'pseudo-ending' can be seen where a storyteller deliberately tries to make a virtue of the fact that nothing has been resolved. The story ends with one or more of the characters moving on into the future, but going nowhere. But because this is presented as a kind of 'moral' to the tale, it purports to give an air of significance to all that has happened.

A story which combines the first two of these 'pseudo-endings' is the play written by Luigi Pirandello in the year before Proust died, *Six Characters in search of an Author* (1921). Actors are in a theatre, preparing to rehearse a play (by Pirandello), when six strangers enter – two older adults, a young man and woman, two children – introducing themselves as the characters in a play who are looking for an author to tell their story. It emerges that they are a father, whose wife has left him and their son to live with another man, with whom she has had three more children. After many years the mother has returned with her children to the city where she previously lived, and has sent her eldest daughter to work in a dress shop, to provide them with money. In reality the shop is the front for a brothel, to which the father comes one day looking for sex. He tries to seduce his own stepdaughter, but in the nick of time is interrupted by the mother, who screams out who he is.

These six characters in fact represent the archetypal family: Father, Mother, Son and Daughter, completed by two versions of the Child, boy and girl, representing the future. But they are divided off from one another by every kind of resentment and unhappiness. Father and mother hate each other. The original son resents his mother for abandoning him. The daughter resents having had to support her family in this degrading way, and in particular her stepfather for the episode where he tried to seduce her. While all this is explained, the two youngest children remain silent.

The 'characters' have no other existence than this wretched drama they have all lived through. Frozen in their appointed roles, incapable of developing, they try to explain what has happened to the play's director and his uncomprehending 'actors'. When the actors clumsily try to recreate the seduction scene, the characters protest they have got it all wrong. The director then asks them to repeat it in a new setting, the garden of the father's house, where suddenly it seems the 'characters' are beginning to break out of their roles. The mother tries to ingratiate herself with the son she had abandoned. He runs away from her to a fountain, where he sees the younger daughter has drowned herself. The younger son then shoots himself. At this shocking irruption of violence, the director no longer knows whether he is watching make-believe or reality, and calls the rehearsal to an end.

439

Through most of the play it has seemed as if the characters, trapped in their ego-roles, are doomed just to go on re-enacting their story in circular fashion for ever.The only hope of release from this treadmill is for something unexpected and violent to happen, as at the end of a Chekhov play. The two characters who have seemed the most helpless victims of all this misery, and who have remained mute, take the only way out. In reality, of course, nothing has been resolved. But at least, as in Chekhov, the play has been given the semblance of a significant ending.

We see a similar combination of endings in a book published four years later, Scott Fitzgerald's *The Great Gatsby* (1925). As the novel concludes, the narrator is musing on the life of Jay Gatsby, the mysterious multi-millionaire who has recently been murdered. He recalls how Gatsby had emerged from obscure beginnings in the American Middle West, and had come east to build up a great fortune, to live in a fine house and to host fabulous parties. For years Gatsby had pursued the vision of Daisy, the beautiful girl he had lost as a young man. But finally he had caught up with her, living nearby and unhappily married to a husband who was having an affair with the wife of a garage mechanic. Just as it seemed the two might at last be brought happily together, Daisy, driving Gatsby's car, had unavoidably run over and killed her husband's mistress. Daisy's husband had then identified Gatsby to the dead woman's husband as the car's owner. The cuckolded husband, thinking Gatsby was his wife's lover, had gone to Gatsby's house and shot him in his swimming pool, before committing suicide. As the story ends, the narrator looks back over Gatsby's life, and how it had all been the vain pursuit of a dream. Beginning thousands of miles away in his humble childhood home, he had worked up to all the splendour of his wealth (albeit achieved by what turned out to be very dubious methods), his fine house, his famous parties (even though he had scarcely known most of his guests, and none had turned up for his funeral). And when he had met Daisy again, his lost *anima*, the ultimate goal of his dream must finally 'have seemed so close that he could hardly fail to grasp it'. Then, in one sudden violent moment, it had all been over. Gatsby had not realised that his dream 'was already behind him', because he had

> 'believed in the green light, the orgastic future that year by year recedes before us. It eluded us then, but that's no matter – tomorrow we will run faster, stretch out our arms further… And one fine morning … so we beat on, boats against the current, borne back ceaselessly into the past.'

Those closing words might have seemed like an echo of the conclusion of Proust's novel, written just four years before.

The third form of 'pseudo-ending', that which tries to make a positive virtue out of the fact that nothing at the end of the story has been resolved, can be seen in Fitzgerald's longest novel, *Tender is the Night* (1934). This was written when Fitzgerald was in his late thirties. The heady days of his early fame were behind him. The 'Jazz Age' to which he had given its name was over. Inwardly wearying of the hectic, rootless life success as a writer had brought him, and of the strain of his marriage to the unstable Zelda, he was taking to drink. His new hero, Dr Dick Diver, is a highly promising young psychiatrist, who has studied in Vienna and

Zurich and has a great future before him. His greatest individual success as a
doctor has been in restoring Nicole, the beautiful, but mentally unstable daughter
of a Chicago millionaire, to apparent health. Under the unwitting influence of
Nicole's older sister Baby, Dick is lured into marrying Nicole, and initially the
marriage appears to be a success. This is the 'dream stage' of the story, when they
are living in the south of France with their two children. Then Rosemary, a new
young Hollywood movie star, enters their life and tries to seduce Dick. At first
it seems out of the question that the happily married hero will give way. But gradually, as his resolve begins to weaken, Nicole simultaneously begins to show
returning signs of her old schizophrenia. For the sake of her sister, Baby puts up
the money for Dick to set up a psychiatric clinic. This places him more than ever
in a state of financial dependence on his wife's family, which emasculates him.
Now in the 'frustration stage', he begins to fall apart. He has a brief, unsatisfactory
affair with Rosemary. He takes to drink, leading to awkward incidents, one of
which forces him to resign from the clinic. This only drives him to drink even
more, pushing him into the 'nightmare stage'. He and Nicole are now miserable
together. He has become a social embarrassment, and she views him with increasing contempt. Conscious that there is now another, more obviously masculine
man who is attracted to her, she feels a new confidence, and tells Dick he has made
a failure of his life. She finally feels liberated, both from the doctor who had once
helped to cure her and from their marriage. Nicole goes off to marry her new
admirer, and the last we hear of Dick is that the once brilliantly promising young
psychiatrist has returned to America, drifting from town to town as a humdrum
general practitioner. He has lost everything: both his manhood and his *anima*.
Nicole, happily cocooned in her new ego-life, sentimentally consoles herself that
he must be merely waiting for some call at last to fulfil his great talents. The truth,
as we know, is that Dr Diver is going nowhere. Six years later his creator was dead,
from excessive drinking, at the age of 44.

## Camus: The egotist as complete outsider

In his novel *L'Etranger* (1938), translated as *The Outsider*, Albert Camus carried
the idea of the egocentric hero totally split off from the Self to its logical conclusion. Not of course that Camus himself would have described it like this. What
inspired him was the idea of a hero who becomes admirable because he finds the
centre of his identity solely within himself. He has been liberated from any sense
of obligation to anyone or anything outside him.

Meursault is a young man in Algeria who has just received news of the death of
his mother in an old people's home. In accordance with convention, he takes
time off work to go to the funeral, but when he arrives at the home he shows
little interest. He smokes in the room where the coffin is lying; gets irritated when
some of her friends begin to cry; and when they process to the cemetery in scorch-
ing sun, he is much more worried about the heat than his mother's death. He then
catches the bus home and looks forward to a long sleep. The next day on the beach

he meets Marie, a girl to whom he is sexually attracted. He suggests they should go to the cinema that evening and she is surprised to hear it is only a day since he lost his mother. After the film, a comedy, she stays the night, but leaves early the next morning. The following weekend they spend another night together, and when Marie asks him whether he loves her, he replies 'No'. She later asks him whether he would marry her, to which he says that he will if she wants it, but that he still does not love her. Shortly afterwards, Meursault is on the beach with Marie and two friends, Raymond and Masson, who have been in a fight with some Arabs. Later Raymond goes looking for the Arabs, and Meursault persuades him to hand over a gun he is carrying. One Arab comes at them with a knife, which gleams in the sun, dazzling Meursault, who impulsively shoots him. Afer a pause, he then fires four more shots into the Arab's body.

Arrested for murder, Meursault is given a lawyer, although he says this will not be necessary. When the lawyer tries to persuade him to plead in mitigation that he has been upset by his mother's death, he dismisses the suggestion, but feels too lazy to explain why. The magistrate produces a crucifix and invites Meursault to repent of his crime, so that God will forgive him. Meursault finds such an idea contemptible. He does not believe in God. He is not sorry for his crime, just annoyed about it. Over the next 11 months, while waiting for his trial, he enjoys sparring with the magistrate, who calls him 'Monsieur Antichrist', and gradually gets used to prison life, even to being deprived of cigarettes and sex (Marie visits him once, but tells him she will not be allowed to come again, because they are not married).

When the trial begins, Meursault is surprised by how many people have turned up. He listens with a sense of bored detachment to the final summing up by the prosecutor, who makes much of his heartlessness over his mother's death and portrays him as a soulless monster. His own lawyer is unimpressive, and Meursault finds the trial depressingly pointless, wishing he could go to sleep. The jury finds him guilty, and sentences him to the guillotine. Waiting in the condemned cell, he three times refuses to talk to the chaplain, explaining that there is no point, since he does not believe in God or any life after death. When the chaplain persists, Meursault becomes angry, saying that it is not an afterlife he wants, but one where he could remember his present one. He says it is the chaplain himself who is dead inside, waiting for his non-existent afterlife. He, Meursault, is the one who has been right all along, living his own life in his own way. No one else's life, death or love is of any concern to him. He falls asleep and wakes up to hear sirens announcing that his execution is imminent. He thinks of his mother, and that no one had any right to cry over her. He feels comfort in the indifference of the world, although he finally hopes that a crowd of people who hate him might turn up to watch him face the guillotine, because then he would feel less alone.

Apart from this final flicker of weakness, Meursault remains cocooned in his egocentric defiance to the end. He has never deliberately set out to do anything wicked, like, say, Dostoyevsky's Raskolnikov. But throughout the story he has shown himself to be totally dead to any normal human feelings, whether towards his mother and his girlfriend, or to the fellow human being he has casually killed without a trace of remorse. He can see nothing outside his own existence as having any significance. In another context, Meursault would have been diagnosed as a psychopath. Yet so far had the 'dark inversion' which had been taking place since the dawn of Romanticism now gone, that he could be presented to the world as a hero: to be admired precisely because he seemed to be a man 'liberated' from all moral, social or religious constraints. Sooner or later, in this process of 'dark inversion', it was logical that a storyteller would one day come up with such a hero. But in terms of how storytelling reflects what happens when the split between ego and Self becomes irretrievable, the process still had one more very significant step to take.

## Samuel Beckett: The end of the road

Two tramps, Vladimir and Estragon, are standing by a roadside in front of a leaf-less tree, engaging in inconsequential chatter. We later learn that they have been together, 'blathering' like this, for 50 years. Suddenly, after they have been dis-cussing Estragon's difficulty in pulling off his boot, in which his friend refuses to help him, Vladimir refers, seemingly apropos of nothing, to the thief crucified alongside Jesus who was saved. 'Suppose we repented' he says. 'Repented what?' replies Estragon. 'Oh', says Vladimir, 'we wouldn't have to go into the details'. He then wonders aloud why only one of the four gospels mentions the thief who was saved, while another says that 'both of them abused him'. 'Abused who?' asks the bored and baffled Estragon. 'The Saviour' comes the reply. 'Why?' 'Because he wouldn't save them'. 'From hell?' 'Imbecile! From death' retorts Vladimir. These Christian references, drawn from Beckett's upbringing by his domineering and 'profoundly religious' Irish-Protestant mother, from whom he spent much of his life trying to escape, serve as prelude to what is to be the central thread of the story. Estragon suggests they should move on. 'We can't' says Vladimir emphati-cally. 'Why not?' 'We're waiting for Godot.'

We are thus introduced to what is really the only significant element of plot in the play. The two tramps, stripped of any social context, are simply two dis-embodied human egos. But the one thing which defines them, it becomes clear, is that they are waiting for the arrival of this mysterious 'Godot'. They know nothing about who, what or where he might be. But gradually we become aware that they look on him as someone of almost cosmic importance. They cannot do anything or go anywhere until they encounter him. If only Godot comes, everything will be different. His arrival is the one thing which could give meaning and purpose to their otherwise empty and hopeless existence.

Eventually diversion arrives in the shape of two more characters, Pozzo driving his servant Lucky in front of him like an animal, on a lead. Their relationship is like a caricature of Lenin's famous question about human society, 'Who? Whom?' Pozzo is the 'above the line' figure who can sit down, picnicking on chicken and a bottle of wine, enjoying a smoke, while treating his wretched, silent, 'below the line' companion like dirt. But then the 'below the line' servant suddenly bursts into a startling flood of pseudo-profound gobbledygook about 'a personal God quaquaquaqua with white beard quaquaquaqua outside time without extension Who from their heights of divine apathia divine athambia divine aphasia loves us dearly with some exceptions for reasons unknown but time will tell …'

and so forth for several minutes, before relapsing into silence. No sooner have the newcomers departed than a boy arrives. He has brought a message from Godot. His master will not be coming today but will definitely come tomorrow. The two tramps discuss hanging themselves from the tree, then Estragon suggests they should move on. 'Yes, let's go' agrees Vladimir, but they do not move. So ends the first act.

The second act, set at the same time and place the following day, is much the same. Pozzo and Lucky eventually return, more briefly, because Pozzo is now blind and Lucky dumb. The boy comes back to say that Godot will not be coming today after all, but will be coming tomorrow. They ask him about his master: 'has he a beard?' 'Yes, sir.' 'Fair … or black?' 'I think it's white, sir' replies the boy, at which Vladimir expostulates 'Christ have mercy on us!' When the boy disappears, the two tramps again discuss hanging themselves from the tree, which now has a few leaves. 'I can't go on like this' says Estragon. 'We'll hang ourselves tomorrow' says Vladimir, adding, after a pause, 'unless Godot comes.' 'And if he comes?' asks Estragon. 'We'll be saved', says Vladimir. Again, as at the end of the first act, they agree to go, and again they do not move. So ends the play.

What makes *Waiting for Godot* exceptional is how, in one particular respect, it characterised the end of that psychological road which storytelling had been travelling since the dawn of Romanticism more profoundly than any other story. Here were two trapped, lost figures, symbolising the inmost essence of human existence when it is reduced to nothing more than the ego. So meaningless has life become that they might as well end it in suicide. Nevertheless, the play's power lies in their awareness that there could be something else. If only they could find whatever it that is symbolised by this mysterious Godot, their world could be transformed. They would be saved.

By definition, neither Beckett nor his characters know anything specific about this elusive missing dimension which could give meaning to their lives. Such fragmentary hints as we are given dress it up in the symbolism associated with religion. Godot's very name, of course, carries the echo of 'God'; and his messenger, the boy-Child, describes him as having a white beard, evoking the Wise Old Man image associated with God to which Lucky explicitly refers in his mad monologue. But everything we hear about this shadowy figure indicates that he represents that archetype which had for so long been dropping ever further out of sight in western storytelling, the transforming power of the Self. The peculiar power of *Waiting for Godot* lies in how it expresses the moment when that process finally hits rock bottom. On a conscious level, we are presented with all the rootless emptiness of life when viewed just through the ego. But so far has its life-giving complement, the Self, now been driven into the unconscious that at last, in shadowy, mysterious form, it reappears; even if only as an off-stage presence with which the characters are doomed never to make contact. One of the central laws governing human psychology is that, whenever any powerful component of the psyche is not integrated, it does not just vanish. It remains buried in the unconscious, ready to re-emerge in some shadowy 'inferior' form; and this is just as true of the most important archetype of them all, that representing human wholeness, as it is of any other. The special contribution of *Waiting for Godot*, which gave it its unique place in twentieth-century storytelling, was precisely that it evoked this missing Self more hauntingly than any other story of the age.

Never again was Beckett's work to refer to the lost Self in this way. From now on his plays merely expressed the emptiness of existence seen through the eyes of the ego, in ever sparser, more concentrated form. As an admirer of Proust, he produced the monologue *Krapp's Last Tape* (1958), in which a shabby old man forlornly tries to recapture the intensity of his earlier life by listening to recordings of his younger self. *Happy Days* (1961) shows an old woman buried up to her waist in a mound, obsessed with the contents of her handbag. *Come and Go* (1966) features three female characters in a text of only 121 words. *Breath* (1969), thirty seconds long, consists only of 'a pile of rubbish, a breath and a cry'. And his final offering, *Not I* (1973), is no more than a 'brief, fragmented, disembodied monologue delivered by an actor of indeterminate sex of whom only the "Mouth" is illuminated'.

In all this we might inescapably have the sense that the tradition of storytelling, which through myths and legends, plays and novels, had for thousands of years provided mankind with its richest single store of meaning, was at last being sucked down into a black hole of nothingness. Indeed, no one expressed this sense of having reached some final void of meaning more eloquently than Beckett himself, in his famous observation:

'we have nothing to say, except that we have nothing to say.'

It was not only in literature that we can see a similar dead end being reached. In twentieth-century art, as the figurative image had begun to dissolve into pure abstractionism, a similar process had finally led by 1950, just three years before the appearance of *Waiting for Godot*, to a painting which was no more than a black canvas. In words remarkably evocative of Beckett's own, its creator, the American abstract expressionist Ad Reinhardt, wrote:

'An artist ... has always nothing to say and he must say that over and over again.'

In 1952, just when Beckett was writing his most famous play, much the same dead end was reached in music, when the American composer John Cage produced his famous work '4.33', consisting solely of four minutes and thirty-three seconds of silence.

Of course the separation of the ego from the Self was to be expressed in twentieth-century storytelling in more ways than this. The most blatant of these will be the subject of the next chapter. But it was not only in 'serious literature', such as the works of Chekhov and Proust, Camus and Beckett, that stories reflected this tendency for their characters and the story itself to end up 'going nowhere'. It also emerged strongly, though perhaps less obviously, in popular storytelling. And we shall end this chapter by looking at three of the most successful Hollywood films of the late-twentieth century.

## Not so close encounters

Much of the appeal of Steven Spielberg, as the most successful popular storyteller of the late twentieth century, lay in the spectacular manner in which his films exploited some of the great archetypal themes of storytelling, such as the Quest, the overcoming of monsters and the hunt for buried treasure.

His first science-fiction film *Close Encounters of the Third Kind* (1977) opens with the discovery in the American desert, in the middle of a mighty sandstorm, of seven World War Two fighter planes, which had mysteriously disappeared with their pilots in 1945. There is no sign of the pilots, but what puzzles their finders is that the aircraft are as good as new, without a trace of rust. Even the oil in their engines is still fresh.

One night shortly afterwards, much of America is amazed by extraordinary displays of lights in the sky, and the appearance of dozens of 'unidentified flying objects'. Our attention is then focused on three people: the hero, an electrical repairman, who lives with his familiy in Indiana; the heroine, a divorced artist; and a child, her young son. There is an eerie scene when the house occupied by the heroine and her son is illuminated by unearthly light, and all the toys in his bedroom begin moving about by themselves. Obviously some more than natural power is at work. Household machines begin to shake, but quite harmlessly and without breaking. The little boy walks out of the house towards the source of the unearthly light, smiling, and disappears.

The following day, quite independently, the hero and the heroine both begin obsessively trying to make models and pictures of a strangely shaped mountain. They behave in other odd ways, as if they are possessed by some power beyond themselves, as when he starts throwing rubbish which should be outside his house in through the windows. Then, still independently, they both see on a television newscast, a picture of the mountain they have become obsessed by. It is called Devil's Peak, in Wyoming, and it seems from the news report that something very odd is going on there.

Both know at once that they must set out for Devil's Peak as the most important thing in their lives. The story thus becomes a Quest, and along their journey to the distant goal they meet and join forces. When they get there, the way has been barred by the US Government with fences and guards, but for some reason they are allowed in, to the foot of the precipitous mountain, where, as night falls, they witness an astonishing spectacle. A gigantic, obviously extra-terrestrial machine, round and glowing with light, glides in over the mountain and lands – on a special airstrip which it seems has been prepared by the US Government. In some way never explained, there seems to be contact between the government and the beings behind this awesome display of interplanetary technology.

The hero and heroine then approach the colossal craft and see, coming out of it, first her son, then the seven pilots of the planes which had disappeared a generation before. Like their aircraft, it is evident that they are not a day older than when they vanished. They have returned from their experience completely unchanged. Then, out of the unearthly light emanating from the spaceship, come the extra-terrestrial beings themselves, like little, smiling human foetuses. They smile to the scientist from the US Government, as if to indicate that they know him. The hero then steps forward and goes off into the spaceship alone, leaving the heroine and the child behind. Forlornly they set off on their journey home, and the story ends.

This curiously unresolved story includes a number of features which may strike us as particularly odd and revealing. In the opening scenes, our expectation is built up that some tremendously important, world-changing event is about to take place. There are miraculous signs – the untouched aircraft found in the desert, the lights in the heavens – which seem to indicate that some stupendous supernatural power is at work. At first we do not know whether it is hostile or friendly, dark or light, although the way the little boy goes off happily into the unearthly light seems to suggest it is benign.

At the point where the hero and heroine separately become possessed by the compulsion to set off on their quest, all our ancient instincts in following stories tell us that they are about to undergo some great, life-transforming experience, an encounter with this colossal but benign and therefore life-renewing power, which has chosen to intervene in worldly affairs and has singled them out for a unique destiny. This is underlined by the fact that the goal of their quest is a mountain, which so often in the storytelling of the world is a symbol of the Self.

But already there are warnings that the story may turn out to deliver less than it promises, not least the mountain's name, Devil's Peak. When they arrive, they find the mountain surrounded by barriers to others, ordinary mortals, but they are let through by some special dispensation, as if to underline their special destiny ('the test which only the true hero or heroine can pass'). The sense of some impending great act of transformation is brought to a climax by the arrival of the huge spaceship: the great, round, glowing object in the heavens, which again is a classic symbol of the Self in all its awesome power. But then the warning signs that all is not going to turn out like this come thick and fast.

The pilots emerge from the spaceship, after their unearthly adventure, completely unchanged (right at the start of the film, the unchanged state of the aircraft had in fact been the first warning sign). The extra-terrestrial beings emerge, not as superhuman, god-like figures, but looking like unborn human children. Most significant of all, the hero steps up into the spaceship alone, parted from the heroine, who presumably had been as much called to the Quest as himself. Unfulfilled, the *anima*-figure goes off home, accompanied by that other great symbol of Rebirth, the Child; so that the hero ends up separated from both the two chief redeeming figures in storytelling. We no longer have the slightest indication that, when he steps up into that spacecraft, anything of real significance will happen to him, any more than it has done to the pilots.

447

In other words, the story has harped on about all the most profound archetypal symbolism of redemption and transformation; yet, because it has been divorced from its inner meaning, nothing really happens at all, apart from a lot of playing with the cinematic tricks of illusion. If there is one lesson above all we learn from stories it is the central symbolic significance of the hero and the heroine being brought together in complete union at the story's end. If for any reason a hero and heroine do not end up together, this always tells us that something has gone seriously amiss. And the film's title is tellingly ironic in that none of its main characters, least of all the hero and heroine, in fact have a 'close encounter' with anyone. Apart from mother and son, everyone remains split off from everyone else.

The second supreme lesson of stories, when they are rooted in the archetypes, is that they are about personal transformation. This is what all the basic plots are about: the inner change in the hero or heroine as they are led from one state to another. When the Roman poet Ovid wrote his book the *Metamorphoses* about myths which showed their central figure being in some fundamental way transformed, or 'metamorphosed', he had to include almost every important story in the Graeco-Roman mythology, because every one of them shows its hero or heroine being changed from one thing to another. Yet in *Close Encounters* no one is changed at all; and the fundamental reason for this is unwittingly reflected in that curious episode when the hero feels compelled to throw all the rubbish which is outside his house in through the windows. It is as if the power which possesses him is trying to tell him that everything which is 'outside' should be 'inside'. This is precisely what has gone astray, not just with this film but with so many other stories of our time. They project outwardly, on a fantasy level, all sorts of things which can only beome real and life-giving when taken symbolically, on an inward level. But this is precisely what happens when the imagining of stories becomes centred on the ego, rather than rooted in that level of the unconscious where the archetypal patterns of storytelling are trying to lead us up to wholeness and connect us with our inmost Self.

## Not so Superman

The defining characteristic of the comic strip hero Superman, of course, which made him one of the great icons of twentieth-century popular culture, is that he is two people in one. In his outward persona, as Clark Kent, he could not be more ordinary, the epitome of Everyman. But he can then be transformed into his other Self, when we see him as the complete archetypal hero: supernaturally strong, but with his strength made lifegiving, because it is dedicated to saving the helpless, battling for the community and righting the world's wrongs. The secret of his appeal is precisely that he seemingly embodies the most fundamental archetype of all: that in each human being the outward, limited, ego-persona is hiding the potential for the true, inner Self within. But when Hollywood translated Superman onto the cinema screen in 1978, we see how sadly the archetype disintegrated.

The opening of the story is mythic in its symbolism.[2] On the planet Krypton, the old order is dying. An imposing, almost god-like Wise Old Man in flowing robes (played by Marlon Brando) warns his elderly and unheeding fellow-members of the ruling council that the end is nigh, and that their world will soon explode. It is that familiar situation we see so often at the start of a story, where the ruling order is decaying and doomed, and the only hope of redemption lies in the emergence of a new young hero. The Wise Old Man and his wife send their infant son to the distant planet Earth, where he is adopted by human parents living on a Middle American farmstead. There is the unmistakable archetypal echo of 'God' sending his son down to earth, to an ordinary humble family, to grow up and save mankind.

Outwardly the young lad seems just like any ordinary American boy. But when, as a teenager, he has his first embarrassing encounter with a girl, he feels the need to show off, and runs home faster than a car or train. His earthly 'father', just before dying, tells him he must have been sent to earth 'for a purpose'. Hearing voices in the night, he is drawn to the barn, where sees a magical rod of crystal glowing in the darkness of a hole in the ground. It is a sign of his awakening destiny as a man, and he goes off, after a touching farewell to 'Mom', on a long journey to the North Pole, where in caves of ice he meets a vision of his real Father, to undergo an initiation rite into manhood.

In fact, he emerges less confident and manly than before, as Clark Kent, the gauche newspaperman in the great city of Metropolis. He is particularly ill-at-ease with Lois, the girl reporter to whom he is attracted. But when Lois gets trapped on top of a skyscraper, in a helicopter which is just about to topple into the street, we see him for the first time transformed into Superman. He swoops up to snatch her from death, in a feat which leaves everyone in the city stunned. Who is this amazing 'Superman'? Lois interviews him in his Superman role and they float around in the clouds, exchanging gooey sentimental platitudes.

We now meet the story's Monster-figure, a super-criminal who lives in a luxurious lair beneath the city, plotting an immense and diabolical crime. He plans to redirect two nuclear rockets to land on California, one targeted on the San Andreas fault, intended to trigger off such an earthquake that the coastal strip of the state will collapse into the sea. Having bought up much of the land to the east of the fault, he will then be fabulously rich. While Lois is away in the desert, investigating his secret land purchases, Superman falls into the super-villain's clutches, and is only rescued from death in the nick of time by the villain's girlfriend, who

---

2. Part of the reason for the emergence of science fiction (which of course has virtually no connection with science fact) is precisely that it has enabled storytellers to imagine stories of mythical dimension. Not only, since H. G. Wells's Martians in *The War of the Worlds*, has this allowed for the creation of 'monsters' just as monstrous as any in the myths of the ancient world. It also, in tales like *Star Wars*, enables storytellers to create alternative realms, peopled by kings, 'dark lords', princesses, knights, goblins, giants and all the archetypal paraphernalia of myth and legend, without seeming to be self-consciously archaic, because such stories are set in 'the future'. In the same way, by calling on the 'magic' of science, it can also, of course, provide heroes with the modern equivalents of those 'magic' weapons used by Perseus and Co. in the myths and legends of yore.

is attracted to him. After his 'thrilling escape' he zooms off, too late to stop one of the rockets exploding, setting off huge earthquakes. By a superhuman feat he manages to stop the San Andreas fault splitting apart, but he cannot stop Lois being engulfed and crushed to death. And at this point the archetypal symbolism of the story finally goes completely haywire.

Superman has at least saved most of the 'kingdom', but he has not overcome the 'shadow' and the *anima* is dead. In this sense the 'shadow' has won. But Superman then uses his supernatural powers to bring her back to life, only to realise to his horror that he has done the one thing he has been forbidden to do by his Father. By bringing Lois back to life, he has 'interfered in human history'. In shame he spirals off up into space, and the film ends on an image of him whizzing round the Earth spinning far below. Even in superficial terms, none of this makes sense. Why should bringing Lois back to life constitute interference in human history, any more than Superman's other feats? What had he been sent to earth for in the first place, except to interfere in history? And what sort of an ending is it when, having brought the heroine back to life, he cannot then be happily reunited with her but must hurtle off into space to behave like the Flying Dutchman?

The key, of course, lies in the fact that, despite his outward guise as Superman, the hero has never been properly a man at all. He is just a two-dimensional fantasy figure, spun out of infantile make-believe. He is unable to relate in any grown-up way to the feminine, either in his gauche Clark Kent *persona* or in his make-believe Superman-role: which is why it is entirely logical that he should end up losing his *anima* to the 'shadow'. When he brings her back to life, while the 'shadow' still lives, this is again just wishful thinking. And, in terms of archetypal symbolism, it is then equally logical that the story should end on the image of this little 'boy hero who cannot grow up' spiralling in futile circles round the Earth, because this is precisely what he has become: a split-off ego circling impotently round the Self; an image of the wholeness with which he no longer has any hope of making contact. It perfectly symbolises all that has been wrong with the story.

### E.T.: The 'Self' from outer space

Even in the Hollywood dream factory, there are of course times when a story makes rather deeper contact with the underlying archetypes. And it may be illuminating to end this section by looking at one such example, by way of contrast, even though this was still a story primarily conceived on no more than a sentimental level. Certainly it was a remarkable achievement to turn a hideous little monster with a wide, bulbous head, huge eyes, a long neck and leathery skin into one of the most lovable characters in modern popular storytelling. But when we consider what the central figure of Steven Spielberg's *E.T.* (1982) really represents, his appeal becomes wholly comprehensible.

The film opens at night with an extra-terrestrial spaceship landing in a Californian forest to study earthly plant-life. Its crew's researches are interrupted by a pack of government scientists and officials, seen menacingly in black silhouette, and the aliens rush back to their spacecraft to escape. But one of them is left behind.

We then meet the hero of the story, 10-year old Elliott, at his home in a nearby town, being excluded from a game played by his older brother and three friends. When they trick him into going outside, he throws a ball into the garage and is startled when it is thrown back at him. Back inside, the sense of Elliott's isolation from his family only deepens when, unwittingly, he lets on to his mother that their father, who has recently left home, has gone to Mexico with his new girl-friend. This makes his mother cry, and his elder brother furious at him for being so tactless. Elliott is a boy seemingly without a friend in the world, but he is about to find one.

That night, sleeping outside, Elliott is disturbed by scuffling noises, turns on his torch and for the first time sees the extraordinary little extra-terrestrial visitor. At first he is terrified, but the creature moves gently forward to touch him with its elongated fingers. Far from being threatening it is offering friendship, rather like Frankenstein's monster when it wakes him from sleep. But, unlike Frankenstein, Elliott reciprocates, protectively leading the 'alien' into the house to hide him in his bedroom. The two begin trying to communicate, with the alien quick to copy everything Elliott does. Next day, Elliott lets his brother and younger sister into the secret, swearing them to secrecy, so they are now a conspiracy of three, led by the formerly excluded Elliott. And they soon discover between them that his new alien friend commands miraculous and life-giving powers.

The biggest surprise is that the alien seems to have established an extraordinary telepathic sympathy with Elliott, so that when the boy is at school, and the alien gets drunk on beer from the fridge back home, Elliott feels drunk at his desk. While this and further telepathically-induced actions are landing Elliott in trouble with the school authorities and his mother, his young sister is teaching the alien to speak. Having returned home in disgrace, Elliott is soon teaching his alter-ego to repeat his new name, 'E.T.', an echo of Elliott's own name. They then learn that E.T. above all wants to contact his far-off planetary home, as he repeats his plaintive new phrase 'E.T., phone home'.

One reason for this is that E.T. is beginning to sicken, from his exposure to life on Earth. He uses his super-intelligence to build a radio-telephone, and after a Hallowe'en party he and Elliott take it into the forest to use it, with E.T. demonstrating his power to make Elliott's bicycle rise magically into the night sky. But when the boy fails to return home, his mother calls the authorities, and we now move into the 'nightmare stage' of the story. First, E.T. seems to be dying. Then menacingly impersonal, space-suited officials and scientists move in to capture him. Finally, he and Elliott are laid out side by side, wired up to a battery of life-support and monitoring devices, not just to study the fast-sinking E.T. himself but the symbiosis between them, which is making the grieving Elliott almost as ill as his friend.

Alone among all the grown-ups who are portrayed in such a threatening, unfeeling way through the story, there is one scientist, Keys, who shows real warmth and understanding. And when E.T. dies, and his body is placed on ice in a sealed container, Keys suggests that Elliott, who, now the symbiosis is broken, suddenly feels much better, might like to be alone with him, before E.T. is taken away to be dissected. Elliott looks in through the inspection-window of the container, and sees from his glowing 'heart light' that his friend has miraculously returned to life. He recruits help from his brother and, when the container is being taken away, they hi-jack the van, with older brother driving while Elliott releases E.T. from his frozen coffin. They are joined by more young friends with bicycles and head off into the forest in a dramatic 'chase sequence', as they are hotly pursued by a horde of police and officials. When their path is blocked by a police barrier, they are saved when, thanks to E.T.'s magic powers, their bicycles simply fly up over it. They arrive at the clearing where the spaceship is just descending to take E.T. back home. There is a touching farewell scene, when E.T. says goodbye to his friends. And these now include not just Elliott, his brother and sister and the other children, but also two grown-ups: Elliott's mother and the friendly scientist Keys, standing beside her. The spacecraft then soars away, leaving a rainbow across the sky.

What makes this story different from any other we have looked at in this chapter is that, as it unfolds, we see a genuine process of transformation taking place. The young hero begins, alone and excluded, in a family under the shadow of his father having selfishly abandoned them all. When this weird alien creature arrives, all normal responses dictate that he should be rejected as a terrifying threat. But when the 'monster' behaves in a friendly fashion, and Elliott responds likewise, it is like one of those moments in a folk tale when a little hero gives food to the animal or 'the little man' he meets in the forest. In establishing that the hero has a kind heart this brings him an ally who is to be the key to his salvation. Indeed we soon see that E.T. is precisely the 'Alter-Ego' Elliott needs to discover himself and to develop a new, deeper sense of his own identity. Everything E.T. does is life-giving and benign and, in this sense, he is more than just Elliott's Alter-Ego: he represents the integrating power of the Self. Thanks to his influence, Elliott finds new strengths in himself and becomes a leader. His divided family gradually knits together, until finally, when E.T. departs, not only are they all united in their love of him: Elliott's mother is now fully integrated with this unifying process, with a new man by her side, the one grown-up in the story who has not behaved like an officious automaton and has shown true human understanding. Whether or not he will become the new 'light' father to replace the 'dark' father who has departed, we cannot know. But what is certain is that Elliott and his family have all been changed for the better by this lovable embodiment of the Self which has come into their midst and now vanished again.[3]

---

3. In archetypal terms, *E.T.* carries clear echoes of the 'Christ myth' (see Chapter 33). Like Jesus, E.T. is a supernaturally intelligent hero who comes to earth from 'somewhere else', performs a series of miracles and builds up a small group of devoted followers. He becomes increasingly at odds with the earthly 'ruling power', which eventually traps him and puts him to death. He is miraculously resurrected and remains for a short further time with his followers, before he leads them out into a lonely place to watch him ascending back into the heaven whence he came.

Thus, even though this may only be another example of Hollywood sentimentality, with the ego borrowing the values of the Self, Spielberg's film at least comes to much more of a genuine resolution than *Close Encounters* or *Superman*. In archetypal terms, indeed, it provides a more substantial ending than the plays of Chekhov, Proust, Beckett or any other story in this chapter. Because their pseudo-endings, going nowhere, are all that stories spun from the ego alone can ever hope to achieve.

## CHAPTER TWENTY-SEVEN

# Why Sex and Violence? The Active Ego

## The Twentieth-Century Obsession:
## From de Sade to The Terminator

'T'will vex thy soul to hear of what I shall speak;
For I must talk of murders, rapes and massacres,
Acts of black night, abominable deeds ...'
Aaron, Titus Andronicus, v.1

'Ne coram populo, pueros Medea trucidet' ('Medea must not kill her children
in sight of the audience').
Horace, Ars Poetica

'The trouble with the modern world is that it has sex on the brain, which is the
wrong place to have it.'
Malcolm Muggeridge, various times in late 1960s

'We have fed the heart on fantasies, the heart's grown brutal from the fare.'
W. B. Yeats, The Stare's Nest by my Window (1922)

Unquestionably the most striking feature of Western storytelling in the closing
decades of the twentieth century was the unprecedented way in which it became
dominated by the imagery of sex and violence. In one sense, of course, sex and
violence had been the stuff of storytelling back into the mists of history. Adultery,
seduction, promiscuity, acts of rape had been a prominent feature of myths all
over the world, from those of ancient Greece to those portrayed on the Hindu
temples of India. The stories of Homer and the Old Testament were as full of
death and destruction as the corpse-laden stages of Elizabethan England. Not even
the twentieth century could offer much competition for the catalogue of horrors
conjured up by the most chilling of Shakespeare's plays, *Titus Andronicus*. These
range from the episode describing how the hero's daughter Lavinia is raped, has
her hands cut off and her tongue cut out, to the later scene where Titus cuts the
throats of the perpetrators of these deeds, so that their blood runs out into a basin
held by Lavinia between her stumps, before he invites their unsuspecting mother
to a dinner party to be served with the bodies of her sons baked into a pie.

But even in this unusually lurid example of pre-twentieth-century sensationalism, the single most shocking incident, the premeditated rape and mutilation of
an innocent young girl, does not take place in front of the audience. In conformity with an age-old code, this would have been categorised as 'obscene', literally
something which must take place, from the Latin '*ob scena*', 'off stage'. As Horace

put it in his *Art of Poetry*, the idea of Medea butchering her children or Atreus cooking a dish of human flesh is so offensive to the moral sense that, although such things can be described by a narrator, they must not be put on public show. A similar taboo, until the twentieth century, generally applied to performances of the sexual act, or exhibitions of female nudity (apart from those depicted as 'ideals of the female form' by serious artists). Socially regarded as 'below the line', such things were confined to brothels or bawdy shows, where their purpose was quite clear. They were regarded as 'pornography', from the Greek word *porne*, 'a prostitute': images designed specifically for the purpose of arousing sexual desire.

What was new about what happened to storytelling in the later decades of the twentieth century was that it was precisely these physical images of sex and violence which emerged into full view. In plays and novels, above all in its display on cinema and television screens, all that subterranean realm of imagery previously hidden away as 'obscene' now came to be regarded as acceptable. Of course, this was only part of a much more general shift in social attitudes. The new freedom with which sexually arousing imagery could be put on public show was by no means confined only to stories. It could be seen in newspapers and advertising, in the nature of women's fashions, in millions of pornographic magazines. But the real reason why all this came about was that it was an entirely natural consequence of that seismic shift which had been taking place in the Western psyche for two centuries, whereby to an unprecedented degree the ego had been losing contact with the deeper archetypal framework of the Self. Inevitably, as stories came increasingly to be spun out of the fantasy level of the mind, centred on the ego, this was where they would one day end up. How and why this should have come about is the theme of this chapter.

### De Sade: The degradation of the feminine

In 1749 an English government official, John Cleland, wrote a short novel entitled *The Memoirs of a Woman of Pleasure, or Fanny Hill*. In the style of the early novels of the time, the story is presented in the form of letters from a young woman, describing how she had come up to London from the country at the age of 15, hoping to make her fortune. She finds lodgings in what turns out to be a high-class brothel, where on her first night she is introduced to lesbian sex by one of the prostitutes. She is then allowed, as a *voyeuse*, to watch the act of sex between a man and a woman, which prompts Fanny herself to masturbate. After an embarrassing encounter with a lecherous old client too incontinent to complete his business with her, she finally loses her virginity to a handsome young man, Charles. There has been such a long build-up of anticipation to this moment that, when it finally arrives and she can fully experience the sensations it brings for the first time, it is like the high point of the story. Indeed, so taken with her is Charles, as she with him, that he sets her up in a flat as his mistress. But he then vanishes abroad, leaving her bereft and miserable, without any means of support.

Forced to make her own way in the world, she moves in with a middle-aged lawyer, although their relationship comes to end when she spies on him seducing another young country girl and takes her revenge by seducing his young protégé.

She then joins the staff of another high-class brothel, where she and her fellow-inmates all enjoy performing with rich young clients in front of each other. When one client is persuaded to pay a particularly high price on being told she is a virgin, she is proud of how she manages to fake the loss of her virginity. Eventually she takes up with a rich elderly bachelor, who rewrites his will to leave her all his fortune and promptly dies, leaving her at the age of 19 a rich woman. Finally, staying in an inn on her way back home to show off her newfound wealth to her family, she runs into her long-lost love Charles, who falls on her with quickly gratified pleasure. We then gather they have got married, had children and are living happily ever after.

In outline this is a classic Rags to Riches story, complete with 'central crisis' and archetypal happy ending. What makes it quite different from any other story we have looked at in this book is that its real purpose is to simply to provide a framework for endless physical descriptions of the sexual act. Each one portrays in detail what it is happening, with the same mechanical descriptions of the man bringing out his 'magnficent machine' or 'weapon', inserting it into the woman's 'delicate slit', surrounded with its 'soft down' of pubic hair, until in each case both parties come to a mechnically perfect mutual climax. The novel is simply a series of erotic daydreams by its author, designed to stimulate similar sexual excitement in the mind of his reader. Although described through the eyes of a woman, it is of course an entirely male fantasy. The purpose of setting it in the framework of a story in which the woman enjoys almost every minute of her sexual transactions as much as the men who are paying her, and in which she ends up rich and respectable, married to the man she loves, is to make these onanistic male daydreams seem more acceptable to the readers, in that the object and vehicle of their desires, Fanny, is portrayed as happily complicit with their own fantasies. Not only does she never really suffer as a result of making herself available to them. She so thrives on it that she can finally be seen enjoying all the outward show of an archetypal happy ending. In this sense, it is a perfect illustration of a story conceived on the sentimental, wishful-thinking level of the mind, in that a book imagined so obviously through the author's own fantasy-self, centred entirely on the ego, can nevertheless end on the image of his pasteboard heroine attaining the state of the fully-developed Self, without having to show her as possessing any of the archetypal qualities necessary to achieve it.

*Fanny Hill* was so obviously written as pornography that it was soon banned, and was to remain suppressed in Britain for more than 200 years. A similar fate was to befall an altogether darker tale written 40 years later, in a Paris prison, by a 47-year old French aristocrat who had narrowly escaped capital punishment for attempting to poison four Marseilles prostitutes with aphrodisiac drugs. The Marquis de Sade had spent most of his adult life on the run, either from the authorities or from enraged fathers, for his callous, violent and perverted treatment of a long succession of women. Having finally had his death sentence for the incident in Marseilles commuted to an indefinite term in prison, he was in the Bastille when, in two weeks in 1787, he dashed off a short novel entitled *The Misfortunes of Virtue*, later revised as *Justine*.

457

The story begins almost like a folk tale, when the death of their parents leaves two teenage girls, Juliette and Justine, orphaned and penniless. The two could not be more contrasted. Juliette, the worldly one, at once embarks on a life of prostitution. After she has been sold to clients as a virgin 80 times, she happily submits to 'criminal refinements, loathsome pleasures, secret, filthy debauches, bizarre tastes, humiliating fancies', all to serve her ruthless desire for worldly advancement. Having ruined three lovers, she marries and murders another to win his title and his fortune. As a rich widow, she plays the role of a fashionable Parisian hostess, while continuing her secret life as an expensive courtesan. She murders two more men for their money and has a string of abortions to keep her figure, until she finally so takes the fancy of one rich 50-year old lover that he takes her on as his wife in all but name. They are just on their way to visit an estate he has bought her in the country when, stopping overnight at an inn, they see a beautiful but poorly dressed girl stepping out of a coach, her hands tied and under police guard. They are so struck by her appearance that they invite her in to explain how she came to be in such a sorry plight.

The girl, who passes under the name of 'Sophie', unfolds a tale of unremitting horror. Having been orphaned in her teens, devout and upright in every way, she had been determined to find honest employment, however lowly. Her first prospective employer, a seemingly respectable man, had offered her a place in his house so long as she was prepared to sleep with highly-placed churchmen. Having turned this down in horror, she is then taken on by an old miser to perform the most menial household tasks, while being treated appallingly, until he orders her to commit a robbery on the man living in the flat above him. When she refuses, the miser hides a diamond in her mattress and summons the police to arrest her for stealing it. She is sentenced to death, and only avoids hanging in the nick of time when a fellow-prisoner, Dubois, an older woman similarly facing execution, sets fire to the prison, allowing them both to escape into a forest. Here Dubois, a hardened criminal, introduces Sophie to her four villainous male accomplices. She offers the innocent young girl a choice. Either she persists in her foolish, doomed desire to live a virtuous life, or she joins the gang. The four drunken ruffians decide to rape Sophie, but fall to blows over who should be first, giving her the chance to make a second escape in the darkness. After sleeping in the undergrowth, she is awakened by the sound of two men nearby, and secretly watches in revulsion while they engage in homosexual intercourse. Of course they then see her, and one, a brutal and vicious young Marquis, threatens to flog her before hanging her from a tree. He eventually relents and takes her home to the chateau where he lives with his mother, a still beautiful Marquise.

Madame de Bressac stands out as one of the few people in the story who is not portrayed as cruel, treacherous and utterly egocentric. She listens to Sophie's awful story, treats her kindly and takes her on as a companion. But this is only to set up the next sequence of horrors, when the utterly debauched young Marquis orders Sophie to poison his mother, to get hold of her money. Although Sophie betrays the plot to her benefactress, the Marquis still manages to murder his mother by other means. He then takes his revenge on Sophie by taking her to the tree where he had earlier threatened to hang her and flogging her within an inch of her life, before leaving her for dead. She crawls to the home of a doctor, who takes her in and heals her wounds. But even he is strangely cold and rough in his manner, and she eventually discovers he has imprisoned a 12-year old girl in his cellar, on whom he plans to carry out a horribly painful and ultimately fatal series of medical experiments. Sophie releases her and the girl runs away. But the doctor and his accomplice revenge themselves on Sophie by cutting off two of her toes, pulling out two of her teeth, branding her with a red-iron iron which imprints her skin with the mark of a convicted prostitute and casting her penniless out into the countryside.

Then follows the longest and most bizarre episode of the whole story. Desperate for somewhere to rest, Sophie is directed to a lonely monastery where she is told there is a small community of particularly holy monks. Arriving at sundown, to the sound of the angelus bell, she is welcomed in, profoundly grateful to have found such a haven from all her nightmarish ordeals. The kindly abbot Father Raphael hears her confession, establishing that there is no one in the world who knows she is there. He then leads her to a room where she sees three middle-aged monks, three beautiful teenage girls and an equally beautiful 30-year old woman all in an advanced state of undress. At inordinate length, we hear how Sophie's own clothes are removed and she is placed in the middle of the room, for the four monks to subject her to every kind of sexual indignity, culminating in Father Raphael himself, a relative of the Pope, exercising his rank by violently removing her virginity. Leaving Sophie moaning with pain and humiliation, the monks then turn their attention to the other girls, before returning to put Sophie through the sexual nightmare again. Finally she is entrusted to the older woman, Omphale, and they are marched off to be locked in for the night.

Sophie discovers, largely from the kindly Omphale, that she has landed up in the worst hell imaginable. The four monks are complete sexual and violent monsters, who treat the girls they have trapped into their prison, all beautiful and from respectable families, simply as objects to gratify their unwearying lust and cruelty. This has been going on for years. From time to time a girl vanishes, almost certainly murdered, to be replaced by others. The author revels for page after page in describing his totally improbable fantasies, of men supposedly capable of indulging in every kind of depravity and violent perversion for days and nights on end. Except for an incident where the monks dress up one girl as the Virgin Mary in order to rape her, and then celebrate Communion using her naked body as an altar, he does not describe these perversions in any detail, but conveys them simply by innuendo and suggestion, with epithets such as 'filthy', 'lascivious', 'lecherous', 'foul', 'impure'. But eventually he faces the problem of how to extricate his heroine from this absurdly over-wrought fantasy prison, in order to save her for yet more horrors. Finally, after Omphale has disappeared to her death, de Sade resorts to a kind of 'with one mighty bound Jack was free' solution. Father Raphael is promoted by the Pope to become head of the Order of St Francis and, when a new abbot arrives, he decides to let all the girls go free, so long as they promise not to tell anyone what has been going on.

In fact, with this episode, de Sade has reached the climax of his fantasy, but remorselessly his narrative continues. Sophie is released with a tiny amount of money, and is almost immediately robbed of it by an old woman whom she tries to help on the road. She goes to bind the wounds of an injured man, who takes her off to his chateau on the edge of a beetling precipice, miles from anywhere. Here she finds she is again a prisoner, stripped naked, having to turn a wheel with other naked women for 12 hours a day, to assist her captor in his task of forging money on a huge scale. Inevitably when his beautiful prisoners are in their cells at night, he rapes them with great violence, letting them know that when they are finally broken by their forced labour and starvation, their bodies will be thrown into a pit. When he goes off to spend his ill-gotten fortune in Venice, the police arrive, to set all the women free.

Sophie again meets the female criminal Dubois, who tries to involve her in stealing a rich man's money. When the honest Sophie warns him what is afoot, the man wants to reward her by proposing marriage, but Dubois manages to poison him. Finally, staying in another inn which catches fire, Sophie bravely tries to rescue a woman's baby from the flames, but stumbles and drops the child to its death, whereupon she is accused by the mother of murder and of having started the fire in the first place. It is for these crimes that Sophie is now being taken for trial under police guard, when she arrives at the hotel to pour out her story to Juliette and her lover. And of course the penny finally drops that her name is not really 'Sophie', but Justine, and that she is Juliette's long-lost sister.

Now blissfully reunited, the two sisters go off to the chateau bought for Juliette by her lover, where they all live happily together until the summer's day when a great storm brews up and a terrified Juliette asks her sister to close the windows. As Justine is wrestling with one window in the wind, a mighty bolt of lightning flashes from the sky and she is hurled lifeless into the middle of the room. Naturally the author is keen to describe how 'the bolt had entered by her right breast, had blasted her thorax and come out again through her mouth, so disfiguring her face that she was hideous to look at'. He has degraded his heroine for the last time. There are no more indignities left for his fantasy-self to heap on her.

## The cult of sensation

These two examples provide a perfect case-study of how the fantasy-self creates stories, as this moves towards its extremes. By the law of the 'dark inversion', the ego takes the archetypal values programmed into the unconscious Self and turns them on their head. The defining feature of Justine is that, in two-dimensional fashion, she represents the essence of what is the highest value in storytelling, the 'light feminine'. She is physically beautiful, pure-minded, good-hearted, spiritually devout. She is the *anima*, the heart and soul of mankind. She is Penelope, Andromeda, Dante's Beatrice, Shakespeare's Perdita, Beethoven's Leonora, Cinderella. She is the 'Princess' whom only the true hero can win, when he has shown himself fit to be united with her because he is himself potentially whole. Yet the whole thrust of de Sade's fantasy is to show this shining symbolic figure being defiled and violated in every way he can imagine, by a series of male and female monsters who in every case end up, he is careful to emphasise, prospering from their villainy. Father Raphael is promoted to one of the highest posts in the Church. The forger enjoys his ill-gotten gains in Venice. The homosexual matricidal Marquis inherits two vast fortunes. The sadistic medical man is appointed doctor to the King of Sweden. Dubois escapes with the money she has stolen. Even Juliette, after her long career as a murderous whore, ends up rich and happy in her pseudo-marriage (although, at the end, it is wholly inconsistent with everything else we know of her character that she should show such compassion and joy in rediscovering her lost sister).

Only the virtuous Justine has to be shown facing endless reverses, betrayals and sufferings, each time precisely because she is virtuous. It is because either she has thrown herself on someone else's mercy or has selflessly tried to help them. Such is the central purpose of de Sade's story, to show virtue defeated and villainy rewarded: to enjoy the thrill which comes from seeing the *anima* degraded and humiliated, through that combination of sex and violence which are the supreme expressions of the human ego when it has broken free from any external restraint. Such are the two most extreme forms of egocentricity through which one human being can relate with another. The ultimate purpose of fantasy is to experience the mental sensation which derives from imagining the assertion of that egocentricity. And the key to understanding how this works is to see how its real driving force is the urge to defy the Self. The Self-defying ego finds its gratification precisely through creating imagery which shows the values of the Self being violated.

We see this clearly illustrated in the nature of those aspects of sexual behaviour from which fantasy derives its thrills. A crucial component in how stories portray the archetype of the Self is the way they resolve on the image of an ideal state of permanent loving union between hero and heroine. As the convention has it, 'they got married and lived happily ever after'. This is why, when the ego sets out to violate the Self, it can only derive its thrills from fantasising about anything but the fulfilled married state. Just as the point about the 'monster' in storytelling is that it can be portrayed as anything but a whole, ideal human being, the same applies when the ego sets out to fantasise about sexual relations. If we look at the imagery such stories feed on, we see how it can be centred on every conceivable aberration from the state of happily married love. It can derive its excitements from extra-marital sex, promiscuity, nymphomania, orgies, fetishism, prostitution, masturbation, homosexuality, lesbianism, sex with children, sex with animals, perversions of all kinds; and the more the sexually-driven ego strains after that sense of lasting resolution it cannot attain, the more likely it is to coalesce with the urge to violence, as it finds expression in sadism, masochism, rape, even murder. The one state from which impersonal fantasy cannot derive gratification is in imagining that state of humdrum 'normality' in which the vast majority of the adult human race has always existed: a secure, unquestioned, lasting marriage.

It is indeed the essence of ego-based fantasies that they feed on images which are unresolved and incomplete. It is the very fact that its images cannot lead to resolution which gives them their power to tease and tantalise and to make them seem more significant than they are. This hugely important aspect of the way the human brain works was recognised by Shakespeare in *A Midsummer Night's Dream* when he wrote how:

'in the night, imagining some fear,
how easy is a bush supposed a bear.'

Because, in the darkness, the brain cannot get enough information to see the bush clearly, it is teased into exaggerating the significance of what it sees, building it up in imagination as a threatening monster. This is the phenomenon we may call a 'nyktomorph', a 'night shape': an image which, because the brain cannot resolve it, becomes invested with far greater power than if it could be clearly seen and understood. And to understand how fantasy works, one must appreciate that it is precisely because it feeds on these nyktomorphic images which cannot reach resolution that it comes to exercise such an obsessive hold over the human mind.

Yet in storytelling the underlying archetypal structures are so constituted that they must always work towards that concluding image which shows us everything in a story being satisfactorily resolved. The mark of a well-constructed story is that every detail in it is contributing in some way towards that final resolution. And this can only come about if the story finally resolves in some image of the Self. Either a light hero and heroine are seen united in perfect love; or a dark hero is brought to destruction, so that light can re-emerge and wholeness be restored. By definition, therefore, where the purpose of the story is to defy the Self, this point can never be reached. The story can only be made up of a series of episodes, each based on building up a sense of anticipation which is spun out as long as possible, finally culminating in some shocking or titillating image which cannot lead to resolution. The only way such a story can 'develop' is by progressively stepping up the degree of violation, so that each episode concludes in an image more sensational than the last.

Such is the 'fantasy spiral': the need constantly to 'up the dose', as with certain types of drug, simply in order to sustain the sense of gratification. In the words of Yeats quoted above 'we have fed the heart on fantasies, the heart's grown brutal from the fare'. Each time the fantasy achieves a mini-climax which cannot lead to resolution, it requires something stronger to achieve the next. As in the tragic 'fantasy cycle', the story's mood thus constantly swings between anticipation and frustration, on an ascending curve. Nevertheless it is notable how, in each of the stories we have been looking at, the ultimate charge of shock is reserved for the moment when heroine finally loses her virginity. In each book, to maintain the sense of anticipation, the moment when this takes place is delayed as long as possible (as it was, even more so, in the novel which appeared the year before *Fanny Hill*, Richardson's *Clarissa*). In the case of *Justine*, it is particularly significant that this act of violation is carried out by four 'holy' monks, representing that symbol of wholeness, the Church, so that the sense of Self-violation is redoubled (just as it is in the incident where the monks are shown raping a girl dressed as the Virgin Mary, before using her bleeding, naked body as a Communion altar). But from this point on in each of the stories, it is hard for the author to sustain the sense of shock, because he has played his trump card. All that is left is to go on repeating more of the same formula, now subject to diminishing returns in terms of its power to shock or thrill, until the moment when the author has to bring his narrative to a conclusion. In *Fanny Hill*, he simply tacks on a sentimental cardboard replica of the archetypal happy ending, which has no connection with the rest of the story. In *The Misfortunes of Virtue*, de Sade produces the only remaining trick he has up his sleeve, in arranging for his hapless heroine to be destroyed, almost literally out of the blue, by as shockingly disfiguring a form of death as he could think of.

Indeed no aspect of this cult of sensation is more revealing than the way it engenders in the ego the illusion that, in escaping from the archetypal constraints of the Self, it can achieve an ever greater state of liberation. In reality, by the law of the 'dark inversion', the very opposite is the case. The further the ego attempts to 'push back the frontiers', the more it becomes boxed into an ever more constricting prison of cliches and stereotypes. To this the plodding, mechanical narratives of Cleland and de Sade have already borne witness. In the rest of this chapter we shall see to just what a limited little wasteland this fantasy of liberation eventually leads.

### Countdown to the explosion: Joyce's *Ulysses*

At the time they were written, in terms of the general landscape of storytelling these two obscure eighteenth-century novels (and others of the time) were no more than faint earth tremors, heralding a subterranean build-up of energies which were only to erupt above the surface far in the distant future. Both books were almost immediately suppressed after they were written. In July 1789, two years after writing *The Misfortunes of Virtue*, de Sade was transferred from prison to the insane asylum at Charenton, where he was eventually to produce an even more lurid version of his tale under the title of *Justine*. Just a week after his move, the Paris mob broke into the Bastille to liberate its remaining prisoners, the event which more than any other marked the onset of the French Revolution.

Europe was plunging into that quarter of a century of upheaval and war which coincided with the dawn of the age of Romanticism. And running through almost every kind of storytelling over the century which followed, as we have seen, was that endless succession of betrayed, imprisoned, violated, dead or dying heroines, summed up by Mario Praz as the image of 'the persecuted maiden': Gretchen, seduced by the hero and brought to a miserable death in Goethe's *Faust*; Lucia *di Lamermoor*, hideously betrayed by her family, driven mad and eventually to her death; the innocent Gilda, unwittingly murdered and thrown into a sack by her father Rigoletto; Dickens's Nancy, battered to death by Bill Sykes; Tess, seduced and driven mad by her double-betrayal, ending up on the scaffold; Madame Butterfly, committing suicide in despair at her heartless abandonment. This constantly recurring image may have been the unconscious reflection of a newly industrialised civilisation losing touch with the *anima* and its roots in the Self. But at least in physical terms these depictions of the violated feminine were presented in an outwardly decorous fashion, designed to tug at the public's heartstrings on a sentimental level without showing anything too explicit. Through the long nineteenth-century heyday of respectable, bourgeois morality, the crude physical details of sex and violence were kept as firmly out of view as those apocryphal piano legs.

Then at the start of the twentieth century, coinciding with a further surge of technological innovation – wireless, motor cars, aeroplanes, skyscrapers – there were signs of a very different age beginning to dawn. It was the time when Freud, then Jung were beginning to reveal how much our conscious life is merely a fragile, superficial construct, at the mercy of immense mysterious forces hidden from view in the unconscious layers of the mind beneath. In all directions, artistically, socially, politically, established forms and structures were suddenly coming to be seen as a prison to the imagination, as constraints to be thrown off. In painting this showed in the tortured Cubist images of Picasso and Braque; in music in the electric energies of Stravinsky, the atonalism of Schoenberg, the syncopated beat of ragtime and jazz; in poetry in the free form of early Eliot. And nowhere did this new mood find more radical expression than in a long novel being written by an Irishman in Trieste, Zurich and Paris over the seven years between 1914 and 1921, just when Eliot was writing *The Waste Land* and Proust in Paris was completing *À La Recherche du Temps Perdu*.

James Joyce intended his *Ulysses* to be read as a modern echo of Homer's *Odyssey*. In reality the contrast between the two stories could scarcely be more profound. As the Quest story beyond compare, the *Odyssey* is entirely shaped by the one overwhelming imperative: that its hero should finally come home, to dispel the terrible shadow which has fallen over his kingdom, to put the forces of darkness to rout and to liberate his faithful Penelope. All of which requires him to become a complete man, finally revealed in his full kingly state. Every detail of the story takes its place in working towards that conclusion, until we are presented with one of the finest pictures in storytelling of a hero developing and maturing to the point where he can achieve the state of Self-realisation.

It would have been hard for Joyce to conceive a story more opposed to this in every respect than his meandering 930-page account of how his little hero Leopold Bloom, a middle-aged, unhappily married, unsuccessful advertising salesman, spends a summer's day drifting aimlessly round the city of Dublin, attending a funeral, swapping trivialities with acquaintances, idly reading newspapers and advertising slogans, having lunch, going for an evening walk on the beach where he masturbates, visiting a brothel and finally returning home, to urinate in the garden with his friend Stephen Daedalus, before tucking up in a foetal position at the end of his wife Molly's bed where he had that afternoon been cuckolded.

Everything about Bloom's day spells defeat, failure, lack of purpose, the trivialised world of the rootless ego divorced from love or any sense of meaning. He is a man frozen in immaturity, incapable of development. And nowhere is this more vividly underlined than at the end of the novel, which becomes a completely inverted caricature of the conclusion of the Odyssey. Odysseus's story comes to its final resolution in the moment when, having returned home and slain the suitors, he and his wife fall into the gold-inlaid bed he had carved years earlier from a single olive tree, to commingle in perfect love, before turning to 'the fresh delights of talk', as they happily wile away much of the rest of the night recalling all that has happened to them since they were last together. Whereas the beaten, exhausted Bloom, after resignedly noting the imprint left on the mattress by his wife's lover earlier in the day, crawls into his corner of the marital bed, to sink, in the pose of an unborn child, into solitary sleep, leaving the unhappy Molly to muse forlornly through the 50-page internal stream of consciousness on which the story ends, fantasising about her past lovers and culminating, as she nostalgically mastur- bates, in a final climactic shout of 'Yes'.

What *Ulysses* illustrates, as vividly as any story, is how once the feminine com- ponents of the overall psychic equation go missing, the values of heart and soul, all that is left are their masculine counterparts, the physical world of the body and the ordering function of the human mind. Few stories have been more self- consciously 'ordered' than *Ulysses*, with its eighteen 'sections', each written in its own style or 'technique', with its own related colour, symbol, organ of the body and supposed correspondence to some episode in the *Odyssey*. As Joyce put in a letter, 'every hour, every organ, every art' is thus 'connected and interrelated in the somatic scheme of the whole'. He explains how Molly's final monologue, con- sisting of eight enormous, rambling, unpunctuated sentences, supposedly corre- sponds to the four 'cardinal points' of womanhood, these 'being the female breasts, arse, womb and cunt'. But compared with the organic complexity of the *Odyssey*, in which each tiny detail grows out of the living whole (e.g., the way those twelve axeheads through which the hero shoots his bow fleeting reflect his twelve ordeals earlier in the story), the structuring of *Ulysses* is like a parody of the order- ing principle of the human brain, when it lacks that 'feminine' power of intuition which can bring it alive and connect it up to meaning. Its endless irresolutions make up a fine example of what D. H. Lawrence called, in a different context, 'masturbating consciousness'. And the sense this gives us of a mind churning away out of contact with meaning is equally reflected in the way the consciousness of the characters wanders on through the book, full of disjointed snippets of knowl- edge, silly puns, compulsive word-play, bits of quotations, empty lists and pseudo- intellectual speculations. As Joyce again put it in a letter:

> 'my head is full of pebbles and rubbish and broken matches and bits of glass picked up 'most everywhere. The task I set myself technically in writing a book from eighteen different points of view ... that and the nature of the legend chosen would be enough to upset anyone's mental balance.'

All this helps to present Joyce's characters as each lost and isolated in their own little ego-world, without understanding. And if this were all there is to *Ulysses*, the book might more appropriately have been discussed in our last chapter. Its characters are just as surely 'going nowhere' as those in Chekhov (Bloom's 'day', 16 June 1904, was set, as it happens, just two weeks before Chekhov died); and it is not irrelevant that, in his later years, Joyce employed Samuel Beckett as his secretary. The inconsequential badinage of the two tramps in *Waiting For Godot* clearly echoes the style of *Ulysses*. In his admiration for Joyce, Beckett simply carried this over onto the stage. But what prompted both the US and British authorities to seize copies of the book when it was published in 1922 by the appro- priately titled Egoist Press, so that for some decades it could not be openly pub- lished in unexpurgated form, was not its spiritual nihilism. It was its obsessive concern with the human body and physical functions, above all its references to the physicality of sex.

As the frustrated Bloom wanders round Dublin, his mind constantly harps on sex. Few passages in the book are unwittingly so comical to a modern reader as the extracts from the supposedly pornographic novel he picks up on a bookstall, which by later standards seem so tame (with supposedly provocative references to a woman's *embonpoint*). Equally startling to later eyes are the mentions of ladies' underwear. References to 'drawers' and 'stays' might have seemed daringly titillatory in Joyce's day, but today such lumpish terms are merely a reminder of just how complete was the repression of such matters to the consciousness of a post-Victorian world. But what is more revealing than anything is the nature of the two sexual episodes which are described in any detail. One is the extraordinary scene as dusk is coming on in the evening, where a young woman, Gerty, and her friends are on the beach, watching a fireworks display. The solitary Bloom, still in his black suit from the funeral, comes up behind Gerty, who becomes aware he is watching her. She deliberately leans over to show him more and more of her thighs, exciting him to the point where he ejaculates in unison with the climax of the firework show. As she walks away, it is clear she has taken pleasure from arousing him in this manner. It is also clear that she is lame.

The second physical episode, forming the climax to the whole book, is that which comes right at the end of Molly's monologue, when she has been remembering, firstly, her lovemaking with Bloom on Ben Howth when they had first met, and then the passion of her first-ever teenage sexual encounter at the top of the Rock in her native Gibraltar. The two memories, interspersed with romantic images of the sun and the monkeys, the tropical vegetation and Moorish white walls of the Mediterranean, excite her too into stimulating herself, so that the book can end on her orgasmic cry of 'Yes'. Two acts of solitary sex, by husband and wife, totally isolated from each other in their unhappiness and frustration. The contrast to the ending of the *Odyssey*, depicting a mature husband and wife in perfect loving union on every level, body, mind, heart and soul, could not be more complete. Yet what we are seeing is an exact reflection of what happens when human consciousness becomes restricted to no more than the ego, and the complexities of human love are reduced to no more than the physicality of the sexual drive. This finds its ultimate expression simply in the physical release of masturbation, stimulated by fantasy images in the mind. Once the sense of the Self and a living connection with the world outside the ego is lost, such is the sterile dead end to which the whole process must inexorably lead.[1]

1. We get a first hint that the whole book is going to be a defiance of the Self when, in its opening paragraph, Buck Mulligan holds up his shaving bowl in a parody of the Latin Mass and intones 'Introibo ad altare Dei' ('I am about to enter before the altar of God'). One puzzle raised by the novel is why Joyce should have been attracted to creating a modern rival to a story of which he seems to have had so little understanding. In Richard Ellmann's biography of Joyce, he cites him asking why was he 'always returning to this theme?' Joyce's answer: 'I find the subject of Ulysses the most human in world literature. Ulysses didn't want to go off to Troy; he knew that the official reason for the war, the dissemination of the culture of Hellas, was only a pretext for the Greek merchants, who were seeking new markets ....' This is bizarre. The 'official' reason for the war was the one described by Homer, that Helen, the wife of the Spartan king Menelaus, had run off with Paris, the son of the Trojan king

## The countdown continues: Lawrence and *Lady Chatterley*

Five years after Joyce completed *Ulysses*, D. H. Lawrence began writing in Tuscany the book which was eventually to make him one of the best-known novelists of the twentieth century. Published in 1928, and almost immediately suppressed in both Britain and America, *Lady Chatterley's Lover* approached what Lawrence called 'the problem of sex' in a way totally different from Joyce. Whereas in *Ulysses*, the sexual act is presented as furtive and solitary, in *Lady Chatterley* the descriptions of the happy coupling of a man and a woman take centre stage. Indeed, scarcely has the novel begun than two things about it become obvious. As we first meet the heroine, Lady Chatterley, 'a ruddy, country-looking girl' with 'big, wondering eyes', and her husband, Sir Clifford Chatterley, with his 'ruddy, healthy-looking face' and 'pale-blue, challenging, bright eyes', it is clear from Lawrence's novelettish tone that this is to be a story conceived on a highly sentimental plane. What is also soon evident is that it is to be a kind of moralistic tract, to argue for a very particular view of the role sex can play in human life. We hear how, when as teenagers, Constance Chatterley and her sister had first experienced 'this sex business' at the hands of German student lovers in Dresden before the war, they felt that men 'insisted on this sex thing like dogs'. For the girls, 'the sex thing had a thrill of its own too; a queer, vibrating thrill inside the body, a final spasm of self-assertion'. But 'women had always known there was something better, something higher'. To put over how much Connie has still to learn about 'this sex business' is the real purpose of the novel.

The role of Clifford Chatterley in the story is to stand as a kind of cardboard amalgam of everything about the modern world and contemporary England that Lawrence wishes to attack, as oppressive, effete and opposed to life. Living in his ancestral home, Wragby Hall, near the coal-mining village with its squalid, brutalised inhabitants which provides his wealth, Sir Clifford represents the privilege and arrogance of the upper classes. He is a capitalist living off the degrading work of others. Paralysed by the wartime injury which confines him to a wheelchair, he is cut off from the physical world. And in his self-centred, unreal way, he lives almost entirely through his mind, writing precious, pseudo-intellectual novels. Trapped in a bloodless marriage to this monster, his young wife Connie, now in her late twenties, feels her youth and spirit fading away, with nothing left to live for. Then Lawrence brings her together with Mellors, the gamekeeper, who stands for everything Sir Clifford is not. He comes from a working-class background, although, as evidence of his manly qualities, he had during the war been made an officer. Bruised by a disastrous marriage, he is a solitary, independent figure, who likes to live apart from society in the natural world of the woods. Above all, he is supremely physical, which is why, before long, he and Connie are falling into each other's arms, to make the mad passionate love which is what the novel is really all about.

---

Priam. Since there is no historical evidence that the Trojan War ever took place, it seems perverse to explain it through a kind of parody of sub-Marxist revisionism. One may well argue that the story of Odysseus is 'the most human in world literature': but not, it seems, for any reason discerned by Joyce, which may further explain why the two stories are so polarically opposed in every way.

What Lawrence wants to show is how the physical act of sex between a man and a woman is the highest, deepest, most life-enhancing experience humanity can know. As he describes the couplings of Constance and Mellors in ever more graphic detail, he wishes to emphasise that this level of sexual intimacy is something which only a minority of people can ever hope to achieve. On p. 140 (Penguin edition), they for the first time enjoy mutual orgasm:

'She turned and looked at him. "We came off together that time", he said.
She did not answer.
"It's good when it's like that. Most folks live their lives through and they never know it", he said, speaking rather dreamily ...
"Don't people often come off together?" she asked with naïve curiosity.
"A good many of them never. You can see by the raw look of them." '

By p. 180, she is enjoying an orgasm far greater than anything she could have imagined possible:

'She quivered again at the potent inexorable entry inside her, so strange and terrible ... she dared let go everything, and be gone in the flood. And it seemed it was like the sea, nothing but dark waves raising and heaving, heaving with a great swell, so that slowly her whole darkness was in motion, and she was ocean rolling its dark, dumb mass. Oh, and far down inside her the deeps parted and rolled asunder, in long, far-travelling billows, and ever, at the quick of her, the depths parted and rolled asunder, from the centre of soft plunging, as the plunger went deeper and deeper, touching lower, and she was deeper and deeper and deeper disclosed, the heavier the billows of her rolled away to some shore, uncovering her, and closer and closer plunged the palpable unknown, and further and further rolled the waves of herself away from herself, leaving her, till suddenly, in a soft, shuddering convulsion, the quick of all her plasm was touched, she knew herself touched, the consummation was upon her, and she was gone. She was gone, she was not, and she was born: a woman.'

The trouble with this stuff, in terms of telling a story, lies in the fact that it cannot lead anywhere. What has brought Lady Chatterley and Mellors together, as Lawrence emphasises, is their sexuality. Theirs is not really a love story, it is a sex story. The part has subsumed the whole. Their relationship is defined by almost nothing else. As social beings they are kept firmly apart, not least by Mellors's insistence on constantly breaking into broad Derbyshire dialect, even though, as an educated former army officer, he is perfectly capable of speaking, when he chooses to, in what is known as 'standard English'. For a while it is possible to sustain the story's momentum by describing further variations on their lovemaking, as when the pair run naked out into the woods in the rain, and Mellors possesses his mistress from behind.[2] The sense of 'upping the ante' is maintained by increasing use of that limited selection of 'shocking' four-letter words for which the novel was eventually to become famous ('fuck', 'cunt', shit', 'piss', 'arse'). The exchanges between the two degenerate more and more into sentimental game-playing, as

2. It was this episode which later prompted John Sparrow, Warden of All Souls College, Oxford, in a famous article in *Encounter*, to claim that Lawrence had intended to show Mellors entering Constance by an act of buggery. As a homosexual Sparrow would not have realised that a man and a woman can quite naturally enjoy intercourse in the fashion Lawrence described.

when they give each other's sexual organs the names of 'John Thomas' and 'Lady Jane', while decorating them with wild flowers.

In story terms, however, the problem is that they *are* social beings, living in a social context. It is one thing to portray them happily lost in their private little ego-world in the woods, enjoying sex. But the demand of any story is that it must develop, to work towards a climax and resolution. And here Lawrence becomes caught up in the conflict between the urge of his fantasy-self to see his hero and heroine heading off for an archetypal happy ending, and those deeper archetypal rules of storytelling which dictate that, because of the way it has been defined, their relationship cannot end that way. Most importantly, both Connie and Mellors are married to other people. And as Lawrence tries to manipulate his plot towards the point where they may be free to come as fully together in the outside world as in the privacy of the bed, the creaking of his stage machinery becomes deafening. Connie is made pregnant by Mellors, then goes off to Venice to provide cover for her story to her husband that the father is someone else. Meanwhile Mellors's harridan wife returns to claim him, creating a scandal about him carrying on with other women which leads to him being fired from his job. The plot spirals into ever more forced improbabilities, above all the wonderfully awful scene in London where Mellors meets Constance's father Sir Malcolm Reid, to win him over to their marriage:

'Sir Malcolm lit a cigar and said, heartily: "Well, young man, and what about my daughter?" The grin flickered on Mellors's face. "Well, Sir, and what about her?"

"You've got a baby in her all right." "I have that honour!" grinned Mellors.

"Honour, by God!" Sir Malcolm gave a little squirting laugh, and became Scotch and lewd. "Honour! How was the going, eh? Good, my boy, what?"

"Good!"

"I'll bet it was! Ha-ha! My daughter, chip of the old block, what! I never went back on a good bit of fucking, myself ... you warmed her up, oh, you warmed her up, I can see that. My blood in her! You set fire to her haystack, all right. Ha-ha-ha! I was jolly glad of it, I can tell you. She needed it ... ha-ha-ha! A game keeper, eh, my boy! Bloody good poacher, if you ask me. Ha-ha! ...." '

Lawrence finally manages to disentangle Constance from the outraged Sir Clifford, who has now sunk into an infantile mother-and-son relationship with an older female servant, Mrs Bolton. She goes to live with her father in Scotland, waiting for the baby and for her divorce. Mellors meanwhile takes a job as a farm labourer, dreaming that he and Constance might one day be able to set up home together on a small farm of their own. The story concludes with a long letter from him to Constance, bemoaning the doomed state of modern civilisation, obsessed with money, cut off from the deeper rhythms of life, and describing how he is hanging onto the memory of that 'little Pentecost flame' they had 'fucked into being' between them. The closing words, 'John Thomas says good night to Lady Jane, a little droopingly, but with a hopeful heart', reflect the wistful mood of sentimentality which is all Lawrence can muster to provide his tale with an ending. Nothing has really been resolved. The story has simply fallen apart, into vague wishful thinking. In trying to evangelise for his belief that physical sexuality between a man and a woman can stand for the totality of love, Lawrence has sought to defy the archetypes. As always, the archetypes have won.

## Shooting Niagara

For more than 30 years unexpurgated versions of these books written in the 1920s remained firmly out of public view. Officially banned on both sides of the Atlantic, like the earlier novels by Cleland and de Sade, they were available only in illicit editions from semi-undergound publishers like the Olympia and Grove Presses, based in Paris and New York. Not only did the law prohibit the publication of such material. Society in general still continued publicly to accept the moral values on which these laws were based. In nothing were those standards more clearly reflected, for instance, than in the Hayes Code, the system of self-censorship voluntarily adopted by the cinema industry in Hollywood, which laid down precise rules as to what could or could not be shown on a movie screen, right down to the maximum number of seconds an actor and actress could be seen making physical contact in a kiss.

Then, in the 1950s, all those strict taboos against the too overt display of sexual imagery, which to a greater or lesser extent had survived through thousands of years, quite suddenly began to crumble. Fuelled by the onset of a material prosperity like nothing known before in history, based on a wave of new technological advances, an immense shift was beginning to take place in the collective psyche of the Western world. This found expression in the emergence around 1955–1958 of the obsessively fashion-conscious new 'youth culture', with its new forms of popular music based on the beat of rock 'n roll, its acceptance of drugs and greater sexual promiscuity, and a rejection of anything identified with the despised 'square' world of their elders. It was heavily reinforced by the presence of powerful new forms of imagery, above all through the suddenly ubiquitous television screen. All this helped create in people's heads a sense that they were entering an entirely new age, in which conventions of thinking and behaviour associated with the past could now be thrown aside as constricting and irrelevant. And nowhere did this heady sense of freedom find more obvious expression than in all those areas of life governed by the rules of what came to be known as 'traditional morality'.

In Britain in 1959, in keeping with the spirit of the times, a Labour politician, Roy Jenkins, passed through Parliament a new law, the Obscene Publications Act. Its intention was to liberalise censorship on books which could be seen as serious 'literature', while continuing to allow that of publications which could be regarded as mere 'pornography'. It was of course impossible to draft any legal definition to distinguish precisely between what was 'art' and what was 'filth'. And it was this Act which in Britain was to prove the watershed, when in 1960 Penguin Books chose to try out the new law by publishing the first general unexpurgated edition of *Lady Chatterley's Lover*.

*Lady Chatterley* seemed the ideal candidate for such a test case (indeed a full version had already been published in America, for similar reasons, the previous year), because Lawrence so clearly intended his book to be considered not as pornography, which he despised, but as a serious work of art. What followed was a battle between two fundamentally opposed mindsets which was to be repeated many times over the years ahead. On one side were the 'progressives', claiming that Lawrence's novel was one of the greatest works of literature of the twentieth century. A prize catch among their witnesses was the Anglican Bishop of Woolwich, who famously claimed in court that Lawrence had portrayed the sex act as a kind of 'holy communion'. On the other were the 'reactionaries', led by their QC, Mervyn Griffiths-Jones, who equally famously asked the jury whether this was really a book they would wish their 'wives or servants to read'.

The delighted howls of scorn this remark aroused from the progressives reflected what had now become a significant psychological feature of their battle to 'push back the frontiers' of what was socially permissible. The progressives actually needed such self-caricaturing expressions of disapproval from the 'reactionary' elements in society, because it helped confirm their conviction that they were involved in a heroic crusade. They needed to be able to deride these reactionaries as 'anti-life', narrow-minded, hidebound, sexually-repressed, as 'prigs', 'Puritans' and 'prudes' whose only concern was to restrict other people's freedom, because this was vital to building up their sense of the moral righteousness of their cause.

But what was the real nature of this 'freedom' for which they imagined they were fighting? Their own view was that, by thrusting aside the old moral conventions, they were moving forwards into a boundless new world in which anything might now be possible. Yet the reality was very different. What they did not realise was that this new realm they were entering would be very much subject to laws and constraints of its own, one of which was the compulsion constantly to push the bounds of what was permissible a little further. The highest terms of praise for a new novel, play or film were that it was 'exciting', 'shocking', 'daring', 'disturbing' or 'sickening', in that it stripped away some further layer of what was considered socially acceptable. But each time the 'frontiers' were pushed back, it would be necessary next time to heighten the dose, to sustain the sense of novelty on which the spiral depended.

The legal battle over *Lady Chatterley's Lover* was not about the story itself. Almost the whole of Lawrence's novel had in fact been freely on sale for many years before 1960; just as Nabokov's *Lolita*, on the face of it a much more 'shocking' story, in that it centred on the sexual relationship of a middle-aged paedophile with a 12-year old girl, had been published uncensored ever since 1955. The only thing 'new' about the version of *Lady Chatterley* on which Penguin Books won its historic court case was that it included the more graphic details of some of the sex scenes; and, more specifically, that it included those publicly taboo (though privately long-familiar) four-letter words. It was these the jury agreed it should now be permissible, under Jenkins's Act, to put into print. So great was the novelty of this that, although one or two newspapers self-consciously printed the 'F' word in reporting on the trial, it was to be quite some time before public use of these words passed into anything like general currency, either in print or on stage or screen. But in essence the floodgates had been opened. Over the years to come, this was to transform the character of storytelling more dramatically than anything in its history.

## Into the twilight world

What happened next can be summed up simply by describing some of the films, plays and novels which in the years that followed came to stand out as particular landmarks, because each in turn was hailed as taking stories a further 'liberating' step into areas of sex and violence hitherto considered forbidden. As we look at these stories, we see a certain pattern emerging.

One of the first landmarks, released in the year *Lady Chatterley* was published in Britain, was Alfred Hitchcock's *Psycho* (1960). Shot, unlike his other recent films, in stark black-and-white, this took mainstream Hollywood movie-making into a dimension of personal violence and sexual voyeurism it had never entered before. Based indirectly on the real-life story of a serial killer, it focused on a pretty young heroine, Marion, who is first seen, in sexy underwear, engaged in an unhappy lunchtime sexual liaison with a married man. In a hopeless bid to lure him into marrying her, she steals a large sum of money from her employer and drives aimlessly off into the middle of nowhere. On the run from the police, she ends up taking a room at a lonely motel, where she is the only guest. She learns that Norman Bates, the creepy young man who owns it, stuffs birds for a hobby and lives with his mad mother in a sinister, dark old house behind the motel (she hears the two of them arguing).

When Marion retires to her cabin to undress to her underwear, we see him spying on her through a hole in the wall. Having decided that next day she will return the stolen money, which is hidden in newspaper, she enters the shower naked. A half-glimpsed grey-haired woman sneaks into the room and, while the shower is running, we then see, to the accompaniment of nerve-jangling music to remind us that this is entertainment, Marion being stabbed fourteen times, sometimes through the shower curtain, sometimes in close-up, sometimes in slow motion, in the most shocking and protracted murder sequence Hollywood had ever shown. When she finally sinks dead to the floor, her blood spiralling down the plughole, Norman comes in to clean up, bundles her body (and the money) into the boot of her car and pushes it into a nearby swamp where it sinks from sight.

A week after Marion has vanished, her sister Lila hires a private detective to find her. He comes to the motel, finds Bates suspiciously evasive, goes away to report what he has discovered, then returns hoping to interview Bates's mysterious mother in the old house. He is climbing the stairs when he is sprung on by a crazed, knife-wielding old woman who repeatedly stabs him to death, in a prolonged murder scene almost bloodier and more violent than the first.

When the detective fails to ring them back, Lila and Marion's lover Sam set out to find what happened to him at the motel. They are particularly disturbed to learn from a local policeman that there is no Mrs Bates. She and her lover had been found dead in suspicious circumstances 10 years earlier. They find suspicious clues that Marion must have stayed in 'Cabin 1'. While Sam holds Bates in conversation, Lila explores the spooky old house, and finally in the cellar finds the old woman sitting in a chair. When she turns Mrs Bates round, Lila sees that she is a mummified corpse. At this moment another old woman appears in the doorway, ready to stab the now terrified Lila with a knife, but is grabbed from behind by Sam and turns out to be Norman in a wig and female clothing. After Bates has been taken to a prison cell and interrogated, a psychiatrist explains how he was a mother's boy so psychotic that it was he who had killed his mother and her lover 10 years before in a jealous rage. He had then dug up and mummified his mother's body and continued to live with her: sometimes as himself, the neurotic son, sometimes taking on the personality of his lost mother. It was in his fantasy-self, disguised as his mother, that he had committed a whole sequence of murders, culminating in those of Marion and the detective. The film ends with Marion's car, her body and the money being recovered from the swamp.

What was new about *Psycho* was its obsessional focusing on the physical details of the two murders. Hitchcock spent two weeks shooting the scene in which the heroine is stabbed in the shower. This is the centrepiece of the film, just as the moment of the heroine's ultimate orgasm had been the centrepiece of *Lady Chatterley*. The gradual working-up of suspense towards this physical image of a naked young woman being brutally murdered provided the story with its shocking highlight, just as in those eighteenth-century novels its equivalent had been the gradual working up to the image of the heroine finally losing her virginity. In a sense the story has become just a frame for these moments of maximum sensation. And although in the end we see Bates in a prison cell, this is scarcely the cathartic destruction of the psychopathic monster which the underlying archetype demands. The interest here lies merely in squeezing a last drop of sensation out of the explanation as to how and why he committed his awful crimes. His subsequent fate is of no concern.

The scale and speed of the change which came over the nature of films and plays between the late 1950s and the mid-1960s was more dramatic than any in the history of storytelling. Within just a few years the sentimental, romantic Hollywood movies and respectable, 'well-crafted' plays of the post-war era were made to seem unimaginably innocent and old-fashioned, as the cinema and the theatre were taken over by a 'new wave' of stories altogether harder, more overtly sensational and more surreal in tone. Leading the field were some of the more 'daring' playwrights of the time, notably in England. In 1962, just when the first James Bond film, presenting its own sanitised version of sex and violence, was being launched in London's Leicester Square, a series of new plays was staged at the nearby Arts Theatre. It opened with Johnny Speight's *The Knacker's Yard*, described by a critic of the time as showing the arrival at a squalid boarding house of 'a mysterious and sinister figure' called Ryder, whose nightly pleasure was

'ritually slashing a series of voluptuous nude pin-ups with a razor on a little patriotic altar of Union Jacks. All of which, plus his large collection of handbags, seems to suggest that he must be the Jack-the-Ripper-like killer in the neighbourhood.'

Ryder ended up by gassing himself. Another play in the series, David Rudkin's *Afore Night Come*, put on by the Royal Shakespeare Company, came to 'a gruesomely compulsive climax involving a ritual murder beneath the poison-sprays of

473

a pest-control helicopter'. A third, Fred Watson's *Infanticide in the House of Fred Ginger*, ended in the gratuitous killing of a child.

Such avant-garde plays were only a small symptom of a much wider and deeper transformation which was now taking place all through Western society, nowhere more obviously than in Britain. This revolution in moral and social attitudes, reflecting what I have analysed elsewhere as a collective fantasy state, came to a head in the extraordinary events of the year 1963. It was a year characterised in Britain by a kind of endless hysteria, most obviously expressed in the explosion of nyktomorphic fantasy surrounding the supposed sex scandals associated with Christine Keeler and Mandy Rice-Davies, and that generated around the emergence of the four Beatles as the 'dream figures' at the centre of the most hypnotically glamorous bubble in the history of show business. It was the year which culminated in what, in terms of its universal personal impact, was the most shockingly sensational event of post-war history, the assassination of that other supreme 'dream figure' of the time, President Kennedy. And this mood of hysteria helped drive the new English drama even further into its violent, sexually-obsessed and freakish fantasy world, as when a few months later the Royal Shakespeare Company staged an 'experimental season' dedicated to the 'Theatre of Cruelty'. This took as its manifesto an excerpt from the book *Le Theatre et Son Double*, written in a lunatic asylum in 1938 by the French psychopath Antonin Artaud:

> 'We need a theatre which wakes us up, nerves and heat … in the anguished catastrophic society we live in, we feel an urgent need for a theatre which events do not exceed … a transcendent experience of life is what the public is fundamentally seeking, through love, crime, drugs, war or insurrection.'

The playlets chosen to open the season included a sketch by Artaud himself, entitled 'The Spurt of Blood' (in which 'colour, light and sound are used expressively'); and another in which an actress representing Christine Keeler performed a 'strip-tease act of grotesque symbolism' standing next to a bath, in what was meant to echo the image of Jacqueline Kennedy looking down into her murdered husband's grave.

But the biggest sensation of the season was a production by Peter Brook, who had first won fame nine years earlier by introducing *Waiting for Godot* to the London stage. Peter Weiss's *Marat/Sade* showed the crazed inmates of Charenton lunatic asylum re-enacting the assassination of the French revolutionary leader Marat, under the direction of their fellow inmate, the Marquis de Sade. This nightmare vision of a twilight world of violence, madness, sexual aggression and revolutionary hysteria, featuring the author of *Justine* as its hero, provoked uproar, led by various impresarios representing the commercial theatre, deploring how the London stage was being taken over by 'filthy plays'. This set off an equally hysterical response from the 'progressives', led by the left-wing politician Michael Foot, who ostentatiously published a telegram:

> 'I CAN SEE THERE IS A RALLY OF THE OLD FORCES TO STOP PEOPLE THINKING STOP BUT IT CAN'T BE DONE STOP IT HAS FAILED EVER SINCE THE SAME RIDICULOUS TRICK WAS PLAYED ON SOPHOCLES.'

One leading 'progressive' critic Penelope Gilliatt solemnly claimed the play 'had the nerve to investigate the sort of violence that Shakespeare himself depicted'. [3]

Another theatrical sensation of 1964 was *Entertaining Mr Sloane*, a 'black comedy' written by Joe Orton, a defiant homosexual who had recently spent nine months in prison for obscenely defacing books from a public library. His 'comedy' showed a mysterious stranger, Mr Sloane, arriving as the new lodger in a house occupied by an unmarried woman in her 30s, her homosexual brother and their father. In the first act Sloane is seduced by the sister. In the next he seduces the brother. The father then identifies him as the man he had seen kicking a pornographer to death, at which Sloane kicks the father to death. The woman then discovers she is pregnant by Sloane, who makes it plain he can think of no fate worse than being tied for life to a woman. The story ends with the prospective mother sucking at a boiled sweet, in a regression to infantilism. Three years later, after writing more plays in similar vein, Orton himself was hacked to death with an axe by his homosexual lover, overcome by a fit of jealous rage.

On both sides of the Atlantic, in 1964, the state tried to mount a last-ditch effort to halt the tide of sex and violence which now seemed to be engulfing storytelling in all directions. When publishers in London and America decided to exploit the new freedom of the times by disinterring *Fanny Hill* from its two centuries of suppressed obscurity, the authorities realised that, if ever they were going to persuade the courts to distinguish between 'literature' and 'pornography', this was the case to go for. Surely no bishops or professors of English literature would rush to defend what no one had ever pretended was anything other than an unashamedly 'dirty book'? In London the magistrates were briefly persuaded by this argument, although their verdict was soon reversed. In America the case actually reached the Supreme Court, where in a historic judgment in 1965 the justices accepted that *Fanny Hill* had 'literary merit' and should no longer be censored.

A more contemporary novel which also briefly faced legal disapproval in 1964 was Hubert Selby Jr's *Last Exit to Brooklyn*. This was excitedly hailed as another triumphant breakthrough in 'pushing back the frontiers', with its unrelievedly black picture of New York slum-life set during a strike in the early 1950s. The plot centres on Harry, a brutal union activist involved in the strike, who begins cheating on his wife with a drug-addict; Georgette, a transvestite homosexual; and a prostitute Tralala, who dreams of escaping from her hopeless day-to-day existence selling her body to men at the back of parking lots. Georgette ends up being crushed to death by a car. Harry, after the strike has come to its climax in a series of explosions when the strikers set fire to a fleet of trucks, is caught attempting to have sex with a young boy from the neighbourhood, and is kicked to death by a gang, who hang up his corpse on a billboard in a parody of the Crucifixion. Finally, as the story's climax, Tralala is subjected to a prolonged and violent gang-rape, before the story ends with the lifting of the strike and the men returning to work.

---

3. This echoed the defence once offered by Ian Fleming to the charge that his James Bond novels were 'pornographic': 'Sex was a perfectly reasonable subject as far as Shakespeare was concerned, and I don't really see why it shouldn't be as far as I'm concerned.'

In Britain the obsession with sexual abnormality and make-believe violence had become so fashionable by the summer of 1965 that the 'daring' new English drama, like the James Bond films, had played an important part in promoting London's image as 'the most swinging city in the world'. In June, to avoid the vestiges of censorship imposed by the Lord Chamberlain, the Royal Court turned itself into a theatre club to stage John Osborne's play *A Patriot for Me*, the main set-piece of which was a lavish homosexual 'drag' ball, before the protagonist, a homosexual spy in decadent Hapsburg Vienna, ends up committing suicide. Centrepiece of the summer season at the Royal Opera House, Covent Garden, was Schoenberg's *Moses and Aaron*, directed by Peter Hall of the Royal Shakespeare Company, featuring an apocalyptic orgy scene and, in what was described as a particularly 'camp' gesture, the casting of four nude Soho strippers as the Four Virgins. At the Aldwych Harold Pinter's *The Homecoming* portrayed a man presenting his new American wife to his father and four brothers, whereupon they take it in turns to have sex with her and plan to set her up as a prostitute. Another vogue film of the summer was Roman Polsanki's *Repulsion*, depicting a young girl's sex and violence obsessed nightmares. In October a young writer who had won the first commission from Britain's new National Theatre (and also scripted the new Beatles film *Help!*) published a solemn article entitled 'My boyhood life and work in the theatre and how I came to be obsessed with sex and violence', including such lines as 'my plays are about filth, filthily. There is a place for filth in the theatre. I've seen it, and lovely cami-knick filth it was.'

In the autumn of 1965, just when this fashionable nervous frenzy was reaching a peak, as in the hysteria which exploded in the first week of November over the appearance of the first mini-skirts, two more new plays aroused the greatest sensations of all. The first, because it was on television, was the BBC's *Up The Junction*, an ostensibly *ciné-vérité* picture of life in working class south London, focusing on the seduction of a teenage girl on a bombsite, and her subsequent horrific back-street abortion. Even a critic normally keen for the BBC to show 'daring' dramas commented:

> 'I suggest that at least part of the object … was a wish, perhaps an unconscious one, to see just how far they could go in a television play with sex and cuss words.'

The other play, first performed on the same evening (November 3), was also ostensibly a picture of working-class life in south London; and again, to stage it, the Royal Court had to turn itself into a club. Edward Bond's *Saved* began with a young couple entering the home where the girl, Pam, a notoriously promiscuous 23-year old, lives with her parents. Len has just picked her up and rather clumsily fails to have sex with her. But we then see him having become her boyfriend and moved in as her parents' lodger.

We now meet, in a café, a gang of young men, one of whom, Pete, is about to attend the funeral of a boy who has been run over. After crude sex jokes, Pete boasts of how he had been responsible for the accident. Seeing the boy run out into the road, he deliberately accelerated his own vehicle to hit the boy, knocking him into the path of an oncoming truck. He did not admit this to the boy's parents or the coroner, We then see that, although Len is still living in her parents' home, Pam has now moved on to another boyfriend, Fred, having had a baby (father unknown, although she thinks it is probably Fred). The baby, throughout the scene, cries pitifully offstage while its mother takes no notice.

We then see Fred and Len fishing in a local park. Pam enters, wheeling a pram, and, after getting into an argument, walks off, followed by Len, abandoning her baby. This leads to the central episode of the play, when the gang of youths we have met earlier, including Pete, join Fred in the park, see the pram and begin pushing it at each other, ever more roughly. They then start to take an interest in the baby. One gives it a punch, followed by another, punching rather harder. They rub its face in its excreta. They flick lighted matches at it. Finally one youth chucks a stone into the pram. The others follow suit, in ever greater frenzy, until the baby is dead. Pam returns to wheel the pram home, not noticing what has happened.

We are never told how Pam discovered her baby was dead, although we see Fred waiting to be tried with the others for the killing, and learn that Len had watched the murder hidden by trees and not intervened to stop it. We then see a scene in which Pam's middle-aged mother is late for a meeting with a friend, but discovers one of her stockings is torn. Len helps to sew it together on her thigh and is so excited by this intimacy that, when she has gone out, he pulls out a handkerchief to masturbate. We then see another scene in the café, where Pam and others are waiting for the gang-members on their release from what seems to have been only a very brief spell of imprisonment. The climax comes with a screaming family row in Pam's home, involving herself, her parents and Len, in which, as Len threatens her father Harry with a knife, Pam despairingly wails 'all my friends gone. Baby's gone. Nothing left but rows … the baby's dead. They're all gone … I can't go on.' Afterwards Harry comes up to Len's room. They engage in trivial chat, as if to imply that they have made up their disagreement. Len muses that he may find somewhere else to live.

Even Penelope Gilliatt, a leading 'progressive' critic with the *Observer*, admitted she had found all this hard to stomach:

> 'I spent a lot of the first act shaking with claustrophobia, and thinking I was going to be sick. The scene where a baby is pelted to death in a pram is nauseating. The swagger of the sex jokes is almost worse….'

In reply, Britain's leading actor Sir Laurence Olivier, now director of the National Theatre, rushed to defend the play, with the claim that Bond 'places his act of violence in the first half of the play, just as Shakespeare does in *Julius Caesar*'. There could have been no clearer measure of just how far contact had now been lost with the psychic roots of storytelling. Firstly Olivier could no longer see that, as a mere 'act of violence', there might be any distinction between the assassination of a supposed Tyrant (after the chief assassin has been shown wrestling with his conscience) and the mindless destruction of a baby by a group of young thugs, so demoralised they are scarcely aware of what they have done. Secondly Olivier seemed oblivious to the fact that, after Caesar's murder, Shakespeare devoted the rest of his play to showing how, in accordance with the archetype, there has to be a counterbalancing 'act of violence', whereby the murderers pay the price with their own deaths.

Nothing, archetypally, was more chilling about Bond's play than the fact that, after the baby's murder, portrayed in such obsessional detail, so little interest is shown in what happens to its perpetrators, apart from their perfunctory prison sentence. Bond's own comment on his play was that it was 'almost irresponsibly optimistic'. Len, as its 'chief character', is 'naturally good'. By creating in the end 'the chance of a friendship with the father', Bond wrote, Len turns what might have been 'the tragic Oedipus pattern of the play' into 'what is formally a comedy'.[4] Truly, in this landmark in the history of storytelling, was the 'dark inversion' complete.

### The limitations of fantasy

In just five short years the great act of 'liberation' had been achieved. Niagara has been shot. Anything, it might have seemed, was now possible. But when we look at what this great leap forward actually led to, nothing is more striking about the brave new world storytelling had now entered than how remarkably limited in scope it turned out to be. When storytelling moves into this realm, as we have seen in this chapter, certain themes continually reappear: the sexual act; nudity; a small number of four-letter words, relating to bodily functions, either sexual or excretory; masturbation; homosexuality; sexual perversions; madness; drug-taking; acts of cruelty and violence; rape; cannibalism; finally violent murder or suicide. Why is it just to this very restricted range of images (often combined with the violation of religious symbols) that stories based on fantasy invariably return?

The starting point for an answer lies in the nature of that most centrally numin-ous figure in storytelling, the archetypal heroine, the *anima*, the ultimate prize the hero has to win. As an embodiment of the feminine she potentially stands for every-thing the opposite sex can represent to a man. Certainly this may begin with the fact that she is physically attractive. But the essence of her role in stories is to represent those 'light feminine' values, feeling for others and seeing whole, which are crucial to escaping from the confines of the ego and to establishing union with the Self. The hero who reaches the ultimate goal in storytelling is he who is worthy to win her,

---

4. Author's note to the published edition of *Saved* (Methuen, London, 1966). A surprising feature of the play in retrospect might be how comparatively mild was its language. It was a tribute to the force of the taboo on 'four-letter words' that, despite the *Lady Chatterley* case five years earlier, the use of such words in public was still at this stage remarkably rare. Indeed another symptom of the hysterical mood of those weeks in the autumn of 1965 was that, only 10 days after the premiere of *Saved*, this taboo was ostentatiously challenged in a carefully set-up BBC television interview with Kenneth Tynan, the leading 'progressive' critic, now literary manager of the National Theatre. Tynan was asked whether he would allow a play to be staged at the National in which 'sexual intercourse took place on the stage?'. This allowed him to give the strangely inconsequential reply 'I doubt if there are any rational people to whom the word "fuck" would be particularly diabolical, revolting or totally forbidden. I think that anything that can be printed or said can also be seen.' In a sense it was the highpoint of Tynan's career. The coup succeeded in its aim of creating a public sensation. The BBC switchboard was jammed with protests. Tynan's fellow-progressives, led by Dr Jonathan Miller and George Melly, rushed publicly to congratulate him. He later compounded his inconse-quentiality by claiming that he had only been 'quoting from the evidence in the *Lady Chatterley* trial'. Only over the next 15–20 years did the use of four-letter words on stage and screen become general. Had Bond written his play later, its dialogue would doubtless have contained little else.

because he represents the 'light masculine', he is both strong and loving. Similarly the light heroine is outwardly feminine and inwardly strong. That is why the sight of a hero and heroine united in love at the end of a story has such power to move us, because unconsciously we recognise this complementary coming together on every level as the image of Self-realisation, complete human fulfilment.

Once stories become centred on nothing higher than the ego, this totality is shut off to them. The ego-transcending feminine values have gone missing. And when fantasy loses touch with the selfless components of love, all that is left to it is to reduce the relationship between men and women to just a physical level. Initially we may get stories like *Fanny Hill* and *Lady Chatterley* which, in their very different ways, show this through the eyes of wish-fulfilment. They are centred on the image of the sexual act, which invariably works with mechanical perfection to the mutual gratification of both parties (as it also does, if less explicitly, in, say, a James Bond film). But in terms of constructing a story, there comes a point where simply to fantasise about the coupling of two people begins to tire. Because it has been cut off from the deeper unconscious purposes of storytelling, it cannot go anywhere.

It may seem easier to sustain the sense of excitement where the actual visual image of the feminine can be used to trigger off male sexual desire, as on a stage or a cinema screen. Men are instinctively programmed to respond to such stimuli, in a way which is ultimately quite impersonal. This is why, through most of human history, women have dressed in such a way as to reveal their faces, that part of them which most completely expresses their individuality, but to conceal the greater part of their bodies from view. Once ego becomes dominant, this creates a pressure for them to reveal more and more of their bodies, to provide stimulus to physical desire. For a long time after the arrival of the cinema, the gentilities were more or less preserved, except in those special circumstances where actresses were permitted to show their legs or cleavage, as in dance or beach sequences, or where they were playing recognisably louche, immoral characters. But when the great psychological watershed was passed in the late 1950s and early 1960s, this inevitably resulted in a compulsion to push display of the female body nearer and nearer to a state of undress: first to underwear, then to half-glimpsed bare breasts, then to full-length nudity. And although, as with a strip-tease act, it may be easy to sustain a sense of arousal and expectation while this process is in its earlier stages, there must eventually come a point where literally all has been revealed. There is nowhere further to go.

So when the ego is denied the only road which can lead to proper fulfilment, where does it then turn? Essentially, as we have seen, it finds three forms of expression. First, when the ego is shut off from any proper loving connection with another person, as we saw in examples from *Ulysses* to *Saved*, the physical urge may simply retreat into the solitary sex of masturbation.[5] Second, as we saw

5. In 1968 the critic Ken Tynan was to launch a campaign to promote the joys of masturbation and to make it 'respectable'. In storytelling this obsession was to reach its most publicised expression in Philip Roth's novel *Portnoy's Complaint* (1969), about a mother-dominated New York Jewish boy who manages to have sexual relations with a number of girls, all non-Jewish, but finds his greatest pleasure in endless, compulsive masturbation. Eventually he goes to Israel where he has an affair with a Jewish girl, whom it would be socially acceptable for him to marry. But his obsession with solitary sex wins out and he returns to mother.

in that 'camp' element which became prominent in so many plays and novels of the 1960s, it finds increasing fascination in variations on the archetypal roles of the sexes, in homosexuality and transvestism: in men who have lost their masculinity and become effeminate, women who have lost their femininity and become possessed by their inner masculine. Finally, most conspicuously of all, the ego frustrated of fulfilment turns in desperation towards violence.

Of course, acts of physical violence have played a prominent part in storytelling since the dawn of time. But when it is shown within the archetypal framework, the exercise of violence is always subject to clear rules. If a dark figure is shown committing a violent act, the archetype dictates that there must always ultimately be a recompense. In the end, the monster, like Macbeth, must always be paid out for his crimes. When light figures resort to violence this is acceptable, because it is always made clear that they are doing so for selfless reasons, on behalf of others. Even when stories first venture onto the fantasy level, taking on a 'sentimental' form, these same rules still hold good. The scenes of violence in a James Bond film may in reality only be included for their sensation value, to excite the audience. But they are still sanctioned in the audience's mind by the fact that Bond is a 'light figure', selflessly risking his life to challenge some monstrous dark figure, the 'good guy' acting to save the world from a megalomaniac super-criminal.

What happens when stories move still further into fantasy, losing contact with their underlying archetypal purpose altogether, is that this opposition between 'light' and 'dark' disappears. Everyone in the story is seen in a twilight. We may see men inflicting violence on each other because they are obviously cruel, vicious and dark. But since there are no 'light' characters to oppose them, such acts of violence become just sensational images for their own sake, designed to excite the audience's horror or disgust.

Where this process becomes even more obviously extreme, however, is when violence becomes entangled with the sexual urge, and is shown being directed against a woman. This is where it at last becomes clear that the real unconscious drive of the process is to turn the archetype upside down, to show the figure who symbolises the highest value in storytelling, the *anima* (and thus the Self), being violated in the most shocking way possible. The value of de Sade's story about Justine is that it illustrates this point so explicitly. Because he was writing in an age when heroines in stories were still generally depicted in their full symbolic *anima*-guise as shining, innocent souls of virtue, to conjure up such a heroine solely in order to show her being repeatedly violated was calculated to give his story the maximum shock-value. It was precisely for this reason that, for nearly two centuries, de Sade's book was regarded as so obviously offensive to the moral sense that it remained buried from view; until society had so changed that the mainstream of storytelling was ready, as it were, to start catching up with him.

It was apt that the trial of *Lady Chatterley's Lover* in 1960 should have coincided almost exactly with the release of *Psycho*, and in particular the scene of a naked young woman being coldly stabbed to death for minutes on end. Hitchcock's heroine was scarcely 'a soul of virtue' in the same way as Justine. But she still, in her vulnerability, symbolised the 'eternal feminine'. Like Justine and countless other 'persecuted heroines' since de Sade's time, Marion represented the defenceless *anima* being violated. And in the way Hitchcock showed it, lingering obsessively over the physical detail of her destruction, he achieved the complete inversion of that archetypal climax to so many of the great stories of the world where, in the nick of time, the hero arrives to save just such a defenceless heroine from destruction. Such is the image which more than any other in storytelling gives us that profound sense of relief and reassurance, that everything is going to turn out, after all, as it should. The fact that Hitchock's film could take such relish in turning that image upside down was a foretaste of what a twilight world storytelling was now beginning to enter.

Over the next few years, as the unconscious pursuit of sensation became ever more intense, we saw the nudity inevitably becoming ever more brazen, the violence ever more extreme. By the time of *Last Exit to Brooklyn*, it was no longer enough for the already degraded heroine to be raped once, by one man. It had to be a mass-rape, going on and on. We saw stories drifting ever more into a strange, dream/nightmare realm of fragmented imagery, often not even attempting to develop any proper sense of plot.[6] We saw all the framework which defines 'reality' and 'normality' disintegrating into a dreamlike twilight where the fantasies of storytellers were drawn, by an entirely consistent internal logic, to explore literally anything that was 'unreal' or 'abnormal'. We saw the difference between the sexes dissolving into a kind of epicene blur. And what above all governed all this seemingly free-play of fantasy was that it was unconsciously driven by only one urge: to defy the rules and values of the Self, and to push that defiance ever further towards its ultimate limits. But, in reality, the further the process travelled into those realms of imagined freedom, so the range of images and situations left for it to play with became ever more limited, repetitive and sterile. Until in 1965 this ended up with the most life-defying, Self-defying image of them all, that of a defenceless baby, the archetypal Child, the supreme image of life renewed, being put casually to death by four young men, so lost in unconsciousness they were not even aware of what they had done. At this point even some of the most determined champions of the new 'freedom' had a sense that they could take no more.

6. One of the more conspicuous features of avant-garde storytelling in the early 1960s was the collapse of plot and structure. Films like *L'Année Dernière à Marienbad* (1961), directed by Alain Resnais and scripted by Alain Robbe-Grillet, or *L'Avventura* (1960) and *L'Eclisse* (1962) by Michelangelo Antonioni were dreamlike in their deliberate inconsequentiality. *Last Year In Marienbad*, shot in an imposing chateau with formal gardens, centred on a beautiful woman ('A') meeting a handsome stranger (X'), who tries to convince her that they had met before, possibly at some resort hotel, possibly in Marienbad, where she may have promised to run away with him. 'A' claims not to remember their meeting, but it is never made clear whether they actually met or not. The key to the film's tantalising power was that it was a nyktomorph. Precisely because it teased its audience by not providing enough information for them to make sense of what was happening, the story, as in a dream, conjured up a sense of some elusive significance which could not be fully grasped. A writer whose work reflected this disintegration rather more simplistically was William Burroughs, an American homosexual and heroin addict, who, after writing a pornographic novel *The Naked Lunch*, went on to experiment with stories in which the sentences were designed to be randomly jumbled up and read in any sequence.

481

## Into the brave new world

Once that psychological watershed had been passed, its consequences for story-telling were inevitably profound. The transformation which had taken place in moral, social and artistic attitudes in those few years between the late 1950s and the mid-1960s reflected a further decisive shift in the relationship between ego and Self which would find expression in stories in many different ways. But nothing was more obviously to characterise the films, plays and novels of the decades which followed than the hitherto unthinkable degree to which the imagery of ego-centred sex and violence had now become an established part of the landscape.

Certain stories would still stand out as landmarks because they managed to come up with some specially 'shocking' new variation on the basic formula. *Bonnie and Clyde* (1967), glamourising the life of two young criminals on the run, caught attention not least because of its brief glimpse at the beginning of the hero-ine standing naked at a window and the much longer sequence at the end showing both her and the hero being riddled with machine gun bullets, their bodies jumping about with the impact as their flesh and clothes became soaked in blood.

Four years later Stanley Kubrick's *A Clockwork Orange* (1971), based on a novel by Anthony Burgess, conjured up so glamorous an image of young men obsessed with sex and violence that the film inspired a rash of imitative crimes in real life, prompting its shaken director to withdraw it from circulation a year after its release. Set in a Britain of 'the near future', the story opens with the hero Alex and his gang of three teenagers, wearing uniforms which emphasise their sexual organs, sitting in a bar furnished with fibreglass figures of naked women in sub-missive poses, drinking drugged milk shakes served from the nipples of more naked female figures and preparing for an evening of their favourite entertain-ment, 'a bit of the old ultra-violence' and 'a bit of the old in-out, in-out' (rape). They first beat up an old tramp, then enter a derelict, abandoned opera house where a young woman is being raped by the members of another gang, with whom they have a stylised knife-fight. Interrupted by the police, they steal a sports car, drive out into the dark countryside and knock on the door of an ultra-modern house where an elderly writer lives with his younger wife. In grotesque, obscene masks, they push the old man to the floor, rhythmically kicking him to the lyric of 'Singin' In The Rain', then tie up both their victims, vandalise the house and finally force the husband to watch the prolonged rape of his wife.

When Alex finally returns home to the dismal tower-block council flat where he lives with his bemused parents, we are treated to his hallucinogenic dreams, including one showing four crucified and bleeding Jesus-figures tap-dancing, another showing men leering at a woman in a white dress dropping through a trapdoor as she is hanged. Alex is visited by his middle-aged male social worker who warns him he risks being arrested by the police, before trying to pull Alex into a homosexual act. To produce a further frisson in violating the values of the Self, the film's more lurid scenes are accompanied by classical music, particularly the 'Ode To Joy' final movement of Beethoven's Ninth, which is implausibly described as exciting Alex like nothing else. He picks up two little teenage nymphets, takes them back to his room to show off his hi-fi system and engages with them in a frenzied sexual orgy, to the sound of the William Tell overture. Alex's gang are getting restive that he does not organise sufficiently lucrative robberies for them, so he leads them off to rob a health farm, run by a rich woman surrounded by gigantic works of pornographic art. Having seen them coming, she rings the police, but when the gang enters Alex bludgeons her to death with a giant sculpted phallus. Police cars arrive and, as the gang flee, one of them deliberately hits Alex in the face with a bottle so that he is caught by the police.

The second half of the film shows Alex in prison, where he is chosen as an ideal subject to test an experimental new rehabilitation technique. This is a drug-based form of aversion therapy which provides an excuse to show yet more filmed images of extreme violence, including the inevitable gang-rape; the idea being that, whenever Alex is tempted to commit sex and violence, the drugs will cause him to vomit in revulsion. When newsreel shots of Nazi violence are accompanied by Beethoven's Ninth, this also inadvertently induces in him a horror of his favourite music. Finally, when it seems he is 'cured', he is returned to society as a kind of brainwashed zombie ('a clockwork orange') where he is subjected to a succession of beatings and humilations by his previous victims. These include the now crippled old writer, who plays Beethoven at him very loudly, prompting Alex to attempt suicide by jumping out of a window.

When he recovers in hospital, he finds the aversion therapy has worn off. But by now he has become famous as an example of the government's new method for treating violent criminals. The film ends with him doing a deal whereby, in return for a well-paid job, he agrees that the government can use him for propaganda purposes, to show what a success its new policy has been. But of course nothing has been resolved since, behind his new persona, he is completely unchanged. He is still the psychopath he always was.[7]

This glossily-packaged commercial for sex and violence coincided in 1971 with Sam Peckinpah's Straw Dogs, also set by a well-known American director in Britain. The hero David, played by Dustin Hoffman, is an American mathematician who has brought his mini-skirted young English wife Amy back home for a year's sabbatical in a lonely farm house, set in a desolate, treeless Cornish landscape. An air of brooding menace centres on the primitive, dirty village nearby, dominated by Tom Venner, a drunken, bullying old patriarch, who holds court in the pub with his brutalised sons and has a would-be-sexy 14-year-old daughter, Janice.

The ineffectual David is so wrapped up in his life of the mind, as he chalks up equations on a blackboard, that his physically frustrated wife deliberately allows a gang of builders to see her standing naked in the hallway. She then arranges for David to be out of the house, so she can receive an old lover, who slaps her about before tearing off her clothes to penetrate her. She is enjoying this when they are interrupted at gunpoint by one of the builders, who takes over, turning adultery to

---

7. In the novel by Anthony Burgess from which Kubrick's film-version was adapted, the effects of the aversion therapy do not wear off, so that Alex remains transformed. Burgess was so angry at Kubrick's rewriting of the story's ending that he withdrew his support from the film version.

rape. Little Janice meanwhile flaunts her sexuality in front of a mentally retarded young man in the village, disappears with him and ends up being strangled.

When the village idiot comes to the farmhouse pleading for sanctuary from her pursuing father and brothers, David agrees to protect him. This prompts the enraged Venner and his sons to storm vengefully up to the house, where Amy wants to hand the murderer over, But, faced with this crisis, her hitherto weak, over-cerebral husband suddenly discovers the physical side of his masculinity, hitherto so conspicuously lacking. As the attackers prepare to break into the house, he slaps his wife into submission and prepares to meet force with force. There is a long, extremely violent battle, which leaves the farmhouse strewn with corpses (the hero-ine herself finally shooting Venner, in an echo of *High Noon*, just as the old monster is about to kill her husband). The triumphant hero is last seen driving off smiling into a fog-shrouded landscape, to hand over the village idiot to the authorities. He has discovered his masculine strength.

In archetypal terms, this is the only interest of the story. Through most of the plot, the hero, lost in his intellectual calculations, is only the indecisive shadow of a man. Everyone else in the story is aggressively physical. The two female charac-ters are sex-mad; the men brutal, violent and also sex-mad. Eventually the scales tip, the ineffectual wimp discovers his manhood and becomes as violent as any of them. This familiar wishful-thinking reversal ('weak, humiliated guy gets his own back on his persecutors') provides the excuse for a prolonged explosion of blood, violence and death, before the story concludes in a typical pseudo-ending with its hero disappearing into the fog. This of course leaves wholly unresolved the ques-tion of how he is going to explain to the police that he and his wife have just been responsible for shooting several people.

A film which aroused a stir the following year was Bernardo Bertolucci's *Last Tango in Paris* (1972), starring Marlon Brando as a middle-aged American ex-patriate living in a dingy quarter of Paris, full of prostitutes and drug-addicts, whose wife has recently committed suicide. He roams the streets and decides to inspect a vacant flat. Jeanne, a French girl barely out of her teens and waiting for her boyfriend to arrive on a train, decides on an impulse to look at the same flat. While she is wandering through the rooms, Brando looms out of the shadows. After sparring over who should get the flat, they are about to leave when they suddenly grab each other and snatch a fumbled act of sex against the wall. This launches a series of further meetings in the all-but empty apartment, each marked by acts of crude, impersonal, unloving copulation which become the main theme of the film. What gave it the frisson of novelty was the sight of two anonymous people, so cut off in their own egos that they never even get to know each other's names, meeting merely to co-operate in the act of sex. An episode which gener-ated a particular stir in 1972 was where Brando used butter to lubricate his entry into the girl's anal passage. Eventually she wearies of participating in this loveless sexual game with an ageing, totally self-absorbed male and brings their meaning-less relationship to an end.

If *Last Tango* 'pushed back the frontiers' in sexual terms, by showing sex for its own sake in the most dehumanised way possible, Tobe Hooper's *The Texas*

*Chainsaw Massacre* (1974) did the same for violence. This was loosely based on the same story of a real-life serial killer which had helped inspire *Psycho*. But the contrast between Hitchcock's version and its successor showed just how far that rising spiral of sensationalism had travelled in just 14 years. A group of five aimless semi-hippies are led by one of them, Sally, to drive off in a van to a remote part of Texas, where in childhood she used to visit her grandfather. The party includes her crippled brother in a wheelchair. On the road an air of gathering menace is built up when they pick up a mad young man who freaks out and slashes himself, before they get rid of him. When they arrive at the grandfather's old house, now abandoned, they hear from a whirring generator that the only other house nearby is occupied. When first one young man, followed by a girl, go to investigate, the film's main action begins.

The house, littered with gnawed bones, is occupied by a family of psychopathic abattoir workers, including the young man they picked up on the road, who it turns out are also cannibals. One of them, Leatherface, wields a screaming chainsaw and wears a face-mask made from human skin. The film's only purpose is to keep the audience's sense of terror, horror, shock and disgust screwed to the highest pitch, as we see Sally's friends one after another hacked to death, dismembered, generally treated like animals in an abattoir (we see the girl being hung from a meat hook before her naked corpse is dumped in a freezer) and finally eaten. A particularly obsessional sequence shows the cripple being chased through the woods in his wheelchair, before he meets the same grisly end as the others.

We eventually see that, living upstairs in the house, is the most horrible monster of them all, the family's patriarchal old grandfather, accompanied, in a self-conscious reference to *Psycho*, by the mummified corpse of his wife, the grandmother. When only Sally is left, the director plays with his audience by allowing her to escape to what she imagines is the safety of a gas station on a nearby road. Except that she then discovers that the man running it is the family's father, who returns her to hellish captivity. Finally she is allowed a second 'thrilling escape' and the film ends with her sitting alone on the back of a truck from which she has thumbed a lift, laughing in hysterical relief.

At least in *Psycho*, beyond the claustrophobic little nightmare world of Norman Bates's motel, there had still been a reassuring framework of normality and social order. The deformed monster could finally be seen being lifted out of his shadowy, nyktomorphic kingdom into the light of common day, sitting as a shrunken, pathetic figure in his prison cell. In *The Texas Chainsaw Massacre* there is scarcely any sense of such a normal, ordered outside world at all. There is no hint of that archetypal ending which would show the monsters being finally brought to book. All that has happened is that one of their victims has escaped, leaving the family of homicidal cannibals to live on in their shadowy kingdom. The film's sole purpose has been to excite its audience by exposing them to as relentless and claustrophobic a stream of life-violating images as its creators' fantasies could come up with. And once the compulsion to 'push back the frontiers' had reached this point, it would not be easy to find many further extremes of fantasy left to explore.

## The heroine as hero

In the closing decades of the twentieth century, the pattern which has been the theme of this chapter worked towards its logical conclusion. The physical imagery of sex and violence, which had once seemed so novel and shocking when confined to just a few trail-blazing examples, gradually became commonplace across large areas of mainstream storytelling. Shots of naked couples engaging in the sexual act became an increasingly familiar feature of films and television dramas. Use of those once-taboo four-letter words became routine on the pages of novels and cinema screens. Horror movies spared no detail in focusing on the dismember-ment of human bodies.

There was one last significant step left for the process to take, and this reflected the dramatic change which was taking place in Western society's view of women, and in women's image of themselves. In parallel with the rise of the feminist movement, the most conspicuous feature of this transformation was a conscious rejection of those values which had traditionally been understood as 'feminine', and a new emphasis on the importance of asserting that 'masculine' element in the female psyche which Jung terms the *animus*. The image of women was becoming de-feminised. No longer were the styles of women's clothing intended to express such traditional feminine attributes as grace, allure, prettiness, elegance: they were designed to be either, in a hard, direct way, sexually provocative, or sexlessly businesslike. The more familiar the sight of the naked female body became on screens and stages, not to mention in newspapers and in millions of pornographic magazines, the more it lost its old aura of hidden female mystery. No longer were female characters in stories expected to display such traditional feminine qualities as innocence, modesty, intuitive understanding, a loving heart.

There was now a premium on showing *animus*-driven women capable of com-peting with men and outperforming them in masculine terms. Female characters were expected to be shown as just as clever and tough as men, mentally and phys-ically. We have already touched on one early example of a film, *Alien* (1979), in which a woman was cast in an archetypally male role, as the central figure in the crew of a spaceship which is invaded by a peculiarly horrible and deadly mon-ster. The basic plot of this film was very similar to that of *The Texas Chainsaw Massacre*. In a terrifyingly claustrophobic, closed little world, we see the seven crew members being picked off one by one, their bodies disintegrating in the most gruesome manner. Eventually only the tough, resourceful heroine is left alive, and in a final shoot-out, worthy of any male hero, she manages in the nick of time to blast the monster into space. The whole point of her part in the story was that nothing about it should be distinctively feminine. She was simply transposed directly into the traditional role of a manly hero.

A rather less straightforward example of the complications this gender-switch could lead to was the horror film *The Silence of the Lambs* (1991). The heroine Clarice Starling, a young police trainee with a psychology degree, is first shown as physically and mentally tough, a match for her all-male fellow-trainees. The emphasis is placed clearly on her masculine rather than feminine attributes. She is then, in a way which would be implausible whatever her gender, pitted by her superior officer in a battle of wits against the most fearsome criminal of the age.

Dr Hannibal Lecter is himself a renowned psychiatrist, but also happens to be serving a life-sentence as a cruel and clever serial killer who likes to eat the bodies of his victims. The purpose of her being sent to interview him in his prison cell is to pick his brains in trying to track down a second serial killer, still at large, who has killed three young women before removing parts of their skin. To build up the horror of what she has to face, when she walks down the corridor of cells to meet the cannibal, another mass-murderer hisses through the bars 'I can smell your cunt' (he later showers her with his semen). Lecter turns out to be a masterful, outwardly courteous, devilishly ingenious representative of the 'dark masculine' possessed by the 'dark feminine'. He has the heartless, intuitive subtlety of a 'Tempter' figure, as he tries to lure the heroine under his spell. In this sense the gender wires begin to get crossed because, although Clarice is meant to represent tough modern womanhood, she finds herself getting drawn by his penetrating intelligence into the more familiar archetypal role of a young woman falling into the power of a male monster.

We then, however, switch to the world of the story's other serial-killer, who we see abducting his fourth prospective victim. This is a young woman whom, as with her predecessors, he plans to keep as a prisoner in a pit in his cellar, until he can kill her and strip off parts of her skin. We thus see the archetypal situation repeated, a second young woman rather more obviously in the power of a ruthless monster. The two elements in the story are then gradually brought together, as Clarice uncovers a direct link between this second monster and Dr Lecter and tries to strike a bargain with him. In return for being taken from his horrible prison cell to more congenial surroundings, he must give her the clues she needs to track down the other killer.

In one sense, her scheme goes hideously wrong, in that this enables Lecter to escape, savagely killing two policemen on the way. In another it works, in that he has given her enough coded clues as to the identity of the second, lesser monster to enable her to track the serial-killer down. This enables her, in classic hero-fashion, to save the girl in the nick of time from a fate worse than death and slay the monster into the bargain. But the fact is that this second killer, a pathetic little obsessional middle-aged man, was only ever small fry. The real monster over-shadowing the story is Lecter who, as we see in the film's closing scene, has escaped to an agreeable Caribbean island. In other words, our heroine has not really fulfilled the proper role of a hero at all. Despite her little cardboard victory over his shadow, the chief figure of darkness in the story has successfully outwitted her. The monster lives on (to allow for him be brought back in the sequel).

## The heroine as monster

In this new age of storytelling where so much of the once clear distinction between 'light' and dark' had been lost, at least some vestige of it remained in stories like this where the conflict centres on a battle between the police, repre-senting the values of the social order, and a psychopathic monster, representing in its most acute form the dark urge to rip all those values to shreds. But even this distinction was open to inversion, as was next year exemplified in another Hollywood film which in a sense brought the story traced in this chapter full circle.

*Basic Instinct* (1992) opens with a shot of an unidentified woman, her face hidden by blonde hair, engaged in passionate sex with a man. She is on top of him, in other words in the 'male' position. As they approach climax we see her tying him down to the bed with a white silk scarf, then secretly reaching for an ice-pick. As they come to frenzied orgasm she plunges the pick repeatedly into her partner, blood spurting everywhere, until he is dead.

Cast in what, in conventional terms, would have been the role of the story's 'hero' is the policeman sent to investigate the crime, Nick Curran of the San Francisco Police Department. His chief antagonist is Catherine, the chief suspect, an ice-cold, beautiful, blonde heiress in her thirties. Everything the detective learns about this lady seems to confirm her guilt. She had been a regular sexual partner of the dead man, not because she loved him, as she makes clear, but simply because she enjoyed 'fucking' him. She has just published a seemingly self-incriminating novel about a woman who murders her lover with an ice-pick, after tying him to the bed with a white silk scarf. Nick discovers that, while she was at college reading psychology (as with Clarice Starling, this is Hollywood shorthand supposed to convey that she has a powerful, 'masculine' intelligence), one of her professors had been found murdered with an ice-pick. There are even suspicions that she had arranged the boating accident which killed her parents, leaving her a rich heiress.

However, Catherine soon begins to run rings round the detective. She deliberately uses her sexuality to draw him under her spell. It seems she knows far too much about his professional and private life, such as that he is former alcoholic and cocaine-user, that his wife committed suicide and that he had been in trouble for accidentally killing some tourists. This is because she has lured one of Nick's fellow policemen into giving her his confidental police file, and when he discovers this, the culprit is soon found shot, leading to Nick's suspension from duty as a suspect. He besottedly tracks Catherine down in a nightclub in a converted church, where he finds her taking cocaine in a lavatory cubicle with a black man, with her lesbian partner standing by. But Catherine takes him home to bed, to engage in frenzied sex, and when she insists on tying him down with a white silk scarf he is so carried away by the excitement he no longer cares whether she is about to murder him or not.

In archetypal terms, Catherine is thus a classic Temptress, beautiful and deadly. Yet, in the spirit of late-twentieth-century 'feminism', she is very much presented as the story's heroine, precisely because she is a strong, clever woman making a fool of all the men around her, above all the weak, bemused hero. And just to neutralise any concerns the audience might have at admiring such a ruthlessly dark figure, the script is then given a cunning twist.

By hints and innuendos, a second woman is built up as Catherine's doppelganger. Nick learns that Beth, his police colleague and former girl friend, had been at college with Catherine, where they read psychology together. They had enjoyed a lesbian affair. They had both dyed their hair blonde, dressed alike and tried to look alike. Had Beth, Nick wonders, killed her husband, just as Catherine killed her parents? When Nick arrives just too late to save his closest friend from being murdered with an ice-pick by a half-glimpsed blonde woman, he then runs into Beth in the same building, seemingly holding a gun, and shoots her. It turns out she had not been holding a gun at all, and her dying words are 'I love you'. So had Beth really committed this latest murder or not? Had she even been responsible, Nick begins to wonder, for all the other murders as well? Or had all the clues pointing to this been planted with devilish cunning by the real murderer, Catherine herself? Deliberately we are denied any of the information which would provide answers to these questions. Then, when Nick finally returns home, he finds Catherine waiting for him. They make passionate love, with her in the 'male' position on top. As the film ends, the camera slides down her side of the bed to the floor, where we see an ice-pick. Is Catherine about to murder the detective in an exact repeat of the film's opening scene? We are left suspecting she might, but we are never allowed to know.

Although the story is thus deliberately turned into a nyktomorph, an image which cannot be resolved, to tease its audience into seeing Catherine as an ambivalent figure who just might not be guilty after all, Yet we have already seen quite enough of her to know that she has all the attributes of a heartless monster. As a metaphorical counterpart to Hannibal Lecter, she is a complete 'man-eater'. She is a supreme example of a woman in the grip of her 'negative *animus*', driven by the masculine component in her personality in the darkest way possible. Using her sexuality as a bait, she is hard, cruel, calculating, predatory, using her power only to destroy. She is egotism incarnate. And in this respect, we have seen the world of fantasy moving from one end of the spectrum to the other. In the beginning was de Sade enjoying the spectacle of Justine, the selfless 'light feminine', being made the helpless victim of a succession of devilish men. The pattern eventually comes full circle, showing a devilish woman, possessed by her inner masculinity in its darkest form, making helpless victims of a succession of weak men. Yet, so far had the 'dark inversion' taken over the fashionable image of womanhood that, unlike her male counterpart Lecter, this glamorous psychopath could somehow be presented to the audience as a heroine to be admired.

What may be seen as a final forlorn footnote to the story traced in this chapter was reflected in a London critic's summary at the end of the century of what he called 'possibly the most significant phenomenon in British theatre since the premiere of John Osborne's *Look Back in Anger* in 1956'. He described how, in the mid-1990s, a 'new breed of writers in their twenties and early thirties' had 'burst through from nowhere', with a new style of play which had been 'quickly dubbed 'in-yer-face' theatre'. This featured such apparent novelties as:

> 'sickening acts of sexual and physical violence, obscene langage and a despairing view of contemporary society that seemed entirely nihilistic ... anal rape, eyeball gouging, on-stage defecation, drug-addicted rentboys, cannibalism and torture became stock ingredients in the dramatic stew.'

Can we not hear a yawn stretching back at least a generation, if not further? After all, had not even Shakespeare included cannibalism in *Titus Andronicus* and eyeball gouging in *King Lear*? Although in his case, of course, these images had merely been incidental to the unfolding of larger and more complete stories, in which the perpetrators of the original shocking acts of violence eventually pay the penalty, according to the pattern of the archetype.

The central figure in this new vogue was a young female playwright, Sarah Kane, whose *Blasted*, written when she was 23, was first staged at London's Royal Court in 1995. Ian, a hardbitten, foul-mouthed tabloid journalist with a liver problem, and Cate, a simple-minded 21-year old who lives with her mum, are in a hotel room. He carries a gun, constantly uses four-letter words and makes racist comments about the hotel's non-white staff. He starts to masturbate in front of Cate, tries to undress her, then forces her to hold his penis while he concludes his masturbation. She says she will not have sex with him because she is not his girl-friend any more and has promised herself to Shaun. They talk inconsequentially about football, her chances of getting a job and whether he has ever killed anyone.

When they wake early next morning, Cate is angry and prepares to leave. He holds his gun at her head, lies between her legs and simulates sex until he ejaculates. He tells her that people are trying to kill him. Cate performs oral sex on him, and ends by biting his penis. They order breakfast. When it arrives, Cate disappears into the bathroom because she feels sick after her sex act. A soldier enters with a rifle. He takes Ian's gun, eats both breakfasts, looks into the bathroom and finds Cate has disappeared. There is a loud explosion. The hotel has been blasted by a mortar bomb, knocking the soldier unconscious. When he comes round, he tells Ian how he and other soldiers had been inspecting a house, where they had only found a small boy. One had shot him through the legs. Then they found three men and four women hiding in the basement. He himself had raped the women, the youngest a girl of twelve:

> 'then she cried. Made her lick me clean ... shot her father in the mouth. Brothers shouted. Hung them from the ceiling by their testicles.'

After more conversation, in which the soldier recalls how his own girlfriend had been buggered, had her throat cut and her ears and nose hacked off and nailed to the front door, he holds the revolver to Ian's head and rapes him, while 'crying his heart out'. The scene ends with the soldier sucking out each of Ian's eyes in turn, and eating it. The final scene opens with the soldier having blown his brains out. Cate enters, soaking wet, carrying a baby a woman has given her to look after. 'Everyone in town is crying ... soldiers have taken over.' The baby is crying for food. Ian wants to kill himself. Cate says this would be wrong, 'God wouldn't like it'. Ian replies:

> 'there isn't one ... no God. No Father Christmas. No fairies. No Narnia. No fucking nothing.'

Ian tries to shoot himself, but the gun doesn't work. Cate discovers the baby is dead. She buries it beneath the floorboards, under a cross made from two pieces of wood, and leaves to find some food. Ian masturbates to the word 'cunt' repeated 11 times. He defecates on the floor, tries to clean it up and then hugs the soldier's corpse. He tears the cross out of the ground, lifts out the baby's body and eats it. He puts the remains back under the floor and climbs into the hole. It rains through a hole in the roof. Cate returns, gives him food and gin, drinks some herself and sits sucking her thumb. At last Ian says 'thank you'. The stage blacks out.

In 1999, as the twentieth century came to its close, the authoress of *Blasted* hanged herself, at the age of 28. Before her death, according to an anthology of contemporary British plays, she had 'established an international reputation as the leading playwright of her generation'. Her 'theatrical gods', according to her director, included Samuel Beckett and Edward Bond. Psychologically, by far the most interesting feature of her best-known play was the character of Cate who, most unusually in stories of this blackness, is shown as essentially good-hearted. She tries to live by some values, has a simple religious sense, cares for the baby, marks its death with a cross, and ends up feeding the eyeless, hopeless Ian like a child. In her mentally retarded state, Cate is a projection of the authoress's own repressed inner femininity. But this part of her is constantly degraded and overridden by the hard, superior masculine element in her personality, the dark *animus* represented by the figure of Ian (which eventually splits into two, with the appearance of the even more brutalised soldier). It is a tragically familiar pattern in real life that, when such a conflict develops in a woman's personality, the aggression of her dark *animus* may eventually turn in on itself, driving her to suicide. In this sense, Sarah Kane's play and her death were a final dark mirror to the inner world of the age: to that psychic disintegration which storytellling had not only reflected but was helping to urge on.

## Re-emergence of the archetype: *The Terminator*

We ended the last chapter with a Hollywood film of the 1980s, *E.T.*, which showed how, even in the least promising surroundings, stories can still, on a sentimental level, recover contact with their fundmental archetypal purpose. At first sight *The Terminator* (1984) might seem just another story relentlessly parading the gratuitous imagery of violence. But, when it is taken together with its sequel, *Judgement Day* (1991), we can see how the unconscious structures ultimately bring this story back to an almost completely archetypal resolution.

The first film opens with the arrival in Los Angeles in 1984 of a truly monstrous figure (played by Arnold Schwarzenegger). Outwardly he appears to be a human being. In fact he is a magically ingenious computer, sent back to contemporary California from a time nearly 50 years into the future, on a deadly errand. That world of the year 2029 is in ruins, after a nuclear war launched in 1997 by a near-omnipotent computer system, Skynet. This autonomous super-intelligence runs the future world like a totalitarian state, and wishes to eliminate human beings altogether. But those humans who survive have launched a heroic war of resistance, under their leader John Connor. The mission of the terminator in returning to 1984 is to seek out Connor's mother, Sarah, and destroy her, before her son can be born.

The terminator is only programmed to do one thing, to kill. It is a perfect representation of the 'masculine' aspects of the human psyche without any 'feminine' balance. Physically and mentally it seems unstoppable, It is so cleverly designed that, even if smashed to pieces, it can immediately restore itself to full working order. But, like any computer, it completely lacks the feminine attributes which would be necessary to make its strength positive. It is totally incapable of feeling, and it lacks intutive understanding, the ability to see whole. It can only see what it has been programmed to see.

The machine's inability to see the wider picture soon becomes apparent when it starts to track down women called Sarah Connor in the telephone book. There are only three of them and, of course, by the storytelling Rule of Three, it coldly wipes out two before finally locking onto the right one. But by this time she has a helper, Kyle, another figure from the future, this time fully human, who has been sent to protect her by the resistance leader, her son, as yet unborn. The Terminator's seeming invincibility, in that it can never be destroyed, is of course, only a reworking in modern terms of that archetypal motif familiar from so many earlier myths and stories, from Hercules's Hydra to Dracula: the monster's capacity, however many times the hero manages to cut off its head or hack it to pieces, simply to re-form itself and reappear as good (or bad) as new. The film thus becomes like one of those Tom and Jerry cartoons in which cat and mouse repeatedly flatten or blow each other to bits, before they jump up again as if nothing has happened.

Eventually the heroine and Kyle escape just long enough for him to make her pregnant, before a final nightmare chase when the machine closes in to destroy them. Kyle manages in a heroic, suicidal gesture to blow both the Terminator and himself to pieces. But still the machine re-emerges, to crawl relentlessly after the heroine through a gigantic metal press. And it is of course she who, according to the late-twentieth-century's gender-reversal, ends up playing the archetypal role of the hero, by managing in the nick of time to bring the press crashing down, imprisoning and crushing the monster beyond repair. It is as if Perseus or St George had been overcome by their monsters, leaving their Princesses to finish it off. But at least our heroine is now pregnant with the hero of the future, and the film ends with her in Mexico, driving off as a great storm brews up, full of foreboding for the future.

*Judgement Day*, set some years later, shows the boy John as a young tearaway who had been adopted after his birth by a suburban family because his mother Sarah is locked away in a lunatic asylum. She had been certified as insane because of her babbling on about how her son's father was a man sent from the future to make her pregnant. Again two figures from the future then appear, but this time both are humanoid computers which have been sent to track John down at all costs.

One is the stony-faced Schwarzenegger, re-born from his earlier destruction. When the other, who can take on the outward appearance of any human being, disguises himself as a policeman, we are meant to assume he must be a new protector-figure, sent to save the young hero from the deadly Terminator. But we then learn, after various exhibitions of mutual violence and mayhem, that their roles are in fact reversed. Our old friend the Terminator is now the 'goody', sent from the future by John in his adult self, to ensure that he survives to play his future role as resistance leader. The 'policeman' is an even more deadly brand of Terminator, sent by the totalitarian computer system to ensure that John and his mother are eliminated. The 'good' Terminator saves Sarah in the nick of time from destruction by his rival in the mental hospital, and escapes with her and the boy to a kind of 'hippy' encampment in Mexico (a typical 'inferior realm' in which the seeds of redemption are destined to germinate). Here he reveals he has been pro-grammed to do anything the boy orders him to do. John's mother, watching them play together, sentimentally muses that he is the ideal, strong, protective 'father' her son never had; although, being a machine, he of course has no comprehension of human feelings and cannot, for instance, understand why they sometimes cry.

Sarah also now discovers that, at this very moment, a brilliant scientist called Dyson, a black American, is putting the final touches to the super-computer system which is destined eventually to launch a nuclear holocaust and take over the world. She realises she must avert this catastrophe by destroying his research institute. And although she storms into Dyson's family home with all the violence of a Terminator herself, she soon convinces him that, for the sake of the future of mankind, his project must be aborted. Although the 'bad' Terminator inevitably tries to stop them, and the 'good' Terminator has now been ordered by young John not to kill any more human beings, there follows yet another luridly violent battle which ends in the institute being destroyed.

This leads to the climactic 'nightmare stage', conveniently ending in a metal foundry, in which the 'bad' Terminator closes in on John, his mother and his 'good' rival. Thanks to Schwarzenegger, the 'bad' Terminator is eventually plunged into a vat of molten metal and is hideously destroyed. But then comes a last twist to the whole story, which shows the power of the archetypal structure once again reasserting itself. In a typically sentimental Hollywood ending, the 'good' Terminator explains to John and his mother that, in order to save mankind, they must help him to be melted down too. Otherwise he and the computer 'super-chip' he is carrying would be enough to ensure that the totalitarian computer-system would still take over the world. As he bids his farewell to them, he says he has at last learned why it is that human beings cry. As a machine, he has at last done the impossible and begun to develop human feelings. That is why he knows he must selflessly sacrifice his own existence, to save humanity. With tears in their eyes, John and his mother see their friendly Terminator dissolving into a molten lake, throwing in the vital chip after him. Humanity has been saved. The values of the Self have won the day.

In rational terms, of course, none of this stands up for a moment. If the dark power of the Terminators has truly been destroyed, then so has the super-computer of the future which created them. They could never have existed in the first place. The world of 2029 could never have materialised in the way it has been described. There would be no nuclear holocaust in 1997; no ruins amid which John could lead his resistance struggle; no John Connor in 2029 to send his father back to the world of 1984 to impregnate his mother. The boy John, whom we have been watching throughout the film, could never have been born. None of this remotely makes sense, but that is not the point.

The point is that, through all this endless parade of make-believe violent imagery, in one of the most relentlessly violent stories ever put on a cinema screen (apart from a Tom and Jerry cartoon), we have seen the two dark versions of the Terminator as personifications of the human ego and the 'masculine' values of physical and mental power, in their most deadly, remorseless guise. We have seen them as agents of an immense, all-knowing totalitarian power, a 'dark Self', dedicated to the extermination of the human race. Yet in the end they have all been destroyed, simply because one of these mechanical embodiments of the human ego has been through a classic Rebirth. Its heart has been awakened, its eyes have been opened to 'see whole'. It has switched from 'dark' to 'light'. And by dying in its ego-self, it has merged with the interests of the true totality; that universal, eternal 'Self' which is the living force behind all the universe. Out of the black depths of such a vision of chaos and destruction, the archetype has again re-formed itself into that image of wholeness which lies at the heart of what our urge to imagine stories is about.

But, if the conclusion of *The Terminator* finally shows the archetype of the Self winning the day, in one sense it always wins the day in stories, because, even on a sentimental level, this is the only way in which any story can be brought to a proper resolution. The archetype cannot be cheated. If it is defied, the story is doomed just to peter out, or to be forced into some implausible 'pseudo-ending' which leaves its audience curiously unsatisfied. None of the other stories we have looked at in this chapter have been able to reach anything like such an all-resolving conclusion. The ending of *Fanny Hill* is just a little cardboard fake; that of *Justine* is like a final despairing gesture of defiance at the values of the Self which the whole novel has tried to deny; that of Ulysses is a last forlorn act of masturbatory make-believe in the meaningless wilderness of the ego. *Lady Chatterley* peters out in vacuous wishful-thinking. At least in *Psycho* the monster is finally shown, in rather half-hearted fashion, as having been brought to justice. By the time we reach *Last Exit to Brooklyn* and *Saved* the values of the Self have passed so far out of sight that their stories scarcely try to resolve at all. In *A Clockwork Orange* the psychopathic hero does eventually seem about to change, but only to re-emerge at the end in the same monstrous state in which he began. In *The Texas Chainsaw Massacre* the monsters simply live on, as they do in *Silence of the Lambs* and *Basic Instinct*. Nothing in any of these stories is ever properly resolved, because their only real purpose has been to titillate the fantasies of their audiences with a stream of Self-defying images which by definition are incapable of leading to a resolution.

The only real value of this explosion of sex and violence in the storytelling of the late twentieth century lies in the evidence it provides of how quickly, when human fantasy ventures down this path, it runs into a dead end. We soon become familiar with the same repetitive handful of clichéd images, mechanically revolving round in the same claustrophobic little circle, unable to lead anywhere and totally divorced from any deeper meaning. But the realm of the imagination open to storytelling is so infinitely larger than this that it is time to return to the wider world.

## CHAPTER TWENTY-EIGHT

# Rebellion Against 'The One'

## *From Job to Nineteen Eighty-Four*

'Then Job answered the Lord, and said: "I know that thou cans't do every thing, and that no thought can be witholden from thee ... I have heard of thee by the hearing of the ear, but now mine eye seeth thee. Wherefore I abhor myself and repent in dust and ashes." '

*Book of Job*, Ch. 42

' "Then you think there is no God?"
"No, I think there quite probably is one."
"Then why ...?"
Mustapha Mond checked him. "But he manifests himself in different ways to different men. In pre-modern days, he manifested himself as the being that's described in these books. Now ..."
"How does he manifest himself now?" asked the Savage.
"Well, he manifests himself as an absence, as though he weren't there at all." '

Aldous Huxley, *Brave New World*

'It was all right, everything was all right, the struggle was finished. He had won the victory over himself. He loved Big Brother.'

George Orwell, *Nineteen Eighty-Four*

In this chapter and the next we shall be looking for the first time at two new plots. Although no survey of the patterns of storytelling would be complete without them, there are good reasons why they should not have been included among the seven central plots which form the core of this book. The Mystery, which we come to in the next chapter, has over the past two centuries provided the basis for one of the most successful genres in modern popular storytelling, the detective story. But, as we shall see, this type of story only emerged as a by-product of that shift in the psychological 'centre of gravity' which has characterised storytelling since the rise of Romanticism.

Similarly the plot which is the theme of this present chapter cannot be described as basic to the understanding of stories, because it only occurs very rarely. Indeed we shall be looking at only three examples. One is ancient, taken from the Bible. The others are two of the best-known novels produced by the twentieth century. But between them they shed a clearer light on a particularly important aspect of human psychology than we see reflected in any other type of story.

The essence of this plot is that it shows us a solitary hero who finds himself being drawn into a state of resentful, mystified opposition to some immense power, which exercises total sway over the world in which he lives. Initially he increasingly feels he is right and that the mysterious power must in some fundamental way be at fault. But suddenly he is confronted by that power in all its awesome omnipotence. The rebellious hero is crushed. He is forced to recognise that his view had been based only on a very limited, subjective perception of reality. He ends accepting the power's rightful claim to rule over the world and himself.

## The Book of Job

The story of Job, probably developed from a Babylonian original around 400 BC, is not like anything else in the Bible. It begins with a hero who is described as 'a perfect and upright' man, 'one that feared God and eschewed evil'. He is rich and powerful, 'the greatest of all the men in the East'. He has 'a very great household', many servants and possessions, and lives happily surrounded by a large family, including seven sons and three daughters. But then Satan, described as a 'son of God', suggests to God that the only reason why Job seems so perfect is that God has 'made a hedge about him'. Of course it is easy for Job to be God-fearing when he enjoys every blessing the world can offer. But Satan throws down a challenge. If God will allow him to undermine Job's prosperity, he will soon win Job away from his perfect loyalty. God agrees to this, on condition that no harm is done to Job physically.

Satan sets about destroying Job's 'kingdom' with a will. Job is robbed of all his possessions. His servants are put to the sword. A mighty wind blows up from nowhere, destroying his eldest son's house and killing all his sons and daughters. In face of all this horrifying news Job remains unshakeable. 'The Lord giveth', he says, 'the Lord taketh away. Blessed be the name of the Lord.' Round one to God. However, Satan then gets permission from God to afflict Job directly, with the worst possible physical torments, so long as he does not actually kill him. Job develops boils all over his body, so agonising that he finally curses the day he was born. He is beginning to crack.

Then follows a long debate between Job and three of his friends, who come to comfort him. Initially he seems to have recovered his philosophical acceptance of what has happened. But gradually he turns on his 'comforters', accusing them of just preaching empty words at him. He muses on how really wicked people, 'those that rebel against the light', so often seem to get away with their crimes, without being punished. He reminisces self-pitifully about how he used to be blessed and respected by all, but now 'they that are younger than me have me in derision'. He begins to list all the virtuous things he has done throughout his life, to show how little he has deserved his terrible fate. Why has God abandoned him? And at this point 'the three men ceased to answer Job because he was righteous in his own eyes'.

Then a fourth, younger man, Elihu, breaks in to reprove not only Job himself but also the three others, because they have so obviously failed in getting Job to understand. 'Job hath spoken without knowledge.' He has dared question the actions and wisdom of the creator of the universe, whose power and knowledge are far greater than any mere mortal can begin to understand. Not only are all men sinners, including Job. He has now added 'rebellion to his sin'. And at this point, in an awesomely dramatic intervention, God himself addresses Job 'out of the whirlwind', in a speech of overwhelming power. 'Who is this that darkeneth counsel without knowledge?' Where were you, he asks Job, 'when I laid the foundations of the earth?' After a long recital demonstrating his omnipotence and omniscience, Job is utterly crushed: 'I know that thou cans't do everything ... I have heard of thee by the hearing of the ear; but now mine eye seeth thee. Wherefore I abhor myself and repent in dust and ashes'. Seeing his abject capitulation, the Lord accepts that the test is over and blesses 'the latter end of Job more than his beginning'. He ends up twice as rich as before, with seven new sons and seven new daughters ('in all the land were no women found so fair') and lives happily for many more years until finally coming to a peaceful end, 'old and full of days'.

### Lesser dark version: *Brave New World*

In the *Book of Job* the omnipotent power is presented as entirely 'light'. The symbolism of light and dark runs through the story. We are never left in any doubt that the only character who is dark and entirely at fault is Job himself. It is his self-justifying ego which blinds his understanding, rendering him unable to see whole. The central point of the story is that his ego has to be crushed and his eyes opened, so he can at last see that he is just a self-centred little mortal creature who has no right to see himself as separate from the all-powerful, all-knowing spirit which created him and everything else, from the stars in heaven to the monsters of the deep. In this sense, Job ends the story entirely at one with the eternal power which lies behind the universe. He has come to see whole. He has at last found his inmost identity, and for this he finds happiness to the end of his days.

In the middle decades of the twentieth century, when civilisation had been through unimaginable changes, two English novelists produced well-known stories based on a dark version of this plot. Each is set in an imaginary future, showing a world which has passed under the control of an immense totalitarian power which purports to be light, and which demands total conformity to its collective ways of thought and behaviour. Each centres on a hero who, like Job, sets out to question that power – until in the end he is crushed into submission.

Like all stories set in some future time, Aldous Huxley's *Brave New World* (1932) is based on projecting into the future certain characteristics of the contemporary world in which the author was writing.[1] In his case these were features of modern Western civilisation which had become increasingly prominent in the 1920s, with

---

1. The first recorded story which was set at a specific date in the future was an English tale published anonymously in London in 1763 entitled *The Reign of George VI 1900-25*. This described how, in the early twentieth century, a 'Patriot King of England' restored the fallen fortunes of his country and defeated an alliance of foreign powers, culminating in victory over a huge Russian army outside Vienna in 1918, making Britain the master of Europe. Although some of the story's coincidences are uncanny, such as its prediction of a great European war ending in 1918, the world it projected into the future looked remarkably like that of the time when the story was written: so that twentieth century wars were supposedly still being fought in eighteenth-century style, with cannons, muskets and cavalry charges.

its technological innovations, material comfort and loosening codes of sexual behaviour. The inhabitants of his 'brave new world' live in a London dominated by a series of huge, shining concrete skyscrapers, set amid trees (along the lines of Le Corbusier's contemporary vision of the 'radiant City' of the future). They are conditioned by drugs and by unconscious brainwashing to see themselves as entirely happy. Their consciousness is shaped entirely by the state, through slogans drilled into their subconscious while they sleep. They are born from test tubes, so that family life has been completely eliminated. The idea that anyone should have a 'Father' and a 'Mother' is regarded as obscene. They have been conditioned to hate anything to do with nature. The world, as they are conditioned to see it, is entirely shaped by man and his technology, just as history has been rewritten to support this view. And the ultimate crime in this society is for any of its members to think or feel for themselves. They must never be alone, except to engage in incessant, promiscuous sex. No one must form a lasting relationship with anyone else.

What this brave new world order represents is a collectivising of the human ego in the name of a selfless totality, except that everything representing the genuine Self has been ruthlessly excluded. Its citizens engage in quasi-religious ceremonies to keep them securely bonded into the collective identity. And what above all binds them together is the collectivising of the physical and mental pleasures of the ego, as the state arranges for them to enjoy an unlimited supply of sex, drugs and rock 'n' roll (or its contemporary equivalent). This is performed in what had formerly been churches, such as Westminster Abbey, now converted into the equivalent of 'discos' as society's central shrines.

The story begins when its hero, Bernard Marx, begins to commit the ultimate offence against this totalitarian order by feeling increasingly resentful of all the techniques used to make him conform. He invites a female colleague to join him on a visit to the 'New Mexico Savage Reservation', inhabited by North American Indians, one of the few places in the world where nature and human beings are still allowed to survive in a 'wild' state. Here, in this 'inferior realm', he meets John, generally described as 'the Savage'. This young man is the son of an English white mother who had been lost and abandoned when she was brought here on a fleeting visit from London, and he has been born and raised among the local Indians. John, 'the Savage', represents everything the World-State has eradicated and suppressed in its conformist subjects. He loves nature. He feels genuine, selfless personal emotions, like his love for his now decaying, dissolute mother. He has educated himself by reading the plays of Shakespeare (totally banned in the outside world). He is, in short, himself.

Marx is permitted to bring the Savage and his mother out of this 'inferior realm' back to the 'above the line' world in London, where John is horrified by everything he sees as being a hideous stultification of human nature. He sees its inhabitants as having been reduced to no more than sleep-walking zombies. At this point, so much clearer is the Savage's perception of how limited the 'ruling consciousness' of this society has become, that he takes over from Bernard Marx as the story's real hero. Finally, in the equivalent of Job's confrontation with God, he and Marx are summoned for an interview with the immensely powerful Mustapha Mond, one of the World Controllers of the universal totalitarian state.

This seemingly benevolent, quasi-god-like figure explains in a fatherly way how he too had once been tempted to rebel against the new world order and to think for himself. He and the Savage even swap quotations from Shakespeare. But the World Controller has now come to appreciate the deeper and wider truth that the highest good for mankind is a completely stable, orderly society in which everyone unthinkingly and happily conforms to the collective stereotype. There can be no place in such a society for family life, great art or any deeper human feelings, because these are individualistic, disruptive and dangerous. The perfect unity of the new world order must at all costs be preserved.[2]

This is why Mond rules that Marx must be sent overseas to one of the remote islands reserved as prison camps for such dissidents. The story's real hero, the Savage, is meanwhile allowed to leave London, to live in a lonely spot in the empty and abandoned countryside of Surrey. Here he becomes a tourist attraction, besieged by hordes of journalists, film cameras and coach parties, peering at him like some bizarre wild animal, Soon he can take no more of this brave new world and hangs himself.

## Full 'dark version': *Nineteen Eighty-Four*

At least in Huxley's version neither Marx nor the Savage end up being crushed into willing submission to the totalitarian power. For the full dark inversion of the Job story we must go to the novel written by George Orwell shortly before his death in 1950. *Nineteen Eighty-Four* (1948) projects into a nearer future a picture of the rundown, bomb-damaged post-World War Two London in which Orwell lived but now ruled by a totalitarian regime far blacker than Huxley's, based more than anything on what was then the contemporary Communist regime of Stalin's Soviet Union.

As in Huxley's version, London is dominated by a handful of huge skyscrapers. But these, inspired by those of Stalin's Moscow, are the ministries through which the 'Party' imposes its ruthless will on the cowed citizens. Orwell's 'brave new world' is the nightmare counterpart to that of which Huxley's pleasure-dominated 'Utopia' had been the dream version. No one in Orwell's world is happy. Spied on by the state through telescreens in every room, people are desperately short of food, perpetually fearful for their lives, and under relentless pressure night and day to conform like zombies to the model of citizenship imposed on them by the Party. They must join in collective hate of its enemies, and demonstrate unceasing collective love for the figure of the Party's remote, mysterious Stalin-like leader 'Big Brother'. In contrast to Huxley's state, family life is still permitted, but only so that children can be encouraged by the state to spy on their parents. Sex is allowed only as a means of reproduction, a 'duty to the Party', never as a source of pleasure.

---

2. This argument echoes that of the speech made by the Grand Inquisitor to Christ in Dostoyevsky's *The Brothers Karamazov*. When Christ returns to earth he is imprisoned by the Spanish Catholic Church because his teaching must be regarded as subversive of the totalitarian social order sanctioned by the Church in the name of Christianity.

Again the story begins when its hero, Winston Smith, whose daily task is to play a tiny part in the Party's incessant rewriting of history, finds himself questioning this totalitarian power which claims sway over every aspect of the world he lives in. It purports to be wholly benign, under the fatherly guidance of Big Brother, 'full of power and mysterious calm' ('My Saviour' shouts one woman when she sees him on the telescreen). All evil and darkness in the world is concentrated in the figure of the shadowy traitor Goldstein and in the country's external enemies. But Winston becomes increasingly aware that the whole system is built on lies, a total dark inversion of the truth. He then surreptitiously meets and falls in love with the heroine, Julia, whom he had initially assumed was a fanatical Party member, but who then becomes a brave, loving *anima*-figure, much more practical and ingenious than himself in knowing how to evade the Party's controls. Their secret commitment to each other is their ultimate act of disobedience to the regime, and as they are drawn ever further into opposition to all it stands for, they come to believe that a seemingly wise, powerful member of the 'Inner Party', O'Brien, is secretly sympathetic to their beliefs. O'Brien encourages them in this, and gives them a book which explains how the Party is in fact 'dark' and Goldstein 'light'.

It seems they are on the edge of an astonishing, life-giving revelation. But suddenly Winston and Julia are arrested, prisoners of the all-seeing Party. Like Job when brought face to face with God, or Marx and the Savage in their interview with the World Controller, they are confronted by O'Brien himself, who turns out to be a senior member of the Thought Police. In the cells of the Ministry of Love O'Brien crushes Winston by physical torture and shows him how the Party is more all-powerful and all-seeing than he had ever imagined. For years he tells Winston:

> 'I have watched over you. Now the turning point has come. I shall save you. I shall make you perfect.'

O'Brien tells Smith he has:

> 'failed in humility ... you would not make the act of submission ... you believe that reality is something objective, external ... but reality exists only in the human mind.'

The aim is to 'cure' a man of such illusions:

> 'We convert him ... we burn all evil and illusion out of him ... we bring him over to our side ... heart and soul.'

Winston asks whether Big Brother will ever die. 'Of course not'. By now, like Job, he has been physically reduced to a rotting 'bag of filth'. He accuses O'Brien of having done this to him. 'No Winston, you reduced yourself to it. This is what you accepted when you set yourself up against the Party'. Although Winston now accepts Big Brother's authority, he still hates him. The time has come for the final ordeal. 'It is not enough to obey Big Brother', says O'Brien, 'you must love him.' Winston must be exposed to that which he fears most in all the world ('he was standing in front of a wall of darkness, and on the other side of was something unendurable, something too dreadful to be faced'). The nature of this ordeal, because it is so profoundly personal, is for each victim different. In Winston's case, it is the sight of giant, ravenous rats ready to gnaw his face. He shouts out that they should do it to Julia rather than himself. He has committed the ultimate betrayal. He has disowned his *anima*. He has submitted to the universal Dark Power. He can be released, to live out his days for a short time as a broken figure, in a kind of limbo. One day he meets Julia. She too has betrayed him and is a broken ghost. Winston waits for the unknown day when he will be summoned to be shot. In the meantime, he feels himself at one with the Party and all it stands for. As the story ends, 'he had won the victory over himself. He loved Big Brother'.

## The Dark Self

In an earlier chapter, 'Going Nowhere', we looked at one way in which twentieth-century storytelling reflected the disappearance of that centrally important archetype of totality, the Self. The human psyche is so constituted that if any of its archetypal components no longer appear on a conscious level, this is not because they have vanished altogether. They regress into the unconscious, to re-emerge in some dark or 'inferior' form. In Beckett's *Waiting for Godot* we saw how the archetype of the Self casts its spell over the entire play in the mysterious off-stage presence of 'Godot'.

Through most of human history, this archetype was nowhere more obviously represented than in the symbolism and myths associated with the world's religions. Their central purpose was to bring human beings into contact with a deeper component in their psyche, which gave them the sense of belonging to something far transcending their own individual ego-existence. Where this level could be reached, it gave a sense of meaning and purpose to life; a sense of connection, not just to other people and all the world but to a dimension beyond time and existence altogether.

We see how this archetype was called into play by the story of Job and how, in the appearance of the all-powerful, all-knowing spirit behind the universe, Job is overwhelmed into a sense of his own utter insignificance. Up to this point, however aware he may have tried to be of some 'higher power' in his life, and of the need to conform his own life with what he imagines to be a pattern dictated by that power, he has still only been able to perceive the world from within his own little bubble of ego-consciousness. But now this bubble has been shattered, showing him how little he has really understood. Compared with the majesty of this super-mind which has created every last, minute detail of the universe, he knows nothing. Yet the very fact that he is part of this creation, that he is part of its complex purposes and that it is somehow concerned with his existence, gives Job a sense that, although in himself he is nothing, he is also identified with something infinitely greater than himself. He is part of the totality, 'the One'. We thus see the immense power which this archetype can generate. But if its original purpose is light, so also it can be taken over by the 'dark inversion'and turned to very different ends. Such is what we see in the other two stories.

The most obvious expression of the Self archetype in the twentieth century was that it shared the same fate as other archetypes. It was taken over by the ego and projected outwards. That once-religious hunger for a sense of totality, to be part of a single all-embracing unity, took on political expression: most notably through those totalitarian political systems which in the twentieth century came to be imposed over large parts of mankind. The whole point of a totalitarian system is that it seeks to control everything in the lives of the individuals who live under it. And it does so precisely because those who create it have become possessed by that unconscious archetype of totality which is now projected onto every detail of the way society is organised. But this is not done in the name of a genuine sense of totality, but only as the expression of a collectivised form of egotism, representing the attempt by one group of human beings to impose their power and control over the rest. The Nazi ideology claimed transcendent justification for imposing on the world the collective will of German nationalism and Aryan racial supremacy. Still more powerfully, Communism claimed universality for its wish to create a new world order in the name of the proletariat, the downtrodden masses. These totalitarian ideologies were unconsciously driven by that archetype of wholeness, but only in the name of part of the whole: as was unconsciously revealed in how they spoke of 'the Party' as the supreme embodiment of their collective will, the 'part' laying claim to the whole. It was the nature of this phenomenon which Orwell portrayed so acutely in *Nineteen Eighty-Four*.

The appeal of Communism lay precisely in the extent to which it was inspired by an image of human totality, personified by Orwell in the all-wise, benevolent, almost god-like father figure of Big Brother. Obviously Communism represented the 'above the line' masculine attributes of strength, power, discipline and order. But it also claimed to speak in the name of the selfless 'feminine' values, the need to fight on behalf of all those 'below the line', to protect the oppressed. In holding out its Utopian vision of the ideal Socialist society, in which all egotism and exploitation have been abolished and all its members can march towards the 'radiant future', bound together in total unity, it projected a universal image of fully-realised humanity: body, mind, heart and soul in perfect balance. But this was no more than a colossal act of make-believe. There was no genuine balance to Communism. Certainly it represented power and organisation. but only as expressions of collectivised egotism, to be imposed on others. It had no life-giving feminine qualities at all. It was utterly heartless and soulless. It represented the 'dark masculine' in the grip of the 'dark feminine', the ego masquerading as the Self.

This is why Orwell's novel is still so powerful, because, without using such language, it captures all this so accurately. Winston Smith comes to recognise that the system is all a lie, a dark inversion of the truth, and it is this which connects him to Julia, the *anima*-figure who represents instinct, individual feeling, everything the system cannot tolerate. But in the end the brutalised 'dark masculine' hits back, crushing them into submission, stamping out their feelings, their desire for truth, every last, selfless 'feminine' quality within them. In this sense, as a complete inversion of the book of *Job*, it can be read as one of the darkest stories ever conceived.

What Orwell was not to know, since he was writing in 1948 when Stalin's tyranny was at its height, was that the time would come, only a few decades later, when

502

the whole of this particular system of tyranny would come tumbling down, for precisely the reasons he intuitively grasped in his novel. All over the Soviet empire, from Solzhenitsyn and Sakharov in Russia to Lech Walesa and the Solidarity movement in Poland, individuals would see how the claims of that ruling consciousness represented by the Party did not match up to the bleak, heartless, soulless reality based on lies they saw all around them. Eventually, from 'below the line', they would develop sufficient inner strength to bring the entire, decayed, corrupt, 'above the line' structure crashing in ruins. In this sense Winston Smith was destined ultimately to win: because, like the Savage in *Brave New World*, he represented that Self, that core of individual human identity, which can never be wholly suppressed. In the end, it will always somehow re-emerge, because the archetypes programmed into the human psyche cannot be cheated and can never die.[3]

3. We saw this pattern reflected in the conclusion of *Judgement Day*, the sequel to *The Terminator*. These films are also shaped by the theme of an individual rebelling in the name of human values against a world-dominating totalitarian system. Other 'science fiction' stories based on this theme include *The Space Merchants* (1953) by Kornbluth and Pohl, in which the world-system is dominated by huge corporations which act to enslave everyone in the world to consumerism through a relentless bombardment of advertising slogans. The hero, a senior copywriter working for one of the two big advertising agencies, joins an underground network of 'conservationists' who are trying to save the world from destruction by over-exploitation of its material resources. He ends by escaping with his wife to Venus to start a new civilisation based on conservation. Another film based on this plot was Francois Truffaut's *Fahrenheit 451* (1966), showing a totalitarian society in which all books are banned as subversive. The hero is a fireman whose job is to seek out any books and burn them (451 degrees Fahrenheit being the burning point of paper). His disillusionment then draws him into joining an underground network of dissidents who aim to overthrow the system.

## CHAPTER TWENTY-NINE

# The Mystery

'Everybody is suspected in turn, and the streets are full of lurking agents whose allegiances we cannot know. Nobody seems guiltless, nobody seems safe; and then, suddenly, the murderer is spotted, and – relief! – he is not, after all, a person like you or me. He is a villain – known to the trade as George Gruesome – and he has been caught by an infallible Power, the supercilious and omniscient detective, who knows exactly where to fix the guilt.'

Edmund Wilson, 'Why do people read detective
stories?', *The New Yorker*, 1944

' "Do you see any clue?"
(Sherlock Holmes) "You have furnished me with seven, but of course I must test them before I can pronounce upon their value."
"You suspect someone?"
(Holmes) "I suspect myself – "
"What?" '

*The Naval Treaty* by Arthur Conan Doyle

One particularly fascinating consequence of the psychological revolution in the way stories are told over the past two centuries is the way it has given rise to a wholly new type of plot. Furthermore, it is one which has provided the modern world with one of its most popular forms of storytelling.

The essence of a story based on the Mystery is that it begins by posing a riddle, usually through the revelation that some baffling crime has been committed. Our interest then centres round the efforts of its central figure to unravel this riddle, as by tracking down the identity of the person responsible for the crime. Obviously this has found its most familiar expression in detective stories, ever since these were first developed by such nineteenth-century writers as Edgar Allan Poe, Wilkie Collins and Conan Doyle.

Stories which centre on a 'detective' working out who was responsible for a crime go very much further back in history than the nineteenth century. The two earliest recorded examples appear in the Apocrypha, the semi-unauthorised appendix to the Old Testament. *The History of Susanna* and *Bel and the Dragon* have been ascribed to the first or second centuries BC. The first of these tells of how a pure and beautiful young married woman, Susanna, went privately into her garden to bathe, naked. Two judges, eminently respectable old men, have secretly been spying on her and become 'inflamed with lust'. They confront Susanna with an ultimatum. Unless she agrees to 'lie with them', they will tell the authorities that they have seen her committing adultery in the garden with a young man, a crime for which she would be punished by death. Susanna views accepting their proposition as a fate worse than death. The vengeful old men therefore make their false report. Everyone, including her husband, is appalled, and she is put on trial for her life. Because the two judges are such respected citizens, the case against her seems unanswerable.

Susanna is about to be sentenced to death when the young hero, Daniel, speaks up, asking for the chance to cross-examine the two accusers separately. He asks each of them just one question: under which tree in the garden did they see Susanna committing her crime? The first confidently answers 'a mastick tree'. When the other is brought in he says 'an oak tree'. The two 'monsters' are thus caught out on their blind spot, by their conflicting evidence, and are sentenced to death in Susanna's place. Daniel, the self-appointed 'detective' (or counsel for the defence), wins universal acclaim and from that day forth 'was held in great reputation in the sight of the people'.

By the time of *Bel and the Dragon* Daniel has risen to become a respected adviser to the greatest ruler of the age, King Cyrus of Babylon. But they fall out, because Daniel, a Jew, refuses to worship the Babylonian god Bel, or Baal. In the city's main temple stands a huge brass image of Bel, and every day a great heap of sacrifices is laid before it: forty sheep, masses of flour, quantities of wine. Regularly each night they disappear, which to the king proves infallibly that Bel is a true, living god. But Daniel only smiles and tells the king he must not be deceived. Cyrus loses his temper and threatens Daniel that, unless he can prove that the god does not eat the food, he will be put to death. Daniel goes to the temple with the king to present the daily offering but, before the door is sealed, he arranges for the floor to be sprinkled with ashes. When, next morning, they return, the king points triumphantly to the evidence that all the food has gone. Daniel invites him to look carefully at the floor. The ashes show the footprints of many men, women and children. The priests of Bel and their families have been creeping in during the night through a secret door, to steal the food. The king orders that those who have deceived him should be put to death and that the statue of Bel should be destroyed. Again Daniel has overcome the 'monster'.

These two tales already include several devices which were to become only too familiar in later detective stories. In particular, there is the figure of the calmly confident, all-seeing detective who has worked out how the crime was committed long before anyone else in the story. Almost equally familiar, of course, was to become the way the finger of suspicion is initially pointed at someone who is innocent, until the detective eventually reveals the true culprit. But there is one crucial difference between these stories and the whodunnits of modern times. For the reader there is no mystery. Right from the start we, the audience, are let in on how the crime was committed, by whom and why: whereas in the modern versions, the true 'Mystery', the whole point is that we do not know these things until they are finally revealed to us and everyone else by that all-seeing detective.

## Where the Mystery began

The writer normally credited with having written the first modern detective story was Edgar Allan Poe, for his *The Murders in the Rue Morgue*, published in 1841. In fact the earliest example of a detective story based on the Mystery plot had already appeared two decades earlier, as one of the tales of the celebrated German early-Romantic writer E. T. A. Hoffmann. His *Fraulein de Scudery* was published as one of the *Serapionsbrüder* between 1819 and 1821. Hoffmann's story is set in Paris in the reign of Louis XIV, and opens with the arrival at midnight of a mysterious, distraught young man at the house of the venerable Mlle de Scudery, a favourite of the king. He wants the great lady to accept a casket. But the servant is reluctant to let him because all Paris has recently been shocked and terrified by a series of horrible murders, They all involve the theft of jewellery made by the most celebrated goldsmith of the day, René Cardillac.

The police, under Desgrais, are at their wits end. Several times a murder has even been witnessed, but each time the murderer has seemed just to melt away into the wall of a house, to the point where it is popularly believed that only the devil himself could be responsible. The plot which follows is complex, just as the mystery behind the thefts and murders remains complete, until the story approaches its climax. This begins when Cardillac, the universally respected jeweller, is himself found murdered, in the presence of his apprentice Olivier Brusson, who is also in love with Cardillac's pure and beautiful daughter, Madélon. Since everything seems to point to Brusson as the murderer, he is arrested. But then Madélon comes to Mlle de Scudery, pleading her lover's innocence. From this moment, the shrewd old lady assumes a detective-like role, as she seeks to unravel the truth of this murky business (thus becoming the prototype for Agatha Christie's spinster-detective Miss Marple). Furthermore, in a fashion which was to become familiar from countless later detective stories, as where Sherlock Holmes was always several jumps ahead of Inspector Lestrade of Scotland Yard, she does this in defiance of Degrais and the police, who persist in their conviction that Brusson is guilty and cannot wait to hurry him to the scaffold.

The horrifying truth the old lady finally uncovers is that the serial-killer responsible for all the murders around Paris had been none other than Cardillac himself. Like Dr Jekyll, the respectable jeweller had developed a dark Alter-Ego, emerging at night like Mr Hyde to commit these fearful crimes. As for his own killer, it turns out the culprit was not Bresson but a captain of the royal guard, who had identified the murderer but wanted to keep his own identity secret. Eventually he comes forward to explain. All is resolved, the hapless Brusson is released to marry the lovely Madélon, and the happy pair go off to start their new life together in another land.

Although Mlle de Scudery's solution of this mystery depends more on a fortuitous series of confessions than on her interpretation of clues, in other respects this story might have provided a model for the vast majority of detective stories which have appeared since. Above all, it is a crucial part of such stories that, as in the tale of Susanna, the suspicions of the authorities should initially be directed at someone who is innocent; and then that the detective should be the only character shrewd enough to 'see whole' in identifying the true criminal.

This was the plot made famous 20 years later by Poe's *The Murders in the Rue Morgue*, which was almost certainly inspired by Hoffmann's tale. The story is narrated by a kind of Doctor Watson-figure, whose role is to be an admiring foil to the genius of his friend Dupuin, the detective. The story begins with a dazzling demonstration of Dupuin's uncanny ability to reconstruct his friend's train of thought as they are strolling through the streets of Paris. The city is then shocked by the discovery of a woman and her daughter having been battered to death and mutilated in a sealed room. The police arrest a young man called Le Bon (his name somewhat crudely signalling that he is 'good', therefore innocent). Dupuin eventually works out from the positioning of finger-marks on the two dead women that the killer cannot have been human, and must have been a giant ape, an orang-outan. Sure enough, precisely such a creature is found to have escaped in the city.

By the 1860s detective stories were becoming particularly fashionable in England, their first leading exponent being Wilkie Collins, notably in *The Moonstone* (1868) in which the detective is for the first time a policeman, Sergeant Cuff. His other best-known novel *The Woman in White* (1860) is also based on the Mystery plot, although it is not strictly a detective story.[1] Collins's friend Dickens used the plot in his last, unfinished novel *The Mystery of Edwin Drood* (1870). In 1887 a young Scottish doctor, Arthur Conan Doyle, published *A Study in Scarlet,* introducing the most famous fictional detective of them all, Sherlock Holmes; and in the 60 Holmes stories he was to publish over the following decades he finally established the genre which in the twentieth century was to find countless practitioners, from Agatha Christie, Dorothy Sayers and G. K. Chesterton to the Belgian writer Simenon and their American contemporaries such as Raymond Chandler.

As we see from *The Woman in White,* it is not only the more obvious type of detective story which can be based on the Mystery plot. It also, for instance, gives rise to a certain type of ghost story, where the mystery centres on tracking down the explanation for some ghostly apparition. But again this usually involves some past tragedy or crime, as in M. R. James's *The Haunted Dolls' House* (1925), written for the library of the Royal dolls' house. A collector buys a beautifully-made antique model of a country house, complete with a set of miniature human

---

1. The initial riddle posed by *The Woman in White* is the apparition on a lonely country road at night of a distraught young woman dressed in white, being chased by mysterious pursuers. In plot terms what is interesting about the complex story which follows is the way this original haunting feminine figure gradually differentiates into three, who are all sisters. The original version, Anne, is simply a weak, helpless victim, who has been incarcerated in a mental asylum by two evil villains, Sir Percy Glyde, a baronet, who is engaged to Anne's sister Laura, and his fat, smooth, sinister friend Count Fosco. They have done this because Anne has discovered an appalling secret about Sir Percy, which he is determined should remain hidden. Laura is stronger than Ann, but the two 'monster-figures' then manage to get her also consigned to the asylum. The key to the story then becomes the third sister Marian, stronger and shrewder than the others, and it is she who, as a fully 'active' heroine, eventually outwits the two villains and puts them to rout. Sir Percy's awful secret, which Marian also discovers, is that he had been born out of wedlock, and is not really a baronet at all. While trying to destroy the evidence for this, he accidentally burns himself to death. Fosco is murdered by an Italian secret society which he has betrayed. In plot terms, the story is thus a combination of Mystery and Overcoming the Monster, and Marian presents us with an unusual pre-modern example of a feminine 'monster-slayer'. The way the '*anima*-figure' in the story develops through three stages, from the original helpless victim Ann into her final manifestation as the tough and resourceful, but still feminine Marian may recall those folk-tales such as *The Three Billy Goats Gruff,* where we see a hero-figure progressively becoming stronger through three incarnations, until he is powerful and mature enough to overcome the monster.

figures, and sets it up in his bedroom. He is awakened in the night by the chiming of a mysterious clock, and sees the dolls' house illuminated as if by moonlight. He then witnesses the unfolding of a ghostly drama, in which the figures in the house commit three murders. Amazed by this apparition, he tries to uncover some historical explanation for these strange events. Eventually he discovers the story of a long-demolished house, in which precisely such a baffling sequence of murders had taken place in the eighteenth century. But only now, two centuries later, have the true identities of the murderers come to light.

## *Citizen Kane*: The Mystery as Tragedy

One well-known but very different type of story based on the Mystery plot was Orson Welles's *Citizen Kane* (1941), The riddle is posed in the film's opening scene when, in a huge and fantastic Californian castle called Xanadu, we see the death of the fabulously rich Charles Foster Kane, owner of a vast newspaper and industrial empire. With his dying breath, he utters the single word 'Rosebud'. A young journalist is so intrigued by this detail, which he senses may contain the clue to Kane's mysterious life, that he sets out to discover what 'Rosebud' may have meant. The framework of the story is provided by the course of his investigation, but within this frame we see the journalist reconstructing Kane's entire life, from the day many years before when a stuffy, self-important lawyer had arrived in falling snow at the humble, remote log cabin where Charles lived as a little boy with his mother, to announce that the boy has been left an immense fortune. Young Charles is playing happily outside in the snow with his friends and is summoned inside, leaving behind his sledge, to be told that the lawyer is now his guardian and will be taking him off to begin a new life as the heir to millions. He is heartbroken to be torn away from his mother and his loving, simple home.

We then follow Kane's astonishing career as he grows up. As a young man he discovers that part of the vast commercial empire he has inherited includes an ailing newspaper, which he decides to edit himself. To the horror of his guardian, Kane transforms it, through muckraking journalism and by buying up all the best journalists of the day, into the most successful newspaper in America. He makes an eminently respectable, unloving marriage to a Senator's daughter, for once approved by his sternly moralistic guardian. He buys more newspapers, becomes ever richer and embarks on a political career which everyone assumes will end in the White House. But in the middle of his first dazzling campaign (when the Dream Stage of his story is at its height), he one night meets in the street a poor, naïve, vulgar young girl, Susan, who has dreams of becoming a professional singer. He becomes infatuated, his political opponents discover his 'secret love nest' and blow it up into a huge scandal, and his political career is in ruins.

Now the pattern of Tragedy is firmly in the ascendant, as Kane divorces his hard, respectable wife, marries the pitiful young Susan and uses his millions in a bid to launch her as an opera singer (hiring a grand opera house and boosting her through his newspapers). She is an appalling, embarrassing flop and takes to drink. Kane immures her in his vast, remote castle, stuffed with so many works of art shipped in from Europe that many have never even been removed from their crates. On the public stage, he cuts an increasingly impotent, absurd figure, richer than ever, but quite unable to exercise any influence on political events, as he wishes. Finally, pathetic, lonely and prematurely aged, he dies, uttering the mysterious word 'Rosebud'; as his fingers let slip a cheap glass paperweight showing a snowstorm, which falls to the floor and shatters.

At the end of his quest, the journalist who has pieced all this story together, still utterly baffled by 'Rosebud', comes to the castle in a last desperate search for clues. He sees an army of workmen sorting through Kane's mountains of possessions and throwing huge quantities of rubbish into a furnace. Among the debris is a child's toboggan and, as it is thrown into the fire, the licking flames illumine the name written on it, 'Rosebud'. The journalist does not even see it. But for us, the audience, the mystery is at last solved. The inner tragedy of Kane's life had begun at that moment when, all those years before, he had been torn away from his happy childish games in the snow and from the softness and love of his mother, to be propelled into the hard, alien, outside world, dominated by the 'masculine' ego-values of money, respectability, power and fame. 'Rosebud' was his soul, the secret heart of the identity he had lost, that he was still hankering for with his dying breath. It symbolised his lost inner feminine, everything the doomed love he had projected onto the little infantile *anima*-figure of Susan, with her vague 'artistic' dreams, had been a last, pitiful attempt to recapture; but which had signalled instead only the onset of his inner ruin, so that he ended like the hero of a dark Rebirth story, trapped in unseeing egotism with no hope of redemption.[2]

2. Another Hollywood director who conspicuously relied on elements of the Mystery plot in many of his films was Alfred Hitchcock. *Rear Window* (1954), for instance, was a straightforward detection mystery in which the hero, a magazine photographer (played by James Stewart) confined by injury to his New York apartment and seeking diversion by spying on his neighbours, is convinced he has seen one of them committing a murder, although there is no sign of the body. Despite initial scepticism, first from his girlfriend, then from his friend in the New York police department, his deductions eventually prove correct and the murderer confesses. A more complex mystery inspired Hitchcock's most popular film, *Vertigo* (1958), in which the hero 'Scottie' (again played by Stewart) is a San Francisco policeman forced into retirement because, following his failure to stop a colleague falling from a roof, he suffers acutely from vertigo. He is commissioned to investigate the strange problem afflicting the wife of a rich friend, who seems to imagine she is the reincarnation of a beautiful and tragic nineteenth-century ancestor who had died young. Stewart falls in love with the wife (Kim Novak) and is led by her to an old Spanish mission station south of the city, which she seems to recall from her previous life. When she ascends the church tower, he is slow to follow her because of his vertigo and sees her falling to her death. Traumatised by his inability to prevent this tragedy, he undergoes hospital treatment but then thinks he sees the dead woman's near-exact double (also Kim Novak). He woos her and gradually comes to suspect that she is the same woman. Having dressed her in the same clothes, he takes her back to the same church. By now he has unravelled the mystery. He had in fact been set up by the husband to provide cover for a murder. The woman he saw falling from the tower had been the man's real wife; the woman played by Kim Novak was his mistress. On the first occasion, when she climbed the tower before him, the husband had already been hiding up there, ready to throw his wife (dressed in identical clothes) off the tower. He had relied on an attack of vertigo to ensure that Scottie would not have been able to climb high enough to see the truth of what happened. He and his mistress had then, unseen, made their escape. When the hero takes the mistress back up the tower, to confront her with the part she had played in this murder, she is so dismayed that, quite accidentally, she falls to her death. But it is never explained why the hero was not asked to identify the original victim's body, at which point the truth would have come out much earlier. But then of course there would have been no story.

## Whodunnit?

The real point of the Mystery story, and what distinguishes it from every other type of story we have looked at in this book, is that the hero – the detective or investigator – is in a peculiar way not directly involved in the central drama of the story. He or she stands outside it, as a kind of voyeur, only intervening, if at all, as a detached, superior *deus ex machina* to sort out what has happened.

In fact, when we examine such stories more carefully, we see that the drama the investigator is observing, like a spectator contemplating a picture or play, is invariably shaped by one of the basic plots we have already looked at, as *Citizen Kane* is shaped by the five-stage plot of Tragedy. In the adventures of Sherlock Holmes, for instance, most begin with the great detective sitting in his cosy Baker Street lodgings. Then some distraught figure intrudes from the outside world, to relate how he or she has been caught up in a terrible drama. The wise, all-seeing Holmes agrees to address his almost supernatural powers to solving the mystery. He eventually unravels the riddle, the shadows are lifted from his distraught client, who expresses undying gratitude, and Holmes returns to his lodgings to smoke his pipe, read the newspaper and await the next case.

The drama in which his clients are caught up always turns out to assume the shape of another plot. It may be an Overcoming the Monster story, as in *The Speckled Band*, where Holmes in fact plays a more than usually central role as the hero who personally overcomes the monster. The distraught client is a young girl, an heiress, who feels threatened by the grim, violent figure of her stepfather, Dr Grimesby Roylott, with whom she lives in the country. Two years earlier her older sister had died in violent and mysterious circumstances in the same house. Holmes inspects the house, in the doctor's absence, and works out how the sister must have been murdered and how his client is now in danger of the same fate. Of course we, the readers, are not told what he has deduced, since this would destroy the suspense. Holmes then secretly returns to the house at night, and in the nick of time manages to send the agent of murder, a deadly snake, back on its tracks up a bell rope and through a specially-contrived hole in the wall to the next room from which it has come. Here it fastens its deadly fangs in the villain who sent it, Dr Roylott, who is after the girl's money. The monster is thus overcome, the beautiful young heroine has been saved; and if this were the usual Overcoming the Monster story we might then expect the brave hero to marry the 'Princess' he has rescued. But here we expect nothing of the kind. The heroine passes out of Holmes's life and he returns to his lodgings quite unchanged by his adventure.

No Holmes adventure is based more overtly on the Overcoming the Monster plot than the novel with which Doyle marked his detective's return to life 11 years after he supposedly fell to his death with Moriarty over the Reichenbach Falls. The suspense of *The Hound of the Baskervilles* (1902) is built up through Doyle's conjuring up the image of a gigantic, luminescent and 'monstrous hound', seemingly supernatural, which roams a fog-wreathed Dartmoor at night and is associated with the mysterious death of a local landowner. Holmes deduces that the 'monster' is not a ghost but a real dog, being used to further a series of crimes, the perpetrator of which he identifies. The climax comes when he manages to shoot the monster, just before its fleeing master is sucked down to his death by a bog (adapting an image borrowed from the climactic episode of R. D. Blackmore's *Lorna Doone* 33 years earlier, when the villain was sucked down to his death in a similar quagmire on Exmoor).

Within the framework of the Mystery, however, other Holmes stories are based on different plots. *The Musgrave Ritual* takes on the shape of a Quest, ending in the discovery at the bottom of a pond of a great treasure, the ancient crown of England. *The Boscombe Valley Mystery* turns out to be shaped by the plot of Comedy, where the dark figures are two fathers, locked in a deadly quarrel, while their two children long to get married but are prevented from doing so by their fathers' feud. One father murders the other, so that suspicion at first falls on the innocent son, which is what brings in Holmes to investigate. The result of his intervention is that the 'hero' and 'heroine' are at last liberated from the shadows and free to get married. But by this time, Holmes has long since returned to Baker Street, to await his next case.

It is this curiously detached role played by the central figure in the Mystery, and his lack of real human involvement with the other characters who pass temporarily under his scrutiny, which really gives us the central clue to what these stories are about.

It is significant that most Mystery stories are concerned with discovering who has been responsible for committing some terrible crime. A great deal of storytelling is concerned in one way or another with the committing of crimes. Although we usually reserve the title of 'murder story' for mysteries or 'whodunnits', much of the great literature of the world is made up of stories in which murders are committed: from the *Oresteia* to *Jack and the Beanstalk*, from *Aladdin* to the tragedies of Shakespeare and the four major novels of Dostoyevsky. But rarely in such stories is there any doubt about who has committed the murder. What they are concerned with is the deeper moral circumstances and consequences of the crime for those involved. Is the killing justified? Will the criminal face up to his guilt? Will he have to pay the price with his own death? Will he go through a change of heart and a period of intense suffering and repentance, so that he can eventually be released?

The difference between these sorts of story and the 'whodunnit' is that the latter is not concerned with such complex issues. It derives its entire appeal from the simple trick of initially hiding the identity of the culprit and then at the end revealing it. We are not really concerned with the finer points of morality involved, or with the other characters acting out the story. They are primarily there just to present us with the basic materials for yet another demonstration of the hero-detective's extraordinary mental powers. And the real point about this figure with whom we identify as the focus of our attention, is that the person who has committed the crime is always someone other than himself. In following the story, we can invariably rest in the comfortable certainty that it will be someone other than the person we are identifying with on whom the guilt will eventually be pinned.

So much do we take this for granted, since it is the whole point of the formula which has given such pleasure to readers since the rise of the modern detective story, that we may see nothing odd about it.

But let us then consider the greatest 'whodunnit' in all literature: a story shaped round the efforts of its central figure to discover who has committed a crime so terrible that it is nothing less than the murder of a king. When we meet the hero, King Oedipus, a fearful curse has fallen on his country, and he is told that it will not be lifted until he has discovered the identity of the man who murdered his predecessor, King Laius. Oedipus sets out, as detective, to unravel this mystery, which of course is only a mystery to him, not to us. He uncovers clue after clue until he is finally brought up against the inexorable realisation that the king's murderer was none other than himself; and, what makes it worse, that the man he killed was none other than his own father.

It is this which places Sophocles's *Oedipus Tyrannos* (which we shall analyse fully in the next chapter) on an infinitely more serious level than any of the other types of 'whodunnit' we have been considering. Instead of just sitting vicarously on the sidelines, cosily identifying with some central figure – Sherlock Holmes, Peter Wimsey, Hercule Poirot – who again and again manages to pin the blame for a crime on someone else, as if by some mechanical formula, we are thrust up against the spectacle of a man going through one of the most profound and uncomfortable experiences any human being can know: having to face up at last to the dark side of his own nature and to recognise his own, irrevocable guilt.

Herein lies the central clue as to why we must consider the modern detective story, and the plot of the Mystery, as in a different category from any other type of story we have looked at in this book. Herein also we may find the reason why even the most devoted readers of detective thrillers often find them ultimately unsatisfying, with a curious sense of flatness each time one of their stories finally reaches its conclusion.

When in 1944 Edmund Wilson famously wrote three critical articles about the passion for detective stories in *The New Yorker*, he was startled by the virulence of the response he received from those who rushed to defend them. What particularly struck him was how these readers seemed to be addicted to detective fiction, as if to a drug, yet seemed to find it remarkably difficult to explain why they liked it so much. One of Wilson's central observations, in his essay 'Who Cares Who Killed Roger Ackroyd?', was how banal, in strictly literary terms, is the style in which most detective stories are written. The characters are just two-dimensional cardboard cutouts, manipulated round a board to serve the story's central purpose, which is to set up what is usually some wholly artificial, improbable puzzle for the detective to solve. Once this conundrum has been solved, or its answer revealed, the story and its characters are of no further interest; any more than is a crossword puzzle once the last clue has been filled in.

The point of detective stories is that they derive from that part of the human psyche, the ordering function of the mind, when this becomes split off from those feminine principles of feeling and intuitive understanding which can connect it to the reality of the living world. It then operates on the level of a fantasy

513

or daydream. This is why such stories are so beguiling to those who, unlike Edmund Wilson, are susceptible to their charms. They create a neat little make-believe world, hermetically sealed from reality, in which the ordering function can set up its riddles, simply by the trick of withholding the information the reader needs to solve the riddle until the author is ready to reveal it. Such is the fantasy realm into which we, the readers, can then have the pleasure of escaping. We first enjoy the frisson of seeing some peaceful, ordered little 'kingdom', such as a traditional English village, a country house or an Oxford college, being upset by a dark and mysterious irruption of evil. We then enjoy the reassuring spectacle of the all-seeing detective moving inexorably, clue by clue, towards the point where the cause of this disorder can safely be pinned on some villainous figure who never really belonged to such a respectable, law-abiding world in the first place. We finally see law and order restored, much as in a story where the values of the Self have eventually triumphed. Except that here the genuine state of all-resolving wholeness represented by the Self plays no part.

The drama has been conceived on that same sentimental level we have seen giving rise to other types of story, where the ego can fantasise about enjoying the rewards of the Self without having to go through the deeper processes required to achieve it. The detective figure is a particular projection of the human ego, or 'super-ego', whose exhibitionistic display of rational intelligence is made morally acceptable because it is serving the wider purpose of ensuring that darkness is exposed and light is victorious. Just as James Bond's indulgence in sex and vio-lence is sanctioned by the fact that he is defending 'our side' against some wicked super-villain, so Sherlock Holmes's outrageous assumption of intellectual super-iority (not to mention his indulgence in cocaine) appears entirely acceptable, because he is using it to expose evil in the name of law, order and truth. We the readers can thus share vicariously in the sight of him showing off in this way, knowing it is all in a higher, righteous cause. And what gives us even more a sense of shared superiority in identifying with the all-seeing central figure in detective stories is that he is always surrounded by those other characters, such as the dim-witted police, who expose the inferiority of their intelligence by invariably jump-ing to the wrong conclusions. The role of the Watson-figure in acting as a bum-bling foil to the detective's brilliance is similarly to reinforce this sense of our hero's awesomely superhuman powers.

All this may seem as harmless a form of self-indulgence as completing a cross-word puzzle. But so little does the unravelling of these self-referential conundrums have to do with the real world, and so much do they rely on the endless recycling of the same set of stereotypes, that there are really only two ways in which the authors of such stories can maintain the illusion of originality necessary to keep their audience's interest alive. The first is through the skill by which they turn their heroes into sufficiently distinctive two-dimensional characters, defined by their quirky habits and catch-phrases; the game at which Conan Doyle in creating Holmes was the supreme master. The other is through the ingenuity with which they can find new intellectual twists to what is essentially such a limited and repetitive formula. This was one reason why Agatha Christie was so successful, in that she managed to come up with one permutation on the basic formula after another: ranging from a story in which every one of the many possible suspects turns out to be equally guilty (*Murder on the Orient Express*) to that in which the culprit turns out to be the story's narrator and the detective's own Watson-like confidant (*The Murder of Roger Ackroyd*).

In a sense the most ingenious twist of all, however, was that used by Agatha Christie in what was to become, in commercial terms, the most successful version of a detective story ever put on the stage. Was it entirely coincidental that this should have been the only example of a modern 'whodunnit' where the person who committed the crime turns out to have been the detective himself? *The Mousetrap* may have no pretensions to psychological profundity or to be considered as great literature. But is it possible that, in this unique twist to the formula, the millions of theatregoers who helped to make it the longest-running stage production in history should have done so because they caught in it just the faintest echo of one of the most profound issues which lie at the heart of storytelling: the real drama implicit in a man discovering not someone else's guilt, which is easy, but his own?[3]

3. Another great work of literature based in part on the Mystery plot was Dostoyevsky's final novel, *The Brothers Karamazov*. We know from the opening paragraph of this long book that it is to be a murder story, involving the death of Fyodor Karamazov, a rich, bullying, debauched landowner. He has had three sons by two young wives, both now dead, but has all but abandoned them. In a way reminiscent of a folk tale, two sons are negative, in opposing respects, the third positive. Dmitri is like his father, a physically strong, drunken bully. Ivan has gone to the opposite masculine extreme, by retreating into the mind, cut off from feeling and reality by his over-dependence on the intellect. The third son, Alyosha, selfless, loving and devout, lives in a monastery with his spiritual mentor Father Zossima (who eventually dies). There is also a shadowy fourth son, Smerdyakov, born from a short-lived illicit affair between old Karamazov and 'stinking Lizaveta', a sad social outcast. From their tortured relationships with their father, it seems that both Dmitri and Ivan might well be tempted to kill the old monster, and when the murder actually takes place, Ivan is at least partly complicit to what has happened (although, as a good intellectual, he has been careful to distance himself from the nasty physical realities of the crime). But it is Dmitri who behaves most suspiciously, and who is therefore arrested and put on trial. Even though the court is presented with evidence that the true murderer was Smerdyakov, the most shadowed son of all, rejected and mentally unstable, this is dismissed, because Smerdyakov had then committed suicide. Dmitri is thus wrongly found guilty. The son who had not been strong enough to prevent any of this happening is Alyosha, the story's hero. But now that his Dark Father is dead, he can set off on the road to Self-realisation by following in the footsteps of his 'light Father-figure', Zossima. At the end of the story, to confirm this image of the Self at last emerging from all the surrounding darkness we also see the condemned but innocent Dmitri, purified by his sufferings, preparing to escape to start a new life in America.

# CHAPTER THIRTY

# The Riddle of the Sphinx
## Oedipus and Hamlet

'Born thus, I ask to be no other man,
Than that I am, and will know who I am.'
Oedipus, Sophocles, *King Oedipus*

'This above all, to thine own self be true,
And it must follow, as the night the day,
Thou canst not then be false to any man.'
Polonius, *Hamlet*, Act I, Scene 3

'What a piece of work is a man, how noble in reason, how infinite in faculties, in form and moving how express and admirable, in action how like an angel, in apprehension how like a god; the beauty of the world, the paragon of animals. And yet to me what is this quintessence of dust?'
*Hamlet*, Act II, Scene 1

'Wonders are many on earth, and the greatest of these is man ... he is master of ageless Earth ... he is lord of all things living ... the use of language, the wind-swift motion of brain he learnt; found out the ways of living together in cities ... there is nothing beyond his power. His subtlety meeteth all chance, all danger conquereth, for every ill he found its remedy, save only death. O wondrous subtlety of man, that draws him either to good or evil ways!'
Sophocles, *Antigone*

We end this third section of the book by looking at what may be regarded as the two supreme puzzle stories in world literature. The first is the Greek myth of Oedipus, as portrayed by Sophocles in the most searching trio of plays to have come down to us from the ancient world. The other is *Hamlet*, the most enigmatic of Shakespeare's tragedies. In unravelling the seeming ambiguity of these tales we return again, more deeply than ever, to the heart of what our need to tell stories is about.

The first puzzle of the Oedipus myth is how it includes two separate stories which in a sense may seem to contradict each other. The first tells how a young man wandering in exile comes to the city of Thebes which is suffering under the shadow of a fearful monster. The Sphinx, literally 'the strangler', is half-woman, half-beast, who lives by the roadside over a precipice near the city. She stops every traveller on the road to pose a riddle. 'What moves on four legs in the morning, two legs in the afternoon and three in the evening?' No traveller can give an answer, and the Sphinx pushes each in turn over the cliff. Finally Oedipus arrives and solves her riddle. The answer of course is 'a man' (who as a baby crawls on all fours and in the evening of his life uses a stick). The enraged Sphinx throws herself off the cliff, and the people of Thebes choose Oedipus by acclamation to be their king, as the great hero who has freed their city from its curse.

Obviously the Sphinx's question stands for something much deeper than just a childhood riddle. The real question she seems to be asking is 'what is a man?', which Oedipus has answered in a way which clearly marks him out as quite exceptional. The fact that he has overcome the 'dark feminine' in this spectacular fashion implies that, like Perseus in slaying Medusa, he has shown himself to be a true man. Indeed, having married Jocasta, widow of its former king, he goes on to rule over Thebes as the greatest king the city ever had. But then begins the more famous part of Oedipus's story, which shows that he has not really become a whole, fully self-aware man at all. Indeed he becomes defined precisely by how much about himself he does not know.

### Oedipus the Tyrant

The opening of Sophocles's *Oedipus Tyrannos* introduces us to the familiar image of a kingdom which has fallen mortally sick. King Oedipus has brought his people fifteen years of peace and prosperity. But now a terrible curse has come upon 'the City of Light'. Crops fail, animals die in the fields, pestilence rages. When the people plead with their king to help them, he promises he will do all in his power to get this shadow lifted. Indeed he has already sent Creon, brother of his wife Jocasta, to ask the Delphic oracle what he should do. Creon returns to report the oracle's pronouncement that the cause of the curse is the presence in Thebes of an 'unclean thing, born and nursed on our soil and now polluting it'. Fifteen years earlier, just before Oedipus arrived in the city, their previous king Laius, on a journey, had been murdered. Only if the murderer can be found and banished can the city be saved. Oedipus promises that all will be 'brought into the light'. He will stop at nothing to track down whoever has been guilty of this unspeakable crime.

Then, at Oedipus's bidding, there arrives the wise old man Teiresias, who is blind. Having lost his outward eyes, he has gained that inward vision which can show him things hidden from normal sight. Three times Teiresias proclaims, to the king's mounting fury, that he, Oedipus, is the 'accursed polluter of this land'; that the killer he is seeking is himself; 'your enemy is yourself'. He ends by prophesying that Laius's killer will one day be driven blind out of the city, having been found to have killed his own father and married his mother. All this strikes Oedipus as no more than the ravings of a foolish old man and, having expressed contempt for Teiresias, he then explodes in fury at Creon, whom he accuses of having set up Teiresias to make these absurd charges as part of a plot to replace him on the throne. But when Jocasta tries to calm him down, we see Oedipus embarking on the three stages through which he pursues his determination to track down the truth of who is to blame for his city's mortal sickness.

First, Jocasta reassures him that he could not possibly have been responsible for her late husband's death, because another oracle had foretold that Laius would die at the hands of his own child. They had only had one child and, when it was three days old, it had been abandoned to die on a mountainside. Anyway, Laius had been killed by a whole gang of robbers, at a place where three roads meet. But this mention of 'three roads' only provokes in Oedipus, for the first time, a terrible doubt. Fiercely he quizzes Jocasta for further details. The more he hears about where this happened and what Laius looked like, the more his fears multiply. Eventually he can hold back no longer. He pours out the story of his life: how, when a young man living in Corinth, he himself had been told by the oracle that he would one day kill his father Polybus and marry his mother; that he had run away from home to ensure that no such horror would ever come to pass; and that when he had come to a place where three roads met, he had encountered a distinguished gentleman in a carriage. This man's servants had pushed him roughly out of the way, their master had viciously lashed out at him as they passed, and, in a fit of rage, Oedipus had killed them all. If it was true that this man was Laius, he cries, 'there is no mortal more wretched than I'.[1]

By this point Oedipus has come to suspect that he himself might have been Laius's killer, but has no idea yet that Laius was his father. But then comes the second stage, when Oedipus recalls Jocasta saying her husband had been killed by a whole gang of robbers, and that there had been a witness, a shepherd, who escaped. Confirming this, Jocasta brightens. 'A fig for this divination', she cries, and sends for the man to repeat his story. First, however, a messenger arrives from Corinth, to announce that Polybus has died a natural death. Oedipus is ecstatic. No longer need he worry about the oracle's prediction that he would kill his father. However, the messenger, only trying to reassure him further, then gives Oedipus the shattering news that Polybus had not been his father anyway. He, the messenger, knew this, because it was he himself who had handed over Oedipus to Polybus as a baby. He had been given the child by one of Laius's servants, the very shepherd now on his way to the court. At this Jocasta finally realises the truth and screams in horror that Oedipus must abandon his search. But saying 'I must pursue this trail to the end', he brutally waves her aside. 'Oh lost and damned' she cries, leaving the stage. 'This is my last and only word to you forever!'

By this point Jocasta can see the whole truth of what has happened, but Oedipus is still blind to his true parentage. Thus begins the third stage, when the shepherd arrives to provide the clinching evidence. He had been ordered to kill the baby, he reveals, because an oracle had foretold that King Laius would be killed by his son. The baby was Laius's own, and he had not had the heart to leave it to die, so he had passed it to this man from Corinth. The icy fear that has been creeping up on Oedipus finally closes round his heart. 'Oh light' he cries, 'never may I look on you again'.

With this third revelation the whole truth is out, and we then hear it reported what this has led to offstage. Oedipus has rushed distracted into the palace to confront Jocasta, only to find her swinging from the rope with which she has killed herself. He has snatched down one of the gold brooches on her dress and

---

1. In a literal sense, of course, it is impossible to believe that Oedipus would not have told Jocasta the story of his life long before, just as it is impossible that he would not have learned the circumstances of Laius's death. But such anomalies are incidental to the deeper drama.

driven its point repeatedly into his eyeballs until his face streams with blood. None of this, of course, has been shown directly, but we then see the state to which it has reduced Oedipus. He stumbles blindly back out into the sunlight, expressing total horror at how he has been guilty of 'all human filthiness in one crime compounded'. He wishes for nothing but death, to be drowned in the depths of the sea.

At this point Creon enters, to take charge. He makes clear he has not come to reprove Oedipus for his misdeeds. He rejects Oedipus's plea that he should be instantly banished. He has already called for Oedipus's two young daughters, Antigone and Ismene, and Oedipus pleads with Creon to look after them, since with so cursed a father, no one will ever want to marry them. As Oedipus turns back towards the palace, his arms round the girls, Creon orders that they must stay behind. Oedipus protests, but Creon insists: 'command no more. Obey. Your rule is ended.' The chorus points the moral by observing how 'this was Oedipus, the greatest of men; he held the key to the deepest mysteries and was envied by all men for his great prosperity'. But 'no one can be called happy until that day when he carries his happiness down to the grave in peace'.

Thus ends the mighty drama which Coleridge described as 'one of the three most perfect plots ever planned' and which Aristotle, in the *Poetics*, mentions more often than any other play as the model of what Tragedy should be. But we may note three points about it.

Firstly, regardless for the moment of the specific nature of what Oedipus has learned about himself, what in general gives the play its unique power is simply that we have seen a man, confronted with a shocking crime, having to go through the acutely painful process of realising that he himself had been responsible. It is the supreme story in the world of a man having to face up to his own guilt, on a cosmic scale. It is no good saying that it was not his fault because he did not know what he was doing, or that he was just the unwitting victim of a malevolent fate. He has offended against one of the most fundamental laws of nature. Indeed, the more he learns about his guilt, the more he discovers that he has been responsible for even worse crimes. It was bad enough that he had killed his father, although there had been mitigating circumstances. Even if he over-reacted, he had only been acting in self-defence, and of course he had not known that Laius was his father. What makes it far worse for Oedipus, as the penny finally drops, is the realisation that he has also then married his own mother and had four children by her, who are not only his sons and daughters but also his brothers and sisters, and on whom he he has thus brought a lifelong curse. Finally, to seal the Tragedy, he has caused the death of his beloved wife and mother. His offence against the laws of nature and of heaven could not be more complete.[2]

2. It has been observed how simply watching this play, showing a man having to face up to his own guilt, can in some spectators evoke a long-repressed sense of guilt about their own lives. I recall how, during a particularly powerful production of the play at Stratford-on-Avon in the 1950s, a good many people in the audience, as the Tragedy moved towards its climax, could evidently take no more and stole out of the theatre. Although these people had not literally killed their fathers and married their mothers, the more general sense of unease the play aroused in them became too much to bear.

When we do then focus on the specific nature of Oedipus's crime, however, what may strike us is how strangely it echoes that basic psychological pattern we analysed in Chapter Twenty which characterises almost every hero of Tragedy. In story after story we saw how the fundamental problem of the tragic hero is that he is frozen into too close a tie with 'Mother' and is therefore locked in opposition to the values of 'Father'.[3] He cannot become fully a man because he cannot 'see whole'. As we saw in Chapter Sixteen, on the 'unrealised value', the hero's opposition to the 'Dark Father-figure' in stories always reflects his own need to develop into the light version of the father: in other words, to become a fully conscious, whole man. And often he achieves this precisely in the act of slaying the Dark Father-figure, symbolising the final elimination of the 'dark masculine' in himself, to replace it with the balanced figure, outwardly strong, inwardly feminine, which he himself has now become.

Certainly King Laius has been a 'dark father-figure' to Oedipus at their only meeting: an arrogant tyrant, behaving in a one-sidedly masculine way as he sweeps the lowly traveller off the road and beats him over the head. But Oedipus has also remained locked into his own incomplete state. He does not know he has killed his father, any more than he is aware that he has married his mother. Precisely because there is so much he does not know, he cannot yet begin to 'see whole'. And this is why we see him so often acting impulsively, disproportionately and in a way which shows him helplessly at the mercy of his own ego: as when, before the play begins, he has lashed out so wildly on the road, killing Laius and his entire party. This is why, even after he has been a revered king for 15 years, he so easily loses his temper when under pressure: again by the Rule of Three, firstly with Teiresias, then with Creon, then with Jocasta. He himself has been carried away by a terrible hubris. He has become a proud, blind, immature Tyrant – until he is finally brought up against the most almighty nemesis any man could ever have to face.

Only when Oedipus realises that he himself has unwittingly been responsible for all his misfortunes is his armour-plated ego at last utterly crushed. But what do we see then? One of the most striking features of the story is what happens to Oedipus at the end. Although this is a tragedy, he does not die. His wife may have committed suicide. His children may be cursed. He himself may have become an object of revulsion to all mankind. But, unlike any other tragic hero, Oedipus is still alive. The most obvious thing which has happened to him is that he has become blind – just like Teiresias. Oedipus can longer see the outward world

---

3. It was this pattern of course which, from his rather narrow perspective, Freud intuitively seized on to provide the basis for his theory of the 'Oedipus complex': the idea that the fundamental psychological problem afflicting many men lies in their inability to resolve their relationship with their mother, leaving them prey to an unconscious 'death wish' against their father. What he had recognised, correctly but without full understanding, was that, in the pattern of human development, a man who has not fully realised his masculinity remains frozen under the spell of the 'Dark Mother'. He thus remains in some way a 'mother's boy', in conflict with the values of 'Father' which represent the masculinity he is unable to develop. This in turn renders him unable properly to develop his *anima*, his own 'inner feminine'. What Freud failed to recognise was the law of the 'unrealised value', by which the figure of the 'Dark Father' represents a negative version of that which the hero needs to make positive in himself in order to succeed, by achieving the full masculine-feminine balance which will allow him to become a 'Light Father'.

because his sight has turned inwards. He can now see those things which were hidden. He had earlier uttered no more hubristic line in the entire story than his contemptuous dismissal of Teiresias, after losing his temper with the old man for speaking what was in fact nothing less than the truth. 'Living in perpetual night' said Oedipus witheringly, 'you cannot harm me, nor any man else that sees the light'. The Tyrant had thought he himself could see the light, just when he was most blind. But now that he too is living in the same perpetual night, he can see. Now his blinding ego has been removed from the equation, he is at last on the way to mature understanding.

## Oedipus the Wise Old Man

When Sophocles wrote *Oedipus Tyrannos* in his late sixties, he intended the play to stand alone in its own right. But 20 years later, when approaching the end of his long life, he produced its sequel. In its austere intensity and sense of eternity, *Oedipus at Colonus* is a typical 'late work' of a great artist, like the late paintings of Titian and Rembrandt or the final quartets of Beethoven.

We now see Oedipus as an old man. For a long time after the catastrophe, Creon had allowed him to continue living in Thebes. But eventually he agreed to the people's demand that he should be banished, and this was supported by Oedipus's two sons, Eteocles and Polynices. They have grown up into proud, arrogant young men, and eventually become locked in deadly rivalry to succeed to their father's former throne, still occupied as regent by the ageing Creon. His loving daughters, Antigone and Ismene, are the very opposite. While Ismene remains in Thebes to keep a watching brief, Antigone has insisted on accompanying her blind father into exile as his faithful guide and companion; and as the play opens we see them arriving at Colonus, a sacred spot outside the city of Athens, where there is a deep cleft in the living rock, shaded by trees (Colonus was where Sophocles himself had been born).

At once the image of the old man and his loving daughter strikes an archetypal chord, as in the sight of Prospero accompanied by Miranda. The people of Colonus discover them and explain that they cannot stay in this holy place. When they learn the identity of this ragged old man, they are horrified. But after Antigone and Oedipus have implored them to have pity on a poor, helpless outcast, they agree that their king, the great Theseus, should be called to pronounce on Oedipus's fate.

At this point the other daughter Ismene arrives and, after all three have expressed joy at being lovingly reunited, she reports how all is far from well in Thebes. Polynices has been driven out of the city by his brother and is even now gathering an army to return to seize the throne. But, what makes it worse, an oracle has pronounced that the future safety of Thebes depends on Oedipus returning to live, die and be buried just outside the city. The brothers know this. Each will therefore be striving to win control of Oedipus, to demonstrate to the people that he alone possesses the talisman which can guarantee the city's prosperity. Thus does it seem that, in his old age, Oedipus is about to become a pawn to the ruthless egotism of his sons. The 'dark masculine' is again very much in the ascendant. Opposed to it but powerless is the 'light feminine', represented by the daughters. In the middle stands the battered, aged hero Oedipus, How will he measure up?

First Theseus enters, with his royal retinue, showing himself at once to be the very model of a 'Good King'. Noble in bearing, strong in authority, he is also entirely sympathetic to Oedipus's plight:

'I do not forget my own upbringing in exile,
Like yours, and how many times I battled, alone,
With dangers to my life in foreign lands.
I could not turn from any fellow-man,
Coming as you come, or deny him help.
I know that I am man; in the day to come
My portion will be as yours, no more, no less.'

When Oedipus explains his situation, Theseus at first cannot understand why he would not wish to return home to Thebes. But Oedipus makes it clear that the only thing he wants is to be allowed to stay right here, in this holy place, 'white Colonus'. He is fearful that his sons will seek him out to abduct him. The compassionate Theseus allows him to remain and promises him complete protection. Armoured with this sense of security, the time has come for Oedipus to be put to the test.

Again shaped by the Rule of Three, the rest of the play shows Oedipus having to go through three ordeals. The first begins with the unexpected arrival from Thebes of King Creon. He makes a long moving speech, declaring how profoundly sorry he is for all that has happened and how, for the sake both of Thebes and Oedipus himself, he must now implore Oedipus to return home with him. It all sounds persuasive, as if Creon is acting only from the highest motives. But the old man is not fooled for a minute. When Creon has finished, Oedipus immediately explodes at him: 'Devil, there is no specious argument you cannot twist to your cunning purposes!' He can see how Creon has only been putting on an act, to trick him into returning to Thebes for Creon's own dark purposes. Sure enough, no sooner has Oedipus called his bluff than Creon reveals the darkness behind his 'light' *persona* by ordering his followers to seize, first Ismene, then her sister and finally Oedipus himself, with the intention of dragging all three back to Thebes by force. In the nick of time, Theseus and his men intervene, Oedipus and his daughters are reunited and Creon is summarily ordered back from where he had come.

The second test immediately follows when Theseus announces that a mysterious young stranger has arrived, begging for a chance to speak to Oedipus. Oedipus at once guesses correctly it is Polynices, his estranged and exiled son, and at first refuses to speak to him. But when Antigone pleads that he should be heard, Polynices also makes a moving speech, expressing deepest sympathy for his father's plight, which he now understands because he is an exile himself. But, he continues, there can now be a happy ending to both their stories. He has summoned an army of allies, led by seven heroic warriors including himself, with which he plans to take Thebes and to restore Oedipus to his home and former glory. Again Oedipus is not fooled. 'Listen scoundrel' he begins, reminding his son that it was he, Polynices, who took the lead in condemning his father to beggary and exile. If Polynices leads his army against Thebes, Oedipus grimly warns, this can only have one outcome: the two brothers will end up killing each other. He dismisses his son with a curse. Antigone explains more gently to her brother that, if he is wise and really has the interests of Thebes at heart, he should stand down his army and return quietly to his new home. Polynices is dumbstruck at seeing his devious plan fall apart. Once an army has been sent home, he explains, it cannot be gathered together again. Despite his father's prophecy, he must now continue his armed advance on Thebes. He must take leave of his sisters forever.

This leads straight into Oedipus's third, very different ordeal, which is heralded by increasingly loud peals of thunder from the heavens. 'God is sending his voice across the sky to summon me to death' says Oedipus, asking for Theseus to be called urgently. When Theseus arrives, Oedipus takes him aside to explain privately that he has a very important secret to impart, which must not be passed on to anyone except Theseus's successors as rulers of Athens. He is about to die in a mysterious way. Only Theseus will see it, and the place and manner of his passing must never be disclosed. So long as this pact is kept, it will guarantee the safety of Athens forever, just as his removal to Thebes would have guaranteed the safety of that city. 'Now' says Oedipus, 'it is time to go: the hand of God directs me'. Calling his daughters to join them, he turns and 'leads the way with slow but sure steps, as one inspired with inward vision'. We only hear at second hand what happens next, as the four of them descend into the sacred cleft in the ground. First Antigone and Ismene wash their father, and dress him in new clothes. He pronounces on them his solemn blessing and says:

'This is the end of all that was I, and the end of your long task of caring for me. I know how hard it was. Yet it was made lighter by one word: love. I loved you as no one else has ever done.'

As a terrifying voice sounds from heaven, calling out 'Oedipus, Oedipus, it is time', he asks Theseus to protect the girls, before asking his daughters to leave, so he can be left alone with Theseus. Then, in a way which cannot be described but which leaves Theseus looking stunned, Oedipus passes from mortal sight:

'Maybe a guiding spirit from the gods took him, or the earth's foundations gently opened and received him with no pain. Certain it is that he was taken without a pang, without grief or agony: a passing more wonderful than that of any other man.'

So, on this sublime note of reconciliation, ends the story of the once-tragic hero Oedipus; leaving his daughters to grieve but to be assured by Theseus that their father is now received by the gods and at peace. 'This is the end of tears' says the Chorus, 'no more lament. Through all the years, immutable stands this event.'

This remarkable episode may remind us how rare it is for the hero of any story to be shown dying peacefully in old age. There are other instances, such as the passing of the great hero King Arthur which in some ways is not unlike that of Oedipus, and to this we shall return. But what makes the death of Oedipus so particularly remarkable is that it should come at the end of the life of someone who has also been the hero of one of the world's greatest tragedies. The natural ending of Tragedy is that its central figure has become so blinded by egotism, so split off from the Self, that he or she must come to a violent death, because this is the only way in which the wider state of wholeness can be restored. We have seen Oedipus at the time in his life where he was blinded by hubris in this way, and certainly this led to catastrophic consequences. But in the final scenes of that tragedy Oedipus himself did not come to a violent end. What happened was that his ego was crushed and his inward eyes were opened, in very much the way we expect to find in a story shaped by the plot of Rebirth.

This is precisely what we see having taken place by the time of *Oedipus at Colonus*, so that the sight of the deposed king wandering the earth with his daughter becomes, like Lear and Cordelia, an image of the Wise Old Man and the Anima. Certainly by the end of the story the physically frail Oedipus is, like Lear, recovering his old kingly authority, but in a wholly new, spiritual way. We are left in no doubt from the supernatural accompaniments to his death that he is fulfilling some extraordinary higher destiny. And when he is at last 'taken by the gods', in a way so miraculous it cannot even be described, this provides one of the most indelible images in literature of a man finally finding his inmost identity as he merges into and becomes one with the universe.

What we also see in *Oedipus at Colonus*, in a way which contrasts it completely with *Oedipus Tyrannos*, is the central opposition throughout the play between the 'dark masculine' and the 'light feminine'. In the earlier play the 'light feminine' value had been conspicuous by its almost complete absence. No one through most of that story had represented love and selfless feeling. No one sees whole until it is too late. Even the increasingly apprehensive Jocasta is presented only really in terms of her own self-interest, wrapped up with the self-interest of her husband. But in the later play, the whole of the action centres round this dramatic contrast. The 'dark masculine' world of the ego is represented by Creon and Polynices, obsessively caught up in the ruthless power struggle raging over who should control Thebes. The 'light feminine' is represented by Antigone and Ismene, acting like twin *anima*-figures to give such powerful emphasis to the feminine through the play. And in between them stands Oedipus, now totally aligned with the 'light feminine', and supported by Theseus, the wise 'Good King' who represents a perfect balance between masculine strength and feminine compassion.

When Oedipus gives way to anger in the earlier play, as he does in turn with Teiresias, Creon and Jocasta, it is always he, blinded by his egotism, who is in the wrong. When he explodes in fury in the later play, as he does with Creon and Polynices, he is expressing righteous anger at the mask of hypocrisy behind which they are each trying to win over his support for their own egocentric ends. The force of Oedipus's rage is shown to be fully justified by the ruthless way in which Creon then abducts the girls. Polynices reveals his obsessional desire to impose his will on Thebes, which, as the wise Oedipus can now see so clearly, can only end in destroying both his sons.

It is precisely this polarity between the 'dark masculine' and the 'light feminine' which so memorably dominates the third play Sophocles wrote on the story of this family. *Antigone* brings the tragic cycle to its conclusion: even though Sophocles wrote it nearly four decades before he was to come to the wonderful point of resolution which he achieved in the story of Oedipus's death and transfiguration, just before his own death.

## Antigone: The triumph of the light feminine

Ten years before writing *Oedipus Tyrannos* Sophocles had already been inspired to write the tragedy which shows how the rest of Oedipus's family ended up. Although this was the first of the three plays to be written, the seeds of its theme are contained in the closing lines of *Oedipus at Colonus*, where Antigone and Ismene are given Theseus's promise of a safe journey back to Thebes, to see whether there is anything they can do to 'stem the tide of blood that dooms our brothers'.

By the time *Antigone* opens, it is too late. Polynices has led his allies, 'seven against Thebes', to storm the seven gates of the city. Their assault has been beaten off but, in the last encounter of a bloody battle, the two brothers, Polynices and Eteocles, had killed each other, exactly as their father foretold. The grim and aged Creon, now the undisputed ruler of the city, orders that the body of Eteocles, as its brave defender, should be given all honourable rites of burial. That of Polynices, as the traitrous invader, must be left unburied on the plain outside the gates, to be picked at by dogs and carrion birds. Anyone who dares disobey this order shall be put to death.

The play begins with Antigone telling her sister Ismene that she intends to defy Creon's order by giving their brother a proper burial. Ismene protests that this would be madness: 'we are women, it is not for us to fight against men'. Antigone says that then she must be left alone with her madness: 'There is no punishment can rob me of my honourable death.'

We then see King Creon telling his council that his highest duty must now be to keep Thebes united . They have seen too much evidence of what disaster can befall the city when it is divided. This is why his will must now be considered as law, and why his first edict has been to prohibit the burial of the traitor Polynices. He has made himself a complete dictator, and while he is thus exemplifying the 'one-sided masculine' belief that, for the sake of the common good, power and order must come above all else, a sentry enters to report that Polynices' corpse has been covered with earth. Creon explodes with rage, and immediately suspects that someone must have been bribed to do this: 'Money's the curse of man, none greater. That's what wrecks cities.' He cannot believe that anyone would have done this for higher reasons. He tells the sentry that unless he can track down the criminal who has defied his edict, the sentry will pay with his life.

Not long afterwards, the sentry returns triumphant. Having removed the earth from the body, and then kept careful watch to see who might cover it up again, he has caught a woman in the act. It is Antigone. The sentry knows she will die, but he will be rewarded with money and, anyway, if he had not caught the culprit, he himself would have been put to death. Creon asks Antigone whether she was aware of his edict. Of course, she replies, but 'that order did not come from God', and 'I did not think your edicts strong enough to overrule the unwritten, unalterable laws of God and heaven, you being only a man'. She knows she will have to die as a result, and Creon had better just get on with killing her. She insists there could be no shame in honouring her brother by giving him proper burial. Creon insists that, on the contrary, to honour a traitor is to dishonour the brother who died to save his country; and that to give 'equal honour to good and bad' is to insult the good. Antigone replies 'my way is to share my love, not share my hate'. 'Go then' says Creon, 'and share your love among the dead. We'll have no woman's law here, while I live.' It is one of several lines in the play where he makes clear that he stands for the stern values of 'man' against those of 'woman'.

Antigone's cause then finds, in succession, three allies. Firstly, Ismene enters, to be addressed by Creon as 'you crawling viper'. He assumes she must have been a partner to her sister's crime. Ismene pleads guilty. 'Yes, if she will let me say so, I am as much to blame as she is'. Antigone hotly protests: 'you would not lend a hand ... you shall not die with me'. Ismene says 'how can I bear to live, if you must die?' Creon's response is to order that Ismene should be arrested too.

Secondly, a more powerful voice is raised on Antigone's behalf. She is engaged to marry Haemon, Creon's own son. When he enters he begins by saying to his father: 'by your wise decisions my life is ruled, and them I shall I always obey. I cannot value any marriage-tie above your own good guidance.' Creon is delighted. 'Rightly said, your father's will should have your heart's first place.' At length he extols the virtues of obedience. All fathers, he says, pray for sons who are obedient and loyal. 'Do not be fooled, my son, by lust and the wiles of a woman.' The important thing for a man is to be 'the righteous master of his house'.

> 'There is no more deadly peril than disobedience;
> States are devoured by it, homes laid in ruins,
> Armies defeated, victory turned to rout.
> While simple obedience saves the lives of hundreds
> Of honest folk. Therefore I hold to the law
> And never will betray it – least of all for a woman.'

But then Haemon cleverly suggests how valuable it can sometimes be to listen to what other people are saying. Of course no one will have questioned his father's judgement to his face: 'your frown is a sufficient silencer of any word that is not for your ears'. But he thinks Creon should know that, behind his back, 'on every side I hear voices of pity for this poor girl, doomed to the cruellest death', and that 'the secret talk about the town' is that, for an action so honourable as burying her brother she would have better deserved 'a crown of gold'. Creon spits out his contempt for the people of Thebes. 'Since when do I take my orders from the people of Thebes?' 'Isn't that rather a childish thing to say?', his son bravely enquires. 'No, I am king and responsible only to myself' says Creon. 'A one-man state? What sort of state is that?' asks Haemon. 'Why' says Creon, 'does not every state belong to its ruler?' 'You'd be an excellent king' says Haemon, 'on a desert island.'

So incensed does Creon become at his son's questioning of his judgement that he finally loses patience and orders that Antigone should immediately be taken to a desert place, to be walled up in a cave. She should be left with enough food to acquit him of any 'blood-guilt' in her death. We then see her brought out under guard, to take her 'last leave of the light of day, going to my rest, where death shall take me alive across the silent river'.

When she has been led away, Creon is confronted by his third challenger: the old sage Teiresias, who tells him that, although 'all men fall into sin', no one is forever lost who does not set his face against repentance. 'Only a fool is governed by self-will.' Creon reveals how completely he is now driven by his own ego, when he accuses Teiresias of only uttering these pious sentiments to make money. Like any real egotist he cannot imagine that others may be motivated by anything higher than their own self-interest. Eventually Teiresias is goaded into delivering his real message: a prophecy that Creon will very soon have to pay the price for his crimes by losing his own son. He departs, leaving Creon so stunned by this prophecy that he immediately orders that Polynices should be given proper burial and Antigone freed from her prison.

But the wise Teiresias never prophesies in vain. We then hear how, after Creon's men have buried Polynices and gone to the cave, they hear the voice of Haemon already inside. They summon Creon, who when the cave is opened sees Antigone swinging from a rope, where she has hanged herself, and Haemon weeping for his lost love. Haemon spits in his father's face, lunges at him with a sword, then plunges it into himself, before dying with his arms round his dead beloved. As this is being reported on stage, Creon's wife Euryidice hears it and leaves without a word. We then hear that, within the palace, she has followed her son's example by driving a sword into her heart. When Creon receives the news he cries 'There is no man can bear this guilt but I ... I am nothing. Lead me away ... I know not where to turn, where look for help.'

What gives *Antigone* its particular force is the absolute starkness of its contrast between the values represented by Creon and those represented by Antigone. Creon adopts all the masculine language of order, the law, obedience, loyalty, the need to preserve the unity of the state and to punish traitors. But behind it, as his son so subtly teases out, is really nothing but Creon's own remorseless will. He is one of the supreme examples in literature of the Tyrant, the flint-hearted *senex*-figure piously pretending to uphold the good of the community when in fact he has confused this entirely with the demands of his own egotism. In contrast, Antigone represents precisely the value which this one-sided masculinity lacks: she is the 'light feminine' who can feel for the humanity of her dead brother and who can 'see whole' above the petty distinctions of worldly loyalties. Certainly in this respect she is feminine. But she also combines this with steely inner strength and resolve. When she talks of burying her brother, she invariably refers to this as giving him 'honourable' burial. She wishes to observe all due honour and pro-priety. These are masculine values, but made life-giving because they are rooted in a loving heart, which cannot see any distinction between traitor and patriot because both are now equal in death and both are her brothers. So inspiringly does Antigone represent the values of the Self in this play that she draws after her Ismene, Haemon, the people of Thebes, even Creon's own wife: everyone except the ever-more isolated figure of the Tyrant himself. They may all by the end have been sucked down into the black hole of his insatiable egotism. But there is no question which figure and whose values shine out at the end of the story as having been its victor. Because that is what storytelling is about. The story could not seem properly resolved or strike such a deep chord of recognition in the human unconscious if it ended any other way.

## *Hamlet*: The original version

Two thousand years after Sophocles's death, the greatest playwright of the modern world produced his own puzzle play. We find *Hamlet* infinitely more perplexing than any other of Shakespeare's tragedies. Why does its clever, thoughtful, engaging hero have to die? Why does he get reduced to such a jelly of indecision over whether he should revenge his murdered father? Why do so many other people in the story get caught up in the resulting mess and also have to die?

There is no better starting point for unravelling the mystery of *Hamlet* than to look at the mediaeval legend from which Shakespeare derived his story. The first thing which may strike us about the plot of *Amleth*, included by the thirteenth-century historian Saxo Grammaticus in his *Gesta Danorum*, a collection of old Danish tales, is how it is a straightforward Overcoming the Monster story, about a hero who overcomes a 'Dark Father-figure' to become king.

Horwendil, a mighty warrior who has defeated and slain the king of Norway in a great battle, is made king of Jutland. He marries the Princess Gerutha (Shakespeare's Gertrude), by whom he has a son, Amleth (Hamlet). But he has a much less brave but crafty brother Feng (Claudius) who, jealous of his brother's renown, treacherously murders him and marries his widow. Prince Amleth sees clearly that Feng, his uncle, now stepfather, is unremittingly evil and fears for his own safety. He protects himself by pretending to be harmlessly mad (the word 'amleth' in old Danish means 'insane'). After three demonstrations of his feigned insanity, one of Feng's courtiers (the Polonius-figure) sets up a trap for Amleth, to test whether he is genuinely mad or not. This involves the old courtier hiding under a pile of straw, to eavesdrop on a private interview between Amleth and his mother. The idea is that, with his mother, whom he loves and trusts, Amleth will drop his guard and show his true character. But when he enters the room, Amleth at once smells a rat, He crows like a cock, jumps on the straw and plunges his sword into something hard he feels beneath it. He pulls out the body of the eavesdropping courtier, cuts it into pieces and throws them into a sewer, to be eaten by pigs. Amleth then returns to his mother and berates her at length for being the 'harlot' who had taken her husband's murderer in 'vile wedlock'.

When Feng discovers what has happened to his courtier, he fears what Amleth may do next and lays an elaborate plot to have him killed. He sends him on an embassy to the King of Britain, accompanied by two courtiers (Shakespeare's Rosencrantz and Guildenstern), carrying a message which asks the king to put the bearer of the message to death. Amleth discovers this and changes the wording, requesting the king to hang the two bearers of the message and to give he who is accompanying them the hand of a princess in marriage.

The British king is deeply impressed when Amleth gives three demonstrations of his second-sight, and does exactly as the message requests. Amleth then returns to Jutland, invites all Feng's noble followers to a highly alcoholic feast and, when they are lying in drunken heaps, burns down the hall with them inside. He is now free to seek out his stepfather in the royal bedchamber and slay him. Amleth then disguises himself to watch for the reaction of the people. When he sees they are all rejoicing that the Tyrant is dead, he throws off his disguise, explains why he had to pretend to be mad to avoid being murdered himself and tells the people that he has slain the Tyrant for their sake. As with Oedipus, the people then acclaim Amleth king, as the hero who has overcome the 'monster' and set them free.

Such is the story on which Shakespeare bases his play, although the original version continues with a new episode in which Amleth marries the Queen of Scotland, defeats the British in a great battle and is finally slain himself in yet another battle, to be buried with honour in Jutland. But the part of the story adapted by Shakespeare, culminating in the hero killing his wicked uncle and succeeding to his father's throne, is thus an archetypal tale of a young hero whose 'light Father' is replaced by a 'dark Father', whom he eventually slays to become king. The fascinating question is why Shakespeare should so dramatically have altered this story (despite retaining many of its details) that he turns it into one totally different. Instead of showing us a young man maturing to the point where he can arrive at the familiar happy ending, the story ends with its hero being destroyed. Why should Shakespeare have wanted to use so much of the original story, only in order to turn it on its head?

### *Hamlet*: The personal drama

The most crucial respect in which Shakespeare's version differs from the original, in that it transforms the character of everything which follows, is how he shows Hamlet conceiving the idea that he must destroy his stepfather. In the original there is never any question that Amleth is justified in killing his stepfather. We have seen his father in life, as a heroic warrior-king and therefore a 'light' figure. There is no doubt he is then treacherously murdered by his weak and crafty brother, who is obviously 'dark', and that Feng may have deadly designs on Amleth too, as a potential rival to the throne. This is why Amleth pretends to be mad, to protect himself, and has every reason for wanting to kill Feng, to preserve his own life.

Shakespeare deliberately shrouds all this in a mysterious fog, where none of these points is anything like so clearly defined. We do not see the old king in life, so we have no direct evidence as to whether he was 'light' or 'dark'. It is not even known that he had been murdered, since it was generally believed that he had died by accident, bitten by a snake. The play opens, at night, with the sentries talking in hushed tones on the battlements about having twice seen his ghost, and all the language used about this apparition makes it seem anything but a figure of light. When Horatio joins the watch, the Ghost makes a third appearance, looking grim and warlike, and disappears when a cock crow heralds the approach of daylight. Clearly this is a creature of darkness; and Horatio notes how, as light dawns, it had 'started like a guilty thing' and scuttled away. Marcellus recalls the old folk belief that, in the nights around Christmas, no ghosts are seen, because the time is 'so hallowed and so gracious' that 'no spirit dare stir abroad'.

The first time we see the play's hero is the following day. Prince Hamlet has been plunged into suicidal depression by the death of his father and his mother's over-hasty remarriage. 'O God, God' he muses:

> 'How weary, stale, flat and unprofitable
> Seem to me all the uses of this world!
> Fie on't, ah, fie, 'tis an unweeded garden
> That grows to seed. Things rank and gross in nature
> Possess it utterly.'

When his friend Horatio breaks in on this morbid soliloquising to tell him about the spectral vision of his father, Hamlet, in his disordered state, cannot wait for the moment when darkness returns and he too may see this creature of the night.

Hamlet's immediate response on seeing the Ghost suggests even more strongly that it is a personification of the dark power. 'Angels and ministers of grace defend us' he cries out, before asking the ghost whether it is a 'spirit of health or goblin damned'. Horatio is fearful that the Ghost may deprive Hamlet of 'the sovereignty of reason' and draw him into madness. Everything is calculated to make us see the Ghost as a deadly presence which bodes nothing but ill for Hamlet, and this is rein-forced when it explains how it has come from a place where it is being fearfully pun-ished for its 'foul crimes'. Although the Ghost speaks of this realm of everlasting fire as if it were purgatory, it sounds more like hell. Then this infernal apparition comes out with its real message. Hamlet must not believe that his father died because he was bitten by a snake. He was treacherously and horribly poisoned by his brother, and it is now Hamlet's duty to 'revenge his foul and most unnatural murder'.

What is so striking is how Shakespeare has taken the original version, based on the familiar symbolism of a son having to kill a 'dark Father' in order to become a 'light Father', and put it so deliberately into the mould of Tragedy. How can it be right for Hamlet to follow the instructions of this messenger from hell? The very course so many heroes need to take in order to reach the happy ending is now presented as the first fatal step on a tragic downward spiral. And once Shakespeare has launched Hamlet on this path, we see how the rest of the play follows the archetypal five-stage tragic pattern,

The first act has been the Anticipation Stage. The Ghost has provided the Focus, and Shakespeare has presented him as a Tempter, egging Hamlet on to do some-thing which is thoroughly dark. The play's second act is the Dream Stage, in which Hamlet pretends to have parted company with reality, as a cover for the deadly course on which he is now set. The height of this comes when he arranges to put on the play which will confirm Claudius's guilt. Even now Hamlet is not certain the Ghost was telling the truth. But *The Mousetrap* is the device in which he will 'catch the conscience of the king'.

As evidence for what is really now happening to Hamlet, we may recall how consistently in Tragedy, as the hero becomes increasingly possessed by darkness, his downward course is symbolised by the deaths of certain key figures who represent aspects of the hero himself. These are the Innocent Young Girl, the Good Old Man and the Light Alter-Ego. The first person to suffer from Hamlet's drift into his dark obsession is the Innocent Young Girl, the 'fair Ophelia', to whom he has lately made 'many tenders' of his affection. Ophelia represents Hamlet's *anima*, his heart and soul. Nothing more chillingly reveals the 'dark inversion' now taking him over than the way he turns so heartlessly against her, mocking her love and innocence with his coarse, stinging jibes.

The 'good old man' (as Claudius explicitly calls him) is Polonius, and he too Hamlet now savagely ridicules. But we are now moving into the Frustration Stage, where what has up to now been no more than cruel mockery and play-acting is about to turn irretrievably nasty. Hamlet's mood of frustration is signalled by the 'to be or not to be' speech, in which he shows his state of extreme inner turmoil. Faced with the kind of outrage he has been subjected to, should he just weakly accept it with Christian forebearance, or should he act resolutely, like a man, and 'take arms' to end it? So intolerable is the choice that it might seem the only way out is to commit suicide. But who knows what hellish punishments this might lead to in an after-life?

> 'Thus conscience does make cowards of us all,
> And thus the native hue of resolution
> Is sicklied o'er with the pale cast of thought'

Reduced to impotence at not knowing which way to turn, Hamlet is temporarily saved from this tortured dithering by the fact that he has already set his 'mousetrap'. His trick with the play succeeds beyond his wildest dreams. As Claudius, sitting in the darkness, sees his hideous secret exposed, he can take no more, leaping up from his chair to shout for light. This reinvigorates Hamlet, who has again just treated Ophelia with such callous contempt; and having been invited by his anguished mother to talk privately about the offence he has given his stepfather, he is now summoning up all his resolve to commit the ultimate act of darkness:

> 'Tis now the very witching time of night,
> When churchyards yawn, and hell itself breathes out,
> Contagion to this world. Now could I drink hot blood
> And do such bitter business as the day
> Would quake to look on.'

What tragic hero in Shakespeare gives more explicit voice to the darkness that has taken over his soul? Yet when Hamlet has the chance to kill Claudius at prayer, he cannot bring himself to do it. He tells himself that this is because, if he kills his stepfather when he is on his knees, Claudius might avoid the ultimate punishment in hell he deserves. However, this seems like rationalisation. Is not the truth that, given the perfect opportunity to do what his darker self is urging, Hamlet is too weak, not manly enough to do it? It is a wonderfully ambiguous moment, exposing just what a 'divided self' Hamlet has become. At this same moment we also see that, for all his show of devotion, Claudius himself knows it is totally empty: 'my words fly up, my thoughts remain below'; and furthermore he has already set in train with Rosencrantz and Guildenstern the plot whereby they will escort Hamlet to England to be murdered. Locked on a collision course, he and Hamlet are now almost equally black in their purposes, except that Hamlet is not man enough to have the full courage of his own dark convictions.

The general mood of frustration deepens when Hamlet, on a sudden violent impulse, stabs the eavesdropping Polonius hidden behind the arras. His only response is frustration at finding his victim is not Claudius, which would have solved his problem. Even when he discovers he has, by mistake, killed the 'good old man', he shows again just how genuinely dark he has become by significantly showing not a flicker of remorse. Instead he lets fly at his mother for her shameless treachery and infidelity (this is where the Freudians, not without justification, see Hamlet reaching the 'Oedipal' impasse, where a weak, unmanly son is fixated on his mother and appalled that she should 'betray' him by her love for the 'father'). All this is taken from the original Amleth story, but given a spin entirely Shakespeare's own. The Ghost, as Tempter, makes one more effort to egg Hamlet on into killing his stepfather; and then, in the most heartlessly comic lines of the play, Hamlet tells Claudius that his 'good old man' is 'at supper': 'not where he eats but where he is eaten. A certain politic convocation of worms are e'en at him' (this closely echoes Amleth feeding the courtier's body into a sewer to be eaten by pigs).

The tragedy is now firmly into its Nightmare Stage, during most of which we do not even see the hero, because he is in England. The image which most chillingly conveys this sense of nightmare, simultaneously betraying what is really going on in Hamlet's inner kingdom, is the heart-rending spectacle of the deranged Ophelia, driven mad by her father's casual murder at the hands of the man she had once loved and hoped to marry. She then drowns as she sings, her flower-strewn body carried away on the stream. Hamlet has lost his soul. Two of the three aspects of his psyche are dead. The only one left is his 'Alter-Ego'.

Laertes is now Hamlet's mirror. Both are young men returned from studying abroad. Both are sons whose fathers have been murdered. Both have lost the feminine other half they loved: except that only one of them has been guilty of her death. And Shakespeare highlights the way in which Laertes has now become Hamlet's 'light rival' in a strange little episode, the significance of which can easily be overlooked. Between Ophelia's 'mad scene' and the news of her death, Claudius and Gertrude are left alone when a messenger bursts in to announce that something akin to a revolution has broken out. Laertes is outside, at the head of an angry mob proclaiming him as king: 'Laertes shall be king'. Laertes himself then bursts in, with some of his followers, to address Claudius as 'O thou vile King'.

What makes this particularly significant is that, in the original story, there is no Laertes-figure. The character whom the people acclaim as king is Amleth himself, after he has slain his stepfather. Shakespeare has thus deliberately split the hero into two, with Laertes as Hamlet's 'light alter ego'. Only now does Claudius tempt

Laertes into his own web of darkness, by offering him the chance to avenge his own father, and this makes the equivalence between Hamlet and Laertes complete.

As Act Five begins, with Hamlet returned from England, the two rivals fight in Ophelia's open grave, grimly foreshadowing how the drama is about to end. Having overcome his conscience and yet realised that he is not going to achieve his purpose, Hamlet is now resigned to his fate. Never has he been more wittily mocking than in the scene where he sends up the hapless Osric, the courtier sent by Claudius to convey the challenge to the fencing match which is to be his downfall. But by now Hamlet and Laertes, who has been in training with 'Lamord' ('La mort'), the finest fencing teacher in Europe, have been wholly transformed into each other's 'dark Alter-Ego'. So far is the distorting power of darkness now in the ascendant, so unable is anyone now to 'see whole', that everything goes as wrong as it possibly could. First Hamlet and Laertes swap their foils, so that both are fatally wounded by the poison intended only for Hamlet. Then Gertrude drinks the poison intended for Hamlet and dies, prompting Hamlet at last to kill his treacherous stepfather. Laertes dies, already repenting of his part in this villainy (as soon as Claudius dies, he begins to move back towards the light). Finally Hamlet follows. The son-hero Prince has killed his 'Dark Father'. But in working towards this he has killed off all those aspects of himself which, if he could have remained at one with them, might have enabled him, had he been 'put on' as king, to have 'proved most royal'.

What we are thus left with is a spectacle unique in storytelling. We have seen a hero setting out to do something which, for so many other heroes, is a natural precondition to their arriving at a happy, light ending. But here this involves him in becoming so possessed by the state of darkness that it destroys him. The intelligent, funny, tortured Hamlet is portrayed so engagingly that we may overlook just how far Shakespeare has shown him turning into a ruthless monster; so that half way through the story, in the scene where Claudius is on his knees, we have the equally rare spectacle of two protagonists, Claudius and Hamlet, who in reality have become as dark as each other: except that Hamlet is not even manly enough to carry out his dark purposes, except when acting on impulse. And to understand just why Shakespeare has wanted to place his characters in this extraordinary situation we must step back from the personal drama of the play, to see how he intends this to be only the central focus for a much more general picture of human nature.

### *Hamlet*: The wider picture

A common misunderstanding about *Hamlet* is reflected in that familiar cliché that something is like 'playing Hamlet without the Prince of Denmark', implying that, without Hamlet, there would be nothing left of the play. It may be the longest stage part in English literature. But not the least fascinating aspect of this story is the extent to which it is not just about the personal problems of its central figure.

Shakespeare is continually at pains to emphasise that his real preoccupation in this play goes much wider than just what is going on in the mind of one individual. As we learn soon after the start of the story, it is not just in Hamlet's mind that 'the time is out of joint'. There is 'something rotten in the state of Denmark' itself. The whole kingdom is sick. Even Elsinore stands for much more than just one little kingdom on the edge of Europe. It has infinitely less to do with the real, geographical Denmark than, say, Julius Caesar's Rome has to with the real Rome, or the 'history plays' with a real England.

Elsinore just happens to be the place on which the spotlight is shining. But we are made continually aware of the rest of the world stretching away into the darkness in all directions. Norway to the north, Paris and Wittenburg to the south, England to the west, Poland to the east: all play their part in the overall story, and in no other of Shakespeare's plays are we made so continually aware of a fever of activity going on off-stage. Right at the start we learn (in a speech inserted by Shakespeare at the last minute, and obviously intended further to underline some general point about the play as a whole) that a major 'crisis' has arisen between Denmark and Norway, and that the people of Denmark are preparing for war. So frenziedly is the country arming that 'the night is made joint labourer with the day', 'Sunday is so no longer divided from the week'. Throughout the play, from the first act to the last, the warlike tramp of armies is continually heard off stage. The little court of Elsinore is thus simply a brightly-lit microcosm, reflecting the general state of the world.

It is against this vast, dark, restless background that Shakespeare focuses on just one human crisis in particular: on the catastrophic events we see unfolding in Elsinore. And if there is one thing above all which marks out the unhappy little group of people we see thrown together in the Danish court it is the way they are all plotting against and spying on each other.

There is scarcely any play of Shakespeare's in which someone does not in some way attempt to trick or deceive someone else, whether it be Iago tricking Othello with the handkerchief or all those heroines in the comedies who appear in male disguise. But no play contains anything like so many plots and stratagems as *Hamlet*: at least nine in all. Scarcely has Polonius seen off Laertes to Paris than he is sending Reynaldo after him to spy on his moral conduct. When Hamlet's old friends Rosencrantz and Guildenstern turn up, they are immediately recruited by Claudius to spy on Hamlet. When the troupe of actors arrives, Hamlet himself immediately sets up the evening's entertainment as his trick to 'catch the conscience of the king'. Polonius and Claudius set Ophelia to waylay Hamlet as he is walking in the palace, then settle behind a pillar to spy on them. Polonius eavesdrops behind the arras, to spy on Hamlet and the Queen. Claudius packs off Hamlet to England with Rosencrantz and Guildenstern, supplied with letters to ensure that Hamlet will be murdered when they get there. Claudius and Laertes finally plot to trap Hamlet with the poisoned foils. While over all this, forming the outlines of the tragedy itself, hang the two greatest plots of all: Claudius's original plot to poison his brother in order to usurp the throne; and Hamlet's own, conceived at the prompting of the Ghost, to murder Claudius.

The significant point, of course, is not just that every one of these schemes is egocentrically motivated but that almost all of them end up producing a result exactly opposite to that intended. As the tragedy darkens, their outcomes become more and more fatal to the plotters themselves. The eavesdropping Polonius is stabbed to death. When Rosencrantz and Guildenstern reach England, thanks to Hamlet's deft footwork, it is they who are executed. It is Gertrude, not Hamlet, who drinks the poisoned cup. Laertes dies poisoned by his own sword. Everything goes exactly as wrong as it could, until finally Claudius and Hamlet are themselves destroyed by the chain of events their own plotting has set in motion. And how keen Shakespeare is to underline this for us as a central key to what the play is really about. It is no accident that we get from Hamlet that most familiar phrase about the way in which, when people set out to deceive others, their devious plans have a habit of rebounding on them: 'the enginer hoist with his own petard'. Again and again, right up to the final curtain, we hear this point being hammered home: how Laertes admits he has been caught 'as a woodock to mine own springe', how 'purposes mistook fall on their inventors' heads', how 'our wills and fates so contrary run, that our devices still are overthrown'.

What Shakespeare is showing us, more searchingly than in any other of his plays, is a human world in which everyone is caught up in the fog of self-deceiving egotism. Everyone is trying to trick someone else. Everyone is in some way pretending to be something other than what they really are. Everyone is hiding from the world behind a false mask, not least Hamlet himself in pretending he is mad. Almost no one in the play is really being true to his or her inmost self. As Polonius himself puts it, 'to thine own self be true', and 'thou cans't not then be false to any man'. If this could only be taken literally, and not just as one of a string of sententious clichés uttered by a pompous old fool, it embodies precisely the truth no one in *Hamlet* is capable of living up to. And what Shakespeare is really telling us is that this is not just a problem affecting one little group of people in Elsinore. It is a problem which is well-nigh universal. The dark side of human nature ordains that people may conceal their egotism behind such masks all their lives, until they end up, like Yorick, as no more than a skull and bones.

What Shakespeare is concerned with here is the infinite capacity of human beings to put on a false front to the world, the seemingly sociable persona behind which they conceal their unremitting egotism. And no passage in the play is more telling in this respect than the churchyard scene, where Hamlet swaps badinage with the gravedigger at the start of the final act. Surrounded with the grisly evidence of how every human being ends up, Hamlet singles out examples of the types of people who most obviously rely on the self-deceiving vanity of the persona. One skull, he suggests, may be that of a politician, someone so false and self-seeking that he 'would circumvent God'. Another could be that of a lawyer. Where now is all that high-flown legal jargon with which he self-importantly protected himself from the human reality of the world? Where now is the courtier, with all his empty flatteries ('Good morrow, sweet lord. How dost thou, sweet lord?')? He is simply the property of 'Lady Worm'. As for all those women who put on a deceiving front to the world with their masks of cosmetics, let them 'paint an inch thick', they will still end up as stinking dust. Even the greatest ones of the earth, in all their power and pomp, Alexander or 'imperious Caesar'; where are they now, but 'dead and turned to clay'.

Like Macbeth in the 'tomorrow and tomorrow' soliloquy at exactly the same stage of his own tragedy, Hamlet now sees the human world as governed by nothing higher than egotism and futile pretence. We are no more than poor ego-driven fools: vain actors strutting and fretting our brief time on the stage of life before we come to 'dusty death'. And this is merely how individuals lead their lives. Behind this picture of human society made up of countless deceiving, scheming little egos, all competing with each other for approval and selfish advantage, lies the wider stage of the world where the collective egos of whole nations compete in the same futile struggle.

Another thread running through *Hamlet* is the wasting of spirit and energy which goes into the rivalry of nations as they battle for empty supremacy over each other, At the start of the play we hear how Denmark is preparing for war against Norway. But we subsequently hear that the two countries have mended this supposedly deadly quarrel, on the payment of a large sum of money, to become allies; and that the Norwegian army under Fortinbras ('strong in arms') is now marching instead against distant Poland: simply to fight over 'a little patch of ground that hath in it no profit but the name'. As Fortinbras's soldiers tramp through Denmark on their way to this foreign war, no one sees more clearly than Hamlet the absurdity of how human beings are prepared 'to find quarrel in a straw when honour's at the stake'. He foresees with horror how these 'twenty thousand men' may be doomed, for a 'mere fantasy and trick of fame' to 'go to their graves like beds'.

Yet no sooner has he expressed his scorn for such self-deceiving madness than he goes on to resolve that, from this moment on, his own thoughts must be similarly 'bloody, or be nothing worth'. We then cut immediately to the sight of Ophelia, now torn apart by that madness to which Hamlet himself has driven her, yet in her derangement speaking limpid truth. How can one tell someone who truly loves, she asks. By his 'cockle hat and staff', the outward signs of a holy pilgrim: one who has surrendered the deceits and self-deceits of the ego for a higher, self-transcending cause. Ophelia has only been driven mad because the world around her is mad. She alone has remained in touch with the world of the Self, where she alone can still see those values of heart and soul which everyone around her has lost.

Yet the fact remains that Shakespeare was inspired to create this unutterably bleak picture of the dark side of human nature by that original legend which simply describes a young man finding his manhood and destiny in the most time-honoured, archetypal fashion, by winning the hand of the Princess and succeeding his father as king. Why has he wanted to make such a shattering break with the archetypal mould?

No idea is more central to storytelling, as we have seen, than that of one generation succeeding to another, and of the need for the hero to reach true maturity so that this can be achieved in the right way. Yet the one thing that is certain about Hamlet is that he cannot make this transition. He is doomed never to grow up. As we see him trapped in his state of tortured irresolution, he cannot relate properly either to his inner feminine or to his masculinity. Like so many other tragic heroes, he thus remains in thrall to his 'unrealised value', trapped in a state of impotent rebellion against the 'Father' of which he cannot turn himself into the light version. What Shakespeare has done is put this archetypal pattern to the test on a still deeper archetypal level, by changing the basis on which it is presented in a particularly significant way.

When the hero of *Jack and the Beanstalk* slays the giant who has murdered his father and stolen his inheritance, we do not for a moment question his right to do so, because the giant is portrayed as nothing but a monstrous personification of human egotism. The giant is unmistakably dark, the hero is light, When Perseus slays his stepfather Polydectes, by showing him the head of the Medusa, this seems wholly justifiable, because Polydectes is a cruel, heartless tyrant. It is the same when Aladdin slays his 'stepfather' and 'uncle' the Sorcerer. It is the same when Nicholas Nickleby's wicked Uncle Ralph, his dead father's brother who has stolen his inheritance, is finally caught out and hangs himself. It is the same when all the countless other dispossessed sons who teem through storytelling manage to overcome the monstrous 'Dark Father' to claim their birthright. But, quite deliberately, Shakespeare varies this pattern. The inspiration for Hamlet's decision to kill his usurping stepfather comes only from the Ghost, who is unrelievedly dark. The result of obeying that temptation is that Hamlet himself becomes overwhelmed by the darkness in his own nature. Clearly the course the Ghost is urging on Hamlet is one he should not follow. So what is Shakespeare trying to tell us?

The clue lies in the nature of what the ghost is urging Hamlet to do. 'Old Hamlet' is not lovingly asking his son to do something which might directly further 'young Hamlet's' own welfare. His sole concern is vengeance for his own death. Having been guilty in life of the 'foul crimes' for which he is now being punished, he is still locked entirely into the world of his own ego and is now instructing his son to commit an equally heartless crime in turn. And what Shakespeare gradually develops from this original core is a picture of a human world in which almost everyone is similarly trapped by the ego, as no one is more acutely aware than Hamlet himself. 'We are arrant knaves all,' he says to Ophelia, 'believe none of us.' 'Use every man after his deserts, and who should 'scape whipping?' Every human being, he implies, is as much in a state of sin as everyone else. 'What news?' Hamlet asks Rosencrantz. 'None, my lord, but that the world's grown honest.' 'Then is doomsday near' replies Hamlet, 'but your news is not true'. Only two figures in the story are not tainted with this relentless, universal curse of egotism. One is the 'faithful Horatio', whose role is simply to be Hamlet's loyal friend. The other, of course, is Ophelia, representing the shining, selfless 'light feminine', which is why she becomes shut out from a world where this is simply not understood, and why Hamlet tells her to retire to a nunnery, since if she does not she will only become a breeder of yet more sinners.

In this respect Ophelia plays much the same role as the heroine in *Antigone*, where the city of Thebes under the Tyrant Creon is, like Elsinore, a microcosm of a world oppressed by the harsh, loveless masculine value, with its talk of honour and vengeance. Thebes too has resounded to the tramp of armed men, with Eteocles and Polynices locked in the egocentric rivalry which was to bring both to their deaths, leaving Antigone as isolated as Ophelia in representing the life-giving feminine value which everyone else lacks (even though Antigone is 'active' and Ophelia 'passive'). *Antigone*, like *Hamlet*, concludes on a stage strewn with corpses, brought about by heartless, vengeance-obsessed, 'eye for an eye' masculine morality. Appropriately Hamlet ends with the sound of military drum beats, as Fortinbras arrives to see the 'dismal sight' of the court of Elsinore reminding him of a battle-field. He orders that Hamlet should be honoured with 'the soldier's music and the rite of war', and the play closes on the line 'Go, bid the soldiers shoot', followed by the noise of cannon-fire. 'Young Hamlet' may have failed to succeed 'Old Hamlet'. But now the warlike 'young Fortinbras', who had succeeded his uncle 'Old Fortinbras', has, with the approval of Hamlet's dying breath, succeeded also to the throne of Denmark. Despite this fearsome illustration of what the loveless pursuit of the one-sided masculine value must in the end lead to, no lesson has been learned. To the sounds of war and death, the vicious circle of human egotism seems destined to carry on, generation succeeding generation, to the crack of doom.

### 'What a piece of work is a man'

It is precisely the seeming ambiguity of *Oedipus Tyrannos* and *Hamlet* which puts them in a dimension of their own; for they tease out the central riddle at the heart of human existence with a depth and subtlety unmatched by any other stories in world literature.

Oedipus is the man who seems to have everything. He is a wise, respected king, surrounded with a loving wife and children. Yet suddenly a crisis arises in his kingdom and he discovers that he really knows nothing about himself at all, and that unwittingly he has become the worst sinner in the world. Hamlet is the prince who seems to have everything: intelligence, wit, unusual gifts, a girl who loves him and whom he loves; everything necessary for him to succeed to manhood and kingship. Yet suddenly a crisis arises in the kingdom, and in the very act of achieving that goal he finds he has irretrievably become a sinner doomed to die.

Was this all that Sophocles and Shakespeare could see in human nature? That there is ultimately nothing higher in human life than to enjoy the empty, self-deceiving exercise of egotism, followed by death? Hamlet himself may have suggested so, in that wonderful, chilling passage where he exclaims:

> 'What a piece of work is a man, how noble in reason, how infinite in faculties, in form and moving how express and admirable, in action how like an angel, in apprehension how like a god; the beauty of the world, the paragon of animals.'

Yet what in the end does all this amount to, he concludes, but a worthless 'quintessence of dust'?

Similarly in *Antigone*, Sophocles's Chorus exclaims how the greatest wonder on earth is man:

> 'master of ageless Earth ... lord of all things living ... the use of language, the wind-swift motion of brain he learnt; found out the ways of living together in cities ... there is nothing beyond his power. His subtlety meeteth all chance, all danger conquereth, for every ill he found its remedy.'

Yet the one thing for which he has no remedy is death. And of all the subtleties of his nature, none is more wondrous, notes the Chorus, than how it can draw him 'either to good or evil ways'.

As it happens, both Sophocles and Shakespeare were eventually able to show us this problem being ultimately resolved. In Sophocles's valedictory play, *Oedipus at Colonus*, we see how his hero, having had his ego utterly crushed, first developed that inner vision which allowed him to see the world straight and whole, and is eventually able to be received back into a state of one-ness with the universe, like no other mortal man,

For the same sense of final resolution in Shakespeare we also have to wait for his last play, *The Tempest*. In crucial respects Prospero is like a light version of the Ghost in *Hamlet*. Like 'Old Hamlet', he has been treacherously dispossessed from his kingdom by a dark, usurping brother. But instead of then turning dark himself, to seek bloody vengeance, he has been through a long process of inner growth and transformation, until he is finally ready to confront his shadow, win him to repentance for his crime and then to forgive him. Thus can the play end on a trumphant note of love and reconciliation, symbolised above all by the union of the young Prince Ferdinand and his Miranda: the very union Prince Hamlet and his Ophelia were so grievously unable to achieve. All Prospero's striving is at an end. The last vestige of his egotism is gone. He has redeemed his inner kingdom, and become whole. Like the wise old Oedipus, he has become one with the universe.

The moment has come at last to step outside this self-contained world of story-telling, and to see how the ways in which we tell stories relate to what we call 'real life'.

# PART FOUR

## *Why We Tell Stories*

'The largest crowds are drawn by the storytellers. It is around them that the people throng most densely and stay longest ... their words come from further off and hang longer in the air than those of ordinary people.'

Elias Canetti, *The Voices of Marrakesh*

# CHAPTER THIRTY-ONE

# Telling Us Who We Are
## Ego versus Instinct

'The difference between men and animals is that men tell stories.'

Source untraced

At the beginning of this book I quoted that haunting little poem by Robert Frost

'We dance around in a ring and suppose,
But the Secret sits in the middle and knows.'

Without in any way wishing to detract from the genius of our great storytellers, if there is one thing we have seen emerging from the past few hundred pages it is the extent to which the stories told by even the greatest of them are not their own. Their skill lies in the power with which they manage to find new outward clothing in which to dress up a theme which is already latent, not only in their own minds but in those of their audience. What we have seen in the first three sections of the book is how stories take shape in the human imagination round certain archetypal patterns and images which are the common property of mankind. Furthermore, at the very deepest level, the essence of the message they are putting across is always the same.

What this points to is something the implications of which are truly awesome. This is the extent to which stories emerge from some place in the human mind which functions autonomously, independent of any storyteller's conscious control. This is not so startling an idea as it might seem, because we are all in a sense familiar with it in the way in which we experience dreams. By definition, the sequences of imagery which make up our dreams are shaped and presented to our conscious awareness (even though we are asleep) by another part of the brain of which we are wholly unconscious. It is true that dreams are more obviously than stories the products of the dreamer's own personal unconscious (although they can often take on a more universal, archetypal dimension); and to compose a story requires a collaboration between the conscious and unconscious levels of the storyteller's mind which cannot apply when we dream. But the real key to understanding stories lies in seeing how they are ultimately rooted in a level of the unconscious which is collective to all humanity; and how the 'Secret' which 'sits in the middle', giving them their underlying shape and purpose, is always trying to put over the same fundamental point.

As we come to this final part of the book we can at last confront what are perhaps the most interesting questions of all. Why has the evolutionary process developed in us this ability and need to imagine stories? What is its purpose? How does the imaginary world conjured up by storytelling relate to what we call 'real life'?

An appropriate starting point from which to answer these questions lies in two specialised types of story we now look at for the first time.

## In the beginning

One of the deepest human needs met by our faculty for imagining stories is our desire for an explanatory and descriptive picture of how the world began and how we came to be in it. There is no culture in the world which does not possess at least one great story to account for how the world came into being, and all such stories have certain things in common. But, broadly speaking, they subdivide into three main categories.

The simplest version is that derived from Jewish mythology and set out at the beginning of the book of *Genesis*. This is untypical because it begins with a conscious power, 'God', who masterminds the whole process of creation in a highly systematic and orderly fashion. He is there before everything else, himself alone. He then creates a duality, heaven and earth. Covered in darkness, the earth is 'without form and void'. The 'Spirit of God' then 'moves upon the face of the waters' and calls Light into being (preceding any source of physical light, such as the sun). This highly significant event (never more dramatically portrayed than by the C Major explosion of sound at the start of Haydn's *Creation*) creates a second duality, between light and dark. God then creates further dualities, between the earth and the sky, land and sea. Finally he proceeds to the orderly creation of the sun, the moon and the stars, followed by all the specific types of living creature which inhabit the earth: plants, fish, reptiles, mammals, birds, culminating in man. Each new species when it is created appears fully-formed. The entire creation is described as having been brought about in six days, and the whole thing has been unrolled as neatly as checking off a shopping list.

Only because in Western culture we are so familiar with this version are we not more generally aware just how untypical it is. The second version, found in almost every other Creation myth in the world, gives the impression of a process infinitely more laborious, mysterious and long drawn-out. There may be some Great Spirit or cosmic mind behind it all, and almost all the different versions begin with an image of dark and formless chaos. But what marks off all these other cosmogonic or Creation myths from the Judaeo-Christian version, is that the emergence of our recognisable world takes place by what we would call an 'evolutionary' process, as each new component develops out of what came before. In a typical myth of the south Pacific, for instance, found among the Ngaitahu people of New Zealand, the original void, without light, heat, sound, form or movement, is 'Po'. We then hear how:

> 'Po begat Light, who begat Daylight, who begat enduring Light, who begat Without-possession, who begat Unpleasant, who begat Wobbly, who begat No-Parents, who begat Damp, who married Huge Light and begat Raki, the Sky.'[1]

1. *Larousse Encyclopaedia of Mythology* (London, 1959), p. 466.

Another variation on this type of myth includes those which feature the emergence of a male and a female being, the 'world parents'. In the Norse version creation begins with the vast, cloudy realm of Niflheim. Here in darkness immense primordial beings eventually heave into view: first a male giant Ymir, who emerges from ice, then a female being, Audumla, the 'world cow'. It is eventually from them that all other beings emerge, including gods, humans and animals.

Perhaps the most widespread version of this type of story, however, found in different cultures all over the world, is that which begins with the image of a single created object set in the primeval void. This 'World Egg' contains within itself the potential for all the diversity that is to come. Variations on this theme have been found everywhere from ancient Egypt to the Pacific islands, from Finland to Japan, from Hindu and Buddhist India to the Orphic mysteries of classical Greece. The 'Egg' then differentiates out of itself, producing a sequence of new entities, often not very clearly defined, which only gradually become such basic splittings into duality as earth and sky, dry land and sea. Almost invariably a crucial event is the coming of Light, creating the polarity of light and dark (which again precedes the arrival of specific sources of light, such as sun and moon). Gradually the details of the creation emerge, as in the appearance of specific creatures. What is important is that each of these evolves from what had come before it.

The third version, probably the most familiar to us today, is that which has been developed in our modern world over the past two centuries. But it is still 'telling a story', and in this sense we can look at it just as we would look at any other type of story.

The 'Big Bang' theory of the creation of the universe suggests that in the beginning there was an agglomeration of hydrogen atoms, so tightly compressed together that it was only millimetres across and of almost infinite mass. This constituted, as it were, a 'Universal Egg', which contained the potential for all that was to follow. At a certain point, somewhere around 15 billion years ago, this 'Egg' exploded, with such force that electrons jumped from one nucleus to another, creating the atoms of all the other elements. These were the atoms which still constitute the physical universe and everything in it, including ourselves. Gradually, as matter exploded outwards from the original 'Egg' at colossal speed, the universe took on a recognisable shape. Billions of galaxies were formed, trillions of stars, innumerable planets, including our own.[2] And as our attention now focuses on one tiny planet, Earth, we see various basic dualities emerging, such as the splitting of gaseous atmosphere from the earth's surface, land from sea.

Then the most startling development of all takes place, the coming not of Light but Life. The first amino-acids are formed, the first self-replicating molecules emerge: and the story of life then becomes rather like a Rags to Riches story, or rather a succession of them, each evolving out of the last. Our hero is originally a little one-celled creature who reveals the potential to multiply and become a

2. Since the 'Big Bang' theory first took shape between the 1920s and the 1950s, various modifications have been put forward, including a hypothesis that the formation of the elements took place a considerable time after the initial explosion. But the above account provides a crude summary of the theory as it originally emerged.

multi-celled creature. Later he is a water creature who reveals the potential to rise from a 'lower' state to a 'higher', by becoming a land creature. At each stage the hero is revealing a 'higher Self' emerging from within his previous, more limited 'inferior Self'. And of course at each stage he is getting nearer to something we can recognise as ourselves.

There is one particularly dramatic episode in the story, in the Mesozoic, when we see a duality emerging between 'the Monster', the slow-witted, cold-blooded dinosaurs, and a new hero, the first little warm-blooded mammals, who rush about like so many Davids in the presence of Goliath: outwardly, physically so much less impressive, but like little David endowed with vastly superior brain-power and ultimately destined to succeed to the kingdom, when the monsters of this mythology, such as *Tyrannosaurus rex*, its Tyrant King, have been mysteriously overthrown.

Finally comes the moment when another hero emerges from the shadow of shambling apes and other mammalian monsters: the first hominids who, after a time of struggling with mammoths, sabre-toothed tigers and other 'dark' figures of our immediate prehistory, turn unto the ultimate hero of the whole story, *Homo sapiens*, ourselves.

Scarcely has the hero emerged from the shadows into his full glorious identity, however, than we find ourselves being drawn into another plot to explain why we have not yet reached the full happy ending.

### The Fall: Ego and imagination

Although every culture in the world has its myths to explain the creation of the universe, there is a second very important type of story which is only found much more rarely. This is the myth which tells how, in the earliest stages of man's arrival in the world, an extraordinary event took place which was to separate him from the rest of creation as being fundamentally different from any other animal.

Again, the version of this story of the 'Fall of Man' with which we are most familiar is that recounted in the book of *Genesis*. This shows us the first man and the first woman, Adam and Eve, originally living in a garden called 'Paradise' (from the old Persian '*pardis*', 'a garden'), in a state of happy and unbroken unity with nature. Everything necessary for their life is available to them. All is well, until they succumb to the temptation of the Serpent and eat of the fruit of the 'Tree of Knowledge'. At this point, several specific things happen to them, transforming their lives. In attaining this mysterious 'knowledge', they realise that what has happened to them is partly a blessing and partly a curse. They are expelled from Paradise. They become aware of a distinction between 'Good and Evil'. They are now superior to all other forms of life, but their existence is filled with new troubles. They have become self-conscious; they are ashamed of their nakedness, and conceal their reproductive organs. Finally they know, for the first time, they are going to die.

Another familiar version of this story is that contained in the complex of Greek myths centred on the figures of Prometheus ('forethought'); his brother Epimetheus ('afterthought'); and the latter's wife Pandora ('giver of all things').

Pandora is given by the gods a mysterious vessel, which she is told on no account to open, just as Eve is told not to eat the fruit of the Tree of Knowledge. She does so and out into the human world pour all sorts of troubles, such as envy, lust, insanity, hatred, lying and war. Prometheus steals from the gods on Olympus the priceless gift of fire, previously the prerogative of the gods alone. For this he is sentenced to a life of endless suffering, as the price of the prize he has won: tied in perpetuity to a great mountain, where every day his liver, supposedly the seat of human contentment, is gnawed by an eagle.

These two myths from the dawn of civilisation represent the most sophisticated attempts by pre-scientific man to account for the fundamental way in which *Homo sapiens* differs from every other species on earth. All other animals live out their lives entirely by instinct. They can only act as they have been genetically programmed to act, by nature. They thus live in a state of complete unity with nature. What marks out mankind from all other species is that, somewhere far back in prehistory, our ancestors began to develop an entirely new level of consciousness which allowed them to step outside that natural frame. For the first time in the history of life on this earth, there was one species which no longer lived entirely in accordance with the dictates of instinct in everything it did. At first almost imperceptibly, then more and more, it began to develop the capacity to choose how to do things differently: as in the way it learned how to use sticks and stones to catch the animals it hunted for its food; to strip off their skins to provide warm clothing; to use fire to make their meat more edible, and language in which to converse.

But along with this new level of consciousness came something else that was entirely new. Each member of this new species now had a sense of its own separate, individual existence. It had what we call an ego. And in this respect it was totally different from any other creature. It is meaningless to speak of an egocentric fish or bee or elephant. But *Homo sapiens*, both individually and collectively, has the capacity to act selfishly. And it is this which has presented him with a problem which is unique in the animal kingdom.

All this is what these stories of the 'Fall' are unconsciously designed to symbolise. When Adam and Eve arrive in Paradise they are in a state of 'innocence', reflecting that state of nature where every animal lives in unthinking obedience to instinct all its life long. In this sense, like any other animals, they are not responsible for their actions, But their expulsion from the garden marks their emergence from this state of nature. It is their new ability to choose between one form of behaviour and another which lies at the root of their sense of a distinction between good and evil. It is their ability to re-order the terms of their relationship with the rest of nature which gives them superiority over all other forms of life. It is this peculiar form of consciousness, standing apart from nature, which makes the human race self-conscious, giving them the sense that they must hide away parts of their body from general view. And it is this sense of their own finite, individual existence which tells each human being that one day its life must come to an end: which is why Adam and Eve know for the first time they will eventually have to die.

The Greek version of the story adds further elements to the message. The names of the two brothers, Prometheus and Epimetheus, 'forethought' and 'afterthought', reflect another extraordinarily important consequence of the emergence of this new form of consciousness. This is that it creates the power of imagination: the ability to create mental images of that which is not present to the physical senses. An animal which lives entirely by instinct can live only in the moment, at one point of time. Although many other species can learn from experience, only human beings can rise above the present moment altogether, to cast their mind's eye forward and back in time: to imagine events which have not yet happened or to summon up memories of that which happened in the past.

But the most significant consequence of all is that symbolised in what happens when Pandora defies the instruction not to open her mysterious sealed 'vase' or vessel. This is not just another image for humanity breaking loose from the confines of nature. It unleashes into the world a range of wholly new troubles, from envy and lust to hatred and war. And all these are by-products of the emergence of the human ego. It is precisely this sense of having a separate ego-centred existence which cuts human beings off from each other, potentially setting them at odds with each other and with nature itself, to a degree which marks them out from any other species. When Prometheus steals 'fire' from the gods, what he is really stealing is that divine spark of consciousness which distinguishes humanity from all those other forms of life which live in unconscious thrall to instinct. Yet for all the new freedom this gives, there is a terrible price to be paid, symbolised in the image of Prometheus stretched out in agony on that Caucasian rock, having his liver eaten away every day by the insatiable eagle. It is the state of perpetual nagging discontent which must follow from that most crucial of all the new faculties that ego-consciouness brings with it: the ability to imagine that things might be different from what they are.

## Ego versus the unconscious

The term 'consciousness' is often used too loosely, as if only man is conscious and all other forms of life live wholly unconsciously. All animals of course possess consciousness to some degree, right down to the humblest amoeba which shows consciousness of the particle of food it tracks down to eat. Higher up the evolutionary ladder, the degree of conscious intelligence shown by, say, dolphins or chimpanzees is enormous. Similarly, the higher we look up the evolutionary ladder, the more we see animals taking on their own individual personality, so that the individual members of a troop of chimpanzees are much more clearly differentiated from each other than, say, a shoal of herrings. Where the distinction lies is in the degree to which the conscious part of any animal's mind, the foreground from which it is perceiving and making sense of the world, remains automatically in harmony with that much larger part of its mind which operates below the level of conscious awareness, and which is governed by all the framework of instinct. In this respect, even the animal species which have the greatest degree of consciousness still operate entirely instinctively; because they do so in such a way that the unconscious and conscious parts of their minds remain wholly integrated and continue to function in perfect accord with each other.

But if the way an animal spends its life, organises its social system and pairs off to reproduce its kind is all dictated by instinct, then, in the broadest sense, the same is true for *Homo sapiens*. The history of mankind shows that he has formed societies, propagated his kind, preserved the chain of life from generation to generation, just like any other species. However, in human societies as in no other, an element of instability has crept in. Human societies are not governed by an unchanging framework of order. They are in perpetual flux. Men do not obtain their food, build their dwellings, order their relationship with the rest of nature according to strict unchanging patterns and laws. They have the power to make choices. The patterns governing their lives change. Above all, every component part of their society, whether it be each individual human being making it up or each collective group within it, each family, community, class, generation, nation and race, becomes conscious of its own identity, separate from the rest.

To understand more clearly how this works requires more a precise definition of just where the difference between men and animals lies. Every animal has what may broadly be described as two complementary sets of instincts. On one hand each individual animal has its physical instincts, such as its need to eat, drink, breathe and sleep, its urge for sexual release. Because these relate only to itself, like the urge to preserve its own life, they can be described as its 'ego' instincts. On the other hand, providing the controlling framework for its existence, are its 'ordering' instincts. These are the genetically coded instructions which enable the individual animal in every way to relate to the world around it. They tell it how to obtain its food, how to form social groups for self-protection, how to pair off with partners to reproduce, how to tend its young until they themselves are ready to mate, and so forth. From the marriage of these two complementary sets of instincts we may conclude that the overriding purpose in any form of life is not so much to survive individually as to preserve its own species. And in the animal kingdom, these two forms of instinct are inseparably integrated. But it is here that in human beings a partial separation has arisen. Their individual physical instincts remain just as automatic as those of the animals. But the controlling framework of their ordering instincts has in some way broken adrift. It is in this separation that the unique element of disintegration in human nature is to be found.

In terms of our physical needs we are just as instinctive as any other creature. The difference lies in how we seek to fulfil those needs. When a lion feels hungry, it knows only one way to satisfy that urge, which is to identify some suitable prey, track it down and kill it. The whole hunting process, from the original desire for food to the method whereby it is obtained, continues to be governed by instinct at every step. When human beings need to satisfy their hunger, so far have they emerged from the state of nature that they have developed a whole range of different ways to obtain their food, from planting seeds in the ground and waiting until they ripen into wheat to visiting a supermarket to buy a chicken frozen in a plastic bag. When a blackbird feels the urge to build a nest to shelter its young, the process is so instinctively driven that all blackbirds' nests look much the same, constructed to the same model. When men build a shelter to protect them from the elements, the results may be a mud hut or a 30-storey tower block, an igloo or the Palace of Versailles.

The difference between men and animals thus lies not in our physical instincts but in all the ways we order our relationship to the world outside us. When it comes to forming social organisations, animals have no choice. The way they relate to each other to promote their common purpose, whether in an ant colony or a herd of elephants, must always follow the same model. When human beings form communities, societies, tribes or nations, the way these are structured becomes infinitely more flexible. Their social groupings can take on a bewildering variety of forms, from a totalitarian dictatorship to a local golf club. It is true that with animal species at the higher end of the evolutionary scale, such as baboons or lions or even chickens, there may be a continual struggle between individuals to establish dominance within the group. But the patterns of this rivalry, and the general form of the social structure in which it takes place, remain strictly dictated by instinct, serving the survival of the group. Similarly, when birds of the same species compete for territory, they may display ritualised aggression towards each other; but at the end of the process, one robin's territory invariably turns out to be much the same size as the next. All this show of competition has determined, in strict accordance with genetic instructions, is how each bird may end up controlling a patch of land just large enough to supply the needs of its family. But when human beings divide up their living space, one family may end up owning a million acres while another has no more than the corner of a room in an overcrowded slum. Instinct no longer plays a part in dictating the pattern of such arrangements, because human behaviour has, in this respect, broken free from the genetic mould.

But of course this breaking adrift is far from total. And here is the crux of the matter. For on one level, and with what must, on the historical evidence of their survival alone, be regarded as the core of their identity, human beings attempt to adhere to their basic instinctive pattern as if no separation from nature had taken place. At this level human beings have always behaved just like any other animal, as if the supreme purpose of their existence is to carry on the chain of life. Their overriding instinct is to reproduce their species, to which end they form mutually supportive social communities, within which males and females of each new generation have the security to pair off to form new families, to mate and then to nurture their children, until they too grow up to the point where they are ready to reproduce in turn. All this is structured into the unconscious of human beings just as instinctively as it is programmed into any other animal.

But then there intrudes that other component in their psychic make-up which is continually urging them away from this unity of purpose. It is this which explains why, to a degree not remotely experienced by any other animals, we see how human beings, individually and collectively, fall prey to every kind of disintegrative impulse: greed, envy, lust, bad temper, hatred, cruelty, violence, the breaking up of families, loneliness, depression, insanity, crime, social injustice, political divisions, revolutions, wars; in short, all those peculiarly human problems which, as the Greek myth had it, were released into the world by the opening of Pandora's 'box'. And all these in one way or another follow from the unique power of ego-consciousness to separate human beings from each other and from nature, and from the breaking down of that natural state of integration between their ego and their deeper unconscious.

Between these two conflicting forces in their psyche, human beings live their lives in a state of constant tension. At the deepest level there is nothing they want more than to re-establish the lost unity between the two parts of their psyche: to live at peace with each other, with nature and with themselves. But to do this they have to make a continual, conscious effort. To assist them in that effort they have evolved a whole array of devices, mechanisms and rituals: from laws and political institutions to codes of morality; from every kind of artistic expression to the framework of religion. What all these creations of human consciousness have in common is that they all originate in a desire to underpin or to re-establish that sense of unity which every animal enjoys without thinking all its life long.

## Life and order

It is remarkable how many of the forms of behaviour which distinguish human beings from all other animals consist of creating a consciously-contrived frame-work for some activity which in the life of every other species is wholly instinctive.

An obvious example is the conscious effort human beings have to make to organ-ise themselves into social groups. The way animals group together is governed entirely by instinct. Every baboon troop or ant colony is hierarchically structured according to the basic model of the species, with a dominant male or queen at its head. Each member of the group is instinctively aware of its role as an integral part of a collective organism much greater than itself, because it has not got the individual consciousness to imagine otherwise. And to a great extent the human counterpart to this is also instinctive. All human beings belong to families, com-munities, tribes or nations which provide them with a central part of their sense of identity. The structure of their social groups is naturally hierarchical, centred on a leader-figure cast more or less successfully in the archetypal role of 'Father', 'Mother' or 'Son-Hero'. But beyond that instinctive core which *Homo sapiens* shares in common with other animals, each human grouping develops its own variations on the basic theme: its own individual forms of organisation, hierarchy and leadership. And to preserve the order of the group against all the disruptive tendencies arising from egotism, it becomes necessary by conscious effort to create elaborate codes of social behaviour, with a framework of laws and punish-ments to enforce them.

Again, as an individual animal matures through its life, it develops through each stage quite naturally. Only human societies have had to evolve a conscious framework for this process, from the formal structures of a child's education to the rites and ceremonies which attend each new step along the way, such as those marking birth, initiation into adulthood, marriage, and finally death. The under-lying purpose of all these rituals is to bring the conscious life of human beings, taken up with all the trivial distractions of the ego, back into harmony with that instinctive, unconscious core which is rooted in the totality of life: reconnecting them with a sense of something deeper and more universal than just their own individual existence.

The need to resolve this psychic split gives rise to other distinctive features of human behaviour for which the animal kingdom offers no real parallels. One conspicuous means whereby human beings sublimate their tendency to egocentricity is through their love of games and sport. Not only does the rivalry between teams and individuals provide a socially acceptable channel for competitive impulses which might otherwise become socially disruptive. By disciplining physical or mental activity within a strict framework of rules, the participants in a game or sport become subordinated to something higher than themselves. A psychological model for all sporting activity is the spiritual discipline of Zen archery, in which the archer's purpose is so to eliminate the distortions arising from his own ego that the arrow naturally flies to its target. Whenever a game is played well it produces those moments when body and mind come into such instinctive co-ordination that the players seem to have been lifted above themselves. This was why, until it became corrupted, the original Olympic Games were one of the central religious ceremonies of the ancient Greek world. The skill of the competitors expressed an ideal of perfection which elevated not only the athletes themselves but all those who watched them. Something of the same sense of transcendence, although it is similarly open to corruption by the ego, accounts for the extraordinary glamour which surrounds sport in our modern world.

An even more significant instance of how human beings express this urge to transcend the limitations of their ego-existence is through every kind of artistic expression. The underlying purpose of all art is to create patterns of imagery which somehow convey a sense of life set in a framework of order. From music to painting, from architecture to poetry, from a finely worked piece of jewellery to the disciplined exuberance of folk-dance, any effective work of art always combines these two elements: on one hand, the imagery of movement, vitality, imagination and colour we associate with the energy of life; on the other, that sense of pattern, rhythm and harmony by which it is structured. Whatever its outward form, the aim of any artistic creation is to weave these essential elements together in a way which gives us a sense of a perfect resolution. Any work of art thus seeks to create a marriage between those complementary aspects of the psyche we see as masculine and feminine. Analyse the appeal of a Beethoven symphony and we see how it is made up of that familiar fourfold combination of strength and mind, heart and soul. The music commands our attention by its masculine power. It appeals to our intellect by the formal subtleties of its structure. It moves us by its feminine grace and delicacy, its flowing life, its appeal to our feelings. It elevates us by evoking something beyond ourselves, a sense of perfect totality. Like all great art it thus harmonises consciousness with the ego-transcending Self.

Any work of art can be analysed along similar lines, even if only in terms of how it may fall short of such perfect balance. Whenever we sense any artistic creation to be in some way deficient, this is either because it somehow lacks life or because it is inadequately organised, or both. Any work of art which succeeds, however, can make us feel mysteriously more alive, by connecting us with the sense of a perfection beyond the limitations of our own ego. Such is what the artistic impulse in mankind is all about. But no device for re-establishing that sense of unity with our inner life is more ingenious than one coded into us by the process of evolution itself: our ability to conjure up inside our heads those patterns of imaginary events we call stories.[3]

## Archetypes: Pictures with a purpose

The evolution of life on this planet has produced countless miracles, from the complex structure of the eye to the even greater complexities of the human brain. But none is more remarkable than this ability of human beings to see organised sequences of pictures in their heads. Even more remarkable, however, is the underlying purpose for which this faculty has evolved.

The real significance of our capacity to imagine stories, as we have seen, lies in the extent to which they emerge from some part of the mind which is beyond the storyteller's conscious awareness. To a great degree stories are thus the product of a controlling power which is centred in the unconscious. The very fact that they follow such identifiable patterns and are shaped by such consistent rules indicates that the unconscious is thus using them for a purpose: to convey to the conscious level of our mind a particular picture of human nature and how it works.

We are of course familiar with the idea that some part of our unconscious has the autonomous power to transmit messages to our consciousness, because it was this which for Freud and Jung lay at the heart of their theorising about why we dream. Our dreams, they suggested, can reveal to us much of what is going on in our psyche below the threshold of consciousness. Nevertheless, it is curious how much of the pioneering work of these two psychoanalysts in opening up our understanding of the unconscious was centred on their study of dreams, without their recognising just how much more systematic a picture of its workings can be derived from analysing the process whereby we imagine stories.

3. Various attempts have been made in recent years to provide a scientific definition of the difference between human consciousness and that of other animals. A fundamental flaw in all of them lies in their failure to take account of the consequences arising from the split between ego and instinct. Michael Tomasello, for instance, in *The Cultural Origins of Human Cognition* (Harvard University Press, 2000), bases his theory on observing the learning processes of apes and human children. He suggests that what makes humans unique is their capacity for empathetic imitation of each other. It is this, he suggests, which enables them to develop and to learn from a continuously evolving 'culture'. Chimpanzees can learn by imitation to make very simple steps outside the frame of instinctive behaviour (as when they learn to use sticks as 'tools' to extract termites from their nests); and, as with other animals, this ability becomes more pronounced when, in captivity, they are trained by human beings to perform non-instinctive actions. But, because their imitation is only based on external imitation and not on empathetic understanding, animals can quickly lose these learned attributes, and cannot develop a 'culture'. Tomasello describes this unique human ability to build on the stored and transmitted experience of previous generations as the 'ratchet' which makes cultural evolution possible. But, in not allowing for the peculiar problems created by the human ego, he fails to recognise that, as each new 'cultural advance' takes *Homo sapiens* further away from nature and the instinctive frame, a large part of what we generally call 'culture' in fact consists of symbolic attempts to reconnect ego-consciousness with the unity of purpose represented by that frame. Nothing reflects this more vividly than our compulsion to imagine stories. In accordance with Tomasello's thesis, stories are certainly based on our capacity to empathise with other human beings (perhaps more graphically than any other expression of the human imagination). But equally they demonstrate that their real symbolic purpose is to overcome the problems created by egotism; and to show how the subjective ego can be reconciled with that 'objective' level of the psyche which empathetically connects human beings with the world outside them, giving them their deepest sense of stability and identity.

Jung, however, went much further in this direction than Freud, above all in seeing how much of our conscious existence is shaped by archetypes: those shadowy elemental structures built into our unconscious which condition so much of our emotional and behavioural response to the world without our being aware of it. This, his central contribution to our understanding of the unconscious, was one of the greatest intuitive discoveries of the twentieth century, ranking alongside those of Einstein and other nuclear physicists, or Watson and Crick's double helix.

The point about the archetypes is that they constitute a crucial legacy from that process whereby human consciousness split off from our unconscious obedience to instinct. The chief archetypes – Mother, Father, *animus* and *anima*, Child – represent all the most basic roles that human beings can be called on to play in that central instinctive process whereby the life of the species is continued, when this is acted out in accordance with the instinctive pattern. But in addition each archetype is two-sided. It contains not only a positive image of how that role should be carried out selflessly in accordance with instinct, but also its negative aspect, reflecting how the intervention of the ego may prevent it being carried out properly.

We are all programmed, for instance, with the set of archetypal impulses surrounding the most basic relationship in all our lives, that with 'Mother'. When a child is born into the world, it is the 'Mother' archetype programmed into its unconscious which leads it instinctively to bond with one single mother-figure (who may not even be biologically its actual mother). Similarly it is the 'Mother' archetype which is activated in a woman as she prepares to give birth to her child, arousing all those loving, protective, practical, selfless maternal instincts which we see in any mother animal in nature. When we see the image of a mother presented in a picture or a story, we can immediately respond to the archetype it represents, just as we can when we recognise that she is a 'Dark Mother'. In this case the ego has intervened, and her role has become not to promote the child's development but in some way to stifle it and hold it back.

Likewise we instinctively respond to the archetype of 'Father' (as in the image of Father Christmas), recognising that his role is to be outwardly strong and masculine, but inwardly open to the feminine, as someone kindly, protective and understanding of those under his care. We can see the 'Father' archetype personified in any older man who is in a position of authority; except that again we may see him as the egocentric 'Dark Father' when, lacking the softer feminine values, he has become a heartless Tyrant. If his deficiency is the other way, in that he lacks masculinity, he shows himself as an immature *puer aeternus*, weak and irresponsible.

For a man no archetype is more powerful than that of the *anima*, that autonomous element in his psyche embodying the qualities of the feminine. His relationship with the *anima* is that which determines his responses to the opposite sex, and much else besides. For a woman the equivalent is her relationship to the *animus*, representing the masculine element in her psyche. Again this determines not just her response to men but also the entire internal balance of her personality.

As an expression of what is the biological goal of the whole instinctive process, we see the power of our response to the archetype of the 'Child'. This arouses in us all those selfless emotions which can be triggered off not only by our own offspring, but by the young of almost any kind.

As an expression of our wish to reintegrate our divided nature, however, no archetype plays a more crucially important role in human psychology than that of the Self. It is this which represents the sense of totality we have lost through our emergence from the state of unconscious unity with creation. It is this archetype which encompasses all the others; which we see at work in the impulse of a story (or any work of art) to come to a perfect resolution; and which governs all human behaviour when, in ways large and small, we sense that our actions are springing from another 'centre' in our personality beyond that of our own ego.

All these archetypal powers in the human psyche were identified by Jung, from his studies of dreams and myths. What he was thus able to show was how the pictures we see in our heads when we dream represent in symbolic form the archetypal elements in our unconscious, holding up a unique mirror to our inner state. But what even he failed fully to appreciate was just how profoundly this also applies to the whole of the process whereby we imagine stories. In fact the archetypal patterns which shape stories provide us with a much more structured picture of the components of the human unconscious than we can derive from dreams. They show us how all the archetypes fit together as part of a dynamic process. And when we learn how to decipher their significance, we begin to see we how it uses stories, ultimately, to put over one central message, the essence of which can be summarised as follows:

## 1. Dark and light

One of the first things we all learn to recognise about the characters we see in stories is that familiar distinction between 'goodies' and 'baddies', heroes and villains. The reason for this division is that it presents to us in symbolic form the split caused in human nature by the separation of ego-consciousness from the selfless unconscious. The chief device the unconscious uses to symbolise this split is by representing it in terms of that central conflict between 'dark' and 'light'.

The 'dark power' in stories, as we have seen, represents the power of the ego, most starkly personified in the archetype of the 'monster'; which is like a symbolic caricature of human nature when deformed by egotism from the state of wholeness it would possess if it was still at one with nature. Hence the way in which the 'monster' is so often seen as a combination of animal and human characteristics. Its animal element represents its unconscious instinctive self. In the greed, cruelty and cunning of its conscious human element, it is twisted and imperfect.[4]

This incomplete creature is immensely powerful and concerned solely with pursuing its own interests, at the expense of everyone else in the world. By showing the 'monster' as casting a shadow over a whole community, the unconscious portrays its egotism as the most life-threatening enemy the human race has to face.

---

4. Hence the irony by which, when human beings behave particularly badly and selfishly, they are likened to 'animals'. They are described as behaving like 'brutes' (or more specifically like 'pigs', 'monkeys', 'asses', etc) when it is precisely the peculiarly human rather than animal part of them which lead them to behave in such an 'inhuman' (i.e., all too human) fashion.

We then, however, see how the 'dark' figures in every other kind of story also display essentially the same psychological characteristics. The first concern of stories is to show us the nature of this power of egocentricity and what it does to human beings. Naturally, since it is heartlessly self-seeking, it isolates the egotist from everyone around him (except those whose own egotism becomes in some way allied to his). But, equally significantly, we see how an inevitable consequence of egocentricity is that it limits and distorts perception. Someone seeing the world through the ego cannot by definition see objectively. He or she becomes cut off from reality. Seeing only what the ego wishes to see, they fall into a state of delusion. But because such a fantasy-state cannot achieve resolution with reality, this creates an unconscious tendency for the ego to step up its demands, taking on the self-destructive pattern we have seen as the 'fantasy spiral'. The egotist is driven ever further into unreality. As we see most obviously mirrored in all the different forms of Tragedy, this puts him increasingly at odds with the world around him, until eventually he is likely to collide with reality in a way which is potentially fatal.

## 2. *Masculine and feminine*

By contrast, stories are then concerned to show what is necessary to counter the distorting power of the human ego. The effect of egocentricity is that it disintegrates the psyche, separating subjective consciousness from the objective unconscious. The ego thus becomes identified with what stories portray to us as 'masculine' characteristics, most obviously representing a self-centred urge for power and control. In so doing it becomes split off from what stories represent to us as the 'feminine' elements in the human psyche. These, combining the capacity to feel sympathetically for others with intuitive understanding, the ability to see objectively and 'whole', are rooted in the instinctive unconscious which is essentially selfless.

Hence that fundamental division in stories between the 'dark masculine' and the 'light feminine', represented by the light heroine. Without the life-giving balance of the selfless values which alone can provide a living connection with other people and with the reality of the world outside it, masculine consciousness must remain cut off and in thrall to the ego. It thus turns into the 'monster' and becomes deadly. To counteract the divisive and destructive power of the ego what is needed is a reintegration of the masculine with the feminine.

## 3. *Above the line/below the line*

One of the subtlest of the devices the unconscious uses to portray this psychic split is the way it presents to us the little world or 'kingdom' of a story divided into two levels: 'above the line' and 'below the line'. This corresponds to the relationship between consciousness and the unconscious in the human psyche.

On the upper level, the world of the story is dominated by a dark figure (or figures), exercising power and control. His, her or their blinkered egocentricity represents the limited vision of ego-consciousness. It is on the 'inferior level', in the shadows cast by the egotism which is dominant on the upper level, that we see those light values of selfless feeling and the ability to see whole which have the potential to bring the upper level back to a state of balance. The world 'below the line' thus represents the unconscious, containing the life-giving values which the ruling consciousness lacks. Eventually, in a fully-resolved story, we see these values emerging from the inferior realm, to dispel the darkness and restore a state of balance. Thus do stories provide a model of how the divided 'kingdom' of the psyche can become reintegrated.

### 4. The unrealised value

The central means whereby stories show this battle for integration being acted out is by setting it in the context of the most fundamental psychological process in every human life: that by which each individual, as he or she emerges into the world representing a new generation, must grow up to replace the generation which came before.

This is why so often at the beginning of stories we see the central figure as young and single. The aim of the story is to show the hero or heroine working towards that state of integration, the balance of masculine and feminine, which will ultimately enable them to succeed in the right way. The Son-Hero must grow up in the right way to unite with a heroine and become a father. The Daughter-Heroine must grow up to marry a hero, to become a mother. Until they are fully ready to succeed, they remain in some way immature and incomplete. But when they finally reach their goal, we see how they have reached that state of psychic wholeness which is maturity.

To achieve this goal they have to work their way through some version of that 'archetypal family drama' which lies at the heart of storytelling. This centres on different aspects of the four archetypal roles which make up the drama of that transition between one generation and the next: Father; Mother; the central figure in the story with whom we identify, its hero or heroine; and finally the 'other half' with whom they are to be united to become whole, to make the process complete.

As we have seen, there is no more ingenious device by which the unconscious makes its point in storytelling than the way it uses dark versions of these four archetypal figures to represent the 'unrealised value': the negative version of that which the hero or heroine need to make positive in themselves in order to succeed. This is why one or more dark figures, such as a 'Dark Father', a 'Dark Mother', a dark 'Alter-Ego' or dark 'Other Half', play such dominant roles through the greater part of most stories, because they each in their different ways correspond to some respect in which the central figure of the story is not yet complete. Only when the hero or heroine themselves reach the point where they are ready for the final state of integration can the darkness be dispelled and the split between 'above the line' and 'below the line' be resolved.

### 5. Self-realisation

The moment in a story when this integration takes place is marked by the final bringing to light of 'that which has been hidden'; the release of the redeeming value from the shadows. This may be symbolised as the uncovering of a buried treasure, or the reaching of some long-pursued goal. More explicitly we see this prize as the liberation of the 'feminine value', as when a heroine is freed from imprisonment by a monster, or emerges from the darkness in which she has been obscured. But essentially this moment is likely to be symbolised in four ways. Firstly, we see, in some way, a coming together of the masculine and feminine values, most obviously symbolised by an image of a hero or heroine being joined with their 'other half' in perfect union. Secondly, we see an image of order restored and life renewed. This may be symbolised in the succession of the hero and heroine to preside over some kind of 'kingdom', having established a new centre to their lives where they can 'live happily ever after'. Thirdly, it is conveyed, they have now reached the centre of their personal identity; they have become most fully themselves. Fourthly, and last, we see how the achieving of this goal may have immense repercussions for the wider community around them. The very fact that they have resolved the problem posed by the dark power and become integrated is portrayed as bringing general benefit to society and humanity as a whole. The 'kingdom' or community which was in the shadows, threatened by egotism, has been brought back into the light and restored to itself. The elimination of the dark power by one individual has consequences felt by all.

All these elements put together represent that state of wholeness which is expressed through the archetypal symbolism of the Self. Such is the archetypal pattern by which the unconscious symbolically shows us how we may restore that unity with our unconscious instinctive programming which first began to split apart with the 'Fall'.

To show the restoration of that state of unity is the only way in which the pattern of a story can be fully resolved; and it must do so according to fundamental rules, which insist that such a resolution can only be achieved under specific conditions, when certain ingredients are in place. If they are not, as in those 'dark versions' of stories where the story is told from an ego-centred point of view, the story cannot achieve a proper resolution.

But of course stories do not just present us with an idealised picture of how human nature can achieve a reintegrated state. They also provide us with a mirror to all those different states of psychological imbalance which can prevent human beings from reaching that state of wholeness in the first place.

### Disintegrated consciousness

The psychic split which distinguishes human beings from other animals is not just a matter of the separation of consciousness from the unconscious. Another consequence of our psychic disintegration is that consciousness itself develops in widely differing ways between one individual and another.

This is why, to a far greater extent than other animals, human beings present such a variety of different personality types. We see some people as having strong personalities, others weak. Some are warm and outgoing, others cold and withdrawn. One person may be naturally practical and down-to-earth, another cerebral and detached, a third romantic and emotional, a fourth imaginative and spiritual.

One of the more obvious ways in which such variations in psychological make-up can be analysed is in terms of those four psychic functions which we see in stories making up the state of human wholeness. In reality these four functions constitute a hierarchy of different types of consciousness, each of which can be viewed in its own right as a distinct form of perception or intelligence.

At the most basic level is physical consciousness, that which relates us to the world through our senses, through our physical needs and capabilities. It is this which anchors us to practical realities and can give a strong physical presence. Mental intelligence provides our cognitive ability to analyse, calculate and discriminate, and generally to organise our perception of the world through the power of the mind. It is from these two forms of consciousness that we derive those two ingredients essential to the effectiveness of almost every aspect of human life: strength and structure. But to become life-giving these functions need to be balanced by the 'feminine' forms of consciousness: the emotional intelligence which gives the capacity for protective and sympathetic feeling; and that imaginative understanding which can look beyond the limitations of sensory and rational perception, to see how things connect up and fit together.[5]

For animals living in a state of nature these functions are so instinctively integrated with each other that there is no real separation between them. And when human beings first begin to emerge from the state of nature, for a long time this remains true. One of the more obvious characteristics of the world's 'primitive' peoples, such as those still at the hunter-gatherer stage of human development, is the extent to which they remain close to the instinctive unity of nature. Although their consciousness is immeasurably more developed than that of animals, the different aspects of their psyche continue to work naturally in concert with each other. The way they relate physically to the world around them; the way they organise their mental perception of the world; their sense of fellow-feeling with each other and their natural surroundings; their intuitive sense of belonging to some indivisible spiritual whole: all these modes of psychic operation remain so closely interwoven that it is hard to separate them. But as civilisation evolves and humanity becomes ever more separated from a state of nature, the more these psychic functions tend to become differentiated from one another. And it is here the imbalances arise which become a key factor in the emergence of different types of human personality, because there is then a tendency in each individual to rely more on some forms of consciousness than others. Those functions which are more strongly developed become superior, the others remain inferior. And, where consciousness becomes unbalanced in this way, people tend to become caught out by those functions in which they are less developed.

We are all familiar with some of the more obvious of these forms of imbalance. A 'sensation type', for instance, someone who primarily relates to the world in a

5. It was one of Jung's most valuable insights, leading to his theory of 'psychological types', that consciousness operates in these four basic ways: through what he called the 'sensation', 'thinking', 'feeling' and intuitive' functions. He noted that most people primarily relate to the world through one, their 'superior' function, while remaining less developed in others. Thus he came to categorise people as 'sensation types', 'thinking types', and so forth, noting also that we tend to get caught out in our relationship to the world by those functions in which we are inferior. But Jung did not develop his observations to the point of recognising, as we can learn from storytelling, how the first two of these functions have an essentially 'masculine' aspect while the other two are essentially 'feminine'. This helps to illuminate both how they can get out of balance with each other and also what is needed for them to brought into that state of balance which allows them to operate effectively.

physical way, may be highly practical but not over-endowed with intellect. Those who are primarily physical may also be caught out by their underdeveloped 'feminine' functions, by a lack of feeling for others or of imaginative understanding. We similarly recognise that 'thinking types', those who one-sidedly relate to the world through their intellect, may be caught out by their inadequacy in relating to the physical world. This deficiency in consciousness renders them uncoordinated and impractical. They may also find it hard to relate to their emotions, making them cold and unfeeling. Even their strongest function, their power to think, unless this is balanced by intuitive understanding, may simply get lost in abstract pattern-making: as we recognise in such stereotypes as the pedantic lawyer, the dry-as-dust academic or the unfeeling bureaucrat.[6]

Wherever people's consciousness becomes too one-sided in this way, their thinking and behaviour become unconsciously influenced in a negative way by those functions in which they are not consciously developed. And in this respect we have to think of unconsciousness in two ways. On one hand there are the deep structures of our unconscious proper, the foundation of our psyche, that 'collective unconscious' which we share in common with the rest of humanity. On the other there is that personal element of unconsciousness made up of the areas in which our own individual functioning is deficient.

Not only do these deficiencies unconsciously influence our thinking and behaviour, because they themselves are not operating to full effect. The resulting imbalances can also interfere with the workings of those functions in which we are more strongly developed. This applies equally to the 'feminine' functions, which cannot find proper expression unless they have the strength and discipline of their 'masculine' balance. Someone who relies primarily on feeling but is weak and lacking in rationality becomes chaotically emotional, lacking the power and discipline to direct their feelings effectively. Someone who is highly intuitive but without controlling reason or a sense of the practical may fall prey to irrational misjudgements, losing precisely that power of understanding which can only be achieved when intuition is disciplined.

There is no one whose personality cannot be analysed in terms of the balance between its 'masculine' and 'feminine' components in this way. A man who is strongly 'masculine' must inevitably, unless this is balanced by the feeling and imagination which represent his *anima*, his 'inner feminine', remain limited,

---

6. The problem with over-reliance on the thinking function is its tendency to what is known as 'cognitive dissonance': the ability to construct rational patterns which may in themselves seem orderly and logical but which do not correspond to the complexities of reality. The scientist, like the bureaucrat or the politician (or indeed any of us), may create a model to explain or replicate the workings of some phenomenon, but which is based on a failure to appreciate all the subtleties of what it involves. In trying to understand the world, ego-consciousness inevitably tends either to over-simplify or to over-complicate. The only remedy to this lies in the power of the intuitive faculty to see 'the wider picture': what the model has missed out or failed to take account of. This is what was symbolised in Greek mythology by Theseus's need for Ariadne's thread to allow him to escape from the Labyrinth. In reality someone whose thinking function is strongly developed often has a poorly developed intuitive function. Hence the hyper-abundance in our world of flawed scientific models, mad bureaucracy, crackpot political schemes and other versions of the Labyrinth, all of which result from the thinking function becoming split off from intuition, feeling and a sense of the practical.

insensitive and self-centred. He is thus likely to become a bully or a tyrant. Conversely, a man weak in his masculinity, a 'mother's boy', cannot develop either side of his personality properly. Taken over by his 'negative *anima*', he becomes, as we say, effeminate. His capacity for feeling may remain self-centred and sentimental, while his repressed masculinity tends to assert itself only in an 'inferior' way, making him feline and petulant.

Similarly a woman's personality needs the balance of the 'inner masculine'. Unless a woman's femininity is given positive balance by the strength of her *animus*, she remains weak, irrational and disorganised. But again, a woman whose femininity becomes overridden by her inner masculinity becomes hard, assertive and domineering. Taken over by her 'negative *animus*', she becomes, as we say, a virago. Quick to find fault or to take offence, eager to pick a quarrel, her negative *animus* speaks in a parody of masculine rationality while talking irrational nonsense.

What all these permutations on the disintegrated psyche have in common is that they are centred on the inability of the ego properly to integrate with the selfless level of the unconscious. They are all therefore different manifestations of immaturity; and certainly nothing provides a clearer mirror than the world of stories to all the ways in which human beings can fall short of that state of integration. But what they also present us with is a model of what is required for any human being to achieve maturity. This means that he or she must consciously have reached a state of harmony with the unconscious. They must have achieved a balance between the masculine and feminine elements in their personality: between body and mind, heart and soul. Only through bringing all these together can anyone rise above the limitations of the ego to become identified with their inmost Self. And to show how this state can be achieved (and how and why human beings fall short of achieving it) is the central purpose of storytelling.

## Patterns for life

When an acorn falls onto the ground, it contains all the genetic information it needs to grow up into a perfect, fully developed oak tree. When a human baby is born, it contains all the genetic programming it needs to develop physically into a fully grown man or woman. What it does not have is the instinctive programming to ensure that it will eventually grow up psychologically into a fully mature human being. It is precisely this lack for which the archetypal patterns which underlie storytelling have emerged through evolution to compensate.

To just what extent these unconscious patterns can be said to be part of the common genetic inheritance of mankind may call for qualification. Almost all the individual stories we have been looking at in this book have been drawn only from one cultural tradition, that of our own Western civilisation, even though this includes by far the most richly developed complex of storytelling in the world and can trace its roots, via Greek and Middle Eastern mythology, far back into pre-history. Some of the story-forms which have evolved within that tradition, such as Comedy, are rarely found outside it. But even when we look outside our own tradition to, say, the mythology and folk tales of the indigenous peoples of Africa or the Americas, we still find that same core of symbolism which forms the basis of all storytelling.

A story told by the tribes who once roamed the Great Plains of the American Middle-West is the tale we know in its Cheyenne form as *Jumping Mouse*. There was once a little mouse, living busily in a forest with all the other mice around him, who one day heard a strange, faint roaring noise, seemingly coming from far away. None of the other mice could hear it, but when it persisted, he eventually set off on his own to see what it was. He runs into a raccoon (in some versions a fox) who guides him nearer and nearer to the source of the roaring, until the little mouse finds himself looking at a mighty river. Here a frog tells him to jump up in the air. When the mouse does so, he falls into the water and gets horribly wet. But while jumping, the mouse has glimpsed far off the most beautiful sight he has ever seen: the 'Sacred Mountains' (in some versions, just one mountain). The frog tells him he has now become 'Jumping Mouse' and he returns to his fellow-mice to tell them of the amazing thing he has seen. They have no idea what he is talking about and dismiss him as mad.

So obsessed has Jumping Mouse become with his Sacred Mountains, however, that he sets off on a long, lonely journey to reach them. He eventually emerges from the forest to the edge of a great open plain, stretching as far as the eye can see. Wheeling in the sky above it are eagles, which would like nothing more than to catch a mouse for their dinner. But he then encounters a bison which has lost its sight. The bison says it has been told that, if only it could be given the eye of a mouse, it would regain its sight. Jumping Mouse hands over one of his eyes and the bison, now able to see, carries him safely over the plain to the foothills of the Sacred Mountains. Here the bison can go no further, but the mouse then runs into a wolf (in some versions a bear) which has also been struck blind. The mouse surrenders its second eye, the wolf regains its sight and carries the mouse, now itself blind, up into the mountains until they reach the shore of a sacred lake, where the wolf leaves the mouse all alone.

As the mouse is abandoned, weak and defenceless, it is not long before a mighty eagle swoops down to attack him. As its talons strike, the mouse feels the shock of death. But he finds himself being carried up into the air and, as he soars up into the heavens, he finds his sight and strength miraculously returning. 'Mouse', the story ends, 'has become Eagle'.

Although this story comes from a cultural tradition which could scarcely be more remote from our own, there is nothing about its fundamental message we cannot immediately recognise. It begins with the group of mice all preoccupied with their busy, mundane, ego-centred existence. Only one has an intuitive apprehension that, somewhere, there is something far more important to life than just this limited little view of the world, and sets out on his long, hazardous Quest to reach it. We recognise the way the hero only makes progress towards his distant goal by self-sacrificing acts of generosity to other animals, who then become his helpers. And obviously the story's main theme, as it describes how an initially ordinary little figure finds himself eventually transformed into something immeasurably greater, is entirely familiar: even if he only becomes at one with the power of the universal life-force at the moment when his separate ego-identity finally dissolves in death.

The essential message of storytelling all over the world is that there are two centres to human nature: and that to become reunited with the totality of life it is necessary to make the long and difficult transition from one to the other. From our earliest years, the first point the unconscious tries to make through stories is that the greatest danger to the human race is its own capacity to think and to act egocentrically. This is why those first properly-formed stories which make sense to us as a child tend to show a little hero or heroine, much like ourselves, venturing out into a mysterious outside world, such as a great forest, where they encounter some terrifying dark figure: a witch, a giant, a wolf or some other monster. The purpose of this is to introduce the child to a personification of that dark power of egotism which it must learn to recognise as its most deadly enemy.

Initially this enemy is shown as something wholly external; and the point of such stories, as we saw, is simply to awaken the child's subconscious awareness to the fact that, in this strange new world it is entering, such a deadly power exists. But progressively, as we grow older, the message is filled out, as it conveys to us with greater subtlety and depth those qualities the hero or heroine must develop for them to reach the complete happy ending; not least when we come to those types of story which show the hero or heroine having to wrestle with that same dark power in themselves.

So, whether we respond to it or not, does the constant feeding of our imagination with stories provide us with a unique mirror to the inner dynamics of human nature. Above all, below the level of our consciousness, the consistency of their symbolism gradually builds up an image of what the pattern of a human life can be, and what happens if we fail.

### The stages of life

We all have in our minds a generalised outline of how a human life unfolds (even if in reality many individual lives vary from it). The pattern begins with the child being born into a family with a mother and a father. Initially living at home in an intimate relationship with its mother, the child then begins to venture into the outside world, embarking on its socialisation and education as part of a wider community. At the end of adolescence, it is ready to go out into the world in a quite different way, as it breaks away from dependence on its parents and begins to establish an independent life. As a young man or woman entering on adult life, they are not only discovering 'what they want to be' but are ready to begin looking for their 'other half' with whom to establish a new home, as the basis on which to start a new family. The preoccupations of this phase of life then become to establish a place in the outside world and to watch over the children as they grow up towards adulthood in turn.

Then, in this idealised picture, comes the moment when the tasks of 'the first half of life' are completed, and now begins the 'second half'. The man or the woman may be able to take on more responsible roles in their work or the wider community, for which they are now equipped by age and experience. They are ready to play their roles as grandparents, reassured at the confirmation this brings that the life for which they have been responsible is continuing into the future. At this point, if they have learned from their experience of life, they know themselves and the ways of the world. They have become fully mature, even wise. Eventually old age overtakes them, they withdraw from the world and prepare for death.

In the light of this outline, we can see how the most comprehensive of the basic plots is Rags to Riches, in that it comes nearest to providing a symbolic model for human life. More consistently than any other, this type of story begins by showing its central figure in childhood. This enables it to set out all the essential stages of human development, as the initially humble and disregarded little hero or heroine embark on the long road to the point where they will eventually be able to identify with that greater 'Self' which has been potentially hidden in them all along.

When we first meet the hero or heroine of a Rags to Riches story, we see them in the situation in which we all begin our lives, overshadowed by the presence of parents and everyone around us. But the vital quality they must be shown as possessing, in contrast to the dark figures around them, is that they are essentially good-hearted, because this shows they are not egocentric. They are in tune with their deeper, selfless instincts, which is the vital precondition of their eventually being qualified to reach the ultimate goal.

The first step, the pattern shows, is for the hero or heroine in childhood to make some venture into the outside world. This symbolises the need for each of us in childhood to establish a secure sense of our own independent identity: the need to build up what the psychologists call our 'ego-complex', that which enables us to relate confidently to the world around us. We all need a strong ego, because it is the centre of our awareness of the world. But the crucial question to be answered is whether that ego is acting only in its own interest, or whether it is acting in harmony with some deeper instinctive pattern which can connect it positively with reality and the world outside itself.

At this early stage of life, like all of us, the hero or heroine are still essentially dependent on the adults around them, which is why they are likely to be overshadowed by 'Dark Father' or 'Dark Mother' figures, representing negative versions of what they themselves must eventually redeem into a positive in order to succeed. But what may carry them through these early stages of life is their alliance with 'helpful animals', like Aladdin's genies (derived from the same root as our word 'genes'), representing all those instinctive gifts and abilities on which we rely in youth, before we can achieve conscious Self-understanding.

Then, at the end of adolescence, comes that second, even more significant act of stepping into the outside world, where we enter on the stage of adult life (which is where so many stories based on other plots begin). And here the story shows how these innate qualities may lead in due course to what seems outwardly like a happy ending, as when, like Aladdin, we may get married and enjoy great success in the outside world. But at this point in the story we come to that highly significant moment in the basic Rags to Riches story which we see as the 'central crisis'.

All that the hero or heroine have so far achieved seems to be snatched away from them, so that in a sense they have to begin the process of working towards their goal all over again. The purpose of this in the story's archetype is to emphasise that the outward fulfilment they have so far enjoyed is not the real goal that they must reach. To reach true maturity requires having to go through the most demanding process of all: to develop that real strength of character based on self-understanding which brings personal autonomy. This can only be achieved by someone who consciously achieves a complete balance of the masculine and feminine components in their personality: who has developed the inner strength which brings authority, combined with that wisdom of heart and soul which can only come from experience.

In this respect the Rags to Riches plot, particularly as set out in its more developed versions, such as *Aladdin, Jane Eyre* or *David Copperfield*, reflects the way in which the process of psychological development in a human life falls into two parts. The overriding task of 'the first half of life' is for us to establish a secure sense of our individual identity while at the same time learning how to accommodate that to the demands of society around us. In youth we have abounding life, energy and dreams of the future, but we need to learn how to control that vitality to the point where we can become established in our adult role in society. In an outward sense, we discover 'what we want to be in life'. We may be able to achieve all those outward goals which conform with the norms of society, such as earning a living, getting married, setting up a new home, establishing a family. But all these landmarks can be achieved without any great depth of self-knowledge. It is possible to achieve them while remaining inwardly immature.

Eventually, however, comes a point where, if we are going to continue on the road of personal development, we must embark on the tasks belonging to 'the second half of life', which are quite different because they require us to look within. They require us to develop much greater Self-understanding. We must learn to see ourselves objectively, recognising not just our strengths but also our deficiencies, our 'shadow', and to work to amend them. Only through such conscious Self-knowledge can anyone develop that inner strength based on emotional and spiritual understanding which is essential to true maturity.

For many people, of course, it is quite possible to go through the second half of life without really embarking on this process at all, so that they remain fundamentally immature and ego-centred, having not really moved forward from where their development stopped in the first half of life. Inwardly they are frozen in a kind of perpetual adolescence, hanging onto the values of youth, as we see in the *puer aeternus*, the 'boy hero who cannot grow up', who often then slips over into that other form of immaturity we see in the archetype of the *senex*: that which characterises those unfulfilled older people who take out their disappointment in life in querulous moralising about the world and reminiscing how much better things were in former times.

For those who do continue to grow inwardly, the ultimate prize is to be brought into a conscious relationship with that archetype which is at the centre of them all, 'the Self': that which is both most completely ourselves, yet not ourselves, because it represents the ultimate state of reintegration between the conscious ego and the selfless objectivity of the unconscious.[7]

Such is the goal which is symbolised at the end of stories by the hero and heroine's final coming together in perfect love and succeeding to rule over a 'kingdom'. Superficially this might be taken to stand for no more than a reflection of that natural, near-universal process whereby the vast majority of the human race eventually leave their parents to pair off in marriage, and to set up their own 'kingdom' in a new home. But from the way the unconscious presents all this to us in stories it is clearly meant to represent something much deeper and more significant; and this is particularly underlined by the archetype of the Quest, the plot which more explicitly than any other presents human life as a journey towards the distant goal of Self-realisation.

Not the least interesting feature of the Quest archetype is that it appears not to be directly concerned with the patterns of psychological development in childhood and early life at all. It is preoccupied with that process of final Self-realisation which really belongs to 'the second half of life'. It is significant that the heroes of Quest stories are often full-grown men, who may well be already married.[8] The problem with which they are confronted is that described by Dante in the opening lines of *The Divine Comedy*, when he recalls how 'midway on the journey of this life, I came to a dark wood where the way was lost'. Their starting point is that they have arrived at that stage in adult life where living unthinkingly in the state of ego-consciousness may suddenly become intolerably constricting. Life in this 'City of Destruction', trapped in a mortal body doomed to die, suddenly seems shallow and oppressive. Is there no escape from this prison? Like the Jumping Mouse, they then have the sense that, far off, there is another, quite different centre to existence, and that to reach it has become the most important thing in their lives.

The archetypal pattern of the Quest shows that the journey they now face is indeed long and arduous, and that it is hard enough simply to get near enough to see the nature of this mysterious ego-transcending goal, the Self. But even when

---

7. This is the two-part pattern to human life which is so imaginatively conveyed in *The Magic Flute*. In the first half of the story, we see young Tamino growing up under the guidance of his 'mother figure', the Queen of the Night, representing the instinctive forces of Mother Nature. But then comes the central shift of emphasis where, to complete his maturing process and win union with Pamina, his *anima*, he must turn his back on unconscious instinct and submit to the equally benign guidance of Sarastro. This priestly 'father figure', serving the goddess of wisdom, represents that which is needed for Tamino to complete the tasks of the 'second half of life'. To reach conscious Self-understanding he must develop the masculine strengths of reason, discipline and self-control which enable him in the end to reach full union with the *anima* and the Self. He thus achieves the purpose symbolised by the magical powers of the flute. The scenes where Tamino and Pamina undergo their final 'ordeals', including the need to pass between the opposites of fire and water, are reminiscent of the Quest. We know that if they pass these tests they will reach the goal. At this point we see the forces of unconscious nature, represented by the Queen of the Night and Monostatos, being overthrown. Tamino has completed the transition from the state of unconsciousness, governed by instinct, in which he began the story, to his final state of fully-realised consciousness.

8. E.g., Odysseus, Aeneas, Christian in *Pilgrim's Progress* (even Babar in *Babar and Father Christmas*). As in Overcoming the Monster stories, but not the other plots, the central figure of a Quest is almost exclusively male, a hero rather than a heroine, because he represents the 'masculinity' of consciousness which needs to find its ultimate fulfilment in union with the 'feminine' unconscious.

this has at last been brought clearly in view, the hardest struggle of all begins. This is the battle with all the temptations and challenges which the ego throws up in a last-ditch bid to defend itself, until the moment when its resistance is finally overcome and it merges with the Self. Such is the moment vividly symbolised in Tolkien's *The Lord of the Rings* when Frodo finally sees Sauron's ring, the ring of the ego, slipping away into the Cracks of Doom. Once again the ego becomes one with that 'ground of being' from which it long ago emerged, leaving the hero with a sense of cosmic liberation he could never have imagined possible.

The Voyage and Return plot is much less ambitious. Here we come back to the type of story where the hero or heroine is usually shown as a young person just setting out on adult life. It is precisely because they are young and as yet without any real Self-understanding that they are shown living fecklessly in a state of ego-consciousness. They think they know who they are, as we all do at the start of adult life. But suddenly the bottom falls out of their world. All the assumptions on which they have based their idea of their own identity are blown apart by their abrupt arrival in a totally unfamiliar world, where they can no longer be sure of anything. The purpose of the Voyage and Return plot is to provide a model for that shocking confrontation between the limited vision of ego-consciousness and the mysterious world of the unconscious. The encounter may at first be exhilarating, but in the end it becomes threatening precisely because their ego–consciousness has not yet got the point and 'seen the light'. Finally the penny drops and the hero or heroine learns in some way to see objectively and whole (as we see even when little Peter Rabbit hops up on that wheelbarrow to get sight of the whole garden). They are finally able to make the 'thrilling escape from death' which can return them to the everyday world. They are at last properly conscious.

At this point, however, compared with the Quest, the Voyage and Return story stops short. It describes that shift of perspective which is a necessary prelude to union with the Self; but, except in rare instances, such as *The Golden Ass*, it does not then continue to the full resounding conclusion we see in, say, the *Odyssey* or *The Divine Comedy*. Indeed a conspicuous feature of this plot is the number of stories it inspires which show their central figure, like the heroes of Evelyn Waugh's novels or Scarlett O'Hara, returning to where they started, from what should have been a life-renewing encounter with the world of the unconscious, but having learned nothing. This may above all be symbolised by the fact that their 'other half', representing their capacity for selfless love and understanding, has been left behind. However entertaining they may be, such stories tell us much more about the particular psychological shortcomings of their authors, such as Waugh or Salinger or Lewis Carroll or J. M. Barrie, than they do about the deeper levels of human nature.

The distinction of Comedy is that the unconscious here particularly focuses on the contagious effect of egotism on a whole group or community of people. Because one dominant figure in particular, on the 'upper level', is in the grip of egotism, this casts a distorting shadow over everyone around them. Everyone in the community is thrown into confusion by the fact that there is something which has not yet come to light, so that they are all stumbling round in a fog of misunderstanding and pretence. Everyone is thus set at odds, in one way or another dominated by the influence of that dark power operating 'above the line', until the moment at the end of the story where everything which has been hidden is revealed, including, usually, the realisation by the central dark figure of how blindly and egocentrically he has been behaving. At this point the selfless power of the unconscious, so often personified in the story's heroine, can finally be released from 'below the line', bringing the community joyfully together. Again the story provides a symbolic model of what can happen when consciousness and the unconscious are at last reintegrated.

Everyone can recall the extraordinary mood which can come over an audience as it leaves a theatre or cinema after seeing a Comedy which has worked its magic. It is no accident that few things in storytelling have greater power to move us. After all the frustrations and confusions which preceded it, the final twists of the plot leave us – and the entire audience – feeling strangely overjoyed and uplifted by the sight of how everything came out miraculously right after all.

The same model, although more specifically focused on what is happening within the psyche of one individual, is that which the unconscious presents to us in the plot of Rebirth. The central figure is shown frozen in ego-consciousness, trapped by limited vision, unable to develop, to the point where this is symbolised as a kind of living death. But eventually, inspired by the redeeming figure who symbolises the selfless power of the unconscious, the prison of ego-consciousness is broken open. Precisely because the hero or heroine have been put back in touch with the deeper level of the unconscious, their hearts and eyes are opened. Because their feeling and understanding have been awoken, they are liberated to become whole.

## Balancing the opposites

Such are the patterns whereby the unconscious shows us how humanity can overcome that fatal separation which took place with the 'Fall'. Before we move on, however, this has one further consequence which is of profound relevance to how we imagine stories. This is the way in which, to make sense of the world, our split-off consciousness needs constantly to see it in terms of opposites.

Nothing is more basic to the processes of human thinking than how we divide everything into oppositions between one thing and another. We orientate ourselves through the world by speaking of up or down, forward or backwards, left or right, over or under, long or short, heavy or light, hot or cold, dry or wet, soft or hard, future or past, good or bad, light or dark, alive or dead. So fundamental is this dualism to the way our consciousness works that we are scarcely aware of what an omnipresent part it plays in our thinking. And this duality is of course one of the crucial ways in which we establish and define our own identity, because we are constantly dividing the world into groups and entities which make us aware that we belong on one side of the line rather than the other. We recognise our own identity in sensing our difference from the 'others'.

Each of us is profoundly aware, for instance, that we are either male or female. We are aware that we belong to one country rather than all the rest, to one part of that country, to one city, town or village, to one family. This sense of belonging to one place or group rather than others, and all the loyalties it brings with it, obviously plays a large part in building up our sense of who we are and how we fit in on this earth. But the most fundamental division of all is that which gives each of us a sense of our own individual identity, separate from everyone and everything else in the world. This is the division which, steming from our ego-consciousness, we again experience to a degree unique in the animal kingdom. And it is this division which more than anything else the patterns of storytelling are designed to overcome, as they work towards a point where the opposites can become reconciled and transcended.

This is why nothing is more central to the way in which stories shape themselves in the human unconscious than the idea of bringing that which is unbalanced and incomplete to a final state of balance and completion. This is why stories are concerned with reconciling dualities, such as masculine and feminine, 'above the line' and 'below the line', ego and Self, in all that they symbolise. This is also why in so many stories we see the need for the hero or heroine to tread a path between two opposites, each of which is negative, inadequate or wrong in its own way.

One of the greatest problems posed to us by the partial nature of our consciousness is the difficulty of judging correctly the point of balance between opposing viewpoints. When we see two people locked in bitter dispute, almost invariably neither is wholly right. Each may be partly right and partly wrong. The truth lies not so much at some halfway point between them as in some third position, from which their opposing views can be seen in a wider and clearer perspective. Again, as with the archetypes themselves, almost everyone and everything in the human world presents both light and dark aspects. Yet it is only too natural to us to oversimplify: to see only the light or only the dark. The truth in human affairs almost invariably lies not on one side or the other of a set of opposites, but in some third position which transcends them both.

Again and again in stories we see that deadly division between two opposing figures, each in their own way 'one-sided'; such as when we see the heroine having fallen into the clutches of a villain or monster, the 'light feminine' in the grip of the 'dark masculine'. We know that such an impasse can only be resolved by the intervention of a third figure, the hero, representing the balance of qualities which can rise above it. Such is the subtlest message of that archetypal 'rule of three'. The way of growth, allowing a story to reach a happy ending, lies not just in taking a middle way between two inadequate extremes; it lies in achieving that third state, transcending both, which alone can bring about the transformation necessary to reconnect with life.

Such was the real reason why the ancient Greeks inscribed over the the temple of Apollo at Delphi, the most sacred spot in the Greek world, their belief that the highest value in life was *meden agan*, 'nothing in excess'.[9] This grew out of the same intuitive process which had led them to develop their belief in the counterpoint of hubris and nemesis. They were aware that hubris, 'stepping over the bounds', represents that imbalance which arises from the inevitable tendency to

---

9. Above it, determined by the Rule of Three, was the most familiar symbol in classical architecture: that triangular pediment of stone in which the two angles at each end of the base give rise to the third point above them, to make a perfect, transcendent whole.

one-sidedness of the human ego: while nemesis represents that inexorable redressing of balance which ensures that the state of cosmic wholeness will eventually be restored.

The 'knowledge' of all this is so deeply imprinted into the human psyche that it unconsciously lies at the heart of storytelling. We cannot imagine stories in any other way. It is precisely to 'remind' us of what our limited state of ego-consciousness so easily overlooks that evolution developed in us the capacity to conjure up these patterns of images. And it is only when we begin to understand how this is their real underlying purpose that we can properly begin to explore the relationship between the imaginary world of storytelling and how we live our lives in what we like to call 'the real world'. Such is the theme of our next chapter.

## CHAPTER THIRTY-TWO

# Into the Real World

## *The Ruling Consciousness*

'The minority is always right ... the majority is always wrong.'

Ibsen, *An Enemy of the People*

'So long as one is within a certain phenomenology one is not astonished, and no one wonders what it is all about. Such philosophical doubt only comes to him who is outside the game.'        C. G. Jung, *Psychology and National Problems*, Collected Works, Vol. XVIII

One of the hardest things to get straight about stories is their relationship with what we call 'real life' and the 'real world' in which we all live. We often hear such dismissive phrases as 'that's only a story' or 'that's just a fairy tale'. When people wish to suggest that something is completely untrue, they say 'it's a myth'. The assumption is that what happens in fact and what happens in fiction are so far apart that they are actually opposed to one another.

It is true the relationship between storytelling and real life may not be immediately obvious. But this may be because we are missing the point of what stories really represent. And the main reason for this is that the only instrument we can use to disentangle the true nature of our ability to imagine stories is that from which they originate in the first place, the human psyche. The problem is that the archetypal patterns and laws which shape storytelling are so deeply embedded in our unconscious that our conscious mind finds it hard to recognise them. So instinctive is it to us that stories should take shape in certain ways that we find it almost impossible to stand sufficiently apart from them to ask why this should be so; why, for instance, they should take these forms and not others. Yet once we do manage to make this leap of understanding, we can also begin to see how these same patterns play a huge part in shaping our thinking and our lives in all sorts of ways which have nothing to do with storytelling. Indeed, the real significance of our ability to tell stories is twofold. Firstly, it provides a uniquely revealing mirror to the inner dynamics of human nature. But secondly, by laying bare the unconscious foundations which underlie so much of the way we view the world, this can in turn cast an extraordinarily revealing light on history, politics, religion, philosophy and almost every aspect of human thought and behaviour.

### *Jack and the Beanstalk*: The Marxist and Freudian versions

One of the starting points for my own interest in why we tell stories was a revue sketch staged in London by an American theatre company in the early 1960s. It showed a meeting which had been called in a small middle-American town to discuss a complaint that the copy of *Jack and the Beanstalk* on the shelves of the local library was a 'subversive book' and should be banned. To discuss this the lady chairman has invited along two professors, a Marxist and a Freudian. The Marxist explains that *Jack and the Beanstalk* is indeed a political tract, nothing less than 'a blueprint for world revolution'. As typical members of the downtrodden rural proletariat in a post-feudal society, Jack and his mother are reduced to such poverty that they are finally forced in desperation to sell the only asset they possess, their cow. The only place they can sell it is on the free market, inevitably used by the rich to exploit the poor. Naturally all Jack gets in return is a worthless handful of beans. But these symbols of their exploitation grow up into 'the mighty beanstalk of the workers' movement'; and when Jack climbs to the top, what does he find but the wicked giant of 'international monopoly capitalism'. Eventually he strikes the revolutionary blow which brings the tyranny crashing down. Having won this glorious victory, the proletariat, represented by Jack and his mother, win the right to live happily ever after.

While this dissertation is proceeding, the Freudian impatiently interrupts to insist that this is just childish hooey. The true meaning of *Jack and the Beanstalk* is that it is no more than 'the simple, rather touching story of a young boy's sexual awakening'. Like any small boy, Jack lives with the person who is closest to him in the world, his mother. But the day comes when he must move on from his initial state of infantile dependence on mother, symbolised by the milk-giving cow. This is when he discovers that he has in his hand beans, 'seminal essences', from which there rises up in front of him 'this thrusting, enormous, towering …'. 'Ye-a-a-s', hastily interjects the lady chairman. Climbing up this symbol of his awakening manhood, the Freudian continues, what does Jack find at the top but the 'non-improjected fantasy image of Father'. 'Father' naturally rejects this challenge to his masculine authority and tries to drive him back down the beanstalk. But eventually our hero hits back by grabbing an axe to eliminate 'Father', so that, in line with his Oedipal urge, he can return to live with mother happily ever after.

Increasingly bemused by the force of the two rival interpretations, the lady chairman sums up by telling the audience that, thanks to their two speakers, 'we now all realise that *Jack and the Beanstalk* is not only subversive. It is also very dirty, and should definitely be taken off our library shelves'.[1]

Obviously what was striking about this sketch was how it brought out such a startling correspondence between the story of *Jack and the Beanstalk* and two of the most influential thought-systems of the twentieth century. But was it possible, I reflected as I watched the sketch, that there might be some deeper reason for these coincidences? Might there be some fundamental structure underlying the way we think about the world which could account for this seemingly remarkable overlap between Marx's analysis of society, Freudian psychology and a centuries-old folk tale? Indeed we can now see that there is an archetypal structure under-

---

1. This sketch was performed by its authors, Bill Alton, Del Close and Mina Kolb of the Second City revue company from Chicago, at the Establishment Club, London, in the autumn of 1962. An edited version was published in the magazine *Private Eye*, 14 December 1962.

lying all of them. And in terms of what this really signifies, in terms of human psychology, we can see how the 'Freudian interpretation', for all its inadequacies, does in fact gets rather closer than the Marxist's to the true underlying meaning of the tale. The story of Jack is indeed rooted in that pattern central to storytelling, showing the pattern of a young man's growing up to maturity. Where the Freudian interpretation begins to fall short, however, is in its inability to recognise the true nature of the giant/Dark Father, as representing the negative version of the Light Father the young hero must eventually become. With its distortingly narrow focus on sexuality, Freudian psychology cannot then offer any proper explanation of the treasures Jack wins from the giant. And although the Freudians may get very excited by the fact that Jack returns at the end to live with mother, they cannot see that the tale ends like this only because it is a version of the archetypal story intended to be told to very young children.

Paradoxically, what is in fact rather more interesting is the way this archetypal story lends itself so neatly to a Marxist interpretation. This is not just because it can show us the psychological foundations which underlie the Marxist view of society. More significantly it opens up the much wider question of how the archetypal structures revealed by storytelling can help us to understand the workings of any human society, and how they shape some of the most fundamental ways in which we view the world around us. This is because, to a far greater degree than we are consciously aware, we look at the world in terms of stories all the time. They are the most natural way in which we structure our descriptions of the world around us. We naturally see our own life as a story, as we do those of others, each made up of an infinite number of subordinate episodes, large and small. Through the media, we view the pageant of public life as a continual kaleidoscope of stories, complete with 'dark' figures and 'light', happy and unhappy endings.

Certainly the Marxist, like any ideologue, interprets how the world works in terms of a basic story: one which can tell him who are the villains, who the heroes, how he would like the plot to end up. But to a great extent, irrespective of our point of view, the same is true for all of us. And nowhere can we see this more clearly than in the unconscious patterns which shape not only how we 'read' the events of politics and history, but how these dramas themselves are acted out.

## Above the line / below the line: right wing / left wing

Apart from a hero or heroine, stories usually present us with the picture of a group of people – a household, a community, a kingdom – which provides the focus of the imaginary world in which the story is set. During much of the story this 'little world' or 'kingdom' may in some way be divided. But if the story comes to a happy ending we see it in some way being brought back to unity. And, as we have seen, there is a close correspondence between the conditions which are necessary for this reintegration to take place and the pattern of integration in the individual human psyche.

In anyone who has achieved personal maturity, we see how this combines strength of character and the capacity for ordered thinking with selfless feeling and the intuitive ability to see objectively and whole. Similarly, in the resolution of a story which comes to a happy ending we see these same essential values being brought together to create an image of 'wholeness' in the wider community. As darkness gives way to light, so we see power in that household, community or kingdom once again being exercised properly and wisely. Order is restored, so that everything and everyone are back in their proper place. Love and reconciliation prevail. That which was hidden has come to light so that, as 'ignorance gives way to knowledge', everything and everyone can at last be seen clearly for what they are.

The significance of this particular combination of values is not just limited to the imaginary world of storytelling. It equally provides an ideal model for the workings of any social grouping in the real world. Every human collectivity, whether it be a nation, a family or any other type of organisation, is by definition hierarchical. One or more figures – a monarch, a tribal leader, a president, a prime minister, a chairman, a general, a father, a mother – are in a position of power, playing the role of leader, exercising authority. When that authority is exercised properly, combining masculine with feminine values, firmness and order united with feeling and understanding, the community itself remains united. But when those in authority fail to exercise power properly what we see is that the community splits in familiar fashion onto two levels, 'above' and 'below the line'.

The fact that on the upper level power is being misused invariably means that it is in some way being exercised selfishly and blindly. Either it is being applied excessively and oppressively, or it is being used weakly and inadequately. Just as in stories, this abuse of power inevitably casts a shadow over those below the line. And it is here, among those in the shadows, that people can see most clearly how they are being misruled, and how what is missing in those 'above the line' is that balance of masculine and feminine qualities which are essential to just and wise governance.

This constitutes what has been the central political fault line in almost every society throughout history. Every society is made up of rulers and ruled, those who govern and those who are governed, and obviously an immense part of human history has been written in the tension and potential conflict between the two. Above the line have been those who wished to hold onto and extend their power: if they were dictators or absolute rulers, through fear and force. From below the line has come a constant pressure to restrain that power and to make the rulers accountable, which has given rise not just to constitutional government, parliamentary democracy and the rule of law but also to all the revolutions and wars of independence in history.

The first thinker who discerned what amounted to an unconscious archetype shaping political behaviour was Plato in Book VIII of his *Republic*. He analysed the tendency of societies to evolve through a cycle which begins with Monarchy, the rule of one leader and father-figure to all his people, the king. But this eventually leads to pressure from those immediately below him to restrain his power, and this emergence of a ruling class made up of a few rich and powerful individuals leads on to the second stage of the cycle, Oligarchy, This in turn leads to pressure from below them for a much wider dispersal of power, where in the name of liberty the people demand the right to participate in framing their laws and calling their government to account. This third stage is Democracy. But the cycle, as Plato described it, does not stop there. The belief in liberty becomes increasingly obsessive, particularly affecting all those who can still be viewed as 'below the line' and oppressed. Women rebel against their roles as wives and mothers; slaves against their masters; children against parents and teachers. People are even expected to respect the 'rights' of animals. The growing disorder of a society in which every kind of rule from above has fallen into disrepute eventually creates pressure for the final phase of the cycle, Tyranny: where again one man imposes his power, to restore order to a society in danger of disintegrating.

In psychological terms it is this same perennial fault line which helps explain that fundamental opposition in politics between 'right' and 'left'. The right wing view rests chiefly on the masculine values, centred on the exercise of power and the maintenance of order; what may be called the values of 'Father'. This is innately conservative because it believes in upholding the established structures and institutions of society. It supports those values which it sees as holding society together: the symbols of the nation state, tradition, patriotism, conventional morality, the family, discipline, the need for strength to defend the existing order against its external and internal enemies. The left wing rests essentially on the feminine values of feeling and understanding, what may be called the values of 'Mother', in which it perceives the ruling order and the right-wing view in general to be so heartlessly deficient. It talks about liberty, compassion and equality. It protests against oppression and the injustices of the system. It proclaims the need to raise up all those whom society places 'below the line', the workers, anyone who can be seen as exploited or as underdogs. It does not wish to preserve a hierarchical order which it sees as corrupt and unjust. It believes in change and the vision of a future society which is fairer and more caring; in which everyone can have an equal chance; which is not bound by narrow exclusive nationalism but sees all humanity as one.[2]

We see this same division between the values of 'Father' and 'Mother' in the way people's political views tend to change over the years: that general human tendency to follow the pattern summed up in the maxim of Huey Long, the one-time governor of Louisiana, that 'every man's political career reads like a book, from left to right'. When people are young, unsettled, just starting on the ladder of life, they are more inclined to take a 'feminine', 'below the line' view; to be idealistic, to feel deeply the injustices of the world, to rebel against what they see as the constraints of discipline, established convention and the stern values of 'Father'. When, as they grow older and more mature, they themselves become more established, with more experience of the world, they are inclined to take a more masculine, 'above the line' view. Idealism gives way, as they would see it, to realism. They come to appreciate the conservative values of discipline, tradition and order. They at last

2. The very fact that we use the terms 'right' and 'left' in this context is itself, of course, significant. Just as right-handedness is considered 'normal' in human beings, so right-sidedness is associated with the ruling order, being 'right' rather than wrong, being on the 'right' side of the law. Left-handedness is looked on as 'abnormal' and the 'left', as we have seen before, is associated with 'below the line' attributes, as in the Russian *na levo*, 'on the left'.

see the point of those values of 'Father' (not least because they may well have been through the educative experience of being a parent themselves). It was this familiar shift taking place in people's psychic perspective which gave rise to Bernard Shaw's famous dictum that 'anyone who is not a socialist at twenty has no heart, anyone who is not a conservative at forty has no head'.[3]

In psychological terms, of course, these two opposing views are simply the two halves of the same whole. To make up the archetype of totality, the Self, each needs the balance of the other. And the more one-sided people's political view becomes, the more they are likely to see the other side in terms of caricature. The right-winger sees the left as 'dangerous anarchists', 'raving Bolsheviks', 'bleeding heart liberals', out to destroy all social order. The left-winger sees the right as 'vicious tyrants', 'racist reactionaries', 'Fascist pigs', whose only concern is to oppress the defenceless and underprivileged. This is not to say that each side may not have justification for its view. But because by definition this kind of division arouses the human ego, each side tends to end up projecting the shadow of its own one-sidedness onto the other. This is why nothing is commoner in political conflict than 'the fallacy of the half-truth', whereby politicians finds it much easier to identify the weaknesses in the position of their opponents than to recognise the deficiencies in their own.

What happens in the archetypal version is that it shows what is necessary for the two sides to become in some way reconciled. The egocentricity and blindness of those exercising power above the line is redeemed by their recognition of the self-less values represented by those below the line. The whole community can thus be brought together in unity. This may, according to the archetypal pattern, be what ought to happen. What in the real world is more likely to happen is that the two sides remain locked in conflict. Those above the line continue to abuse their power; and in extreme cases this may eventually provoke in those below the line a dream of rising up in an attempt to overthrow the power of their oppressors by force. This is because, in the real world, those below the line are not necessarily just embodiments of the selfless redeeming values, as they are in a story. They may well become just as much possessed by collective egotism as those above the line. However genuine and justified their demands for truth, justice and compassion may originally have been, these may no longer be entirely selfless and absolute. In becoming politicised they have also become sentimentalised, hi-jacked by the collective ego to justify its drive to power.

---

3. The archetypes underlying politics relate also to the archetypal basis for the way we perceive the symbolism of colour. Archetypally red relates to the female, unconscious end of the colour spectrum, while conscious, masculine values are associated with the opposite blue end. Hence the historical association of left-wing political groups, promoting the values of 'Mother', with red (Communism, the Red Flag) and that of right-wing groups, representing the values of 'Father', with blue (e.g. the British Conservative Party). Where we find red in stories it is often associated with the 'Dark Mother' (e.g., Lady de Winter in *The Three Musketeers*, the Red Queen and the Queen of Hearts in Carroll's Alice stories). Green at the centre of the spectrum represents the un-differentiated, instinctive balance of masculine and feminine (as in nature). The most consciously, fully differentiated marriage of masculine and feminine attributes unites the two ends of the spectrum in purple: hence the association of this colour with royalty and the Self. White, as a blend of all the colours, is of course associated with light, purity and innocence, and black, the absence of colour, with darkness.

It is here we see the emergence of that Utopian revolutionary mindset, as in Marxism, which comes to see the existing power structure as so oppressive and corrupt that it is beyond redemption. It must be torn down altogether and replaced by a new one. In their fantasies the revolutionaries become driven by a projected vision of the Self, a new order in which society can be remade and reintegrated in a perfect form, where power can be exercised justly and wisely to the benefit of all. In reality this vision of the Self has been taken over by the collectivised ego. All those who, for whatever reason, cannot subscribe to this vision must be crushed and eliminated, as 'enemies of the people'.

Thus do we see the emergence of that familiar 'dark inversion' whereby, in the name of creating the ideal state, bringing justice and liberty for society's dispossessed, a totalitarian new order emerges, much more ruthless and oppressive than that which it has replaced. What has happened is that the forces below the line, consciously motivated by the feminine values, have become unconsciously possessed by a dark version of precisely that masculine drive to power and control they so resent in those above the line. And at this point we see how the archetype which has really taken over is that of Tragedy. We see just why any revolutionary dream inevitably becomes self-defeating. Indeed it is here in the archetype of Tragedy that we can at last begin to unravel the true relationship between the unconscious patterns which shape stories and those which shape human behaviour in real life.

### The fantasy cycle in history

It is no accident that so many of the world's best-known fictional tragedies were originally inspired by historical events, or by events which actually occurred in real life: Shakespeare's *Julius Caesar*, *Antony and Cleopatra* and *Richard III*, Tolstoy's *Anna Karenina*, Flaubert's *Madame Bovary*, Stendhal's *Le Rouge et Le Noir*, the film *Bonnie and Clyde*, to name but a few. The reason why these episodes translated so neatly into fictional form was that the way they unfolded in real life (or at least as they were presented by historians) so closely followed the pattern of the tragic archetype. And the reason they did so was that this five-stage tragic cycle is not just an arbitrary construct of the human imagination. It is a pattern we see constantly being acted out in the world around us, because it is the pattern of what may follow whenever people, whether individually or collectively, are drawn to embark on a course of action based on ego-centred fantasy.

Exactly as in any fictional version, this is likely in some way to be based either on a desire for power (or money, a version of the same thing), or on sexuality. It may involve the planning of a crime or the start of an illicit love affair. It may be any scheme which involves deceiving others or any kind of reckless gamble. There will invariably be some form of Anticipation Stage when those possessed by the power of fantasy are looking for a Focus. When they find it, they commit the act which launches them irretrievably on their dark course. For a while, because they have taken the initiative or because what they are up to remains undetected, all seems to go well (Dream Stage). They seem to be getting away with it. But because what they are acting out is ultimately based on defying their surrounding framework of reality, they begin to run into difficulties. Other people and events begin to constellate against them (Frustration Stage). In an increasingly desperate attempt to keep the fantasy in being they push on, committing further dark acts, or attempting to cover up what they have done, as reality closes in on them (Nightmare Stage). Finally comes that moment when the fantasy collides with reality, bringing about their downfall or destruction.

Looking at history, we see how this cycle repeats itself again and again. We may see it in what happens to individual politicians, as when in 1972 President Nixon connived in the burglary of his opponents' headquarters at the Watergate. What eventually forced him two years later to become the first American President in history to resign from office was not so much this original 'dark act' but the way he became increasingly caught out by his efforts to deny and to hide his involvement in what had happened. Repeatedly in the history of politics we see that what destroys a politician's career is not so much his initial error as his subsequent attempts to cover it up. It is the increasingly contorted web of deceit involved in the cover-up which eventually brings him to the Nightmare Stage, leading to his exposure and downfall.[4]

Again we see this tragic pattern in the fate of every failed rebellion against a ruling order, from the revolt of Spartacus against Rome in 73 BC to the English Peasants' Revolt of 1381, from Pugachev's rebellion in Russia in 1773 to the Hungarian rising against the Communists in 1956 or Che Guevara's attempt to overthrow the Bolivian Government in 1967. In each case, if we examine the course taken by such a rebellion, we see how it is shaped by the five-stage pattern. Initially the rebels win such support that they dream they can actually overthrow the ruling power. As that power gathers its forces to crush them, the rebels experience increasing frustration, Finally there is the Nightmare Stage when reality closes in on them and it is clear their rebellion has failed. Their leaders and many of their followers are killed.

Where revolutions are apparently successful, we see the five-stage pattern taking a different form. It was the American historian Crane Brinton, in his book *The Anatomy of Revolution* (1938), who first analysed what might be described the 'revolutionary archetype', as he traced the remarkable parallels between the three most influential revolutions in history, those in England in the seventeenth century, France at the end of the eighteenth century, and Russia in the years after 1917. In each case the course of events was unconsciously dictated by what we can now see was that archetypal five-stage pattern.

When in 1789 the French people rose up in the name of liberty against the excessive power and privileges of Louis XVI and the French aristocracy, there was a Dream Stage when it seemed the old order, the *ancien régime*, was just disintegrating before them. They soon won all the liberties they were demanding. But it is in the nature of fantasy, whether in politics, sex or anything else, that it cannot reach a satisfactory point of resolution. Once unleashed, it becomes unconsciously driven

4. In recent British political history, this was the pattern which, for instance, accounted for the resignations or disgrace of John Profumo, John Stonehouse, Jeremy Thorpe, Jeffrey Archer, Peter Mandelson, Stephen Byers and many others. Similar examples can be found in political life all over the world.

to make ever more extreme demands. In Paris in the early 1790s, as the promised Utopia failed to materialise, with the king, the Father-figure of his country, still on the throne, the relatively moderate Girondins gave way to the more extreme Jacobins, who unleashed an orgy of killing, its symbolic centrepiece in 1793 being the execution of the king and his family. But this only led on to the Terror, the Nightmare Stage, when the revolution turned inward on itself and began, in the famous phrase, to 'eat its own children'. As the revolutionaries set up their fearsome dictatorship under the Committee of Public Safety – what Robespierre called 'the despotism of liberty against tyranny' – it was now they themselves who were being murdered and guillotined in ever greater numbers, culminating in 1794 in the execution by his own Revolutionary Tribunal of Robespierre himself.

This was the shocking event which brought the nightmarish explosion of violence and the five-stage cycle to its climax. France fell back into a state of nervous exhaustion and uneasy calm, characterised also by a frenzied pursuit of sexual and other egocentric pleasures (the unleashing of fantasy in a new and different form) until eventually a new 'dream figure' emerged, the successful young general Napoleon. In 1799, when he established himself as his country's new strong man, a new collective fantasy began to take shape. A new five-stage cycle had begun.

The Napoleonic fantasy reached the height of its Dream Stage during the years between 1805 and 1812 when, as self-proclaimed Emperor, he seemed to have all Europe at his feet. In 1812, when his fantasies over-reached themselves in his invasion of Russia, this entered its Frustration Stage, forcing him eventually into humiliating retreat. By now, in the shadows cast over Europe by his vainglorious tyranny, countervailing forces were beginning to constellate against him. This led to the Nightmare Stage of the next two years as his armies suffered a series of defeats, leaving him a powerless prisoner. In 1815 the 'Hundred Days' when he escaped from exile in Elba constituted another, lesser five-stage cycle, beginning with the Dream Stage of his euphoric progress through France to reclaim his throne and culminating in his nightmare at Waterloo. Finally his fantasy-career was brought to its devastating conclusion when he was taken off to that bleak and remote islet in the South Atlantic where, six years later, broken in health and spirit, he died.

As Brinton traced in his book, we can see how a remarkably similar basic pattern shaped the revolutions which took place in England in the 1640s and Russia in 1917. In each case, after a long Anticipation Stage, those who saw themselves in the shadows cast by the excessive power of a King/Father-figure eventually rose up to challenge him. In each case, as the existing order was overthrown, there was a Dream Stage when it seemed as though sufficient restraints had been placed on kingly power and liberty had been won. But in each case the demands of the revolutionaries then became more extreme. In England, the victory of the parliamentary forces in the Civil War led to the desire for a completely new type of political order. In Russia, Kerensky's moderate parliamentary government was overthrown by Lenin's Bolsheviks. In each case the unconscious logic of the fantasy led eventually to the murder of the King/Father, and in the name of liberty the new regime then rapidly evolved into a tyranny far more oppressive and dictatorial than the one it had replaced. Eventually, after Cromwell's premature death, the English people welcomed back their monarchy in an explosion of rejoicing. In Russia, after the nightmare of civil war and the rise of the Bolshevik dictatorship, Lenin came to a premature death: but only to be succeeded by Stalin, under whose even darker tyranny the revolution was to continue to 'eat its own children' for decades to come.[5]

Perhaps the most vivid historical example of the way events in real life are unconsciously shaped by this archetypal pattern was that supreme defining drama of the twentieth century, the Second World War (it was no accident, as we have noted, that this was to inspire more fictional stories than any other event in history). More specifically, we can see the pattern of that drama in terms of the rise and fall of its central actor, Adolf Hitler.

If we look at the rise and fall of Nazi Germany as an archetypal story, then the role of Hitler is that of a Tempter. The blow the German people had suffered to their collective national ego through their humiliating defeat in the First World War, followed by years of weak, unmasculine government under the Weimar Republic, led them to see their once proud, militaristic nation as having been reduced to a state of impotence and economic depression. Hitler emerged as the visionary and orator who could awaken Germany's dark, resentful nationalist energies. With his election as leader of the nation in 1933, the Anticipation Stage found its Focus. This launched the Dream Stage of Nazi rule which was to develop through the rest of the 1930s. Inspired by its 'dream leader', the fantasy grew in confidence round projections of the masculine values of power and order, constantly extending its appetites as it began to take over one neighbouring country after another. When in 1939 his invasion of Poland led other countries for the first time to threaten resistance to his demands, this led to war. But in 1940 the Dream Stage reached its height, when his armies were able to march into Denmark, Norway, Belgium, Holland and France almost unopposed. A first momentary check on his ambitions was the emergence of Churchill and the failure of his plan to invade England. But it was in the nature of Hitler's dream-state that this merely fired up his fantasy to yet greater heights, as when in 1941 he invaded, firstly, Yugoslavia and Greece, and finally, in his greatest gamble of all, the Soviet Union. This was to mark the onset, over the next two years, of the Frustration Stage. Every fantasy, because it cannot reach any satisfactory resolution, must consist of swings

---

5. To a much less violent degree, this alternation of illusion and disillusion typifies the pattern of political life even in a peaceful democracy. Almost every successful political leader has a 'shelf life', whereby initially he or she commands respect and seems to represent the qualities the country needs. But eventually the very qualities which once seemed so admirable show their shadowy underside and come to be viewed as discreditable. The same kind of switch into its opposite applies to the popularity of political parties. A party may successfully hold sway for a long period, but eventually it seems tired, no longer capable of governing effectively or in touch with the social forces which put it in power. This helps to generate a sense of optimism that the party which is its main rival can provide a new government which is quite different: energetic, efficient, honest, more in tune with the country's needs. Its election to power is hailed as marking the start of a new, more hopeful era. For a while the new reforming government may enjoy a Dream Stage, when it seems it can do no wrong. But it gradually moves into a Frustration Stage, when its errors and deficiencies seem to multiply. Finally, as the mood of the country shifts irreversibly against it, it enters a Nightmare Stage where it can do nothing right; and by now, of course, the familiar momentum of optimism is building up around its opponents until the moment when they can sweep into power. Thus does the cycle of illusion and disillusion begin again.

between anticipation and frustration; and the middle phase of the fantasy cycle marks that moment when frustration begins to outweigh anticipation. The initial euphoria of Hitler's advance into Russia (and the start of a new, more murderous phase in his drive to exterminate the Jews and other 'below the line' *untermenschen*) was succeeded by the setback of the first Russian winter and the entry into the war of the United States. This was followed by the even more breathtaking advances of his armies in the summer of 1942, both in Russia and North Africa; succeeded in that autumn and winter by his first really crushing reverses at Stalingrad and El Alamein. Again, as we see in so many stories, external forces were at last constellating in serious opposition to the dark central figure, and by the summer of 1943, with the defeat of his last great Russian offensive at Kursk, coinciding with the allied invasion of Sicily, the mass-sinking of his U-boats in the Atlantic and the unleashing of day-and-night assault by allied bomber fleets on the cities of Germany itself, Hitler's dream was moving into its Nightmare Stage. By the summer and autumn of 1944, with enemies now closing in from three sides, he was in exactly that position in which we see the hero by the end of the fourth act in a Shakespearian tragedy such as *Macbeth* or *Richard III*: a cornered rat without hope of escape. In 1945 the final act of the drama wound to its archetypal conclusion when, amid the rubble of the one-time capital of his great European empire, he, like so many central figures of Tragedy before him, took his own life.

At this point, for all those hundreds of millions of people who had been drawn into the conflict against him, the archetypal response which now shaped their emotions more than anything else was that which we see enacted at the end of an Overcoming the Monster story. For six years Hitler had loomed up in their consciousness just like any monster in storytelling, vested with all the psychological characteristics of a mythical monster. He had seemed invincibly powerful, utterly heartless, devilishly ingenious: the complete personification of all that is twisted and dark in human nature. Yet now at last the monster was dead. By a titanic concentration of masculine values, strength, will and organisation, reinforced by the selflessness of the allied cause, this quintessence of evil had been overcome. And ultimately it could be seen how, like any monster in fiction, his central failing, his fundamental flaw, was that he was blind. Possessed by unconscious forces, he had, as he himself once put it, been a 'sleepwalker', leading his people into a colossal act of collective make-believe. As the archetype dictates, this cosmic act of hubris had eventually aroused its inevitable nemesis. Cosmic balance had been restored. Yet, for all the mighty wave of relief and rejoicing which engulfed humanity, this was not of course the end of the story, even when, a few months later, the Nazis' collective alter-ego on the other side of the world met similar nemesis in those mushroom clouds rising over the cities of Hiroshima and Nagasaki.

For millions of those who had suffered under Hitler's shadow, the slaying of the monster did not bring the unalloyed victory for light that we see at the end of a fictional version of the story. For half the peoples of Europe, the end of one tyranny meant only their falling under the advancing shadow of another, that of Stalin's Communism. Even for many in the West, the time after the war was still bleak, as they struggled out of the ruins to live through years of austerity. For the fact was that, although it had been natural to view the events of those wartime years as like living through a gigantic, real-life Overcoming the Monster story, this had only been a projection onto the outer world of an archetype the true essence of which lies within. Certainly Hitler and his Nazi followers had been a supreme embodiment of everything the archetypal 'monster' represents.[6] But ultimately the archetype, as we see it expressed in stories, stands not for the overcoming of any specific external monster. It runs much deeper than that, as an expression of the human need to overcome the very principle of egotism, as this operates in every one of us. In this sense, we are reminded that the real purpose of these great archetypes in storytelling is not to describe what happens in the outside world, but to show us the patterns which shape what goes on within, in that inner psychic realm from which all our behaviour in the outside world originates. It is this which explains why we so often get the impression that what happens in stories is quite different from what happens in real life: because we are looking in the wrong place for what stories really represent. This does not mean that these great archetypal patterns embedded in our unconscious do not influence how we view the outside world. They do so in countless ways all the time. But the most obvious means whereby they do so lies in how we project them outwardly onto the world, in a manner which misses their true inner purpose. And it is this which inevitably leads to frustration, when they seem never quite to fulfil the expectations we have placed on them: leading us to suppose that what only happens in 'a story' and what happens in 'real life' are two quite different things.

## Projections and disappointments

In 1336 the Italian poet Petrarch and his brother climbed to the summit of Mont Ventoux in Provence. Doubtless many people, shepherds and others, had ascended mountains before. But this was the first occasion in history when the climbers were sufficently self-conscious about what they were doing to record the event. Since then, and particularly in the last two centuries, climbing to the tops of mountains such as Everest, 'because they are there', has become a commonplace. But it is a uniquely human thing to want to do. Animals feel no urge to reach the tops of mountains except in pursuit of food, and the question arises 'why do human beings do it?' Why should they wish to make long, arduous journeys, often

6. So compellingly did the Nazis represent the archetypal image of the 'monster' that they would continue to play this role in storytelling of all kinds for decades. Even half a century later, they helped inspire two of Steven Spielberg's most successful films of the 1990s, *Saving Private Ryan* (1997) and *Schindler's List* (1993). Loosely adapted from a real-life wartime episode, turned into a novel in the 1980s by Thomas Kenneally, *Schindler's List* was in plot terms a combination of Rebirth and Thrilling Escape From Death. The hero, Oskar Schindler, was an amoral businessman who, by currying favour with the Nazis in occupied Poland, recruited dispossessed Jews as cheap labour to help him build up a lucrative manufacturing business. As persecution of the Jews becomes ever more ruthless, Schindler begins to develop 'light' qualities, in contrast to the monstrous command-ant of a concentration camp from which he draws some of his workforce. At the story's climax, Schindler risks his own life in saving hundreds of Jews from the gas-chambers, by smuggling them to a new factory in his Czech home town. Here they learn the war is over. Schindler disappears. The film ends with a ceremony in Jerusalem decades later, after Schindler's death, when his body has been reburied in a Jewish cemetery. Survivors and their families meet to honour his memory as 'a just gentile'.

risking death, to reach such arbitrary points on our Earth's surface as the North and South Poles? Clearly there is a parallel between the obsessive human desire to achieve such purely symbolic physical goals and that overwhelming sense of compulsion to achieve a single, central purpose we see evoked by the archetype of the Quest. It is no accident that, when we read an account of some expedition to conquer Everest, land on the Moon or reach any other physical goal hard to attain, the story should draw us on in precisely the same way as a fictional Quest, because both are rooted in the same archetype.

The reason why our unconscious has been coded with this pattern, preconditioning us to this sense that somewhere there is a goal of immense significance which will require a long and difficult journey to reach is that it relates to our inner psychological development. The goal on which the Quest archetype is centred symbolises the state of psychic 'wholeness'. As with any other archetype, however, it can also be projected onto the outer world. Even though those who set out to climb Everest or reach the North Pole may derive immense personal satisfaction from achieving their goal, they have not reached that ego-transcending inner goal with which the pattern coded into our unconscious is really concerned. What has happened is that their ego has become identified with a pattern which actually originates in the drive to reach an internal goal and projected it externally. And herein lies the clue to the most obvious way in which most of the archetypal patterns of storytelling unconsciously influence our lives and thinking in the 'real world'.

In fact the only archetypal pattern which directly shapes events in the real world in precisely the sense the archetype intends is that of Tragedy. Those who seek to further their ego-centred desires by way of fantasy, whether individual or collective, do unconsciously find themselves acting out that five-stage pattern leading to destruction, exactly as we see in a story. In this sense there is no difference between the pattern as represented in fiction and that we see unfolding in real life. But the point about Tragedy is that it is the only archetypal plot which is not concerned with showing how its central figure or figures can eventually transcend egotism. All the others are concerned with this, and therefore they are essentially concerned with what is going inside the hero or heroine. But where an archetype is projected externally, it inevitably becomes itself an expression of the ego. The result is that it misses the real underlying point of why that pattern is programmed into our unconscious in the first place.

We have already seen how this works in terms of the archetype of Overcoming the Monster. Whenever someone in real life becomes possessed by an extreme form of egotism, they will inevitably be seen as a 'monster' by all those in the shadow cast by their egotism. Hitler, as merely one extreme example, was seen as a monster because he displayed all the psychological characteristics of the archetypal monster; and inevitably the colossal struggle required to defeat him came to be seen by all those involved as precisely like the acting out of a fictional Overcoming the Monster story, with the corresponding sense of cosmic liberation when the battle was finally over. But the fundamental purpose of the Overcoming the Monster archetype is to show that central internal conflict which exists inside each human individual, the potential battle between the power of the ego and the deeper Self. And this means that whenever the archetype is projected out onto the outside world, it ceases to be an idealised pattern and becomes prone to all the distortions which can arise when we see all the properties of the monster in someone else, without recognising that we may have the seeds of those same failings in ourselves.

We saw a vivid example of this in the contrast between the stories of Goliath and Samson, as they are presented in Jewish folklore in the Bible. Because we are shown the story of Goliath, the strong man of the Philistines, from a Jewish point of view, he is presented as an archetypal monster: immensely strong, boastful, heartless and stupid. Everything about him is dark, because he is the champion of the other side. But then we come to the story of Samson, Israel's own strong man. To his own people, Samson was seen as nothing but a shining hero, prepared to sacrifice his own life in slaying 3000 Philistines. To the Philistines, however, he would have seemed a heartless and murderous monster. They would have seen him exactly as the children of Israel saw the Philistines' own hero Goliath. And we saw a striking echo of this thousands of years later when, at the start of the twenty-first century, the people of Israel faced a horrifying challenge from Palestinian suicide bombers. To the Israelis they were nothing but ruthless terrorists. To the Palestinians they were selfless heroes. But when the great Jewish hero Samson pulled down the pillars of the hall, to be crushed along with all those Philistines, what was he himself but the historical equivalent of a suicide bomber?

We can see the Overcoming the Monster archetype shaping human responses to real-life situations all through history. One example was the British response to the Argentinian seizure of the Falklands in 1982. The pattern of the drama which unfolded as the British task force set out to wrest the islands back from the sinister Buenos Aires junta was precisely that of an Overcoming the Monster story (although, as the British forces journeyed across half the world to face their worst ordeals as they finally secured their goal, it also included a strong element of the Quest). From the Argentinians' point of view, of course, the pattern of those two months exactly matched the five-stage cycle of a fantasy, ending in nightmare and disaster.

An even more vivid example was the response of the Western allies to Saddam Hussein's seizure of Kuwait in 1990. The Iraqui leader, with his vast armies, missiles and poison gas, was built up in Western eyes as an archetypal monster; and the frustration felt by so many when the allied forces halted their advance in southern Iraq instead of driving on to take Baghdad derived precisely from their intuitive sense that the story had not been carried forward to its proper archetypal conclusion. How could this be a happy ending when the monster was left still brooding balefully in his lair? [7]

7. In January 1991, as the first Gulf War began, I noted as a journalist how the spectacle of allied forces travelling across half the world to confront Saddam Hussein provided a curious echo of the oldest recorded story in the world, the episode in the *Epic of Gilgamesh* when the heroes set out across the world to confront the monstrous giant Humbaba. It was of course from Mesopotamia, now Iraq, that this ancient story originated. Twelve years later, in 2003, it seemed very possible that the sense of an archetypal pattern having been left complete played a significant part in prompting George Bush Jr to invade Iraq, to complete the business left unfinished by his father.

In the weeks following the terrorist attacks on New York and Washington on 11 September 2001, we saw Western consciousness building up Osama bin Laden, with his worldwide terrorist organisation, into another archetypal monster, even to the point where he was imagined directing his murderous operations from that classic monster's lair, a cave. But what we also saw was how, across the Moslem world and elsewhere, the same archetype was evoked to build up President Bush's America into an equally classic monster, heartless and blind, using its colossal power to dominate the rest of mankind. And in that sense the stand-off between the two camps presented a perfect example of mutual projection, with each side projecting all the darkness in the world onto the other.

Another archetype which in its projected form exercises particularly powerful sway over our imagination is that of Rags to Riches. Few things have more consistently appealed to the fantasies of mankind than the dream of emerging from obscurity to fame and fortune. We see it in people's perennial dream of having their humdrum lives miraculously transformed by a lottery win, or conceiving some idea which will bring them fabulous riches, or simply being plucked out from the anonymous crowd to become the focus of attention as a celebrity.

In our modern world we see this Rags to Riches pattern acted out incessantly, as young men and women emerge from humble anonymity to receive obsessive adulation as film stars, pop singers, supermodels, sporting heroes. But the real reason why this archetype exercises such a hold over our imagination is that, as in a fairy tale, it shows the pattern of an individual being inwardly transformed, to the point where he or she can finally be revealed in glory as their fully-realised Self. That final outward transformation we see when Cinderella or Dick Whittington appear centre-stage in their fine clothes, to mark their winning of great position and wealth, is only an outward symbol of how they have realised their full inner potential. When the archetype comes to be projected outwardly, however, as no more than a vehicle for the ego, the external transformation is all that is left. The inner transformation has been lost sight of. This is why our newspapers delight in telling us what happens to so many of the real-life Rags to Riches heroes and heroines of our time when, having apparently attained all the prizes the outward world can offer, they end up with all the problems of drink, drugs, failed relationships and general disillusionment which result from having been led on by the ego into chasing such an unreal and hollow dream.

The plot least obviously open to outward projection is Voyage and Return, because of all the archetypal patterns this is the one which has least of a purposive drive. The whole point of Voyage and Return stories is that their central figures' sudden, disconcerting plunge into a strange, unfamiliar world happens to them without their wishing it. This has little to appeal to the ego and it therefore lacks the compelling unconscious power of the other patterns to take over our lives, although something of the archetype remains in our desire to plunge into the adventure of an unfamiliar world when we go on holiday.

The archetype of Rebirth, however, is certainly one which can exercise an enormously compelling hold over the ego, as we see whenever people imagine that they can escape in an outward fashion from some way of life that has become like a prison to them. They may imagine that by bailing out from an unsatisfactory marriage or job without properly understanding the reasons why their life has been unsatisfactory, they can 'make a new start' which will solve all their difficulties. They may imagine that if they in some way 'project a new image' or elect a new government their fortunes may be miraculously transformed, simply because they are changing the externals without identifying the true cause of their problems. And nowhere does the power of this projection become potentially more damaging and disillusioning than when the ego becomes unconsciously possessed by the archetype of the Self, usually as a result of being drawn into identification with the collective ego of some religious or political group. The victims imagine they have gone through some profound religious or political 'conversion' and for a while enjoy the Dream Stage of viewing the world in a dramatically new way, convinced they have 'seen the light'. But all this 'ego-Self confusion' has really brought them is an inflation of the ego, without properly discovering their individual inner self at all.

The most significant way in which the archetypal plots can tell us about the real world, however, is not when we see them projected outwards, but when we return to their original meaning and use them as a guide to understanding how human behaviour actually works. In this respect we have already seen something of how events in real life are shaped by the pattern of Tragedy. But, oddly enough, we can learn as much about the workings of human nature from that plot which seems, with all its absurdities and artificial conventions, less obviously related to the real world than any of them: the plot of Comedy.

### The *persona*

There are two particular respects in which Comedy sheds invaluable light on human behaviour, both relating to the light it can shed on that crucially important factor in human psychology, the *persona*.

If human egotism is all-but universal and has the potential to create such immense problems, the chief reason why it is not more obviously intrusive in all our lives lies in the extent to which it can be hidden from view. This is one purpose of that social front we all put up to the world, the *persona*, when we use it as a device to reduce social stresses and strains by concealing our true feelings. In this respect we use it not just to provide a socially convenient disguise for our own egotism but to hide from other people the extent to which we have noticed theirs.

We are familiar with the image of what may happen when someone is rung on the telephone by a caller who is tiresome or unwanted. Down the line to the caller, the recipient may seem the soul of patience and politeness. But to other people in the room, he or she may be grimacing or cupping a hand over the mouthpiece to make a sense of irritation only too clear. At this level, the *persona*, the mask we put on for other people, is invaluable, as a means to avoid giving offence and generally to make it easier for us to relate with each other. In this respect, the *persona* is a social device we employ all the time, to curb our impulses to aggression, to appear friendly and sociable, to conceal the extent to which we ourselves are ego-centred.

At a deeper level, however, people may come to adopt a *persona* more unconsciously, and it then becomes more a matter of self-deception than of deceiving others. This is where we can talk about someone having 'a *persona* problem', one test of which is what other people say about them when they are not present. If there is a serious gap between anyone's conscious view of themselves and what others say behind their back, this is likely to be because they are in the grip of negative aspects of their personality of which they themselves are unconscious. Such is the shadow cast by their one-sided egotism. Everyone around them can see a truth to which they themselves are oblivious. And this crucial feature of human psychology is of course particularly strongly reflected in Comedy, because a large part of the appeal of this type of story down the ages has lain in how it simultaneously shows us both sides of the picture. On one hand we see characters self-deludingly relating to the world 'above the line', through their image of themselves. On the other, we the audience can see only too clearly what, behind their social mask, these people are really like.

All the great comic characters in storytelling are defined by the fact that they are living in an ego-centred dream world, from which they are then brought abruptly down to earth. We see the 'foolish knight' Don Quixote, hubristically fantasising that he is slaying monsters with his rusty lance, and constantly having to be brought back to earth by his resolutely commonsensical squire Sancho Panza. We see the gullible Bertie Wooster constantly having to be reconnected to the real world by his shrewd but ever-tactful servant Jeeves. We see Thurber's Walter Mitty spiralling off into one daydream after another until in each case he is brought back to reality with a bump. This is the pattern of countless television situation comedies: the fanciful Tony Hancock being brought to earth by his shrewdly cynical friend Sid James; Captain Mainwaring, the Home Guard commander in *Dad's Army*, having to be brought to earth by his lugubrious second-in-command, Sergeant Wilson; Sergeant Bilko constantly trying to outwit his colonel and his fellow soldiers with some new money-making scheme and invariably being caught out; Basil Fawlty, constantly trying to preserve his *persona* as an efficient hotel manager, pretending to his guests that everything is under control, when behind the scenes we see only too clearly it is in chaos.

In each case the central joke of the story is the way we see how the mask keeps slipping, until the denouement when the delusions of the central figure are finally irretrievably exposed. And because the central purpose of Comedy is to show up this two-sidedness of human nature in a playful manner, no one usually ends up getting too badly hurt. Where we see the problem of the *persona* presented in a much darker light, of course, is in Tragedy. As we saw in Chapter Nine, 'The Divided Self', it is a crucial part of the make-up of most tragic heroes and heroines that, consciously or unconsciously, they try to hide the dark side of their nature from the world behind a 'light' mask of respectability. This is the two-sidedness so vividly personified in *Dr Jekyll and Mr Hyde*, where the hero's *persona* and his shadow are actually split into two separate characters. But we can see the same split between the 'light' outward persona and the shadowy ego-self behind it in almost any of the central figures in tragedies. And equally we can see it all around us in real life.

Each of us to a greater or lesser degree has an ego-centred 'shadow self' which we would like to keep hidden from public view. Although we may continually be aware of it in our own heads, we try to conceal it from other people behind a mask of sociability. But there are occasions when the mask slips, as when someone loses their temper and starts shouting in an uncontrollably ego-centred manner, or is in some other respect caught out acting badly, in a way they would normally wish to hide from the world.

We then see the 'dark self' out in the open, in all its unattractive horror. And the essence of all those tragic situations in real life where people bring disaster on themselves is that their 'dark self' has taken them over to such a degree that it can no longer be hidden. In this way Comedy and Tragedy are merely looking in different ways at the same aspect of human nature. No one was more keenly aware of this universal feature of human psychology than that master of both types of story, Shakespeare. In *Hamlet* we hear the hero say of Claudius how 'you may smile and smile and be a villain'. In *The Merchant of Venice* Antonio speaks of the 'villain with a smiling cheek ... O, what a goodly outside falsehood hath'. In *Pericles* Cleon says 'who makes the fairest show means most deceit'.

Here, of course, as in so many other respects, stories merely provide us with a mirror to how human nature actually works. And this leads on to another very important aspect of human psychology to which Comedy again provides the clue.

A recurring feature of Comedy is the way it shows us a particular group of people whose lives are shadowed by the presence in their midst of an egocentric dark figure. Thus the lecherous Count Almaviva dominates his household, the jealous King Leontes dominates his court, Napoleon in *War and Peace* dominates Russia, and so forth. So overpowering is the force of their egotism that it has the effect of casting everyone else into shadow, making it difficult for other people to be properly themselves.

This is precisely the effect we can see in real life whenever any social group or organisation becomes dominated by one strongly egotistical personality. We can see it in a family, a place of work, a village, street or town, any form of community, even a whole nation. The power of such egotists to dominate the lives of all those around them is enormous. They may do it in a 'dark masculine' way, by open bullying and aggression, in a 'dark feminine' way, by devious scheming and plotting, or by a combination of both. They may be aided by a group of accomplices or toadies around them, who act like extensions of their ego. But the effect of their behaviour is exactly as we see it reflected in so many comedies. It casts a malign spell on everyone in its shadow. It makes other people uneasy, miserable, fearful. It makes it hard for them to act to their full potential. And it wastes their time. Whenever we come across people who represent an extreme case of egotism, one of its most noticeable consequences is the strain this imposes on other people's time and energy, as they try to meet the egotists' demands or to operate around them, to an extent of which the egotists themselves are blithely unaware.

This is of course because, in being taken in by their own self-image, such egotists are largely unconscious. By definition they are blind. And one of the things to which they are particularly blind, as we have noted, is what other people say and think about them behind their back. They live in a little bubble of self-esteem, either imagining that others take them at their own face value or heedless of what these others think anyway, because such people are 'below the line'. The views and feelings of these others are therefore of no account. Unconsciously, the egotist sees the world around him in exactly the terms in which we see it presented in a Comedy. He himself (or she) is 'above the line' and therefore, to those whom he sees as similarly above the line, on his own level, he can be polite, humorous, generous, even deferential. But everyone else, 'below the line', can be disregarded, bullied, exploited or treated with contempt. And it is they, his victims, who see most clearly just what a blindly self-centred and immature human being they are having to cope with.

We may all have come across extreme examples of this kind of egotism in our own lives and be grateful that on the whole they are exceptions. But the real reason for this type of two-facedness is that it reflects what happens to human nature whenever ego-consciousness becomes split off from the ability for selfless feeling and objective awareness. And in this respect it provides us with a model which applies not just to the psychology of individuals but also to human beings collectively.

## The ruling consciousness

The real problem with the ego, as the only part of our psyche through which we can be conscious of the world, is that it is so structured that its awareness must always be limited. However much we may try to eliminate its distortions and to dissolve its conflict with the objective unconscious, some element of subjective distortion and blindness must inevitably remain. And just as this applies to the consciousness of the individual ego, so it equally applies to that collective consciousness which tends to develop in any human group or society. Of course no group of human beings can establish a single, undifferentiated consciousness, through which each member of the group views the world in exactly the same way. But in any group or society it is possible to discern certain prevailing tendencies of view, even if the views of a minority of members of the group may conflict with them. Groups of human beings develop a sense of common identity, shared values, shared assumptions of what they believe to be true or important. And in this respect they develop a collective ego-consciousness.

We see this most obviously when they are swept up in some great shared emotion, as in the collective state of hysteria which grips a crowd at a football match or the sense of collective unity associated with times of war. But in any group it is possible to discern what may be called its ruling state of consciousness: that which determines what views, values and behaviour are at any time generally considered acceptable, and those which are regarded as beyond the pale, condemned as disruptive, eccentric, alien or mad. And one has only to consider what extraordinary changes come over the state of consciousness prevailing in any society through different times in history (the dramatic variations in what is considered acceptable that we see in everything from patterns of moral behaviour to fashions in clothes) to see that there cannot be any time when the ruling consciousness is objectively right, by some absolute standard, in everything it holds to be important or true.

It is naturally easiest to appreciate this in societies where the prevailing consciousness is furthest removed from our own. Until the fifteenth and sixteenth centuries, for instance, the ruling consciousness decreed that the earth was flat and that the sun went round it. To challenge that consciousness, even though it had no basis in fact, was virtually unthinkable. As the old song had it, 'They all laughed at Christopher Columbus, when he said the world was round'.

For challenging the received wisdom that it was the sun which moved while the earth stood still, Galileo faced such duress from the Papal inquisition that publicly he conceded the point (even though, as he did so, he was said to have muttered under his breath 'but it still moves').

We may today laugh knowledgeably at the blindness and arrogance of those inquisitors, because we have inherited the new prevailing wisdom which Galileo helped to shape; just as we may express moral outrage at all those who became rich from the eighteenth-century slave trade in the days before moral perceptions changed and the inhuman cruelty of the slave-system became obvious for all to see. But what we may not recognise is just how many firmly-held convictions making up the prevailing consciousness of our own time are just as ill-founded as the belief in a flat earth or the social acceptability of slavery: because the point about any state of ruling consciousness is that it is based on unconscious assumptions so deep and all-pervading that they are taken for granted. In any society, organisation or group, the unconscious psychological pressure to accept those assumptions is so great that only a few outsiders have the clarity of vision to perceive from 'below the line' how baseless and unjustified they are.

In fact the ruling consciousness of any group with a sense of common identity provides an exact parallel to the state of consciousness in individual human beings. Because it is centred on a collective ego, it can exhibit precisely the same tendency to distortion and subjectivity that we see in human individuals. As we see in, say, a political party, there will thus be a significant element of unconsciousness in the way that group behaves, whereby it remains collectively unaware of its own deficiencies. Just as we see in an individual, the more one-sided the ruling consciousness becomes, the greater the area of shadow its one-sidedness creates. And the denser those shadows, the more we are likely to find within them people who represent those values and that wider awareness which, 'above the line', in the ruling consciousness, have gone missing.

It was his perception of this psychological characteristic of human groups which Ibsen summarised in those words from *An Enemy of the People* quoted at the head of this chapter: 'the majority is always wrong' and 'the minority is always right'. This is an observation which on the face of it might seem perverse, contrary to common sense, inviting the ridicule of all received opinion. But it is precisely 'received opinion', the ruling consciousness, which by definition can never grasp the subtle truth of the point Ibsen was trying to make. He is not of course saying that whenever the majority of the human race agree on something they must in all cases be wrong. Most people accept, for instance, that it is undesirable for human beings to go around killing each other. They are not misguided in this belief just because they are a majority. There are many issues on which the majority of people hold similar beliefs and are right to do so. But at any given time, in any human group, large or small, there will be a generally prevailing state of consciousness which in very significant respects will be blind; which will be unable to see the world objectively. It is in this sense that, as Ibsen put it, the 'majority', the ruling consciousness, is always wrong. And there should be nothing particularly surprising about this, since it is self-evident that in any collection of human beings there will be only a minority who have achieved that degree of self-understanding which can allow them to see the world without their perception being in some way fogged or skewed by unconscious subjectivity.[8]

The question then arises: if in this sense the majority is always likely to be wrong, what steps are open to humankind to try to counter this tendency to remain imprisoned in egotism and perpetual immaturity? Is there no alternative to being carried away into bubbles of fantasy and wishful thinking, followed eventually by inevitable disillusionment? We have already seen how it is precisely this question which the archetypal structure of storytelling is designed to answer. But no analysis of the hidden purpose of storytelling would be complete without seeing how it has been complemented throughout human history by another archetypal process programmed into our unconscious, in which the telling of stories also plays a central part. Such is the theme of our next chapter.

8. This was the point so memorably crystallised in Hans Christian Andersen's fable *The Emperor's New Clothes*. The 'ruling consciousness' is happy to agree that the Emperor is dressed in magnificent clothes. Only the small boy in the crowd, not affected by the collective consciousness, points out that he is naked. The child, 'below the line', represents that minority which is always right.

## CHAPTER THIRTY-THREE

# Of Gods and Men

## *Reconnecting with 'The One'*

'God created man in order to tell stories.'
Hasidic saying quoted by Franz Kafka

'Because of our traditions everyone knows who he is and what God expects him to do.'                     *Fiddler on the Roof*, adapted by Joseph Stein
from stories by Sholem Aleichem

'Try to submerge yourself in that light, giving up all belief in a separate self, all attachment to the illusory ego. Recognise that the boundless Light of this true Reality is your own true self, and you shall be saved!'
*Tibetan Book of the Dead*

'Who sees the variety and not the unity must wander on from death to death.'
*Katha Upanishad*

In 1988 two archaeologists reported on a remarkable discovery they had made in a cave complex in the Pyrenees which contained Palaeolithic paintings. They noticed that the places where the images were most thickly clustered, some tucked away in narrow side passages, awkward to reach, all had one thing in common. If a note was sung in them by the human voice, the sound gave off a resonance, more obviously than anywhere else in the caves.[1]

These and other Palaeolithic paintings are the earliest records we have of the human ability to conjure up images of the world around us: the basis on which we create stories. The pictures they show, of men and animals and even dots apparently representing the monthly cycle of the moon, are the beginning of narrative. And although we do not know why our ancestors around 20,000 years ago should have devoted so much skill to inscribing these particular images on the rock-faces of pitch-black underground caverns, the fact that they particularly chose to do so in places where the sound of the human voice reverberates may provide a significant clue. Because when we experience that kind of resonance with our surroundings, we have the sense of being in touch with an unearthly 'other dimension'. Whatever the conscious purpose of those paintings, it seems that what lay behind it was their creators' sense that, in making them, they were in some way being brought 'into tune' with something larger than themselves.

1. Reznikoff, Iegor, and Dauvois, Michel (1988), *Bulletin de la Societe Prehistorique Francaise* (85,238-246). Their discovery was subsequently confirmed by study of other cave complexes (*cf.* Devereux, Paul, and Richardson, Tony (2001), *Stone Age Soundtracks: The Acoustic Archaeology of Ancient Sites*, (Vega)).

Nothing has fascinated us more about our prehistoric ancestors, as they progressively emerged from the state of unconscious unity with nature, than their more spectacular artefacts. We endlessly speculate, for instance, as to why the ancient Egyptians built their mighty pyramids or why the Neolithic inhabitants of Britain raised up their great stone circles at Stonehenge and Avebury. Certainly these awe-inspiring structures show the organising and ordering function of human consciousness already developed to a very high degree. But what is also obvious about them is that they were designed as symbols. The three pyramids of Giza are based on a combination of those familiar archetypal numbers three and four, four triangles arranged in a quaternity to make a symbolic whole: three becoming four to make one. The stones of Stonehenge, including the tripartite structures known as 'trilithons', were not only composed in a series of concentric circles but aligned with the rising and the setting of the sun on the longest and shortest days of the year.[2] What these structures had in common was that, like cave paintings more than 10,000 years earlier, they were designed to give the people who made them a sense of connection with something infinitely greater than themselves. And nothing struck in them a deeper chord of recognition than the patterns they discerned in the movement of those mysterious sources of light wheeling silently through the heavens above them; the life-giving sun defining the lengths of their days and years, the waxing and waning moon defining their months, the constellations of stars progressing with unfailing regularity across the night sky. It was to harmonise their own lives on earth with these indications of heavenly pattern and purpose that those Palaeolithic artists recorded the lunar cycle on their cave walls, that those Neolithic builders designed Stonehenge to accord so precisely with the yearly cycle of the sun.

What our prehistoric ancestors were doing was to try to reconnect themselves with that sense of unity from which they had been exiled by the emergence of their new type of consciousness. The structures they created to that end we recognise from storytelling as representations of the archetype of the Self. They stood for that sense of 'wholeness' which we derive from the Greek *holos*, which also gives us 'holy' and 'holiness'. In creating these 'holy' symbols they were trying to establish a correspondence between their own lives and the totality of the cosmos.

However, in the thousands of years which elapsed between the painting of those cave walls in the Old Stone Age and the raising of these vast monumental structures in the New Stone Age, the consciousness of *Homo sapiens* had in fact been through a revolution as profound as any in the history of our species.

### From Mother Earth to sky gods

The earliest artefacts we recognise as unmistakably religious in purpose were a large number of clay and stone figurines which have been found all across Europe from Spain to Siberia. The late Palaeolithic hunter-gatherers who made them

2. Although it was long supposed that the chief alignment of Stonehenge was with the rising of the sun at the summer solstice, this has been questioned by the observations of Professor John North in *Stonehenge: Neolithic Man and the Cosmos* (HarperCollins, London, 1997), who suggests that a more accurate alignment might have been with the sun's setting at the winter solstice. But he accepts that alignments of various kinds with movements of heavenly bodies was the prime purpose of the stones' layout.

often placed them in caves which seem to have been used as sanctuaries or 'holy places'. The word 'religion' comes from the Latin *ligare*, to bind, as in ligature and ligament. The prefix 're-' implies the re-establishing of a connection which has been lost. The vast majority of these statuettes show a woman in all her rounded, nurturing, protective, life-giving female-ness, emphasising the curves of breasts, belly, buttocks and vulva. They are generally described as symbolising the Great Mother, Mother Earth, the Mother Goddess. They were symbols of fertility: that Mother Nature who must be treated with holy awe because it was from her that all life emerged, and on her that the creators of these figures depended for the animals and plants which supplied all their food, clothing and shelter.[3]

By the time we arrive at the height of the 'New Stone Age' or Neolithic period, between 4000 and 2500 BC, which created the great stone monuments of Egypt, Britain and elsewhere, a psychological earthquake has taken place. As men have further emerged from their original state of nature, they are no longer dependent on hunting wild animals for their survival. They have become herdsmen and cultivators of the soil. They are no longer so directly dependent on Mother Nature, as something of which they are still unconsciously a part. They are now much more consciously separated from nature. They have developed a degree of conscious control over the natural world around them. And to match this mighty advance in consciousness, they are now looking upwards to the sky, the source of light. The Greek and Latin words for 'god', *theos* and *deus*, derive from the same Sanskrit root *dyaus* from which we get the word 'day'. Originally this meant simply 'that which shines': that from which light comes. Certainly it was from the sky that light came, not least in the life-giving warmth of the sun. It was also the sky which provided life-giving rain. As men now planted seeds in the earth, which the powers of sun and rain would assist to grow, the relationship of man to nature had become more like that of a marriage, with the earth as the unconscious female partner, fertilised by a masculine alliance between human consciousness and those powers deriving from the sky above.

In fact, as we can see from various cosmologies of that period, the more advanced agricultural peoples had come to see the world as divided into three levels. In the middle was the mundane, earthly level on which they lived their lives. But above them now was the sky, the heavens, the source of light, corresponding to a higher state of consciousness; while below them, corresponding to the dark unconscious, was a shadowy underworld. And in the way that is natural to the human unconscious, as it reveals its workings to the conscious mind through symbolism, they had come to see each of these levels peopled with mysterious supernatural beings, personifying the forces which shaped their lives.[4]

3. See *The Great Mother: An Analysis of the Archetype* by Erich Neumann (Routledge and Kegan Paul, London, 1955), particularly the chapter on 'The Primordial Goddess'.
4. It was the Sumerian builders of the first cities in Mesopotamia who first gave the names of their gods to the five planets nearest to earth. These were later translated into their Greek and Roman equivalents with the names we still give them today: Mercury, Venus, Mars, Jupiter and Saturn. The Mesopotamians particularly believed there was an intimate connection between the dispositions of heavenly bodies and events on earth, and that the spirits embodied in planets, stars, comets, sun and moon could not only influence earthly events but foretell what was going to happen in the future. It was they who divided the sky into the 12 signs of the Zodiac, thus establishing that link between

These powers came under two main headings. On one hand they represented external, natural forces, such as the Sun, the Moon, air, wind, fire, water, thunder, lightning. On the other they were projections of those internal psychic forces and states which govern human emotions and actions, such as love, justice, war, wisdom. Each of these powers was personified in its own way by its own 'god', 'goddess' or spirit. Because what these figures represented were the forces which dominate human life they took on a numinous power, that which pertains to a 'god'. It was natural that they should be treated with awe and reverence and that efforts should be made to harmonise with the forces they represented or to placate them by ritual acts of worship and sacrifice. What they also had in common was that woven around them was a great web of myth. For our prehistoric ancestors, the most profound way in which they could express their sense of how they should relate to these mysterious powers governing their lives was through their ability to imagine stories.

One of the earliest cosmologies we know was that of the civilisation of ancient Egypt, which teemed with more than 700 separate divinities. Increasingly, however, these came to be dominated by a central quartet of figures. The great god Osiris represented the masculine principle. It was he, according to the myth, who had originally brought order and civilisation to the Egyptian people, instructing them in law and justice, teaching them the arts of fishing and agriculture, introducing them to religion, building the first temples. The great goddess Isis, his wife and sister, represented the feminine principle. She brought them all the arts of home-making, nurturing children, spinning, weaving, and grinding corn. She was also the goddess of wisdom. The son-god Horus was born as their Eternal Child. And as a shadowy fourth came Osiris's brother Set, who was jealous, twisted and dark. It was the treacherous Set who eventually slew Osiris, cutting him into 14 pieces, twice the magical number seven. It was the wise and loving Isis who brought them together again and miraculously reimbued them with life. It was Horus, the redeeming Child, who finally avenged his father by slaying Set. This myth provides the earliest example we know of the God who dies and is reborn. And although its cycle of death and rebirth was associated with similar patterns in nature, such as the nightly death and rebirth of the sun or the yearly alternation of drought and flood which restored life-giving fertility to the valley of the Nile, there can be no mistaking that the cause of Osiris's death was that dark power in human nature which it was the purpose of Set to personify.

### The archetype of the city

No creations marking this dawn of human civilisation were more spectacular than the first cities. It was Lewis Mumford in *The History of the City* who first observed that there seems to be a universal archetype behind the idea of the city. Wherever we look in the world at the remains of the earliest cities, in the plains of

---

the Zodiac and astrology which persists in popular folklore to this day. So preoccupied were they with astronomical observation that it was they who divided the lunar month into four weeks of seven days, each day into 24 hours of 60 minutes, and the circumference of the horizon (or a circle) into 360 degrees.

Mesopotamia or the jungles of central America, we see them exhibiting certain common characteristics. They are laid out according to geometric, formal patterns, often clearly marked off from the surrounding countryside, as by walls. And they are centred on symbolic monumental structures which represent a combination of spiritual and earthly power: such as the temple-palaces of Babylon, Nineveh, Nippur and Ur, with their ziggurats, or stepped pyramid-like towers made from sun-baked brick, soaring over the rooftops of the city to bring its priest-kings closer to the heavens.[5] By definition a city stands for the four-sided totality of human functioning. It represents the masculine principles of power and order, both of which have been required to build such a monumental creation in the first place. But these are made life-giving by the feminine way it provides nurture for the citizens under its protection, and feeds their spiritual life as a storehouse of their collective wisdom and as a symbol of totality. A city implies a complete hierarchy of social organisation, made up of all the classes and groups whose contribution is necessary to keep its complex life functioning, from those 'above the line' who represent its ruling consciousness down to the helot class 'below the line' at the bottom who help maintain it with their physical labour. As we say of a city, 'all human life is there'. All those who belong to a city are potentially enlarged by the sense of being part of a mighty organism much greater than any of its constituent parts. In this sense it is not surprising that all the way through the history of storytelling we see the city itself symbolising the archetype of the Self, as 'the centre', the place where heroes and heroines can realise their full human potential (unless like Chekhov's three sisters they cannot get there). Something else we soon recognise when we study the earliest cities, like those of Mesopotamia, Egypt or Greece, is how each had its own story, to explain its origins; and how each had its tutelary deity or deities in whose honour those great central symbolic structures were raised to the sky. But there was one thing above all which distinguished these heavenly beings from the human beings who viewed them with such awe. The gods were immortal. Mankind was not.

### The hunger for eternal life

There was a second obvious purpose for which our prehistoric ancestors created imposing symbolic structures. This was to house the remains of their dead. What all these burial places had in common, from the royal tombs of the Valley of the Kings to the barrows and tumuli of Salisbury Plain, was the belief that, after death, their occupants might somehow live on, in some other dimension.

---

5. At this stage of human development, the exercise of spiritual and secular power was still very much conjoined. One ritual purpose of the ziggurats, we know from Herodotus and other authors, was to enable a priest-king to engage in sacred sexual intercourse on the top, or a priestess to enact the same. This was the *hieros gamos* or 'holy marriage', symbolising the reunion of heaven and earth, masculine and feminine, consciousness and the unconscious. Recent discoveries in fact seem to indicate that the first cities may not have been those built by the Mesopotamian civilisation but those built thousands of years earlier on the coast of India and submerged by the rise in sea-levels at the end of the last glacial period. However the ruins found beneath the sea off north-west and southern India include monumental symbolic structures which parallel those we associate with the cities of Mesopotamia.

In the ancient Middle Eastern legend of the Fall, one of the most significant consequences of Adam and Eve emerging to a new kind of self-consciousness was that for the first time knew they were going to die. Because, in emerging from the instinctive state of nature, human beings had developed a sense of their own individual, ego-centred existence, separate from the unity of all life, they now knew, unlike any other animals, that this would one day come to an end. Yet still within them was the half-remembered knowledge that they were part of that total-ity of life which continues in 'eternity', irrespective of the finite little lives of each separate organism which temporarily embodies it. Out of this sense that they were part of that 'eternity' came the belief that those who died might be reunited with it; and this belief took two forms, each of which was to have enormous influence on the developing consciousness of mankind.

The first of these beliefs, essentially collective, reflected the attitude of the living towards those who had died before them. One of the most widespread character-istics of societies in the earlier stages of humanity's emergence from a state of nature was their intimate sense of being part of a chain of life stretching back into the past. As can still be seen in certain parts of the world today, such cultures are marked by a profound reverence for the 'ancestors', who are looked on as a living presence. The highest duty of the living is to please the ancestors, by maintaining those inherited customs and beliefs which enshrine the tribe's collective spiritual identity. This gives significance to every aspect of their lives. In such a culture the death of any individual is seen merely as marking the moment when he or she merges back into a collective whole, which connects them in turn to the spirit which animates the universe.[6]

Eventually, however, a second attitude towards death began to emerge, centred more on the attitude of individuals to their own death, and on the possibility that they themselves might survive death in some personal form. It was this which in early Neolithic times, as we see in Egypt and across Europe, led to the practice of placing of food and other 'grave goods' in their tombs, to assist them on their jour-ney after death. So haunting did this dream of personal immortality become that it plays a key part in that first story of which we have historical record, thought to date back at least to the third millennium BC.

The *Epic of Gilgamesh* was the central inspiring myth of the civilisation which sprang up in the fertile, originally forested plains between the two great rivers which defined Mesopotamia. The story of the great hero Gilgamesh, two thirds divine and a third human, divides into three main parts. He begins as an unruly king, physically strong and powerful, but entirely at the mercy of his physical appetites, such as insisting on the right to deflower every maiden in his kingdom as she reaches the time of marriage. He is an embodiment of the untrammelled human ego. The turning point is when the gods arrange for him to meet Enkidu,

---

6. Even at the end of the twentieth century an old Kalahari bushman could be filmed for television explaining how ritual dance was so important to his people because 'our dancing makes the ances-tors happy, which in turn makes God happy. So our dancing makes a link between us, our ancestors and our God'. (Roy Sesana, filmed in 1997, shown in 2002 as part of *The Last Dance of the Bushmen*, made for the BBC by James Smith).

a true child of nature who has grown up with wild beasts and never been part of human society. Enkidu is tamed when a harlot is sent out into the wilderness to seduce him. When she exposes her naked beauty to him he succumbs, with the result that all the wild creatures flee from him. He has emerged from the state of nature to become human. But his real role in the story is to represent the hero's shadowy alter-ego. Enkidu is as strong and unruly as Gilgamesh, and when they first meet they fight. But after this they are so inseparable they are like two halves of one person, making a new whole. By thus splitting into two, confronting his 'natural self' and becoming self-aware, Gilgamesh begins to mature, to develop a sense of selfless responsibility. And it is this which, when his kingdom falls under the shadow of a mysterious and deadly evil, inspires Gilgamesh and Enkidu to make the long 'forest journey' half across the world to track down and slay the source of that evil, the monstrous Humbaba, the 'guardian of the forest'.

However, when Enkidu strikes the third and fatal blow which kills Gilgamesh's Humbaba, we see the giant's death has been far from an unmixed blessing. Gilgamesh and Enkidu go on to fell all the trees of that great forest of which Humbaba had been the guardian. Nature is being forced into retreat before the growing power of men to subdue it. This may have seemed a triumph for advancing human consciousness. But, as we now know, it was that clearing of the Mesopotamian forests to make way for agriculture which was eventually to reduce those lands through soil erosion to arid desert, bringing an end to the civilisations they had supported. Humbaba had not in fact been so much a personification of human egotism as a spirit of unconscious nature, crushed by the ego-consciousness of man.

This leads on to the next episode, which shows the Queen of Heaven, Ishtar, angry at the slaying of Humbaba, deciding to tempt Gilgamesh by offering herself to him as a bride. If only he will succumb to her embraces, she promises him riches, glory and power over all the earth. But Gilgamesh rejects her, pointing out that everyone else she has ever seduced has ended up being emasculated or humiliated. Ishtar is here like the Queen of the Night in *The Magic Flute*, playing the role of the Temptress/Dark Mother, that Mother Nature from whom the hero must escape if he is to reach fully conscious autonomy. In vengeance for Gilgamesh's rejection she sends the Bull of Heaven to kill him, and after it has launched two ferocious assaults, inflicting death on many of his warriors, the third encounter ends in glorious victory as, with Enkidu's help, the bull is slain. For this triumph, Gilgamesh and Enkidu are acclaimed by the people as the greatest of heroes. But Ishtar is so enraged that she wins agreement from the other gods that one of the two must die. The price of separation from nature is the knowledge that we are mortal. The episode ends with Enkidu sinking to his death, leaving Gilgamesh to grieve bitterly over the 'brother' he has lost. The great hero, who has enjoyed such earthly glory, is now all alone, facing the realisation that he too must one day die. He has come to his 'central crisis'. Having lost that which was most dear to him, facing the certainty of extinction, he must now confront the central task of the 'second half of life', as he sets out on his own on a long hazardous Quest for the secret of immortality.

The final episode shows Gilgamesh wandering despairingly through the wilderness and eventually coming to a great mountain whose twin peaks rise to heaven and whose roots reach far down into the underworld. This is the Self, combining the consciousness of the heavenly upper world with the dark unconscious, buried from view. Gilgamesh enters the mountain, where for 12 leagues he journeys underground through impenetrable darkness, where no mortal man has travelled before. After travelling ever further into the unconscious, he finally emerges into blazing light and the 'garden of the gods' and here he has three encounters. Each of the three people he meets exclaims in turn how worn and starved Gilgamesh is looking, and to each he explains how the death of Enkidu has brought home to him that he must die. The first is Shamash, god of the sun, justice and wisdom, attributes of full-developed consciousness. The second is a young woman Siduri, an *anima*-figure tending her vineyard and making wine, who tells him he must seek out Utnapishtim, the only mortal who has ever been granted eternal life. The third is the ferryman who can carry him over the waters of death to meet Utnapishtim.

After further ordeals, Gilgamesh finally reaches his goal and meets Utnapishtim, 'the far off one', who tells him how he came to enjoy immortality. This was the episode which particularly electrified the Victorian public when George Smith unveiled his translation of the story in 1872, because what Utnapishtim describes was the Sumerian version of the Biblical myth of Noah's flood. He recalls how the human world had become a babel of pride and greed, how the gods had decided that mankind must be punished for its wickedness with a great flood and how they had ordered him alone to build a boat to enable him to survive. The god Enlil, born of a marriage between earth and air, then unleashed the deluge which covered the earth. After seven days the rains ceased and, as the waters went down, Utnapishtim found, like Noah, that his boat had grounded at the top of a high mountain. He then, like Noah, sent out a succession of birds, ending in a raven, which told him, after seven more days, that dry land was re-emerging. The god Ea, the supreme god of wisdom 'who alone knows all things', told Enlil he had gone too far. Although it is right that sinners should be punished, they must not be driven too hard or they will die. Relenting a little, Enlil therefore decided that Utnapishtim and his wife should become immortal.

In answer to Gilgamesh's plea that he too should be given the secret of eternal life, Utnapishtim sets him a test. He can have what he craves if he can survive for seven nights and six days without sleeping. Long before the seventh day it is clear that Gilgamesh, filthy and worn out from his ordeals, has hopelessly failed. But Utnapishtim too now relents, and promises that at least Gilgamesh can be made to look fresh and young again for his return to Uruk. After an intervention by his wife, Utnapishtim relents still further and tells Gilgamesh how he can obtain the secret of eternal youth, by diving down into water and plucking a magical herb. The hero does this and sets on his long journey home. But eventually he wearies and falls asleep by a well, from which a serpent emerges, 'sensing the sweetness of the flower', and snatches the herb away. From that day forth, snakes had the power to renew themselves, by sloughing off their old skin to emerge looking fresh and young. But Gilgamesh had to return home empty-handed. He was hailed as the king who had been on a long journey, 'who was wise, who knew mysteries and secret things'. But now he was 'worn out with labour', and so he died, the greatest of heroes.

This great Sumerian epic brilliantly reflected how far mankind had travelled since it began the long process of emerging from unconscious dependence on instinct and nature. It tells the story of a man who begins at the mercy of his egocentric physical appetites, without any controlling discipline or self-understanding. To reach maturity and self-awareness it is first necessary for him to begin an inner dialogue, which is what is represented by the arrival of his shadowy alter-ego Enkidu. Just as Enkidu has emerged from the state of nature, so the two-in-one hero now overcomes Humbaba, further representing the unconscious state of nature which has to be subdued to make the self-advancement of mankind possible. This is repeated in their victory over Ishtar. But all these victories for ego-consciousness, marking an ever greater emancipation from unity with nature, also bring with them an awareness of the inevitability of death. Gilgamesh then has to set out on his lonely quest, symbolised as an outward journey, in fact an inner journey, in search of that lost connection with the totality of life. Although, as he grows physically old and weary, he at least seems to come near to grasping the elusive secret he is seeking, it slips away from him. At last, full of years, he is forced to accept that which he has dreaded so long: the extinction of his separate conscious existence.

In showing how its hero eventually dies a natural death of old age, the epic of Gilgamesh was in fact to remain highly unusual in the history of storytelling. The riddle of how humankind was to cope with this new realisation that each individual centre of consciousness must die was one to which it would continue to come up with differing answers. But what was to remain crucial to how this riddle was resolved was whether those answers ultimately stemmed from the ego, or were drawn from the deeper, universal realm of the Self.

## Understanding the Greek gods

While the civilisations of Mesopotamia and Egypt were at their zenith, the more primitive tribes of a peninsula hundreds of miles to the west and north of them were evolving a new mythology much more complex than anything which had gone before. The stories of Greek mythology have continued to resonate through the history of our Western civilisation like no others. So rich was the archetypal imagery with which they reflected the human condition that it still haunts our thinking to this day, as when we refer to a 'labyrinth', a 'Herculean task', a 'hydra-headed monster', 'cleansing the Augean stables', a 'Gorgon', an 'Oedipus complex', 'narcissism', an 'echo', an 'atlas', 'panic', 'tantalising', a 'Trojan horse'.

Considering the unique subtlety with which the Greek imagination tapped into the collective unconscious, it may not be surprising that this was the people whose literature was the first to present us with stories based on all the archetypal plots we have been looking at in this book. Starting with what is arguably the world's most profound Quest story, it contains examples of all the others, culminating in their invention of Comedy and Tragedy. Nevertheless, the foundations of all this wealth of storytelling lay in their myths. And the world these conjured up contains one feature which we find particularly puzzling. Most of the better-known stories are centred on mythic human heroes and heroines, representing the four central roles in the archetypal family drama, as kings, queens, princes or princesses. Theseus, Perseus, Odysseus, Agamemnon, Jason, Medea, Oedipus are all familiar examples. But whichever basic plot is shaping the story, we are almost invariably made aware of the presence of one or more of the Greek gods or goddesses, hovering on the edge of the action. These supernatural beings are either able to give the hero or heroine assistance, as by providing them with advice or with magic weapons; or to hinder them by placing obstacles in their path. But they are not able to intervene in the action directly. Once we appreciate the hidden significance of the role the gods play in these stories, however, the true purpose of Greek mythology emerges in a striking new light.

Like other cultures, the Greeks imagined the world as divided into three levels, each peopled with a mass of divinities. In the centre was the everyday earthly world in which they lived. This was inhabited by many lesser spirits associated with the natural features which connected the visible, 'conscious' world with some more mysterious 'unconscious' dimension: such as the nymphs associated with springs gushing water from some invisible underground source, or the echo which reverberated from cliffs or hillsides. Below the visible conscious world was the shadowy underworld, ruled over by divinities of its own, such as the god Hades or Pluto. It was here that human beings went when they died. A few, if they had per-formed heroically on behalf of their community, enjoyed bliss in the Elysian fields. Another minority, those who had been particularly wicked and egotistical, was doomed to eternal punishment, like Sisyphus, eternally pushing his stone up a hill, only for it to roll down again; or Tantalus, constantly hoping to seize the grapes which would quench his terrifying thirst, only for them to be snatched away. Most former mortals spent their time in eternity just as bloodless shades, ghosts of their former selves.

By far the most important set of divinities, however, were those inhabiting the uppermost level, the 12 supreme gods: those who were 'above mankind' because they lived in the sky or on the snow-capped summit of Greece's highest mountain, Olympus. These represented an exact balance of masculine and feminine. Six were male, six female. King of the gods was Zeus, whose name derived from the same root, *dyaus*, the source of light, as the Greek *theos*. He represented the masculine principle, above all kingly and fatherly authority. His queen Hera, whose name derived from the Sanskrit *svar*, the sky, similarly represented the feminine principle, presiding over marriage and motherhood. Alongside Zeus were five other gods, each representing a particular aspect of masculinity: his son Apollo, god of light and order (and therefore consciousness), also of youthful energy and male physical perfection[7]; Poseidon and Ares, gods of the sea and of war; Hephaestus, god of

---

7. Apollo was also god of music, which unites life-energy and emotion with order; of healing, the restoration to physical health or 'wholeness'; and of prophecy and oracles, the means whereby rational consciousness can divine from the irrational 'underworld' what is to happen in the future.

craftsmanship, who presided over the use of fire to work metal; and finally Hermes, the divine messenger. Alongside Hera were five goddesses, each representing a particular aspect of femininity: Aphrodite, goddess of love; Athene, goddess of wisdom; Artemis, the huntress; Hestia, who presided over home-making and the domestic use of fire for cooking and warming; and Ceres, or Demeter, presiding over fertility, natural growth and cultivation of the soil. Ranked below them was an array of lesser divine beings, all with their own role to play in the life of mankind, ranging from gods personifying the forces of nature, such as Aeolus, god of the winds, to the nine Muses, personifying different forms of artistic inspiration and learning.

Around all these figures the Greeks wove an immense thicket of stories, which really come under two headings. Firstly, there are stories just about the inter-relationships of the gods themselves. But alongside them are all those myths which, although centred on human heroes and heroines, also feature the gods in their mysteriously influential role on the edge of the action. And it is here we see that the true purpose of these supernatural beings is to personify all those dynamic forces in the psyche which govern human emotions and behaviour.

The key to understanding the role of the Greek gods is to see how they appear in a story at just the moment when the particular psychic force they represent becomes relevant to the action which is about to unfold. They thus give us a clue as to what psychic powers are in play: either to help the heroes and heroines on their way to success, or to personify the nature of the challenges they will have to face. One of the most crucial figures in this respect, as we have already seen several times in this book, is Poseidon. As Zeus's brother, the god who lives in the mysterious depths of the sea represents, in his dark aspect, the negative, 'inferior' version of full-grown masculinity. In this aspect he thus becomes the 'Dark Father'. Whenever a hero in some way comes into conflict with Poseidon or one of his agents, we know he is going to have to show himself to be his 'light opposite': fully masculine but also balanced, open to the feminine values of selfless feeling and intuition.

Thus when Theseus sets out for Crete to confront the power of the Tyrant Minos, the chief physical opponent he is about to face, the Bull, is a creation of Poseidon. But as Theseus embarks, the protective deity hovering over him is Aphrodite, goddess of love. This tells us that the loving feminine will somehow prove the key to overcoming the dark masculine he is setting out to challenge; as we see when, on his arrival, Ariadne falls in love with him and supplies all he needs to overcome the monster and escape the labyrinth.

When Danae is shut away in a tower by her tyrannical father Acrisius, it is the king of the gods, Zeus, representing 'light masculinity', who impregnates her, disguised as a shining shower of gold. Like many mythic heroes, her child Perseus is thus half-man, half-god; and we then see him – with the help of Hermes, Athene and Pluto – winning his manhood by overcoming the Gorgon, representing the emasculating power of the dark feminine. His final task, to show that his man-hood is fully balanced, is to rescue Andromeda, the *anima*, from the sea-monster, which is again a creation of Poseidon.

Similarly, Poseidon is the hero's chief opponent all through the *Odyssey*, deter-mined that he should not reach his goal. It is Poseidon who has fathered Odysseus's most terrifying opponent, Polyphemus. What Odysseus needs to survive this ordeal is the intuition which eventually teaches him how to outwit the foolish giant (whose inner blindness is then symbolised by the outer blindness Odysseus inflicts on him).[8] All through the story Odysseus's chief ally is Athene, the goddess of wisdom, representing precisely that feminine value which Odysseus needs to overcome the blind and heartless masculinity represented by Poseidon. Gradually, under Athene's tutelage, we see Odysseus developing his understanding and self-control, until at last he is ready for that showdown with the suitors which shows he has reached fully-balanced maturity.

One of the most ingenious of the Greek gods is Hermes, best-known in his role as the divine messenger. But he had many more roles than this; and once we see what they all have in common, we begin to recognise just what a subtle part Hermes played in the Greeks' understanding of human psychology. Essentially Hermes is the god who presides over transitions between one state and another. This is why, for instance, he was the god of travellers and of sailors, each of which imply movement between one place and another. He was also the god of merchants, markets and buying and selling, as goods and property are transferred from one person to another. For the same reason he was the god of thieves. But at a deeper level, Hermes is the god who presides over all transitions between what is known and what is unknown; what is visible and what is invisible; between the world of consciousness and the unconscious. This is why he was the god of twilight, the transition from day to night; and the god presiding over burials and graveyards, the transition from life to death. He was also the god of dreams, images passed from our unconscious to consciousness. He was the god representing our sense of intuition, which is why he was also the god of gambling and luck. And it was in this respect that he was the carrier of messages from the gods to men; because he is the god who presides over all that vital process whereby the objective unconscious tries to inform us of that which our subjective consciousness is blocking out. In archetypal terms he thus plays the role of the 'Trickster', not dissimilar to that played by Ariel in *The Tempest*.[9]

There is no more crucial moment in the *Odyssey* than that on Circe's island, where Odysseus's men have been trapped by the witch-goddess's enchantments. For the first time we have seen Odysseus developing the self-protective understanding which has led him only to send half his men forward to explore the

8. This is an example of how the meaning of symbolism can sometimes be interpreted only by seeing it in context. The blindness of Polyphemus, after Odysseus has rammed a red-hot stake into his single eye, stands for the opposite of the self-inflicted blindness of Oedipus, when he gouges out his own eyes. Oedipus's outer blindness reflects his attainment of inner vision, in parallel to the blindness of the wise Teiresias. Polyphemus's blindness acts merely to confirm the lack of vision he has already shown in being outwitted by Odysseus.

9. In this way Hermes represented the act or process of intuition, the intuitive 'flash' which gives consciousness a glimpse of that which has been unconscious (it was this 'quicksilver' property which led the Romans to use their version of his name to describe the metal Mercury). But he did not represent that deeper state of understanding which the intuitive link with the unconscious can lead to. This was reserved for Athene in her role as goddess of wisdom. This is why both of them can appear in the same story, as they do to Perseus and Odysseus, because what they stand for is subtly different.

island, while he remains behind. At this point who should turn up in the forest but Hermes, giving Odysseus a magic herb and the advice he needs to withstand Circe's magic. This is really the turning point of the story, because from now on Odysseus becomes more and more conscious of what he has to do. Once mastered, Circe shows him how to get in touch with the spirits of the underworld, including Teiresias, symbolising his new contact with the wisdom of the unconscious. He develops that self-control he has previously lacked, and which will eventually carry him to his goal.

The greatest of the Greek mythic heroes was Heracles or Hercules who, like Perseus, was the son of Zeus and a mortal mother: half-man, half-god. The complex of legends which eventually accumulated round Hercules begin when his birth arouses the rage and jealousy of Zeus's queen Hera, who thus takes on her negative aspect as the 'Dark Mother'.[10] Faced with the deadly enmity of the 'dark feminine', his task is thus to win his full manhood from the power of unconsciousness she represents. He wins his first victory when, as a newborn baby, he strangles the two deadly serpents Hera has sent to kill him (rather like Tamino overcoming the serpent at the start of *The Magic Flute*). He grows up to adulthood, winning several more symbolic battles, and is rewarded by being given the Theban princess Megara as his wife. But then comes the 'central crisis' when, rendered 'unconscious' by a fit of madness inflicted on him by Hera, he murders his wife and children, thus losing all that is most dear to him.

To learn how he can expiate this dreadful crime, he visits Delphi to consult the oracle of Apollo. This again always symbolises the obtaining of wisdom from the unconscious, because Apollo, the god of light and consciousness, is served by priestesses who pass up messages from that mysterious dark underworld with which they are in contact. The oracle tells him the only way he can remedy his offence is to embark on the series of 12 tasks for which he is famous (the Greek for these is *athloi*, meaning 'ordeals which offer a great prize', from which we derive 'athlete'). He nominally has to carry these out at the behest of Eurystheus, king of Tiryns, in the north-east Peloponnese, who is presented as an unmanly, cowardly creature, the negative opposite of the fully-masculine figure Hercules is to become. The pattern of these ordeals, to show how Hercules is growing in stature as they progress, is that they gradually widen out geographically from Tiryns. The first five, including the slaying of several monsters, such as the Nemean lion and the many-headed Hydra of the Lernean marshes, all take place not far from Tiryns. The sixth, the cleansing of the Augean stables at Elis, takes Hercules to the other side of the Peloponnese; and from here the circle grows ever wider. He is taken in turn to Crete, to Thrace in the north of Greece, to the Black

---

10. It is no accident that the two gods we see most often in their dark, negative aspects are Hera and Poseidon, because they then represent those key archetypal figures, the 'Dark Mother' and the 'Dark Father'. But of course each can also appear in a light aspect: Hera when she plays a positive role as loving wife and mother; Poseidon when we see him in his 'above the line' role as sea god, benignly presiding over 'calm seas and prosperous voyages'. It is only when he assumes his 'below the surface' role that we see him as the angry 'Dark Father', whether he is sending storms at sea or creating monsters.

Sea, to win the girdle of the queen of the Amazons; to the westernmost end of the Mediterranean (hence 'the Pillars of Hercules' as the ancient name for the straits of Gibraltar); and then even further to the west, the direction of the setting sun and of death, to seize the golden apples from the remote Garden of the Hesperides (this also requires him to visit Africa to see the giant Atlas who carries the world on his shoulders, hence, of course, our word 'atlas'). Hercules's final ordeal takes him down to the underworld itself, to seize the monstrous Cerberus, which he does with the aid of both Hermes and Athene, the god and goddess who supremely represent that those powers of intuition and wisdom only available to those who are most closely in harmony with the unconscious.

In mastering the terrifying guardian of the kingdom of Hades, Hercules has conquered death. And although in his mortal self he must eventually die, poisoned by the blood of the Hydra, he is taken up into heaven. Here he is finally reconciled with Hera, who gives him in marriage her daughter Hebe, the handmaiden of the gods, associated with eternal youth. United with his *anima*, he has become one of the immortals.

All these myths emerge from the mists of Greek prehistory, anonymous products of the Greek collective unconscious. But we finally come to the two epics which are the first Greek stories ascribed to a named author, dating back to the dawn of post-Mycaenean Hellenic civilisation at the end of the Bronze Age. One of these, like *Gilgamesh* the individual story of a great hero, we have already looked at many times in this book, as the first and greatest of all stories based on the archetype of the Quest. Homer's other epic poem, the *Iliad*, concentrates on only a comparatively small part of what had become the central collective legend of the Greek peoples, as it describes how they united, under the leadership of kings and heroes from all over Greece, to fight a mighty war with their greatest external enemy. Despite archaeological evidence that there was a succession of cities on the site of Troy in Asia Minor, there is no historical evidence that a war such as that described in the story ever took place. But what is significant is the basic symbolism behind it.

The story of this great conflict begins with rivalry on Olympus when the three leading goddesses; Hera, Athene and Aphrodite, decide to ask the young Trojan prince, Paris, to judge which of them is most beautiful. For him, as a handsome young man, love is to be preferred above motherhood or wisdom, and he awards the prize to Aphrodite. This provokes Hera to vengeful 'dark feminine' fury, and she arranges that Paris shall be paid out for his folly by falling in love with the wife of one of the greatest of the Greek kings, Menelaus of Sparta, and abducting her back to Troy. The Greeks all join together to win her back, and we thus see in the essential story of the Trojan war that all too familiar archetypal scenario which shows a group of heroes setting out to challenge a 'dark power' which has in its grip the shining feminine, the *anima*, the spirit of life. As they lay siege to the monster's citadel, it is to be a long and fiercely fought struggle. But the Greek heroes have one ultimate advantage. Their protective deity is Athene, the goddess of wisdom. It is she who in the end, after all their direct assaults on the city have been in vain, guides them to realise that the only way to win this war is through cunning. They trick the

Trojans into accepting the gift of the wooden horse, so that the Greek warriors concealed within it can win access to the city. Within a short time, thanks to their 'feminine' guile, all they have failed to achieve by mere masculine heroics has been delivered up to them. Troy lies in ruins, its brave defenders slain. Helen, the 'eternal feminine', has been liberated from her imprisonment.

But this is not of course the end of the story. So curious was the Greek intelligence that, as we have seen, they were always wanting to know what happened before the beginning of a story, and what came after it ended. That central legendary event of their history, the Trojan war, gave rise to a host of ancillary tales. Some of these described events which took place in the run-up to the great siege, such as those featuring the sacrifice of Agamemnon's daughter Iphigenia. Even more described the fate of the various heroes on their return from the war, such as that which befell Agamemnon on his return to Mycenae, when he was murdered by his adulterous wife Clytemnestra, then avenged by his son Orestes. This particular cycle was to end when Athene, as goddess of wisdom, was called in to rule that Orestes had finally expiated his crime. But the greatest of these stories was that describing the return home of Odysseus. And of course this, like the story of the war itself, ends in a last great battle to liberate the *anima* from the deadly grip of the dark power.

One of the most striking features of Greek mythology was the way it, for the first time, gave a central place to the 'feminine value', personified above all in that goddess of wisdom who was revered so highly that she gave her name to the foremost city of Greek civilisation, and whose greatest temple, looking down over that city from the mighty rock of the Acropolis, remains alongside the pyramids of Egypt as the most famous single building of the ancient world. In myth after myth we see the release of the 'eternal feminine' from the grip of darkness as the moment of ultimate fulfilment, when the true hero reaches the state of wholeness.

Such was the power of this body of stories that when the civilisation centred on Athens achieved its finest flowering in the fifth century BC, it continued to shape many of those tragedies which represented the first great written literature of the Western world. The Greeks looked back to that dawn-time when the gods mingled with those legendary heroes who had created their world centuries before, and found in these ancient stories, like those of Orestes or Oedipus or Medea, the themes of human folly and redemption which could provide them with catharsis: that purification of the emotions and the soul described by Aristotle, which comes from watching the acting out in a theatre of the most profound psychological patterns in human life.

But in some quarters there was already a sense that there was something archaic about this way of looking at the world; that all this profusion of mythical beings belonged to a former, more primitive age. Already, more than two centuries earlier, the poet Hesiod had portrayed the history of mankind as having unfolded through four ages, Once, in the beginning, had been the Golden Age, when men had lived happily and innocently at one with nature and each other, with all their needs taken care of. Then had come a Silver Age, when men had become proud, rebelling against the gods, eventually provoking Zeus to such anger that he destroyed many of them. Then had come the age of Bronze, when men had turned on each other, using their new weapons to kill and wage war. This had eventually led to the Heroic Age, a kind of interlude, the time of the Trojan and Theban wars, when at least the great warrior heroes had redeemed themselves by their nobility. But now had come the worst time of all, the age of Iron, when humanity had sunk back from this heroic level and become petty, mean, greedy, lustful, vain and quarrelsome, without any real redeeming features. And at this point Hesiod personified that principle of 'wholeness' from which men had so fallen short as one single 'God'.

This picture of how, following his emergence from a state of nature, man's increasing consciousness had progressively brought him more and more problems long pre-dated the flowering of Athenian civilisation between 600 and 400 BC. But during this period a new impulse was beginning to show itself in the psyche of mankind which was to come up with a quite different way of looking at the relationship of human beings to that state of 'wholeness' from which they felt exiled. What if, behind all this profusion of anthropomorphic gods personifying the forces shaping human thinking and behaviour, there was only One? What if, behind all the multitude of creatures on this earth and beyond it, there was just one immeasurably mysterious, all-powerful and omniscient Spirit or Mind, responsible for creating the entire universe and everything in it; and of which all created things, including human beings themselves, were in some way just transitory physical embodiments?

A further great earthquake was taking place in human consciousness: as great as the one which had given rise to the sky gods two or three thousand years earlier.

### Tao, the universal soul and 'the one'

In all the more advanced civilisations of the world at this time we can see an impulse to unify: to imagine all the bewildering variety of creation as being governed not by a range of separate divinities but by one Ultimate Power, Spirit or Principle. We see this not just in the west, where Hesiod had already written of a single God as ruling over the affairs of mankind. It emerges even more dramatically in the world's two most populous civilisations, those of China and India.

Just as in Greece and Egypt, the prehistoric mythologies of China and India had developed a dazzling multiplicity of deities to explain the invisible forces which presided over human affairs. In the early period of the Chinese empire, the chief god was the August Personage of Jade.[11] He was seen as like a heavenly version of the emperor, surrounded by his court, living in a jade palace on top of a fabulous mountain. This imperial god ruled over a vast heavenly government, made up of bureaucratic 'ministries' responsible for all areas of natural and human existence. The rule they represented to mankind was known as 'T'ien Ming' or 'the Mandate of Heaven'. Eventually the Chinese devised an equally bureaucratic version of hell: an underworld complete with its own law courts and carefully prescribed punishments for each form of failure to obey the Mandate of Heaven; while those self-

---

11. Although even he was part of a trinity, the Supreme Triad. This included his predecessor, the Heavenly Master of the First Origin, and the Heavenly Master of the Dawn of Jade of the Golden Door who would one day succeed him, so that the three gods represented past, present and future.

less, virtuous mortals who did fulfil it might be rewarded after their death by being admitted to the gardens of the heavenly palace, to eat the fruit of the Peach Tree of Immortality.

The peoples of India had already begun weaving the most convoluted mythic web of all, out of which were eventually to spring several different religions, including the various forms of Hinduism, Buddhism and Jainism. In earliest times the Zeus-figure of their pantheon was the sky god, Indra, celebrated in Vedic hymns before 1000 BC, associated with explosive masculine power, god of thunder and war, bringer of fertility by his splitting of mountains and clouds to provide rivers, sunshine and rain. He was associated with another great god, Viruna, representing that cosmic principle of order which governs both the workings of the universe and the moral law written in the hearts of mankind. They were accompanied by innumerable lesser divinities, from among whom two more great gods gradually came to the fore, Siva and Vishnu, 'creator, preserver and destroyer of worlds'. These were eventually joined by a third, Brahma, to form the celebrated Hindu trinity, *trimurti*. According to one version Brahma describes how he observed:

'the great Narayana, the soul of the universe, with a thousand omniscient eyes, at once being and not-being, brooding over the waters without form, supported by the thousand-headed snake of the infinite.'

But when Brahma addresses this apparently supreme being, the voice which answers is that of Vishnu:

'Do you not know that it is I who am Narayana, creator, preserver and destroyer of worlds, the eternal male, immortal source and centre of the universe? You yourself were born from my imperishable body.'

Eventually Siva joins them and is welcomed by Vishnu as the 'god of gods'. Siva ends his reply:

'I, the supreme indivisible Lord, am three ... Brahma, Vishnu and Siva: I create, I preserve, I destroy.'

The three great Hindu divinities have by this time become virtually interchangeable aspects of each other, like three different faces of the same single god.

During the centuries between 700 BC and 500 BC this tendency for all the multiplicities of gods to dissolve in favour of a single supreme being was gathering momentum in many different cultures. And this brought with it a wholly new perception of how mankind should relate to the unseen dimension beyond his mortal, physical existence.

In China in the sixth century, we see this in the teachings of Lao-Tzu, a pupil of Confucius. The Chinese had already begun to view everything in the universe as being made up of the interplay between two opposing principles, the yang and the yin: male and female, light and dark, strong and weak, dominant and submissive, upper and lower, solid and fluid, hot and cold. There was nothing which could not be seen in these terms. Yang was creation, yin was completion, yang was the idea, yin its material realisation. Yet the two opposites were always two halves of one whole. If, in any context, one principle predominated, this was because the state of cosmic balance had been lost; and there would then be a tendency for it to become unbalanced in the opposite direction. The teaching of Lao-Tzu was that the only way to understand life and the universe was to see that everything in them ultimately belongs to a single, indivisible, living entity: 'the One'. The central principle of life is 'Tao', 'the Way', to become at one with the One, which implies rising above all opposites, because the Tao is the state of perfect balance in which the opposites no longer exist. In the Tao the yin and the yang are one. All partial views and divisions are illusory. All sense of separate existence must be transcended, to achieve union with the One that is eternal.

A remarkably similar perception was being arrived at in India through the body of Hindu teachings known as the *Upanishads*, which were being set down from around 700 BC onwards. The divided nature of human consciousness means that we are imprisoned in maya, that state of illusion which comes from seeing the world in terms of opposites, which are always getting out of balance. But within us is the atman, our true Self, that part of us which is part of the Atman, the Universal Soul. The only way to escape imprisonment in maya is to reach the state where all individual appetites and distortions of subjective consciousness are transcended. This is the state of nirvana, where all personal attachments end, and where the individual atman can be rejoined in perfect union with the Atman which is the state of perfect consciousness ruling the universe.

Until the reaching of nirvana, the Hindus believed, each separate individual soul is doomed to continue being reborn, taking on different bodily forms, as humans or as animals, until it has reached the state of 'enlightenment' or complete consciousness which can enable it to released into the One. To work towards that state of illumination is the purpose of meditation or yoga, from the Sanskrit word for 'union' (from which we also get 'yoke', that which 'joins together'). In the sixth century BC, there grew up in India the legend of a particular hero, a prince, who managed through his meditation to become so liberated from his lower, individual self, so dedicated to love, selflessness and the light, that midway through life he attained 'enlightenment'. He was thus ready to be taken up into heaven and to become immortal, as part of the Universal Soul. But selflessly he remained on earth for another 40 years to spread his teachings as to how this state of perfect light can be achieved. This was the Buddha, who became the central exemplary figure of a whole new religious tradition.

We see a parallel development in sixth century Persia, where the prophet Zoroaster taught that a single spirit of light rules the universe, dispelling the darkness of illusion which shrouds all material existence. In the Mesopotamian civilisation now dominated by the great city of Babylon, the old polytheism had given to a form of monotheism centred on a single supreme spirit, Marduk or Baal, of whom lesser gods were considered to represent particular aspects. In northern Mesopotamia, dominated by the Assyrians, the same tendency centred on their supreme god Ashur. Even in the Mediterranean Greek world, where officially the traditional divinities still held sway, philosophers such as Heraclitus, Empedocles, Pythagoras and Parmenides were wrestling intellectually and spiritually with prob-

OF GODS AND MEN

lems strikingly similar to those which were being confronted by the religions of the east. How, if all created things are in a permanent state of flux, growth and decay, can we see behind them something which is changeless and eternal? How, since the world consists of a myriad separate entities, can we see that they all ulti-mately resolve in the One? [12]

Meanwhile the new religious impulse of the time was finding its most dramatic expression in the Greek world in the 'Orphic mysteries', centred on the cult of the god Dionysus. This son of Zeus had long been part of Greek mythology, asso-ciated particularly with the effect of wine to 'take men out of themselves', and many stories had been woven around him, not least that of how he had been put to death by the jealousy of the other gods, then brought back to life again, through his father Zeus. But now he had changed his character. He had come to be seen in a new, more serious, more cosmic guise, as if he had been re-conceived as a new and more significant divinity altogether. He aroused in his followers that state of 'enthusiasm' or *entheosiasmos* which literally means 'being possessed by the god'. And the key to the power he exercised over them, in the words of the historian Plutarch, was that he was:

'the god who is destroyed, who disappears, who relinquishes life and then is born again.'

Dionysus, in whose honour in fifth century Athens were staged the great reli-gious theatrical festivals which inspired Aeschylus, Sophocles and Euripides to conceive some of the greatest plays ever written, had come to be viewed as a symbol of everlasting life.

## 'The one true God'

There was one racial group in the ancient world which had seen the universe as ruled by a single divine being long before the others, back into the mists of prehistory. This was that branch of the Semitic peoples living at the eastern end of the Mediterranean who called themselves the 'children of Israel'. As with all other peoples, the chief way

12. As an expression of this new phase in the evolution of human consciousness, the parallels between east and west are particularly striking since culturally they were wholly independent of each other. To Heraclitus, living in Asia Minor around 500 BC, there was a supreme unity, the One, which he also called 'God', but made up from the reconciliation of all opposites. 'All things emerge from the One and the One emerges out of all things.' Only 'the One' is ultimately real. All oppositions or separate forms of existence to which it gives rise are by definition less real: just as in India at the same time the Hindus were coming to see the world of maya, governed by the interplay of opposites, as illusion. At much the same time, in China, Lao Tzu was writing in similar vein that 'the myriad creatures are only alive by virtue of the One'; 'all the myriad creatures in the world are born from Something, and Something from Nothing', and 'the Tao begets One, one begets two, two begets three; three begets all the myriad creatures'. Lao Tzu also observed the tendency of all imbalances to produce a contrary impulse which eventually leads to an imbalance in the opposite direction, echoing Heraclitus's law of *enantiodromia*, whereby everything in the created world has a tendency to 'run about into its opposite'. This is the pattern which two thousand years later Hegel was to identify as the 'dialectic', whereby 'thesis' produces 'antithesis' which leads to 'synthesis'. But from the way in which this pattern appears in storytelling we can see it is an arche-typal response by the human unconscious to that innate tendency of ego-consciousness to perceive the world in terms of opposites which inevitably swing between extremes before finding a point of balance.

611

in which they sought to define their identity was through telling stories. And the most important form these took was to rehearse the history of their tribe, generation by generation, back to the beginning: to that moment when the world was called into being by a single Creator-spirit, their god Jaweh. But between these Jewish stories and those of other cultures lay two significant differences.

The first was the degree to which Jaweh was seen as very much the proprietary god of the people of Israel themselves. Although he begins as a universal, world-creating spirit, by the time their world-history reaches the legends of Abraham, Isaac and Jacob, it is obvious that a special relationship has been established between Jahweh and the people who believe that he has singled them out for a unique destiny. Their most holy religious object, which their temple in Jerusalem was built to house, was the 'ark' or chest containing a record of the 'covenant' between them and God; the bond which had been cemented in the story of Moses leading the 'chosen people' out of captivity in Egypt into the Promised Land. We have already looked at that episode in *Deuteronomy* where Moses reminds his followers how he had climbed the great mountain to receive from God the rules which they must obey. At first sight these might be taken as ten absolute laws, intended to govern all human behaviour. But Moses goes on to explain that when the Jews reach the Promised Land they will find it full of other peoples for whom it is already their homeland, and that they must be shown 'no mercy'. The law does not apply to these alien tribes. They must be killed, their land taken from them and the altars of their gods overthrown. In other words the 'one true God' is seen as above all a Jewish god. The Jews are set apart from and above all other races. All other gods are just 'false idols', to be treated with contempt.

The other distinctive feature of the Jewish story recorded in what Christians call the Old Testament is the exceptional degree to which it is dominated by masculine values. We have seen how the Jewish Creation myth is unique in the orderly way in which God sets out his created world in six days like checking off a shopping list. This 'Father God' is the ordering function of human consciousness personified. There is none of that female creative process associated with the cosmogonic myths of other cultures, where the created world is gradually, laboriously evolved out of a dark, unconscious matrix. And what is striking about the stories which follow is how often in them the feminine value is absent or downplayed; or, if it is has to be present, is personfied in a male rather than female character. This is particularly noticeable when we compare these Old Testament stories to the Greek myths, where female figures such as Athene, Ariadne or Penelope play such a central role in symbolising the life-giving feminine value. In the story of Joseph, for instance, when it is necessary for the feminine values of love and seeing whole to be called into play to bring about the reconciliation of Joseph and his brothers, this is not personified in a feminine figure. It has to be conjured up by the tortured device of turning 'little Benjamin' back into an archetypal Child. The story of the journey to the Promised Land, as we have seen, is in many ways an archetypal Quest. But where, at the end of a Quest story, one could normally expect a symbolic union with the feminine, to convey the image of completion and fulfilment, the nearest the story can come up with to a feminine image is to portray the goal, in soft, welcoming guise, as a land 'flowing with milk and honey'.[13] In the story of David, although Saul rewards him for his victory over Goliath with the hand of the Princess Michal, she plays little further part. David's real reward is his loving friendship with her brother Jonathan, as his alter-ego. In fact the feminine element in this story is chiefly personified in the character of David himself, so carefully depicted as combining both masculine and feminine qualities.

This preponderance of the masculine value of course colours much of the history of the Jewish people presented by the Old Testament. Two features of this story are particularly familiar to us. The first is how much of it is taken up by the endless violent struggle of 'God's chosen people' to defend themselves against their enemies, notably the Philistines, but also those neighbouring civilisations which twice took them into captivity, the Egyptians and the Babylonians. The other is how their rigid, legalistic morality rested ultimately on the unyielding masculine principle of the *lex talionis*: the idea that a crime must be paid out by identical retribution, an eye for an eye, a tooth for a tooth. There is little place in the 'ruling consciousness' of this people for the softer feminine values of compassion, mercy and understanding. Where women do play a significant role in these stories, they tend to be presented negatively (e.g., the Temptress Delilah, the raging virago Jezebel) or in an 'active' masculine fashion like Deborah, portrayed as tough matriarchal leader of her people in the *Book of Judges*, or Esther, wife of the Persian emperor Xerxes, who saves her Jewish compatriots from a treacherous massacre through her brave ingenuity. There are exceptions, as in the *Book of Ruth*, where the widowed non-Jewish heroine movingly insists on accompanying her mother-in-law back to Judaea (where she marries a Jewish husband); and the *Song of Solomon* where, untypically, the feminine is mystically portrayed in her full, inspiring *anima* role as the soul of man.[14] In general, however, the picture we are given by their storytelling is of a people outwardly dominated by the hard masculine values of strength and order. The most important defining characteristic of their individual identity was their membership of the tribal group, set apart from all others. In archetypal terms, they had thus become a people whose stern, unrelenting 'Father God' represented not so much the Universal Self, of equal relevance to all mankind, but more an expression and sanctification of their own collective ego-identity.

13. The archetypal role of the feminine remains vestigially present in this story, in the part played, as a symbolic figure helping the Israelites on towards their goal, by 'Rahab the harlot'. Betraying her own people, she assists the Israelites when they are besieging the city of Jericho, by letting down a rope from its walls. But Rahab represents the feminine in very much an 'inferior' guise. Her walk-on part as a traitrous prostitute hardly equates to the inspiring central roles played in Greek myth by figures such as Athene or Ariadne; and her part in the story is not even crucial to its outcome. What wins the victory for Joshua's followers is not her betrayal but the trumpet blast which brings down the city walls.

14. The feminine value is also presented positively in the 'books of wisdom', *Proverbs* and *Ecclesiastes*. The first nine books of *Proverbs* take the form of a 'hymn to Wisdom' who is personified in *anima*-guise as a woman, like the Greek Sophia or Athene. This book also contains the famous passage in praise of the perfect wife, whose 'price is above rubies'.

## Man becomes god

The Jews were not the only people whose storytelling reflected a bias towards masculine consciousness. When the Romans took over their pantheon of gods and much of their mythology from the Greeks, it is noticeable how the role the Greeks accorded to the feminine became less prominent. The most famous city of the Greek world may have been named after the goddess of wisdom, but when the Romans renamed Athene as Minerva she became markedly less significant in their collective life. Much of the subtlety with which the Greek mythology had personified the dynamic forces in the human psyche becomes blurred over. In making Neptune their sea-god, the Romans lost sight of that hugely important role played by his predecessor Poseidon as symbolic of the 'Dark Father'. The role of Jupiter, as the incarnation of masculine power and authority, becomes markedly more dominant and less open to challenge than that which the Greeks had given to Zeus. The role of Mars, equating to Ares as god of war, also becomes more prominent. On all sides we see a shift of the masculine-feminine balance in favour of the masculine, and this can be seen clearly reflected in the greatest single Roman poem, Virgil's *Aeneid*, their equivalent to the *Odyssey*.

The Romans evolved two quite separate stories to explain the origins of their city. One was the legend of how the orphaned twin babies Romulus and Remus had been suckled and brought up by a she-wolf. This obscurely recalled the primordial emergence of humankind from the state of nature; and Romulus eventually grew up to found the city which took his name. The other 'national myth', so powerfully developed by Virgil, told how the Romans were really descended from the Trojans, and how their city had been founded by Aeneas after he had escaped from the smoking wreck of Troy. There had been no subtler element in the *Odyssey* than the contest between Poseidon and Athene. One is the hero's chief antagonist, trying to prevent him reaching home, the other his chief ally, putting him in touch with the self-knowledge which eventually enables him to reach his goal. In the *Aeneid*, the hero's chief antagonist is Juno, queen of the gods, the Roman Hera, in her role as 'Dark Mother'. It is she, for instance, who arranges for him to fall in love with the widowed Queen Dido, whose emasculating charms are almost enough to make Aeneas forget his mission to establish a new city. This shows us, in archetypal terms, that Aeneas's task is not to discover self-knowledge. It is to win his independent manhood from the 'dark feminine'. And his chief ally is not the goddess of wisdom but Venus, the goddess of love.

As the story approaches its climax, it carries echoes of the 'children of Israel' arriving in the Promised Land. The main task of Aeneas and his men is to overcome the opposition of all the tribes already living there, to establish their new city. But as a token of their eventual success Aeneas has already won the support of one of the most powerful Italian tribes, by promising to marry Lavinia, their king's daughter. This is why the tutelary goddess hovering over the action in Aeneas's showdown with Turnus, the leader of the opposing tribes, is Venus. When he is finally victorious, we imagine he will go on to marry Lavinia and found his new city, and that this is to be the happy ending of the story. But we are only left to assume this. We are not shown it. The story ends simply with Turnus's death. Compare this with the resounding conclusion Homer provides to the *Odyssey*, and we see just how much more profoundly the Greek version succeeds in exploring the underlying archetype. One story shows its hero developing to the most complete state of personal maturity of which an individual human being is capable. The other in comparison is no more than a two-dimensional strip cartoon or a Hollywood film: entertaining propaganda designed to reinforce the collective self-image of the Romans just when they had established the most powerful empire the world had ever seen.

The qualities which enabled the Romans to do this were above all those masculine values of strength and order, power and organisation, with which Roman civilisation has been identified all through subsequent history. When we think of Rome, we think of Roman legions, die-straight roads carving across the landscape, superb engineering, Roman law, triumphant monuments to military conquests. We think of a highly materialistic civilisation, dedicated also to physical pleasures, hot baths and spectacular entertainments, to 'bread and circuses': a civilisation which eventually decayed because it became soft within, losing the virility and unity of will which had enabled it to dominate the world and choked by that proliferating bureaucracy which was the negative side of the Roman ability to organise. But all this was still far ahead when Virgil spent the last 11 years of his life writing his great epic poem in celebration of Roman power, before his death in 19 BC.

Eight years earlier Virgil's friend Octavian, who had become de facto leader of Rome in the years of civil war which followed the assassination of his uncle Julius Caesar in 44 BC, was granted by the Senate the title of *Augustus Imperator*, 'the most august leader'. This made him the first Roman Emperor. In 12 BC, to complete his attainment of supreme earthly power, Augustus also became *Pontifex Maximus*, the official head of the Roman religion. Increasingly he was being revered by his millions of subjects as a semi-divine figure. On his death in 14 AD the transformation became complete, when he was officially declared to have become a god.

Other priest-kings in earlier civilisations, notably the Phaoroahs of Egypt, had been accorded divine status, because of their ceremonial closeness to the unseen supernatural beings who ruled the world. But this was the first time in history that the principle had applied the other way round: where a mere mortal had become so identified with his unprecedented earthly power that he was elevated to become a god in his own right. By that principle which Heraclitus had recognised as the tendency of everything when it reaches its extreme to produce its opposite, at that very moment in a remote village in Augustus's vast empire an obscure young boy was growing up whose billions of followers over the centuries ahead would declare that he was not 'man made god' but 'God made man'.

### God becomes man

If we look at the story of Jesus in terms of its underlying archetypes, we can do so under three related headings. First, there is what may be called the 'Christ myth', those elements in the story which are of familiar mythic dimension. Second, there is what his actions and teachings represent in terms of archetypal psychology.

615

Thirdly, there is the way in which all this was interpreted by his followers after his death.

The 'mythic' element in the story of Christ's life itself centres on three chief episodes. Easily the most important of these are the events surrounding each end of his life, his birth and death. But between them comes the curiously revealing episode which shows his temptations by 'the Devil'.

## 1. The Birth

With Jesus's birth we are at once on familiar archetypal ground. Like other mythic heroes before him, such as Perseus and Hercules, the sons of Zeus, he is born the son of a divine father and a human mother. He is therefore half-god, half-mortal. In the imagery associated with his birth, what we see coming into the world is that archetypal redeeming figure, the Eternal Child: that image of defenceless innocence symbolising the renewal of life which evokes one of the deepest archetypal responses we know.

At a still deeper archetypal level, the image of Christ's nativity is that conveyed by Rembrandt in his painting of the scene in the National Gallery. The infant Jesus in his cradle is softly illuminated while everything else in the picture is almost invisible in surrounding darkness. Christ is represented as the 'treasure in the cave', the source of light shining in the darkness of the world.

Another crucial feature of the symbolism of the birth is the way it takes place 'below the line'. 'Above the line', the Emperor Augustus himself, representing the ruling consciousness at the very pinnacle of earthly power, has decreed a census or roll-call of everyone in the Roman empire. Below the line, in faraway Palestine, an insignificant couple, Joseph and Mary, are thus forced to travel from their village to register in Bethlehem, where so many others are doing the same that they are pushed even further beyond the social pale, in being forced to find shelter in a mere stable for animals. The only people who recognise the cosmic significance of what is going on are a group of humble shepherds: until later they are joined by 'wise men from the East', from that Mesopotamian civilisation which finds spiritual guidance in the movement of heavenly bodies, and who represent that 'higher consciousness' which recognises it is 'below the line' that truth is to be found.

A final archetypal element is the determined effort by King Herod shortly after Jesus's birth to have him killed. Again, as in the myths of Zeus, Perseus, Hercules, Romulus and others, we recognise the pattern whereby the life of the new-born hero is threatened by the dark power. The 'Dark King' is attempting to stifle the 'Light King'. But in a 'thrilling escape from death', the baby is carried by his parents to safety in Egypt. He thus fulfils yet another recurring ingredient in the 'hero archetype': that which dictates that the hero destined to become king, like Theseus, Oedipus and others, should spend time in his youth exiled from his homeland.

## 2. The temptations: ego versus Self

The hero grows up to manhood in normal fashion, marked out only by the episode when, in his early teens, he astonishes the elders in his local synagogue by the authority with which he expounds the scriptures. But then, when he is finally ready to reveal his message to the world, comes the second 'mythic' passage in the story, the dream-like episode when goes out alone into the wilderness to be put to the test by the Devil. He is offered three temptations: that he should use his divine power to turn stones into bread; that he should throw himself off the temple roof, so that he can demonstrate his power by being saved by angels; and that, when he is taken up 'into a high place' to be shown 'all the kingdoms of the world', he can be given the power to rule over them.

This is a significant moment in the history of the human imagination. The figure of 'Satan', as 'God's opposite', has appeared before in Jewish legend, most notably in the story of Job.[15] But never before has this Tempter-figure emerged so openly and in such uncompromisingly personal guise. He is a complete personification of all the treacherous, self-deceiving, self-destructive power of the human ego. And the reason he can be now be portrayed in such an extreme way, as a 'dark opposite' to the hero, is that in no story before has the hero ever been portrayed so uncompromisingly as a personification of the Self (perhaps the only exception is the Indian legend of the Buddha). In rejecting the three temptations out of hand, Jesus shows he is so completely identified with the Self that he has no ego to be tempted. Of course he will not turn stones into bread, because what he stands for has nothing to do with gaining advantage in the outward, material world. He is concerned solely with the internal realm of the human spirit. Equally he will not be party to a spectacular demonstration of his power simply in the name of saving himself. Again he has no interest in exercising power over the 'kingdoms of the world' because his message is concerned with a wholly different 'kingdom': that spiritual domain within each human individual which has nothing to do with the exercise of power over other people.

What was revolutionary about this message was that it was directed so precisely to that central problem of human psychology at which, because it is also the central problem addressed by storytelling, we have been looking at all through this book. He was not concerned with his hearers' outward status, or to which race or social grouping they belonged. He was addressing each as an individual, on that inner level where all human beings start off on completely equal terms (exactly as we see them portrayed in stories). On this level, the only question which matters, whether someone is ruler of the Roman empire or a humble fisherman, is what sort of a person they are. How do they measure up inwardly to the challenge of what it is to be human? Are they centred on the ego or on the Self? Are they weak, self-centred, heartless, greedy, vain, proud, cruel, treacherous, mean-spirited, lustful, bad-tempered, vengeful, intolerant, narrow-minded, humourless, lazy, irresponsible and ultimately immature? Or are they centred on that deeper ego-transcending level of the personality which can make them strong, selfless, loving, generous, modest, self-effacing, compassionate, loyal, understanding, good-humoured, self-disciplined, even-tempered, merciful, tolerant, hard-working, responsible and ultimately mature?

15. Satan also, of course, became later identified with the serpent which tempted Eve in the Garden of Eden, although in the original account in *Genesis* this personification of ego-consciousness is given no name.

The essence of Jesus's message, much of it put across in the form of parables or stories, was that, for any of us, this is the only test which matters. Is our personality centred on the ego or the Self? And it was because he viewed this distinction as of such crucial importance that he was able to come up with that other revolutionary idea at the heart of his message: that the first responsibility of those who heard it was to 'repent' of their 'sins' (for which, as we have seen, his word in Greek was *hamartia*, 'missing the mark'). What this meant was that they must develop the self-awareness to recognise just how all-pervasive a part egocentricity plays in all our human thinking and behaviour. Only through this self-understanding can we properly appreciate the other 'centre' in our nature: and how far egotism holds us back from 'hitting the mark', in realising that which we have the potential to become. Only then can we appreciate what Jesus constantly proclaimed as the two supreme human values, love and truth: the capacity for selfless love and the ability to see the world objectively, free from subjective distortion. In other words, precisely those two key principles we see represented all through storytelling as 'the feminine value': selfless feeling and the ability to 'see whole'. And to achieve the state where this can be realised, he insisted, requires real strength of will and self-discipline: in other words, those values which stories represent as masculine. The essence of his message was thus that the highest state of individual human development can only be achieved through a combination of masculine and feminine qualities. One cannot be fully developed without the other. It is simply another version of that message we see at the heart of the archetypal patterns of storytelling (and which, as we see in the *Odyssey* and other examples, both western and eastern, was evident long before Christianity).

A third echo of the archetypal structure of storytelling was Jesus's insistence that the only way for people to realise their full human potential is by avoiding all the psychological pitfalls associated with living 'above the line'. This is why he constantly reiterated that only those who inwardly have a 'below the line' view of themselves can inherit that 'kingdom of heaven' which lies within: those whom he portrayed as the 'poor' and the 'meek', those who are not proud, those who think and feel 'as little children'. In outward terms, Jesus had no argument with that worldly power which is 'above the line'. He respected the Roman centurion as one 'in authority'. When they brought him a coin bearing the image of the emperor, hoping he might pass some subversive comment, he did not hesitate in saying it was right to 'render unto Caesar what is Caesar's'. In the outward world, as one exercising power and authority, Caesar should be respected and obeyed. But it was vital to make the distinction between that outer kingdom which was Caesar's and that inner kingdom of the psyche, which should be ruled only by God. And the greatest obstacles to recognising that inner kingdom, he constantly pointed out, are all those temptations to egotism which inevitably come with riches, worldly power, social position, priestly rank or any of the outward *persona* trappings which can so easily engender a sense of superiority to others and of being 'above the line'.

Reading the stories of Jesus wandering through Palestine in the years when he was putting over his message, the central impression they convey is how he is portrayed as psychologically complete. In terms of the four functions shown in stories as making up human wholeness, he scores fully on all counts. He is always shown as strong and commanding, speaking with authority. He is disciplined, with an exact sense of order; his mind whenever he is challenged or questioned is razor sharp. He is wholly selfless: loving, compassionate and sensitive to the needs of others, as when he invariably tries to help the suffering or heal the sick. And he always shows that intuitive understanding which enables him to relate everything which happens to one unified view of the world, centred on that God whom he portrays as like an ideal human father.

In fact the image of God presented by Jesus had no real precedent, in that it combines in such perfect balance the four archetypal attributes of the Self. The picture he conveyed of this mysterious presence ruling the universe was of a being which is somehow all-powerful, all-knowing, all-loving and all-seeing: displaying strength, order, compassion and understanding, in perfect equation. The power of Jesus's own image lies in how he is portrayed in the Gospels as a human embodiment of the same balance of attributes. So completely is he identified with the state of 'wholeness' which is the Self that when he speaks of himself as 'the way, the truth and the life', he uses the word 'way' much as the Lao-Tzu speaks of 'Tao'. He himself represents that state of totality to which all human beings can aspire. This was why his 'first commandment' to his followers was that they must love God with the same equation of attributes: 'with all thy heart, with all thy soul, with all thy mind and with all thy strength'.

But such a symbol of wholeness is, by definition, an affront to the ego, something the ruling consciousness cannot understand. What we see next, when Jesus's three years of teaching are up, is what happens when the ruling consciousness finally loses patience with the challenge this presents.

### 3. Death and resurrection: the immortal Self

The final mythic episode in the story is that which centres on the last week of Jesus's earthly life. He travels up to Jerusalem, the holy city which is the symbolic centre of the Jewish world. And what we then see unfolding is a perfect example of the archetypal five-stage cycle of Tragedy. The Anticipation Stage has been his preparation for this supreme moment. We see the Dream Stage when, as he enters the city on a donkey, he is welcomed by wildly cheering crowds. The Frustration Stage reaches its height in the air of foreboding which hangs over the Last Supper, and when, in the garden of Gethesamane, he must inwardly face up to the horror of what lies ahead. The forces of opposition are constellating against him. The Nightmare Stage begins with his betrayal by Judas and his arrest by the High Priest's armed guards. It continues with his one-sided trial for blasphemy, his subjection to physical torture and his interrogation by the decent but weak Roman governor Pontius Pilate, with the mob outside howling for his blood. The Destruction Stage begins when he is led out of the city to be crucified by Roman soldiers between two common criminals and, after three hours of agony, he meets his death.

What is so striking is that this appears to be such a complete inversion of what the pattern of Tragedy is about. The purpose of the tragic archetype is to show what happens when human beings become so possessed by the darkness of the

619

ego that in the end they bring about their own destruction, so that unity can be restored and light triumph over darkness. Yet Jesus, as portrayed in the story, is wholly ego-free. The darkness in the story is all outside him. Thus his death on the cross seems to be a total victory for darkness. But herein, of course, lies the point. Although the dark power may have managed to kill him in his earthly outward state, this is not his true identity, which lies in the fact that he is so completely at one with the Self: that totality which is eternal and which cannot be destroyed. Accordingly, when the third day comes, he reappears, bathed in that soft light of eternity which characterises all his appearances after the resurrection. He has overcome death because in reality he has always been part of that which cannot die. And he is then taken up into heaven to merge with the One.[16]

Thus ends the most famous of all those myths, found in many parts of the world, telling of the god who dies and is reborn. In the Egyptian version, the great god Osiris had been put to death by the dark part of himself, his brother Set, but then brought to life again. It was his son Horus who had completed the story, by avenging his father and thus overcoming the cause of death. In the Greek version it was Dionysus, also the 'son of god', who had been put to death and then been brought back to life by his father, representing the boundless power of life which cannot be destroyed.

In archetypal terms, the myth of Jesus shows how, in acting out the pattern of Tragedy, he acted out the pattern of how all human beings imprisoned in ego-consciousness must die. Yet it also shows how, if only they can make contact with the selfless part of themselves which lies beyond ego-consciousness, that state of 'sin' which only came into the world with the 'Fall' and mankind's emergence from unconscious unity with nature, they can be reunited with that state of One-ness which cannot die because it is eternal. In the words of St Paul used in the Christian burial service, 'as in Adam all die, even so in Christ shall all be made alive'. In this respect, acting out his own statement that 'greater love hath no man than that he lay down his life for his friends', Jesus's death also represents that other great recurring feature in the religions of the world, the practice of offering life as a 'sacrifice', a 'making whole'. In innumerable religions, the lives of animals and humans have been ritually offered to the gods as a way of healing the separation between gods and men. The sacrificial animal, like the scapegoat, was supposed to carry with it all the offences and imperfections of the tribe or the individual, thus leaving those who had offered the sacrifice 'cleansed' and restoring the unity which had been broken.[17] In taking upon himself the 'sin' of all mankind, the story ran, Jesus had 'redeemed' the whole world. But this kind of interpretation

---

16. A striking feature of the story of Jesus, as presented in the Gospels, is how consistently it is structured round the Rule of Three. We see this in the original triad of Mary, Joseph and Jesus; the three wise men; the three temptations; the three years of his teaching; the three crosses; the three hours of his death agony, his resurrection on the third day. After 40 days, a multiplication of four as the number of completion, he ascends into heaven, to become part of the Trinity. He lived on earth for 33 years, and chose the archetypal number of 12 apostles, multiplying three by four.

17. It was precisely this which first gave rise to the Greek word 'tragedy', derived from τραγως, a 'goat'. The tragic figure is the 'scapegoat' whose death purges the community of darkness, so that light and wholeness can be restored.

belongs not so much to the story itself as to what was to be made of it in later years, when the myth of the God who had died and been reborn became the central inspiration for something rather different: the story of the religion known as 'Christianity'.

## Christianity 'above the line'

Over the next three centuries, although the story of 'the man-God who died and was reborn' spread all over the Roman empire and even to India and China, the religion of those who followed 'the Way' remained very much 'below the line'. In the catacombs of Rome these new 'Christians' literally went underground. During that time the new faith, built on the stories of Jesus's life, gradually built up its own collective consciousness. Paul, a Jew from the heavily Greek-influenced region of Asia Minor, played a key part in shaping the message, emphasising what a break it marked from traditional Judaism, in that its God was equally 'father' to every member of the human race, 'Jew or Gentile, slave or free'. Its central ritual was formalised round the act of sharing bread and wine, symbolising the coming together of all Christians in the 'one-ness' of Christ's 'mystical body'. The other supreme Christian symbol was the cross, representing not just the instrument of his 'act of atonement' or 'at-One-ment' between God and all mankind, but as itself a four-cornered symbol of wholeness; so that, as Christians made the 'sign of the cross', they were 'centring' themselves in an act which marks a bringing together of the four components of the human personality: body, mind, heart and soul.[18]

In obvious respects the new religion inherited from Judaism its 'masculine' bias, in that it centred on a male trinity of 'Father', 'Son' and 'Holy Spirit', regarded, like other divine trinities elsewhere in the world, as three different aspects of one single God. But behind this, reflecting the central significance of the 'feminine' in Christ's own teaching, a fourth figure soon became closely related to the male trinity, Mary, 'wife of the Father', 'Mother of the Son', representing all the archetypal attributes of an idealised, loving human mother. After the crucifixion itself, no image was to play a more central part in Christian symbolism than the representation of the 'Holy Mother and Child'; although, as a virgin, Mary also represents the *anima*. Equally significant was the enigmatic nature of the third member of the trinity, the Holy Spirit. As its name implies, this mysterious being represents the 'spirit of wholeness', all those psychic forces which draw human beings towards integration with the One. In terms of its underlying archetype, the 'holy spirit' thus represents the dynamic power of the Self. But since no archetype symbolises this more completely than the *anima*, as supreme embodiment of the feminine

18. As a four-cornered mystical symbol of 'wholeness', sometimes representing the four points of the compass, the cross in numerous forms is found in different cultures all over the world. It was a holy symbol in Egypt millennia before Christ. To the Aztecs it was a sign of Quetzalcoatl the creator, master of life and god of the four winds. One ancient form, found widely, was the cross as a symbol of the sun, with arms trailing backwards from the four points as if it is revolving clockwise. This was known in Sanskrit as *sv-astika* from *sv-asti*, 'well-being'. In the old Teutonic religion the trailing arms were reversed, so that they look either as if they are revolving anti-clockwise or are like menacing hooks. This was the form adopted by Hitler's Nazis, whose *hakenkreuz*, or 'hooked cross' thus inverted the ancient symbol of 'well-being'.

value, the 'holy spirit' must by definition include a strong, if disguised, feminine component. This was later to become manifest when individual Christians sought to personify the spiritual power guiding them to wholeness, as when the fourth century writer Boethius imagined the awe-inspiring figure opening his eyes to the 'light' of spiritual understanding as 'Sophia'. She was as much a feminine embodiment of the spirit of wisdom as Athene had been to the Greeks. And it was apt that the greatest Christian shrine in the Greek world, in that new centre of the Roman empire set up on the banks of the Bosphorus by the emperor Constantine, was to be a cathedral dedicated to Hagia Sophia, 'holy wisdom'.

In the early years of the fourth century AD, just after the emperor Diocletian had made a last ruthless but forlorn effort to re-establish the status of the old Graeco-Roman gods, came the dramatic moment in 312 when, on the eve of the battle of the Milvian Bridge which was finally to confirm him as sole ruler of the Roman empire, Constantine had a dream of the cross of Christ, accompanied by the legend '*In hoc vinces*': 'in this sign you shall conquer'. The following year, in his Edict of Milan, for the first time Christians were given full civil rights throughout the empire which had put the founder of their religion to death three centuries before. In 324 Constantine declared Christianity to be its official religion, and six years later established his 'city of Constantine', Constantinople, as its new capital. In one mighty bound, Christianity had finally moved from 'below the line' to being so 'above the line' that it was to shape the ruling consciousness of European civilisation for much of the next 2000 years.

## Heaven, hell and judgement

Even in the century before Constantine, the Roman empire had already been under attack from that other presence which the Roman world viewed as 'below the line': those troublesome tribes of Goths, Vandals, Franks, Alemanni and Huns who inhabited the 'badlands' of central and eastern Europe beyond its frontiers. A century later the great secular power which had dominated the Mediterranean world and half of Europe for seven centuries was in terminal disintegration. The city of Rome itself was repeatedly sacked and pillaged by the 'barbarian hordes', until in 476 the last western emperor, tellingly named after the city's founder Romulus, was deposed. In the west the only ghostly legacy of Rome's imperium was the Papacy, which remained the ruling power of the Christian church. The eastern empire, centred on Constantinople, lived on to enjoy a last sunset moment of glory in the early sixth century, in the reign of Justinian, before beginning its long fade into that twilight which would only end 900 years later.

From the deserts of the Arabian peninsula to the south, the seventh century saw the sudden meteoric rise of the world's last great new monotheistic religion. Islam (meaning 'submission' of the individual ego to the will of God) took on elements of both Judaism and Christianity, while omitting others. Born in the harsh world of the desert, the new religion shared the overtly 'masculine' character of Judaism, with its emphasis on obedience, rituals, law and discipline. It thus had little place for that emphasis on love and compassion by which Christianity had softened and 'feminised' the Judaism from which it originally sprang. But, unlike Judaism, Islam did not see itself as the religion just of one tribal group. It shared with Christianity a missionary zeal to convert the whole of mankind. Indeed, such was the power of the explosive new spiritual force unleashed by the prophet Mohammed that, within a century of his death, his armed followers had not only swept through North Africa and Spain but seemed on the verge of taking over much of western Europe, until in 732 their advance was halted by the Franks at Tours. But in many ways, with its intellectual vitality, its art, architecture and mathematics and its preservation of Greek learning, the consciousness of this new southern civilisation was to outshine the rest of the western world for 300 years.

Bereft of that unifying power which for so long had brought it order and civilisation, western Europe was now firmly plunged into what became known as the Dark Ages. The remains of the Roman cultural inheritance rapidly crumbled before the expansionism of those Germanic and Norse peoples who had never been part of the Roman empire: the Franks, who gave their name to France; the Angles and Saxons who occupied much of the island of Britain; Jutes, Danes, Swedes and Vikings from Scandinavia. But even in these dark and confused times, Christianity continued to make its own advances, as when in the seventh century the new Anglo-Saxon rulers of what would eventually be named after them as 'England' were converted to Christianity, abandoning the Teutonic gods after whom the English-speaking world still names its days of the week.[19] And out of the mists shrouding those centuries have survived some remarkable stories, not least that Anglo-Saxon epic dating from the eighth century with which this book began, *Beowulf*.

The story of Beowulf falls into two parts. The first tells of how its hero comes from overseas to save the land of Heorot by overcoming two deadly monsters: first the semi-human Grendel, then his even more terrible mother, after a mighty battle at the bottom of the lake which had been their lair. After this victory, Beowulf is rewarded with finely-wrought gold and made king over his own people, whom he rules as their loved and revered leader for 50 years. In archetypal terms, this first half of the story has shown Beowulf defeating that symbolic dark

19. The central day of the Anglo-Saxon week was reserved for Woden, chief of the Germanic gods. 'Woden's day' (Wednesday) is flanked by those named after gods representing the masculine values: 'Tiw's day' (Tuesday) after the god of justice, law and order, and 'Thor's day' (Thursday) after the god of thunder, battles and physical strength. On each side of them are days dedicated to female divinities, the Moon goddess (Monday) and Freya (Friday) commemorating the wife of Woden, representing the feminine attributes of love, beauty, marriage and care for the sick. The week ends on 'Surtur's day', named after the god who, like his Roman equivalent Saturn, presided over the transition between endings and beginnings (which was why the Roman festival of the winter solstice, marking the transition from the old year to the new, was the Saturnalia). Surtur plays a similar role in Norse/Teutonic mythology (hence, as we shall see, the crucial part he plays in the events of Ragnarok/*Gottderdammerung*, the end of the world). Thus Saturday marks the moment when the old week ends, followed by the resurrection of the 'Sun' to mark the first day of the next (in Russian, Sunday is still named 'resurrection day'). This also links up with the Christian 'Easter', the festival marking Christ's resurrection, named after the place where the sun rises: in the east, from the original Sanskrit *usra*, 'the dawn' (from which the Greeks also derived their word for 'dawn', 'eos', beloved by Homer). Thus Christ, like the Sun, is the source of light which dies and is then resurrected, on Easter Sunday morning (just as Christian churches are aligned east-west, so that the sun rises over the altar).

combination of 'son and mother' which represents immaturity. As a young man he has demonstrated those attributes of fully developed manhood which qualify him to become a strong, wise and mature father-figure. But then, when he is old and nearing the end of his days, comes a new episode, quite different in its character. A fearful dragon, guarding a great treasure in an undergound cave in his kingdom, is disturbed from its long sleep. The monster flaps forth from its lair, wreaking devastation on the kingdom, even burning Beowulf's great hall with its fiery breath. Beowulf summons up his strength and prepares for his last great battle, accompanied by his brave young kinsman Wiglaf. After two bouts, Beowulf has succeeded in inflicting mortal wounds on the dragon, when his mighty ancestral sword shatters in pieces. The monster unleashes its third attack, filling Beowulf with deadly poison. Rushing to the rescue, young Wiglaf helps Beowulf to finish off the monster and the dying hero gazes on the mighty corpse of the 'Worm' they have slain, exulting at how they have liberated the treasure it was guarding, for the benefit of his people. He declares Wiglaf worthy to succeed him to the kingdom, then dies. His sorrowing people place his body on a pyre and bury his ashes in a great barrow on a headland looking over the sea, 'the finest vault that men could build'. Apart from recalling his manly deeds, they also remember how 'of all kings' he had been 'the gentlest and most gracious of men, and kindest to his people'.

What is remarkable about this concluding episode is how the dragon clearly personifies death itself Its first stirring from sleep to wreak devastation over Beowulf's kingdom represents the physical effects of advancing age, and eventually Beowulf is forced to succumb to its irresistible power. But even as he dies he also knows that he has slain his fearful antagonist, thus winning the great treasure of life for his people. And he has done so with the aid of the young hero who, in assisting him to win this mighty victory, has shown himself worthy to succeed to the kingdom.

In this respect, the story of Beowulf, written by a Christian (as we can see from internal evidence in the poem), echoes the story of Christ, in showing a mighty hero who, in dying himself, at the same time overcomes death. But apart from a perfunctory reference to his 'soul leaving his body to receive the reward of the just', there is no further indication that, as a result, Beowulf himself 'lives on' in any more obvious personal sense. In essence his ending is not portrayed very differently from that 3000 years before of the great hero Gilgamesh who, having sought in vain for the secret of immortal life, dies of old age, physically worn out but mourned by his people as their greatest and wisest king. Indeed this may also recall just how unusual it is in the history of storytelling to see a story which ends with its hero's death from old age. Infinitely more familiar are those two great archetypal endings which show the hero either ending up happily united with the heroine and 'living happily ever after', or dying 'tragically' and prematurely as a result of his 'missing the mark'. And at this point we must consider just how the immense changes in consciousness which had come about in the preceding 1000 years had provided answers to that perennial puzzle: what happens to human beings when they die?

The orthodox Christian answer to this question was that, following Christ's death and resurrection, everything was now different. According to the Christian creed, dating back to the year after Constantine made Christianity the official religion of the Roman empire, after Christ's crucifixion he had 'descended into hell' to confront the power of death. But on 'the third day' he had risen again, having conquered death, as a result of which every Christian could look forward to sharing in his resurrection to enjoy eternal life. Based on various of the reported teachings of Jesus himself, this belief had then been further refined. As each person died, their 'soul' – the non-physical essence of their personality – would face a divine judgement as to how they had lived on earth. If they were found to have lived well, according to the Christian way, they could look forward to being received into heaven, to enjoy eternal happiness with God. If they were found to have failed, or to have 'missed the mark', they faced 'damnation', doomed to be sent down to hell to face the horror of eternal punishment with the devil.

In fact there was nothing uniquely Christian about this idea. Behind it lay an archetypal model which went back into the mists of history. In ancient China, well over 1000 years earlier, there had already been a belief that when individuals died they faced a judgement as to how well they had lived in accordance with the 'Mandate of Heaven'. If approved, they could live in the heavenly garden surrounding the palace of the gods, eating from the Peach Tree of Immortality. If they failed, they faced appropriate punishment in the underworld. The ancient Greeks envisaged a similar form of judgement, whereby those who had lived particularly heroically could share eternity in the Elysian Fields, while those who had been particularly wicked, like Sisyphus, faced eternal punishment in the kingdom of Hades. For the majority there was nothing but limbo, where the shades of the dead lived in an insubstantial twilight, only able to speak if some earthly visitor, such as Odysseus, was able to animate them by giving them human blood to drink (as if the dead can only be brought back briefly to a semblance of life when they are remembered by those still alive on earth). Very rarely there were also mortals, such as Hercules, whose performance on earth was so exceptionally heroic that, when they died, they were allowed to join the gods, to be numbered among the 'immortals'.

According to the religious tradition of India, another form of 'judgement' awaited the dead in that, according to how they had lived, they could expect to be reincarnated in some other physical existence, either as a human being, higher or lower in status than their previous existence, or as some form of animal.[20] Only those exceptional spirits who had reached complete 'enlightenment', that nirvana which marked the transcending of all earthly attachments, could hope for release from mortal existence altogether, in merging back into indivisible union with the World Soul.

---

20. This belief in the 'transmigration of souls' through a series of bodily incarnations was also shared by some in the west, most notably by the followers of Pythagoras, as Shakespeare quizzically reflected in *Twelfth Night*:

  '*Clown*: What is the opinion of Pythagoras concerning wild fowl?
  *Malvolio*: That the soul of our grandam might haply inhabit a bird.
  *Clown*: What thinkest thou of his opinion?
  *Malvolio*: I think nobly of the soul, and no way approve his opinion.'

In terms of the fundamental archetype underlying these various mind-pictures, we can see how they were constantly trying to reconcile two very different perspectives. On one hand it was only when mankind became separated from all other animals in emerging from unconscious unity with nature that this problem had arisen in the first place. Only then had individual human beings begun to develop that sense of their own separate existence, centred on the ego, which made them aware that one day this existence must come to an end. Yet the fundamental drive behind men's religious impulse was to resolve that split between ego-consciousness and the selfless level of their psyche which still identified with the 'One'. What the unconscious was trying to tell them, not least through the imagery of storytelling, was that living through the 'darkness' of the ego must lead eventually to death, and that only by transcending ego-consciousness was it possible to reconnect with the 'light' of that unity which is eternal and indestructible.

By this first view, therefore, human beings are merely fleeting embodiments of that universal spirit which lies behind all creation, like bubbles coming to the surface of a pool. With death the individuality of each bubble dissipates, but the pool it emerged from remains. This view is summed up in the instruction given to Buddhist monks in the words from the *Tibetan Book of the Dead* quoted at the head of this chapter:

> 'Try to submerge yourself in that light, giving up all belief in a separate self and all attachment to the illusory ego. Recognise that the boundless Light of this true Reality is your own true self, and you shall be saved.'

On the other hand, so all-pervasive is the power of ego-consciousness and the sense that each human being enjoys a unique existence, that it has been difficult to shake off the hope that in some way death might not mark the extinction of the *individual* personality; and that some non-physical essence of each person, the 'soul', might still carry on after death. This was why those prehistoric tombs had contained food and other material possessions, to assist the dead when they crossed over into that mysterious 'other world' beyond the grave. This was why one religion after another had conceived of an 'after-life', where individual souls or spirits might live for eternity. And this became further refined by the idea that they would here be rewarded or punished according to how they had lived their lives on earth. This sprang from that archetypal pattern, coded into the unconscious, which tells us that to live by the ego must lead ultimately to destruction, whereas to live in accordance with the Self reconnects us with 'the One' which is eternal. Hence the idea in folklore that the hero or heroine who meet all the archetypal requirements which connect them to the Self will 'live happily ever after': because they are now identified with that ego-transcending part of them which lives forever.

In the eastern religions this sense that all life is ultimately one and indivisible had been expressed through the belief that, as each human being relinquishes its hold on life, so that indestructible substance takes on new bodily form through its 're-incarnation' in another creature. But even here the power of ego-consciousness retained its hold, in that the soul which passes from one physical body to another was still viewed as possessing its own individual essence; unless or until that moment comes when it attains such complete consciousness that it can merge back into indistinguishable unity with the World Soul, the universal light.

How this great question was answered therefore lay ultimately in whether the answer was coming from the ego or the Self. And although the ruling consciousness now emerging in the West might have seemed to be offering its own unequivocal response, as we can see from two of the greatest stories arising from the centuries which followed the answer which emerged from the unconscious was not always so clear cut.

### 'The love that moves the sun and the other stars'

By the eleventh century, we can begin to speak of a 'Christian Europe', and the emergence of that civilisation we associate with the 'Middle Ages'. At its centre, now acknowledged all over Europe as the supreme source of spiritual authority, stood the Papacy, still based on Rome. Its secular counterpart, at least in theory, was the 'Holy Roman Empire', centred on Germany and established since the crowning of Charlemagne as its first 'emperor' in 800. For the people of Europe, from kings and feudal lords to the humblest serf, the symbols and rituals of the Christian religion had come to provide a transcendent framework to every aspect of their lives, from birth and marriage to death and beyond. And in nothing was this more conspicuously made manifest than in those mighty buildings now beginning to soar hundreds of feet into the sky above the rooftops of Europe's cities, the 'Romanesque', later 'Gothic' cathedrals, standing at the centre of their citizens' consciousness as great symbolic embodiments of the inspiring totality of the Self.

In the twelfth and thirteenth centuries we see the heyday of that greatest cycle of mediaeval storytelling, originally derived from British legend and set in an imaginary Britain of the dark ages, but developed to some of its highest literary expressions in France and Germany: the complex of stories centred round the life and reign of the fabulous King Arthur and his knights of the Round Table. So rich was the imagery of chivalry and romance conjured up by these tales that they would continue to inspire poets, composers, painters and film-makers for centuries to come; not least through some of those subsidiary stories which grew out of the main narrative, such as the quest for the Holy Grail, the tragedy of Tristan and Isolde, the rebirth and redemption story of Parsifal. But the central story of the life of Arthur himself falls into three main stages. The first is the archetypal Rags to Riches story of Arthur's initial emergence from obscurity, until he is established in his role as an idealised 'Good King'. The second includes all the different stories centring on Camelot and that shining image of the Self, the Round Table, around which his legendary knights are drawn together, and from which they can then sally forth to perform their chivalric tasks, such as rescuing 'damsels in distress' or seeking the Grail. But the closing stage of the story shows Arthur's kingdom beginning to decay and lose its unifying power. This includes the episodes describing how Arthur falls out irreparably with his most loved knight, Sir Lancelot, who has been locked in the long-standing love affair with Arthur's Queen Guinivere which is eventually to end for both on a note of wistful tragedy. Before this, however, comes the strange episode which marks the end of Arthur's own long, heroic life.

A shadow has intruded on the ageing king, that of his nephew Mordred, his name echoing that of death. In a premonitory fit of dread, Arthur had sought to preserve his kingdom by ordering that a group of children should be sent into exile on a ship, which is then wrecked. The only survivor of this wreck, unknown to Arthur, is Mordred, who grows up in secret until, now a man, he returns with a foreign army to seek vengeance. So successfully does Mordred win over the people that he is crowned king, forcing Arthur to retreat deep into the west of his island kingdom. In a final great battle, sometimes interpreted as the last stand of Celtic Britain against the advancing Saxon invaders. Arthur strikes down the usurper. But, just as Beowulf is mortally wounded in his victorious battle with the dragon, Arthur too is dealt a fatal wound. Just as Beowulf loses his great sword, so Arthur now orders the faithful Sir Bedevere to throw his mighty sword Excalibur into a western lake, where it is caught by an arm clothed in white samite and drawn down into the depths. Then in the mists across the lake comes a boat draped in deepest black, crewed by three weeping feminine figures. Arthur enters the boat and disappears from view into the mist and gathering darkness. The story-tellers suppose that he passed from there into the mysterious Isle of Avalon, where it is eternal summer. But folklore also dictates that, when his nation again one day has need of its greatest hero, he will return.

The odd thing about this ending is that, although the story grows out of the heart of the Christian Middle Ages and is so full of Christian imagery, there should be so little that is overtly Christian about Arthur's death. Certainly, archetypally, the closing episodes of his life provide echoes of the death of Beowulf. Both are great heroes who, when full of years, are confronted by a treacherous enemy representing death. Each in his last great battle is mortally wounded but at the same time wins the victory, overcoming his antagonist. At least in Beowulf's case we know he is physically dead, as we see his ashes consumed on a funeral pyre. But Arthur simply passes from sight, merging into some new state of wholeness and light, accompanied by that shining threefold presence of the 'feminine'. Whatever the nature of this blessed world he has passed into, it is not the orthodox Christian heaven. There is no sign of God, or angels, or judgement. And in this sense he might simply be taken to have merged mystically with the One. Yet it then appears this is not the end of Arthur's story. He has seemingly survived in his full individual identity, to such effect that he may one day 'awaken', to return as redeemer of his nation: although not as a spiritual saviour but as the warlike hero he had been in life. As a compromise between ego and Self, it was a brilliantly fudged formula. The one thing it was not was a Christian answer to that perennial riddle.[21]

The story which did provide a Christian answer, more profoundly than any other, was the long poem written in the early years of the fourteenth century by a Florentine scholar, soldier, diplomat, politician and philosopher, Dante Alighieri. *The Divine Comedy* was one of the towering imaginative achievements of the

---

21. There is a semi-archetypal influence at work behind the desire to believe that a great national leader may one day return to assist his country in its hour of need. Such beliefs are not uncommon in history: Frederick Barbarossa, James IV of Scotland, Sebastian of Portugal, Alexander I of Russia and Francis Drake were among those who inspired such legends.

Middle Ages. In three books, describing Dante's journey down through Hell and up through Purgatory to Paradise, it is constructed as completely around the Rule of Three as any story in the world. Each book is divided into thirty-three cantos, plus one more as a prologue to the whole poem, making a hundred in all. His narrative famously begins with those words 'Midway through the journey of this life I found myself in a dark wood where the way was lost'. Outwardly this referred back to the time in his own life when, in his mid-thirties, as one of the civic leaders of his city-state, he had become caught up in a violent political conflict which resulted in his expulsion from the city. Cast penniless into exile, his world seemed in ruins. But inwardly Dante was describing that 'central crisis', where a hero suddenly finds himself forced to set out from the 'City of Destruction' on a Quest for the innermost meaning of human existence.

At the start of the first book, the *Inferno*, Dante sees before him a great mountain, rising out of darkness into sunlight far above. He sets off to climb it, but finds his way barred in turn by three fierce animals, a leopard, a lion and a wolf. As he runs away, stumbling in his desperation to escape, he is confronted by an imposing figure who turns out to be Virgil, revered in the Middle Ages above all other pre-Christian writers. This 'wise old man', who is to be Dante's guide through the first part of his journey, tells him that, if he wishes to escape from this savage place, he will have to take another road:

'This beast [the ego] which makes you weep does not allow anyone to pass by her, but so entangles them that she kills them; and she has a nature so perverse and vicious that her craving appetite can never be satisfied, so that after feeding she is hungrier than before.'

Dante cannot hope to climb the mountain without first going down through all the nine circles of Hell which contain those shades condemned to eternal punishment for their sins on earth. Virgil leads him to a grim gateway, bearing the legend 'Abandon hope all ye who enter here'. As they go through, his guide tells him:

'"We are come to the place where, as I said, you would see the wretched people who have lost the good of their understanding" … here sighs, cries and deep wailings resounded through the starless air, at first bringing tears to my eyes. Strange tongues, horrible outcries, words of pain, tones of anger, voices deep and hoarse … made a tumult which echoes forever through that tainted air, like the whirlwind eddies of desert sand.'

They see queues of newly-arrived souls miserably waiting to be ferried across a black river into the underworld, and Virgil arranges for them to cross over. Before reaching the pit of Hell proper, they first pass through Limbo where, in meadows around a seven-walled, seven-gated castle, they meet 'the virtuous pagans', noble figures from pre-Christian and even post-Christian times, such as Aeneas, Orpheus, Socrates, Plato, Euclid, Heraclitus, Saladin and Averroes,[22] who could not hope to enter heaven because they had not had the benefit of Christian salvation. But from

---

22. Averroes (1126-98), the Moslem scholar and philosopher, born in Spain, was exceptional among Western thinkers in believing that there was no such thing as personal immortality for individual souls, but that each human being merges back after death into an eternal whole.

here, as they enter the true Inferno, 'a place where nothing shines', Virgil begins to lead Dante down, level by level, through a carefully structured portrayal of all the gradations of human egotism.

As they travel downwards through an ever darker and more nightmarish landscape, with its fogs, marshes, beetling cliffs and stinking pools, each new circle represents states of separation from 'wholeness' more extreme than those which came before. The three animals Dante had encountered characterised the general nature of these sins. The topmost three circles, symbolised by the untamable leopard, contain those who have committed sins associated with 'incontinence', lack of self-control. The first, dedicated to those who have given way to lust, contains pairs of illicit lovers, such as Paolo and Francesca of Rimini. Trapped in marriage to a monster, she had sought refuge in a love affair with her brother-in-law until her husband murdered them both. But at least the sin of these couples had been based on a shared love. The second circle contains those who allowed their physical appetites to run to excess in greed or gluttony. But again this can at least imply a measure of sociability. The third contains those who had lived enslaved to material wealth, as hoarders or spendthrifts, and below them, in a fourth, transitional circle, are those whose lives had become consumed by anger. Here the states of egocentricity are becoming more obviously and aggressively turned against other people. Dante and Virgil then come to the gates of the infernal city, 'lower Hell', where three more circles, symbolised by the raging lion, contain those who had been guilty of crimes of violence: first those murderers and torturers who had been violent against others; then the suicides who had committed violence against themselves; finally those who had violated nature, as 'sodomites' or by living parasitically on the efforts of others through usury.

The last two circles, symbolised by the ravening wolf, contain those who lived by deceiving others. One includes a bewildering variety of sinners, from those whose deceit had lain in seduction or flattery to those whose offence had been hypocrisy or fraud. The lowest circle includes those guilty of betraying a fundamental loyalty or trust: those who had betrayed their kin or their country; those who had violated the trust of hospitality by betraying their guests; lastly those who had betrayed their lord. At this deepest part of Hell, Dante and Virgil are finally confronted by the terrifying figure of the Devil himself, a huge monster with three faces, each munching the shade of a particularly notorious traitor, Brutus and Cassius, the treacherous assassins of Caesar, and Judas, the betrayer of Christ. And at this point, when they begin to clamber down the Devil's immense body, comes that dazzling stroke whereby, as they continue to descend ever deeper, they suddenly sense they are no longer moving downwards. Having reached the very centre of the earth, they are now climbing upwards: until, in the book's closing lines, they glimpse, shining far above them, the light of the stars. Their hellish slog through the claustrophobic underworld of the ego is over. They are at the start of the next stage of their journey, at the foot of the towering mountain of Purgatory.

The next book, *Purgatorio*, is devoted to those who, although they had lived selfishly on earth, still had enough good in them or sense of remorse to hope for eventual salvation. The first two 'terraces' of the precipitous mountain contain the shades of those excommunicated by the Church, or who for some reason, such as sudden death, had not repented of their sins before dying. Then, through Peter's Gate, Dante and Virgil come to the seven cornices inhabited by those who are painfully working off their indulgence in each of the seven deadly sins: pride, envy, anger, sloth, covetousness, gluttony, lust. Each is presided over by an angel representing the 'light' opposite to its particular form of egotism: humility, generosity of spirit, peace, zeal, acceptance, temperance, chastity. Higher and higher Dante mounts until he finds himself in a place of flowers, trees and running water, the garden of mankind's innocence before the Fall, the earthly Paradise. Here an amazing pageant unfolds before him, and while he is gazing at it, transfixed, he realises his guide Virgil has silently departed. As he weeps at his loss, he realises he is now looking instead at the visionary beauty of Beatrice, the woman who has been the central inspiration of his life ever since their first childhood meeting in Florence, personifying his *anima*, the carrier of his soul. It is she who, unknown to him, has arranged from on high that he can make this journey, and that for the first part he should be accompanied by Virgil, representing spiritual wisdom on earth. But now Dante is ready for the next stage, which begins when, enlightened by all he has seen, he is finally overwhelmed by a sense of his own unworthiness. He faints at the horror of his past blindness and inadequacy, but regains consciousness to find he is being dragged across Lethe, the river of Forgetfulness, which blots out all his unhappy recollections. Beatrice leads him past the Tree of Knowledge, which bursts into blossom, he drinks of the waters of Good Remembrance and now, purged and filled with a sense of heavenly peace, he feels reborn, 'pure and prepared to leap up to the stars'. The second book thus ends on the same starry image as the first. He is ready for his *anima* to lead him on to the final stage.

The third book, the *Paradiso*, begins with a mystical vision as Dante sees Beatrice gazing into the light of the sun, hears the music of the heavenly spheres, finds himself surrounded by a shimmering sea of light and flame and realises that they have floated weightless above the earth. They rise into the first of nine heavens, each presided over by one of the nine orders of angelic beings. The first heaven, that of the Moon, is guarded by the lowest order of angels, those who watch over each individual through life. The second, that of Mercury, is guarded by the archangels who protect whole nations and bring tidings of great import to mankind, as Gabriel brought news to Mary that she was to give birth to Jesus. Here Dante talks to the Emperor Justinian, as an ideal Christian ruler and lawgiver. This takes them on to the third heaven, that of Venus, guarded by the beings known as 'Principalities', who preside over just and well-ordered earthly government. The fourth heaven, that of the Sun, is guarded by the 'Powers', images of divine power in combating the powers of darkness. Here Dante sees a dazzling array of philosophers, moral teachers, wise men and saints, from Thomas Aquinas to Solomon. The fifth heaven, Mars, guarded by the 'Virtues', the angelic images of strength and fortitude, is peopled by righteous warrior-leaders, from Joshua to Charlemagne. The sixth heaven, Jupiter, guarded by 'Dominions' representing justice and the ultimate dominion of God over the world, includes King David and the first

Christian Emperor Constantine. The seventh, Saturn, guarded by 'Thrones', represents divine steadfastness and self-discipline, personified in saintly contemplatives such as Benedict, founder of Christian monasticism.

Here, appropriately, Saturn marks the end of one sequence and the beginning of another, as Dante and Beatrice ascend a Celestial Ladder to the final two heavens. The previous five have represented different aspects of power, justice and self-discipline, the masculine virtues. Now at last we come to the feminine values, beginning in the eighth heaven, that of the fixed stars guarded by Cherubim, representing Divine Wisdom. Here Dante is quizzed by St Peter, St James and John on the meaning of the three supreme Christian virtues, Faith, Hope and Love. When they ascend to the ninth heaven, guarded by Seraphim, the highest angelic order, representing Divine Love, this turns out to be the prelude to their ascent onto yet another level, incomparably different from all those which have preceded it. First they see a point of intense light, surrounded by nine concentric rings, which Beatrice explains is a vision of God, surrounded by the nine orders of angels. Dante sees her beauty now so transfigured that it is beyond his powers to describe, and bathed in such light that he is temporarily blinded. She tells him they have come into the Empyrean and, as he recovers his sight, he sees rising above them a great shining mystical rose. Here, in the snow-white petals of this mighty symbol of heavenly totality are tier upon tier of the souls of the blessed, bathed in peace and love. Dante turns to Beatrice for an explanation, to find she has gone and been replaced by a figure who looks on him with immense benevolence. It is St Bernard, his third and final guide, who shows him Beatrice now enthroned in the rose, crowned in glory, while higher up sits the Queen of Heaven herself, the Virgin Mary, attended by countless angels.

Dante is then confronted with a final astonishing vision: three spheres of radiant light, all distinct, but all occupying the same space: an emblem of the Trinity and of that number which is the archetype of growth and transformation. While he is gazing at it, trying to puzzle out with his intellect how the three spheres can be separate yet one, he suddenly feels he is able to let go. He no longer has any separate will or mind or existence. Dante feels his entire being taken over, by the power of a love so total that it is beyond all comprehension.

'As a wheel moves smoothly, free from jars,
My will and my desire were turned by love.
The love that moves the sun and the other stars.'

So the story ends, on this breathtaking image in which Dante sees love as the power which ultimately gives purpose, meaning and connection to everything in the universe. What is particularly striking about this vision is that the 'love that moves the sun and the other stars' is seen not just as a force which can bind animate creatures together, but as the all-uniting power which shapes and impels all inanimate matter as well. For Dante, at the end of his mighty inner journey, imagines his own separate existence finally dissolving into the light of that single mind which called everything into being in the first place. He is portraying the entire universe as a just a single great thought, based on unimaginable love. In all storytelling it is the supreme example of a hero finally merging into the One.

## 'Man is the measure of all things'

Immeasurably remote though it now seems to us, the world-picture developed by mediaeval Christendom was one of the most remarkable achievements of the human imagination. For the peoples of Christian Europe it provided a psychological framework which could explain and give meaning to the entire way in which they viewed their existence. The picture of the world it presented was made up of two separate but interfused dimensions, one material, the other spiritual. On the outward, worldly plane, the earth was the centre of the universe. Europe stood at its centre. Its secular society, with its feudal system, was built around a hierarchy which gave each person an allotted place, owing loyalty to their lord and their king (even, in parts of Europe, to that ghostly echo of a long-vanished political unity, the 'Holy Roman Emperor'). But this outward world was subordinate to the unseen eternal dimension which was viewed as the true reality. Although this was visibly represented by the Church, with its ranks of priests, monks and bishops rising to the Pope at its head, these were mere earthly intermediaries for the heavenly hierarchy of saints and angels, centred on the power which had created the universe and which ruled over all earthly existence. In itself such a power might have seemed so immense as to be unimaginable. Yet it had become possible for people to relate to it inwardly through the humanising of God in the figure of Christ himself, representing a projection of human nature in its most perfect state. The purpose of prayer and Christian ritual was to dissolve the barrier between ego and Self, to bring people into contact with that level of their psyche which transcended the imperfect ego, thus linking them back to the unseen totality.

So all-embracing was this 'Christian myth' that it could give a sense of significance to every aspect of individual and collective life. And not the least reflection of its power was the way, for hundreds of years, the chief visual self-expression of European civilisation, alongside its churches and cathedrals, was centred on a particular set of images, endlessly painted, sculpted and depicted in stained-glass, the purpose of which was constantly to focus people's minds on this other dimension to their lives. These stylised icons of the crucified Christ and the Mother and Child made no attempt to relate to the imperfect, everyday, material world. They were windows onto that eternal plane of perfection which was regarded as the only true reality.

One of the earliest signs of how all this was to change began to appear at the very time Dante was writing his *Divine Comedy*. In the paintings of a fellow Florentine who was his almost exact contemporary, we see Western art at last bursting out of that two-dimensional iconographic frame which had constrained it for so long as, with a mighty leap of the imagination, Giotto brought the central events of the Christian story out into the visible, material world: a world of sky and hills, trees and buildings, peopled by real three-dimensional human beings showing real human emotions. Just when the power of that all-unifying world-picture was reaching its zenith in Dante's vision, we see the beginnings of another great shift in consciousness which was eventually to reshape the human world more fundamentally than anything which had come before.

The disintegration of the mediaeval world-image was to be a centuries-long process. But an early reflection of it was the way in which, in the two centuries following Giotto, artists took the subject matter of their paintings ever further out into the earthly world. Their pictures remained centred on Christian imagery. But as artists such as Masaccio and Piero della Francesca, Ucello and Jan van Eyck developed an ever greater 'realism' in the way they portrayed the physical world, a profound shift was taking place in where that 'reality' was perceived to lie. Their art was still subordinated to a vision of heavenly perfection. Through images of Christ's suffering on the cross which represented humanity's struggle to escape the imperfections of the ego, it was still imbued with the transcendent values of the Self. But the spiritual dimension was now coming to be expressed through an ever more life-like recreation of the world of physical appearances. And, as they steadily widened the range of their subject matter in painting landscapes, secular portraits and even scenes from classical mythology, it was no longer necessary that their sources of inspiration should be explicitly Christian at all.

Equally significant was the way this shift in consciousness was reflected in architecture. Nothing had more majestically expressed the transcendent world-view of the Christian Middle Ages than its great cathedrals, with their dark, mysterious interiors leading up towards the central focus of the high altar, their luminous stained-glass windows, their spires and towers soaring heavenwards. Their purpose, reinforced by music, incense and the profusion of holy images, was to lead worshippers into the presence of an unearthly spiritual mystery. But quite suddenly, around the end of the fifteenth century, the Gothic style which had expressed this all but vanished from view. Taking conscious inspiration from the pre-Christian civilisation of Greece and Rome, the dominant buildings of the new age, like St Peter's, Rome, sought, like the temples of the ancient world, to express perfection in more earthly form, as ideal images based on the language of symmetry, harmony and intellectual order.

There is no better clue to the new spirit underlying the Renaissance than the great staircase designed by Piero della Francesca for the palace of the Duke of Urbino in the mid-fifteenth century. The steps are so arranged that it is impossible to descend them except in the most stately and dignified fashion. Merely to walk down a set of stairs gives a sense of elevation and nobility. One cannot do so without having to 'walk tall'. The Renaissance was thus inspired by a vision of man being drawn up to his fullest stature, realising the highest potential of which he was capable: as we see in the lofty view of humanity conveyed by those grave and luminous figures in Piero's own paintings. It was in this sense that Kenneth Clark identified the essence of the Renaissance in the words of Plato's *Protagoras*: 'man is the measure of all things'. It was this vision of human nature at its most ideal, with all darkness and deformity purged away, which inspired the artists of the later Renaissance, such as Leonardo and Michelangelo. It was a new vision of the perfection of the Self. But it was far removed from that world-view of the Middle Ages in the time of Dante only 200 years before, with its image of a fallen humanity which could only hope to be made perfect on the plane of eternity.

A further great hole was punched in the frame of that mediaeval world-picture by the great voyages of exploration at the end of the fifteenth century, which opened up the realisation that whole 'new worlds' lay beyond the confines of Christian Europe, above all those vast unknown continents across the Atlantic. But just as important as these discoveries themselves was that, in order to make them, men were coming to rely on a new perception of what constituted 'reality', as something which lay in the outward, physical world. In doing so, they were learning to reject that central assumption of the mediaeval world-picture that the earth was flat in favour of a new, empirical realisation that it was round.

Another significant chunk of the unified world-picture slipped away when, all over northern Europe in the first half of the sixteenth century, men challenged the authority of the Papacy to rule over Western Christendom. No longer were they prepared just blindly to accept the rule of a system which had become only too obviously worldly and corrupt. Like Luther when he declared 'here I stand, I can say no other', they had found a new source of authority in their own judgement, as they looked anew at the image of Jesus presented in the Bible, the book on which Christianity rested. Possessed by this new vision of the Self, they set about destroying all those outward trappings which had been designed to convey religion as the gateway to an other-worldly spiritual dimension. In their newfound zeal, they tore down statutes of the saints and images of the Virgin, poured contempt on the belief in Purgatory, and lectured bemused worshippers that unless they were among the 'elect', chosen by God, they faced eternal damnation. But as they did so they became all too easily inflated by that self-righteousness which arises from confusing ego with Self, potentially the most deadly form of egotism of all.

Yet another shock came from the discovery of the later sixteenth century, with the aid of new scientific inventions such as the telescope, that the earth did not stand at the centre of the universe. Again, this derived from the growing perception that true 'reality' could only be established through understanding the structures of the outward, physical world. But the way this shook the foundations of Western man's sense of identity was caught by one of the most intelligent thinkers of the early seventeenth century, John Donne:

> 'And new philosophy calls all in doubt,
> The element of fire is quite put out;
> The sun is lost; and th'earth; and no man's wit
> Can well direct him where to look for it.
> And freely men confess that this world's spent,
> When in the planets and the firmament,
> They seek so many new; they see that this
> Is crumbled out again to his atomies.
> 'Tis all in pieces, all coherence gone.'[23]

When Donne spoke of how 'all coherence' had been lost, what he was really talking about was the disintegration of that mediaeval world-picture which had seemed to explain so perfectly how everything fitted together with everything else,

---

23. Donne, *An Anatomy of the World, First Anniversary* (1611).

in that unified and universal image which was unconsciously a projection of the totality of the Self. But just when Donne was lamenting how, thanks to the 'new philosophy'. everything seemed to be falling apart, a wholly new vision of that totality had lately been emerging through the imagination of one of Donne's contemporaries and fellow-countrymen. Originally it had been the visual arts which first expressed the disintegration of that mediaeval world-view, while at the same time conjuring up a new, more earthly vision of the Self. Now the torch of achieving a new synthesis passed to a different art-form, literature: most notably through the works of just one writer, Shakespeare.

What above all made Shakespeare's tragedies and comedies unique was how they sprung from a vision of the world which was so completely unified. From his sense of the fundamental patterns governing human behaviour down to the unerringly exact observation of his individual images, the essence of his greatness lay in his ability to portray the world as it is, unclouded by any subjective notion of how it might be. 'Life with Shakespeare' as the writer Christopher Hollis put it, 'is not a debate on principles. The principles are settled. Life is the pageant of men living up to them or failing to live up to them.' To Shakespeare those principles were the outward expression of a living framework of order which equally encompassed personal morality, the social order and the natural order of the universe, all making up a harmonious whole which can only be flouted at ultimately fatal risk. And the reason he was able to see the world so clearly was because, more than any other author, he was so instinctively at one with the values of the Self.

In that famous speech of Ulysses in *Troilus and Cressida*, Shakespeare showed that he had just as comprehensive a sense of a universal order as anything conceived in the Middle Ages.

> 'The heavens themselves, the planets and this centre,
> Observe degree, priority and place,
> Insisture, course, proportion, season, form,
> Office and custom in all line of order ...'

The same kind of order governed the affairs of mankind. Yet when its balance becomes disturbed, 'when the planets in evil mixture to disorder wander', then:

> 'What plagues and what portents, what mutiny,
> What raging of the sea, shaking of earth,
> Commotion in the winds, frights, changes, horrors,
> Divert and crack, rend and deracinate
> The unity and married calm of states.'

When human affairs thus become disintegrated, nothing reflects this more clearly than the way in which each component part rebels against the whole: that unleashing of the power of individual and collective egotism which Shakespeare so vividly portrays in each of his tragedies:

> 'Take but degree away, untune that string,
> And hark what discord follows! Each thing meets
> In mere oppugnancy ...'

until:

> 'Every thing includes itself in power,
> Power into will, will into appetite,
> And appetite, an universal wolf …
> Must make perforce an universal prey,
> And last eat up himself.'

Nowhere else in his plays does Shakespeare so explicitly summarise the fundamental world-view which underlies them all. Ulysses's speech sets out that cosmic polarity between the Self and the ego which informs almost every line Shakespeare wrote, and which no other writer has ever explored with such penetrating depth. And he did so, not with the aid of some external, projected model of the kind which had provided the inspiration of the Middle Ages, but because, more than any other storyteller, his conscious mind was so instinctively at one with the objective unconscious within him: that 'Secret' which 'sits in the middle and knows'.[24]

In this respect Shakespeare's plays demonstrate how, as it emerged from the constraints of the mediaeval world-picture, it was possible for the consciousness of Western man to reach a depth of psychological understanding which hitherto would have been impossible. In Shakespeare's perception of human nature, the fourfold components of totality, strength, mind, heart and soul, could still be held in perfect balance. But within 20 years of his death the French philosopher Descartes gave an early indication of the way the consciousness of Western man was now moving when he proclaimed 'I think, therefore I am'. He did not say, as the Middle Ages might have had it, 'God thinks, therefore I am'. For Descartes, the greatest riddle in human nature was to unravel the distinction between body and mind. For him the heart and the soul had begun to drop out of the picture. As Western civilisation moved still further from the Middle Ages, consciousness centred on the ego was now beginning to split off from the unconscious in a way which was wholly new.

In the later seventeenth century Newton's discovery of the law of gravitation paved the way for a new mental image of the universe, whereby it could be seen as essentially an immense physical mechanism which was open to understanding by the human mind because its workings were governed by wholly consistent physical laws. Newton himself was deeply religious and for him this vision of a perfectly-ordered universe was merely confirmation that it must be the creation of a supernatural mind. The more his own intelligence came to understand how physical creation fitted together, the more he was awed by its unity ('nature', as he put it 'is very consonant and conformable with itself'). Yet, equally, the more he discovered, the more he sensed just how little of the workings of the physical universe the human mind could ever hope to understand. As he also put it in a famous passage:

---

24. As William Hazlitt put it: 'the striking peculiarity of Shakespeare's mind was its generic quality, its power of communication with all other minds, so that it contained a universe of thought and feeling within itself, and had no particular bias or exclusive excellence more than another. He was just like any other man, but that he was like all other men. He was the least of an egotist that it was possible to be.' (*On Shakespeare and Ben Jonson*).

'I seem to have been only like a boy playing on the sea-shore, and diverting myself in now and then finding a smoother pebble or a prettier shell than ordinary, while the great ocean of truth lay all undiscovered before me.'

By the mid-eighteenth century, however, we see a world in which even this sense of awe before an immense mystery has begun to vanish. 'Above the line' we see a civilisation bathed in the confident light of a consciousness which is based above all on the ordering function of the human mind. Its architecture is harmonious and orderly, its painting and literature likewise. When it observes nature it does so by means of classification and taxonomy. Its thinkers imagine there is no problem confronting mankind, from the making of political constitutions to increasing the productivity of agriculture, which cannot be resolved by use of the human intellect to perceive the laws and principles which lie behind it. So bright now is the 'light of reason' that the remnants of that old mediaeval sense of a transcendent, supernatural dimension to human existence are beginning to fade away into little more than high-minded sentimentality. The spirit ruling this world has come to be seen as no more than a 'benevolent Deity'. Yet when we look at this 'age of enlightenment' in terms of its storytelling, we see how much of what constitutes psychic totality had now dropped out of view.

It was revealing that such a characteristic plot of stories in the eighteenth century was the 'Voyage and Return', describing the adventures of travellers such as Gulliver, Robinson Crusoe, Candide, Rasselas and the Ancient Mariner venturing into unknown realms.This was not just because the eighteenth century, with its voyages into the uncharted southern hemisphere, was one of the great ages of European exploration in the outward, physical world. The essence of this type of story is that it shows someone living in a state of limited consciousness suddenly falling through the floor into some hidden realm which contains a whole dimension of existence of which they were previously unaware. The appearance of this plot (as in the novels of Kafka, Evelyn Waugh or J. D. Salinger) is always a sign that consciousness has become dangerously one-sided and split off from the unconscious. And nothing is more striking about eighteenth-century storytelling than the extent to which it manages to diminish or shut out the dark side of human nature. The Overcoming the Monster plot in its more grotesque expressions virtually drops out of western storytelling (except occasionally in pastiche form, as in the sea-monster which appears in Mozart's opera *Idomeneo*). The eighteenth century was much more naturally at home with the cosy, optimistic world of comedy. So ill at ease was it with the darker spirit of Tragedy that attempts were even made to rewrite the tragedies of Shakespeare to give them happy endings, such as the famous reworking of *King Lear* by Nahum Tate, defended by Dr Johnson, which showed Lear and Cordelia surviving to take a final curtain.

Beneath the harmoniously ordered surface of this civilisation, however, behind the elegant crescents of Bath, the calmly rational prose of the French Encyclopaedists, the dancers circling to a stately minuet beneath the chandeliers of a Viennese ballroom, the well-bred pleasure those English aristocrats took in going on their 'Grand Tours' of the classical sites of Italy, subterranean energies were stirring which were about to unleash an even greater earthquake in the collective psyche of the western world than anything seen so far.

## Revolution and Romanticism: The unleashing of the ego

The theme of this chapter has been the most obvious of the ways in which, since far back into prehistory, human beings have tried to reconcile the psychic split which arose from the moment they began emerging from a state of nature. Its central importance to human civilisation could be seen in how its symbolic structures dominated the settlements of almost every culture in the world, from the cathedrals of Europe to the ziggurats and minarets of the Middle East, from the pagodas of Asia to the carved totems of North America.

Closely allied to religion, however, as these structures showed, was that other chief means whereby human beings had used imagination to connect their conscious lives with the ego-transcending realm of the unconscious: through the power of art.

During the Middle Ages the art form which most dramatically expressed this desire for re-connection to the Self was architecture, in those Gothic cathedrals. But over the centuries which followed the central focus of that imaginative effort had moved at different times from one art form to another. As the European imagination broke out from its mediaeval frame, it initially found its most complete psychological expression in the new styles of painting which produced the glories of the fifteenth and early sixteenth-century Renaissance. By the early seventeenth century, the focus had moved to literature acted out on a stage. It was the plays of Shakespeare which now showed the greatest ability to penetrate to the objective level of the human psyche (although the isolated genius of Rembrandt, a little later, matched his depth of insight). By the eighteenth century, literature and painting were no longer capable of reaching such psychological and spiritual depths. The form which now most profoundly conveyed the power of the Western imagination to express psychic totality was music. In the age first of Bach and Handel, then of Haydn and Mozart, finally of Beethoven and Schubert, it was music, the most inward and abstract of all the arts, which most completely expressed that power by which great art harmonises consciousness with the Self. And no composer was more consciously aware of the significance of this than the towering figure who stood at the end of this period when, psychologically, music stood unrivalled among the arts. In Beethoven's own words:

'like all the arts music is founded on the exalted symbols of the moral sense; all true invention is a moral progress. To submit to its inscrutable laws, and by means of these laws to tame and guide one's own mind, so that the manifestations of art may pour out: this is the isolating principle of art ... so art always represents the divine, and the relationship of men towards art is religion: what we obtain through art comes from God ... thus every genuine product of art is independent, more powerful than the artist himself ... connected with men only inasmuch as it bears witness to the divine of which they are a medium. Music relates the spirit to harmony.' [25]

25. Recorded by Bettina von Brentano in a letter to Goethe, May 1810.

In fact, at a less rarified level, the same principle governed those more popular forms of art which had entertained and uplifted the great mass of ordinary people for thousands of years, from the songs and dances associated with all the world's rich traditions of folk music to the skills of the popular storytellers.[26] It is no accident that so much of this book has been taken up with discussing stories derived from folk tales, those anonymous products of the collective imagination of mankind whose origins are so mysterious that we can usually only track them down to the forms in which they were first collected. By the time at the end of the seventeenth century when the Frenchman Charles Perrault first came to publish versions of such folk tales as *Sleeping Beauty, Red Riding Hood, Bluebeard* and *Cinderella*,[27] or when the Grimm brothers produced their collection of German folk tales in the early nineteenth century, many centuries had probably elapsed since most of these stories had first begun to evolve, to be passed on by oral retelling through many generations.

In psychological terms these tales provide as perfect a reflection of the underlying archetypes of storytelling as anything we find in more self-consciously sophisticated forms of literature, which is why in this book we have returned to such examples as *Cinderella* or *Jack and the Beanstalk* again and again. There is nothing overtly religious or 'Christian' about these stories (indeed variations of them are found in cultures all over the world). But they can be seen to reflect the same fundamental picture of human nature as that which underlies Christianity or other religions, because they spring so directly from the same archetypal roots. Just as surely as we see expressed through the religious impulse in mankind, they reflect the patterns whereby humanity can transcend the limitations of the ego to make contact with the Self. In that respect the folk tales which were so important to the 'below the line' culture of mediaeval and post-mediaeval Europe were as much part of the psychological framework which helped connect people to the values of the Self as religion itself.

In the centuries following the Middle Ages, as European civilisation began to discover a quite different basis on which to look at the world, the imaginative and cultural framework created to provide this sense of unity in people's lives had begun subtly to disintegrate. For a long time the outward signs of this might not have seemed too obvious. But towards the end of the eighteenth century three developments coincided which were to mark the onset of a wholly new phase in the psychic development of mankind.

The first stemmed from all those advances in scientific knowledge and technological skill which were bringing about the industrial revolution. It is hard to exaggerate the psychological impact of the change this was to bring about in Western civilisation, as it began to become ever more dependent on the machine. The new machines, combining unprecedented power with the rigid repetitive patterns

---

26. As Tolstoy wrote in *What Is Art?*, 'Only two kinds of art can be considered good art in our time ... first, art transmitting feelings from a religious perception of man's position in the world, in relation to God and his neighbour ... secondly, art transmitting the simplest feelings of common life, such as are accessible to all men throughout the world: the art of common life, the art of the people, universal art.'
27. *Histoire ou Contes du Temps Passé* (1695).

of mechanical order, helped to reinforce the masculine element in the collective psyche like nothing in human experience. They provided the means whereby civilisation could amass unheard of new wealth, reshaping the world with great new cities, joined together by such triumphs of nineteenth-century engineering as the railways, steam trains, steamships, great metal bridges. The effect of all this was immense, not least because it created the sense that men were now as never before emerging from their old dependence on nature to become masters of the world around them, controlling it to their own purposes. This was reinforced by that radical new mind-picture, first put forward by Erasmus Darwin and others before the end of the eighteenth century, which showed how life on earth had evolved over millions of years, from lower forms of life to higher, until it culminated in *Homo sapiens*. All this helped build up what over the next 100 years was, 'above the line', to be seen as the new 'religion of progress', portraying the entire history of the world as a long and painful upward climb from darkness into light, of which nineteenth-century man, with all his newfound power and mental ingenuity, was the crowning achievement.

But 'below the line' this triumphant onward march of human consciousness cast a long shadow. As people were drawn off the land in their millions to crowd into the cities and factories, many were forced to live out their lives in surroundings more oppressive and dehumanised than anything experienced by human beings before. They were becoming cut off from the living rhythms of nature in a way that was entirely new. And that ingenuity which was creating the new machines and new wealth was also creating new weapons of mass-destruction which would eventually exact a terrible price.

A second, more specific break with the past at the end of the eighteenth century was exemplified in the tumultuous events of the French Revolution. More self-consciously than any generation before them, the French revolutionaries saw themselves as launching a wholly new era in the life of mankind, putting behind them all the darkness and superstition of the past. They were determined to tear down not just the monarchy and the social hierarchy which had ruled France since far back into the Middle Ages, but also the entire legacy of the Christian religion. Their revolution was seen as marking a final victory for that spirit of rationalism which had found expression in the eighteenth-century Enlightenment. The idea of a transcendent God was to be replaced by a new 'Supreme Being', the 'Goddess of Reason': a glorified projection of the power of human consciousness. And nothing better symbolised this triumph for the ordering function of the human brain than the desire of the new revolutionary rulers to force the people of France to live in a new mental universe. They were to have a new calendar, replacing the dating of years from the birth of Christ with a new system which began with 1792 as 'Year One' of the Revolution. There were to be new names for their months; a new decimal week, replacing the Babylonian week of seven 24-hour days with one of 10 days, each divided into 10 hours; a new decimal currency. Above all they were to have a new system of weights and measures. The confusion of old traditional measures was to be replaced by a perfectly rational system in which all weights and measures would be defined in terms of the new 'metre', precisely equivalent to one ten-millionth of a quarter of the circumference of the earth, In 1799, after two leading French savants had spent seven years meticulously measuring every inch of the distance between Dunkirk and Barcelona, to establish the exact length of this new standard, a huge crowd assembled in Paris to see the unveiling of the platinum bar which was to define the length of the metre for all time. It was the most holy object of the Revolution: the central symbol of how the world had been made new.

But again, to all this triumphant celebration of human consciousness there was a dark underside. For the privilege of living in this new era of liberty and equality, the people of France paid in a sea of blood, starting with the heady spectacle of thousands of aristocrats being sent to the guillotine, ending in the deaths of millions on the battlefields of the revolutionary and Napoleonic wars. When the churches of France were rededicated as 'Temples of Reason', the role of the 'Goddess' was more than once acted out by a local prostitute, paraded in triumph through the streets before being enthroned on the high altar of the cathedral. So mad was the new revolutionary calendar that within only a year or two it had been shame-facedly abandoned. As for the hubris which inspired that sacred symbol of the revolutionaries' brave new world, the platinum metre, it was somehow appropriate that one of the two *savants* employed to ensure that it precisely corresponded to that fraction of the earth's circumference had secretly discovered that his sums did not add up, provoking him to a nervous breakdown. Rather than admit the truth, he falsified his figures: with the result that the strip of metal defining what is still to this day the metre's length all over the world, is a fraction of a millimetre short of what it should be. The entire metric system, symbol of the power of human reason to make the world anew, is based on a tiny but symbolic lie.[28]

The third fundamental break with the past taking place towards the end of the eighteenth century was in important respects related to the other two. The extraordinary drama of the French Revolution had sent a psychic shock wave through Europe, the repercussions of which ran much wider and deeper than just the world of politics. As William Wordsworth wrote in his famous lines remembering the euphoric mood of that revolutionary time:

> 'Bliss was it in that dawn to be alive,
> But to be young was very heaven!'

A generation later, lecturing in *On the Living Poets* (1818), William Hazlitt recalled how:

> 'There was a mighty ferment in the heads of statesmen and poets, kings and people. According to the prevailing notions, all was to be natural and new. Nothing that was established was to be tolerated ... authority ... elegance or arrangement were hooted out of countenance ... everyone did that which was good in his own eyes ... the licentiousness grew extreme ... it was a time of promise, a renewal of the world.'

28. A fascinating historical account of this triumph of ego-consciousness is given in *The Measure of All Things* by Ken Alder (2002). He goes on to describe how in 1801 Napoleon decreed that exclusive use of the metric system should be compulsory throughout France. But this led to such chaos and proved so unpopular that in 1812 he allowed the French to return to their traditional measures. The French government only reimposed the metric system in 1840.

One of the poets about whom Hazlitt was writing, Wordsworth himself, had written in the immediate aftermath of the French Revolution of how:

'A multitude of causes, unknown to former times, are now acting with a combined force to blunt the discriminating powers of the mind, and ... to reduce it to a state of almost savage torpor. The most effective of these causes are the great national events which are daily taking place, and the increasing accumulation of men in cities, where the uniformity of their occupations produces a craving for extraordinary incident which the rapid communication of intelligence hourly gratifies. To this tendency ... the literature and theatrical exhibitions of the country have conformed themselves. The invaluable works of our older writers ... are driven into neglect by frantic novels, sickly and stupid German tragedies, and deluges of idle and extravagant stories.'[29]

Nothing indeed was more expressive of Hazlitt's 'mighty ferment' than that great fever which had already begun to sweep through the artistic imagination of Europe and that was to be associated with all the dreams, delusions and excesses we associate with the phenomenon known as Romanticism. And nowhere was this upheaval more evident, as we have already seen, than in the shift which was taking place around that time in the psychic centre of gravity from which writers imagined stories. It is here we can see more clearly reflected than anywhere else how what was happening in Western civilisation was a new kind of split developing between the ego and the Self. As all the cultural framework of beliefs and customs which provided people with a spiritual and mental centre to their lives was being dismantled, what was emerging was storytelling of a kind which had never been seen before.

The ego was slipping its leash. It was the beginning of that new phase in the psychic evolution of mankind with which we are still living two centuries later.

---

29. Preface to second edition of *Lyrical Ballads* (1800).

CHAPTER THIRTY-FOUR

# The Age of Loki

## *The Dismantling of the Self*

'When the Way was lost, there was virtue; when virtue was lost there was benevolence; when benevolence was lost there was rectitude; when rectitude was lost there were the rites; the rites are the wearing thin of loyalty and good faith and the beginning of disorder.'     Lao Tzu, *Tao Te Ching*, XXXVIII

'Things fall apart; the centre cannot hold;
Mere anarchy is loosed upon the world.
The blood dimmed tide is loosed; and everywhere
The ceremony of innocence is drowned;
The best lack all conviction, while the worst
Are full of passionate intensity ...
And what rough beast, its hour come round at last,
Slouches towards Bethlehem to be born?'

W. B. Yeats, *The Second Coming*

'Take but degree away, untune that string,
And, hark, what discord follows! Each thing meets
In mere oppugnancy ...
Strength should be lord of imbecility ...
Force should be right, or rather, right and wrong ...
Should lose their names ...
Then every thing includes itself in power,
Power into will, will into appetite,
And appetite, an universal wolf ...
Must make perforce an universal prey,
And last eat up himself.'

Ulysses, *Troilus and Cressida*, I.iii

There is one mythological tradition in human history which stands separate from all the others. This is the web of myths which we can piece together from various epics of the pre-Christian peoples of northern Europe, which show the whole adventure of life on earth ending in a mighty, all-consuming catastrophe: the Teutonic *Gotterdammerung*, the Norse *Ragnarok*, the passing of the gods and the destruction of the world. There is one particular feature of this story which makes it an apt prologue to our final chapter, which looks at how storytelling has reflected the evolving consciousness of Western civilisation over the past 200 years.

Like many others before it, the Norse mythology saw the world as divided into three levels. That inhabited by mankind was Midgard or Middle Earth. Above it, in the heavens, was Asgard, home of the gods, the Aesir, presided over from his great hall, Valhalla, by the wise 'All-Father' Odin. The dim underworld of Helheim (from which we get our word 'hell') was where all human beings went after their death, except those killed in battle who ascended to Valhalla. In addition to these three familiar levels, separated from Midgard and Asgard by mountains, was the mysterious realm of Jotunheim, inhabited by giants. Although closely related to the gods, these often brutal, treacherous beings with supernatural powers were the Aesir's worst enemies. If the gods represented 'upper world' consciousness, the giants represented their menacing shadow.

Some time after the creation of the world and all its inhabitants, while Odin and his brother are wandering through Midgard, on a forest path near the borders of Jotunheim they meet a handsome young man with twinkling eyes and a mischievous expression, who introduces himself as their 'cousin' Loki.

Loki becomes the most interesting figure in the story. Although he is of giant stock, the gods welcome him, because he is charming and cleverer than any of them. But there is something deeply ambivalent about his nature. In the perpetual rivalry between the Aesir and the giants, Loki's ingenuity extricates the gods from one difficult situation after another, even though it is often Loki's own two-sided nature which has created the problem in the first place. His trickery proves so useful to the gods that they invite him to become one of their own number. But somehow it seems there is always a catch to what their crafty new companion is up to; some hidden price to be paid for the benefits he brings them.

The dark side of Loki's nature is confirmed when one day he disappears and Odin, looking down from the lofty eyrie from which he can view all the world, is eventually horrified to spy him in Jotunheim, playing with three young monsters. It turns out that Loki has sneaked off to have an affair with a giantess, and that these are their offspring: Hela, half a living woman, half a decaying corpse; Jormengand, a fast-growing serpent; and Fenris, a ferocious wolf. The news strikes the Aesir like a thunderclap. Are these hideous creatures destined some day to play a part in the long-prophesied end of the world, *Ragnarok*, the Last Great Battle? At the urging of Thor, god of physical strength and battles, the gods take steps to neutralise these fearsome new arrivals. Hela is sent down to preside over the underworld. Thor hurls Jormengand into the sea, only for the monster to coil itself round the earth as the Midgard Serpent. The Fenris Wolf is eventually chained up on an island. But from now on the gods live in perpetual fear that, when the day of *Ragnarok* arrives, the terrifying power of these monsters will be unleashed.

Loki revenges himself for what has been done to his offspring by secretly cutting off the shining golden hair of Thor's wife. When Thor guesses who is responsible, Loki attempts to appease his wrath by persuading the dwarves who fashion gold and wondrous inventions deep in the mountains to make a succession of miraculous gifts. One of these is new hair for Thor's wife, spun from purest gold. They also include a gold ring which has the power to multiply itself, thus guaranteeing infinite riches, and a set of magic weapons: a spear for Odin which always returns to his hand after he has thrown it; a boat which can travel by sea, land

and air; and a mighty hammer for Thor, so powerful that it will overwhelm any opponent. But the presentation of these gifts itself leads to a further row, which ends in one of the dwarves angrily sewing up the loquacious Loki's mouth with leather. The other gods all laugh, at seeing him for once unable to speak. When Loki tears off the thong, it leaves his mouth scarred and his smile twisted. From now on he and the Aesir are set ever more at odds.

The showdown comes when it is announced that Baldur, Odin's youngest son and the most loved of all the gods, has been made invulnerable to attack by any weapon made from a substance which originated in the earth. So dark has Loki now become that, by 'dark inversion', he develops a passionate hatred for the perfect young hero. He discovers that the one substance which can harm Baldur is mistletoe, because it grows on trees and therefore not directly from the earth. He hardens a twig of mistletoe into a dart and persuades Baldur's blind brother to throw it. To the horror of the Aesir, the most loved of their number falls dead. They soon realise who is guilty of this crime and Loki is taken to a cave to be imprisoned, like Prometheus, in perpetual agony, pinned to a rock with venom ceaselessly dripping onto his skin.

How the story eventually ends is only known from a wise old woman who can see the future. She tells Odin that there will be three years of perpetual cold and darkness, the Fimbull Winter. Then the Last Great Battle will begin, when Loki and his three monsters break their bonds, joining the Giants and all the dark forces of the earth in unleashing a fearful assault on Asgard. Looking down on this twilight of the gods will be Surtur who, like his Roman equivalent Saturn, presides over endings and beginnings. After a mighty struggle, Thor and the great Midgard Serpent will kill each other; Odin will be eaten by the ravening Fenris Wolf, now grown to enormous size, although it in turn will then be slain by Odin's son Vidar. Loki will engage in mortal combat with another of the Aesir, Heimdall the Watchman, ending in both their deaths. Surtur will then spread fire over all the earth, and everything living will perish.

At this point, says the prophetess, 'darkness descends and I can see no more'. But then Odin himself has a vision. First he sees the earth covered with a great waste of storm-tossed waters. Then, rising out of the sea, he sees a new earth, covered in forests, meadows and rivers. There standing in the sunshine are his two older sons, together with the sons of Thor, and they are joined by Baldur, returned from Helheim. Down in Midgard, it seems that two members of the human race, hiding away in a dark cave, have also escaped Surtur's holocaust, and they too emerge to begin repopulating the earth. Soon new halls are rising in Asgard, children are playing and Odin weeps for joy. At last he knows the meaning of the mysterious word he had whispered into Baldur's ear as his dead son lay on his funeral ship. The word had been 'rebirth'.

What makes the role played by Loki in this sequence of stories so significant is precisely his remarkable ambivalence. He is endlessly inventive, yet strangely amoral. Directly or indirectly he provides the gods with immense benefits. He brings them great riches, security, peace and prosperity, an array of fearsome weapons, magical new modes of transport. But always there is that shadowy underside to his feats of ingenuity, that hidden price to be paid, and nothing more so than the dreadful monsters he brings to birth which, although for a long time they can be kept out of sight and under control, are eventually destined to play a crucial part in destroying the world.

The function of Loki, who like Prometheus was associated with fire, is to personify ego-consciousness[1]; that inventive capacity of the human brain which, never more than in the past two centuries, has given *Homo sapiens* astonishing prosperity and the power to transform the earth to his own material advantage on an unprecedented scale. Yet for every new advance made possible by the onward march of one-sided human consciousness there has been a price to be paid: not least, of course, that it has brought that unprecedented command over the forces of nature which has the potential to destroy the earth and all the life it contains a thousand times over.

It is in this respect that the character of Loki provides an appropriate introduction to this final chapter, as we look at what the storytelling of the past 200 years reveals of the lengthening shadow cast by mankind's triumphantly evolving consciousness.

### The nineteenth-century watershed: Imagination and fantasy

In Part Three we saw how, in the decades around 1800, a remarkable change began to come over Western storytelling. Up to that time the vast majority of stories imagined by mankind had reflected an instinctive harmony with the values of the Self. But now something unprecedented happened. In many instances, the archetypal patterns underlying stories began to be refracted through the storyteller's ego, and this had two consequences.

Firstly, it produced a 'dark inversion' of the types of story which archetypally show selfless heroes or heroines coming to a happy ending. We now see a new type of hero appearing in such stories, who is himself egocentric; but in thus defying the values of the Self, he cannot ultimately reach the goal.

Secondly, as stories lost touch with the deeper values of the Self, they became sentimentalised. Even where they try to act out the outward form of an archetypal pattern, because they are no longer concerned with the inner transformation of their central figures they become mere 'entertainments'. They still manage to play on their audience's archetypally-conditioned emotional responses, but only in an outward, make-believe fashion. Their characters become no more than two-dimensional stereotypes.

Such a psychic earthquake could not have come completely out of nowhere. Its premonitory tremors were felt long before the emergence of Romanticism proper.

---

1. One episode in which Loki plays his familiar role is that from the *Prose Edda* centred on a ring stolen by Loki from Andvari the dwarf. As usual, Loki has got the gods into trouble, by killing one of the sons of Hreidmar, and steals the ring to buy off Hreidmar's wrath. But Andvari places a curse on anyone who owns the ring, and this leads to one of Hreidmar's two remaining sons, Fafnir, killing his brother and turning into a monster. Fafnir is eventually killed by Sigurd the Volsung, giving rise to the saga which was to inspire Wagner's *Ring of the Nibelungen* and, less directly, Tolkien's *The Lord of the Rings*. It is apt that the image of a cursed ring symbolising the power of the ego should thus have originated in association with Loki.

Even today, for instance, it would be very unusual to find a story which featured a wholly dark heroine and heroine coming to a triumphant happy ending. But such a story appeared as early as 1643, in a work written at the end of his life by Claudio Monteverdi, the first composer of full-scale operas. The *Coronation of Poppaea* begins by showing the emperor Nero enjoying an adulterous affair with a new mistress, Poppaea, who is engaged to marry young Otho. Seeing the supreme prize almost within her grasp, Poppaea is determined that Nero should leave his wife Octavia and make her his empress. When the wise old philosopher Seneca advises against this, Nero orders him to commit suicide. Poppaea rejoices, but Octavia persuades Otho to murder her in revenge for her faithlessness. The murder plot comes unstuck, and Otho is banished. Octavia resigns herself to her fate. The monstrous hero crowns his scheming mistress as empress of Rome, and they sing an ecstatic duet to celebrate the triumph of their love.

At exactly the same period of that turbulent epoch of the mid-seventeenth century, John Milton was working on the first sketches for his dramatic poem, *Paradise Lost*. So attractive and plausible did he make his story's central character and God's chief antagonist, the fallen angel Satan, that this was later to prompt William Blake to his famous comment that Milton was 'of the Devil's party without knowing it'.

It was not until a century later, however, that more direct precursors of the great Romantic upheaval began to appear, one of the first being that early novel which caused such a stir across Europe in 1748, Richardson's *Clarissa*. This account of a dark hero obsessively setting out to deflower a chaste and virtuous heroine, eventually drugging and raping her to succeed in his quest, marked the appearance of that figure who over the following 100 years was to become the supreme expression of the Romantic inversion in Western storytelling: the 'persecuted maiden', the violated *anima*.

In the 1760s Horace Walpole's *The Castle of Otranto: A Gothic Story* (1765) was the first of those 'Gothic novels' which within a few decades would become one of the dominant genres in European storytelling. Complete with all the later familiar stage-machinery of gloomy vaults, ghostly apparitions, sinister forests and bleeding statues, this sensationalist fantasy excited huge fashionable attention by bringing back into storytelling the type of dark supernatural imagery which previously, in the rational 'age of the Enlightenment', had virtually dropped out of sight. But it did so in a curiously artificial fashion. What was happening was that the supernatural dimension to human existence which, since the Middle Ages, had been gradually pushed down into the unconscious by the increasingly one-sided consciousness of western civilisation was now re-emerging, but in a sentimentalised, 'inferior' form, merely to provide entertainment. Again, at the story's climax, we see the violation of the *anima* when the Tyrant hero rushes to a graveyard at night in the hope of stabbing to death the innocent and persecuted heroine, only to find, like the later hero of Verdi's *Rigoletto*, that he has inadvertently murdered his own daughter. It was a premonition of that melodramatic twilight world, playing on the emotions to maximum sentimental effect, which was to become commonplace in nineteenth-century storytelling, not least in opera.

Another foretaste of the earthquake to come was the *Sturm und Drang* movement of the early 1770s, of which the most celebrated product was Goethe's sentimental fantasy *The Sorrows of Young Werther*. For the first time we see the 'dark inversion' taking over the plot of Tragedy. The audience is invited so to identify with the foolish young central figure in his infatuation with the cardboard heroine that his self-deluding immaturity supposedly becomes heroic.

In the 1780s, as France moved towards the cataclysm of its revolution, de Sade's *Misfortunes of Justine* was in psychological terms as black a story as the world had yet seen: centred entirely on the mental sensations its author derived from fantasising about the prolonged sadistic and sexual degradation of the pure and selfless *anima*-figure who gave the book its title.

The revolutionary 1790s brought that deluge of 'frantic' and 'extravagant' stories which inspired such contempt in Wordsworth, none more fantastic than those 'Gothic novels' which were the best-sellers of the decade. In 1794 Anne Radcliffe's *The Mysteries of Udolpho* won a then-record advance for a novel (£500), describing how its orphaned young heroine is kidnapped by her villainous uncle and imprisoned in a remote, mysterious castle in the Apennines. Here he subjects her to every kind of indignity and horror, some seemingly supernatural, in his efforts to force her to surrender her virtue and her fortune. She eventually makes a 'thrilling escape' and finally comes to a pasteboard happy ending in being reunited with the young man she loves. Two years later M. G. Lewis's *The Monk* was a similar commercial success, describing a worthy Spanish abbot who becomes corrupted by a woman possessed by the devil, who has entered his monastery disguised as a male novice. Now utterly depraved, he relentlessly pursues a pious young girl who has come to him for absolution. Finally, to avoid detection, he murders her, but is caught and tortured by the Inquisition. He escapes burning by making a pact with the devil, but ends being cast into the fires of hell.

What marked out all these stories from almost anything the world had seen before (except those melodramatic early 'novels' which circulated during the later Roman empire) was something sensed by Wordsworth and his friend Coleridge when, in the early years of the nineteenth century, they tried to draw a distinction between 'imagination' and 'fancy' (or fantasy). There is a fundamental distinction between the psychological process which gives rise to these fantasy-based types of story, and that which created, say, the plays of Shakespeare (or, for that matter, the novels Jane Austen was beginning to write just when the vogue for 'Gothic horror' was at its height). Shakespeare's plays stem from a genuinely creative imagination which connects with our inner reality and that of the world around us, based on profound observation and an intuitive understanding of human nature. By contrast, the stories of de Sade or the 'Gothic novelists' were created not from imagination but from fantasy, which operates in a quite different way.

Imagination, as Coleridge puts it in his *Biographia Literaria* (1817), is a living thing, producing original observations and images which heighten and deepen our perception and understanding of the world. But the fantasy or daydreaming level of the mind is not concerned with understanding. It is two-dimensional. It deals in fixed, 'dead' images, which can be used to trigger off in our consciousness a desired effect but which have no connection with the 'real world'. They are no more than the play of shadows on a wall, which is why stories based on fantasy present us with such cardboard characters and provide only the counterfeit of human emotion.

The effect of fantasy on our minds can be extraordinarily powerful, but this relies on the way that, like day-dreaming, it operates by suggestion. It feeds on nykto-morphs, those shadowy, unresolved images which arouse an emotional response for the very reason that they tease our brain by giving it insufficient information fully to get hold of them. One of the most obvious tricks of fantasy-based writing is the way it uses particular words to trigger off such an automatic response. With the addition of a few suggestively incomplete words such as 'measureless' or 'sun-less', for instance, the otherwise straightforward image of a stream flowing under-ground may be conjured (by Coleridge himself, in the most overtly dreamlike of all his poems) into lines as powerful as:

'Where Alph the *sacred* river ran
Through *caverns measureless* to man
Down to a *sunless* sea.'

Take away from Romantic storytelling or poetry all such nyktomorphic trigger words as nameless, infinite, weird, mysterious, strange, faery, enchanted, ghostly, gloomy, phantom, wraith-like, dream-like, nebulous, unearthly, lurking, haunting, trembling, obscure, tempestuous, ghastly, fearful, dread, etc, and what was left of many admired stories and poems would be no more interesting and a good deal less meaningful than the telephone directory. Thus in *A Vision of the Sea* Shelley writes:

'… where the *hum* of the *hot blood* that *spouts* and *rains*
Where the *gripe* of the *tiger* has wounded the veins
*Swollen* his *rage*, strength and effort; the *whirl* and the *splash*
As of some *hideous engine* whose *brazen teeth smash*
The *thin* winds and *soft* waves into *thunder*.'

In reality this is no more than a catalogue of suggestive imagery and violent sounds working themselves into a frenzy that is ultimately meaningless (e.g., 'the hum of the hot blood'). But on a fantasy level it achieves its effect, which was why Wordsworth wrote of Shelley's poetry that it was:

'what astrology is to natural science – a passionate dream, straining after impossibilities, a record of fond conjectures, a confused embodying of vague abstraction – a fever of the soul, thirsting and craving after what it cannot have, indulging its love of power and novelty at the expense of truth and nature.'

Certainly the 'Gothic novels' which launched literary Romanticism on its way achieved their effect through an abundance of such nyktomorphic imagery, which often makes it difficult for the reader to work out exactly what is going on. But the appeal of such stories was not that they cast a clearer light on the world. It was that they provided the reader with a stream of mental sensations: images which trigger a thrill in the mind precisely because they are not resolved.

When we recall that the archetypal purpose of stories is to achieve a perfect resolution, and that the point at which such a story reaches its fullest resolution is where the hero can liberate and be united with the 'light feminine', as the highest value in storytelling, we can see why there was no more revealing feature of this new type of story than how obsessively it focused on the image of the abused heroine.

In itself there was nothing new about the sight of a story's heroine being mal-treated. But when Othello murders Desdemona or Hamlet rejects Ophelia or Lear rejects Cordelia, the real significance of this is what it reveals of what is going on inside the hero. It shows more clearly than anything how he has become cut off from true feeling and understanding: the feminine values of the Self. When de Sade fantasises about the cruelties and sexual degradations inflicted on Justine, his only concern is the thrill this can excite in his own mind. The essence of that sensation is the gratification the fantasy-level of the mind derives from con-templating the violation of the *anima*, as the highest aspect of the Self. By the 'dark inversion', the ego no longer subordinated to the Self thus derives its greatest energy from rejecting and violating the very thing it has escaped from.

So subtle are the workings of the unconscious, however, that its response, like a self-correcting mechanism, is then to show that the only way such a course can ultimately end is in death and destruction. Such is the pattern we see emerging in those stories which reflected the darker side of Romanticism as it swept through the collective unconscious of Europe in the early decades of the nineteenth century.

Mary Shelley's *Frankenstein: The Modern Prometheus* (1817) was above all remarkable, as we have seen, in showing a dark hero bringing to birth a monster who represents his rejected Self in shadowy 'inferior' form. In every other respect it was a typical 'Gothic' fantasy, with its routine array of sensational 'Gothic' imagery and its cast of cardboard characters. What makes the story so unusual is that we see the monster as initially benevolent. Then, as the blind and heartless hero rejects his shadow three times, that benign monster becomes ever darker, until on the third occasion it turns on its creator and destroys him.

One of the more revealing features of Stendhal's *The Scarlet and the Black* (1830) was the way its egocentric and ambitious hero was obsessed with Napoleon. The image of Napoleon had burned itself into the consciousness of his time like no one else in history. The way he had sprung from nowhere to become the ruler of Europe made him in his own way one of the supreme embodiments of the Romantic move-ment. The French Revolution had pulled down all the old collective framework symbolising the Self, from the monarchy to the Christian religion. And there into the void it left rose this glamorous dream figure, seeming to symbolise a new synthesis: power and youthful energy married to an altruistic new social order, based on liberty, equality and brotherhood. It was not surprising that he exercised such an obsessive hold over the fantasies of millions of his contemporaries.

Even when Napoleon's ambition swelled into megalomania, as he declared him-self emperor and began imposing his will by force over a whole continent, there were many who continued to see him as the most heroic figure of the age. Even when his fantasy-career had run its full five-stage course, ending in humiliating downfall, he still inspired admiration as the model of what an individual human being could achieve, if only he were great enough to throw off all constraint in rising above the mass of mankind. It was such a vision which would inspire

Raskolnikov to murder old ladies (although this would be portrayed by Dostoyevsky from the perspective of the Self). And it was such a vision which inspired Stendhal, when he came to fantasise his extended day-dream of a Rags to Riches hero even more ruthlessly egocentric than himself. Even as Julien Sorel stretched out for that make-believe image of the Self subordinated to his own ego, the unconscious intervened, to bring him to a destruction more violent than that which had awaited his hero Napoleon.

But by now, regardless, the Romantic movement was in full swing all over Europe. Thus began that chapter in the evolution of western consciousness which was to lead up to the present day: the history of which we can follow in five stages.

## 1. The golden age of romanticism: 1830–1890

Storytelling was not the only form of artistic expression which went through this kind of transition in the early nineteenth century. We see it in all the arts, from painting to poetry to architecture, but in none more acutely than music, which in the eighteenth and early nineteenth centuries had been the last art-form to express complete harmony with the values of the Self. In the music of Bach and Handel, Mozart and Haydn, Beethoven and Schubert, European music had developed to the point where it was able to express those values to the fullest extent of which the Western imagination had yet shown itself capable. One reflection of this was the archetypal structure underlying 'sonata form', which was at the centre of classical music during the decades when it reached its zenith. This usually showed an assertive, essentially masculine thematic 'first subject' being followed by a more graceful, essentially feminine 'second subject', the two then combining and inter-weaving through the 'development' section, to return at the end transformed, bringing the movement to a perfect resolution.

In the early decades of the nineteenth century, however, there were clear signs in the work of younger composers that the formal structures of the classical era were becoming blurred and sentimentalised by the approach of the age of Romanticism. No composer had ever won such world-wide popularity as Rossini in the decade after 1810. The dazzlingly catchy themes from Rossini's operas, as his hero-worshipping biographer Stendhal observed, were hailed from New York to St Petersburg, from Buenos Aires to Sydney. Yet no one was more keenly aware that this signalled a profound shift taking place in the nature of contemporary music than Beethoven, as when he observed in 1824 that, 'in this age of Rossini, true music has little welcome'. [2]

In his novel *Doctor Faustus*, Thomas Mann describes the narrator and his friends attending a lecture by a wise old music teacher, who plays and expounds to them the closing arietta of Beethoven's last piano sonata, Opus 111. They are deeply moved. When he has completed the final bars he bangs shut the piano, pronouncing 'thus ends the sonata'; by which he means not just that this particu-

---

2. From a conversation with Beethoven in 1824 recorded by Johann August Stumpff. Rossini at this time was at the height of his fame. Beethoven was still to write the final sequence of quartets, stretching the framework of the classical style to its ultimate imaginative extreme, which brought his life's work to such a perfect resolution.

lar sonata in C Minor is concluded but sonata form in general, and all that it represented. The classical age in music, which had plumbed the heights and depths of the human spirit like nothing else, was over (apart from the glorious sunset of Beethoven's own final works before his death in 1827, and the magical twilight of Schubert, who died the following year).

Suddenly music changed, even more dramatically than storytelling. However gifted composers such as Berlioz and Schumann, Liszt and Wagner, Brahms and Verdi might be, their music was no longer shaped by that instinctive harmony between conscious and unconscious which had raised the works of Bach, Mozart and Beethoven to such a transcendent perfection. The direct contact with the Self had been lost. The mould was broken. The ego had intruded. And with it came all the cloudy sentimentality, the disintegration of form, the sensational striving for effect which we associate with the age of Romanticism.

There could be no neater image of the difference between the power of true imagination and the artifice of fantasy than Berlioz's comment, in a letter to Wagner, 'I can only paint the moon when I see her at the bottom of a well'. Beethoven had not just believed in the divine power of the Self as the centre of his inspiration. He experienced it so directly he had no need to paint its reflection in a well. The difference between Beethoven and his successors, one might jokingly observe, was that Beethoven believed in God, Brahms believed in Beethoven and Wagner believed in Wagner. But in this declension we can also see the essence of what was happening in the nineteenth century to Western man's relationship with the instinctive totality of the Self.

Outwardly, the most obvious contrast between the civilisation of the nineteenth century and that of the century which preceded it lay in the astonishing transformation produced by the industrial revolution. The coming of the age of steam power and the machine, factory-based mass-production, the railways and the telegraph bridging distances with unimaginable speed, was suddenly carrying humanity much further from a state of nature than ever before. With this came an unprecedented sense that civilisation was moving forwards and upwards: that belief in 'progress' which was reinforced by the new doctrine of evolution. People came to see history as a long climb out of the darkness of mankind's primitive, superstitious past into the glorious light of modern nineteenth-century civilisation.

Yet, even as this materially triumphant age cut them off from nature and the past to an unprecedented degree, so they hankered for the lost certainties of a vanished time when their ancestors had been able to enjoy the sense of an unshakeable spiritual centre and transcendent dimension to life. Few aspects of the nineteenth century were more remarkable than the extraordinary revival of interest in the imagery of the Middle Ages. At the very time when Western civilisation was making such dramatic material advances, so we see this wholesale gazing backward to the outward forms of mediaeval Christian Europe, in the hugely fashionable novels of Walter Scott, in the paintings of the pre-Raphaelites, in the poems of Tennyson, and above all in the revival of Gothic styles of architecture, so long derided as barbarous and primitive. A fashion which had begun almost playfully, heralding the approach of Romanticism in secular buildings such as Horace Walpole's Strawberry Hill and Beckford's Fonthill, now covered Europe in new Gothic churches and cathedrals, not to mention some of its most important secular buildings such as the Palace of Westminster.

The Gothic Revival expressed a sentimental desire to recreate the symbolism of the Self. It was accompanied, of course, by that widespread revival of religious observance which became one of the defining characteristics of nineteenth-century Europe. This in turn was coupled with the emergence of that 'Victorian' or 'bourgeois' morality, which rested on strict codes of sexual and social behaviour, with 'respectability' as one of its highest values. Yet in all this too there was a strong element of mawkish sentimentality, to cover up the repression of everything from sexuality to the awareness of death. To a great degree, the ruling consciousness of the age was adopting the values of the Self as a *persona*, an outward mask.

For all its Gothic spires, stained glass windows and loving recreations of mediaeval Christian imagery, the Victorian age, with its grim factories belching out stinking smoke over foetid slums to create wealth for the respectable new-rich bourgeoisie, was scarcely a rebirth of the Middle Ages. It is curious how the evolving spiritual consciousness of the previous three centuries had echoed the pattern of that passage from Lao Tsu at the head of this chapter. If the crumbling apart of the religious world-image of mediaeval Christendom had been the moment when 'the way was lost', then the stern moralists of the sixteenth and seventeenth century Reformation had replaced it with 'virtue'. This in turn had been replaced in the religion of the rational, de-spiritualised eighteenth century by 'benevolence'. Now, in the sentimental nineteenth century, this had given way to 'rectitude'. And if this was what seemed to rule 'above the line', nowhere was its shadow more clearly reflected than in some of the ways in which the nineteenth century told stories.

As always, there is no clearer key to what storytelling can tell us about the inner life of the age which produced it than the way in which it presents the *anima*, personifying the feminine value and ultimately the 'soul'. The literary form which came closest to conveying the values of the Self in the nineteenth century was the novel; but even in the greatest novels of the time, such as those of Tolstoy and Dostoyevsky, let alone those of Dickens or George Eliot, we can often discern more than a hint of sentimentality. When Tolstoy tried at the end of *Anna Karenina* to describe the religious awakening of his hero Levin, in contrast to the damnation and destruction of the story's heroine, it was Dostoyevsky who found Levin's new-found faith so unconvincing that he described as likely to 'rip apart on the first nail it encountered'. Yet carrying scarcely more conviction is the religious conversion inspired in Raskolnikov by the little prostitute Sonia at the end of *Crime and Punishment*. Dostoyevsky hardly develops his redeeming figure into more than a rather thin and pallid ghost of the *anima*, and it is telling that, when he comes to showing how she transformed his hero's life, he leaves off by suggesting that this is really the subject for another story.

As the archetypes became projected outwards onto the material world, it is noticeable how often storytellers, to convey the numinosity of their *anima*-heroines, made them into heiresses. In earlier times, the numinosity of the heroine would often have been conveyed, as in myths and folk tales, simply by making her a 'Princess'. But now, as in Stendhal or Balzac, *Nicholas Nickleby* or *Jane Eyre*, she is either rich to begin with, or she inherits money towards the end of the story, to symbolise her value. In stories written by female authors, the poor but virtuous heroine often falls in love with an *animus*-hero whose numinosity is heightened by the fact that he is of higher social standing, such as Jane Eyre's Mr Rochester or Elizabeth Bennett's Mr D'Arcy.

Much more significant as a revelation of the psychic state of nineteenth century civilisation, however, was that persistent obsession with the image of the 'persecuted maiden', the trapped, violated or dying heroine who continues to appear in so many guises throughout the age of Romanticism. We see her in the mad scene of Donizetti's *Lucia di Lammermoor*; in that whole sequence of unhappy and fated Verdi heroines, from the innocent Gilda stabbed by her father in *Rigoletto* to the consumptive Viola in *La Traviata*; in Puccini's consumptive Mimi and the piteous Madam Butterfly. In Romantic ballet we see her as the elusive *anima*, dying broken-hearted in *Giselle*, and again as the betrayed and doomed Swan Queen Odette in *Swan Lake*. We see her in countless novels of the time, including several by Dickens, notably in Little Nell, whose heart-tugging death in *The Old Curiosity Shop* provoked an almost hysterical reaction from Britain's reading public in 1841, and in Sykes's bludgeoning to death of Nancy in *Oliver Twist*.

In Britain in the 1860s came the vogue for what came to be known at the time as the 'sensation novel': highly melodramatic tales which reached an enormous mass audience through their serialisation in newspapers and magazines. What titillated the fantasies of the Victorian public in these tales was their exploitation of such 'self-violating' themes as bigamy and adultery. But a central role in almost all these successors to the Gothic novels of 70 years earlier was played by the maltreated *anima*. The fashion was set by Wilkie Collins's *The Woman in White* (1860), which begins with the seemingly supernatural apparition on a road outside London of the young woman who, it turns out, has been incarcerated in a mental asylum to prevent her stumbling on the guilty secret of the evil baronet Sir Percy Glyde. The most famous of all these fantasy concoctions was *East Lynne* (1861) by Mrs Henry Wood. So relentlessly does she heap suffering and indignity on her heroine that Lady Isabel ends up hideously disfigured by the accident in which her illegitimate daughter has died, desperately seeking employment as a governess in the home of her ex-husband. She does this only to be reunited with her children, but it then leads to her having to watch incognito over her son as he dies of a fatal disease ('dead, and never called me mother'), before she expires herself.[3]

---

3. Lady Isobel Vane, Mrs Wood's heroine, having been left poor and alone by her father's death, marries the ambitious young lawyer who has bought the family's home East Lynne, even though she has already fallen in love with another man. Despite giving birth to three children, she feels neglected by her husband, whom she falsely suspects of being unfaithful. She eventually elopes to France with her lover, by whom she has an illegitimate daughter, but he abandons her. Isobel and her daughter become the victims of a railway accident, which kills the child and leaves Isobel hideously crippled and disfigured. Desperate to see her children again, and disguised by her maiming, Isobel implausibly wins the post of governess in her old home. She first has to endure the sight of her former husband living happily with his new wife, and then has to watch her son falling so ill

At the end of this period a particularly notable example of the suffering *anima* is Hardy's favourite heroine, Tess. More than anything this story shows us why Hardy's novels provide such a revealing mirror to the underside of an age which, on the surface, imagined itself to be emerging into the light from all the primitive darkness of former times. We see an author whose first stories had shown him still able to cling on sentimentally to the simplicities and certainties of the rooted rustic world in which he grew up. But then, as the socially emancipated Hardy himself became ever more detached from that world, his stories turn ever darker, their heroes and heroines ever more fatally plagued by an inability to find their right 'other half', until he ends by showing his tortured *anima* so distracted that she is driven to that desperate act which can only precipitate her own death on the gallows.

In this sense, as we saw, the progression of Hardy's novels reflected something which was happening much more generally to western civilisation in the nineteenth century. No novel more powerfully conveyed the sense of the 'dark inversion' than *Moby Dick*, with its picture of a crazed hero, surrounded by a cosmopolitan crew from all over the world, symbolising mankind, obsessively seeking to find and destroy the mysterious White Whale which stood for the power of nature at one with itself: a living image of the Self. Yet so firmly was Melville himself in the grip of the Romantic dark inversion that, although he intuitively sensed that he had written 'a wicked book', he felt as 'spotless as the lamb'.

Another symptom of the psychic disintegration of the age was the curious fate of the Comedy plot, as it split into two quite separate types of story: on the one hand, inspiring some of the most serious novels of the age, such as *War and Peace* and *Middlemarch*; on the other, as in Viennese operetta, Parisian farce or the 'light operas' of Gilbert and Sullivan, retaining its frivolous, implausible surface, while losing touch altogether with that serious, unsentimental core which had made the comedies of Shakespeare or Mozart such archetypally complete creations of the human imagination.

More than any age before it, beneath its gravely respectable, materially successful, brilliantly innovative surface, the nineteenth century was two-sided. Behind its church-building shows of piety, it was an age more than ever losing that contact with the Self which inspires a genuine religious sense: an age in which Matthew Arnold could only hear faith's 'melancholy, long, withdrawing roar'; in which Nietzsche could confidently proclaim 'God is dead'. One of the more obvious underlying reasons why Darwin won such a welcome for his theory of natural selection was that it made the whole evolutionary process seem impersonal and self-referential, without the need to imagine that behind it was any transcendent power or guiding mind.

---

that, despite her loving care, he dies ('dead, and never called me mother' was introduced in the stage version). Isobel then dies herself, but not before she has revealed her true identity to her former husband. Naturally he forgives her to provide a 'happy ending'.

Novels of this genre, so popular in the 1860s, were satirised in W. S. Gilbert's musical comedy *A Sensation Novel* (1871), in which, foreshadowing Pirandello by half a century, the stock characters of a melodramatic novel step outside their fictional roles, to comment scornfully on what a silly piece of make-believe they have become caught up in.

Behind the grandiose new civic buildings which stood proudly at the centre of the great new industrial cities, expressing their unprecedented wealth, were those miles of belching factories and stinking slums, where millions of workers lived their lives wracked by poverty and disease. In the shadows cast 'below the line' by all this oppressive one-sidedness, a new vision of the 'Self' was emerging, projected onto the potential power of these dispossessed masses.

Into the minds of men such as Karl Marx and his fellow socialists and revolutionaries came the dream that they might one day rise up to sweep away all that corrupt and privileged world 'above the line', in the name of a perfect new society, in which the downtrodden peoples of the world could once again be united, in one selfless common purpose. Drawing on precisely those archetypal wellsprings which in previous ages had found religious expression, they projected that spiritual image of totality out onto the material world (as in the synthesis which would emerge from 'dialectical materialism'). In fact these dreamers had become possessed by the archetypal power of a story, with its plot set in the future: a nyktomorphic vision which, in the century which lay ahead, was destined to become the single most influential legacy of nineteenth-century Romanticism.

## 2. The birth of 'modernism': 1890–1918

One of the more interesting episodes in the evolution of storytelling was that moment in the 1890s when, quite independently, three British storytellers almost simultaneously conceived stories which disinterred the archetypal vision of the monster. For centuries, as advancing Western ego-consciousness had gradually lost touch with the sense of a supernatural dimension to life, the grotesque monsters of the old legends and mythologies had faded into the distant past, as no more than historical curiosities. But all of a sudden they re-emerged. H. G. Wells's Martians, heaving out of a pit in the cosy, bourgeois Surrey countryside with their leathery skin and tentacles, Bram Stoker's Dracula, crawling like a bat across the wall of his Transylvanian castle, M. R. James's nightmarish apparition rising out of the pages of an old book in the Pyrenees, created almost overnight that modern tradition of the nyktomorphic monster which was to become such a significant presence in the popular storytelling of the twentieth century.

In the very years when these monstrous creations were emerging from the unconscious minds of their authors, Sigmund Freud was working in Vienna on his magnum opus *The Interpretation of Dreams* (1900). This was the book which more than anything else was to open the eyes of the twentieth century to the idea that our consciousness is only a relatively small and fragile superstructure to all that goes on in the unconscious levels of our brain; and that to understand human nature properly we must recognise how much of the way we think and behave is shaped by forces buried behind our conscious awareness.

James's first horror story, Stoker's *Dracula* and Wells's *War of the Worlds* were conceived merely as entertainments. But why in the last decade of the nineteenth century should these menacing embodiments of evil have floated up into the fantasies of storytellers all at much the same time? The archetype of the monster personifies the darkest side of human nature. What did it say about the state of mankind that these fearsome apparitions, representing the power of the human ego in its most grotesque form, should have simultaneously emerged from the collective unconscious just as the new century approached?[4]

It is remarkable just how many of the features which were to define twentieth-century civilisation as unlike any period in history before first appeared in the years around 1900. The most obvious are the dazzling array of technological discoveries which appeared at this time: the internal combustion engine in the 1880s followed by the first motor cars; the first wireless signals, with Marconi's transmissions across the Atlantic in 1901; the Wright brothers' flight in 1903 and the first aeroplanes; the gramophone and recorded music; the first moving pictures and the beginnings of the cinema; the first skyscrapers soaring above the skyline of New York and Chicago. In Zurich in 1905 the young Einstein published the formula $e = mc^2$, heralding the birth of that nuclear age which within decades was to see *homo sapiens* unlocking the secret power of the most elemental physical unit in the universe.

At much the same time, emerging from the blues and the gospel-singing of the black communities of New Orleans and the southern states of the USA, the hypnotic, fantasy-exciting syncopation of ragtime and jazz were introducing what was to become the single most defining feature of twentieth-century popular music. The campaign for women's suffrage in the early years of the new century heralded the new spirit of female assertiveness which would lead to a radical realignment in the relationship between the sexes. In Russia in 1902 Lenin published *What Then Must Be Done?*, the pamphlet which more than anything else was to set out his blueprint for the revolution by which, from 'below the line', he planned to save Russia and perhaps the world.

The arts at this time were going through a transformation which reflected another decisive extension of that psychic shift which had given rise to the Romantic movement a century earlier. In painting, the light, evanescent imagery of French Impressionism (in the wake of Turner) had for decades been promoting liberation from the heavy, sentimental formalities of nineteenth-century academicism. But in the early years of the new century these already dissolving figurative images suddenly gave way to the much more dramatically abstract pictures of the Cubists, Fauvists and Futurists. Figurative imagery was finally disintegrating altogether in a haze of suggestive nyktomorphs. It was telling that one of the landmark canvases in this evolution, Picasso's *Les Demoiselles D'Avignon* (1907), showed a group of prostitutes: a subject which would have been unthinkable to any 'above the line' nineteenth-century academician, except that Picasso's contemporaries might have found it hard to decipher from the fragmented new 'Cubist' style quite what his image was meant to represent at all.

---

4. Another instance can be seen in Wells's short story *The Time Machine*, where the society of the future is shown as divided between the 'above the line' daylight world inhabited by the infantile, pleasure-loving, fruit-eating Eloi, and the subterranean 'below the line' world, in which the flesh-eating Morlocks live in darkness, working at machines, before coming out at night to terrorise and prey on the Eloi. As a late nineteenth-century Socialist, Wells would probably have seen this as a parable of how the division of society between the privileged, effete upper-classes and the industrial proletariat would eventually separate them, in effect, into separate species.

In music, the ponderous, overblown Romanticism of Brahms, Bruckner and their late nineteenth-century contemporaries suddenly gave way to the revolutionary 'new music' represented by the stark atonal experiments of Schoenberg, Webern and Berg, the nervously exciting rhythms and dissonant polytonalities of Stravinsky.

Meanwhile in storytelling, no writer was to reflect the shift towards twentieth-century sensibility more significantly than Chekhov, with his creation of a new twilight world in which the clear archetypal contrast between light figures and dark dissolved into a grey twilight. Chekov's plays, in which everyone was trapped in a little prison of the ego, lacking in any spiritual centre, where human life was portrayed as no more than the muddled, altruistic dreams of youth decaying into the egocentric disillusionments of old age, marked the beginning of that new genre of storytelling, where the narrative could have no end other than a despairing shot offstage, or merely a curtain coming down to indicate that the story was over, with nothing resolved. Three years after Chekhov's death in 1904, Proust began that immense essay in self-absorbed futility which would only be finished 15 years later, and which was to represent a new extreme in the shift of the psychic centre of storytelling from the Self to the ego. But by that time the dream of the ninteenth-century age of progress had exploded into reality, with the greatest explosion of violence the human race had ever experienced.

In many ways it is possible to see the holocaust of the First World War as a kind of judgement on the different forms of hubris European civilisation had enjoyed in the nineteenth century. For decades the Western nations had been using their new technological might to develop ever more destructive means of waging war; but the very fact that these had not been deployed in earnest for nearly half a century before 1914 meant that few people realised how terrible might be the consequences if they were. The stoking up of nationalistic self-esteem, and the imperialist adventures in which the technological superiority of the great powers had allowed them to indulge around the globe, had produced a psychic inflation and a sense of rivalry between their collective egotisms which was tipping towards danger point.

Socially in the years leading up to 1914 we can see all sorts of stresses developing which indicated the onset of a collective psychic fever sweeping through Europe, manifesting itself in everything from the rise of new mass labour movements, demanding radical political change, to the new assertiveness of women. Everywhere the 'above the line' established order was under challenge. And this was equally reflected in that disintegration of the old forms and unleashing of new nervous energy which was revolutionising the arts. No artistic event was more symptomatic of the mood of the time than the Paris première of Stravinsky's ballet *The Rite of Spring* in 1913, which provoked a storm of controversy by showing the frenzied ritual sacrifice of a young girl, accompanied by music more wildly dissonant than anything its audience had heard before.

Three years earlier, another musician, Edward Elgar, composer of that great nationalistic British anthem 'Land of Hope And Glory', had written with foreboding, 'we walk like ghosts'. In August 1914 vast cheering crowds gathered in the capital cities of Europe, as their countries sleepwalked into war. On the Somme, at Verdun and Tannenburg, the nineteenth-century age of Romanticism finally disintegrated in four years of nightmarish slaughter. Great empires crumbled. In Russia the heirs of Marx, led by Lenin, stormed the Winter Palace to proclaim the Dictatorship of the Proletariat.

After all that heady, century-long dream of progress, the spirit of Loki had brought the human race to catastrophe on a scale it had never experienced.

### 3. Brave New World: 1918–1939

As the peoples of Europe finally stumbled out of the darkness into the wan light of peace, the country which for the first time was to make the running in dictating the spirit of the era just beginning was America.

It was the US President Woodrow Wilson who took the lead in setting up the League of Nations: that idealistic experiment in international co-operation which was to ensure that 'the war to end wars' was never repeated. And as a new decade began it would be from America that so many of the phenomena which were to become inseparable with its image originated (even though, in almost every case, these had first appeared in embryo before the war).

The prevailing mood of the 'Roaring Twenties' was that of a great burst of liberated energy, reflected in all the nervous frenzy and hedonistic materialism of Scott Fitzgerald's 'Jazz Age'. It was the age of 'flappers' and the Charleston; of the unprecedented share boom on Wall Street, when millions of ordinary folk could for the first time hope to become rich by investing in the stocks of America's leading companies; the heyday of Henry Ford's 'Model T', when for the first time millions could afford to buy motor cars. It was the age when those soaring skyscrapers, pioneered in the years before 1914, now turned the Manhattan skyline into one of the most powerfully familiar images in the world. It was the first heyday of telling stories through the medium of the cinema, making Hollywood the world centre of mass-entertainment, peopling the fantasies of millions with the dream images of the first 'movie stars'.

The thread running through all these manifestations of the spirit of the age was their sanctioning of a newly assertive kind of self-expression, nowhere made more visible than in the rivalry of those New York developers to outvie each other in raising the tallest structures ever seen, culminating at the decade's end in the New Empire State building. This was accompanied by a radical transformation in the appearance of women, as the long flowing dresses, elaborate hairstyles and parasols of pre-war times suddenly gave way to the leg-revealing short skirts, cropped hair and flaunted cigarette holders associated with the young flappers of the Jazz Age. Never in history had there been such a dramatically sudden change in women's fashions. But the new 'mannishness' of their short hair and emancipated attitudes was matched by a corresponding 'feminisation' of their male counterparts such as Rudolf Valentino, whose rouged and powdered image aroused mass-hysteria when, in films like *The Sheikh*, he was magnified by the silver screen into the romantic heart-throb of the age.

In counterpoint to all this 'mass-individualism', the 1920s was also marked by an extraordinary wave of Utopian idealism, its tone set by that which inspired the

League of Nations itself, as the supposed guarantee of a new age of international peace and brotherhood. In the mid-1920s, the statesmen of France and Germany dreamed of joining together to build a new 'United States of Europe'. In Russia, after the horrors of revolution and civil war, Lenin's Bolsheviks were setting out to create an ideal Communist society, of a kind the world had never seen before, in which all the oppressive old hierarchical order centred on the 'Little Father', the Czar, had been torn down, and where all its citizens would now be equal.

In Paris the visionary architect Le Corbusier dreamed of tearing down all the old historic cities, starting with Paris itself, and replacing them with his Utopian new 'City of the Future', planned down to the tiniest detail, in which vast, shining white concrete skyscrapers would stand amid grass and trees. For millennia, centred on great temples and cathedrals, the city had been a symbolic image of human totality, the Self. Le Corbusier's vision of his 'radiant city', laid out on a perfect four-sided geometric grid, surrounded by woods and fields, was a projection of the same archetype. But by a telling inversion, instead of having a mighty cathedral at its heart, the ultimate focal point of Le Corbusier's city was its central transport 'node'; the intersection of its grid of motorways, with above them its main railway station and central airport. Instead of his city being centred on a cathedral spire and high altar, symbolising some ultimate point of inner peace and union with the 'One', its centre represented the point of maximum external noise and restlessness. Obsessed as he was with the new aeroplanes, racing cars, ocean liners and other technological wonders of the age, Le Corbusier's dream was that his new type of city would in itself be the means to bring about a revolution, in that it would soon mould its inhabitants into a new type of man and woman, fit to live in 'the age of the machine'.

What was happening in the 1920s was that, as technological innovations created the sense that society was being carried forward into an era different from anything known before, that traditional framework of social and moral constraints which for centuries had held the power of the human ego in check was beginning to crumble as never before. The ego was being liberated. At the same time, in the upsurge of collectivist Utopianism, the power of the displaced archetype of the Self was being projected outwards, in dreams of humanity being brought together as one, in different visions of selfless totality.

All this was reflected in the decade's storytelling. On the face of it, nothing seemed to capture the mood of youthful hedonism that was sweeping through new-rich America better than the novels of Scott Fitzgerald. In Britain their counterparts were the novels of Evelyn Waugh, celebrating the brittle chatter of the upper-class 'bright young things', and the 'daring' plays of the young Noel Coward, such as *The Vortex*, with its hero the drug-addicted son of an adulterous mother. In Italy Pirandello seemed to be pioneering the advance of the drama into even more 'experimental' realms, promising some immense nyktomorphic significance. And there were no more celebrated manifestos of the sexual revolution, throwing off the prudish inhibitions of 'Victorian morality', than those two most daring novels of the decade, Joyce's *Ulysses* and Lawrence's *Lady Chatterley*, so uninhibited that the authorities rushed to suppress them. This in itself only heightened

662

the impression that these books must be striking a brave blow for life, 'honesty' and the future against all that deadening edifice of authoritarianism and sexual repression which now seemed outmoded.

It might not have taken long to discern the dark underside of all this fictional excitement. Fitzgerald's Gatsby, the mysterious millionaire party-giver, his grand house constantly filled with fashionable socialites, turns out to be a lost soul, living behind a carefully concocted *persona* and ending up riddled with bullets in his own swimming pool. Pirandello's *Six Characters*, behind the artifice of its framing device, with fictional characters taking over their own story, turns out to centre on no more than a dismal little fantasy of a father meeting his daughter as a prostitute, winding up with the trick-sensational conclusion of having the two children come to violent deaths. *Ulysses*, hailed as the bible of post-Freudian sexual liberation, ends up with its two emotionally-inadequate central figures engaging in solitary acts of self-abuse. *Lady Chatterley*, acclaimed as an even more heroic call to liberation, ends with its two ill-assorted central figures apart and alone, with its pasteboard hero fantasising sadly over a lost sexual adventure whose heady physical pleasures have long faded and which has ruined both their lives.

Not for nothing did Lawrence himself, often shrewder about the work of others than his own, issue that trenchant verdict on the spirit of the 1920s quoted earlier:

> 'Never was any age more sentimental, more devoid of real feeling, more exaggerated in false feeling than our own ... the radio and the film are mere counterfeit emotion all the time, the current press and literature the same. People wallow in emotion, counterfeit emotion. They lap it up, they live in it and on it ... and at times they seem to get on very well with it all. And then, more and more, they break down. They go to pieces.' [5]

As for those collectivist Utopias of the future which held such a fascination for the 1920s, there were already storytellers pointing out how these dreams too might lead to nightmares. Fritz Lang's film *Metropolis* (1926) showed a kind of Le Corbusier-like city of the future, full of colossal concrete buildings with aeroplanes flying between them: except that he portrayed it as a dehumanised slave-state, with serried armies of regimented workers having to toil ceaselessly at machines in a 'below the line' underworld, to serve the 'above the line' elite who ruled this hellish new society. Six years later Aldous Huxley delivered his own verdict on the 1920s in *Brave New World*, extrapolating the obsessive hedonism of those years into the basis for a future World State. Here, again in a Le Corbusier-like city of immense buildings set amid trees, the Alphas were kept by drugs in constant mindless pursuit of promiscuous self-indulgence. Again this was made possible by regimented slave-armies of Betas, Gammas, Deltas and Epsilons

---

5. One artistic product of the 1920s which reflected this in its own way was Ravel's *Bolero* (1922), musically expressing the need of any pattern based on fantasy to create a rising spiral of sensations. The same tune, almost indefinitely repeated to a hypnotically insistent rhythm, rises ever louder through a Dream Stage, but towards what? How could Ravel bring his fantasy pattern to a climax and a resolution? In the closing bars we hear how, in desperate pursuit of that elusive climax, he is finally driven to change key (Frustration Stage). This only makes the search for a climax even more frantic. The piece falls into a series of jagged discords (Nightmare Stage), before finally collapsing into the cacophony by which the fantasy destroys itself. By such a pattern does fantasy demonstrate the way in which it ultimately develops its own 'death wish'.

'below the line'. Above them all, the tiny, shadowy elite who were the real rulers of Huxley's nightmare world strove to ensure that no one should ever develop individual thoughts or feelings, because for everyone to be kept unthinkingly at one with the collective consciousness was the fundamental principle on which this totalitarian state rested.

In fact, by the time Huxley's book was published, the Dream Stage of the 1920s which inspired it had already come abruptly to an end. In November 1929 the Wall Street crash heralded the greatest economic slump in history, with tens of millions unemployed all across the Western world. Amid the gloom of the Great Depression, Fitzgerald laboured at his last complete novel, *Tender is the Night*, reflecting how his own 1920s euphoria had soured into a nightmare of failed dreams and alcoholic depression. Meanwhile in Russia and Germany two genuinely totalitarian systems were now in the ascendant, each in its own way darker than anything Huxley had conceived of, and which, in the years ahead, were to cast a shadow extending over the whole of mankind.

The dream of a Communist Utopia which took over Russia in 1917, as we have seen, was the most extreme expression of that collective fantasy which had begun to emerge in the minds of Marx and other early Socialists in the nineteenth century, in response to the one-sidedness of mass-industrialisation. They became gripped by the vision of the downtrodden proletariat rising up from 'below the line' to sweep away all the oppressive old political and social structure, to build a perfect society in which everyone could be equal. The hypnotic appeal of this vision derived precisely from the extent to which it unconsciously drew on the power of the archetype of the Self. In claiming to act in the interests of all mankind, it tapped into that sense of moral righteousness which could be generated around the dream of building a community which transcended selfish interests, when in fact it was only expressing the collective egotism of a particular group.

Every group-fantasy – such as Communism – depends on three factors. The first is the particular dream or collective act of make-believe which binds its followers together. The second is its need for 'dream heroes' who are inflated to superhuman stature because they embody and act as projections of the fantasy. The third, playing a crucial role in reinforcing the sense of collective identity of those caught up in the fantasy, as Dostoyevsky portrayed in *The Possessed* and as Orwell was later to show in *Nineteen Eighty Four*, is the need for 'enemies' and 'hate-figures': those outside the fantasy against whom they can work up feelings of aggression. Caricaturing the 'enemies' as darkly and negatively as possible plays a key part in helping those within the fantasy to see their own role in a heroic, idealised light.

For Russia, in the years after 1917, the dream was to 'construct Socialism', leading ultimately to the achievement of the perfect Communist state. The first 'dream heroes' whose iconic images were soon to proliferate all over Russia were Marx and Lenin, joined in the mid-1920s by Stalin. The necessary hate-figures were all those 'enemies of the revolution' who needed to be rooted out and crushed, from the remnants of the discredited social order defeated in Russia's Civil War to the 'wreckers', 'saboteurs' and 'reactionaries' of whom the years which followed would provide a limitless supply.

A striking feature of Communism was the speed at which, having torn down Russia's old social order, centred on a religiously-sanctioned autarchy, it replaced it with a caricature of what it had destroyed. In place of the absolute rule of the Czar came the absolute rule of the Communist dictators, Lenin and Stalin. In place of the old aristocracy emerged the new ruling elite of 'the Party'. In place of that Christian Orthodoxy which had provided the people of Russia with an explanation for the world and the faith they should live by came the new Marxist-Leninist orthodoxy, seeking to do precisely the same.

Initially Communism had been a below-the-line, 'left-wing fantasy', associated with all the 'progressive' tendencies of the early twentieth century, from avant-garde painting and 'modernism' in architecture to a belief in 'free love'. Within a few years the new Soviet Union had officially reinstated a belief in marriage and the family as a keystone of Communist society. It had imposed on its artists and writers the rigid doctrines of 'Socialist Realism', whereby their only duty was to produce films, novels, plays, paintings, statues, buildings and musical compositions designed, in crudely sentimental fashion, to extol the glories of Communism and the heroic achievements of the proletariat.

As with any fantasy, Soviet Communism was based on building up a state of expectation which was unable to resolve with reality. It therefore needed constantly to be fed with new promises of glorious achievements to come, along with new excuses as to why it had so far failed to deliver on its earlier promises. At the end of the 1920s, Stalin unveiled the first of his 'Five Year Plans', holding out the Utopia which would arrive when he had taken the Soviet Union's agriculture into state ownership and completed his visionary programme for dragging his backward country into the age of heroic industrialism. The first class of 'enemies' and 'wreckers' who were demonised as obstacles to achieving this were the *kulaks*: all those peasants with their little plots of land who still clung onto a belief in private property. Millions were either murdered directly, or died in the mass famine which followed when the land confiscated from them failed to produce food. In the late 1930s, frustrated by his continuing failure to achieve the Communist Utopia, Stalin switched the blame onto his own followers, as millions of Party members and officers of the Red Army were either shot or deported to die more slowly in the slave camps of Siberia.

The infection of one group-fantasy often helps to set off another. By this time, partly in response to the spread of Communist ideas across Europe, a new group-fantasy had taken possession of Germany: the virulence of which would before long pose a threat to the entire continent.

We traced earlier how Hitler's career as Nazi leader followed the five-stage fantasy pattern. The Anticipation Stage lasted through his rise to power in 1933. From then onwards he entered the Dream Stage in which everything seemed to be miraculously going his way. The key to the hold he exercised over Germany was the way he managed to collectivise the egos of his followers behind that particular projection of the Self archetype which was identified with German nationhood. By playing on the archetypal elements which provided the German people with the emotional core of their collective sense of identity, Hitler welded them into a single totality, obedient to his will: not least through the skilful use of quasi-religious imagery, from the swastika symbol to that 'cathedral of light' which was Speer's masterpiece in stage-managing the Nuremberg rallies.

Like Communism, Nazism was dependent on those same three factors displayed by any group-fantasy. The collective act of make-believe which bound its followers together was the dream of Germany reborn from its post-war humiliations, as the 'Fatherland' of a 'master race' equipped to take on the world. Its supreme 'dream hero' was the spell-binding, superhuman Fuehrer himself. The role of the 'hate-figures' needed to fuel its aggression was played, initially, by the Communists and the Jews, then by any 'lesser breeds' from outside Germany who dared stand in its way.

If Communism had begun as a 'left-wing' fantasy, centring its appeal on raising up the oppressed and building a classless, internationalist new world order, Nazism, like Fascism, was more obviously a 'right-wing' fantasy, centred on nationalism, racial superiority and myths from the past, and the masculine values of power and strength, discipline and order. But it had not taken long for Communism to demonstrate that, behind its outward show of altruistic concern for the underdog, it was really driven just as much by an obsession with power and order as its right-wing 'opposites'. Similarly Nazism pretended to have the caring 'feminine' values, in its relentless sentimentalisation of *kinder und kuche*, the role of 'Aryan womanhood' and blond, blue-eyed children.

For both ideologies, their supreme mode of self-expression was staging spectacular displays of war machines and serried ranks of uniformed men marching with mechanical precision, to demonstrate total obedience to the 'dream hero' leader. Based on a 'dark inversion' of the Self, Communism and Nazism were equally totalitarian, seeking to control the inner life of each individual citizen and every aspect of collective life. Inevitably both were implacably atheistic, seeing religion as their despised and hated 'opposite'.

Just as any fantasy to stay in being must step up its demands, so the most obvious characteristic of Hitler in the 1930s was his need constantly to expand his power: firstly by building up his armed might within Germany itself, then, as Predator, by seizing one neighbouring country after another.

In the fast-lengthening shadow cast by this colossal projection of collective egotism, the other nations of Europe in the late 1930s seemed weak, effete and powerless. Their well-meaning leaders seemed paralysed, unable to summon up any 'masculine' strength of character in response. The Western world in general, as it slowly emerged from the trauma of the Great Depression, had become preoccupied with the material pleasures of returning prosperity.

In the cinema, it took refuge in the sugary escapism of Fred Astaire and Busby Berkeley musicals, and by 1939 in two of the most successful escapist movies of all time, each centred on a female character. *Gone with the Wind*, centred on a beautiful heroine caught between two men who, for opposing reasons, were both inadequate, carried audiences back to the romantic lost world of the Southern States aristocracy before the American Civil War, and ended on the despairing pseudo-optimism of its lost and battered heroine proclaiming 'tomorrow is another day'. *The Wizard of Oz*, centred on the child-star Judy Garland, carried them off to the infantile Technicolor-fantasy world of Munchkin-land, the Yellow Brick Road and a 'wise old man' who turned out to be a silly old fraud, accompanied by the equally sentimental pseudo-optimism of 'Somewhere, over the rainbow'.

Confronted by the gravest threat Western civilisation had ever faced, the peace-loving democracies, it seemed, had gone soft. What happened next was to provide the greatest psychological reversal of the past 200 years.

## 4. The re-emergence of the Self: 1940–1955

A measure of the psychic shift which was to follow was the contrast between the thin, defeated voice in which Neville Chamberlain informed his fellow-country-men on 3 September 1939 that Britain was 'now at war with Germany' and the masculine rhetoric in which, within nine months, Winston Churchill would be inspiring them to one of the greatest acts of national defiance shown by any people in history.

On 24 August 1939 the two great totalitarian powers of Europe had joined forces in the Nazi-Soviet pact, to divide up Poland. A week later, Britain and France finally accepted that they could appease Hitler no longer. Thus began the six months Anticipation Stage of the 'phoney war', as armies massed along the Western front for the immense conflict which now seemed inevitable. On 10 May, following his lightning seizure of Denmark and Norway, Hitler launched his blitz-krieg on Holland, Belgium and France. In London the discredited Chamberlain gave way to the towering figure who was to lead his country through the next five years. That summer, as the skies of southern England provided the stage for the Battle of Britain, giving way in the autumn and winter of 1940 to Hitler's blitz on London and other cities, Churchill's rock-like presence focused his countrymen's resolve with a manly strength they had not known in their leaders for decades.

The prevailing archetype in British life changed with startling speed. The heroes of the hour were the gallant young pilots of the RAF; the sailors of the Royal Navy who had already raised the spirits of the nation by pulling off such dazzling victories as that over the pocket-battleship *Graf Spee*; the troops and the crews of the 'little ships' who turned defeat into moral victory at Dunkirk.

In archetypal terms what these new national heroes represented was the 'light masculine': strength and bravery made positive by the fact that, like the indomitable will of Churchill himself, it was being exercised selflessly. But behind this was the spirit of a whole nation, welded together in common cause, showing 'the spirit of the Blitz' and determined that, come what may, it would stand up to this assault by the forces of darkness until final victory was assured.

The real archetype now coming into play in British life was that of the Self: giving each individual a part to play in a cosmic battle between the powers of dark-ness and those of light. Men were again liberated to play a fully masculine role. Women could again become feminine, courageously representing those values of heart and soul for which so much was now being risked. Everyone was caught up in the new-found national spirit. From the King and Queen, venturing out from a bomb-damaged Buckingham Palace to tour the blitzed slums of London's East End, down to a country village clustered round its ancient church or the shipyards of the 'Red Clyde', the British people had never before felt so united: as was nowhere better symbolised than by the eagerness with which they clustered round radio sets to listen to the speeches of the robust 'father-figure' who was now their leader.

The reason why an entire nation could become possessed by the archetype in this way was that the 'dark power' they were up against so obviously represented its opposite: a complete inversion of the Self. Much more than in the First World War, the 'enemy', personified in Hitler's evil genius, now represented unalloyed darkness. By so clearly representing the extreme dark pole of the human psyche, this had now constellated in the hearts and minds of the British people the archetype which was its light opposite.

We have noted before how the Second World War was to give rise to immeasurably more 'stories', from fictional films and novels to factual documentaries, than any other event in history. One reason for this was that, in real life, the war was made up of countless individual episodes, air and sea battles, campaigns on land, each of which in due course could lend itself to retelling as a story in its own right. But what really made this possible, apart from the fact that advances in technology made World War Two much more far-reaching and fast-moving than its predecessor, was precisely that the conduct of the Germans and their Japanese allies, so much more obviously than in World War One, cast them so unequivocally into the archetypal role of the 'monster'.

This was why, first for the British, then for their other allies, the pattern which shaped their emotional response to the war was that of participation in a huge, real-life Overcoming the Monster story: an archetypal drama in which everyone felt involved, and which would not be over until the monster was finally tracked down to his lair and slain. Even when that distant prospect of victory was as yet almost unthinkable, the war gave rise to a host of fictional stories, all of which, more than almost any conceived in the inter-war decades, were firmly rooted in the values of the Self.

As early as 1940, Paul Gallico's *The Snow Goose* wove out of the tragedy of Dunkirk an extraordinary parable of light and dark, centred on a hero who was portrayed as completely light, in a world where darkness seemed to reign supreme. Yet even in his death, ran the message of the story, life and light were triumphant (as in the story of Christ). In the same years, welling up from the unconscious of an Oxford professor of Anglo-Saxon literature, was that huge story of how two little, very English heroes, Frodo and Sam, eventually saved Middle Earth from the terrifying monster whose world-conquering ambitions were casting such a shadow over it from the east.

Nowhere, however, was the change which had come over storytelling more immediately obvious than in the cinema, In 1942 Noel Coward, whose pre-war plays about drug-addiction and divorce had made him synonymous with modern 'decadence', came up with one of the most robustly patriotic films of the war. *In Which We Serve* moved audiences with its tribute to the selfless courage of those enduring terrifying ordeals at sea, and the equally selfless strength of character shown by those they loved at home. Other popular wartime films drew on Britain's history to centre on such manly national heroes from the past as Nelson, Pitt the Younger and Henry V, in Laurence Olivier's unashamedly morale-boosting version of Shakespeare's play. Carol Reed's *The Way Ahead* (1944) told the story of how a group of British soldiers rebuilt their morale after defeat at Dunkirk, to end with their part in the victory over Rommel at El Alamein. *The Way to the Stars* (1944) centred on a love affair between a young airman and a girl representing the 'eternal feminine', who eventually had to come to terms with the news that, like so many of his comrades, he had made the supreme sacrifice in a raid on a German city.

Of course to the inhabitants of those German cities which between 1942 and 1945 allied bombers were reducing to rubble, as for those once all-conquering German armies now in retreat all over Europe, the plot they were caught up in was very different. It was that of Tragedy, as Hitler's fantasy gradually moved from its dream stage to frustration in 1941–1942, then to the nightmare which, from 1943 onwards, closed in on Germany from all sides.

Archetypally, a significant moment of the war came in the Soviet Union in 1942, when Stalin, reeling from his Red Army's initial catastrophic reverses, dropped the slogans of Communism and appealed to all the most atavistic patriotic instincts associated by his people with 'Mother Russia'. Persecution of the Church ceased. Army officers could again wear uniforms to mark them out from their men. The Russian people were now engaged in 'the Great Patriotic War'. At least in propaganda terms, Stalin had reversed something of Communism's 'dark inversion', and sought to play on precisely those archetypal emotions centred around the collective symbolism of the Self which for two decades he had done everything to root out and destroy.[6]

When America's entry into the war was precipitated by the Japanese attack on Pearl Harbour in December 1941, it did not take long for her national mood to go through much the same transformation as that which had already overtaken Britain. Her people became caught up by the same sense that they were involved in a cosmic struggle for the forces of light against darkness. There was the same realignment of archetypal values, soon reflected by Hollywood, reinstating to a place of honour those masculine virtues which were now identified with heroic young American servicemen, and the firm, 'fatherly' leadership of their President, Franklin D. Roosevelt. In 1945 the image of US Marines raising the Stars and Stripes over Iwo Jima became for their compatriots the war's supreme icon of idealised American manhood, just as for the British the iconic image of their indomitable island spirit had been the shot of St Paul's standing unbowed amid the fire and smoke of the London Blitz.

Then, in August 1945, came another unforgettable image for all mankind: that of the fireball and mushroom cloud rising over Hiroshima. Guided by the ambiguous 'spirit of Loki', *Homo sapiens* had finally learned how to unlock the

---

6. Interestingly this switch was unconsciously foreshadowed by the great Soviet film-maker Sergei Eistenstein, whose *Alexander Nevsky* in 1938 had returned to the Russian Middle Ages to show a devout Russian king eventually leading his people to a heroic victory over Germanic invaders from the West. Eisenstein's previous films, such as *The Battleship Potemkin*, had been largely Communist propaganda, exalting the triumphs of the Bolshevik revolutionaries.

most basic power of the universe, to bring the greatest war in history to an abrupt end.[7] The shock which forced the surrender of Japan saved many more lives than those lost in the pulverisation of two of her cities. Even the firestorm which engulfed Dresden in the closing weeks of the European war might have seemed justified when allied troops uncovered the unimaginable horrors of the extermination camps in which Hitler and his followers had murdered millions of victims. By a collective demonstration of that combination of archetypal qualities required in any hero of myth, the 'monster' had finally been overcome. But as humanity stumbled out into the dawn of a fragile peace, it was haunted by the knowledge that advancing consciousness had now called into being a monster potentially even more terrifying, with the power to destroy life many times over.

In many ways, the realignment of the prevailing archetypes which had so changed the mood of the Western world during the war years persisted through the decade that followed. America assumed the role of the west's superpower, the bastion of freedom and democracy against the new 'dark empire' of Communism which had taken over half of Europe, followed by the country containing a quarter of the world's population, China. Toughened by war, America's leaders, under Presidents Truman and Eisenhower, seemed appropriately masculine and mature for their new role. And, as her economy again took off into the greatest material prosperity the world had ever known, her storytelling mirrored a society still at home with those conservative values of the Self which were symbolised in Norman Rockwell's covers for the *Saturday Evening Post*, showing an idealised family of loving father and mother gathered with their smiling, well-dressed children round the Christmas tree in a neat, 'all-American' suburban home.

From *It's a Wonderful Life* (1946) through *High Noon* (1952) to *Ben Hur* (1959), the ethos which governed post-war Hollywood movies still held to those values by which stars such as James Stewart (himself a wartime bomber pilot), Gary Cooper, Cary Grant, John Wayne and Charlton Heston could be shown as men who were unmistakably masculine, brave, decent, good-hearted, chivalrous to women. Their unmistakably feminine counterparts, in flowing calf-length 'New Look' dresses, were stars such as Marilyn Monroe, Ava Gardner, Grace Kelly, Audrey Hepburn, Debbie Reynolds, Doris Day, Kim Novak, Sophia Loren. Similar values shaped the Rogers and Hammerstein and Cole Porter musicals which so dominated post-war entertainment, such as *Oklahoma, South Pacific, The King and I, Paint Your Wagon, Kiss Me Kate* and *Call Me Madam*. Sentimental they may have been, but in almost all such stories, the uplift of the archetypal happy ending, the uniting of hero and heroine before the curtain fell, had become almost synonymous with storytelling.

In Britain, amid the austerities of the immediate post-war period, a new Labour government seemed to continue that sense of communal idealism generated by the war, as it set out to build a selfless, fair new world supposedly dedicated to the interests of all 'the People'. In the early 1950s, Churchill returned to 10 Downing Street, to preside over his country's gradual return to prosperity. In 1953, the ancient

---

7. It was telling that, after the first nuclear test at Alamagordo, on 16 July 1945, Robert J. Oppenheimer, scientific director of the Manhattan Project, resorted to religious imagery to express his awe. Quoting Shiva from the Baghavadh Gita, he exclaimed 'I am become death, the destroyer of worlds.'

pageantry surrounding the Coronation of a new young Queen, attended by representatives from Britain's Empire and Commonwealth, projected an extraordinary image of a worldwide 'family', gathered together to pay homage to the archetypal symbols of its collective Self. British society, its class structure still largely intact, still held together by a framework of traditional social and sexual morality, seemed to be returning to a conservative 'normality'.

All this was reflected in the post-war years by the British cinema, happily projecting a particular view of Britain as it had emerged from its heroic wartime ordeal, keenly aware of class differences but still a society bound together by shared traditional values. It was the heyday of Ealing comedies, such as *Passport to Pimlico*, *Kind Hearts and Coronets*, *The Lavender Hill Mob*; of films like *The Blue Lamp*, with Jack Warner creating the idealised fatherly policeman later to become the hero of a 1950s television series *Dixon of Dock Green*; of the classic film versions of Dickens's nineteenth-century novels, such as *Great Expectations* and *Oliver Twist*. The events of the war itself did not much feature on the screen until, in the early 1950s, a flood of films appeared recreating heroic British wartime episodes, from the Battle of Britain, the Dambusters raid and the sinking of the *Graf Spee* to prison-camp escape stories.

In the theatre it was the heyday of West End 'drawing room comedy', Terence Rattigan, T. S. Eliot's *The Cocktail Party*: thoughtful, undisturbing plays for respectable middle-class audiences, about the lives of socially 'above the line' people like themselves. Evelyn Waugh, the provocative young novelist of the 1920s, had embarked on his earnest trilogy about the war, *Sword of Honour*, partly inspired by his conversion to Roman Catholicism; while his longest novel, *Brideshead Revisited* (1945) was like a serious revisiting of the plot of his first, *Decline and Fall* (1928), replacing its sardonic satire of the amoral 1920s with a haunting portrait of an old upper-class Catholic family in its decadence, clinging on to a sentimentalised version of its Catholic faith as the rising tide of modern barbarism consigned it to the past. Even Waugh's contemporary, Graham Greene, although he specialised in portraying the social and moral twilight world dubbed 'Greeneland', clung on to his own sentimental version of Catholicism, as offering the hope that there was light flickering somewhere in the darkness.[8]

---

8. Greene's two most overtly 'Catholic' novels – *The Power and the Glory* (1938) and *The Heart of the Matter* (1948) – centre on a hero who has in reality lost his faith but clings on in desperation to an idea of Catholicism, as embodying the Self with which he no longer has any living contact. When it comes to a final test, Greene's 'whisky priest' in *The Power and the Glory* faces the firing squad unable to pray. In *The Heart of the Matter*, Scobie, the policeman whose life has fallen apart, escapes the problems he has brought on himself by suicide, which his Church teaches is the ultimate mortal sin. In each case Greene tries to end his story with a positive 'Catholic' twist. Despite the Church's apparent defeat in the priest's execution by an atheist regime, the novel ends with the secret arrival of a new priest, to show that the Church goes on forever. When Scobie dies, the book ends with a priest saying he was sure that Scobie 'really loved God', while Scobie's wife agrees that 'he certainly loved no one else'. Apart from these sentimental conclusions, the picture of human nature given by the two novels is unrelievedly bleak. Their characters are shown as confused or empty, lost in a moral twilight. In later years Greene abandoned his attempt to use 'Catholicism' as an image of 'saving grace' in his books, and, in proclaiming sympathy for various Communist regimes, appeared to have switched his sentimental projection of the 'Self' from Catholicism to a fuzzy Marxism.

However much some were still holding to the imagery and symbolism of the past in their search for meaning, the world in that first post-war decade was changing rapidly. It was symbolically apt that the crowning of a new Queen in the mediaeval setting of Westminster Abbey should have been the occasion which more than anything else introduced the people of Britain to the new medium of television. On all sides the pace of technological innovation was now transforming human life more rapidly than ever before: the first jet airliners; transistors; new wonder-drugs like penicillin, which promised a revolution in man's ability to combat disease; new pesticides like DDT, which promised a worldwide revolution in food production; nuclear fission producing electric power; the first rockets reaching into space.

By the mid-1950s there was a growing sense that humanity was standing at the dawn of a wholly new era, with a power to command the forces of nature which would dwarf anything which had gone before. Nowhere was this more obvious than in America, now, under the presidency of the elderly and conservative wartime general Eisenhower, indisputably the richest, most powerful, most technologically advanced nation in the world. But along with this vision of a shining future had come the uncomfortable awareness that it cast a long shadow. The advance of nuclear physics had already produced the hydrogen bomb. Those advances in rocket science were creating missiles capable of carrying such weapons halfway across the globe. The dreams of mankind were now becoming haunted by a barely imaginable new nightmare.

At least on the surface such fears could be turned into popular entertainment. Both in America and Britain, the early 1950s saw a rash of science fiction horror stories showing humanity facing some final catastrophe: either through its own technological ingenuity having created monsters which run out of control, or through the arrival of aliens from outer space bent on taking over planet Earth. The power of stories such as John Wyndham's *The Day of the Triffids* or Nigel Kneale's *Quatermass* serials for television derived from the way they began by showing their characters living in a peaceful, everyday contemporary world of the 1950s, and how this peace was then suddenly shattered by the terrifying irruption of some dark and monstrous power. Invariably, just when the nightmare reached its height and mankind seemed doomed, the hero and his companions either managed to destroy the monster, or at least to escape from its clutches, in a way which offered hope that humanity could survive and that the reign of darkness could one day be brought to an end.

The prevailing archetype in the societies of the West was again about to go through a startling change.

## 5. The re-emergence of the ego (I): 1955–1980

'When the mood of the music changes, the walls of the city shake.'
(Late 1960s slogan, attributed to Plato.[9])

9. Plato's original version was: 'A change to a new type of music is something to beware of as a hazard to all our fortunes. For the modes of music are never disturbed without unsettling of the most fundamental political and social conventions' (*The Republic*, Book IV).

The psychic upheaval about to engulf the Western world first showed in the younger generation. By the mid-1950s various films were catching a newly restive mood now affecting many of those on the verge of adult life, who 10 years earlier would have been preoccupied with fighting World War Two. In 1953 *The Wild One* featured Marlon Brando as the leader of an aggressive gang of leather-jacketed 'ton-up kids' descending on a California town (and ended with him being accused of murder). Two years later teenage American movie-goers were hypnotised by a new young Hollywood star James Dean in *Rebel Without a Cause* (1955), playing a speed-crazed hero who ended up killing himself in a car crash (only months before Dean died in identical fashion in real life). Across the Atlantic Federico Fellini's *I Vitelloni* (1954) centred on a bored, sensation-seeking bunch of Italian teenagers, showing, like the contemporary 'Teddy boy' craze in Britain, that, as the shadows of the war receded, the new hunger for excitement was not confined only to America.

The first real sign of the scale of the earthquake to come, however, was the reaction in 1956 to the movie *Rock Around the Clock*, starring a group known as Bill Haley and the Comets (who had briefly featured the previous year in a film about violence in a New York slum school, *Blackboard Jungle*). Their music aroused such excitement that it set off riots. In south London a mob of three thousand 'Teddy boys' rampaged through the streets for several hours, leaving a trail of devastation. Within months Haley was overshadowed by another new cult hero, Elvis Presley, the epitome of rampant young male sexuality. The pounding beat of rock 'n' roll became the most feverish craze in popular music since the 1920s.

At much the same time, apparently unconnected, a new play in London, by an unknown young playwright, became overnight the theatrical sensation of the year. John Osborne's *Look Back in Anger*, showing its bored, angry, 'lower-class' young hero Jimmy Porter in a seedy Midlands flat, ranting at the middle-class, Establishment values which he saw as suffocating English life, was unlike anything audiences had seen before. It was hailed by critics like Ken Tynan as roaring like a gale of fresh air through the stifling conservative conventions which had dominated English drama since the war. Soon Osborne and other new, young, 'below the line' writers, such as the novelists Kingsley Amis and John Braine, had been dubbed by the press as 'angry young men'.

A remarkable feature of the last four decades of the twentieth century was the extent to which they would be characterised by a set of values and attitudes which came into being in the space of just a few years, between the middle of the 1950s and the late 1960s. Already by the mid-1960s it was being observed that a 'revolution' had taken place in the Western world, exemplified in everything from popular music, the rise of 'youth culture' and 'sexual liberation' to the new omnipresence of television and the rise of the 'consumer society'. The transformation this had brought about in the way people thought and behaved would last to the end of the century and beyond. But essentially it had begun at that moment in 1955–1956 when 'the mood of the music' changed.

Over the next few years a distinct new 'sub-culture' emerged among the young of the Western democracies, whereby they saw themselves as in rebellion against the older generation and all it stood for. Bonded together by their new music, their fashions in clothes and jazz-derived American slang ('cool', 'crazy', 'rave', 'wild', 'freaky', 'kicks'), their collective mood exhibited all the familiar symptoms of a group-fantasy: rigidly conformist, centred on rock 'n' roll singers as its iconic dream heroes, and exhibiting a sense of aggression towards the 'boring', 'repressive' values of all those outside their fantasy-community, who were dismissed as 'squares'. In America the mood of this new 'beat generation' found expression in Jack Kerouac's novel *On the Road* (1957). In Britain a middle-aged novelist Colin MacInnes tried to capture this dream-state in *Absolute Beginners* (1959), as he described his young hero looking down on London from a plate-glass window:

> 'pressed up so close it was like I was out there in the air, suspended above the city, and I swore by Elvis and all the saints that this last teenage year of mine was going to be a real rave. Yes, man, come whatever, this last year of the teenage dream I was out for kicks and fantasy.'

By the late 1950s, however, it was not only the young who had the sense that some extraordinary new world was opening up. What was happening was that, after that revival of the values of the Self which had characterised the war years, the mood of the age was picking up where it left off in the 'Roaring Twenties': and this was now generating different bubbles of expectation which overlapped and soon began to merge with each other.

Underpinning it all was the exhilarating pace of technological change, which for most people in the richer countries of the West was bringing an entirely new kind of material prosperity. 'Affluence' had arrived. As millions bought their first cars and refrigerators, the coming of the first motorways, the first neon-lit supermarkets, above all the now ubiquitous television screens were filling people's heads with a new vision of 'modernity'. Symbolically, the feel of city life was being transformed as massive new metal, glass and concrete towers (again picking up on ideas from the 1920s) began to rise above skylines until now dominated by the towers, spires and domes of churches.

So headily all-pervasive was the sense that society was being carried into a new, exciting future that, even more obviously than in the 1920s, this brought an urge for liberation from all that framework of social and moral structures inherited from the past. From the class structure to sex, long-established constraints and attitudes seemed suddenly restrictive, outmoded, irrelevant to the needs of the new world technology was making possible.

In 1950 an American sociologist, David Riesman, had published a prescient book, *The Lonely Crowd*, identifying three basic ways in which human beings formed their values and attitudes to life. The first was what Riesman described as the 'tradition-directed' society, in which people in general inherited conventions and belief-systems passed on to them by their parents and by previous generations. The second was the 'other-directed' society, in which people took on the fashion-based values dictated by their peer-group and by all the pressures of the contemporary world around them. A third, much rarer category included those 'inner-directed' individuals who gradually discover their own autonomous inner 'centre', evolving values based on their own experience and understanding.

The change coming over Western society around 1960 represented a move on an unprecedented scale away from a 'tradition-directed' society to one in which people were becoming 'other-directed'. Reinforced by the new power of advertising, the pace of technological change, reflected in everything from the contraceptive pill to the new architecture, helped to create the sense that a wholly new type of society was coming to birth: free-thinking, classless, sexually emancipated. People were at last being liberated to express their own 'individuality': but only so long as this conformed with the collective norms dictated by the new ruling consciousness. In the slang of the time, the need was to be 'with it'. No one could have defined precisely what 'it' was; but everyone knew intuitively what was meant.

In the wider world there was an awakening desire for liberation among all those who saw themselves as 'below the line', such as the black population of the USA and those countries which could now look forward to independence from European colonial rule. When Britain's prime minister Harold Macmillan remarked, as the new decade of the 1960s began, that 'a wind of change' was blowing through Africa, he might have been speaking not just of Africa but for humanity as a whole. A new archetype was in the ascendant, which everywhere was promoting the imagery of youth, vitality, freedom, excitement and the future against structures of thought and behaviour which seemed suddenly oppressive and to belong to a dead past. It was the power of this new imagery over people's minds which was now going to shape their thinking in everything from social attitudes to politics for a long time to come. And as usual nothing reflected the psychic upheaval more vividly than the way in which this new age told stories.

As the world stood on the edge of the 1960s, one group of storytellers who picked up the new mood to particular effect were the young film-makers of the *nouvelle vague* in France. Jean-Luc Godard's *Breathless* (1959), Francois Truffaut's *Shoot the Pianist* (1960) and *Jules et Jim* (1962) were strange dream-like narratives which each began in a mood of reckless youthful euphoria. But each then gradually turned to a puzzling nightmare, ending abruptly in a sudden, shocking death.

In Britain in 1960 it was appropriate that it should have been that most 'daring' novel of the 1920s, *Lady Chatterley's Lover*, which reappeared to become the focus of the new battle for sexual liberation. But it was telling that the essence of this battle against the 'reactionary prudes' and 'killjoys', at a time when *Playboy* magazine was pioneering the drive to make pornographic pictures of naked women socially acceptable, lay in the urge to enjoy not so much sexual gratification itself as the mental image of sex.[10] In the same year, the impact of Hitchcock's *Psycho* was so great because its central image of a naked young woman being sadistically stabbed to death provided such a shocking contrast to the decorous image of womanhood familiar from films of the post-war era.

10. Another feature of *Lady Chatterley* echoed in other novels and plays by 'lower-class' writers in the late 1950s, was the way it centred on Lawrence's fantasising about his socially 'below the line' hero dominating an aristocratic 'above the line' heroine. An important ingredient in *Look Back in Anger* was the verbal raping by Osborne's assertively 'lower-class' hero of his submissive 'upper-class' wife. Similarly John Braine in *Room at the Top* fantasised about his ambitious young working-class hero sweeping off her feet and dominating the millionaire's daughter he was set on marrying (an echo of Stendhal's fantasising about his hero Sorel sexually humiliating Mathilde in *Le Rouge et Le Noir*).

However, the event of 1960 which most vividly reflected the arrival of the 'Sixties dream' was the American presidential election which, thanks for the first time to the power of the televised image, led to the replacement of America's oldest-ever President with her youngest. John F. Kennedy's charismatic good looks and 'dynamism' immediately made him the new decade's first 'dream hero' (as the novelist Norman Mailer excitably put it, 'Superman comes to Supermarket!'). Within months this had provoked growing tension between the glamorous new young leader of the free world and his ageing counterpart in the Soviet Union, Nikita Khruschev. In 1961 Kennedy's failed invasion of the Soviet empire's satellite in Cuba was followed by Khruschev's Berlin Wall, provoking the worst crisis of the Cold War. In October 1962 came the even more dangerous crisis when Khruschev's dispatch of nuclear rockets to Cuba brought the world to the edge of nuclear catastrophe.

The mood of the times was becoming ever more feverish. In November 1962, within weeks of the Cuba crisis, London saw the premiere of the first James Bond film *Dr No* (coincidentally featuring a monstrous villain who, from his lair on a Caribbean island, planned the nuclear destruction of the West). This coincided in London with a clutch of nightmarishly sensational new plays (referred to in Chapter 27), centred on the imagery of sex and violence. In the same month the hitherto staid and deferential BBC introduced the 'satire craze' to a mass-audience with *That Was The Week That Was*, mocking everything established and traditional in British national life, not least the government headed by the now seemingly antiquated and 'upper class' father-figure, Macmillan. The same weeks saw the first entry into the charts of a new rock 'n' roll-based 'pop group' from Liverpool, the Beatles.

One of the most acclaimed 'art films' of 1962 was the Italian director Michelangelo Antonioni's *Eclipse*, a drifting nightmare which ended in a cloud covering the sun, throwing the world into a silent twilight. Through 1963, as Macmillan's Conservative government disintegrated in a cloudy miasma of rumour and scandal, the hysteria surrounding the Beatles, the epitome of 'classless', 'irreverent' youthful energy bubbling up from socially 'below the line', grew ever more deafening. In Washington in September another 'dream hero' of the early 1960s, Martin Luther King, led a million protestors through 'above the line' Washington in an unprecedented demonstration for the civil rights of America's black minority. Then, on 22 November, after a year when the headlines had been dominated by one sensation after another, came the most shocking moment of the post-war era: the assassination of President Kennedy.

In the aftermath of this eruption of 'shadow', America's own mood turned darker. Over the next two years, it was to become dominated by race riots in her cities and, increasingly, the catastrophe unfolding in Vietnam. But in these same years it became obvious that the psychic upheaval which began at the time of rock 'n' roll in the mid-1950s had produced a remarkable change in the character and mood of Western life, nowhere more obviously than in London.

As obsessive attention centred on its classless 'new aristocracy' of pop singers, model girls, actors, photographers and dress-designers, it emerged in 1964 and 1965 that Britain was leading the way in promoting that bubble of image-based fantasy which caused London to be hailed as 'the most swinging city in the world'. On the surface there was an almost child-like innocence about the crazes and fashions which swept through London's boutiques, discotheques and glossy magazines, from the dazzling patterns of Op Art to the shiny PVC uniforms, mini-skirts and little white boots which depersonalised young girls into throwaway sex toys, But in an earlier chapter we traced how this remorseless pursuit of novelty was accompanied by the drift of plays, films and novels into an ever more sensational twilight world, preoccupied with sex and violence and culminating in November 1965 in the spectacle of young men stoning a baby to death in its pram.[11]

By the beginning of 1966, a curious change of mood was taking place. The new craze among the pop culture's elite was the psychedelic drug LSD, which helped to inspire a new interest in the imagery and message of Eastern religions. As the now bearded and kaftanned Beatles sat at the feet of their guru, the Maharishi, and strummed their sitars with Ravi Shankar, they had travelled a long way in just five short years from the leather-jacketed suburban teenagers who had first earned a living together imitating American rock 'n' roll in the nightclubs of Hamburg's red-light district.

Psychologically what was happening was that, for those at the heart of the fantasy bubble, the untrammelled egotism it represented had now gone so far that it was producing that familiar unconscious reversal. The archetype of the Self was returning in an 'inferior' form. The craze for 'Eastern mysticism' represented a form of 'ego-Self confusion', whereby the ego, having wearied of all the novelties of overt ego-gratification, now wanted a sentimental version of its ego-transcending opposite. In 1967 this took on more widespread form in the craze which swept young people across the Western world for the hippie bells, joss sticks, 'peace and love' of the 'flower power' movement, which had originated in San Francisco. Pseudo-religious cults flourished, invariably centred on some darkly charismatic leader-figure and based on the ruthless separation of their members from the rest of society.

---

11. Nothing better reflected the changing mood of these years when the Sixties fantasy was at its height than the way the words of the pop songs of the period reflected the five stages of the fantasy cycle. Early Beatles songs, such as 'Love Me Do' and 'Please, Please Me', expressed the mood of an Anticipation Stage. The projected *anima* was still to be won. The Dream Stage, as their fame took off in 1963, was expressed in the child-like euphoria of songs such as 'She Loves You' and 'I Wanna Hold Your Hand' (the girl was theirs, the *anima* had been won). By 1964 and early 1965, as the strain of their fame and new life-style began to tell, the mood changed to one of frustration ('A Hard Day's Night') and loss ('Help!'). The Frustration Stage, as the dreamed-of resolution proved ever more elusive, was never better expressed than in the Rolling Stones' 1965 hit 'I Can't Get No Satisfaction'. Shortly afterwards, the Nightmare Stage (now fuelled in America by the growing real-life nightmare of Vietnam) inspired a despairing American hit-song proclaiming 'We're on the eve of destruction'. This was followed, as Britain's chief pop-craze in the autumn of 1965, by the frantic, auto-destructive guitar-smashing of The Who, as they screamed out in 'My Generation' how 'I wanna die before I get old'. In three years, the fantasy had travelled from naive and euphoric anticipation to death wish.

Although there was a general tendency for the films, plays and novels of the time to become more violent and sexually explicit, and for their narratives and imagery to become more fragmented and surreal (e.g., the Beatles films *A Hard Day's Night* and *Help!*, *The Knack*, *What's New Pussycat?*), there were of course exceptions. Two major Hollywood successes of these years were *My Fair Lady* (1964) and *The Sound of Music* (1965), based on more conventional musicals dating from the earlier tradition of the 1950s.

In 1968 the prevailing fashion again mutated, as mobs of unkempt students demonstrated, half-angrily, half-playfully, across the world against any symbol of the adult, established order, from the Vietnam war to their university curriculum. As they mouthed the slogans of Trotskyite revolution, decorated their rooms with iconic posters of the dead Cuban revolutionary Che Guevara and daubed walls with such graffiti as 'make love, not war', this coincided with the news from the USA of the assassinations of two more 'sixties dream heroes', Martin Luther King and President Kennedy's younger brother Bobby. The following year in California, the story of one particularly dark quasi-religious cult ended in hideous catas-trophe, when Charles Manson, leader of 'The Family', egged on his followers to an orgy of violence which led to the murder of the film actress Sharon Tate. By fearful symmetry, she was married to one of the decade's most obsessive creators of the imagery of sex-and-violence, Roman Polanski, the director of *Repulsion* (1965) and *Rosemary's Baby* (1966), centred on a pregnant young mother who gives birth to the devil.

With these visions of a world turned to nightmare, the great 1960s hysteria was in fact running out of steam. Psychologically it had been one of the most extra-ordinary episodes in the history of mankind (comparable perhaps only with the much more violent frenzy which gripped France in the 1790s). But the cultural legacy it left behind, in everything from the rhythmic beat of its music to the acceptance of sexual promiscuity, from the importance of drugs to the fashionable orthodoxy of an anti-establishment, 'left-wing' attitude to authority was going to remain at the heart of Western life for many decades to come.

The decade which followed was like a prolonged hangover from the excesses of the 1960s. The self-destructive power of the mass-neurosis unleashed in those years was reflected in the deaths of several of its drug-addicted dream heroes, from Janis Joplin and Jimi Hendrix to Elvis Presley and John Lennon. Lesser stars con-tinued to emerge to feed the collective youthful fantasy. New films, such as *A Clockwork Orange*, *Straw Dogs*, *Last Tango in Paris* and *The Texas Chainsaw Massacre* ratcheted up the sensationalism with which the cinema fed the appetite for the imagery of sex and violence. But the outlines of how the group-fantasy continued to evolve were all by now well-established. And in some respects the 1970s saw a reaction to the relentless neophilia of the previous decade, nowhere more conspicuously than in the widespread revulsion against the inhuman envir-onments created by the megalomaniac architectural revolution of the 1960s. The gargantuan housing estates and concrete tower blocks which had so powerfully expressed the hubris of the sixties now came widely to be seen as ugly, soulless and a social disaster. Many films and television commercials reflected a sentimental nostalgia for the imagery of earlier times, before the modern age, when the world had seemed quieter, more ordered, more colourful and more innocent.

This nostalgia for the world as it had been before the rise of modern technology had already found expression in the late 1960s in the remarkable revival of interest in Tolkien's *The Lord of the Rings*, for its conjuring up of an entire pseudo-mythic world set in an imaginary pre-mechanical age, when battles were still fought with swords and axes, bows and arrows. *Watership Down* similarly became one of the best-sellers of the 1970s by conjuring up a natural world in which anthropomorphic animals could be portrayed as relying on basic human qualities, and in which the creations of modern human technology – cars, barbed wire, bulldozers – were seen as monstrous and destructive intrusions. Even in one of the most futuristically technological fantasies of the decade, *Star Wars*, the make-believe hardware and dazzling special effects only provided the outward clothing for an essentially timeless story in which knights of old fought hand-to-hand duels to save the Princess from imprisonment and the kingdom from destruction.

Another respect in which the headlong rush of technological advance was now inspiring a reaction – although again its origins first appeared in the 1960s – lay in the growing sense that it represented a collective hubris which was threatening to destroy all life on earth. Increasingly prominent in the 1970s was the worldwide environmental movement, which had developed its own 'narrative' centred on what it saw as man's reckless over-exploitation of the earth's natural resources and the ever-increasing pollution of land, sea and air caused by the waste products of his material self-indulgence. As the world's forests were laid waste, as human activity led each year to the extinction of thousands of other species, as the earth's atmosphere (according to the narrative) became subject to potentially disastrous chemical changes, humanity's defiance of nature for its own egocentric advantage was casting *Homo sapiens* as a cosmic 'cuckoo in the nest': the ultimate 'monster'. And nowhere was the ambivalence of 'the spirit of Loki' more obvious than in the way dramatic advances in medical knowledge and agricultural technology were helping to promote an explosion in the world's human population. Whenever in nature such an exponential rise was observed in the numbers of any other species, this was invariably the prelude to a devastating population collapse.

No single image did more to bring all this home than the picture taken in 1969 by the first men to land on the moon, showing the Earth rising above the lifeless lunar landscape. There floating, unimaginably beautiful, in the blackness of space was the soft blue image of the world they had left: the place which was home to themselves and to every known form of life; the only true source of their identity; the living centre of all meaning and existence. In that unforgettable image Earth became a symbol of the Self. Yet now, through that same hyper-developed consciousness which had enabled *Homo sapiens* for the first time to step outside the confines of the Earth where nature had placed him, an ever-lengthening shadow was stretching across all those fragile eco-systems and natural balances which allowed life on that planet to survive. The Earth itself had become a symbol of that wholeness against which the collective ego of mankind was now in potentially catastrophic rebellion.

The response to this awakening perception was, on the one hand, an apocalyptic sense that, unless the human race took the most drastic steps to mend its ways and curb its material appetites, life on Earth must be doomed to destruction. On the other, there was no sign that the measures humanity was prepared to take to reduce its despoliation of the natural world were anything more than sentimental gestures. 'Environmentalism' thus became another expression of 'ego-Self confusion'. A vocal minority worked up a tremendous sense of self-righteousness about the need to 'save the planet'; while mankind as a whole (including most of the would-be planet-savers themselves) carried on consuming and destroying its natural resources at a greater rate than ever.

## The 'age of Mother'

The two decades which followed the late 1950s had seen a shift in the ruling consciousness of the Western world which was without precedent. We can catch a little glimpse of this change in comparing two British films made twenty years apart but each based on the same event, the sinking of the Titanic in 1912.

*A Night to Remember* (1958), recreated this familiar tragic story according to the values dominant during the Second World War and the decade which followed. The film showed the liner's passengers as a microcosm of pre-First World War society, divided between an 'upper world' of aristocrats and millionaires travelling in first-class luxury and the Irish and working-class emigrants travelling 'below the line' in steerage. But when disaster strikes, almost everyone, 'upper class' and 'lower ' alike, is portrayed as acting bravely and unselfishly, displaying that 'stiff upper lip' courage still familiar from the war years. The ship's captain and his officers (led by Kenneth More) are shown playing a positive masculine role, concerned only to do their duty in an honourable, humane fashion, just as their Second World War equivalents (also not infrequently played by Kenneth More) had been shown doing in so many other films of the 1950s.

Twenty years later, *S.O.S. Titanic* (1979) presented a startlingly different picture. No longer are the liner's occupants seen as a single community, united by a common danger. The privileged upper classes inhabiting the 'above the line' world are now caricatured as cold, spoiled egotists, concerned only with saving themselves. The captain and his officers are shown as weak and vacillating. The only group now shown as warm, human and heroic are those trapped 'below the line' in the bowels of the ship, notably the Irish, sentimentally portrayed as doomed victims of a heartless class system and arrogant British imperialism.

The shift of perspective reflected in these two versions of the same tale conveys how far the prevailing archetype of the time had changed. Up to the late 1950s Western society had still managed to preserve an idealised image of its own totality, corresponding to the Self. Vital to this had been those ruling masculine principles of order, discipline and hierarchy which archetypally constituted the 'values of Father'. The institutions and conventions traditionally regarded as essential to holding society together had generally remained intact. Importance was still attached to such concepts as 'duty', 'responsibility' and 'good manners'. The social order still rested on the respect accorded to 'authority figures': from parents to political leaders, from teachers to policemen. A framework of sanctions still existed to uphold sexual discipline and the central importance of marriage, from laws prohibiting homosexuality to social taboos on promiscuity and adultery.

One of the more obvious features of the change which came over society after the late 1950s had been the extent to which all this was rejected. All that complex of 'masculine' principles associated with duty, discipline, hierarchy, tradition and authority came to be perceived as oppressive and life-denying. The new ruling consciousness was one which promoted 'below the line' values at the expense of those 'above the line'; the attributes of youth over those of maturity; liberation over constraint; 'lower class' over 'upper'; the future over the past. A dominant archetype of the age – personified in such hero-figures as Elvis Presley or the Beatles – became that of the rebellious *puer aeternus*, 'the boy hero' frozen in immaturity. No longer was it generally taken for granted that the ultimate goal of human life was to work towards the wisdom of age. What mattered in an age of incessant change was to remain in touch with the new: to aspire to a state of perpetual youth. And again, as we see from stories, wherever the archetype of the immature 'boy hero' is in the ascendant, never far away is the archetype of the emasculating 'Dark Mother'.

Certainly in all the transformation which had taken place in the 1960s and 1970s the 'values of Father' had in many ways been replaced by the more liberal, more indulgent values of 'Mother'. This found every kind of expression, not least in the qualities shown by the political leaders of the time, as the dominant figures shaped by the war, such as Churchill, Eisenhower and de Gaulle, gave way to a new generation of politicians who seemed by comparison softer, weaker and more lightweight, typified in the new age of television more by a self-regarding concern with 'image' than by strength of character.

What more than anything else lay behind the psychological change which had come over the Western world was a consequence of all those technological advances which had brought an entirely new kind of prosperity. It was this which had turned its inhabitants into 'consumers'. It was this all-providing technological 'machine' which could now gratify their every material need: from the supermarkets which provided their frozen, plastic-wrapped food to the machines which washed their clothes; from the heating which kept them warm to the cars and jet airliners which carried them about; from the blaze of electric light which turned night into day in their homes to the hypnotic presence of the television screen through which they now derived much of their entertainment and their picture of the world.

Never before had any civilisation been so cocooned from nature. Never before had human beings been so dependent for their comfort on something so vast and impersonal outside themselves that they could survive through much of their everyday lives without having to take any real direct responsibility (other than knowing which buttons to press). Without being aware of it, they were being infantilised, reduced psychologically to a child-like state of dependence on that 'Great Mother' which had been called into being by late-twentieth-century technology. And an inevitable consequence was that the traditional constraints on the gratifications of the ego were being eroded as never before.

On the surface, the prevailing mood of the years since the 1950s had been one of liberation. For most people, life had in so many ways become easier, materially more comfortable, morally more relaxed, less constrained by social conventions. But in all directions this was accompanied by a social disintegration which manifested itself in the soaring incidence of crime; in the breakdown of discipline in families, communities and schools; in addiction to drugs and pornography. One of its more conspicuous features was an unprecedented increase in the breakdown of marriages, and of that basic family unit which had been the bedrock of every human society since the dawn of recorded time.

Another phenomenon reflecting the new prominence now given to the ego was the cult of 'celebrity'. Athough this was a process which had begun in the earlier decades of the twentieth century, not least with the worldwide fame won by the first movie stars, the glamour and deference once attached to royalty and those occupying leading positions of responsibility in society now increasingly centred on a new fantasy-community of 'celebrities', blurring together actors, sportsmen, pop singers and other 'personalities' created by the media. Although those inhabiting this unreal bubble did occasionally include politicians, by definition they were responsible to no one. Most were in reality very ordinary, shallow individuals whose only claim on public attention was that they appeared on television, and, in the words of Daniel J. Boorstin, had become 'famous for being famous'.[12]

At the end of the 1970s, the writer Tom Wolfe, writing about the ego-obsessed culture of contemporary America, preoccupied by personal vanity, reflected in anything from slimming and physical fitness regimes to the vogues for self-regarding psychobabble and pseudo-spirituality, summed up these years as 'The Me Decade'. But no one cast a more questioning eye on what had happened to Western civilisation since the 1950s than the Russian writer Alexander Solzhenitsyn, after his exile in 1974 from the Soviet Union.

In 1978 Solzhenitsyn delivered the verdict of a shocked outsider on the culture he had found on arriving in his new home, America.[13] His first surprise was the lack of 'civil courage' and moral character he saw in those who were supposed to be society's leaders: their air of weak geniality and a tendency to say only what people might want to hear. Another, in a society which gave its citizens a degree of material comfort which 30 years earlier would have seemed inconceivable, was how strained and unhappy so many people looked. A third was the emphasis now placed on people's 'rights', rather than their duties and obligations. A fourth, which shocked him as much as anything on his emergence from a tyranny where every public word was controlled by the state, was the relentless triviality and conformism of the supposedly 'free' Western media.

The picture Solzhenitsyn painted was of a society of spoiled children, sunk in mindless egotism. No longer, he said, could he recommend the western way of life as a model for the transformation of the Russia he had escaped from. 'Through intense suffering' he went on, 'our country has now achieved a spiritual development of such intensity that the western system in its present state of spiritual exhaustion' looked singularly unattractive. 'A fact which cannot be disputed is the weakening of human beings in the west, while in the east they are becoming firmer and stronger ... life's complexity and mortal weight have produced stronger, deeper and more interesting characters than those generated by standardised western well-being'.

12. Daniel J. Boorstin, *The Image: What Happened to the American Dream* (London, Weidenfeld and Nicolson, 1961). His epigraph was taken from the Swiss novelist and playwright Max Frisch: 'Technology ... the knack of so arranging the world that we don't have to experience it.'
13. Solzhenitsyn offered his analysis in a speech at Harvard University in June 1978.

At the time Solzhenitysn was speaking, it seemed as though the empire of Communism, which in the 1970s had taken over ten more countries in Africa and Asia, its greatest advance since the late 1940s, was better placed to challenge American hegemony than ever before. As if desperate to provoke some response in the complacency of his audience, he went on:

> 'There are meaningful warnings which history gives to a threatened or perishing society. Such as, for instance, the decadence of art or the lack of great statesmen. There are open and evident warnings too. The centre of your democracy and your culture is left without electric power for a few hours only, and all of a sudden American citizens start looting and creating havoc ... The fight for our planet, physical and spiritual, a fight of cosmic proportions, is not a vague matter of the future. It has already started. The forces of evil have begun their decisive offensive, you can feel their pressure, and yet your screens and publications are full of prescribed smiles and raised glasses. What is the joy about?'

Solzhenitsyn's comments might have acted as a reminder that, for the people living over a large part of the globe, the experience of the previous 30 years had been very different.

## The re-emergence of the Self (II)

> 'The lack of bitter experience of people in the west makes them incapable of imagining tragedy.'                                   Vladimir Bukovsky, BBC TV, 1980

By the end of the 1970s, more than a quarter of mankind had spent the decades since the Second World War living under the tyranny of darkness to a degree which was almost beyond the comprehension of people living in the West. By the time of Stalin's death in 1953, he had already been responsible for the deaths of anything up to 20 million of his own people. Millions more were barely surviving in the slave camps of 'the Gulag archipelago'. In China Mao-tse-Tung's dictatorship had in 1949 established the terror which over the next three decades would kill tens of millions more.

One of the few westerners who had early developed an intuitive understanding of the realities of life under Communism was George Orwell, whose *Nineteen Eighty Four* (1949) held up such a vivid mirror to how such a supposedly idealistic system worked in practice. In particular, with his picture of the totalitarian rule of 'the Party', centred on the ubiquitous image of 'Big Brother', the incessant lying propaganda, the 'two-minute hate', 'thoughtcrime' and 'newspeak', he showed how such a regime set up a complete dark inversion of the Self; and how its central aim was to deny its people any right to individuality or an inner life. As Orwell showed in the crushing of his hero, each citizen had to be forced into subjection to the collective consciousness and to that projection of the collectivised Self the Party had created.

In the closing years of the 1950s, however, a novel smuggled to the West showed that, behind the monolithic propaganda surface of the Soviet Union, there were still individuals with an inner life, capable of thinking for themselves. What made Boris Pasternak's *Dr Zhivago* (1958) so subversive that the Soviet authorities immediately suppressed it was that it looked back to the Russia of the revolutionary years around 1917, not according to the prescribed Party line, but through the private life and sufferings of its strictly non-ideological hero.

Stripped to its essence, the story of Yuri Zhivago was that of a decent, intelligent, spiritually-sensitive man whose outer and inner life had been destroyed by the chaos of the revolution. Before it, he had been a promising young middle-class doctor, conventionally married, with a small son. Called up into the army, he then meets and falls in love with the bewitching Lara. Zhivago returns to his family in Moscow, but when they retreat to the country he again meets Lara and they begin an affair, which he eventually breaks off and admits to his wife. He is then conscripted to serve with Communist partisans in Russia's civil war, after which he resumes his affair with Lara. Despite the deprivations of the time, they spend several happy months together but eventually, to save her life, he tricks her into fleeing under protection to a safer part of Russia. His wife and child have by now disappeared into exile abroad. Yuri returns to Moscow, where he begins living with a third woman, by whom he has two more children. Two male friends tell him he must choose between his new mistress and his wife. Amid the miseries and cold of post-revolutionary Moscow he is lucky to get a menial job. On his way to start work he collapses in the street with a heart attack and dies. At his funeral Lara turns up, mysteriously asking Yuri's half-brother if there is any way to track down a child who has been given away to strangers. She disappears, and is supposed eventually to have died in a slave-camp (it was from *Dr Zhivago* that Western readers first learned the word 'Gulag'). Serving in the army in World War Two, after themselves spending years in the Gulag, Zhivago's two friends meet a laundry-girl, Tanya, who tells them her horrendous life story. Abandoned by her mother as a child, and after then becoming involved in an episode of chilling violence, she had been cast out on the world without family, friends or support. From her evidence they guess she must be the daughter of Yuri and Lara, and arrange measures whereby her life may now modestly improve.

In archetypal terms, what was significant about this bleak tale was the way it showed Russia's revolution and civil war as the cause of the hero's disintegration. From being happily married, with a son, he is first guiltily divided when he becomes bewitched by the elusive *anima*-figure of Lara. He attempts to behave responsibly by returning to his wife, but is then bewitched again. He again attempts to behave selflessly by sending Lara to safety, but when this leaves him unhappy, confused and alone, he takes up with a third woman, by whom he has children. His friends confront him with the need to resolve the crisis brought on by how his *anima* is now split three ways. Symbolically, his heart gives way under the strain. The real carrier of his *anima* mysteriously rematerialises at his funeral, only to slip back into the unconscious, where she is crushed by the new tyranny of the proletarian state. We are left years later with the image of Tanya, the tragic, orphaned *anima*-figure who is the sole relic of their love – although a final sentimental twist gives the tale some vestige of a positive ending.

Decades later, it may seem hard to recall why the publication of this novel created such a stir in the West (where it later became the basis of an even more sentimentalised film version), let alone why it seemed to pose such a challenge to the Soviet system that it was instantly suppressed. But, along with the release of millions of Stalin's prisoners from the Gulag archipelago in the mid-1950s and Khruschev's secret attack on Stalin's tyranny at the 1956 Communist Party Congress, the very fact that such a private book could have been written marked a faint but striking crack in the seemingly all-powerful Communist monolith.

Five years later came another, when Khruschev permitted the publication of *One Day in the Life of Ivan Denisovich* (1962), the first story by one of those millions of *zeks* or prisoners who had been released from Soviet labour camps in the post-Stalin 'thaw'. On the face of it, Solzhenitysn's novella was a slight tale, merely describing a single day in the life of an anonymous *zek*. The hero wakes up in his bunk early in the morning, freezing, ill and utterly miserable. We follow him into a hellish day, being bullied by guards, as he works at laying bricks for a wall. Gradually his mood changes. He finds himself taking pleasure in the neatness with which he is laying his bricks. He forgets his illness. In the evening a fellow *zek* gives him a fragment of sausage. By the time he is ready for sleep, he is surprisingly content. He has been through a kind of Rebirth. Inwardly, in his own tiny way, he has triumphed over the system.

So powerfully did the waves which flowed from the publication of this story establish Solzhenitsyn as everything the Soviet system did not want him to be, as his own man, implacably tough and devoutly religious, that over the next few years, through further books smuggled out to the West, including in 1974 *The Gulag Archipelago*, he established himself as the central inspiration for Russia's burgeoning 'dissident' movement. He and other brave individuals, such as the nuclear physicist Andrei Sakharov, were now ready to challenge the system and all its lies head on.

What was happening in the Communist empire in the 1960s and 1970s offered a curious parallel to what had happened to Britain in 1940. After decades when the force of the Soviet totalitarian system had succeeded in crushing its subjects into submission, the very fact that it constituted such an extreme psychological pole was now provoking an equal and opposite reaction. Here and there individuals were now appearing for whom its very power was concentrating their human and spiritual energies into its opposite. Confronted by this collectivised outward projection of the 'dark Self', they were discovering the power of the 'light Self' within themselves. It became one of the paradoxes of this period of history that it was those societies governed by a system dedicated to eradicating human individuality which ended up by producing some of the outstanding individuals of the age. Not least among them was the Polish bishop, Karol Woityla, whose faith and character had been forged in opposition to both Nazi and Communist regimes; and whose elevation to the Papacy in 1978 and first triumphant return to his homeland the following year did much to inspire that heroic resistance to Poland's Communist government in 1980 which would eventually play a key symbolic part in bringing about the downfall of the entire Soviet system.

One of the most remarkable books written in the twilight years of Communism was the autobiography of Eugenia Ginsburg, smuggled out to the West to be published in two volumes in the 1960s and 1970s as *Into the Whirlwind* and *Within the Whirlwind*. Although her book was based on fact, Ginsburg's story reads with all the imaginative power of a novel. She described how, in the 1930s, she had been the wife of a leading Party official in a provincial Soviet capital, enjoying a privileged life 'above the line'. In 1937, like so many others, she and her husband were arrested by the secret police in the first of Stalin's great purges. She found *herself* disappearing through the floor of Soviet society into the foetid, violent underworld of its vast prison system. Much of her book described the horrendous sufferings she endured in this twilight world, subjected to Kafkaesque interrogations by the NKVD and spells of solitary confinement, ending eventually in a hellish succession of slave camps in the icy wastes of the Soviet Far East.

What makes her book exceptional is the way we see her experience turning into an inner journey, as she develops the kind of understanding which enables her immediately to capture the human essence of each person she meets. Just as in a fictional story, we can see at once whether each new character she meets is 'dark' or 'light': devious, bullying and ego-centred, or honest, goodhearted and selfless. As the story nears its end, she comes to work with a fellow-prisoner, a German doctor, who shines out as a moral giant, strong, compassionate, wise and revered by all around him. The two are separated, but when they meet again we at once know, as they walk towards each other through a raging blizzard, that they love each other and are not going to be parted again.

This memorable scene is like a positive opposite to that which ends *The Third Man*, where the uncomprehending hero sees the elusive *anima*-figure of Anna walking towards him through falling leaves in the wintry cemetery, then straight past him without a look. In Ginsburg's version the hero and heroine, purged of egotism by their suffering, are finally united in the complete, mature love of two people who have grown up. Since her husband has long since died on some other island of the Gulag archipelago, she and her hero can marry, and the story ends on a true note of liberation as they joyfully regain their limited freedom in the grey post-Stalinist world of Russia in the mid-1950s.

In the spiritual depth of this story, as in other books and novels which emerged from the darkness of the Soviet empire in the 1960s and 1970s, we see something of why, when Solzhenitsyn was sent into exile by the Soviet regime in 1974, he was so startled by what he found in the West: the world of *A Clockwork Orange, Last Tango in Paris* and *The Texas Chainsaw Massacre*, in which the 'dark inversion' appeared to have taken over storytelling and much else besides.

### The re-emergence of the ego (II): 1980 onwards

By the closing decades of the twentieth century, there were many respects in which Western storytelling reflected the psychological twilight into which mankind had been heading, but perhaps the most obvious was the continuing obsession of so many film-makers, playwrights and novelists with the imagery of sex and violence. Psychologically, as we have seen, this was the natural outcome of that process which had begun 200 years earlier when stories began to be refracted through the ego and conceived on the level of fantasy rather than imagination.

For two centuries or more, as the consciousness of Western civilisation had continued to travel ever further from unity with nature, its central tendency had been to reinforce those 'masculine' physical and mental aspects of the human psyche which are identified with the ego, at the expense of the 'feminine' instincts of selfless feeling and intuitive understanding. All the emphasis of this advance had been on extending man's command over nature and to achieve an ever greater understanding of how it worked through the ordering function of the human mind. The most obvious prize this had yielded was to enable part of the human race (but by no means all) to enjoy a materially comfortable existence, catering for its every physical need. But part of the price paid for this one-sidedness had been to cut people off from those deeper 'feminine' instincts which can give them the sense of belonging to something larger and more significant than themselves – as could still be seen among those less 'developed' peoples of the world who continued to live physically taxing but dignified and uncomplaining lives much closer to nature.

A similar limitation could be seen in how people in the developed world looked for their understanding of how the world worked. For centuries Western civilisation had increasingly sought to rest such explanations on that analytical function of the human mind which could supposedly provide objective, 'scientific' answers to every question. This had created a hugely impressive assemblage of knowledge of the physical mechanisms whereby life and the universe operated. But it had become ever harder to hold all this knowledge together in a way which gave any sense of unified meaning. The more the human mind focused on the material details of existence, the more detached it became from those deeper levels of the psyche which alone can provide it with a real sense of meaning and purpose. Yet it is from precisely those deeper levels of the psyche that our archetypal urge to imagine stories originates, and it is only when human beings can make contact with them that they can reach proper maturity.

This had profound relevance to another significant development mirrored by storytelling in the closing decades of the twentieth century: the change which was now coming over the relationship between the sexes and the relationship of men and women to the internal balance of their own gender attributes. An inevitable corollary of the difficulty people in the West were now finding in achieving psychological maturity was the tendency for men to become softer and less overtly masculine, while the effect on women was the opposite.

The new assertiveness of women became particularly obvious from the late 1960s onwards, with the rise of the 'Women's Lib' movement. Like so many other features of twentieth-century life, this tendency had first begun to appear in the years before the First World War, with the campaign for women's suffrage; and before that in the writings of the early 'feminists', such as Mary Woolstonecraft, at the time of that psychic upheaval which had coincided with the French Revolution and the dawn of Romanticism. But much more aggressively than ever before, the new feminists of the 1960s and 1970s could see women only as oppressed victims, in a world dominated by men, treated as mentally and socially inferior, as little more than 'sex objects' and slaves. They indiscriminately projected onto the male sex the archetype of the 'dark masculine'; seeing men as wholly egocentric, either as bullying Tyrants or as insensitive, immature 'little boys', or both.

Even more than in its earlier manifestations, the new feminism was concerned not with promoting the importance of 'femininity' but the reverse. It despised the 'feminine' values of feeling and intuition. Its central drive was to show women as equal to men in masculine terms. Despite their contempt for men and for the 'values of Father', the feminists had become dominated by the *animus*: that masculine component in a woman's psyche which can give her the strength and rational intelligence which is necessary for psychological balance, but which, if it is allowed to override her femininity, renders her negative, hard and combative.[14]

In no sense was possession by the negative *animus* a new phenomenon. More than 2000 years earlier it had been portrayed by Aristophanes in his *Thesmophoriazusae*, showing the pack of Athenian women driven by their collective negative *animus* into wishing to kill Euripides for the dismissive way in which he presented women in his plays. It was memorably depicted by Shakespeare in *The Taming of the Shrew* and had been portrayed in many other stories down the ages, showing a virago having to be 'tamed' back into contact with her femininity. What that was new about its late-twentieth-century manifestation was the scale on which it was now becoming adopted by the ruling consciousness of the time. Never before had the idea of women behaving so egocentrically on behalf of their sex become so acceptable.

This new female assertiveness did produce one episode of considerable psychological irony. A particular grievance of the feminists was the extent to which men dominated the world of power and politics. Yet when, in 1979, Britain became the first major country to elect a woman as its prime minister, the feminists were appalled. In all respects but her gender, they saw Margaret Thatcher as representing everything they abhorred.

Mrs Thatcher's significance as a leader was that, at a time when male politicians had been losing their masculinity, she stood for masculine qualities in politics more effectively than any of the men around her (as we have seen from stories, when the hero is weak, it can often fall to the heroine to supply the masculine strength he lacks). With her strength of character and firmness of principle, her opposition to dependence on the 'Great Mother' of the state and her belief in individual self-reliance, she stood for the 'values of Father' more than any other

14. This was well illustrated by one of the books which helped to inspire the 'women's movement', Germaine Greer's *The Female Eunuch* (1970). The book laid all its emphasis on the ability of women to compete with men in terms of the 'masculine' functions of the psyche, while dismissing the 'feminine' functions as unimportant. Greer was eager to claim, for instance, that women could outperform men in 'cognitive abilities like counting, mathematical reasoning, spatial cognition, abstract reasoning, set-breaking and restructuring'. She followed this by listing women who had successfully competed with men in the business world, and like other feminists of the time she laid great emphasis on the 'clitoral orgasm', centred on the female equivalent of the male sex organ. But of the 'feminine values', Greer was witheringly scornful. Women who became nurses, for instance, were only fooled by men into 'feeling good because they are relieving pain' so that they could be overworked and underpaid (which left them 'tired, resentful and harried'). As for the intuitive function which is crucial to objective understanding, she dismissed this in typically 'pseudo-masculine' terms as no more than 'a faculty for observing tiny insignificant aspects of behaviour and forming an empirical conclusion which cannot be syllogistically examined'. Greer unconsciously revealed the roots of her own difficulty in relating positively to either the 'masculine' or 'feminine' components of her personality by describing how she was the child of a weak, self-centred father and a domineering mother. She was thus not provided by either of her parents with a mature gender model.

politician of her generation. This was reflected in the virulence with which her left-wing opponents saw her as 'heartless' and in her opposition to the Soviet Communists, who first nicknamed her 'the Iron Lady'. It was seen supremely in the masculine role she played in taking back the Falklands, the most successful military operation Britain had mounted since World War Two.

In 1981 Thatcher was joined in championing the 'values of Father' by President Ronald Reagan, who had first won fame in the 1940s and 1950s by playing 'masculine' roles in Hollywood films (he was thus the first major political figure in history to have founded his career on acting out characters in fictional stories). Their partnership through the 1980s was defined not least by their opposition to the 'evil empire' of Soviet Communism, now under such pressure from its internal contradictions that by the end of the decade it was disintegrating. Almost Mrs Thatcher's last act as a world leader was to supply the masculine resolve which persuaded Reagan's successor President Bush to deploy overwhelming military force against that archetypal 'monster-figure' and tyrant Saddam Hussein.

With her departure, Western politics settled back to their domination in the 1990s by 'mother's boys', the first generation of leaders whose coming to adulthood had been shaped by the values prevailing in the late 1960s and 1970s. Conspicuously lacking in any firm moral 'centre', these were exemplified by the vain, promiscuous President Clinton, and later by the *puer aeternus* figure of Tony Blair who, as much as any politician before him, relied on projecting a fantasy-image of himself which bore scant relation to reality.

The 'feminisation' of men and the 'masculinisation' of women had already become a central feature of that new ideological orthodoxy which was sweeping the Western world under the name of 'political correctness'. In psychological terms, this was a 'left-wing' phenomenon and one of the most remarkable developments of the twentieth century. The kind of self-righteous intolerance once associated with the more puritanical forms of religion and the more extreme forms of Socialism now reappeared to promote the 'rights' of women, homosexuals, racial minorities, the disabled and any group of people who could be portrayed as being 'below the line' and therefore discriminated against. Closely allied to this was the new social pressure for the power of 'Mother State' to be used to regulate to protect its citizens from any conceivable risk, however imaginary. The key to the nature of this new secular puritanism was the degree of self-righteous inflation it inspired in its adherents. Like their religious and political forerunners they presented a classic study in 'ego-Self confusion'. Unconsciously they were using the belief that they were acting in the name of selfless moral principle simply as a cloak for asserting their ego, and as a means to enjoy feelings of moral superiority. In the cause of 'toleration' and promoting collective 'rights', they had become possessed by a fanatical and humourless intolerance.[15]

15. In many ways the emergence of this collectivist new orthodoxy recalled Plato's description in Book VIII of *The Republic* of the final stages of his political cycle where, as 'democracy' becomes increasingly obsessed with the 'rights' of those below the line, it mutates into 'tyranny'. There were many signs of a new phase of 'tyranny' appearing in western societies at the end of the twentieth century, not least in the increasingly technocratic nature of government, manifested, for instance, in the rise of the European Union.

So deeply did political correctness permeate the ethos of the time that it inevitably found reflection in storytelling, in no respect more obviously than the urge to reverse what became known as the 'gender stereotyping' which had characterised stories since the dawn of civilisation. An early example, as we saw, was the science-fiction horror film *Alien* (1979), a classic Overcoming the Monster story in which the archetypally masculine role of the monster-slaying hero was deliberately given to a forceful heroine, representing the 'new woman'. Many other examples were to follow, not least in the role of monster-slayer played by the heroine in *The Terminator* (1984).

As became evident, however, to defy the unconscious pull of the archetypes is not easy. We saw, for instance, how in *The Silence Of The Lambs* (1991), the attempt to give the archetypal hero-role to a 'new woman' was subtly undermined when the power of the repulsively dark but devilishly charming and clever male villain eventually proved too much for her. She ended up being outwitted and allowing him to escape. *Basic Instinct* (1991) carried the sexual inversion to its ultimate, by featuring a wholly dark heroine, possessed by her negative *animus*, who succeeds in mastering and making a fool of the inadequate hero. But even here, so remorselessly did the film attempt to turn the archetypes upside down, that its makers could not quite bring themselves to press their inverted logic to its full conclusion, leaving the ending tellingly ambiguous.

Equally revealing of the underlying power of the archetypes was the way some of the more popular films of this period managed to challenge the new orthodoxy of the times head on. *Crocodile Dundee* (1986) and *The Thomas Crown Affair* (1968, new version 1999), for instance, each featured a heroine who was a model of the new, assertive 'post-feminist' career woman. But in each story the hero manages to display such a masterful combination of 'masculine' strength of character with 'feminine' emotional intelligence that this eventually proves enough to free the heroine from the stifling grip of her *animus*. Her suppressed femininity is brought to life, and hero and heroine are united in an archetypal happy ending.

Another aspect of how storytelling reflected the psychological twilight of the time was the extraordinary popularity in the second half of the twentieth century of the 'soap opera', simple, untaxing dramas regularly broadcast on radio or television portraying the everyday lives of a community of 'ordinary' people. From the 1960s onwards, no form of television entertainment attracted a larger or more devoted following, from *I Love Lucy* through *Dallas* to *Friends*, from *Coronation Street* and *Eastenders* to *Neighbours*.

The most obvious feature of the soap opera was the way it used the power of stories like a mental drug, addicting its audiences and keeping them hooked by playing sentimentally on their emotions. Soap operas exploited all the basic archetypal material of storytelling by reducing it to a mechanical formula, designed to set up a continual stream of teasing or heart-tugging suspense. Boy meets girl. Boy betrays girl. Can they make it up? Man intent on behaving badly seeks to deceive. Man is caught out in his deception. Will he get away with it? Not only is every situation in a soap opera stereotyped, so is the language in which it is couched. No character ever speaks except in clichés. In real life 'ordinary' people often use unexpected or quirky turns of phrase. In a soap opera they never say anything which has not been said a million times before. But in plot terms the most significant characteristic of soap operas is that their stories never truly resolve. The aim of the industrial process which creates them is to produce an unending succession of emotional cliff-hangers, to keep the audience switching on to see what happens next – whereas the archetypal purpose of any proper story is that it must eventually work up to a full-scale climax, followed by a conclusion which resolves everything that has gone before.[16]

Related to the soap opera, although less mechanical in its construction, was its more obviously episodic counterpart, the situation comedy, usually centred on the life of a particular family or a small group of people who had for some reason been brought intimately together. A study carried out in the late 1980s of the 25 most popular situation comedies on American television which centred on the life of a family found that in 24 of them the most intelligent and sensible member of the family was the mother, followed by her children, The stupidest family member, most prone to act foolishly, was the father.

At the end of the century this was echoed in the most popular cartoon sitcom ever produced by American television, *The Simpsons*, where the self-deluding schemes of the father, Homer, made him the perpetual fall-guy. He was followed in stupidity by his son Bart, whose bright younger sister Lisa was so much more on the ball (as even, on occasion, was his dummy-sucking baby sister Maggie). The long-suffering mother of the family, Marge, was invariably shown as most sensible of all. But it would be a mistake to see these characterisations as simply reflecting post-feminist political correctness. In archetypal terms, *The Simpsons* could scarcely have been more traditional. The role of the obsessively self-deceiving father, as a representation of the deluded ruling consciousness, has been basic to Comedy back to the time of Aristophanes, The son, Bart, represented a lesser version of the blindness of ego-centred masculinity. The female members of the family represented that wider 'feminine' vision which we invariably see in stories emanating from 'below the line', centred particularly (as in, say, *A Winter's Tale* or *The Marriage of Figaro*) on the bright Daughter/Princess and the put-upon but emotionally wise Mother/Queen.[17]

In this respect *The Simpsons* took its place in the mainstream of a tradition of storytelling which could be traced back through more than two and a half thou-

---

16. A rare exception was the massacre by which the scriptwriters eventually ended *Dallas*. The origins of using the appeal of stories to keep an audience spellbound in this way went back to the nineteenth century, when magazines serialised novels by authors such as Dickens or Hardy in regular instalments, each ending on some highpoint of emotional suspense to ensure that readers would buy the next issue. Certain authors developed this technique for getting their readers hooked by producing a whole sequence of novels centred around the same group of characters. In this sense Trollope's Palliser novels constituted high-grade 'soap opera', as later did Galsworthy's novels about the Forsyte family and Anthony Powell's *Dance to the Music of Time*.

17. In 2004 a poll carried out among young people by the Anglican Mothers' Union found that Marge Simpson scored more highly than anyone else, real or fictional, as 'the best mother in public life'. As an ideal role model, she was admired for her 'down-to-earth approach', for the way she held her family together and for her advice to her children such as 'listen to your heart, not the voices in your head' (*The Times*, 17 March 2004).

sand years. But the very fact that probably not one of the countless millions of people watching the series were aware of this (any more, one suspects, than were its authors) was in itself a measure of just how unconscious is the process whereby human beings are carried along by a story. We can follow hundreds of different versions of the same archetypal plot, each reflecting something profoundly significant about how our own psyche works. Yet so beguiled are we by the magic of storytelling that we do not even notice that fundamentally they are all telling us the same story.

If the evolution of human consciousness is really concerned with developing a clearer understanding of how we and the world work, perhaps the time has come when we should begin to appreciate what this astonishing faculty we each possess is really about: this mystery so close beneath our noses that we do not even recognise it to be a mystery at all.

### The story of mankind

The fact that, as the year 2000 began, almost the entire human race celebrated the start of a new millennium, was itself a tribute to the power of a story. Even though Christianity was still, statistically, the world's leading religion, it had retreated a long way from the overwhelming dominance it once exercised over the individual and collective life of the inhabitants of a mainly European 'Christendom'. For most people in the Europe of the early twenty-first century, the nearest they still came to observing Christian rituals was the continuing, largely secularised role played by the celebration of Christmas (although this too reflected the archetypal hold over the human imagination of a story). As Lao Tsu had put it, when 'rectitude' was lost, all that was left were those outward 'rites' which mark 'the wearing thin of loyalty and good faith and the beginning of disorder'.

Quite apart from religion itself, however, all across the world the traditional frameworks of belief and symbolism designed to integrate human beings with the idea of the Self had long been in retreat against the advancing forces of secularism, the primary psychological effect of which was to promote the power and influence of the ego. Yet at the same time, the very fact that even those parts of the world which had never been predominantly Christian joined in marking the onset of the new millennium reflected the extraordinary speed with which in recent years the human world had seemed to shrink. What had brought it together as never before were the innovations in technology. Not only had the increased speed and ease of physical travel now made it possible for people to move around the globe in unprecedented numbers. Even more dramatic was the way in which satellite communications, global television coverage and the Internet had transformed it into what Marshall McLuhan called 'the electronic village'. Much more obviously than ever before, the entire human race was now involved in the same common story.

As the twenty-first century began, three particular ways could be singled out in which the urge to see life in terms of stories might help to shed light on the state in which mankind now found itself.

The first was that, thanks again to technology, stories were now more freely accessible than ever before in history. One of the more prominent forms this took, although not normally recognised as such, was the unprecedented ubiquity of 'news'. Never had people been bombarded with such a plethora of 'stories', reflecting the daily drama of human life as it unfolded in all parts of the globe. But obviously only the tiniest fraction of what was actually going on in the world was deemed worthy to be considered as 'news'. It was noticeable how much of what was considered appropriate for this treatment – political dramas, tragic accidents, the committing of crimes, the doings and misdoings of celebrities – was now presented through the new intimacy made possible by the modern media as if it were a kind of continuous soap opera. And the values which lay behind this were much the same as those which determined the contents of fictional soap operas. What made 'news' were not the routine events of life but anything unusual which disturbed the order of the human world; anything which conjured up images of conflict, dissension, violence or abnormality, as was reflected in those familiar trigger words done to death in newspaper headlines such as 'crisis', 'storm', 'row', 'rift', 'shock', 'horror', 'crackdown', 'blitz', 'bombshell'. Just as in a soap opera, there would always be room for episodes which played sentimentally on the public's emotions: a man and woman in love; the birth of a baby; an act of heroism. But essentially the purpose of 'news' was to appeal to the fantasy-level of the mind, in much the same way as a fictional story might do, by setting off a stream of titillatory mental sensations. And, just as in their fictional counterpart, this was most effectively achieved by conjuring up almost any image which represented some assertion of the ego which violated the totality of the Self.

Inevitably many of the fictional stories of the time reflected the same values, and with them all the ego-based obsessions, confusions and immaturities of the contemporary world. But what might have been thought remarkable was the degree to which, despite all the shattering changes which had taken place in how people now led their outward lives, the underlying patterns of the tales which held their attention were much the same as those which had held their ancestors spellbound for thousands of years.

Nothing might have seemed more peculiarly modern, for instance, than the 'interactive' games millions were now able to play on their computer screens. Yet the form many of these took was only too familiar. The player would identify with a 'hero' (or a super-feminist heroine, such as Lara Croft), through whom he or she would then have to overcome dragons and super-villains, venture on complex quests or thread the way through some treacherous labyrinth, in order to reach the ultimate goal of the game – which might well be the need to free a Princess (or mankind) from the clutches of a Monster.

In the years around the turn of the new millennium a series of stories which had begun being scribbled out by a single mother living on income support struck such a chord with millions of readers and cinemagoers across the world that, within less than a decade, they had made their authoress J. K. Rowling one of the richest women in Britain. Yet with their combination of wizards and magic, trolls, overcoming monsters, quests, light triumphing over darkness and a seemingly ordinary little hero turning out to be extraordinary, the essential symbolism of the Harry Potter stories was again entirely familiar.

Most remarkable of all was the impact between 2001 and 2003 of the three-part film version of *The Lord of the Rings*, a phenomenon which had no real parallel in the history of the cinema.

The circumstances in which this film came about were themselves unprecedented. A story originally created by an Oxford professor of literature was taken on half a century later by a young film director, Peter Jackson, living in New Zealand at the other end of the world, and turned into a project involving literally thousands of artists, craftsmen and technicians from different nations. The task of welding all their skills together to produce such a monumental work of the human imagination was not unreminiscent of the teamwork which had gone into building a great mediaeval cathedral.

The *Lord of the Rings* trilogy could not have been created without the tricks of the latest computer technology, from its breathtaking battle scenes featuring thousands of participants to the haunting visualisation of the deformed little creature Gollum. Yet, even more than in the Harry Potter films, the actual contents of the story could not have been more timelessly archetypal.

For those who fell under the spell of *The Lord of the Rings* (and of course there were those who did not), Jackson's film version only reinforced the sense that this story, with all the epic grandeur of its theme set in a vast mythic landscape, was cast on a scale which somehow set it apart from any other. But the real reason for the power of its appeal was that it drew so deeply on the wellsprings of all that storytelling has been about ever since stories were first told.

As we saw in Chapter 19, *The Lord of the Rings* is one of those rare stories big enough to incorporate all the seven basic plots of storytelling at once. It presents the central battle between darkness and light in the most cosmic way imaginable. Frodo's quest is a symbolic struggle to get rid of the beguiling power of the ego. At the heart of the story we see a perfect golden ring, seemingly so small, so attractive, so harmless. Yet through it can be summoned up all the immense, shadowy power of Sauron, the ultimate representative of all that is evil in the world: the bringer of darkness, destruction and death. We see Sauron only as one enormous, burning eye, at the top of his proud tower, symbolising the single-eyed tunnel-vision of the human ego. Under his sway, vast regimented legions of deformed human monsters can be launched against the frail forces of decent, honourable, loving humanity, destroying the ordered peace of their homes and communities, putting innocents to the sword, just as the world has seen so often through history, and never more than in the twentieth century.

In the earlier stages of his journey, Frodo has loyal companions and the guidance of the Wise Old Man Gandalf and the Anima Galadriel, between them representing that power of spiritual human maturity which must inspire him on his way. In its closing stages, accompanied only by the faithful Sam, but now dogged also by Gollum, representing the obsessive inner state of someone who has fallen irreparably into the grip of the ego, Frodo personifies all the loneliness of humanity's struggle to be free of egocentricity. Yet it is the very fact that he and Sam are so selfless in serving their cosmic, ego-transcending cause which enables them in the end to reach their goal.

The nearer Frodo gets to the end of his Quest, the more his story is paralleled by the equally timeless story of a man who, after long exile from his home, is at last ready to claim his kingdom. Like Odysseus, Aragorn is returning from long wanderings through the world, to seize back his kingdom from the impostors who have usurped it. Only when he has proved himself ready and worthy will he emerge in all his kingly majesty, to be brought together with the feminine 'other half' who will make him whole. Aragorn's story is that of every man who, after years when he has been lost because the inner kingdom of his soul has been under inadequate rule, is finally ready, in *The Return of the King*, to reach that state of maturity which means that he knows who he is.

In this final episode the two dramas coincide. Only when Frodo has succeeded in the inner drama of destroying the ego, is the darkness which has cast its shadow over the world finally dispelled. In all directions, light and life return. On the outward stage Aragorn can now succeed to his kingdom, marry his Princess and become at one with himself and the world. And again we see it symbolised, as in so many other stories before, how each victory by one individual over the power of darkness can somehow take on a cosmic significance. As an old Vietnamese put it to a *Guardian* journalist, when his country was being torn apart by the unimaginable hell of war in the late 1960s:

'Humanity is one. Each of us is responsible for his personal actions and his actions towards the rest of humanity. All we can do is hold back our own brand from the fire. Pull it back, do not add to the flame.'

As crowds emerged from watching *The Lord of the Rings* in the first years of the twenty-first century, they might have felt just as mysteriously elevated by the immense drama they had just witnessed as their predecessors emerging from a theatre in sixteenth century London or Athens of the fifth century BC, or an audience hearing of the battle between Gilgamesh and Humbaba in some city of ancient Mesopotamia; even though, outwardly, the world they emerged into seemed so unrecognisably different. But what they would then also have found was that this world was itself now acting out its own version of the cosmic drama they had just been following; except that it was by no means so clear where the powers of darkness and light lay.

When on 11 September 2001 images flashed round the globe of the airliners crashing into the towers of New York's World Trade Center, the single most shocking event since the Kennedy assassination, mankind was drawn into a conflict which could only be properly understood by recognising the extent to which all the different players were projecting onto it their own versions of precisely those same archetypes which shape storytelling.

From the point of view of George W. Bush, he was involved in a battle with the supreme embodiment of evil: that many-headed monster of global terrorism which initially centred on the invisible figure of Osama bin Laden, lurking like the bearded Saruman in his cave. But it then appeared that bin Laden, like Saruman, was only a front for an even more deadly figure of evil. Now Sauron himself could be seen casting his threatening shadow over the world, from the centre of his dark empire in Baghdad.

For Bush and his allies, a good part of the power of the archetypal narrative now calling them to action was the memory of how his father had failed to press his earlier bid to overcome Saddam Hussein to its proper archetypal conclusion. In 1991, after the heroes had set out, like Gilgamesh and Enkidu, to travel half across the world to slay the monster, they had at the last minute stayed their hand, leaving the monster untouched. Now Bush the son set out to complete his father's story. When in 2003 his forces had won their brilliant military victory, and Saddam was finally pulled like a shrivelled monster from his hole in the ground, it might have seemed the tale was finally over.

But already it was apparent that the plot was not quite so simple. This was to become even more obvious when it emerged just how far Bush and his faithful companion Tony Blair had, in projecting onto Saddam rather more power to threaten the world than reality justified, been emulating Don Quixote and Sancho Panza, launching a ferocious assault on giants and discovering them to be only windmills.

From another point of view, of course, it was not Saddam who was the monster of the story at all. For many this archetype was now projected on America and Bush himself, representing that ruling consciousness which, from 'above the line', cannot see the truth of what is going on in the shadows cast by its egocentric power. The United States was now the one undisputed global superpower, in a way the world had never seen before. But 'below the line', in the world of Islam, in Europe, in the awakening giant of China, all sorts of forces were beginning to constellate in resentment at their perception of how one-sided America's domination had become.

Nowhere, however, was the balance of power more intractably one-sided than in that country allied to America which had only come into being because of a story: Israel. In the first half of the twentieth century, the Jews of Europe had become the supreme example of 'below the line' victims, first persecuted and driven into exile by the Russian empire, then falling prey to the genocidal madness which possessed Hitler's Nazis, the darkest tyranny of the age. But in the second half of the century, the aftermath of this astonishing tragedy was to be an uncanny re-enactment of that story recounted through much of the Old Testament when, following the arrival of 'the children of Israel' in their 'promised land', they had found it inhabited by all those people for whom it was already their home. In ancient times this had led to all those centuries of violence which were only to end when, first, the Jewish people were taken into captivity in Babylon, and then, after their return, saw their homeland taken over by the Roman empire, which in 70 AD sent them again into an exile which was to last for nearly two thousand years.

After 1948 when, with the aid of terrorism, those European Jews who had been returning to Palestine since the 1890s set up their new state of Israel in the land which for centuries had been home to the Palestinian Arabs, they provided yet another example of what can happen when people once 'below the line' then manage to rise 'above the line' to a position of dominance. The new state displayed

towards the dispossessed Palestinians all the archetypal characteristics of a tyrannical ruling power. It was now the turn of the Arabs to be cast in the role of
victims, as Israel created a society just as firmly divided into two groups, above
and below the line, as that of South Africa during the years of apartheid. Inevitably
such one-sidedness threw a shadow across the Middle East which lay at the heart
of much of the tension and instability which was to plague that region through the
next half century, leading to five successive wars – and which perpetually threatened one day to explode into a catastrophe which could draw in much of the rest
of the world.[18]

All this leads on to a third way in which the understanding of stories can help
to shed light on the state of mankind at the start of the twenty-first century. If
we are to look on the entire history of the human race as itself a colossal story,
what is the archetypal pattern which is shaping that story? How is the story likely
to end?

The starting point must be that *Homo sapiens* is the one form of life on
earth which has stepped outside the instinctive frame of nature to develop ego-
consciousness. It is this which, to an ever greater degree, has enabled it to enjoy
such success in bending the powers of nature to its own advantage. But with every
advance in consciousness it has lost more of its innocence and cast an ever longer
shadow. There is always some price to be paid. Each time consciousness has
expanded, so in another sense it has become more limited. And eventually its
ingenuity has created the potential to destroy all life on earth, including itself.
Although mankind has no obvious external rival, apart from the power of those
humblest of organisms, viruses and bacteria, its greatest potential enemy is its
own divided nature.

Looked at from another perspective, this breaking out of from a state of nature
has been like an ever-greater act of rebellion against the unity of nature. And if
we see characters behaving like this in a story, we know that such hubris will in
the end contrive to bring about its own nemesis, so that cosmic balance can be
restored. Which brings us back to the story of Loki, the original stealer of the ring
which inspired Tolkien's story: the ring of ego-consciousness which gives great
power but carries with it the fatal curse which, in Wagner's version, eventually
brings about the twilight of the gods and the ending of the world.

In the original Norse version, the story does not end like this. Loki eventually
calls into being those three monsters which are to play their part in the ending of

18. The heart of the Israeli/Palestinian problem lay in that ego-Self confusion which led the Jews so
rigidly to identify their collective identity with race and religion. Although Israel was set up as a
'democracy', it thus could not develop into a liberal society based on that principle of assimilation
which would allow its two main racial groups gradually to come together (as in other societies
across the world where different races and cultures had eventually achieved a *modus vivendi*). The
exclusion of the Arabs inevitably set up a classic confrontation between irreconcilable 'opposites',
each of which, according to the archetypal pattern, was driven to become ever more extreme: the
Israelis in their relentless assertion of dominance and expansion into the Palestinian lands
surrounding the original territory of Israel, the Palestinians in their increasingly desperate and
suicidal opposition to the ruling power. This in turn polarised the outside world into two camps,
supporting each side, creating an impasse which, according to the archetype, offered no hope of
resolution other than some eventual catastrophe. .

the world, just as our own ego-consciousness has called into being those 'weapons of mass destruction' – biological, chemical and nuclear – which could bring about the destruction of our own world. But on the far side of the eternal winter and holocaust of fire which marks the final catastrophe, comes Odin's vision of some strange and wonderful rebirth.

The truth is that we can dream dreams, we can paint word-pictures, we can imagine stories – but they cannot tell us for certain how the story of mankind will end, let alone what form such a 'rebirth' might take. As Robert Frost had it:

> 'Some say the world will end in fire,
> Some say in ice.
> From what I've tasted of desire,
> I hold with those who favour fire.
> But if it had to perish twice,
> I think I know enough of hate,
> To say that, for destruction, ice
> Is also great
> And would suffice.'

What stories can tell us, however, much more profoundly than we have realised, is how our human nature works, and why we think and behave in this world as we do. That is why I believe that to arrive at a proper understanding of why our species has the compulsion to imagine stories is as important a riddle as there is left for mankind to solve on this earth.

Even if it cannot save us from ourselves, it may help us to understand why Dante ended his great poem on that most extraordinary thought of all: his vision that, even when life is ended, we can still be absorbed back into that unimaginable power which ultimately holds all the universe together and which continues for ever: 'the love that moves the sun and the other stars'.

# The Light and the Shadows
# on the Wall

'First people deny a thing; then they belittle it; then they say it was known all along.'                                                    Alexander von Humboldt

One of the most profound stories in the world is really no more than an elaborate image: Plato's Parable of the Cave.[1] He conjures up the picture of a row of men, imprisoned in a cave, their gaze forcibly fixed in only one direction. Here on the wall in front of them they see a constant play of shadows as figures and objects pass in front of a fire behind them; and, since this is all they ever see, they take it for the reality of the world in which they live.

One of them then finds himself free to look around and move from his place. He dimly sees above and behind them what appears to be a purer, stronger light than that of the flickering fire. He makes the rough and steep ascent up to its source, to discover that it is coming from the mouth of the cave. He steps out into the daylight, where he sees the sun. At first its light is so bright that he is blinded. But as he gradually becomes accustomed to it, he can for the first time gaze on the real world outside the cave and all that is in it.

Dazzled by what he has seen, he makes his way back down into the darkness to where his old companions are still transfixed, like a modern television audience, by the play of shadows on the wall. He tries to explain to them the wonder of what he has witnessed, but there is no way they can understand what he is talking about. The dancing shadows on the wall are the only reality they know. They laugh at him, imagine he is making up his story about what he has seen, and call him mad. He, on the other hand, can now see the shapes on the wall clearly for what they are, as no more than shadows and illusions. He can longer share his companions' commendation of each other for all their clever observations about the shadows, and what they represent, because he has glimpsed 'reality'.

The archetypal essence of this story is much the same as that symbolised in the Cheyenne story of *Jumping Mouse*. When Jumping Mouse returns to the dark forest and tries to tell his fellow mice about his journey to the great river, and how he had caught a far-off glimpse of the 'Sacred Mountain', they cannot understand what he is talking about and scorn him.

The forest-dwelling mice, like Plato's cave-dwellers, represent collective ego-consciousness. They are naturally sure the world they see around them is real,

---

1. *The Republic*, Book VII.

because it is all their limited state of consciousness allows them to see. The hero of each of these stories has found that the walls of his consciousness have suddenly fallen away, allowing him to glimpse something immeasurably more real. But having been through such an inspiring experience, there is no way he can communicate it to his companions, because their vision is still bound by the limitations of the ego. As the Argentine novelist Jorge Luis Borges once put it, for a believer to try to communicate to an atheist what is meant by 'God' is like trying to explain to a blind man what is meant by the colour yellow.

One day, I believe, it will eventually be seen that for a long time one of the most remarkable failures of our scientific approach to understanding the world was not to perceive that our urge to imagine stories is something just as much governed by laws which lay it open to scientific investigation as the structures of the atom or the genome.

The paradox, as is mirrored by Plato's Parable, is that it is the very nature of our limited ego-consciousness which stands in the way of our seeing how much stories can teach us about the limitations on our consciousness.

That is why among those who will unconsciously experience the greatest resistance to the approach put forward by this book are those critics and specialists in 'literature' who are already sure that they know what stories are about. Many of the interpretations of individual stories in these pages will contradict views they have already formed and would find it hard to abandon.

But in the end, however inadequately I may have argued the case, the general approach to stories set out in this book will come to be widely accepted, simply because it opens up our understanding of why we tell stories in a way which makes it scientifically comprehensible. However many examples the hypothesis is tested against, the laws hold. These are the shapes around which our mind creates stories. This is why we respond to them in the way we do.

Obviously a crucial moment in the narrative we have been following is the change which has come over storytelling in the past 200 years. It is the very fact that so many stories have 'lost the plot' in this way, reflecting such a fundamental psychic shift in our culture, which has made it possible to see much more clearly just what is the purpose of the archetypal patterns underlying stories when they are functioning properly. In Dr Salk's words, 'it is where life's normal structures are disturbed that we come to know the essential laws of the species'.

There is nothing with which stories are more intimately concerned, as we have seen, than the conflict between 'dark' and 'light'. Yet, in the words quoted earlier from Laurence Whistler, 'the light needs the dark to become articulate'. The very reason why we see the world in terms of this contrast stems from the fact that our consciousness has become separated from its instinctive unity with nature. And certainly in some respects, the further we move away from that unity, as the history of the past two centuries shows, the more confused and lost we become. But the more we experience the darkness and spiritual void this leads to, the easier in some ways it becomes to recognise what it is we have become exiled from. As we explore the shallowness and limitations of the world into which we are unconsciously led by the darkness of the human ego, the more consciously we can appreciate the 'light', in ways which would never have been possible had we not been separated from it.

Dante needed to travel down to the very lowest point of hell before he could begin the climb up to Paradise. Odysseus needed to go through the hell and darkness of his twelve ordeals before he was ready to reclaim his 'other half' and his kingdom. Christ needed to die in his 'ego self' before he could be resurrected in the Self that is eternal. In our own time, those Soviet 'dissidents' needed to endure the Communist tyranny of lies at its worst, before they could become inwardly strong enough to recognise the truth.

Whatever the power that created the universe, what more extraordinary act of the imagination could there be than that it should create a tiny part of that material universe which took on its own separate existence, in a way which enabled it to reproduce itself, creating life? And then that this strange new entity should gradually differentiate out of itself, becoming more and more complex, until it required two different individual organisms of the same species to join together to produce a third – which would then have to unite with a fourth for the process to be repeated. And then that part of this entity, life, should eventually become so unimaginably more complex that it developed a unique new form of consciousness, enabling it not only to step outside its unconscious obedience to instinct but to use it to speculate as to where it had come from and why it had been created.

Many of these new individual organisms might conclude that their only function in existing was to live separately from that totality of life from which they had emerged, and to enjoy the pleasures of gratifying their instincts until the time came for them to be extinguished. Eat, drink and be merry, for tomorrow we die. Others, however, might look on the world and the universe into which they had been born with a sense of holy awe, as the miraculous totality of which their own individual consciousness was just a fleeting, miniscule expression.

The cosmic mind which had originally set all this in motion had at last created an organism which could, however dimly, share a tiny bit of its own consciousness; which could become aware of its own transcendent existence; which could sense that behind all creation and all the universe was one unifying power which bound it all together, as one substance, one structure, one all-connecting impulse and one spirit which, because it transcended matter, was eternal: that four-in-one quaternity which the human mind was to translate into the terms of its own understanding as body, mind, heart and soul. And one way in which it would do this was by imagining it in terms of stories.

In the end we are all of us in a sense experts on stories, because nothing is closer to us than to see the world in the form of stories. Not only are our heads full of stories all the time; we are each of us acting out our own story throughout our lives. Outwardly male or female, we are each of us, like David Copperfield, cast as the hero of the story of our own life – just as we are equally its heroine. And the aim of our life, as we see from stories, is that those two should become one, to 'live happily ever after'.

Wherever possible, I have tried in this book to supply the original thought behind all the terms we use when we are talking about stories: hubris, nemesis, denouement, catastrophe. The only words for which no dictionary seems to provide the original root idea are in a way the most important of all: those words 'hero' and 'heroine' themselves. But, after many years working on this book, I am convinced that, lost in the mists of history, they must be closely related in some way to our word 'heir'. In other words, the hero or the heroine is he or she who is born to inherit; who is worthy to succeed; who must grow up as fit to take on the torch of life from those who went before.

Such is the essence of the task laid on each of us as we come into this world. That is what stories are trying to tell us.

# Author's Personal Note

When in the autumn of 1969 it was first decided that I should write this book, I had little idea that 34 years would elapse before it was finished. To spend half a lifetime writing a single book is obviously ridiculous, and my first debt is to all those people during the decades between who, when told that I was working on a book on 'the basic plots of storytelling', greeted the idea that anyone should attempt such a project with such enthusiasm. Their warm response gave me more encouragement than they can have known; even though, as the years went by, not a few began to express a suspicion that, like Dr Casaubon's 'key to all mythologies', my efforts would never see the light of day.

The idea for the book originated when I was working on a book called *The Neophiliacs*, analysing the changes which had taken place in English life in the 1950s and 1960s. By the time this was published in October 1969 I had already seen enough of the unconscious patterns underlying the way in which we imagine stories to wish to explore them more systematically. At dinner with my then-agent Diana Crawfurd, in a long-vanished restaurant off Buckingham Gate, we agreed that I should follow that impulse; and I set to work, knowing that my first task would be to read through a wide variety of stories, to see how the idea might develop.

The following year I gave a talk on *Hamlet* and the underlying pattern of Tragedy at my old school, Shrewsbury, and parts of that lecture have been incorporated into Chapter 30 as the oldest surviving chunk of the book's final text. Within 18 months, having filled a pile of notebooks with synopses, I had completed a first draft outline of 'the seven basic plots', already recognising two general principles on which it would be advisable to choose examples to illustrate the theme.

Firstly, to convey the 'universality' of these recurring patterns behind storytelling it would be necessary to include as wide a range of story-types as possible, from myths and folk tales, through the plays and novels of 'great literature', to the Hollywood films, thrillers and science fiction of the present day. But, secondly, to prevent the argument becoming clogged with endless obscure plot-summaries, it would be desirable wherever possible to use stories which were already familiar to the greatest number of potential readers. This would means keeping in general within the Western cultural tradition of storytelling, only mentioning instances outside it where this was necessary to underline the ubiquity of a particular theme.

One enormous debt I owed at this early stage was to the Penguin Classics series, launched in 1944 by E. V. Rieu whose translation of the *Odyssey* was a particular inspiration for this book, and co-edited at this time by Betty Radice (who, as it happened, had written me a very generous letter about *The Neophiliacs*). More than 300 of these volumes have lined the shelves around my desk throughout the writing of this book, ranging all through the ages from *The Epic of Gilgamesh* to the novels and plays of the nineteenth century. Without the easy access to world literature they made possible, it would have been infinitely harder to carry out the basic groundwork for this project (just as, decades later, it would have been difficult to track down detailed summaries of many films without the blessings of the Internet).

It soon became clear that my first draft was only an inadequate overture. Through the 1970s I was having to get more closely to grips with how far the symbolism of storytelling derived from archetypal structures within the human unconscious, and here I benefited hugely from reading through the works of Jung; although I could already see that a proper understanding of stories might make it possible to develop his intuitive approach to the workings of the psyche into something rather more systematically structured than the form in which he had left it. By the end of that decade I was well into a second draft, enough to begin discussing the book with potential publishers, one of whom, Richard Cohen, was to remain tirelessly encouraging for several years.

Only when this draft itself became bogged down in chaotic detail did I finally start again on what was to be the third and final draft. Athough this emerged with painful slowness, by the end of the 1980s I had completed the introductory chapters on the 'seven basic plots' (constituting most of Part One of the final version), foolishly thinking that I had almost finished the book. One particular benefit of these years was the opportunity to study in detail just how my two young sons took to being told stories, watching out for what it is, particularly in early years, which first draws us all into the world of storytelling, and what are the patterns a child is unconsciously looking for. But at the end of this second decade, I had no idea how much work was still to come.

By the mid-1990s what was originally a single concluding chapter had developed into the whole of Part Two, deciphering the basic symbolic language from which stories are constructed; and I was now aware that a further huge section of the book would be required to deal with the immense change which has come over storytelling in the past 200 years. Fortunately it was at this time that, again with profound gratitude, I could at last transfer the book onto a computer screen. Until now, to allow for endless modification of the text, every page had had to be typed not once but in many cases scores of times. Now, like many authors, I was liberated by the electronic revolution in a way which made one wonder how we all managed to write books before.

By the end of the 1990s I could at last begin to see how the book should develop towards its conclusion with Part Four. I was now halfway into Part Three, dealing with the changes in storytelling in the past two centuries, when I ran into a mental block in having to cope with writing about Proust (whose *Remembrance of Times Past* was at the time being hailed on all sides as 'the greatest novel of the twentieth century'). Once surmounted, this proved to be the final logjam. The remainder of Part Three emerged with gratifying speed, including the exhilaration of writing the chapter on Oedipus and *Hamlet*, which incorporated material first drafted for that school lecture 30 years earlier.

By now, as I approached the final chapters, relating our capacity to imagine stories to the 'real world', I was relieved to realise that it would really have been difficult to complete a book dealing so intimately with the patterns of human psychology at any earlier stage in my life. For years I had been frustrated by how long it all seemed to take (another author might have got there much sooner). But I had needed those years of experience of the world to puzzle out some of the deeper riddles presented by storytelling, in a way which earlier would not have been possible. By the time I came to its concluding chapters this project had taken half my time on earth, which might to anyone seem excessive. But at least, with all its imperfections, the project was now complete.

Inevitably through all those years countless people have made comments or suggestions which, often without their knowing it, have proved invaluable in helping to shape a thought or to provide an example or quotation which appears in the final text. I cannot do justice to them all, but in particular I would like to thank the following:

Richard Ingrams (for drawing my attention to the quotation from Boswell's life of Dr Johnson which stands at the beginning of the book); Sara Meyer (for giving me *The Golden Ass*); Tony and Jill Jay; Barry Fantoni; Andrew Osmond; Christine Stone (for widening my horizons); Bennie Gray; Mary Booker; Arianna Stassinopoulos; Professor Robert Donington; Dr Anthony Stevens; Christopher Hogwood (for drawing my attention to the shortcomings of *Amadeus*); Robert McCrum; Richard Cohen; Anne Baring; Hella Adler; my sons Nicholas and Alexander Booker (for all they taught me without realising it); Robert Temple; Esther Eidinow (for her paper on the origins of hubris); Sir Laurens van der Post; Patricia Ashby; Sir Laurence Whistler; Charlie Paton (for giving me *The Voices of Marrakesh*); Ian Hislop; Richard North (not least for *The Terminator*); Helen Szamuely; Anna Duda; Ed Howker (who was first to read the final draft); John Gibbons; and finally my patient, if battered, publisher Robin Baird-Smith.

Among too many other duties neglected during the years of my preoccupation with the book were those I owed to my godchildren. Very belatedly I now offer it to them as containing something of what I should have passed on to them in other ways: Tom Winnifrith, Sam Eidinow, Toby Baring, Sam Holden, David Jay, Honor Baldry, Eleanor Percival, Storm Boyle and Tom Bishop.

My final debt is to Valerie, for allowing me to sit for years in the peace of my study, happily lost in a struggle I still cannot quite believe is over.

Litton, 6 March 2004

# Glossary of Terms

Inevitably, in attempting to open up such a wide and complex field to scientific study, this book uses a good many 'technical terms'. This is a brief guide to the more significant of those referred to in the text. Some are adapted from Jungian psychology, others are new.

*Archetypes*: Jung's term to identify the structures programmed into the unconscious levels of our psyche, related to our core instincts, and which shape much of our response to the world.

    The main archetypal complexes centre round the key roles played by human beings in the 'archetypal family drama' (see below) – Father, Mother, Son/Hero, Daughter/Heroine and Child. Stories are centred round these archetypes, along with those representing the ego and 'the Self' (see below).

    The patterns shaping stories, as this book shows, are themselves archetypal.

*Archetypal Family Drama*: term used in this book to describe the process, central to story-telling and to human life, whereby each generation grows up to succeed to that which came before. Each person begins life as a child, created by the pairing off of a father and mother. A central preoccupation of stories is the process whereby their hero or heroine learns to pair off with their right 'other half', thus continuing the chain of life.

*The ego/Self split*: the key to why evolution has given human beings the capacity to imagine stories. This stems from the division in our psyche, unique in the animal kingdom, between the ego and 'the Self' – and the need to reconnect the two.

*Ego*: the centre of our consciousness, that part of our psyche through which we perceive the world and our own part in it. Due to the 'ego/Self split', human beings, unlike other animals, can think and act egocentrically.

*Self*: term used by Jung and others to identify that deeper centre of the human personality which connects us with our selfless core instincts. It is the Self which links us with the totality of life outside the demands of the ego. The underlying purpose of our ability to imagine stories is to show how the two can be re-integrated.

*Dark and Light*: the means whereby stories distinguish whether a character is centred on the ego or the Self.

    'Dark figures' in stories (exemplified most obviously in the 'monster') are egocentric, heartless and in some way blind to the reality of the world around them. This symbolises the power of the ego to distort perception and limit understanding.

    The 'light' in stories symbolises the power connecting a character to the Self.

    All the archetypal figures have both 'light' and 'dark' aspects.

*Fantasy*: make-believe or wishful thinking originating from the ego, essentially different in character from imagination.

*Fantasy cycle*: the five-stage pattern which shapes the attempt to live out an ego-based fantasy when pressed to its conclusion (Anticipation – Dream Stage – Frustration – Nightmare Stage – Destruction). The basis of Tragedy.

*Nyktomorph*: literally a 'night shape'. Term used to describe the way in which fantasy feeds on incomplete images, which exercise their suggestive power over the mind from the fact that it lacks enough information fully to resolve them. This is helpful to understanding the psychological mechanism behind the appeal of fantasy-based storytelling, e.g. horror stories, pornography.

*Masculine and Feminine*: terms used in this book in a specific sense, unconnected to whether someone is outwardly male or female. A man or a woman can display both 'masculine' and 'feminine' attributes (or the lack of them).

The 'masculine values' relate to power or strength, and to the ordering or 'rational' function of the human mind. These can most naturally become allied to ego-consciousness.

The 'feminine values', rooted in the Self, represent selfless or sympathetic feeling and intuitive understanding, the ability to 'see whole'.

*Anima*: Jung's term to define the feminine component in a man's psyche which shapes his response to the opposite sex and his relationship to the 'feminine values'. Anima-figures personifying the feminine value (such as the heroine or a 'Princess') play a central part in storytelling.

*Animus*: the corresponding masculine component in a woman's psyche. This similarly determines her relationship to the male sex and to the 'masculine values'. In stories where the central figure is a heroine, the animus is personified by the hero (or a 'Prince').

*Dark Masculine*: this represents the masculine values of power and order when they are cut off from the connecting feminine and centred on the ego.

*Dark Feminine*: this represents the feminine when it is taken over by the ego. Behind an outward show of 'feminine' attributes, it becomes driven by the dark masculine.

*'Unrealised value'*: term used to describe the way in which 'dark figures' in stories (e.g. 'Dark Father', 'Dark Mother', 'Dark Alter-ego', 'Dark Other Half') represent the negative version of those qualities which the hero or heroine must make positive in themselves to achieve maturity and thus to reach a 'happy ending'.

*Shadow*: Jung's term to describe the negative elements called into play when psychic development becomes unbalanced and 'one-sided'. The 'shadow' includes all those elements of which ego-consciousness is not aware. This may result in 'projection of the shadow' onto others (see below). When people are caught out by these limitations on their awareness they 'fall into their shadow' (see Tragedy).

*Projection*: the ability of the psyche to 'project' onto the external world those archetypal elements which should be internal. E.g. we talk of 'anima projection' when someone falls foolishly in love; or 'shadow projection' when people display irrational antagonism to those who embody their own failings ('mote and beam syndrome').

*Ego/Self confusion*: describes the unconscious process whereby the urge to totality represented by the Self can be hijacked by the ego (individually or collectively). This leads to 'ego inflation', as the ego then claims the moral superiority of acting in some higher, selfless cause. Invaluable to understanding a wide range of social and political phenomena, from puritanical self-righteousness in religion to Marxism, from the more extreme forms of environmentalism to political correctness.

*Sentimentality*: another expression of 'ego/Self confusion', where the ego enjoys a make-believe version of non-egocentric qualities associated with the Self. It takes on their outward form, but separated from their inner reality. As Hollywood long since discovered, any loving emotion can be sentimentally appropriated in this way, such as love between man and woman, between parents and children, love of country, nature or God. Helpful in understanding the appeal of all types of fantasy-based storytelling and art.

*Inferior*: the positive elements needed to make up a deficiency caused by psychological one-sidedness may often appear in some 'inferior' (i.e. undeveloped, weak or distorted) form. They thus point up that which needs to be consciously developed for integration to be achieved (e.g. the role played by 'helpful animals' in folk tales).

*Above the Line/Below The Line*: centrally important feature of storytelling which shows the 'little world' of a story divided onto two levels. In archetypal terms, this division represents the psychic split created by ego-consciousness.

'Above the line' we see initially dominant 'dark' characters whose egocentricity throws into shadow 'below the line' those characters who represent the 'light'. The archetypal structure of stories shows these 'light' elements finally emerging from the shadows, to eliminate the distortions of egocentricity and thus to integrate the two levels.

*Ruling Consciousness*: the state of collective ego-consciousness which characterises every social group, establishing its prevailing attitudes and values. Since ego-consciousness is by definition 'one-sided', this invariably casts a shadow which (a) it projects onto other groups, and (b) obscures those members of the group 'below the line' who represent values missing from its ruling mindset.

*'Change of Heart'*: centrally important motif in stories, showing the process whereby a 'dark' character may switch to the side of 'light'. This invariably involves a radical shift in both feeling and awareness. The heart is opened to selfless feeling, and the eyes to objective understanding or 'seeing whole'.

*Thrilling Escape From Death*: one of the commonest devices used in a story (particularly at its climax), to show the hero or heroine miraculously escaping from the clutches of the 'dark power'.

*The Archetypal Happy Ending*: for a story to reach a completely 'happy ending' the masculine and feminine values must be brought into perfect balance. This is supremely symbolised by the image of a man and a woman being brought together in loving union, representing integration with the Self.

# Bibliography

Most of the hundreds of individual stories cited in this book as examples are not listed here, because either they are so well-known that they have been published in many editions, or they are more familiar in non-literary form, as films, operas or ballets. I have, however, included a number of stories which did not originate in English, to specify the translations used (although even here the translations have on occasion been very slightly modified, to clarify their meaning in sympathy with the original text).

Aeschylus, *The Oresteian Trilogy*, translated by Philip Vellacott, Penguin Classics, 1956.
Afanas'ev, Alexsandr, *Russian Fairy Tales*, translated by Norbert Guterman, Sheldon Press, London, 1976.
Andersen, Hans, *Fairy Tales and Legends*, Hodder and Stoughton, 1924.
Apuleius, *The Golden Ass*, translated byRobert Graves, Penguin Classics, 1950.
Aristophanes, *The Wasps* and *The Poet and the Women* (*Thesmophoriazusae*), translated by David Barrett, Penguin Classics, 1964.
Aristophanes, *Lysistrata*, translated by Alan H. Sommerstein, Penguin Classics, 1973.
Aristotle, *The Poetics*, translated by T. S. Dorsch, Penguin Classics, London, 1965.
Beckett, Samuel, *Waiting For Godot*, Faber and Faber, London, 1955.
*Beowulf*, translated by David Wright, Penguin Classics, 1957.
Bettelheim, Bruno, *The Uses of Enchantment: The Meaning and Importance of Fairy Tales*, Thames and Hudson, London, 1976.
Booker, Christopher, *The Neophiliacs: A Study of the Revolution in English Life in the 1950s and 1960s*, Collins, London, 1969.
Brinton, Crane, *The Anatomy of Revolution*, W. W. Norton.New York, 1938.
Campbell, Joseph, *The Hero With A Thousand Faces*, Bollingen Foundation, New York, 1949.
Canetti, Elias, *The Voices of Marrakesh*, Marion Boyars, London, 1978
Chekhov, Anton, *Plays*, translated by Elizaveta Fen, Penguin Classics, 1959.
Dante, Alighieri, *The Divine Comedy* (3 vols.), translated by Dorothy L. Sayers, Penguin Classics, 1955.
Donington, Robert, *Wagner's Ring and Its Symbols*, Faber and Faber, London, 1963.
Fiedler, Leslie, *Love and Death In The American Novel*, Jonathan Cape, London, 1967.
Frye, Northrop, *Anatomy of Criticism*, Princeton University Press, 1957
*Gilgamesh, The Epic of*, an English version by N. K. Saunders, Penguin Classics, 1960.
Gittings, Robert, *The Younger Hardy* and *The Older Hardy*, Heinemann, London, 1975/1978.

Goethe, J. W., *The Sorrows of Young Werther*, translated by Catherine Hutter, New American Library (Signet Classic) New York, 1962.

Graves, Robert, *The Greek Myths*, Pelican Books, London, 1955

Grimm, Jakob and Wilhelm, *The Complete Grimm's Fairy Tales*, Routledge and Kegan Paul, London, 1975,

Holden, Amanda (ed.), *The Penguin Opera Guide*, Penguin Books, 1997.

Holmes, Richard, *Shelley: The Pursuit*, Weidenfeld and Nicolson, 1974.

Homer, *The Odyssey*, translated by E. V. Rieu, Penguin Classics, 1946.

Ibsen, Henrik, *Peer Gynt*, translated by Peter Watts, Penguin Classics, 1966

James, M. R., *The Ghost Stories*, Edward Arnold, 1931.

Jung, Carl, Collected Works, published 1953–1979 by Routledge, Kegan Paul (London), particularly:

Vol. 5 (II), *Symbols of Transformation*; Vol.6, *Psychological Types*; Vol.7, *Two Essays On Analytical Pychology*; Vol.8, *The Structure And Dynamics Of The Psyche*; Vol. 9 (I), *The Archetypes And The Collective Unconscious*; Vol. 9 (II), *Aion*; Vol. 10, *Civilisation In Transition*.

Kane, Sarah, Blasted, *Modern Drama: Plays of the 1980s and 1990s*, the Methuen Book of Modern Drama, Methuen, London, 2001

Lancelyn Green, Roger, *Myths of the Norsemen*, Puffin Books, London, 1960

Lao Tzu, *Tao Te Ching*, translated by D. C. Lau, Penguin Classics, London, 1963.

*Larousse Encyclopaedia of Mythology*, Batchworth Press, London, 1959

Lawrence, D. H., *A Propos of Lady Chatterley's Lover*, Penguin Books, 1961.

Lawrence, D. H., *Studies in Classical American Literature*, Penguin Books, London, 1971.

Longus, *Daphnis and Chloe*, translated by Paul Turner, Penguin Classics, 1956

Lucas, George, *Star Wars, A Novel*, Ballantine Books, New York, 1976.

Mann, Thomas, *Doctor Faustus*, translated by H. T. Lowe-Porter, Secker and Warburg, London, 1949.

Maugham, Somerset, *Ten Novels And Their Authors*, Heinemann, 1954.

Menander, *Plays and Fragments*, translated by Philip Vellacott, Penguin Classics, 1967.

Moliere, *The Miser and Other Plays*, translated by John Wood, Penguin Classics, 1953.

Moliere, *The Misanthrope and Other Plays*, translated by John Wood, Penguin Classics, 1959.

Mumford, Lewis, *The City In History*, Pelican Books, London, 1966.

Neumann, Erich, *The Great Mother Archetype*, Routledge, Kegan Paul, London, 1955.

Neumann, Erich, *The Origins And History of Consciousness*, Princeton University, 1954.

Opie, Peter and Iona, *The Classic Fairy Tales*, Oxford University Press, 1974.

Painter, George, *Marcel Proust: A Biography* (2 vols.), Chatto and Windus, 1959.

Pearson, John, *The Life of Ian Fleming*, Cape, London, 1966

Pirandello, Luigi, *Three Plays*, J. M. Dent, London, 1929.

Plato, *The Republic*, translated by H. D. P. Lee, Penguin Classics (London, 1955).

Plautus, *The Pot Of Gold and Other Plays*, translated by E. F. Watling, Penguin Classics, 1975.

Praz, Mario, *The Romantic Agony*, Oxford University Press, 1933.

Proust, Marcel, *Remembrance of Things Past* (3 vols.), translated by C. K. Scott Moncrieff and Terence Kilmartin, Chatto and Windus, London, 1981.

*Quest Of The Holy Grail*, translated by P. M. Matarasso, Penguin Classics, 1969.

Sade, Marquis de, *The Misfortunes of Virtue*, translated by David Coward, Oxford World Classics, 1992.

Sophocles, *The Theban Plays*, translated by E. F. Watling, Penguin Classics, London, 1947.

Spielberg, Steven, *Close Encounters Of The Third Kind*, Sphere Books, London, 1978.

Stendhal, *Scarlet and Black (Le Rouge et Le Noir)*, translated by Margaret Shaw, Penguin Classics, 1953

*Tales From The Thousand and One Nights*, translated by N. J. Dawood, Penguin Classics, London, 1955.

Tomasello, Michael, *The Cultural Origins of Human Cognition*, Harvard University Press, 2000.

Upanishads, The, translated by Juan Mascaro, Penguin Classics, London, 1965.

Van der Post, Laurens, *The Heart Of The Hunter*, Hogarth Press, 1968.
Van der Post, Laurens (with Jane Taylor), *Testament To The Bushmen*, Viking, London, 1984.
Virgil, *The Aeneid*, translated by W. Jackson Knight, Penguin Classics, London, 1956.
Vyvyan, John, *The Shakespearian Ethic*, Chatto and Windus, 1959.
Whistler, Laurens, *Scenes and Signs on Glass*, John Murray, 1985.
Whitmont, Edward, *The Symbolic Quest*, Barrie and Rockliff, London, 1969.
Wilson, Edmund, *Classics and Commercials: A Literary Chronicle of the 1940s*, W. H. Allen, London, 1950.

# Index of Stories Cited

# General Index

Temptress, as 'dark feminine', 75, 248–249, 259–260, 280–281, 283, 306, 334, 336, 338, 409, 599
Tennyson, Alfred, 654
Teutonic gods (and days of week), 623fn
Thatcher, Margaret, 688–689
Thinking (ordering) function, 558–559 and fn
Thor, 646–647
Three (archetypal significance of in stories): 229–235; becomes four, 282, 229, 313–315; in Dante, 628–632
Three levels of existence in world mythologies, 602, 595–596, 645–646
'Thrilling escape' (from death), 45–48, 85fn, 87, 106, 212
Thurber, James, 587
Tibetan Book of the Dead, The, 626
Titanic, films about sinking of, 680
Tokens, to show true identity, 113, 127, 131
Tolkien, J. R. R., 316 et seq.
Tolstoy, Leo, 136–138, 139, 153, 162–164, 267, 399, 419, 640, 655
Totality (four-sided), 552
Tragedy, as archetype, 153–192, 224–226; derivation of, 191; 329–343; shaping events in real life, 577 et seq.; Greek, 601, 607–608
Tragic cycle, in Christ 'myth', 619–620
Transformation, need for and lack of, 353, 367, 379–381, 447–448
Treasure,as symbol of Self, 22–23, 25, 71, 269
Trickster, as archetype, 308–309, 323–324, 604
Triffids, 28
Trojan War, 466–467fn, 606–607
Truffaut, Francois, 161-2, 503fn, 675
Trollope, Anthony, 136
Twain, Mark, 383
Twelve, as archetypal number, 235fn
'Twenties', 661–663, 674
Tynan, Ken, 478fn, 479fn, 673
Tyrant, as archetype, 247–248, 251, 258, 260, 261, 265, 277, 290fn; and daughter 292–293; 296, 301, 306, 325

Uccello, Paolo, 634
Unconscious, as source of dreams and stories, 543, 554
Underworld, journey to, 76–77; images of, 595, 602, 606, 625
Unreconciled dark figures, 119–120, 132
Unrealised value, 277 et seq.; examples 283–288, 291, 321, 340; as defining component of stories, 556
'Unrelenting father' (or parent), 110–111, 122–123, 133, 150, 256, 261
Ulysses speech (Troilus and Cressida), 267, 636–637, 645
Upanishads, The, 593, 610

Updike, John, 383
Ur, 597
Utopianism, as projection of Self, 661–662, 664–667

Valentino, Rudolf, 142, 661
Valhalla, 646
Van Eyck, Jan, 634
Verdi, Giuseppe, 402–404, 418, 649, 654, 656
Verne, Jules, 84, 92
Virgil, 69, 70, 73, 222, 614–615; as guide to Dante, 629–630
Virginity, loss of as climax of story, 385–386, 457, 459, 449, 522–526
Voltaire, 91
Voyage And Return, as archetype, 87–106; summing up, 105–106; 223–224, 250–252, projected, 566–567; reflecting one-sided consciousness of 18th c., 638
Vyvyan, John, 13
Van der Post, Laurens, 287

Wagner, Richard, 6, 25, 185, 404–406, 407, 648, 654, 697
Walesa, Lech, 593
Walpole, Horace, 649, 655
Waugh, Evelyn, 4, 87, 93, 395, 567, 638, 662, 671
Wayne, John, 670
Welles, Orson, 509
Wells, H.G., 28, 39, 45, 92, 658, 659fn
Whistler, Laurence, 277, 700
Wilde, Oscar, 141–142, 153, 158–159, 215, 396, 409, 411
Wilder, Billy, 147
Wilson, Edmund (on detective stories), 505, 513
'Wise Old Man', as archetype, 77–78, 264; defined, 297–299; 302, 306–307; Prospero as, 322–325; Sarastro as, 325–327; 335, 382, 394. See also Gandalf, Teiresias
Witch, as 'dark feminine', 22–23, 241, 244, 248–249, 251, 279–280
Wodehouse, P. G., 6, 108, 145–147, 255, 397
Woityla, Karol (Pope John-Paul II), 685
Wolfe, Tom, 682
Women, de-feminisation of in 20th c., 486, 660–661, 687–689
'World egg', 545
World, end of, 406, 647, 679, 697–698
Wordsworth, William, 642–643, 650
Wyndham, John, 40–41

Yeats, W. B., 455
Yin and Yang, 609–610

Zeus, 23, 602–607, 611, 614, 616
Ziggurats, 597fn
Zoroaster, 610